Stan Lee
PRESENTS

MARVEL TEAM-UP

VOL. 1

ESSENTIAL

MARVEL TEAM-UP #1-24

ESSENTIAL MARVEL® TEAM-UP VOL. 1. Contains material originally published in magazine form as MARVEL TEAM-UP #1-24. First printing. April 2002. ISBN# 0-7851-0828-9. Published by MARVEL COMICS, a division of MARVEL ENTERTAINMENT GROUP, INC. OFFICE OF PUBLI-CATION: 10 EAST 40th STREET, NEW YORK, NY 10016. Copyright © 1972, 1973,1974 and 2002 Marvel Characters, Inc. All rights reserved. Price $14.95 in the U.S. and $23.95 in Canada (GST# R127032852). No similarity between any of the names, characters, persons, and/or insti-tutions in this publication with those of any living or dead person or institutions is intended, and any such similarity which may exist is purely coincidental. This publication may not be sold except by authorized dealers and is sold subject to the conditions that it shall not be sold or dis-tributed with any part of its cover or markings removed, nor in a mutilated condition. SPIDER-MAN, HUMAN TORCH, X-MEN, VISION, THING, THOR, HELLCAT, IRON MAN, INHUMANS, WEREWOLF BY NIGHT, CAPTAIN AMERICA, SUB-MARINER, GHOST RIDER, CAPTAIN MARVEL, MR. FANTASTIC, HULK, KA-ZAR, BLACK PANTHER, DOCTOR STRANGE, HAWKEYE, ICEMAN and BROTHER VOODOO (including prominent charac-ters featured in this publication and the distinctive likenesses thereof) are trademarks of MARVEL CHARACTERS, INC. Printed in Canada. PETER CUNEO, Chief Executive Officer; AVI ARAD, Chief Creative Officer; GUI KARYO, Chief Information Officer; STAN LEE, Chairman Emeritus.

10 9 8 7 6 5 4 3 2 1

ESSENTIAL MARVEL TEAM-UP VOL. 1

MARVEL TEAM-UP #1
WRITER: ROY THOMAS
PENCILER: ROSS ANDRU
INKER: MIKE ESPOSITO
LETTERER: ART SIMEK

MARVEL TEAM-UP #2
WRITER: GERRY CONWAY
PENCILER: ROSS ANDRU
INKER: JIM MOONEY
LETTERER: SAM ROSEN

MARVEL TEAM-UP #3
WRITER: GERRY CONWAY
PENCILER: ROSS ANDRU
INKER: FRANK GIACOIA
LETTERER: ART SIMEK

MARVEL TEAM-UP #4
WRITER: GERRY CONWAY
PENCILER: GIL KANE
INKER: STEVE MITCHELL
LETTERER: JOHN COSTANZA

MARVEL TEAM-UP #5
WRITER: GERRY CONWAY
PENCILER: GIL KANE
INKER: MIKE ESPOSITO
LETTERER: JOHN COSTANZA

MARVEL TEAM-UP #6
WRITER: GERRY CONWAY
PENCILER: GIL KANE
INKER: MIKE ESPOSITO
LETTERER: JEAN IZZO

MARVEL TEAM-UP #7
WRITER: GERRY CONWAY
PENCILER: ROSS ANDRU
INKER: JIM MOONEY
LETTERER: ART SIMEK

MARVEL TEAM-UP #8
WRITER: GERRY CONWAY
ILLUSTRATOR: JIM MOONEY
LETTERER: CHARLOTTE JETTER

MARVEL TEAM-UP #9
WRITER: GERRY CONWAY
PENCILER: ROSS ANDRU
INKER: FRANK BOLLE
LETTERER: CHARLOTTE JETTER

MARVEL TEAM-UP #10
WRITER: GERRY CONWAY
PENCILER: ROSS ANDRU
INKER: FRANK GIACOIA
LETTERER: CHARLOTTE JETTER

MARVEL TEAM-UP #11
PLOT: GERRY CONWAY
SCRIPT: LEN WEIN
PENCILER: JIM MOONEY
INKER: MIKE ESPOSITO
LETTERER: JOHN COSTANZA

MARVEL TEAM-UP #12

PLOT: GERRY CONWAY
SCRIPT: LEN WEIN
PENCILER: ROSS ANDRU
INKER: DON PERLIN
LETTERER: CHARLOTTE JETTER

MARVEL TEAM-UP #13

WRITER: LEN WEIN
PENCILER: GIL KANE
INKER: FRANK GIACOIA
LETTERER: JUNE BRAVERMAN

MARVEL TEAM-UP #14

WRITER: LEN WEIN
PENCILER: GIL KANE
INKER: WAYNE HOWARD
LETTERER: JOHN COSTANZA

MARVEL TEAM-UP #15

WRITER: LEN WEIN
PENCILER: ROSS ANDRU
INKER: DON PERLIN
LETTERER: JOHN COSTANZA

MARVEL TEAM-UP #16

WRITER: LEN WEIN
PENCILER: GIL KANE
INKER: JIM MOONEY
LETTERER: ART SIMEK

MARVEL TEAM-UP #17

WRITER: LEN WEIN
PENCILER: GIL KANE
INKERS: SAL TRAPANI, FRANK GIACOIA & MIKE ESPOSITO
LETTERER: JEAN IZZO

MARVEL TEAM-UP #18

WRITER: LEN WEIN
PENCILER: GIL KANE
INKERS: FRANK GIACOIA & MIKE ESPOSITO
LETTERER: JEAN IZZO

MARVEL TEAM-UP #19

WRITER: LEN WEIN
PENCILER: GIL KANE
INKER: FRANK GIACOIA
LETTERER: DAVE HUNT

MARVEL TEAM-UP #20

WRITER: LEN WEIN
PENCILER: SAL BUSCEMA
INKERS: FRANK GIACOIA & MIKE ESPOSITO
LETTERER: ART SIMEK

MARVEL TEAM-UP #21

WRITER: LEN WEIN
PENCILER: SAL BUSCEMA
INKER: FRANK GIACOIA & DAVE HUNT
LETTERER: DAVE HUNT

MARVEL TEAM-UP #22

WRITER: LEN WEIN
PENCILER: SAL BUSCEMA
INKER: FRANK GIACOIA
LETTERER: DAVE HUNT

MARVEL TEAM-UP #23

WRITER: LEN WEIN
PENCILER: GIL KANE
INKER: MIKE ESPOSITO
LETTERER: CHARLOTTE JETTER

MARVEL TEAM-UP #24

WRITER: LEN WEIN
PENCILER: JIM MOONEY
INKER: SAL TRAPANI
LETTERER: JOHN COSTANZA

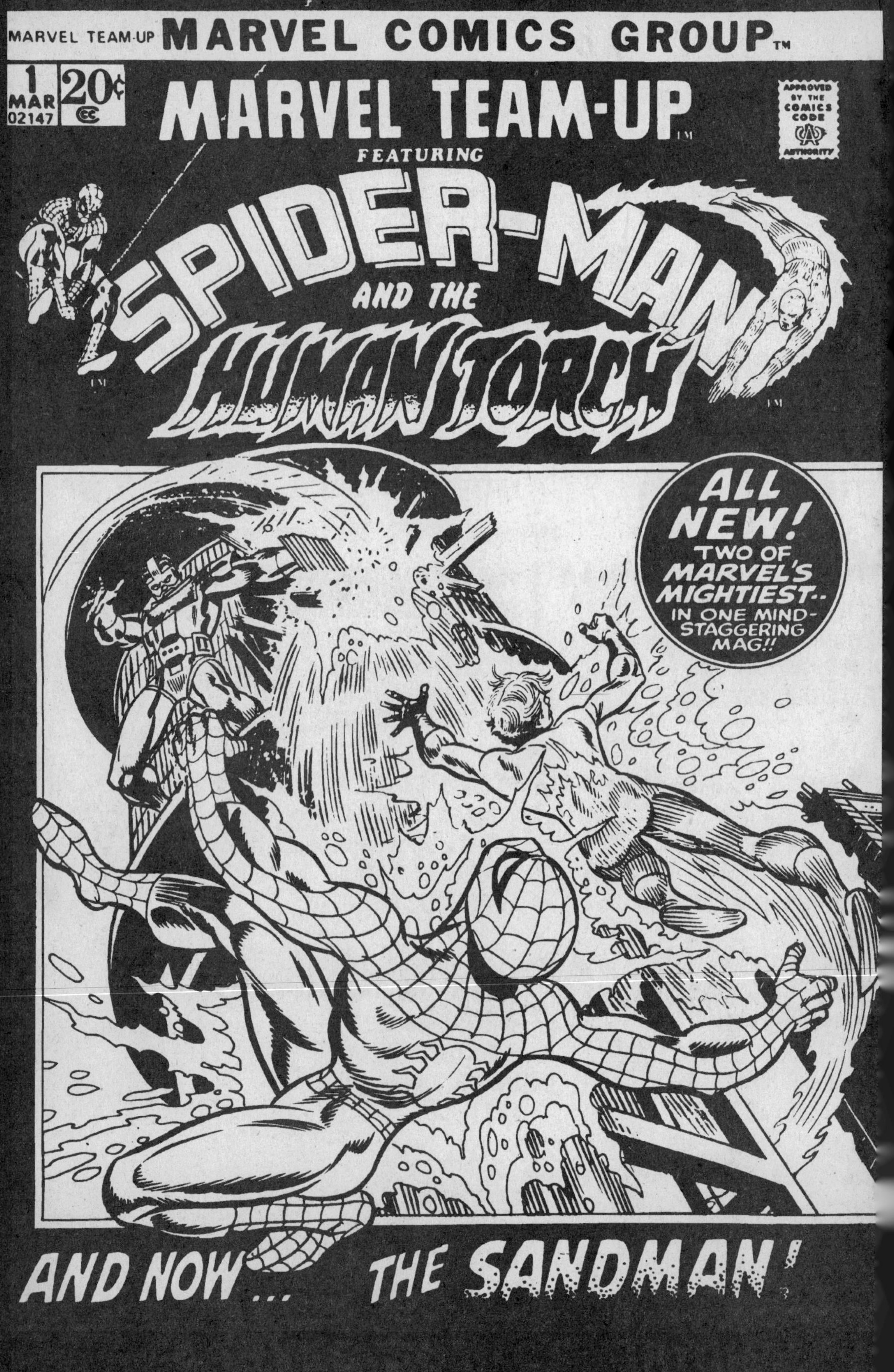
MARVEL TEAM-UP MARVEL COMICS GROUP TM
1 MAR 02147
20¢ CC
MARVEL TEAM-UP
APPROVED BY THE COMICS CODE AUTHORITY
FEATURING
SPIDER-MAN
AND THE
HUMAN TORCH
ALL NEW! TWO OF MARVEL'S MIGHTIEST-- IN ONE MIND-STAGGERING MAG!!
AND NOW... THE SANDMAN!

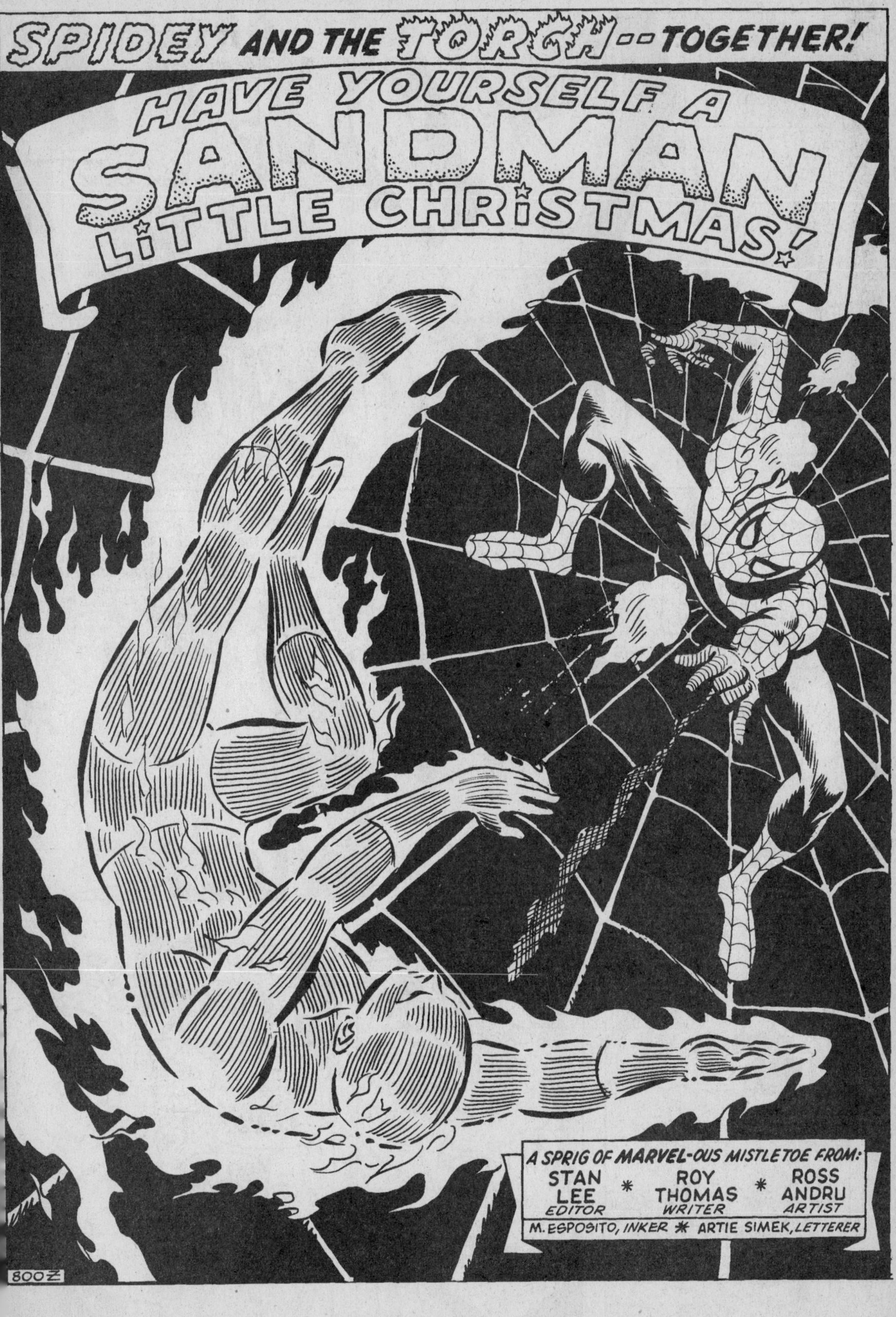
SPIDEY AND THE TORCH--TOGETHER!
HAVE YOURSELF A SANDMAN LITTLE CHRISTMAS!
A SPRIG OF MARVEL-OUS MISTLETOE FROM:
STAN LEE EDITOR * ROY THOMAS WRITER * ROSS ANDRU ARTIST
M. ESPOSITO, INKER * ARTIE SIMEK, LETTERER
800Z

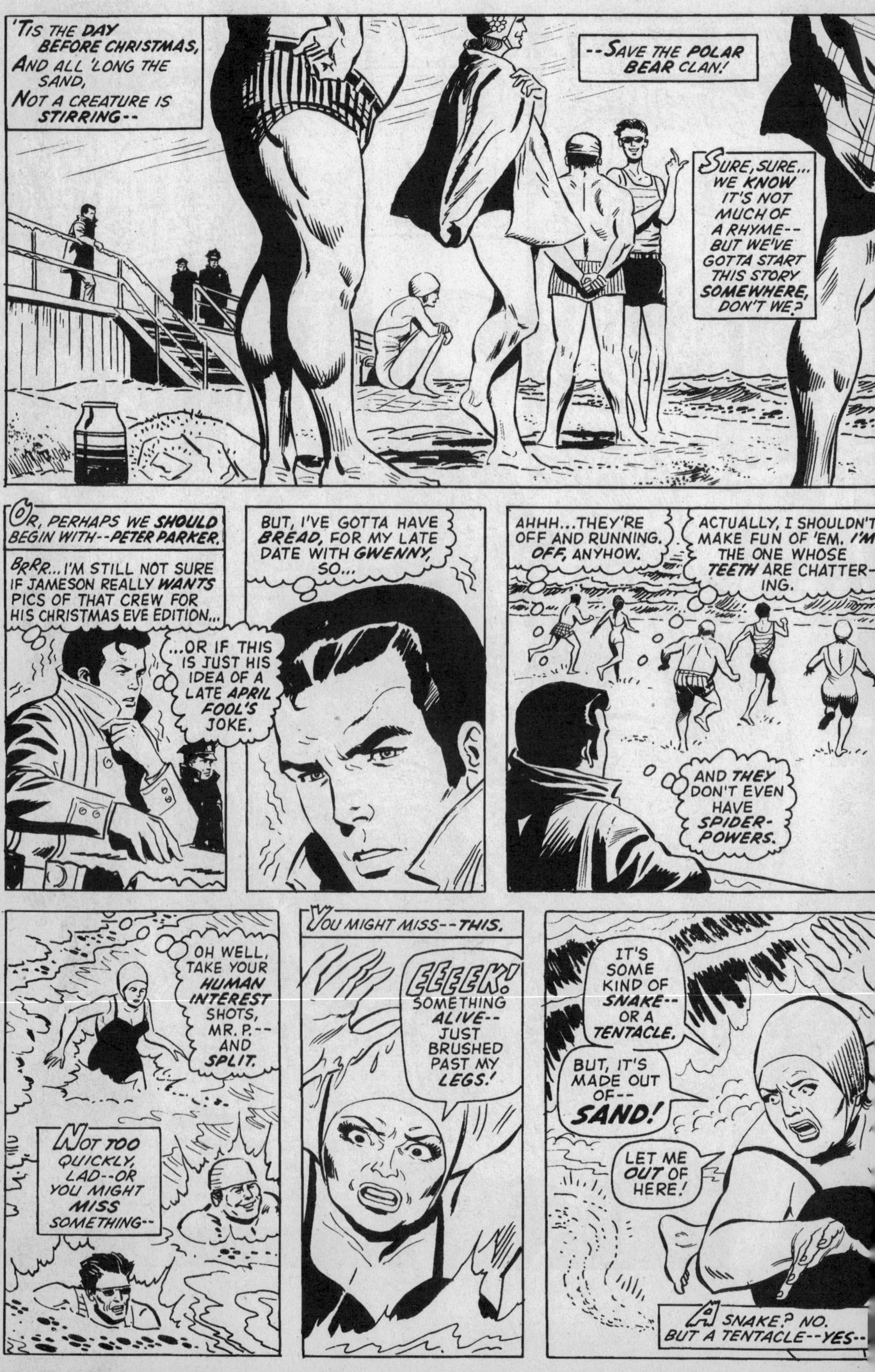
'TIS THE DAY BEFORE CHRISTMAS, AND ALL 'LONG THE SAND, NOT A CREATURE IS STIRRING--
--SAVE THE POLAR BEAR CLAN!
SURE, SURE... WE KNOW IT'S NOT MUCH OF A RHYME--BUT WE'VE GOTTA START THIS STORY SOMEWHERE, DON'T WE?
OR, PERHAPS WE SHOULD BEGIN WITH--PETER PARKER.
BRRR... I'M STILL NOT SURE IF JAMESON REALLY WANTS PICS OF THAT CREW FOR HIS CHRISTMAS EVE EDITION...
...OR IF THIS IS JUST HIS IDEA OF A LATE APRIL FOOL'S JOKE.
BUT, I'VE GOTTA HAVE BREAD, FOR MY LATE DATE WITH GWENNY, SO...
AHHH... THEY'RE OFF AND RUNNING. OFF, ANYHOW.
ACTUALLY, I SHOULDN'T MAKE FUN OF 'EM. I'M THE ONE WHOSE TEETH ARE CHATTERING.
AND THEY DON'T EVEN HAVE SPIDER-POWERS.
OH WELL, TAKE YOUR HUMAN INTEREST SHOTS, MR. P.--AND SPLIT.
NOT TOO QUICKLY, LAD--OR YOU MIGHT MISS SOMETHING--
YOU MIGHT MISS--THIS.
EEEEK! SOMETHING ALIVE--JUST BRUSHED PAST MY LEGS!
IT'S SOME KIND OF SNAKE--OR A TENTACLE.
BUT, IT'S MADE OUT OF--SAND!
LET ME OUT OF HERE!
A SNAKE? NO. BUT A TENTACLE--YES--

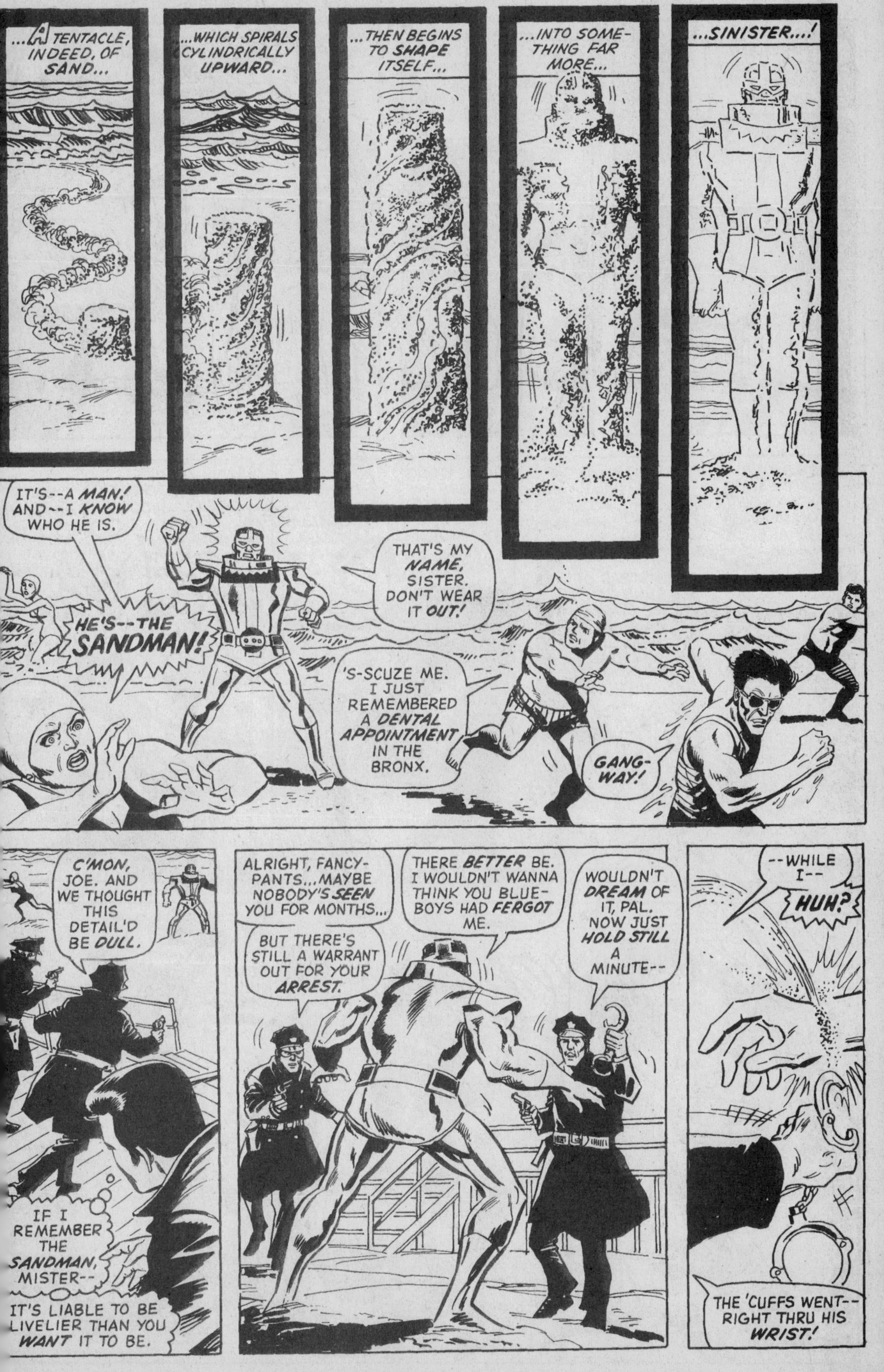

...A TENTACLE, INDEED, OF SAND...
...WHICH SPIRALS CYLINDRICALLY UPWARD...
...THEN BEGINS TO SHAPE ITSELF...
...INTO SOMETHING FAR MORE...
...SINISTER...!
IT'S--A MAN! AND--I KNOW WHO HE IS.
HE'S--THE SANDMAN!
THAT'S MY NAME, SISTER. DON'T WEAR IT OUT!
'S-SCUZE ME. I JUST REMEMBERED A DENTAL APPOINTMENT IN THE BRONX.
GANGWAY!
C'MON, JOE. AND WE THOUGHT THIS DETAIL'D BE DULL.
IF I REMEMBER THE SANDMAN, MISTER--
IT'S LIABLE TO BE LIVELIER THAN YOU WANT IT TO BE.
ALRIGHT, FANCY-PANTS... MAYBE NOBODY'S SEEN YOU FOR MONTHS...
BUT THERE'S STILL A WARRANT OUT FOR YOUR ARREST.
THERE BETTER BE. I WOULDN'T WANNA THINK YOU BLUE-BOYS HAD FERGOT ME.
WOULDN'T DREAM OF IT, PAL. NOW JUST HOLD STILL A MINUTE--
--WHILE I--
HUH?
THE 'CUFFS WENT--RIGHT THRU HIS WRIST!

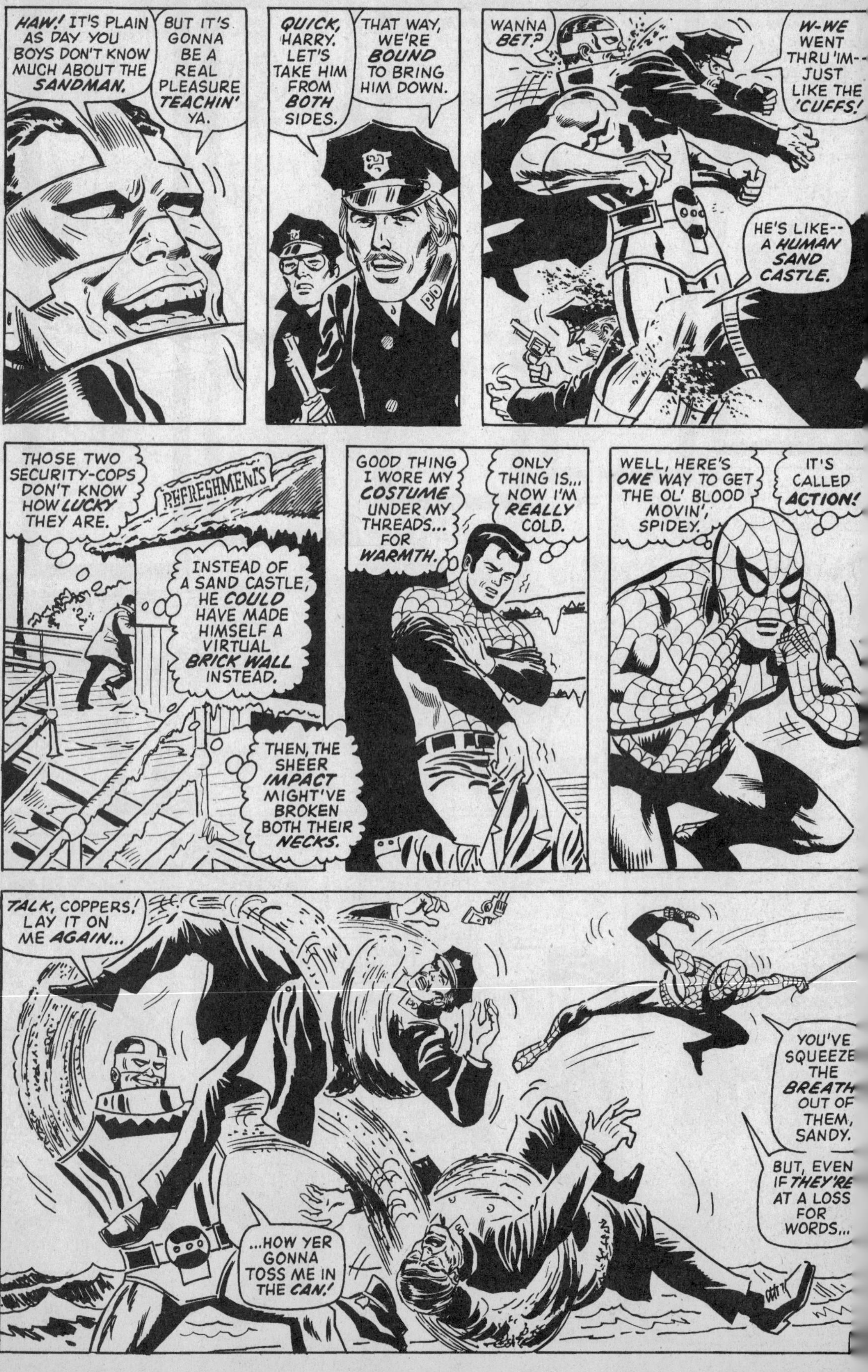
HAW! IT'S PLAIN AS DAY YOU BOYS DON'T KNOW MUCH ABOUT THE SANDMAN.
BUT IT'S GONNA BE A REAL PLEASURE TEACHIN' YA.
QUICK, HARRY. LET'S TAKE HIM FROM BOTH SIDES.
THAT WAY, WE'RE BOUND TO BRING HIM DOWN.
WANNA BET?
W-WE WENT THRU 'IM-- JUST LIKE THE 'CUFFS!
HE'S LIKE-- A HUMAN SAND CASTLE.
THOSE TWO SECURITY-COPS DON'T KNOW HOW LUCKY THEY ARE.
REFRESHMENTS
INSTEAD OF A SAND CASTLE, HE COULD HAVE MADE HIMSELF A VIRTUAL BRICK WALL INSTEAD.
THEN, THE SHEER IMPACT MIGHT'VE BROKEN BOTH THEIR NECKS.
GOOD THING I WORE MY COSTUME UNDER MY THREADS... FOR WARMTH.
ONLY THING IS... NOW I'M REALLY COLD.
WELL, HERE'S ONE WAY TO GET THE OL' BLOOD MOVIN', SPIDEY.
IT'S CALLED ACTION!
TALK, COPPERS! LAY IT ON ME AGAIN...
...HOW YER GONNA TOSS ME IN THE CAN!
YOU'VE SQUEEZE THE BREATH OUT OF THEM, SANDY.
BUT, EVEN IF THEY'RE AT A LOSS FOR WORDS...

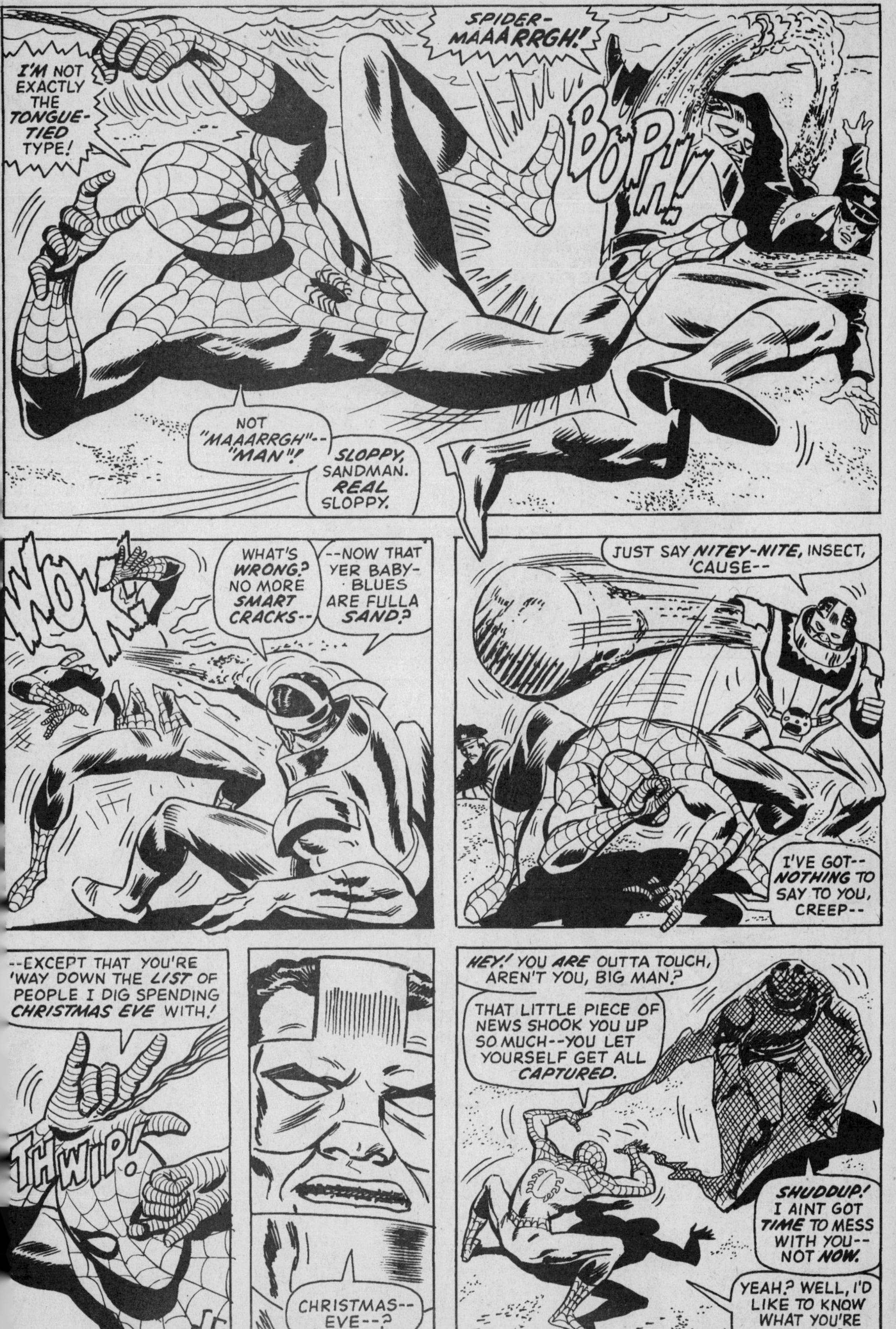
I'M NOT EXACTLY THE TONGUE-TIED TYPE!
SPIDER-MAAARRGH!
BOPH!
NOT "MAAARRGH"--"MAN"!
SLOPPY, SANDMAN. REAL SLOPPY.
WHOK!
WHAT'S WRONG? NO MORE SMART CRACKS--
--NOW THAT YER BABY-BLUES ARE FULLA SAND?
JUST SAY NITEY-NITE, INSECT, 'CAUSE--
I'VE GOT--NOTHING TO SAY TO YOU, CREEP--
--EXCEPT THAT YOU'RE 'WAY DOWN THE LIST OF PEOPLE I DIG SPENDING CHRISTMAS EVE WITH!
THWIP!
CHRISTMAS--EVE--?
HEY! YOU ARE OUTTA TOUCH, AREN'T YOU, BIG MAN?
THAT LITTLE PIECE OF NEWS SHOOK YOU UP SO MUCH--YOU LET YOURSELF GET ALL CAPTURED.
SHUDDUP! I AINT GOT TIME TO MESS WITH YOU--NOT NOW.
YEAH? WELL, I'D LIKE TO KNOW WHAT YOU'RE GONNA DO--

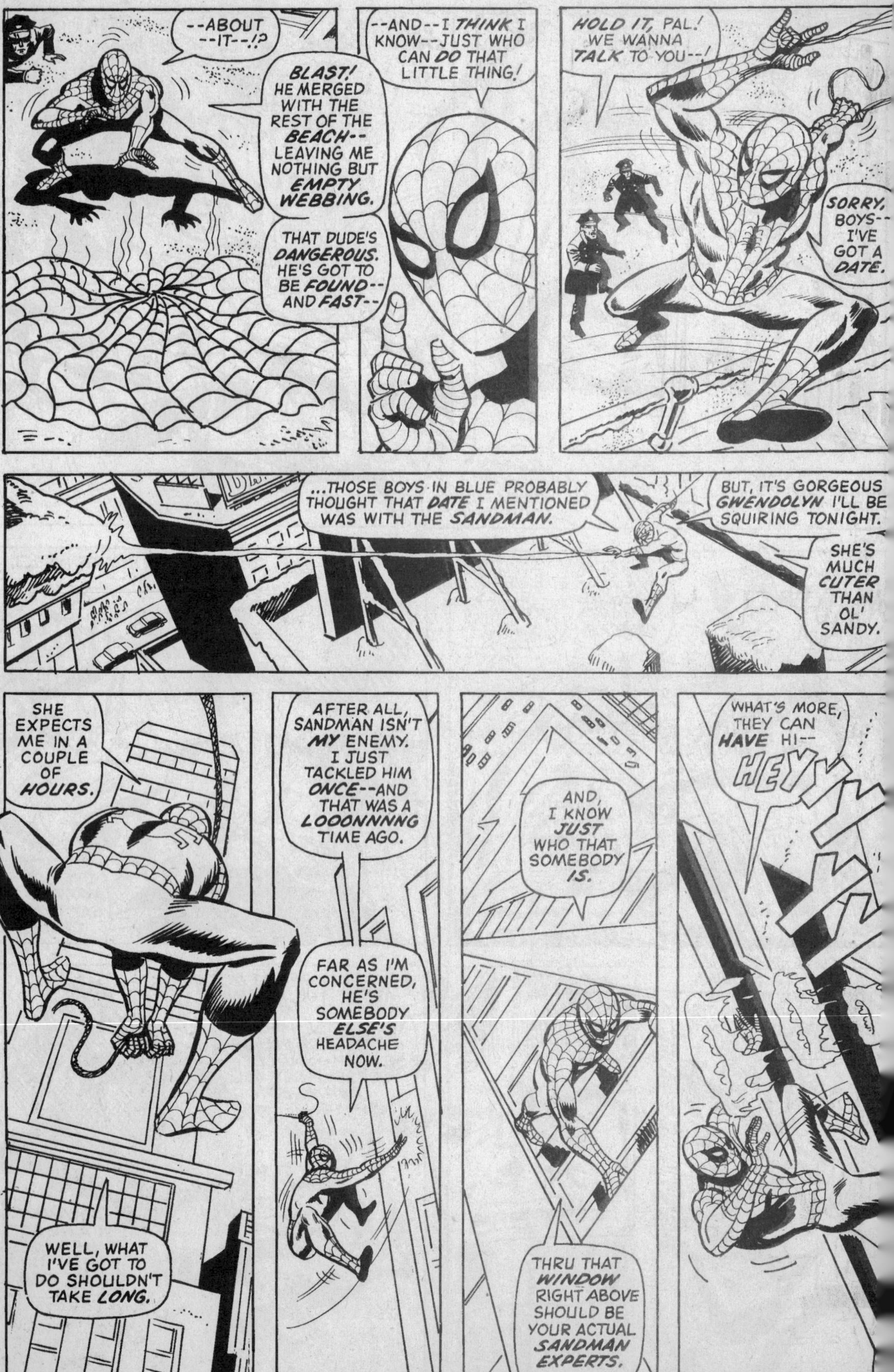
--ABOUT --IT--!?
BLAST! HE MERGED WITH THE REST OF THE BEACH-- LEAVING ME NOTHING BUT EMPTY WEBBING.
THAT DUDE'S DANGEROUS. HE'S GOT TO BE FOUND-- AND FAST--
--AND--I THINK I KNOW--JUST WHO CAN DO THAT LITTLE THING!
HOLD IT, PAL! WE WANNA TALK TO YOU--!
SORRY, BOYS-- I'VE GOT A DATE.
...THOSE BOYS IN BLUE PROBABLY THOUGHT THAT DATE I MENTIONED WAS WITH THE SANDMAN.
BUT, IT'S GORGEOUS GWENDOLYN I'LL BE SQUIRING TONIGHT.
SHE'S MUCH CUTER THAN OL' SANDY.
SHE EXPECTS ME IN A COUPLE OF HOURS.
WELL, WHAT I'VE GOT TO DO SHOULDN'T TAKE LONG.
AFTER ALL, SANDMAN ISN'T MY ENEMY. I JUST TACKLED HIM ONCE--AND THAT WAS A LOOONNNNG TIME AGO.
FAR AS I'M CONCERNED, HE'S SOMEBODY ELSE'S HEADACHE NOW.
AND, I KNOW JUST WHO THAT SOMEBODY IS.
THRU THAT WINDOW RIGHT ABOVE SHOULD BE YOUR ACTUAL SANDMAN EXPERTS.
WHAT'S MORE, THEY CAN HAVE HI--
HEYY

THIS *ISN'T* QUITE-- WHAT I HAD IN *MIND*--

--AND *SOMEBODY'S* GONNA *PAY* FOR IT-- *NOW!*

JOHNNY STORM! YOU FLAMIN' *FREAK-OUT!* WHAT'S THE BIG IDEA OF SHOOTING *FIRE-RINGS* AT ME?

HUH? SORRY, SPIDER-MAN... I DIDN'T KNOW YOU WERE *OUT* THERE.

C'MON *IN.*

WHAT'S *WITH* YOU, TORCH? YOU'RE BEING HALFWAY *CIVIL.*

AND WHERE'S THE *REST* OF YOUR FAR-OUT *FOUR-SOME?*

IT'S *CHRISTMAS EVE,* Y'KNOW.

SO THEY *TELL* ME.

AND, BEFORE YOU START ASKIN' SUBTLE QUESTIONS ABOUT WHY *I'M* NOT AT *WHISPER HILL* WITH THE OTHERS...

...I'LL GIVE IT TO YOU STRAIGHT! I'VE GOT *GIRL PROBLEMS.*

YOU AND THE *REST* OF THE CIVILIZED WORLD.

WELL, MAYBE *THIS* LITTLE TIDBIT WILL TAKE YOUR MIND OFF YOUR TROUBLES!

THE *SANDMAN'S* BACK IN TOWN!

THE *SANDMAN?* THEN WHAT'RE YOU DOING *HERE?* WHY AREN'T YOU--?

WHOA, FELLA. HE'S NOT *MY* RESPONSIBILITY.

I JUST DROPPED BY TO CLUE YOU IN--AND LET *YOU* TAKE IT FROM THERE.

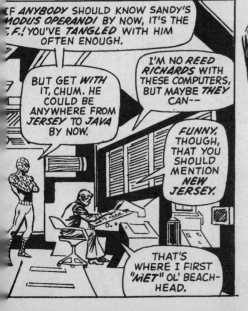

IF *ANYBODY* SHOULD KNOW SANDY'S *MODUS OPERANDI* BY NOW, IT'S THE *F.F.!* YOU'VE *TANGLED* WITH HIM OFTEN ENOUGH.

BUT GET *WITH* IT, CHUM. HE COULD BE ANYWHERE FROM *JERSEY* TO *JAVA* BY NOW.

I'M NO *REED RICHARDS* WITH THESE COMPUTERS, BUT MAYBE *THEY* CAN--

FUNNY, THOUGH, THAT YOU SHOULD MENTION *NEW JERSEY.*

THAT'S WHERE I FIRST "MET" OL' BEACH-HEAD.

WELL... NOT *IN* JERSEY, EXACTLY.

IT WAS MORE LIKE ON TOP OF THE *GEORGE WASHINGTON BRIDGE*-- BUT HE WAS HEADIN' INTO THE CITY FROM *THAT SIDE* OF THE HUDSON RIVER.*

*'WAY BACK IN *STRANGE TALES #115.* --STAN.

7.

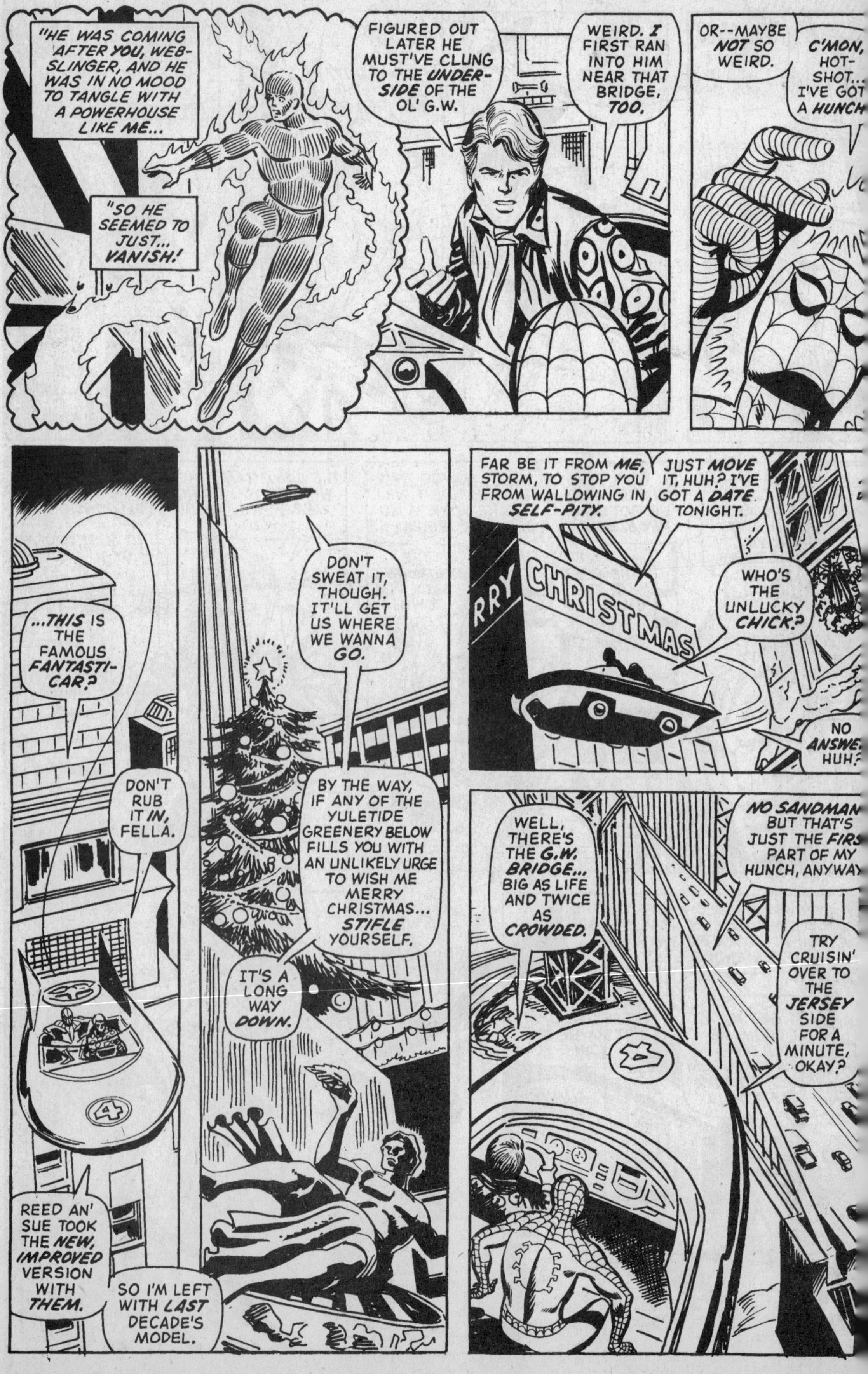
"HE WAS COMING AFTER YOU, WEB-SLINGER, AND HE WAS IN NO MOOD TO TANGLE WITH A POWERHOUSE LIKE ME...
"SO HE SEEMED TO JUST... VANISH!
FIGURED OUT LATER HE MUST'VE CLUNG TO THE UNDER-SIDE OF THE OL' G.W.
WEIRD. I FIRST RAN INTO HIM NEAR THAT BRIDGE, TOO.
OR--MAYBE NOT SO WEIRD.
C'MON, HOT-SHOT... I'VE GOT A HUNCH
...THIS IS THE FAMOUS FANTASTI-CAR?
DON'T RUB IT IN, FELLA.
REED AN' SUE TOOK THE NEW, IMPROVED VERSION WITH THEM.
SO I'M LEFT WITH LAST DECADE'S MODEL.
DON'T SWEAT IT, THOUGH. IT'LL GET US WHERE WE WANNA GO.
BY THE WAY, IF ANY OF THE YULETIDE GREENERY BELOW FILLS YOU WITH AN UNLIKELY URGE TO WISH ME MERRY CHRISTMAS... STIFLE YOURSELF.
IT'S A LONG WAY DOWN.
FAR BE IT FROM ME, STORM, TO STOP YOU FROM WALLOWING IN SELF-PITY.
JUST MOVE IT, HUH? I'VE GOT A DATE TONIGHT.
RRY CHRISTMAS
WHO'S THE UNLUCKY CHICK?
NO ANSWE HUH?
WELL, THERE'S THE G.W. BRIDGE... BIG AS LIFE AND TWICE AS CROWDED.
NO SANDMAN BUT THAT'S JUST THE FIRS PART OF MY HUNCH, ANYWAY
TRY CRUISIN' OVER TO THE JERSEY SIDE FOR A MINUTE, OKAY?

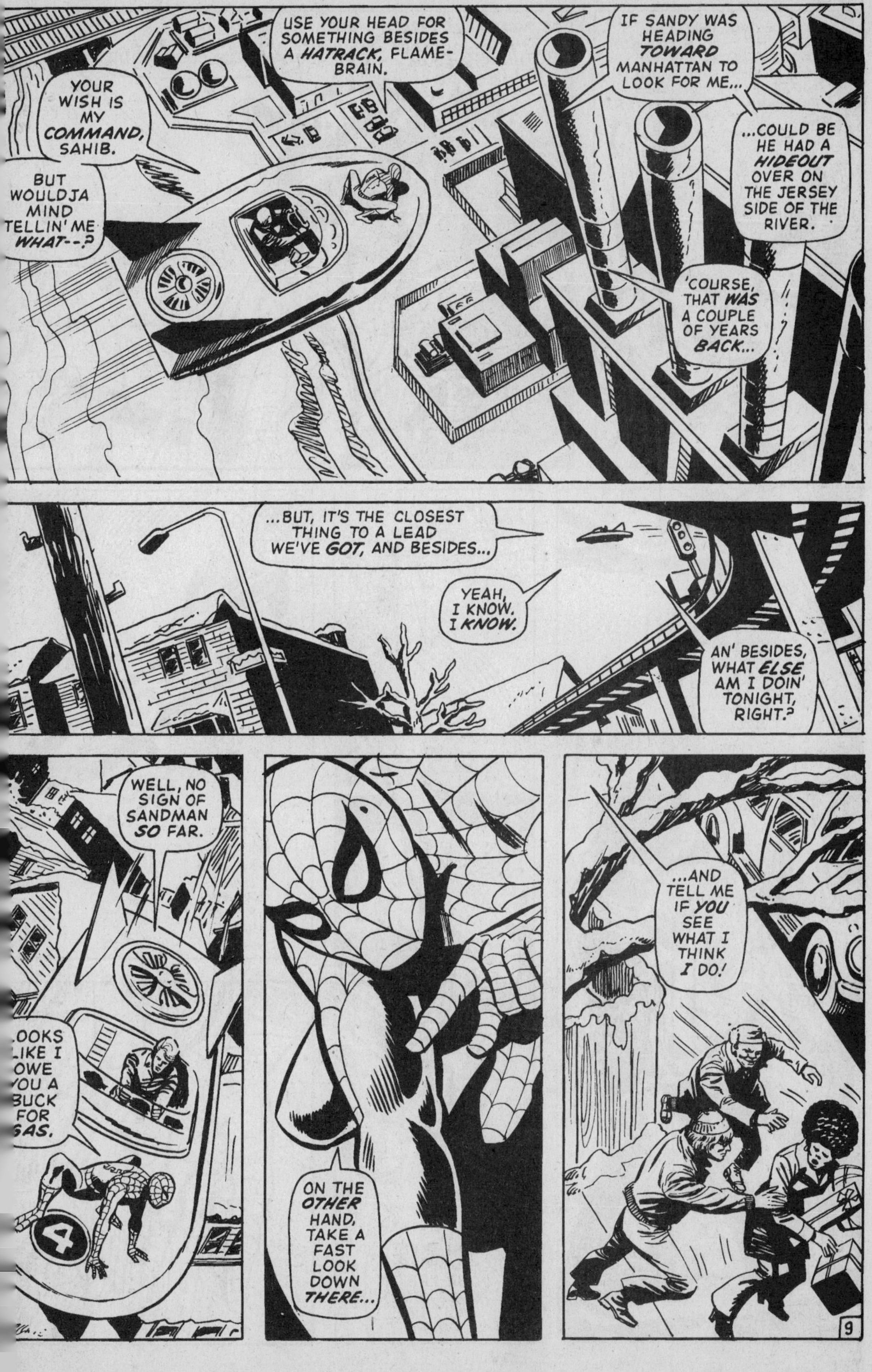
USE YOUR HEAD FOR SOMETHING BESIDES A HATRACK, FLAME-BRAIN.
YOUR WISH IS MY COMMAND, SAHIB.
BUT WOULDJA MIND TELLIN' ME WHAT--?
IF SANDY WAS HEADING TOWARD MANHATTAN TO LOOK FOR ME...
...COULD BE HE HAD A HIDEOUT OVER ON THE JERSEY SIDE OF THE RIVER.
'COURSE, THAT WAS A COUPLE OF YEARS BACK...
...BUT, IT'S THE CLOSEST THING TO A LEAD WE'VE GOT, AND BESIDES...
YEAH, I KNOW. I KNOW.
AN' BESIDES, WHAT ELSE AM I DOIN' TONIGHT, RIGHT?
WELL, NO SIGN OF SANDMAN SO FAR.
LOOKS LIKE I OWE YOU A BUCK FOR GAS.
ON THE OTHER HAND, TAKE A FAST LOOK DOWN THERE...
...AND TELL ME IF YOU SEE WHAT I THINK I DO!
9

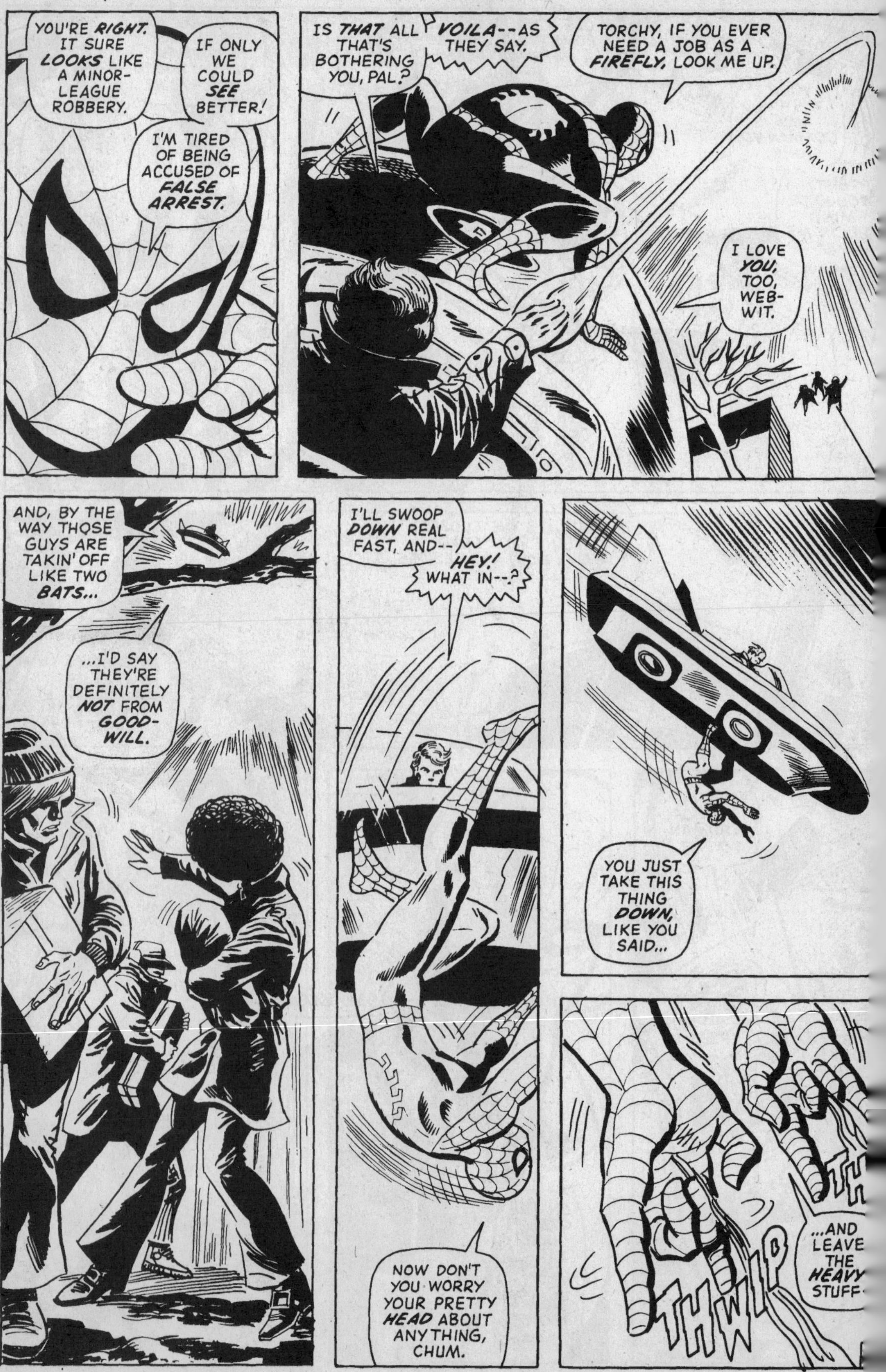

YOU'RE RIGHT. IT SURE LOOKS LIKE A MINOR-LEAGUE ROBBERY.
IF ONLY WE COULD SEE BETTER!
I'M TIRED OF BEING ACCUSED OF FALSE ARREST.
IS THAT ALL THAT'S BOTHERING YOU, PAL?
VOILA--AS THEY SAY.
TORCHY, IF YOU EVER NEED A JOB AS A FIREFLY, LOOK ME UP.
I LOVE YOU, TOO, WEB-WIT.
AND, BY THE WAY THOSE GUYS ARE TAKIN' OFF LIKE TWO BATS...
...I'D SAY THEY'RE DEFINITELY NOT FROM GOOD-WILL.
I'LL SWOOP DOWN REAL FAST, AND--
HEY! WHAT IN--?
NOW DON'T YOU WORRY YOUR PRETTY HEAD ABOUT ANYTHING, CHUM.
YOU JUST TAKE THIS THING DOWN, LIKE YOU SAID...
THWIP
...AND LEAVE THE HEAVY STUFF

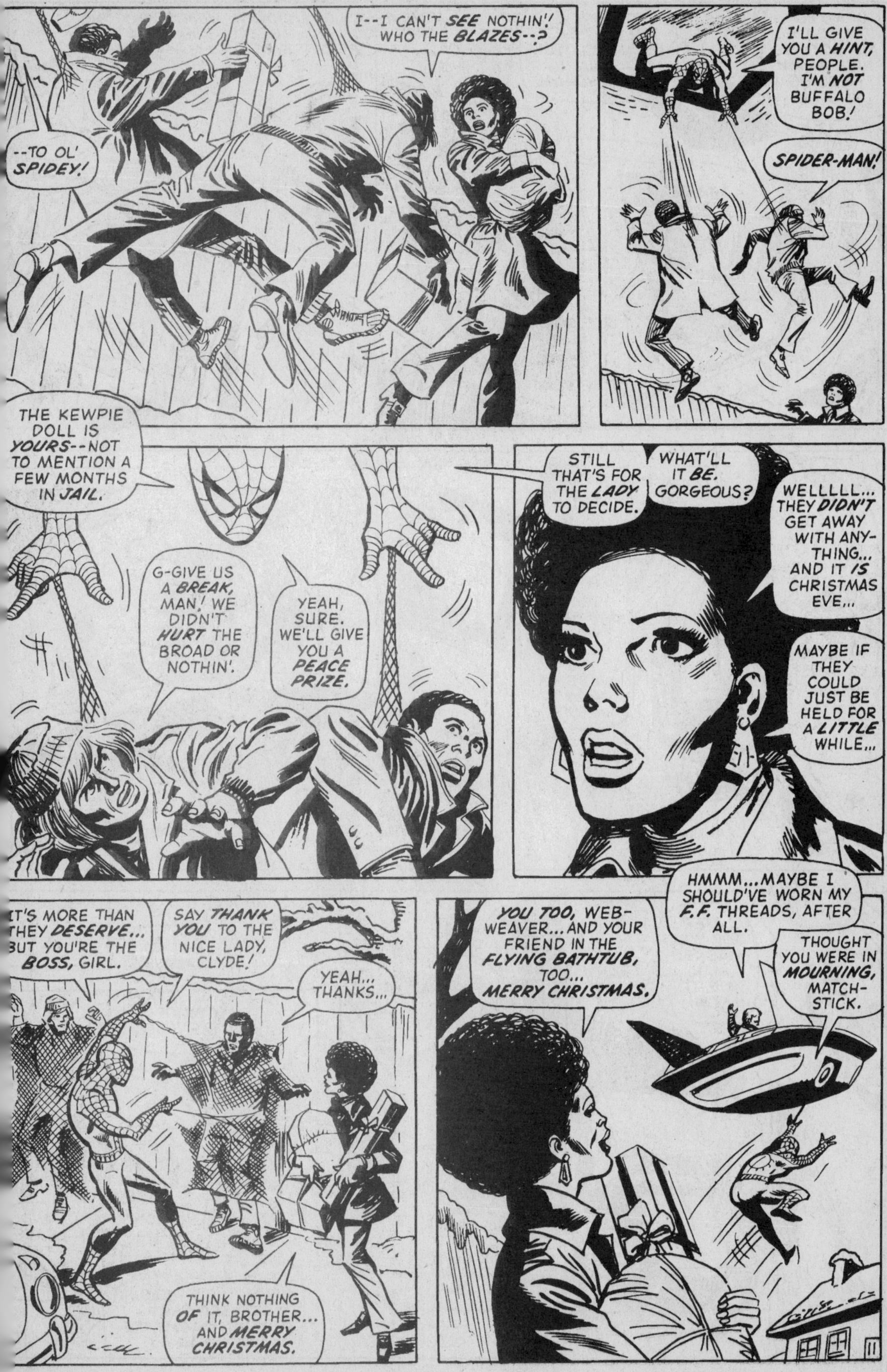
--TO OL' SPIDEY!
I--I CAN'T SEE NOTHIN'! WHO THE BLAZES--?
I'LL GIVE YOU A HINT, PEOPLE. I'M NOT BUFFALO BOB!
SPIDER-MAN!
THE KEWPIE DOLL IS YOURS--NOT TO MENTION A FEW MONTHS IN JAIL.
G-GIVE US A BREAK, MAN! WE DIDN'T HURT THE BROAD OR NOTHIN'.
YEAH, SURE. WE'LL GIVE YOU A PEACE PRIZE.
STILL THAT'S FOR THE LADY TO DECIDE.
WHAT'LL IT BE, GORGEOUS?
WELLLLL... THEY DIDN'T GET AWAY WITH ANY-THING... AND IT IS CHRISTMAS EVE...
MAYBE IF THEY COULD JUST BE HELD FOR A LITTLE WHILE...
IT'S MORE THAN THEY DESERVE... BUT YOU'RE THE BOSS, GIRL.
SAY THANK YOU TO THE NICE LADY, CLYDE!
YEAH... THANKS...
THINK NOTHING OF IT, BROTHER... AND MERRY CHRISTMAS.
YOU TOO, WEB-WEAVER... AND YOUR FRIEND IN THE FLYING BATHTUB, TOO... MERRY CHRISTMAS.
HMMM... MAYBE I SHOULD'VE WORN MY F.F. THREADS, AFTER ALL.
THOUGHT YOU WERE IN MOURNING, MATCH-STICK.
11

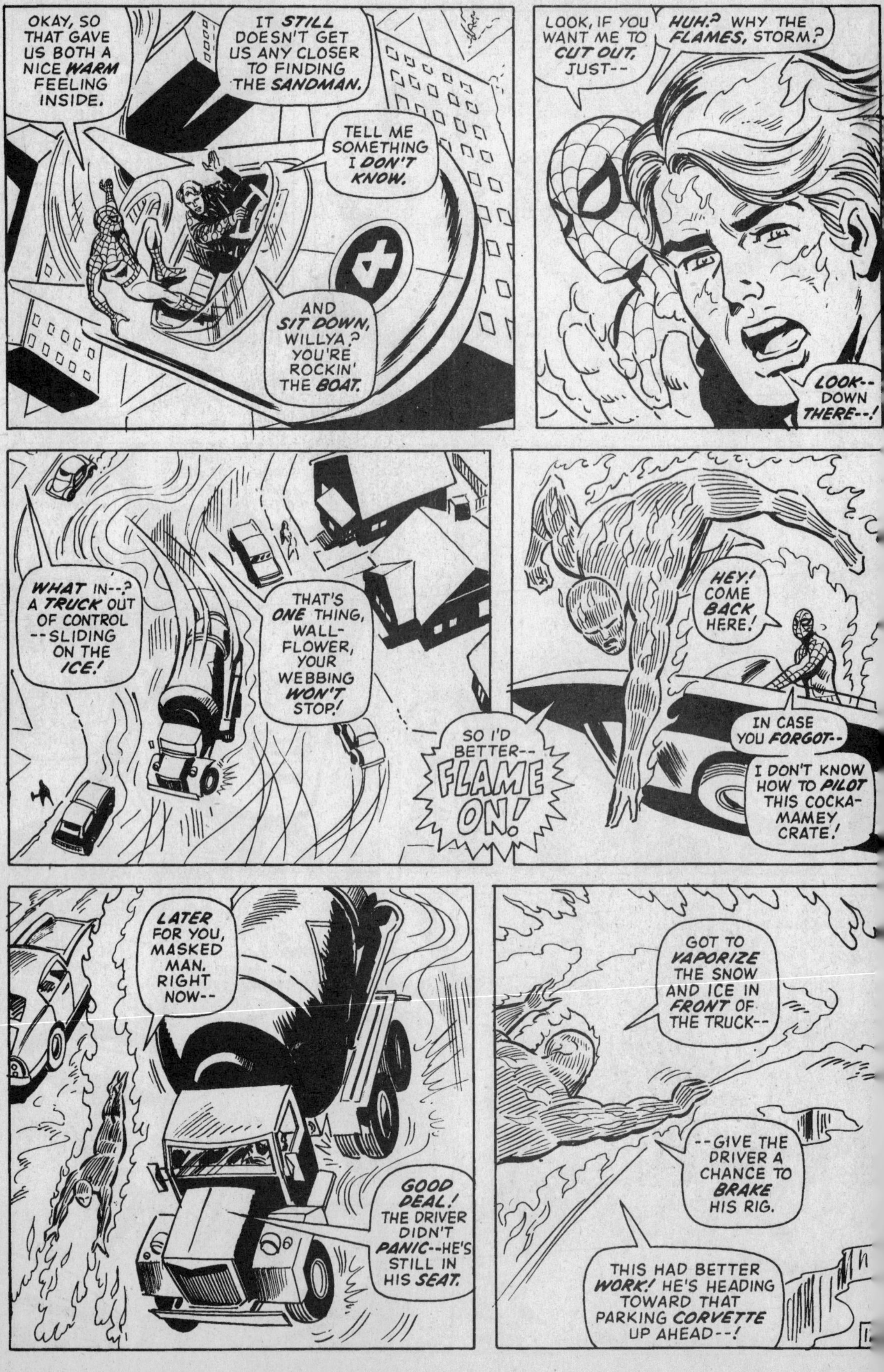

OKAY, SO THAT GAVE US BOTH A NICE WARM FEELING INSIDE.
IT STILL DOESN'T GET US ANY CLOSER TO FINDING THE SANDMAN.
TELL ME SOMETHING I DON'T KNOW.
AND SIT DOWN, WILLYA? YOU'RE ROCKIN' THE BOAT.
LOOK, IF YOU WANT ME TO CUT OUT, JUST--
HUH? WHY THE FLAMES, STORM?
LOOK--DOWN THERE--!
WHAT IN--? A TRUCK OUT OF CONTROL --SLIDING ON THE ICE!
THAT'S ONE THING, WALL-FLOWER, YOUR WEBBING WON'T STOP!
SO I'D BETTER--
FLAME ON!
HEY! COME BACK HERE!
IN CASE YOU FORGOT--
I DON'T KNOW HOW TO PILOT THIS COCKA-MAMEY CRATE!
LATER FOR YOU, MASKED MAN. RIGHT NOW--
GOOD DEAL! THE DRIVER DIDN'T PANIC--HE'S STILL IN HIS SEAT.
GOT TO VAPORIZE THE SNOW AND ICE IN FRONT OF THE TRUCK--
--GIVE THE DRIVER A CHANCE TO BRAKE HIS RIG.
THIS HAD BETTER WORK! HE'S HEADING TOWARD THAT PARKING CORVETTE UP AHEAD--!

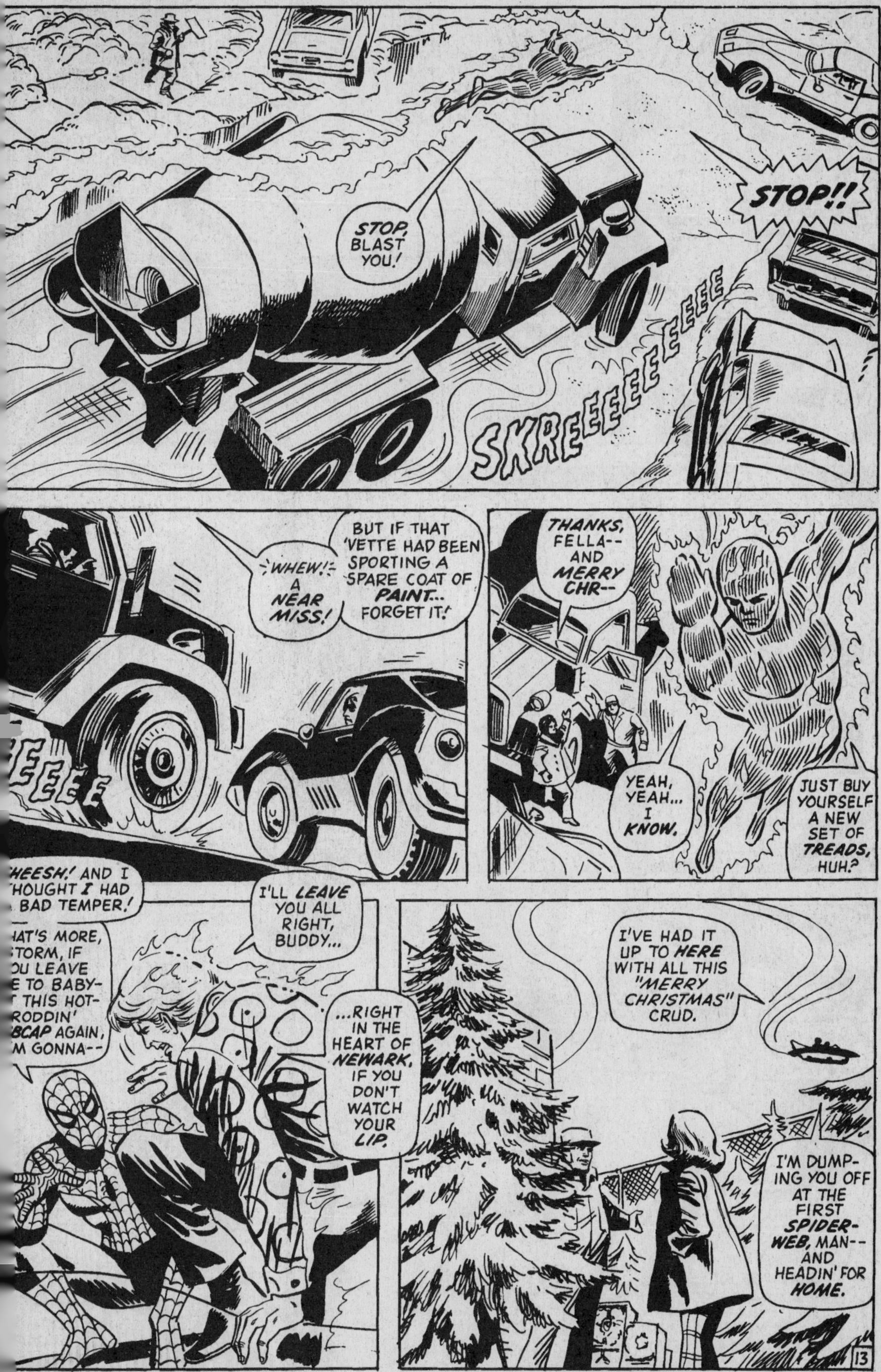
STOP, BLAST YOU!
STOP!!
SKREEEEEEEEEE
WHEW! A NEAR MISS!
BUT IF THAT 'VETTE HAD BEEN SPORTING A SPARE COAT OF PAINT... FORGET IT!
EEEEE
THANKS, FELLA-- AND MERRY CHR--
YEAH, YEAH... I KNOW.
JUST BUY YOURSELF A NEW SET OF TREADS, HUH?
HEESH! AND I THOUGHT I HAD BAD TEMPER!
HAT'S MORE, STORM, IF OU LEAVE E TO BABY- T THIS HOT- RODDIN' BCAP AGAIN, M GONNA--
I'LL LEAVE YOU ALL RIGHT, BUDDY...
...RIGHT IN THE HEART OF NEWARK, IF YOU DON'T WATCH YOUR LIP.
I'VE HAD IT UP TO HERE WITH ALL THIS "MERRY CHRISTMAS" CRUD.
I'M DUMPING YOU OFF AT THE FIRST SPIDER-WEB, MAN-- AND HEADIN' FOR HOME.
13

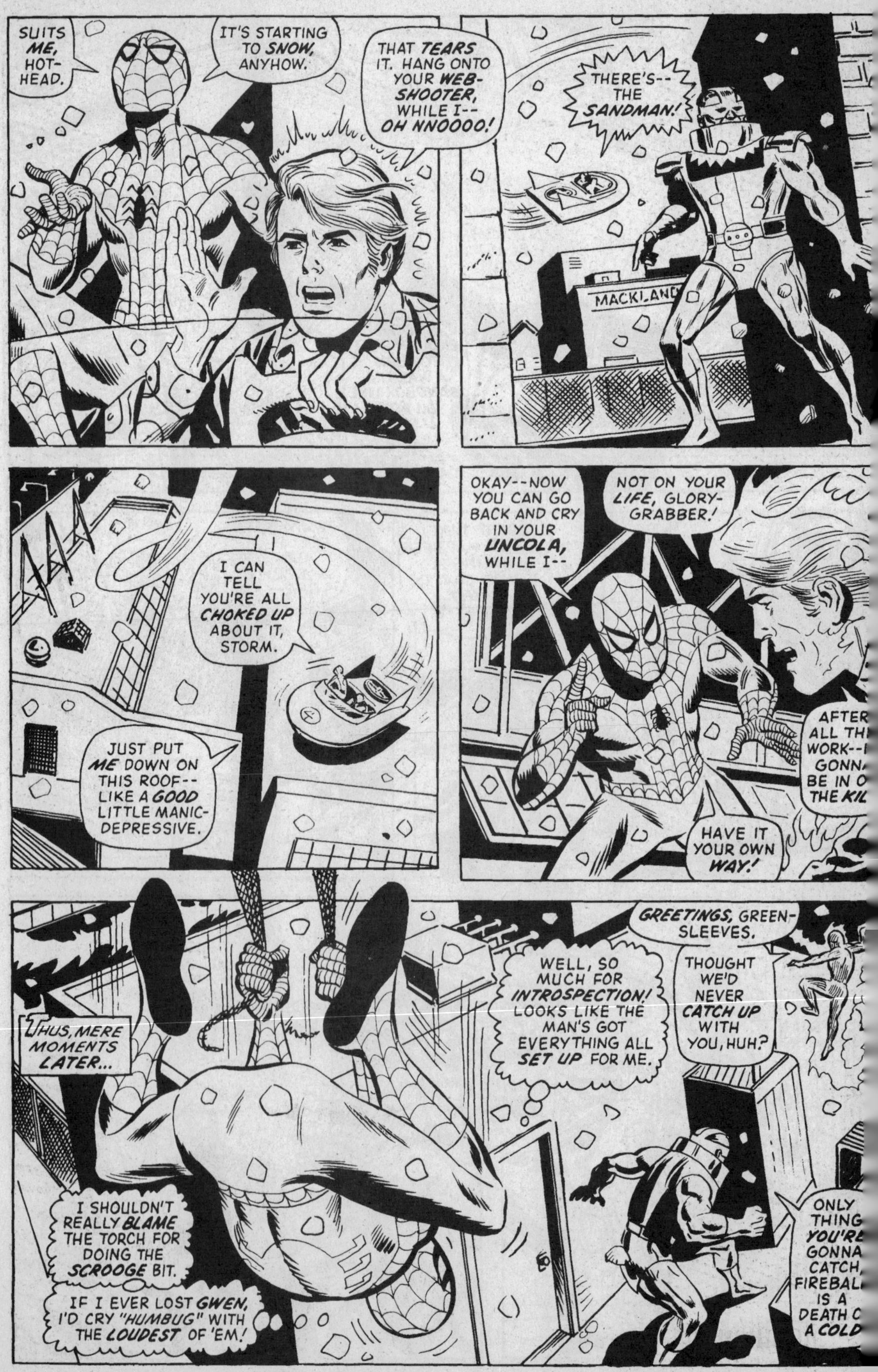

SUITS ME, HOT-HEAD.
IT'S STARTING TO SNOW, ANYHOW.
THAT TEARS IT. HANG ONTO YOUR WEB-SHOOTER, WHILE I-- OH NNOOOO!
THERE'S-- THE SANDMAN!
MACKLAND
I CAN TELL YOU'RE ALL CHOKED UP ABOUT IT, STORM.
JUST PUT ME DOWN ON THIS ROOF-- LIKE A GOOD LITTLE MANIC-DEPRESSIVE.
OKAY--NOW YOU CAN GO BACK AND CRY IN YOUR UNCOLA, WHILE I--
NOT ON YOUR LIFE, GLORY-GRABBER!
HAVE IT YOUR OWN WAY!
THUS, MERE MOMENTS LATER...
I SHOULDN'T REALLY BLAME THE TORCH FOR DOING THE SCROOGE BIT.
IF I EVER LOST GWEN, I'D CRY "HUMBUG" WITH THE LOUDEST OF 'EM!
WELL, SO MUCH FOR INTROSPECTION! LOOKS LIKE THE MAN'S GOT EVERYTHING ALL SET UP FOR ME.
GREETINGS, GREEN-SLEEVES.
THOUGHT WE'D NEVER CATCH UP WITH YOU, HUH?

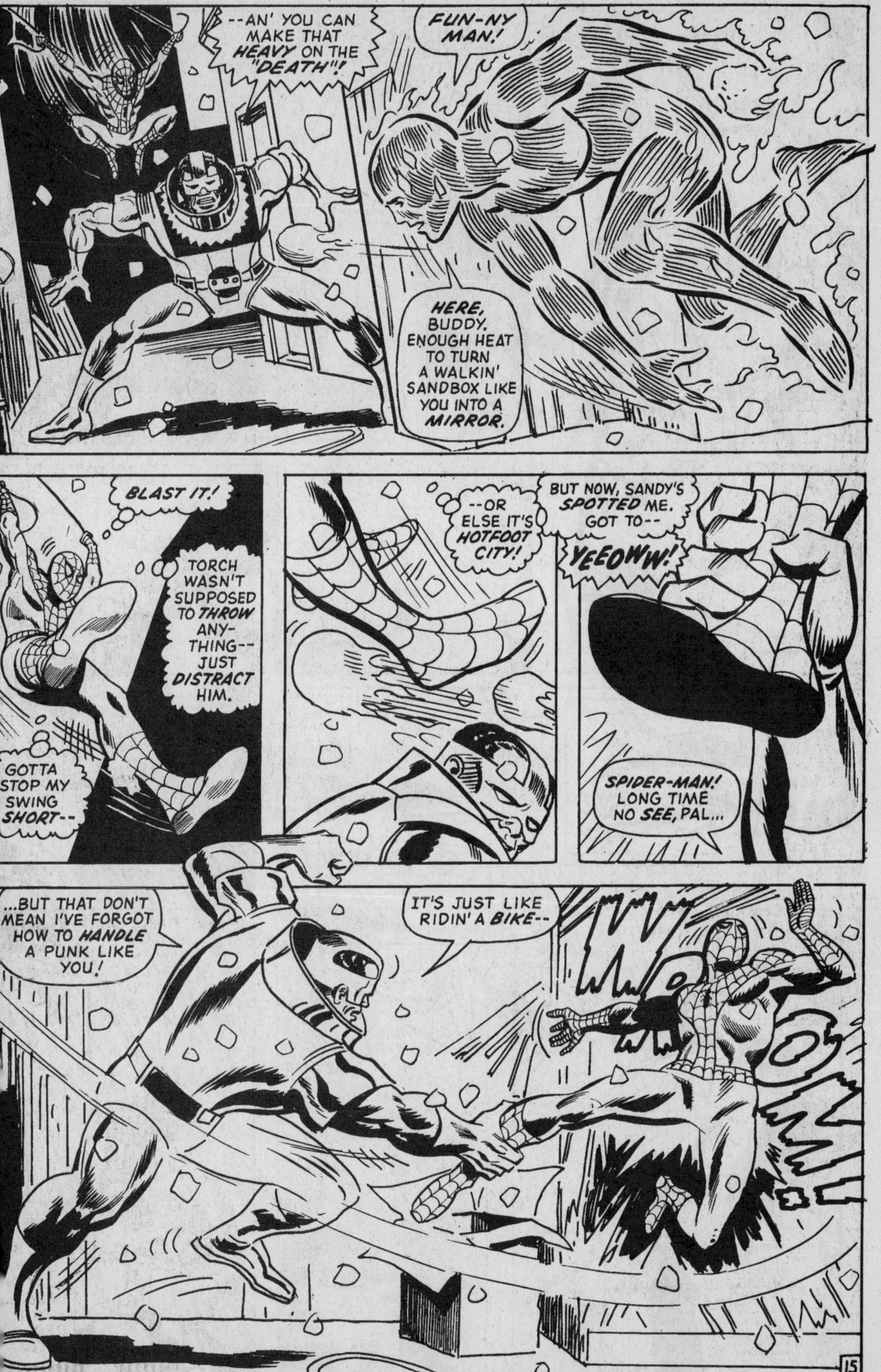

--AN' YOU CAN MAKE THAT HEAVY ON THE "DEATH"!
FUN-NY MAN!
HERE, BUDDY. ENOUGH HEAT TO TURN A WALKIN' SANDBOX LIKE YOU INTO A MIRROR.
BLAST IT!
TORCH WASN'T SUPPOSED TO THROW ANY-THING--JUST DISTRACT HIM.
GOTTA STOP MY SWING SHORT--
--OR ELSE IT'S HOTFOOT CITY!
BUT NOW, SANDY'S SPOTTED ME. GOT TO--
YEEOWW!
SPIDER-MAN! LONG TIME NO SEE, PAL...
...BUT THAT DON'T MEAN I'VE FORGOT HOW TO HANDLE A PUNK LIKE YOU!
IT'S JUST LIKE RIDIN' A BIKE--

...IT *DOES* COME BACK TO YA!

AND *THIS,* CLAYFACE, IS GONNA COME BACK TO *YOU...*

FLORIDA NOW!

...LIKE, RIGHT ON YOUR SANDY *LOCKS!*

RIGHT NOW!

NO! NOT WHEN I'M *THIS* CLOSE...

NUTHIN'S GONNA STOP ME NOW...

NOT SINCE THE *WIZARD* HELPED ME RIG UP THESE LITTLE *BUTTONS...*

KRAASH

...WHICH TURN ME *HARD* FASTER'N YOU CAN SAY *CEMENT BLOCK!*

NOT THE SO-CALLED *AMAZIN'* SPIDER-MAN...

...AN' *CERTAINLY* NOT THE HALF-BAKED *HUMAN TORCH!*

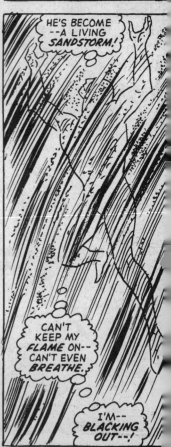

HE'S BECOME --A LIVING *SANDSTORM!*

CAN'T KEEP MY *FLAME* ON-- CAN'T EVEN *BREATHE.*

I'M-- *BLACKING OUT--!*

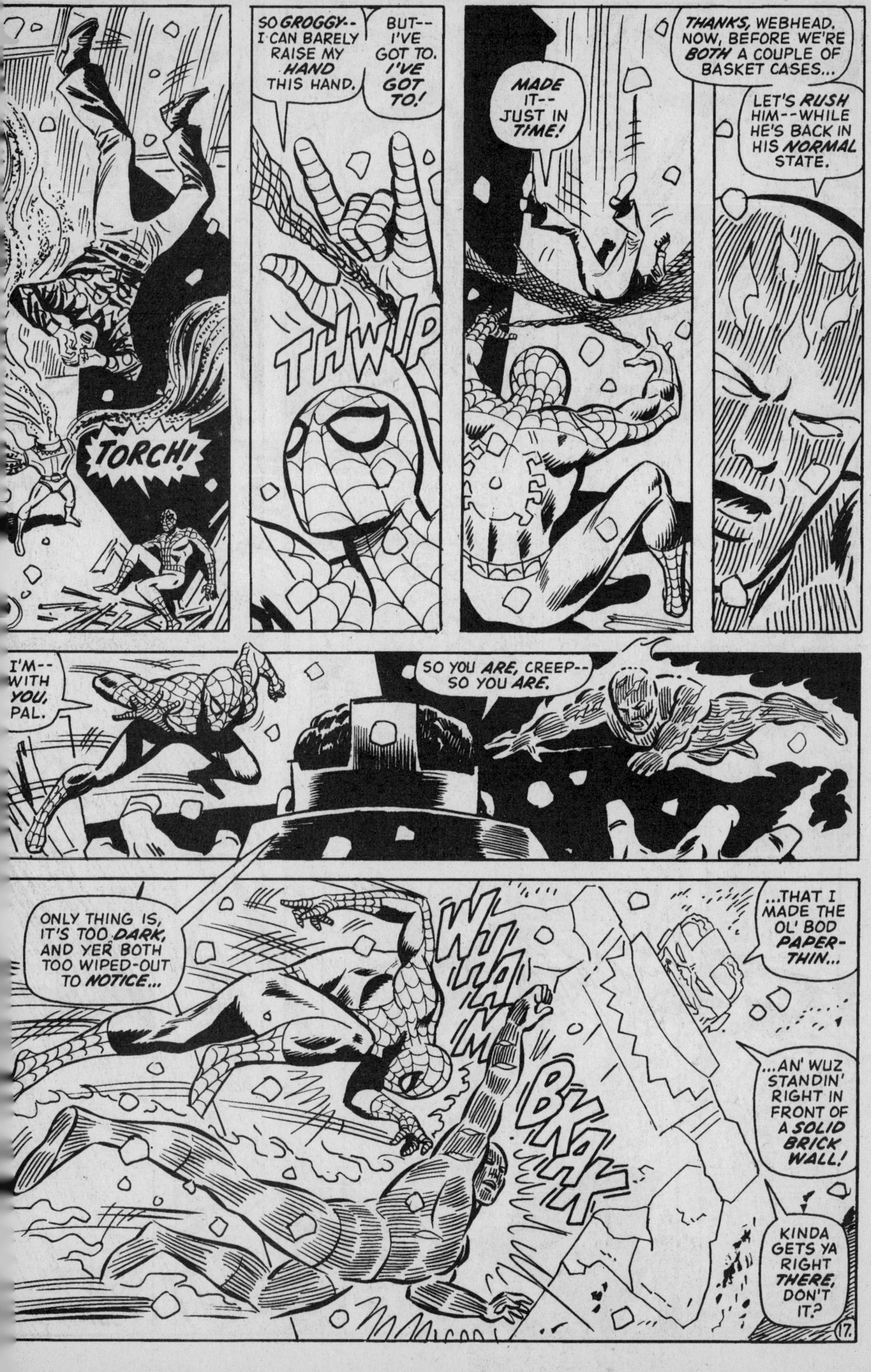
TORCH!
SO GROGGY-- I CAN BARELY RAISE MY HAND THIS HAND.
BUT-- I'VE GOT TO. I'VE GOT TO!
THWIP
MADE IT-- JUST IN TIME!
THANKS, WEBHEAD. NOW, BEFORE WE'RE BOTH A COUPLE OF BASKET CASES...
LET'S RUSH HIM--WHILE HE'S BACK IN HIS NORMAL STATE.
I'M-- WITH YOU, PAL.
SO YOU ARE, CREEP-- SO YOU ARE.
ONLY THING IS, IT'S TOO DARK, AND YER BOTH TOO WIPED-OUT TO NOTICE...
...THAT I MADE THE OL' BOD PAPER-THIN...
WHAMM
BKAK
...AN' WUZ STANDIN' RIGHT IN FRONT OF A SOLID BRICK WALL!
KINDA GETS YA RIGHT THERE, DON'T IT?
17

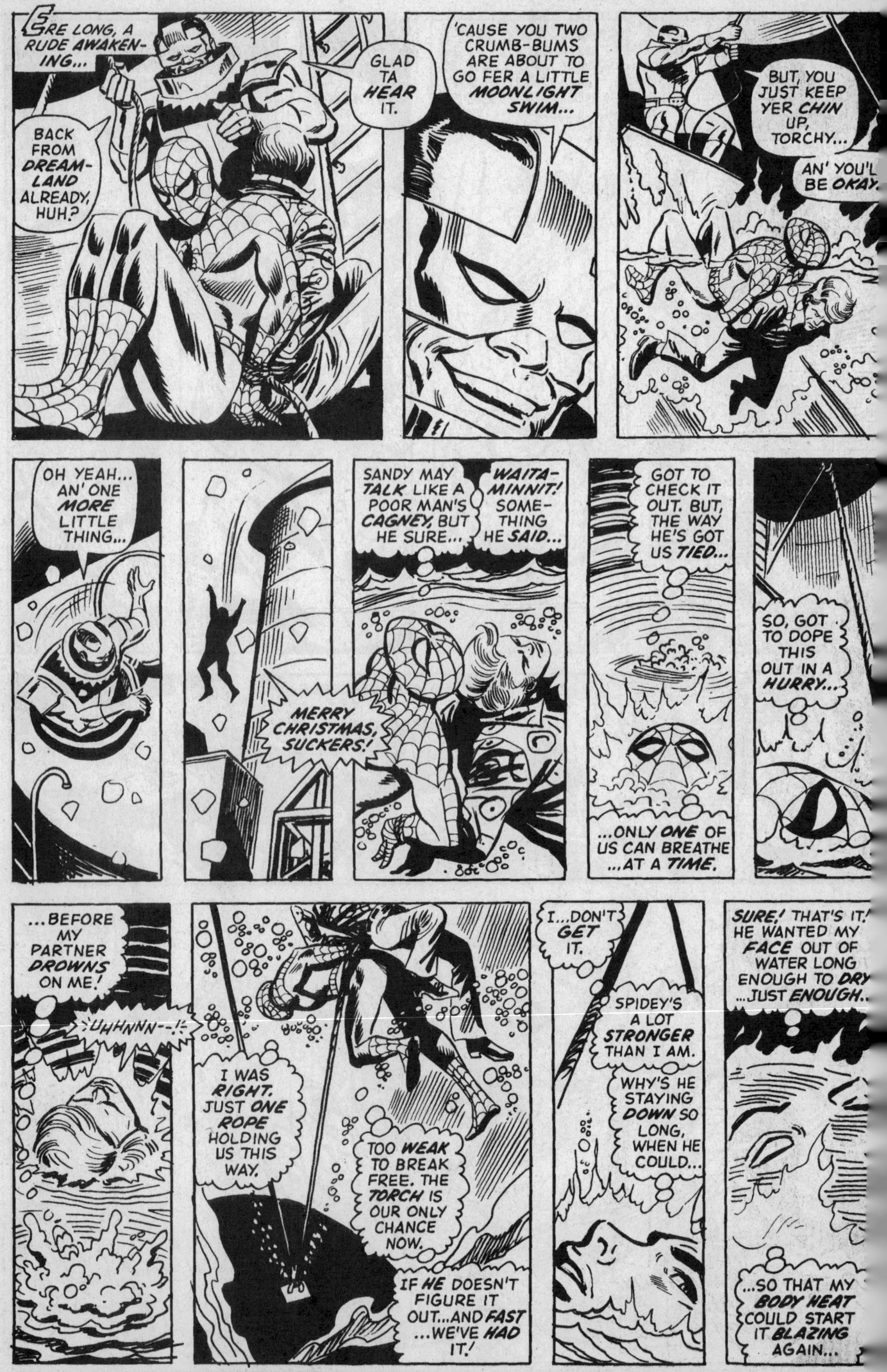
ERE LONG, A RUDE AWAKENING...
BACK FROM DREAMLAND ALREADY, HUH?
GLAD TA HEAR IT.
'CAUSE YOU TWO CRUMB-BUMS ARE ABOUT TO GO FER A LITTLE MOONLIGHT SWIM...
BUT, YOU JUST KEEP YER CHIN UP, TORCHY...
AN' YOU'LL BE OKAY.
OH YEAH... AN' ONE MORE LITTLE THING...
MERRY CHRISTMAS, SUCKERS!
SANDY MAY TALK LIKE A POOR MAN'S CAGNEY, BUT HE SURE...
WAITA-MINNIT! SOME-THING HE SAID...
GOT TO CHECK IT OUT. BUT, THE WAY HE'S GOT US TIED...
...ONLY ONE OF US CAN BREATHE ...AT A TIME.
SO, GOT TO DOPE THIS OUT IN A HURRY...
...BEFORE MY PARTNER DROWNS ON ME!
UHHNNN--!
I WAS RIGHT. JUST ONE ROPE HOLDING US THIS WAY.
TOO WEAK TO BREAK FREE. THE TORCH IS OUR ONLY CHANCE NOW.
IF HE DOESN'T FIGURE IT OUT...AND FAST ...WE'VE HAD IT!
I...DON'T GET IT.
SPIDEY'S A LOT STRONGER THAN I AM.
WHY'S HE STAYING DOWN SO LONG, WHEN HE COULD...
SURE! THAT'S IT! HE WANTED MY FACE OUT OF WATER LONG ENOUGH TO DRY ...JUST ENOUGH...
...SO THAT MY BODY HEAT COULD START IT BLAZING AGAIN...

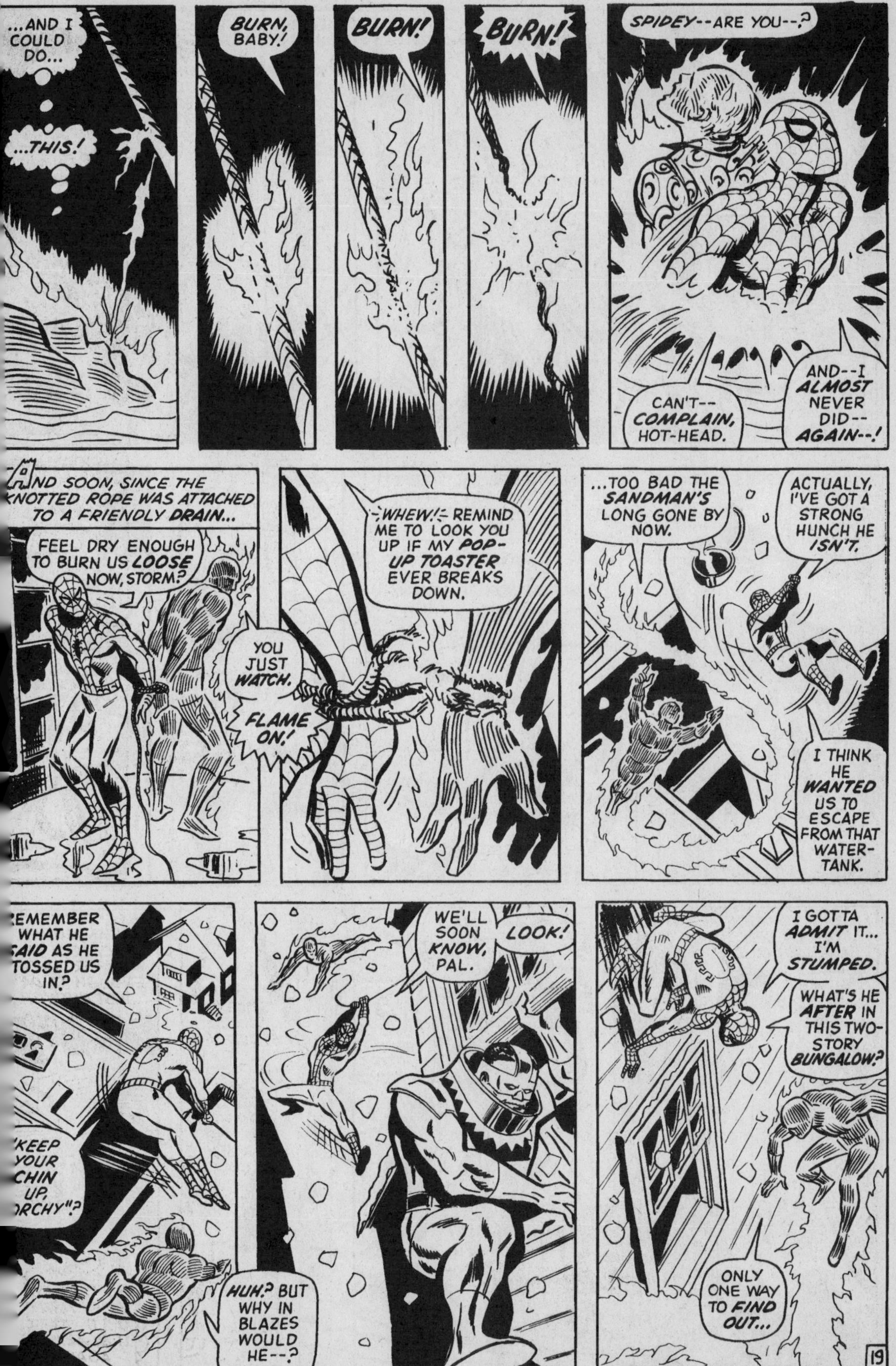
...AND I COULD DO...
...THIS!
BURN, BABY!
BURN!
BURN!
SPIDEY--ARE YOU--?
CAN'T-- COMPLAIN, HOT-HEAD.
AND--I ALMOST NEVER DID-- AGAIN--!
AND SOON, SINCE THE KNOTTED ROPE WAS ATTACHED TO A FRIENDLY DRAIN...
FEEL DRY ENOUGH TO BURN US LOOSE NOW, STORM?
YOU JUST WATCH.
FLAME ON!
WHEW! REMIND ME TO LOOK YOU UP IF MY POP-UP TOASTER EVER BREAKS DOWN.
...TOO BAD THE SANDMAN'S LONG GONE BY NOW.
ACTUALLY, I'VE GOT A STRONG HUNCH HE ISN'T.
I THINK HE WANTED US TO ESCAPE FROM THAT WATER-TANK.
REMEMBER WHAT HE SAID AS HE TOSSED US IN?
"KEEP YOUR CHIN UP, TORCHY"?
HUH? BUT WHY IN BLAZES WOULD HE--?
WE'LL SOON KNOW, PAL.
LOOK!
I GOTTA ADMIT IT... I'M STUMPED.
WHAT'S HE AFTER IN THIS TWO-STORY BUNGALOW?
ONLY ONE WAY TO FIND OUT...
19

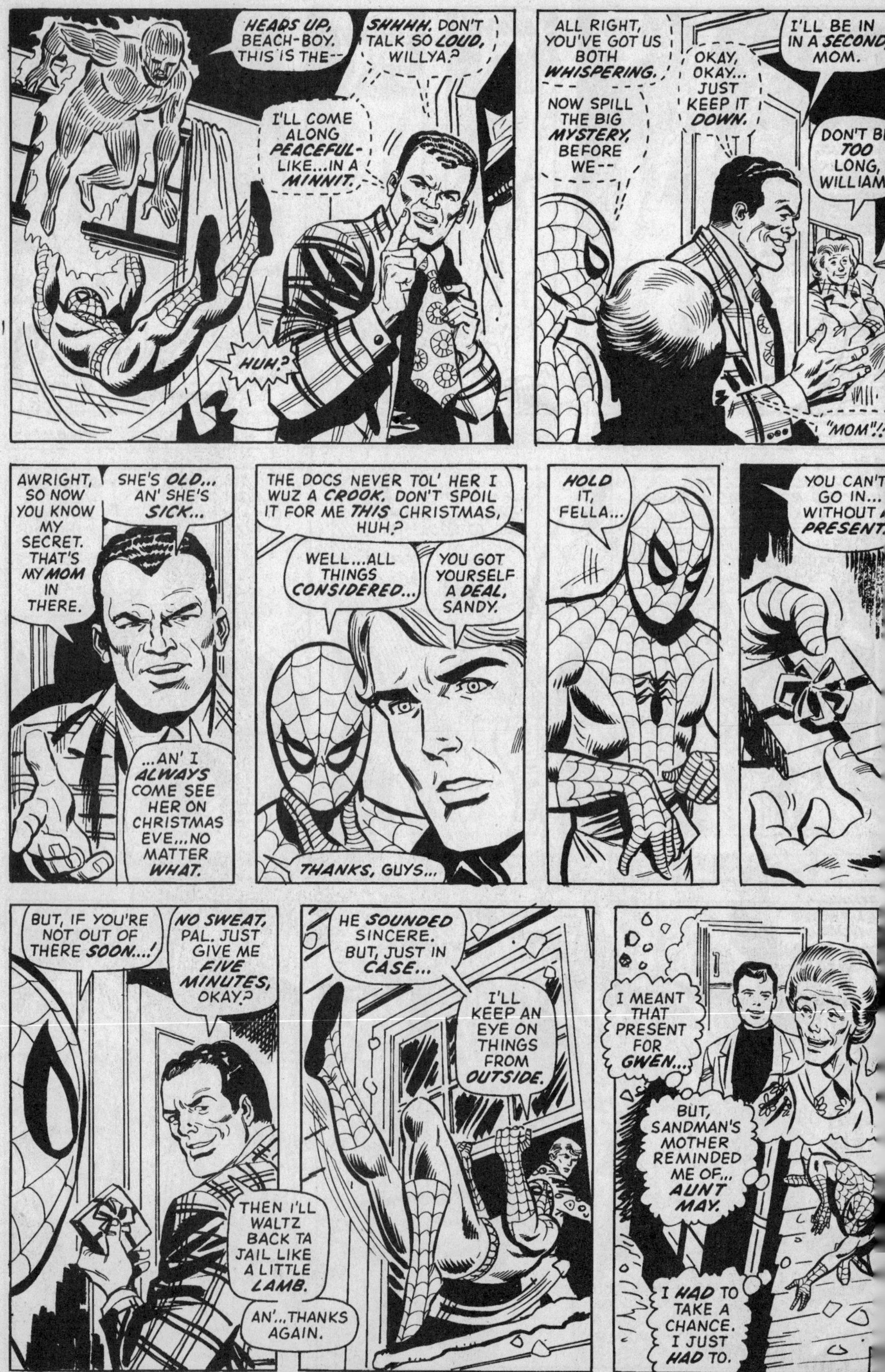

HEADS UP, BEACH-BOY. THIS IS THE--
SHHHH. DON'T TALK SO LOUD, WILLYA?
I'LL COME ALONG PEACEFUL-LIKE...IN A MINNIT.
HUH?
ALL RIGHT, YOU'VE GOT US BOTH WHISPERING.
NOW SPILL THE BIG MYSTERY, BEFORE WE--
OKAY, OKAY... JUST KEEP IT DOWN.
I'LL BE IN IN A SECOND, MOM.
DON'T BE TOO LONG, WILLIAM.
"MOM"!?
AWRIGHT, SO NOW YOU KNOW MY SECRET. THAT'S MY MOM IN THERE.
SHE'S OLD... AN' SHE'S SICK...
...AN' I ALWAYS COME SEE HER ON CHRISTMAS EVE...NO MATTER WHAT.
THE DOCS NEVER TOL' HER I WUZ A CROOK. DON'T SPOIL IT FOR ME THIS CHRISTMAS, HUH?
WELL...ALL THINGS CONSIDERED...
YOU GOT YOURSELF A DEAL, SANDY.
THANKS, GUYS...
HOLD IT, FELLA...
YOU CAN'T GO IN... WITHOUT A PRESENT.
BUT, IF YOU'RE NOT OUT OF THERE SOON...!
NO SWEAT, PAL. JUST GIVE ME FIVE MINUTES, OKAY?
THEN I'LL WALTZ BACK TA JAIL LIKE A LITTLE LAMB.
AN'...THANKS AGAIN.
HE SOUNDED SINCERE. BUT, JUST IN CASE...
I'LL KEEP AN EYE ON THINGS FROM OUTSIDE.
I MEANT THAT PRESENT FOR GWEN...
BUT, SANDMAN'S MOTHER REMINDED ME OF... AUNT MAY.
I HAD TO TAKE A CHANCE. I JUST HAD TO.

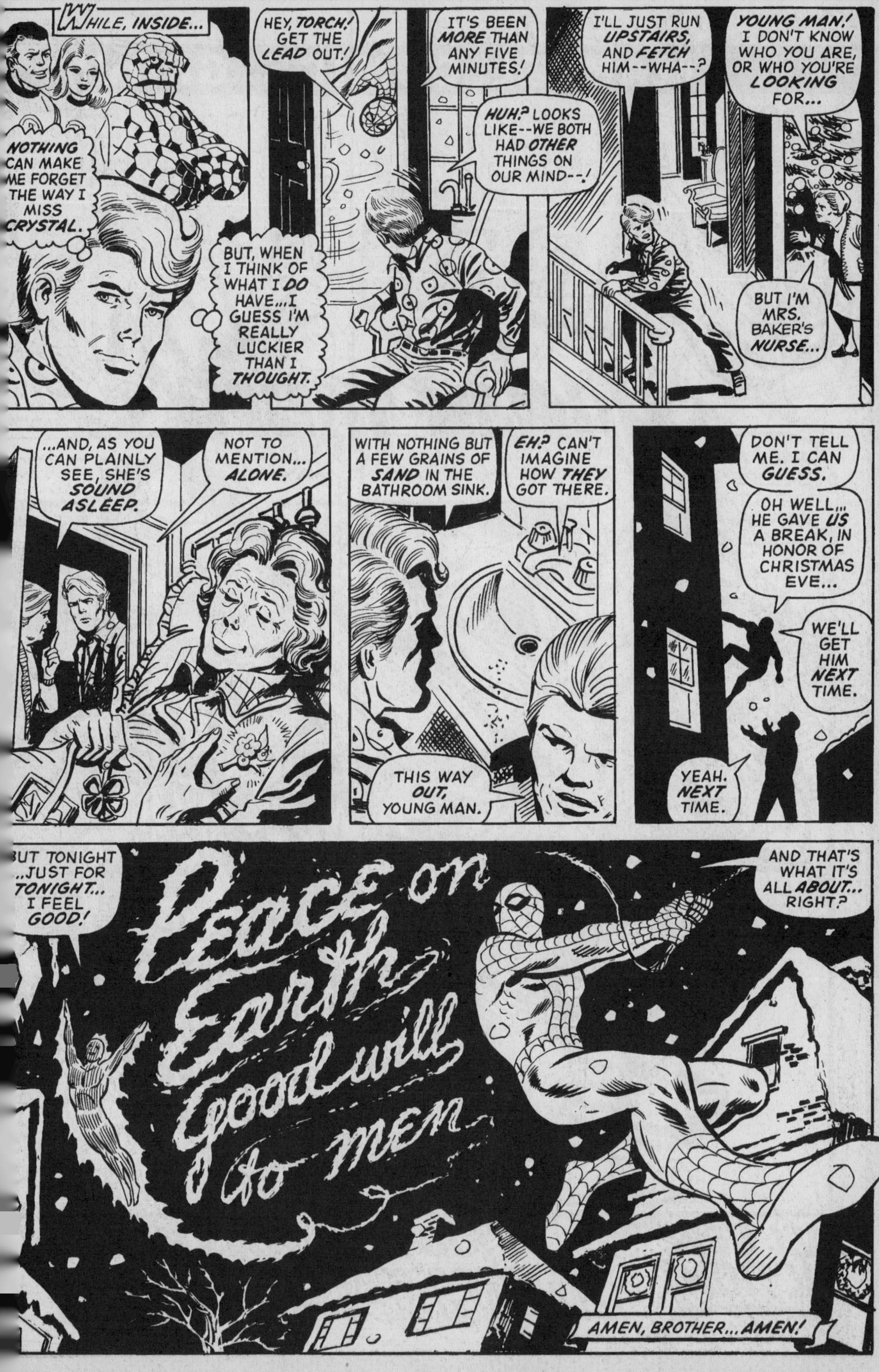

WHILE, INSIDE...
NOTHING CAN MAKE ME FORGET THE WAY I MISS CRYSTAL.
BUT, WHEN I THINK OF WHAT I DO HAVE... I GUESS I'M REALLY LUCKIER THAN I THOUGHT.
HEY, TORCH! GET THE LEAD OUT!
IT'S BEEN MORE THAN ANY FIVE MINUTES!
HUH? LOOKS LIKE--WE BOTH HAD OTHER THINGS ON OUR MIND--!
I'LL JUST RUN UPSTAIRS, AND FETCH HIM--WHA--?
YOUNG MAN! I DON'T KNOW WHO YOU ARE, OR WHO YOU'RE LOOKING FOR...
BUT I'M MRS. BAKER'S NURSE...
...AND, AS YOU CAN PLAINLY SEE, SHE'S SOUND ASLEEP.
NOT TO MENTION... ALONE.
WITH NOTHING BUT A FEW GRAINS OF SAND IN THE BATHROOM SINK.
EH? CAN'T IMAGINE HOW THEY GOT THERE.
THIS WAY OUT, YOUNG MAN.
DON'T TELL ME. I CAN GUESS.
OH WELL... HE GAVE US A BREAK, IN HONOR OF CHRISTMAS EVE...
WE'LL GET HIM NEXT TIME.
YEAH. NEXT TIME.
BUT TONIGHT ...JUST FOR TONIGHT... I FEEL GOOD!
Peace on Earth Good will to men
AND THAT'S WHAT IT'S ALL ABOUT... RIGHT?
AMEN, BROTHER... AMEN!

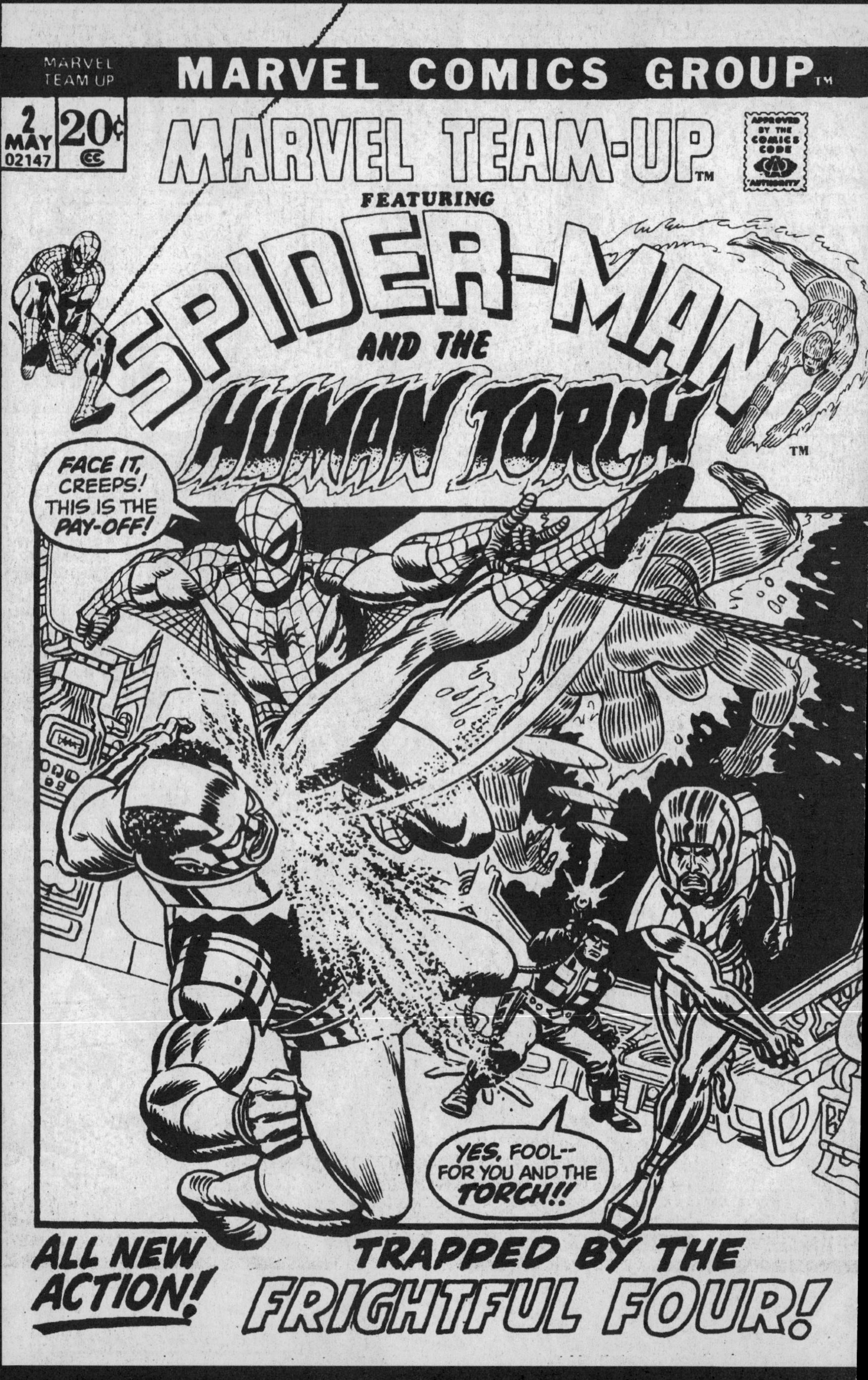

MARVEL TEAM UP
MARVEL COMICS GROUP™
2 MAY 02147
20¢ CC
APPROVED BY THE COMICS CODE AUTHORITY
MARVEL TEAM-UP™
FEATURING
SPIDER-MAN AND THE HUMAN TORCH™
FACE IT, CREEPS! THIS IS THE PAY-OFF!
YES, FOOL-- FOR YOU AND THE TORCH!!
ALL NEW ACTION!
TRAPPED BY THE FRIGHTFUL FOUR!

SPIDEY AND THE TORCH--TOGETHER!™

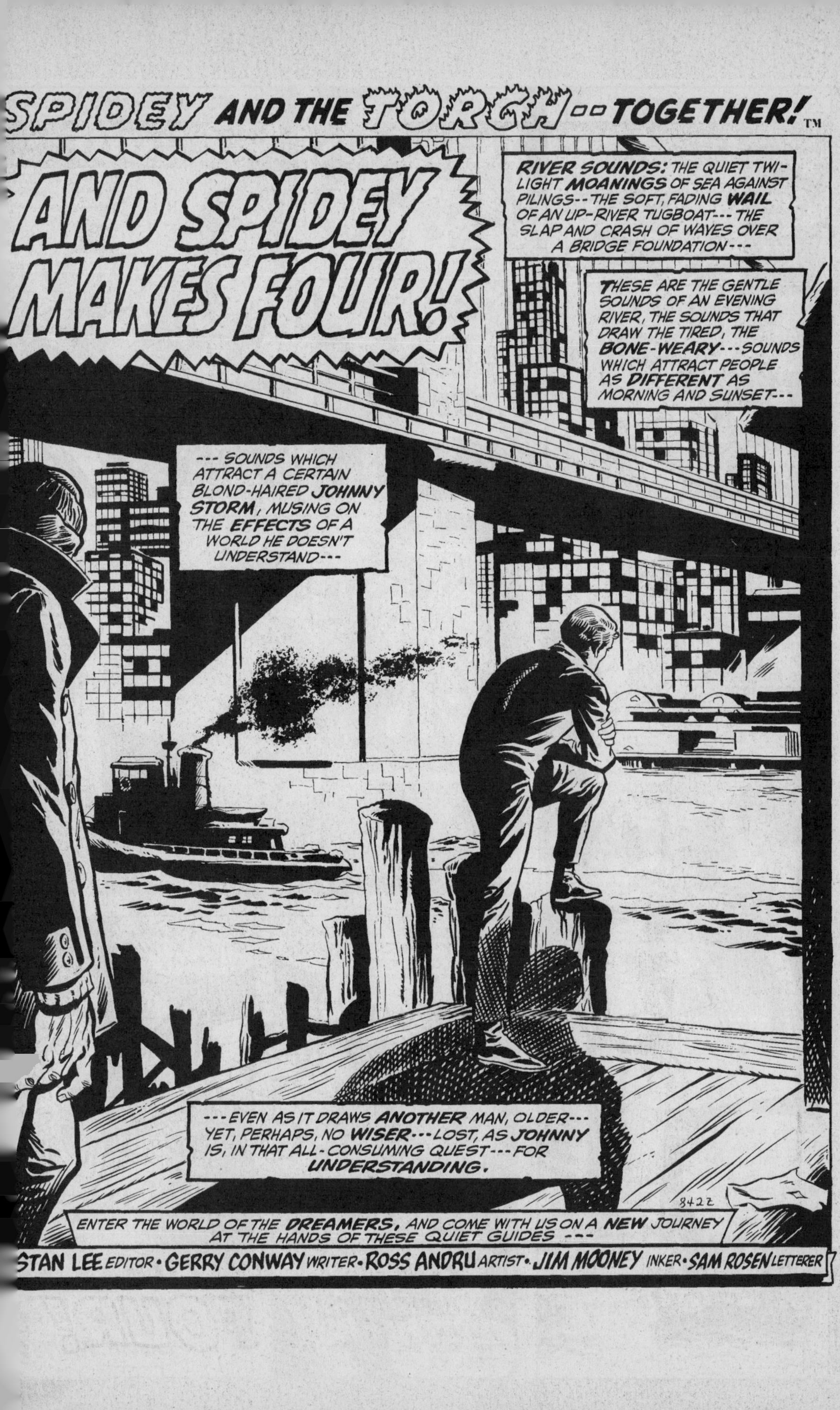
AND SPIDEY MAKES FOUR!
RIVER SOUNDS: THE QUIET TWILIGHT MOANINGS OF SEA AGAINST PILINGS--THE SOFT, FADING WAIL OF AN UP-RIVER TUGBOAT---THE SLAP AND CRASH OF WAVES OVER A BRIDGE FOUNDATION---
THESE ARE THE GENTLE SOUNDS OF AN EVENING RIVER, THE SOUNDS THAT DRAW THE TIRED, THE BONE-WEARY---SOUNDS WHICH ATTRACT PEOPLE AS DIFFERENT AS MORNING AND SUNSET---
---SOUNDS WHICH ATTRACT A CERTAIN BLOND-HAIRED JOHNNY STORM, MUSING ON THE EFFECTS OF A WORLD HE DOESN'T UNDERSTAND---
---EVEN AS IT DRAWS ANOTHER MAN, OLDER---YET, PERHAPS, NO WISER---LOST, AS JOHNNY IS, IN THAT ALL-CONSUMING QUEST---FOR UNDERSTANDING.
8422
ENTER THE WORLD OF THE DREAMERS, AND COME WITH US ON A NEW JOURNEY AT THE HANDS OF THESE QUIET GUIDES---
STAN LEE EDITOR • GERRY CONWAY WRITER • ROSS ANDRU ARTIST • JIM MOONEY INKER • SAM ROSEN LETTERER

AND WHAT DOES HE **THINK** ABOUT? THE LOSING OF A **LOVE**, AND, YES,--- THE **MEANING** OF THAT LOVE---

--THOUGHTS ABRUPTLY **BROKEN**, WHEN---

'ERE, LAD--- WHAT'S THE **PROBLEM**, 'EY?

--WHO?

THE TAG'S **NATHANIEL**, LAD -- YE'LL WANT NO MORE THAN **THAT**, I'LL WAGER.

YE LOOK FIT TO BUST A **CORKIN'**, YE DO--- WHAT'S **WRONG** WITH YE, SON?

WRONG WHAT **ISN'T**

AH, IT'S **THAT** WAY, IS IT? A SAD THING, 'TIS INDEED, FOR A YOUNGSTER YER AGE TO BE SO **BITTER**.

WHY, LOOK AT OLD **NATHANIEL**-- NOT A SORE BONE IN 'IS BODY, NOT A **ONE**!

AYE, I KNOW THAT LOOK, LAD --YE THINK I'M JUST A BLIND OL' **SOT**, DON'T YE NOW? WELL MAYBE **SO**---

--BUT THAT DON'T MEAN I HAVEN'T A GOOD **WORD** FOR YE, LAD!

I WAS YOUNG ONCE **TOO** Y'KNOW--- WE **ALL** ARE, THEY TELL ME.

RIGHT NOW, YE'RE SAYIN' TO YERSELF-- "WHAT'S THE POINT IN IT ALL? WHAT'S IT ALL BLOOMIN' **MATTER**?"

IT **MATTERS**, LAD. IF ONLY TILL YOU GAIN YOURSELF A **MATE** --

--A FRIEND YE CAN **TRUST**. THAT'S WHAT MAKES IT **COUNT**!

A **FRIEND**? MAYBE YOU'VE **GOT** SOMETHING THERE, OLD TIMER.

SURE AN' I **DO**, LAD.

ASK **ANY** OLD SALT. 'E'LL TELL YE.

WELL, I'VE NO TIME FOR **THAT**, OLD MAN---

GUESS I'LL JUS' TAKE YOUR **WOR**'

WAIT, LAD-- DON'T Y' DO ANYTHING **RASH**

LADDIE, **WAIT**!

LORD-- HE'S BLINKIN' GOING TO *JUMP!*

I'VE *KILLED* HIM, I HAVE!

NOT *QUITE,* NATHANIEL--

SAINTS BE PRAISED.

NOT WHEN YOUR LAD'S NAME IS---

THE HUMAN TORCH!

NAT, METHINKS YE'D BETTER GO ON THE *WAGON* AG'IN.

YER EYES ARE TREATIN' YE NONE TOO *GOOD--!*

--AN' JUST SO YE DON'T GO TAKIN' THE PLEDGE TOO *LIGHTLY...*

-- LET'S *SEAL* IT WIT' A *DRINK!*

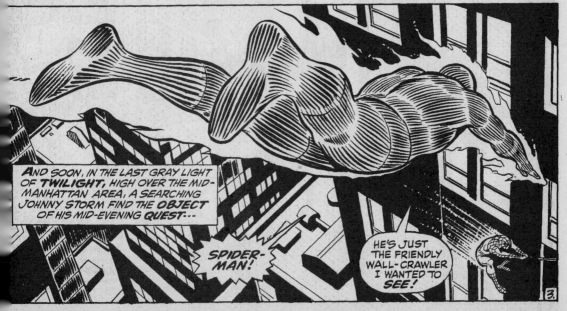

AND SOON, IN THE LAST GRAY LIGHT OF TWILIGHT, HIGH OVER THE MID-MANHATTAN AREA, A SEARCHING JOHNNY STORM FIND THE OBJECT OF HIS MID-EVENING QUEST---

SPIDER-MAN!

HE'S JUST THE FRIENDLY WALL-CRAWLER I WANTED TO *SEE!*

3.

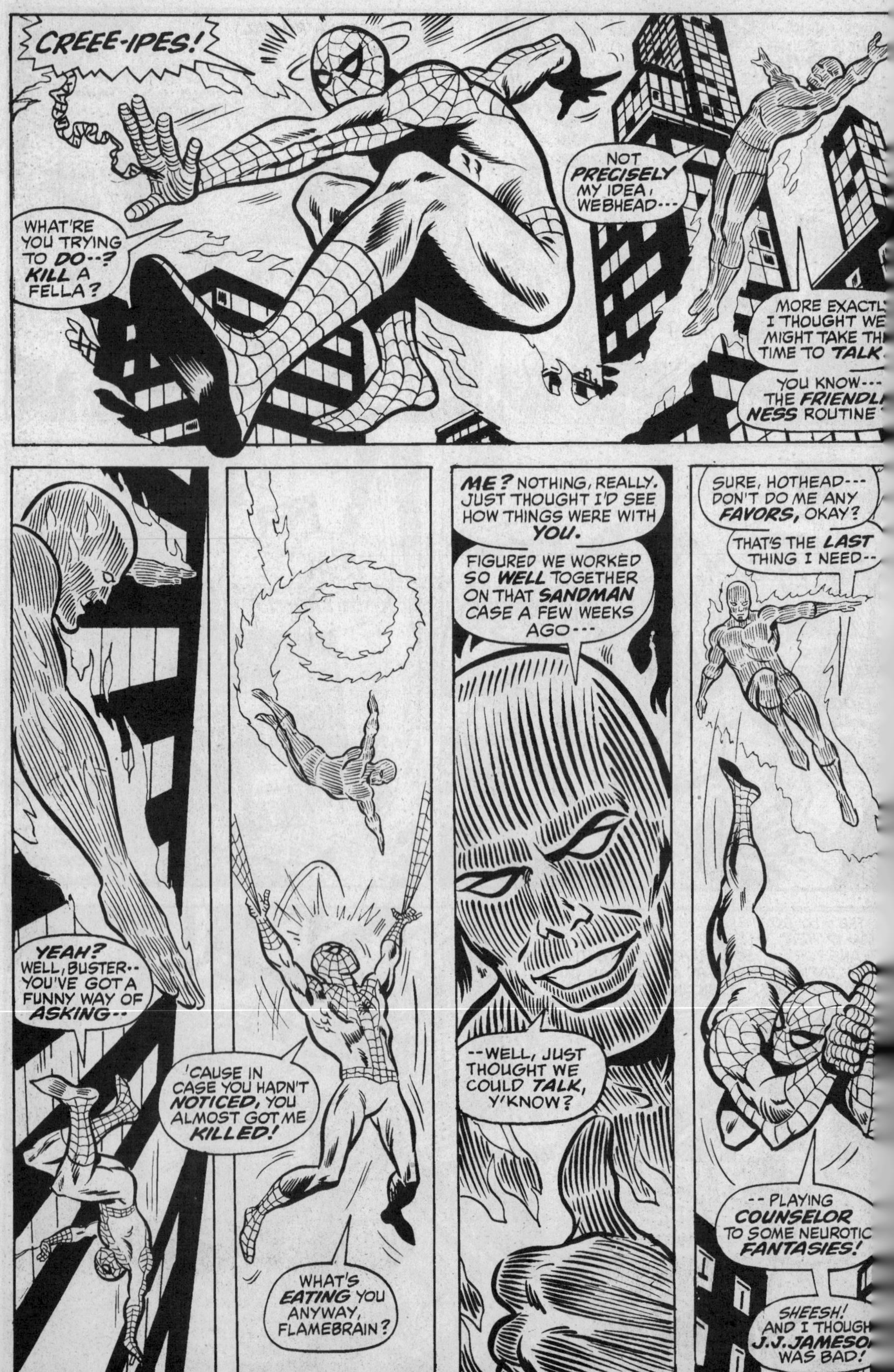
CREEE-IPES!
WHAT'RE YOU TRYING TO DO--? KILL A FELLA?
NOT PRECISELY MY IDEA, WEBHEAD---
MORE EXACTL I THOUGHT WE MIGHT TAKE TH TIME TO TALK
YOU KNOW--- THE FRIENDL NESS ROUTINE
YEAH? WELL, BUSTER-- YOU'VE GOT A FUNNY WAY OF ASKING--
'CAUSE IN CASE YOU HADN'T NOTICED, YOU ALMOST GOT ME KILLED!
WHAT'S EATING YOU ANYWAY, FLAMEBRAIN?
ME? NOTHING, REALLY. JUST THOUGHT I'D SEE HOW THINGS WERE WITH YOU.
FIGURED WE WORKED SO WELL TOGETHER ON THAT SANDMAN CASE A FEW WEEKS AGO---
--WELL, JUST THOUGHT WE COULD TALK, Y'KNOW?
SURE, HOTHEAD--- DON'T DO ME ANY FAVORS, OKAY?
THAT'S THE LAST THING I NEED--
-- PLAYING COUNSELOR TO SOME NEUROTIC FANTASIES!
SHEESH! AND I THOUGH J.J. JAMESO WAS BAD!

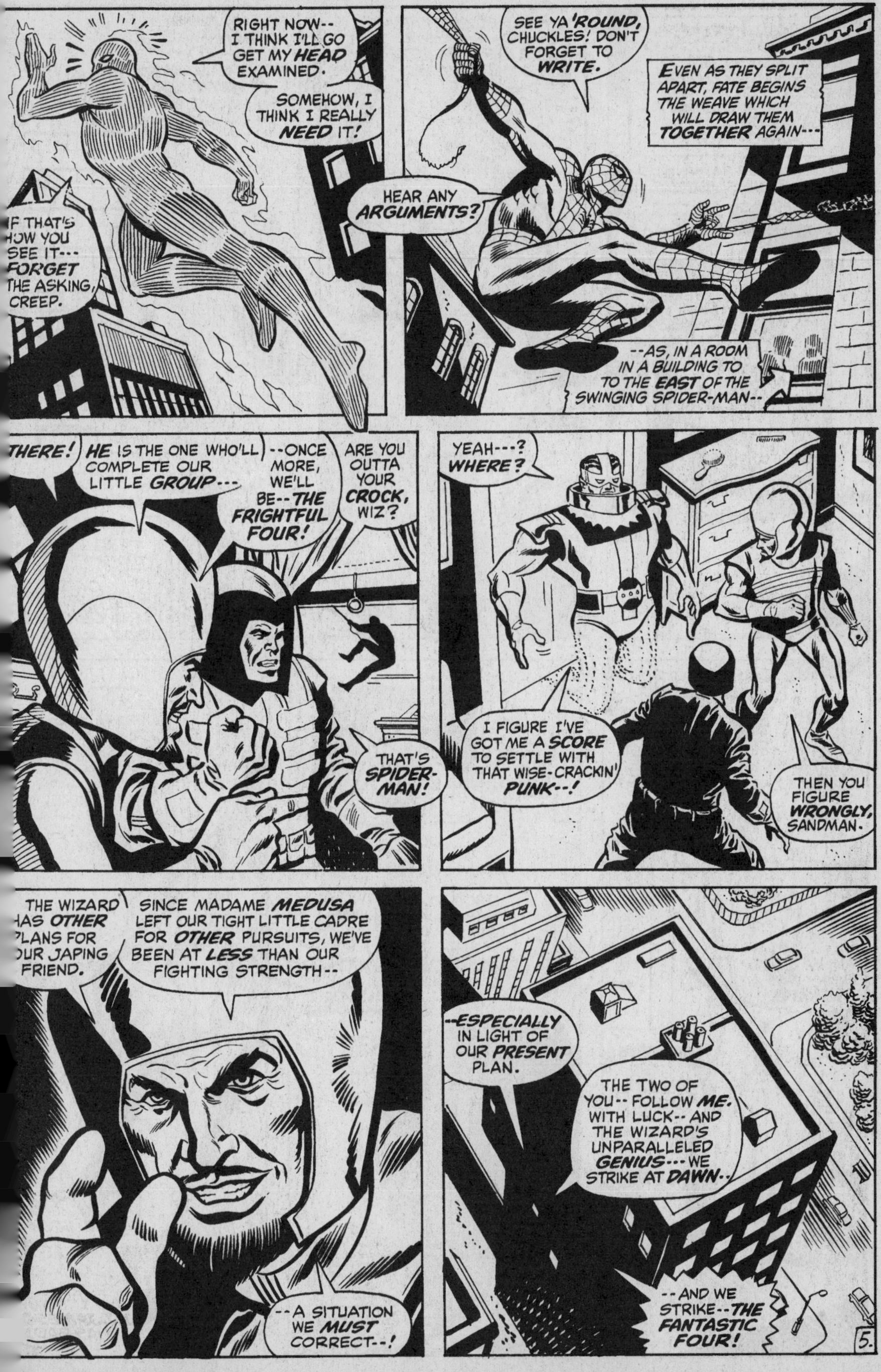

RIGHT NOW-- I THINK I'LL GO GET MY HEAD EXAMINED.
SOMEHOW, I THINK I REALLY NEED IT!
IF THAT'S HOW YOU SEE IT--- FORGET THE ASKING, CREEP.
SEE YA 'ROUND, CHUCKLES! DON'T FORGET TO WRITE.
HEAR ANY ARGUMENTS?
EVEN AS THEY SPLIT APART, FATE BEGINS THE WEAVE WHICH WILL DRAW THEM TOGETHER AGAIN---
--AS, IN A ROOM IN A BUILDING TO TO THE EAST OF THE SWINGING SPIDER-MAN--
THERE!
HE IS THE ONE WHO'LL COMPLETE OUR LITTLE GROUP---
--ONCE MORE, WE'LL BE--THE FRIGHTFUL FOUR!
ARE YOU OUTTA YOUR CROCK, WIZ?
THAT'S SPIDER-MAN!
YEAH---? WHERE?
I FIGURE I'VE GOT ME A SCORE TO SETTLE WITH THAT WISE-CRACKIN' PUNK--!
THEN YOU FIGURE WRONGLY, SANDMAN.
THE WIZARD HAS OTHER PLANS FOR OUR JAPING FRIEND.
SINCE MADAME MEDUSA LEFT OUR TIGHT LITTLE CADRE FOR OTHER PURSUITS, WE'VE BEEN AT LESS THAN OUR FIGHTING STRENGTH--
--A SITUATION WE MUST CORRECT--!
--ESPECIALLY IN LIGHT OF OUR PRESENT PLAN.
THE TWO OF YOU-- FOLLOW ME. WITH LUCK-- AND THE WIZARD'S UNPARALLELED GENIUS--- WE STRIKE AT DAWN..
--AND WE STRIKE--THE FANTASTIC FOUR!

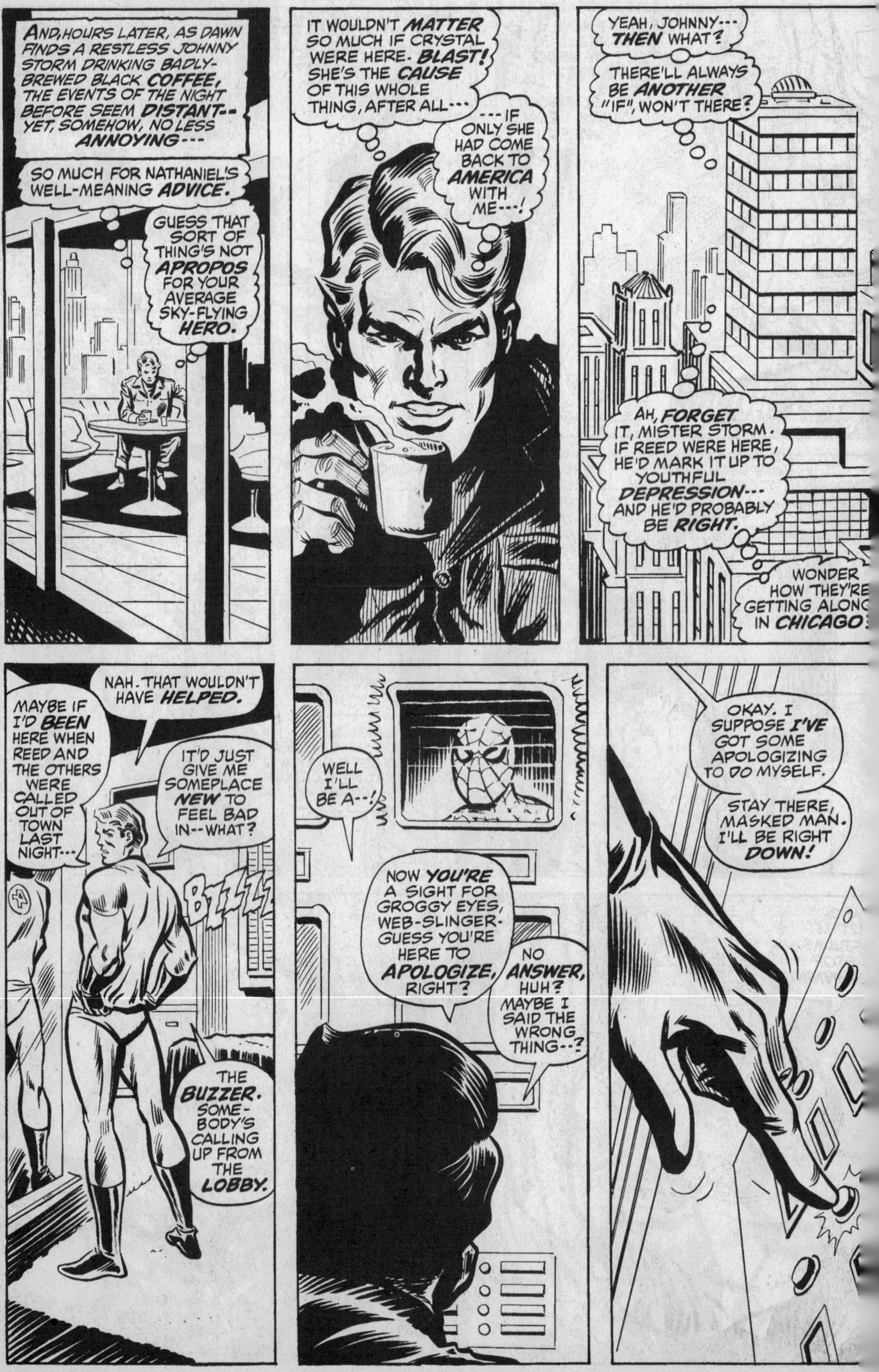
AND, HOURS LATER, AS DAWN FINDS A RESTLESS JOHNNY STORM DRINKING BADLY-BREWED BLACK COFFEE, THE EVENTS OF THE NIGHT BEFORE SEEM DISTANT--YET, SOMEHOW, NO LESS ANNOYING---
SO MUCH FOR NATHANIEL'S WELL-MEANING ADVICE.
GUESS THAT SORT OF THING'S NOT APROPOS FOR YOUR AVERAGE SKY-FLYING HERO.
IT WOULDN'T MATTER SO MUCH IF CRYSTAL WERE HERE. BLAST! SHE'S THE CAUSE OF THIS WHOLE THING, AFTER ALL---
---IF ONLY SHE HAD COME BACK TO AMERICA WITH ME---!
YEAH, JOHNNY--- THEN WHAT?
THERE'LL ALWAYS BE ANOTHER "IF", WON'T THERE?
AH, FORGET IT, MISTER STORM. IF REED WERE HERE, HE'D MARK IT UP TO YOUTHFUL DEPRESSION--- AND HE'D PROBABLY BE RIGHT.
WONDER HOW THEY'RE GETTING ALONG IN CHICAGO?
MAYBE IF I'D BEEN HERE WHEN REED AND THE OTHERS WERE CALLED OUT OF TOWN LAST NIGHT---
NAH. THAT WOULDN'T HAVE HELPED.
IT'D JUST GIVE ME SOMEPLACE NEW TO FEEL BAD IN--WHAT?
BZZZ
THE BUZZER. SOMEBODY'S CALLING UP FROM THE LOBBY.
WELL I'LL BE A--!
NOW YOU'RE A SIGHT FOR GROGGY EYES, WEB-SLINGER-- GUESS YOU'RE HERE TO APOLOGIZE, RIGHT?
NO ANSWER, HUH? MAYBE I SAID THE WRONG THING--?
OKAY. I SUPPOSE I'VE GOT SOME APOLOGIZING TO DO MYSELF.
STAY THERE, MASKED MAN. I'LL BE RIGHT DOWN!

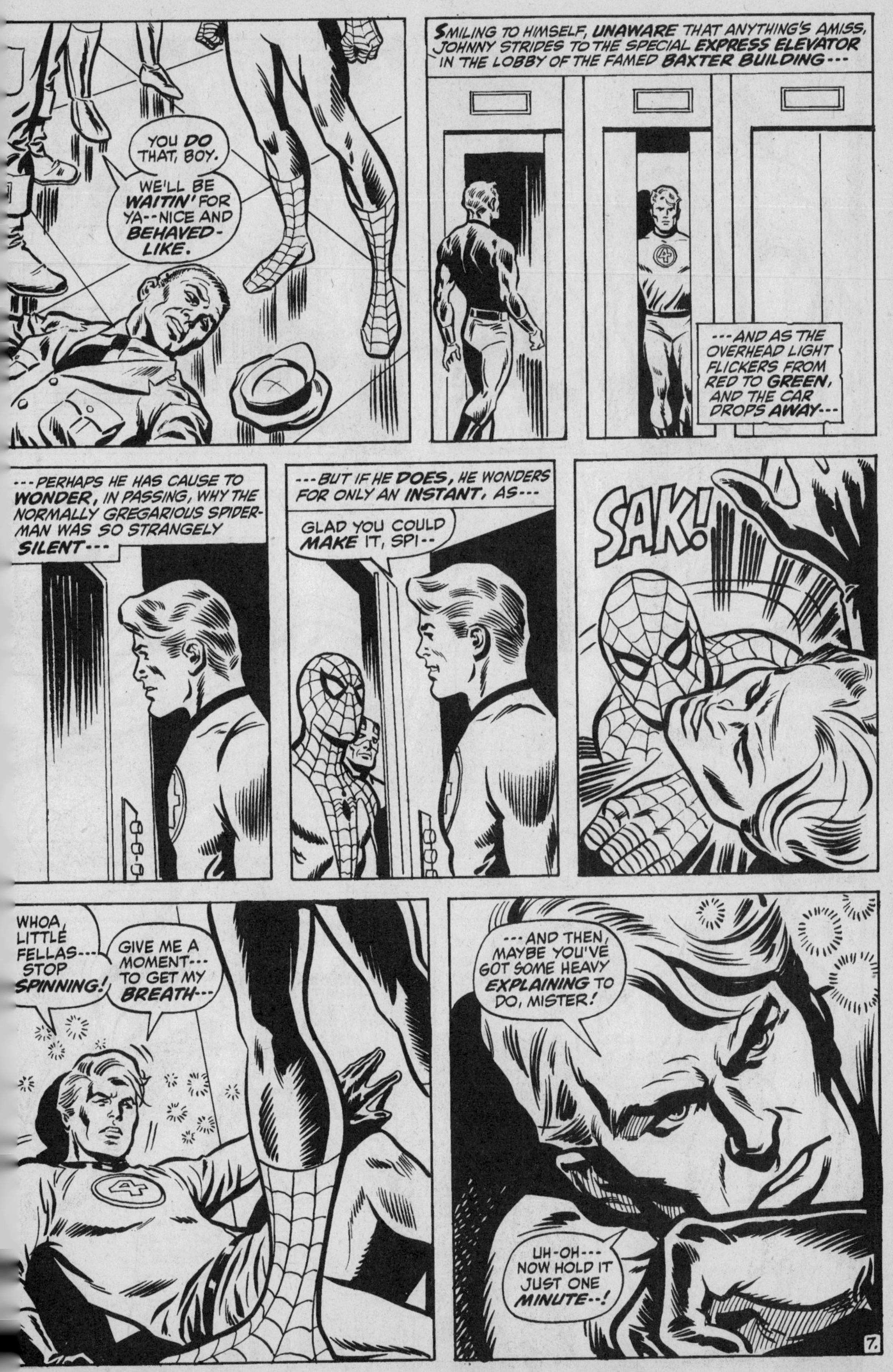
YOU DO THAT, BOY.
WE'LL BE WAITIN' FOR YA--NICE AND BEHAVED-LIKE.
SMILING TO HIMSELF, UNAWARE THAT ANYTHING'S AMISS, JOHNNY STRIDES TO THE SPECIAL EXPRESS ELEVATOR IN THE LOBBY OF THE FAMED BAXTER BUILDING---
---AND AS THE OVERHEAD LIGHT FLICKERS FROM RED TO GREEN, AND THE CAR DROPS AWAY---
---PERHAPS HE HAS CAUSE TO WONDER, IN PASSING, WHY THE NORMALLY GREGARIOUS SPIDER-MAN WAS SO STRANGELY SILENT---
---BUT IF HE DOES, HE WONDERS FOR ONLY AN INSTANT, AS---
GLAD YOU COULD MAKE IT, SPI--
SAK!
WHOA, LITTLE FELLAS--- STOP SPINNING!
GIVE ME A MOMENT--- TO GET MY BREATH---
---AND THEN, MAYBE YOU'VE GOT SOME HEAVY EXPLAINING TO DO, MISTER!
UH-OH--- NOW HOLD IT JUST ONE MINUTE--!
7.

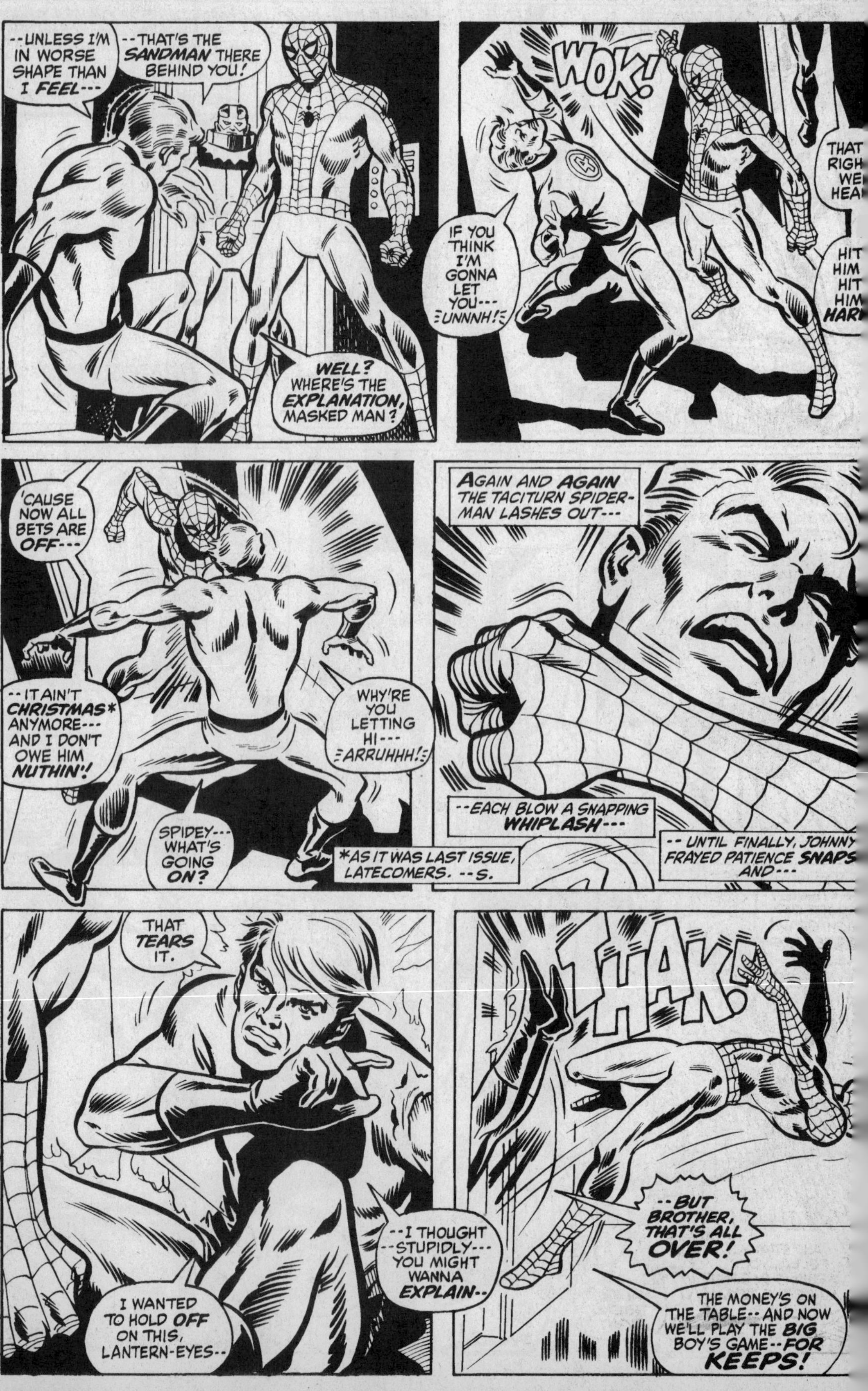
--UNLESS I'M IN WORSE SHAPE THAN I FEEL---
--THAT'S THE SANDMAN THERE BEHIND YOU!
WELL? WHERE'S THE EXPLANATION, MASKED MAN?
WOK!
IF YOU THINK I'M GONNA LET YOU--- UNNNH!
'CAUSE NOW ALL BETS ARE OFF---
--IT AIN'T CHRISTMAS* ANYMORE--- AND I DON'T OWE HIM NUTHIN'!
WHY'RE YOU LETTING HI--- ARRUHHH!
SPIDEY--- WHAT'S GOING ON?
*AS IT WAS LAST ISSUE, LATECOMERS. --S.
AGAIN AND AGAIN THE TACITURN SPIDER-MAN LASHES OUT---
--EACH BLOW A SNAPPING WHIPLASH---
-- UNTIL FINALLY, JOHNNY FRAYED PATIENCE SNAPS AND---
THAT TEARS IT.
I WANTED TO HOLD OFF ON THIS, LANTERN-EYES--
--I THOUGHT --STUPIDLY--- YOU MIGHT WANNA EXPLAIN--
THAK!
--BUT BROTHER, THAT'S ALL OVER!
THE MONEY'S ON THE TABLE-- AND NOW WE'LL PLAY THE BIG BOY'S GAME--FOR KEEPS!

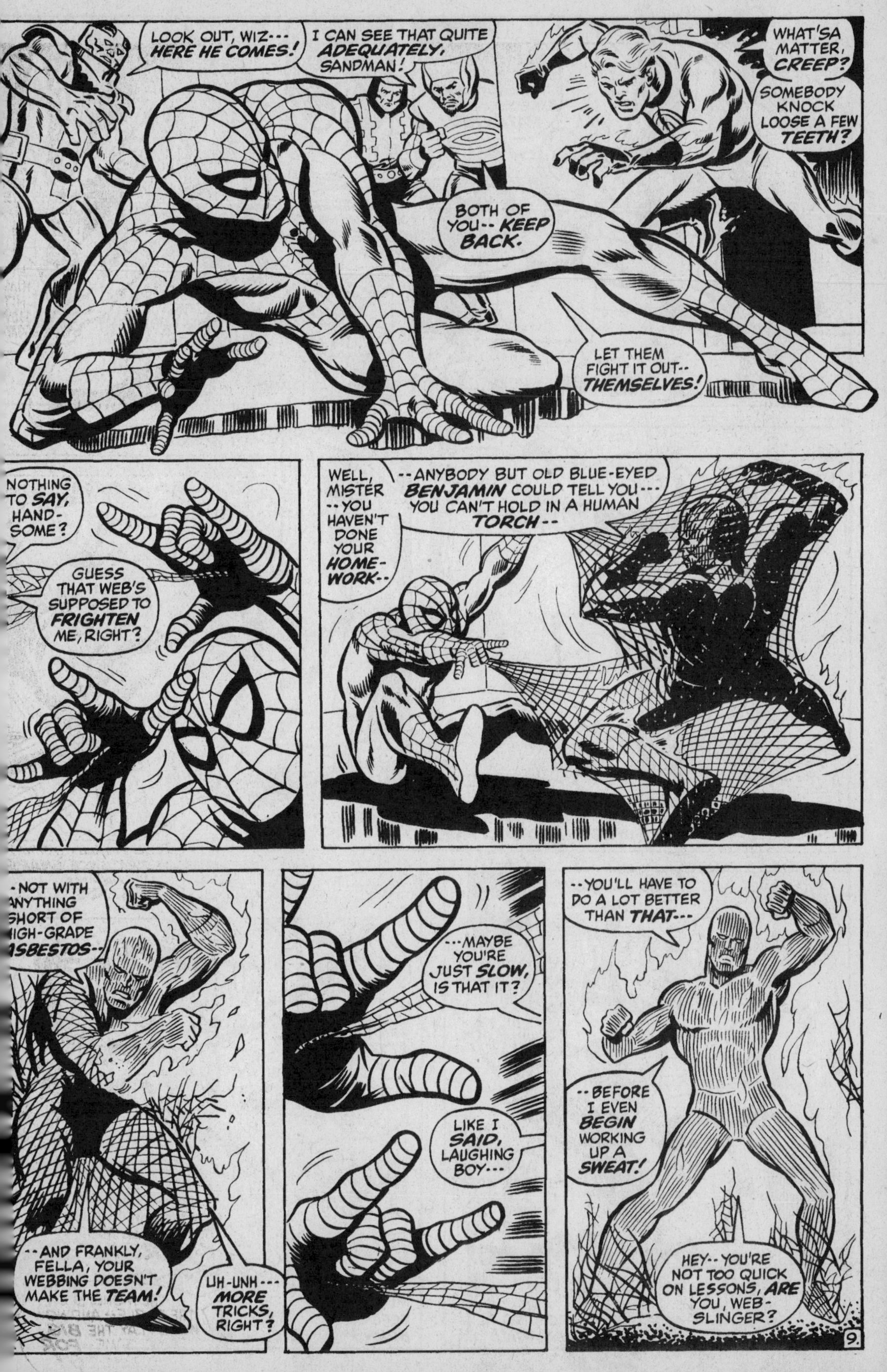

LOOK OUT, WIZ--- HERE HE COMES!
I CAN SEE THAT QUITE ADEQUATELY, SANDMAN!
WHAT'SA MATTER, CREEP?
SOMEBODY KNOCK LOOSE A FEW TEETH?
BOTH OF YOU-- KEEP BACK.
LET THEM FIGHT IT OUT-- THEMSELVES!
NOTHING TO SAY, HAND-SOME?
GUESS THAT WEB'S SUPPOSED TO FRIGHTEN ME, RIGHT?
WELL, MISTER --YOU HAVEN'T DONE YOUR HOME-WORK--
--ANYBODY BUT OLD BLUE-EYED BENJAMIN COULD TELL YOU--- YOU CAN'T HOLD IN A HUMAN TORCH--
-NOT WITH ANYTHING SHORT OF HIGH-GRADE ASBESTOS--
--AND FRANKLY, FELLA, YOUR WEBBING DOESN'T MAKE THE TEAM!
---MAYBE YOU'RE JUST SLOW, IS THAT IT?
LIKE I SAID, LAUGHING BOY---
UH-UNH--- MORE TRICKS, RIGHT?
--YOU'LL HAVE TO DO A LOT BETTER THAN THAT---
--BEFORE I EVEN BEGIN WORKING UP A SWEAT!
HEY-- YOU'RE NOT TOO QUICK ON LESSONS, ARE YOU, WEB-SLINGER?
9.

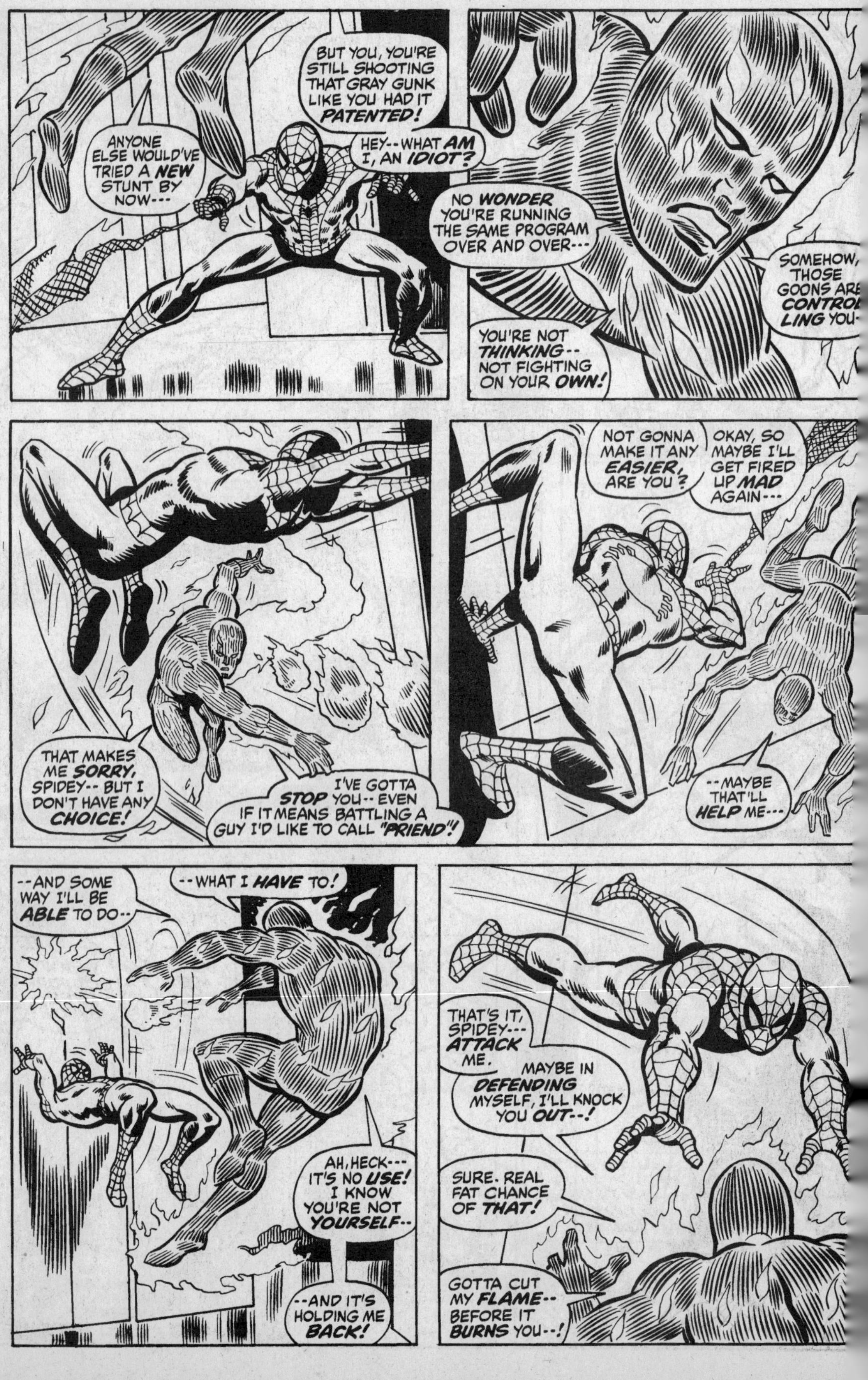
ANYONE ELSE WOULD'VE TRIED A NEW STUNT BY NOW---
BUT YOU, YOU'RE STILL SHOOTING THAT GRAY GUNK LIKE YOU HAD IT PATENTED!
HEY--WHAT AM I, AN IDIOT?
NO WONDER YOU'RE RUNNING THE SAME PROGRAM OVER AND OVER---
YOU'RE NOT THINKING--NOT FIGHTING ON YOUR OWN!
SOMEHOW, THOSE GOONS ARE CONTROL-LING YOU--
THAT MAKES ME SORRY, SPIDEY--BUT I DON'T HAVE ANY CHOICE!
I'VE GOTTA STOP YOU--EVEN IF IT MEANS BATTLING A GUY I'D LIKE TO CALL "FRIEND"!
NOT GONNA MAKE IT ANY EASIER, ARE YOU?
OKAY, SO MAYBE I'LL GET FIRED UP MAD AGAIN---
--MAYBE THAT'LL HELP ME---
--AND SOME WAY I'LL BE ABLE TO DO--
--WHAT I HAVE TO!
AH, HECK---IT'S NO USE! I KNOW YOU'RE NOT YOURSELF--
--AND IT'S HOLDING ME BACK!
THAT'S IT, SPIDEY--ATTACK ME.
MAYBE IN DEFENDING MYSELF, I'LL KNOCK YOU OUT--!
SURE. REAL FAT CHANCE OF THAT!
GOTTA CUT MY FLAME--BEFORE IT BURNS YOU--!

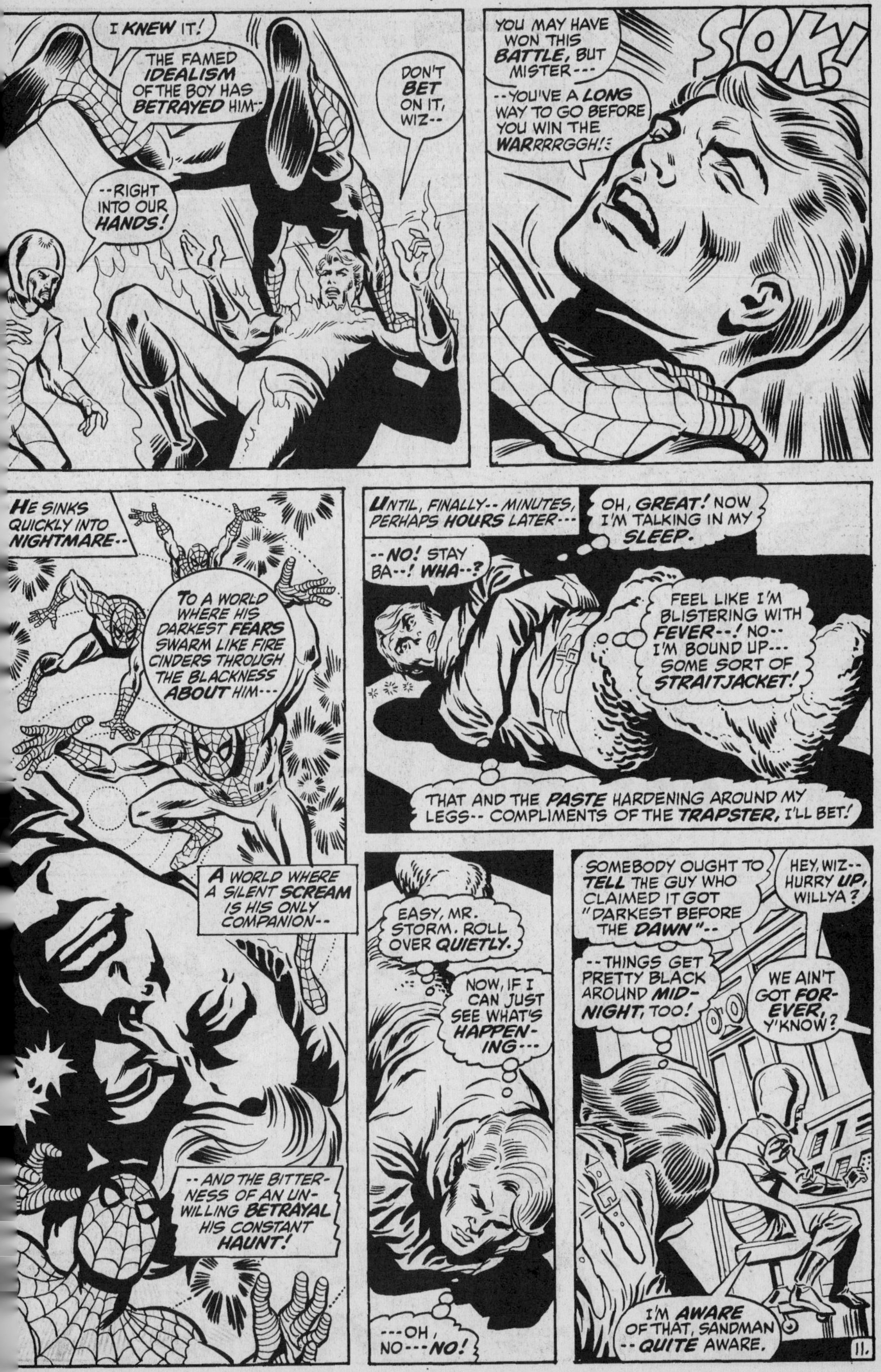

I KNEW IT!
THE FAMED IDEALISM OF THE BOY HAS BETRAYED HIM--
--RIGHT INTO OUR HANDS!
DON'T BET ON IT, WIZ--
YOU MAY HAVE WON THIS BATTLE, BUT MISTER---
--YOU'VE A LONG WAY TO GO BEFORE YOU WIN THE WARRRRGGH!!
SOK!
HE SINKS QUICKLY INTO NIGHTMARE--
TO A WORLD WHERE HIS DARKEST FEARS SWARM LIKE FIRE CINDERS THROUGH THE BLACKNESS ABOUT HIM---
A WORLD WHERE A SILENT SCREAM IS HIS ONLY COMPANION--
--AND THE BITTERNESS OF AN UNWILLING BETRAYAL HIS CONSTANT HAUNT!
UNTIL, FINALLY-- MINUTES, PERHAPS HOURS LATER---
OH, GREAT! NOW I'M TALKING IN MY SLEEP.
--NO! STAY BA--! WHA--?
FEEL LIKE I'M BLISTERING WITH FEVER--! NO-- I'M BOUND UP--- SOME SORT OF STRAITJACKET!
THAT AND THE PASTE HARDENING AROUND MY LEGS-- COMPLIMENTS OF THE TRAPSTER, I'LL BET!
EASY, MR. STORM. ROLL OVER QUIETLY.
NOW, IF I CAN JUST SEE WHAT'S HAPPENING---
---OH, NO---NO!
SOMEBODY OUGHT TO TELL THE GUY WHO CLAIMED IT GOT "DARKEST BEFORE THE DAWN"--
--THINGS GET PRETTY BLACK AROUND MIDNIGHT, TOO!
HEY, WIZ-- HURRY UP, WILLYA?
WE AIN'T GOT FOREVER, Y'KNOW?
I'M AWARE OF THAT, SANDMAN --QUITE AWARE.
11.

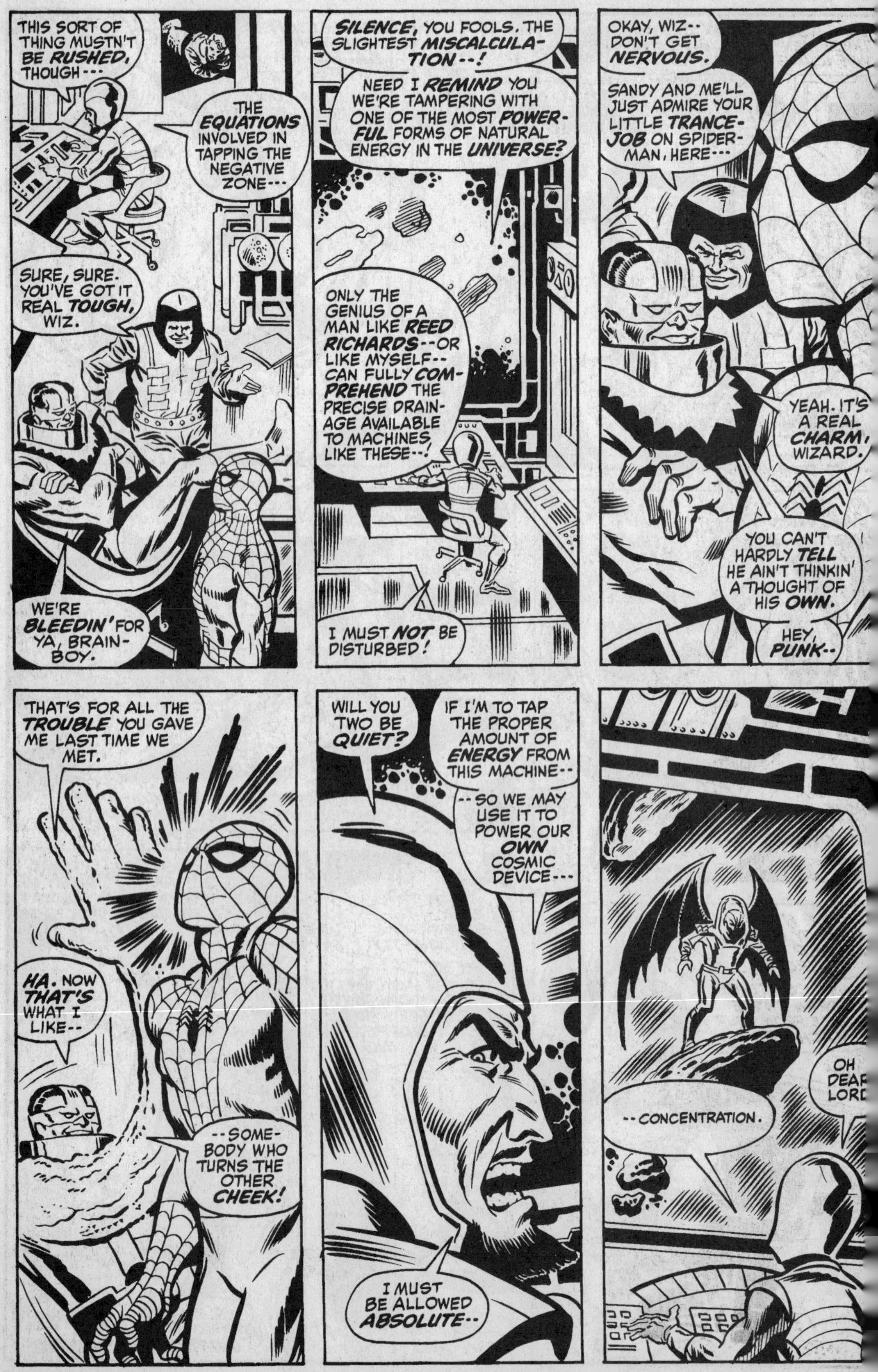
THIS SORT OF THING MUSTN'T BE RUSHED, THOUGH---
THE EQUATIONS INVOLVED IN TAPPING THE NEGATIVE ZONE---
SURE, SURE. YOU'VE GOT IT REAL TOUGH, WIZ.
WE'RE BLEEDIN' FOR YA, BRAIN-BOY.
SILENCE, YOU FOOLS. THE SLIGHTEST MISCALCULATION--!
NEED I REMIND YOU WE'RE TAMPERING WITH ONE OF THE MOST POWERFUL FORMS OF NATURAL ENERGY IN THE UNIVERSE?
ONLY THE GENIUS OF A MAN LIKE REED RICHARDS--OR LIKE MYSELF--CAN FULLY COMPREHEND THE PRECISE DRAINAGE AVAILABLE TO MACHINES LIKE THESE--!
I MUST NOT BE DISTURBED!
OKAY, WIZ--DON'T GET NERVOUS.
SANDY AND ME'LL JUST ADMIRE YOUR LITTLE TRANCE-JOB ON SPIDER-MAN, HERE---
YEAH. IT'S A REAL CHARM, WIZARD.
YOU CAN'T HARDLY TELL HE AIN'T THINKIN' A THOUGHT OF HIS OWN.
HEY, PUNK--
THAT'S FOR ALL THE TROUBLE YOU GAVE ME LAST TIME WE MET.
HA. NOW THAT'S WHAT I LIKE--
--SOMEBODY WHO TURNS THE OTHER CHEEK!
WILL YOU TWO BE QUIET?
IF I'M TO TAP THE PROPER AMOUNT OF ENERGY FROM THIS MACHINE--
--SO WE MAY USE IT TO POWER OUR OWN COSMIC DEVICE---
I MUST BE ALLOWED ABSOLUTE--
--CONCENTRATION.
OH DEAR LORD

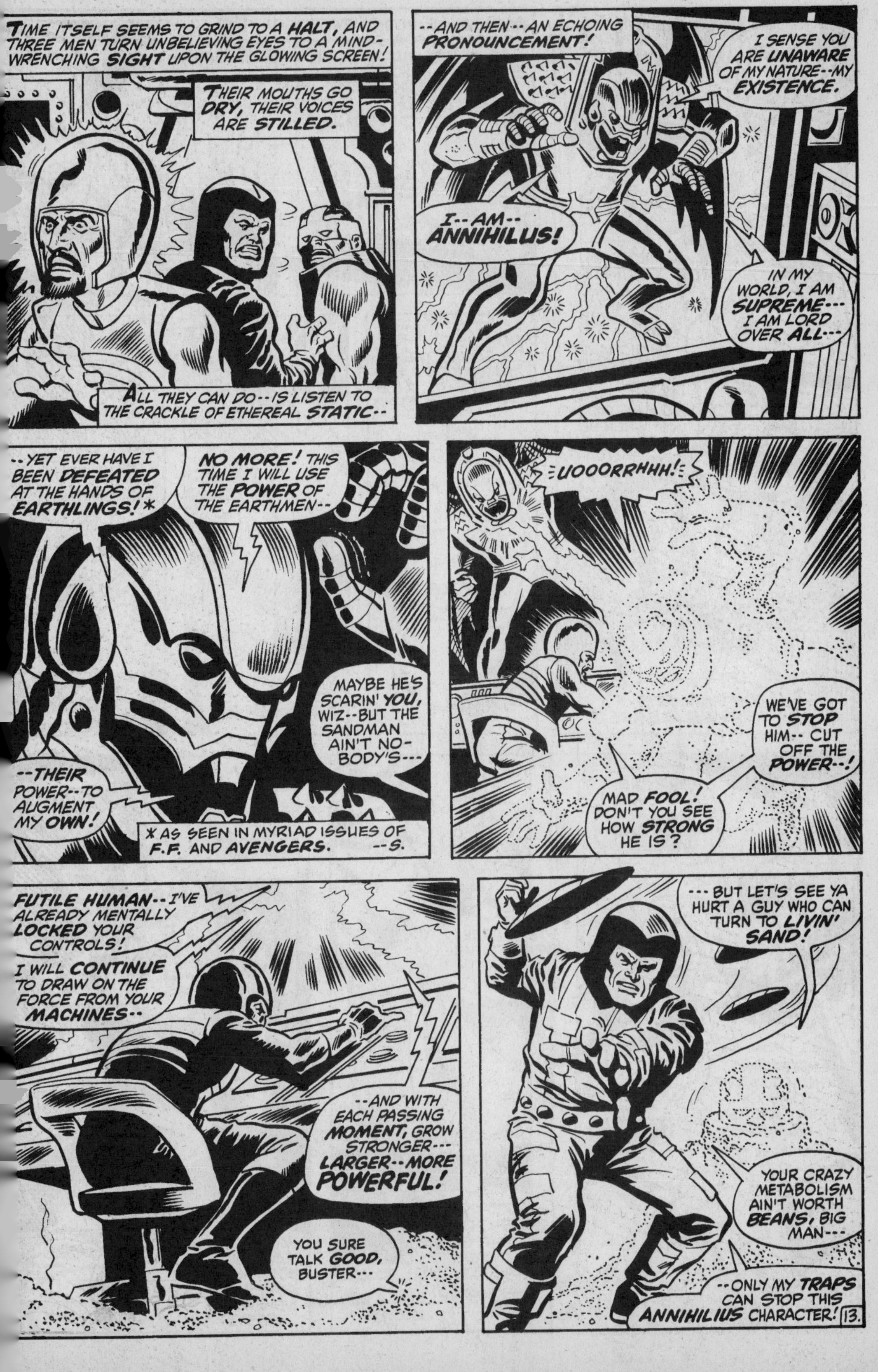
TIME ITSELF SEEMS TO GRIND TO A HALT, AND THREE MEN TURN UNBELIEVING EYES TO A MIND-WRENCHING SIGHT UPON THE GLOWING SCREEN!
THEIR MOUTHS GO DRY, THEIR VOICES ARE STILLED.
ALL THEY CAN DO--IS LISTEN TO THE CRACKLE OF ETHEREAL STATIC--
--AND THEN--AN ECHOING PRONOUNCEMENT!
I SENSE YOU ARE UNAWARE OF MY NATURE--MY EXISTENCE.
I--AM--ANNIHILUS!
IN MY WORLD, I AM SUPREME--- I AM LORD OVER ALL---
--YET EVER HAVE I BEEN DEFEATED AT THE HANDS OF EARTHLINGS!*
NO MORE! THIS TIME I WILL USE THE POWER OF THE EARTHMEN--
MAYBE HE'S SCARIN' YOU, WIZ--BUT THE SANDMAN AIN'T NO-BODY'S---
--THEIR POWER--TO AUGMENT MY OWN!
*AS SEEN IN MYRIAD ISSUES OF F.F. AND AVENGERS. --S.
UOOORRHHH!
WE'VE GOT TO STOP HIM-- CUT OFF THE POWER--!
MAD FOOL! DON'T YOU SEE HOW STRONG HE IS?
FUTILE HUMAN--I'VE ALREADY MENTALLY LOCKED YOUR CONTROLS!
I WILL CONTINUE TO DRAW ON THE FORCE FROM YOUR MACHINES--
--AND WITH EACH PASSING MOMENT, GROW STRONGER--- LARGER--MORE POWERFUL!
YOU SURE TALK GOOD, BUSTER---
---BUT LET'S SEE YA HURT A GUY WHO CAN TURN TO LIVIN' SAND!
YOUR CRAZY METABOLISM AIN'T WORTH BEANS, BIG MAN---
--ONLY MY TRAPS CAN STOP THIS ANNIHILIUS CHARACTER!
13.

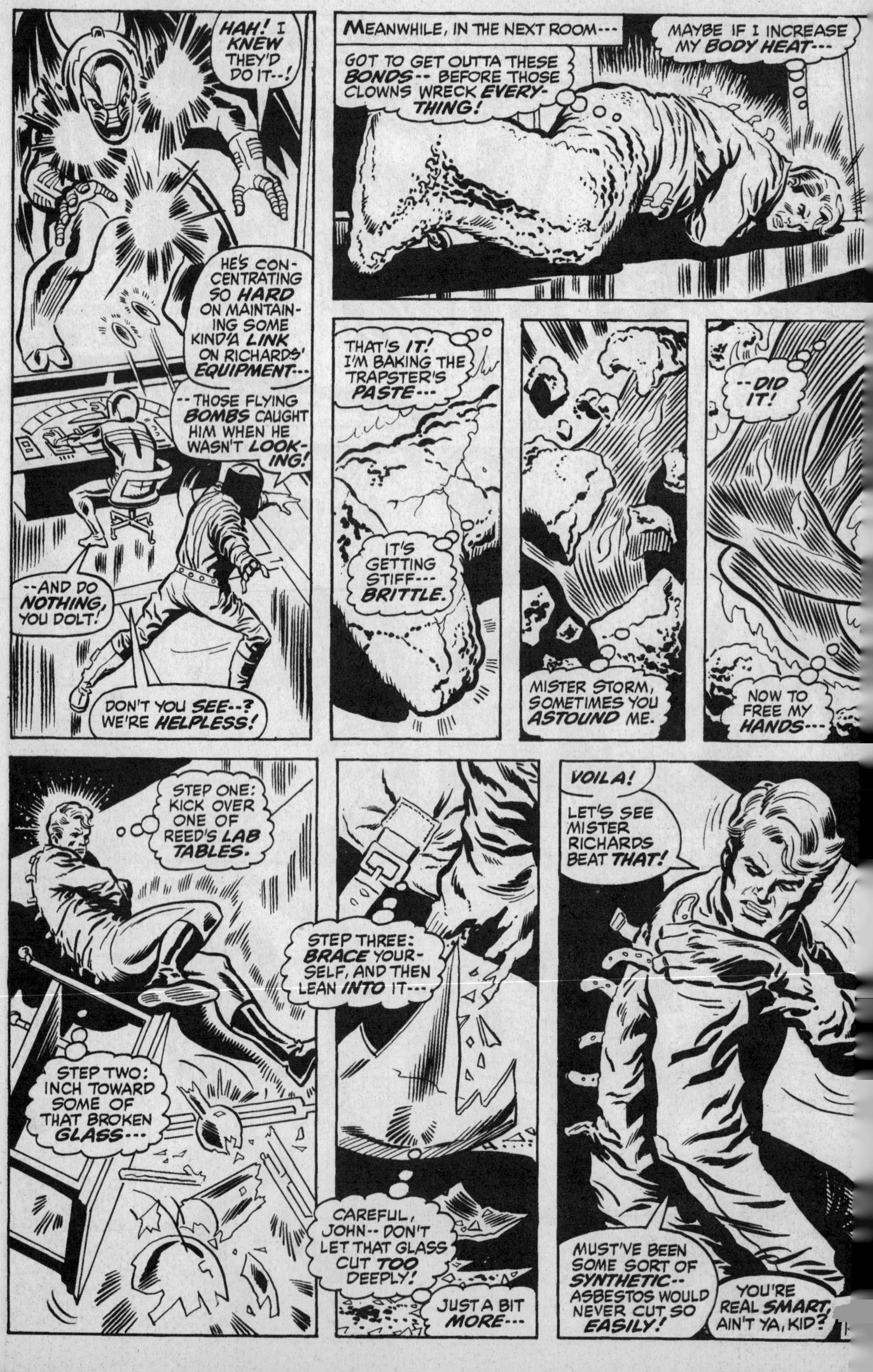
HAH! I KNEW THEY'D DO IT--!
HE'S CONCENTRATING SO HARD ON MAINTAINING SOME KIND'A LINK ON RICHARDS' EQUIPMENT---
--THOSE FLYING BOMBS CAUGHT HIM WHEN HE WASN'T LOOKING!
--AND DO NOTHING, YOU DOLT!
DON'T YOU SEE--? WE'RE HELPLESS!
MEANWHILE, IN THE NEXT ROOM---
GOT TO GET OUTTA THESE BONDS-- BEFORE THOSE CLOWNS WRECK EVERYTHING!
MAYBE IF I INCREASE MY BODY HEAT---
THAT'S IT! I'M BAKING THE TRAPSTER'S PASTE---
IT'S GETTING STIFF--- BRITTLE.
MISTER STORM, SOMETIMES YOU ASTOUND ME.
--DID IT!
NOW TO FREE MY HANDS---
STEP ONE: KICK OVER ONE OF REED'S LAB TABLES.
STEP TWO: INCH TOWARD SOME OF THAT BROKEN GLASS---
STEP THREE: BRACE YOURSELF, AND THEN LEAN INTO IT---
CAREFUL, JOHN-- DON'T LET THAT GLASS CUT TOO DEEPLY!
JUST A BIT MORE---
VOILA!
LET'S SEE MISTER RICHARDS BEAT THAT!
MUST'VE BEEN SOME SORT OF SYNTHETIC-- ASBESTOS WOULD NEVER CUT SO EASILY!
YOU'RE REAL SMART, AIN'T YA, KID?

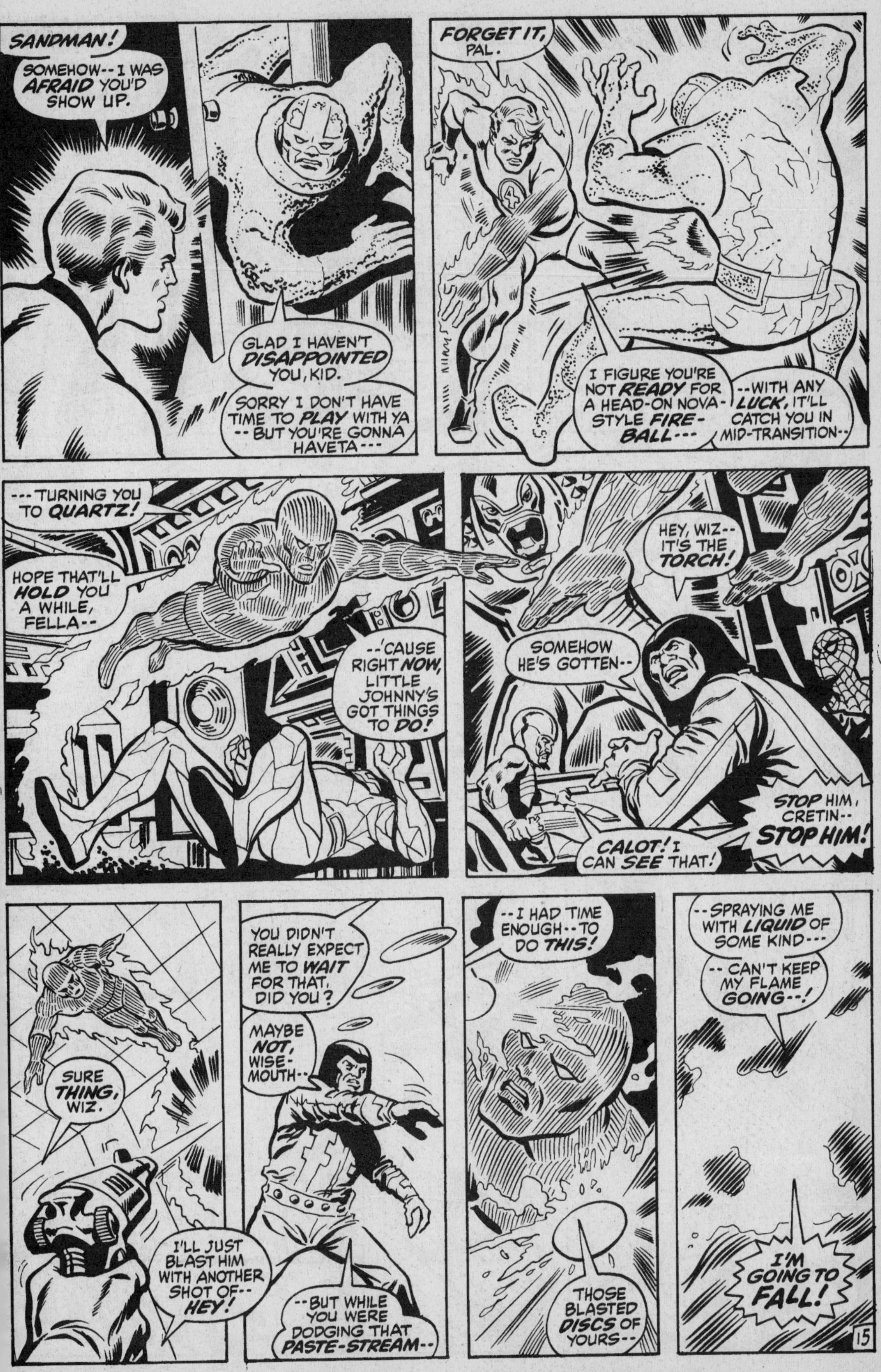
SANDMAN!
SOMEHOW-- I WAS AFRAID YOU'D SHOW UP.
GLAD I HAVEN'T DISAPPOINTED YOU, KID.
SORRY I DON'T HAVE TIME TO PLAY WITH YA -- BUT YOU'RE GONNA HAVETA---
FORGET IT, PAL.
I FIGURE YOU'RE NOT READY FOR A HEAD-ON NOVA-STYLE FIRE-BALL---
--WITH ANY LUCK, IT'LL CATCH YOU IN MID-TRANSITION--
---TURNING YOU TO QUARTZ!
HOPE THAT'LL HOLD YOU A WHILE, FELLA--
--'CAUSE RIGHT NOW, LITTLE JOHNNY'S GOT THINGS TO DO!
HEY, WIZ-- IT'S THE TORCH!
SOMEHOW HE'S GOTTEN--
STOP HIM, CRETIN-- STOP HIM!
CALOT! I CAN SEE THAT!
SURE THING, WIZ.
I'LL JUST BLAST HIM WITH ANOTHER SHOT OF-- HEY!
YOU DIDN'T REALLY EXPECT ME TO WAIT FOR THAT, DID YOU?
MAYBE NOT, WISE-MOUTH--
--BUT WHILE YOU WERE DODGING THAT PASTE-STREAM--
--I HAD TIME ENOUGH-- TO DO THIS!
THOSE BLASTED DISCS OF YOURS--
--SPRAYING ME WITH LIQUID OF SOME KIND---
--CAN'T KEEP MY FLAME GOING--!
I'M GOING TO FALL!
15

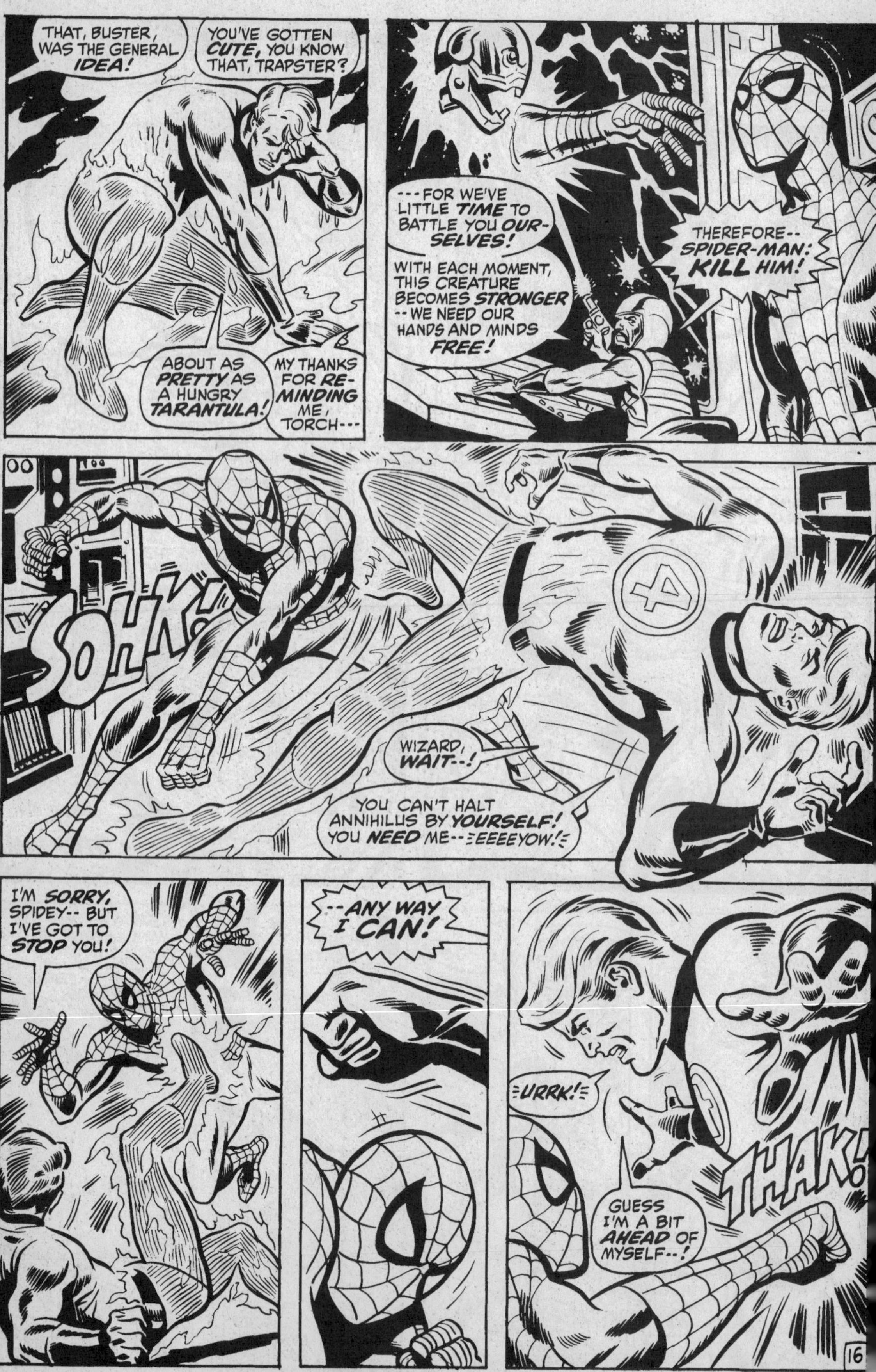
THAT, BUSTER, WAS THE GENERAL IDEA!
YOU'VE GOTTEN CUTE, YOU KNOW THAT, TRAPSTER?
ABOUT AS PRETTY AS A HUNGRY TARANTULA!
MY THANKS FOR RE-MINDING ME, TORCH---
---FOR WE'VE LITTLE TIME TO BATTLE YOU OUR-SELVES!
WITH EACH MOMENT, THIS CREATURE BECOMES STRONGER --WE NEED OUR HANDS AND MINDS FREE!
THEREFORE-- SPIDER-MAN: KILL HIM!
SOHK!
WIZARD, WAIT--!
YOU CAN'T HALT ANNIHILUS BY YOURSELF! YOU NEED ME---EEEEYOW!
I'M SORRY, SPIDEY-- BUT I'VE GOT TO STOP YOU!
--ANY WAY I CAN!
URRK!
THAK!
GUESS I'M A BIT AHEAD OF MYSELF--!
16

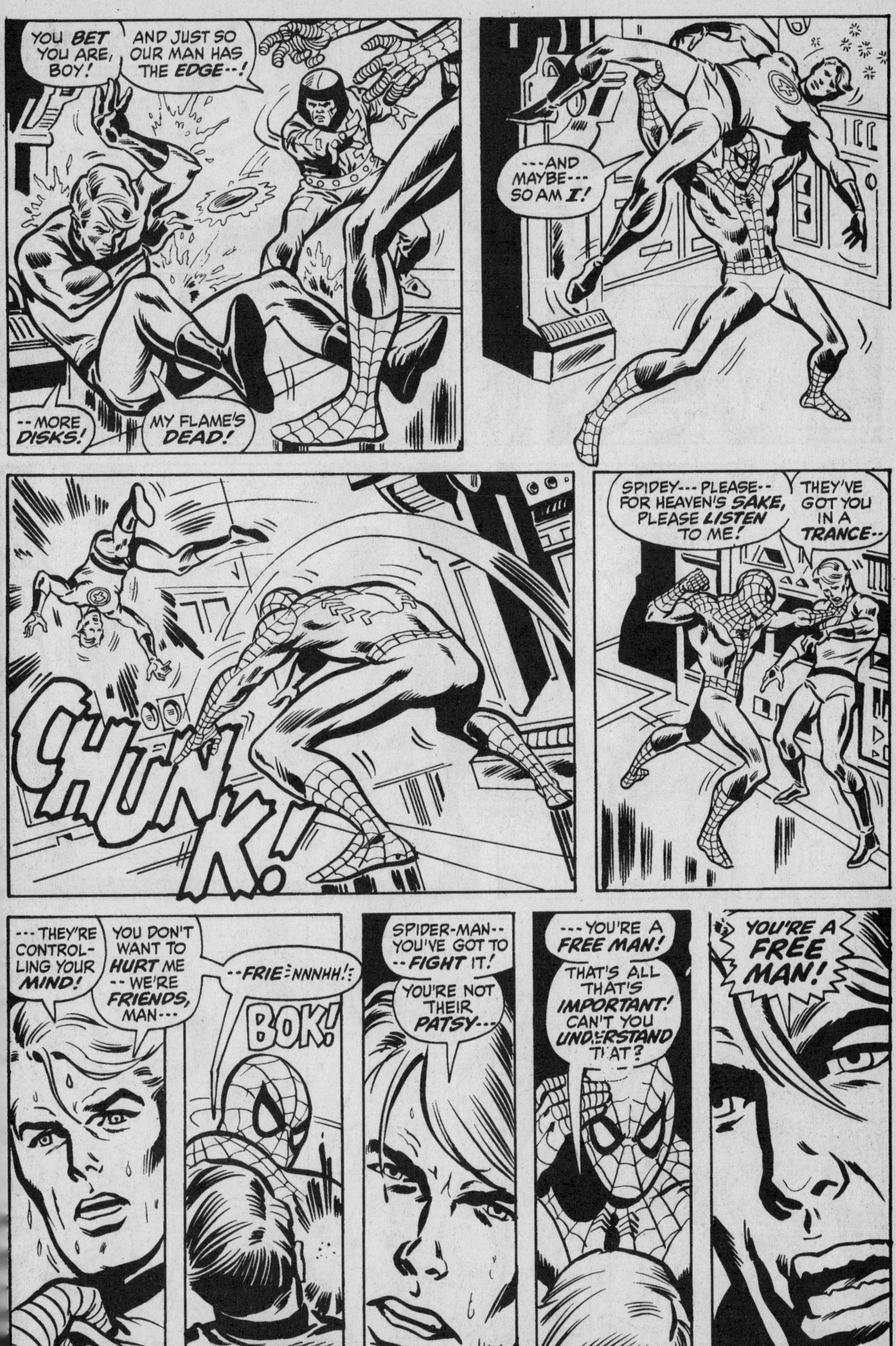

YOU BET YOU ARE, BOY!
AND JUST SO OUR MAN HAS THE EDGE--!
--MORE DISKS!
MY FLAME'S DEAD!
---AND MAYBE--- SO AM I!
CHUNK!
SPIDEY--- PLEASE-- FOR HEAVEN'S SAKE, PLEASE LISTEN TO ME!
THEY'VE GOT YOU IN A TRANCE--
---THEY'RE CONTROL-LING YOUR MIND!
YOU DON'T WANT TO HURT ME --WE'RE FRIENDS, MAN---
--FRIE-NNNHH!--
BOK!
SPIDER-MAN-- YOU'VE GOT TO --FIGHT IT!
YOU'RE NOT THEIR PATSY---
---YOU'RE A FREE MAN!
THAT'S ALL THAT'S IMPORTANT! CAN'T YOU UNDERSTAND THAT?
YOU'RE A FREE MAN!
17.

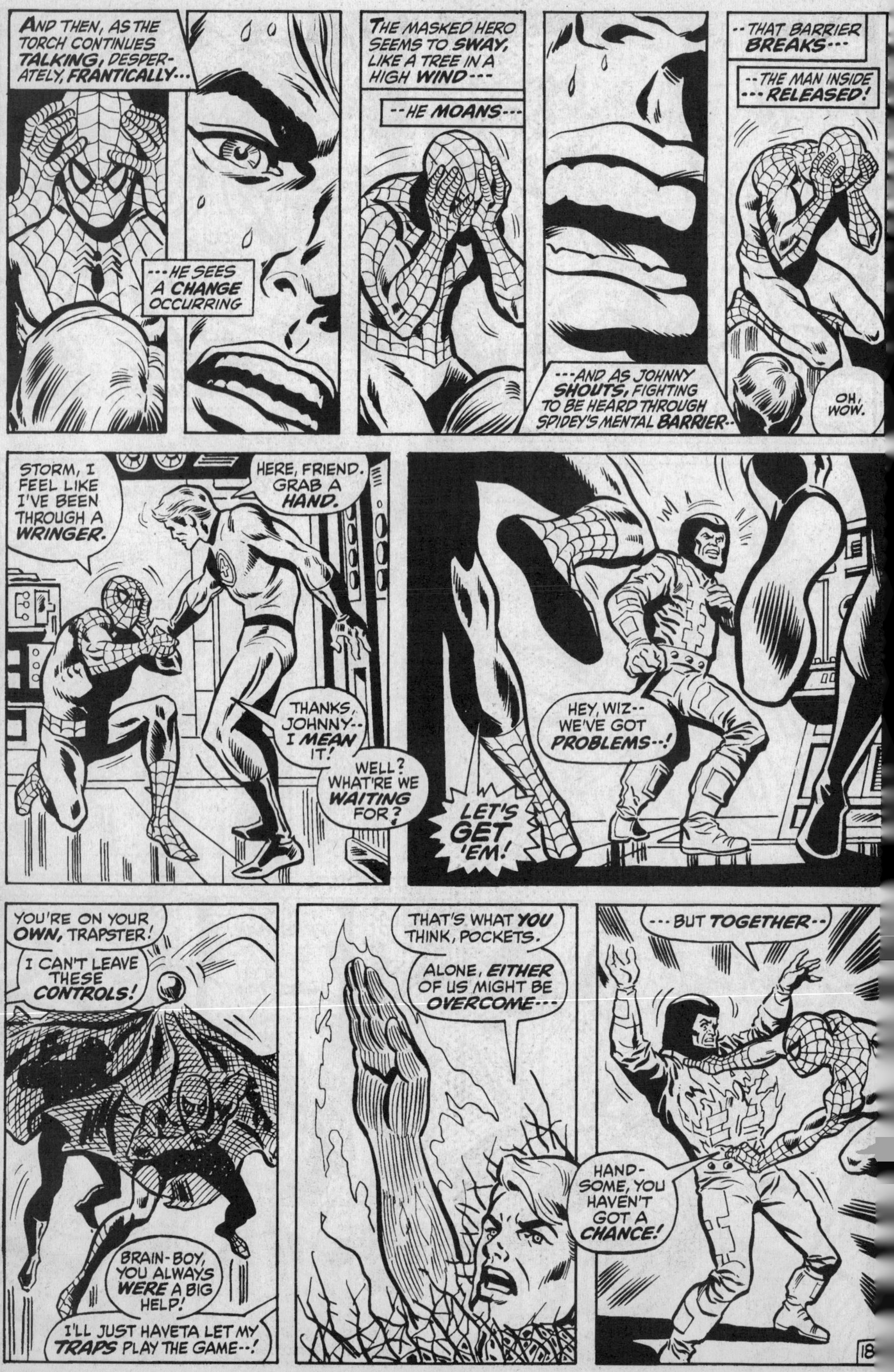
AND THEN, AS THE TORCH CONTINUES TALKING, DESPERATELY, FRANTICALLY...
...HE SEES A CHANGE OCCURRING
THE MASKED HERO SEEMS TO SWAY, LIKE A TREE IN A HIGH WIND---
--HE MOANS---
---AND AS JOHNNY SHOUTS, FIGHTING TO BE HEARD THROUGH SPIDEY'S MENTAL BARRIER--
--THAT BARRIER BREAKS---
--THE MAN INSIDE ---RELEASED!
OH, WOW.
STORM, I FEEL LIKE I'VE BEEN THROUGH A WRINGER.
HERE, FRIEND. GRAB A HAND.
THANKS, JOHNNY-- I MEAN IT!
WELL? WHAT'RE WE WAITING FOR?
LET'S GET 'EM!
HEY, WIZ-- WE'VE GOT PROBLEMS--!
YOU'RE ON YOUR OWN, TRAPSTER!
I CAN'T LEAVE THESE CONTROLS!
BRAIN-BOY, YOU ALWAYS WERE A BIG HELP!
I'LL JUST HAVETA LET MY TRAPS PLAY THE GAME--!
THAT'S WHAT YOU THINK, POCKETS.
ALONE, EITHER OF US MIGHT BE OVERCOME---
---BUT TOGETHER--
HAND-SOME, YOU HAVEN'T GOT A CHANCE!
18

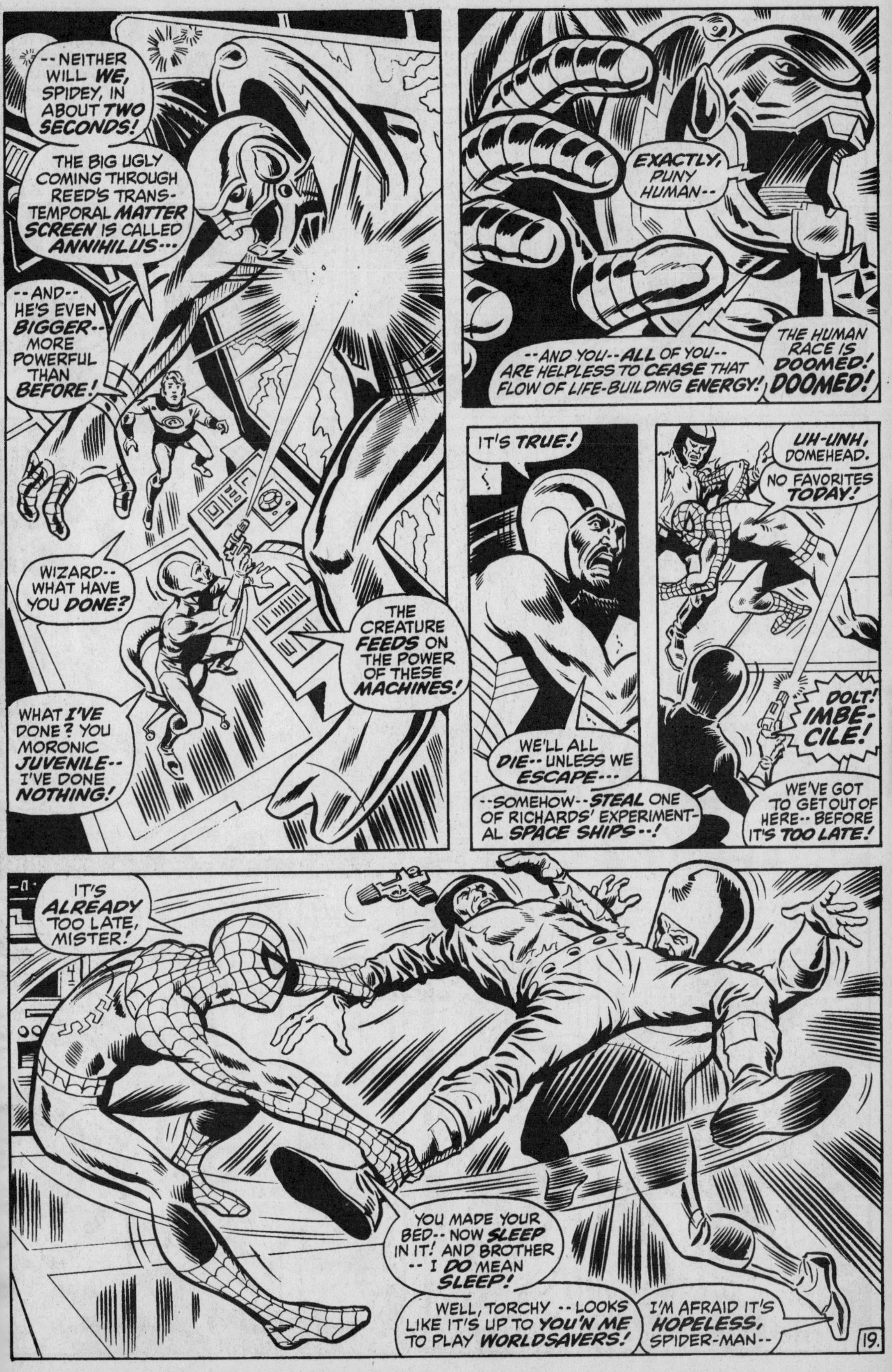
--NEITHER WILL WE, SPIDEY, IN ABOUT TWO SECONDS!
THE BIG UGLY COMING THROUGH REED'S TRANS-TEMPORAL MATTER SCREEN IS CALLED ANNIHILUS---
--AND-- HE'S EVEN BIGGER-- MORE POWERFUL THAN BEFORE!
WIZARD-- WHAT HAVE YOU DONE?
THE CREATURE FEEDS ON THE POWER OF THESE MACHINES!
WHAT I'VE DONE? YOU MORONIC JUVENILE-- I'VE DONE NOTHING!
EXACTLY, PUNY HUMAN--
--AND YOU--ALL OF YOU-- ARE HELPLESS TO CEASE THAT FLOW OF LIFE-BUILDING ENERGY!
THE HUMAN RACE IS DOOMED! DOOMED!
IT'S TRUE!
WE'LL ALL DIE-- UNLESS WE ESCAPE---
--SOMEHOW--STEAL ONE OF RICHARDS' EXPERIMENT-AL SPACE SHIPS--!
UH-UNH, DOMEHEAD.
NO FAVORITES TODAY!
DOLT! IMBE-CILE!
WE'VE GOT TO GET OUT OF HERE-- BEFORE IT'S TOO LATE!
IT'S ALREADY TOO LATE, MISTER!
YOU MADE YOUR BED-- NOW SLEEP IN IT! AND BROTHER -- I DO MEAN SLEEP!
WELL, TORCHY --LOOKS LIKE IT'S UP TO YOU'N ME TO PLAY WORLDSAVERS!
I'M AFRAID IT'S HOPELESS, SPIDER-MAN--
19.

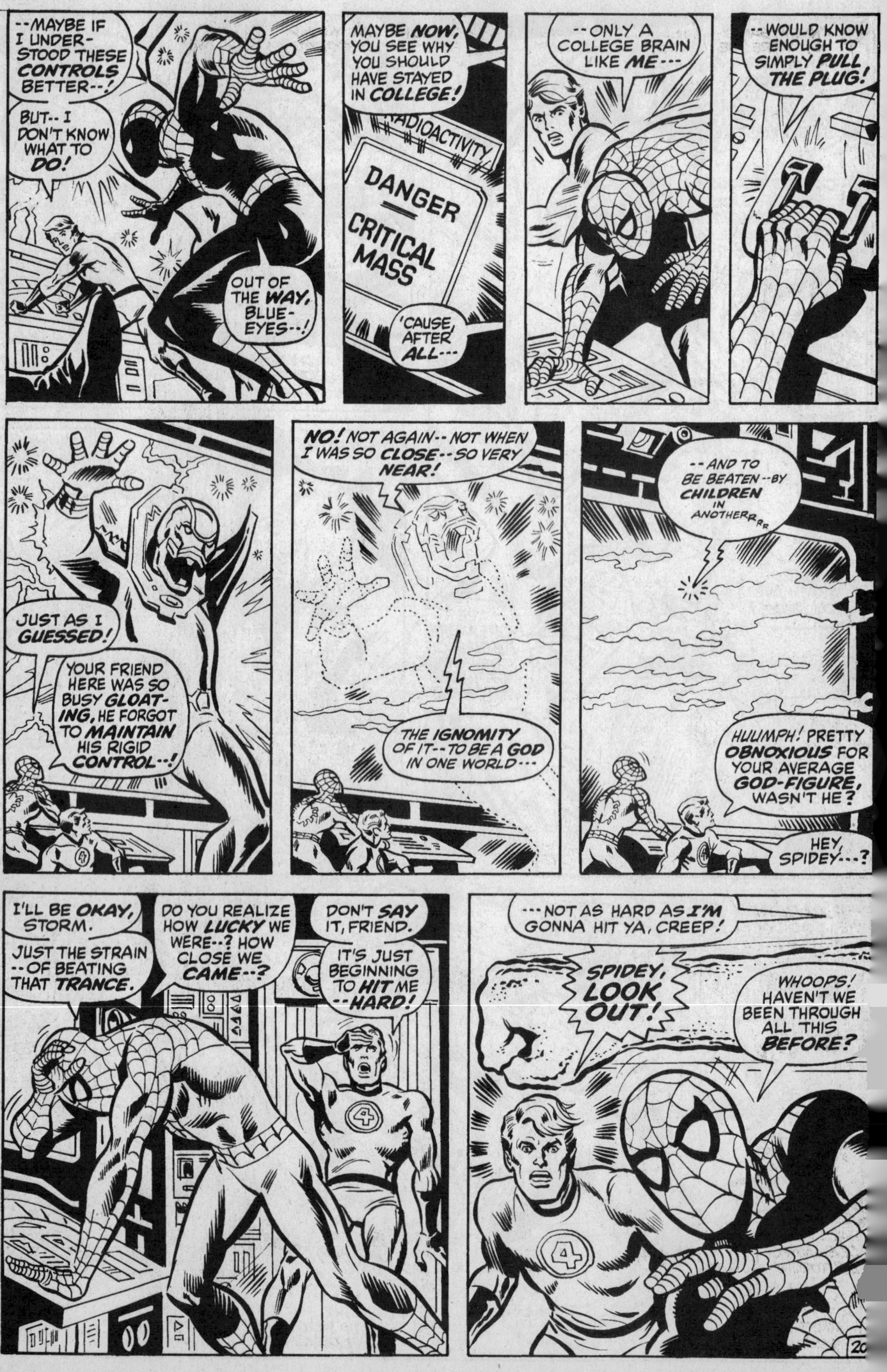
--MAYBE IF I UNDER-STOOD THESE CONTROLS BETTER--!
BUT-- I DON'T KNOW WHAT TO DO!
OUT OF THE WAY, BLUE-EYES--!
MAYBE NOW, YOU SEE WHY YOU SHOULD HAVE STAYED IN COLLEGE!
RADIOACTIVITY
DANGER
CRITICAL MASS
'CAUSE, AFTER ALL---
--ONLY A COLLEGE BRAIN LIKE ME---
--WOULD KNOW ENOUGH TO SIMPLY PULL THE PLUG!
JUST AS I GUESSED!
YOUR FRIEND HERE WAS SO BUSY GLOATING, HE FORGOT TO MAINTAIN HIS RIGID CONTROL--!
NO! NOT AGAIN-- NOT WHEN I WAS SO CLOSE--SO VERY NEAR!
THE IGNOMITY OF IT--TO BE A GOD IN ONE WORLD---
--AND TO BE BEATEN--BY CHILDREN IN ANOTHERRRR
HUUMPH! PRETTY OBNOXIOUS FOR YOUR AVERAGE GOD-FIGURE, WASN'T HE?
HEY, SPIDEY---?
I'LL BE OKAY, STORM.
JUST THE STRAIN --OF BEATING THAT TRANCE.
DO YOU REALIZE HOW LUCKY WE WERE--? HOW CLOSE WE CAME--?
DON'T SAY IT, FRIEND.
IT'S JUST BEGINNING TO HIT ME --HARD!
---NOT AS HARD AS I'M GONNA HIT YA, CREEP!
SPIDEY, LOOK OUT!
WHOOPS! HAVEN'T WE BEEN THROUGH ALL THIS BEFORE?
20

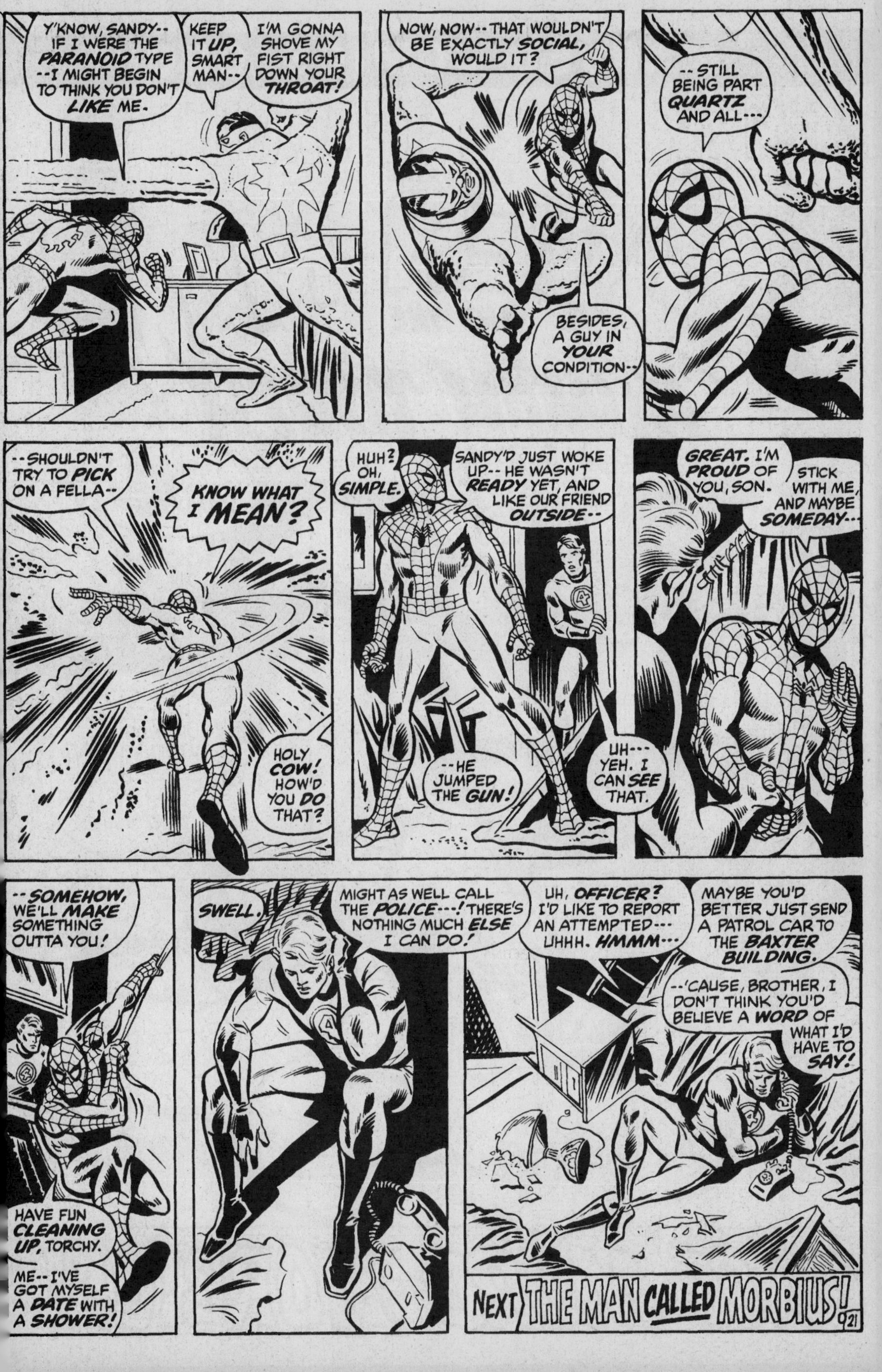
Y'KNOW, SANDY-- IF I WERE THE PARANOID TYPE --I MIGHT BEGIN TO THINK YOU DON'T LIKE ME.
KEEP IT UP, SMART MAN--
I'M GONNA SHOVE MY FIST RIGHT DOWN YOUR THROAT!
NOW, NOW-- THAT WOULDN'T BE EXACTLY SOCIAL, WOULD IT?
BESIDES, A GUY IN YOUR CONDITION--
--STILL BEING PART QUARTZ AND ALL---
--SHOULDN'T TRY TO PICK ON A FELLA--
KNOW WHAT I MEAN?
HOLY COW! HOW'D YOU DO THAT?
HUH? OH, SIMPLE.
SANDY'D JUST WOKE UP-- HE WASN'T READY YET, AND LIKE OUR FRIEND OUTSIDE--
--HE JUMPED THE GUN!
UH--- YEH. I CAN SEE THAT.
GREAT. I'M PROUD OF YOU, SON.
STICK WITH ME, AND MAYBE SOMEDAY---
--SOMEHOW, WE'LL MAKE SOMETHING OUTTA YOU!
HAVE FUN CLEANING UP, TORCHY.
ME-- I'VE GOT MYSELF A DATE WITH A SHOWER!
SWELL.
MIGHT AS WELL CALL THE POLICE---! THERE'S NOTHING MUCH ELSE I CAN DO!
UH, OFFICER? I'D LIKE TO REPORT AN ATTEMPTED--- UHHH. HMMM---
MAYBE YOU'D BETTER JUST SEND A PATROL CAR TO THE BAXTER BUILDING.
--'CAUSE, BROTHER, I DON'T THINK YOU'D BELIEVE A WORD OF WHAT I'D HAVE TO SAY!
NEXT THE MAN CALLED MORBIUS!
21

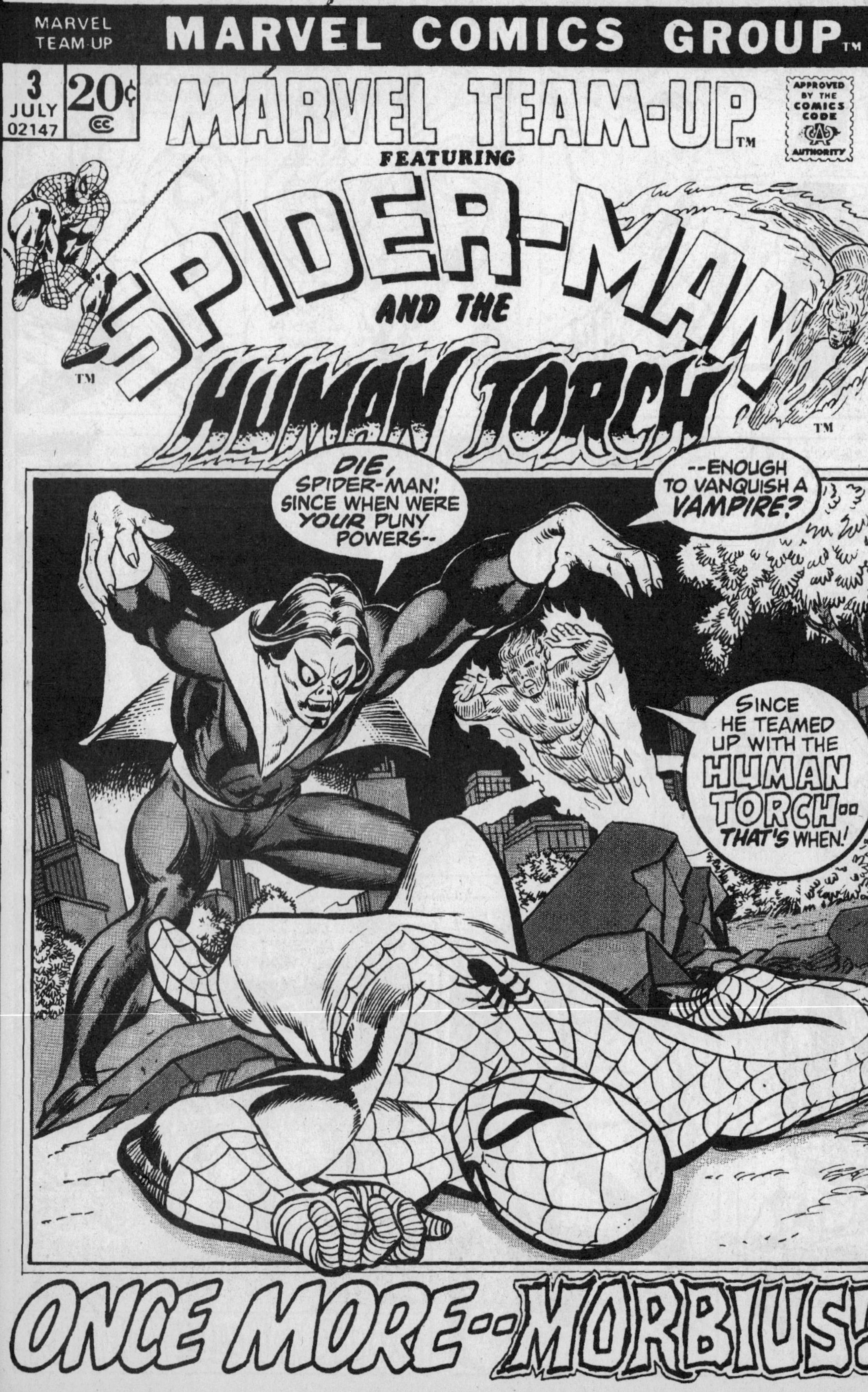
MARVEL TEAM-UP
MARVEL COMICS GROUP™
3 JULY 02147
20¢ CC
APPROVED BY THE COMICS CODE AUTHORITY
MARVEL TEAM-UP™
FEATURING
SPIDER-MAN™
AND THE
HUMAN TORCH™
DIE, SPIDER-MAN! SINCE WHEN WERE YOUR PUNY POWERS--
--ENOUGH TO VANQUISH A VAMPIRE?
SINCE HE TEAMED UP WITH THE HUMAN TORCH-- THAT'S WHEN!
ONCE MORE--MORBIUS!

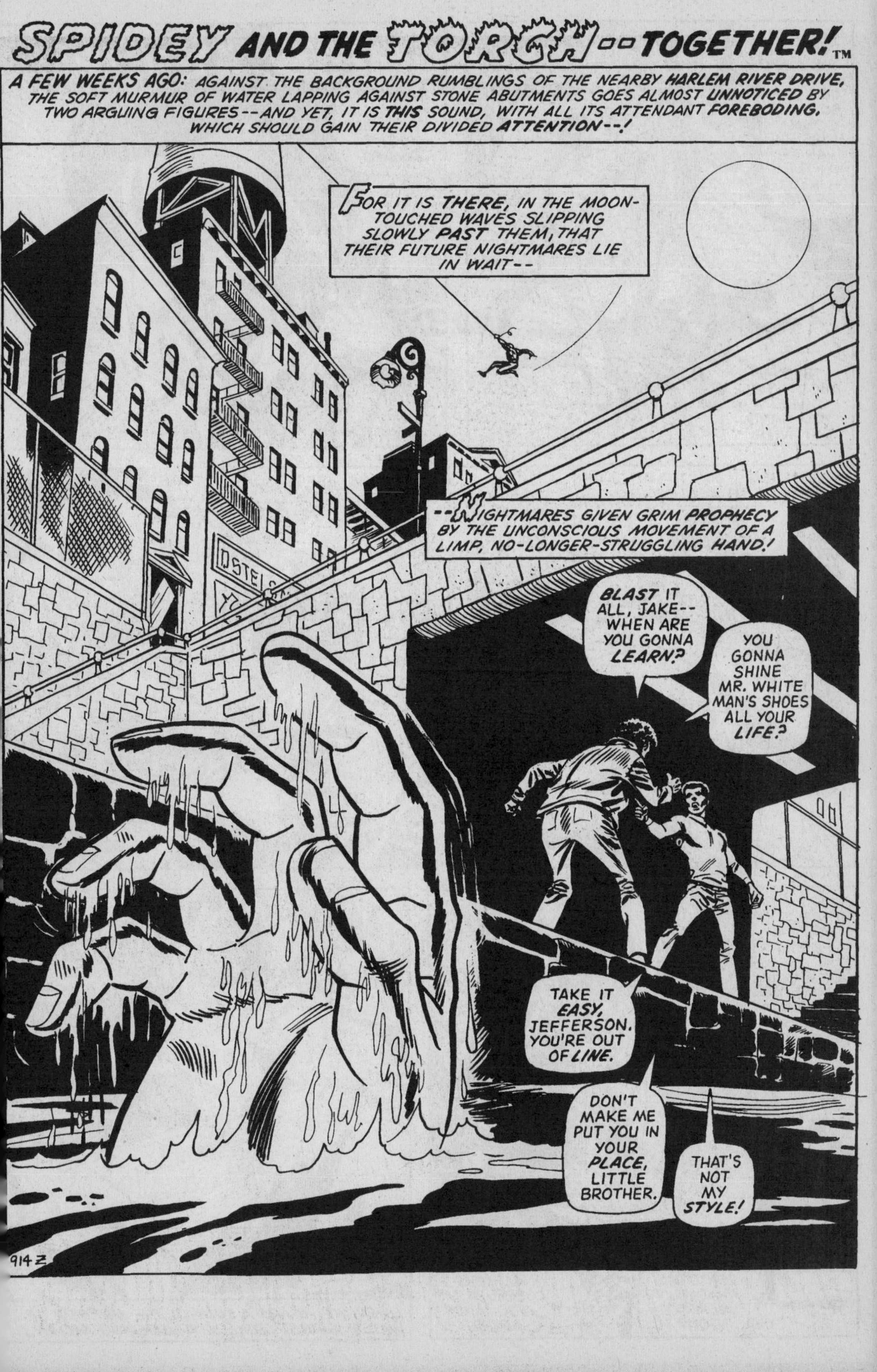
SPIDEY AND THE TORCH--TOGETHER! TM
A FEW WEEKS AGO: AGAINST THE BACKGROUND RUMBLINGS OF THE NEARBY HARLEM RIVER DRIVE, THE SOFT MURMUR OF WATER LAPPING AGAINST STONE ABUTMENTS GOES ALMOST UNNOTICED BY TWO ARGUING FIGURES--AND YET, IT IS THIS SOUND, WITH ALL ITS ATTENDANT FOREBODING, WHICH SHOULD GAIN THEIR DIVIDED ATTENTION--!
FOR IT IS THERE, IN THE MOON-TOUCHED WAVES SLIPPING SLOWLY PAST THEM, THAT THEIR FUTURE NIGHTMARES LIE IN WAIT--
--NIGHTMARES GIVEN GRIM PROPHECY BY THE UNCONSCIOUS MOVEMENT OF A LIMP, NO-LONGER-STRUGGLING HAND!
BLAST IT ALL, JAKE--WHEN ARE YOU GONNA LEARN?
YOU GONNA SHINE MR. WHITE MAN'S SHOES ALL YOUR LIFE?
TAKE IT EASY, JEFFERSON. YOU'RE OUT OF LINE.
DON'T MAKE ME PUT YOU IN YOUR PLACE, LITTLE BROTHER.
THAT'S NOT MY STYLE!
914 Z

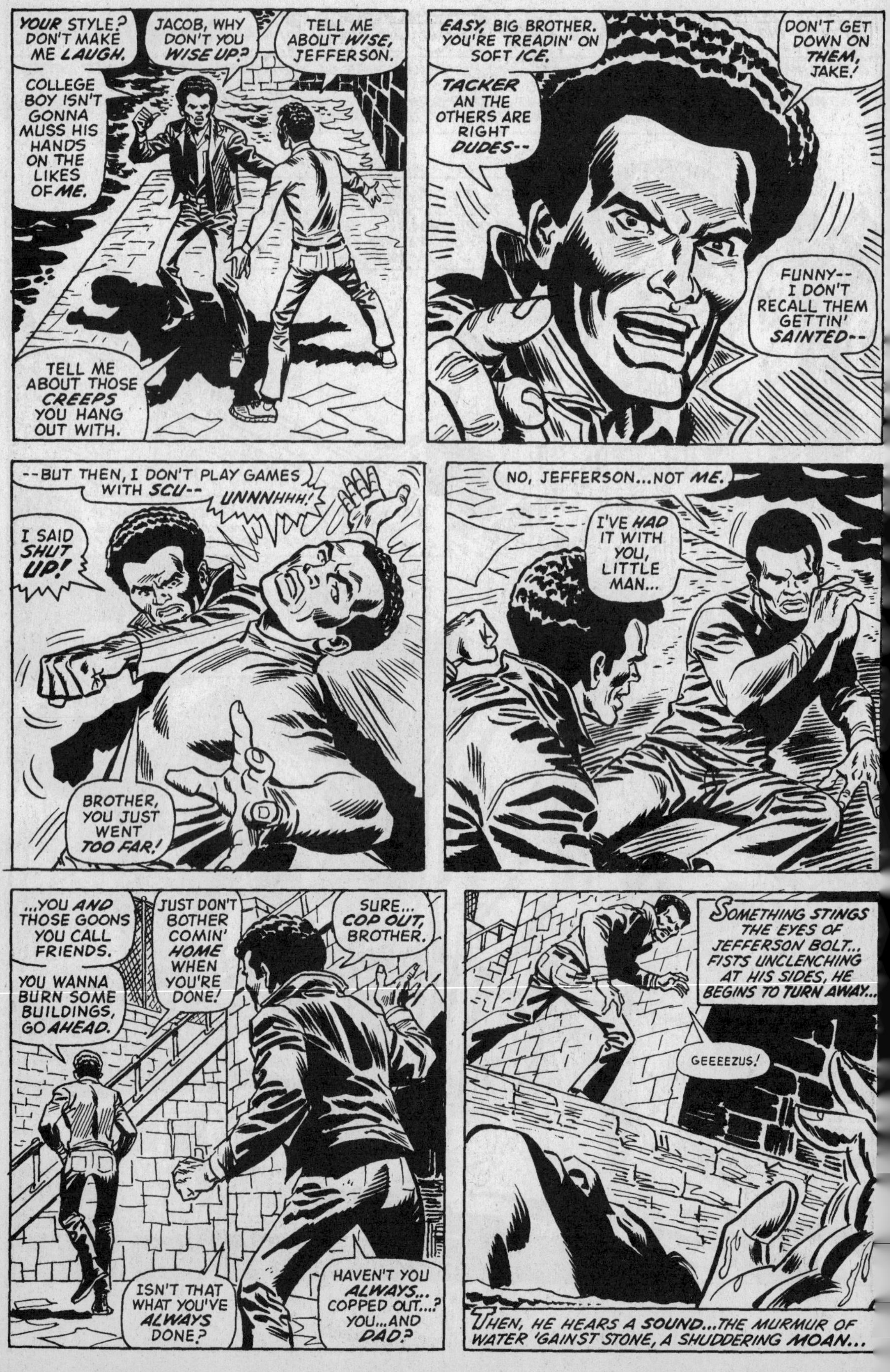
YOUR STYLE? DON'T MAKE ME LAUGH.
JACOB, WHY DON'T YOU WISE UP?
TELL ME ABOUT WISE, JEFFERSON.
COLLEGE BOY ISN'T GONNA MUSS HIS HANDS ON THE LIKES OF ME.
TELL ME ABOUT THOSE CREEPS YOU HANG OUT WITH.
EASY, BIG BROTHER. YOU'RE TREADIN' ON SOFT ICE.
TACKER AN THE OTHERS ARE RIGHT DUDES--
DON'T GET DOWN ON THEM, JAKE!
FUNNY-- I DON'T RECALL THEM GETTIN' SAINTED--
--BUT THEN, I DON'T PLAY GAMES WITH SCU--
UNNNHHH!
I SAID SHUT UP!
BROTHER, YOU JUST WENT TOO FAR!
NO, JEFFERSON...NOT ME.
I'VE HAD IT WITH YOU, LITTLE MAN...
...YOU AND THOSE GOONS YOU CALL FRIENDS.
YOU WANNA BURN SOME BUILDINGS, GO AHEAD.
JUST DON'T BOTHER COMIN' HOME WHEN YOU'RE DONE!
SURE... COP OUT, BROTHER.
ISN'T THAT WHAT YOU'VE ALWAYS DONE?
HAVEN'T YOU ALWAYS... COPPED OUT...? YOU...AND DAD?
SOMETHING STINGS THE EYES OF JEFFERSON BOLT... FISTS UNCLENCHING AT HIS SIDES, HE BEGINS TO TURN AWAY...
GEEEEZUS!
THEN, HE HEARS A SOUND...THE MURMUR OF WATER 'GAINST STONE, A SHUDDERING MOAN...

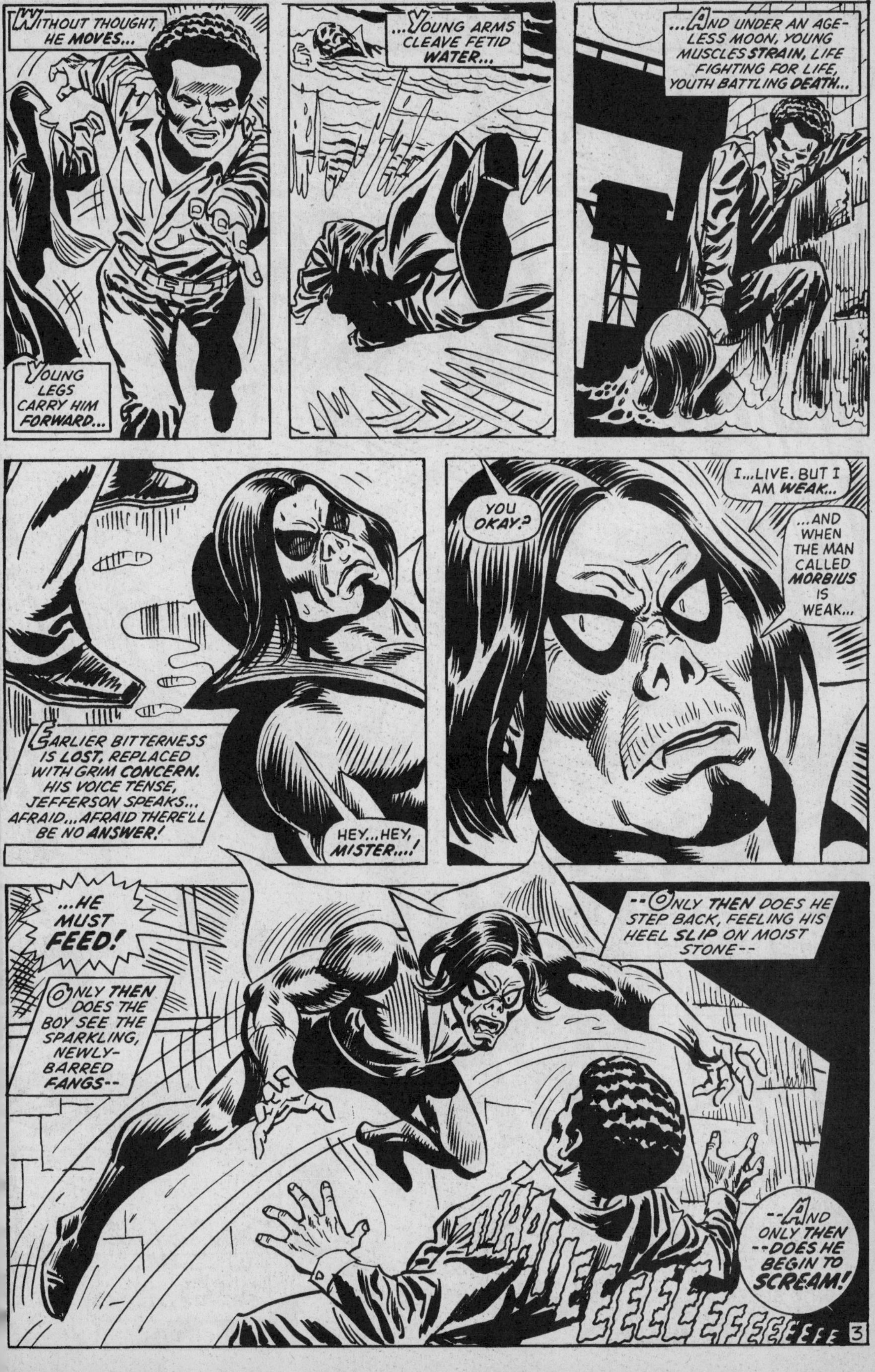
WITHOUT THOUGHT, HE MOVES...
YOUNG LEGS CARRY HIM FORWARD...
...YOUNG ARMS CLEAVE FETID WATER...
...AND UNDER AN AGE-LESS MOON, YOUNG MUSCLES STRAIN, LIFE FIGHTING FOR LIFE, YOUTH BATTLING DEATH...
EARLIER BITTERNESS IS LOST, REPLACED WITH GRIM CONCERN. HIS VOICE TENSE, JEFFERSON SPEAKS... AFRAID...AFRAID THERE'LL BE NO ANSWER!
HEY...HEY, MISTER...!
YOU OKAY?
I...LIVE. BUT I AM WEAK...
...AND WHEN THE MAN CALLED MORBIUS IS WEAK...
...HE MUST FEED!
ONLY THEN DOES THE BOY SEE THE SPARKLING, NEWLY-BARRED FANGS--
--ONLY THEN DOES HE STEP BACK, FEELING HIS HEEL SLIP ON MOIST STONE--
--AND ONLY THEN --DOES HE BEGIN TO SCREAM!
AAIEEEEEEEEEEEE

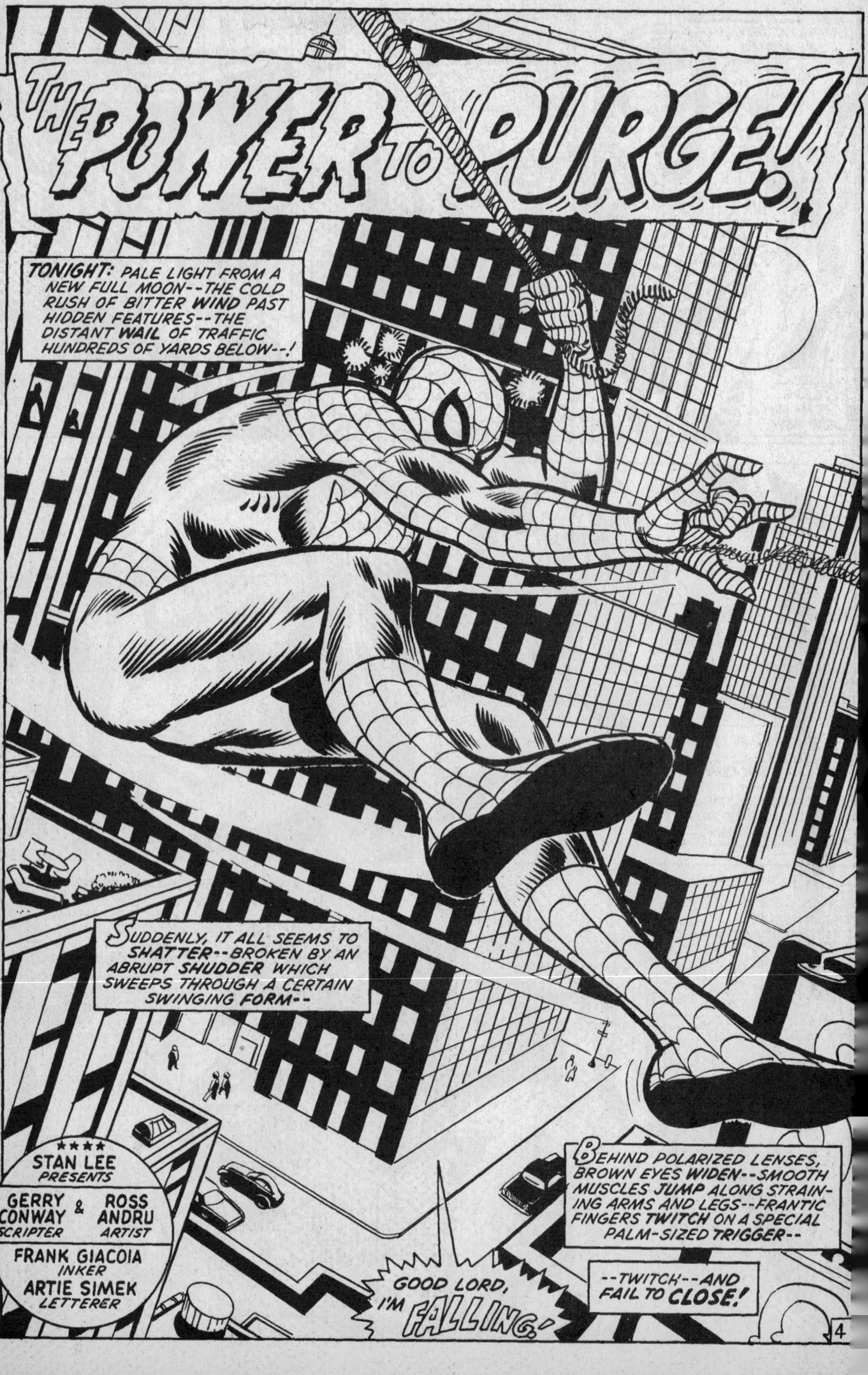

THE POWER TO PURGE!
TONIGHT: PALE LIGHT FROM A NEW FULL MOON--THE COLD RUSH OF BITTER WIND PAST HIDDEN FEATURES--THE DISTANT WAIL OF TRAFFIC HUNDREDS OF YARDS BELOW--!
SUDDENLY, IT ALL SEEMS TO SHATTER--BROKEN BY AN ABRUPT SHUDDER WHICH SWEEPS THROUGH A CERTAIN SWINGING FORM--
★★★★ STAN LEE PRESENTS
GERRY CONWAY SCRIPTER & ROSS ANDRU ARTIST
FRANK GIACOIA INKER
ARTIE SIMEK LETTERER
BEHIND POLARIZED LENSES, BROWN EYES WIDEN--SMOOTH MUSCLES JUMP ALONG STRAINING ARMS AND LEGS--FRANTIC FINGERS TWITCH ON A SPECIAL PALM-SIZED TRIGGER--
GOOD LORD, I'M FALLING!
--TWITCH--AND FAIL TO CLOSE!

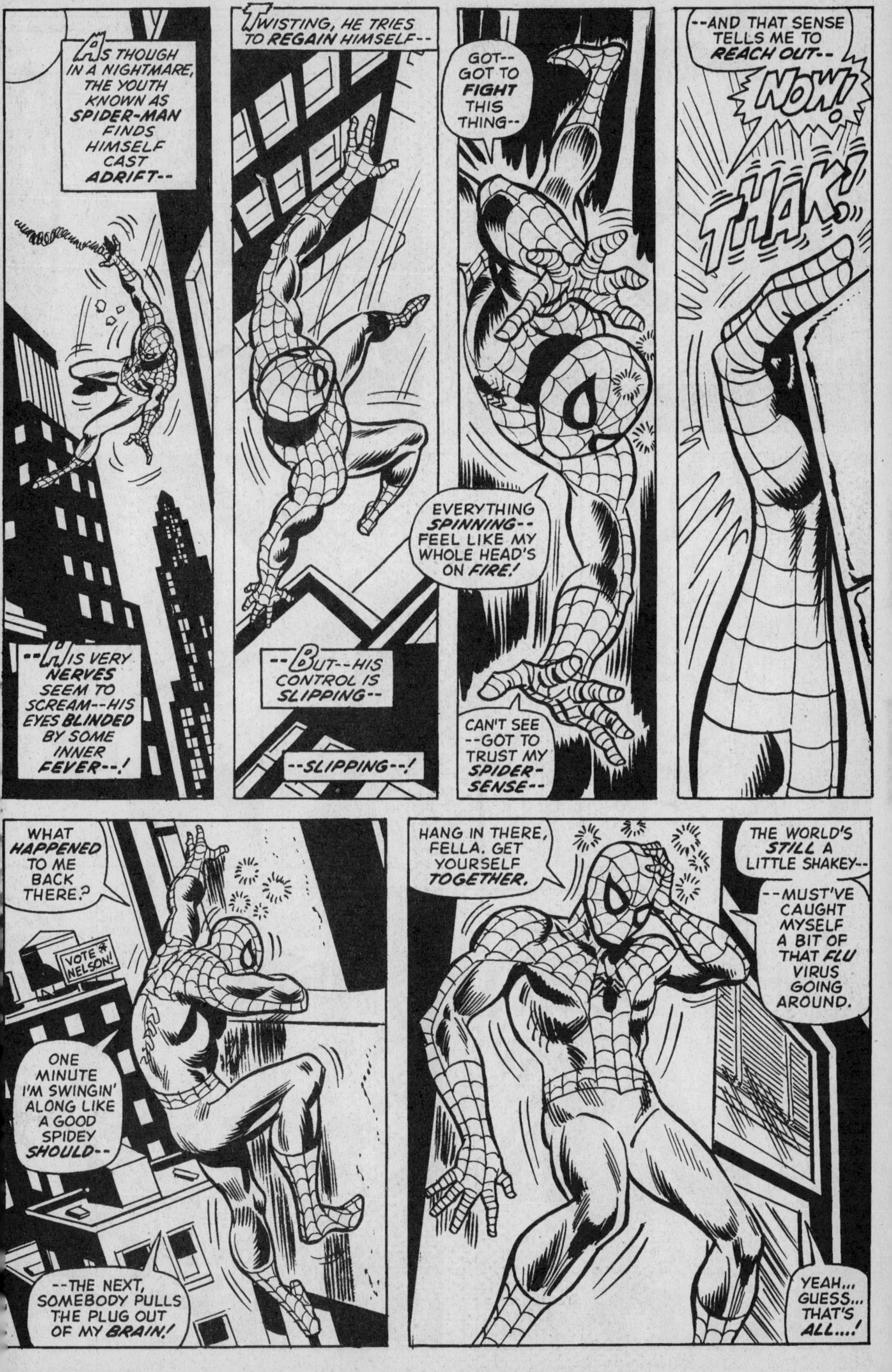
AS THOUGH IN A NIGHTMARE, THE YOUTH KNOWN AS SPIDER-MAN FINDS HIMSELF CAST ADRIFT--
--HIS VERY NERVES SEEM TO SCREAM--HIS EYES BLINDED BY SOME INNER FEVER--!
TWISTING, HE TRIES TO REGAIN HIMSELF--
--BUT--HIS CONTROL IS SLIPPING--
--SLIPPING--!
GOT-- GOT TO FIGHT THIS THING--
EVERYTHING SPINNING-- FEEL LIKE MY WHOLE HEAD'S ON FIRE!
CAN'T SEE --GOT TO TRUST MY SPIDER-SENSE--
--AND THAT SENSE TELLS ME TO REACH OUT--
NOW!
THAK!
WHAT HAPPENED TO ME BACK THERE?
VOTE NELSON!
ONE MINUTE I'M SWINGIN' ALONG LIKE A GOOD SPIDEY SHOULD--
--THE NEXT, SOMEBODY PULLS THE PLUG OUT OF MY BRAIN!
HANG IN THERE, FELLA. GET YOURSELF TOGETHER.
THE WORLD'S STILL A LITTLE SHAKEY--
--MUST'VE CAUGHT MYSELF A BIT OF THAT FLU VIRUS GOING AROUND.
YEAH... GUESS... THAT'S ALL...!

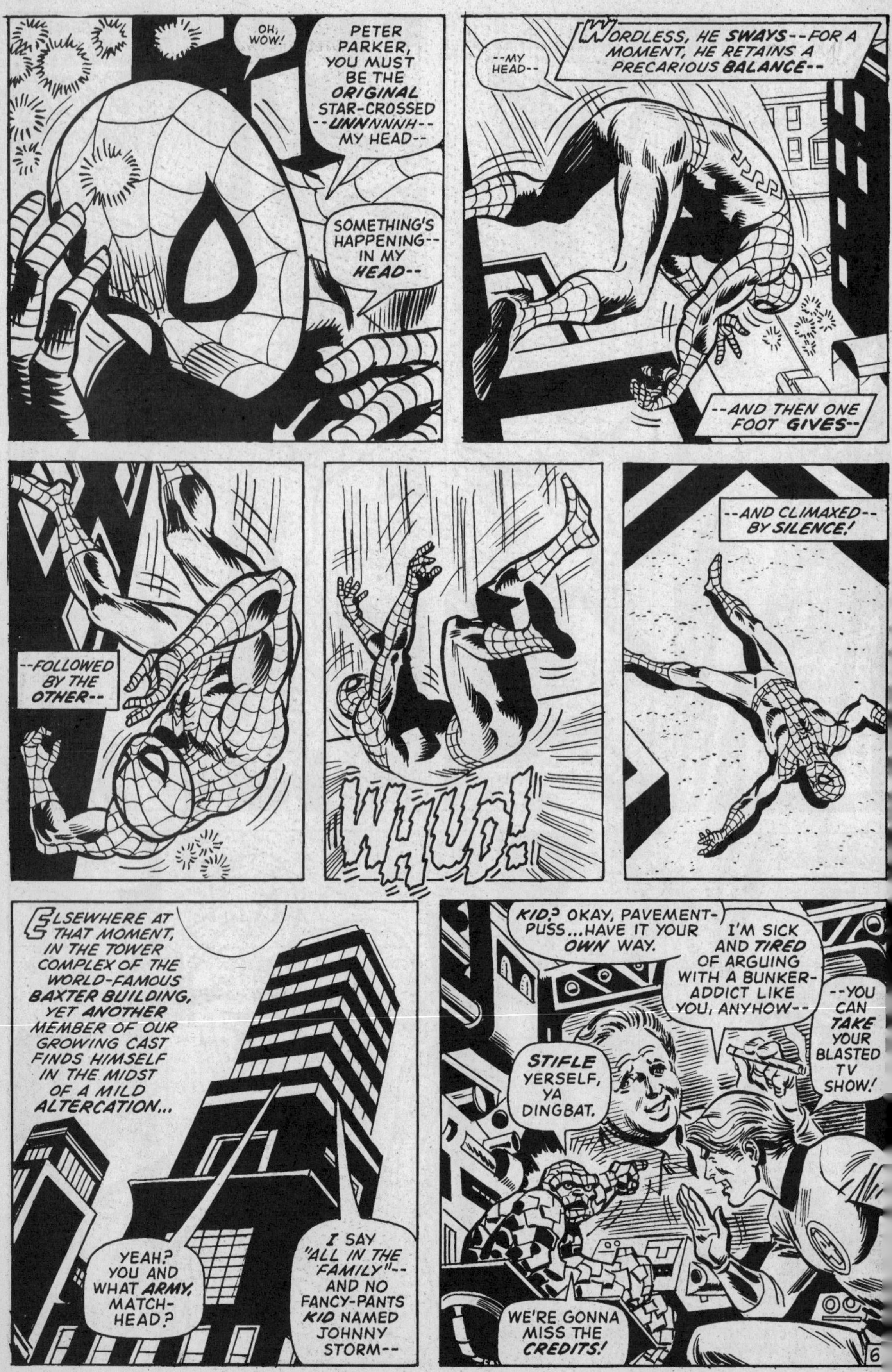
OH, WOW!
PETER PARKER, YOU MUST BE THE ORIGINAL STAR-CROSSED --UNNNNNH-- MY HEAD--
SOMETHING'S HAPPENING-- IN MY HEAD--
WORDLESS, HE SWAYS--FOR A MOMENT, HE RETAINS A PRECARIOUS BALANCE--
--MY HEAD--
--AND THEN ONE FOOT GIVES--
--FOLLOWED BY THE OTHER--
WHUD!
--AND CLIMAXED BY SILENCE!
ELSEWHERE AT THAT MOMENT, IN THE TOWER COMPLEX OF THE WORLD-FAMOUS BAXTER BUILDING, YET ANOTHER MEMBER OF OUR GROWING CAST FINDS HIMSELF IN THE MIDST OF A MILD ALTERCATION...
YEAH? YOU AND WHAT ARMY, MATCH-HEAD?
I SAY "ALL IN THE FAMILY"--AND NO FANCY-PANTS KID NAMED JOHNNY STORM--
KID? OKAY, PAVEMENT-PUSS...HAVE IT YOUR OWN WAY.
I'M SICK AND TIRED OF ARGUING WITH A BUNKER-ADDICT LIKE YOU, ANYHOW--
--YOU CAN TAKE YOUR BLASTED TV SHOW!
STIFLE YERSELF, YA DINGBAT.
WE'RE GONNA MISS THE CREDITS!
6

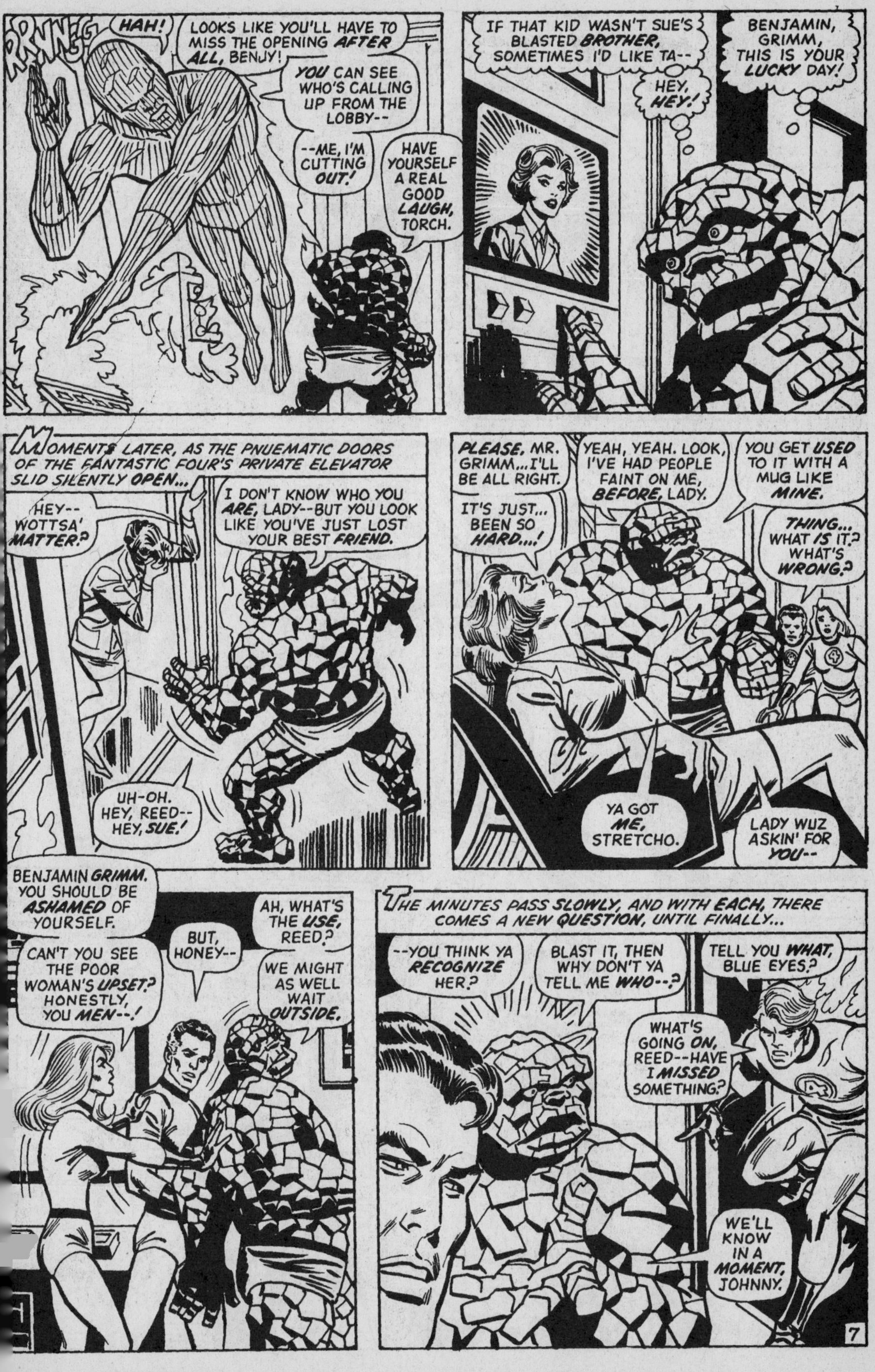

PRWNG
HAH!
LOOKS LIKE YOU'LL HAVE TO MISS THE OPENING AFTER ALL, BENJY!
YOU CAN SEE WHO'S CALLING UP FROM THE LOBBY--
--ME, I'M CUTTING OUT!
HAVE YOURSELF A REAL GOOD LAUGH, TORCH.
IF THAT KID WASN'T SUE'S BLASTED BROTHER, SOMETIMES I'D LIKE TA--
HEY, HEY!
BENJAMIN, GRIMM, THIS IS YOUR LUCKY DAY!
MOMENTS LATER, AS THE PNUEMATIC DOORS OF THE FANTASTIC FOUR'S PRIVATE ELEVATOR SLID SILENTLY OPEN...
HEY-- WOTTSA' MATTER?
I DON'T KNOW WHO YOU ARE, LADY--BUT YOU LOOK LIKE YOU'VE JUST LOST YOUR BEST FRIEND.
UH-OH. HEY, REED-- HEY, SUE!
PLEASE, MR. GRIMM... I'LL BE ALL RIGHT.
IT'S JUST... BEEN SO HARD...!
YEAH, YEAH. LOOK, I'VE HAD PEOPLE FAINT ON ME, BEFORE, LADY.
YOU GET USED TO IT WITH A MUG LIKE MINE.
THING... WHAT IS IT? WHAT'S WRONG?
YA GOT ME, STRETCHO.
LADY WUZ ASKIN' FOR YOU--
BENJAMIN GRIMM. YOU SHOULD BE ASHAMED OF YOURSELF.
CAN'T YOU SEE THE POOR WOMAN'S UPSET? HONESTLY, YOU MEN--!
BUT, HONEY--
AH, WHAT'S THE USE, REED?
WE MIGHT AS WELL WAIT OUTSIDE.
THE MINUTES PASS SLOWLY, AND WITH EACH, THERE COMES A NEW QUESTION, UNTIL FINALLY...
--YOU THINK YA RECOGNIZE HER?
BLAST IT, THEN WHY DON'T YA TELL ME WHO--?
TELL YOU WHAT, BLUE EYES?
WHAT'S GOING ON, REED--HAVE I MISSED SOMETHING?
WE'LL KNOW IN A MOMENT, JOHNNY.

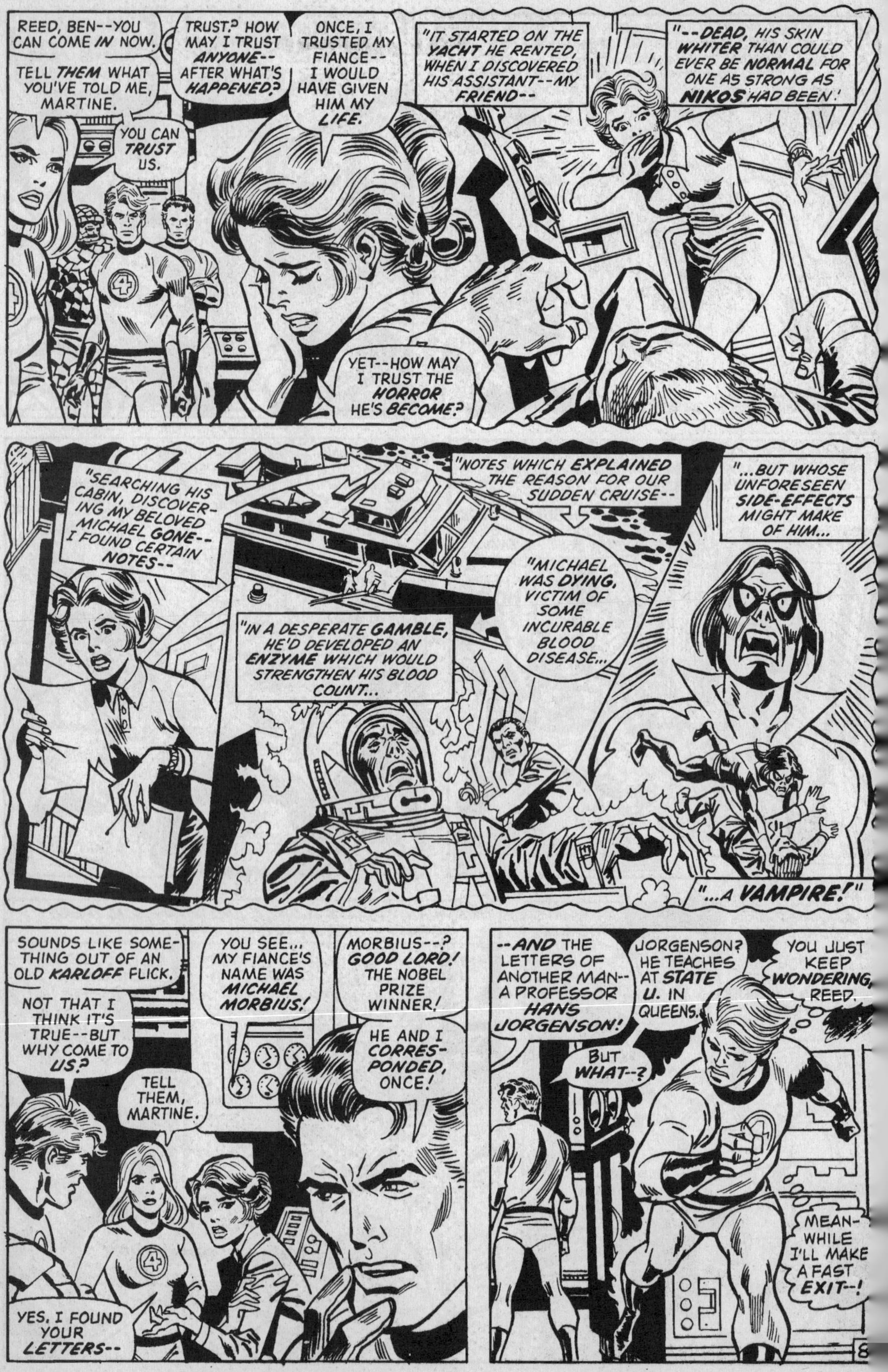
REED, BEN--YOU CAN COME IN NOW.
TELL THEM WHAT YOU'VE TOLD ME, MARTINE.
TRUST? HOW MAY I TRUST ANYONE-- AFTER WHAT'S HAPPENED?
YOU CAN TRUST US.
ONCE, I TRUSTED MY FIANCE-- I WOULD HAVE GIVEN HIM MY LIFE.
YET--HOW MAY I TRUST THE HORROR HE'S BECOME?
"IT STARTED ON THE YACHT HE RENTED, WHEN I DISCOVERED HIS ASSISTANT--MY FRIEND--
"--DEAD, HIS SKIN WHITER THAN COULD EVER BE NORMAL FOR ONE AS STRONG AS NIKOS HAD BEEN!
"SEARCHING HIS CABIN, DISCOVERING MY BELOVED MICHAEL GONE--I FOUND CERTAIN NOTES--
"NOTES WHICH EXPLAINED THE REASON FOR OUR SUDDEN CRUISE--
"MICHAEL WAS DYING, VICTIM OF SOME INCURABLE BLOOD DISEASE...
"IN A DESPERATE GAMBLE, HE'D DEVELOPED AN ENZYME WHICH WOULD STRENGTHEN HIS BLOOD COUNT...
"...BUT WHOSE UNFORESEEN SIDE-EFFECTS MIGHT MAKE OF HIM...
"...A VAMPIRE!"
SOUNDS LIKE SOMETHING OUT OF AN OLD KARLOFF FLICK.
NOT THAT I THINK IT'S TRUE--BUT WHY COME TO US?
TELL THEM, MARTINE.
YES, I FOUND YOUR LETTERS--
YOU SEE... MY FIANCE'S NAME WAS MICHAEL MORBIUS!
MORBIUS--? GOOD LORD! THE NOBEL PRIZE WINNER!
HE AND I CORRESPONDED, ONCE!
--AND THE LETTERS OF ANOTHER MAN--A PROFESSOR HANS JORGENSON!
JORGENSON? HE TEACHES AT STATE U. IN QUEENS.
BUT WHAT--?
YOU JUST KEEP WONDERING, REED.
MEAN-WHILE I'LL MAKE A FAST EXIT--!
8

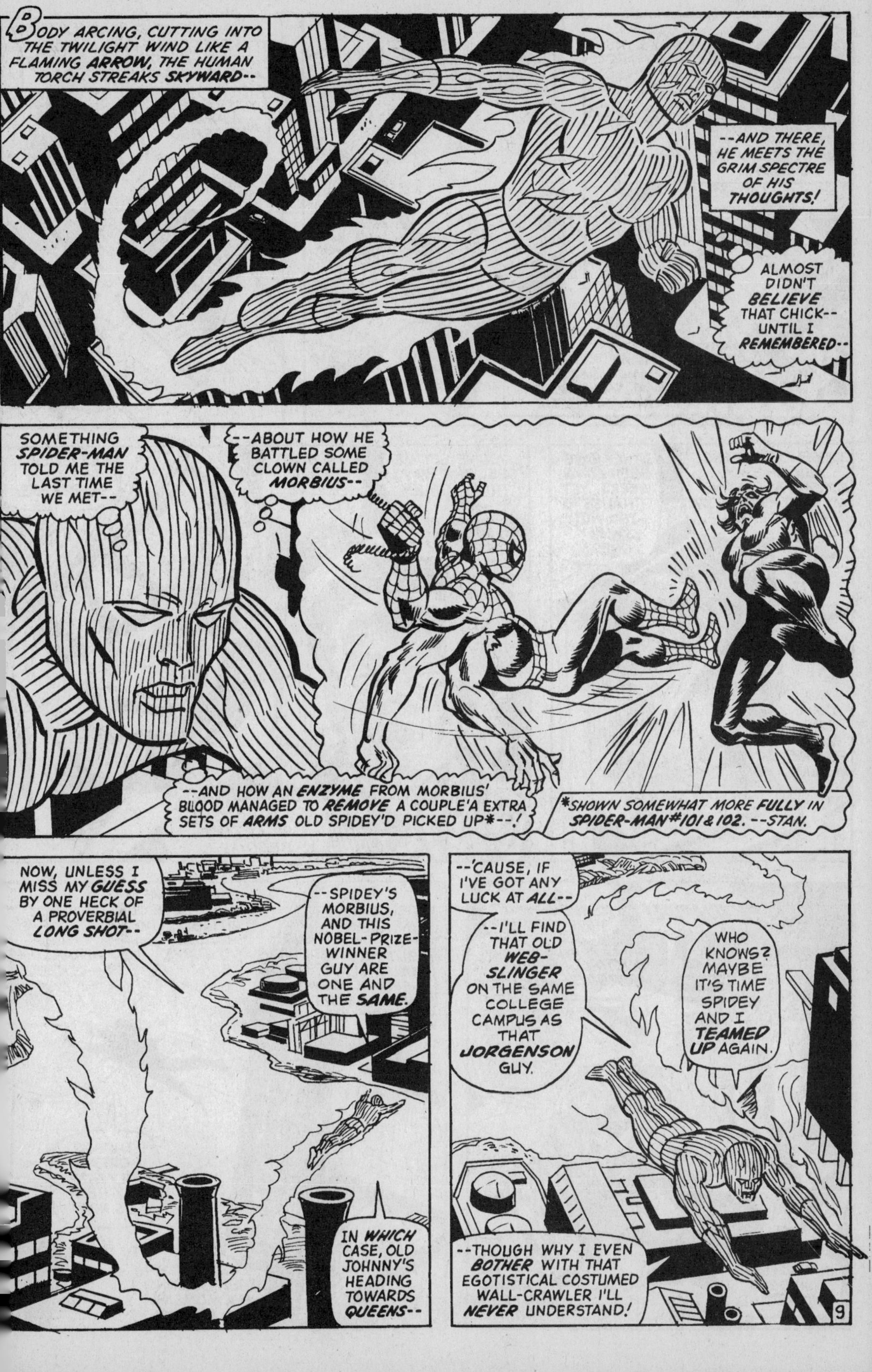
BODY ARCING, CUTTING INTO THE TWILIGHT WIND LIKE A FLAMING ARROW, THE HUMAN TORCH STREAKS SKYWARD--
--AND THERE, HE MEETS THE GRIM SPECTRE OF HIS THOUGHTS!
ALMOST DIDN'T BELIEVE THAT CHICK-- UNTIL I REMEMBERED--
SOMETHING SPIDER-MAN TOLD ME THE LAST TIME WE MET--
--ABOUT HOW HE BATTLED SOME CLOWN CALLED MORBIUS--
--AND HOW AN ENZYME FROM MORBIUS' BLOOD MANAGED TO REMOVE A COUPLE'A EXTRA SETS OF ARMS OLD SPIDEY'D PICKED UP*--!
*SHOWN SOMEWHAT MORE FULLY IN SPIDER-MAN #101 & 102. --STAN.
NOW, UNLESS I MISS MY GUESS BY ONE HECK OF A PROVERBIAL LONG SHOT--
--SPIDEY'S MORBIUS, AND THIS NOBEL-PRIZE-WINNER GUY ARE ONE AND THE SAME.
IN WHICH CASE, OLD JOHNNY'S HEADING TOWARDS QUEENS--
--'CAUSE, IF I'VE GOT ANY LUCK AT ALL--
--I'LL FIND THAT OLD WEB-SLINGER ON THE SAME COLLEGE CAMPUS AS THAT JORGENSON GUY.
WHO KNOWS? MAYBE IT'S TIME SPIDEY AND I TEAMED UP AGAIN.
--THOUGH WHY I EVEN BOTHER WITH THAT EGOTISTICAL COSTUMED WALL-CRAWLER I'LL NEVER UNDERSTAND!
9

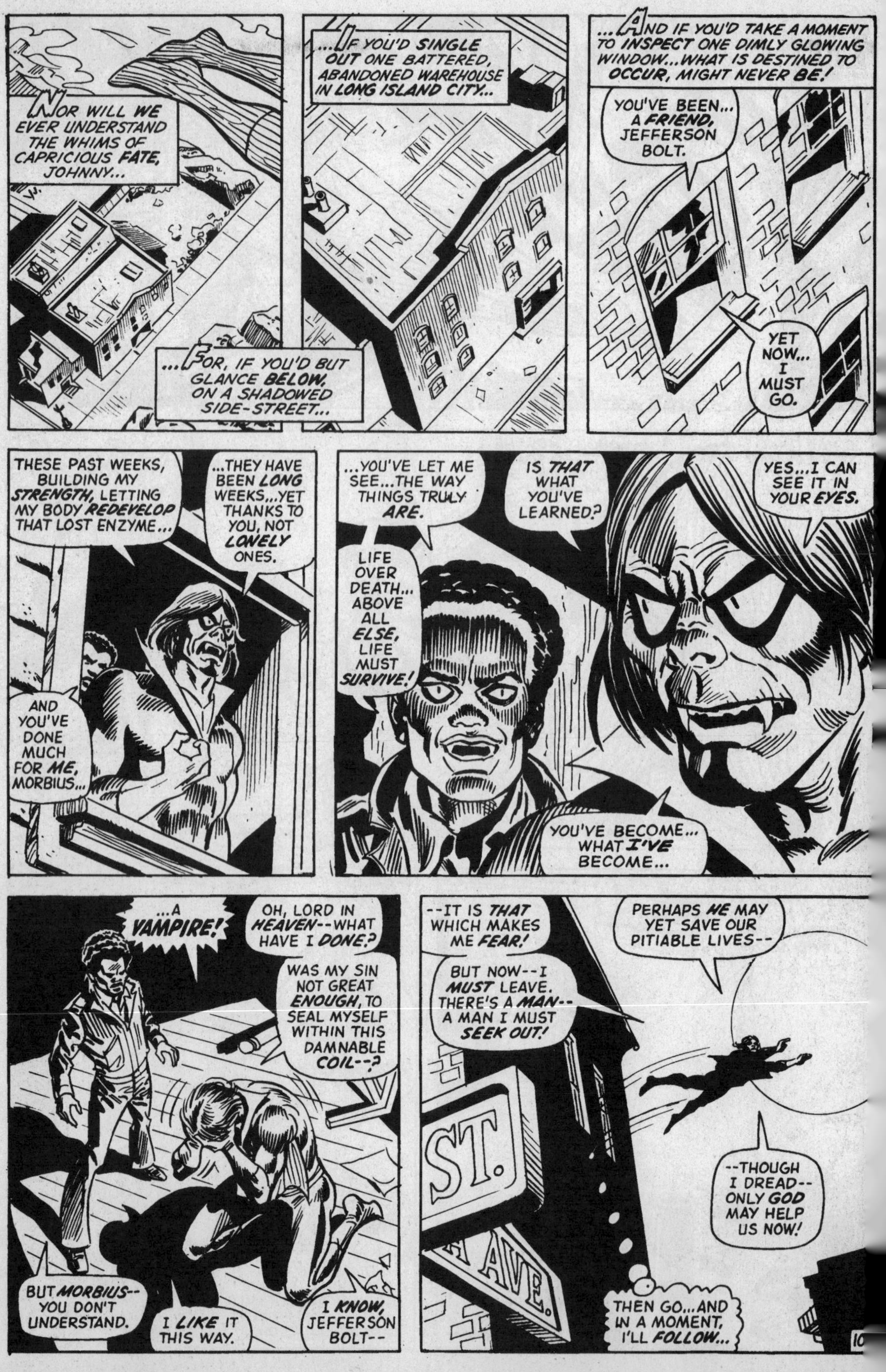
NOR WILL WE EVER UNDERSTAND THE WHIMS OF CAPRICIOUS FATE, JOHNNY...
...FOR, IF YOU'D BUT GLANCE BELOW, ON A SHADOWED SIDE-STREET...
...IF YOU'D SINGLE OUT ONE BATTERED, ABANDONED WAREHOUSE IN LONG ISLAND CITY...
...AND IF YOU'D TAKE A MOMENT TO INSPECT ONE DIMLY GLOWING WINDOW...WHAT IS DESTINED TO OCCUR, MIGHT NEVER BE!
YOU'VE BEEN... A FRIEND, JEFFERSON BOLT.
YET NOW... I MUST GO.
THESE PAST WEEKS, BUILDING MY STRENGTH, LETTING MY BODY REDEVELOP THAT LOST ENZYME...
...THEY HAVE BEEN LONG WEEKS...YET THANKS TO YOU, NOT LONELY ONES.
AND YOU'VE DONE MUCH FOR ME, MORBIUS...
...YOU'VE LET ME SEE...THE WAY THINGS TRULY ARE.
LIFE OVER DEATH... ABOVE ALL ELSE, LIFE MUST SURVIVE!
IS THAT WHAT YOU'VE LEARNED?
YES...I CAN SEE IT IN YOUR EYES.
YOU'VE BECOME... WHAT I'VE BECOME...
...A VAMPIRE!
OH, LORD IN HEAVEN--WHAT HAVE I DONE?
WAS MY SIN NOT GREAT ENOUGH, TO SEAL MYSELF WITHIN THIS DAMNABLE COIL--?
BUT MORBIUS-- YOU DON'T UNDERSTAND.
I LIKE IT THIS WAY.
I KNOW, JEFFERSON BOLT--
--IT IS THAT WHICH MAKES ME FEAR!
BUT NOW--I MUST LEAVE. THERE'S A MAN-- A MAN I MUST SEEK OUT!
ST.
AVE.
PERHAPS HE MAY YET SAVE OUR PITIABLE LIVES--
--THOUGH I DREAD-- ONLY GOD MAY HELP US NOW!
THEN GO...AND IN A MOMENT, I'LL FOLLOW...

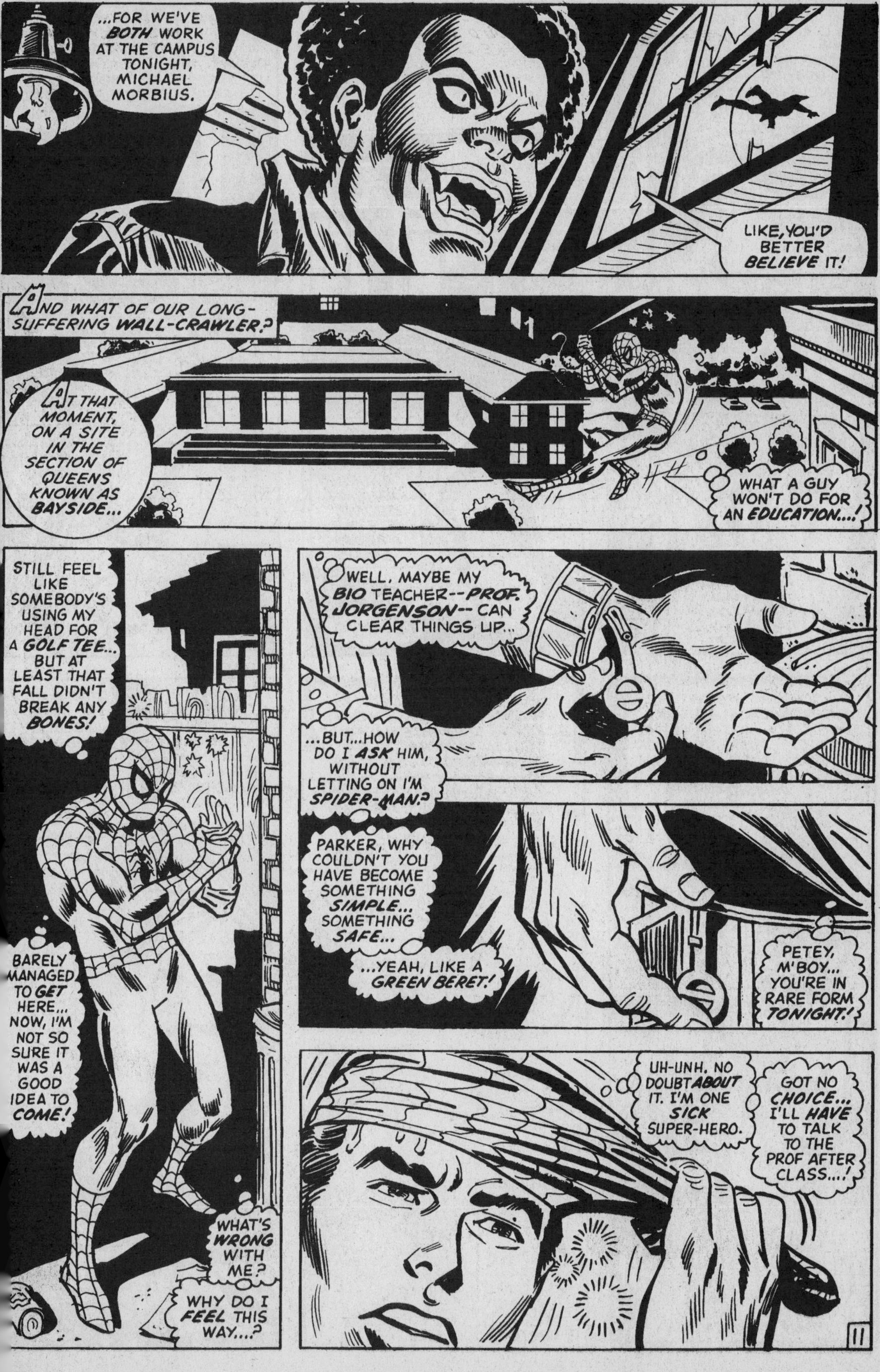
...FOR WE'VE BOTH WORK AT THE CAMPUS TONIGHT, MICHAEL MORBIUS.
LIKE, YOU'D BETTER BELIEVE IT!
AND WHAT OF OUR LONG-SUFFERING WALL-CRAWLER?
AT THAT MOMENT, ON A SITE IN THE SECTION OF QUEENS KNOWN AS BAYSIDE...
WHAT A GUY WON'T DO FOR AN EDUCATION...!
STILL FEEL LIKE SOMEBODY'S USING MY HEAD FOR A GOLF TEE... BUT AT LEAST THAT FALL DIDN'T BREAK ANY BONES!
BARELY MANAGED TO GET HERE... NOW, I'M NOT SO SURE IT WAS A GOOD IDEA TO COME!
WHAT'S WRONG WITH ME?
WHY DO I FEEL THIS WAY...?
WELL, MAYBE MY BIO TEACHER--PROF. JORGENSON--CAN CLEAR THINGS UP...
...BUT...HOW DO I ASK HIM, WITHOUT LETTING ON I'M SPIDER-MAN?
PARKER, WHY COULDN'T YOU HAVE BECOME SOMETHING SIMPLE... SOMETHING SAFE...
...YEAH, LIKE A GREEN BERET!
PETEY, M'BOY... YOU'RE IN RARE FORM TONIGHT!
UH-UNH. NO DOUBT ABOUT IT. I'M ONE SICK SUPER-HERO.
GOT NO CHOICE... I'LL HAVE TO TALK TO THE PROF AFTER CLASS...!

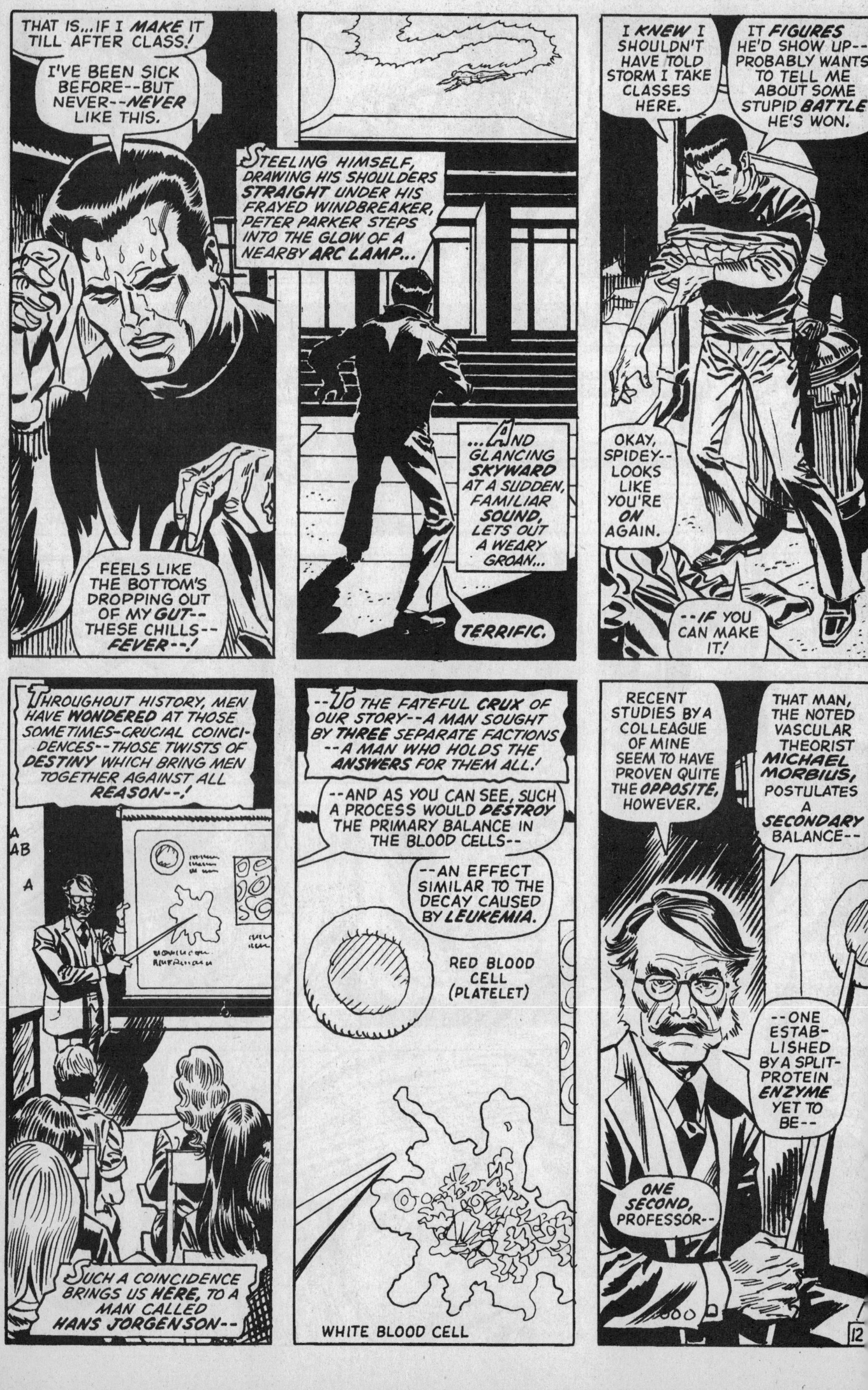

THAT IS...IF I MAKE IT TILL AFTER CLASS!
I'VE BEEN SICK BEFORE--BUT NEVER--NEVER LIKE THIS.
FEELS LIKE THE BOTTOM'S DROPPING OUT OF MY GUT-- THESE CHILLS-- FEVER--!
STEELING HIMSELF, DRAWING HIS SHOULDERS STRAIGHT UNDER HIS FRAYED WINDBREAKER, PETER PARKER STEPS INTO THE GLOW OF A NEARBY ARC LAMP...
...AND GLANCING SKYWARD AT A SUDDEN, FAMILIAR SOUND, LETS OUT A WEARY GROAN...
TERRIFIC.
I KNEW I SHOULDN'T HAVE TOLD STORM I TAKE CLASSES HERE.
IT FIGURES HE'D SHOW UP-- PROBABLY WANTS TO TELL ME ABOUT SOME STUPID BATTLE HE'S WON.
OKAY, SPIDEY-- LOOKS LIKE YOU'RE ON AGAIN.
--IF YOU CAN MAKE IT!
THROUGHOUT HISTORY, MEN HAVE WONDERED AT THOSE SOMETIMES-CRUCIAL COINCIDENCES--THOSE TWISTS OF DESTINY WHICH BRING MEN TOGETHER AGAINST ALL REASON--!
SUCH A COINCIDENCE BRINGS US HERE, TO A MAN CALLED HANS JORGENSON--
--TO THE FATEFUL CRUX OF OUR STORY--A MAN SOUGHT BY THREE SEPARATE FACTIONS --A MAN WHO HOLDS THE ANSWERS FOR THEM ALL!
--AND AS YOU CAN SEE, SUCH A PROCESS WOULD DESTROY THE PRIMARY BALANCE IN THE BLOOD CELLS--
--AN EFFECT SIMILAR TO THE DECAY CAUSED BY LEUKEMIA.
RED BLOOD CELL (PLATELET)
WHITE BLOOD CELL
RECENT STUDIES BY A COLLEAGUE OF MINE SEEM TO HAVE PROVEN QUITE THE OPPOSITE, HOWEVER.
THAT MAN, THE NOTED VASCULAR THEORIST MICHAEL MORBIUS, POSTULATES A SECONDARY BALANCE--
--ONE ESTABLISHED BY A SPLIT-PROTEIN ENZYME YET TO BE--
ONE SECOND, PROFESSOR--
12

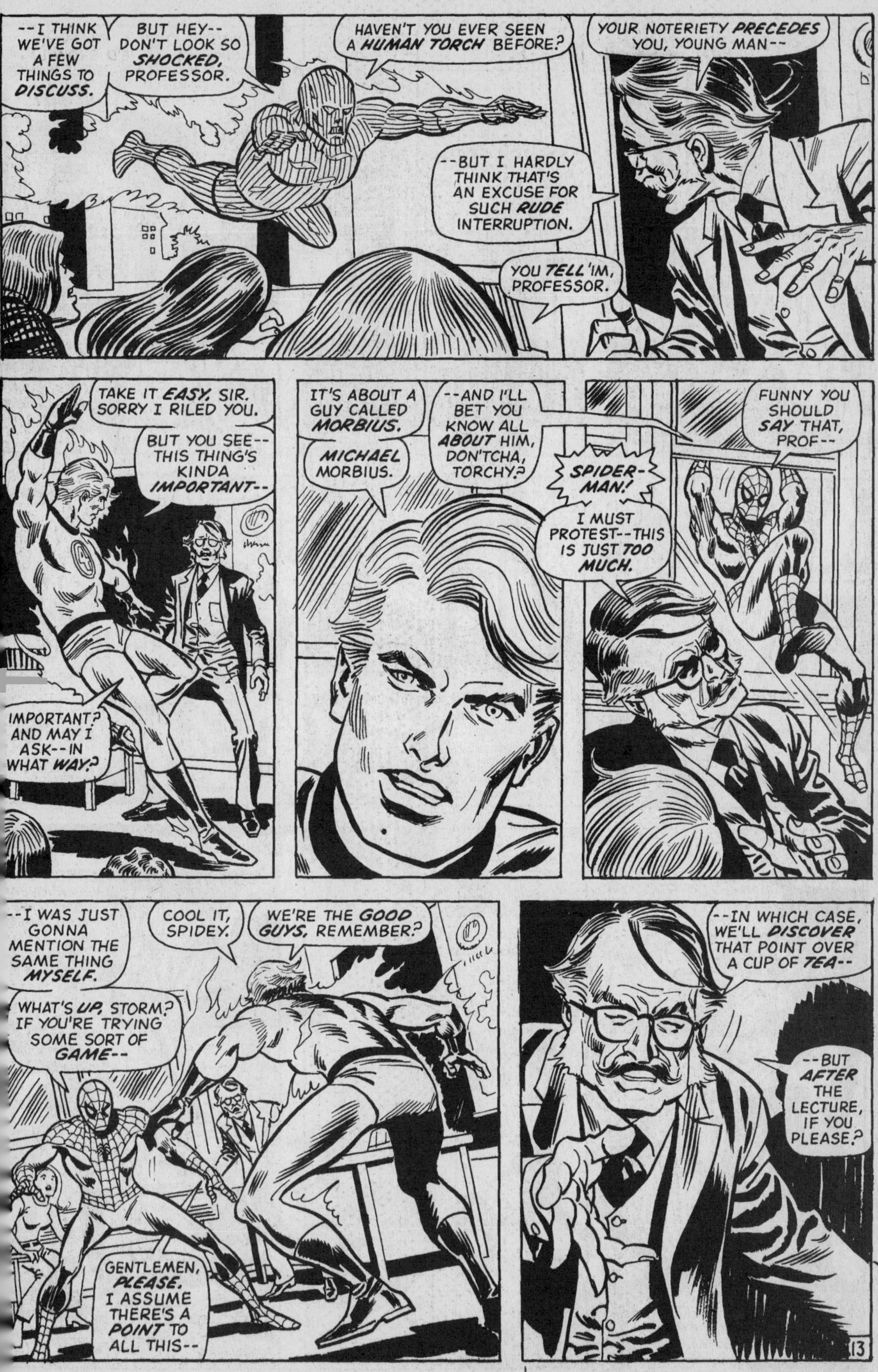
--I THINK WE'VE GOT A FEW THINGS TO DISCUSS.
BUT HEY-- DON'T LOOK SO SHOCKED, PROFESSOR.
HAVEN'T YOU EVER SEEN A HUMAN TORCH BEFORE?
YOUR NOTERIETY PRECEDES YOU, YOUNG MAN--
--BUT I HARDLY THINK THAT'S AN EXCUSE FOR SUCH RUDE INTERRUPTION.
YOU TELL 'IM, PROFESSOR.
TAKE IT EASY, SIR. SORRY I RILED YOU.
BUT YOU SEE-- THIS THING'S KINDA IMPORTANT--
IMPORTANT? AND MAY I ASK--IN WHAT WAY?
IT'S ABOUT A GUY CALLED MORBIUS.
MICHAEL MORBIUS.
--AND I'LL BET YOU KNOW ALL ABOUT HIM, DON'TCHA, TORCHY?
SPIDER-MAN!
I MUST PROTEST--THIS IS JUST TOO MUCH.
FUNNY YOU SHOULD SAY THAT, PROF--
--I WAS JUST GONNA MENTION THE SAME THING MYSELF.
COOL IT, SPIDEY.
WE'RE THE GOOD GUYS, REMEMBER?
WHAT'S UP, STORM? IF YOU'RE TRYING SOME SORT OF GAME--
GENTLEMEN, PLEASE. I ASSUME THERE'S A POINT TO ALL THIS--
--IN WHICH CASE, WE'LL DISCOVER THAT POINT OVER A CUP OF TEA--
--BUT AFTER THE LECTURE, IF YOU PLEASE?
13

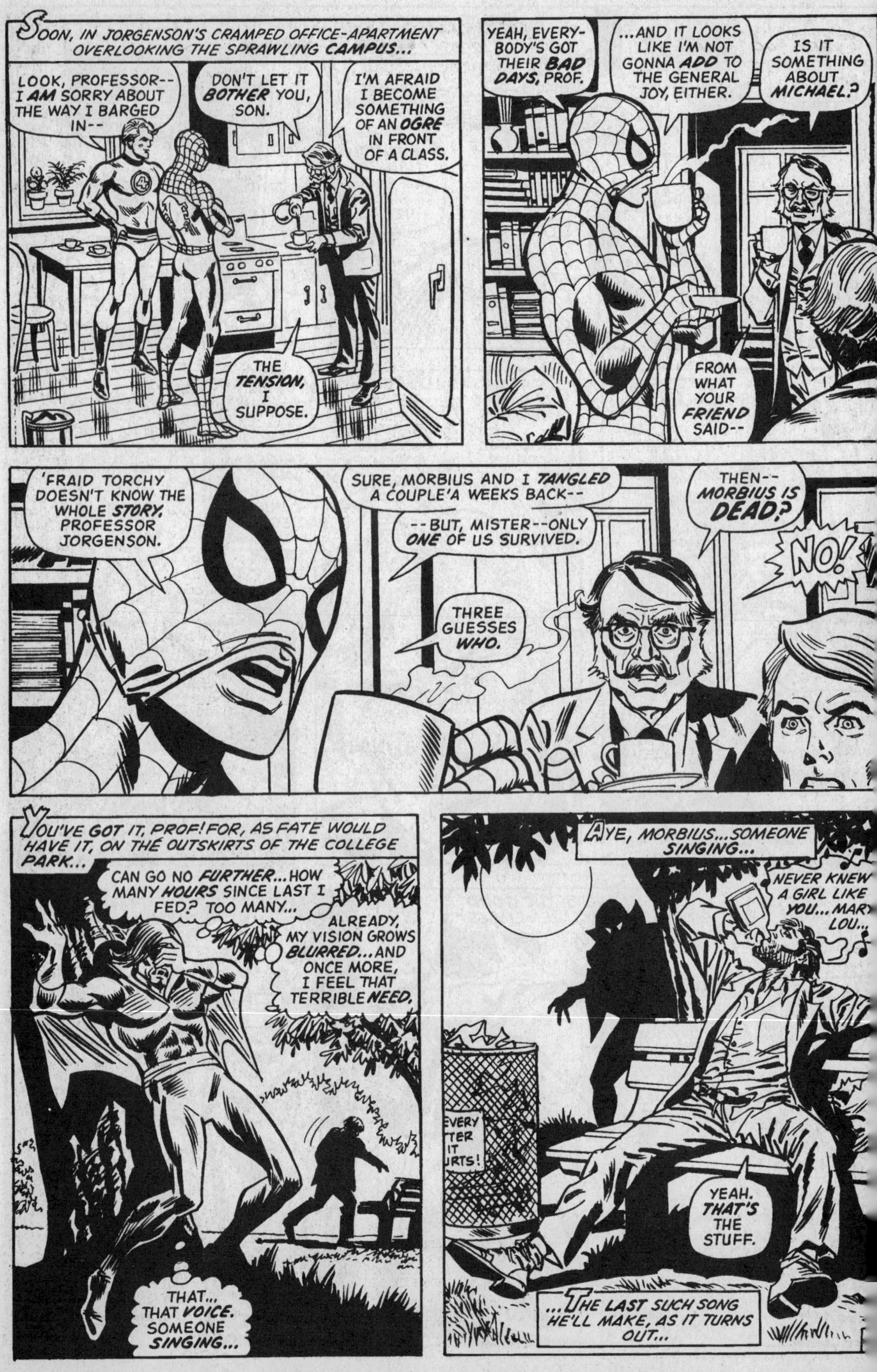
SOON, IN JORGENSON'S CRAMPED OFFICE-APARTMENT OVERLOOKING THE SPRAWLING CAMPUS...
LOOK, PROFESSOR-- I AM SORRY ABOUT THE WAY I BARGED IN--
DON'T LET IT BOTHER YOU, SON.
I'M AFRAID I BECOME SOMETHING OF AN OGRE IN FRONT OF A CLASS.
THE TENSION, I SUPPOSE.
YEAH, EVERYBODY'S GOT THEIR BAD DAYS, PROF.
...AND IT LOOKS LIKE I'M NOT GONNA ADD TO THE GENERAL JOY, EITHER.
IS IT SOMETHING ABOUT MICHAEL?
FROM WHAT YOUR FRIEND SAID--
'FRAID TORCHY DOESN'T KNOW THE WHOLE STORY, PROFESSOR JORGENSON.
SURE, MORBIUS AND I TANGLED A COUPLE'A WEEKS BACK--
--BUT, MISTER--ONLY ONE OF US SURVIVED.
THREE GUESSES WHO.
THEN-- MORBIUS IS DEAD?
NO!
YOU'VE GOT IT, PROF! FOR, AS FATE WOULD HAVE IT, ON THE OUTSKIRTS OF THE COLLEGE PARK...
CAN GO NO FURTHER... HOW MANY HOURS SINCE LAST I FED? TOO MANY...
ALREADY, MY VISION GROWS BLURRED... AND ONCE MORE, I FEEL THAT TERRIBLE NEED.
THAT... THAT VOICE. SOMEONE SINGING...
AYE, MORBIUS... SOMEONE SINGING...
NEVER KNEW A GIRL LIKE YOU... MARY LOU...
YEAH. THAT'S THE STUFF.
...THE LAST SUCH SONG HE'LL MAKE, AS IT TURNS OUT...

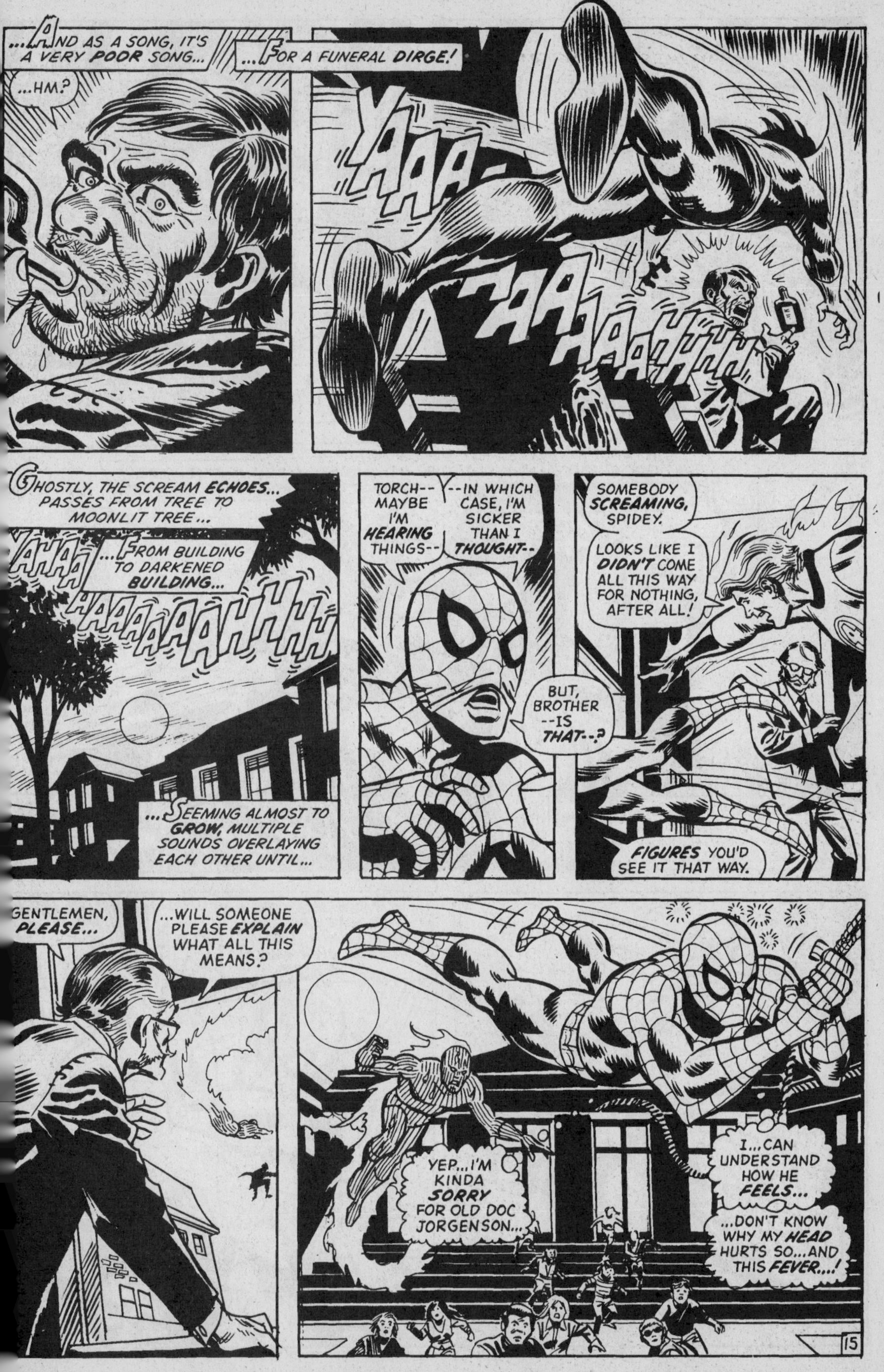

...AND AS A SONG, IT'S A VERY POOR SONG...
...HM?
...FOR A FUNERAL DIRGE!
YAAA-
ZAAAAAAHHHH
GHOSTLY, THE SCREAM ECHOES... PASSES FROM TREE TO MOONLIT TREE...
...FROM BUILDING TO DARKENED BUILDING...
AHAAAAAAAAHHHH
...SEEMING ALMOST TO GROW, MULTIPLE SOUNDS OVERLAYING EACH OTHER UNTIL...
TORCH-- MAYBE I'M HEARING THINGS--
--IN WHICH CASE, I'M SICKER THAN I THOUGHT--
BUT, BROTHER --IS THAT--?
SOMEBODY SCREAMING, SPIDEY.
LOOKS LIKE I DIDN'T COME ALL THIS WAY FOR NOTHING, AFTER ALL!
FIGURES YOU'D SEE IT THAT WAY.
GENTLEMEN, PLEASE...
...WILL SOMEONE PLEASE EXPLAIN WHAT ALL THIS MEANS?
YEP...I'M KINDA SORRY FOR OLD DOC JORGENSON...
I...CAN UNDERSTAND HOW HE FEELS...
...DON'T KNOW WHY MY HEAD HURTS SO...AND THIS FEVER...!
15

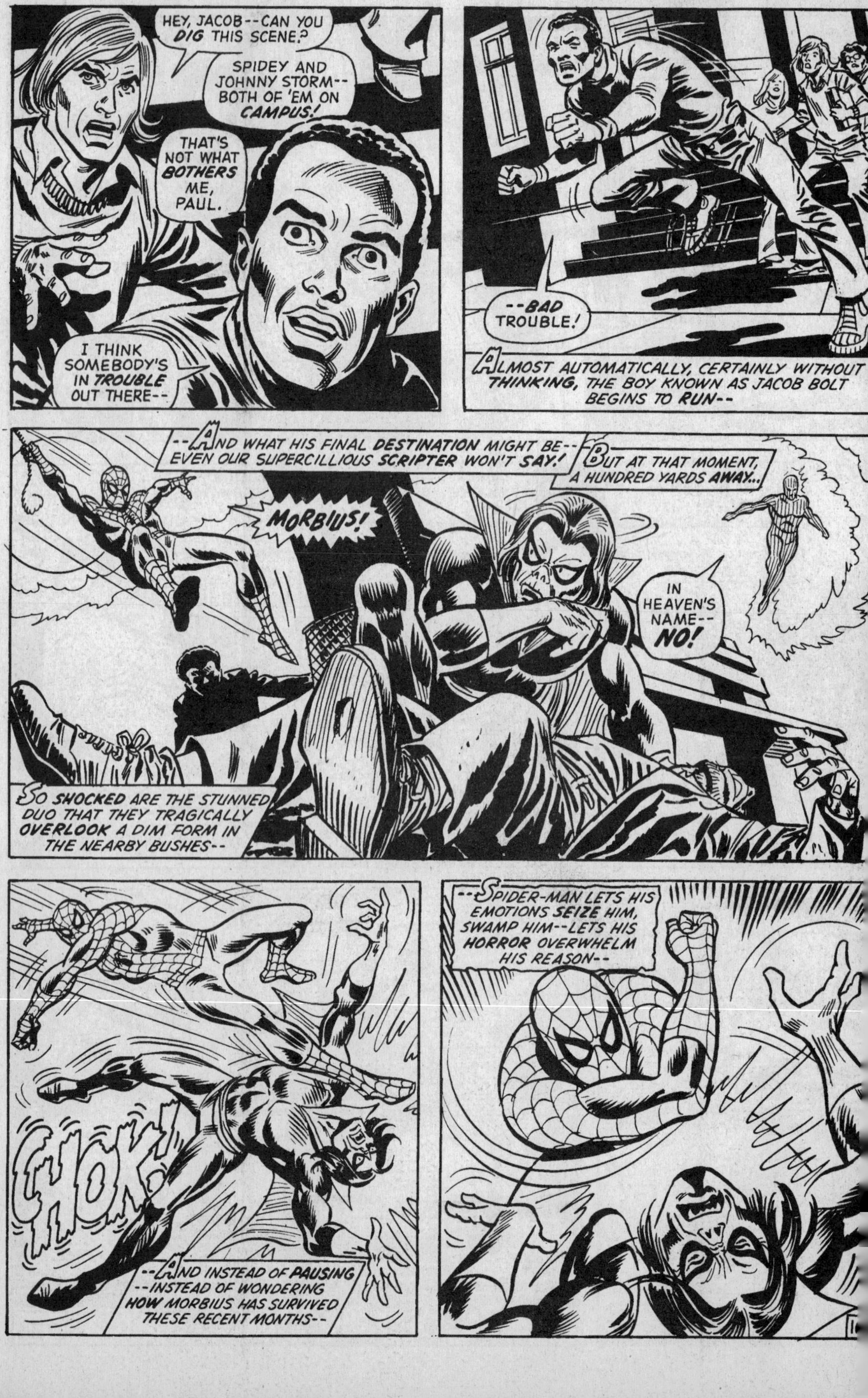
HEY, JACOB--CAN YOU DIG THIS SCENE?
SPIDEY AND JOHNNY STORM--BOTH OF 'EM ON CAMPUS!
THAT'S NOT WHAT BOTHERS ME, PAUL.
I THINK SOMEBODY'S IN TROUBLE OUT THERE--
--BAD TROUBLE!
ALMOST AUTOMATICALLY, CERTAINLY WITHOUT THINKING, THE BOY KNOWN AS JACOB BOLT BEGINS TO RUN--
--AND WHAT HIS FINAL DESTINATION MIGHT BE--EVEN OUR SUPERCILLIOUS SCRIPTER WON'T SAY!
BUT AT THAT MOMENT, A HUNDRED YARDS AWAY...
MORBIUS!
IN HEAVEN'S NAME--NO!
SO SHOCKED ARE THE STUNNED DUO THAT THEY TRAGICALLY OVERLOOK A DIM FORM IN THE NEARBY BUSHES--
CHOK!
--AND INSTEAD OF PAUSING--INSTEAD OF WONDERING HOW MORBIUS HAS SURVIVED THESE RECENT MONTHS--
--SPIDER-MAN LETS HIS EMOTIONS SEIZE HIM, SWAMP HIM--LETS HIS HORROR OVERWHELM HIS REASON--

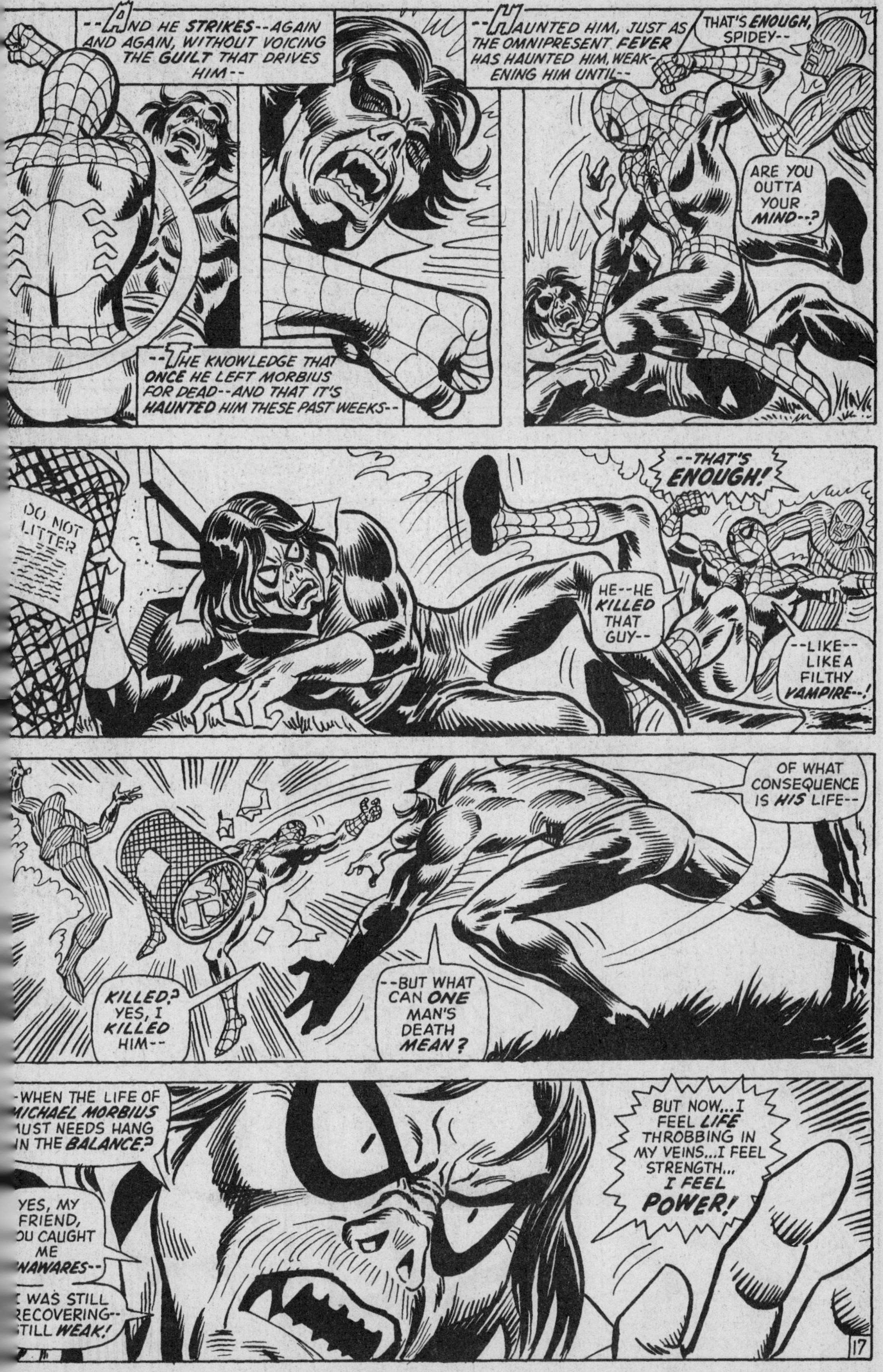
--AND HE STRIKES--AGAIN AND AGAIN, WITHOUT VOICING THE GUILT THAT DRIVES HIM--
--THE KNOWLEDGE THAT ONCE HE LEFT MORBIUS FOR DEAD--AND THAT IT'S HAUNTED HIM THESE PAST WEEKS--
--HAUNTED HIM, JUST AS THE OMNIPRESENT FEVER HAS HAUNTED HIM, WEAKENING HIM UNTIL--
THAT'S ENOUGH, SPIDEY--
ARE YOU OUTTA YOUR MIND--?
DO NOT LITTER
--THAT'S ENOUGH!
HE--HE KILLED THAT GUY--
--LIKE--LIKE A FILTHY VAMPIRE--!
OF WHAT CONSEQUENCE IS HIS LIFE--
KILLED? YES, I KILLED HIM--
--BUT WHAT CAN ONE MAN'S DEATH MEAN?
-WHEN THE LIFE OF MICHAEL MORBIUS MUST NEEDS HANG IN THE BALANCE?
BUT NOW...I FEEL LIFE THROBBING IN MY VEINS...I FEEL STRENGTH... I FEEL POWER!
YES, MY FRIEND, YOU CAUGHT ME UNAWARES--
I WAS STILL RECOVERING--STILL WEAK!
17

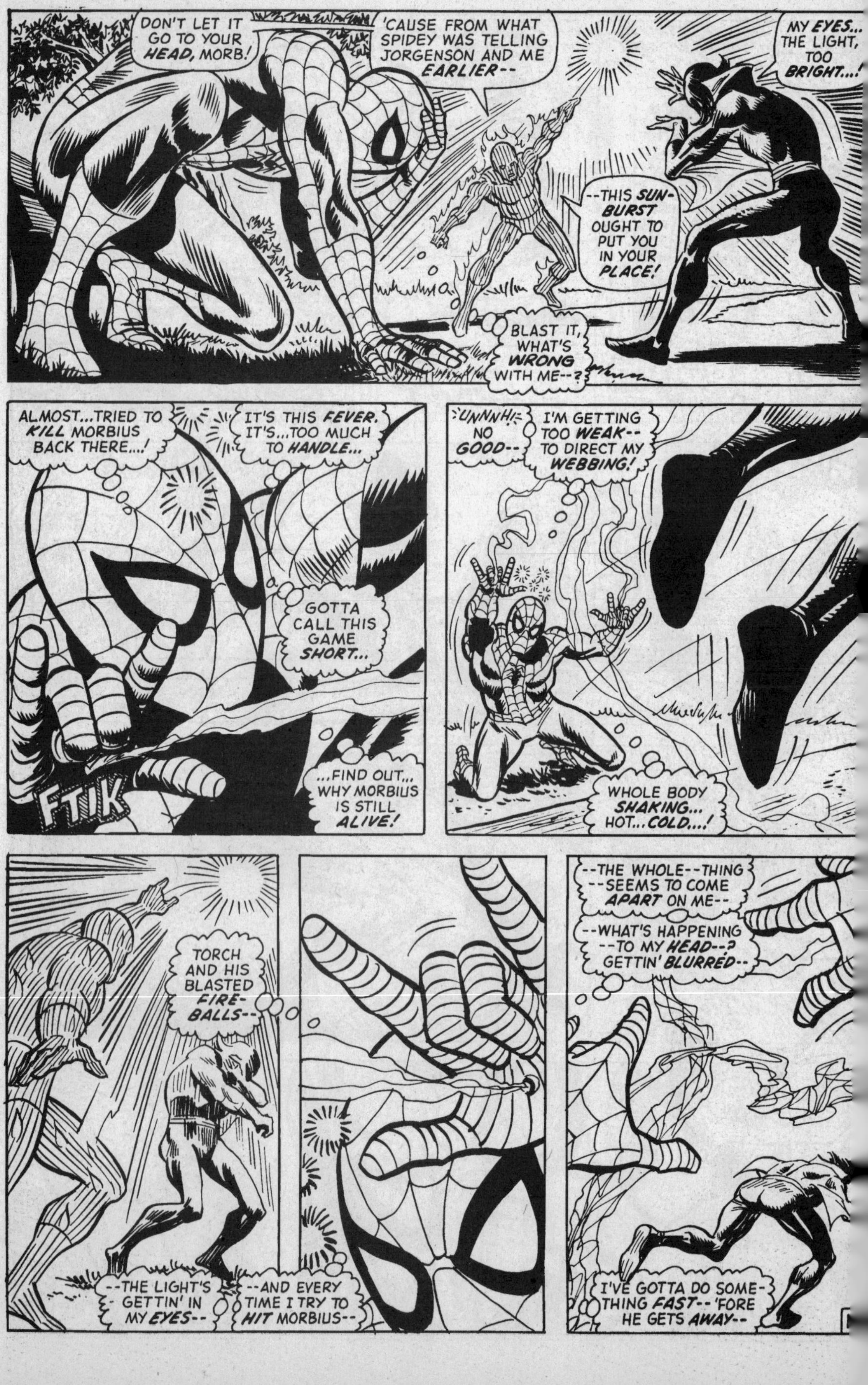
DON'T LET IT GO TO YOUR HEAD, MORB!
'CAUSE FROM WHAT SPIDEY WAS TELLING JORGENSON AND ME EARLIER--
--THIS SUN-BURST OUGHT TO PUT YOU IN YOUR PLACE!
MY EYES... THE LIGHT, TOO BRIGHT...!
BLAST IT, WHAT'S WRONG WITH ME--?
ALMOST...TRIED TO KILL MORBIUS BACK THERE....!
IT'S THIS FEVER. IT'S...TOO MUCH TO HANDLE...
GOTTA CALL THIS GAME SHORT...
...FIND OUT... WHY MORBIUS IS STILL ALIVE!
FTIK
UNNNH! NO GOOD--
I'M GETTING TOO WEAK-- TO DIRECT MY WEBBING!
WHOLE BODY SHAKING... HOT... COLD...!
TORCH AND HIS BLASTED FIRE-BALLS--
--THE LIGHT'S GETTIN' IN MY EYES--
--AND EVERY TIME I TRY TO HIT MORBIUS--
--THE WHOLE--THING --SEEMS TO COME APART ON ME--
--WHAT'S HAPPENING --TO MY HEAD--? GETTIN' BLURRED--
I'VE GOTTA DO SOME-THING FAST--'FORE HE GETS AWAY--

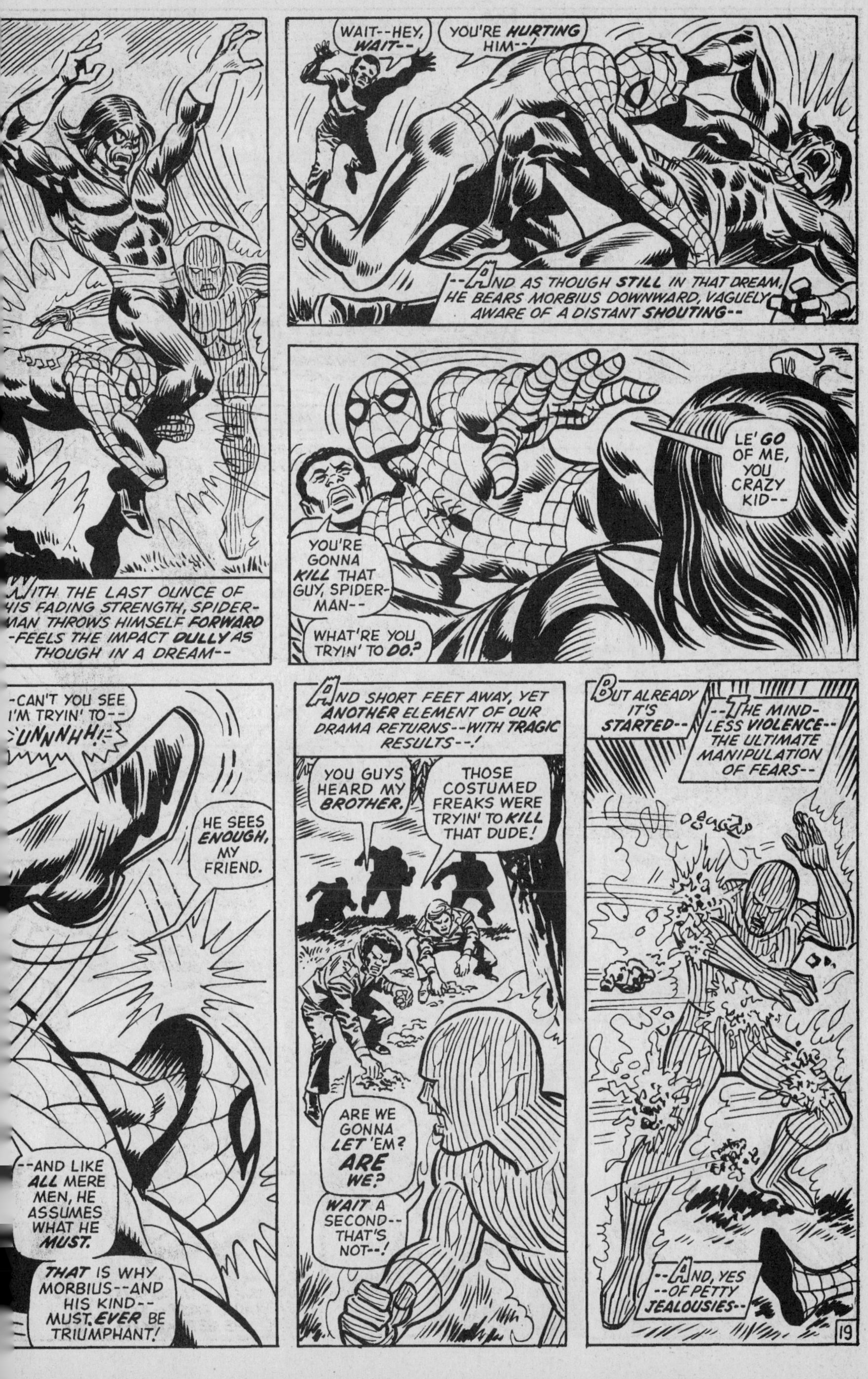

WAIT--HEY, WAIT--
YOU'RE HURTING HIM--!
--AND AS THOUGH STILL IN THAT DREAM, HE BEARS MORBIUS DOWNWARD, VAGUELY AWARE OF A DISTANT SHOUTING--
WITH THE LAST OUNCE OF HIS FADING STRENGTH, SPIDER-MAN THROWS HIMSELF FORWARD -FEELS THE IMPACT DULLY AS THOUGH IN A DREAM--
LE' GO OF ME, YOU CRAZY KID--
YOU'RE GONNA KILL THAT GUY, SPIDER-MAN--
WHAT'RE YOU TRYIN' TO DO?
--CAN'T YOU SEE I'M TRYIN' TO--
UNNHH!
HE SEES ENOUGH, MY FRIEND.
--AND LIKE ALL MERE MEN, HE ASSUMES WHAT HE MUST.
THAT IS WHY MORBIUS--AND HIS KIND--MUST EVER BE TRIUMPHANT!
AND SHORT FEET AWAY, YET ANOTHER ELEMENT OF OUR DRAMA RETURNS--WITH TRAGIC RESULTS--!
YOU GUYS HEARD MY BROTHER.
THOSE COSTUMED FREAKS WERE TRYIN' TO KILL THAT DUDE!
ARE WE GONNA LET 'EM? ARE WE?
WAIT A SECOND--THAT'S NOT--!
BUT ALREADY IT'S STARTED--
--THE MINDLESS VIOLENCE--THE ULTIMATE MANIPULATION OF FEARS--
--AND, YES--OF PETTY JEALOUSIES--

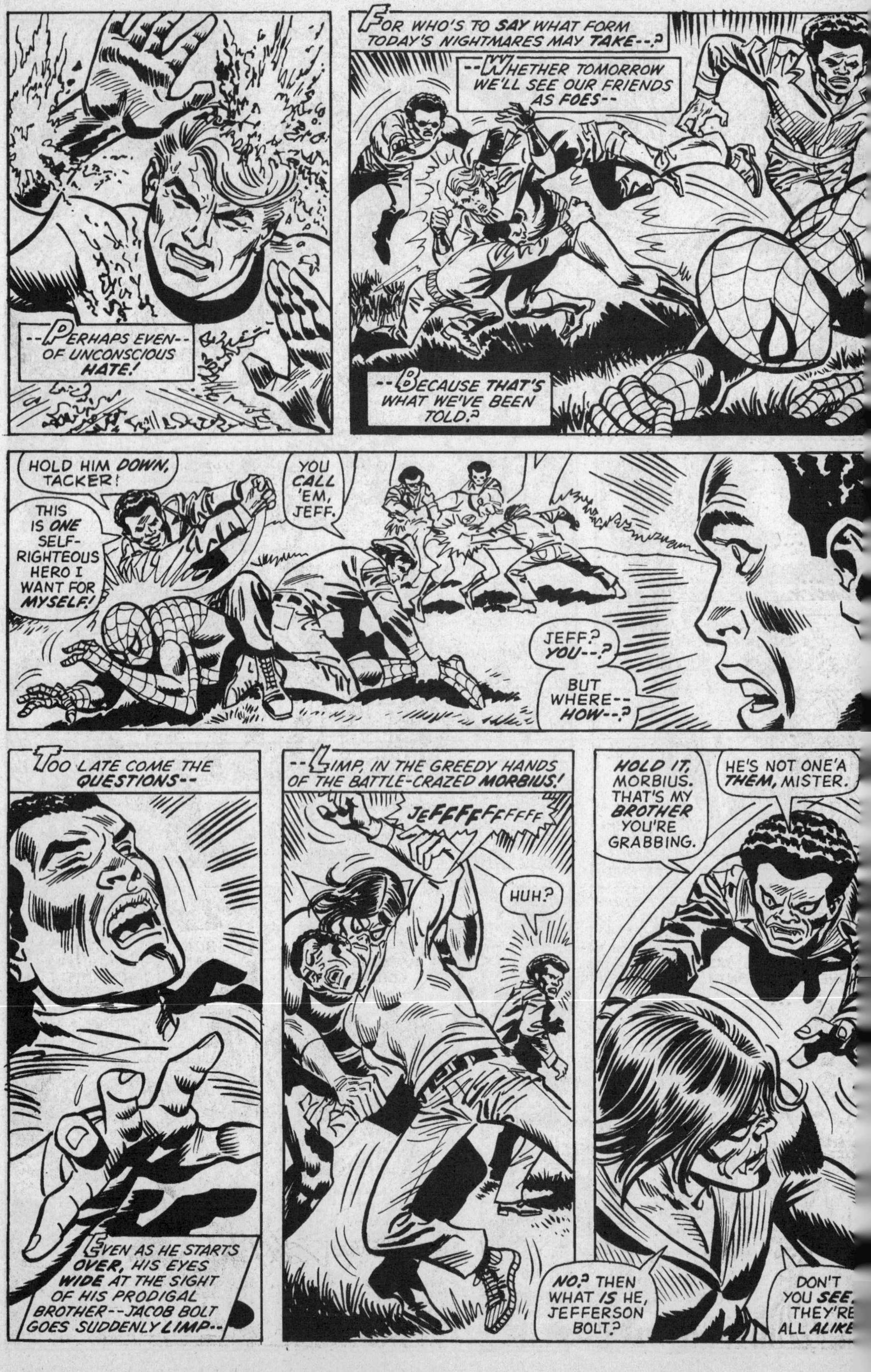
--PERHAPS EVEN--
OF UNCONSCIOUS
HATE!
FOR WHO'S TO SAY WHAT FORM
TODAY'S NIGHTMARES MAY TAKE--?
--WHETHER TOMORROW
WE'LL SEE OUR FRIENDS
AS FOES--
--BECAUSE THAT'S
WHAT WE'VE BEEN
TOLD?
HOLD HIM DOWN,
TACKER!
THIS
IS ONE
SELF-
RIGHTEOUS
HERO I
WANT FOR
MYSELF!
YOU
CALL
'EM,
JEFF.
JEFF? YOU--?
BUT WHERE--
HOW--?
TOO LATE COME THE
QUESTIONS--
EVEN AS HE STARTS
OVER, HIS EYES
WIDE AT THE SIGHT
OF HIS PRODIGAL
BROTHER--JACOB BOLT
GOES SUDDENLY LIMP--
--LIMP, IN THE GREEDY HANDS
OF THE BATTLE-CRAZED MORBIUS!
JEFFFFFFFFFF
HUH?
HOLD IT,
MORBIUS.
THAT'S MY
BROTHER
YOU'RE
GRABBING.
HE'S NOT ONE'A
THEM, MISTER.
NO? THEN
WHAT IS HE,
JEFFERSON
BOLT?
DON'T
YOU SEE.
THEY'RE
ALL ALIKE

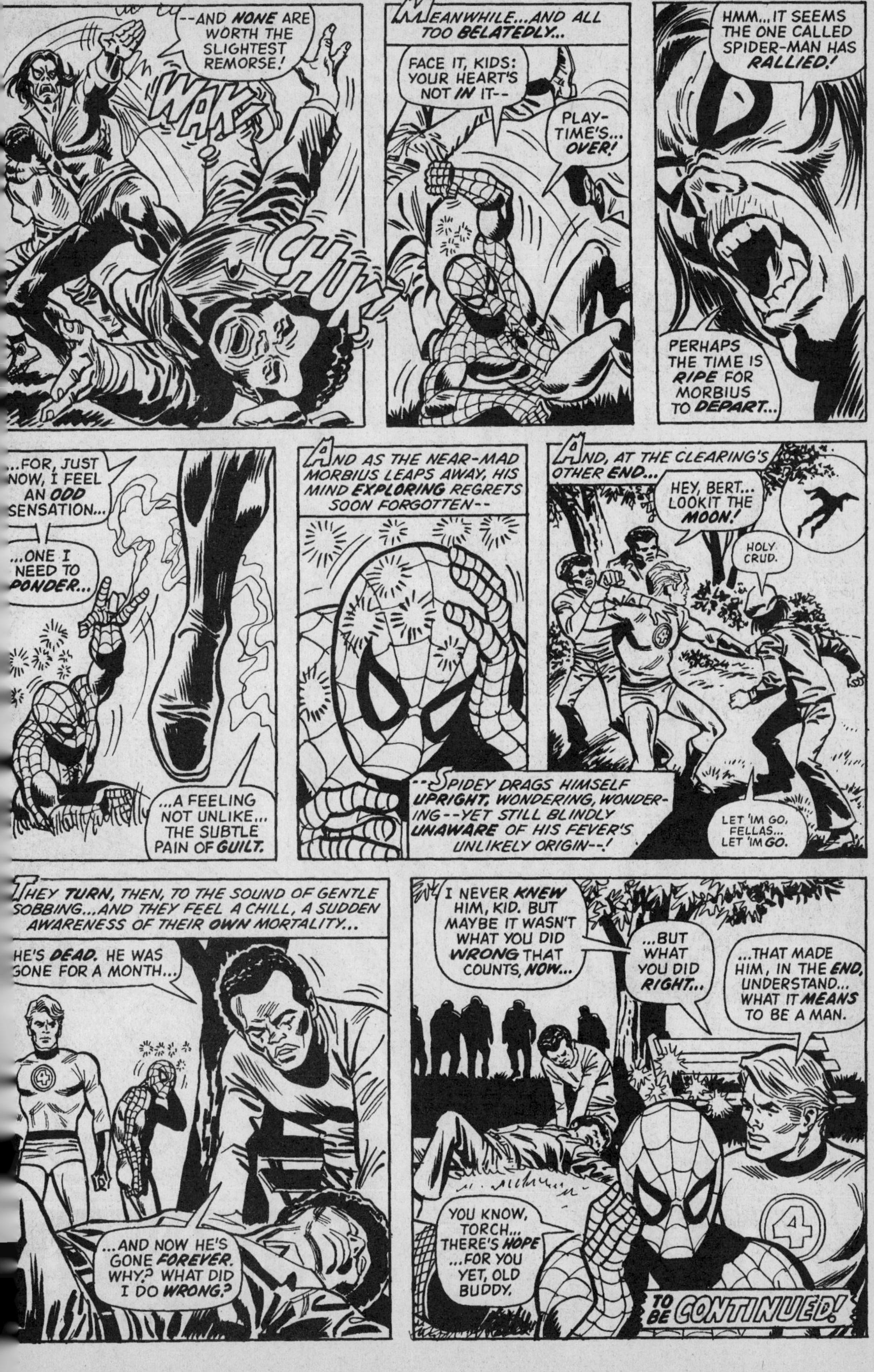
--AND NONE ARE WORTH THE SLIGHTEST REMORSE!
WAK
CHUK
MEANWHILE...AND ALL TOO BELATEDLY...
FACE IT, KIDS: YOUR HEART'S NOT IN IT--
PLAY-TIME'S... OVER!
HMM...IT SEEMS THE ONE CALLED SPIDER-MAN HAS RALLIED!
PERHAPS THE TIME IS RIPE FOR MORBIUS TO DEPART...
...FOR, JUST NOW, I FEEL AN ODD SENSATION...
...ONE I NEED TO PONDER...
...A FEELING NOT UNLIKE... THE SUBTLE PAIN OF GUILT.
AND AS THE NEAR-MAD MORBIUS LEAPS AWAY, HIS MIND EXPLORING REGRETS SOON FORGOTTEN--
--SPIDEY DRAGS HIMSELF UPRIGHT, WONDERING, WONDERING--YET STILL BLINDLY UNAWARE OF HIS FEVER'S UNLIKELY ORIGIN--!
AND, AT THE CLEARING'S OTHER END...
HEY, BERT... LOOKIT THE MOON!
HOLY CRUD.
LET 'IM GO, FELLAS... LET 'IM GO.
THEY TURN, THEN, TO THE SOUND OF GENTLE SOBBING...AND THEY FEEL A CHILL, A SUDDEN AWARENESS OF THEIR OWN MORTALITY...
HE'S DEAD. HE WAS GONE FOR A MONTH...
...AND NOW HE'S GONE FOREVER. WHY? WHAT DID I DO WRONG?
I NEVER KNEW HIM, KID. BUT MAYBE IT WASN'T WHAT YOU DID WRONG THAT COUNTS, NOW...
...BUT WHAT YOU DID RIGHT...
...THAT MADE HIM, IN THE END, UNDERSTAND... WHAT IT MEANS TO BE A MAN.
YOU KNOW, TORCH... THERE'S HOPE ...FOR YOU YET, OLD BUDDY.
TO BE CONTINUED!

MARVEL TEAM-UP
MARVEL COMICS GROUP
APPROVED BY THE COMICS CODE AUTHORITY
4 SEPT 02147
20¢
MARVEL TEAM-UP
FEATURING
SPIDER-MAN AND THE X-MEN
THEY'RE BACK! IN ALL NEW, ALL-GREAT ACTION!
THIS TIME YOU PUSHED US TOO FAR, WALL-CRAWLER!
NO, SCOTT! DON'T BLAST HIM--NOT NOW-- OR HE'LL FALL TO HIS DEATH!!
TOO LATE, LADY! SCRATCH ONE SPIDER-MAN!!
THE MARK OF THE MUTANTS!

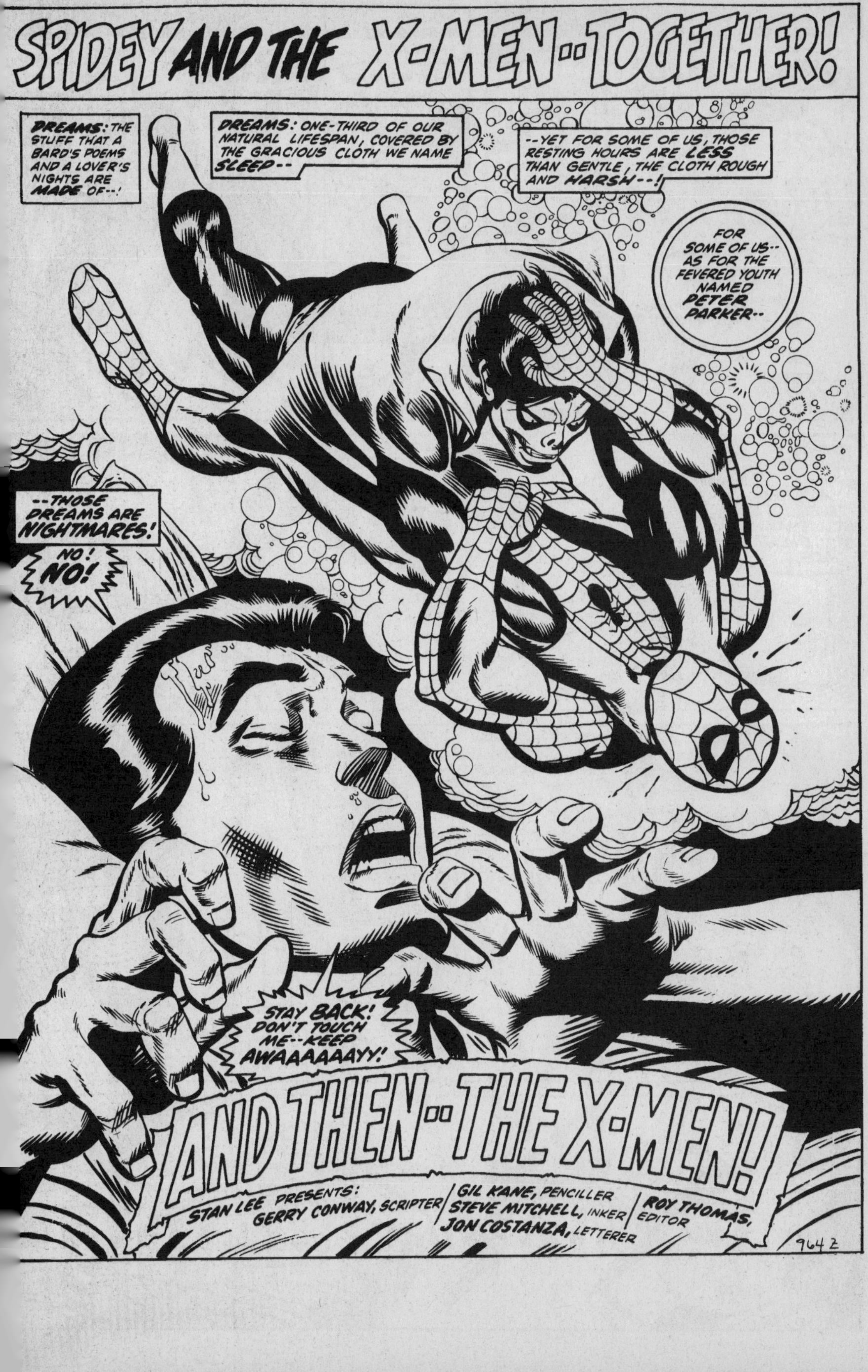

SPIDEY AND THE X-MEN--TOGETHER!
DREAMS: THE STUFF THAT A BARD'S POEMS AND A LOVER'S NIGHTS ARE MADE OF--!
DREAMS: ONE-THIRD OF OUR NATURAL LIFESPAN, COVERED BY THE GRACIOUS CLOTH WE NAME SLEEP--
--YET FOR SOME OF US, THOSE RESTING HOURS ARE LESS THAN GENTLE, THE CLOTH ROUGH AND HARSH--!
FOR SOME OF US--AS FOR THE FEVERED YOUTH NAMED PETER PARKER--
--THOSE DREAMS ARE NIGHTMARES!
NO! NO!
STAY BACK! DON'T TOUCH ME--KEEP AWAAAAAAAYY!
AND THEN--THE X-MEN!
STAN LEE PRESENTS: GERRY CONWAY, SCRIPTER
GIL KANE, PENCILLER
STEVE MITCHELL, INKER
JON COSTANZA, LETTERER
ROY THOMAS, EDITOR
9642

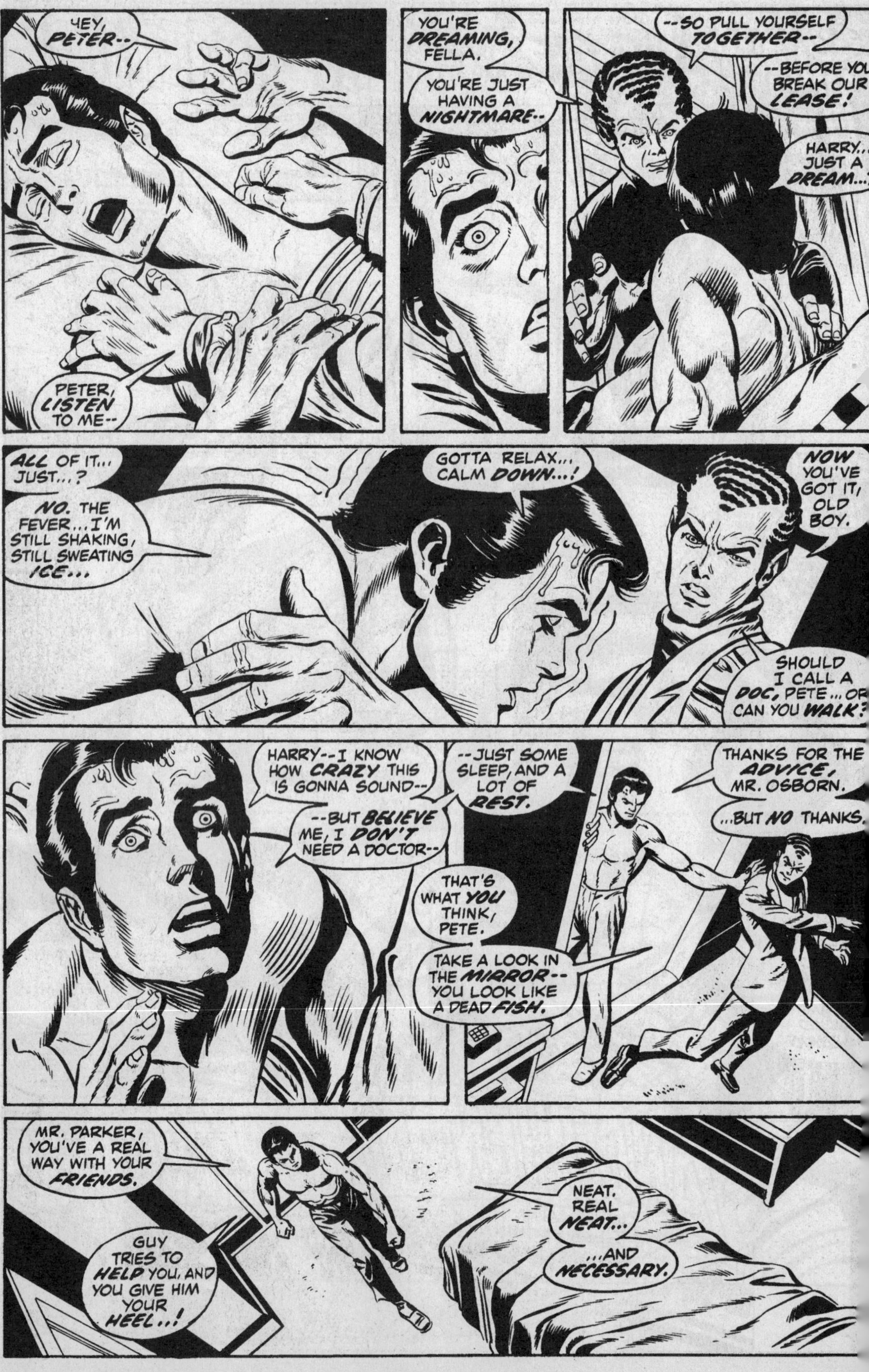
HEY, PETER--
PETER, LISTEN TO ME--
YOU'RE DREAMING, FELLA.
YOU'RE JUST HAVING A NIGHTMARE--
--SO PULL YOURSELF TOGETHER--
--BEFORE YOU BREAK OUR LEASE!
HARRY... JUST A DREAM...?
ALL OF IT... JUST...?
NO. THE FEVER... I'M STILL SHAKING, STILL SWEATING ICE...
GOTTA RELAX... CALM DOWN...!
NOW YOU'VE GOT IT, OLD BOY.
SHOULD I CALL A DOC, PETE... OR CAN YOU WALK?
HARRY--I KNOW HOW CRAZY THIS IS GONNA SOUND--
--BUT BELIEVE ME, I DON'T NEED A DOCTOR--
--JUST SOME SLEEP, AND A LOT OF REST.
THAT'S WHAT YOU THINK, PETE.
TAKE A LOOK IN THE MIRROR-- YOU LOOK LIKE A DEAD FISH.
THANKS FOR THE ADVICE, MR. OSBORN.
...BUT NO THANKS.
MR. PARKER, YOU'VE A REAL WAY WITH YOUR FRIENDS.
GUY TRIES TO HELP YOU, AND YOU GIVE HIM YOUR HEEL..!
NEAT. REAL NEAT...
...AND NECESSARY.

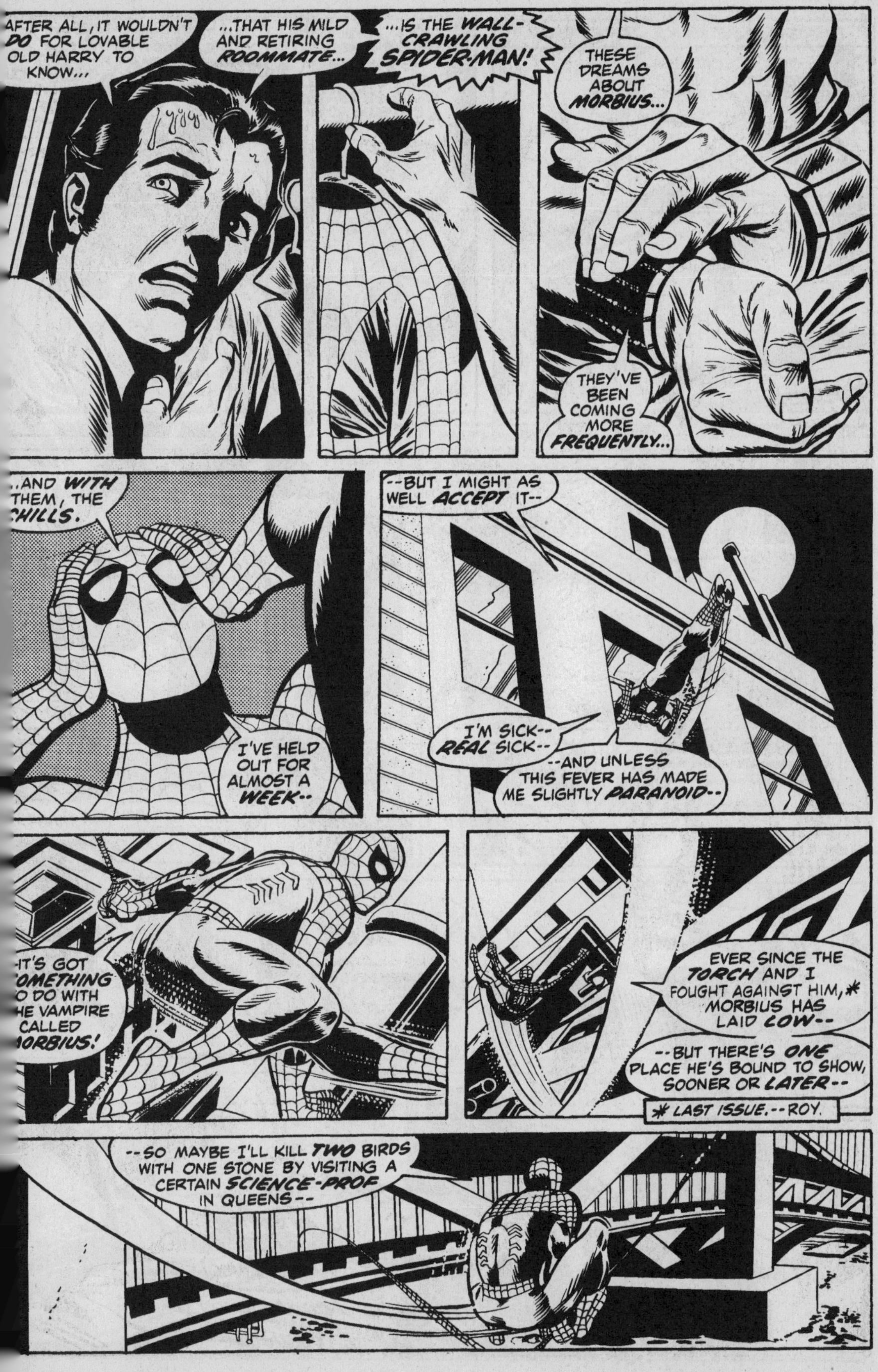
AFTER ALL, IT WOULDN'T DO FOR LOVABLE OLD HARRY TO KNOW...
...THAT HIS MILD AND RETIRING ROOMMATE...
...IS THE WALL-CRAWLING SPIDER-MAN!
THESE DREAMS ABOUT MORBIUS...
THEY'VE BEEN COMING MORE FREQUENTLY...
..AND WITH THEM, THE CHILLS.
I'VE HELD OUT FOR ALMOST A WEEK--
--BUT I MIGHT AS WELL ACCEPT IT--
I'M SICK-- REAL SICK--
--AND UNLESS THIS FEVER HAS MADE ME SLIGHTLY PARANOID--
IT'S GOT SOMETHING TO DO WITH THE VAMPIRE CALLED MORBIUS!
EVER SINCE THE TORCH AND I FOUGHT AGAINST HIM,* MORBIUS HAS LAID LOW--
--BUT THERE'S ONE PLACE HE'S BOUND TO SHOW, SOONER OR LATER--
* LAST ISSUE.--ROY.
--SO MAYBE I'LL KILL TWO BIRDS WITH ONE STONE BY VISITING A CERTAIN SCIENCE-PROF IN QUEENS--

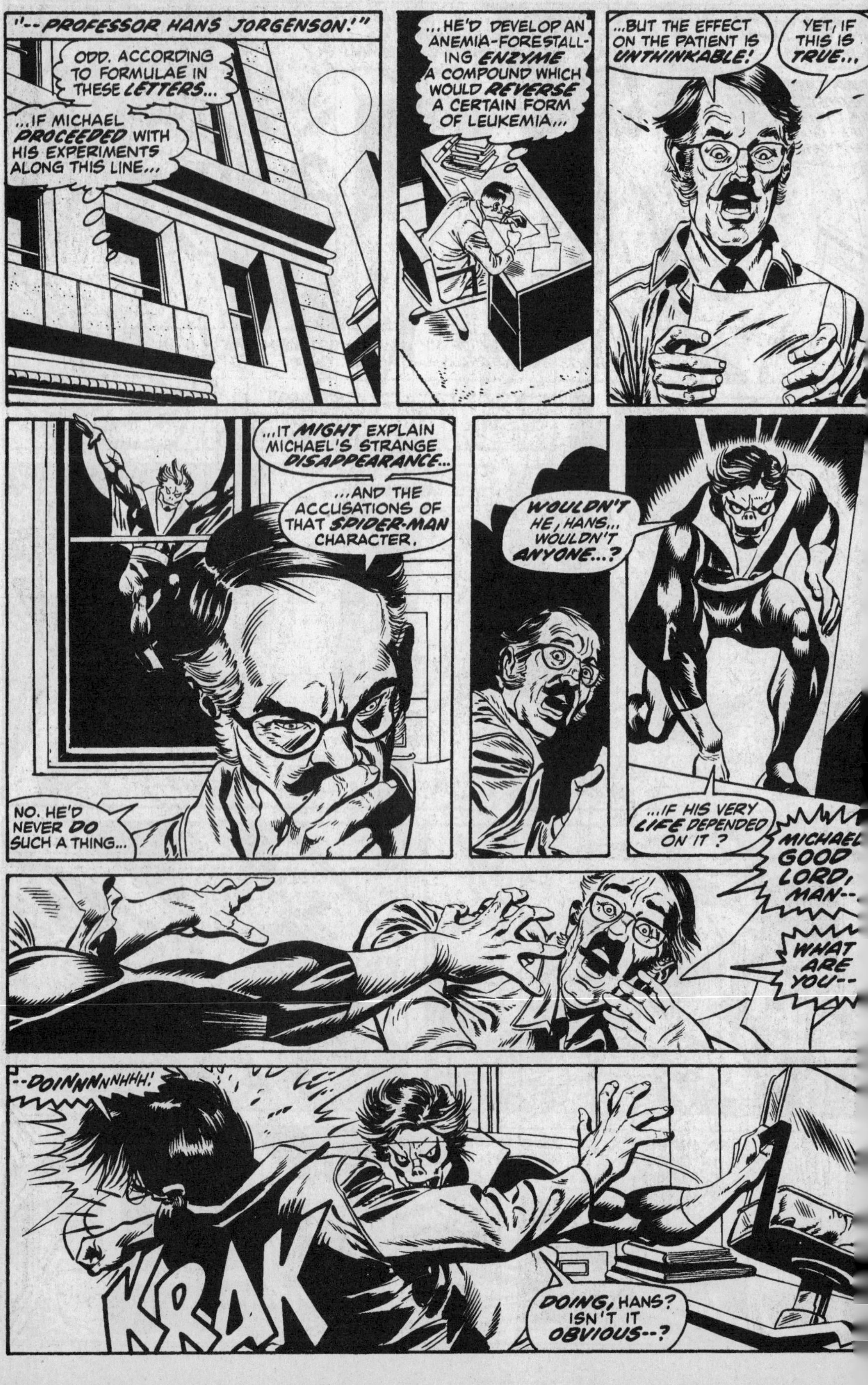
"--PROFESSOR HANS JORGENSON!"
ODD. ACCORDING TO FORMULAE IN THESE LETTERS...
...IF MICHAEL PROCEEDED WITH HIS EXPERIMENTS ALONG THIS LINE...
...HE'D DEVELOP AN ANEMIA-FORESTALLING ENZYME A COMPOUND WHICH WOULD REVERSE A CERTAIN FORM OF LEUKEMIA...
...BUT THE EFFECT ON THE PATIENT IS UNTHINKABLE!
YET, IF THIS IS TRUE...
...IT MIGHT EXPLAIN MICHAEL'S STRANGE DISAPPEARANCE...
...AND THE ACCUSATIONS OF THAT SPIDER-MAN CHARACTER.
NO. HE'D NEVER DO SUCH A THING...
WOULDN'T HE, HANS... WOULDN'T ANYONE...?
...IF HIS VERY LIFE DEPENDED ON IT ?
MICHAEL GOOD LORD, MAN--
WHAT ARE YOU--
--DOINNNNNHHH!
KRAK
DOING, HANS? ISN'T IT OBVIOUS--?

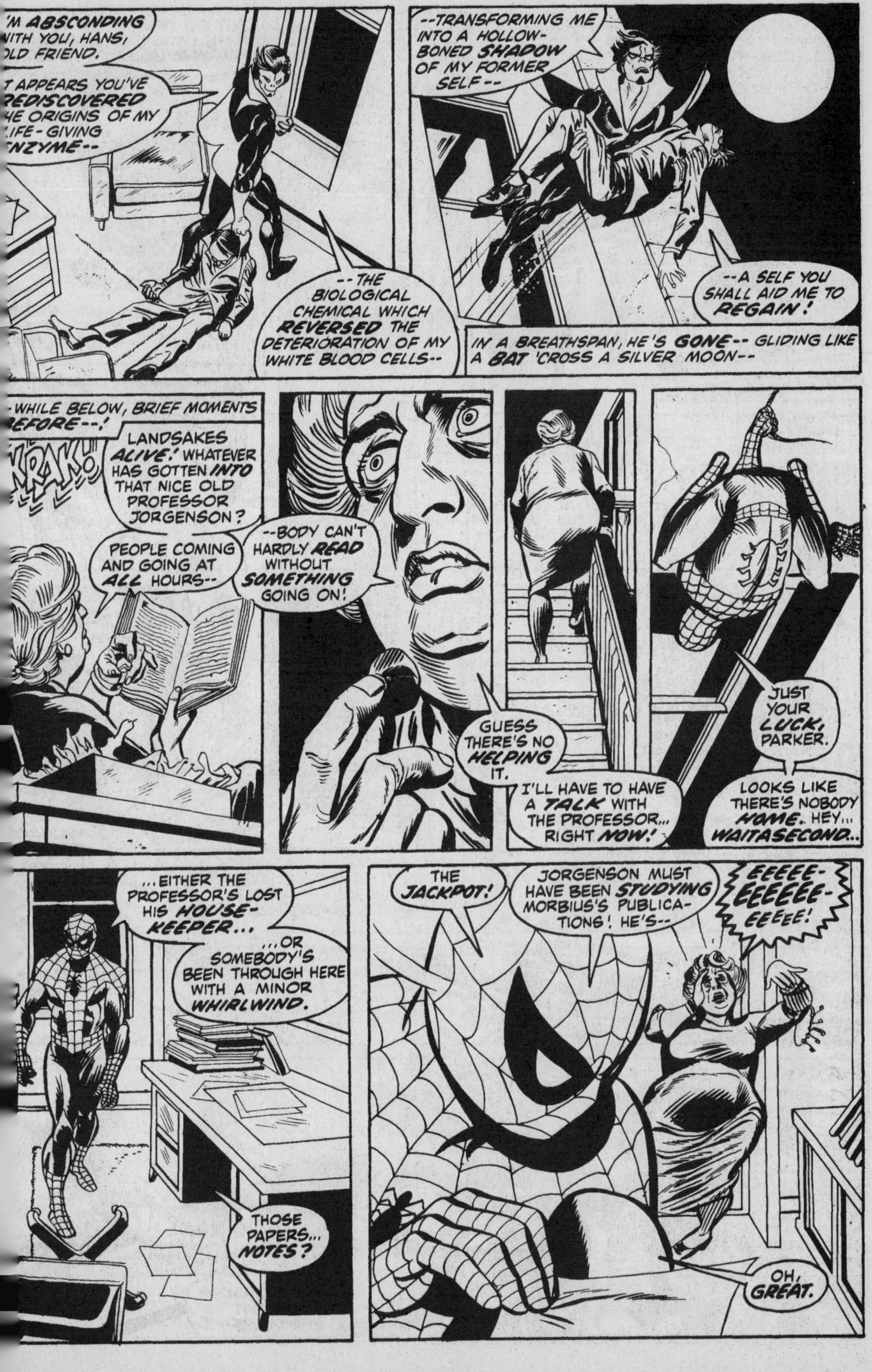
'M ABSCONDING WITH YOU, HANS, OLD FRIEND.
T APPEARS YOU'VE REDISCOVERED HE ORIGINS OF MY LIFE-GIVING ENZYME--
--THE BIOLOGICAL CHEMICAL WHICH REVERSED THE DETERIORATION OF MY WHITE BLOOD CELLS--
--TRANSFORMING ME INTO A HOLLOW-BONED SHADOW OF MY FORMER SELF--
--A SELF YOU SHALL AID ME TO REGAIN!
IN A BREATHSPAN, HE'S GONE-- GLIDING LIKE A BAT 'CROSS A SILVER MOON--
-WHILE BELOW, BRIEF MOMENTS BEFORE--!
KRAK!
LANDSAKES ALIVE! WHATEVER HAS GOTTEN INTO THAT NICE OLD PROFESSOR JORGENSON?
PEOPLE COMING AND GOING AT ALL HOURS--
--BODY CAN'T HARDLY READ WITHOUT SOMETHING GOING ON!
GUESS THERE'S NO HELPING IT.
I'LL HAVE TO HAVE A TALK WITH THE PROFESSOR... RIGHT NOW!
JUST YOUR LUCK, PARKER.
LOOKS LIKE THERE'S NOBODY HOME.. HEY... WAITASECOND...
...EITHER THE PROFESSOR'S LOST HIS HOUSE-KEEPER...
...OR SOMEBODY'S BEEN THROUGH HERE WITH A MINOR WHIRLWIND.
THOSE PAPERS... NOTES?
THE JACKPOT!
JORGENSON MUST HAVE BEEN STUDYING MORBIUS'S PUBLICA-TIONS! HE'S--
EEEEE-EEEEEE-EEEEE!
OH, GREAT.

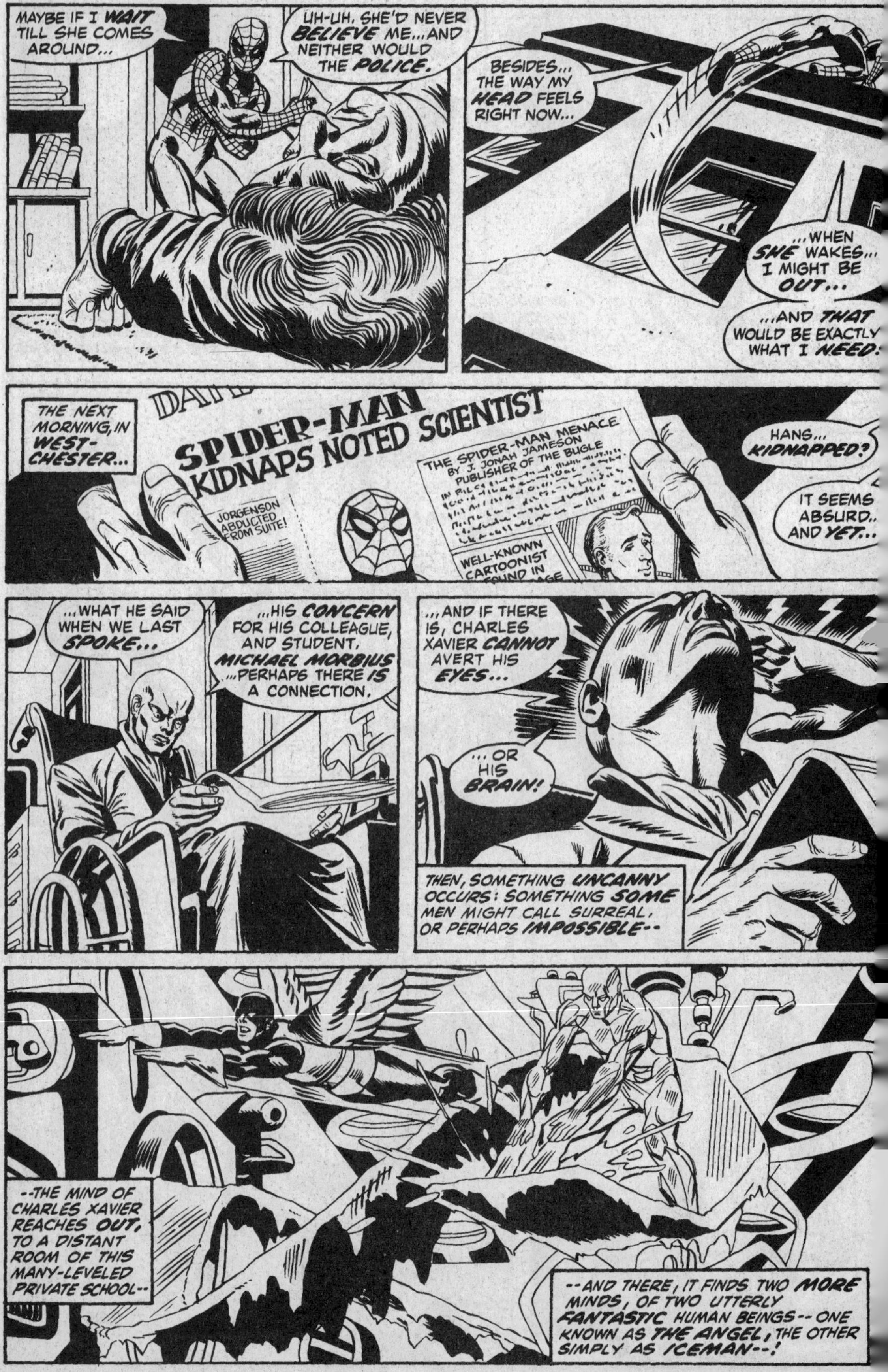

MAYBE IF I WAIT TILL SHE COMES AROUND...
UH-UH. SHE'D NEVER BELIEVE ME...AND NEITHER WOULD THE POLICE.
BESIDES... THE WAY MY HEAD FEELS RIGHT NOW...
...WHEN SHE WAKES... I MIGHT BE OUT...
...AND THAT WOULD BE EXACTLY WHAT I NEED!
THE NEXT MORNING, IN WEST-CHESTER...
SPIDER-MAN KIDNAPS NOTED SCIENTIST
THE SPIDER-MAN MENACE BY J. JONAH JAMESON PUBLISHER OF THE BUGLE
JORGENSON ABDUCTED FROM SUITE!
WELL-KNOWN CARTOONIST FOUND IN
HANS... KIDNAPPED?
IT SEEMS ABSURD... AND YET...
...WHAT HE SAID WHEN WE LAST SPOKE...
...HIS CONCERN FOR HIS COLLEAGUE, AND STUDENT, MICHAEL MORBIUS ...PERHAPS THERE IS A CONNECTION.
...AND IF THERE IS, CHARLES XAVIER CANNOT AVERT HIS EYES...
...OR HIS BRAIN!
THEN, SOMETHING UNCANNY OCCURS: SOMETHING SOME MEN MIGHT CALL SURREAL, OR PERHAPS IMPOSSIBLE--
--THE MIND OF CHARLES XAVIER REACHES OUT, TO A DISTANT ROOM OF THIS MANY-LEVELED PRIVATE SCHOOL--
--AND THERE, IT FINDS TWO MORE MINDS, OF TWO UTTERLY FANTASTIC HUMAN BEINGS-- ONE KNOWN AS THE ANGEL, THE OTHER SIMPLY AS ICEMAN--!

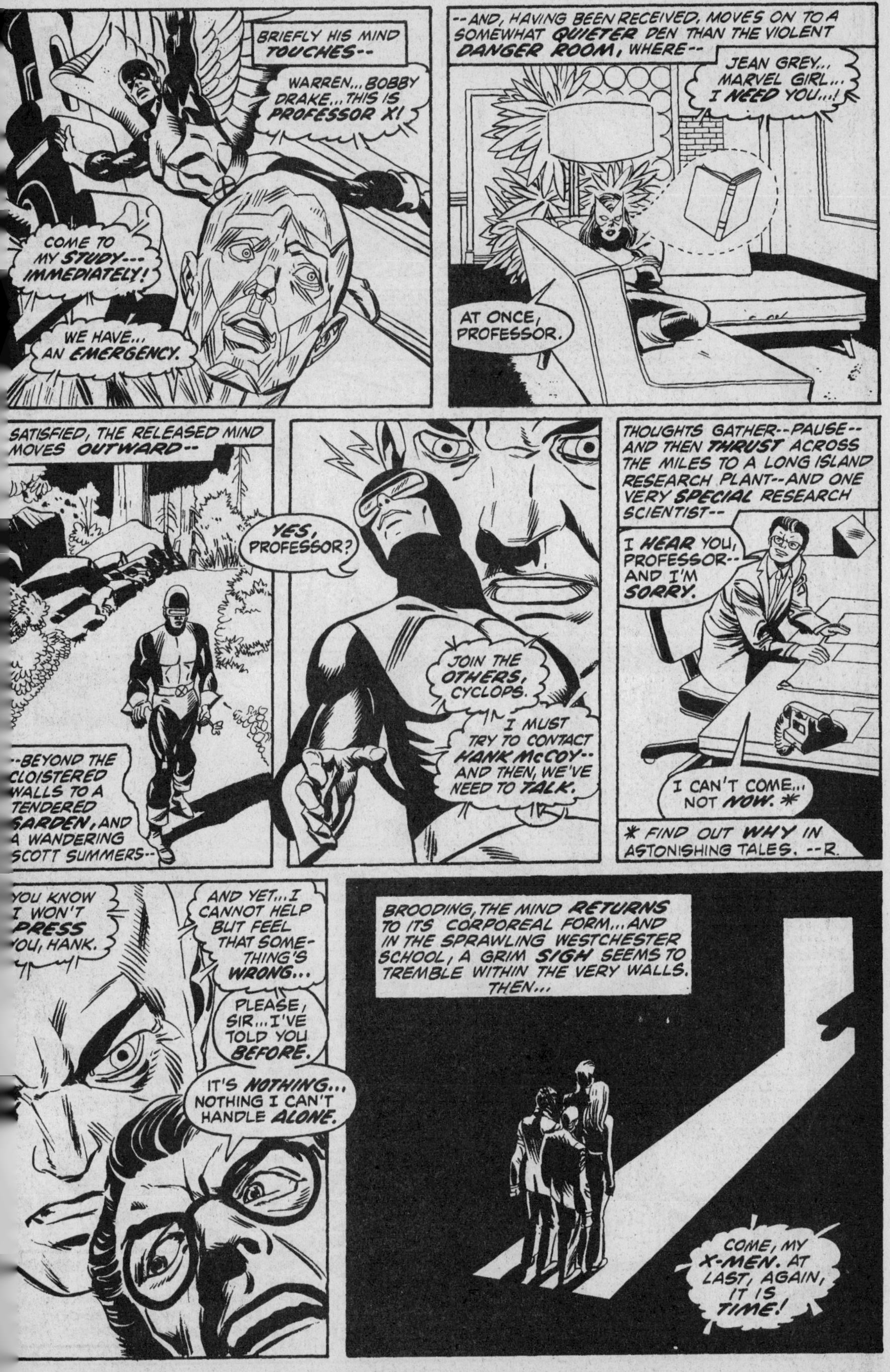

BRIEFLY HIS MIND TOUCHES--
WARREN... BOBBY DRAKE... THIS IS PROFESSOR X!
COME TO MY STUDY--- IMMEDIATELY!
WE HAVE... AN EMERGENCY.
--AND, HAVING BEEN RECEIVED, MOVES ON TO A SOMEWHAT QUIETER DEN THAN THE VIOLENT DANGER ROOM, WHERE--
JEAN GREY... MARVEL GIRL... I NEED YOU...!
AT ONCE, PROFESSOR.
SATISFIED, THE RELEASED MIND MOVES OUTWARD--
--BEYOND THE CLOISTERED WALLS TO A TENDERED GARDEN, AND A WANDERING SCOTT SUMMERS--
YES, PROFESSOR?
JOIN THE OTHERS, CYCLOPS.
I MUST TRY TO CONTACT HANK McCOY-- AND THEN, WE'VE NEED TO TALK.
THOUGHTS GATHER--PAUSE-- AND THEN THRUST ACROSS THE MILES TO A LONG ISLAND RESEARCH PLANT--AND ONE VERY SPECIAL RESEARCH SCIENTIST--
I HEAR YOU, PROFESSOR-- AND I'M SORRY.
I CAN'T COME... NOT NOW. *
* FIND OUT WHY IN ASTONISHING TALES. --R.
YOU KNOW I WON'T PRESS YOU, HANK.
AND YET... I CANNOT HELP BUT FEEL THAT SOME-THING'S WRONG...
PLEASE, SIR... I'VE TOLD YOU BEFORE.
IT'S NOTHING... NOTHING I CAN'T HANDLE ALONE.
BROODING, THE MIND RETURNS TO ITS CORPOREAL FORM... AND IN THE SPRAWLING WESTCHESTER SCHOOL, A GRIM SIGH SEEMS TO TREMBLE WITHIN THE VERY WALLS. THEN...
COME, MY X-MEN. AT LAST, AGAIN, IT IS TIME!

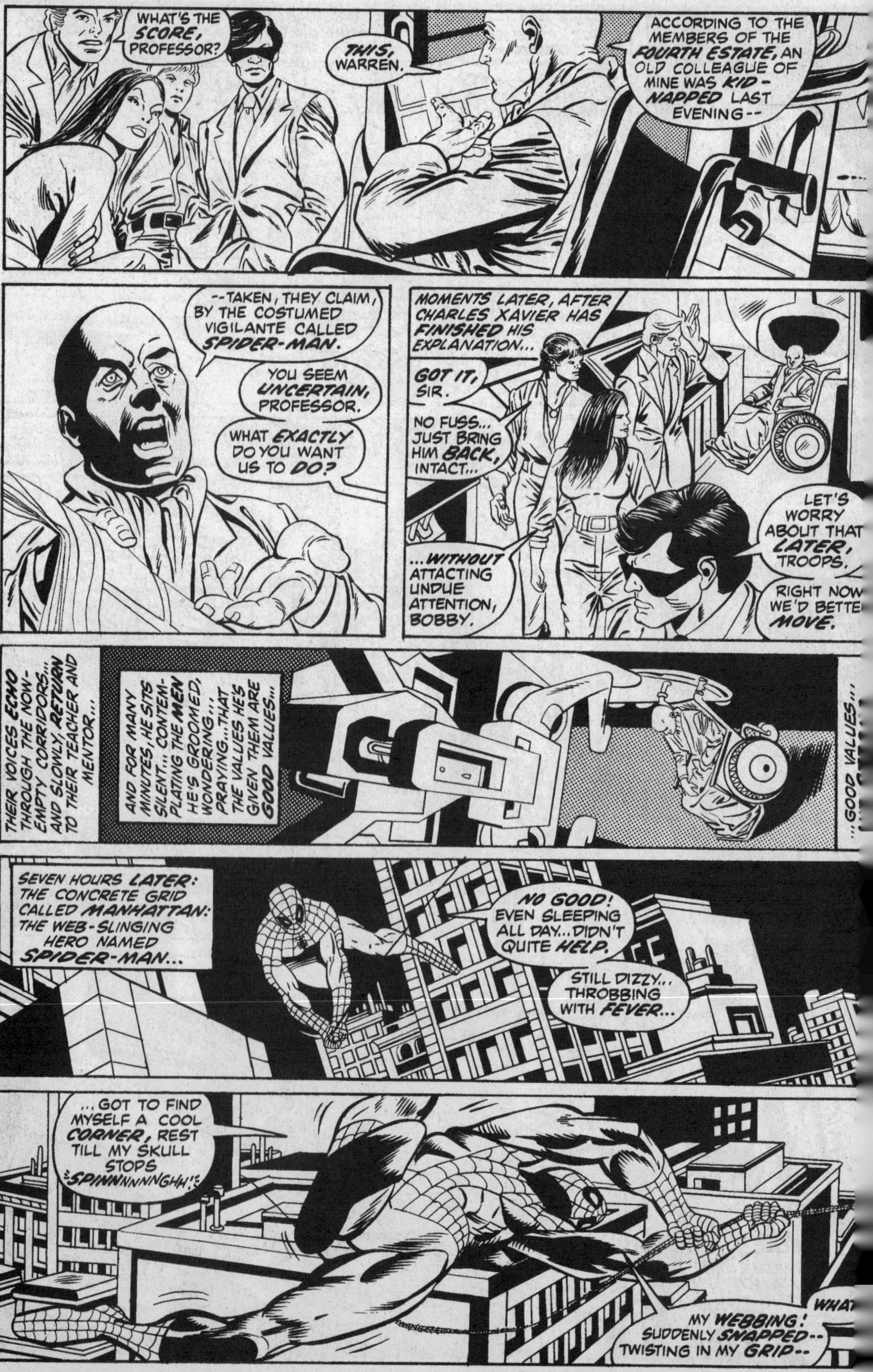
WHAT'S THE SCORE, PROFESSOR?
THIS, WARREN.
ACCORDING TO THE MEMBERS OF THE FOURTH ESTATE, AN OLD COLLEAGUE OF MINE WAS KID-NAPPED LAST EVENING--
--TAKEN, THEY CLAIM, BY THE COSTUMED VIGILANTE CALLED SPIDER-MAN.
YOU SEEM UNCERTAIN, PROFESSOR.
WHAT EXACTLY DO YOU WANT US TO DO?
MOMENTS LATER, AFTER CHARLES XAVIER HAS FINISHED HIS EXPLANATION...
GOT IT, SIR.
NO FUSS... JUST BRING HIM BACK, INTACT...
...WITHOUT ATTACTING UNDUE ATTENTION, BOBBY.
LET'S WORRY ABOUT THAT LATER, TROOPS.
RIGHT NOW WE'D BETTE MOVE.
THEIR VOICES ECHO THROUGH THE NOW-EMPTY CORRIDORS... AND SLOWLY, RETURN TO THEIR TEACHER AND MENTOR...
AND FOR MANY MINUTES, HE SITS SILENT... CONTEMPLATING THE MEN HE'S GROOMED, WONDERING... PRAYING... THAT THE VALUES HE'S GIVEN THEM ARE GOOD VALUES...
...GOOD VALUES...
SEVEN HOURS LATER: THE CONCRETE GRID CALLED MANHATTAN: THE WEB-SLINGING HERO NAMED SPIDER-MAN...
NO GOOD! EVEN SLEEPING ALL DAY... DIDN'T QUITE HELP.
STILL DIZZY... THROBBING WITH FEVER...
...GOT TO FIND MYSELF A COOL CORNER, REST TILL MY SKULL STOPS SPINNNNNNGHH!
WHAT
MY WEBBING! SUDDENLY SNAPPED--TWISTING IN MY GRIP--

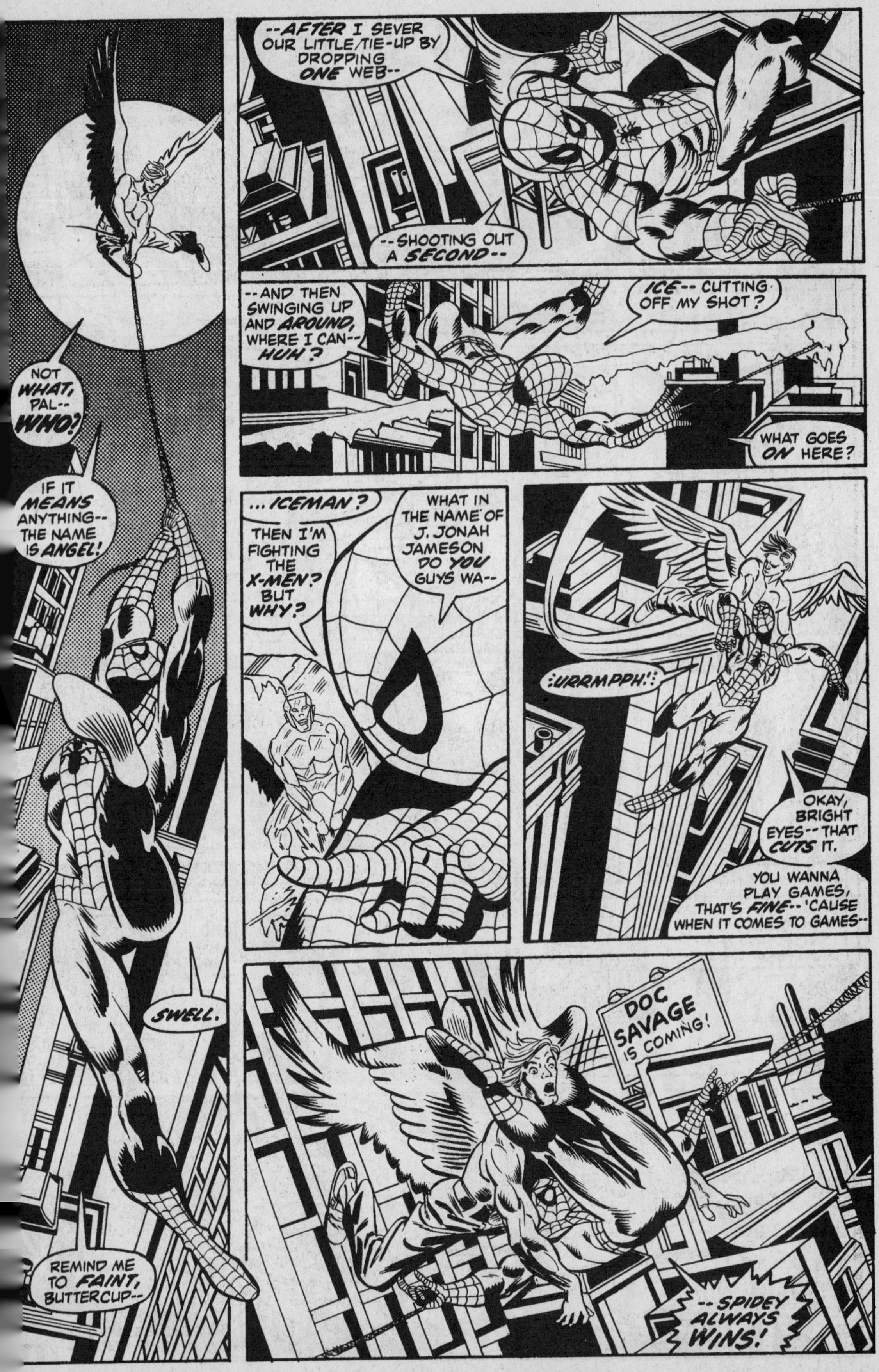
NOT WHAT, PAL-- WHO?
IF IT MEANS ANYTHING-- THE NAME IS ANGEL!
SWELL.
REMIND ME TO FAINT, BUTTERCUP--
--AFTER I SEVER OUR LITTLE TIE-UP BY DROPPING ONE WEB--
--SHOOTING OUT A SECOND--
--AND THEN SWINGING UP AND AROUND, WHERE I CAN-- HUH?
ICE-- CUTTING OFF MY SHOT?
WHAT GOES ON HERE?
...ICEMAN?
THEN I'M FIGHTING THE X-MEN? BUT WHY?
WHAT IN THE NAME OF J. JONAH JAMESON DO YOU GUYS WA--
URRMPPH!
OKAY, BRIGHT EYES-- THAT CUTS IT.
YOU WANNA PLAY GAMES, THAT'S FINE-- 'CAUSE WHEN IT COMES TO GAMES--
DOC SAVAGE IS COMING!
--SPIDEY ALWAYS WINS!

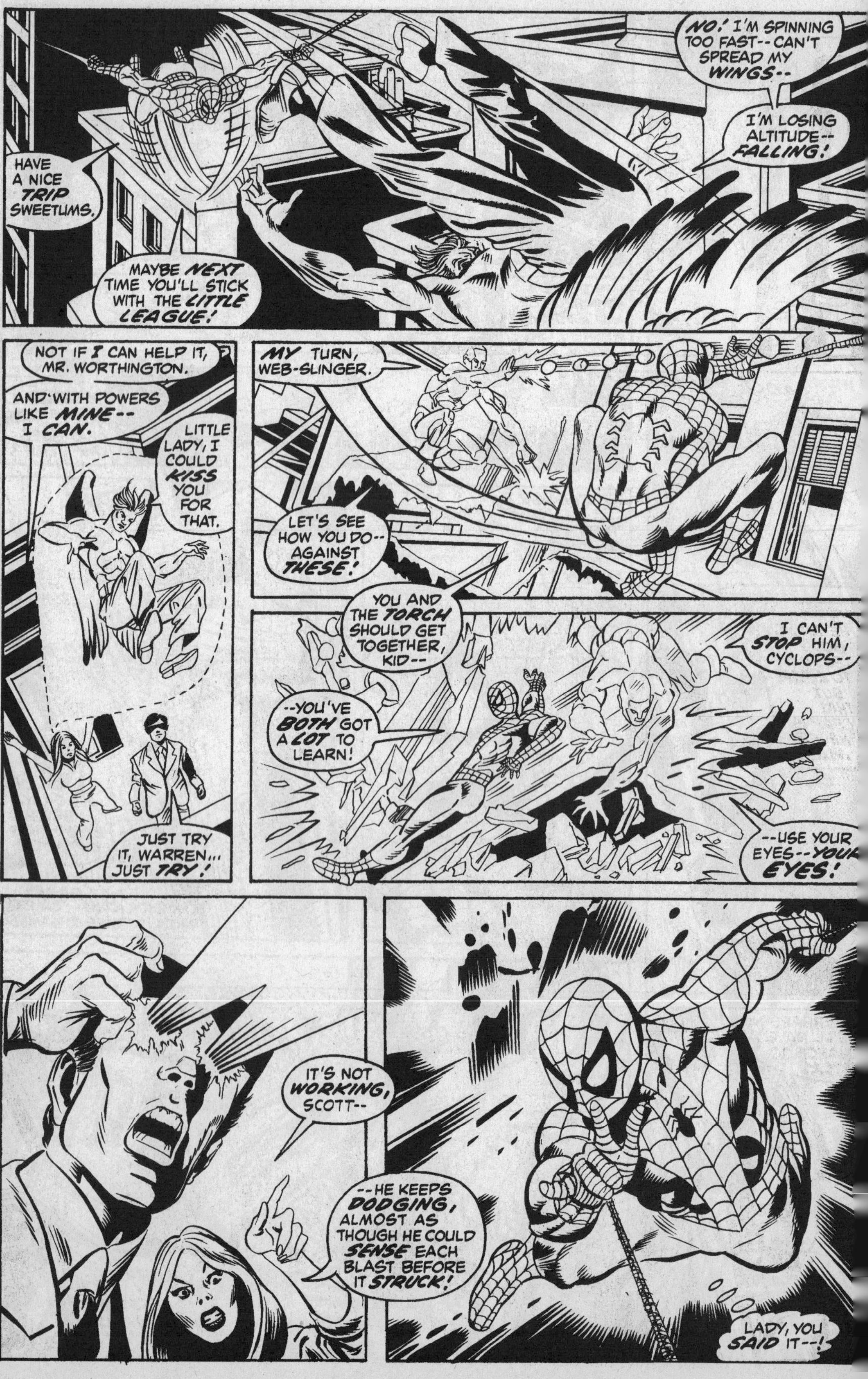

NO! I'M SPINNING TOO FAST--CAN'T SPREAD MY WINGS--
I'M LOSING ALTITUDE--FALLING!
HAVE A NICE TRIP SWEETUMS.
MAYBE NEXT TIME YOU'LL STICK WITH THE LITTLE LEAGUE!
NOT IF I CAN HELP IT, MR. WORTHINGTON.
AND WITH POWERS LIKE MINE--I CAN.
LITTLE LADY, I COULD KISS YOU FOR THAT.
JUST TRY IT, WARREN... JUST TRY!
MY TURN, WEB-SLINGER.
LET'S SEE HOW YOU DO--AGAINST THESE!
YOU AND THE TORCH SHOULD GET TOGETHER, KID--
--YOU'VE BOTH GOT A LOT TO LEARN!
I CAN'T STOP HIM, CYCLOPS--
--USE YOUR EYES--YOUR EYES!
IT'S NOT WORKING, SCOTT--
--HE KEEPS DODGING, ALMOST AS THOUGH HE COULD SENSE EACH BLAST BEFORE IT STRUCK!
LADY, YOU SAID IT--!

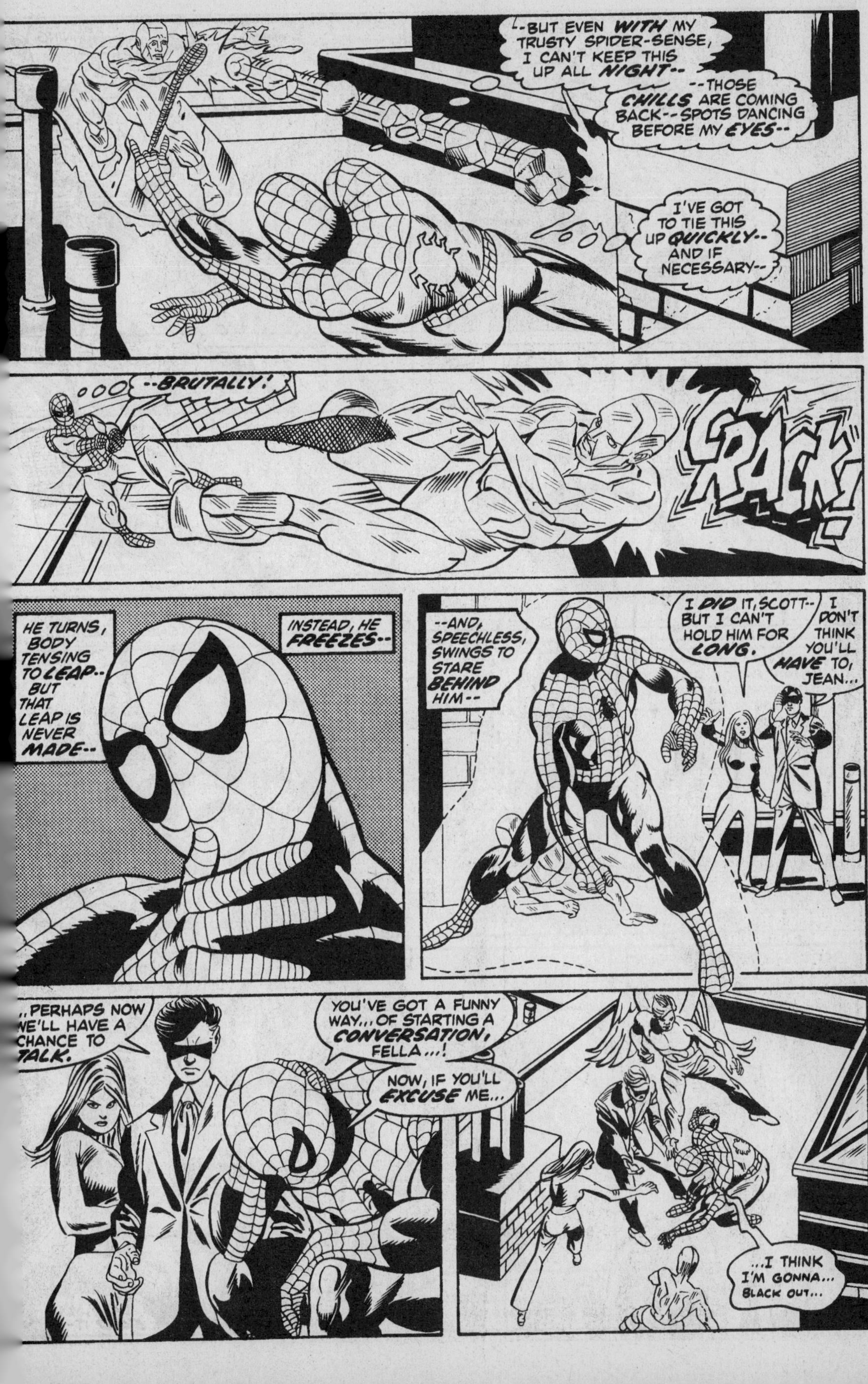
--BUT EVEN WITH MY TRUSTY SPIDER-SENSE, I CAN'T KEEP THIS UP ALL NIGHT--
--THOSE CHILLS ARE COMING BACK--SPOTS DANCING BEFORE MY EYES--
I'VE GOT TO TIE THIS UP QUICKLY--AND IF NECESSARY--
--BRUTALLY!
CRACK!
HE TURNS, BODY TENSING TO LEAP--BUT THAT LEAP IS NEVER MADE--
INSTEAD, HE FREEZES--
--AND, SPEECHLESS, SWINGS TO STARE BEHIND HIM--
I DID IT, SCOTT--BUT I CAN'T HOLD HIM FOR LONG.
I DON'T THINK YOU'LL HAVE TO, JEAN...
...PERHAPS NOW WE'LL HAVE A CHANCE TO TALK.
YOU'VE GOT A FUNNY WAY... OF STARTING A CONVERSATION, FELLA...!
NOW, IF YOU'LL EXCUSE ME...
...I THINK I'M GONNA... BLACK OUT...

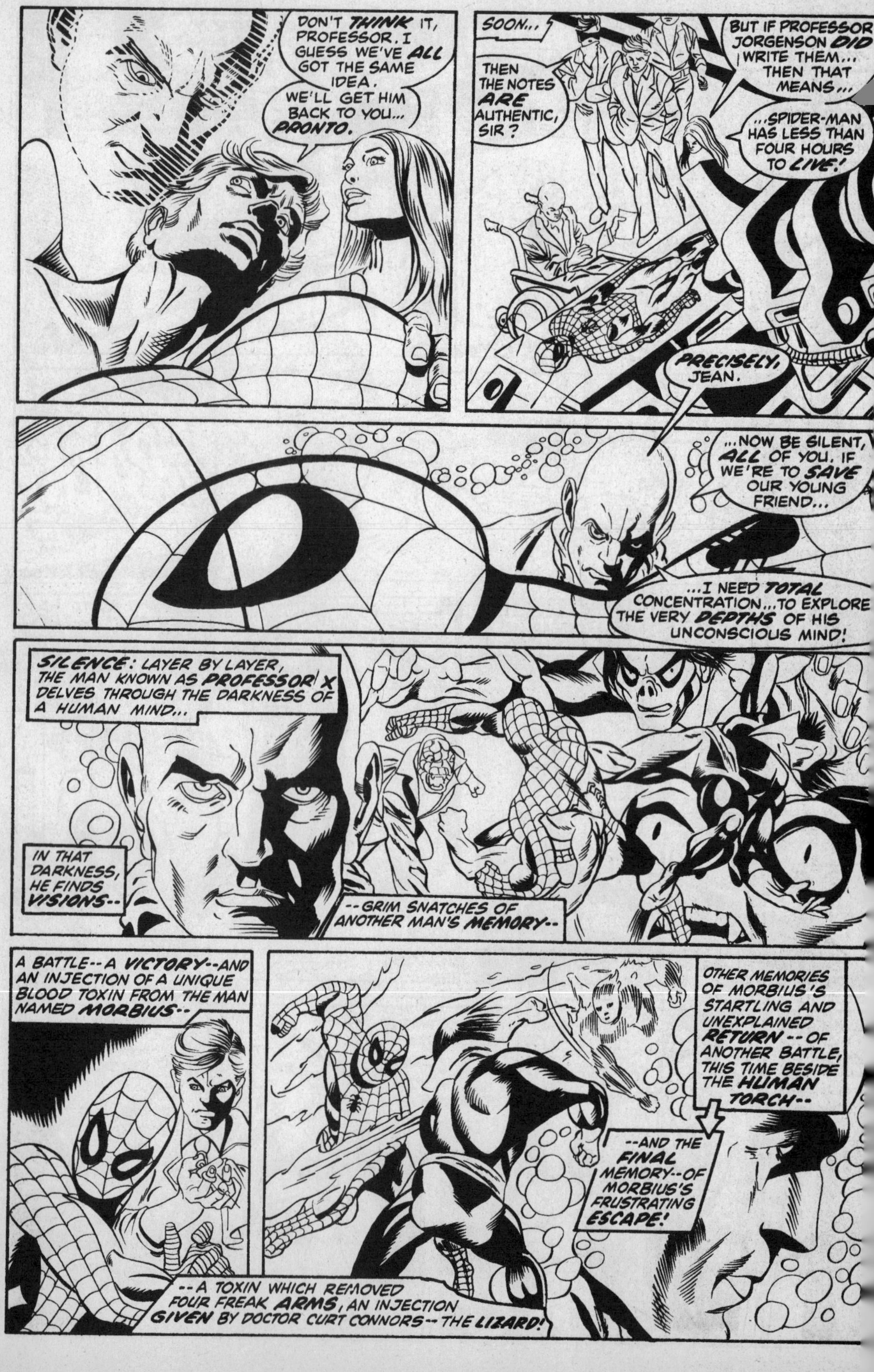
DON'T THINK IT, PROFESSOR. I GUESS WE'VE ALL GOT THE SAME IDEA. WE'LL GET HIM BACK TO YOU... PRONTO.
SOON...
THEN THE NOTES ARE AUTHENTIC, SIR?
BUT IF PROFESSOR JORGENSON DID WRITE THEM... THEN THAT MEANS...
...SPIDER-MAN HAS LESS THAN FOUR HOURS TO LIVE!
PRECISELY, JEAN.
...NOW BE SILENT, ALL OF YOU. IF WE'RE TO SAVE OUR YOUNG FRIEND...
...I NEED TOTAL CONCENTRATION...TO EXPLORE THE VERY DEPTHS OF HIS UNCONSCIOUS MIND!
SILENCE: LAYER BY LAYER, THE MAN KNOWN AS PROFESSOR X DELVES THROUGH THE DARKNESS OF A HUMAN MIND...
IN THAT DARKNESS, HE FINDS VISIONS--
--GRIM SNATCHES OF ANOTHER MAN'S MEMORY--
A BATTLE--A VICTORY--AND AN INJECTION OF A UNIQUE BLOOD TOXIN FROM THE MAN NAMED MORBIUS--
--A TOXIN WHICH REMOVED FOUR FREAK ARMS, AN INJECTION GIVEN BY DOCTOR CURT CONNORS--THE LIZARD!
OTHER MEMORIES OF MORBIUS'S STARTLING AND UNEXPLAINED RETURN--OF ANOTHER BATTLE, THIS TIME BESIDE THE HUMAN TORCH--
--AND THE FINAL MEMORY--OF MORBIUS'S FRUSTRATING ESCAPE!

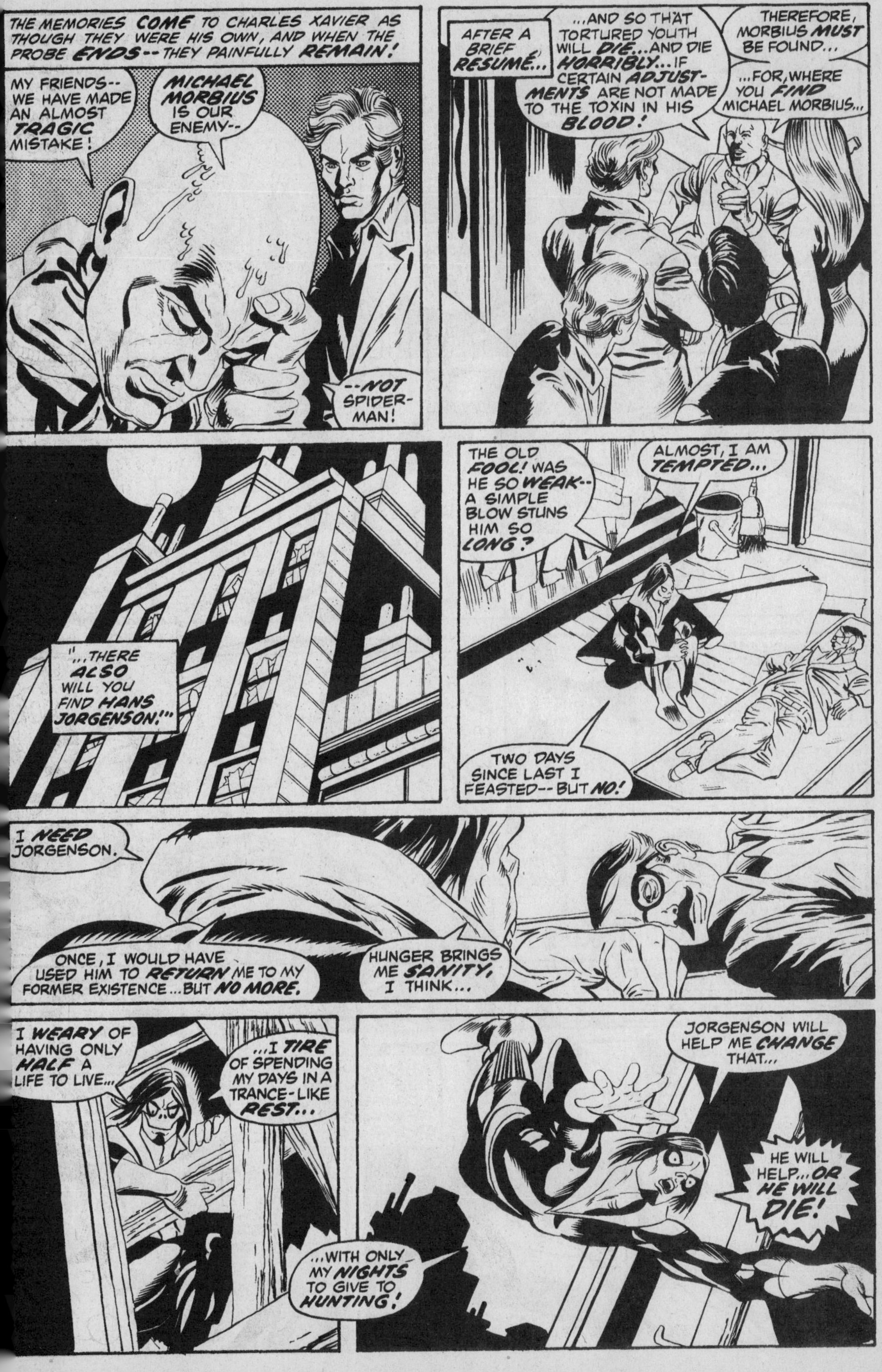

THE MEMORIES COME TO CHARLES XAVIER AS THOUGH THEY WERE HIS OWN, AND WHEN THE PROBE ENDS-- THEY PAINFULLY REMAIN!
MY FRIENDS-- WE HAVE MADE AN ALMOST TRAGIC MISTAKE!
MICHAEL MORBIUS IS OUR ENEMY--
--NOT SPIDER-MAN!
AFTER A BRIEF RESUMÉ...
...AND SO THAT TORTURED YOUTH WILL DIE...AND DIE HORRIBLY...IF CERTAIN ADJUSTMENTS ARE NOT MADE TO THE TOXIN IN HIS BLOOD!
THEREFORE, MORBIUS MUST BE FOUND...
...FOR, WHERE YOU FIND MICHAEL MORBIUS...
"...THERE ALSO WILL YOU FIND HANS JORGENSON!"
THE OLD FOOL! WAS HE SO WEAK-- A SIMPLE BLOW STUNS HIM SO LONG?
ALMOST, I AM TEMPTED...
TWO DAYS SINCE LAST I FEASTED-- BUT NO!
I NEED JORGENSON.
ONCE, I WOULD HAVE USED HIM TO RETURN ME TO MY FORMER EXISTENCE...BUT NO MORE.
HUNGER BRINGS ME SANITY, I THINK...
I WEARY OF HAVING ONLY HALF A LIFE TO LIVE...
...I TIRE OF SPENDING MY DAYS IN A TRANCE-LIKE REST...
...WITH ONLY MY NIGHTS TO GIVE TO HUNTING!
JORGENSON WILL HELP ME CHANGE THAT...
HE WILL HELP...OR HE WILL DIE!

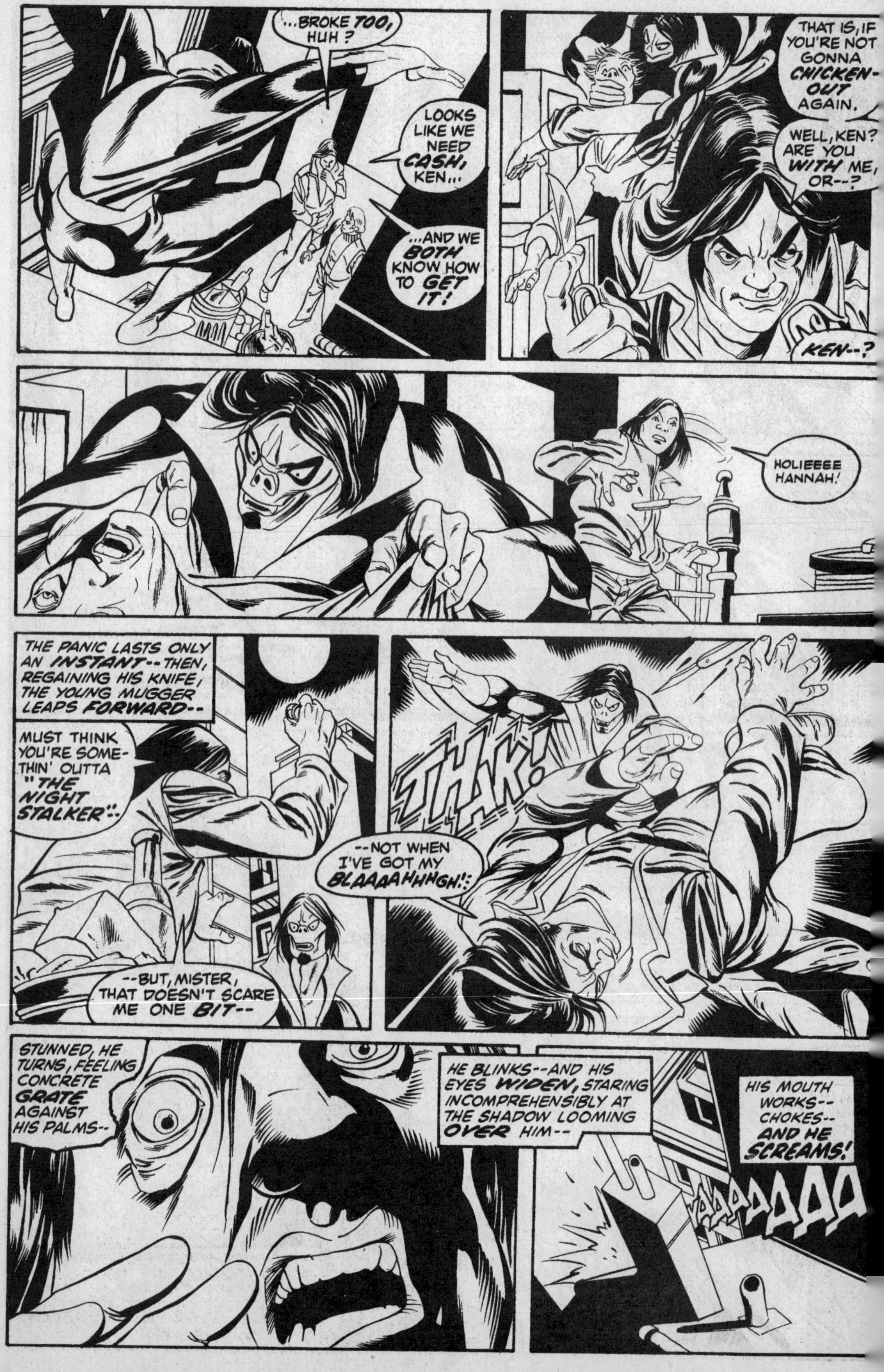
...BROKE TOO, HUH?
LOOKS LIKE WE NEED CASH, KEN...
...AND WE BOTH KNOW HOW TO GET IT!
THAT IS, IF YOU'RE NOT GONNA CHICKEN-OUT AGAIN.
WELL, KEN? ARE YOU WITH ME, OR--?
KEN--?
HOLIEEEE HANNAH!
THE PANIC LASTS ONLY AN INSTANT--THEN, REGAINING HIS KNIFE, THE YOUNG MUGGER LEAPS FORWARD--
MUST THINK YOU'RE SOMETHIN' OUTTA "THE NIGHT STALKER"--
--BUT, MISTER, THAT DOESN'T SCARE ME ONE BIT--
THAK!
--NOT WHEN I'VE GOT MY BLAAAAHHHGH!!
STUNNED, HE TURNS, FEELING CONCRETE GRATE AGAINST HIS PALMS--
HE BLINKS--AND HIS EYES WIDEN, STARING INCOMPREHENSIBLY AT THE SHADOW LOOMING OVER HIM--
HIS MOUTH WORKS--CHOKES--AND HE SCREAMS!
YAAAAAAA

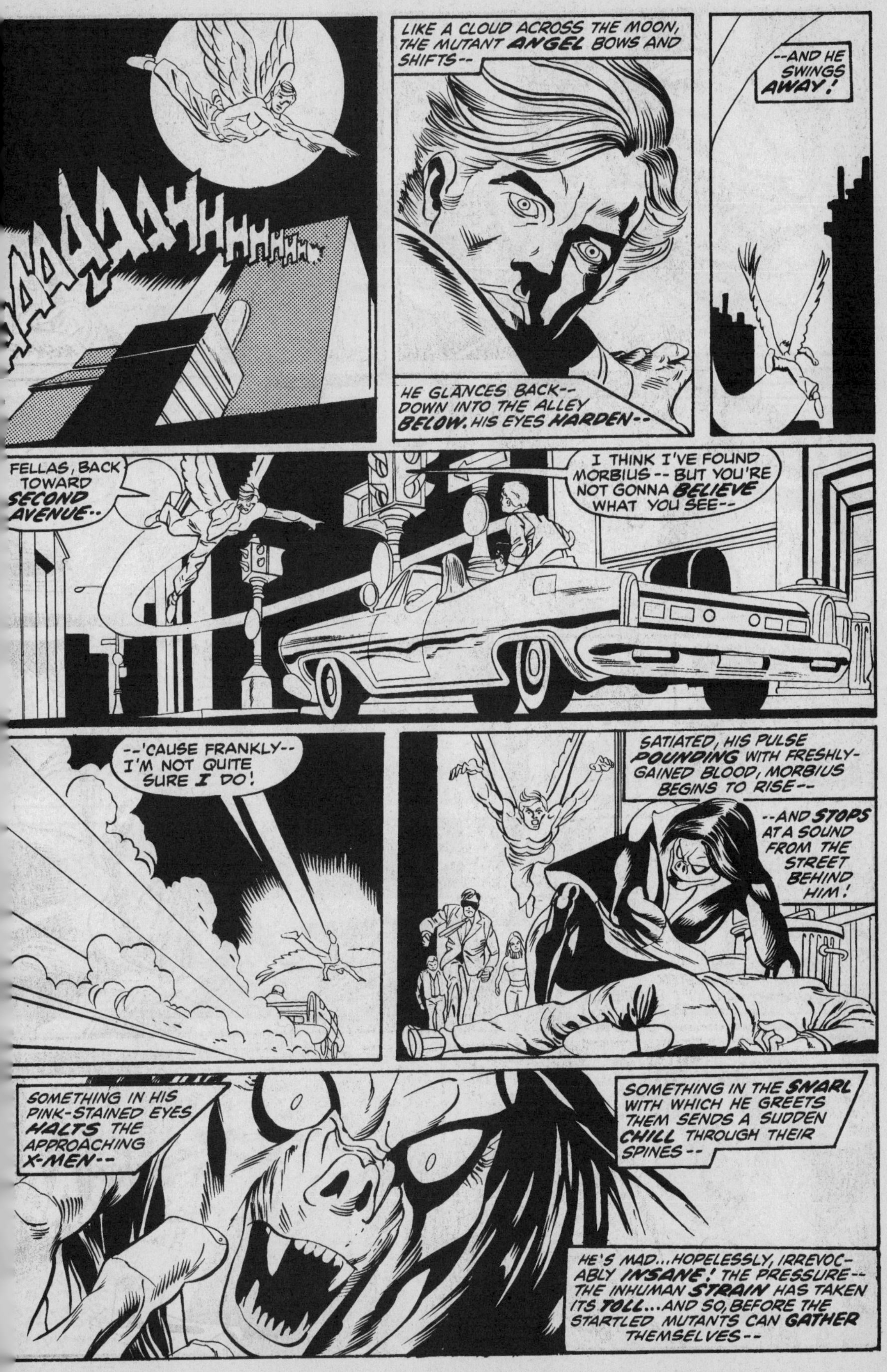
AAAAAAAHHHHHH
LIKE A CLOUD ACROSS THE MOON, THE MUTANT ANGEL BOWS AND SHIFTS--
HE GLANCES BACK-- DOWN INTO THE ALLEY BELOW. HIS EYES HARDEN--
--AND HE SWINGS AWAY!
FELLAS, BACK TOWARD SECOND AVENUE--
I THINK I'VE FOUND MORBIUS -- BUT YOU'RE NOT GONNA BELIEVE WHAT YOU SEE--
--'CAUSE FRANKLY-- I'M NOT QUITE SURE I DO!
SATIATED, HIS PULSE POUNDING WITH FRESHLY-GAINED BLOOD, MORBIUS BEGINS TO RISE--
--AND STOPS AT A SOUND FROM THE STREET BEHIND HIM!
SOMETHING IN HIS PINK-STAINED EYES HALTS THE APPROACHING X-MEN--
SOMETHING IN THE SNARL WITH WHICH HE GREETS THEM SENDS A SUDDEN CHILL THROUGH THEIR SPINES--
HE'S MAD...HOPELESSLY, IRREVOCABLY INSANE! THE PRESSURE-- THE INHUMAN STRAIN HAS TAKEN ITS TOLL...AND SO, BEFORE THE STARTLED MUTANTS CAN GATHER THEMSELVES--

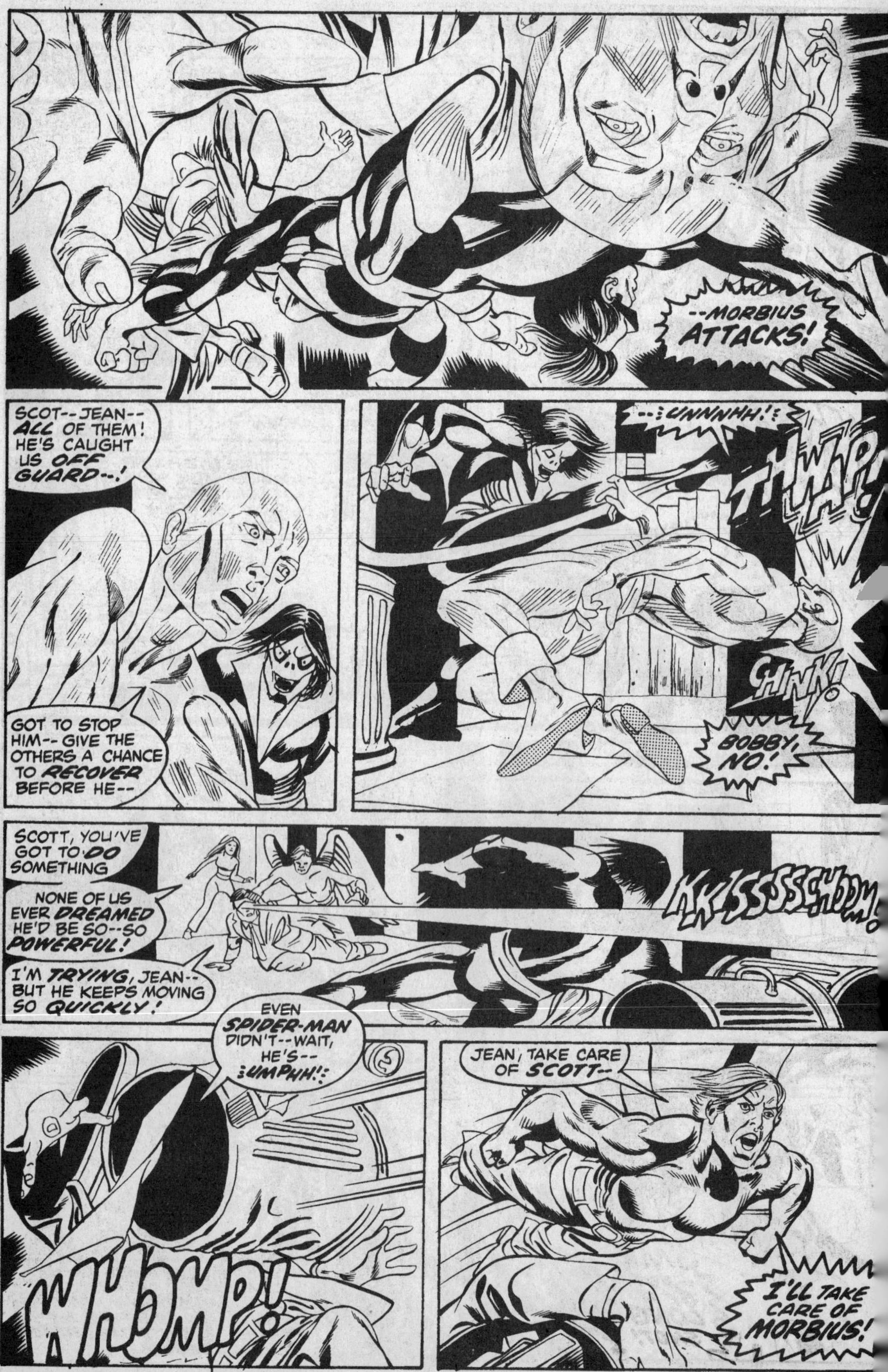
--MORBIUS ATTACKS!
SCOT--JEAN--ALL OF THEM! HE'S CAUGHT US OFF GUARD--!
GOT TO STOP HIM--GIVE THE OTHERS A CHANCE TO RECOVER BEFORE HE--
--UNNNHH!--
THWAP!
CHINK!
BOBBY, NO!
SCOTT, YOU'VE GOT TO DO SOMETHING
NONE OF US EVER DREAMED HE'D BE SO--SO POWERFUL!
I'M TRYING, JEAN--BUT HE KEEPS MOVING SO QUICKLY!
KKISSSSCHOOM!
EVEN SPIDER-MAN DIDN'T--WAIT, HE'S----UMPHH!--
WHOMP!
JEAN, TAKE CARE OF SCOTT--
I'LL TAKE CARE OF MORBIUS!

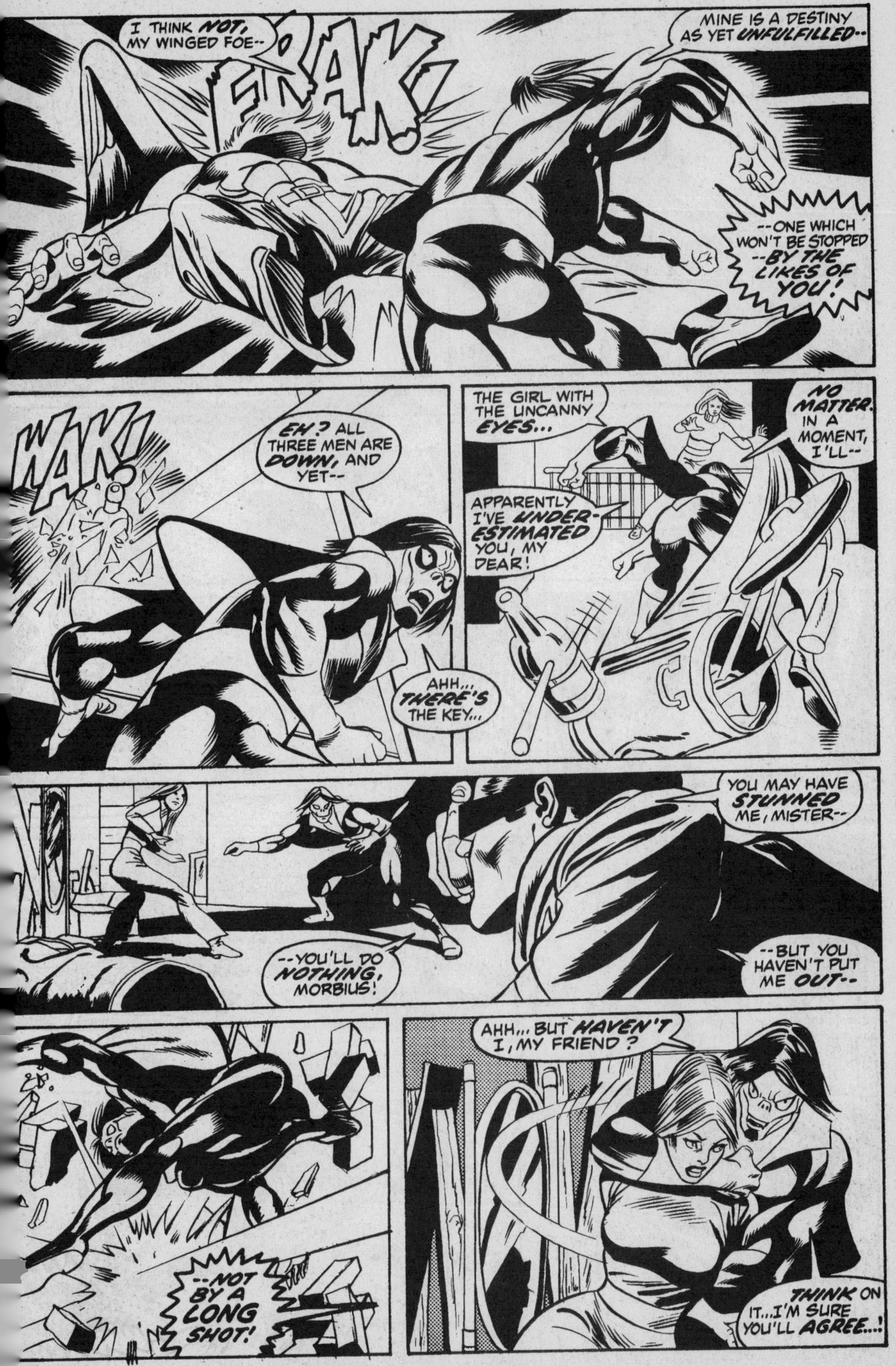
I THINK NOT, MY WINGED FOE--
FRAK
MINE IS A DESTINY AS YET UNFULFILLED--
--ONE WHICH WON'T BE STOPPED --BY THE LIKES OF YOU!
WAK!
EH? ALL THREE MEN ARE DOWN, AND YET--
AHH... THERE'S THE KEY...
THE GIRL WITH THE UNCANNY EYES...
APPARENTLY I'VE UNDER-ESTIMATED YOU, MY DEAR!
NO MATTER. IN A MOMENT, I'LL--
--YOU'LL DO NOTHING, MORBIUS!
YOU MAY HAVE STUNNED ME, MISTER--
--BUT YOU HAVEN'T PUT ME OUT--
--NOT BY A LONG SHOT!
AHH... BUT HAVEN'T I, MY FRIEND?
THINK ON IT...I'M SURE YOU'LL AGREE...!

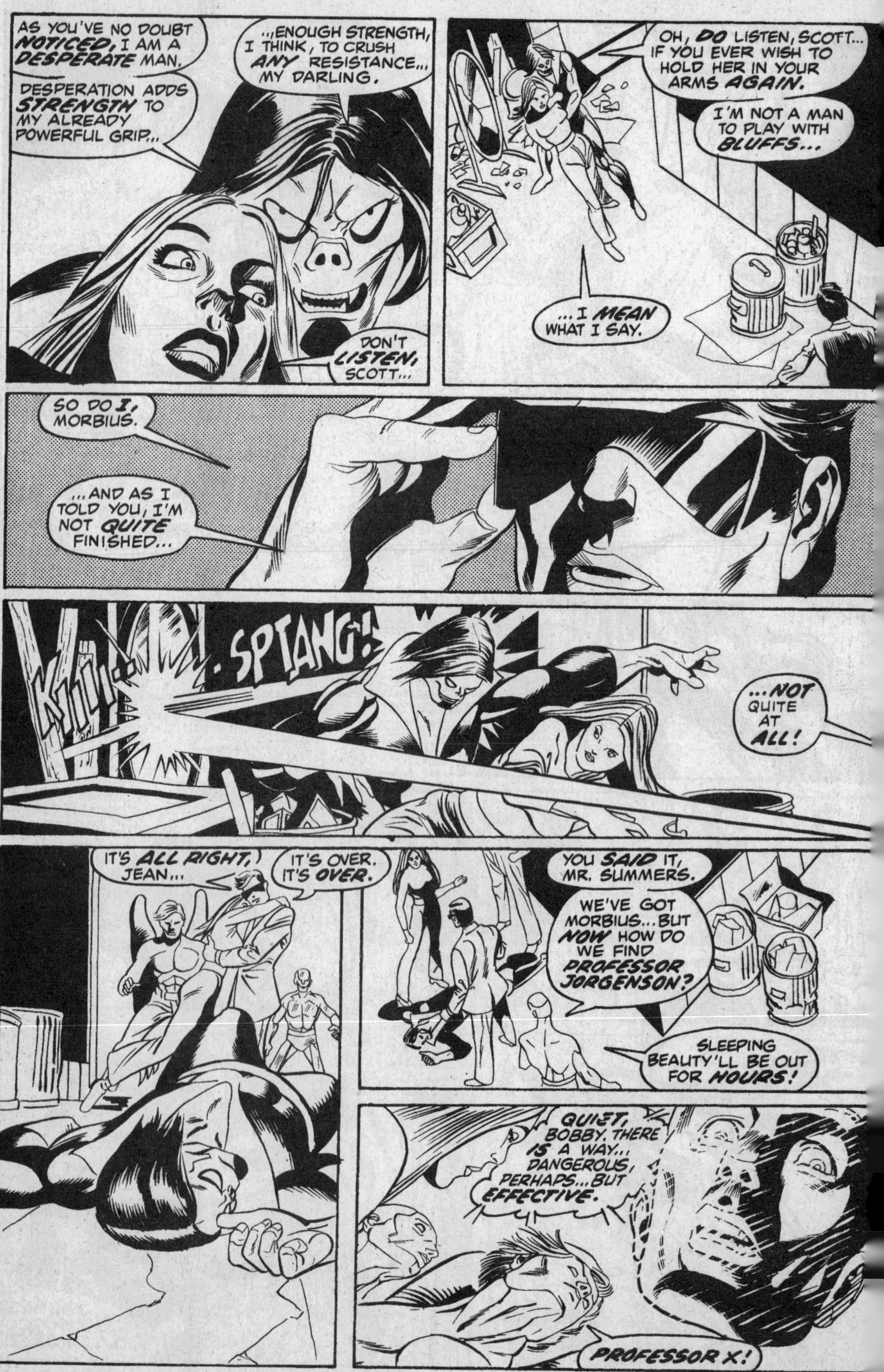
AS YOU'VE NO DOUBT NOTICED, I AM A DESPERATE MAN.
DESPERATION ADDS STRENGTH TO MY ALREADY POWERFUL GRIP...
...ENOUGH STRENGTH, I THINK, TO CRUSH ANY RESISTANCE... MY DARLING.
DON'T LISTEN, SCOTT...
OH, DO LISTEN, SCOTT... IF YOU EVER WISH TO HOLD HER IN YOUR ARMS AGAIN.
I'M NOT A MAN TO PLAY WITH BLUFFS...
...I MEAN WHAT I SAY.
SO DO I, MORBIUS.
...AND AS I TOLD YOU, I'M NOT QUITE FINISHED...
SPTANG!
...NOT QUITE AT ALL!
IT'S ALL RIGHT, JEAN...
IT'S OVER. IT'S OVER.
YOU SAID IT, MR. SUMMERS.
WE'VE GOT MORBIUS... BUT NOW HOW DO WE FIND PROFESSOR JORGENSON?
SLEEPING BEAUTY'LL BE OUT FOR HOURS!
QUIET, BOBBY. THERE IS A WAY... DANGEROUS, PERHAPS... BUT EFFECTIVE.
PROFESSOR X!

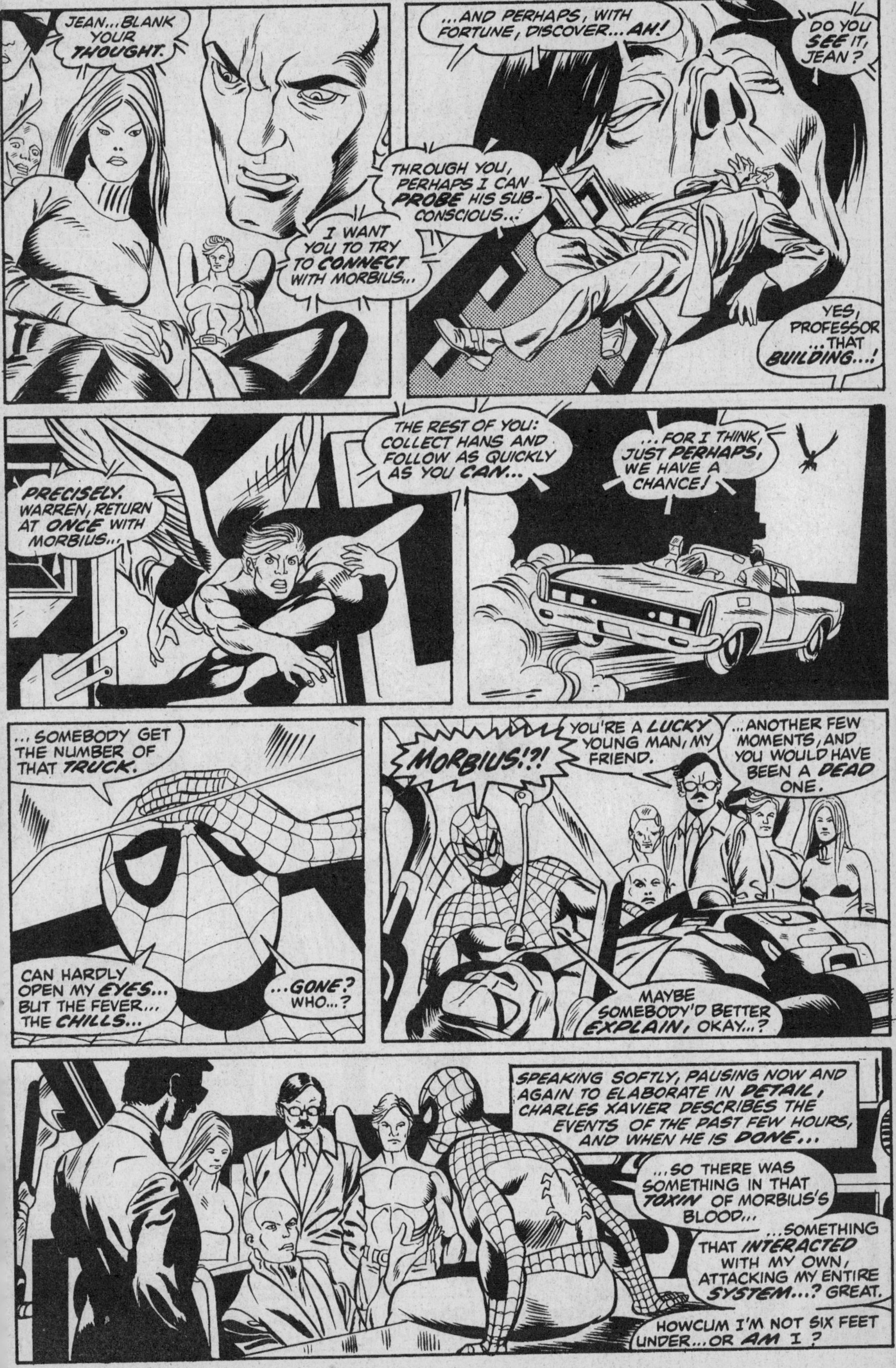
JEAN... BLANK YOUR THOUGHT.
I WANT YOU TO TRY TO CONNECT WITH MORBIUS...
THROUGH YOU, PERHAPS I CAN PROBE HIS SUB-CONSCIOUS...
...AND PERHAPS, WITH FORTUNE, DISCOVER... AH!
DO YOU SEE IT, JEAN?
YES, PROFESSOR ...THAT BUILDING...!
PRECISELY. WARREN, RETURN AT ONCE WITH MORBIUS...
THE REST OF YOU: COLLECT HANS AND FOLLOW AS QUICKLY AS YOU CAN...
...FOR I THINK, JUST PERHAPS, WE HAVE A CHANCE!
... SOMEBODY GET THE NUMBER OF THAT TRUCK.
CAN HARDLY OPEN MY EYES... BUT THE FEVER... THE CHILLS...
...GONE? WHO...?
MORBIUS!?!
YOU'RE A LUCKY YOUNG MAN, MY FRIEND.
...ANOTHER FEW MOMENTS, AND YOU WOULD HAVE BEEN A DEAD ONE.
MAYBE SOMEBODY'D BETTER EXPLAIN, OKAY...?
SPEAKING SOFTLY, PAUSING NOW AND AGAIN TO ELABORATE IN DETAIL, CHARLES XAVIER DESCRIBES THE EVENTS OF THE PAST FEW HOURS, AND WHEN HE IS DONE...
...SO THERE WAS SOMETHING IN THAT TOXIN OF MORBIUS'S BLOOD...
...SOMETHING THAT INTERACTED WITH MY OWN, ATTACKING MY ENTIRE SYSTEM...? GREAT.
HOWCUM I'M NOT SIX FEET UNDER... OR AM I?

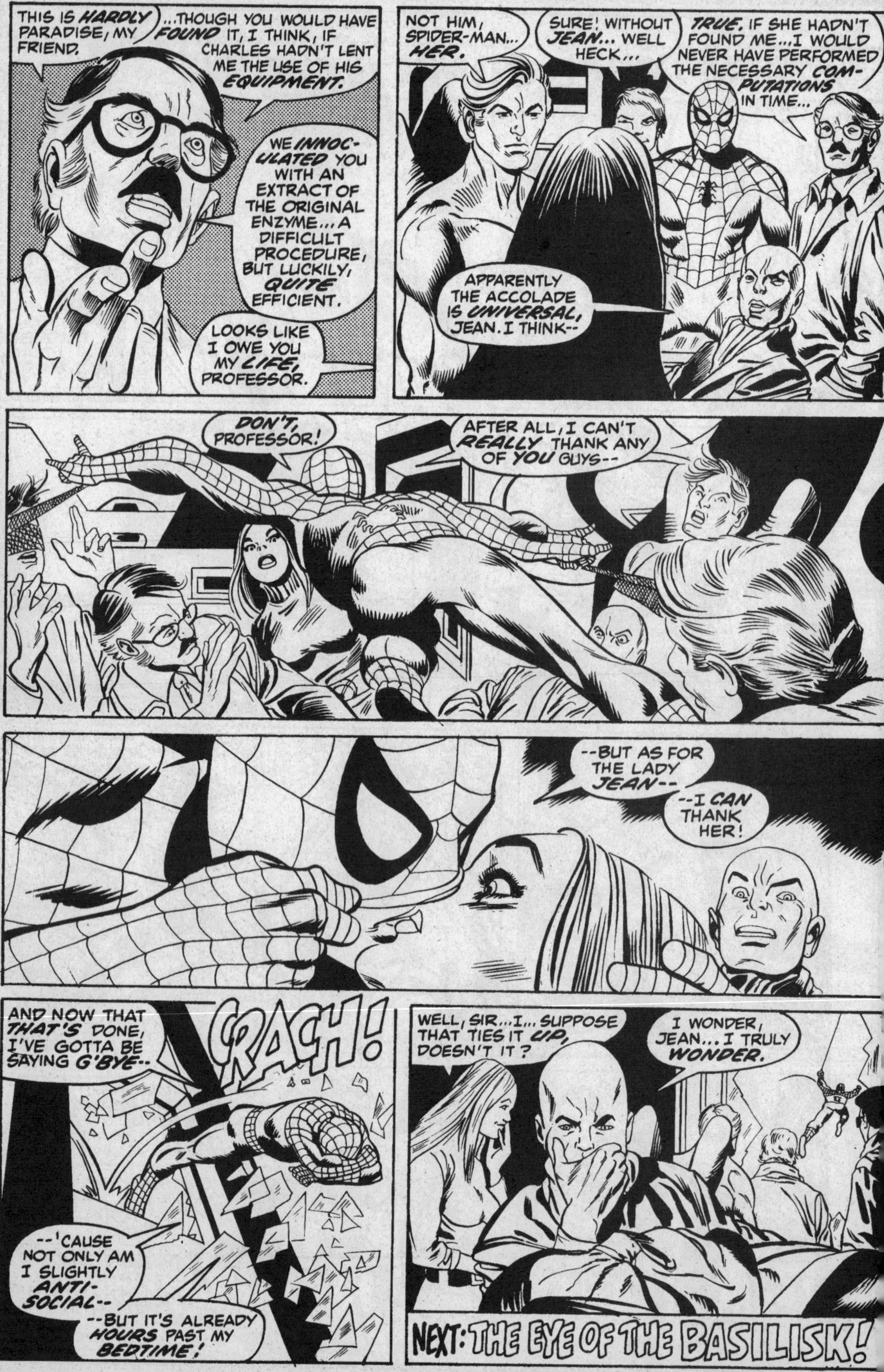
THIS IS HARDLY PARADISE, MY FRIEND.
...THOUGH YOU WOULD HAVE FOUND IT, I THINK, IF CHARLES HADN'T LENT ME THE USE OF HIS EQUIPMENT.
WE INNOCULATED YOU WITH AN EXTRACT OF THE ORIGINAL ENZYME...A DIFFICULT PROCEDURE, BUT LUCKILY, QUITE EFFICIENT.
LOOKS LIKE I OWE YOU MY LIFE, PROFESSOR.
NOT HIM, SPIDER-MAN... HER.
SURE! WITHOUT JEAN... WELL HECK...
TRUE. IF SHE HADN'T FOUND ME...I WOULD NEVER HAVE PERFORMED THE NECESSARY COMPUTATIONS IN TIME...
APPARENTLY THE ACCOLADE IS UNIVERSAL, JEAN. I THINK--
DON'T, PROFESSOR!
AFTER ALL, I CAN'T REALLY THANK ANY OF YOU GUYS--
--BUT AS FOR THE LADY JEAN--
--I CAN THANK HER!
AND NOW THAT THAT'S DONE, I'VE GOTTA BE SAYING G'BYE--
CRACH!
--'CAUSE NOT ONLY AM I SLIGHTLY ANTI-SOCIAL--
--BUT IT'S ALREADY HOURS PAST MY BEDTIME!
WELL, SIR...I... SUPPOSE THAT TIES IT UP, DOESN'T IT?
I WONDER, JEAN... I TRULY WONDER.
NEXT: THE EYE OF THE BASILISK!

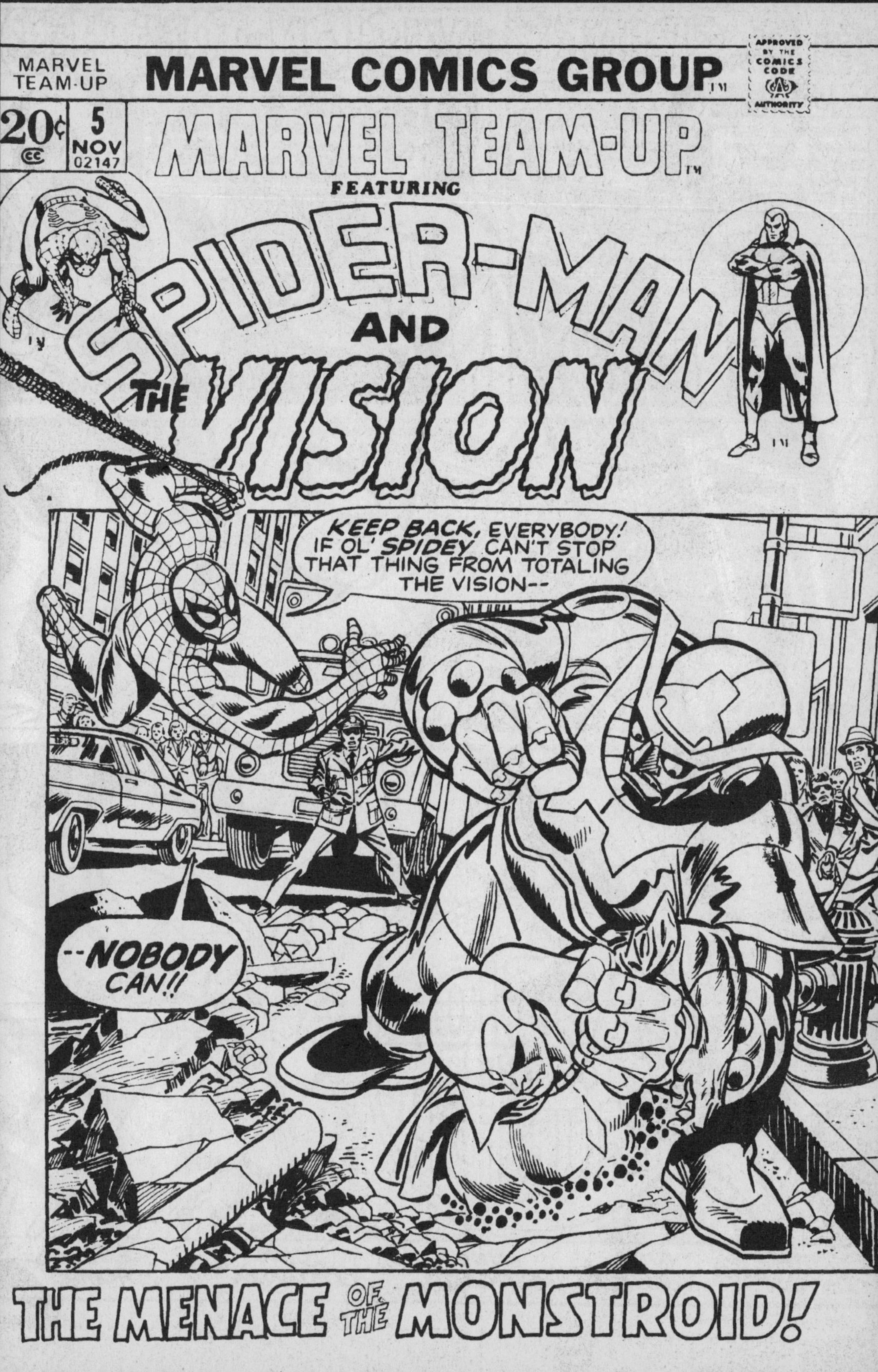
MARVEL TEAM-UP
MARVEL COMICS GROUP
APPROVED BY THE COMICS CODE AUTHORITY
20¢ 5 NOV 02147
MARVEL TEAM-UP
FEATURING
SPIDER-MAN
AND
THE VISION
KEEP BACK, EVERYBODY! IF OL' SPIDEY CAN'T STOP THAT THING FROM TOTALING THE VISION--
--NOBODY CAN!!
THE MENACE OF THE MONSTROID!

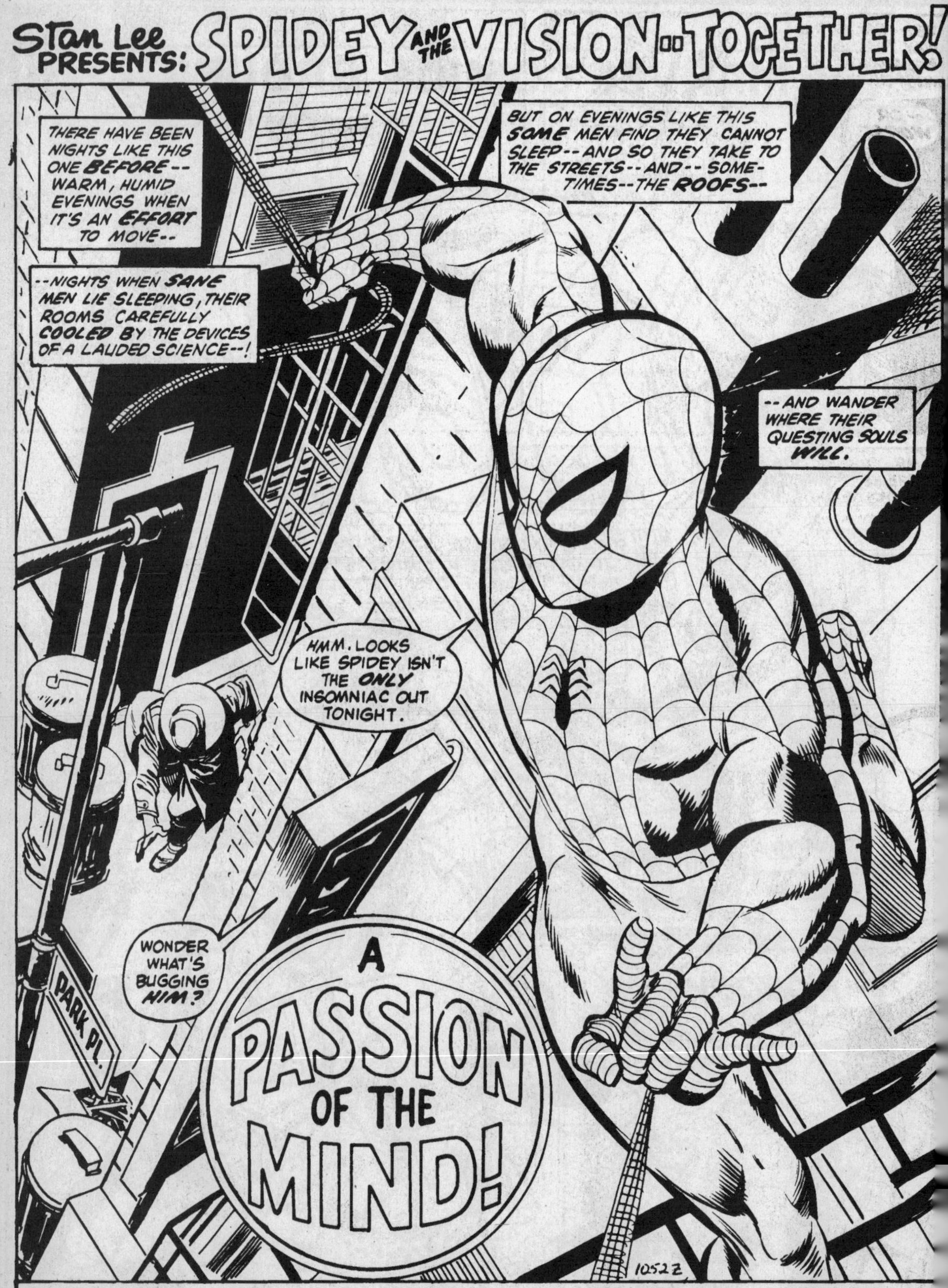

Stan Lee PRESENTS: SPIDEY AND THE VISION--TOGETHER!
THERE HAVE BEEN NIGHTS LIKE THIS ONE BEFORE-- WARM, HUMID EVENINGS WHEN IT'S AN EFFORT TO MOVE--
--NIGHTS WHEN SANE MEN LIE SLEEPING, THEIR ROOMS CAREFULLY COOLED BY THE DEVICES OF A LAUDED SCIENCE--!
BUT ON EVENINGS LIKE THIS SOME MEN FIND THEY CANNOT SLEEP-- AND SO THEY TAKE TO THE STREETS-- AND-- SOMETIMES-- THE ROOFS--
--AND WANDER WHERE THEIR QUESTING SOULS WILL.
HMM. LOOKS LIKE SPIDEY ISN'T THE ONLY INSOMNIAC OUT TONIGHT.
WONDER WHAT'S BUGGING HIM?
PARK PL.
A PASSION OF THE MIND!
GERRY CONWAY script · GIL KANE art · MIKE ESPOSITO inks · JOHN COSTANZA letterer · ROY THOMAS editor

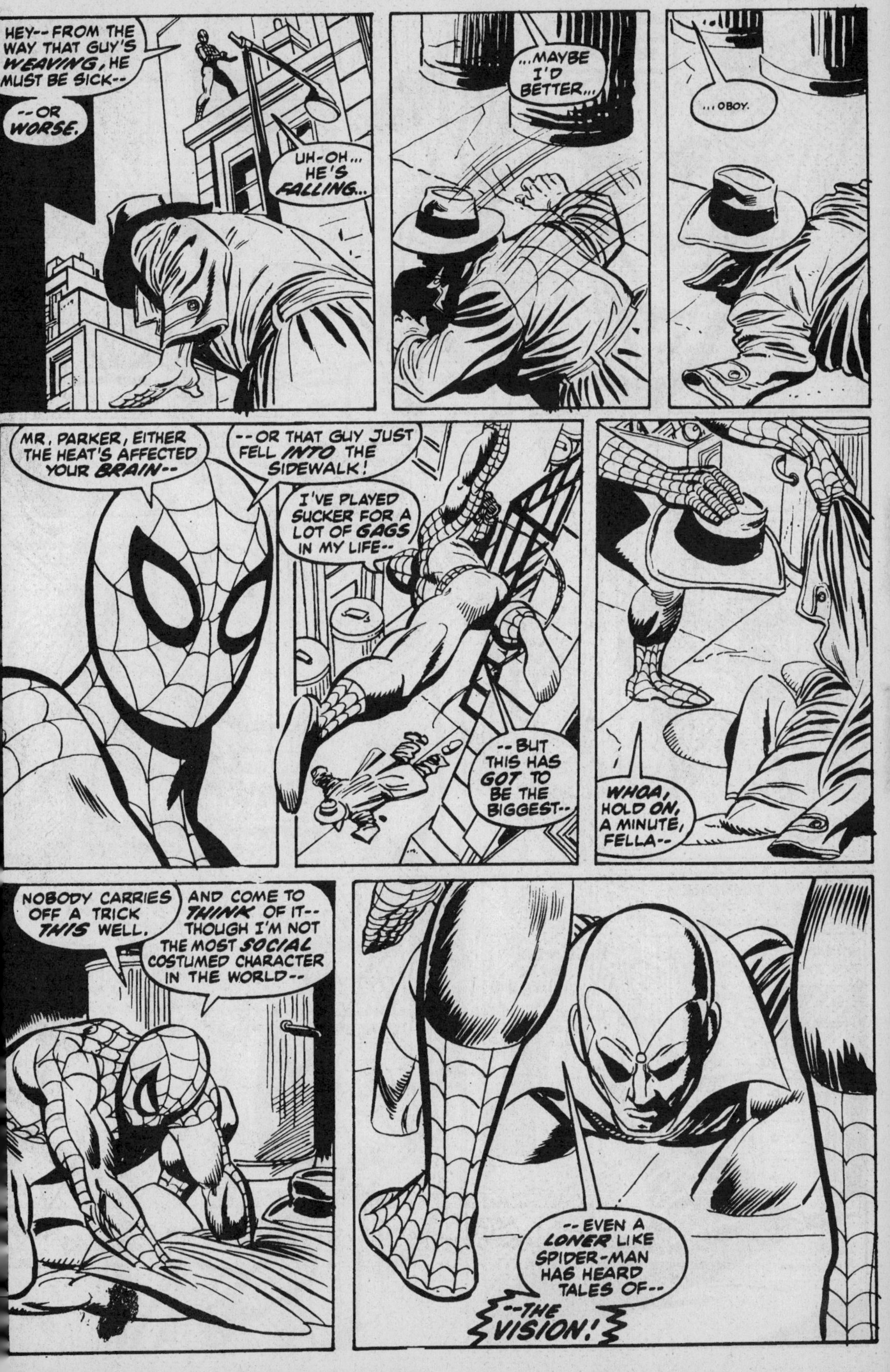
HEY--FROM THE WAY THAT GUY'S WEAVING, HE MUST BE SICK--
--OR WORSE.
UH-OH... HE'S FALLING...
...MAYBE I'D BETTER...
...OBOY.
MR. PARKER, EITHER THE HEAT'S AFFECTED YOUR BRAIN--
--OR THAT GUY JUST FELL INTO THE SIDEWALK!
I'VE PLAYED SUCKER FOR A LOT OF GAGS IN MY LIFE--
--BUT THIS HAS GOT TO BE THE BIGGEST--
WHOA, HOLD ON, A MINUTE, FELLA--
NOBODY CARRIES OFF A TRICK THIS WELL.
AND COME TO THINK OF IT-- THOUGH I'M NOT THE MOST SOCIAL COSTUMED CHARACTER IN THE WORLD--
--EVEN A LONER LIKE SPIDER-MAN HAS HEARD TALES OF--
--THE VISION!

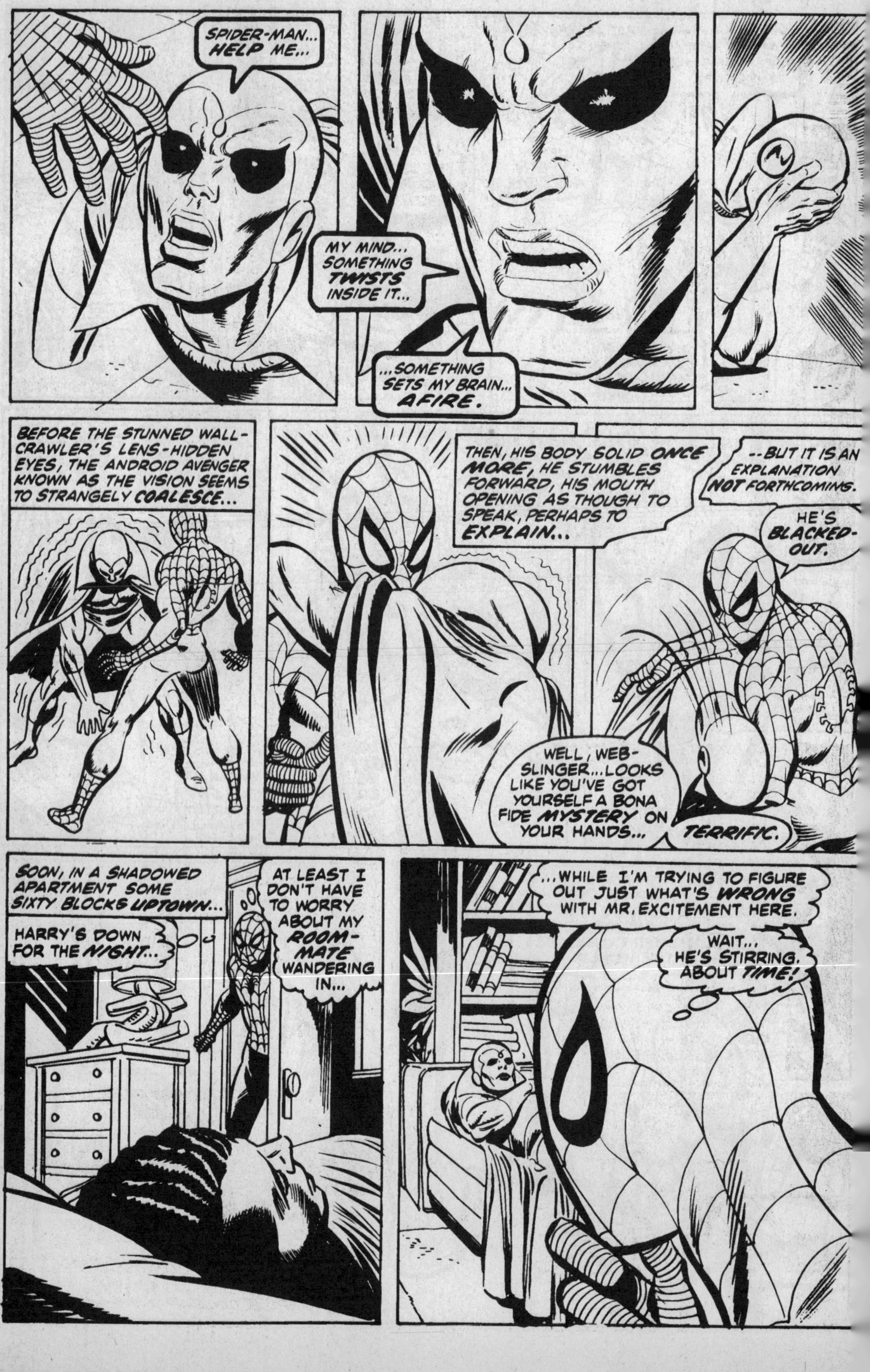

SPIDER-MAN... HELP ME...
MY MIND... SOMETHING TWISTS INSIDE IT...
...SOMETHING SETS MY BRAIN... AFIRE.
BEFORE THE STUNNED WALL-CRAWLER'S LENS-HIDDEN EYES, THE ANDROID AVENGER KNOWN AS THE VISION SEEMS TO STRANGELY COALESCE...
THEN, HIS BODY SOLID ONCE MORE, HE STUMBLES FORWARD, HIS MOUTH OPENING AS THOUGH TO SPEAK, PERHAPS TO EXPLAIN...
--BUT IT IS AN EXPLANATION NOT FORTHCOMING.
HE'S BLACKED-OUT.
WELL, WEB-SLINGER...LOOKS LIKE YOU'VE GOT YOURSELF A BONA FIDE MYSTERY ON YOUR HANDS...
TERRIFIC.
SOON, IN A SHADOWED APARTMENT SOME SIXTY BLOCKS UPTOWN...
HARRY'S DOWN FOR THE NIGHT...
AT LEAST I DON'T HAVE TO WORRY ABOUT MY ROOM-MATE WANDERING IN...
...WHILE I'M TRYING TO FIGURE OUT JUST WHAT'S WRONG WITH MR. EXCITEMENT HERE.
WAIT... HE'S STIRRING. ABOUT TIME!

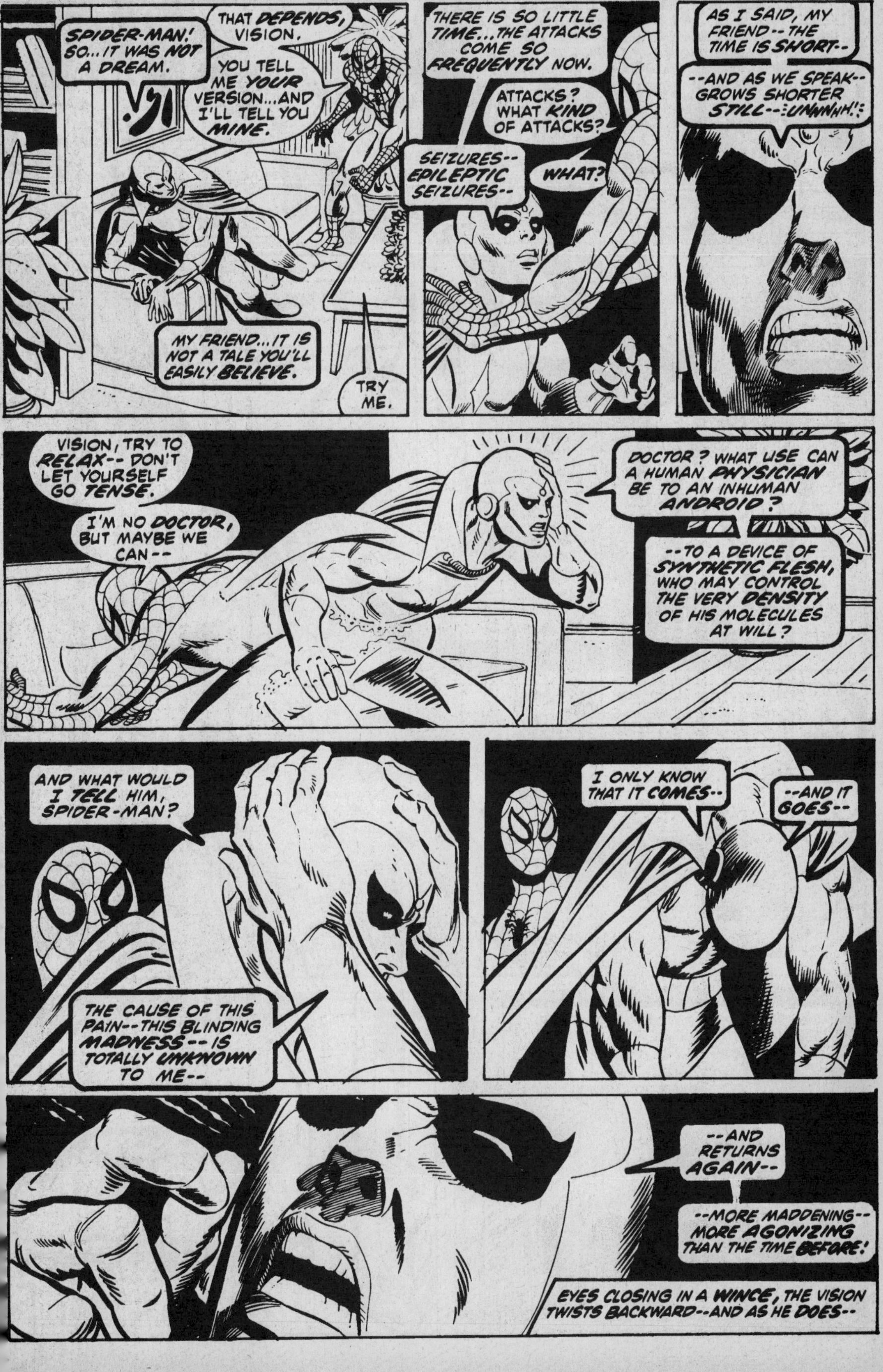
SPIDER-MAN! SO... IT WAS NOT A DREAM.
THAT DEPENDS, VISION.
YOU TELL ME YOUR VERSION...AND I'LL TELL YOU MINE.
MY FRIEND...IT IS NOT A TALE YOU'LL EASILY BELIEVE.
TRY ME.
THERE IS SO LITTLE TIME...THE ATTACKS COME SO FREQUENTLY NOW.
ATTACKS? WHAT KIND OF ATTACKS?
SEIZURES-- EPILEPTIC SEIZURES--
WHAT?
AS I SAID, MY FRIEND--THE TIME IS SHORT--
--AND AS WE SPEAK-- GROWS SHORTER STILL--UNNNHH!
VISION, TRY TO RELAX--DON'T LET YOURSELF GO TENSE.
I'M NO DOCTOR, BUT MAYBE WE CAN--
DOCTOR? WHAT USE CAN A HUMAN PHYSICIAN BE TO AN INHUMAN ANDROID?
--TO A DEVICE OF SYNTHETIC FLESH, WHO MAY CONTROL THE VERY DENSITY OF HIS MOLECULES AT WILL?
AND WHAT WOULD I TELL HIM, SPIDER-MAN?
THE CAUSE OF THIS PAIN--THIS BLINDING MADNESS--IS TOTALLY UNKNOWN TO ME--
I ONLY KNOW THAT IT COMES--
--AND IT GOES--
--AND RETURNS AGAIN--
--MORE MADDENING--MORE AGONIZING THAN THE TIME BEFORE!
EYES CLOSING IN A WINCE, THE VISION TWISTS BACKWARD--AND AS HE DOES--

--WE TAKE THIS OPPORTUNITY TO SEEK OUR ANSWERS *ELSEWHERE,* TURNING OUR ATTENTION EASTWARD, TO LONG ISLAND'S *NORTH SHORE,* WHERE IN A DARKENED *LABORATORY*--

--THE MAN KNOWN ONLY AS *THE PUPPET MASTER* LABORS IN BROODING SILENCE.

TIME AND AGAIN, HE GLANCES FROM HIS WORK TO ITS LIFESIZE *MODEL*--

--AND WHEN HE DOES, HIS LIPS CURL IN A NARROW *SMILE*--

--AND HE RESUMES HIS WORK, ONCE MORE.

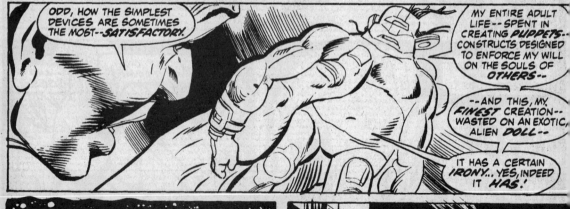

ODD, HOW THE SIMPLEST DEVICES ARE SOMETIMES THE MOST--*SATISFACTORY.*

MY ENTIRE ADULT LIFE-- SPENT IN CREATING *PUPPETS*-- CONSTRUCTS DESIGNED TO ENFORCE MY WILL ON THE SOULS OF *OTHERS*--

--AND THIS, MY *FINEST* CREATION-- WASTED ON AN EXOTIC, ALIEN *DOLL*--

IT HAS A CERTAIN *IRONY*... YES, INDEED IT *HAS!*

HIS THOUGHTS FLIT *BACKWARD,* THROUGH THE HOURS, THE DAYS, THE *WEEKS* TO THE MOMENT WHEN HE FIRST *GLIMPSED* THAT ALIEN ROBOT--

PLUNGING OUT OF THE MID-NIGHT HEAVENS, A GLEAMING *CHROMALLOY SHADOW* STREAKING TO THE SEA--

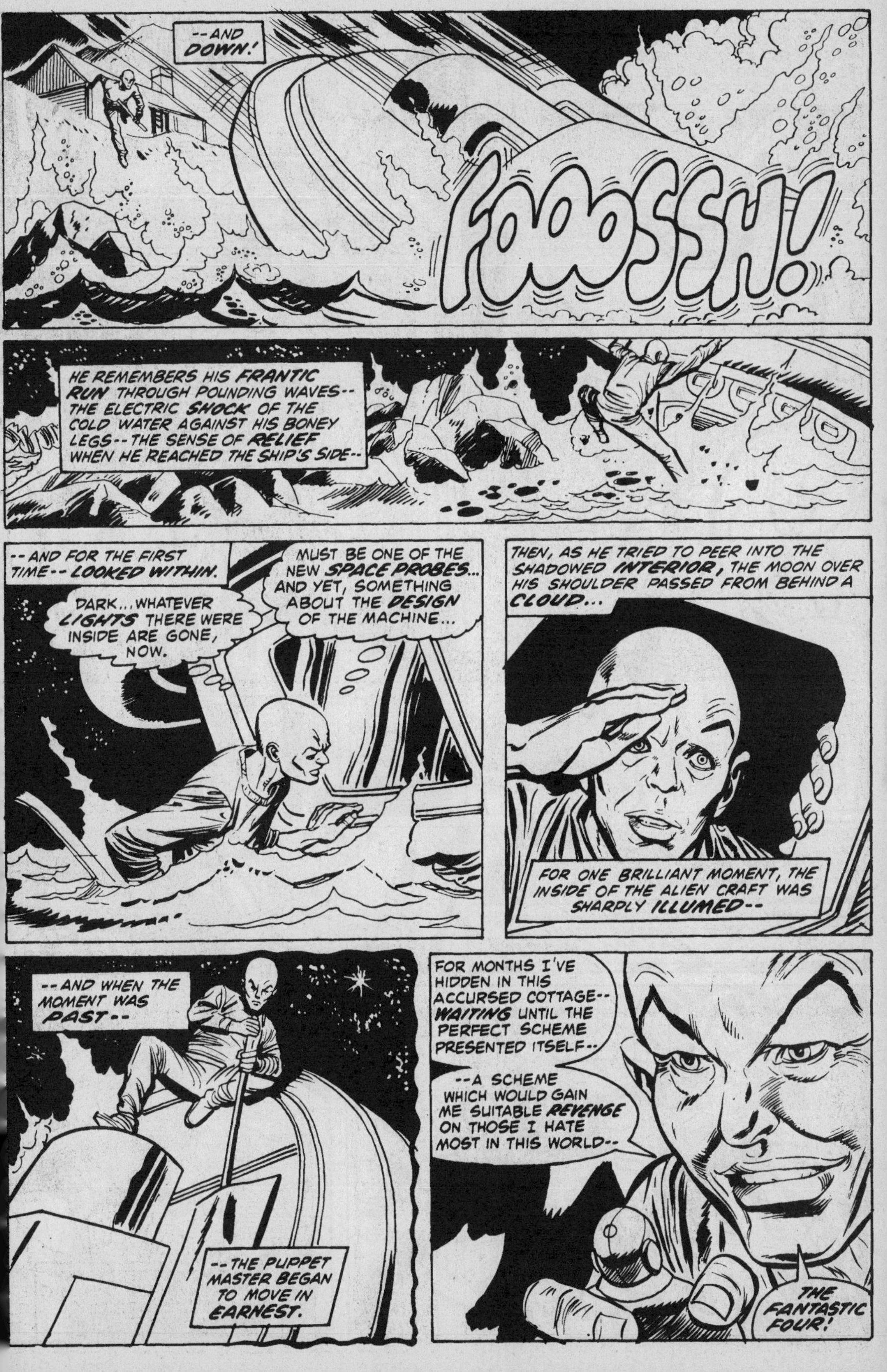
--AND DOWN!
FOOOSSH!
HE REMEMBERS HIS FRANTIC RUN THROUGH POUNDING WAVES--THE ELECTRIC SHOCK OF THE COLD WATER AGAINST HIS BONEY LEGS--THE SENSE OF RELIEF WHEN HE REACHED THE SHIP'S SIDE--
--AND FOR THE FIRST TIME--LOOKED WITHIN.
DARK...WHATEVER LIGHTS THERE WERE INSIDE ARE GONE, NOW.
MUST BE ONE OF THE NEW SPACE PROBES... AND YET, SOMETHING ABOUT THE DESIGN OF THE MACHINE...
THEN, AS HE TRIED TO PEER INTO THE SHADOWED INTERIOR, THE MOON OVER HIS SHOULDER PASSED FROM BEHIND A CLOUD...
FOR ONE BRILLIANT MOMENT, THE INSIDE OF THE ALIEN CRAFT WAS SHARPLY ILLUMED--
--AND WHEN THE MOMENT WAS PAST--
--THE PUPPET MASTER BEGAN TO MOVE IN EARNEST.
FOR MONTHS I'VE HIDDEN IN THIS ACCURSED COTTAGE--WAITING UNTIL THE PERFECT SCHEME PRESENTED ITSELF--
--A SCHEME WHICH WOULD GAIN ME SUITABLE REVENGE ON THOSE I HATE MOST IN THIS WORLD--
THE FANTASTIC FOUR!

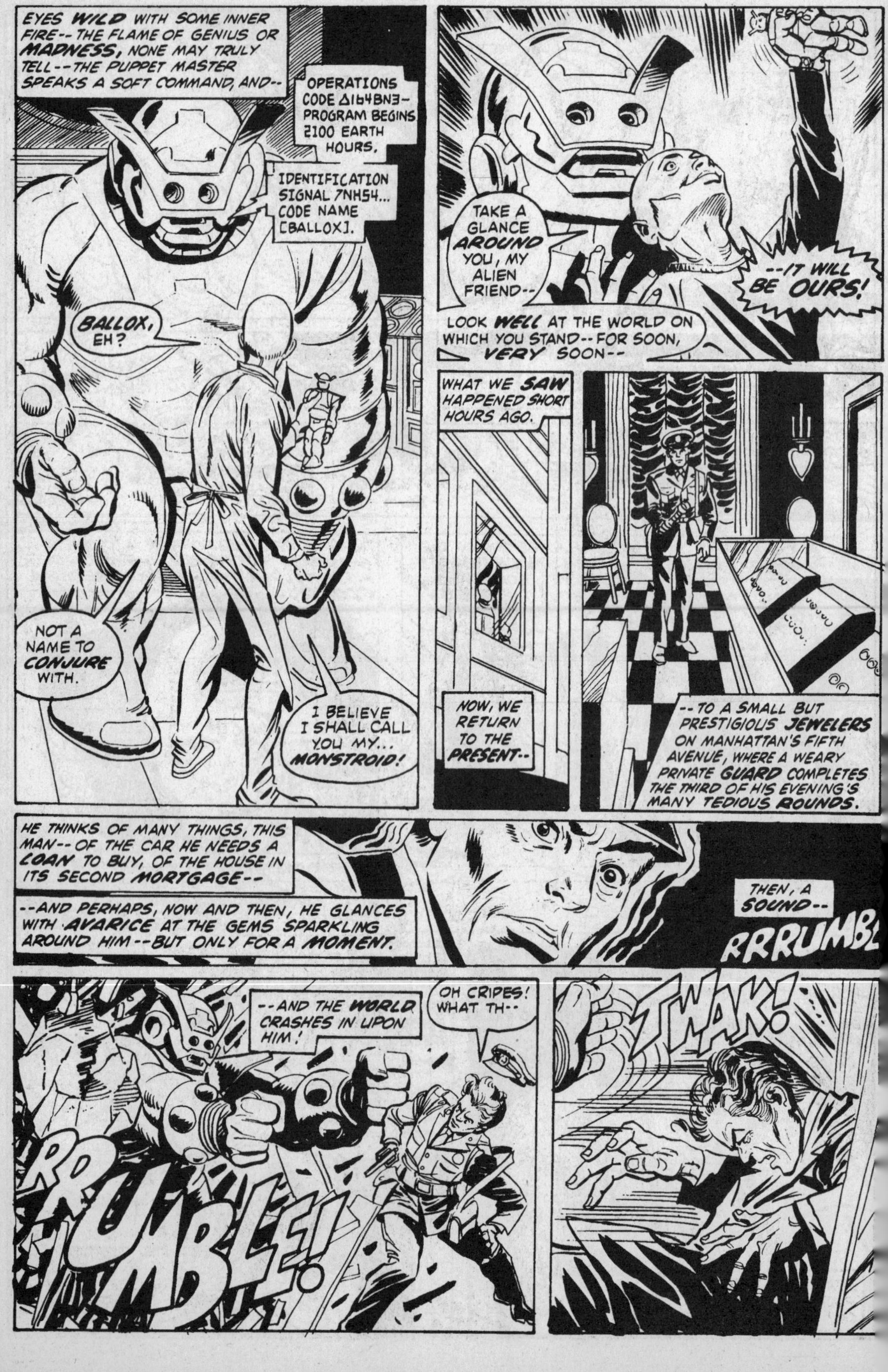
EYES WILD WITH SOME INNER FIRE--THE FLAME OF GENIUS OR MADNESS, NONE MAY TRULY TELL--THE PUPPET MASTER SPEAKS A SOFT COMMAND, AND--
OPERATIONS CODE Δ164BN3-- PROGRAM BEGINS 2100 EARTH HOURS.
IDENTIFICATION SIGNAL 7NH54... CODE NAME [BALLOX].
BALLOX, EH?
NOT A NAME TO CONJURE WITH.
I BELIEVE I SHALL CALL YOU MY... MONSTROID!
TAKE A GLANCE AROUND YOU, MY ALIEN FRIEND--
LOOK WELL AT THE WORLD ON WHICH YOU STAND--FOR SOON, VERY SOON--
--IT WILL BE OURS!
WHAT WE SAW HAPPENED SHORT HOURS AGO.
NOW, WE RETURN TO THE PRESENT--
--TO A SMALL BUT PRESTIGIOUS JEWELERS ON MANHATTAN'S FIFTH AVENUE, WHERE A WEARY PRIVATE GUARD COMPLETES THE THIRD OF HIS EVENING'S MANY TEDIOUS ROUNDS.
HE THINKS OF MANY THINGS, THIS MAN--OF THE CAR HE NEEDS A LOAN TO BUY, OF THE HOUSE IN ITS SECOND MORTGAGE--
--AND PERHAPS, NOW AND THEN, HE GLANCES WITH AVARICE AT THE GEMS SPARKLING AROUND HIM--BUT ONLY FOR A MOMENT.
THEN, A SOUND--
RRRUMBL
--AND THE WORLD CRASHES IN UPON HIM!
OH CRIPES! WHAT TH--
RRUMBLE!
THAK!

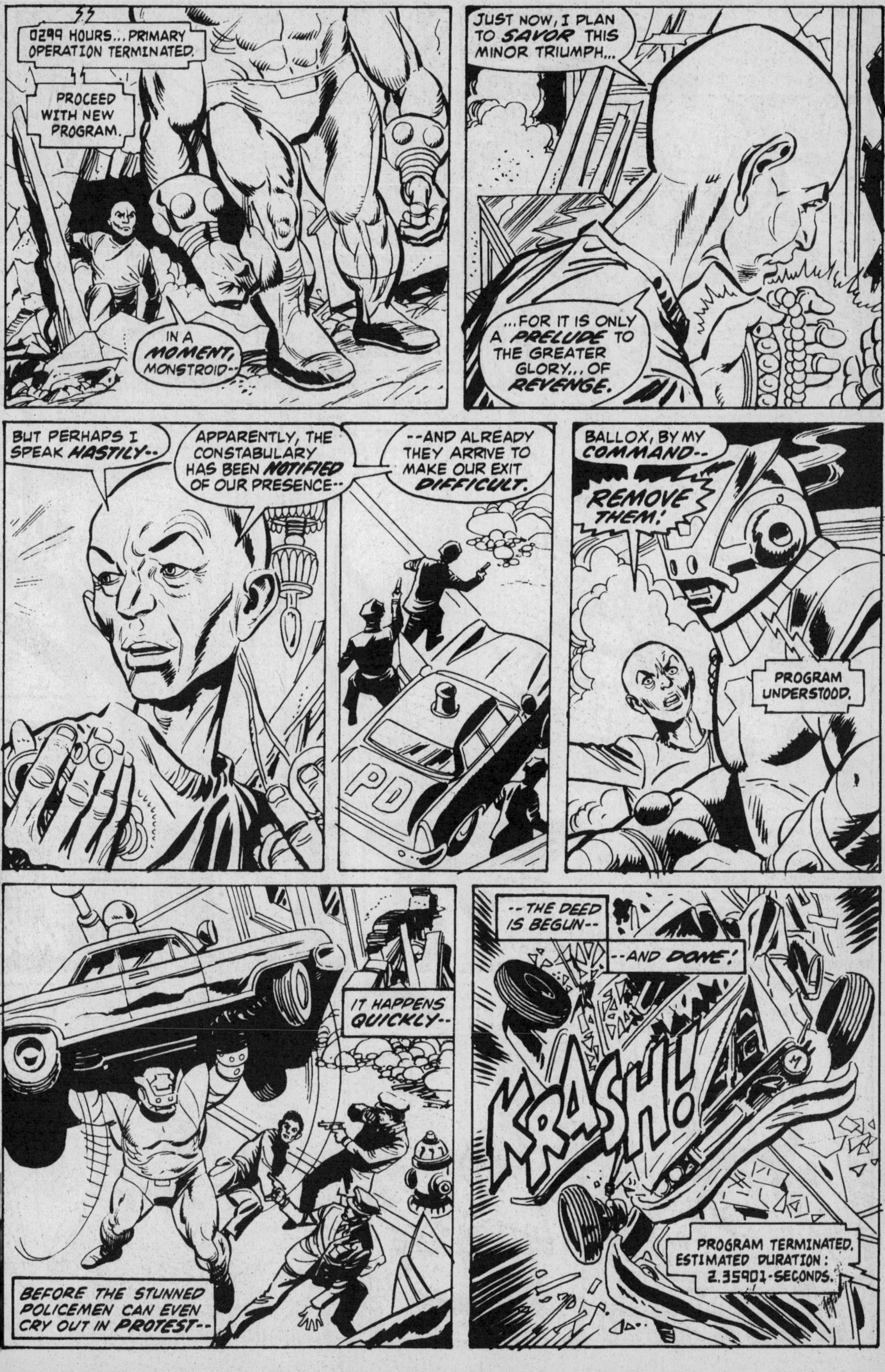
0299 HOURS... PRIMARY OPERATION TERMINATED.
PROCEED WITH NEW PROGRAM.
IN A MOMENT, MONSTROID--
JUST NOW, I PLAN TO SAVOR THIS MINOR TRIUMPH...
...FOR IT IS ONLY A PRELUDE TO THE GREATER GLORY... OF REVENGE.
BUT PERHAPS I SPEAK HASTILY--
APPARENTLY, THE CONSTABULARY HAS BEEN NOTIFIED OF OUR PRESENCE--
--AND ALREADY THEY ARRIVE TO MAKE OUR EXIT DIFFICULT.
PD
BALLOX, BY MY COMMAND--
REMOVE THEM!
PROGRAM UNDERSTOOD.
IT HAPPENS QUICKLY--
BEFORE THE STUNNED POLICEMEN CAN EVEN CRY OUT IN PROTEST--
--THE DEED IS BEGUN--
--AND DONE!
KRASH!
PROGRAM TERMINATED. ESTIMATED DURATION: 2.35901-SECONDS.

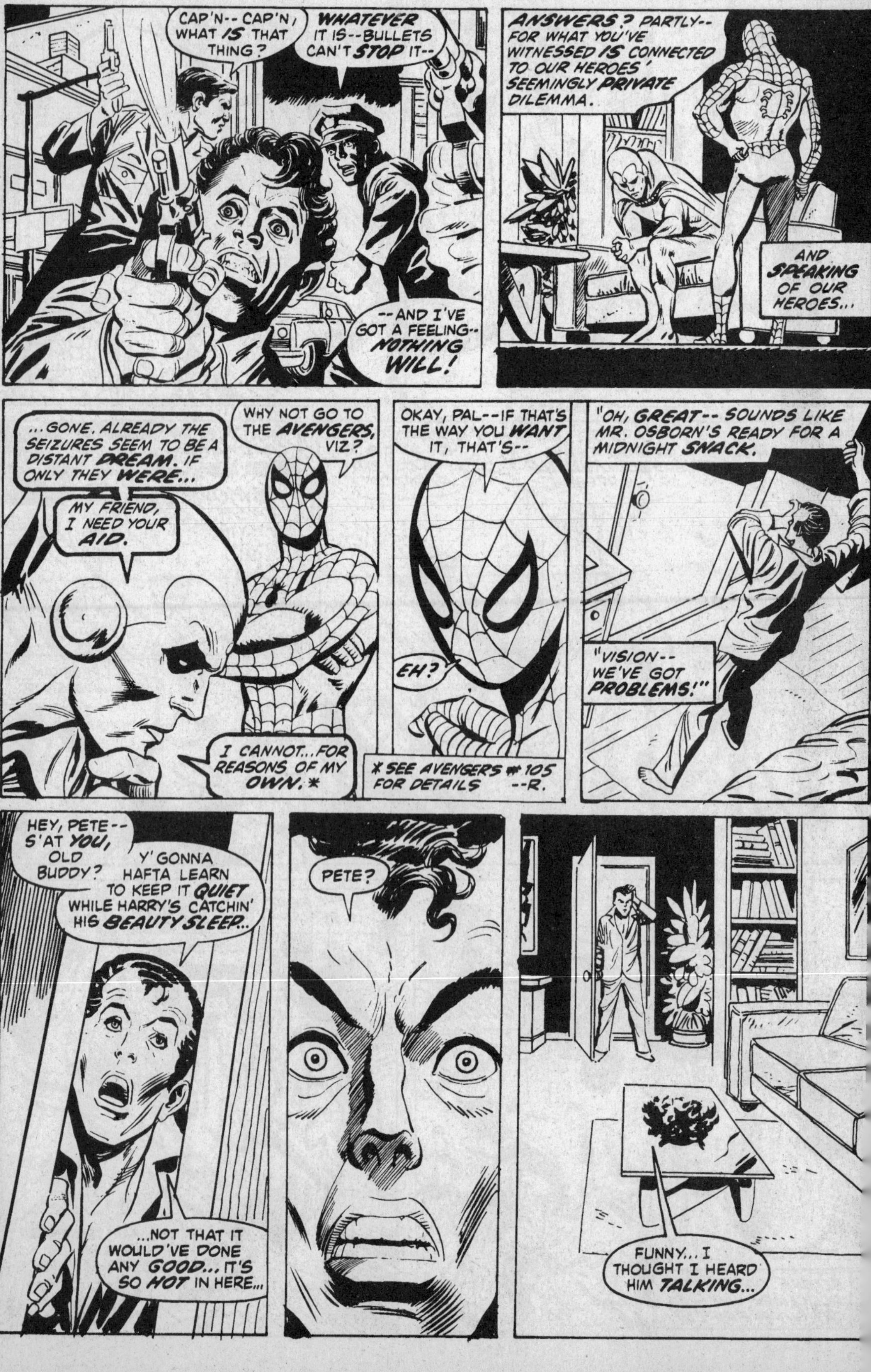

CAP'N-- CAP'N, WHAT IS THAT THING?
WHATEVER IT IS--BULLETS CAN'T STOP IT--
--AND I'VE GOT A FEELING-- NOTHING WILL!
ANSWERS? PARTLY-- FOR WHAT YOU'VE WITNESSED IS CONNECTED TO OUR HEROES' SEEMINGLY PRIVATE DILEMMA.
AND SPEAKING OF OUR HEROES...
...GONE. ALREADY THE SEIZURES SEEM TO BE A DISTANT DREAM. IF ONLY THEY WERE...
MY FRIEND, I NEED YOUR AID.
WHY NOT GO TO THE AVENGERS, VIZ?
I CANNOT...FOR REASONS OF MY OWN.*
OKAY, PAL--IF THAT'S THE WAY YOU WANT IT, THAT'S--
EH?
*SEE AVENGERS #105 FOR DETAILS --R.
"OH, GREAT-- SOUNDS LIKE MR. OSBORN'S READY FOR A MIDNIGHT SNACK.
"VISION-- WE'VE GOT PROBLEMS!"
HEY, PETE-- S'AT YOU, OLD BUDDY?
Y'GONNA HAFTA LEARN TO KEEP IT QUIET WHILE HARRY'S CATCHIN' HIS BEAUTY SLEEP...
...NOT THAT IT WOULD'VE DONE ANY GOOD... IT'S SO HOT IN HERE...
PETE?
FUNNY... I THOUGHT I HEARD HIM TALKING...

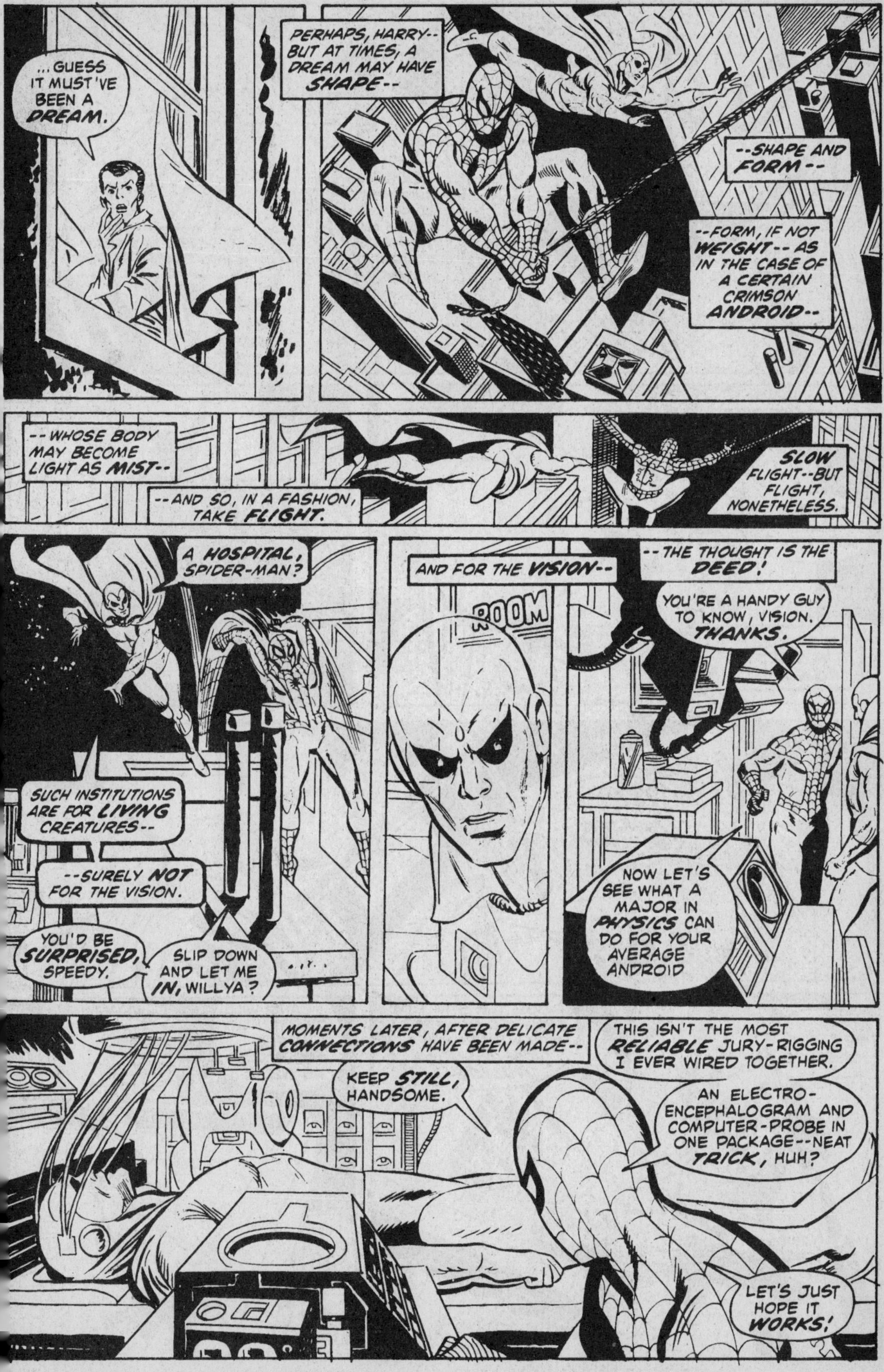
...GUESS IT MUST'VE BEEN A DREAM.
PERHAPS, HARRY-- BUT AT TIMES, A DREAM MAY HAVE SHAPE--
--SHAPE AND FORM--
--FORM, IF NOT WEIGHT-- AS IN THE CASE OF A CERTAIN CRIMSON ANDROID--
--WHOSE BODY MAY BECOME LIGHT AS MIST--
--AND SO, IN A FASHION, TAKE FLIGHT.
SLOW FLIGHT--BUT FLIGHT, NONETHELESS.
A HOSPITAL, SPIDER-MAN?
SUCH INSTITUTIONS ARE FOR LIVING CREATURES--
--SURELY NOT FOR THE VISION.
YOU'D BE SURPRISED, SPEEDY.
SLIP DOWN AND LET ME IN, WILLYA?
AND FOR THE VISION--
--THE THOUGHT IS THE DEED!
BOOM
YOU'RE A HANDY GUY TO KNOW, VISION. THANKS.
NOW LET'S SEE WHAT A MAJOR IN PHYSICS CAN DO FOR YOUR AVERAGE ANDROID
MOMENTS LATER, AFTER DELICATE CONNECTIONS HAVE BEEN MADE--
KEEP STILL, HANDSOME.
THIS ISN'T THE MOST RELIABLE JURY-RIGGING I EVER WIRED TOGETHER.
AN ELECTRO-ENCEPHALOGRAM AND COMPUTER-PROBE IN ONE PACKAGE--NEAT TRICK, HUH?
LET'S JUST HOPE IT WORKS!

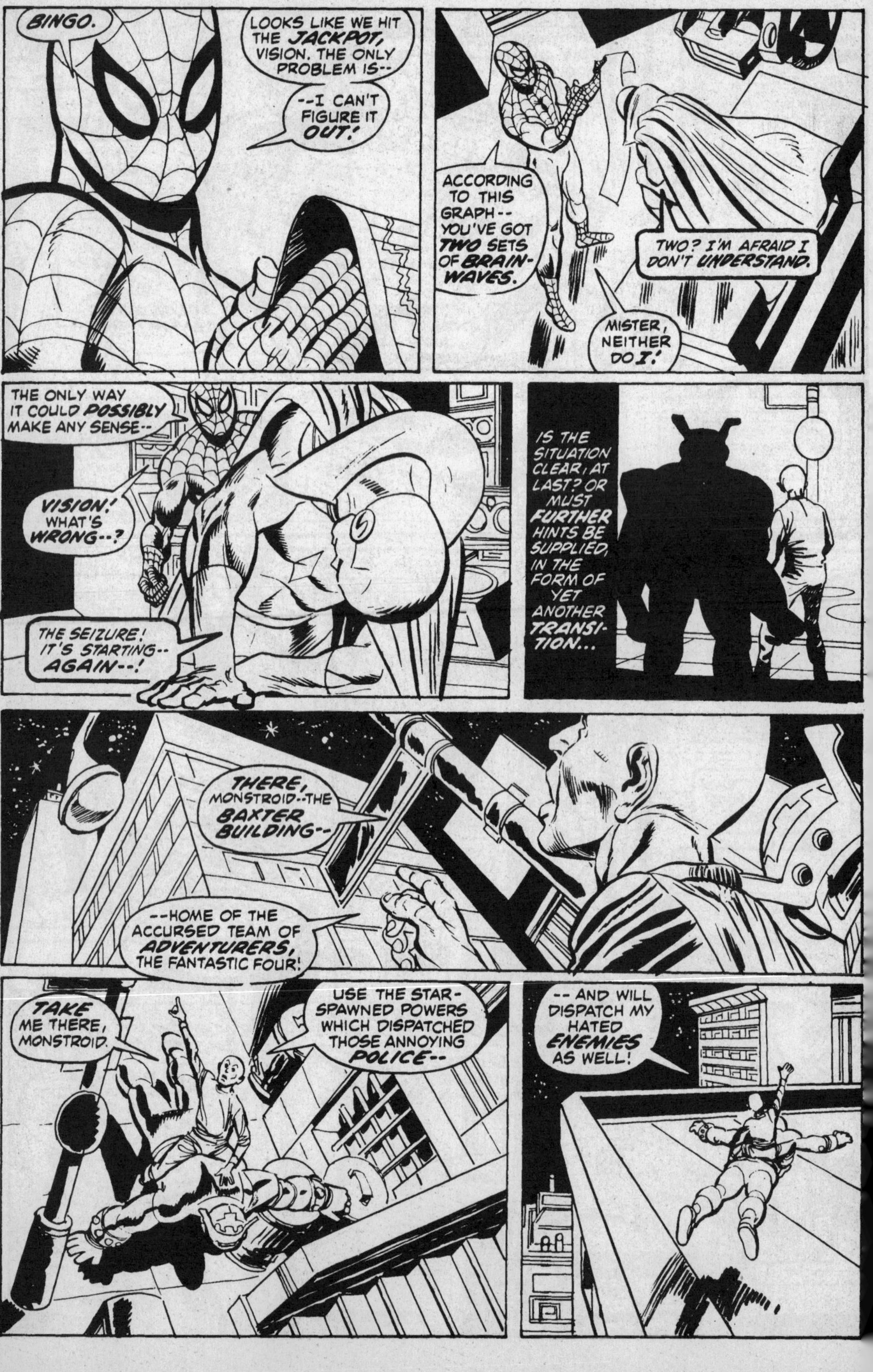
BINGO.
LOOKS LIKE WE HIT THE JACKPOT, VISION. THE ONLY PROBLEM IS--
--I CAN'T FIGURE IT OUT!
ACCORDING TO THIS GRAPH-- YOU'VE GOT TWO SETS OF BRAIN-WAVES.
TWO? I'M AFRAID I DON'T UNDERSTAND.
MISTER, NEITHER DO I!
THE ONLY WAY IT COULD POSSIBLY MAKE ANY SENSE--
VISION! WHAT'S WRONG--?
THE SEIZURE! IT'S STARTING-- AGAIN--!
IS THE SITUATION CLEAR, AT LAST? OR MUST FURTHER HINTS BE SUPPLIED, IN THE FORM OF YET ANOTHER TRANSI-TION...
THERE, MONSTROID--THE BAXTER BUILDING--
--HOME OF THE ACCURSED TEAM OF ADVENTURERS, THE FANTASTIC FOUR!
TAKE ME THERE, MONSTROID.
USE THE STAR-SPAWNED POWERS WHICH DISPATCHED THOSE ANNOYING POLICE--
-- AND WILL DISPATCH MY HATED ENEMIES AS WELL!

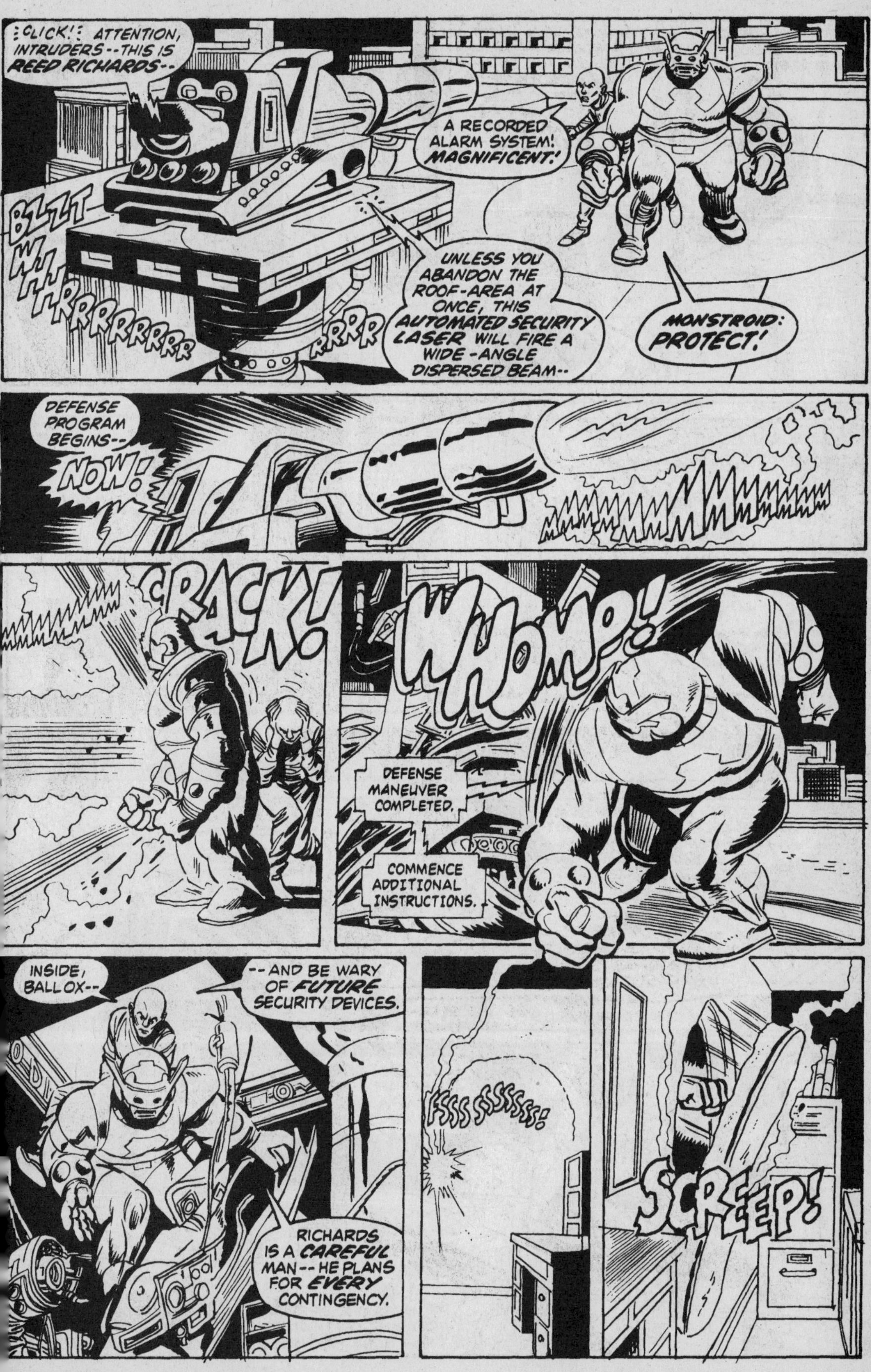
:CLICK!: ATTENTION, INTRUDERS--THIS IS REED RICHARDS--
A RECORDED ALARM SYSTEM! MAGNIFICENT!
BZZT
WHHRRRRRRRRR
UNLESS YOU ABANDON THE ROOF-AREA AT ONCE, THIS AUTOMATED SECURITY LASER WILL FIRE A WIDE-ANGLE DISPERSED BEAM--
RRRR
MONSTROID: PROTECT!
DEFENSE PROGRAM BEGINS--
NOW!
CRACK!
WHOMP!
DEFENSE MANEUVER COMPLETED.
COMMENCE ADDITIONAL INSTRUCTIONS.
INSIDE, BALLOX--
--AND BE WARY OF FUTURE SECURITY DEVICES.
RICHARDS IS A CAREFUL MAN--HE PLANS FOR EVERY CONTINGENCY.
FSSS SSSSSSS!
SCREEP!

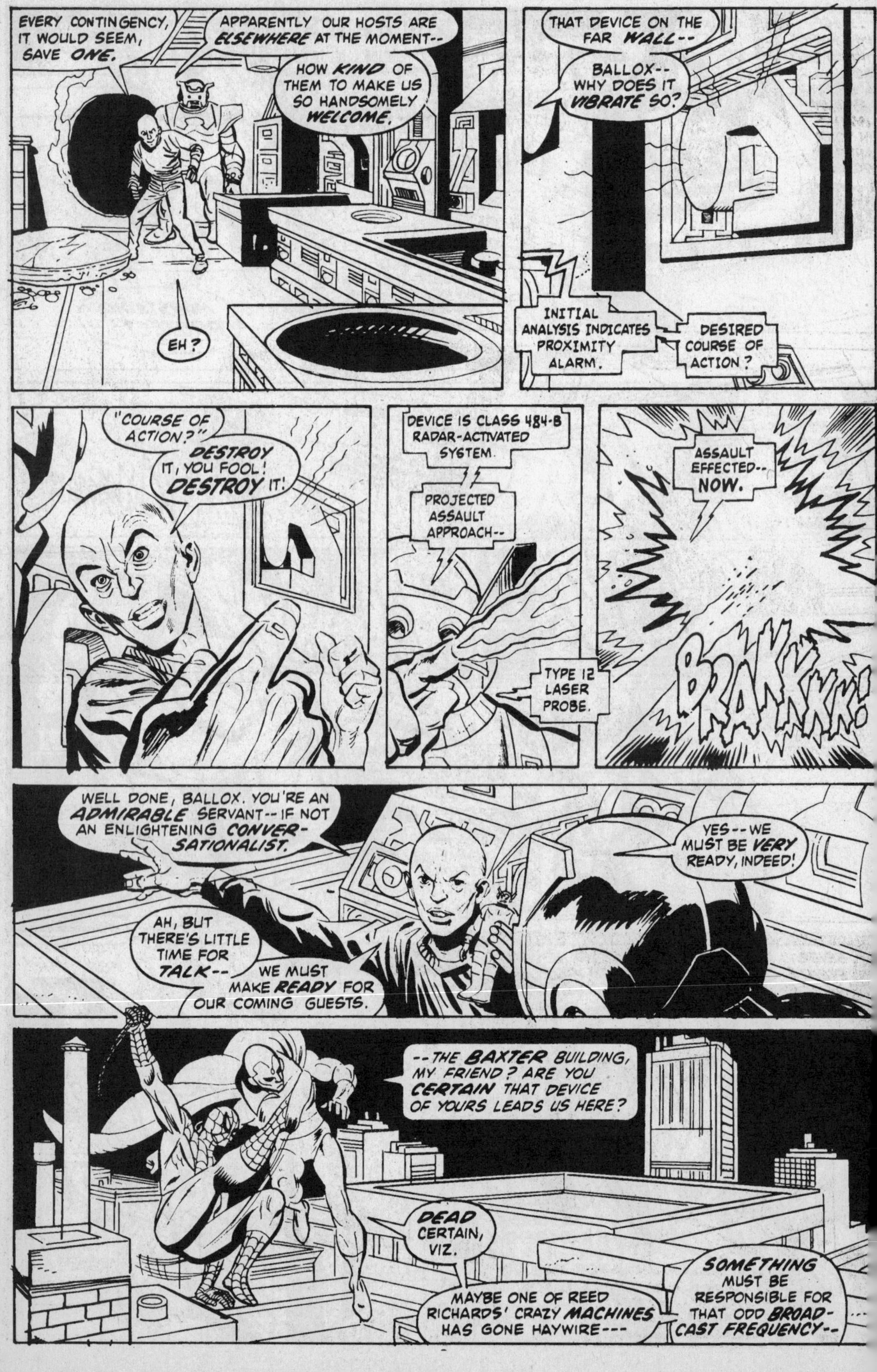
EVERY CONTINGENCY, IT WOULD SEEM, SAVE ONE.
APPARENTLY OUR HOSTS ARE ELSEWHERE AT THE MOMENT--
HOW KIND OF THEM TO MAKE US SO HANDSOMELY WELCOME.
EH?
THAT DEVICE ON THE FAR WALL--
BALLOX-- WHY DOES IT VIBRATE SO?
INITIAL ANALYSIS INDICATES PROXIMITY ALARM.
DESIRED COURSE OF ACTION?
"COURSE OF ACTION?"
DESTROY IT, YOU FOOL! DESTROY IT!
DEVICE IS CLASS 484-B RADAR-ACTIVATED SYSTEM.
PROJECTED ASSAULT APPROACH--
TYPE 12 LASER PROBE.
ASSAULT EFFECTED-- NOW.
BRAKKKK!
WELL DONE, BALLOX. YOU'RE AN ADMIRABLE SERVANT-- IF NOT AN ENLIGHTENING CONVER-SATIONALIST.
AH, BUT THERE'S LITTLE TIME FOR TALK--
WE MUST MAKE READY FOR OUR COMING GUESTS.
YES-- WE MUST BE VERY READY, INDEED!
--THE BAXTER BUILDING, MY FRIEND? ARE YOU CERTAIN THAT DEVICE OF YOURS LEADS US HERE?
DEAD CERTAIN, VIZ.
MAYBE ONE OF REED RICHARDS' CRAZY MACHINES HAS GONE HAYWIRE---
SOMETHING MUST BE RESPONSIBLE FOR THAT ODD BROAD-CAST FREQUENCY--

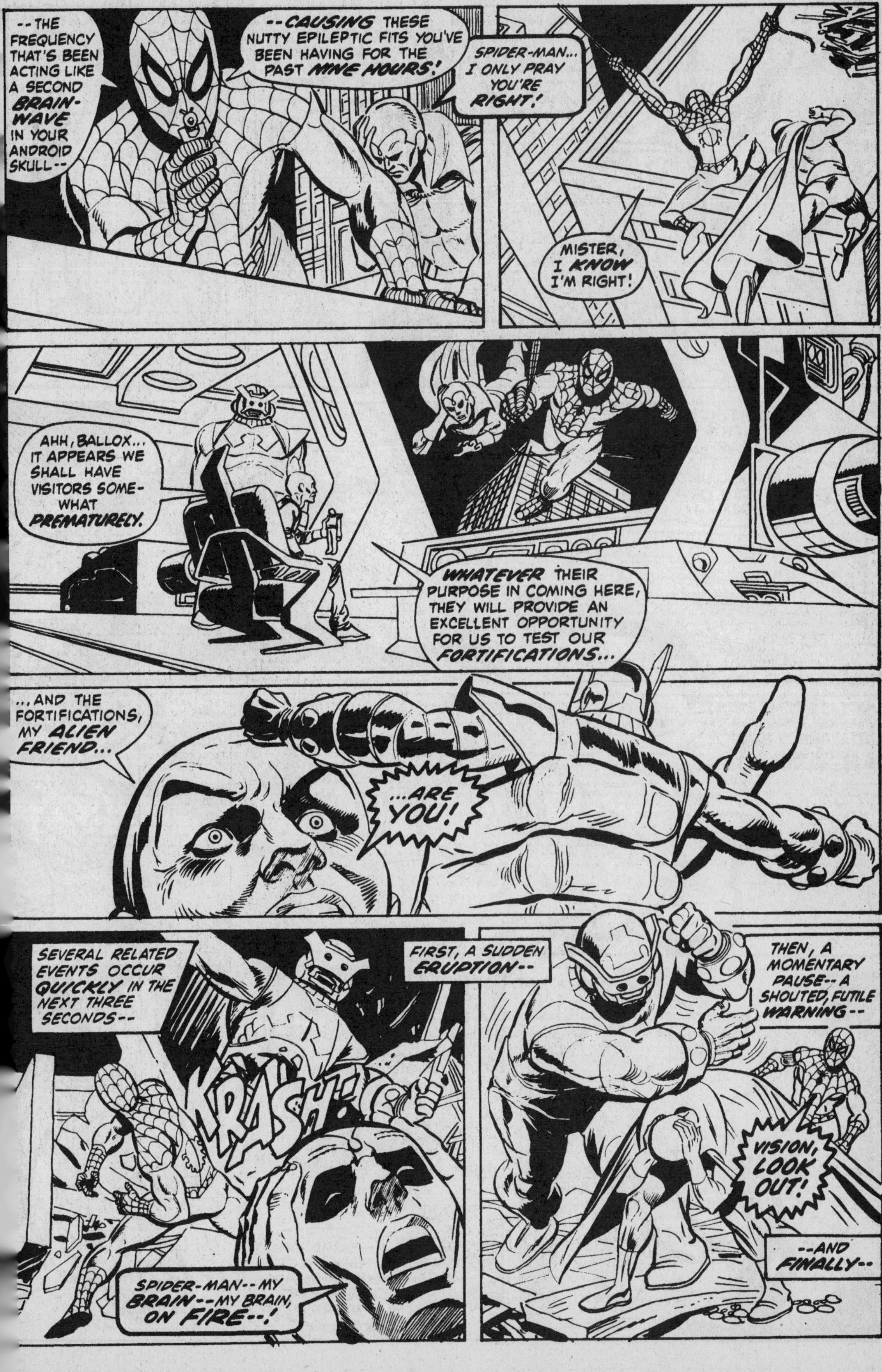
--THE FREQUENCY THAT'S BEEN ACTING LIKE A SECOND BRAIN-WAVE IN YOUR ANDROID SKULL--
--CAUSING THESE NUTTY EPILEPTIC FITS YOU'VE BEEN HAVING FOR THE PAST NINE HOURS!
SPIDER-MAN... I ONLY PRAY YOU'RE RIGHT!
MISTER, I KNOW I'M RIGHT!
AHH, BALLOX... IT APPEARS WE SHALL HAVE VISITORS SOME-WHAT PREMATURELY.
WHATEVER THEIR PURPOSE IN COMING HERE, THEY WILL PROVIDE AN EXCELLENT OPPORTUNITY FOR US TO TEST OUR FORTIFICATIONS...
..., AND THE FORTIFICATIONS, MY ALIEN FRIEND...
...ARE YOU!
SEVERAL RELATED EVENTS OCCUR QUICKLY IN THE NEXT THREE SECONDS--
FIRST, A SUDDEN ERUPTION--
KRASH!
SPIDER-MAN--MY BRAIN--MY BRAIN, ON FIRE--!
THEN, A MOMENTARY PAUSE--A SHOUTED, FUTILE WARNING--
VISION, LOOK OUT!
--AND FINALLY--

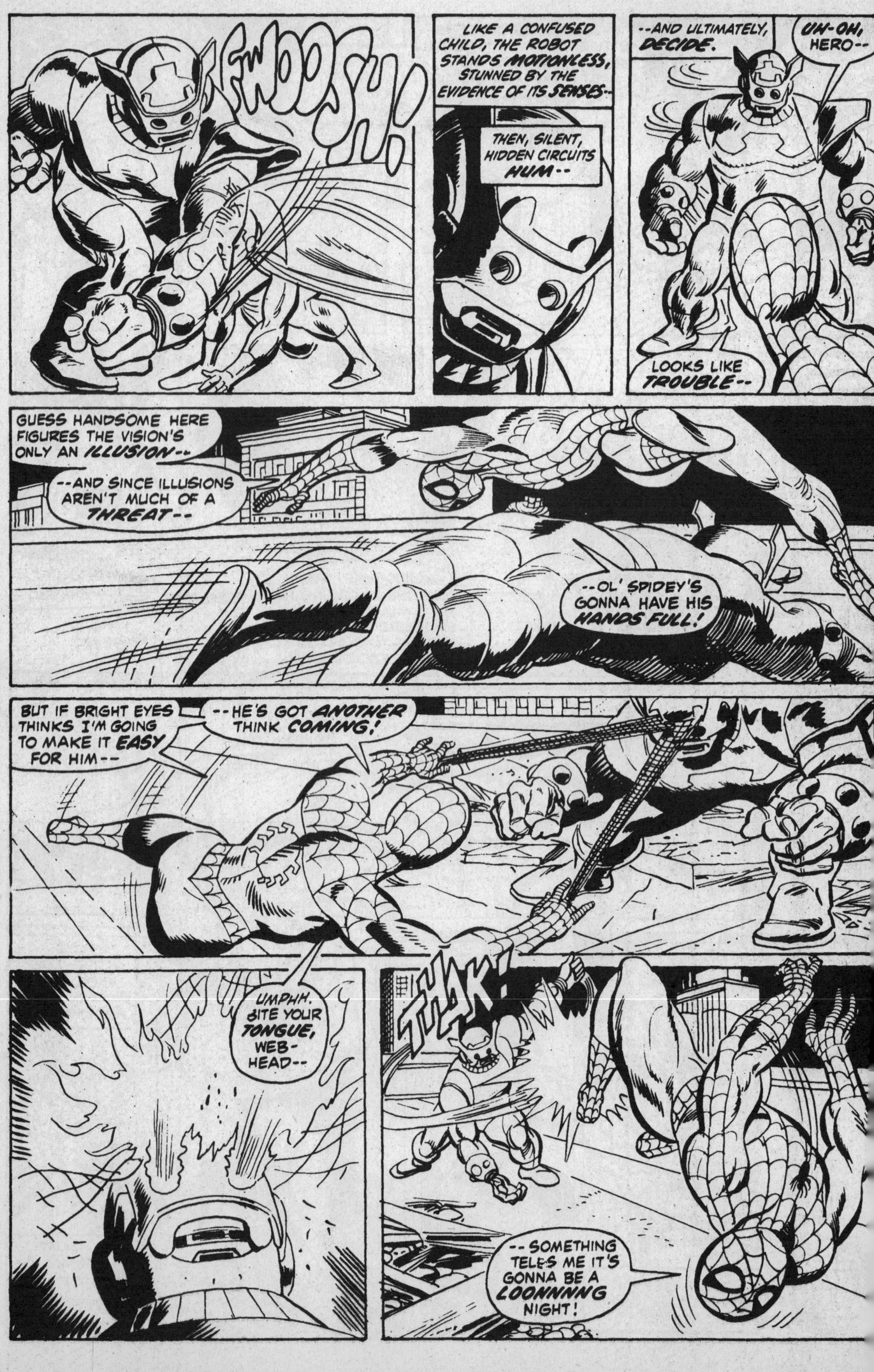
FWOOSH!
LIKE A CONFUSED CHILD, THE ROBOT STANDS MOTIONLESS, STUNNED BY THE EVIDENCE OF ITS SENSES--
THEN, SILENT, HIDDEN CIRCUITS HUM--
--AND ULTIMATELY, DECIDE.
UH-OH, HERO--
LOOKS LIKE TROUBLE--
GUESS HANDSOME HERE FIGURES THE VISION'S ONLY AN ILLUSION--
--AND SINCE ILLUSIONS AREN'T MUCH OF A THREAT--
--OL' SPIDEY'S GONNA HAVE HIS HANDS FULL!
BUT IF BRIGHT EYES THINKS I'M GOING TO MAKE IT EASY FOR HIM--
--HE'S GOT ANOTHER THINK COMING!
UMPHH. BITE YOUR TONGUE, WEB-HEAD--
THAK!
--SOMETHING TELLS ME IT'S GONNA BE A LOONNNNG NIGHT!

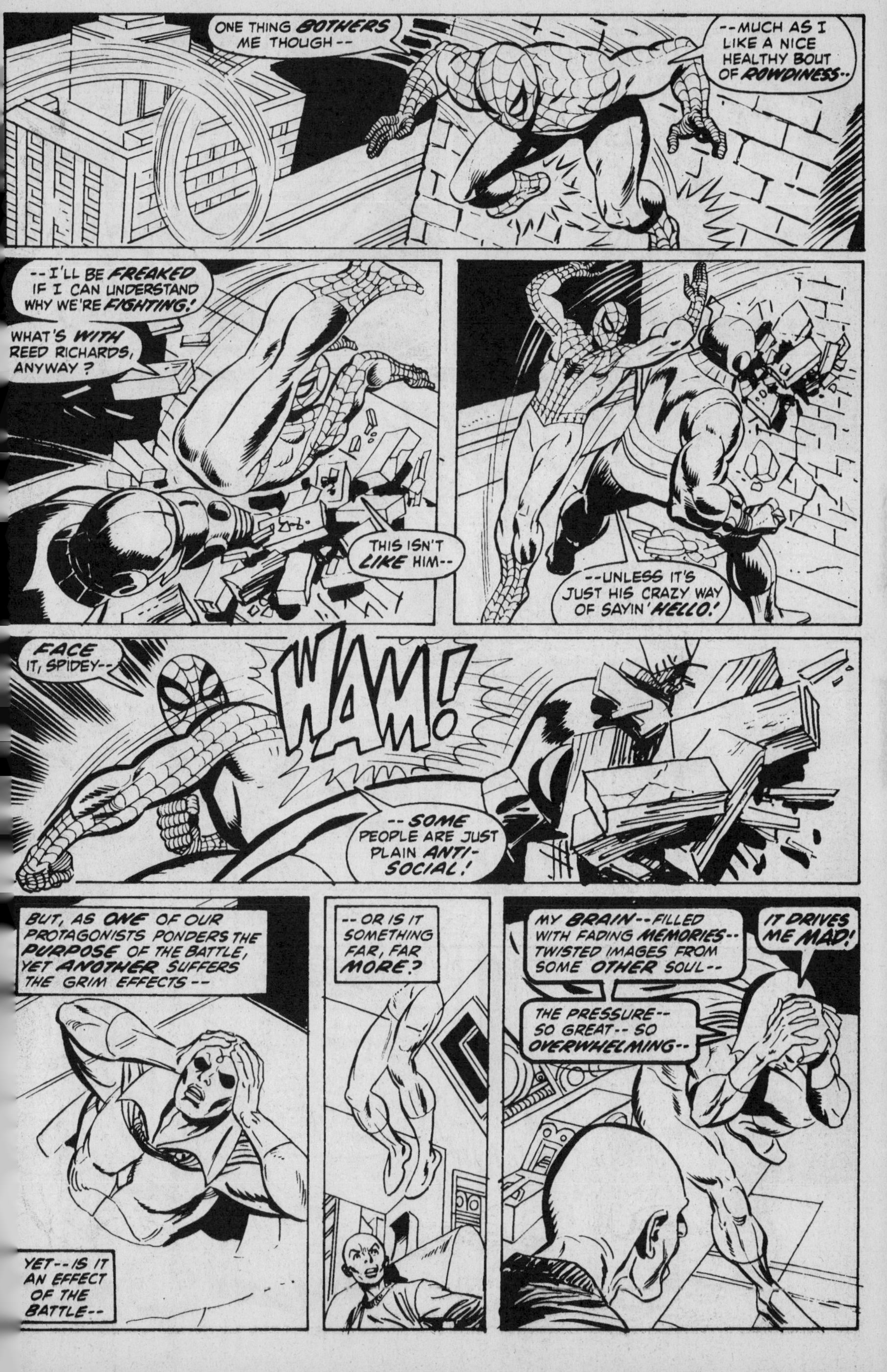
ONE THING BOTHERS ME THOUGH--
--MUCH AS I LIKE A NICE HEALTHY BOUT OF ROWDINESS--
--I'LL BE FREAKED IF I CAN UNDERSTAND WHY WE'RE FIGHTING!
WHAT'S WITH REED RICHARDS, ANYWAY?
THIS ISN'T LIKE HIM--
--UNLESS IT'S JUST HIS CRAZY WAY OF SAYIN' HELLO!
FACE IT, SPIDEY--
WAM!
--SOME PEOPLE ARE JUST PLAIN ANTI-SOCIAL!
BUT, AS ONE OF OUR PROTAGONISTS PONDERS THE PURPOSE OF THE BATTLE, YET ANOTHER SUFFERS THE GRIM EFFECTS--
YET--IS IT AN EFFECT OF THE BATTLE--
--OR IS IT SOMETHING FAR, FAR MORE?
MY BRAIN--FILLED WITH FADING MEMORIES--TWISTED IMAGES FROM SOME OTHER SOUL--
THE PRESSURE--SO GREAT--SO OVERWHELMING--
IT DRIVES ME MAD!

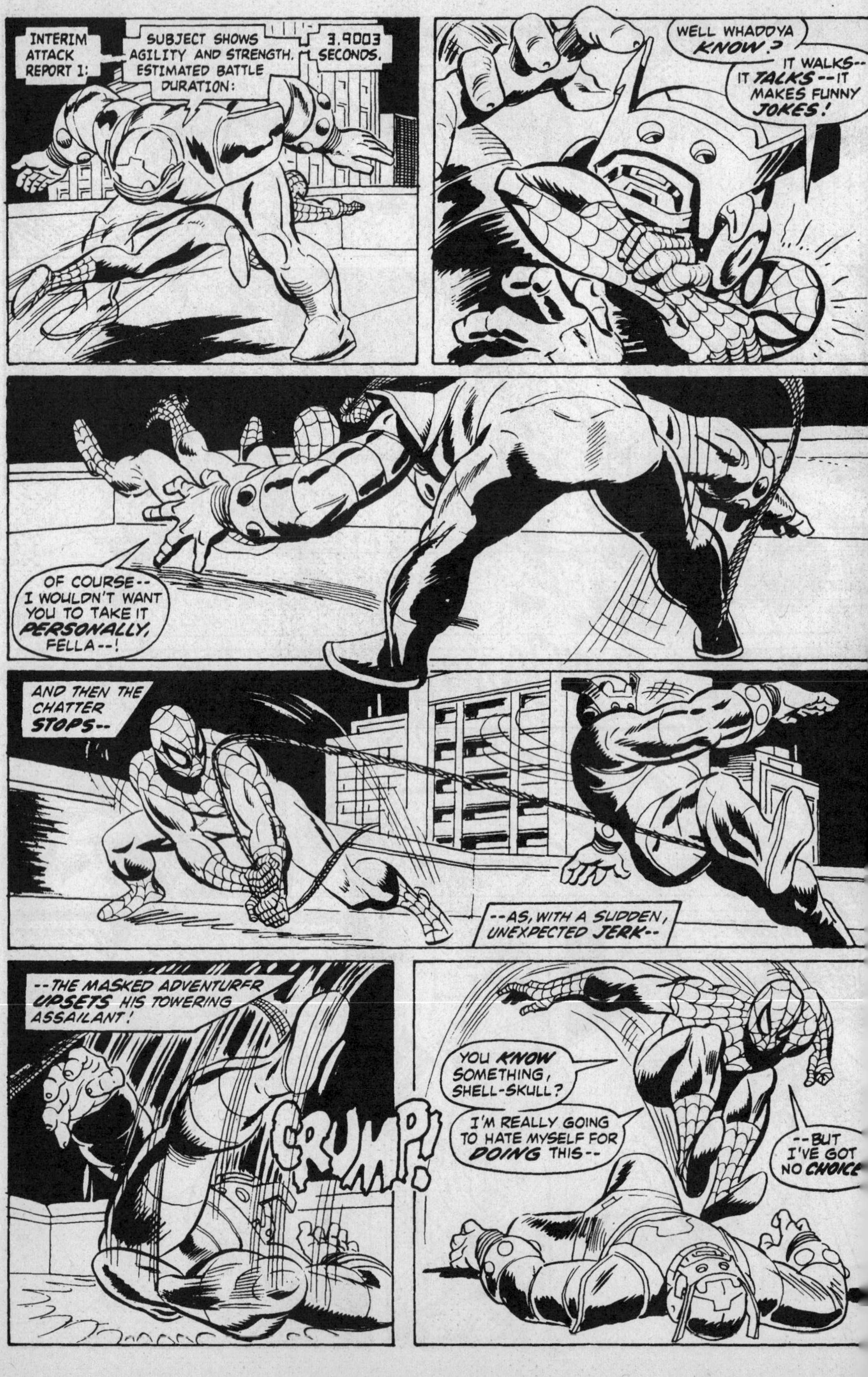
INTERIM ATTACK REPORT 1:
SUBJECT SHOWS AGILITY AND STRENGTH. ESTIMATED BATTLE DURATION:
3.9003 SECONDS.
WELL WHADDYA KNOW?
IT WALKS-- IT TALKS--IT MAKES FUNNY JOKES!
OF COURSE-- I WOULDN'T WANT YOU TO TAKE IT PERSONALLY, FELLA--!
AND THEN THE CHATTER STOPS--
--AS, WITH A SUDDEN, UNEXPECTED JERK--
--THE MASKED ADVENTURER UPSETS HIS TOWERING ASSAILANT!
CRUMP!
YOU KNOW SOMETHING, SHELL-SKULL?
I'M REALLY GOING TO HATE MYSELF FOR DOING THIS--
--BUT I'VE GOT NO CHOICE

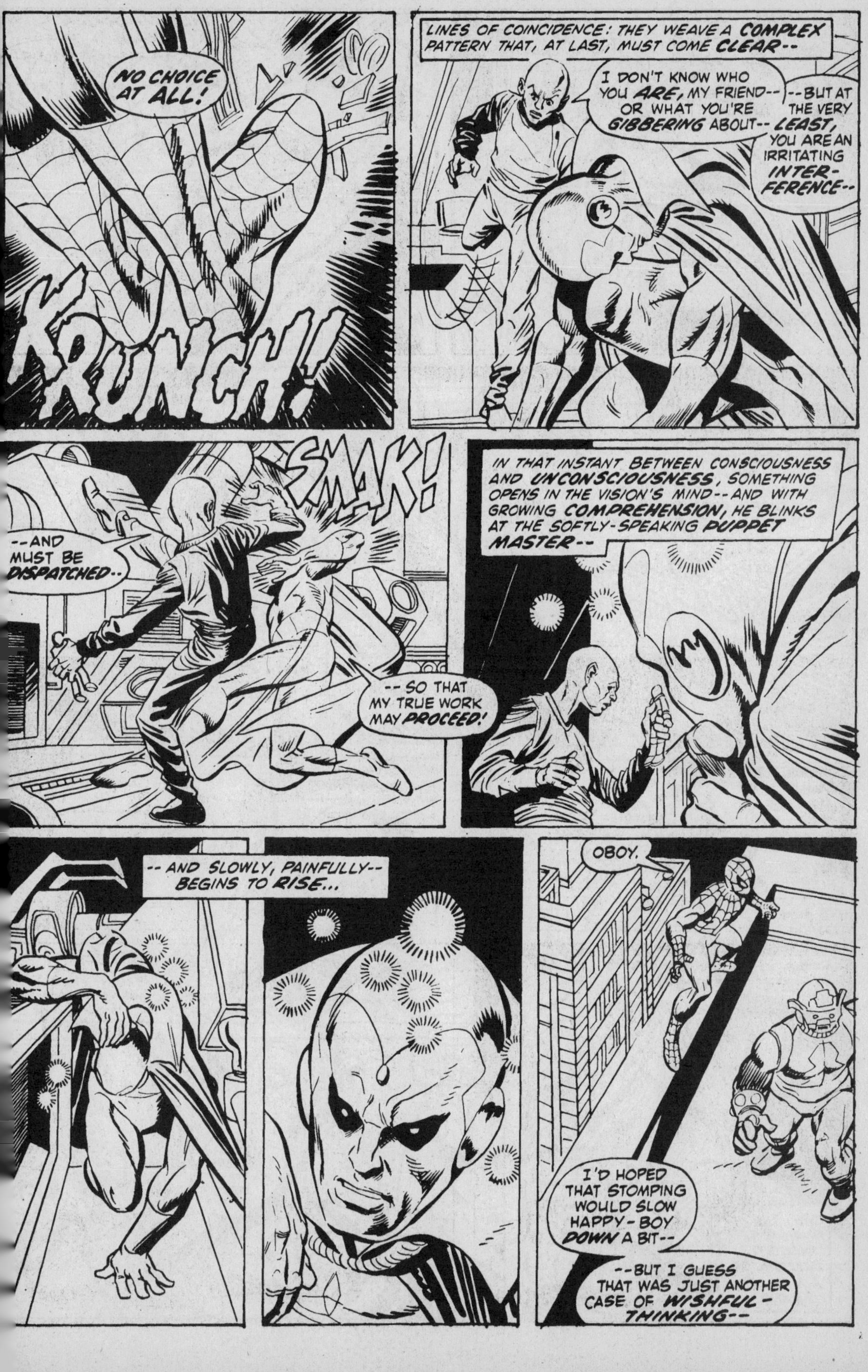
NO CHOICE AT ALL!
KRUNCH!
LINES OF COINCIDENCE: THEY WEAVE A COMPLEX PATTERN THAT, AT LAST, MUST COME CLEAR--
I DON'T KNOW WHO YOU ARE, MY FRIEND-- OR WHAT YOU'RE GIBBERING ABOUT--
--BUT AT THE VERY LEAST, YOU ARE AN IRRITATING INTER-FERENCE--
SMAK!
--AND MUST BE DISPATCHED--
--SO THAT MY TRUE WORK MAY PROCEED!
IN THAT INSTANT BETWEEN CONSCIOUSNESS AND UNCONSCIOUSNESS, SOMETHING OPENS IN THE VISION'S MIND--AND WITH GROWING COMPREHENSION, HE BLINKS AT THE SOFTLY-SPEAKING PUPPET MASTER--
-- AND SLOWLY, PAINFULLY-- BEGINS TO RISE...
OBOY.
I'D HOPED THAT STOMPING WOULD SLOW HAPPY-BOY DOWN A BIT--
--BUT I GUESS THAT WAS JUST ANOTHER CASE OF WISHFUL-THINKING--

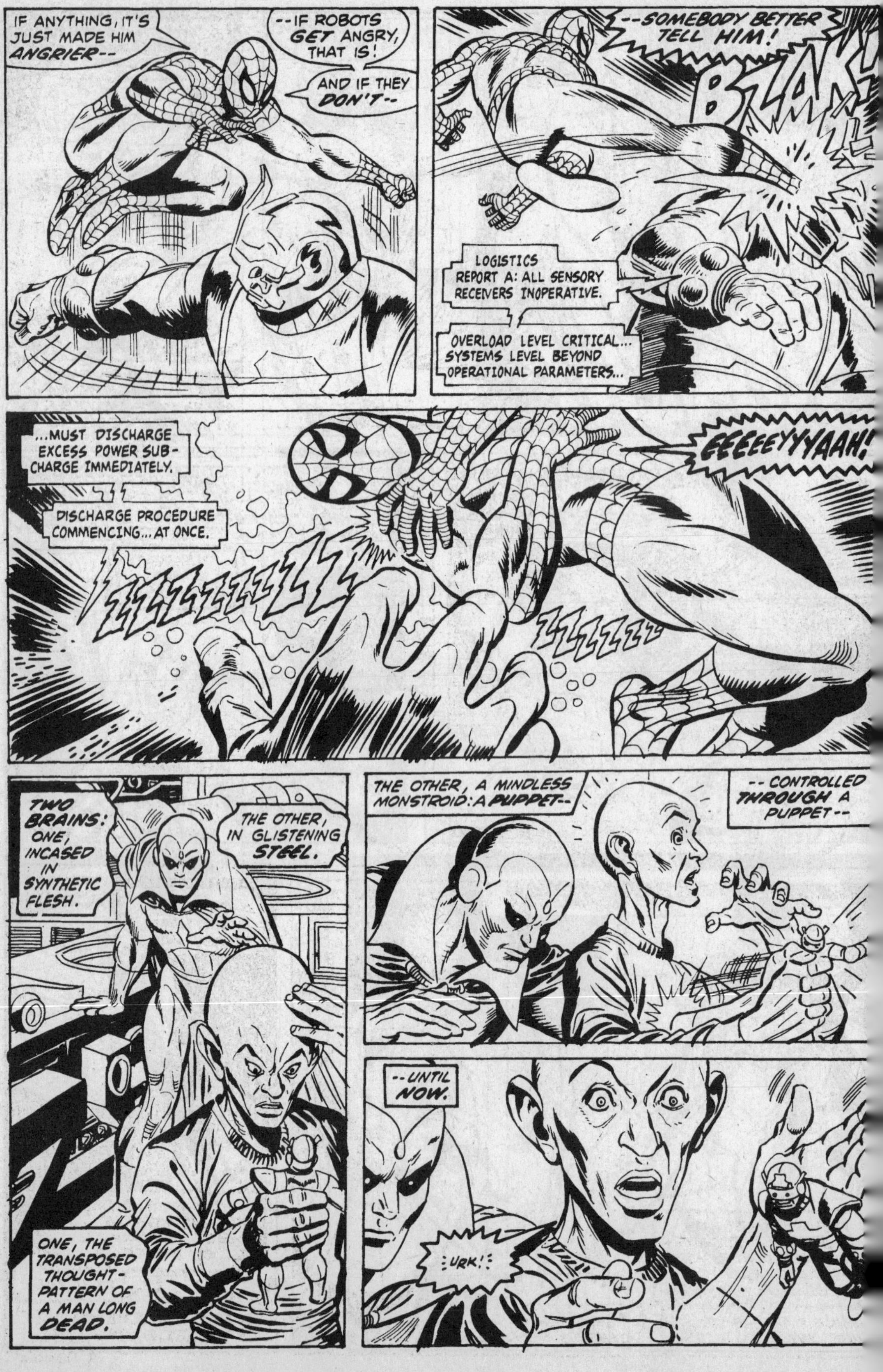
IF ANYTHING, IT'S JUST MADE HIM ANGRIER--
--IF ROBOTS GET ANGRY, THAT IS!
AND IF THEY DON'T--
--SOMEBODY BETTER TELL HIM!
BLAM!
LOGISTICS REPORT A: ALL SENSORY RECEIVERS INOPERATIVE.
OVERLOAD LEVEL CRITICAL... SYSTEMS LEVEL BEYOND OPERATIONAL PARAMETERS...
...MUST DISCHARGE EXCESS POWER SUB-CHARGE IMMEDIATELY.
DISCHARGE PROCEDURE COMMENCING... AT ONCE.
EEEEEYYYAAH!
ZZZZZZZZZ
ZZZZZZZ
TWO BRAINS: ONE, INCASED IN SYNTHETIC FLESH.
THE OTHER, IN GLISTENING STEEL.
ONE, THE TRANSPOSED THOUGHT-PATTERN OF A MAN LONG DEAD.
THE OTHER, A MINDLESS MONSTROID: A PUPPET--
--CONTROLLED THROUGH A PUPPET--
--UNTIL NOW.
URK!

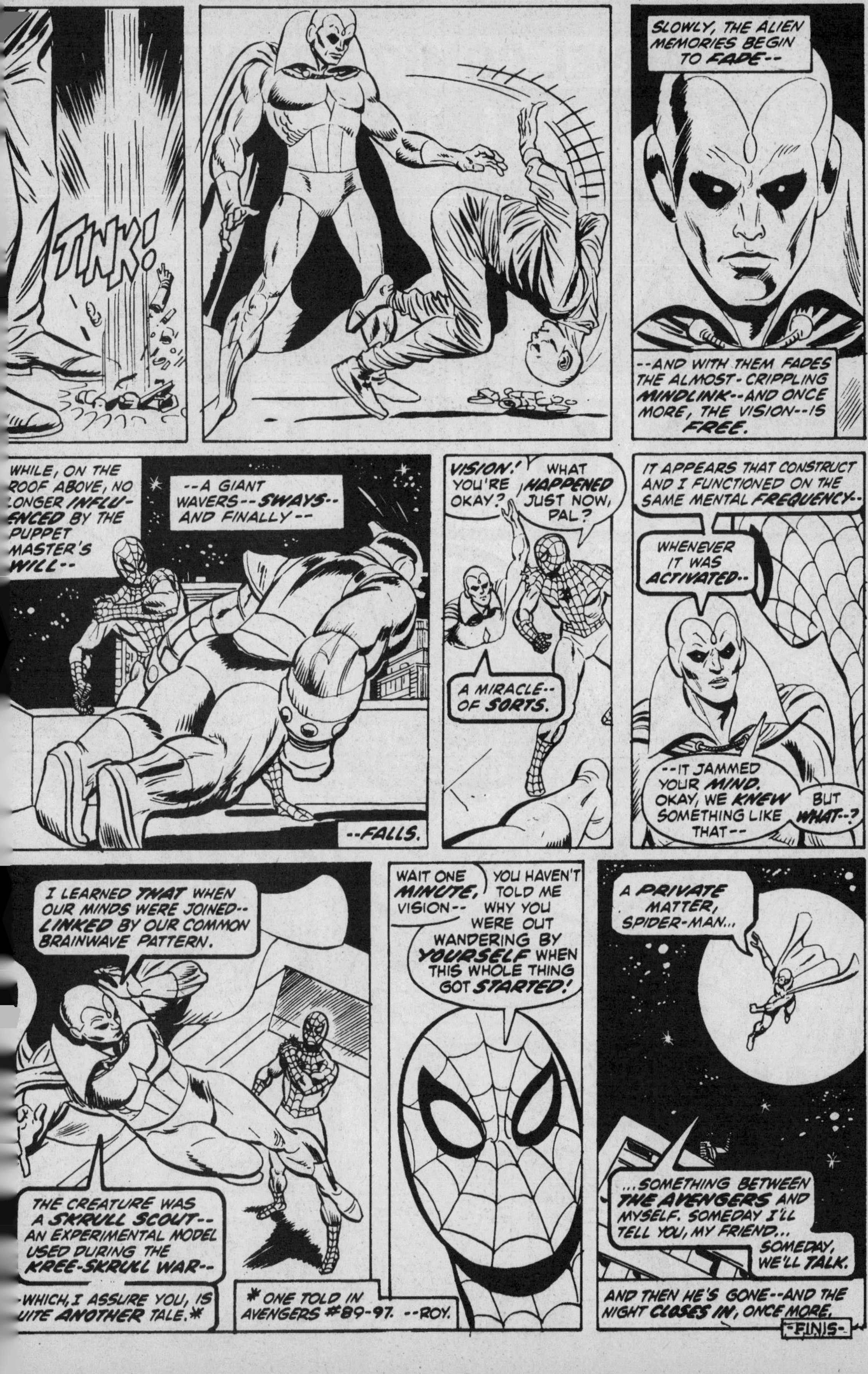
TINK!
SLOWLY, THE ALIEN MEMORIES BEGIN TO FADE--
--AND WITH THEM FADES THE ALMOST-CRIPPLING MINDLINK--AND ONCE MORE, THE VISION--IS FREE.
WHILE, ON THE ROOF ABOVE, NO LONGER INFLU-ENCED BY THE PUPPET MASTER'S WILL--
--A GIANT WAVERS--SWAYS--AND FINALLY--
--FALLS.
VISION! YOU'RE OKAY?
WHAT HAPPENED JUST NOW, PAL?
A MIRACLE--OF SORTS.
IT APPEARS THAT CONSTRUCT AND I FUNCTIONED ON THE SAME MENTAL FREQUENCY--
WHENEVER IT WAS ACTIVATED--
--IT JAMMED YOUR MIND. OKAY, WE KNEW SOMETHING LIKE THAT--
BUT WHAT--?
I LEARNED THAT WHEN OUR MINDS WERE JOINED--LINKED BY OUR COMMON BRAINWAVE PATTERN.
THE CREATURE WAS A SKRULL SCOUT--AN EXPERIMENTAL MODEL USED DURING THE KREE-SKRULL WAR--
-WHICH, I ASSURE YOU, IS UITE ANOTHER TALE.*
WAIT ONE MINUTE, VISION--
YOU HAVEN'T TOLD ME WHY YOU WERE OUT WANDERING BY YOURSELF WHEN THIS WHOLE THING GOT STARTED!
* ONE TOLD IN AVENGERS #89-97. --ROY.
A PRIVATE MATTER, SPIDER-MAN...
...SOMETHING BETWEEN THE AVENGERS AND MYSELF. SOMEDAY I'LL TELL YOU, MY FRIEND...
SOMEDAY, WE'LL TALK.
AND THEN HE'S GONE--AND THE NIGHT CLOSES IN, ONCE MORE.
-FINIS-

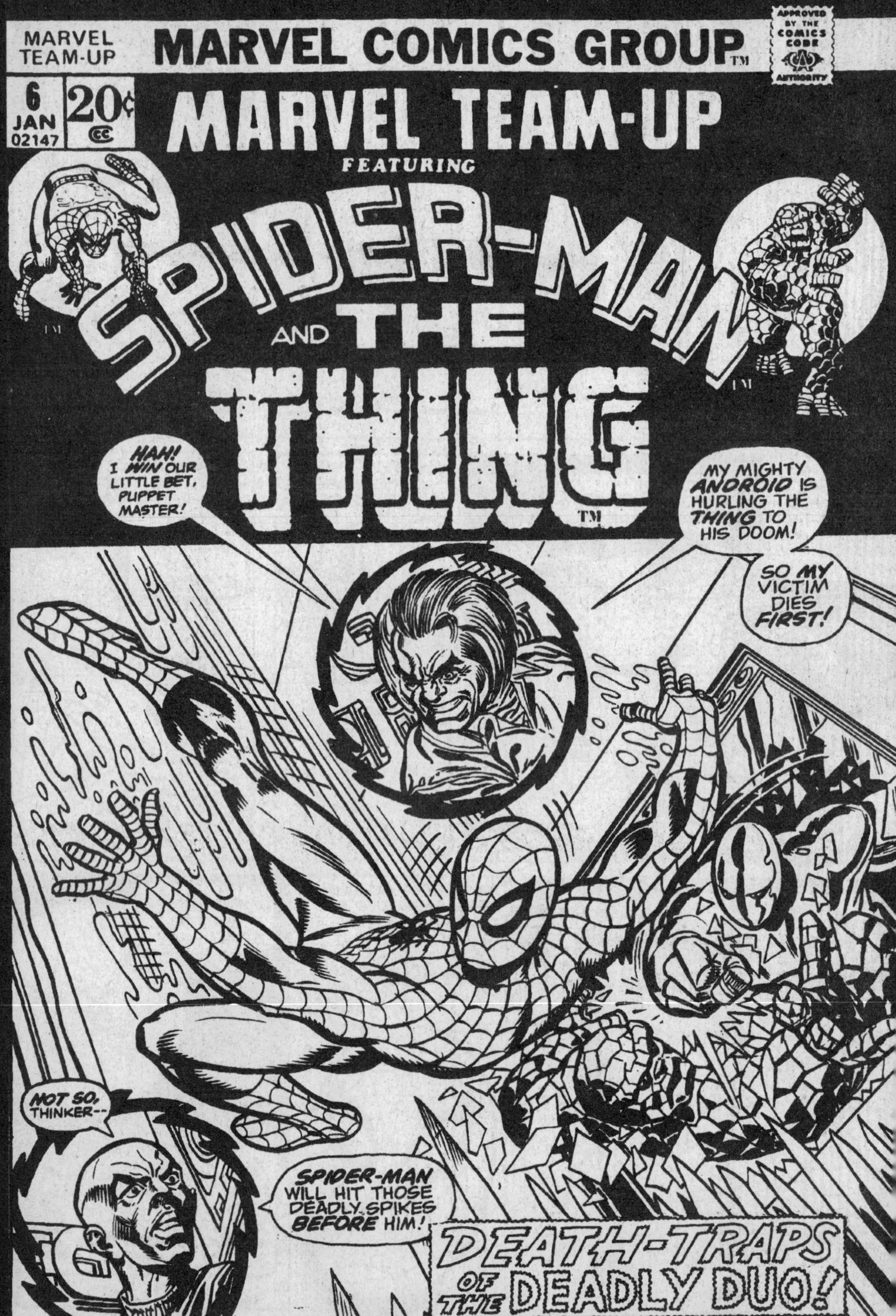
MARVEL TEAM-UP
MARVEL COMICS GROUP
APPROVED BY THE COMICS CODE AUTHORITY
6 JAN 02147
20¢
MARVEL TEAM-UP
FEATURING
SPIDER-MAN AND THE THING
HAH! I WIN OUR LITTLE BET, PUPPET MASTER!
MY MIGHTY ANDROID IS HURLING THE THING TO HIS DOOM!
SO MY VICTIM DIES FIRST!
NOT SO, THINKER--
SPIDER-MAN WILL HIT THOSE DEADLY SPIKES BEFORE HIM!
DEATH-TRAPS OF THE DEADLY DUO!

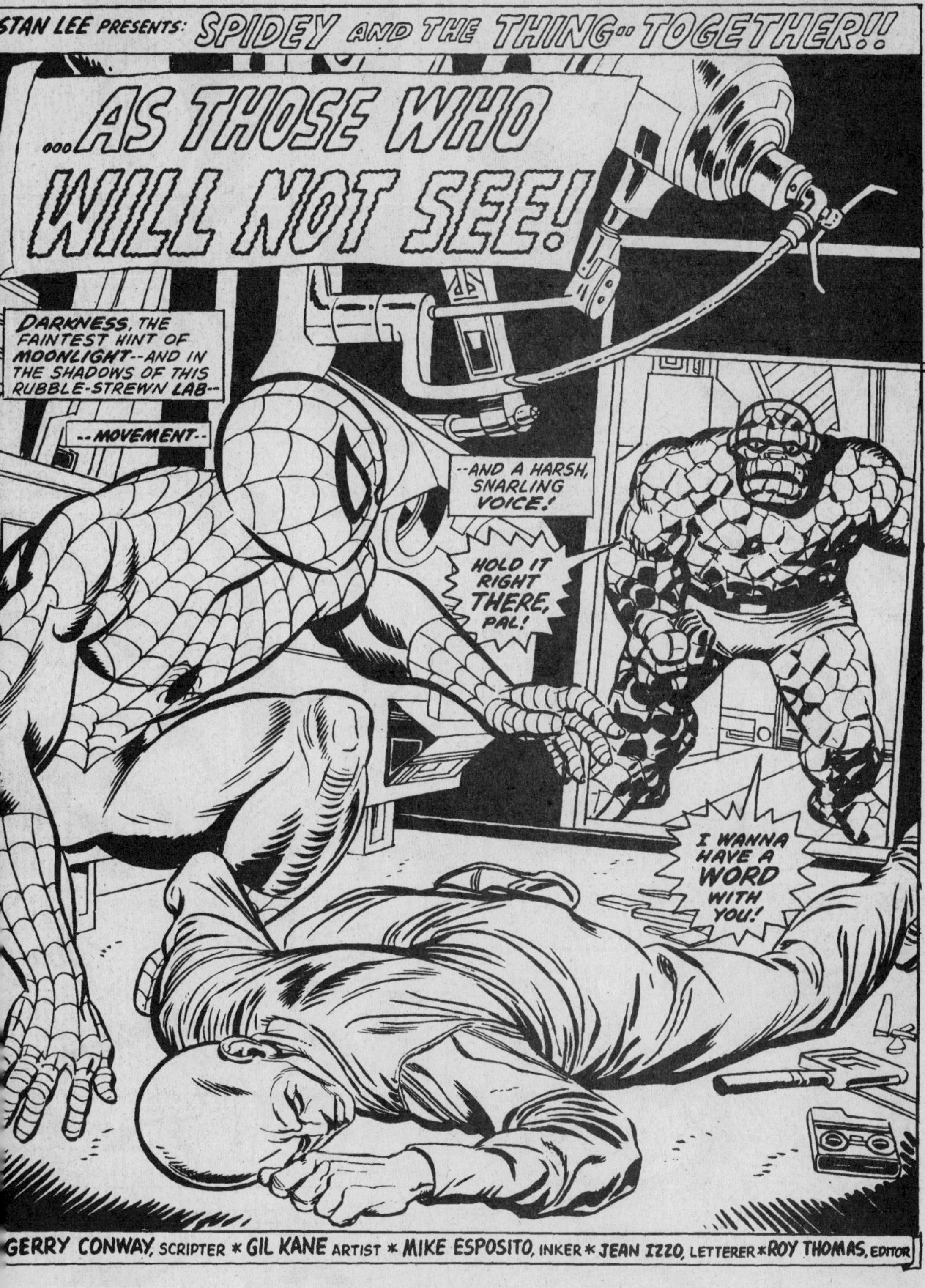
STAN LEE PRESENTS: SPIDEY AND THE THING.. TOGETHER!!
...AS THOSE WHO WILL NOT SEE!
DARKNESS, THE FAINTEST HINT OF MOONLIGHT--AND IN THE SHADOWS OF THIS RUBBLE-STREWN LAB--
--MOVEMENT--
--AND A HARSH, SNARLING VOICE!
HOLD IT RIGHT THERE, PAL!
I WANNA HAVE A WORD WITH YOU!
GERRY CONWAY, SCRIPTER * GIL KANE ARTIST * MIKE ESPOSITO, INKER * JEAN IZZO, LETTERER * ROY THOMAS, EDITOR

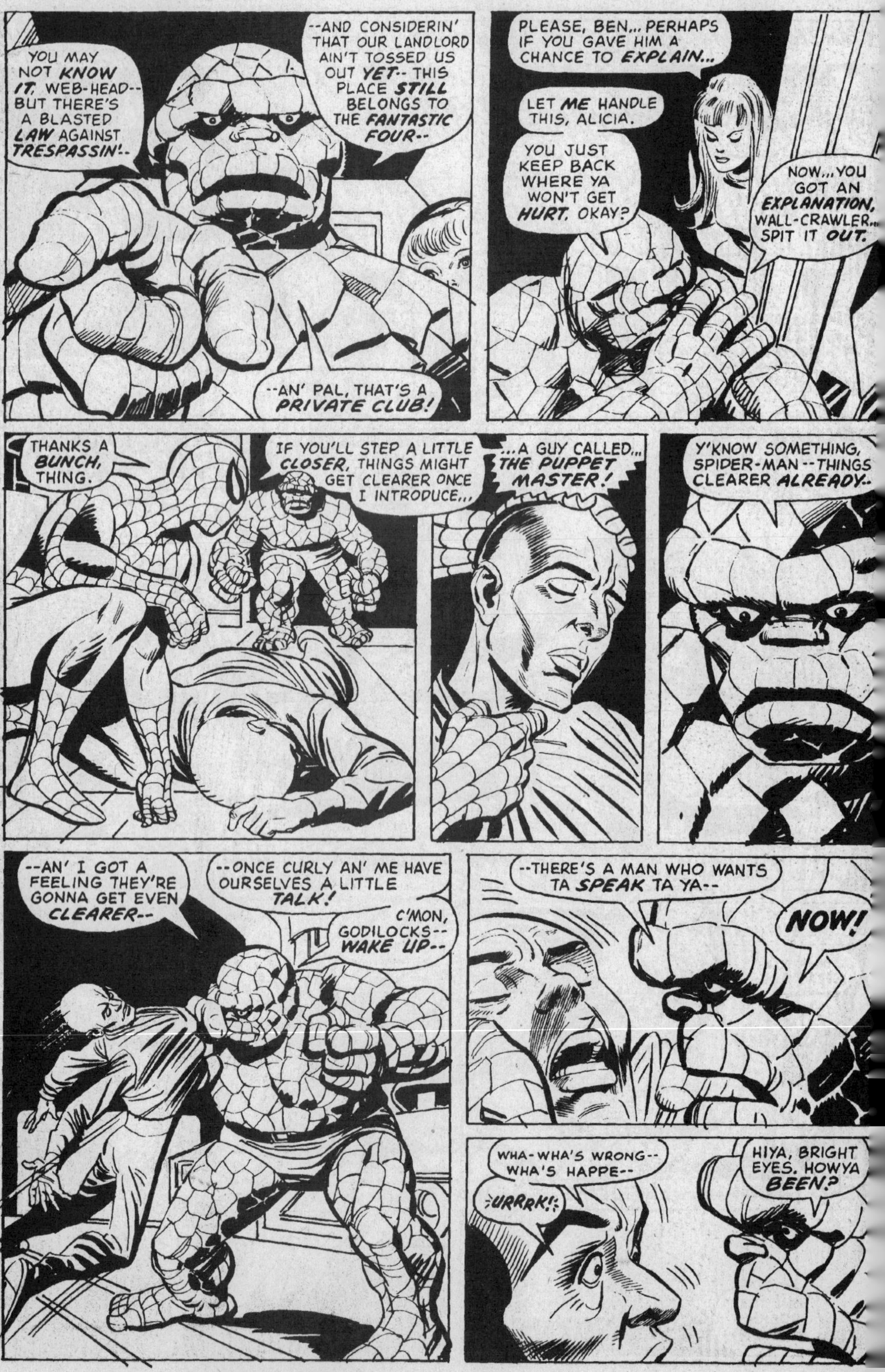
YOU MAY NOT KNOW IT, WEB-HEAD-- BUT THERE'S A BLASTED LAW AGAINST TRESPASSIN'--
--AND CONSIDERIN' THAT OUR LANDLORD AIN'T TOSSED US OUT YET-- THIS PLACE STILL BELONGS TO THE FANTASTIC FOUR--
--AN' PAL, THAT'S A PRIVATE CLUB!
PLEASE, BEN... PERHAPS IF YOU GAVE HIM A CHANCE TO EXPLAIN...
LET ME HANDLE THIS, ALICIA.
YOU JUST KEEP BACK WHERE YA WON'T GET HURT, OKAY?
NOW... YOU GOT AN EXPLANATION, WALL-CRAWLER... SPIT IT OUT.
THANKS A BUNCH, THING.
IF YOU'LL STEP A LITTLE CLOSER, THINGS MIGHT GET CLEARER ONCE I INTRODUCE...
...A GUY CALLED... THE PUPPET MASTER!
Y'KNOW SOMETHING, SPIDER-MAN --THINGS CLEARER ALREADY--
--AN' I GOT A FEELING THEY'RE GONNA GET EVEN CLEARER--
--ONCE CURLY AN' ME HAVE OURSELVES A LITTLE TALK!
C'MON, GODILOCKS-- WAKE UP--
--THERE'S A MAN WHO WANTS TA SPEAK TA YA--
NOW!
WHA-WHA'S WRONG-- WHA'S HAPPE--
URRRK!
HIYA, BRIGHT EYES. HOWYA BEEN?

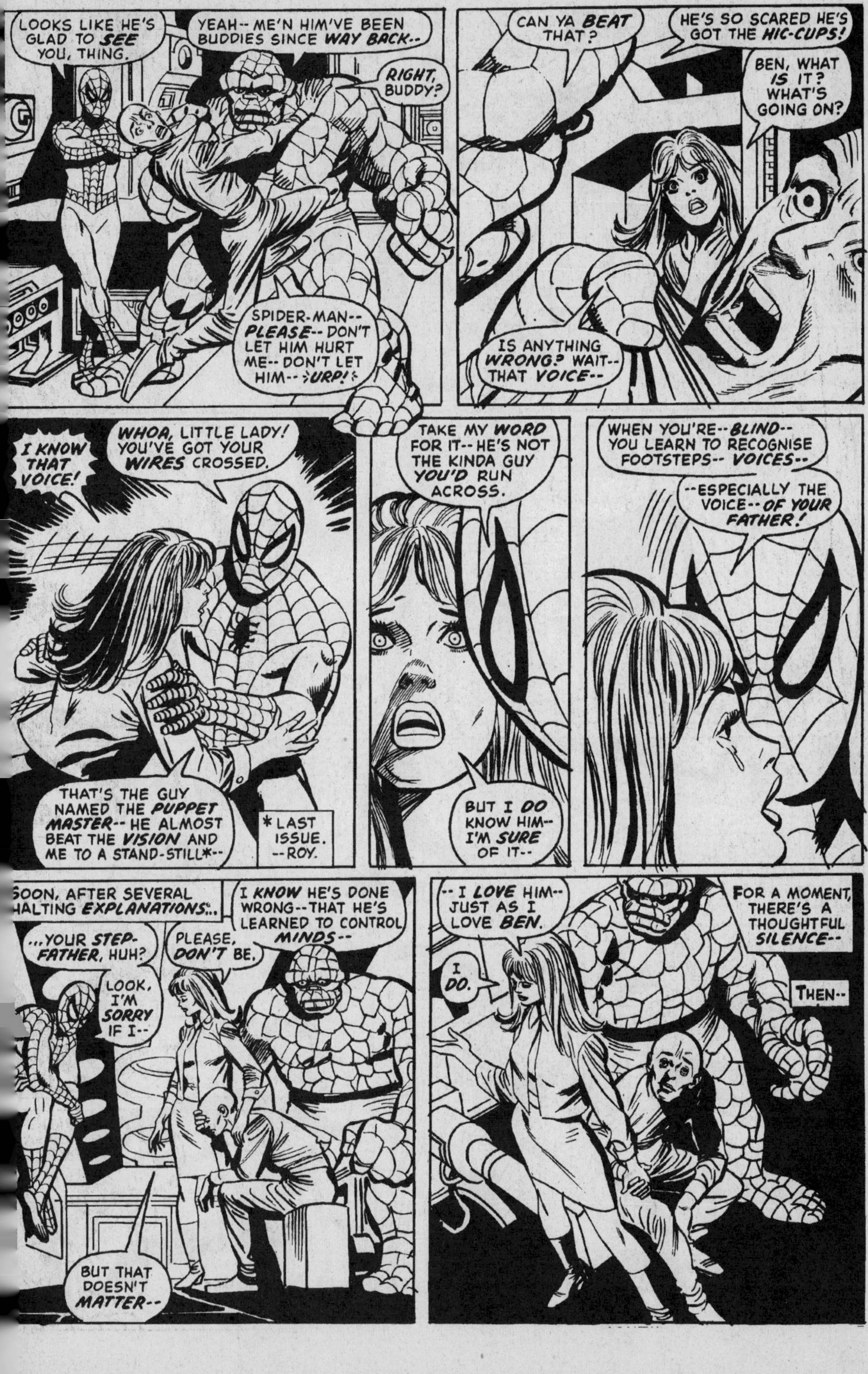
LOOKS LIKE HE'S GLAD TO SEE YOU, THING.
YEAH-- ME'N HIM'VE BEEN BUDDIES SINCE WAY BACK--
RIGHT, BUDDY?
SPIDER-MAN-- PLEASE-- DON'T LET HIM HURT ME-- DON'T LET HIM-- URP!
CAN YA BEAT THAT?
HE'S SO SCARED HE'S GOT THE HIC-CUPS!
BEN, WHAT IS IT? WHAT'S GOING ON?
IS ANYTHING WRONG? WAIT-- THAT VOICE--
I KNOW THAT VOICE!
WHOA, LITTLE LADY! YOU'VE GOT YOUR WIRES CROSSED.
THAT'S THE GUY NAMED THE PUPPET MASTER-- HE ALMOST BEAT THE VISION AND ME TO A STAND-STILL*--
*LAST ISSUE. --ROY.
TAKE MY WORD FOR IT-- HE'S NOT THE KINDA GUY YOU'D RUN ACROSS.
BUT I DO KNOW HIM-- I'M SURE OF IT--
WHEN YOU'RE-- BLIND-- YOU LEARN TO RECOGNISE FOOTSTEPS-- VOICES--
--ESPECIALLY THE VOICE-- OF YOUR FATHER!
SOON, AFTER SEVERAL HALTING EXPLANATIONS...
...YOUR STEP-FATHER, HUH?
LOOK, I'M SORRY IF I--
PLEASE, DON'T BE.
I KNOW HE'S DONE WRONG-- THAT HE'S LEARNED TO CONTROL MINDS--
BUT THAT DOESN'T MATTER--
-- I LOVE HIM-- JUST AS I LOVE BEN.
I DO.
FOR A MOMENT, THERE'S A THOUGHTFUL SILENCE--
THEN--

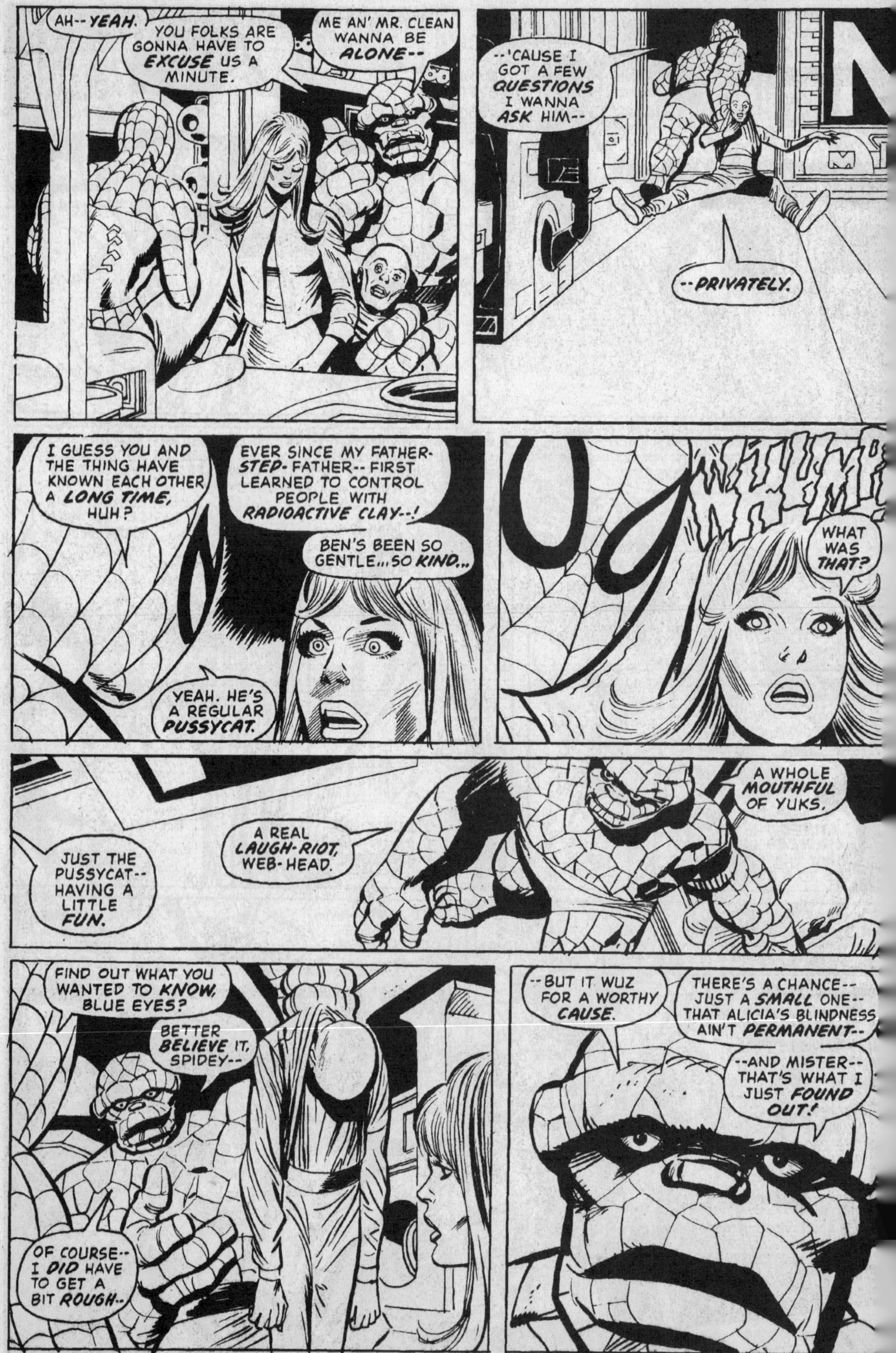
AH--YEAH.
YOU FOLKS ARE GONNA HAVE TO EXCUSE US A MINUTE.
ME AN' MR. CLEAN WANNA BE ALONE--
--'CAUSE I GOT A FEW QUESTIONS I WANNA ASK HIM--
--PRIVATELY.
I GUESS YOU AND THE THING HAVE KNOWN EACH OTHER A LONG TIME, HUH?
EVER SINCE MY FATHER-STEP-FATHER--FIRST LEARNED TO CONTROL PEOPLE WITH RADIOACTIVE CLAY--!
BEN'S BEEN SO GENTLE...SO KIND...
YEAH. HE'S A REGULAR PUSSYCAT.
WHUMP!
WHAT WAS THAT?
JUST THE PUSSYCAT--HAVING A LITTLE FUN.
A REAL LAUGH-RIOT, WEB-HEAD.
A WHOLE MOUTHFUL OF YUKS.
FIND OUT WHAT YOU WANTED TO KNOW, BLUE EYES?
BETTER BELIEVE IT, SPIDEY--
OF COURSE--I DID HAVE TO GET A BIT ROUGH--
--BUT IT WUZ FOR A WORTHY CAUSE.
THERE'S A CHANCE--JUST A SMALL ONE--THAT ALICIA'S BLINDNESS AIN'T PERMANENT--
--AND MISTER--THAT'S WHAT I JUST FOUND OUT!

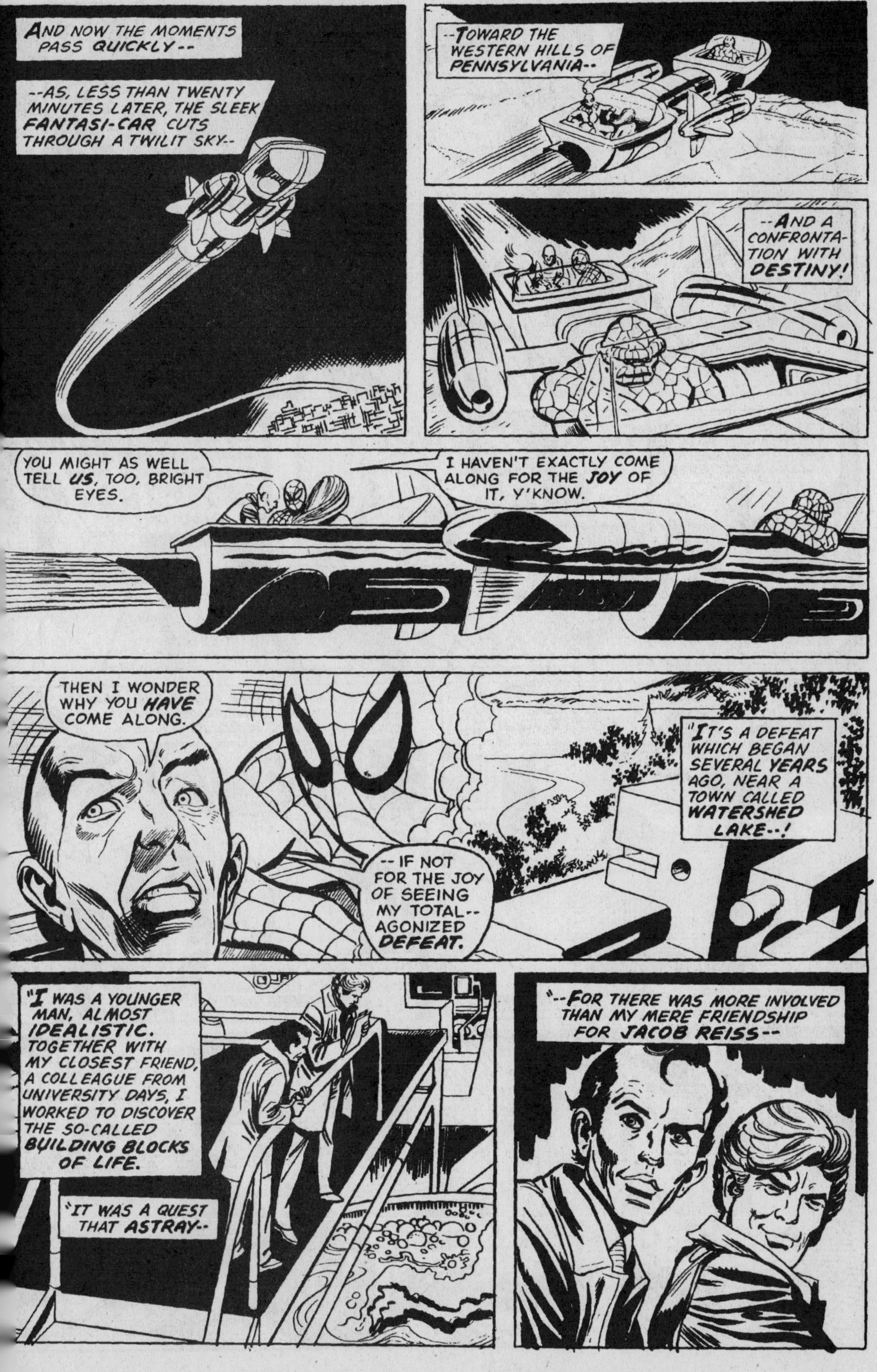
AND NOW THE MOMENTS PASS QUICKLY--
--AS, LESS THAN TWENTY MINUTES LATER, THE SLEEK FANTASI-CAR CUTS THROUGH A TWILIT SKY--
--TOWARD THE WESTERN HILLS OF PENNSYLVANIA--
--AND A CONFRONTATION WITH DESTINY!
YOU MIGHT AS WELL TELL US, TOO, BRIGHT EYES.
I HAVEN'T EXACTLY COME ALONG FOR THE JOY OF IT, Y'KNOW.
THEN I WONDER WHY YOU HAVE COME ALONG.
--IF NOT FOR THE JOY OF SEEING MY TOTAL--AGONIZED DEFEAT.
"IT'S A DEFEAT WHICH BEGAN SEVERAL YEARS AGO, NEAR A TOWN CALLED WATERSHED LAKE--!
"I WAS A YOUNGER MAN, ALMOST IDEALISTIC. TOGETHER WITH MY CLOSEST FRIEND, A COLLEAGUE FROM UNIVERSITY DAYS, I WORKED TO DISCOVER THE SO-CALLED BUILDING BLOCKS OF LIFE.
"IT WAS A QUEST THAT ASTRAY--
"--FOR THERE WAS MORE INVOLVED THAN MY MERE FRIENDSHIP FOR JACOB REISS--

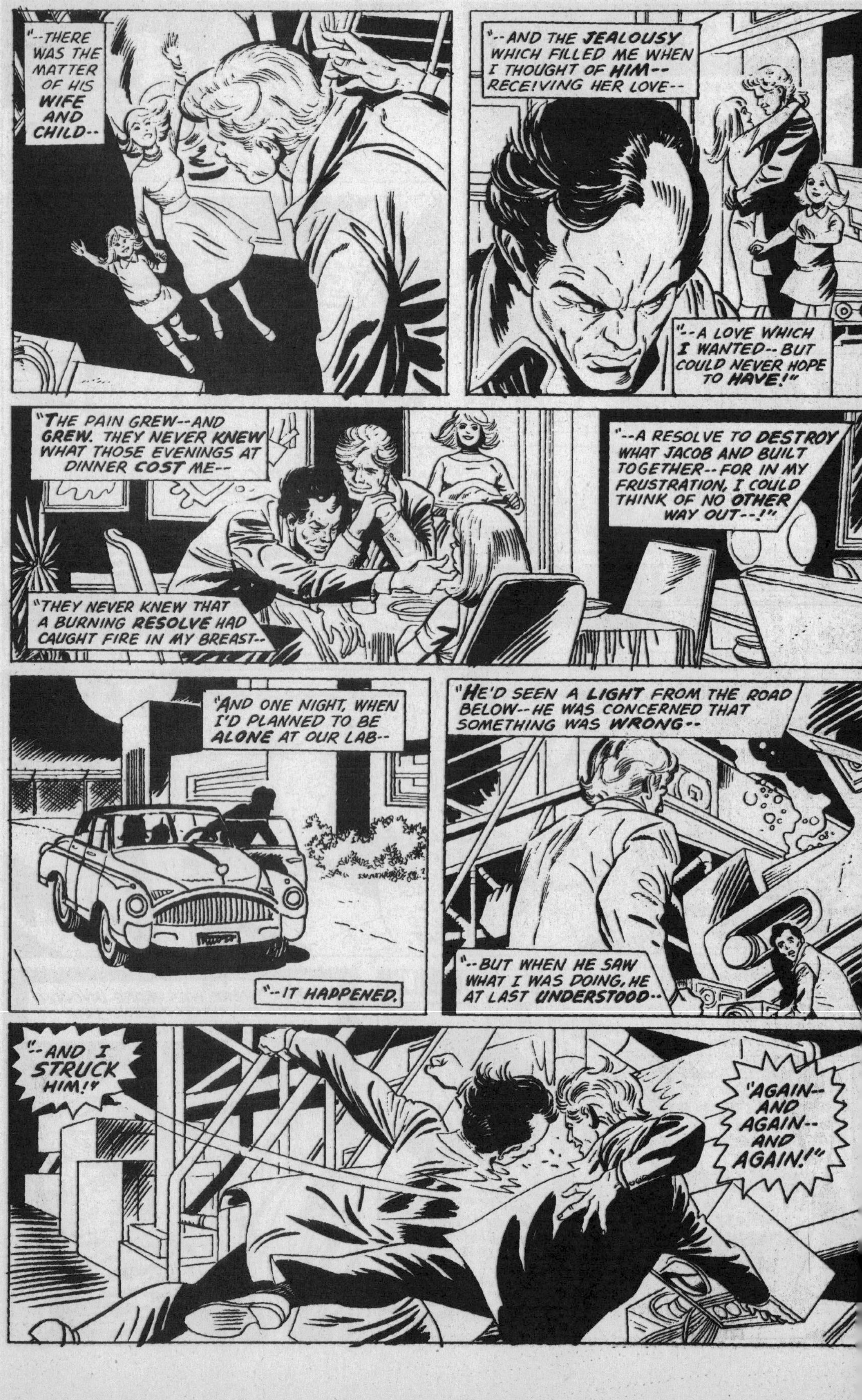
"--THERE WAS THE MATTER OF HIS WIFE AND CHILD--
"--AND THE JEALOUSY WHICH FILLED ME WHEN I THOUGHT OF HIM--RECEIVING HER LOVE--
"--A LOVE WHICH I WANTED--BUT COULD NEVER HOPE TO HAVE!"
"THE PAIN GREW--AND GREW. THEY NEVER KNEW WHAT THOSE EVENINGS AT DINNER COST ME--
"THEY NEVER KNEW THAT A BURNING RESOLVE HAD CAUGHT FIRE IN MY BREAST--
"--A RESOLVE TO DESTROY WHAT JACOB AND BUILT TOGETHER--FOR IN MY FRUSTRATION, I COULD THINK OF NO OTHER WAY OUT--!"
"AND ONE NIGHT, WHEN I'D PLANNED TO BE ALONE AT OUR LAB--
"--IT HAPPENED.
"HE'D SEEN A LIGHT FROM THE ROAD BELOW--HE WAS CONCERNED THAT SOMETHING WAS WRONG--
"--BUT WHEN HE SAW WHAT I WAS DOING, HE AT LAST UNDERSTOOD--
"--AND I STRUCK HIM!"
"AGAIN--AND AGAIN--AND AGAIN!"

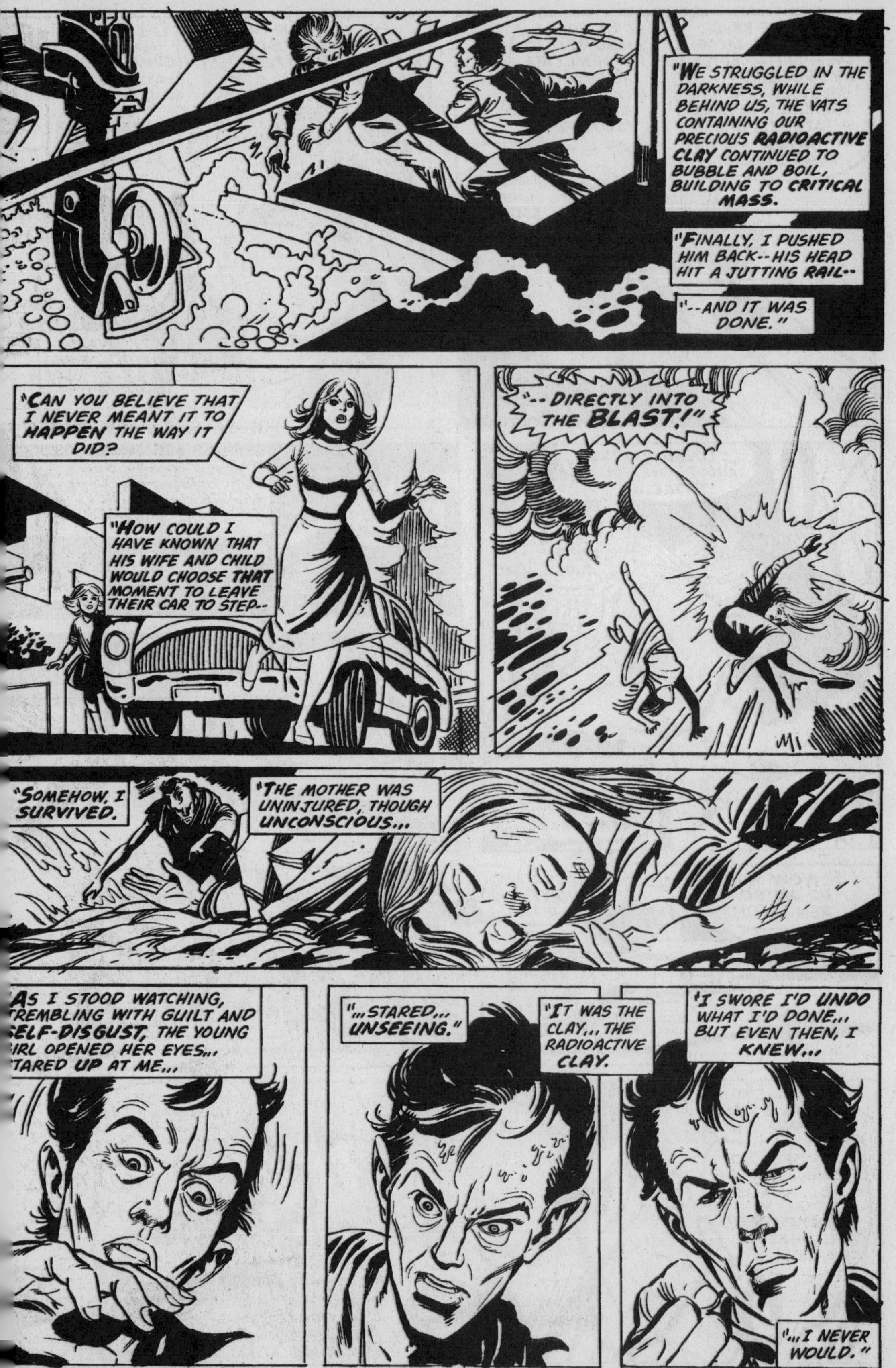
"WE STRUGGLED IN THE DARKNESS, WHILE BEHIND US, THE VATS CONTAINING OUR PRECIOUS RADIOACTIVE CLAY CONTINUED TO BUBBLE AND BOIL, BUILDING TO CRITICAL MASS.
"FINALLY, I PUSHED HIM BACK--HIS HEAD HIT A JUTTING RAIL--
"--AND IT WAS DONE."
"CAN YOU BELIEVE THAT I NEVER MEANT IT TO HAPPEN THE WAY IT DID?
"HOW COULD I HAVE KNOWN THAT HIS WIFE AND CHILD WOULD CHOOSE THAT MOMENT TO LEAVE THEIR CAR TO STEP--
"--DIRECTLY INTO THE BLAST!"
"SOMEHOW, I SURVIVED.
"THE MOTHER WAS UNINJURED, THOUGH UNCONSCIOUS...
AS I STOOD WATCHING, TREMBLING WITH GUILT AND SELF-DISGUST, THE YOUNG GIRL OPENED HER EYES... STARED UP AT ME...
"...STARED... UNSEEING."
"IT WAS THE CLAY... THE RADIOACTIVE CLAY.
'I SWORE I'D UNDO WHAT I'D DONE... BUT EVEN THEN, I KNEW...
"...I NEVER WOULD."

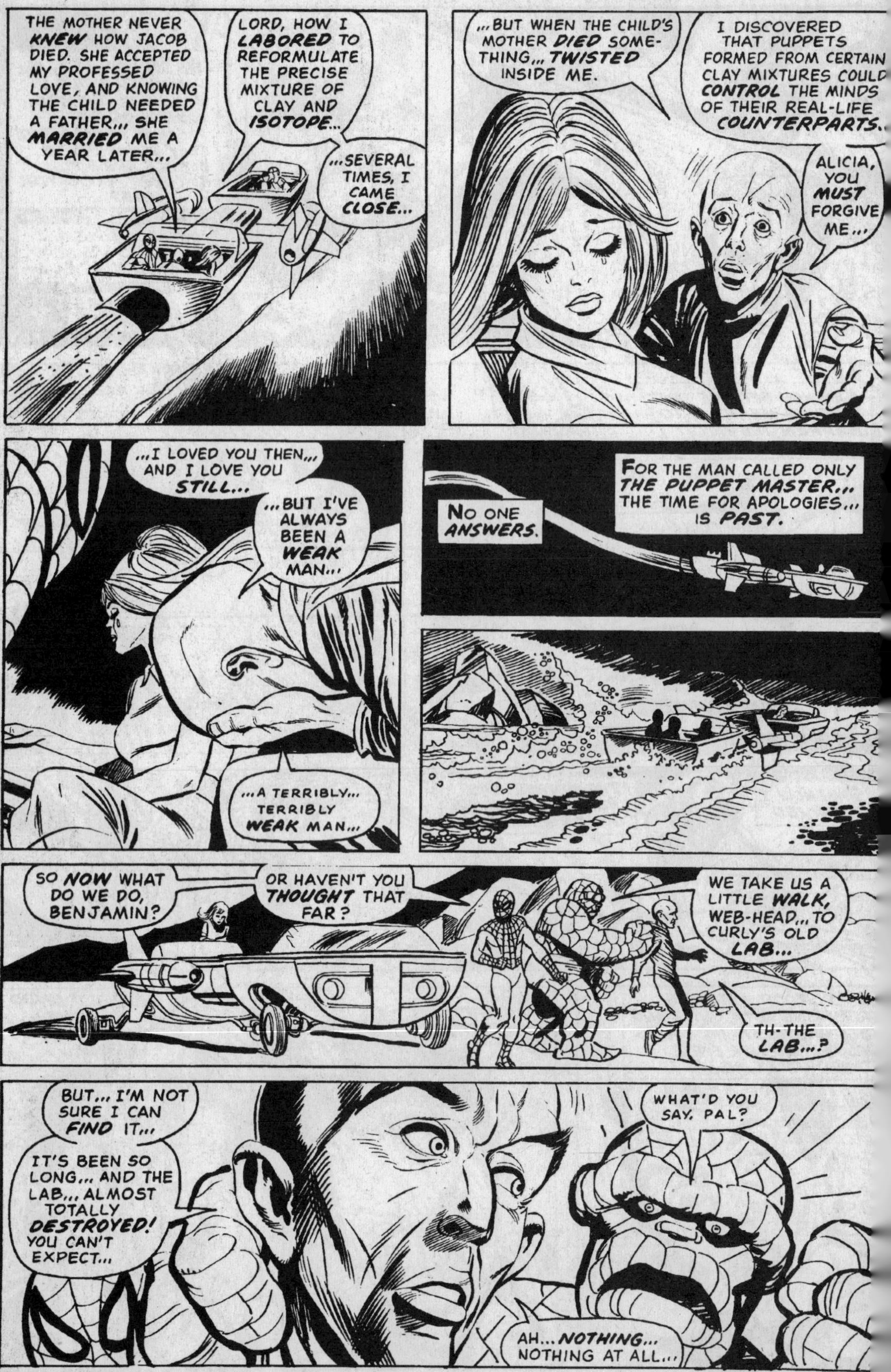
THE MOTHER NEVER KNEW HOW JACOB DIED. SHE ACCEPTED MY PROFESSED LOVE, AND KNOWING THE CHILD NEEDED A FATHER... SHE MARRIED ME A YEAR LATER...
LORD, HOW I LABORED TO REFORMULATE THE PRECISE MIXTURE OF CLAY AND ISOTOPE...
...SEVERAL TIMES, I CAME CLOSE...
...BUT WHEN THE CHILD'S MOTHER DIED SOMETHING... TWISTED INSIDE ME.
I DISCOVERED THAT PUPPETS FORMED FROM CERTAIN CLAY MIXTURES COULD CONTROL THE MINDS OF THEIR REAL-LIFE COUNTERPARTS...
ALICIA, YOU MUST FORGIVE ME...
...I LOVED YOU THEN... AND I LOVE YOU STILL...
...BUT I'VE ALWAYS BEEN A WEAK MAN...
...A TERRIBLY... TERRIBLY WEAK MAN...
NO ONE ANSWERS.
FOR THE MAN CALLED ONLY THE PUPPET MASTER... THE TIME FOR APOLOGIES... IS PAST.
SO NOW WHAT DO WE DO, BENJAMIN?
OR HAVEN'T YOU THOUGHT THAT FAR?
WE TAKE US A LITTLE WALK, WEB-HEAD... TO CURLY'S OLD LAB...
TH-THE LAB...?
BUT... I'M NOT SURE I CAN FIND IT...
IT'S BEEN SO LONG... AND THE LAB... ALMOST TOTALLY DESTROYED! YOU CAN'T EXPECT...
WHAT'D YOU SAY, PAL?
AH... NOTHING... NOTHING AT ALL...

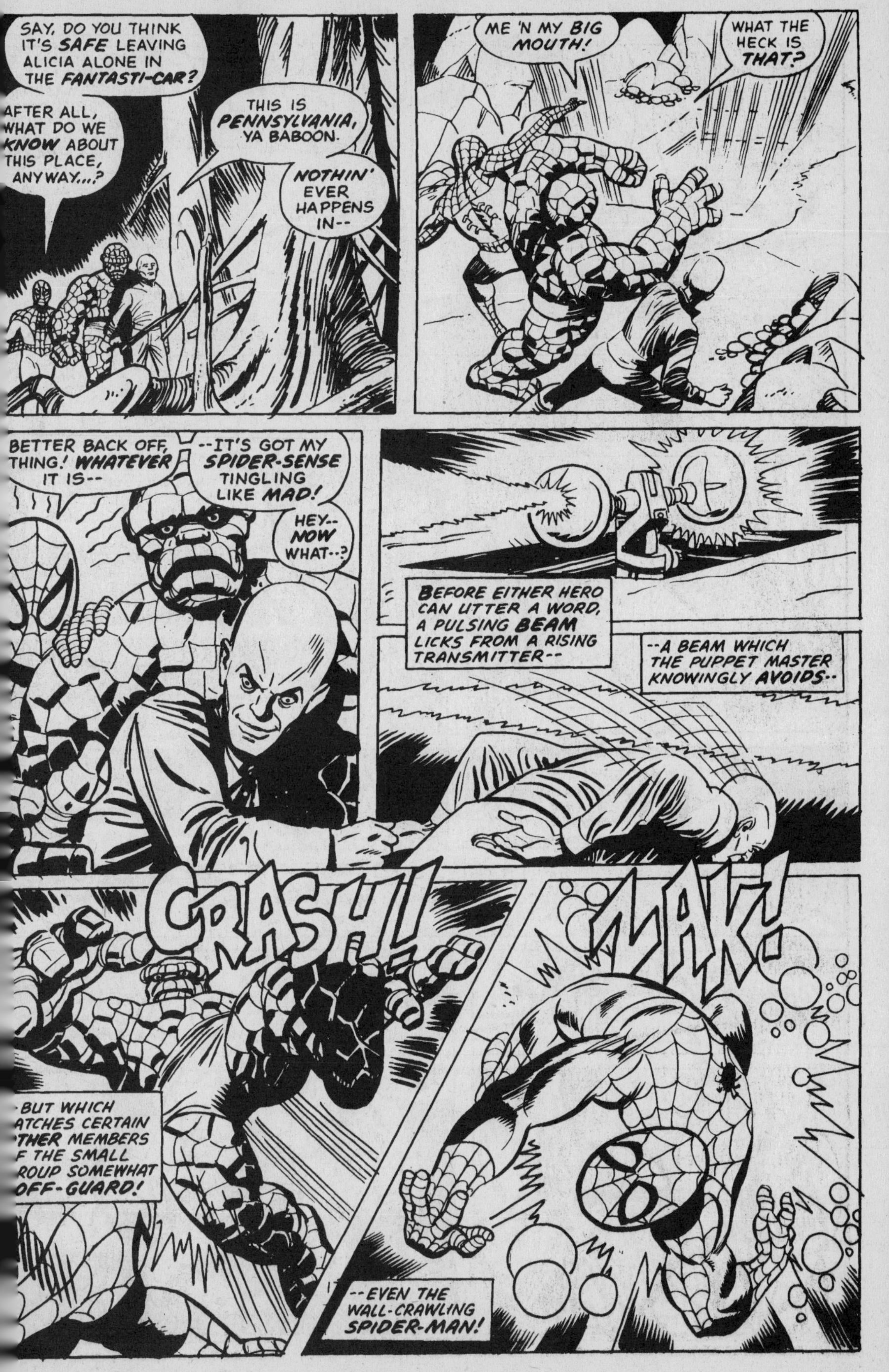
SAY, DO YOU THINK IT'S SAFE LEAVING ALICIA ALONE IN THE FANTASTI-CAR?
AFTER ALL, WHAT DO WE KNOW ABOUT THIS PLACE, ANYWAY...?
THIS IS PENNSYLVANIA, YA BABOON.
NOTHIN' EVER HAPPENS IN--
ME 'N MY BIG MOUTH!
WHAT THE HECK IS THAT?
BETTER BACK OFF, THING! WHATEVER IT IS--
--IT'S GOT MY SPIDER-SENSE TINGLING LIKE MAD!
HEY-- NOW WHAT--?
BEFORE EITHER HERO CAN UTTER A WORD, A PULSING BEAM LICKS FROM A RISING TRANSMITTER--
--A BEAM WHICH THE PUPPET MASTER KNOWINGLY AVOIDS--
CRASH!
ZZAK!
BUT WHICH ATCHES CERTAIN THER MEMBERS F THE SMALL ROUP SOMEWHAT OFF-GUARD!
--EVEN THE WALL-CRAWLING SPIDER-MAN!

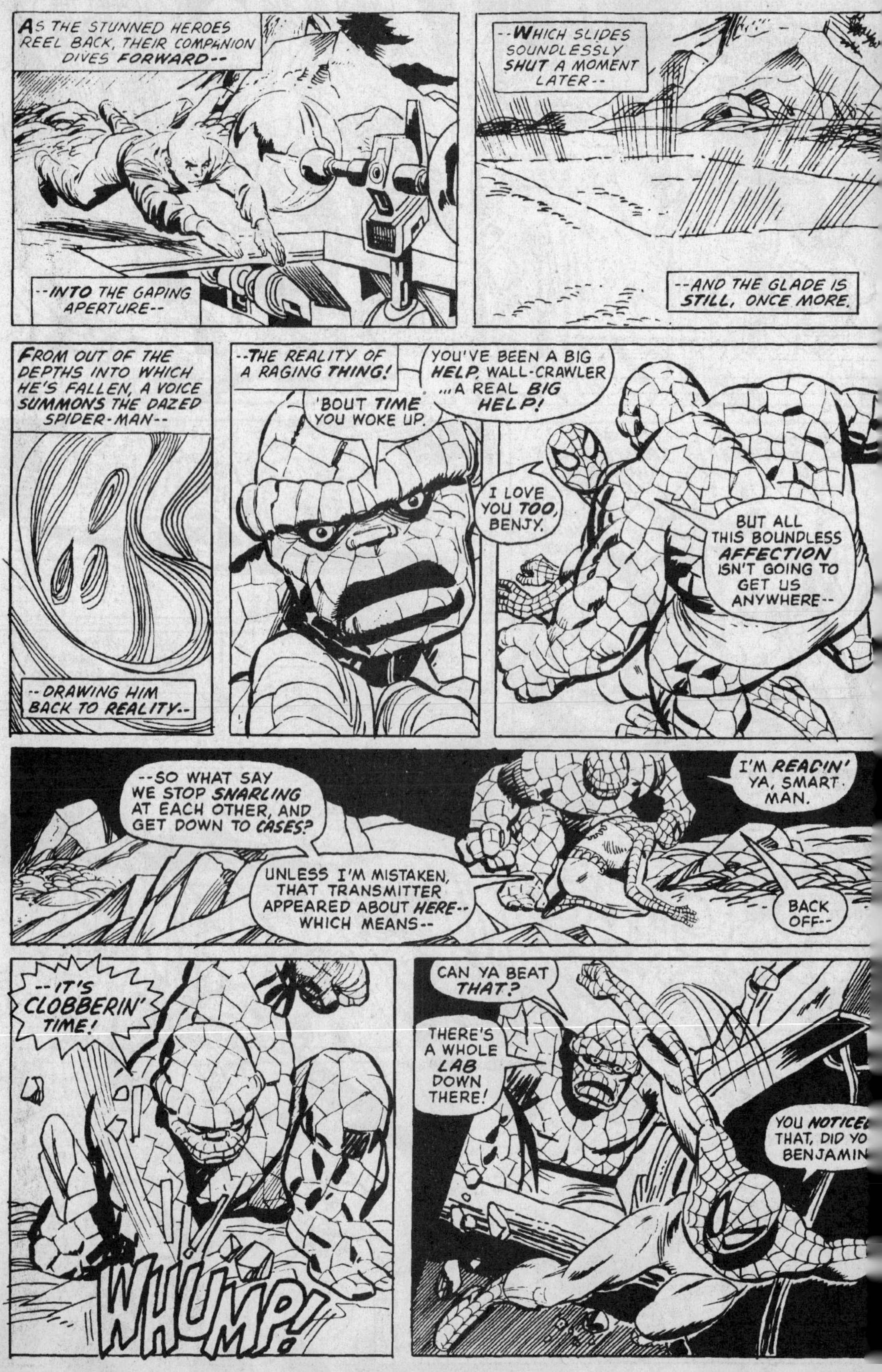
AS THE STUNNED HEROES REEL BACK, THEIR COMPANION DIVES FORWARD--
--INTO THE GAPING APERTURE--
--WHICH SLIDES SOUNDLESSLY SHUT A MOMENT LATER--
--AND THE GLADE IS STILL, ONCE MORE.
FROM OUT OF THE DEPTHS INTO WHICH HE'S FALLEN, A VOICE SUMMONS THE DAZED SPIDER-MAN--
--DRAWING HIM BACK TO REALITY--
--THE REALITY OF A RAGING THING!
'BOUT TIME YOU WOKE UP.
YOU'VE BEEN A BIG HELP, WALL-CRAWLER ...A REAL BIG HELP!
I LOVE YOU TOO, BENJY.
BUT ALL THIS BOUNDLESS AFFECTION ISN'T GOING TO GET US ANYWHERE--
--SO WHAT SAY WE STOP SNARLING AT EACH OTHER, AND GET DOWN TO CASES?
UNLESS I'M MISTAKEN, THAT TRANSMITTER APPEARED ABOUT HERE-- WHICH MEANS--
I'M READIN' YA, SMART MAN.
BACK OFF--
--IT'S CLOBBERIN' TIME!
WHUMP!
CAN YA BEAT THAT?
THERE'S A WHOLE LAB DOWN THERE!
YOU NOTICED THAT, DID YO BENJAMIN

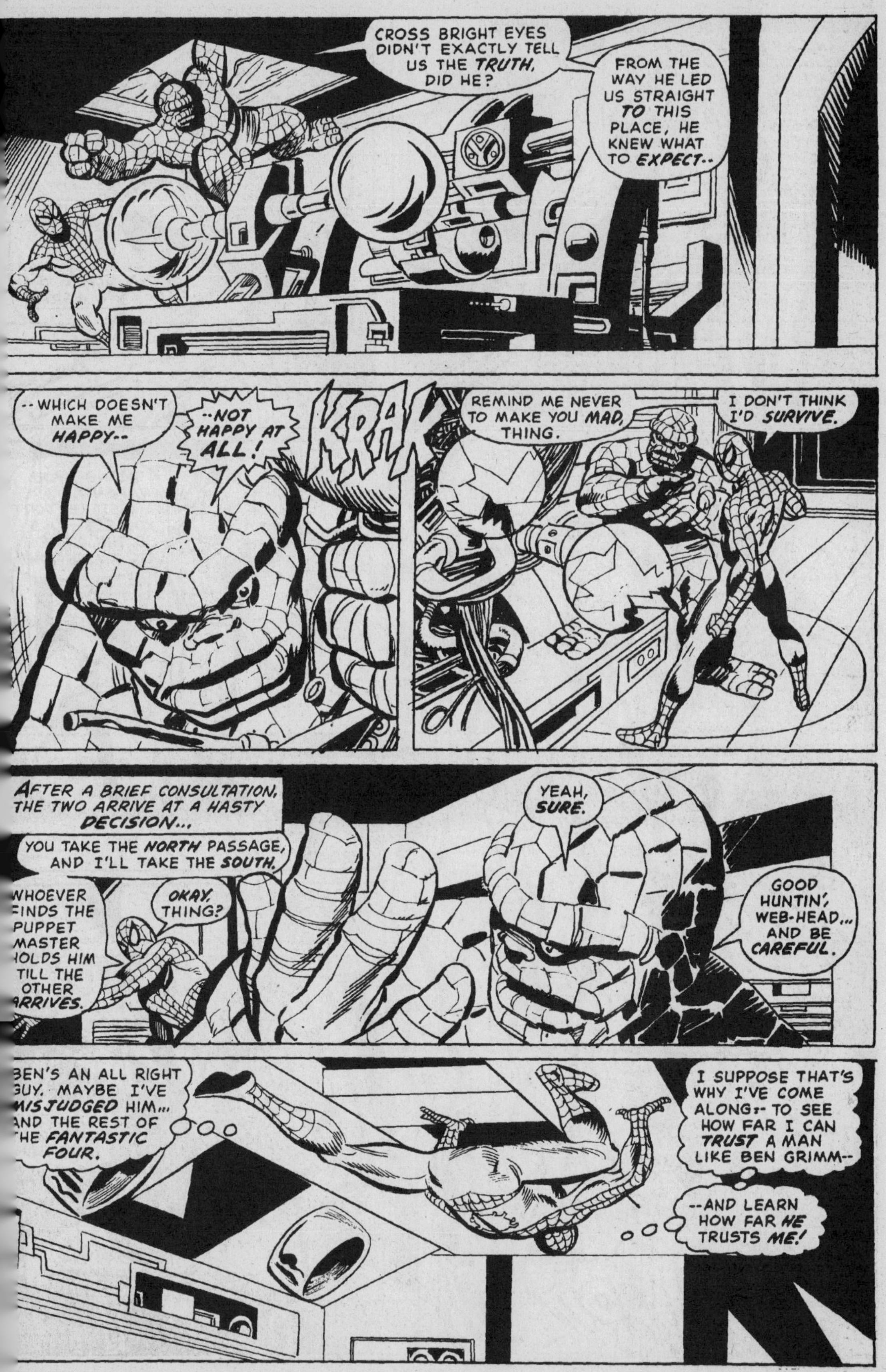
CROSS BRIGHT EYES DIDN'T EXACTLY TELL US THE TRUTH, DID HE?
FROM THE WAY HE LED US STRAIGHT TO THIS PLACE, HE KNEW WHAT TO EXPECT..
--WHICH DOESN'T MAKE ME HAPPY--
--NOT HAPPY AT ALL!
KRAK
REMIND ME NEVER TO MAKE YOU MAD, THING.
I DON'T THINK I'D SURVIVE.
AFTER A BRIEF CONSULTATION, THE TWO ARRIVE AT A HASTY DECISION...
YOU TAKE THE NORTH PASSAGE, AND I'LL TAKE THE SOUTH.
WHOEVER FINDS THE PUPPET MASTER HOLDS HIM TILL THE OTHER ARRIVES.
OKAY, THING?
YEAH, SURE.
GOOD HUNTIN', WEB-HEAD,... AND BE CAREFUL.
BEN'S AN ALL RIGHT GUY. MAYBE I'VE MISJUDGED HIM... AND THE REST OF THE FANTASTIC FOUR.
I SUPPOSE THAT'S WHY I'VE COME ALONG;- TO SEE HOW FAR I CAN TRUST A MAN LIKE BEN GRIMM--
--AND LEARN HOW FAR HE TRUSTS ME!

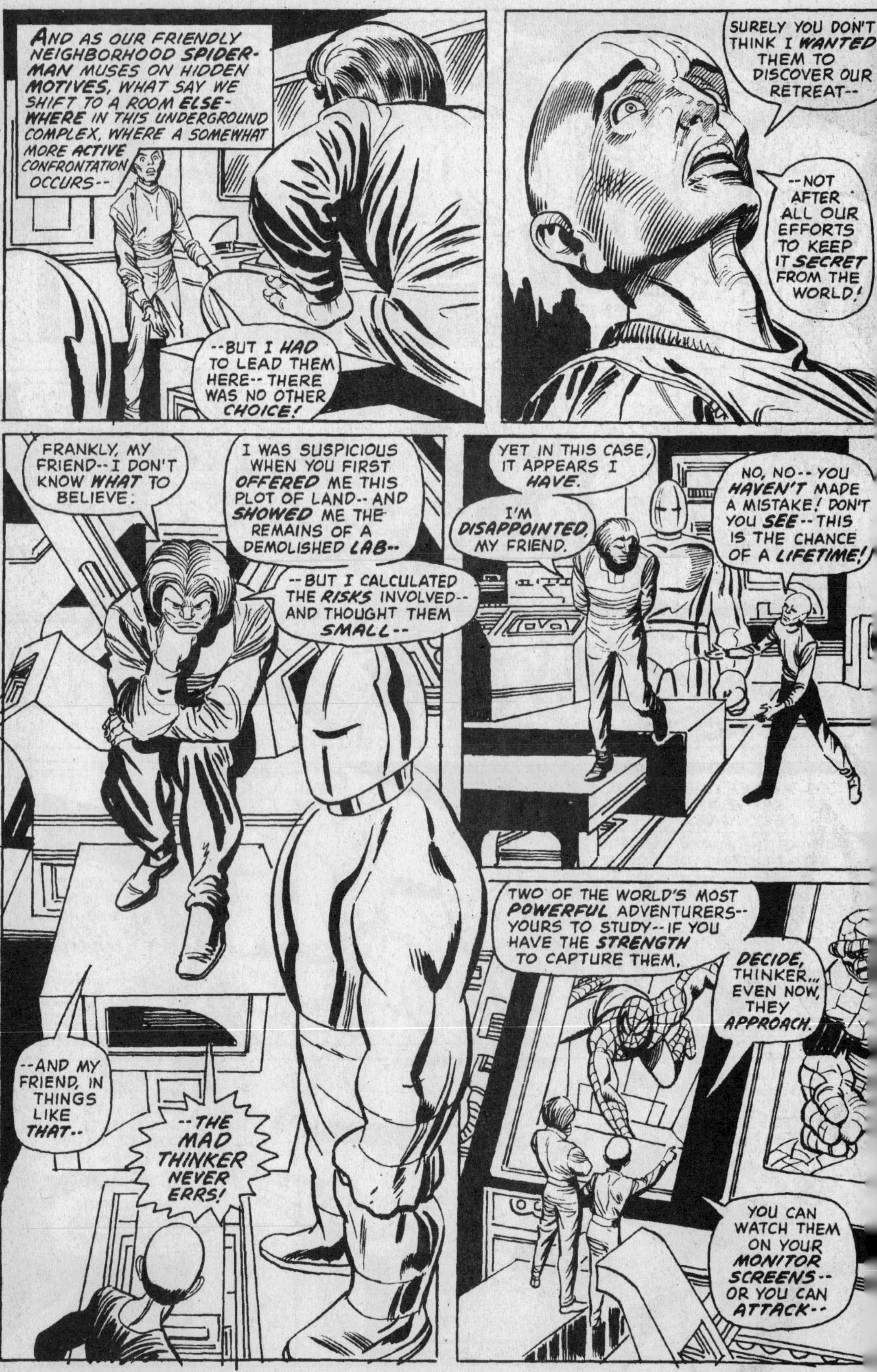
AND AS OUR FRIENDLY NEIGHBORHOOD SPIDER-MAN MUSES ON HIDDEN MOTIVES, WHAT SAY WE SHIFT TO A ROOM ELSEWHERE IN THIS UNDERGROUND COMPLEX, WHERE A SOMEWHAT MORE ACTIVE CONFRONTATION OCCURS--
--BUT I HAD TO LEAD THEM HERE--THERE WAS NO OTHER CHOICE!
SURELY YOU DON'T THINK I WANTED THEM TO DISCOVER OUR RETREAT--
--NOT AFTER ALL OUR EFFORTS TO KEEP IT SECRET FROM THE WORLD!
FRANKLY, MY FRIEND--I DON'T KNOW WHAT TO BELIEVE:
I WAS SUSPICIOUS WHEN YOU FIRST OFFERED ME THIS PLOT OF LAND--AND SHOWED ME THE REMAINS OF A DEMOLISHED LAB--
--BUT I CALCULATED THE RISKS INVOLVED--AND THOUGHT THEM SMALL--
--AND MY FRIEND, IN THINGS LIKE THAT--
--THE MAD THINKER NEVER ERRS!
YET IN THIS CASE, IT APPEARS I HAVE.
I'M DISAPPOINTED, MY FRIEND.
NO, NO--YOU HAVEN'T MADE A MISTAKE! DON'T YOU SEE--THIS IS THE CHANCE OF A LIFETIME!
TWO OF THE WORLD'S MOST POWERFUL ADVENTURERS--YOURS TO STUDY--IF YOU HAVE THE STRENGTH TO CAPTURE THEM.
DECIDE, THINKER... EVEN NOW, THEY APPROACH.
YOU CAN WATCH THEM ON YOUR MONITOR SCREENS--OR YOU CAN ATTACK--

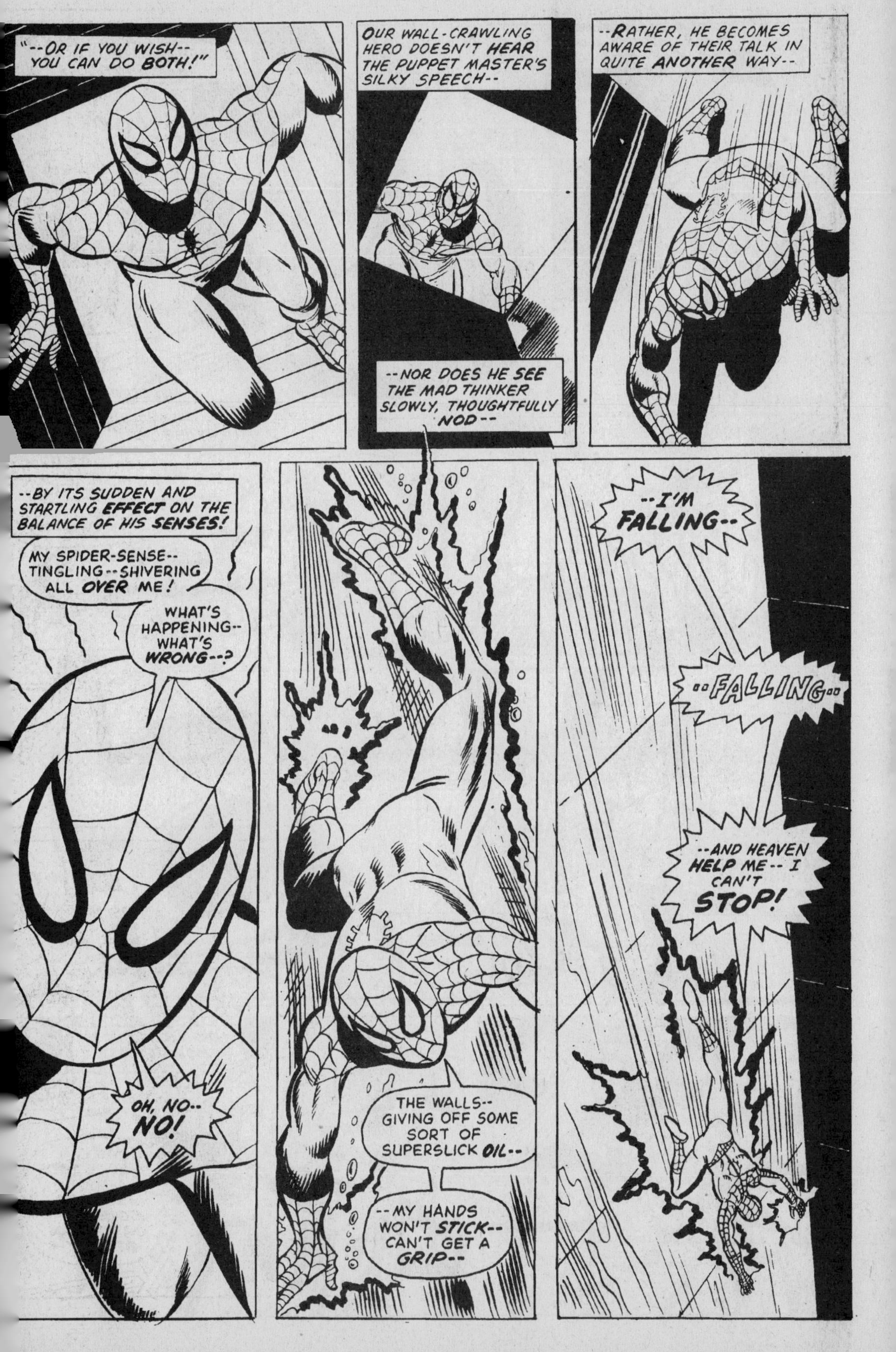
"--OR IF YOU WISH-- YOU CAN DO BOTH!"
OUR WALL-CRAWLING HERO DOESN'T HEAR THE PUPPET MASTER'S SILKY SPEECH--
--NOR DOES HE SEE THE MAD THINKER SLOWLY, THOUGHTFULLY NOD--
--RATHER, HE BECOMES AWARE OF THEIR TALK IN QUITE ANOTHER WAY--
--BY ITS SUDDEN AND STARTLING EFFECT ON THE BALANCE OF HIS SENSES!
MY SPIDER-SENSE-- TINGLING--SHIVERING ALL OVER ME!
WHAT'S HAPPENING-- WHAT'S WRONG--?
OH, NO-- NO!
THE WALLS-- GIVING OFF SOME SORT OF SUPERSLICK OIL--
--MY HANDS WON'T STICK-- CAN'T GET A GRIP--
--I'M FALLING--
--FALLING--
--AND HEAVEN HELP ME-- I CAN'T STOP!

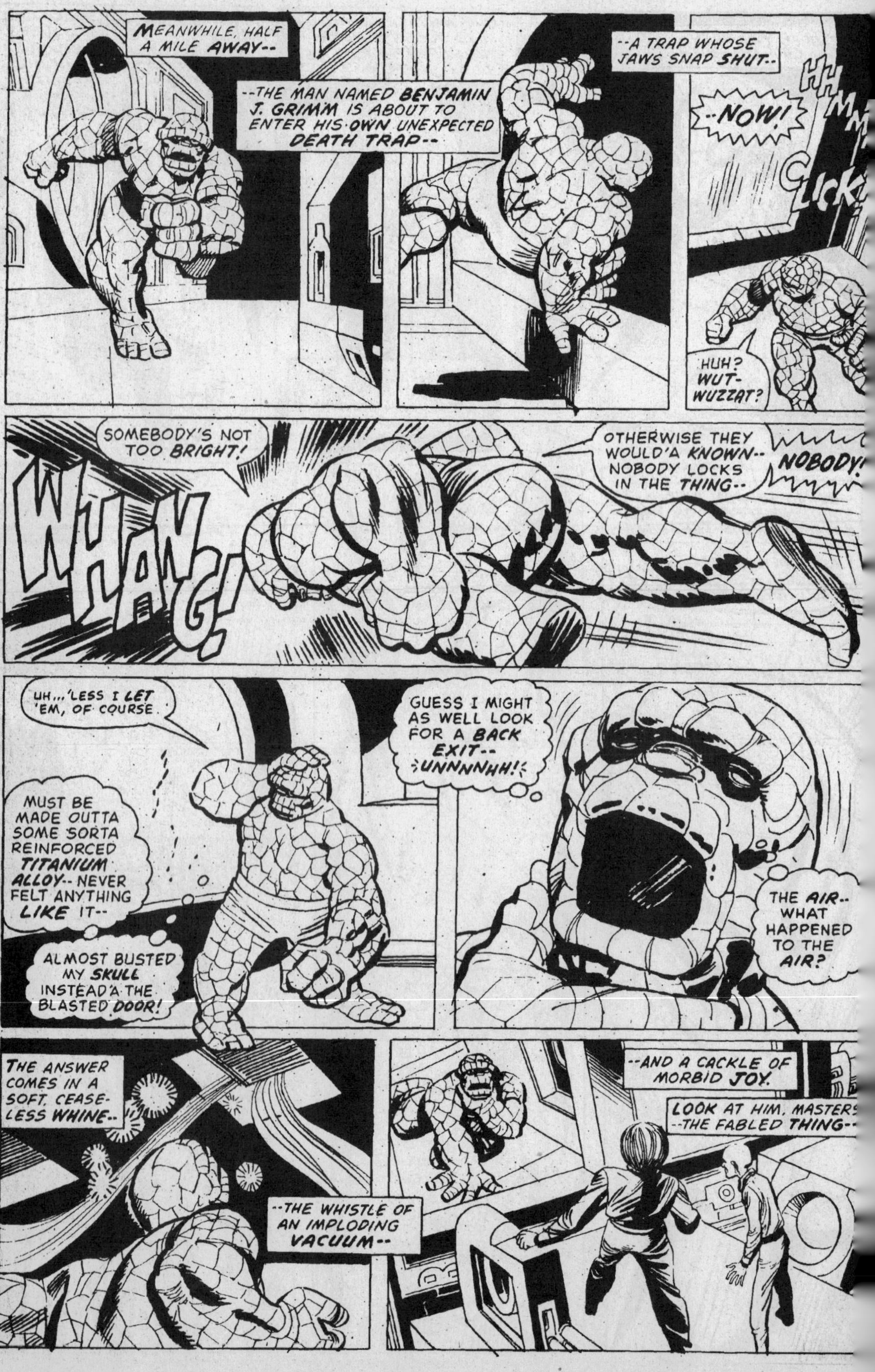
MEANWHILE, HALF A MILE AWAY--
--THE MAN NAMED BENJAMIN J. GRIMM IS ABOUT TO ENTER HIS OWN UNEXPECTED DEATH TRAP--
--A TRAP WHOSE JAWS SNAP SHUT--
--NOW!
CLICK!
HUH? WUT-WUZZAT?
SOMEBODY'S NOT TOO BRIGHT!
WHANG!
OTHERWISE THEY WOULD'A KNOWN-- NOBODY LOCKS IN THE THING--
NOBODY!
UH... 'LESS I LET 'EM, OF COURSE.
MUST BE MADE OUTTA SOME SORTA REINFORCED TITANIUM ALLOY-- NEVER FELT ANYTHING LIKE IT--
ALMOST BUSTED MY SKULL INSTEAD A THE BLASTED DOOR!
GUESS I MIGHT AS WELL LOOK FOR A BACK EXIT-- UNNNNHH!
THE AIR-- WHAT HAPPENED TO THE AIR?
THE ANSWER COMES IN A SOFT, CEASE-LESS WHINE--
--THE WHISTLE OF AN IMPLODING VACUUM--
--AND A CACKLE OF MORBID JOY.
LOOK AT HIM, MASTERS --THE FABLED THING--

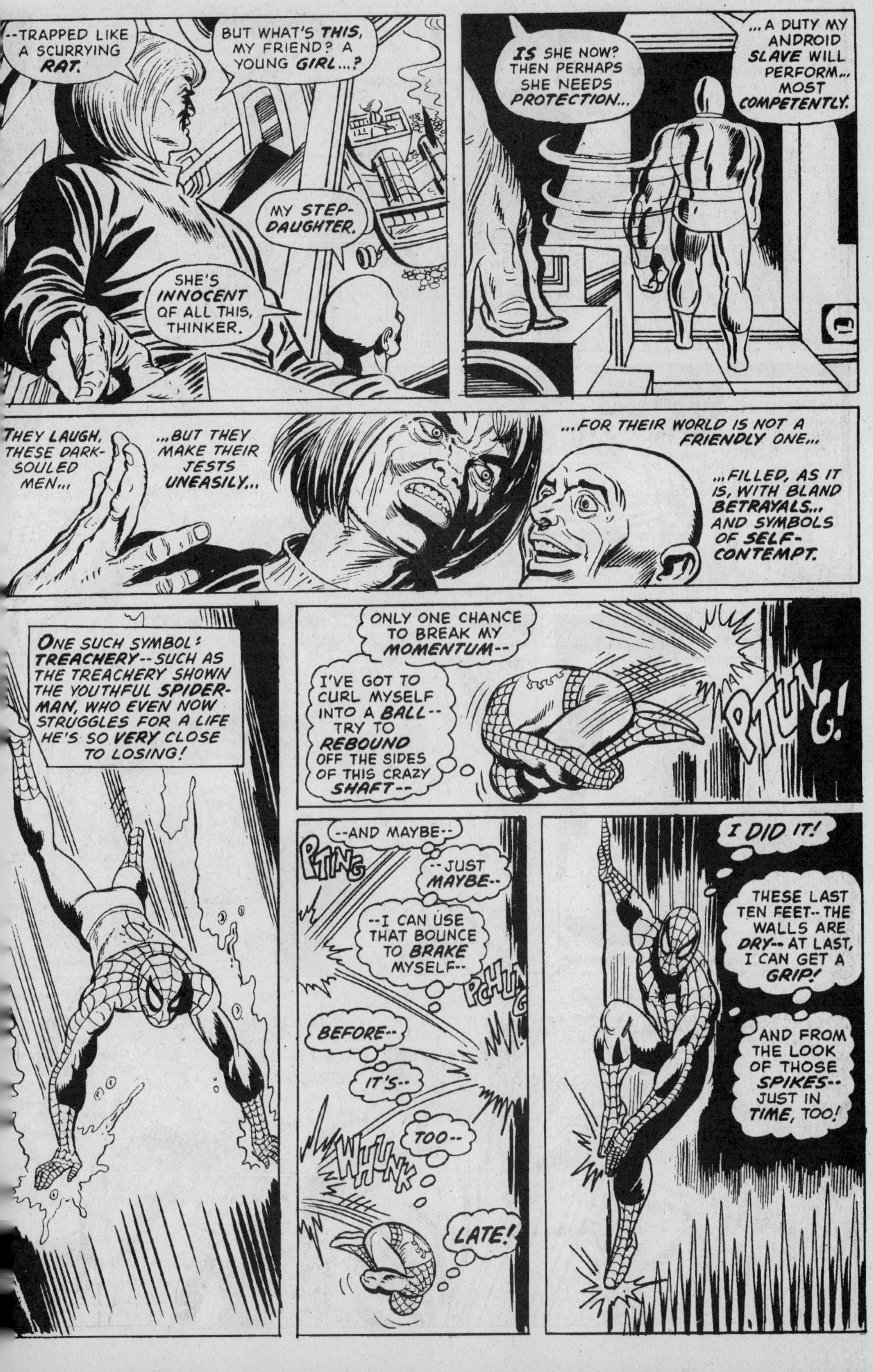
--TRAPPED LIKE A SCURRYING RAT.
BUT WHAT'S THIS, MY FRIEND? A YOUNG GIRL...?
MY STEP-DAUGHTER.
SHE'S INNOCENT OF ALL THIS, THINKER.
IS SHE NOW? THEN PERHAPS SHE NEEDS PROTECTION...
...A DUTY MY ANDROID SLAVE WILL PERFORM... MOST COMPETENTLY.
THEY LAUGH, THESE DARK-SOULED MEN...
...BUT THEY MAKE THEIR JESTS UNEASILY...
...FOR THEIR WORLD IS NOT A FRIENDLY ONE...
...FILLED, AS IT IS, WITH BLAND BETRAYALS... AND SYMBOLS OF SELF-CONTEMPT.
ONE SUCH SYMBOL: TREACHERY--SUCH AS THE TREACHERY SHOWN THE YOUTHFUL SPIDER-MAN, WHO EVEN NOW STRUGGLES FOR A LIFE HE'S SO VERY CLOSE TO LOSING!
ONLY ONE CHANCE TO BREAK MY MOMENTUM--
I'VE GOT TO CURL MYSELF INTO A BALL--TRY TO REBOUND OFF THE SIDES OF THIS CRAZY SHAFT--
PTUNG!
--AND MAYBE--
PTING
--JUST MAYBE--
--I CAN USE THAT BOUNCE TO BRAKE MYSELF--
PCHUNG
BEFORE--
IT'S--
TOO--
WHUNK
LATE!
I DID IT!
THESE LAST TEN FEET--THE WALLS ARE DRY--AT LAST, I CAN GET A GRIP!
AND FROM THE LOOK OF THOSE SPIKES--JUST IN TIME, TOO!

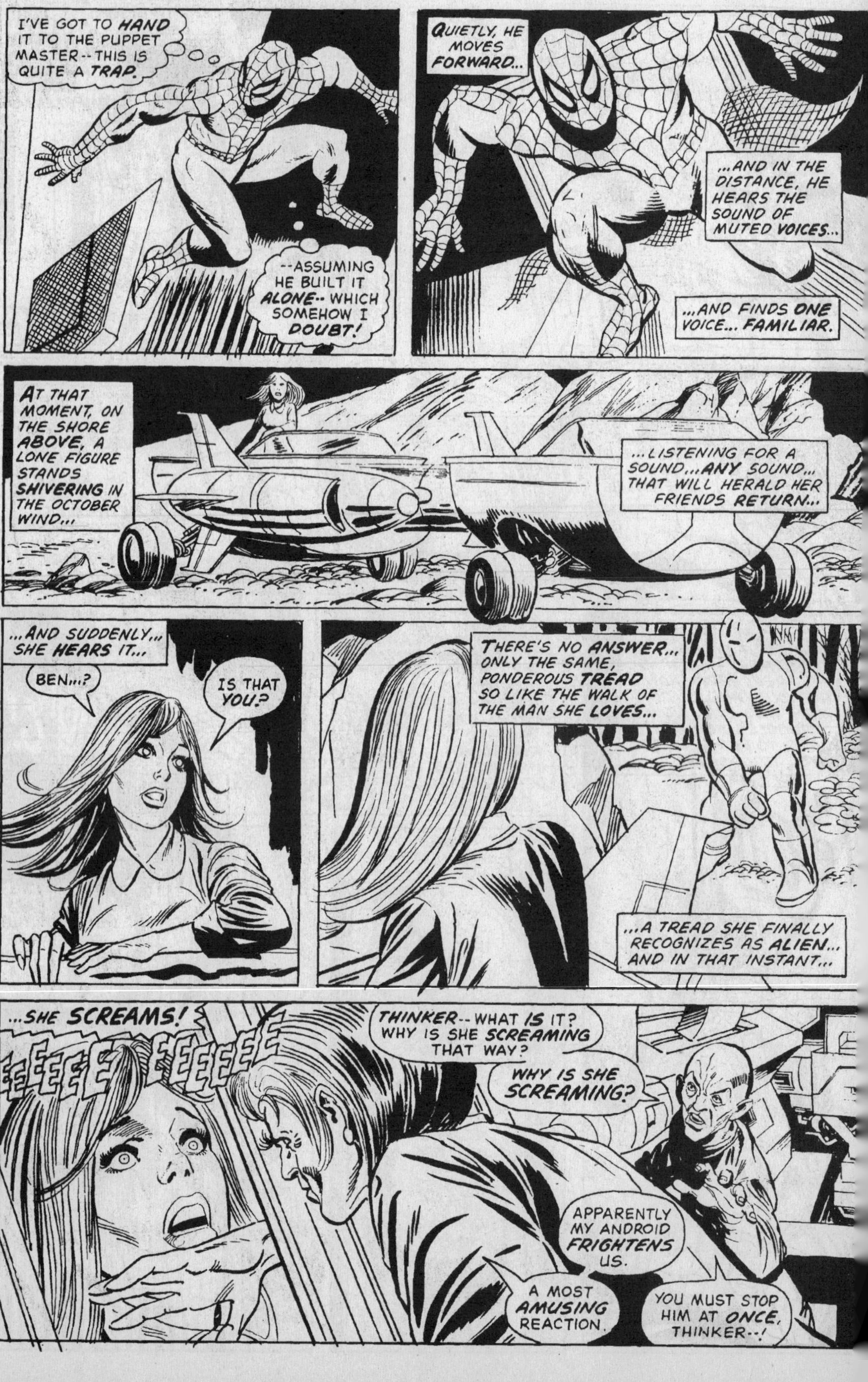
I'VE GOT TO HAND IT TO THE PUPPET MASTER--THIS IS QUITE A TRAP.
--ASSUMING HE BUILT IT ALONE-- WHICH SOMEHOW I DOUBT!
QUIETLY, HE MOVES FORWARD...
...AND IN THE DISTANCE, HE HEARS THE SOUND OF MUTED VOICES...
...AND FINDS ONE VOICE... FAMILIAR.
AT THAT MOMENT, ON THE SHORE ABOVE, A LONE FIGURE STANDS SHIVERING IN THE OCTOBER WIND...
...LISTENING FOR A SOUND... ANY SOUND... THAT WILL HERALD HER FRIENDS RETURN...
...AND SUDDENLY... SHE HEARS IT...
BEN...?
IS THAT YOU?
THERE'S NO ANSWER... ONLY THE SAME, PONDEROUS TREAD SO LIKE THE WALK OF THE MAN SHE LOVES...
...A TREAD SHE FINALLY RECOGNIZES AS ALIEN... AND IN THAT INSTANT...
...SHE SCREAMS!
EEEEEEEEEEE
THINKER--WHAT IS IT? WHY IS SHE SCREAMING THAT WAY?
WHY IS SHE SCREAMING?
APPARENTLY MY ANDROID FRIGHTENS US.
A MOST AMUSING REACTION.
YOU MUST STOP HIM AT ONCE, THINKER--!

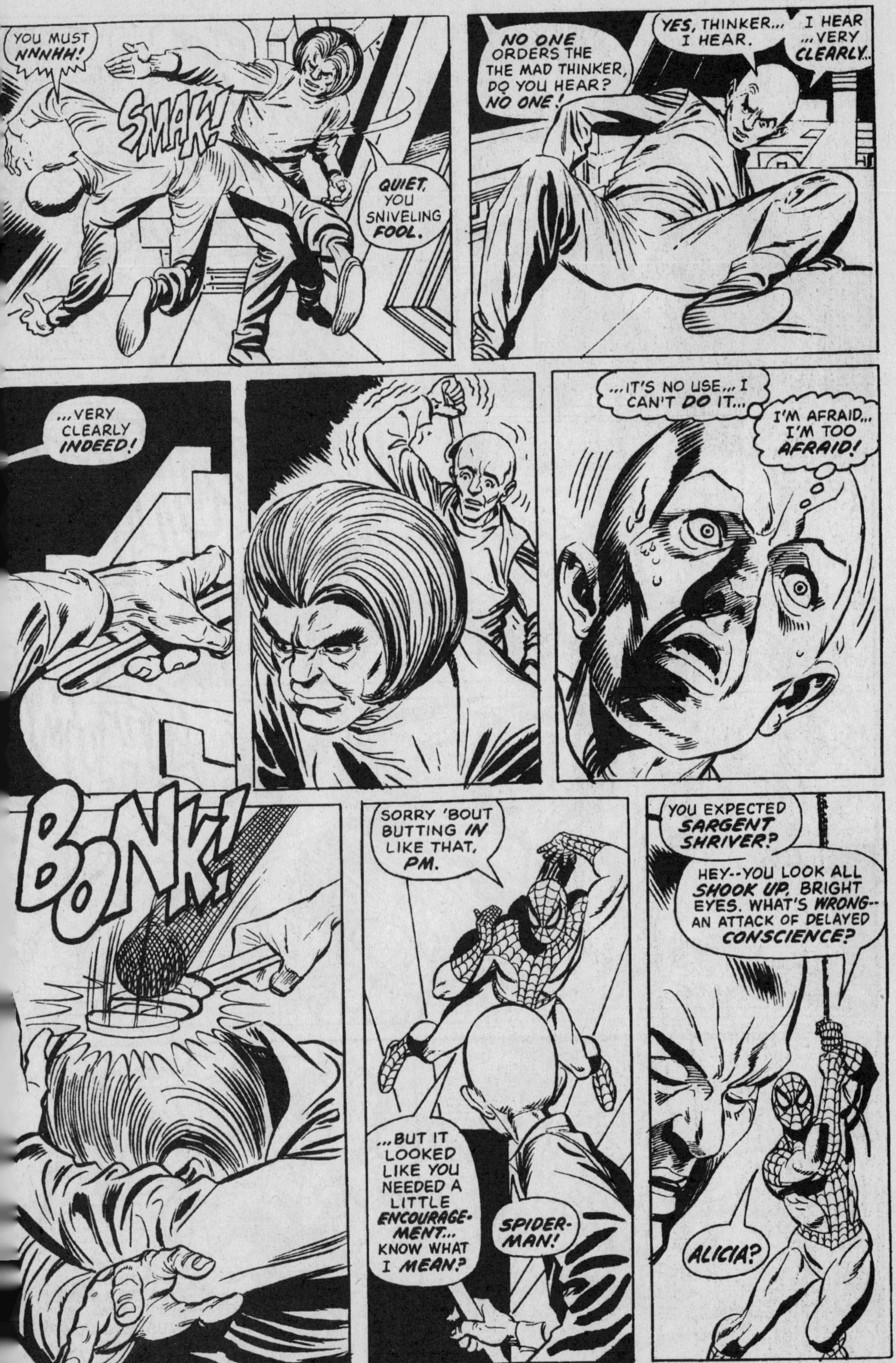

YOU MUST NNNHH!
SMAK!
QUIET, YOU SNIVELING FOOL.
NO ONE ORDERS THE THE MAD THINKER, DO YOU HEAR? NO ONE!
YES, THINKER... I HEAR.
I HEAR ...VERY CLEARLY...
...VERY CLEARLY INDEED!
...IT'S NO USE... I CAN'T DO IT...
I'M AFRAID... I'M TOO AFRAID!
BONK!
SORRY 'BOUT BUTTING IN LIKE THAT, PM.
...BUT IT LOOKED LIKE YOU NEEDED A LITTLE ENCOURAGE-MENT... KNOW WHAT I MEAN?
SPIDER-MAN!
YOU EXPECTED SARGENT SHRIVER?
HEY--YOU LOOK ALL SHOOK UP, BRIGHT EYES. WHAT'S WRONG--AN ATTACK OF DELAYED CONSCIENCE?
ALICIA?

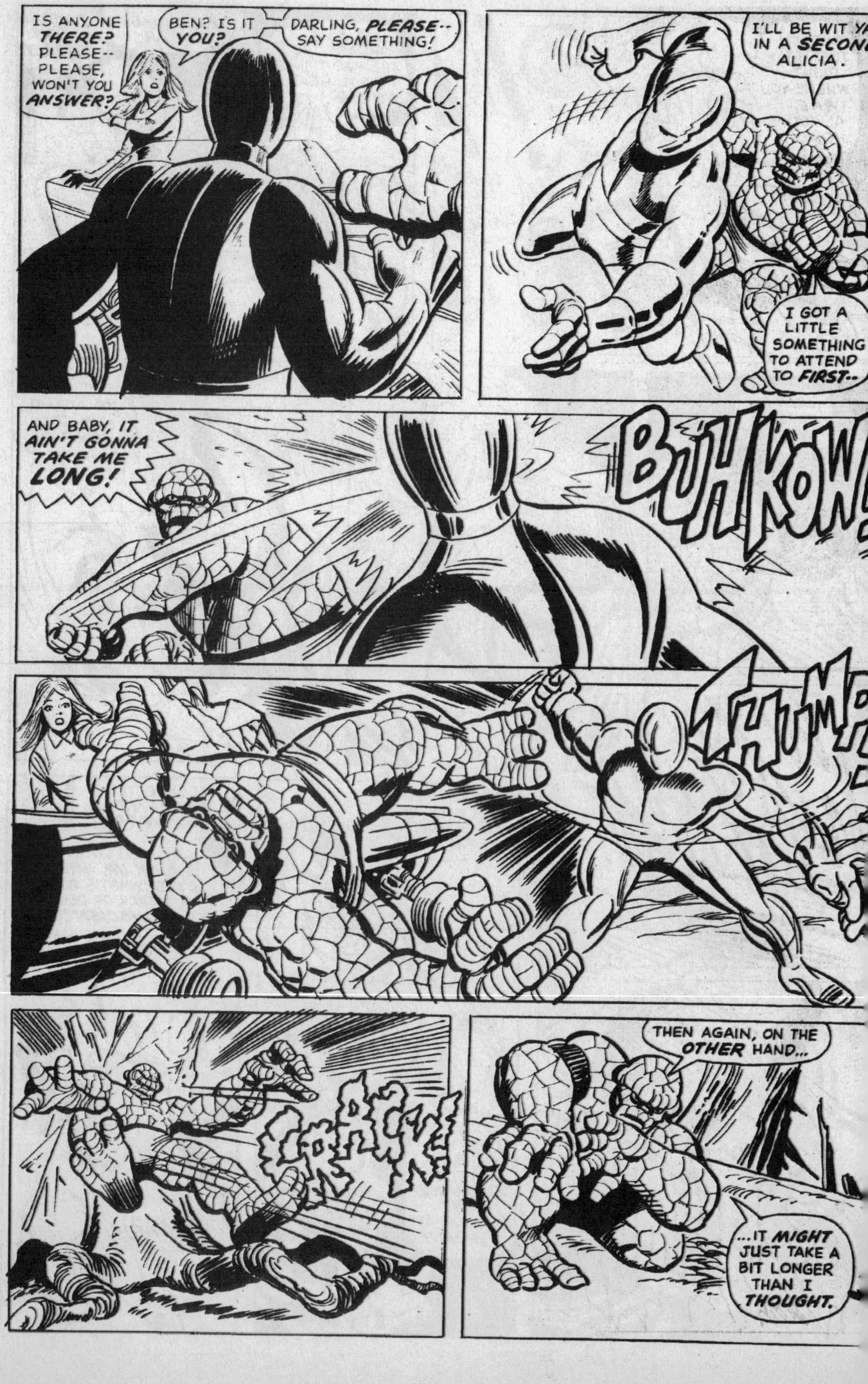
IS ANYONE THERE? PLEASE-- PLEASE, WON'T YOU ANSWER?
BEN? IS IT YOU?
DARLING, PLEASE-- SAY SOMETHING!
I'LL BE WIT YA IN A SECOND ALICIA.
I GOT A LITTLE SOMETHING TO ATTEND TO FIRST--
AND BABY, IT AIN'T GONNA TAKE ME LONG!
BUHKOW
THUMP
CRACK!
THEN AGAIN, ON THE OTHER HAND...
...IT MIGHT JUST TAKE A BIT LONGER THAN I THOUGHT.

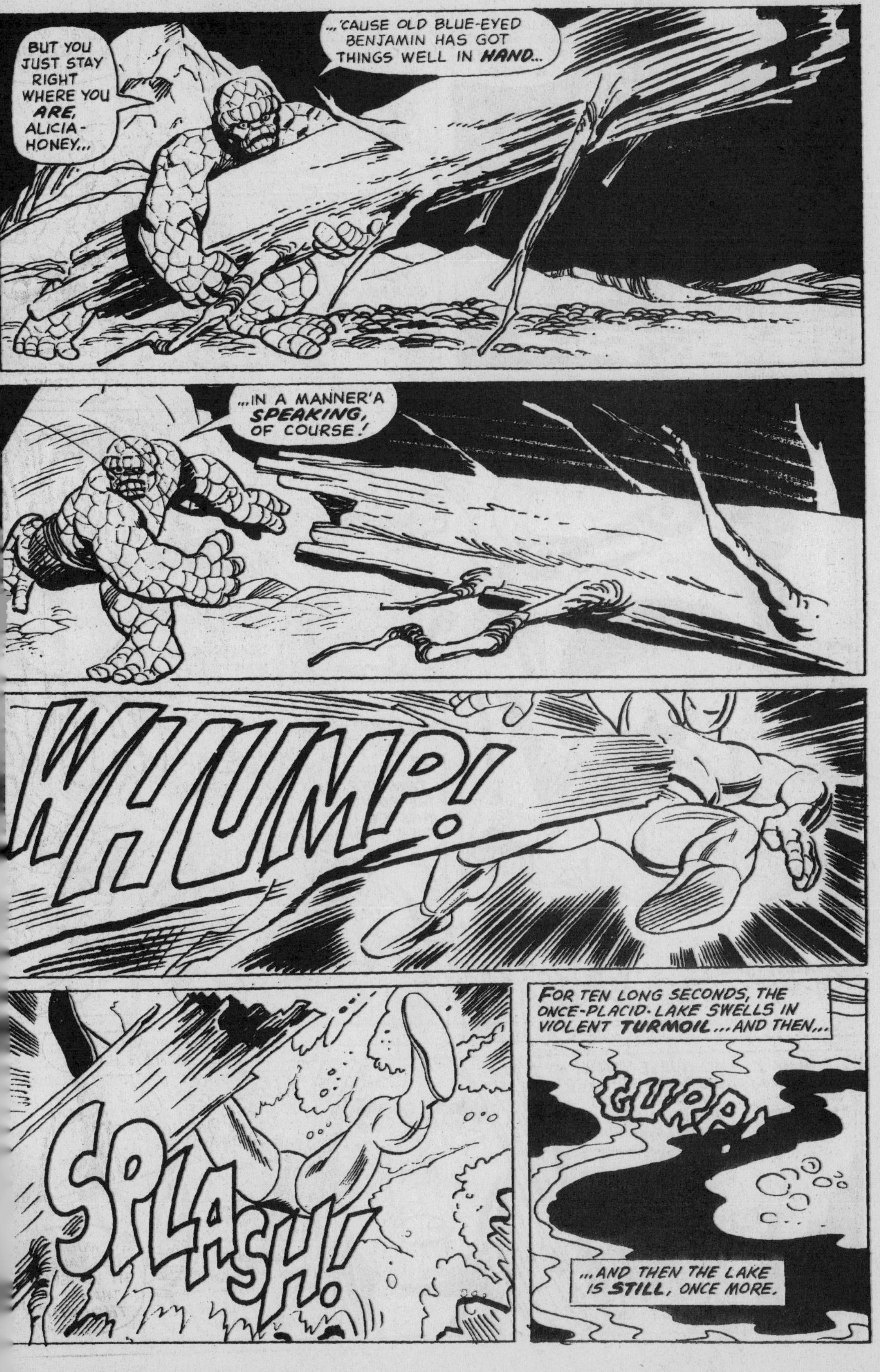

BUT YOU JUST STAY RIGHT WHERE YOU ARE, ALICIA-HONEY...
...'CAUSE OLD BLUE-EYED BENJAMIN HAS GOT THINGS WELL IN HAND...
...IN A MANNER'A SPEAKING, OF COURSE!
WHUMP!
SPLASH!
FOR TEN LONG SECONDS, THE ONCE-PLACID LAKE SWELLS IN VIOLENT TURMOIL...AND THEN...
GURP.
...AND THEN THE LAKE IS STILL, ONCE MORE.

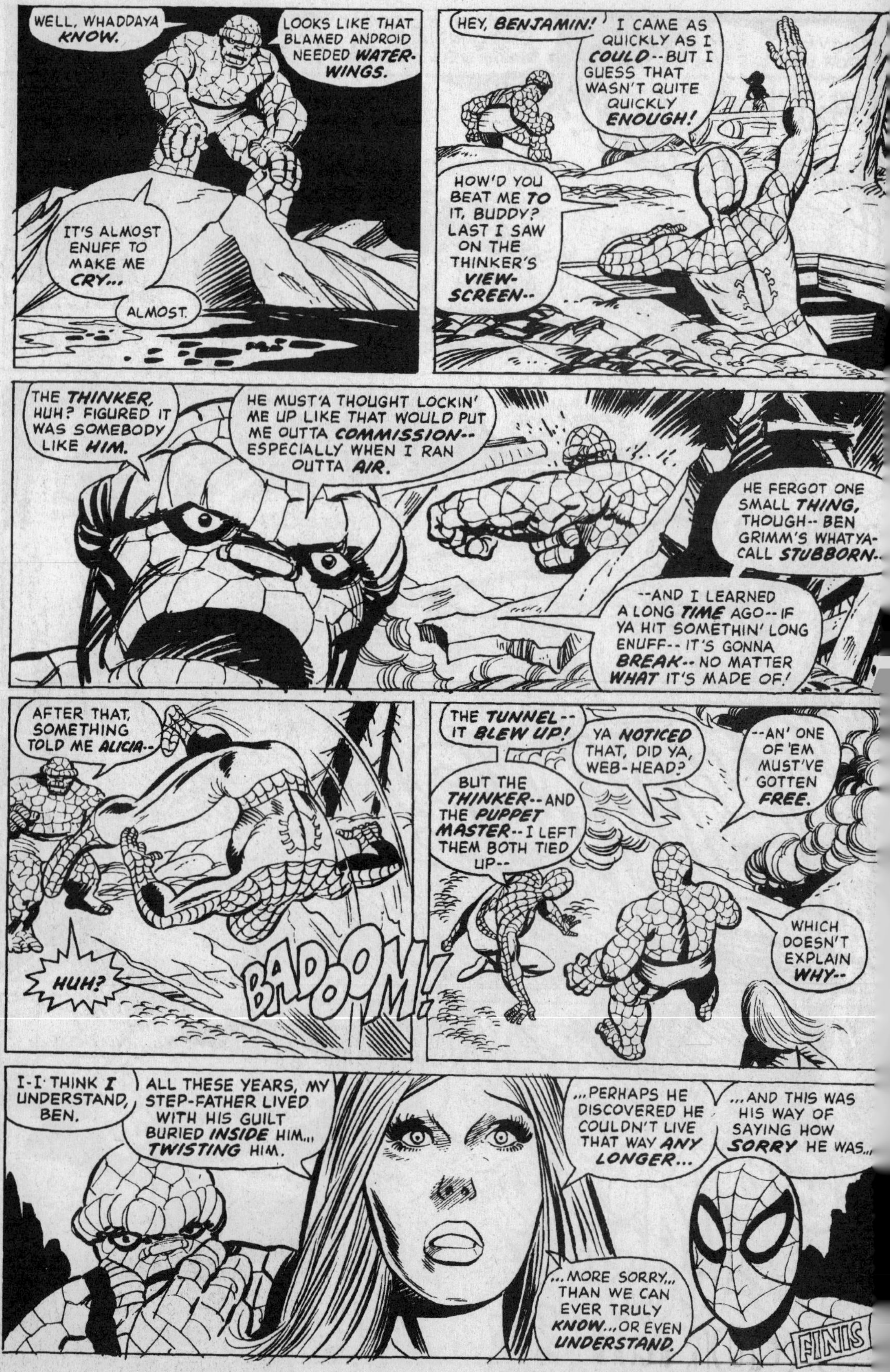

WELL, WHADDAYA KNOW.
LOOKS LIKE THAT BLAMED ANDROID NEEDED WATER-WINGS.
IT'S ALMOST ENUFF TO MAKE ME CRY...
ALMOST.
HEY, BENJAMIN!
I CAME AS QUICKLY AS I COULD--BUT I GUESS THAT WASN'T QUITE QUICKLY ENOUGH!
HOW'D YOU BEAT ME TO IT, BUDDY? LAST I SAW ON THE THINKER'S VIEW-SCREEN--
THE THINKER, HUH? FIGURED IT WAS SOMEBODY LIKE HIM.
HE MUST'A THOUGHT LOCKIN' ME UP LIKE THAT WOULD PUT ME OUTTA COMMISSION--ESPECIALLY WHEN I RAN OUTTA AIR.
HE FERGOT ONE SMALL THING, THOUGH--BEN GRIMM'S WHATYA-CALL STUBBORN--
--AND I LEARNED A LONG TIME AGO--IF YA HIT SOMETHIN' LONG ENUFF--IT'S GONNA BREAK--NO MATTER WHAT IT'S MADE OF!
AFTER THAT, SOMETHING TOLD ME ALICIA--
HUH?
BADOOOM!
THE TUNNEL--IT BLEW UP!
YA NOTICED THAT, DID YA, WEB-HEAD?
BUT THE THINKER--AND THE PUPPET MASTER--I LEFT THEM BOTH TIED UP--
--AN' ONE OF 'EM MUST'VE GOTTEN FREE.
WHICH DOESN'T EXPLAIN WHY--
I-I-THINK I UNDERSTAND, BEN.
ALL THESE YEARS, MY STEP-FATHER LIVED WITH HIS GUILT BURIED INSIDE HIM... TWISTING HIM.
...PERHAPS HE DISCOVERED HE COULDN'T LIVE THAT WAY ANY LONGER...
...AND THIS WAS HIS WAY OF SAYING HOW SORRY HE WAS...
...MORE SORRY... THAN WE CAN EVER TRULY KNOW...OR EVEN UNDERSTAND.
FINIS

MARVEL
TEAM-UP
MARVEL COMICS GROUP™
APPROVED BY THE COMICS CODE AUTHORITY
20¢
7
MAR
02147
MARVEL TEAM-UP™
FEATURING
SPIDER-MAN™
AND
THE MIGHTY
THOR®
THUNDER GOD OR HUMAN SPIDER-- NOTHING CAN STAND AGAINST KRYLLK!
FIRST EARTH SHALL FALL--AND THEN ASGARD ITSELF!!
TWO WORLDS TO CONQUER!

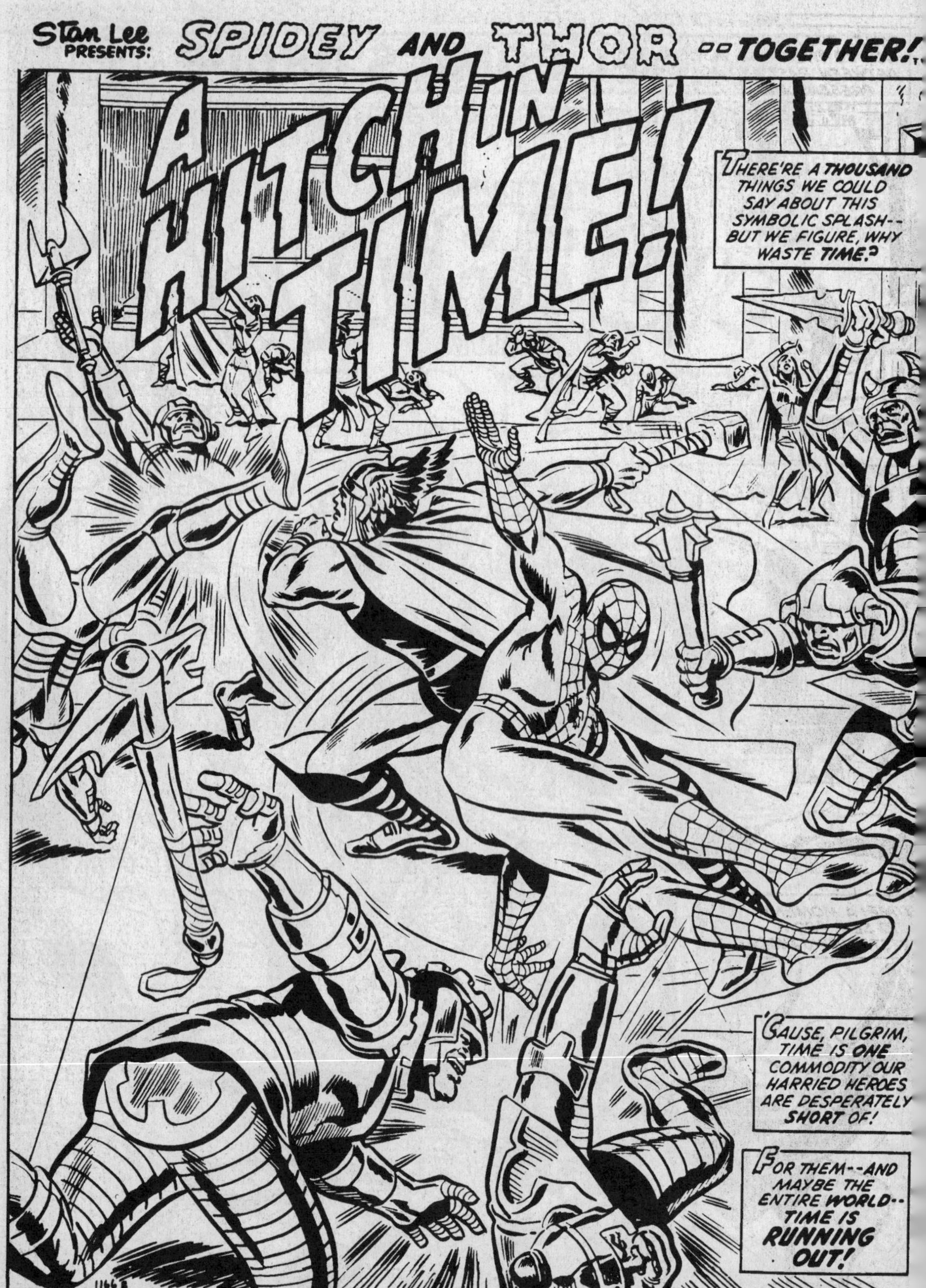
Stan Lee PRESENTS: SPIDEY AND THOR --TOGETHER!
A HITCH IN TIME!
THERE'RE A THOUSAND THINGS WE COULD SAY ABOUT THIS SYMBOLIC SPLASH--BUT WE FIGURE, WHY WASTE TIME?
'CAUSE, PILGRIM, TIME IS ONE COMMODITY OUR HARRIED HEROES ARE DESPERATELY SHORT OF!
FOR THEM--AND MAYBE THE ENTIRE WORLD--TIME IS RUNNING OUT!
GERRY CONWAY SCRIPTER / ROSS ANDRU ARTIST / JIM MOONEY INKER / ARTIE SIMEK LETTERER / ROY THOMA EDITOR

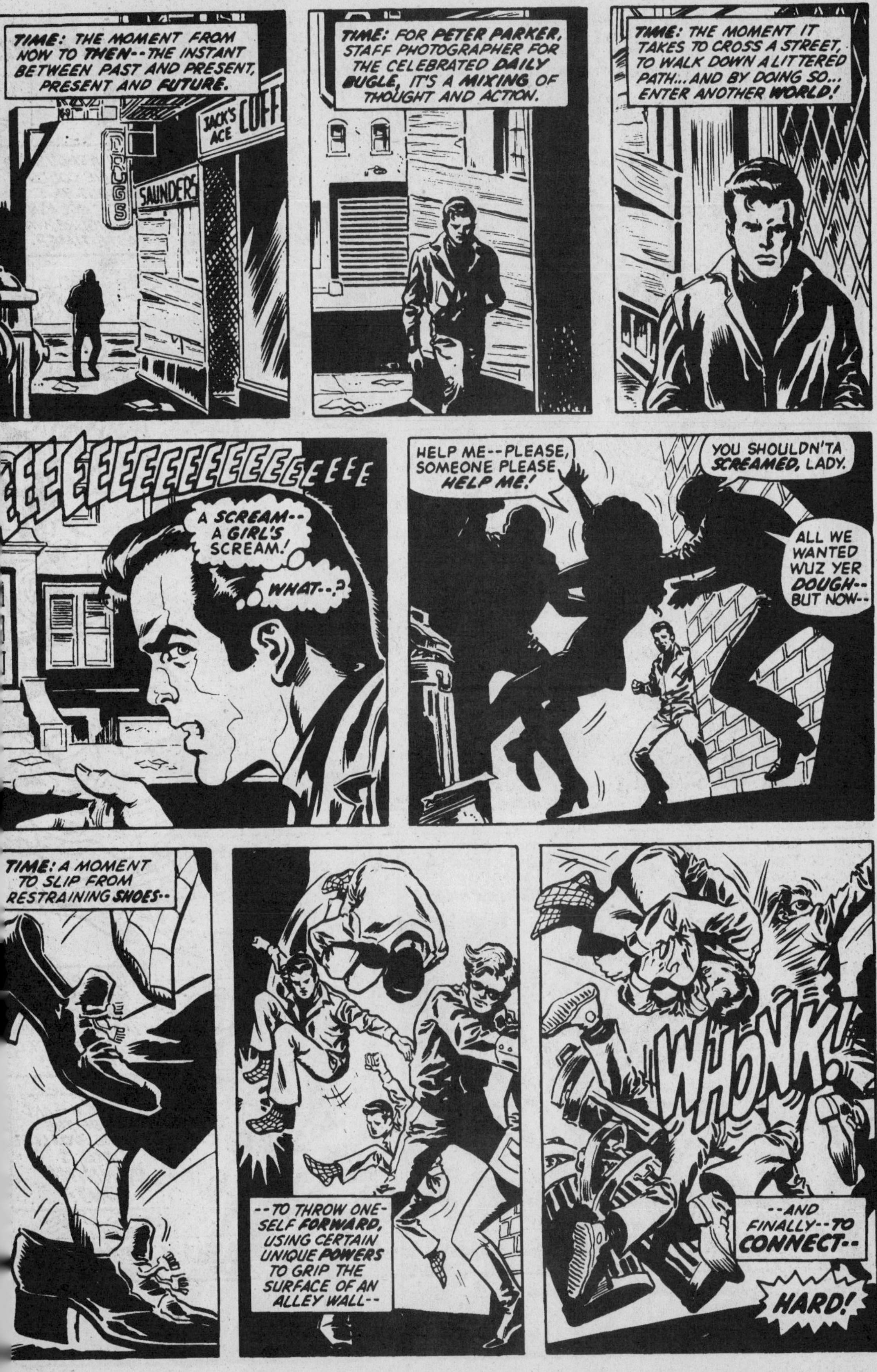

TIME: THE MOMENT FROM NOW TO THEN--THE INSTANT BETWEEN PAST AND PRESENT, PRESENT AND FUTURE.
JACK'S ACE
COFF
DRUGS
SAUNDERS
TIME: FOR PETER PARKER, STAFF PHOTOGRAPHER FOR THE CELEBRATED DAILY BUGLE, IT'S A MIXING OF THOUGHT AND ACTION.
TIME: THE MOMENT IT TAKES TO CROSS A STREET, TO WALK DOWN A LITTERED PATH... AND BY DOING SO... ENTER ANOTHER WORLD!
EEEEEEEEEEEEEEEEE
A SCREAM-- A GIRL'S SCREAM!
WHAT--?
HELP ME--PLEASE, SOMEONE PLEASE HELP ME!
YOU SHOULDN'TA SCREAMED, LADY.
ALL WE WANTED WUZ YER DOUGH-- BUT NOW--
TIME: A MOMENT TO SLIP FROM RESTRAINING SHOES--
--TO THROW ONE-SELF FORWARD, USING CERTAIN UNIQUE POWERS TO GRIP THE SURFACE OF AN ALLEY WALL--
WHONK!
--AND FINALLY--TO CONNECT--
HARD!

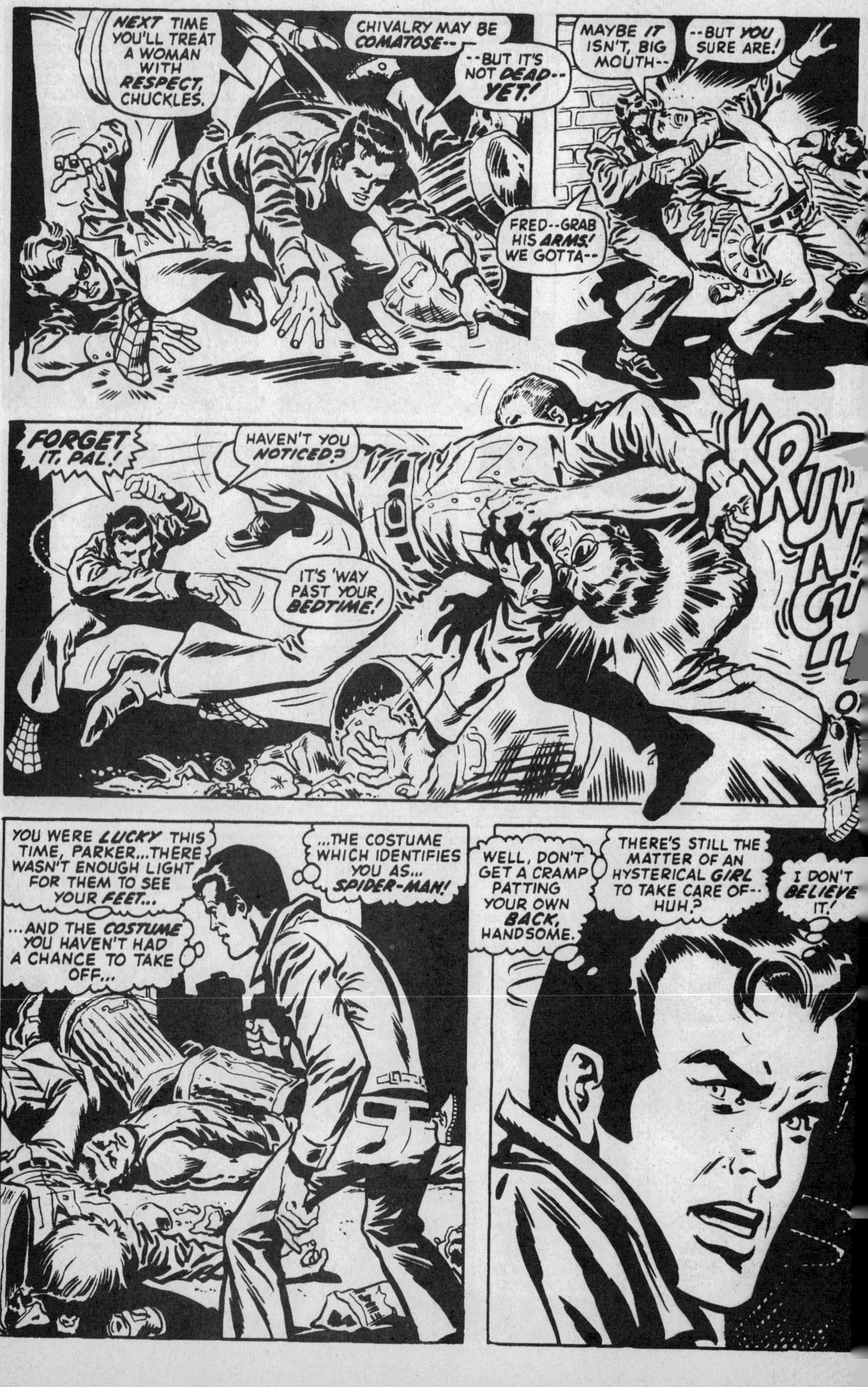
NEXT TIME YOU'LL TREAT A WOMAN WITH RESPECT, CHUCKLES.
CHIVALRY MAY BE COMATOSE--
--BUT IT'S NOT DEAD--YET!
MAYBE IT ISN'T, BIG MOUTH--
--BUT YOU SURE ARE!
FRED--GRAB HIS ARMS! WE GOTTA--
FORGET IT, PAL!
HAVEN'T YOU NOTICED?
IT'S 'WAY PAST YOUR BEDTIME!
KRUNNACH!
YOU WERE LUCKY THIS TIME, PARKER...THERE WASN'T ENOUGH LIGHT FOR THEM TO SEE YOUR FEET...
...AND THE COSTUME YOU HAVEN'T HAD A CHANCE TO TAKE OFF...
...THE COSTUME WHICH IDENTIFIES YOU AS... SPIDER-MAN!
WELL, DON'T GET A CRAMP PATTING YOUR OWN BACK, HANDSOME.
THERE'S STILL THE MATTER OF AN HYSTERICAL GIRL TO TAKE CARE OF-- HUH?
I DON'T BELIEVE IT!

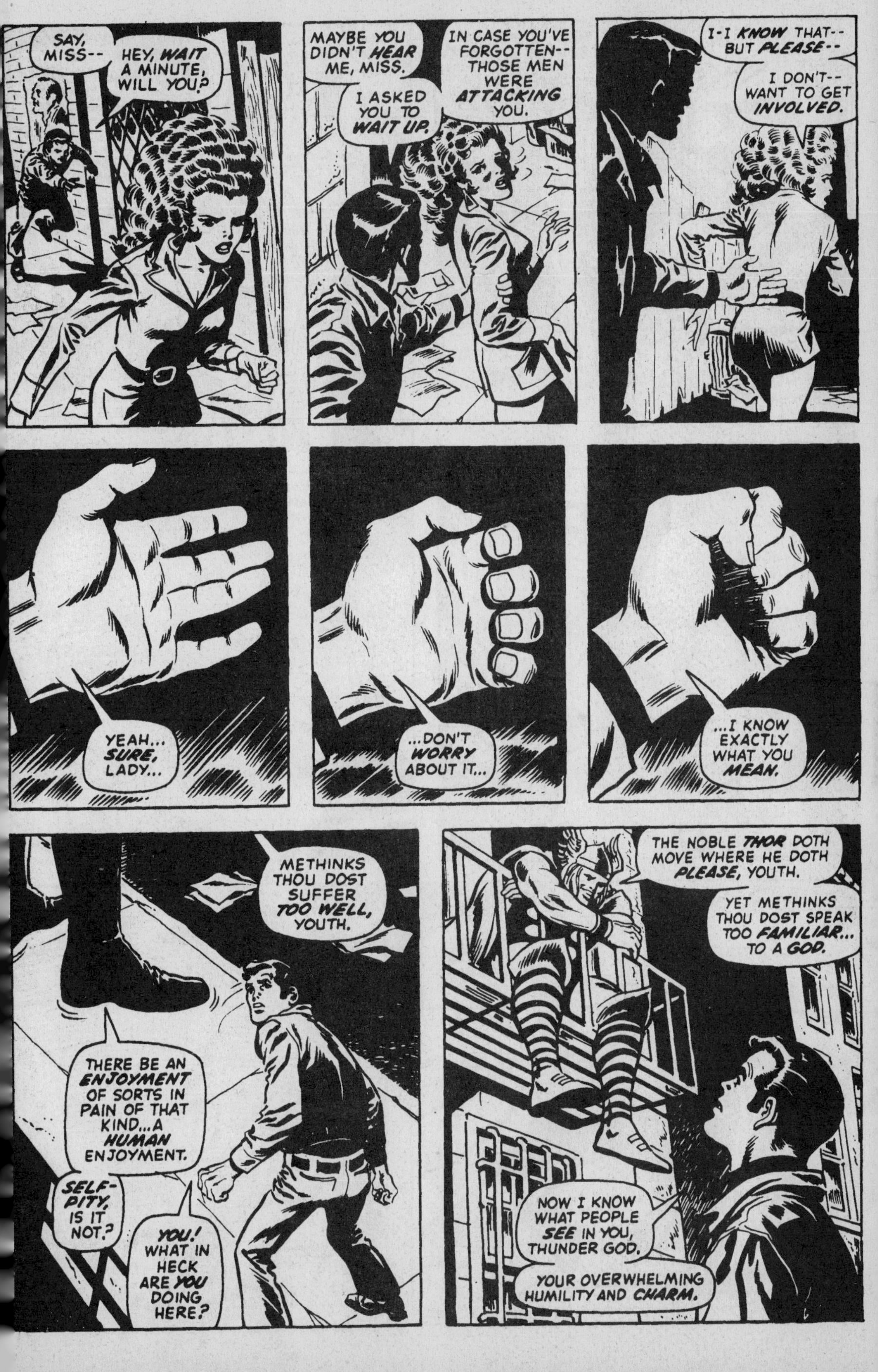

SAY, MISS--
HEY, WAIT A MINUTE, WILL YOU?
MAYBE YOU DIDN'T HEAR ME, MISS.
I ASKED YOU TO WAIT UP.
IN CASE YOU'VE FORGOTTEN-- THOSE MEN WERE ATTACKING YOU.
I-I KNOW THAT-- BUT PLEASE--
I DON'T-- WANT TO GET INVOLVED.
YEAH... SURE, LADY...
...DON'T WORRY ABOUT IT...
...I KNOW EXACTLY WHAT YOU MEAN.
METHINKS THOU DOST SUFFER TOO WELL, YOUTH.
THERE BE AN ENJOYMENT OF SORTS IN PAIN OF THAT KIND...A HUMAN ENJOYMENT.
SELF-PITY, IS IT NOT?
YOU! WHAT IN HECK ARE YOU DOING HERE?
THE NOBLE THOR DOTH MOVE WHERE HE DOTH PLEASE, YOUTH.
YET METHINKS THOU DOST SPEAK TOO FAMILIAR... TO A GOD.
NOW I KNOW WHAT PEOPLE SEE IN YOU, THUNDER GOD.
YOUR OVERWHELMING HUMILITY AND CHARM.

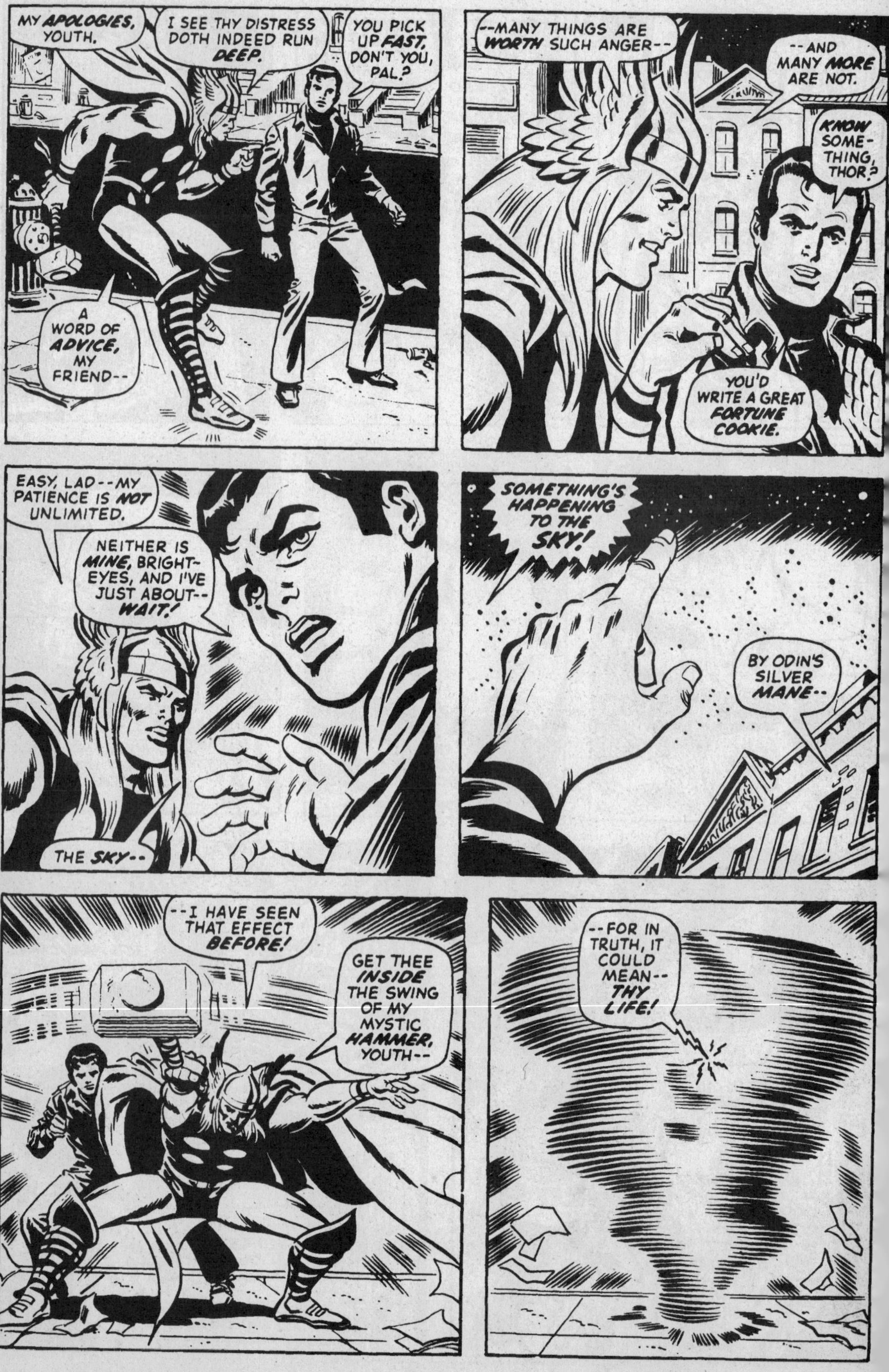
MY APOLOGIES, YOUTH.
I SEE THY DISTRESS DOTH INDEED RUN DEEP.
YOU PICK UP FAST, DON'T YOU, PAL?
A WORD OF ADVICE, MY FRIEND--
--MANY THINGS ARE WORTH SUCH ANGER--
--AND MANY MORE ARE NOT.
KNOW SOMETHING, THOR?
YOU'D WRITE A GREAT FORTUNE COOKIE.
EASY, LAD--MY PATIENCE IS NOT UNLIMITED.
NEITHER IS MINE, BRIGHT-EYES, AND I'VE JUST ABOUT--WAIT!
THE SKY--
SOMETHING'S HAPPENING TO THE SKY!
BY ODIN'S SILVER MANE--
--I HAVE SEEN THAT EFFECT BEFORE!
GET THEE INSIDE THE SWING OF MY MYSTIC HAMMER, YOUTH--
--FOR IN TRUTH, IT COULD MEAN--THY LIFE!

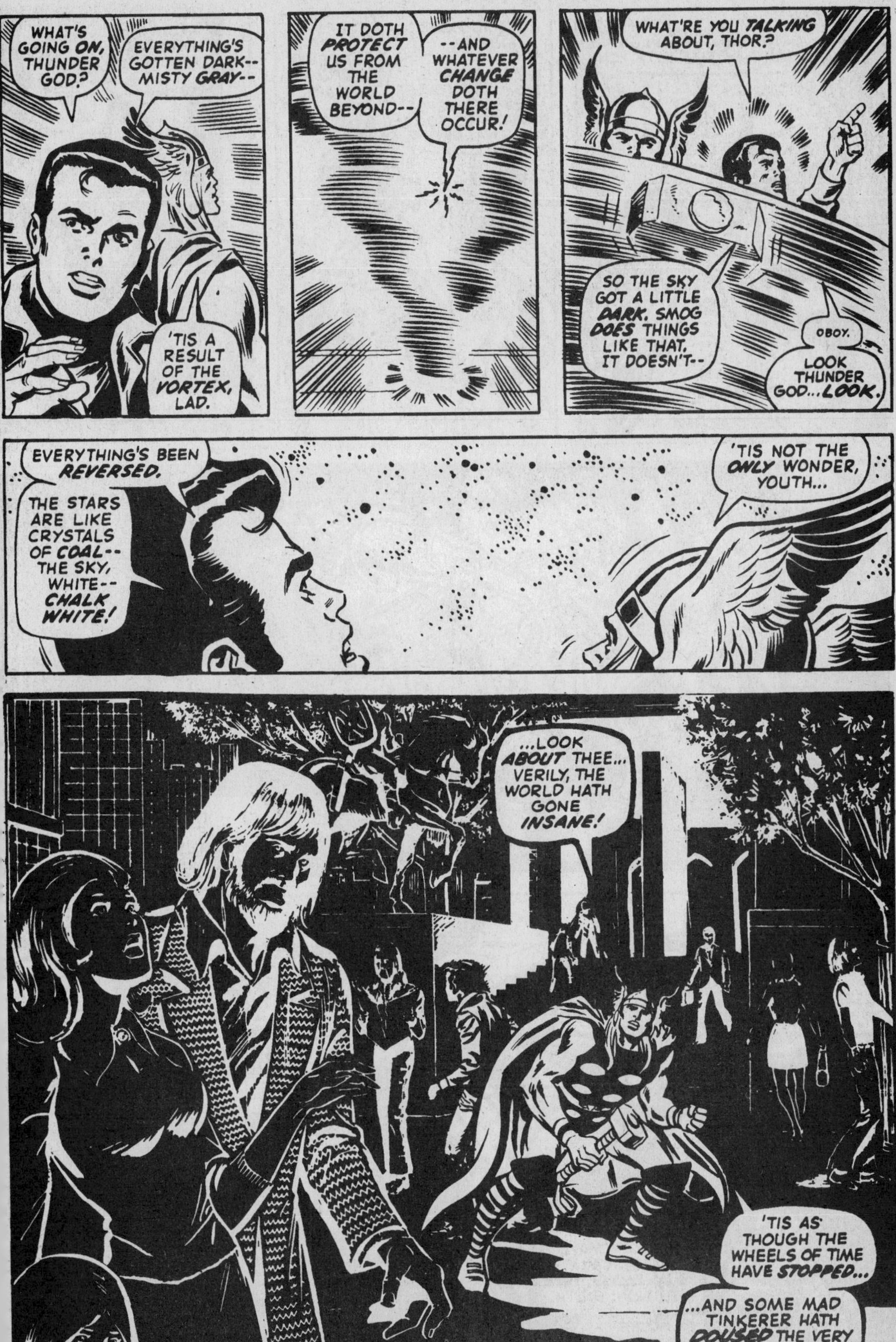

WHAT'S GOING ON, THUNDER GOD?
EVERYTHING'S GOTTEN DARK-- MISTY GRAY--
'TIS A RESULT OF THE VORTEX, LAD.
IT DOTH PROTECT US FROM THE WORLD BEYOND--
--AND WHATEVER CHANGE DOTH THERE OCCUR!
WHAT'RE YOU TALKING ABOUT, THOR?
SO THE SKY GOT A LITTLE DARK. SMOG DOES THINGS LIKE THAT. IT DOESN'T--
OBOY.
LOOK THUNDER GOD...LOOK.
EVERYTHING'S BEEN REVERSED.
THE STARS ARE LIKE CRYSTALS OF COAL-- THE SKY, WHITE-- CHALK WHITE!
'TIS NOT THE ONLY WONDER, YOUTH...
...LOOK ABOUT THEE... VERILY, THE WORLD HATH GONE INSANE!
'TIS AS THOUGH THE WHEELS OF TIME HAVE STOPPED...
...AND SOME MAD TINKERER HATH DOUSED THE VERY LIGHT OF REALITY!

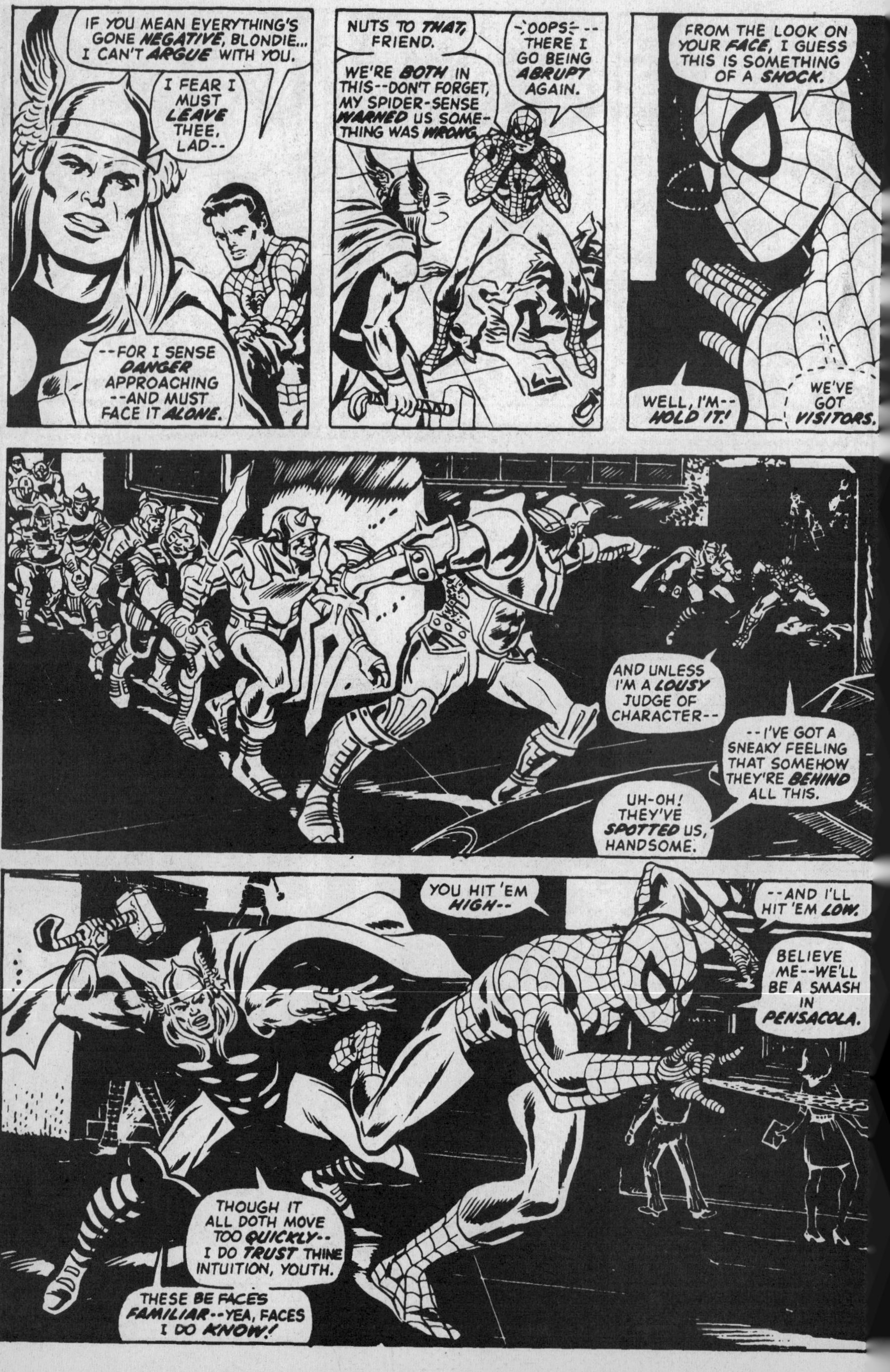
IF YOU MEAN EVERYTHING'S GONE NEGATIVE, BLONDIE... I CAN'T ARGUE WITH YOU.
I FEAR I MUST LEAVE THEE, LAD--
--FOR I SENSE DANGER APPROACHING --AND MUST FACE IT ALONE.
NUTS TO THAT, FRIEND.
WE'RE BOTH IN THIS--DON'T FORGET, MY SPIDER-SENSE WARNED US SOMETHING WAS WRONG.
OOPS-- THERE I GO BEING ABRUPT AGAIN.
FROM THE LOOK ON YOUR FACE, I GUESS THIS IS SOMETHING OF A SHOCK.
WELL, I'M-- HOLD IT!
WE'VE GOT VISITORS.
AND UNLESS I'M A LOUSY JUDGE OF CHARACTER--
--I'VE GOT A SNEAKY FEELING THAT SOMEHOW THEY'RE BEHIND ALL THIS.
UH-OH! THEY'VE SPOTTED US, HANDSOME.
YOU HIT 'EM HIGH--
--AND I'LL HIT 'EM LOW.
BELIEVE ME--WE'LL BE A SMASH IN PENSACOLA.
THOUGH IT ALL DOTH MOVE TOO QUICKLY-- I DO TRUST THINE INTUITION, YOUTH.
THESE BE FACES FAMILIAR--YEA, FACES I DO KNOW!

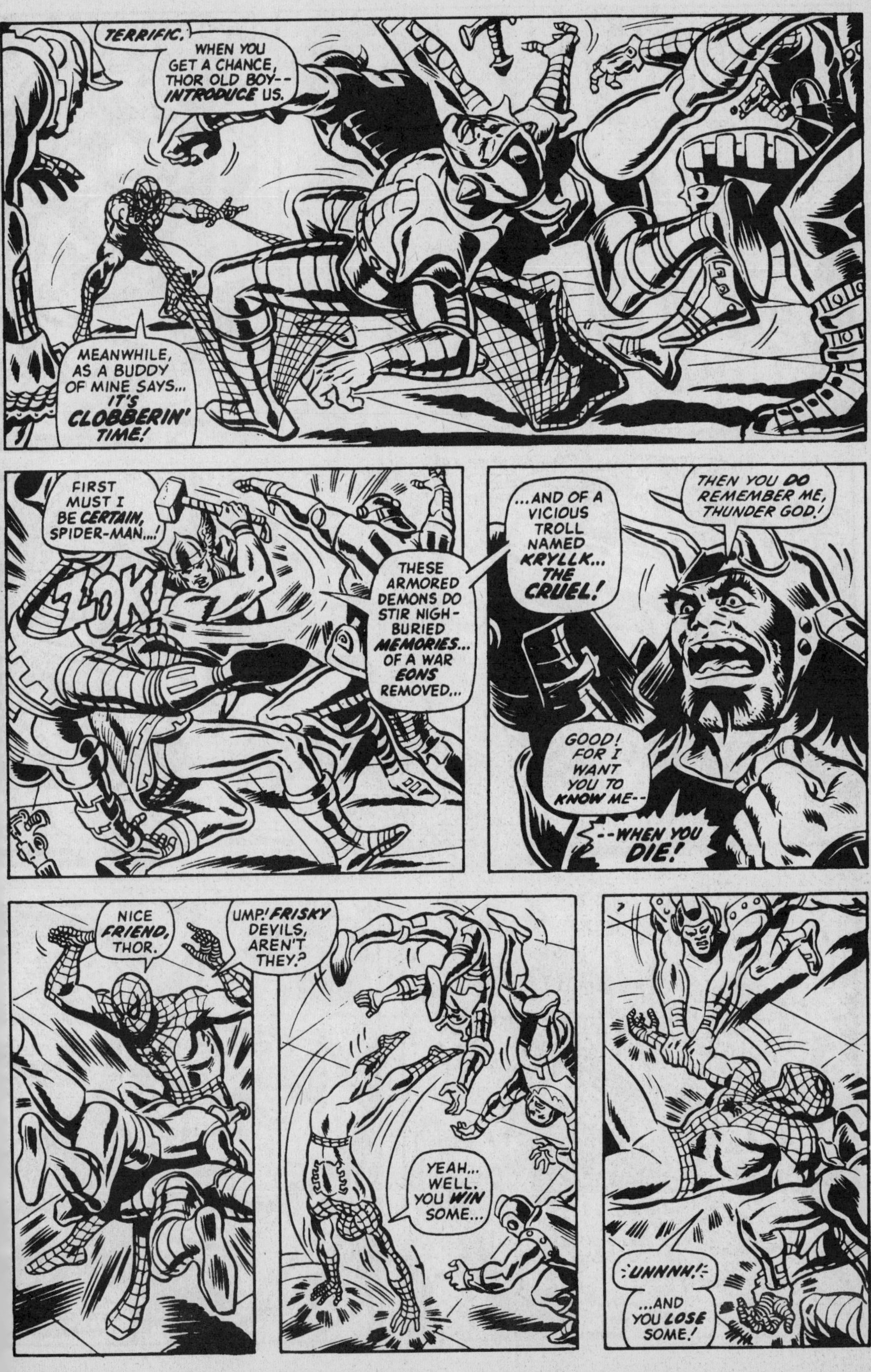
TERRIFIC.
WHEN YOU GET A CHANCE, THOR OLD BOY--INTRODUCE US.
MEANWHILE, AS A BUDDY OF MINE SAYS... IT'S CLOBBERIN' TIME!
FIRST MUST I BE CERTAIN, SPIDER-MAN...!
ZOK!
THESE ARMORED DEMONS DO STIR NIGH-BURIED MEMORIES... OF A WAR EONS REMOVED...
...AND OF A VICIOUS TROLL NAMED KRYLLK... THE CRUEL!
THEN YOU DO REMEMBER ME, THUNDER GOD!
GOOD! FOR I WANT YOU TO KNOW ME--
--WHEN YOU DIE!
NICE FRIEND, THOR.
UMP! FRISKY DEVILS, AREN'T THEY?
YEAH... WELL. YOU WIN SOME...
UNNNH!
...AND YOU LOSE SOME!

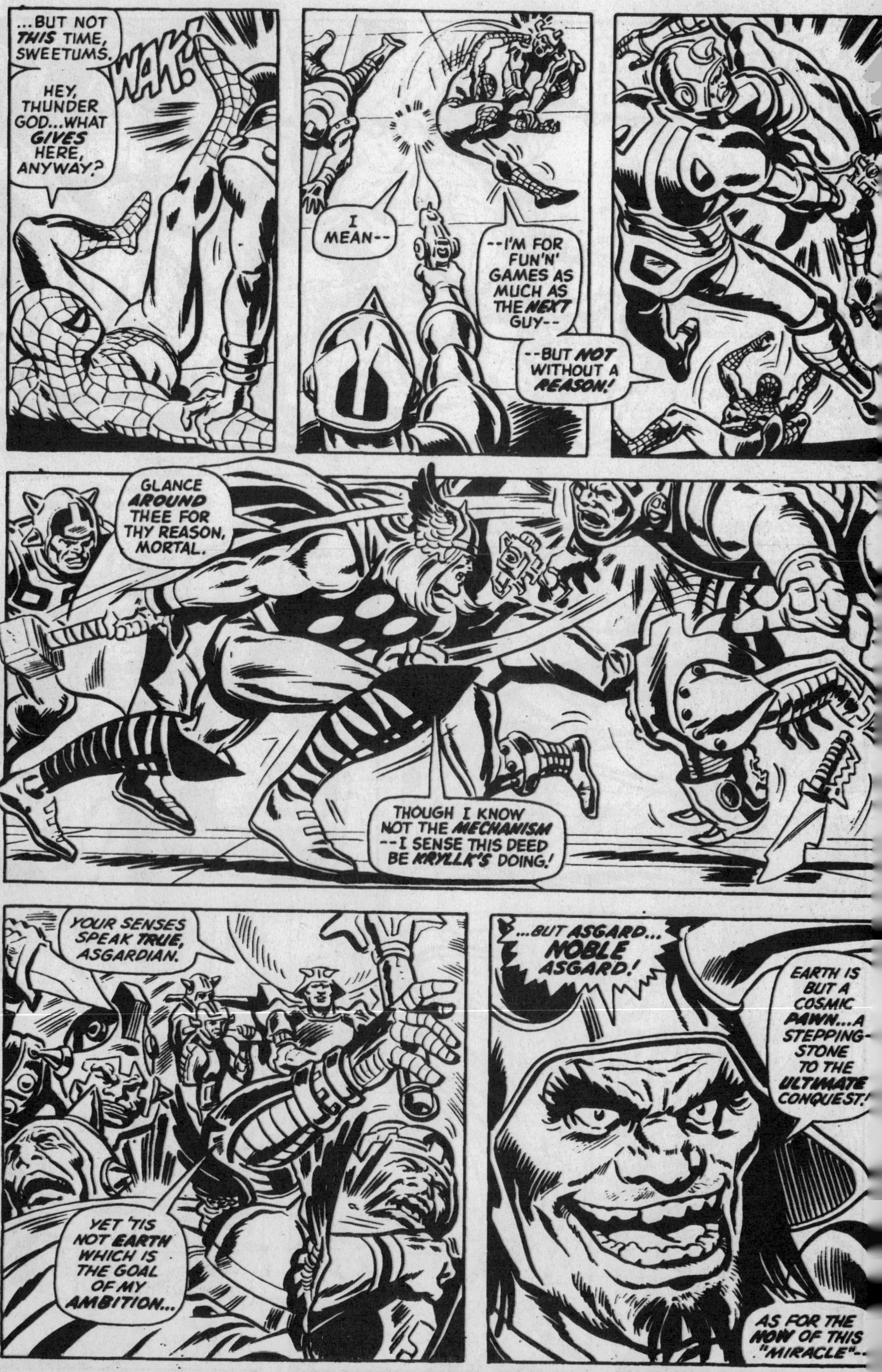
...BUT NOT THIS TIME, SWEETUMS.
WAK!
HEY, THUNDER GOD...WHAT GIVES HERE, ANYWAY?
I MEAN--
--I'M FOR FUN'N' GAMES AS MUCH AS THE NEXT GUY--
--BUT NOT WITHOUT A REASON!
GLANCE AROUND THEE FOR THY REASON, MORTAL.
THOUGH I KNOW NOT THE MECHANISM --I SENSE THIS DEED BE KRYLLK'S DOING!
YOUR SENSES SPEAK TRUE, ASGARDIAN.
YET 'TIS NOT EARTH WHICH IS THE GOAL OF MY AMBITION...
...BUT ASGARD... NOBLE ASGARD!
EARTH IS BUT A COSMIC PAWN...A STEPPING-STONE TO THE ULTIMATE CONQUEST!
AS FOR THE HOW OF THIS "MIRACLE"--

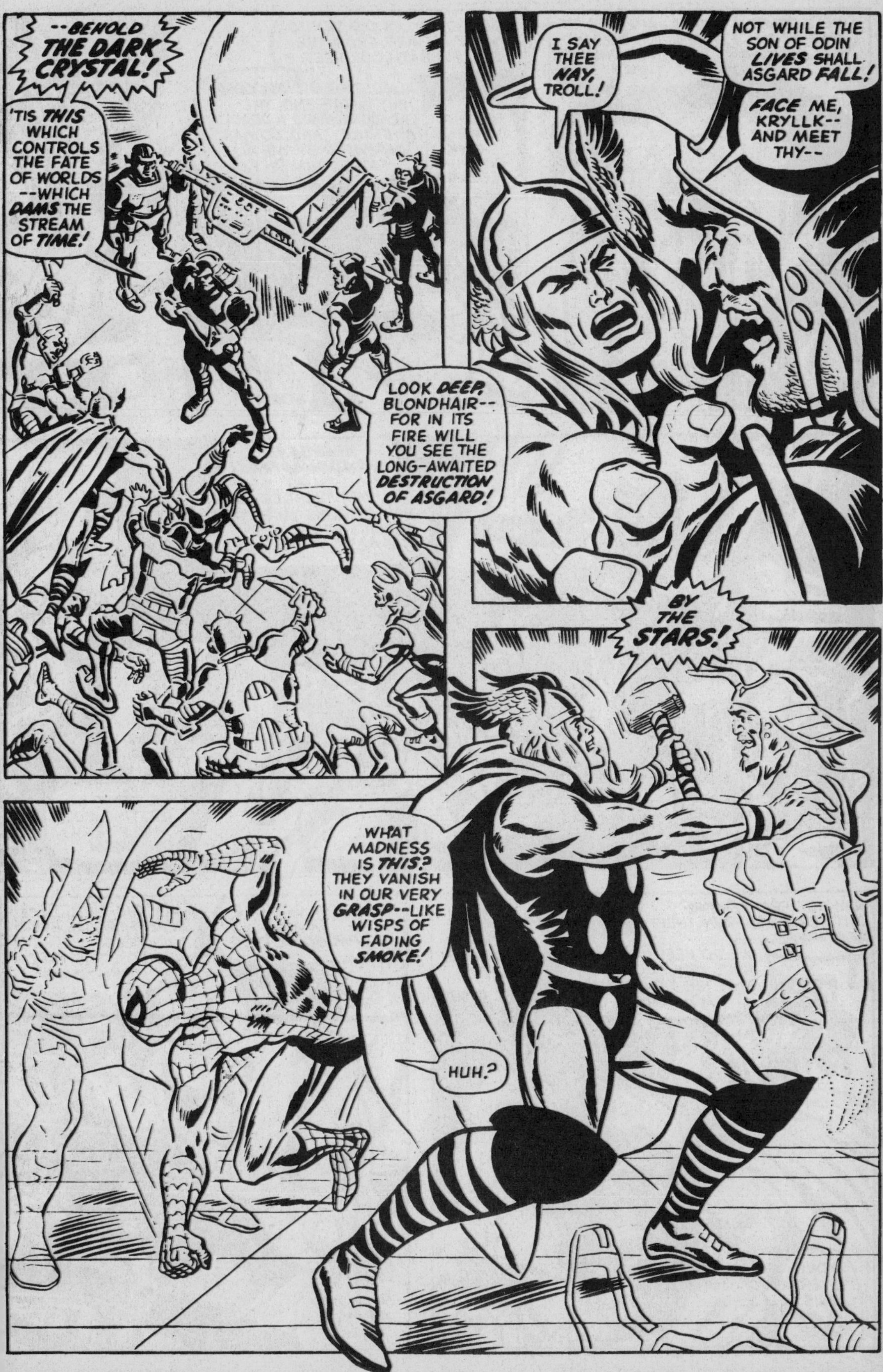
--BEHOLD THE DARK CRYSTAL!
'TIS THIS WHICH CONTROLS THE FATE OF WORLDS --WHICH DAMS THE STREAM OF TIME!
LOOK DEEP, BLONDHAIR-- FOR IN ITS FIRE WILL YOU SEE THE LONG-AWAITED DESTRUCTION OF ASGARD!
I SAY THEE NAY, TROLL!
NOT WHILE THE SON OF ODIN LIVES SHALL ASGARD FALL!
FACE ME, KRYLLK-- AND MEET THY--
BY THE STARS!
WHAT MADNESS IS THIS? THEY VANISH IN OUR VERY GRASP--LIKE WISPS OF FADING SMOKE!
HUH?

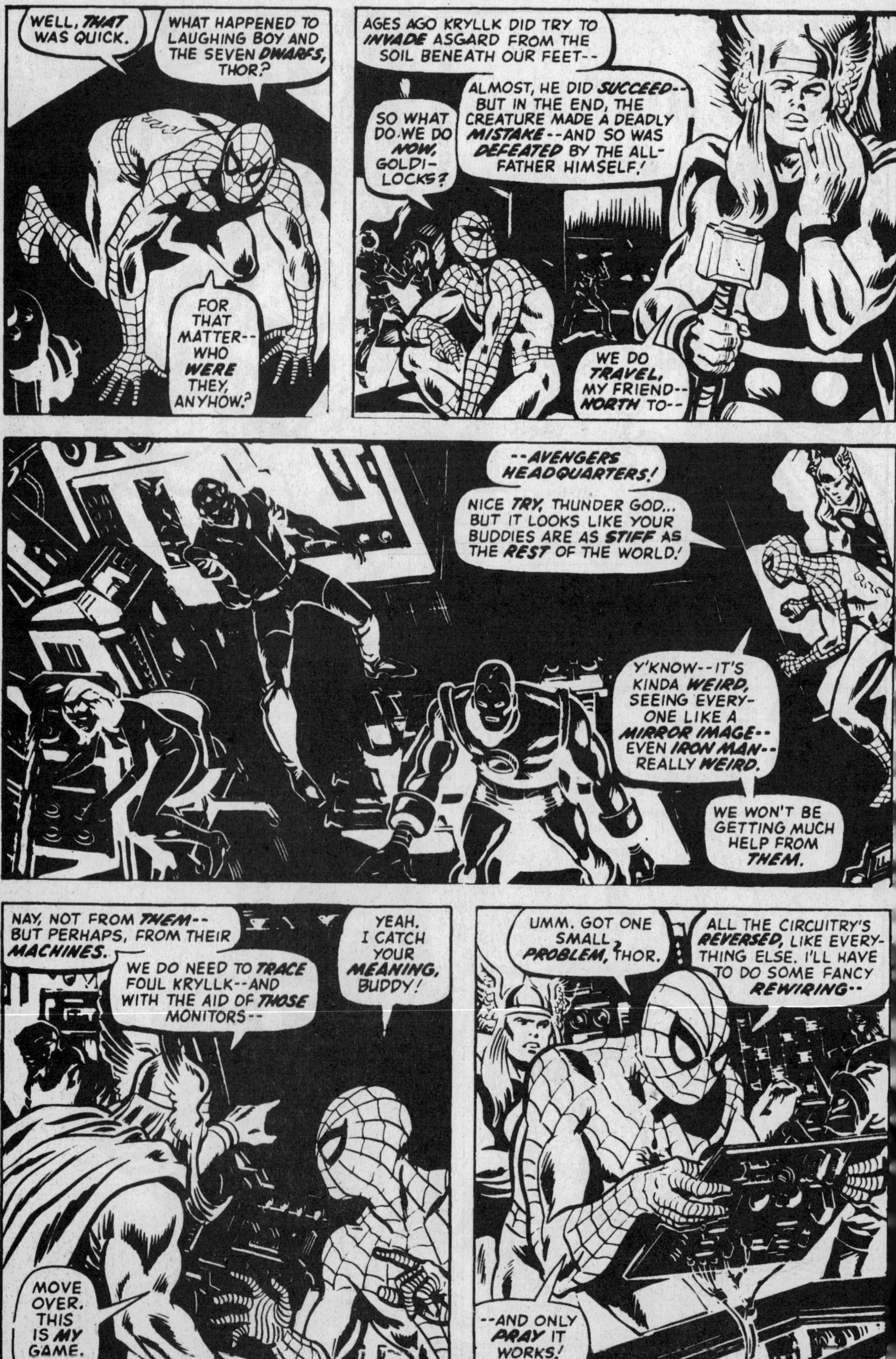

WELL, THAT WAS QUICK.
WHAT HAPPENED TO LAUGHING BOY AND THE SEVEN DWARFS, THOR?
FOR THAT MATTER--WHO WERE THEY, ANYHOW?
AGES AGO KRYLLK DID TRY TO INVADE ASGARD FROM THE SOIL BENEATH OUR FEET--
ALMOST, HE DID SUCCEED--BUT IN THE END, THE CREATURE MADE A DEADLY MISTAKE--AND SO WAS DEFEATED BY THE ALL-FATHER HIMSELF!
SO WHAT DO WE DO NOW, GOLDI-LOCKS?
WE DO TRAVEL, MY FRIEND--NORTH TO--
--AVENGERS HEADQUARTERS!
NICE TRY, THUNDER GOD... BUT IT LOOKS LIKE YOUR BUDDIES ARE AS STIFF AS THE REST OF THE WORLD!
Y'KNOW--IT'S KINDA WEIRD, SEEING EVERY-ONE LIKE A MIRROR IMAGE--EVEN IRON MAN--REALLY WEIRD.
WE WON'T BE GETTING MUCH HELP FROM THEM.
NAY, NOT FROM THEM--BUT PERHAPS, FROM THEIR MACHINES.
WE DO NEED TO TRACE FOUL KRYLLK--AND WITH THE AID OF THOSE MONITORS--
YEAH. I CATCH YOUR MEANING, BUDDY!
MOVE OVER. THIS IS MY GAME.
UMM. GOT ONE SMALL PROBLEM, THOR.
ALL THE CIRCUITRY'S REVERSED, LIKE EVERY-THING ELSE. I'LL HAVE TO DO SOME FANCY REWIRING--
--AND ONLY PRAY IT WORKS!

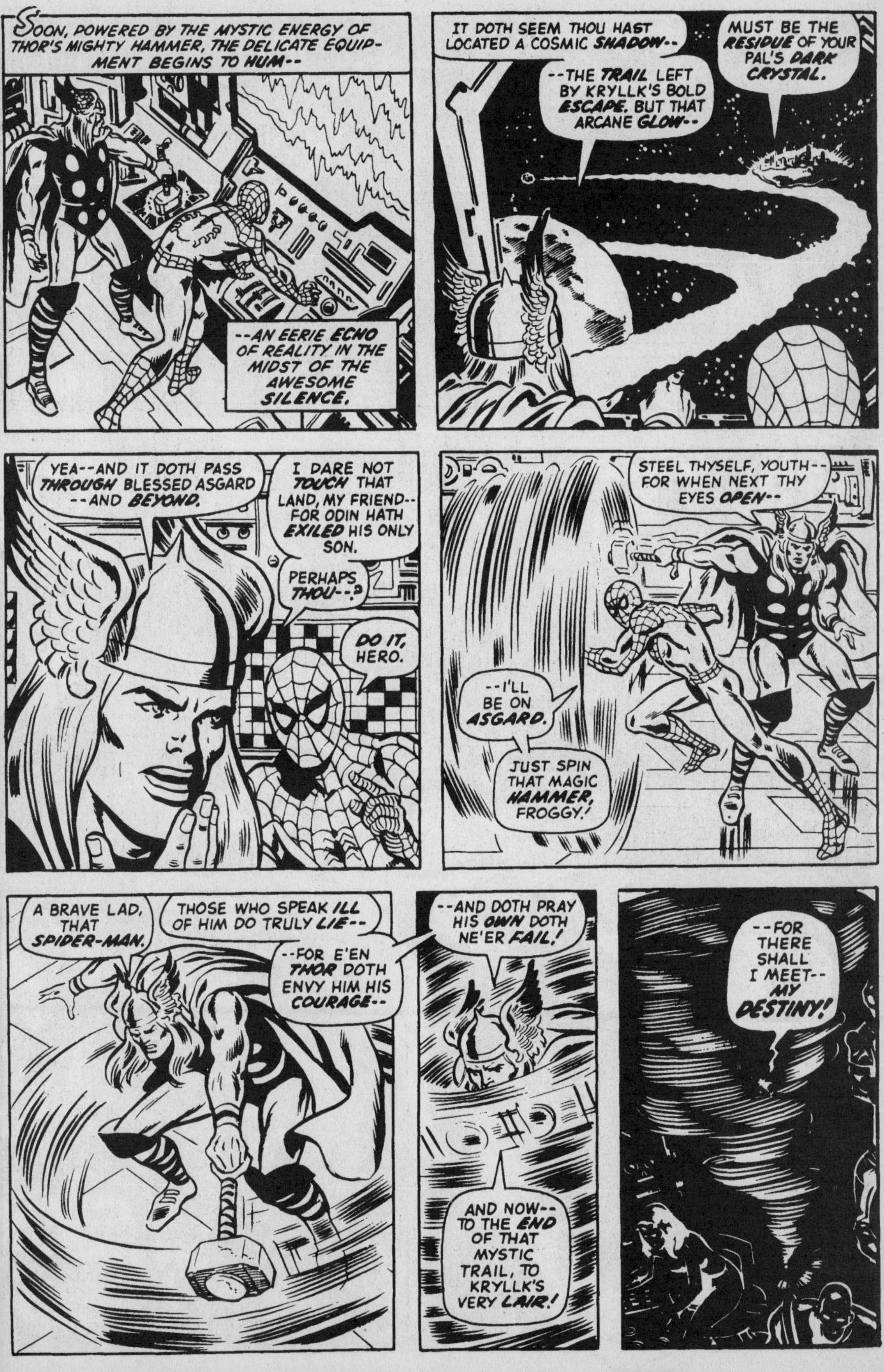
SOON, POWERED BY THE MYSTIC ENERGY OF THOR'S MIGHTY HAMMER, THE DELICATE EQUIPMENT BEGINS TO HUM--
--AN EERIE ECHO OF REALITY IN THE MIDST OF THE AWESOME SILENCE.
IT DOTH SEEM THOU HAST LOCATED A COSMIC SHADOW--
--THE TRAIL LEFT BY KRYLLK'S BOLD ESCAPE. BUT THAT ARCANE GLOW--
MUST BE THE RESIDUE OF YOUR PAL'S DARK CRYSTAL.
YEA--AND IT DOTH PASS THROUGH BLESSED ASGARD --AND BEYOND.
I DARE NOT TOUCH THAT LAND, MY FRIEND--FOR ODIN HATH EXILED HIS ONLY SON.
PERHAPS THOU--?
DO IT, HERO.
STEEL THYSELF, YOUTH--FOR WHEN NEXT THY EYES OPEN--
--I'LL BE ON ASGARD.
JUST SPIN THAT MAGIC HAMMER, FROGGY!
A BRAVE LAD, THAT SPIDER-MAN.
THOSE WHO SPEAK ILL OF HIM DO TRULY LIE--
--FOR E'EN THOR DOTH ENVY HIM HIS COURAGE--
--AND DOTH PRAY HIS OWN DOTH NE'ER FAIL!
AND NOW--TO THE END OF THAT MYSTIC TRAIL, TO KRYLLK'S VERY LAIR!
--FOR THERE SHALL I MEET--MY DESTINY!

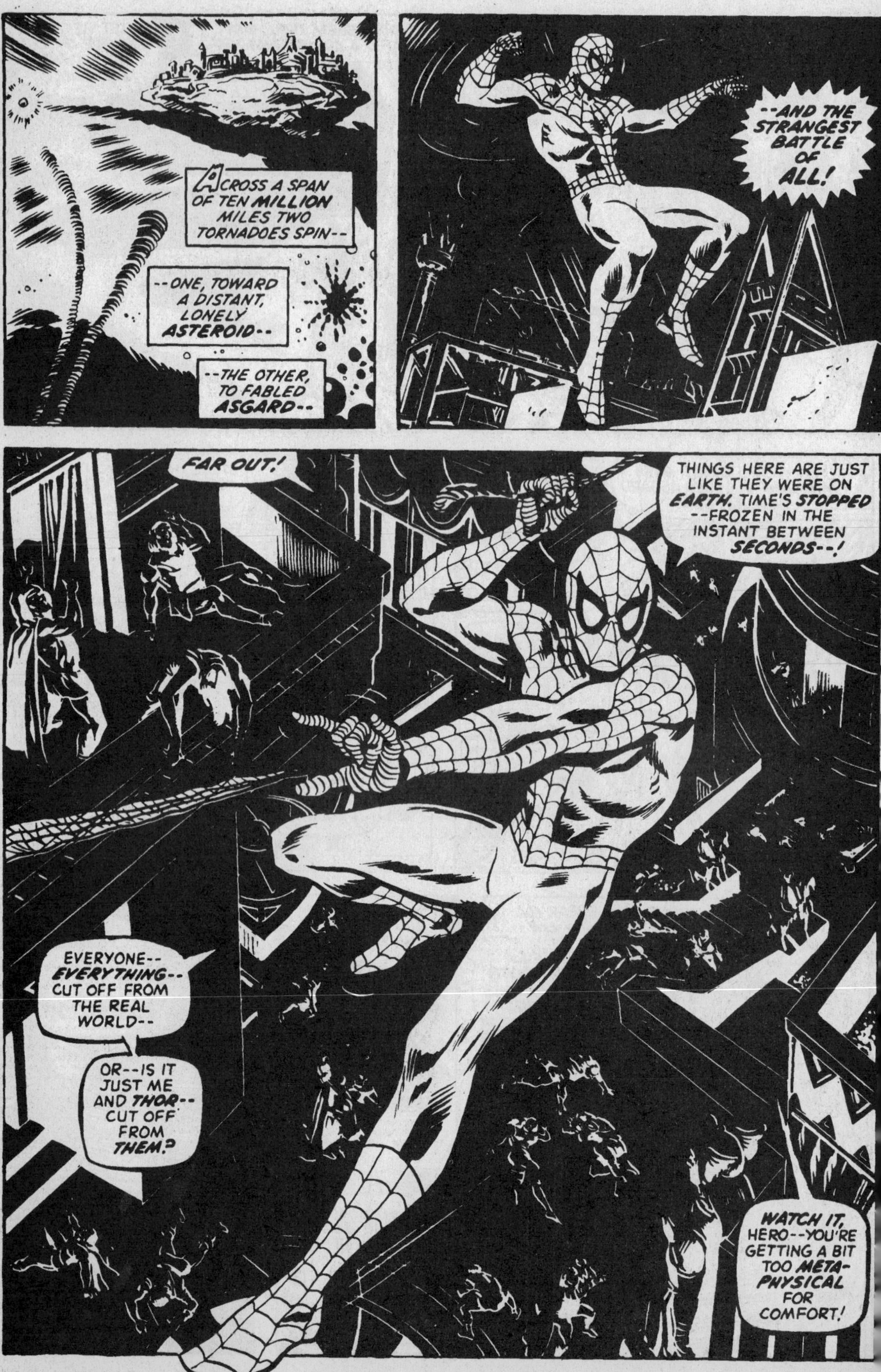
ACROSS A SPAN OF TEN MILLION MILES TWO TORNADOES SPIN--
--ONE, TOWARD A DISTANT, LONELY ASTEROID--
--THE OTHER, TO FABLED ASGARD--
--AND THE STRANGEST BATTLE OF ALL!
FAR OUT!
THINGS HERE ARE JUST LIKE THEY WERE ON EARTH. TIME'S STOPPED --FROZEN IN THE INSTANT BETWEEN SECONDS--!
EVERYONE--EVERYTHING--CUT OFF FROM THE REAL WORLD--
OR--IS IT JUST ME AND THOR--CUT OFF FROM THEM?
WATCH IT, HERO--YOU'RE GETTING A BIT TOO META-PHYSICAL FOR COMFORT!

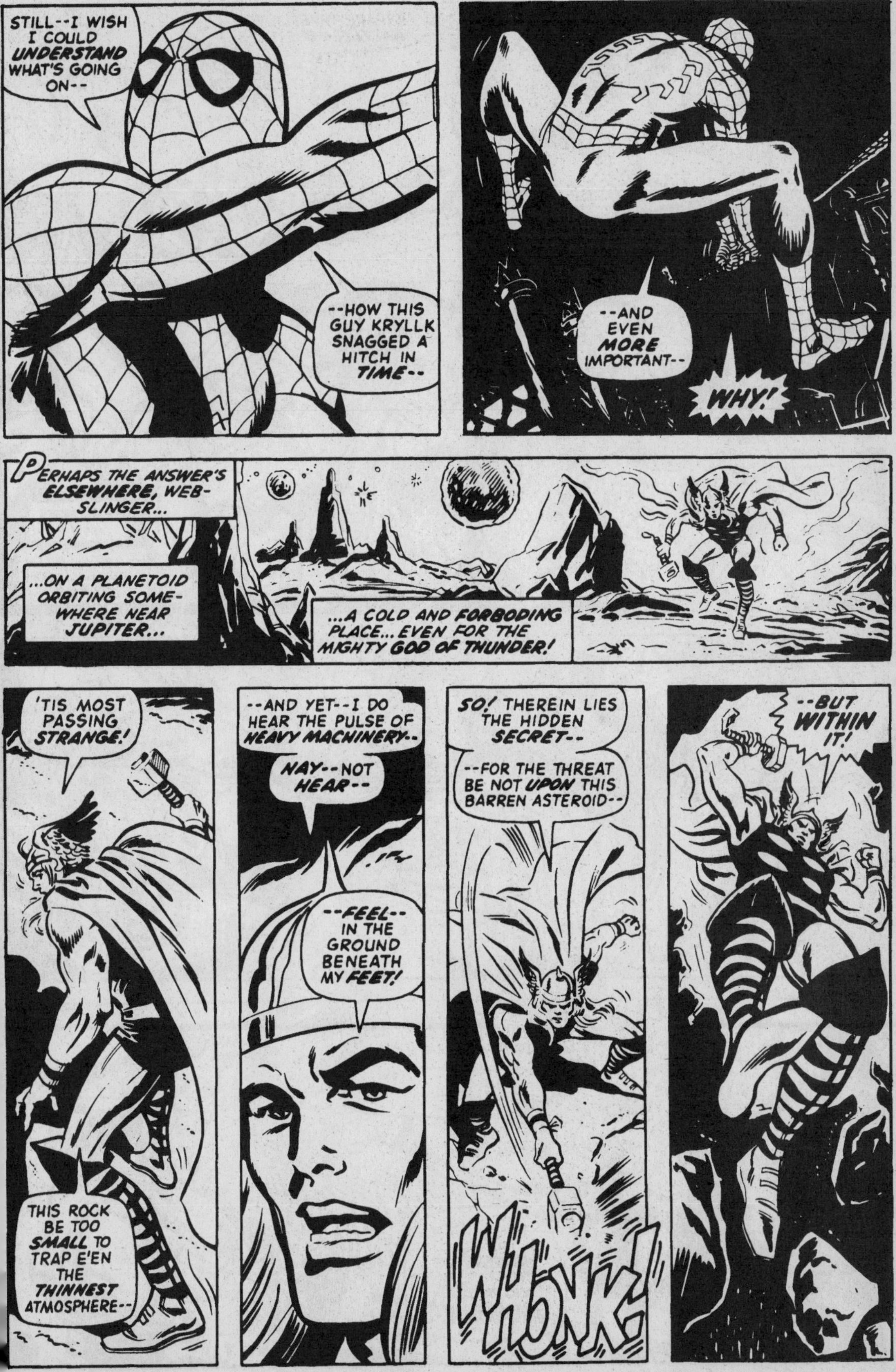
STILL--I WISH I COULD UNDERSTAND WHAT'S GOING ON--
--HOW THIS GUY KRYLLK SNAGGED A HITCH IN TIME--
--AND EVEN MORE IMPORTANT--
WHY!
PERHAPS THE ANSWER'S ELSEWHERE, WEB-SLINGER...
...ON A PLANETOID ORBITING SOMEWHERE NEAR JUPITER...
...A COLD AND FORBODING PLACE... EVEN FOR THE MIGHTY GOD OF THUNDER!
'TIS MOST PASSING STRANGE!
THIS ROCK BE TOO SMALL TO TRAP E'EN THE THINNEST ATMOSPHERE--
--AND YET--I DO HEAR THE PULSE OF HEAVY MACHINERY--
NAY--NOT HEAR--
--FEEL--IN THE GROUND BENEATH MY FEET!
SO! THEREIN LIES THE HIDDEN SECRET--
--FOR THE THREAT BE NOT UPON THIS BARREN ASTEROID--
WHONK!
--BUT WITHIN IT!

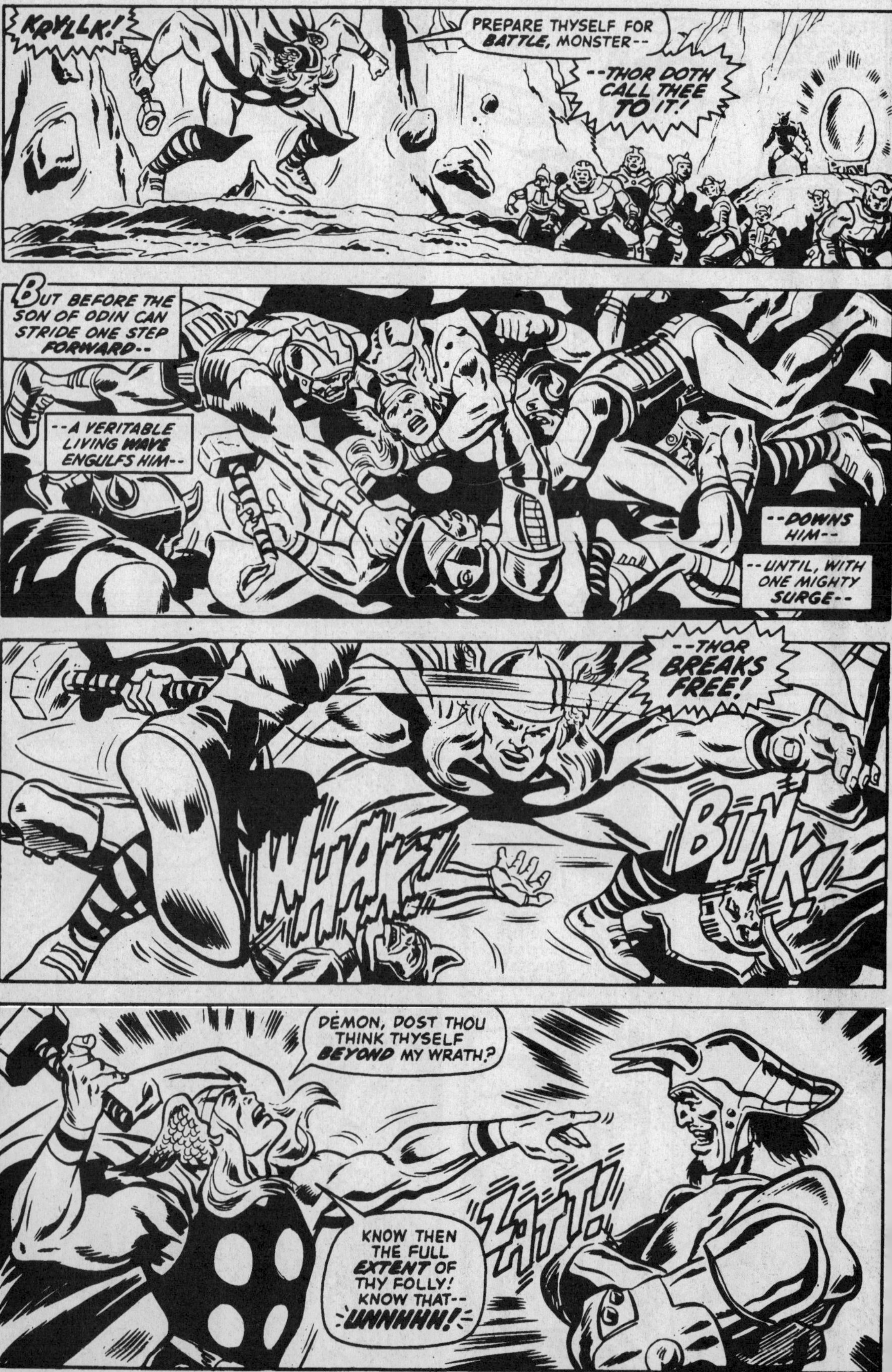
KRYLLK!
PREPARE THYSELF FOR BATTLE, MONSTER--
--THOR DOTH CALL THEE TO IT!
BUT BEFORE THE SON OF ODIN CAN STRIDE ONE STEP FORWARD--
--A VERITABLE LIVING WAVE ENGULFS HIM--
--DOWNS HIM--
--UNTIL, WITH ONE MIGHTY SURGE--
--THOR BREAKS FREE!
WHAP!
BINK!
DEMON, DOST THOU THINK THYSELF BEYOND MY WRATH?
KNOW THEN THE FULL EXTENT OF THY FOLLY! KNOW THAT-- -UNNHHH!-
ZATT!

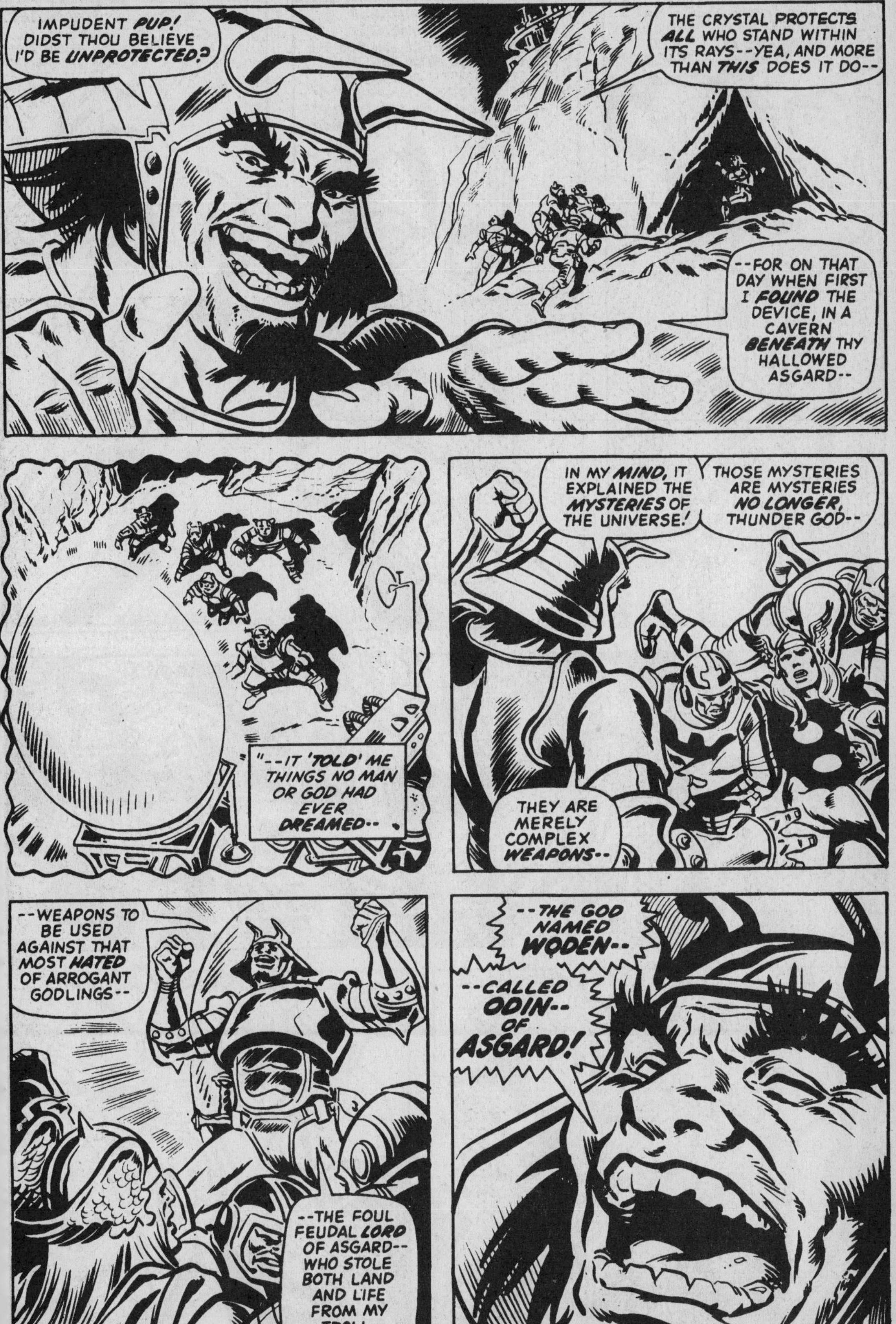
IMPUDENT PUP! DIDST THOU BELIEVE I'D BE UNPROTECTED?
THE CRYSTAL PROTECTS ALL WHO STAND WITHIN ITS RAYS--YEA, AND MORE THAN THIS DOES IT DO--
--FOR ON THAT DAY WHEN FIRST I FOUND THE DEVICE, IN A CAVERN BENEATH THY HALLOWED ASGARD--
"--IT 'TOLD' ME THINGS NO MAN OR GOD HAD EVER DREAMED--
IN MY MIND, IT EXPLAINED THE MYSTERIES OF THE UNIVERSE!
THOSE MYSTERIES ARE MYSTERIES NO LONGER, THUNDER GOD--
THEY ARE MERELY COMPLEX WEAPONS--
--WEAPONS TO BE USED AGAINST THAT MOST HATED OF ARROGANT GODLINGS--
--THE FOUL FEUDAL LORD OF ASGARD--WHO STOLE BOTH LAND AND LIFE FROM MY TROLL BRETHREN--
--THE GOD NAMED WODEN--
--CALLED ODIN-- OF ASGARD!

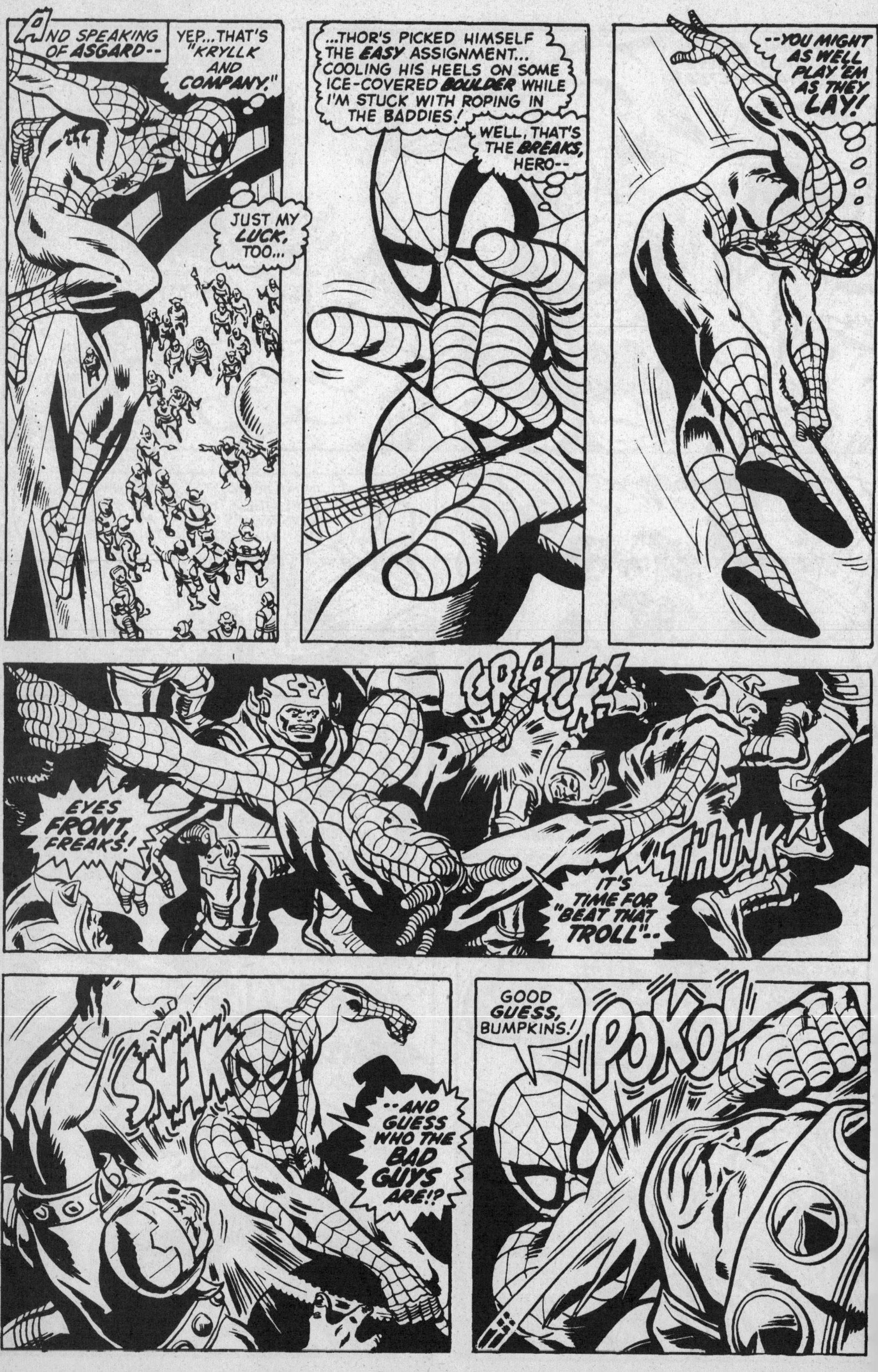

AND SPEAKING OF ASGARD--
YEP...THAT'S "KRYLLK AND COMPANY."
JUST MY LUCK, TOO...
...THOR'S PICKED HIMSELF THE EASY ASSIGNMENT... COOLING HIS HEELS ON SOME ICE-COVERED BOULDER WHILE I'M STUCK WITH ROPING IN THE BADDIES!
WELL, THAT'S THE BREAKS, HERO--
--YOU MIGHT AS WELL PLAY 'EM AS THEY LAY!
CRACK!
EYES FRONT, FREAKS!
THUNK!
IT'S TIME FOR "BEAT THAT TROLL"--
SNAK
--AND GUESS WHO THE BAD GUYS ARE!?
GOOD GUESS, BUMPKINS!
POKO!

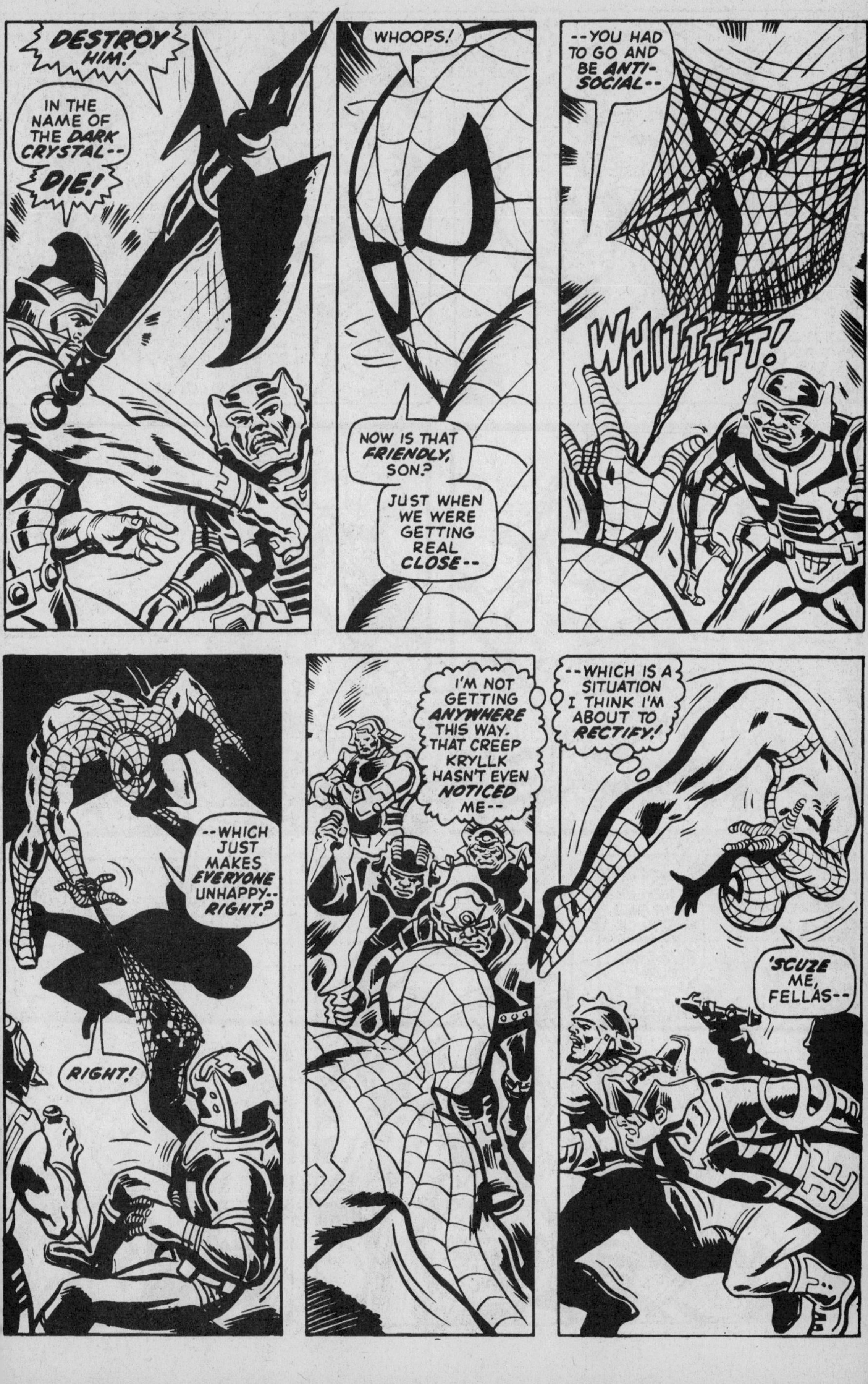
DESTROY HIM!
IN THE NAME OF THE DARK CRYSTAL--
DIE!
WHOOPS!
NOW IS THAT FRIENDLY, SON?
JUST WHEN WE WERE GETTING REAL CLOSE--
--YOU HAD TO GO AND BE ANTI-SOCIAL--
WHITTTTT!
--WHICH JUST MAKES EVERYONE UNHAPPY-- RIGHT?
RIGHT!
I'M NOT GETTING ANYWHERE THIS WAY. THAT CREEP KRYLLK HASN'T EVEN NOTICED ME--
--WHICH IS A SITUATION I THINK I'M ABOUT TO RECTIFY!
'SCUZE ME, FELLAS--

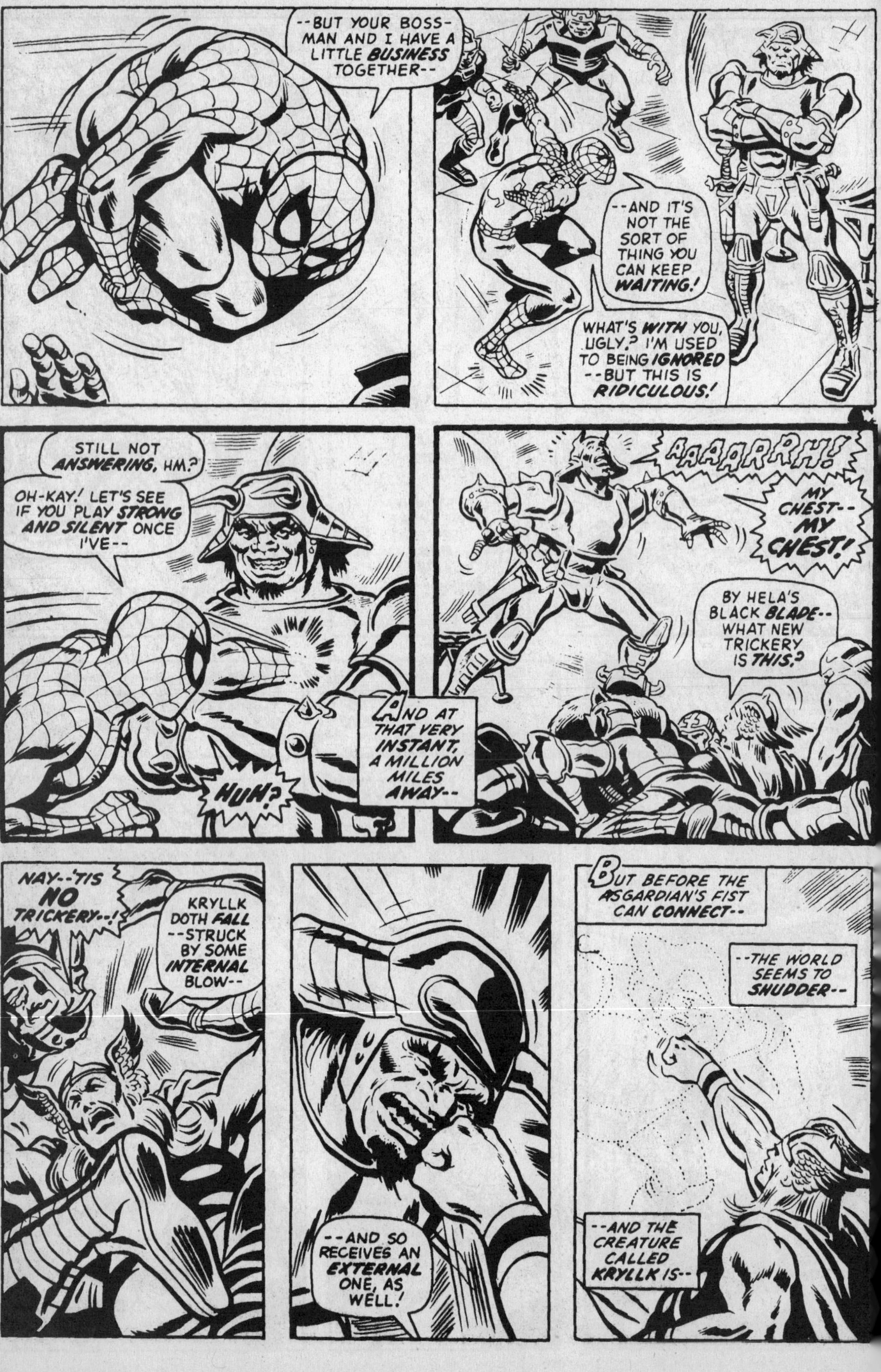

--BUT YOUR BOSS-MAN AND I HAVE A LITTLE BUSINESS TOGETHER--
--AND IT'S NOT THE SORT OF THING YOU CAN KEEP WAITING!
WHAT'S WITH YOU, UGLY? I'M USED TO BEING IGNORED --BUT THIS IS RIDICULOUS!
STILL NOT ANSWERING, HM?
OH-KAY! LET'S SEE IF YOU PLAY STRONG AND SILENT ONCE I'VE--
HUH?
AND AT THAT VERY INSTANT, A MILLION MILES AWAY--
AAAARRRH!
MY CHEST-- MY CHEST!
BY HELA'S BLACK BLADE-- WHAT NEW TRICKERY IS THIS?
NAY--'TIS NO TRICKERY--!
KRYLLK DOTH FALL --STRUCK BY SOME INTERNAL BLOW--
--AND SO RECEIVES AN EXTERNAL ONE, AS WELL!
BUT BEFORE THE ASGARDIAN'S FIST CAN CONNECT--
--THE WORLD SEEMS TO SHUDDER--
--AND THE CREATURE CALLED KRYLLK IS--

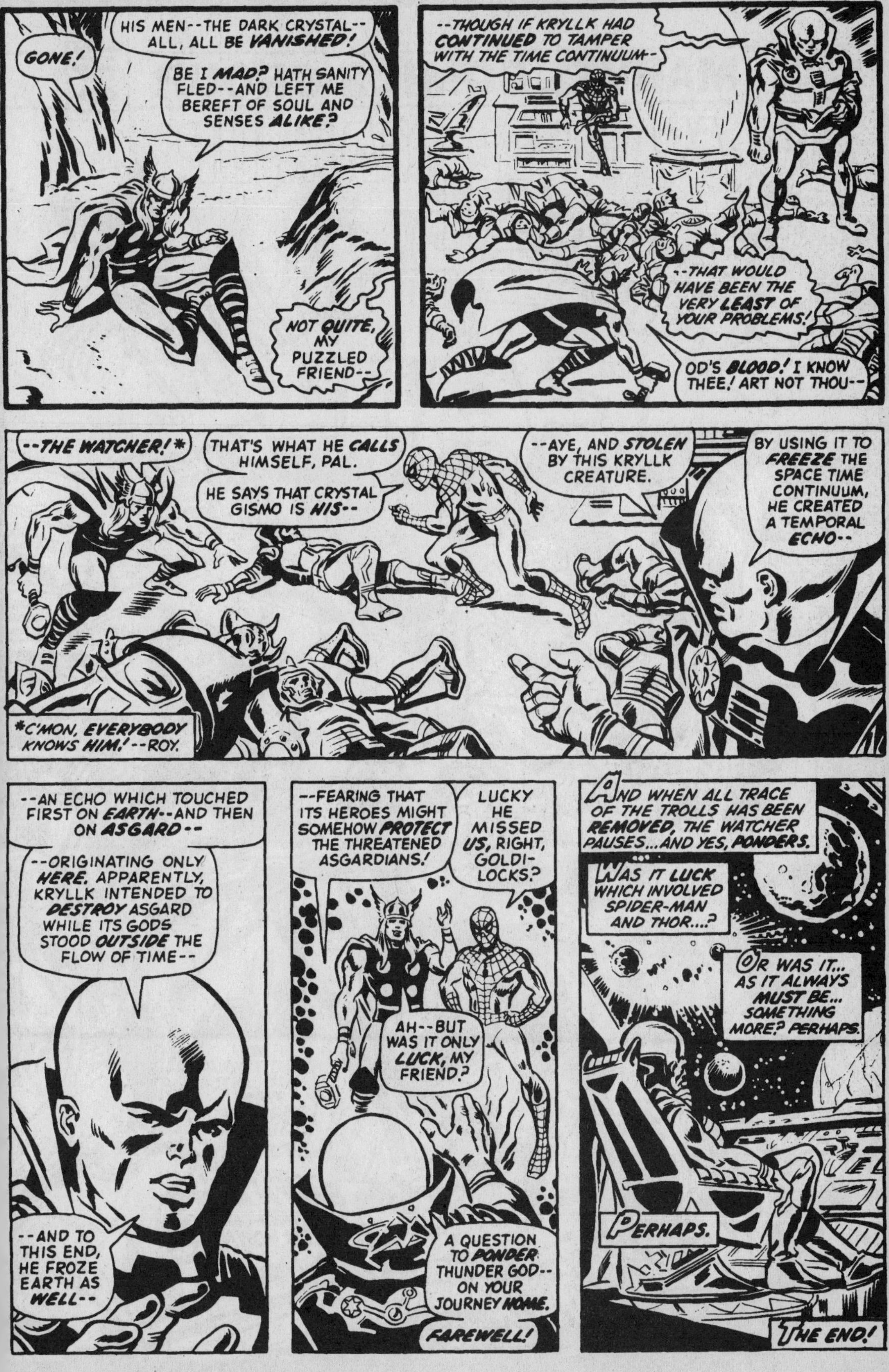
GONE!
HIS MEN--THE DARK CRYSTAL--ALL, ALL BE VANISHED!
BE I MAD? HATH SANITY FLED--AND LEFT ME BEREFT OF SOUL AND SENSES ALIKE?
NOT QUITE, MY PUZZLED FRIEND--
--THOUGH IF KRYLLK HAD CONTINUED TO TAMPER WITH THE TIME CONTINUUM--
--THAT WOULD HAVE BEEN THE VERY LEAST OF YOUR PROBLEMS!
OD'S BLOOD! I KNOW THEE! ART NOT THOU--
--THE WATCHER!*
THAT'S WHAT HE CALLS HIMSELF, PAL.
HE SAYS THAT CRYSTAL GISMO IS HIS--
--AYE, AND STOLEN BY THIS KRYLLK CREATURE.
BY USING IT TO FREEZE THE SPACE TIME CONTINUUM, HE CREATED A TEMPORAL ECHO--
*C'MON, EVERYBODY KNOWS HIM!--ROY.
--AN ECHO WHICH TOUCHED FIRST ON EARTH--AND THEN ON ASGARD--
--ORIGINATING ONLY HERE. APPARENTLY, KRYLLK INTENDED TO DESTROY ASGARD WHILE ITS GODS STOOD OUTSIDE THE FLOW OF TIME--
--AND TO THIS END, HE FROZE EARTH AS WELL--
--FEARING THAT ITS HEROES MIGHT SOMEHOW PROTECT THE THREATENED ASGARDIANS!
LUCKY HE MISSED US, RIGHT, GOLDI-LOCKS?
AH--BUT WAS IT ONLY LUCK, MY FRIEND?
A QUESTION TO PONDER THUNDER GOD--ON YOUR JOURNEY HOME.
FAREWELL!
AND WHEN ALL TRACE OF THE TROLLS HAS BEEN REMOVED, THE WATCHER PAUSES...AND YES, PONDERS.
WAS IT LUCK WHICH INVOLVED SPIDER-MAN AND THOR...?
OR WAS IT... AS IT ALWAYS MUST BE... SOMETHING MORE? PERHAPS.
PERHAPS.
THE END!

MARVEL TEAM-UP
MARVEL COMICS GROUP
APPROVED BY THE COMICS CODE AUTHORITY
20¢
8 APR
02147
MARVEL TEAM-UP
FEATURING
SPIDER-MAN
AND
THE CAT
ENTER: THE MURDEROUSLY MAGNIFICENT GAL THEY CALL MAN-KILLER!
KEEP YOUR COOL, CAT-LADY! THE OLE WALL-CRAWLER COMETH!
NO WAY, MAN!
IF YOU BUTT YOUR WAY INTO THIS GRUDGE MATCH--
--WE'LL BOTH MOP UP THE FLOOR WITH YOU!!

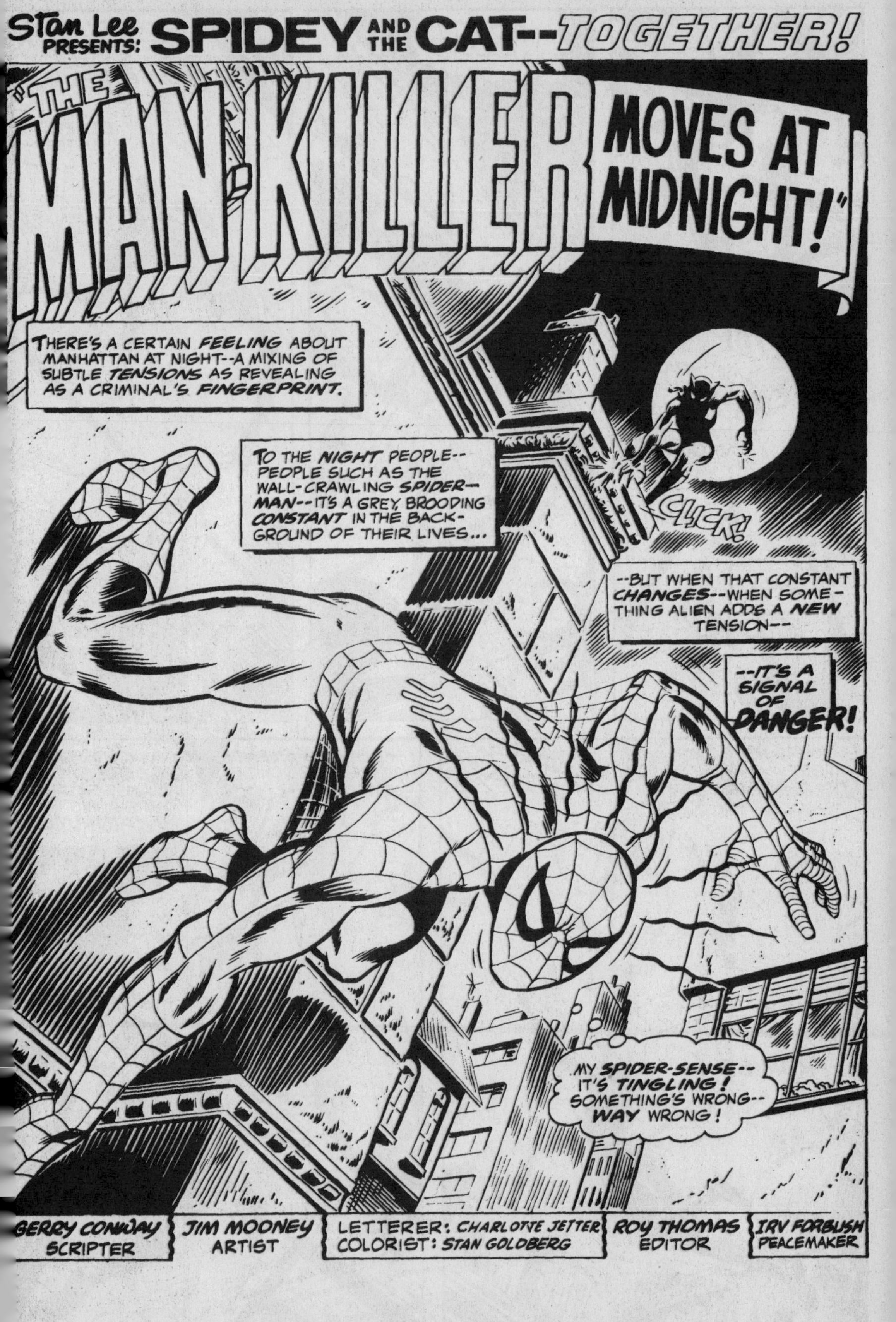
Stan Lee PRESENTS: SPIDEY AND THE CAT--TOGETHER!
"THE MAN-KILLER MOVES AT MIDNIGHT!"
THERE'S A CERTAIN FEELING ABOUT MANHATTAN AT NIGHT--A MIXING OF SUBTLE TENSIONS AS REVEALING AS A CRIMINAL'S FINGERPRINT.
TO THE NIGHT PEOPLE--PEOPLE SUCH AS THE WALL-CRAWLING SPIDER-MAN--IT'S A GREY, BROODING CONSTANT IN THE BACKGROUND OF THEIR LIVES...
CLICK!
--BUT WHEN THAT CONSTANT CHANGES--WHEN SOMETHING ALIEN ADDS A NEW TENSION--
--IT'S A SIGNAL OF DANGER!
MY SPIDER-SENSE--IT'S TINGLING! SOMETHING'S WRONG--WAY WRONG!
GERRY CONWAY SCRIPTER
JIM MOONEY ARTIST
LETTERER: CHARLOTTE JETTER COLORIST: STAN GOLDBERG
ROY THOMAS EDITOR
IRV FORBUSH PEACEMAKER

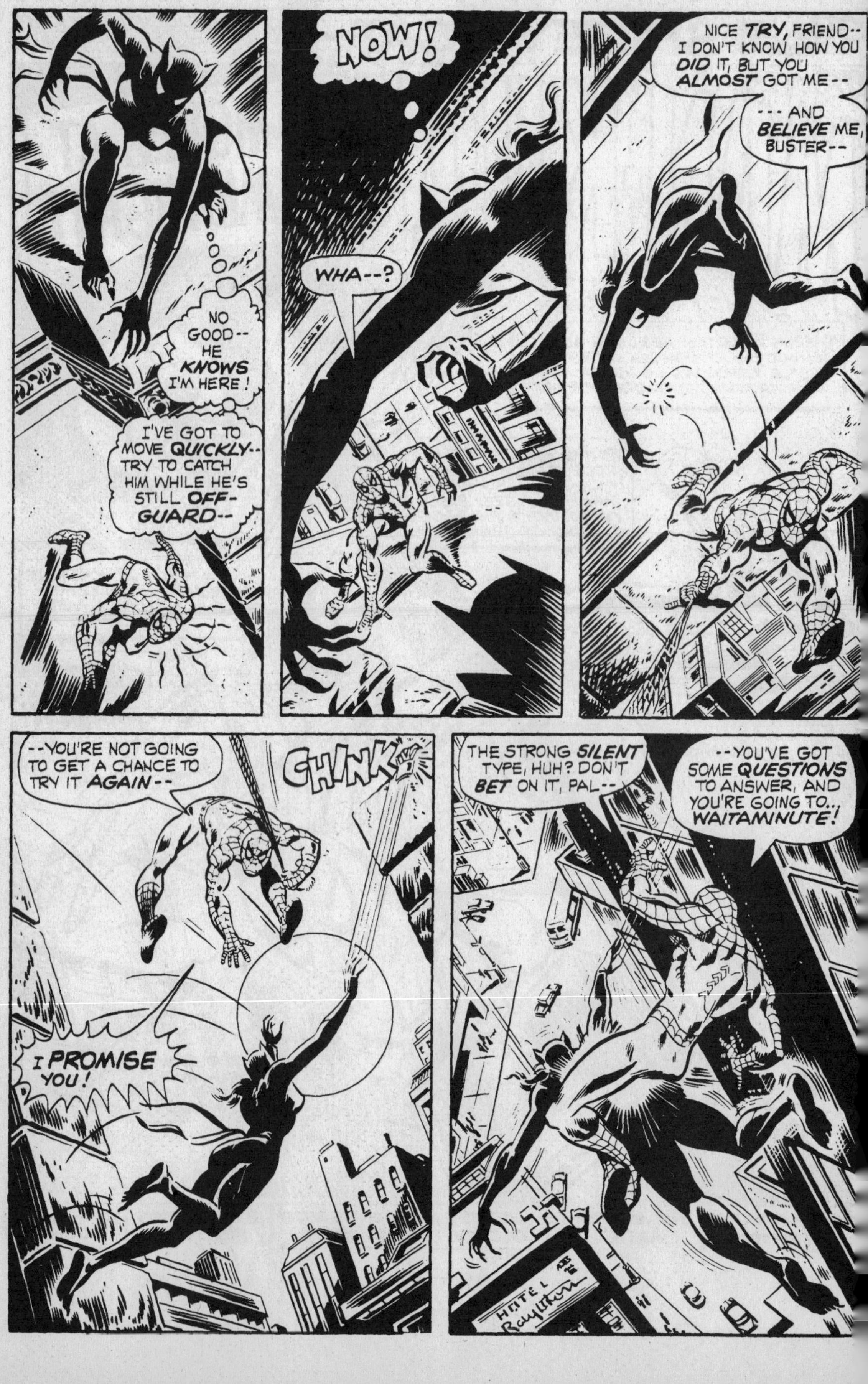
NO GOOD-- HE KNOWS I'M HERE!
I'VE GOT TO MOVE QUICKLY-- TRY TO CATCH HIM WHILE HE'S STILL OFF-GUARD--
NOW!
WHA--?
NICE TRY, FRIEND-- I DON'T KNOW HOW YOU DID IT, BUT YOU ALMOST GOT ME--
--- AND BELIEVE ME, BUSTER--
--YOU'RE NOT GOING TO GET A CHANCE TO TRY IT AGAIN--
CHINK
I PROMISE YOU!
THE STRONG SILENT TYPE, HUH? DON'T BET ON IT, PAL--
--YOU'VE GOT SOME QUESTIONS TO ANSWER, AND YOU'RE GOING TO... WAITAMINUTE!

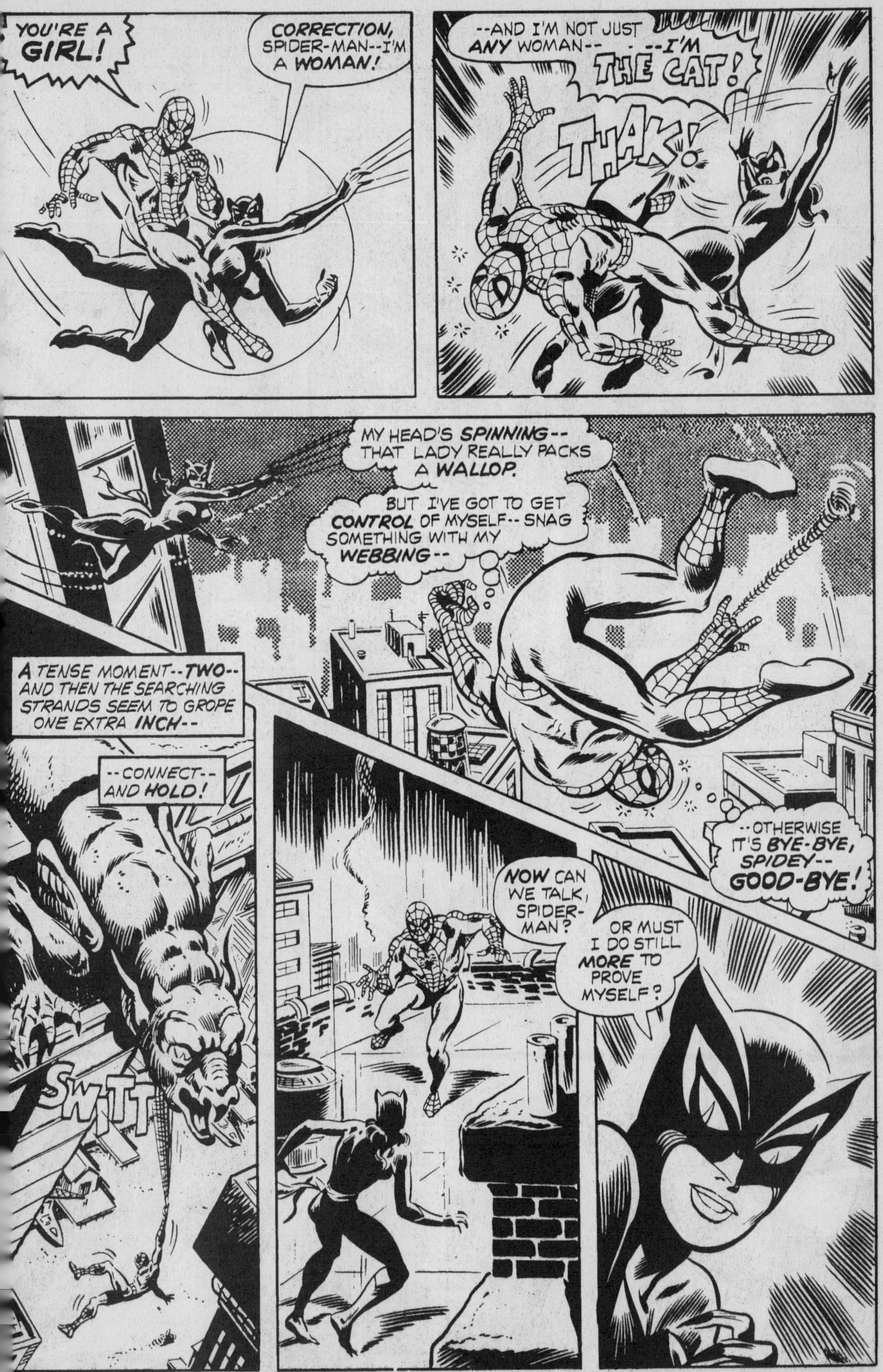

YOU'RE A GIRL!
CORRECTION, SPIDER-MAN--I'M A WOMAN!
--AND I'M NOT JUST ANY WOMAN--
--I'M THE CAT!
THAK!
MY HEAD'S SPINNING-- THAT LADY REALLY PACKS A WALLOP.
BUT I'VE GOT TO GET CONTROL OF MYSELF-- SNAG SOMETHING WITH MY WEBBING--
--OTHERWISE IT'S BYE-BYE, SPIDEY-- GOOD-BYE!
A TENSE MOMENT--TWO-- AND THEN THE SEARCHING STRANDS SEEM TO GROPE ONE EXTRA INCH--
--CONNECT-- AND HOLD!
SWITT
NOW CAN WE TALK, SPIDER-MAN?
OR MUST I DO STILL MORE TO PROVE MYSELF?

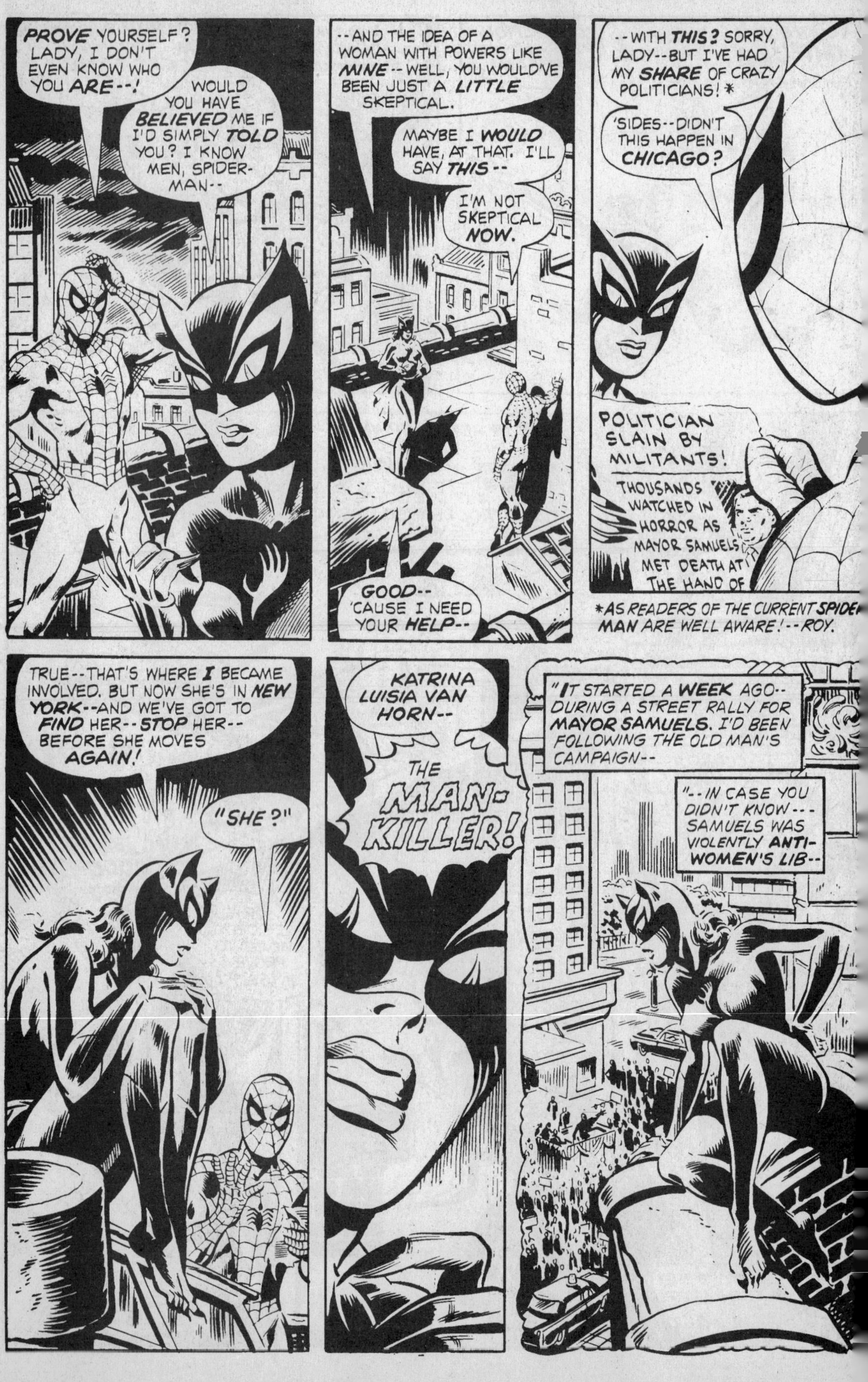
PROVE YOURSELF? LADY, I DON'T EVEN KNOW WHO YOU ARE--!
WOULD YOU HAVE BELIEVED ME IF I'D SIMPLY TOLD YOU? I KNOW MEN, SPIDER-MAN--
--AND THE IDEA OF A WOMAN WITH POWERS LIKE MINE--WELL, YOU WOULD'VE BEEN JUST A LITTLE SKEPTICAL.
MAYBE I WOULD HAVE, AT THAT. I'LL SAY THIS--
I'M NOT SKEPTICAL NOW.
GOOD-- 'CAUSE I NEED YOUR HELP--
--WITH THIS? SORRY, LADY--BUT I'VE HAD MY SHARE OF CRAZY POLITICIANS! *
'SIDES--DIDN'T THIS HAPPEN IN CHICAGO?
POLITICIAN SLAIN BY MILITANTS!
THOUSANDS WATCHED IN HORROR AS MAYOR SAMUELS MET DEATH AT THE HAND OF
*AS READERS OF THE CURRENT SPIDER-MAN ARE WELL AWARE!--ROY.
TRUE--THAT'S WHERE I BECAME INVOLVED. BUT NOW SHE'S IN NEW YORK--AND WE'VE GOT TO FIND HER--STOP HER--BEFORE SHE MOVES AGAIN!
"SHE?"
KATRINA LUISIA VAN HORN--
THE MAN-KILLER!
"IT STARTED A WEEK AGO--DURING A STREET RALLY FOR MAYOR SAMUELS. I'D BEEN FOLLOWING THE OLD MAN'S CAMPAIGN--
"--IN CASE YOU DIDN'T KNOW---SAMUELS WAS VIOLENTLY ANTI-WOMEN'S LIB--

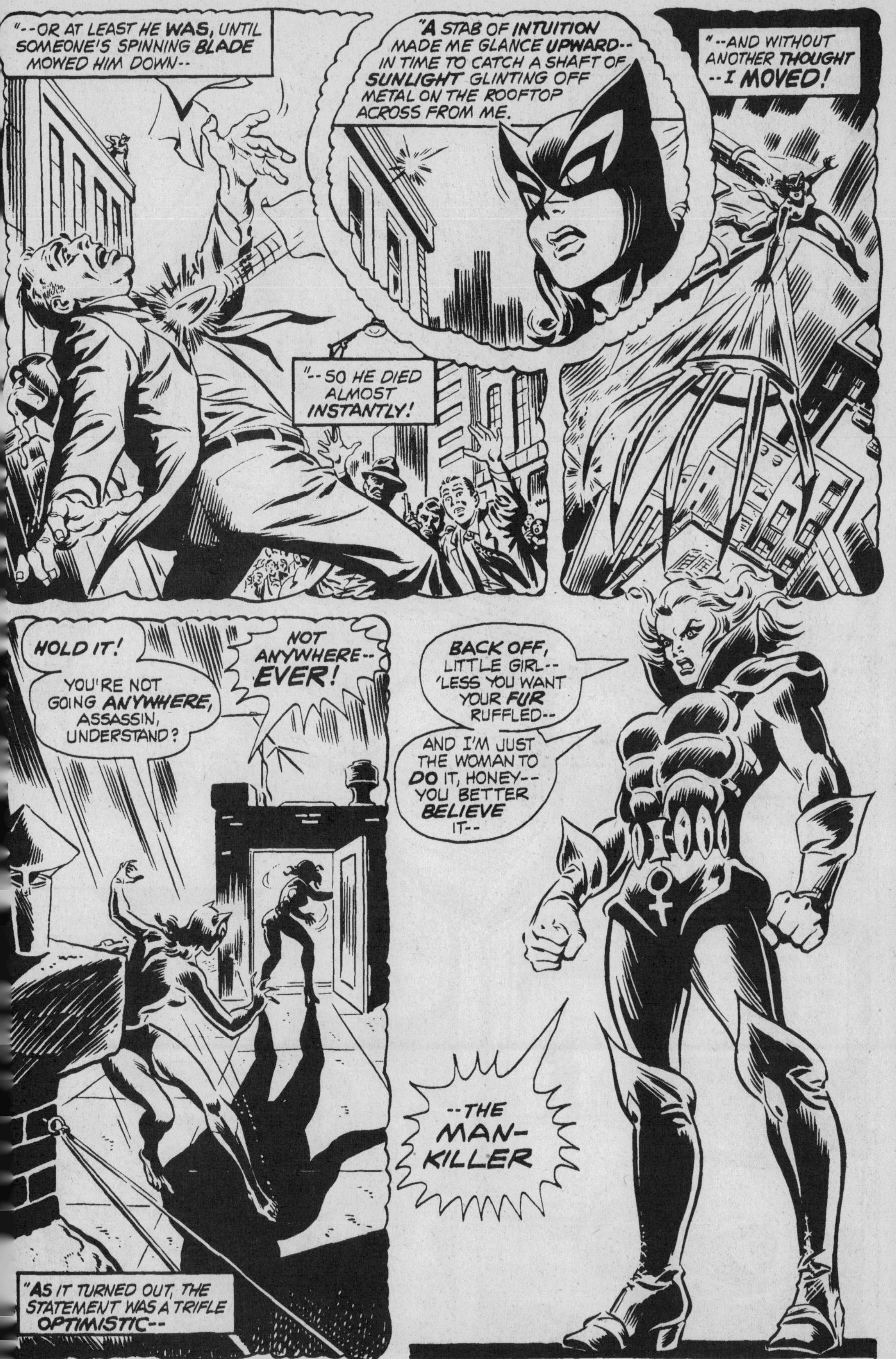
"--OR AT LEAST HE WAS, UNTIL SOMEONE'S SPINNING BLADE MOWED HIM DOWN--
"A STAB OF INTUITION MADE ME GLANCE UPWARD-- IN TIME TO CATCH A SHAFT OF SUNLIGHT GLINTING OFF METAL ON THE ROOFTOP ACROSS FROM ME.
"--SO HE DIED ALMOST INSTANTLY!
"--AND WITHOUT ANOTHER THOUGHT --I MOVED!
HOLD IT!
YOU'RE NOT GOING ANYWHERE, ASSASSIN, UNDERSTAND?
NOT ANYWHERE-- EVER!
"AS IT TURNED OUT, THE STATEMENT WAS A TRIFLE OPTIMISTIC--
BACK OFF, LITTLE GIRL-- 'LESS YOU WANT YOUR FUR RUFFLED--
AND I'M JUST THE WOMAN TO DO IT, HONEY-- YOU BETTER BELIEVE IT--
--THE MAN-KILLER

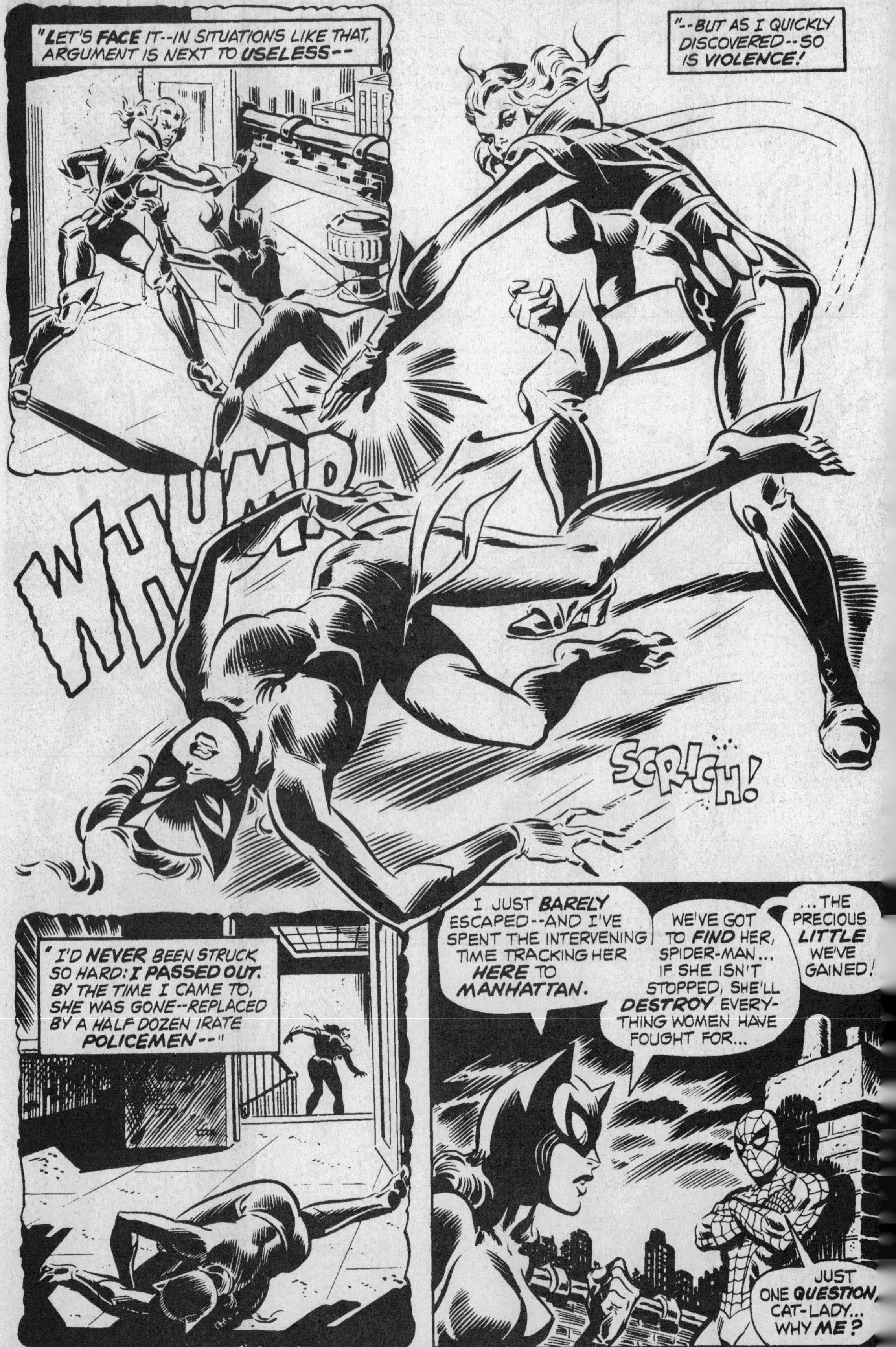
"LET'S FACE IT--IN SITUATIONS LIKE THAT, ARGUMENT IS NEXT TO USELESS--
"--BUT AS I QUICKLY DISCOVERED--SO IS VIOLENCE!
WHUMP
SCRITCH!
" I'D NEVER BEEN STRUCK SO HARD: I PASSED OUT. BY THE TIME I CAME TO, SHE WAS GONE--REPLACED BY A HALF DOZEN IRATE POLICEMEN--"
I JUST BARELY ESCAPED--AND I'VE SPENT THE INTERVENING TIME TRACKING HER HERE TO MANHATTAN.
WE'VE GOT TO FIND HER, SPIDER-MAN... IF SHE ISN'T STOPPED, SHE'LL DESTROY EVERY-THING WOMEN HAVE FOUGHT FOR...
...THE PRECIOUS LITTLE WE'VE GAINED!
JUST ONE QUESTION, CAT-LADY... WHY ME?

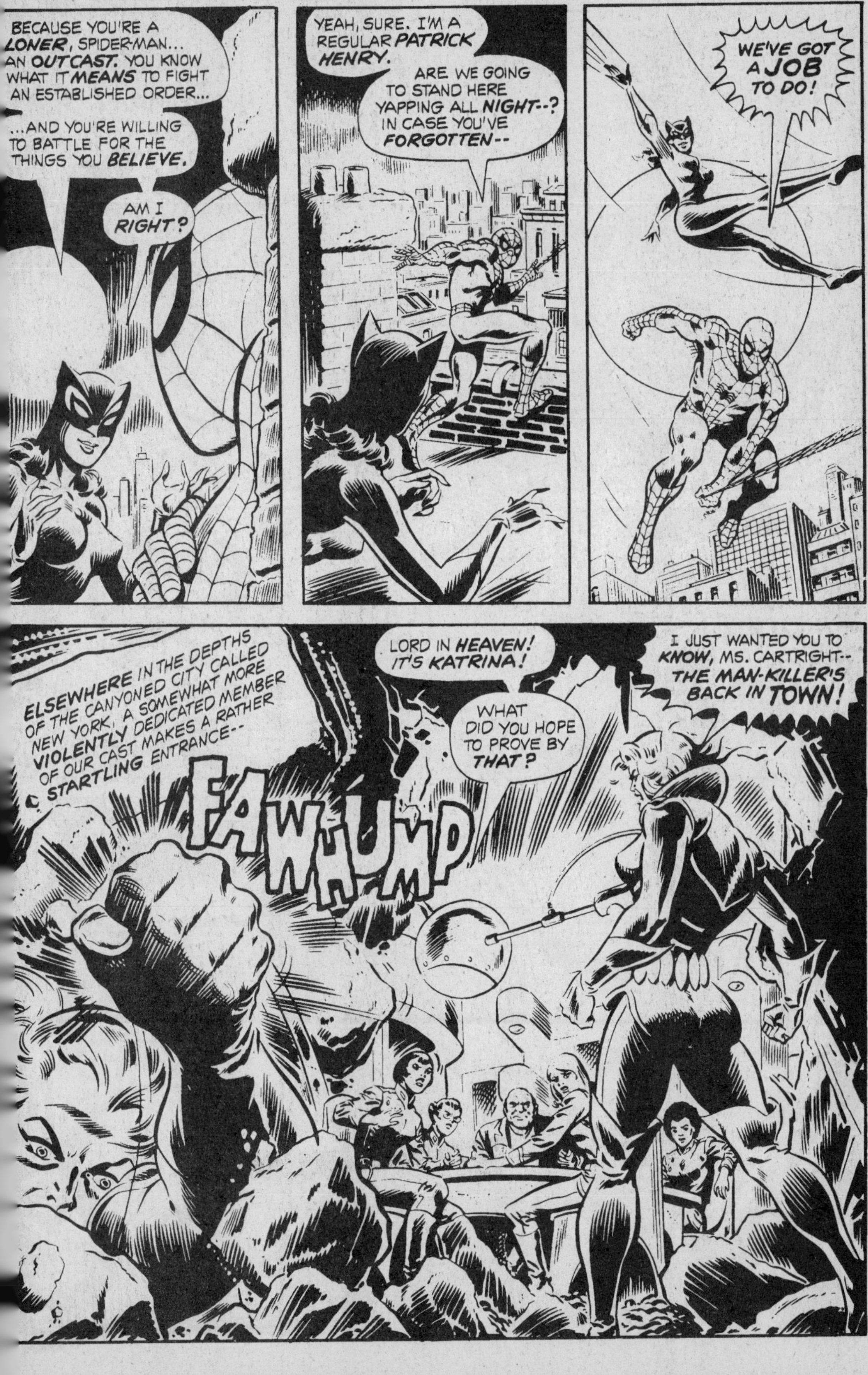
BECAUSE YOU'RE A LONER, SPIDER-MAN... AN OUTCAST. YOU KNOW WHAT IT MEANS TO FIGHT AN ESTABLISHED ORDER...
...AND YOU'RE WILLING TO BATTLE FOR THE THINGS YOU BELIEVE.
AM I RIGHT?
YEAH, SURE. I'M A REGULAR PATRICK HENRY.
ARE WE GOING TO STAND HERE YAPPING ALL NIGHT--? IN CASE YOU'VE FORGOTTEN--
WE'VE GOT A JOB TO DO!
ELSEWHERE IN THE DEPTHS OF THE CANYONED CITY CALLED NEW YORK, A SOMEWHAT MORE VIOLENTLY DEDICATED MEMBER OF OUR CAST MAKES A RATHER STARTLING ENTRANCE--
FAWHUMP
LORD IN HEAVEN! IT'S KATRINA!
WHAT DID YOU HOPE TO PROVE BY THAT?
I JUST WANTED YOU TO KNOW, MS. CARTRIGHT-- THE MAN-KILLER'S BACK IN TOWN!

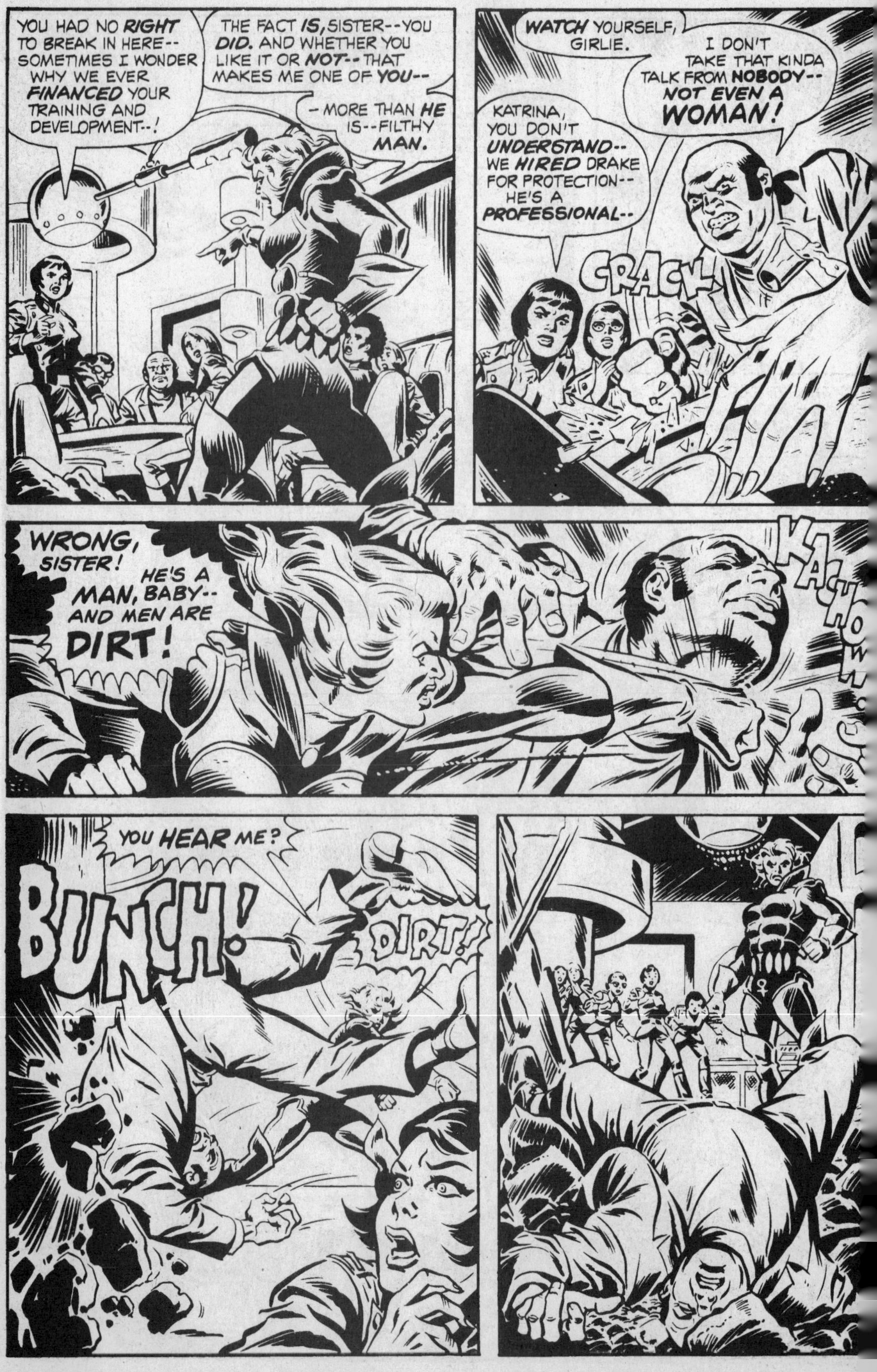
YOU HAD NO RIGHT TO BREAK IN HERE-- SOMETIMES I WONDER WHY WE EVER FINANCED YOUR TRAINING AND DEVELOPMENT--!
THE FACT IS, SISTER--YOU DID. AND WHETHER YOU LIKE IT OR NOT--THAT MAKES ME ONE OF YOU--
--MORE THAN HE IS--FILTHY MAN.
WATCH YOURSELF, GIRLIE.
I DON'T TAKE THAT KINDA TALK FROM NOBODY-- NOT EVEN A WOMAN!
KATRINA, YOU DON'T UNDERSTAND-- WE HIRED DRAKE FOR PROTECTION-- HE'S A PROFESSIONAL--
CRACK
WRONG, SISTER!
HE'S A MAN, BABY-- AND MEN ARE DIRT!
KACHOWW
YOU HEAR ME?
BUNCH!
DIRT!

SEE WHAT I *MEAN?*

AND THE SISTERS DO SEE--THEY SEE THE BUILDING IMAGE OF *NIGHTMARE*--

--A NIGHTMARE WHICH *BEGAN* TWO YEARS AGO, DURING THE *WINTER OLYMPICS*-- WHERE A EUROPEAN SKIER NAMED KATRINA LUISA VAN HORN MADE HER FIRST --MOST *FATEFUL* APPEARANCE--

WOMEN ATHLETES? THE IDEA'S *ABSURD!*

ONLY *MEN* CAN BE TRULY COMPETITIVE-- IT'S OUR *NATURE*, YOU KNOW. WOMEN SHOULD REMAIN WITH *CHILDREN!*

NO WOMAN CAN EVER BEAT A MAN--A *TRUE* MAN---IN ATHLETIC COMPETITION.

WOULD YOU CARE TO *BET* ON THAT, HERR LUBBINGS?

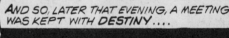

AND SO, LATER THAT EVENING, A MEETING WAS KEPT WITH *DESTINY*....

...AS EGO MATCHED WITH *EGO*...

..IN A CONTEST ONLY THE *DEVIL* COULD WIN.

AH...*FREULEIN VAN HORN.* PERHAPS I WILL *ACCEPT* YOUR CHALLENGE---

WOULDN'T YOU *AGREE*, HERR LUBBINGS.. THAT REMAINS TO BE *SEEN?*

--FOR I AM, I ASSURE YOU, THE FAR *BETTER* SKIER.

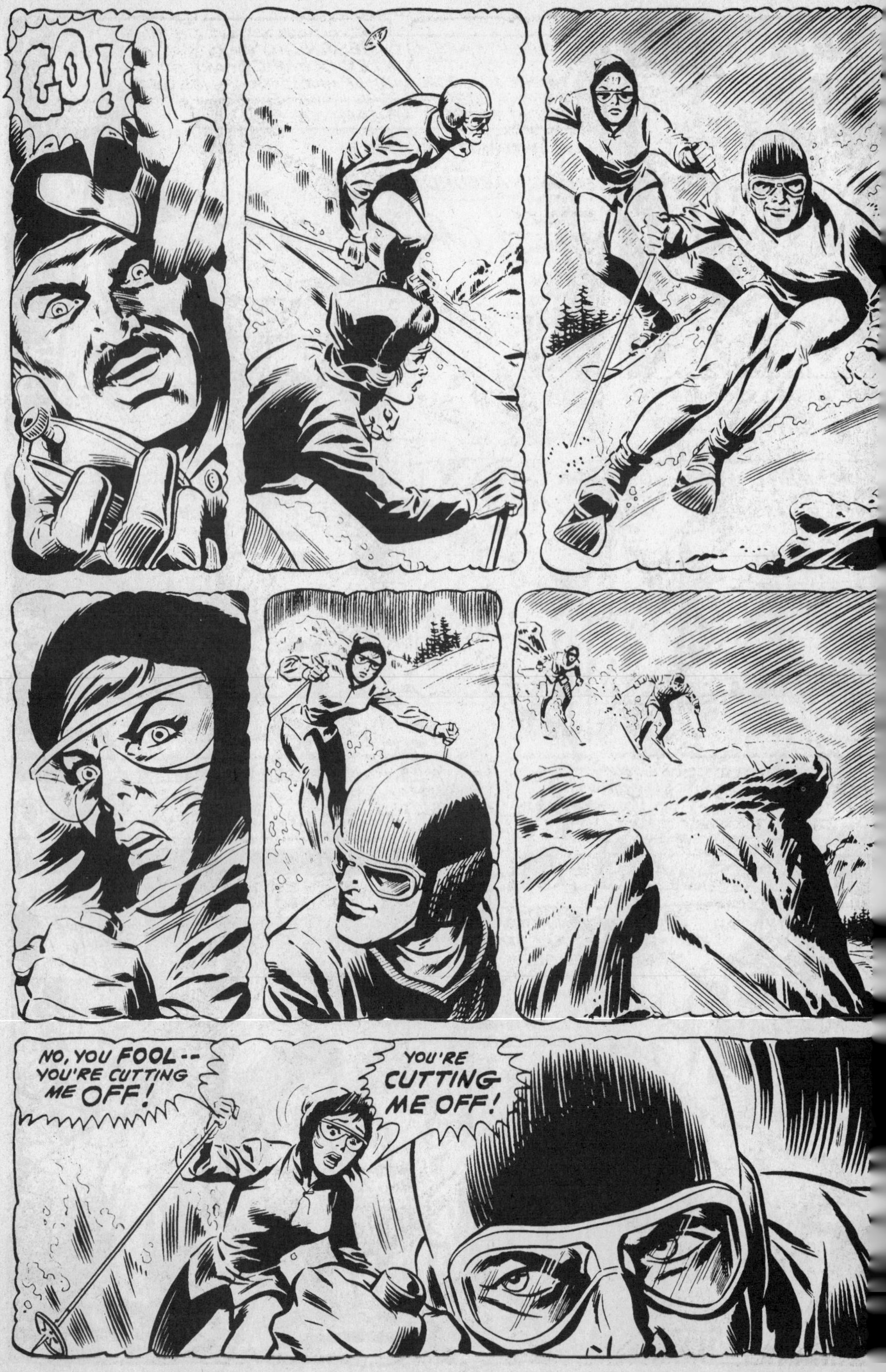
GO!
NO, YOU FOOL-- YOU'RE CUTTING ME OFF!
YOU'RE CUTTING ME OFF!

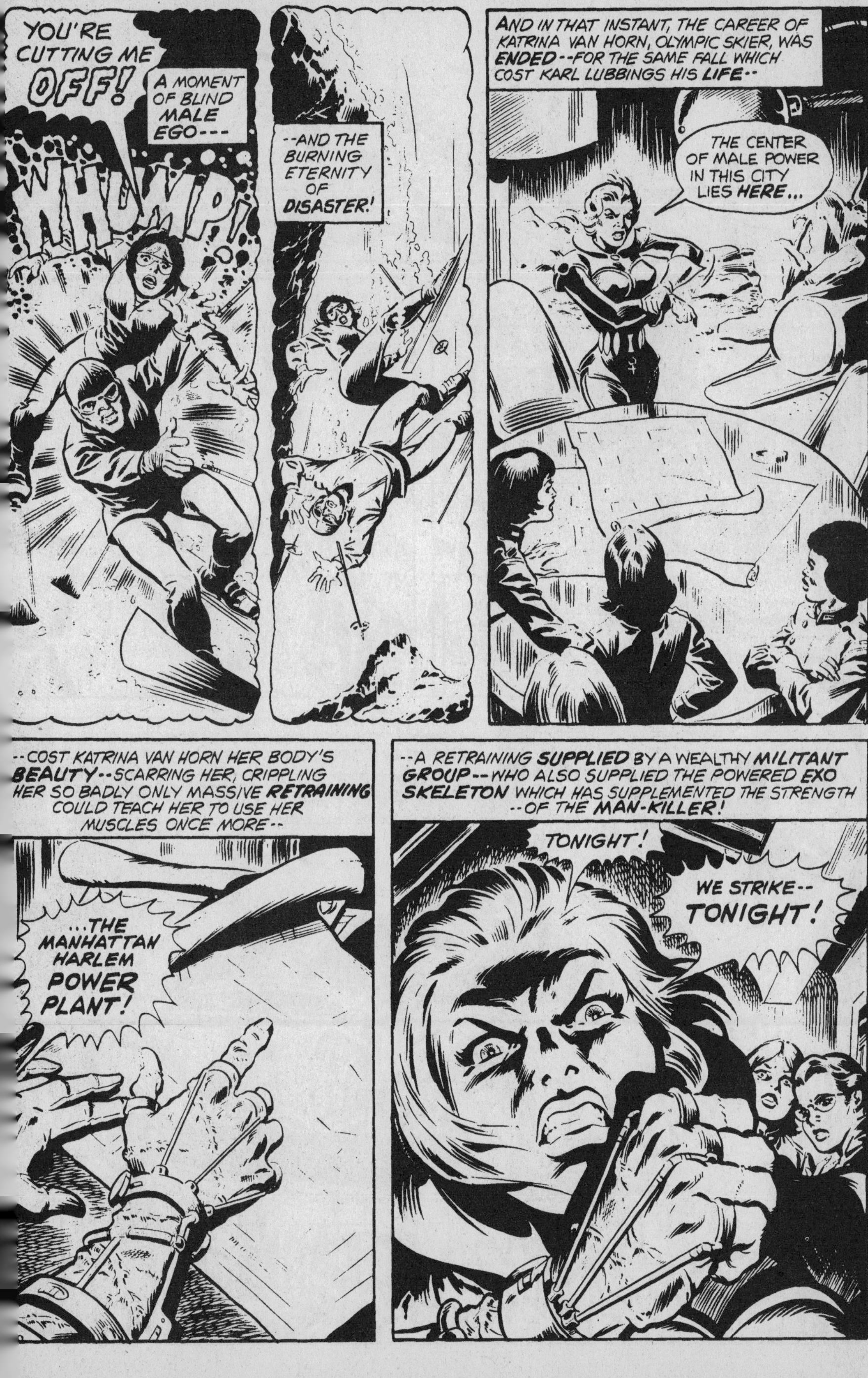
YOU'RE CUTTING ME OFF!
A MOMENT OF BLIND MALE EGO---
WHUMP!
--AND THE BURNING ETERNITY OF DISASTER!
AND IN THAT INSTANT, THE CAREER OF KATRINA VAN HORN, OLYMPIC SKIER, WAS ENDED--FOR THE SAME FALL WHICH COST KARL LUBBINGS HIS LIFE--
THE CENTER OF MALE POWER IN THIS CITY LIES HERE...
--COST KATRINA VAN HORN HER BODY'S BEAUTY--SCARRING HER, CRIPPLING HER SO BADLY ONLY MASSIVE RETRAINING COULD TEACH HER TO USE HER MUSCLES ONCE MORE--
...THE MANHATTAN HARLEM POWER PLANT!
--A RETRAINING SUPPLIED BY A WEALTHY MILITANT GROUP--WHO ALSO SUPPLIED THE POWERED EXO SKELETON WHICH HAS SUPPLEMENTED THE STRENGTH --OF THE MAN-KILLER!
TONIGHT!
WE STRIKE--TONIGHT!

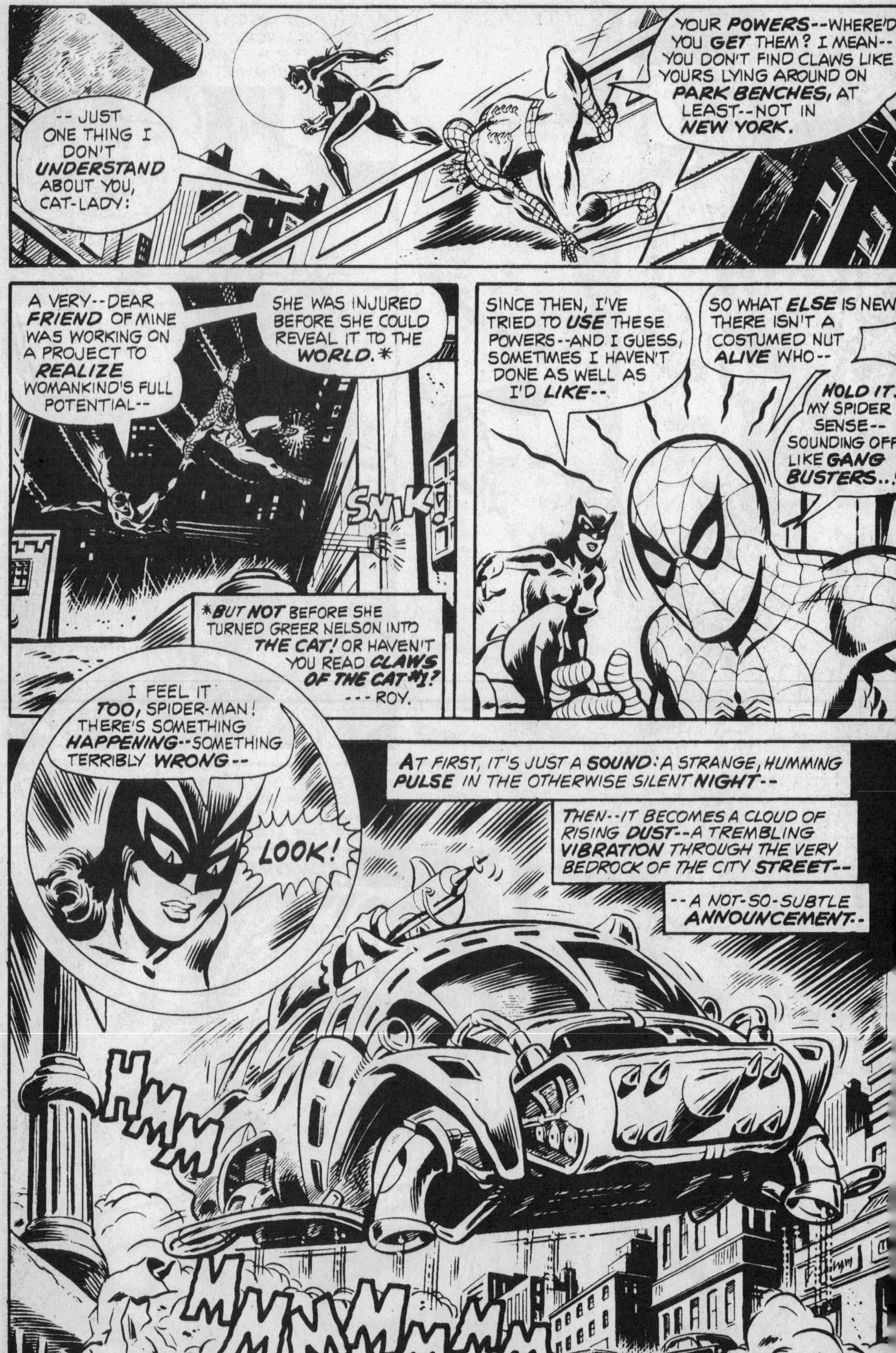
-- JUST ONE THING I DON'T UNDERSTAND ABOUT YOU, CAT-LADY:
YOUR POWERS--WHERE'D YOU GET THEM? I MEAN--YOU DON'T FIND CLAWS LIKE YOURS LYING AROUND ON PARK BENCHES, AT LEAST--NOT IN NEW YORK.
A VERY--DEAR FRIEND OF MINE WAS WORKING ON A PROJECT TO REALIZE WOMANKIND'S FULL POTENTIAL--
SHE WAS INJURED BEFORE SHE COULD REVEAL IT TO THE WORLD.*
SNIK!
*BUT NOT BEFORE SHE TURNED GREER NELSON INTO THE CAT! OR HAVEN'T YOU READ CLAWS OF THE CAT #1? ---ROY.
SINCE THEN, I'VE TRIED TO USE THESE POWERS--AND I GUESS, SOMETIMES I HAVEN'T DONE AS WELL AS I'D LIKE--
SO WHAT ELSE IS NEW THERE ISN'T A COSTUMED NUT ALIVE WHO--
HOLD IT! MY SPIDER SENSE--SOUNDING OFF LIKE GANG BUSTERS..!
I FEEL IT TOO, SPIDER-MAN! THERE'S SOMETHING HAPPENING--SOMETHING TERRIBLY WRONG--
LOOK!
AT FIRST, IT'S JUST A SOUND: A STRANGE, HUMMING PULSE IN THE OTHERWISE SILENT NIGHT--
THEN--IT BECOMES A CLOUD OF RISING DUST--A TREMBLING VIBRATION THROUGH THE VERY BEDROCK OF THE CITY STREET--
--A NOT-SO-SUBTLE ANNOUNCEMENT--
HMMM
MMMMMMMMMMMM

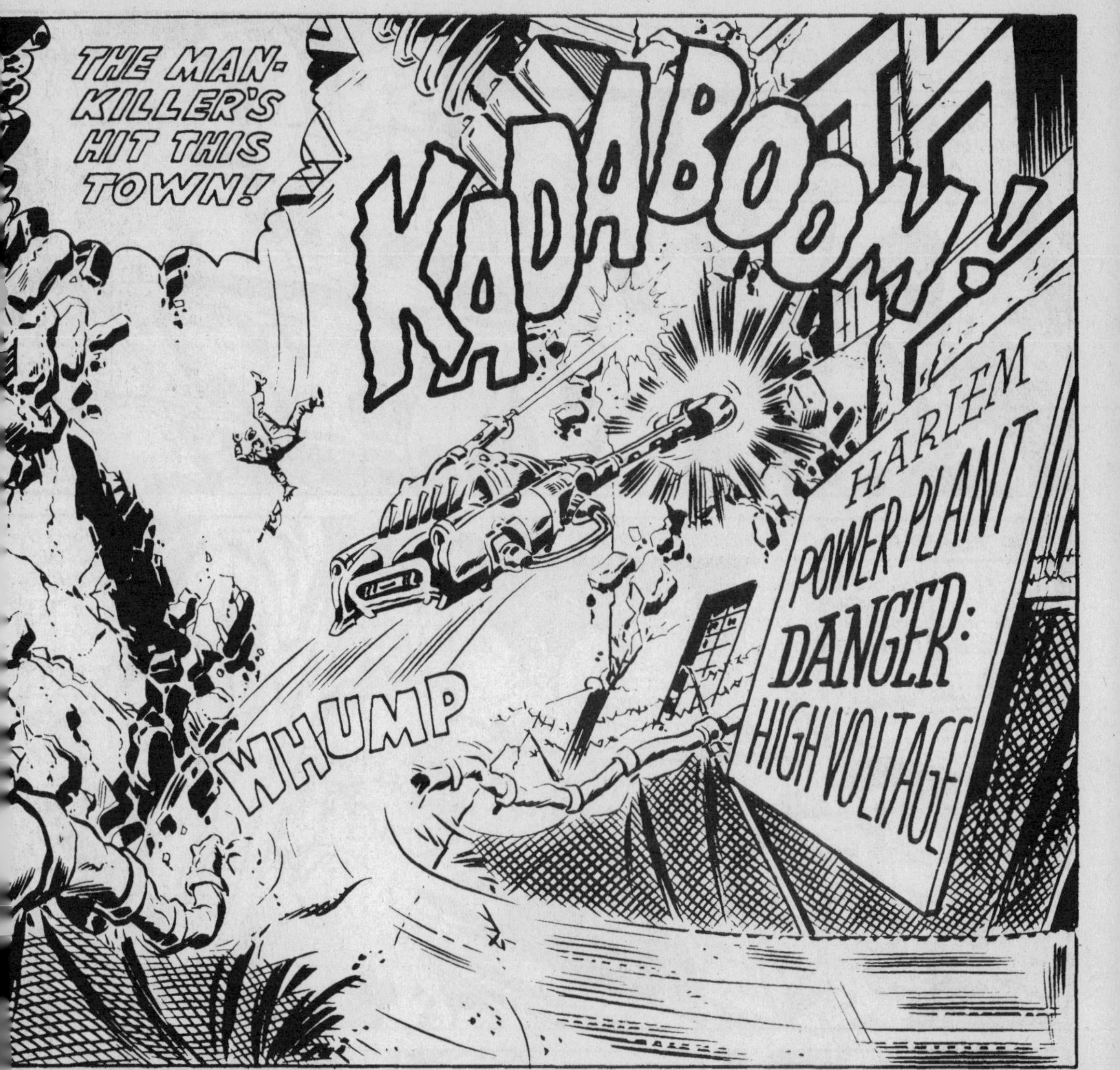
THE MAN-KILLER'S HIT THIS TOWN!
KADABOOM!
HARLEM POWER PLANT
DANGER: HIGH VOLTAGE
WHUMP

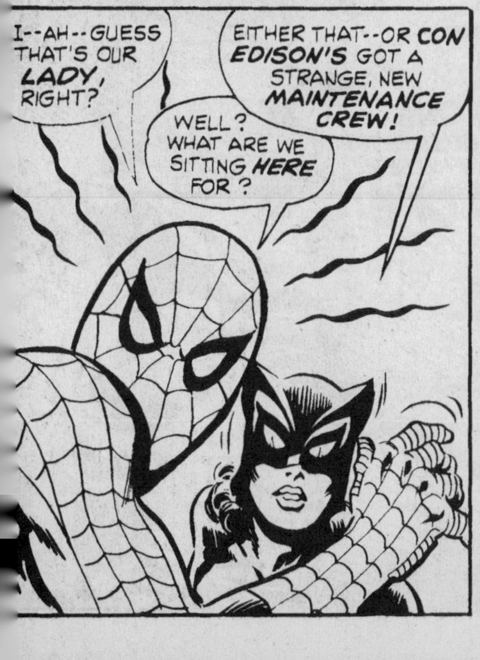
I--AH--GUESS THAT'S OUR LADY, RIGHT?
EITHER THAT--OR CON EDISON'S GOT A STRANGE, NEW MAINTENANCE CREW!
WELL? WHAT ARE WE SITTING HERE FOR?

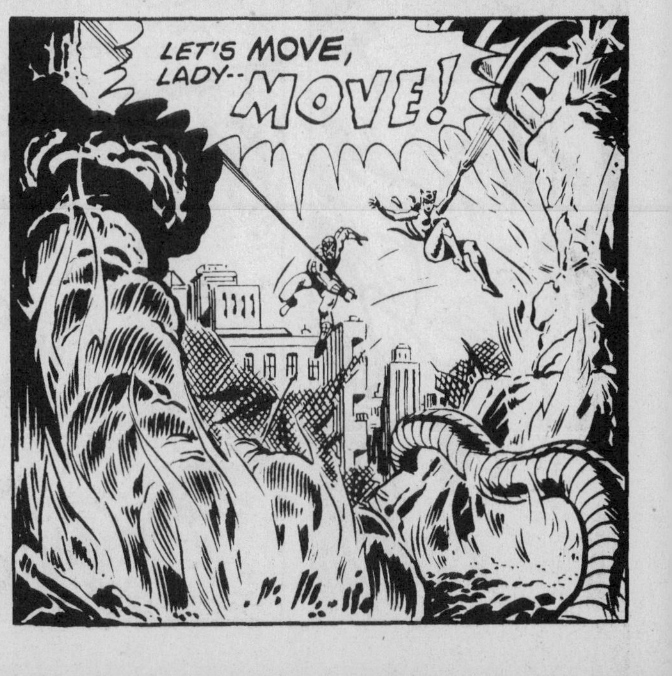
LET'S MOVE, LADY--MOVE!

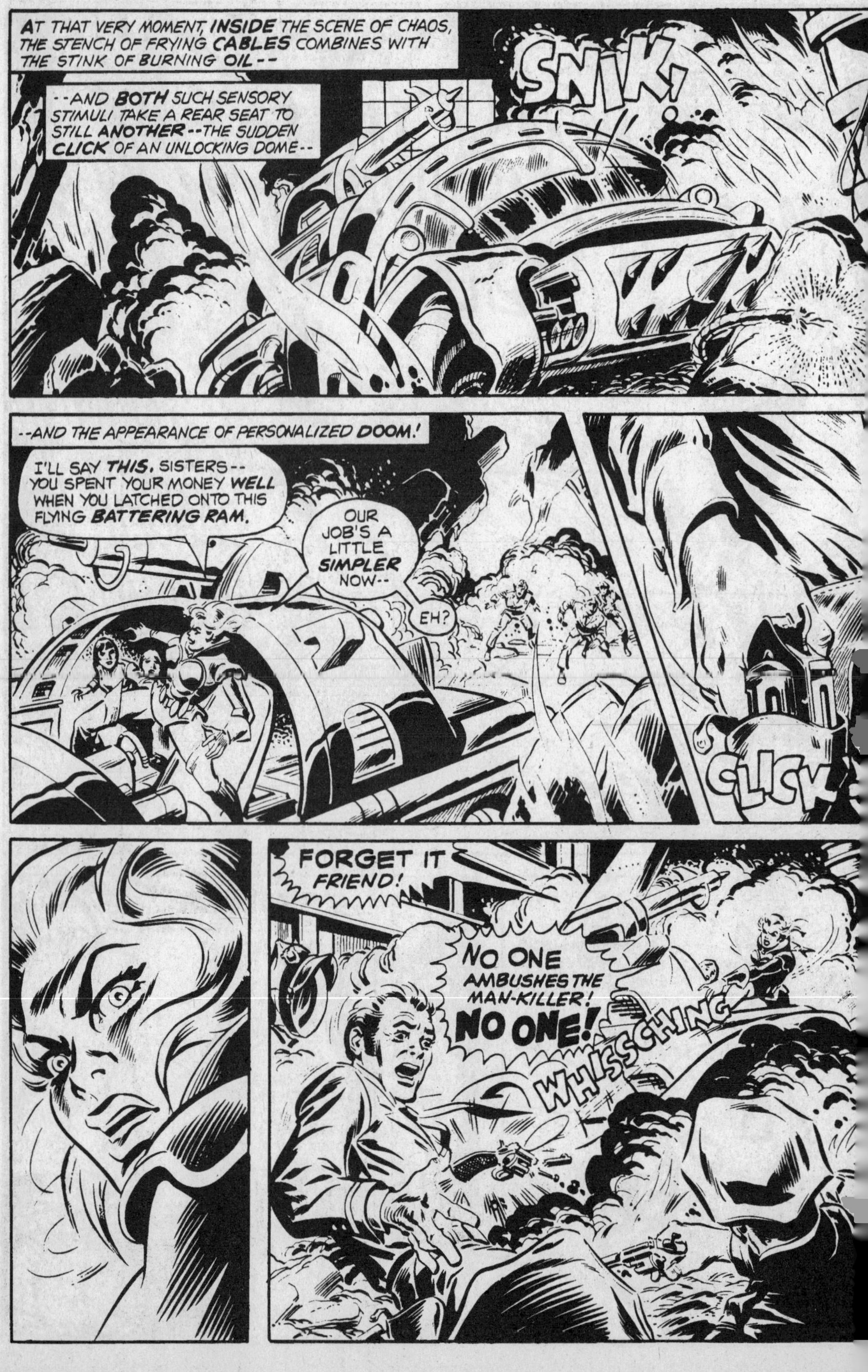
AT THAT VERY MOMENT, INSIDE THE SCENE OF CHAOS, THE STENCH OF FRYING CABLES COMBINES WITH THE STINK OF BURNING OIL--
SNIK,
--AND BOTH SUCH SENSORY STIMULI TAKE A REAR SEAT TO STILL ANOTHER--THE SUDDEN CLICK OF AN UNLOCKING DOME--
--AND THE APPEARANCE OF PERSONALIZED DOOM!
I'LL SAY THIS, SISTERS-- YOU SPENT YOUR MONEY WELL WHEN YOU LATCHED ONTO THIS FLYING BATTERING RAM.
OUR JOB'S A LITTLE SIMPLER NOW--
EH?
CLICK
FORGET IT FRIEND!
NO ONE AMBUSHES THE MAN-KILLER! NO ONE!
WHISSCHING

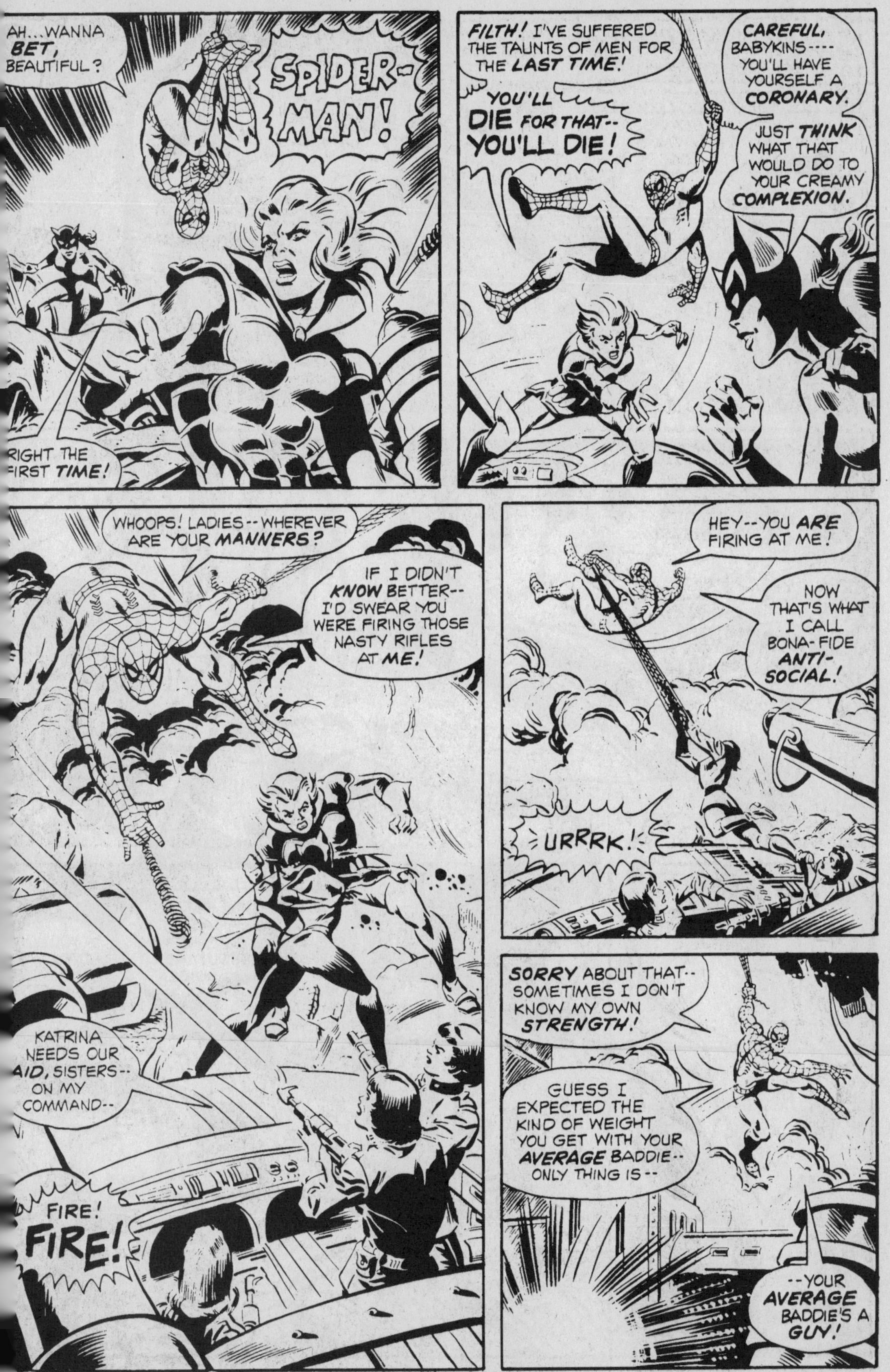
AH...WANNA BET, BEAUTIFUL?
SPIDER-MAN!
RIGHT THE FIRST TIME!
FILTH! I'VE SUFFERED THE TAUNTS OF MEN FOR THE LAST TIME!
YOU'LL DIE FOR THAT-- YOU'LL DIE!
CAREFUL, BABYKINS---- YOU'LL HAVE YOURSELF A CORONARY.
JUST THINK WHAT THAT WOULD DO TO YOUR CREAMY COMPLEXION.
WHOOPS! LADIES--WHEREVER ARE YOUR MANNERS?
IF I DIDN'T KNOW BETTER-- I'D SWEAR YOU WERE FIRING THOSE NASTY RIFLES AT ME!
KATRINA NEEDS OUR AID, SISTERS-- ON MY COMMAND--
FIRE! FIRE!
HEY--YOU ARE FIRING AT ME!
NOW THAT'S WHAT I CALL BONA-FIDE ANTI-SOCIAL!
URRRK!
SORRY ABOUT THAT-- SOMETIMES I DON'T KNOW MY OWN STRENGTH!
GUESS I EXPECTED THE KIND OF WEIGHT YOU GET WITH YOUR AVERAGE BADDIE-- ONLY THING IS--
--YOUR AVERAGE BADDIE'S A GUY!

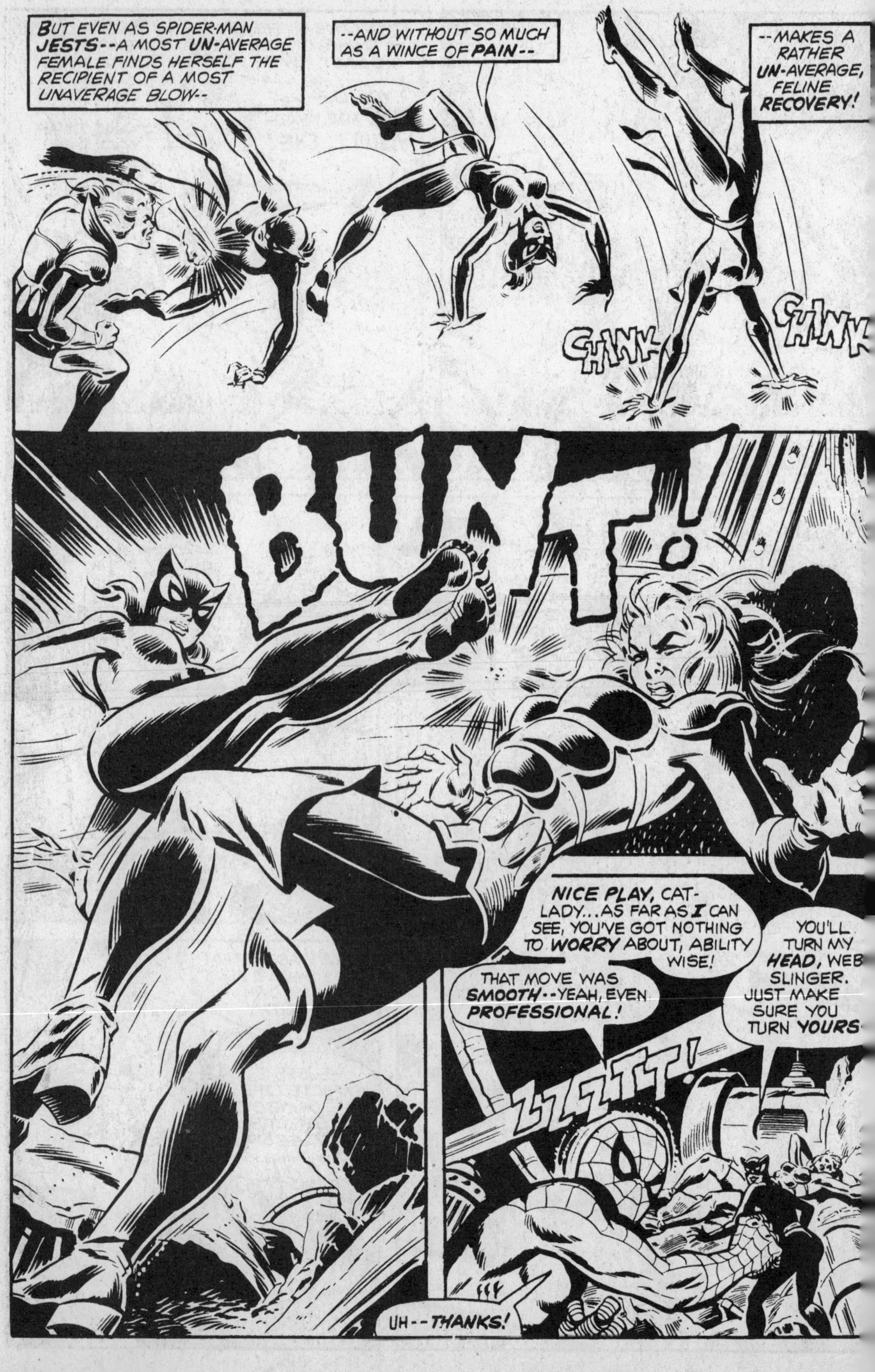
BUT EVEN AS SPIDER-MAN JESTS--A MOST UN-AVERAGE FEMALE FINDS HERSELF THE RECIPIENT OF A MOST UNAVERAGE BLOW--
--AND WITHOUT SO MUCH AS A WINCE OF PAIN--
--MAKES A RATHER UN-AVERAGE, FELINE RECOVERY!
CHINK
CHINK
BUNT!
NICE PLAY, CAT-LADY...AS FAR AS I CAN SEE, YOU'VE GOT NOTHING TO WORRY ABOUT, ABILITY WISE!
THAT MOVE WAS SMOOTH--YEAH, EVEN PROFESSIONAL!
YOU'LL TURN MY HEAD, WEB SLINGER. JUST MAKE SURE YOU TURN YOURS
ZZZTTT!
UH--THANKS!

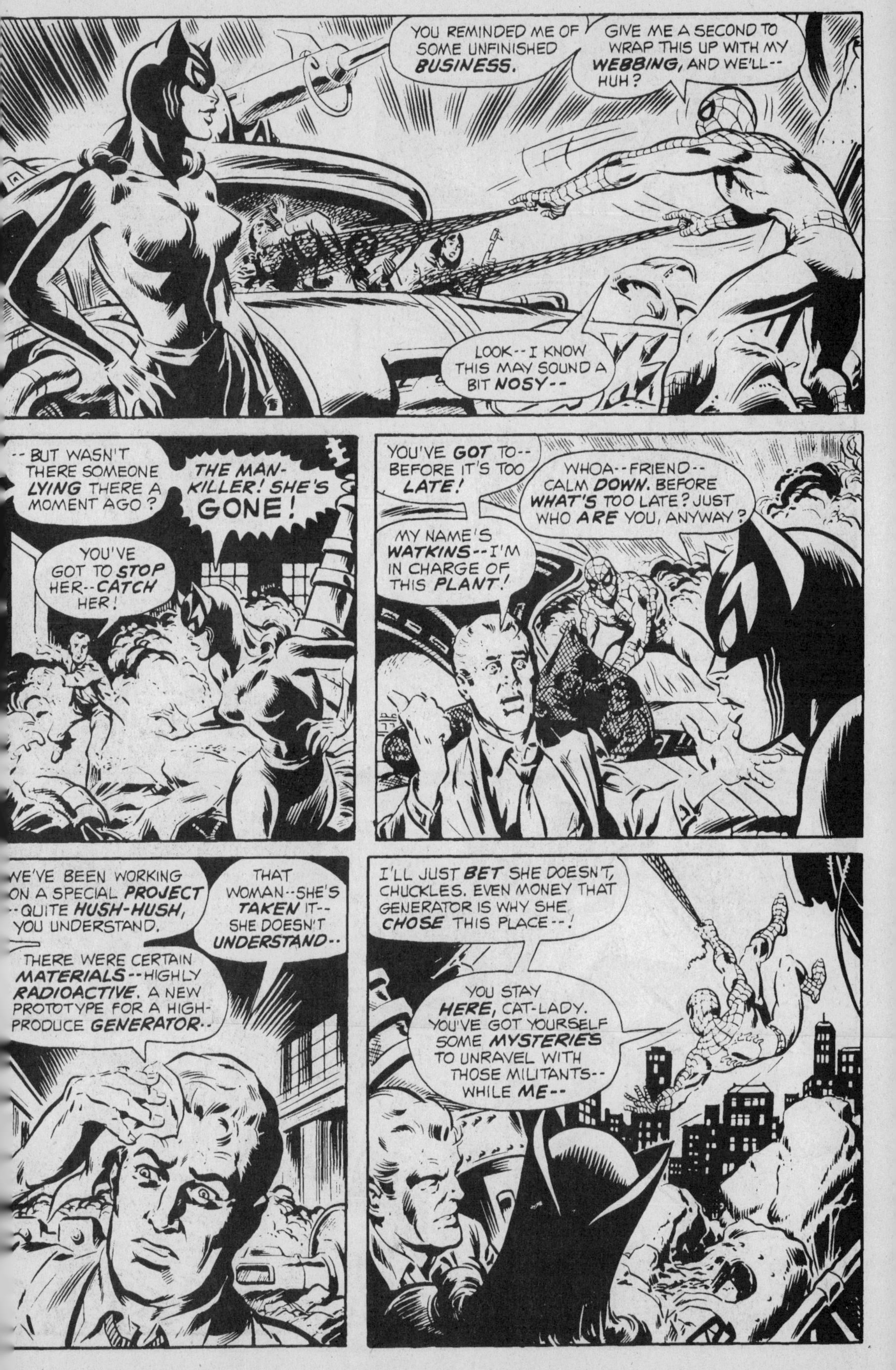
YOU REMINDED ME OF SOME UNFINISHED BUSINESS.
GIVE ME A SECOND TO WRAP THIS UP WITH MY WEBBING, AND WE'LL-- HUH?
LOOK--I KNOW THIS MAY SOUND A BIT NOSY--
--BUT WASN'T THERE SOMEONE LYING THERE A MOMENT AGO?
THE MAN-KILLER! SHE'S GONE!
YOU'VE GOT TO STOP HER--CATCH HER!
YOU'VE GOT TO--BEFORE IT'S TOO LATE!
WHOA--FRIEND--CALM DOWN. BEFORE WHAT'S TOO LATE? JUST WHO ARE YOU, ANYWAY?
MY NAME'S WATKINS--I'M IN CHARGE OF THIS PLANT!
WE'VE BEEN WORKING ON A SPECIAL PROJECT --QUITE HUSH-HUSH, YOU UNDERSTAND.
THERE WERE CERTAIN MATERIALS--HIGHLY RADIOACTIVE. A NEW PROTOTYPE FOR A HIGH-PRODUCE GENERATOR..
THAT WOMAN--SHE'S TAKEN IT-- SHE DOESN'T UNDERSTAND..
I'LL JUST BET SHE DOESN'T, CHUCKLES. EVEN MONEY THAT GENERATOR IS WHY SHE CHOSE THIS PLACE--!
YOU STAY HERE, CAT-LADY. YOU'VE GOT YOURSELF SOME MYSTERIES TO UNRAVEL WITH THOSE MILITANTS--WHILE ME--

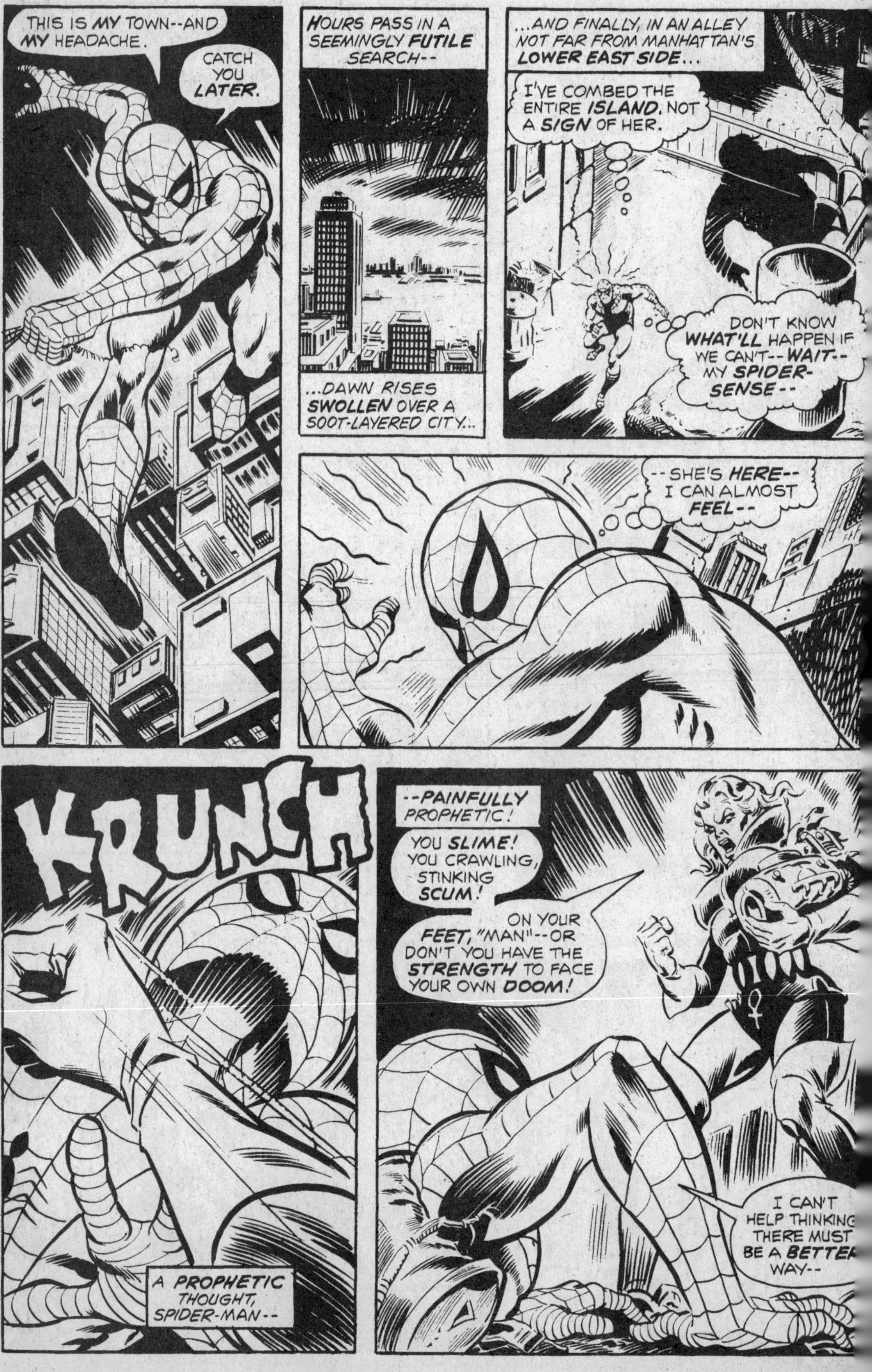
THIS IS MY TOWN--AND MY HEADACHE.
CATCH YOU LATER.
HOURS PASS IN A SEEMINGLY FUTILE SEARCH--
...DAWN RISES SWOLLEN OVER A SOOT-LAYERED CITY...
...AND FINALLY, IN AN ALLEY NOT FAR FROM MANHATTAN'S LOWER EAST SIDE...
I'VE COMBED THE ENTIRE ISLAND. NOT A SIGN OF HER.
DON'T KNOW WHAT'LL HAPPEN IF WE CAN'T--WAIT--MY SPIDER-SENSE--
--SHE'S HERE-- I CAN ALMOST FEEL--
KRUNCH
A PROPHETIC THOUGHT, SPIDER-MAN--
--PAINFULLY PROPHETIC!
YOU SLIME! YOU CRAWLING, STINKING SCUM!
ON YOUR FEET, "MAN"--OR DON'T YOU HAVE THE STRENGTH TO FACE YOUR OWN DOOM!
I CAN'T HELP THINKING THERE MUST BE A BETTER WAY--

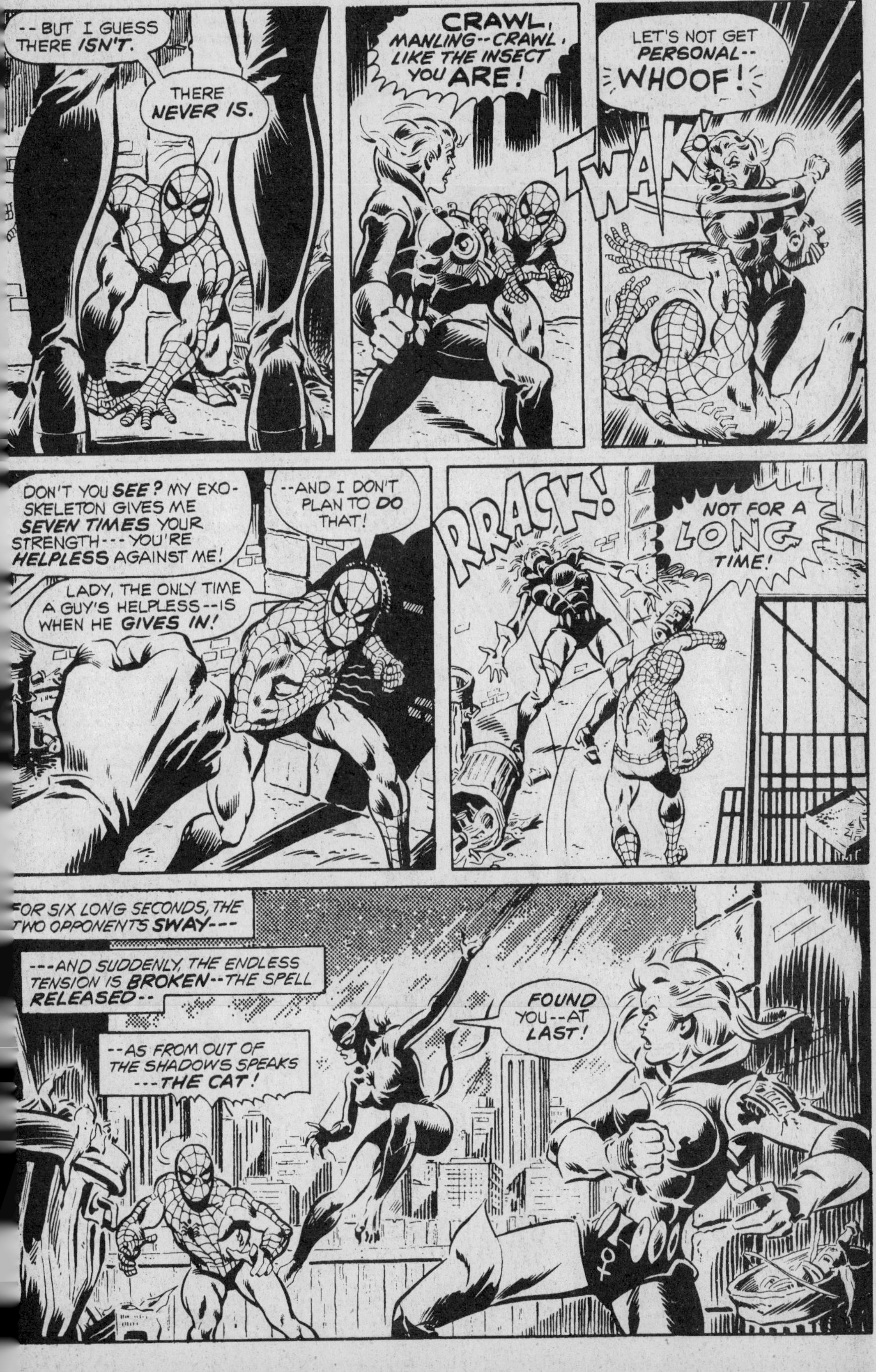
-- BUT I GUESS THERE ISN'T.
THERE NEVER IS.
CRAWL, MANLING--CRAWL, LIKE THE INSECT YOU ARE!
LET'S NOT GET PERSONAL-- WHOOF!
TWAK!
DON'T YOU SEE? MY EXO-SKELETON GIVES ME SEVEN TIMES YOUR STRENGTH--- YOU'RE HELPLESS AGAINST ME!
LADY, THE ONLY TIME A GUY'S HELPLESS--IS WHEN HE GIVES IN!
--AND I DON'T PLAN TO DO THAT!
RRACK!
NOT FOR A LONG TIME!
FOR SIX LONG SECONDS, THE TWO OPPONENTS SWAY---
---AND SUDDENLY, THE ENDLESS TENSION IS BROKEN--THE SPELL RELEASED--
--AS FROM OUT OF THE SHADOWS SPEAKS ---THE CAT!
FOUND YOU--AT LAST!

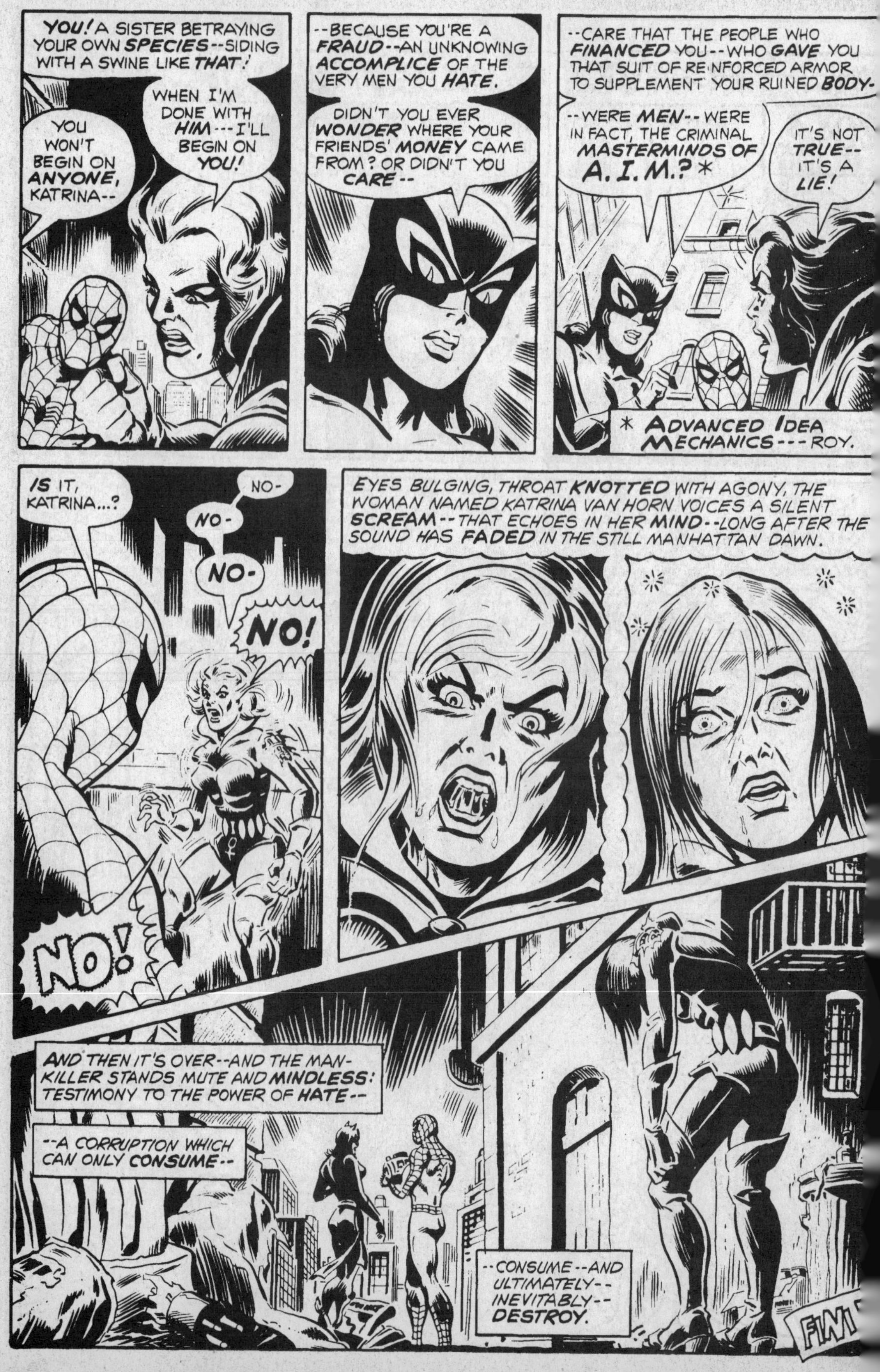

YOU! A SISTER BETRAYING YOUR OWN SPECIES--SIDING WITH A SWINE LIKE THAT!
WHEN I'M DONE WITH HIM---I'LL BEGIN ON YOU!
YOU WON'T BEGIN ON ANYONE, KATRINA--
--BECAUSE YOU'RE A FRAUD--AN UNKNOWING ACCOMPLICE OF THE VERY MEN YOU HATE.
DIDN'T YOU EVER WONDER WHERE YOUR FRIENDS' MONEY CAME FROM? OR DIDN'T YOU CARE--
--CARE THAT THE PEOPLE WHO FINANCED YOU--WHO GAVE YOU THAT SUIT OF RE-INFORCED ARMOR TO SUPPLEMENT YOUR RUINED BODY-
--WERE MEN--WERE IN FACT, THE CRIMINAL MASTERMINDS OF A.I.M.? *
IT'S NOT TRUE--IT'S A LIE!
* ADVANCED IDEA MECHANICS---ROY.
IS IT, KATRINA...?
NO-
NO-
NO-
NO!
NO!
EYES BULGING, THROAT KNOTTED WITH AGONY, THE WOMAN NAMED KATRINA VAN HORN VOICES A SILENT SCREAM--THAT ECHOES IN HER MIND--LONG AFTER THE SOUND HAS FADED IN THE STILL MANHATTAN DAWN.
AND THEN IT'S OVER--AND THE MAN-KILLER STANDS MUTE AND MINDLESS: TESTIMONY TO THE POWER OF HATE--
--A CORRUPTION WHICH CAN ONLY CONSUME--
--CONSUME--AND ULTIMATELY--INEVITABLY--DESTROY.
FINI

MARVEL TEAM-UP
MARVEL COMICS GROUP
20¢
9 MAY 02147
MARVEL TEAM-UP
FEATURING
SPIDER-MAN
AND
THE INVINCIBLE
IRON MAN
WH--? WHERE IN BLAZES ARE WE, WALL-CRAWLER?
WELL-- WE CAME FROM TODAY--
--AND THIS SURE AIN'T YESTERDAY--
SO, OFFHAND I'D SAY WE'RE SMACK-DAB IN THE MIDDLE OF--
...The TOMORROW WAR!

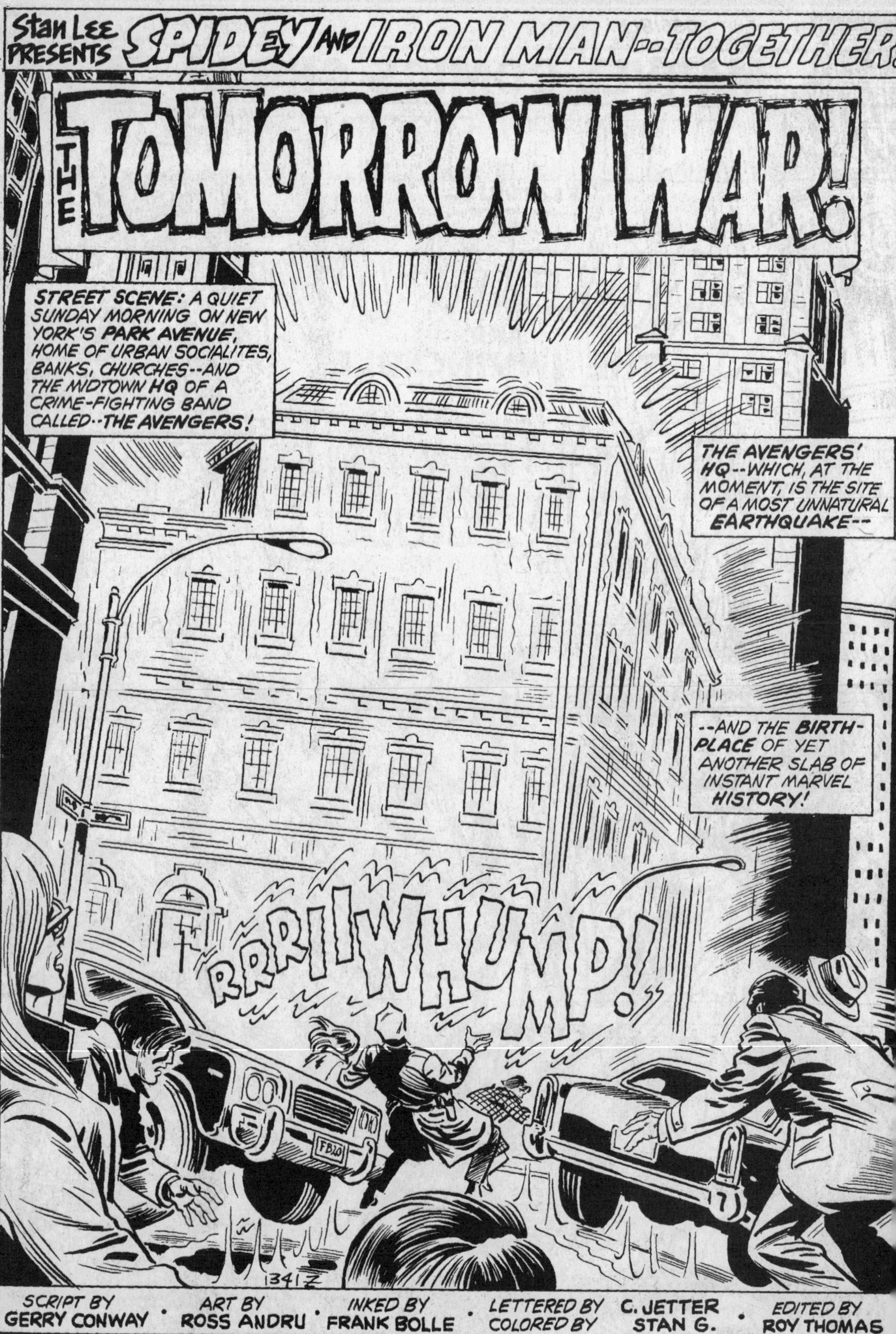
Stan Lee PRESENTS SPIDEY AND IRON MAN--TOGETHER!
THE TOMORROW WAR!
STREET SCENE: A QUIET SUNDAY MORNING ON NEW YORK'S PARK AVENUE, HOME OF URBAN SOCIALITES, BANKS, CHURCHES--AND THE MIDTOWN HQ OF A CRIME-FIGHTING BAND CALLED--THE AVENGERS!
THE AVENGERS' HQ--WHICH, AT THE MOMENT, IS THE SITE OF A MOST UNNATURAL EARTHQUAKE--
--AND THE BIRTH-PLACE OF YET ANOTHER SLAB OF INSTANT MARVEL HISTORY!
RRRIWHUMP!
FB20
SCRIPT BY GERRY CONWAY • ART BY ROSS ANDRU • INKED BY FRANK BOLLE • LETTERED BY C. JETTER COLORED BY STAN G. • EDITED BY ROY THOMAS

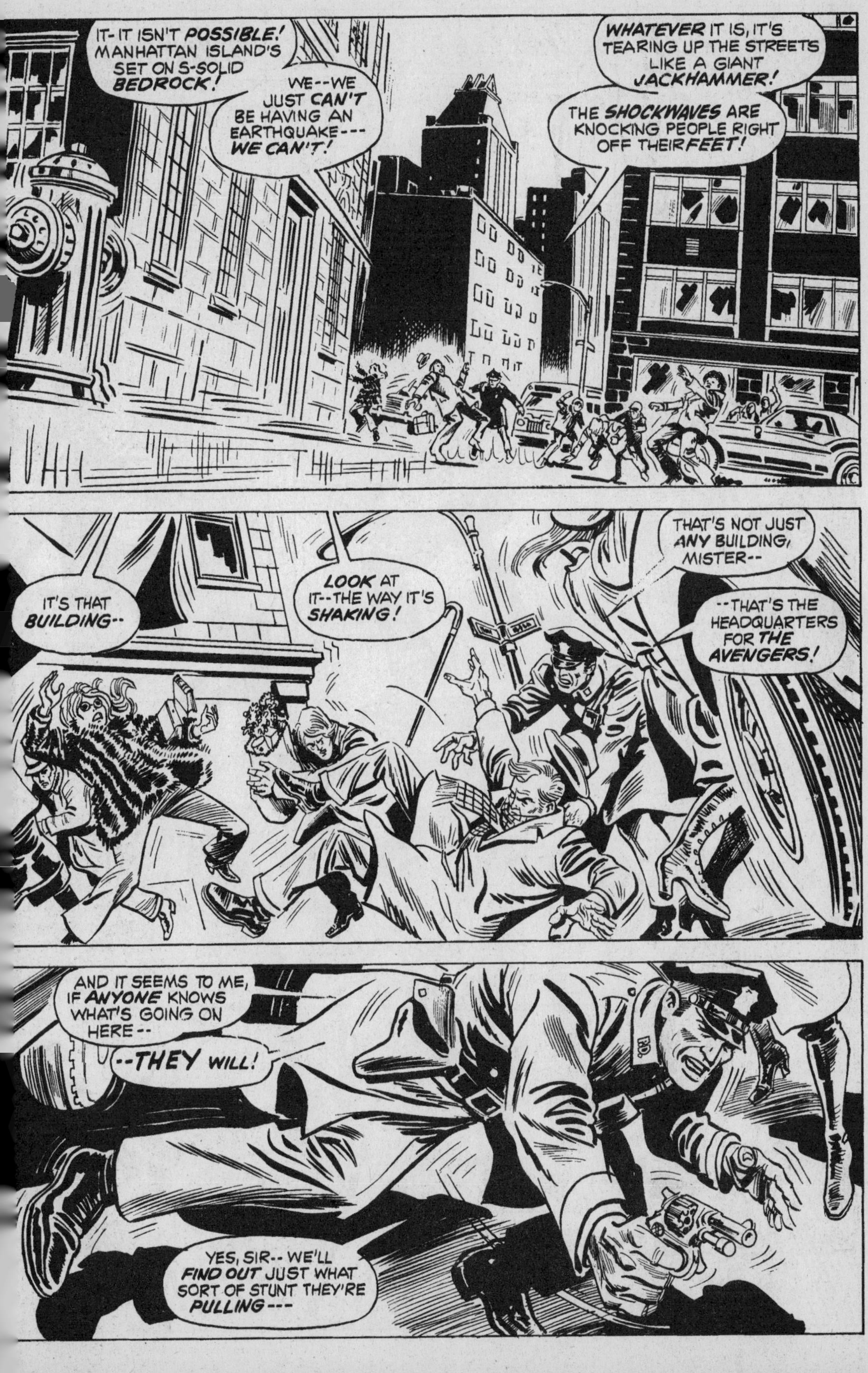

IT- IT ISN'T POSSIBLE! MANHATTAN ISLAND'S SET ON S-SOLID BEDROCK!
WE--WE JUST CAN'T BE HAVING AN EARTHQUAKE--- WE CAN'T!
WHATEVER IT IS, IT'S TEARING UP THE STREETS LIKE A GIANT JACKHAMMER!
THE SHOCKWAVES ARE KNOCKING PEOPLE RIGHT OFF THEIR FEET!
IT'S THAT BUILDING--
LOOK AT IT--THE WAY IT'S SHAKING!
THAT'S NOT JUST ANY BUILDING, MISTER--
--THAT'S THE HEADQUARTERS FOR THE AVENGERS!
AND IT SEEMS TO ME, IF ANYONE KNOWS WHAT'S GOING ON HERE --
--THEY WILL!
YES, SIR-- WE'LL FIND OUT JUST WHAT SORT OF STUNT THEY'RE PULLING---

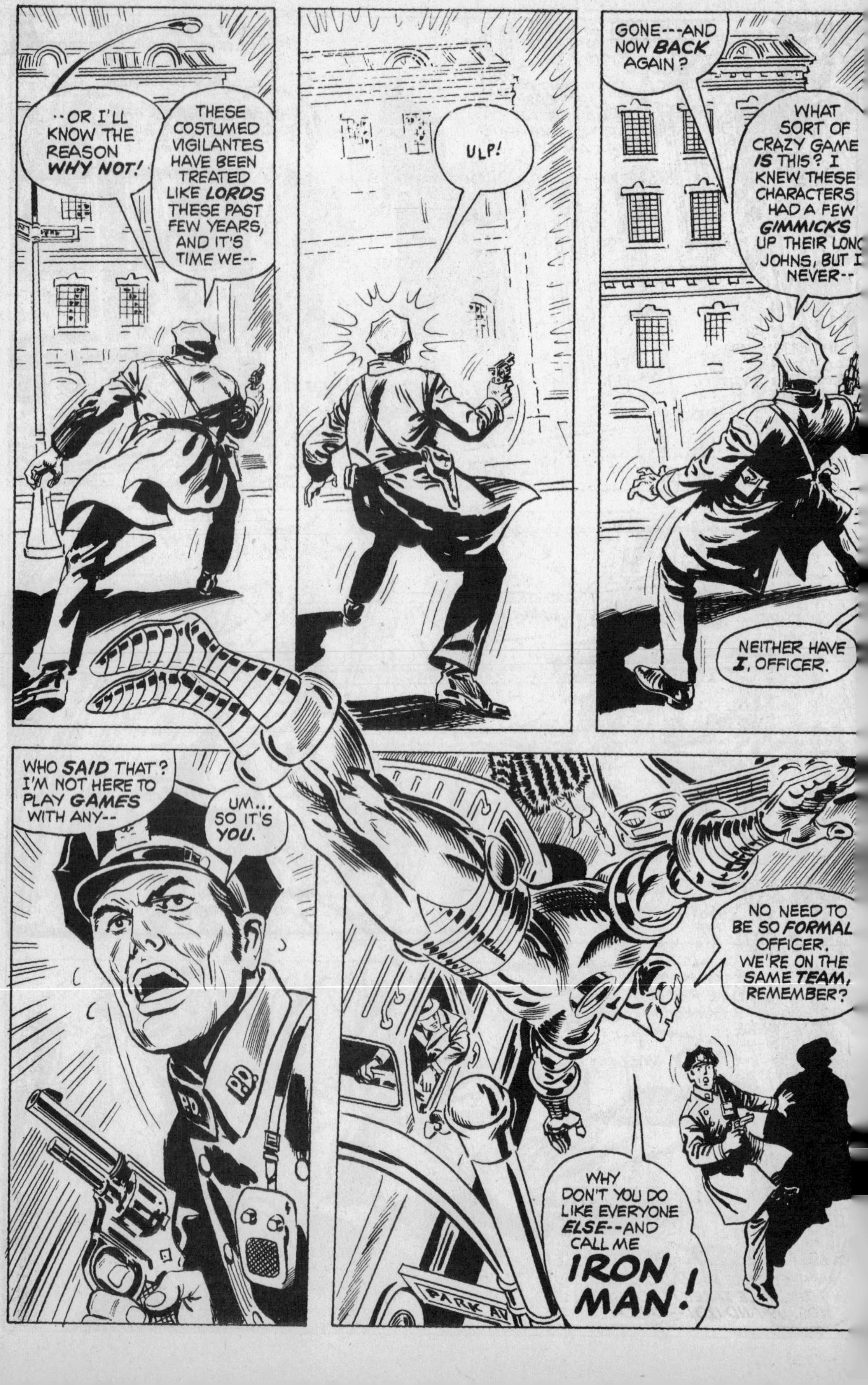

..OR I'LL KNOW THE REASON WHY NOT!
THESE COSTUMED VIGILANTES HAVE BEEN TREATED LIKE LORDS THESE PAST FEW YEARS, AND IT'S TIME WE--
ULP!
GONE---AND NOW BACK AGAIN?
WHAT SORT OF CRAZY GAME IS THIS? I KNEW THESE CHARACTERS HAD A FEW GIMMICKS UP THEIR LONG JOHNS, BUT I NEVER--
NEITHER HAVE I, OFFICER.
WHO SAID THAT? I'M NOT HERE TO PLAY GAMES WITH ANY--
UM... SO IT'S YOU.
NO NEED TO BE SO FORMAL OFFICER. WE'RE ON THE SAME TEAM, REMEMBER?
WHY DON'T YOU DO LIKE EVERYONE ELSE--AND CALL ME IRON MAN!
PARK AV

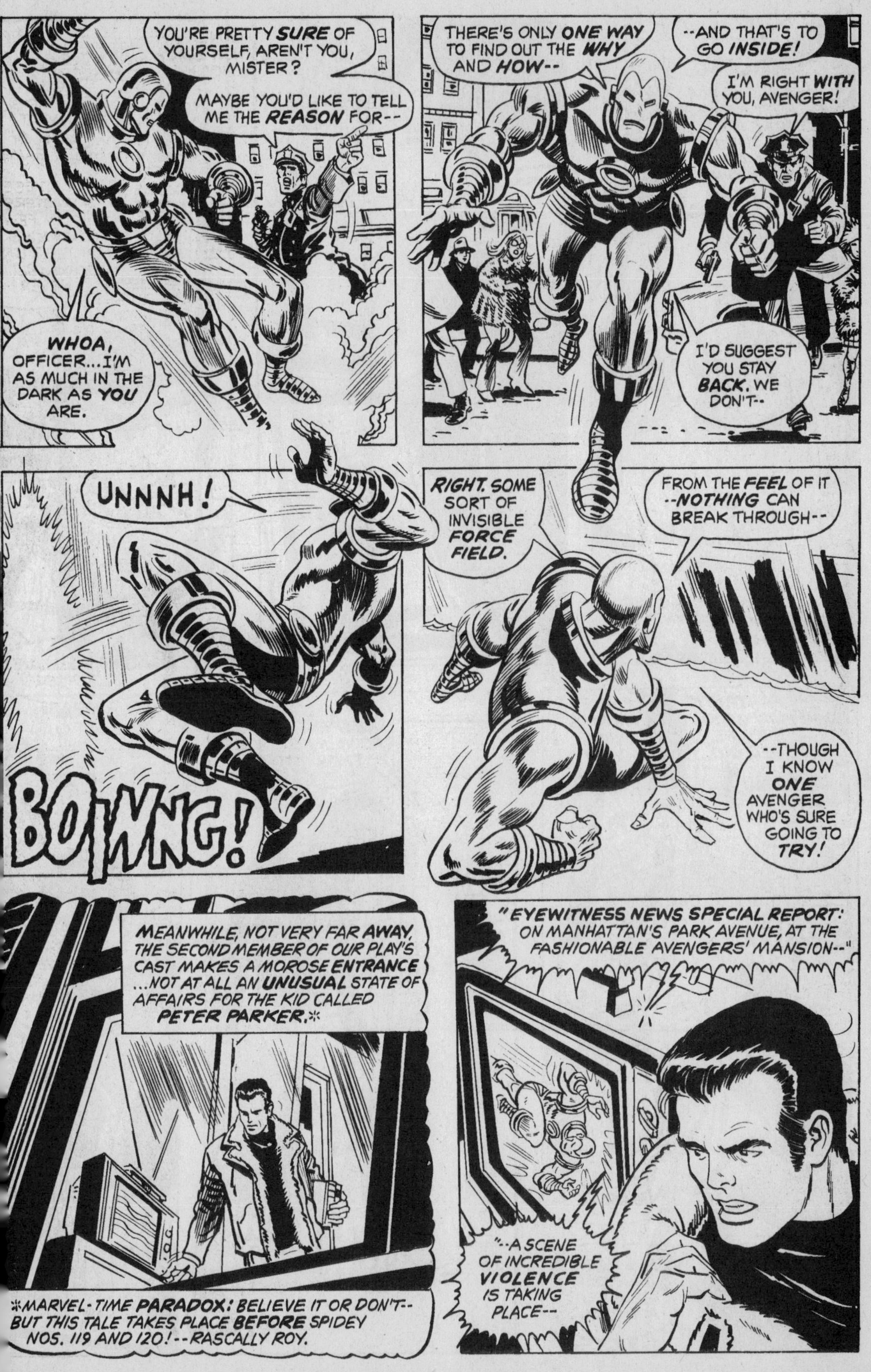
YOU'RE PRETTY SURE OF YOURSELF, AREN'T YOU, MISTER?
MAYBE YOU'D LIKE TO TELL ME THE REASON FOR--
WHOA, OFFICER...I'M AS MUCH IN THE DARK AS YOU ARE.
THERE'S ONLY ONE WAY TO FIND OUT THE WHY AND HOW--
--AND THAT'S TO GO INSIDE!
I'M RIGHT WITH YOU, AVENGER!
I'D SUGGEST YOU STAY BACK. WE DON'T--
UNNNH!
BOWNG!
RIGHT. SOME SORT OF INVISIBLE FORCE FIELD.
FROM THE FEEL OF IT --NOTHING CAN BREAK THROUGH--
--THOUGH I KNOW ONE AVENGER WHO'S SURE GOING TO TRY!
MEANWHILE, NOT VERY FAR AWAY, THE SECOND MEMBER OF OUR PLAY'S CAST MAKES A MOROSE ENTRANCE ...NOT AT ALL AN UNUSUAL STATE OF AFFAIRS FOR THE KID CALLED PETER PARKER.*
*MARVEL-TIME PARADOX: BELIEVE IT OR DON'T-- BUT THIS TALE TAKES PLACE BEFORE SPIDEY NOS. 119 AND 120! --RASCALLY ROY.
"EYEWITNESS NEWS SPECIAL REPORT: ON MANHATTAN'S PARK AVENUE, AT THE FASHIONABLE AVENGERS' MANSION--"
"--A SCENE OF INCREDIBLE VIOLENCE IS TAKING PLACE--

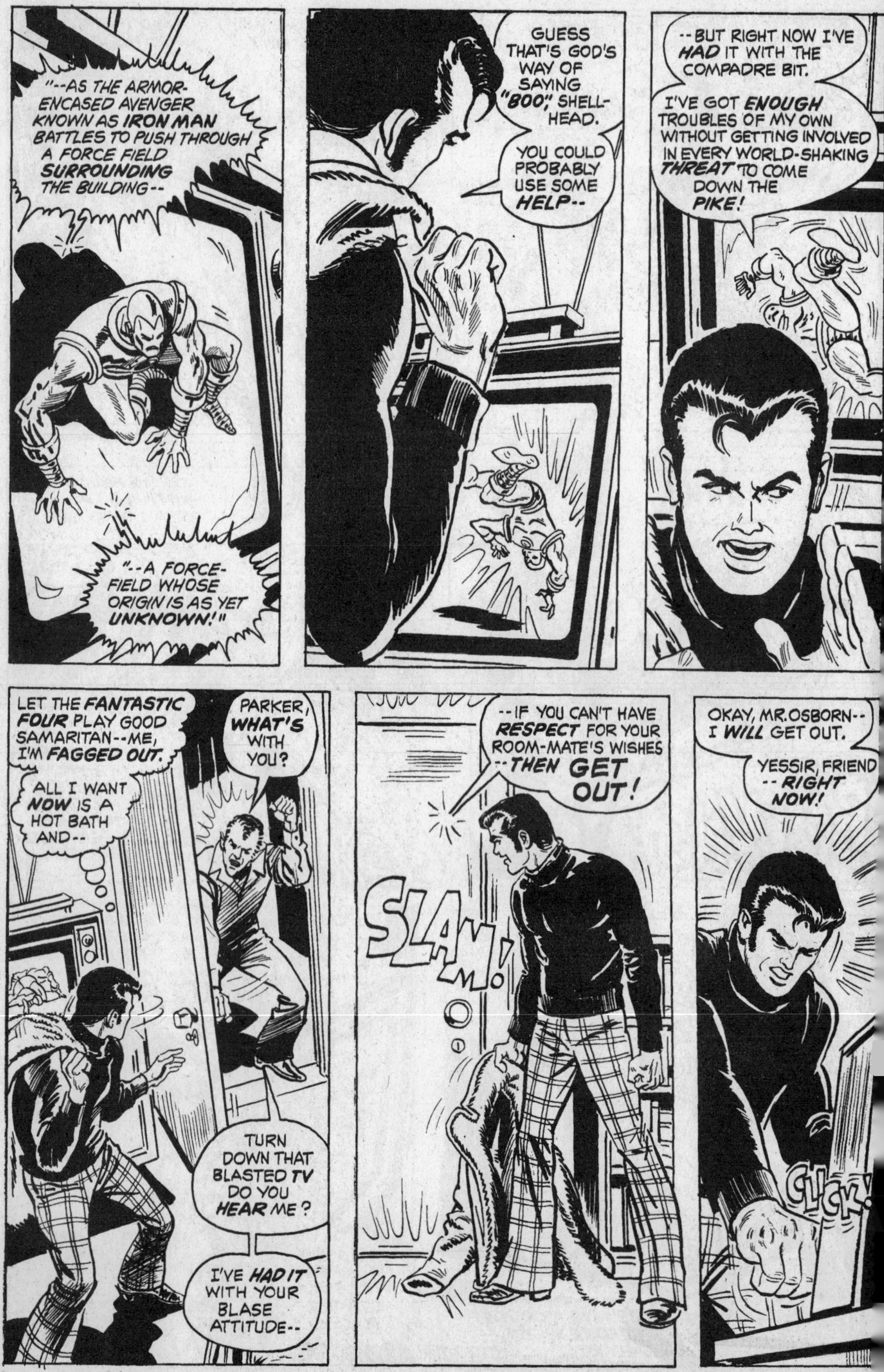
"--AS THE ARMOR-ENCASED AVENGER KNOWN AS IRON MAN BATTLES TO PUSH THROUGH A FORCE FIELD SURROUNDING THE BUILDING--
"--A FORCE-FIELD WHOSE ORIGIN IS AS YET UNKNOWN!"
GUESS THAT'S GOD'S WAY OF SAYING "BOO," SHELL-HEAD.
YOU COULD PROBABLY USE SOME HELP--
--BUT RIGHT NOW I'VE HAD IT WITH THE COMPADRE BIT.
I'VE GOT ENOUGH TROUBLES OF MY OWN WITHOUT GETTING INVOLVED IN EVERY WORLD-SHAKING THREAT TO COME DOWN THE PIKE!
LET THE FANTASTIC FOUR PLAY GOOD SAMARITAN--ME, I'M FAGGED OUT.
ALL I WANT NOW IS A HOT BATH AND--
PARKER, WHAT'S WITH YOU?
TURN DOWN THAT BLASTED TV DO YOU HEAR ME?
I'VE HAD IT WITH YOUR BLASE ATTITUDE--
--IF YOU CAN'T HAVE RESPECT FOR YOUR ROOM-MATE'S WISHES --THEN GET OUT!
SLAM!
OKAY, MR. OSBORN-- I WILL GET OUT.
YESSIR, FRIEND --RIGHT NOW!
CLICK!

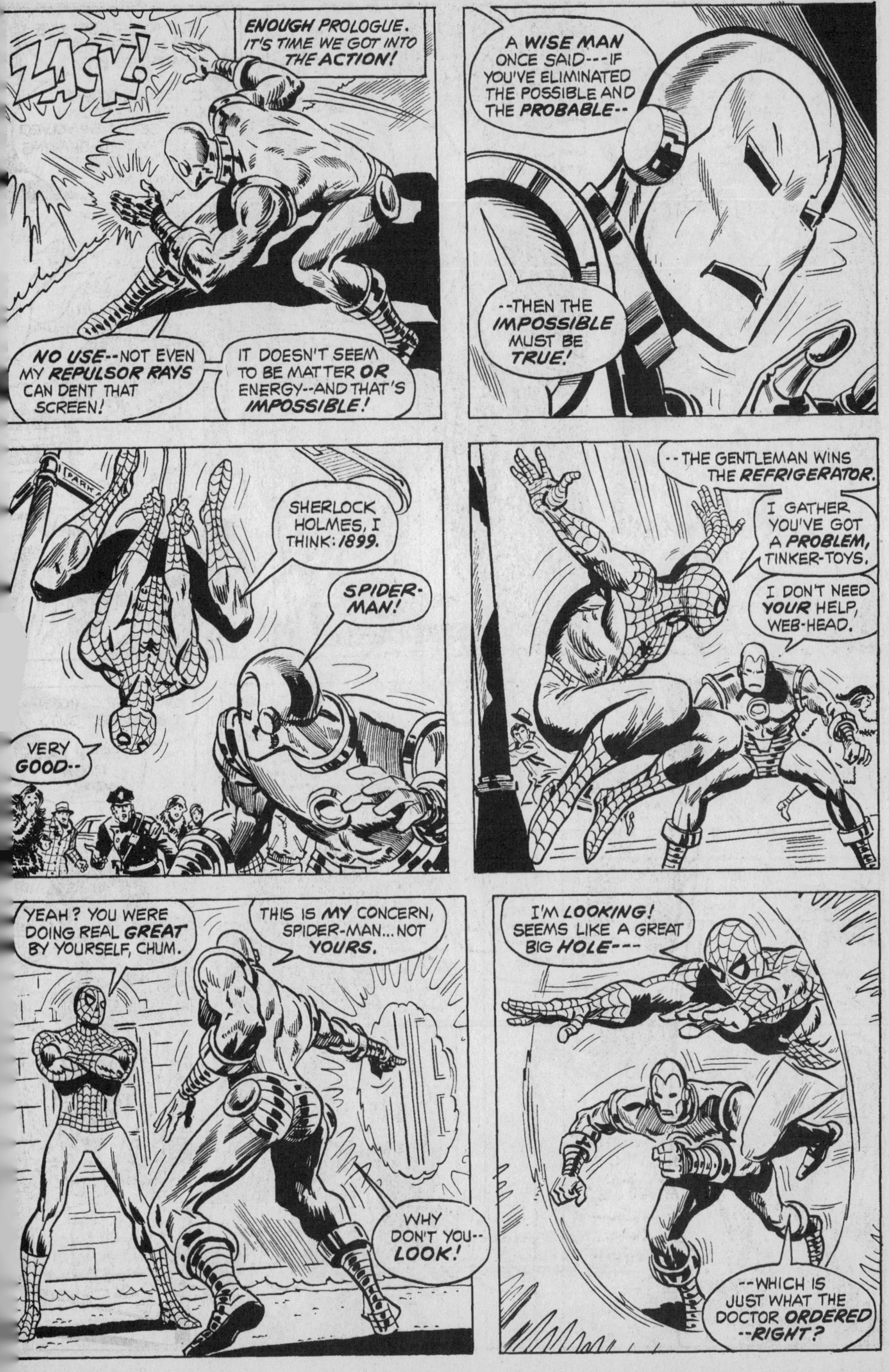
ZACK!
ENOUGH PROLOGUE. IT'S TIME WE GOT INTO THE ACTION!
NO USE--NOT EVEN MY REPULSOR RAYS CAN DENT THAT SCREEN!
IT DOESN'T SEEM TO BE MATTER OR ENERGY--AND THAT'S IMPOSSIBLE!
A WISE MAN ONCE SAID---IF YOU'VE ELIMINATED THE POSSIBLE AND THE PROBABLE--
--THEN THE IMPOSSIBLE MUST BE TRUE!
PARK
SHERLOCK HOLMES, I THINK: 1899.
SPIDER-MAN!
VERY GOOD--
--THE GENTLEMAN WINS THE REFRIGERATOR.
I GATHER YOU'VE GOT A PROBLEM, TINKER-TOYS.
I DON'T NEED YOUR HELP, WEB-HEAD.
YEAH? YOU WERE DOING REAL GREAT BY YOURSELF, CHUM.
THIS IS MY CONCERN, SPIDER-MAN... NOT YOURS.
WHY DON'T YOU--LOOK!
I'M LOOKING! SEEMS LIKE A GREAT BIG HOLE---
--WHICH IS JUST WHAT THE DOCTOR ORDERED --RIGHT?

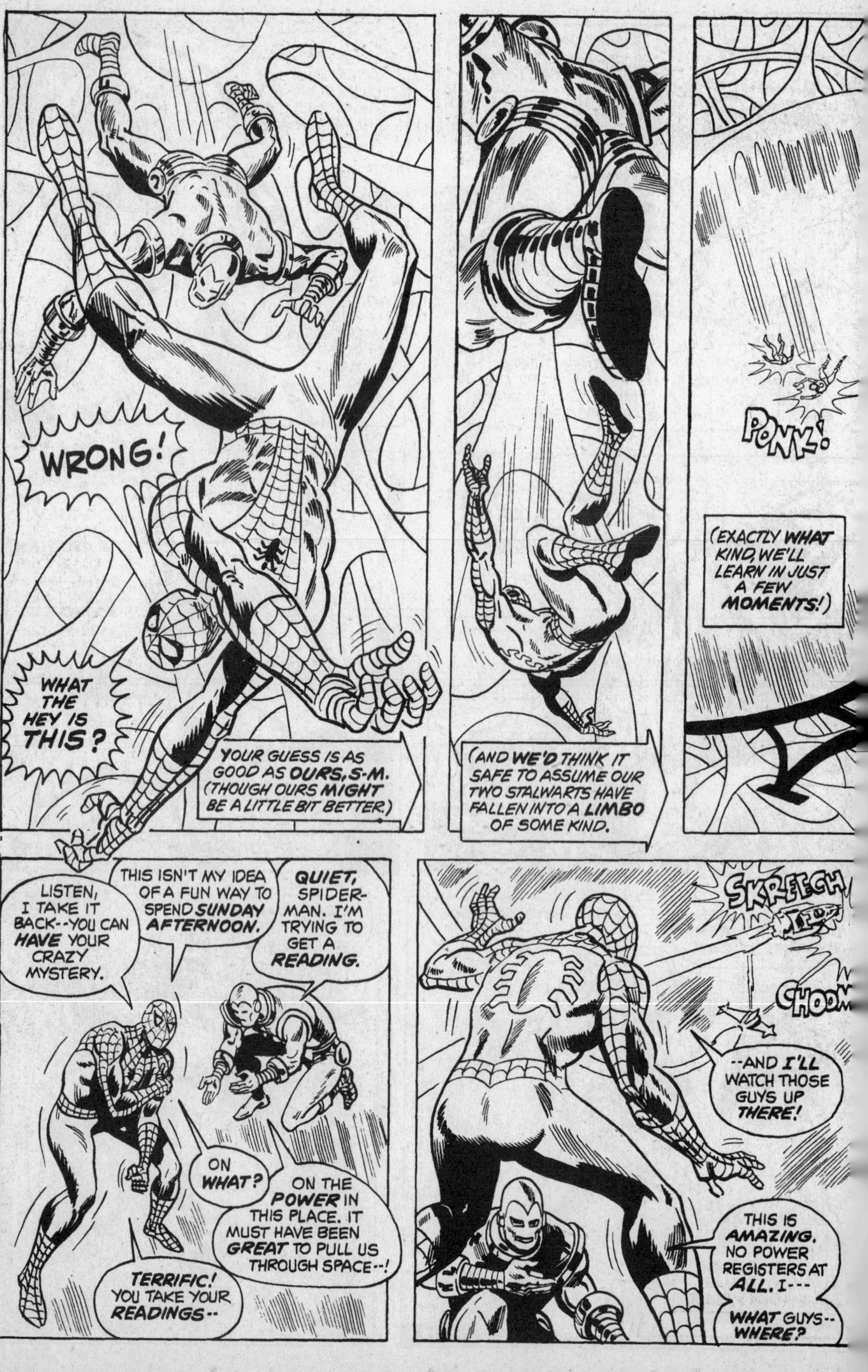
WRONG!
WHAT THE HEY IS THIS?
YOUR GUESS IS AS GOOD AS OURS, S-M. (THOUGH OURS MIGHT BE A LITTLE BIT BETTER.)
(AND WE'D THINK IT SAFE TO ASSUME OUR TWO STALWARTS HAVE FALLEN INTO A LIMBO OF SOME KIND.
PONK!
(EXACTLY WHAT KIND, WE'LL LEARN IN JUST A FEW MOMENTS!)
LISTEN, I TAKE IT BACK--YOU CAN HAVE YOUR CRAZY MYSTERY.
THIS ISN'T MY IDEA OF A FUN WAY TO SPEND SUNDAY AFTERNOON.
QUIET, SPIDER-MAN. I'M TRYING TO GET A READING.
ON WHAT?
ON THE POWER IN THIS PLACE. IT MUST HAVE BEEN GREAT TO PULL US THROUGH SPACE--!
TERRIFIC! YOU TAKE YOUR READINGS--
SKREECH
--AND I'LL WATCH THOSE GUYS UP THERE!
THIS IS AMAZING. NO POWER REGISTERS AT ALL. I---
WHAT GUYS--WHERE?

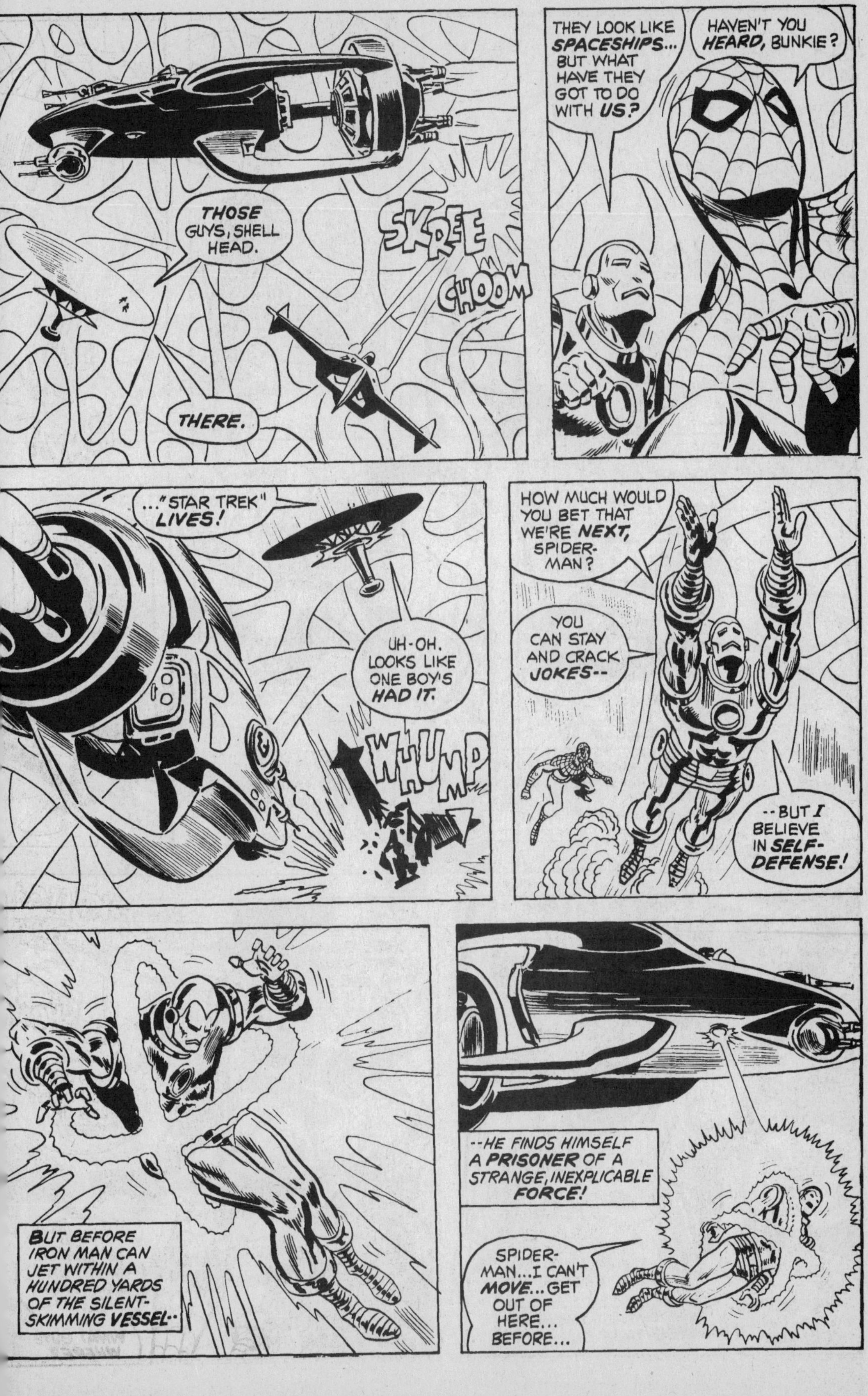
THOSE GUYS, SHELL HEAD.
THERE.
SKREE
CHOOM
THEY LOOK LIKE SPACESHIPS... BUT WHAT HAVE THEY GOT TO DO WITH US?
HAVEN'T YOU HEARD, BUNKIE?
..."STAR TREK" LIVES!
UH-OH. LOOKS LIKE ONE BOY'S HAD IT.
WHUMP
HOW MUCH WOULD YOU BET THAT WE'RE NEXT, SPIDER-MAN?
YOU CAN STAY AND CRACK JOKES--
--BUT I BELIEVE IN SELF-DEFENSE!
BUT BEFORE IRON MAN CAN JET WITHIN A HUNDRED YARDS OF THE SILENT-SKIMMING VESSEL--
--HE FINDS HIMSELF A PRISONER OF A STRANGE, INEXPLICABLE FORCE!
SPIDER-MAN...I CAN'T MOVE...GET OUT OF HERE... BEFORE...

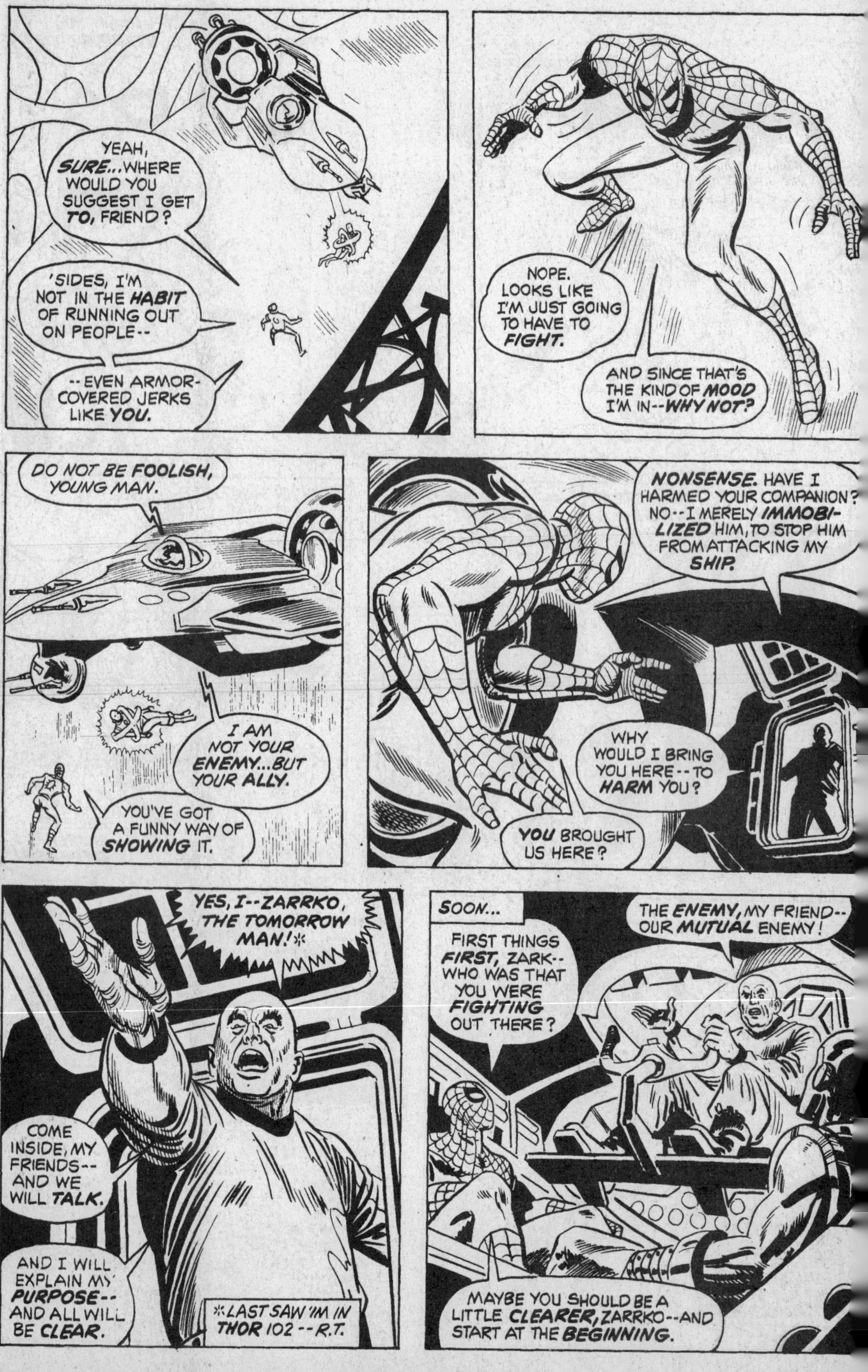
YEAH, SURE...WHERE WOULD YOU SUGGEST I GET TO, FRIEND?
'SIDES, I'M NOT IN THE HABIT OF RUNNING OUT ON PEOPLE--
--EVEN ARMOR-COVERED JERKS LIKE YOU.
NOPE. LOOKS LIKE I'M JUST GOING TO HAVE TO FIGHT.
AND SINCE THAT'S THE KIND OF MOOD I'M IN--WHY NOT?
DO NOT BE FOOLISH, YOUNG MAN.
I AM NOT YOUR ENEMY...BUT YOUR ALLY.
YOU'VE GOT A FUNNY WAY OF SHOWING IT.
NONSENSE. HAVE I HARMED YOUR COMPANION? NO--I MERELY IMMOBILIZED HIM, TO STOP HIM FROM ATTACKING MY SHIP.
WHY WOULD I BRING YOU HERE--TO HARM YOU?
YOU BROUGHT US HERE?
YES, I--ZARRKO, THE TOMORROW MAN!*
COME INSIDE, MY FRIENDS--AND WE WILL TALK.
AND I WILL EXPLAIN MY PURPOSE--AND ALL WILL BE CLEAR.
*LAST SAW 'IM IN THOR 102 --R.T.
SOON...
FIRST THINGS FIRST, ZARK--WHO WAS THAT YOU WERE FIGHTING OUT THERE?
THE ENEMY, MY FRIEND--OUR MUTUAL ENEMY!
MAYBE YOU SHOULD BE A LITTLE CLEARER, ZARRKO--AND START AT THE BEGINNING.

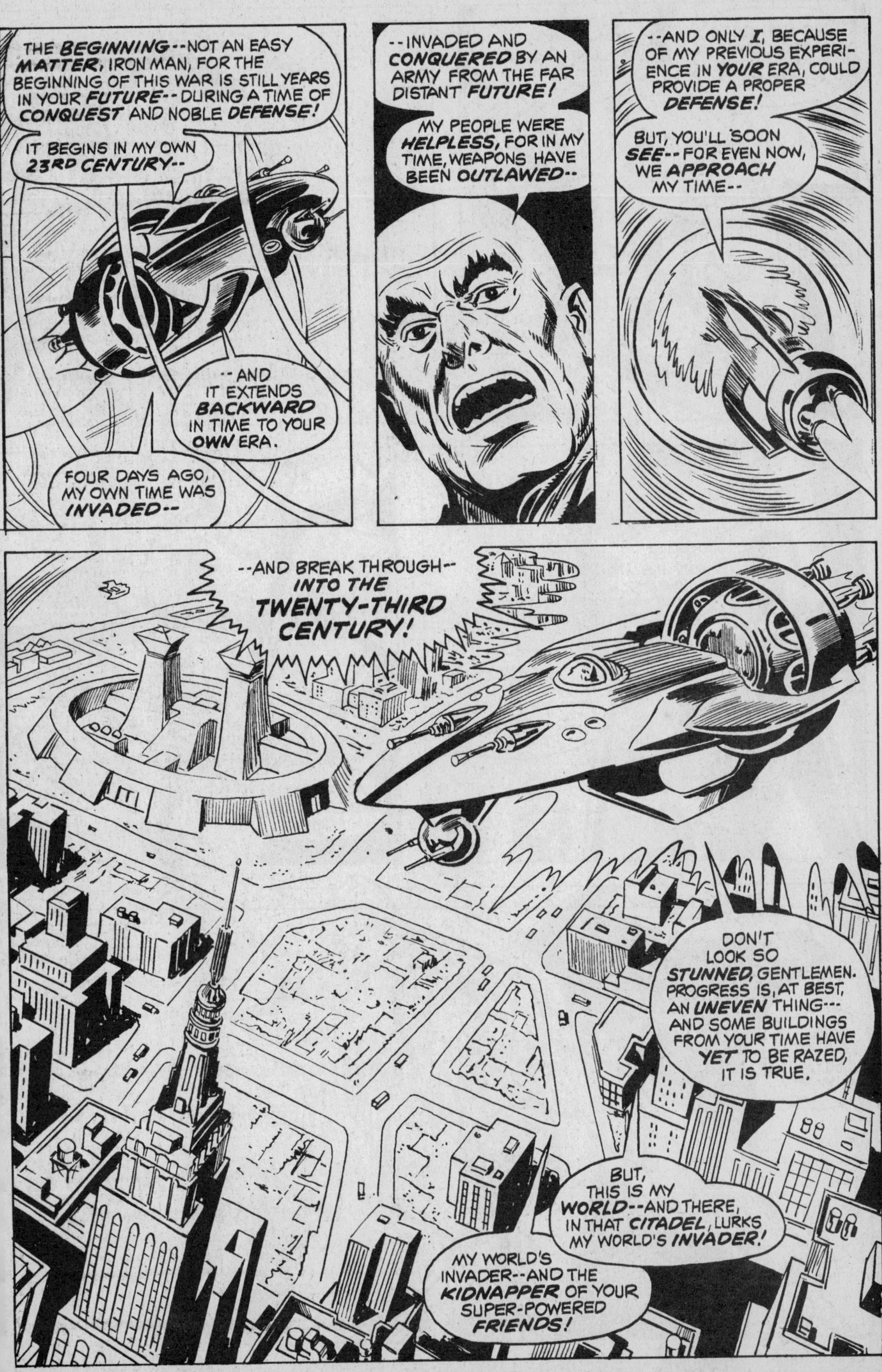
THE BEGINNING--NOT AN EASY MATTER, IRON MAN, FOR THE BEGINNING OF THIS WAR IS STILL YEARS IN YOUR FUTURE--DURING A TIME OF CONQUEST AND NOBLE DEFENSE!
IT BEGINS IN MY OWN 23RD CENTURY--
--AND IT EXTENDS BACKWARD IN TIME TO YOUR OWN ERA.
FOUR DAYS AGO, MY OWN TIME WAS INVADED--
--INVADED AND CONQUERED BY AN ARMY FROM THE FAR DISTANT FUTURE!
MY PEOPLE WERE HELPLESS, FOR IN MY TIME, WEAPONS HAVE BEEN OUTLAWED--
--AND ONLY I, BECAUSE OF MY PREVIOUS EXPERIENCE IN YOUR ERA, COULD PROVIDE A PROPER DEFENSE!
BUT, YOU'LL SOON SEE--FOR EVEN NOW, WE APPROACH MY TIME--
--AND BREAK THROUGH--INTO THE TWENTY-THIRD CENTURY!
DON'T LOOK SO STUNNED, GENTLEMEN. PROGRESS IS, AT BEST, AN UNEVEN THING---AND SOME BUILDINGS FROM YOUR TIME HAVE YET TO BE RAZED, IT IS TRUE.
BUT, THIS IS MY WORLD--AND THERE, IN THAT CITADEL, LURKS MY WORLD'S INVADER!
MY WORLD'S INVADER--AND THE KIDNAPPER OF YOUR SUPER-POWERED FRIENDS!

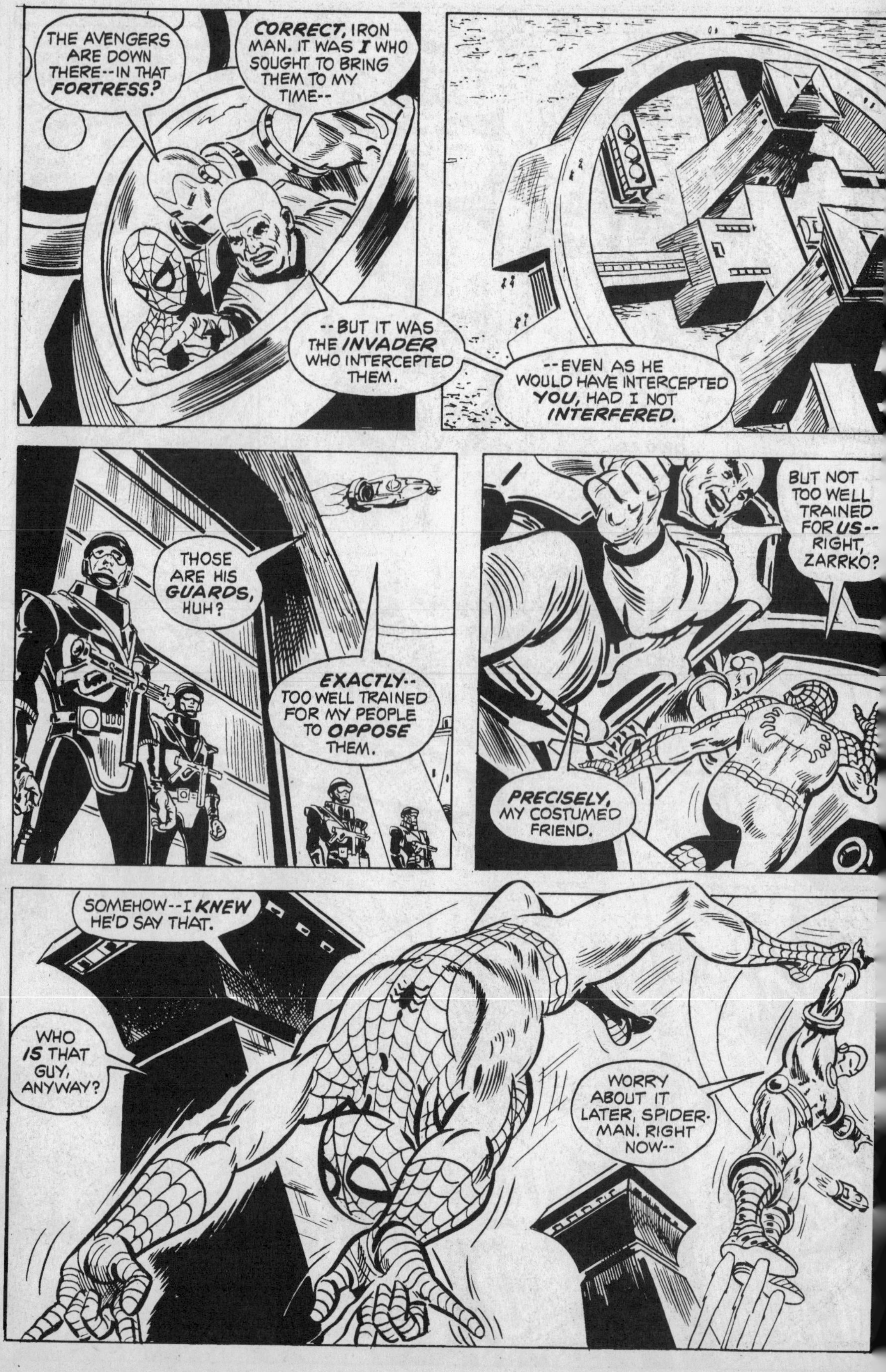
THE AVENGERS ARE DOWN THERE--IN THAT FORTRESS?
CORRECT, IRON MAN. IT WAS I WHO SOUGHT TO BRING THEM TO MY TIME--
--BUT IT WAS THE INVADER WHO INTERCEPTED THEM.
--EVEN AS HE WOULD HAVE INTERCEPTED YOU, HAD I NOT INTERFERED.
THOSE ARE HIS GUARDS, HUH?
EXACTLY--TOO WELL TRAINED FOR MY PEOPLE TO OPPOSE THEM.
BUT NOT TOO WELL TRAINED FOR US--RIGHT, ZARRKO?
PRECISELY, MY COSTUMED FRIEND.
SOMEHOW--I KNEW HE'D SAY THAT.
WHO IS THAT GUY, ANYWAY?
WORRY ABOUT IT LATER, SPIDER-MAN. RIGHT NOW--

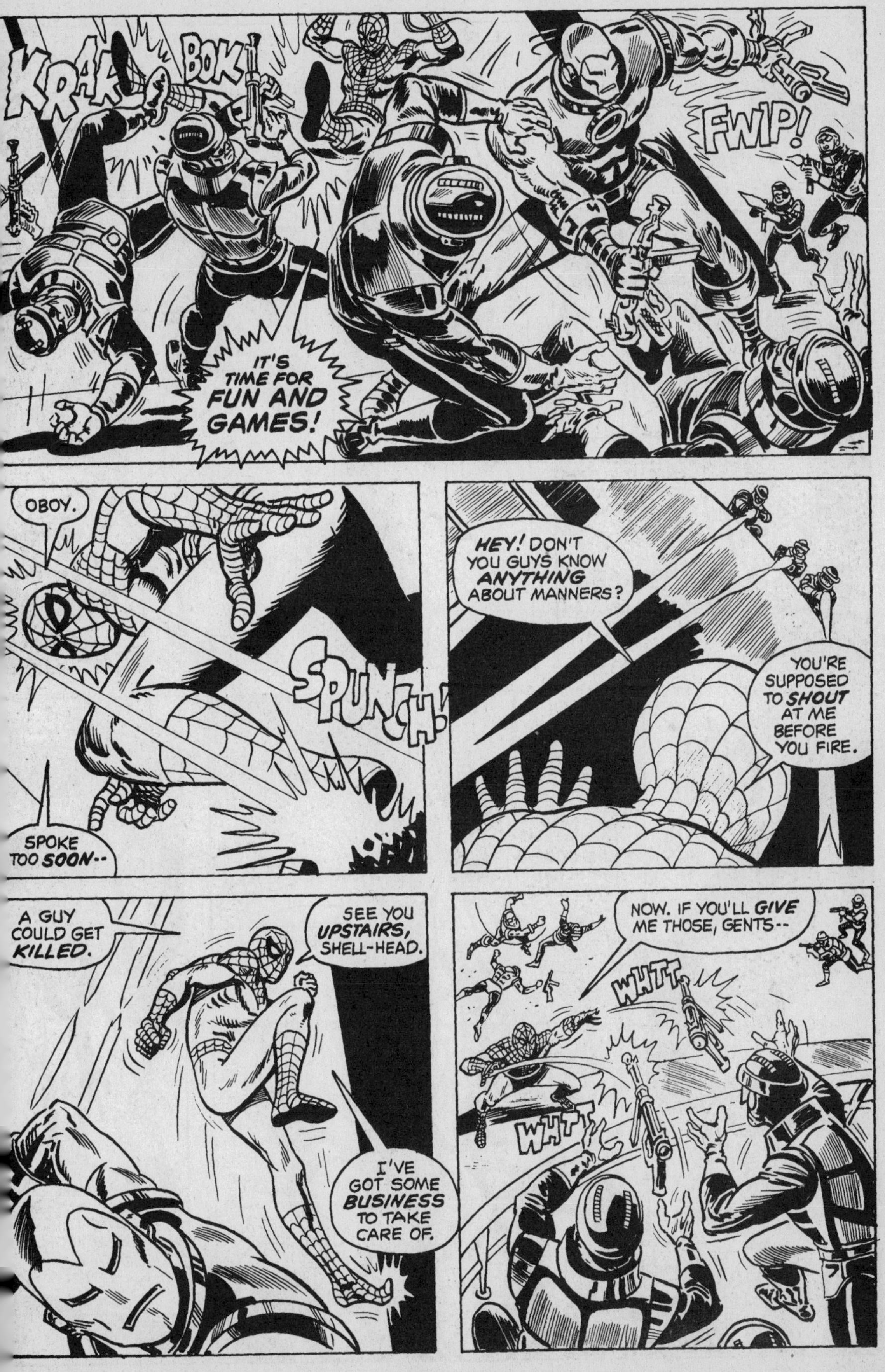
KRAK
BOK
FWIP!
IT'S TIME FOR FUN AND GAMES!
OBOY.
SPUNCH!
SPOKE TOO SOON--
HEY! DON'T YOU GUYS KNOW ANYTHING ABOUT MANNERS?
YOU'RE SUPPOSED TO SHOUT AT ME BEFORE YOU FIRE.
A GUY COULD GET KILLED.
SEE YOU UPSTAIRS, SHELL-HEAD.
I'VE GOT SOME BUSINESS TO TAKE CARE OF.
NOW. IF YOU'LL GIVE ME THOSE, GENTS--
WHTT
WHTT

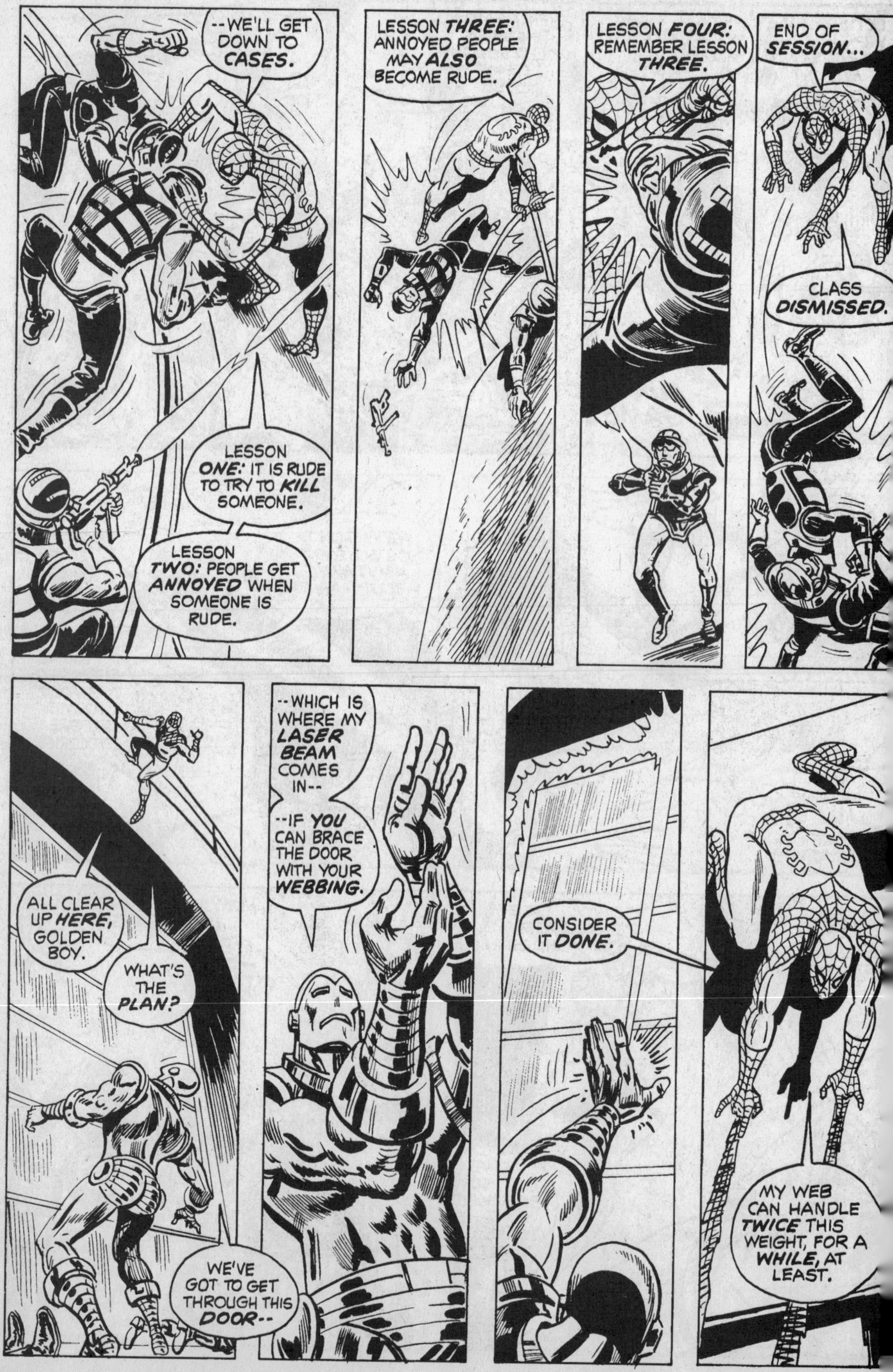
--WE'LL GET DOWN TO CASES.
LESSON ONE: IT IS RUDE TO TRY TO KILL SOMEONE.
LESSON TWO: PEOPLE GET ANNOYED WHEN SOMEONE IS RUDE.
LESSON THREE: ANNOYED PEOPLE MAY ALSO BECOME RUDE.
LESSON FOUR: REMEMBER LESSON THREE.
END OF SESSION...
CLASS DISMISSED.
ALL CLEAR UP HERE, GOLDEN BOY.
WHAT'S THE PLAN?
WE'VE GOT TO GET THROUGH THIS DOOR--
--WHICH IS WHERE MY LASER BEAM COMES IN--
--IF YOU CAN BRACE THE DOOR WITH YOUR WEBBING.
CONSIDER IT DONE.
MY WEB CAN HANDLE TWICE THIS WEIGHT, FOR A WHILE, AT LEAST.

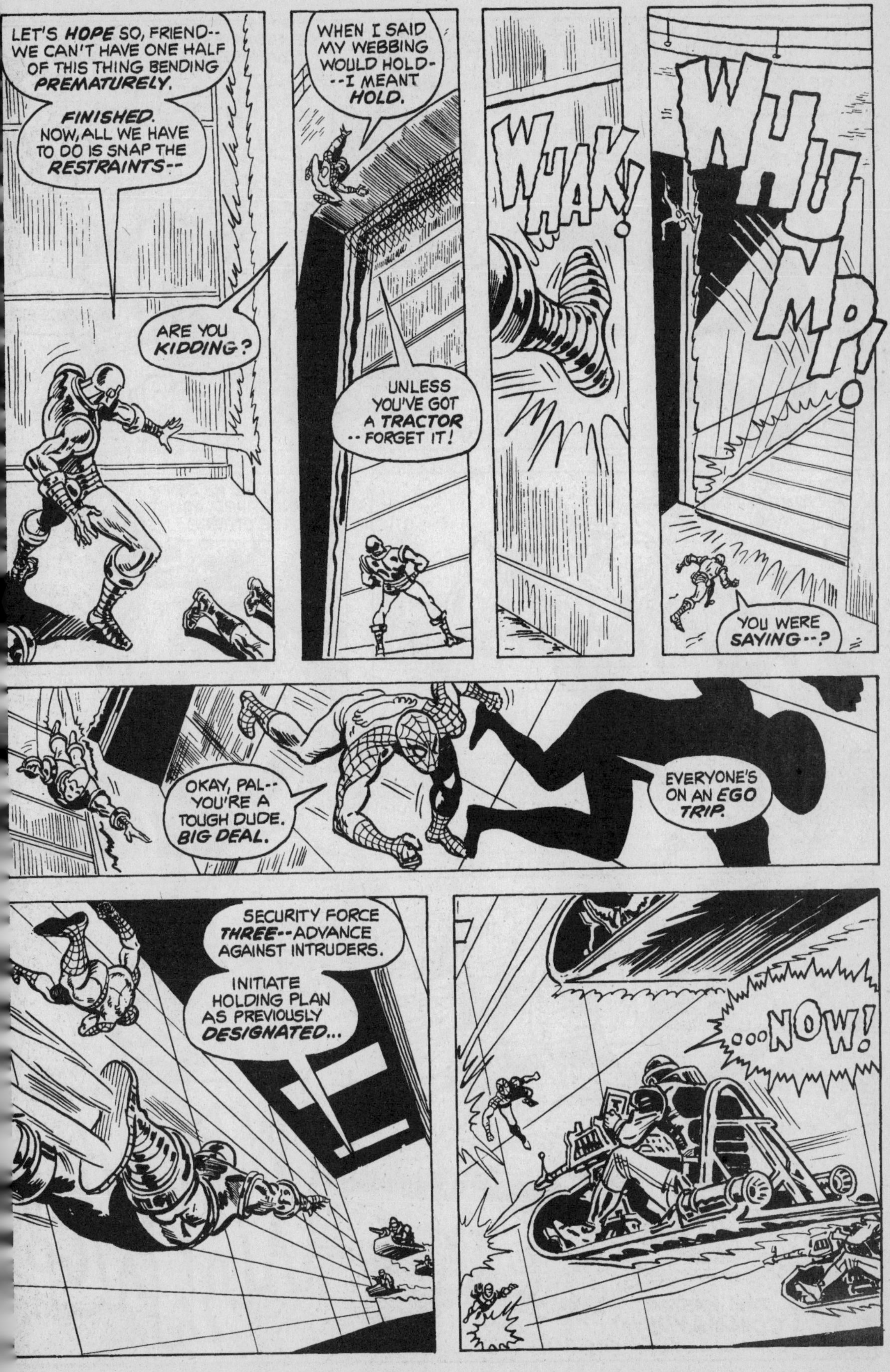

LET'S HOPE SO, FRIEND-- WE CAN'T HAVE ONE HALF OF THIS THING BENDING PREMATURELY.
FINISHED. NOW, ALL WE HAVE TO DO IS SNAP THE RESTRAINTS--
ARE YOU KIDDING?
WHEN I SAID MY WEBBING WOULD HOLD- --I MEANT HOLD.
UNLESS YOU'VE GOT A TRACTOR --FORGET IT!
WHAK!
WHUMP!
YOU WERE SAYING--?
OKAY, PAL-- YOU'RE A TOUGH DUDE. BIG DEAL.
EVERYONE'S ON AN EGO TRIP.
SECURITY FORCE THREE--ADVANCE AGAINST INTRUDERS.
INITIATE HOLDING PLAN AS PREVIOUSLY DESIGNATED...
ooo NOW!

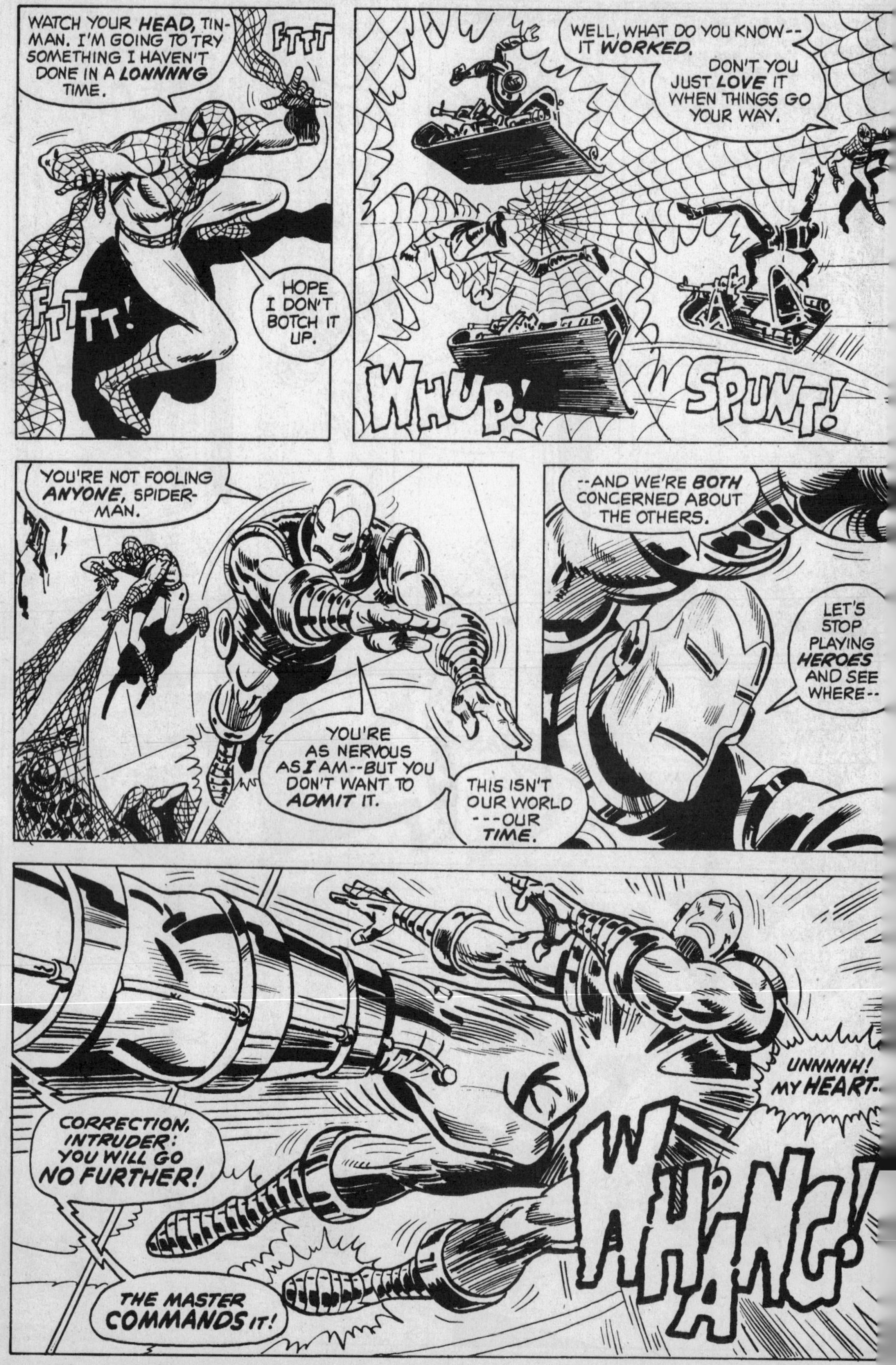

WATCH YOUR HEAD, TIN-MAN. I'M GOING TO TRY SOMETHING I HAVEN'T DONE IN A LONNNNG TIME.
FTTT
FTTTT!
HOPE I DON'T BOTCH IT UP.
WELL, WHAT DO YOU KNOW-- IT WORKED.
DON'T YOU JUST LOVE IT WHEN THINGS GO YOUR WAY.
WHUP!
SPUNT!
YOU'RE NOT FOOLING ANYONE, SPIDER-MAN.
YOU'RE AS NERVOUS AS I AM--BUT YOU DON'T WANT TO ADMIT IT.
THIS ISN'T OUR WORLD ---OUR TIME.
--AND WE'RE BOTH CONCERNED ABOUT THE OTHERS.
LET'S STOP PLAYING HEROES AND SEE WHERE--
UNNNNH! MY HEART--
CORRECTION, INTRUDER: YOU WILL GO NO FURTHER!
THE MASTER COMMANDS IT!
WHANG!

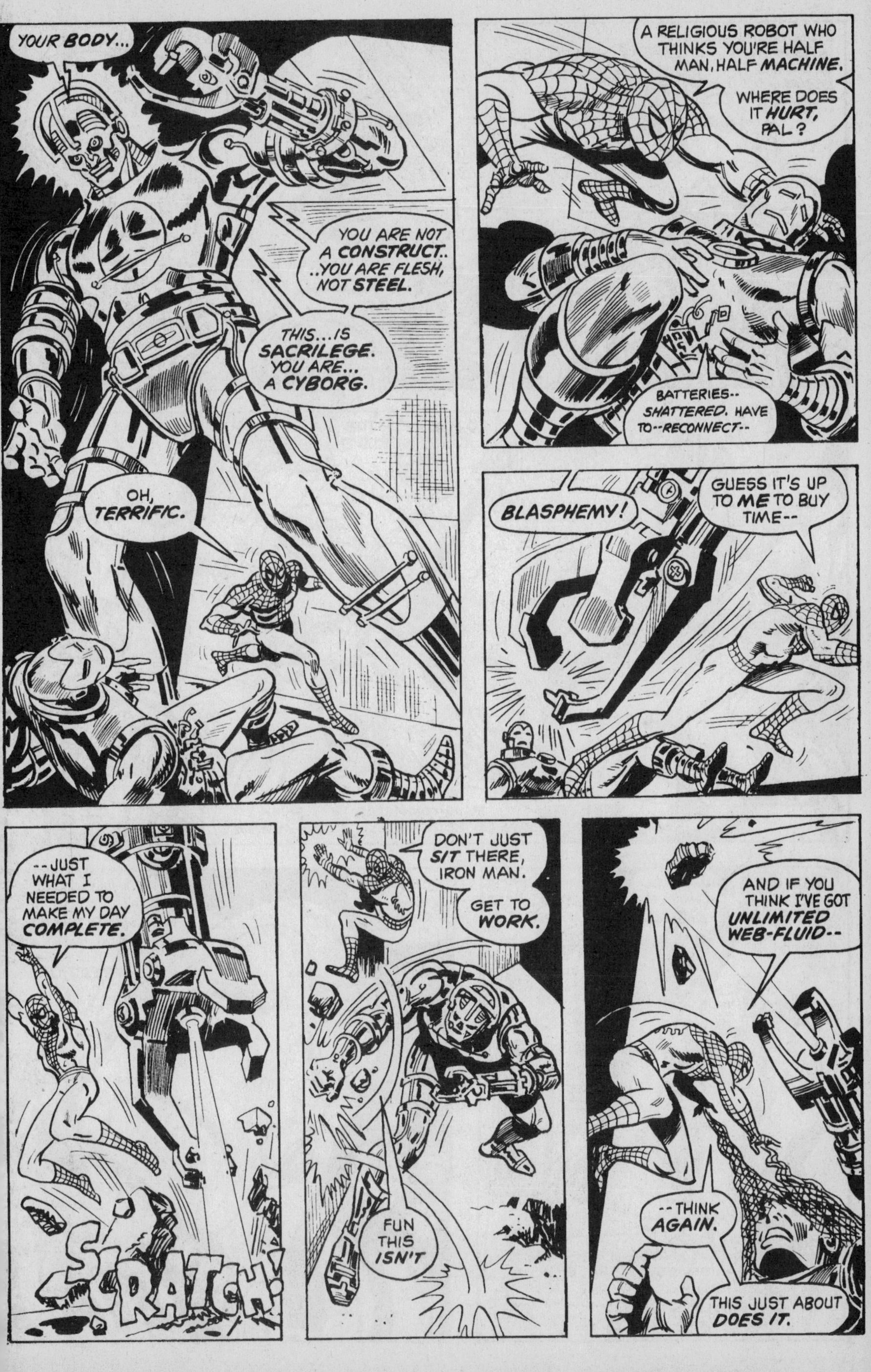
YOUR BODY...
YOU ARE NOT A CONSTRUCT.. ..YOU ARE FLESH, NOT STEEL.
THIS... IS SACRILEGE. YOU ARE... A CYBORG.
OH, TERRIFIC.
A RELIGIOUS ROBOT WHO THINKS YOU'RE HALF MAN, HALF MACHINE.
WHERE DOES IT HURT, PAL?
BATTERIES-- SHATTERED. HAVE TO--RECONNECT--
BLASPHEMY!
GUESS IT'S UP TO ME TO BUY TIME--
--JUST WHAT I NEEDED TO MAKE MY DAY COMPLETE.
SCRATCH!
DON'T JUST SIT THERE, IRON MAN.
GET TO WORK.
FUN THIS ISN'T
AND IF YOU THINK I'VE GOT UNLIMITED WEB-FLUID--
--THINK AGAIN.
THIS JUST ABOUT DOES IT.

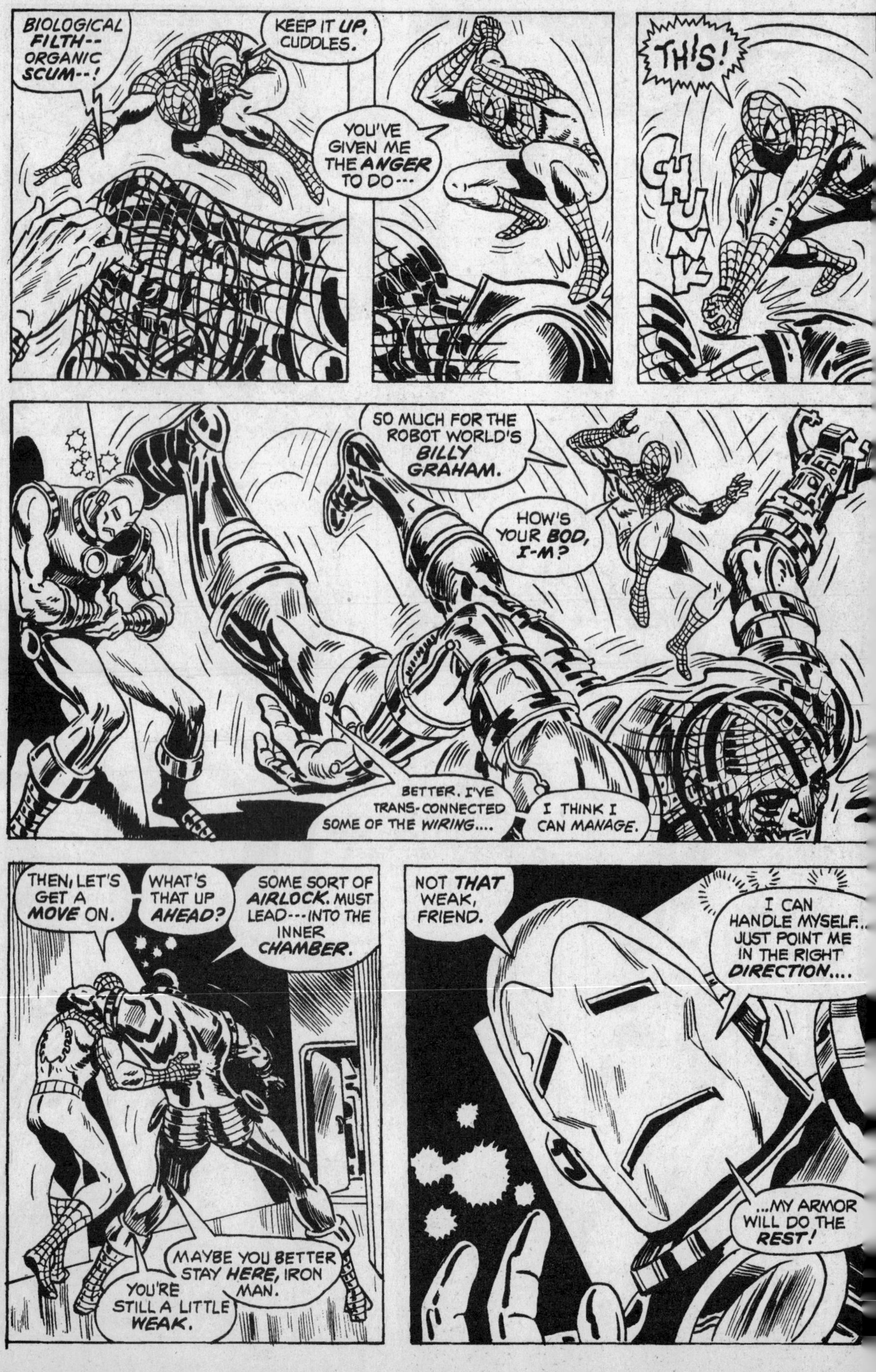
BIOLOGICAL FILTH-- ORGANIC SCUM--!
KEEP IT UP, CUDDLES.
YOU'VE GIVEN ME THE ANGER TO DO---
THIS!
CHUNK
SO MUCH FOR THE ROBOT WORLD'S BILLY GRAHAM.
HOW'S YOUR BOD, I-M?
BETTER. I'VE TRANS-CONNECTED SOME OF THE WIRING....
I THINK I CAN MANAGE.
THEN, LET'S GET A MOVE ON.
WHAT'S THAT UP AHEAD?
SOME SORT OF AIRLOCK. MUST LEAD---INTO THE INNER CHAMBER.
MAYBE YOU BETTER STAY HERE, IRON MAN.
YOU'RE STILL A LITTLE WEAK.
NOT THAT WEAK, FRIEND.
I CAN HANDLE MYSELF... JUST POINT ME IN THE RIGHT DIRECTION....
...MY ARMOR WILL DO THE REST!

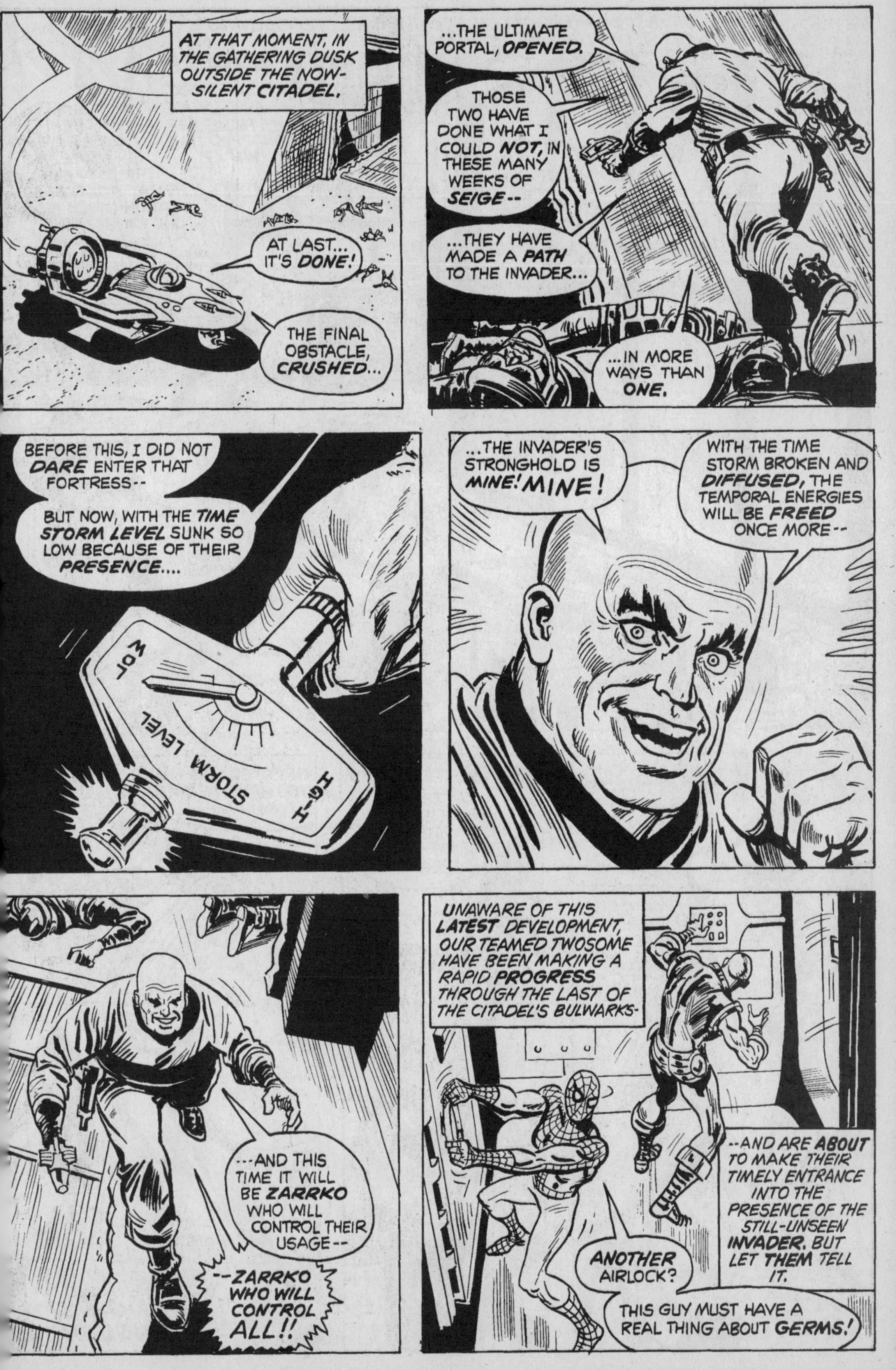
AT THAT MOMENT, IN THE GATHERING DUSK OUTSIDE THE NOW-SILENT CITADEL.
AT LAST... IT'S DONE!
THE FINAL OBSTACLE, CRUSHED...
...THE ULTIMATE PORTAL, OPENED.
THOSE TWO HAVE DONE WHAT I COULD NOT, IN THESE MANY WEEKS OF SEIGE--
...THEY HAVE MADE A PATH TO THE INVADER...
...IN MORE WAYS THAN ONE.
BEFORE THIS, I DID NOT DARE ENTER THAT FORTRESS--
BUT NOW, WITH THE TIME STORM LEVEL SUNK SO LOW BECAUSE OF THEIR PRESENCE....
LOW
STORM LEVEL
HIGH
...THE INVADER'S STRONGHOLD IS MINE! MINE!
WITH THE TIME STORM BROKEN AND DIFFUSED, THE TEMPORAL ENERGIES WILL BE FREED ONCE MORE--
---AND THIS TIME IT WILL BE ZARRKO WHO WILL CONTROL THEIR USAGE--
--ZARRKO WHO WILL CONTROL ALL!!
UNAWARE OF THIS LATEST DEVELOPMENT, OUR TEAMED TWOSOME HAVE BEEN MAKING A RAPID PROGRESS THROUGH THE LAST OF THE CITADEL'S BULWARKS-
--AND ARE ABOUT TO MAKE THEIR TIMELY ENTRANCE INTO THE PRESENCE OF THE STILL-UNSEEN INVADER. BUT LET THEM TELL IT.
ANOTHER AIRLOCK?
THIS GUY MUST HAVE A REAL THING ABOUT GERMS!

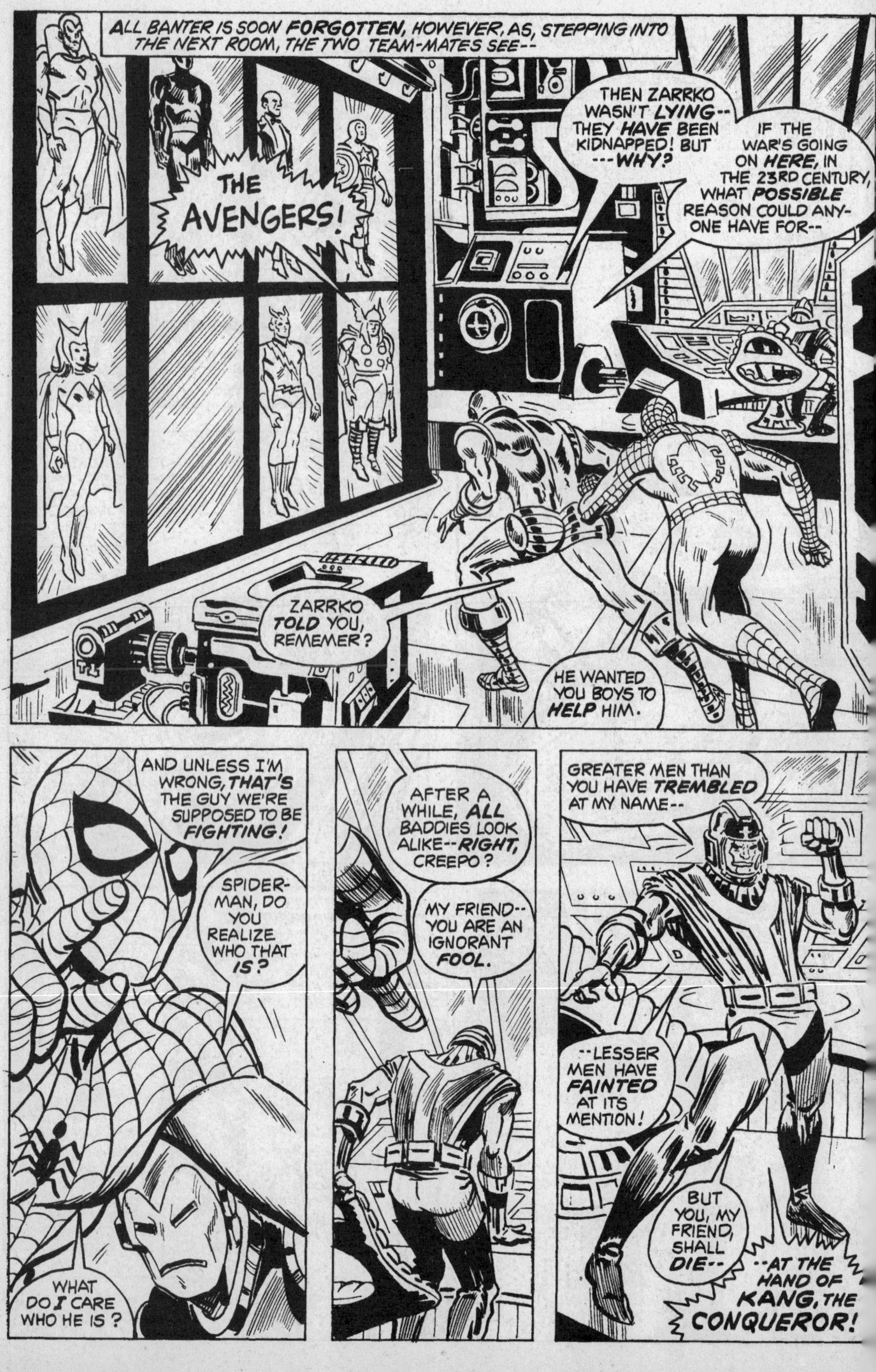

ALL BANTER IS SOON FORGOTTEN, HOWEVER, AS, STEPPING INTO THE NEXT ROOM, THE TWO TEAM-MATES SEE--
THE AVENGERS!
THEN ZARRKO WASN'T LYING-- THEY HAVE BEEN KIDNAPPED! BUT ---WHY?
IF THE WAR'S GOING ON HERE, IN THE 23RD CENTURY, WHAT POSSIBLE REASON COULD ANY-ONE HAVE FOR--
ZARRKO TOLD YOU, REMEMER?
HE WANTED YOU BOYS TO HELP HIM.
AND UNLESS I'M WRONG, THAT'S THE GUY WE'RE SUPPOSED TO BE FIGHTING!
SPIDER-MAN, DO YOU REALIZE WHO THAT IS?
WHAT DO I CARE WHO HE IS?
AFTER A WHILE, ALL BADDIES LOOK ALIKE--RIGHT, CREEPO?
MY FRIEND-- YOU ARE AN IGNORANT FOOL.
GREATER MEN THAN YOU HAVE TREMBLED AT MY NAME--
--LESSER MEN HAVE FAINTED AT ITS MENTION!
BUT YOU, MY FRIEND, SHALL DIE--
--AT THE HAND OF KANG, THE CONQUEROR!

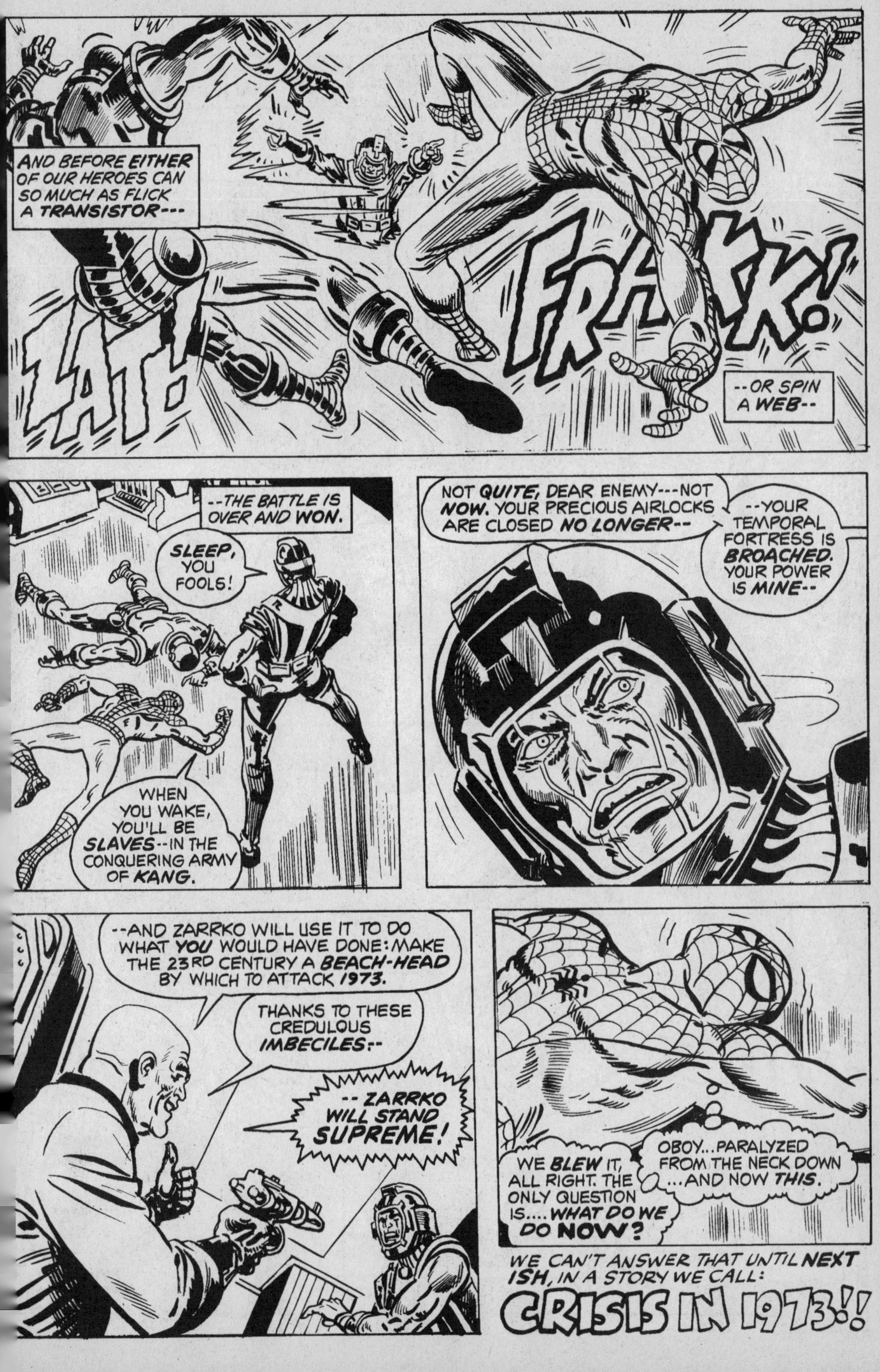

AND BEFORE EITHER OF OUR HEROES CAN SO MUCH AS FLICK A TRANSISTOR---
ZAT!
FRAKK!
--OR SPIN A WEB--
--THE BATTLE IS OVER AND WON.
SLEEP, YOU FOOLS!
WHEN YOU WAKE, YOU'LL BE SLAVES--IN THE CONQUERING ARMY OF KANG.
NOT QUITE, DEAR ENEMY---NOT NOW. YOUR PRECIOUS AIRLOCKS ARE CLOSED NO LONGER--
--YOUR TEMPORAL FORTRESS IS BROACHED. YOUR POWER IS MINE--
--AND ZARRKO WILL USE IT TO DO WHAT YOU WOULD HAVE DONE: MAKE THE 23RD CENTURY A BEACH-HEAD BY WHICH TO ATTACK 1973.
THANKS TO THESE CREDULOUS IMBECILES:-
-- ZARRKO WILL STAND SUPREME!
OBOY...PARALYZED FROM THE NECK DOWN ...AND NOW THIS.
WE BLEW IT, ALL RIGHT. THE ONLY QUESTION IS.... WHAT DO WE DO NOW?
WE CAN'T ANSWER THAT UNTIL NEXT ISH, IN A STORY WE CALL:
CRISIS IN 1973!!

MARVEL TEAM-UP
MARVEL COMICS GROUP™
20¢
10
JUNE
02147
MARVEL TEAM-UP
APPROVED BY THE COMICS CODE AUTHORITY
FEATURING
SPIDER-MAN™
AND THE
HUMAN TORCH™
IN THE CLUTCHES OF
KANG
THE
CONQUEROR!
WAR
--ACROSS A
THOUSAND
CENTURIES!
ALL THIS-- AND THE TOMORROW MAN! TOO! ('NUFF SAID?)

Stan Lee PRESENTS: SPIDEY AND THE HUMAN TORCH - TOGETHER! TM
TIME BOMB!
THE TIME: THE 23RD CENTURY!
THE PLACE: THE FORTRESS HEADQUARTERS OF AN INVADER FROM THE 41ST CENTURY-- KANG, THE CONQUEROR!
THE SITUATION: PERILOUS!
ZARRKO-- YOU ABYSMAL FOOL! PUT DOWN THAT WEAPON!
YOU CAN'T HOPE TO DEFEAT ME WITH YOUR PITIABLY BARBARIC TOYS!
NEED I POINT OUT-- I ALREADY HAVE!
JUST AS YOU HAVE DEFEATED OUR MUTUAL ENEMIES --INCLUDING THAT CURSED INTERLOPER--
--SPIDER-MAN!
GERRY CONWAY SCRIPTER
JIM MOONEY, ARTIST
F. GIACOIA INKER
C. JETTER, LETTERER STAN G., COLORIST
ROY THOMAS, EDITOR

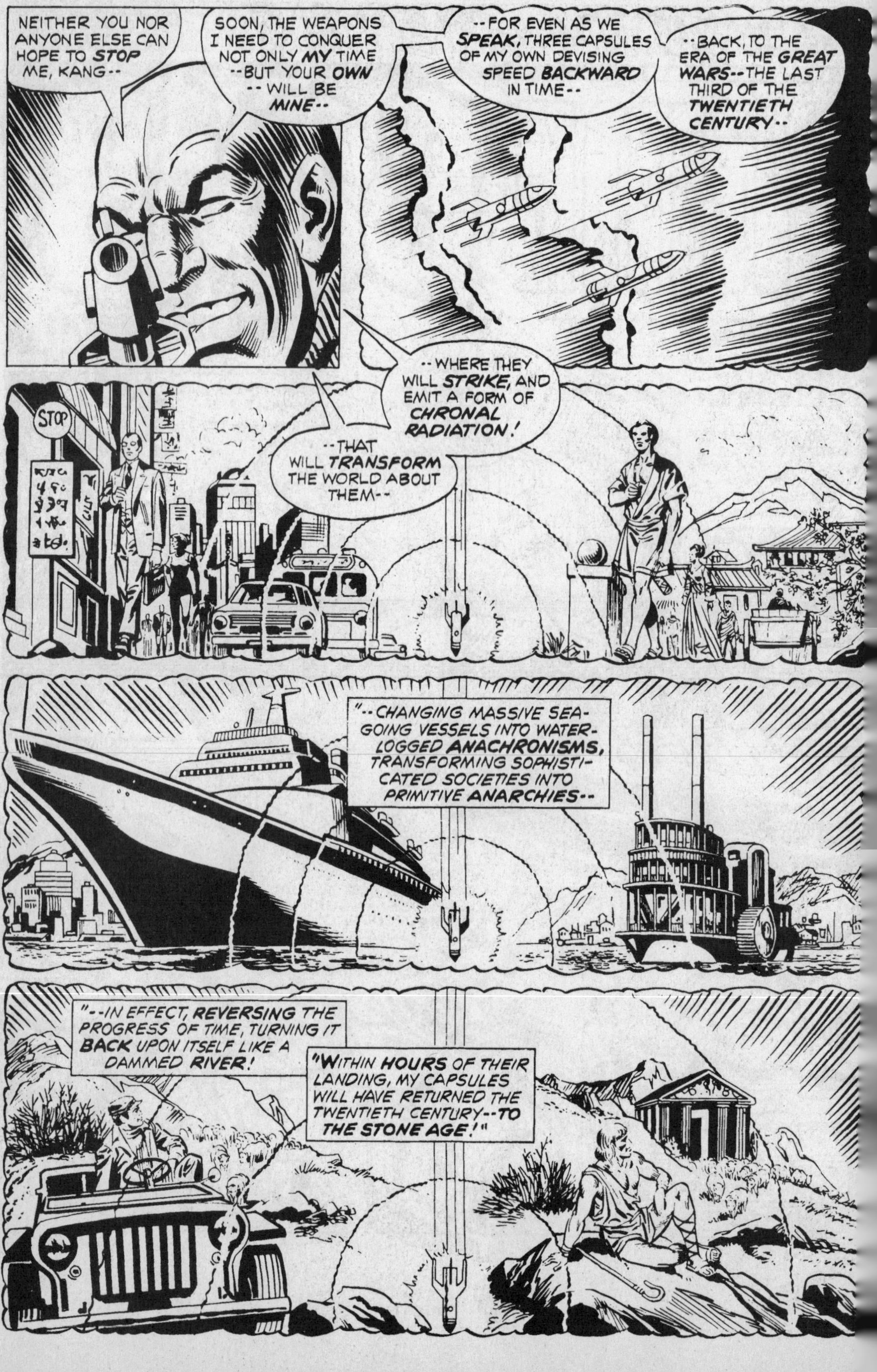

NEITHER YOU NOR ANYONE ELSE CAN HOPE TO STOP ME, KANG--
SOON, THE WEAPONS I NEED TO CONQUER NOT ONLY MY TIME --BUT YOUR OWN -- WILL BE MINE--
--FOR EVEN AS WE SPEAK, THREE CAPSULES OF MY OWN DEVISING SPEED BACKWARD IN TIME--
--BACK, TO THE ERA OF THE GREAT WARS--THE LAST THIRD OF THE TWENTIETH CENTURY--
--WHERE THEY WILL STRIKE, AND EMIT A FORM OF CHRONAL RADIATION!
--THAT WILL TRANSFORM THE WORLD ABOUT THEM--
STOP
"--CHANGING MASSIVE SEA-GOING VESSELS INTO WATER-LOGGED ANACHRONISMS, TRANSFORMING SOPHISTICATED SOCIETIES INTO PRIMITIVE ANARCHIES--
"--IN EFFECT, REVERSING THE PROGRESS OF TIME, TURNING IT BACK UPON ITSELF LIKE A DAMMED RIVER!
"WITHIN HOURS OF THEIR LANDING, MY CAPSULES WILL HAVE RETURNED THE TWENTIETH CENTURY--TO THE STONE AGE!"

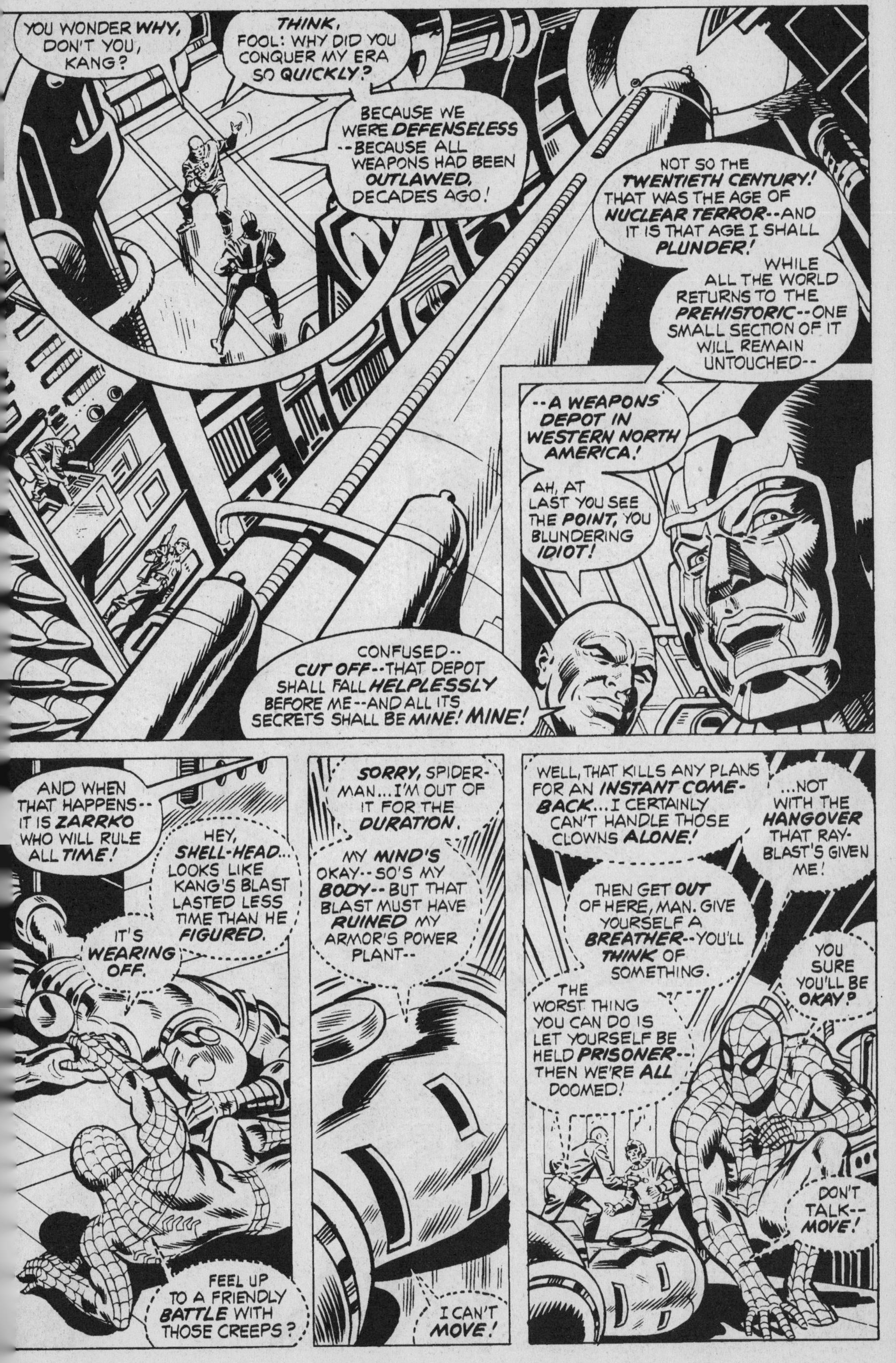
YOU WONDER WHY, DON'T YOU, KANG?
THINK, FOOL: WHY DID YOU CONQUER MY ERA SO QUICKLY?
BECAUSE WE WERE DEFENSELESS --BECAUSE ALL WEAPONS HAD BEEN OUTLAWED, DECADES AGO!
NOT SO THE TWENTIETH CENTURY! THAT WAS THE AGE OF NUCLEAR TERROR--AND IT IS THAT AGE I SHALL PLUNDER!
WHILE ALL THE WORLD RETURNS TO THE PREHISTORIC--ONE SMALL SECTION OF IT WILL REMAIN UNTOUCHED--
--A WEAPONS' DEPOT IN WESTERN NORTH AMERICA!
AH, AT LAST YOU SEE THE POINT, YOU BLUNDERING IDIOT!
CONFUSED-- CUT OFF--THAT DEPOT SHALL FALL HELPLESSLY BEFORE ME--AND ALL ITS SECRETS SHALL BE MINE! MINE!
AND WHEN THAT HAPPENS-- IT IS ZARRKO WHO WILL RULE ALL TIME!
HEY, SHELL-HEAD... LOOKS LIKE KANG'S BLAST LASTED LESS TIME THAN HE FIGURED.
IT'S WEARING OFF.
FEEL UP TO A FRIENDLY BATTLE WITH THOSE CREEPS?
SORRY, SPIDER-MAN... I'M OUT OF IT FOR THE DURATION.
MY MIND'S OKAY--SO'S MY BODY--BUT THAT BLAST MUST HAVE RUINED MY ARMOR'S POWER PLANT--
I CAN'T MOVE!
WELL, THAT KILLS ANY PLANS FOR AN INSTANT COME-BACK... I CERTAINLY CAN'T HANDLE THOSE CLOWNS ALONE!
...NOT WITH THE HANGOVER THAT RAY-BLAST'S GIVEN ME!
THEN GET OUT OF HERE, MAN. GIVE YOURSELF A BREATHER--YOU'LL THINK OF SOMETHING.
THE WORST THING YOU CAN DO IS LET YOURSELF BE HELD PRISONER-- THEN WE'RE ALL DOOMED!
YOU SURE YOU'LL BE OKAY?
DON'T TALK-- MOVE!

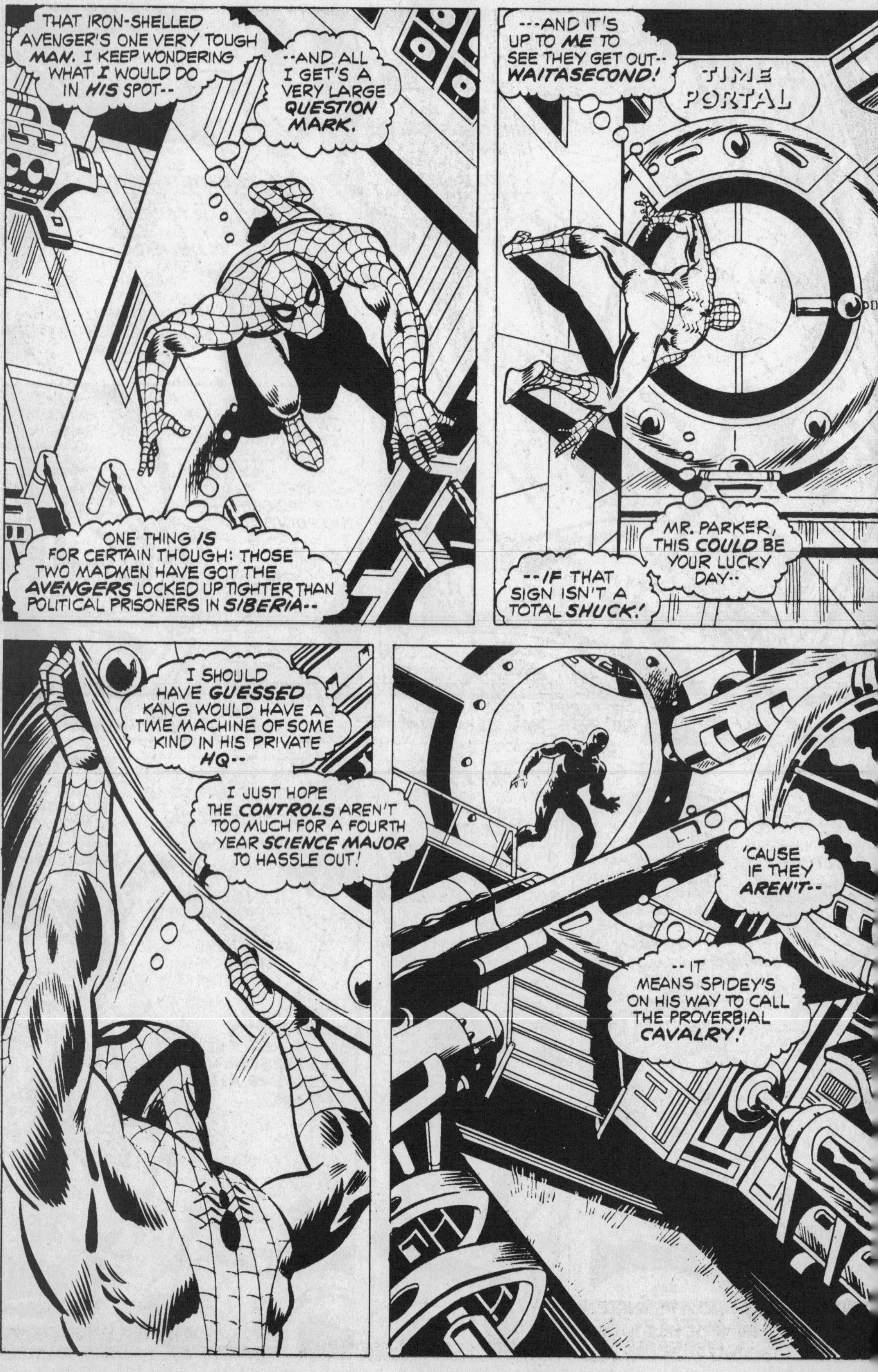
THAT IRON-SHELLED AVENGER'S ONE VERY TOUGH MAN. I KEEP WONDERING WHAT I WOULD DO IN HIS SPOT--
--AND ALL I GET'S A VERY LARGE QUESTION MARK.
ONE THING IS FOR CERTAIN THOUGH: THOSE TWO MADMEN HAVE GOT THE AVENGERS LOCKED UP TIGHTER THAN POLITICAL PRISONERS IN SIBERIA--
---AND IT'S UP TO ME TO SEE THEY GET OUT-- WAITASECOND!
TIME PORTAL
MR. PARKER, THIS COULD BE YOUR LUCKY DAY--
--IF THAT SIGN ISN'T A TOTAL SHUCK!
I SHOULD HAVE GUESSED KANG WOULD HAVE A TIME MACHINE OF SOME KIND IN HIS PRIVATE HQ--
I JUST HOPE THE CONTROLS AREN'T TOO MUCH FOR A FOURTH YEAR SCIENCE MAJOR TO HASSLE OUT!
'CAUSE IF THEY AREN'T--
--IT MEANS SPIDEY'S ON HIS WAY TO CALL THE PROVERBIAL CAVALRY!

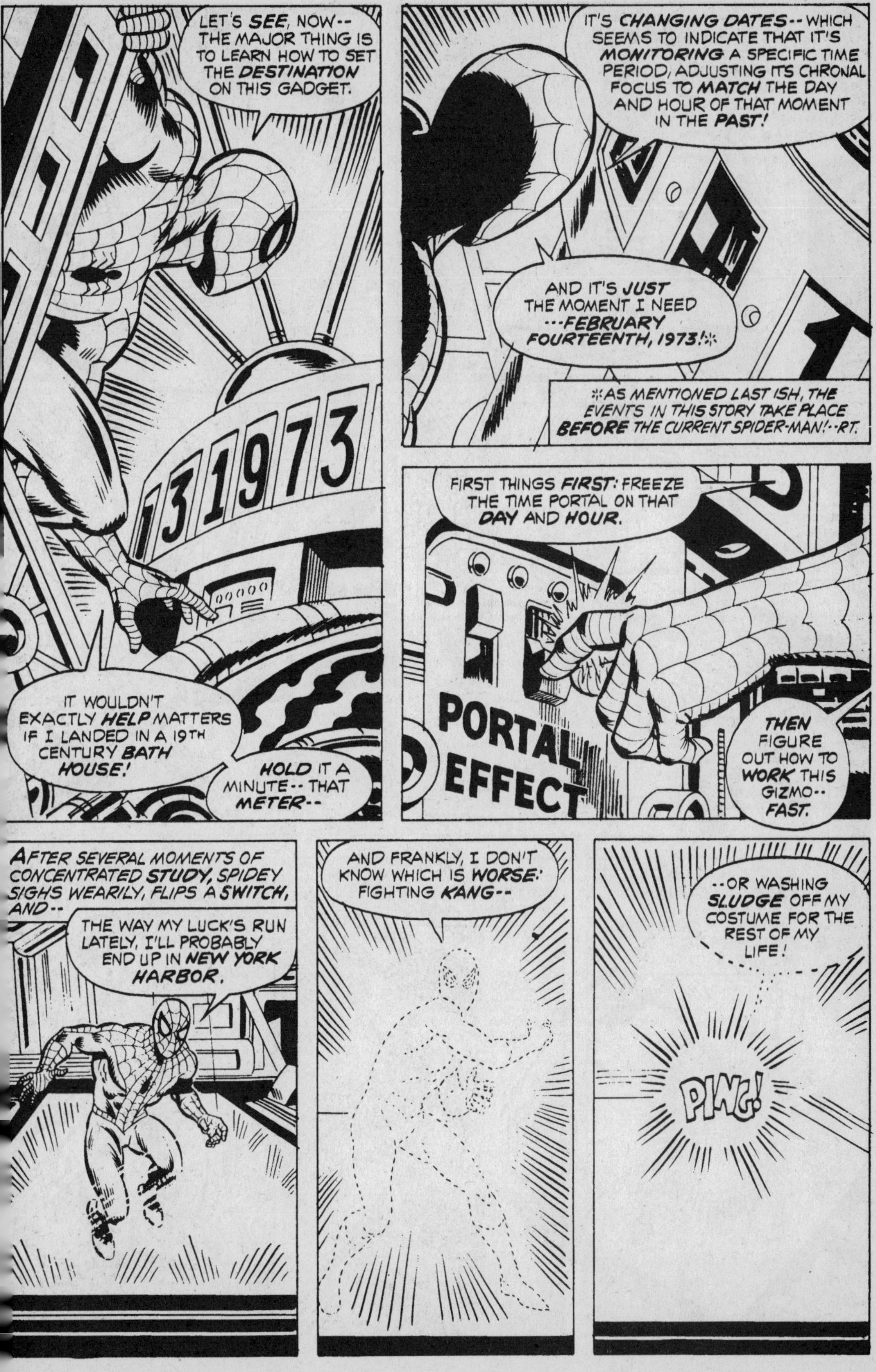
LET'S SEE, NOW-- THE MAJOR THING IS TO LEARN HOW TO SET THE DESTINATION ON THIS GADGET.
IT WOULDN'T EXACTLY HELP MATTERS IF I LANDED IN A 19TH CENTURY BATH HOUSE!
HOLD IT A MINUTE-- THAT METER--
IT'S CHANGING DATES-- WHICH SEEMS TO INDICATE THAT IT'S MONITORING A SPECIFIC TIME PERIOD, ADJUSTING ITS CHRONAL FOCUS TO MATCH THE DAY AND HOUR OF THAT MOMENT IN THE PAST!
AND IT'S JUST THE MOMENT I NEED ---FEBRUARY FOURTEENTH, 1973!*
*AS MENTIONED LAST ISH, THE EVENTS IN THIS STORY TAKE PLACE BEFORE THE CURRENT SPIDER-MAN!--RT.
FIRST THINGS FIRST: FREEZE THE TIME PORTAL ON THAT DAY AND HOUR.
PORTAL EFFECT
THEN FIGURE OUT HOW TO WORK THIS GIZMO-- FAST.
AFTER SEVERAL MOMENTS OF CONCENTRATED STUDY, SPIDEY SIGHS WEARILY, FLIPS A SWITCH, AND--
THE WAY MY LUCK'S RUN LATELY, I'LL PROBABLY END UP IN NEW YORK HARBOR.
AND FRANKLY, I DON'T KNOW WHICH IS WORSE: FIGHTING KANG--
--OR WASHING SLUDGE OFF MY COSTUME FOR THE REST OF MY LIFE!
PING!

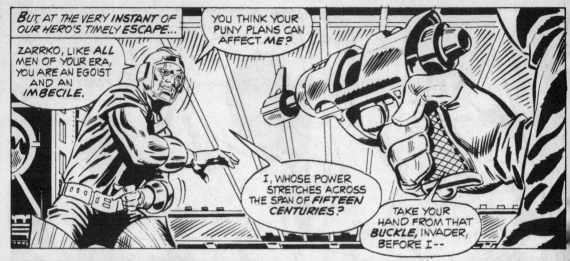

BUT, AT THE VERY INSTANT OF OUR HERO'S TIMELY *ESCAPE...*

ZARRKO, LIKE *ALL* MEN OF YOUR ERA, YOU ARE AN *EGOIST* AND AN *IMBECILE.*

YOU THINK YOUR *PUNY* PLANS CAN AFFECT *ME?*

I, WHOSE POWER STRETCHES ACROSS THE SPAN OF *FIFTEEN CENTURIES?*

TAKE YOUR HAND FROM THAT *BUCKLE,* INVADER, BEFORE I --

YOU'LL DO *NOTHING,* ZARRKO. YOUR EFFORTS ARE *FINISHED.*

THE SAME RAY WHICH STUNNED MY *PREVIOUS* GUESTS WILL HOLD YOU *NICELY,* WHILE I --

EH?

SOMEONE'S ATTEMPTING TO ENTER THROUGH THE *AIRLOCK* -- THE THOUGHTLESS *BABOONS!*

ENTER, YOU -- *NO!*

NO, IT CANNOT *BE!*

NOT YOU! NOT *YOU!*

WE'LL HAVE TO WAIT UNTIL *NEXT ISSUE* TO LEARN THE IDENTITY OF KANG'S *NEW* ASSAILANT -- BUT IN THE MEANTIME, LET'S DROP BACK IN TIME THREE HUNDRED YEARS --

PING!

-- TO A ROOM IN A BUILDING IN MANHATTAN'S *MIDTOWN* AREA --

-- AND THE *REAPPEARING* FIGURE -- OF *SPIDER-MAN!*

I *DID* IT --

THE *QUESTION* IS -- WHERE DID I DO IT *TO?*

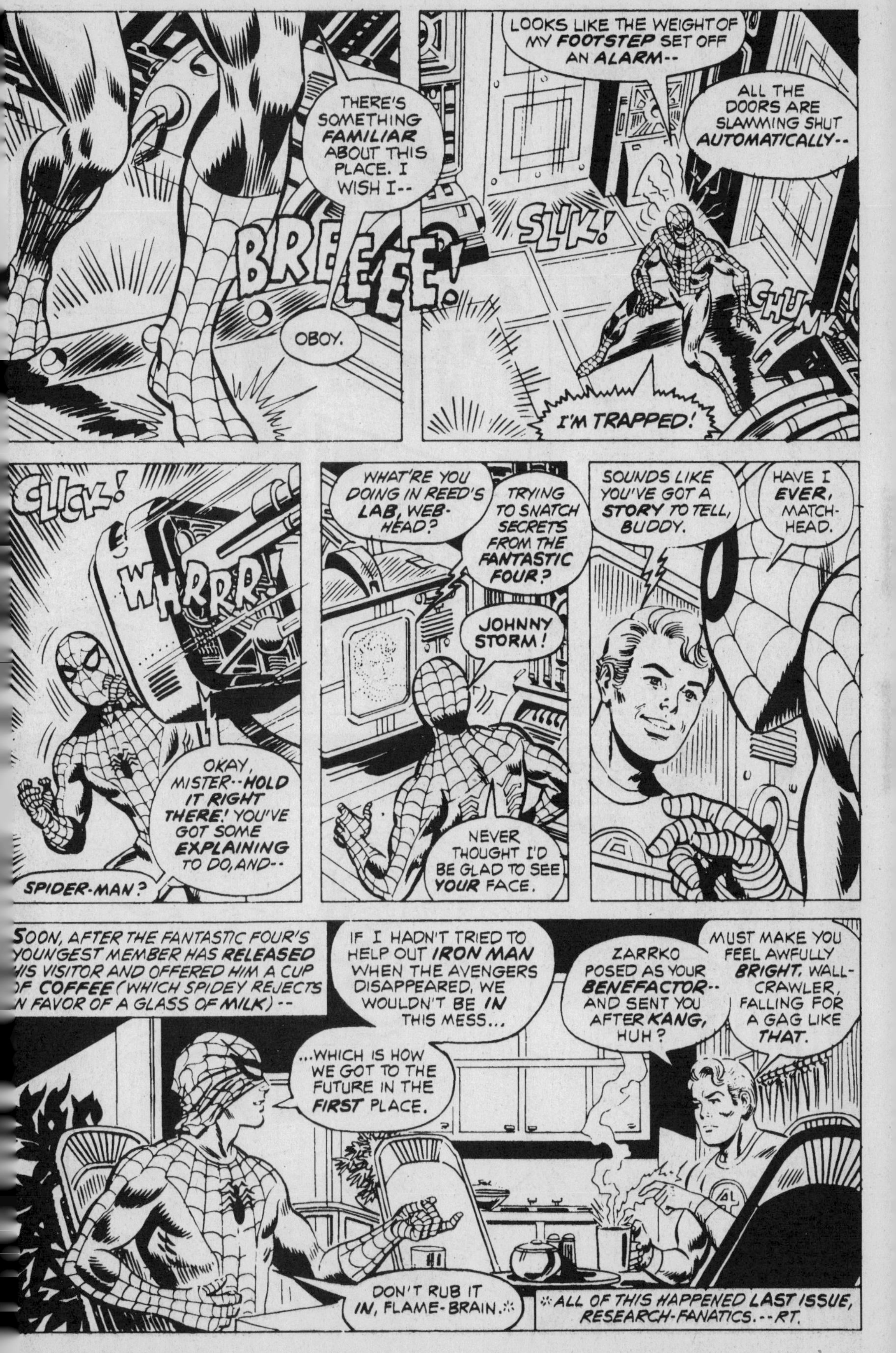

THERE'S SOMETHING FAMILIAR ABOUT THIS PLACE. I WISH I--
BREEEEE!
OBOY.
LOOKS LIKE THE WEIGHT OF MY FOOTSTEP SET OFF AN ALARM--
ALL THE DOORS ARE SLAMMING SHUT AUTOMATICALLY--
SLIK!
CHUNK!
I'M TRAPPED!
CLICK!
WHRRR!
OKAY, MISTER--HOLD IT RIGHT THERE! YOU'VE GOT SOME EXPLAINING TO DO, AND--
SPIDER-MAN?
WHAT'RE YOU DOING IN REED'S LAB, WEB-HEAD?
TRYING TO SNATCH SECRETS FROM THE FANTASTIC FOUR?
JOHNNY STORM!
NEVER THOUGHT I'D BE GLAD TO SEE YOUR FACE.
SOUNDS LIKE YOU'VE GOT A STORY TO TELL, BUDDY.
HAVE I EVER, MATCH-HEAD.
SOON, AFTER THE FANTASTIC FOUR'S YOUNGEST MEMBER HAS RELEASED HIS VISITOR AND OFFERED HIM A CUP OF COFFEE (WHICH SPIDEY REJECTS IN FAVOR OF A GLASS OF MILK) --
IF I HADN'T TRIED TO HELP OUT IRON MAN WHEN THE AVENGERS DISAPPEARED, WE WOULDN'T BE IN THIS MESS...
...WHICH IS HOW WE GOT TO THE FUTURE IN THE FIRST PLACE.
ZARRKO POSED AS YOUR BENEFACTOR--AND SENT YOU AFTER KANG, HUH?
MUST MAKE YOU FEEL AWFULLY BRIGHT, WALL-CRAWLER, FALLING FOR A GAG LIKE THAT.
DON'T RUB IT IN, FLAME-BRAIN.*
*ALL OF THIS HAPPENED LAST ISSUE, RESEARCH-FANATICS.--RT.

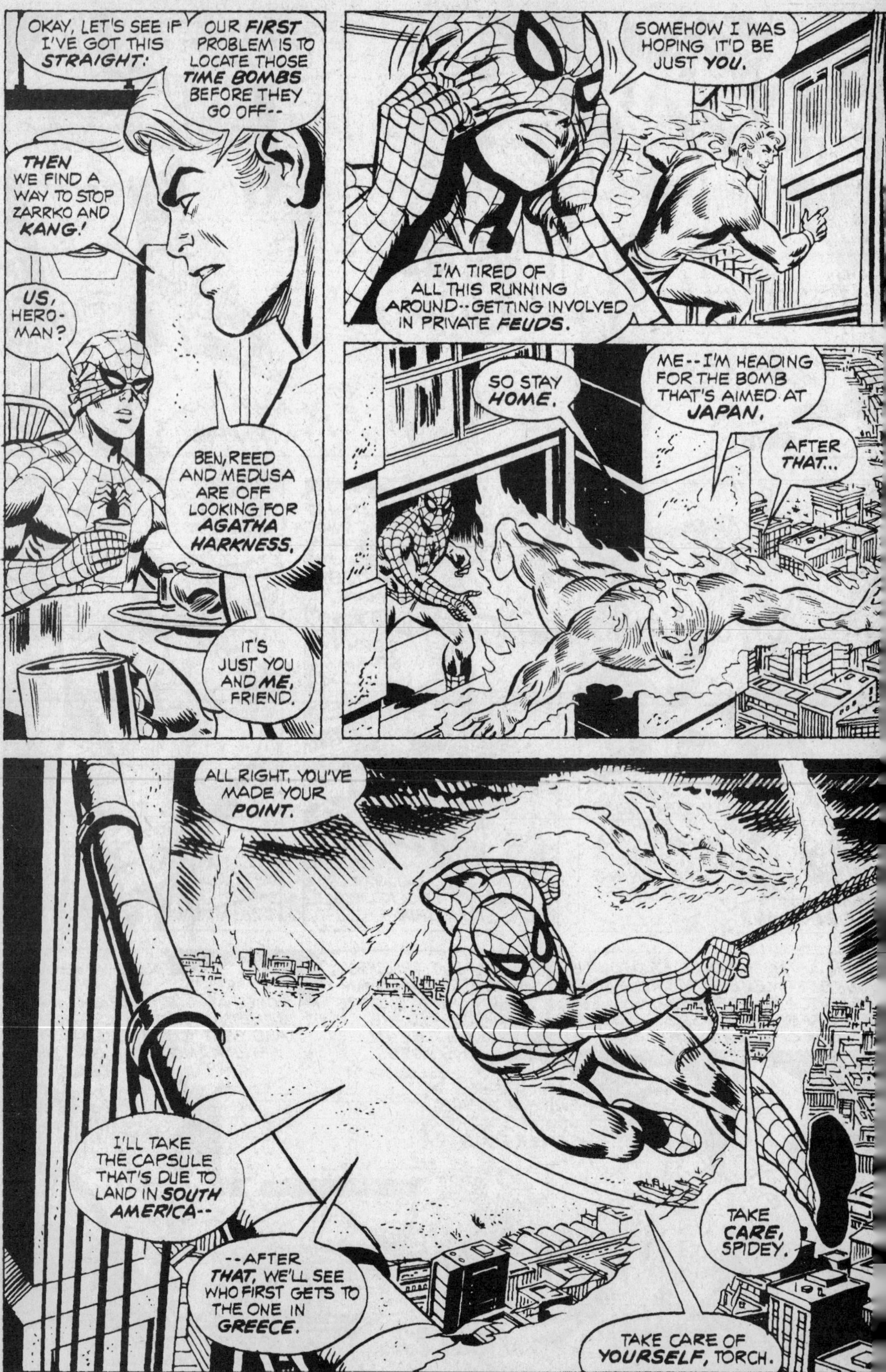

OKAY, LET'S SEE IF I'VE GOT THIS STRAIGHT:
OUR FIRST PROBLEM IS TO LOCATE THOSE TIME BOMBS BEFORE THEY GO OFF--
THEN WE FIND A WAY TO STOP ZARRKO AND KANG!
US, HERO-MAN?
BEN, REED AND MEDUSA ARE OFF LOOKING FOR AGATHA HARKNESS.
IT'S JUST YOU AND ME, FRIEND.
SOMEHOW I WAS HOPING IT'D BE JUST YOU.
I'M TIRED OF ALL THIS RUNNING AROUND--GETTING INVOLVED IN PRIVATE FEUDS.
SO STAY HOME.
ME--I'M HEADING FOR THE BOMB THAT'S AIMED AT JAPAN.
AFTER THAT...
ALL RIGHT, YOU'VE MADE YOUR POINT.
I'LL TAKE THE CAPSULE THAT'S DUE TO LAND IN SOUTH AMERICA--
--AFTER THAT, WE'LL SEE WHO FIRST GETS TO THE ONE IN GREECE.
TAKE CARE, SPIDEY.
TAKE CARE OF YOURSELF, TORCH.

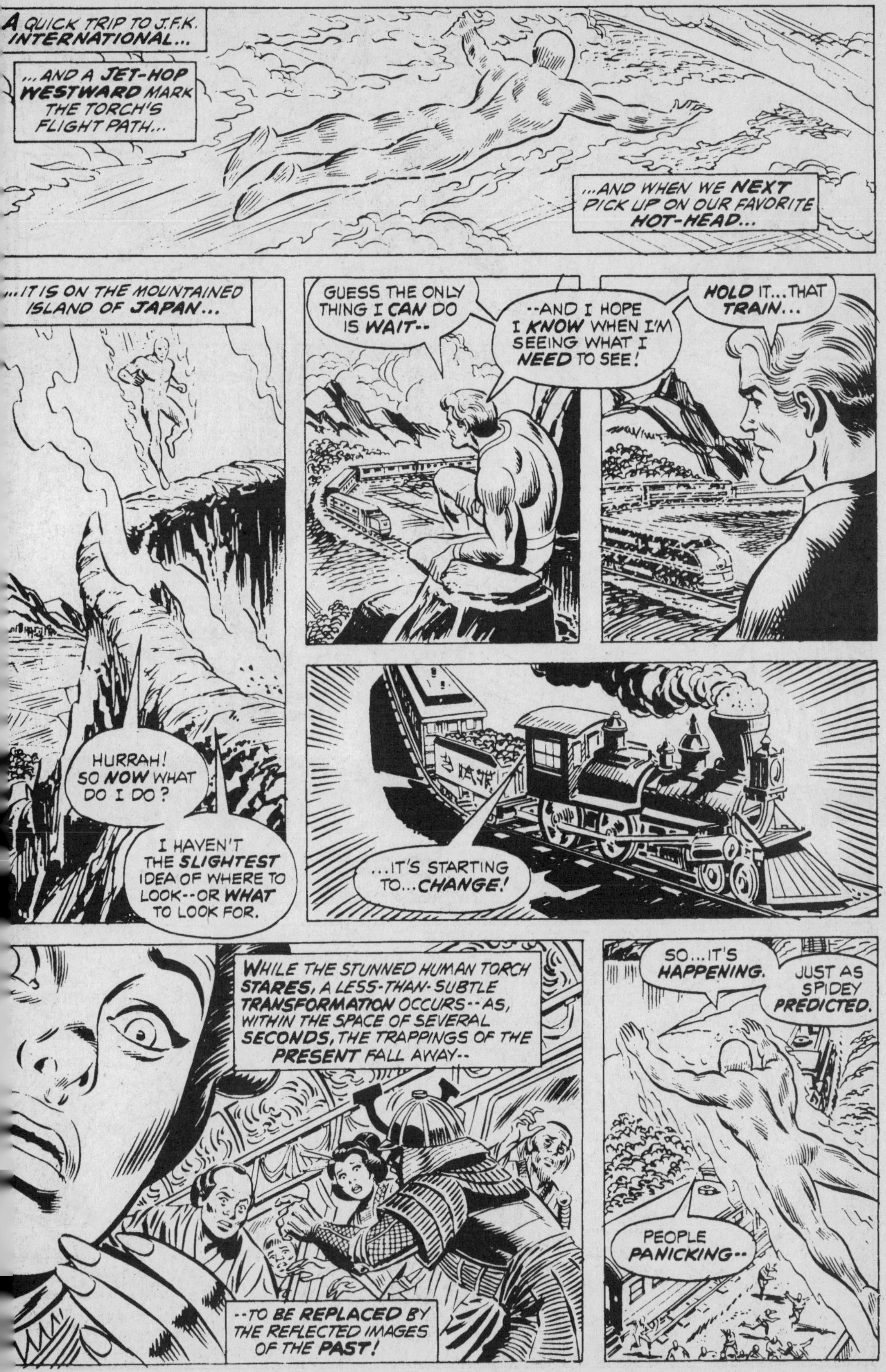
A QUICK TRIP TO J.F.K. INTERNATIONAL...
...AND A JET-HOP WESTWARD MARK THE TORCH'S FLIGHT PATH...
...AND WHEN WE NEXT PICK UP ON OUR FAVORITE HOT-HEAD...
...IT IS ON THE MOUNTAINED ISLAND OF JAPAN...
HURRAH! SO NOW WHAT DO I DO?
I HAVEN'T THE SLIGHTEST IDEA OF WHERE TO LOOK--OR WHAT TO LOOK FOR.
GUESS THE ONLY THING I CAN DO IS WAIT--
--AND I HOPE I KNOW WHEN I'M SEEING WHAT I NEED TO SEE!
HOLD IT...THAT TRAIN...
...IT'S STARTING TO...CHANGE!
WHILE THE STUNNED HUMAN TORCH STARES, A LESS-THAN-SUBTLE TRANSFORMATION OCCURS--AS, WITHIN THE SPACE OF SEVERAL SECONDS, THE TRAPPINGS OF THE PRESENT FALL AWAY--
--TO BE REPLACED BY THE REFLECTED IMAGES OF THE PAST!
SO...IT'S HAPPENING.
JUST AS SPIDEY PREDICTED.
PEOPLE PANICKING--

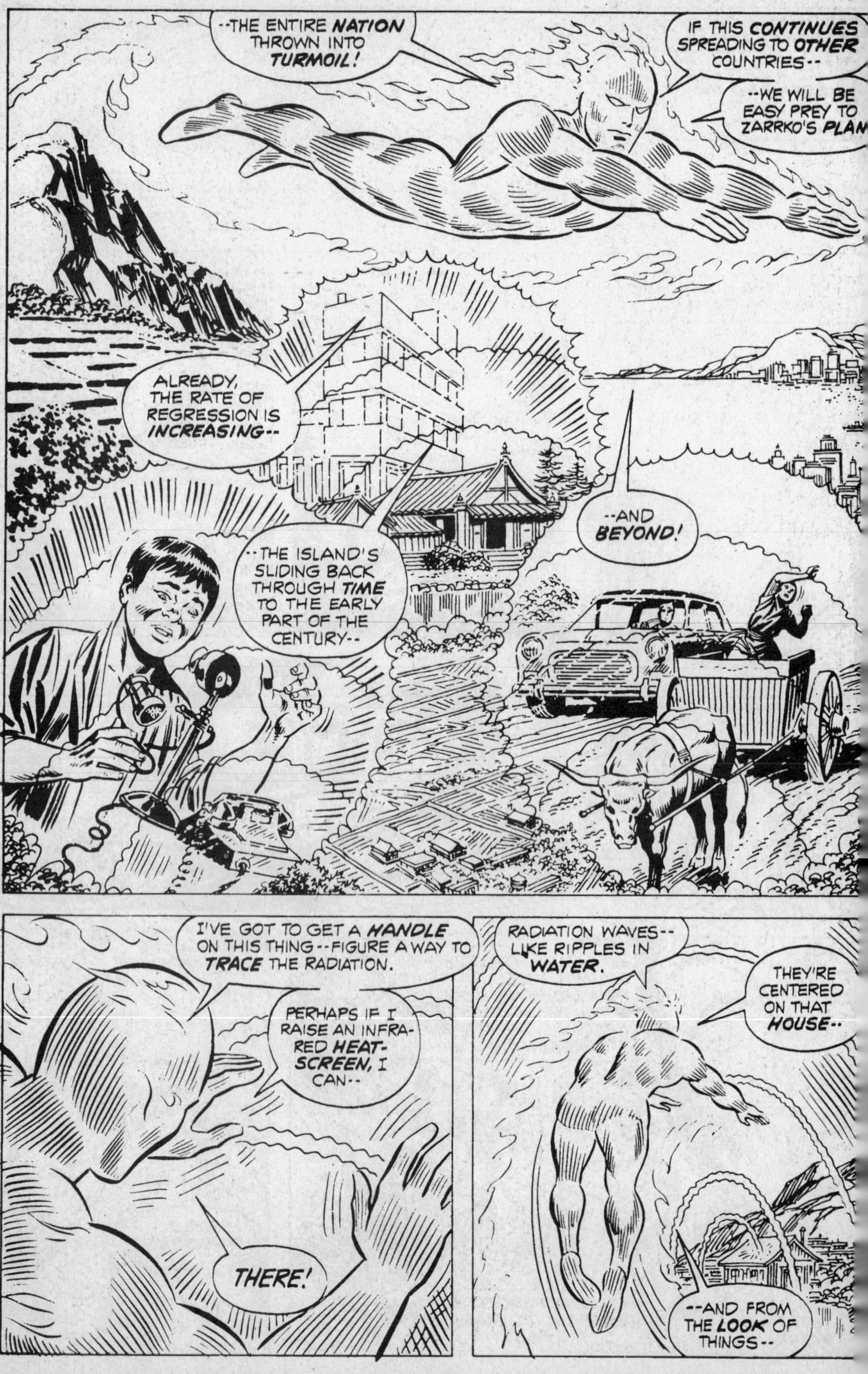

--THE ENTIRE NATION THROWN INTO TURMOIL!
IF THIS CONTINUES SPREADING TO OTHER COUNTRIES--
--WE WILL BE EASY PREY TO ZARRKO'S PLAN
ALREADY, THE RATE OF REGRESSION IS INCREASING--
--THE ISLAND'S SLIDING BACK THROUGH TIME TO THE EARLY PART OF THE CENTURY--
--AND BEYOND!
I'VE GOT TO GET A HANDLE ON THIS THING--FIGURE A WAY TO TRACE THE RADIATION.
PERHAPS IF I RAISE AN INFRA-RED HEAT-SCREEN, I CAN--
THERE!
RADIATION WAVES--LIKE RIPPLES IN WATER.
THEY'RE CENTERED ON THAT HOUSE--
--AND FROM THE LOOK OF THINGS--

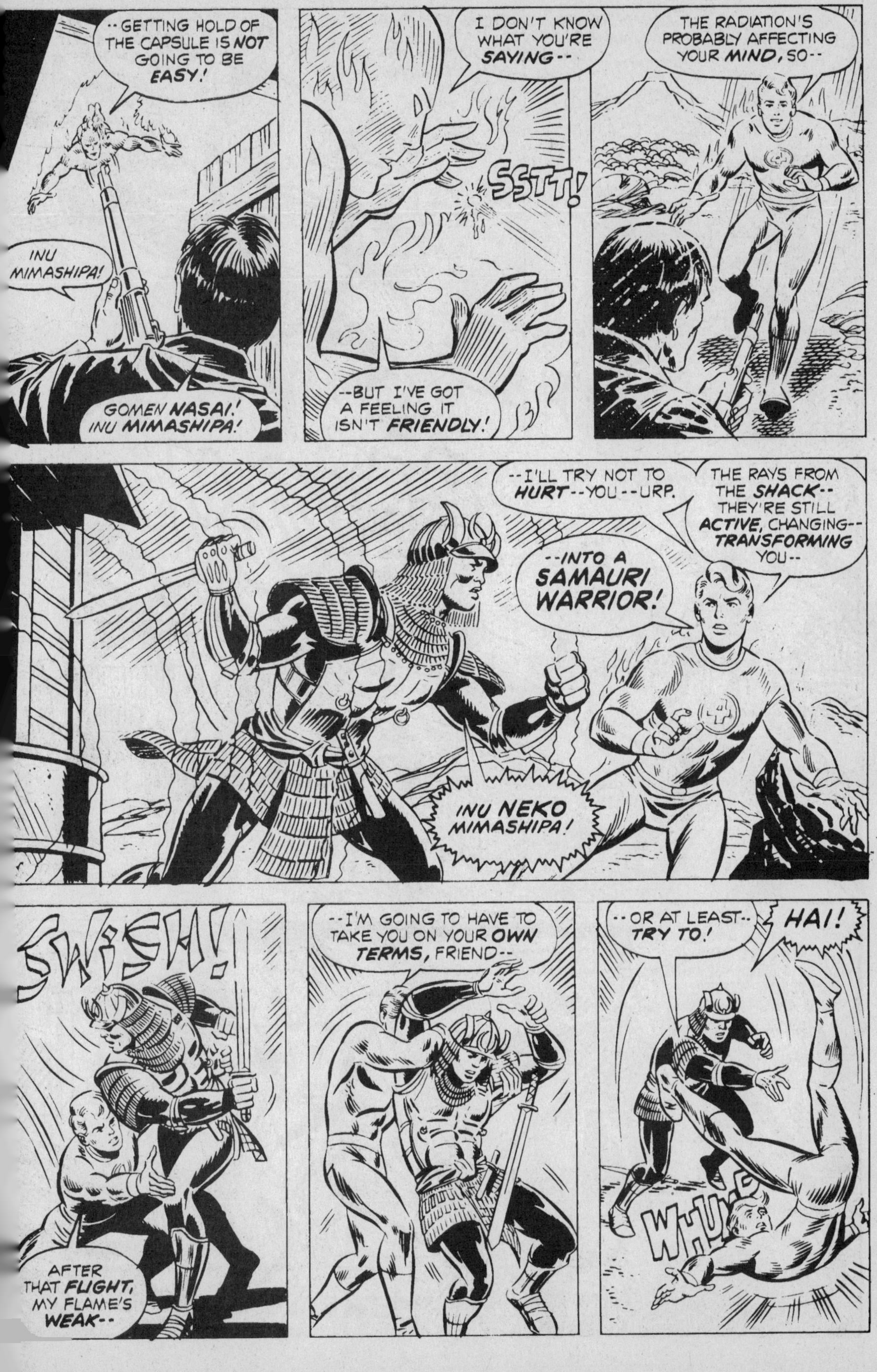

--GETTING HOLD OF THE CAPSULE IS NOT GOING TO BE EASY!
INU MIMASHIPA!
GOMEN NASAI! INU MIMASHIPA!
I DON'T KNOW WHAT YOU'RE SAYING--
SSTT!
--BUT I'VE GOT A FEELING IT ISN'T FRIENDLY!
THE RADIATION'S PROBABLY AFFECTING YOUR MIND, SO--
--I'LL TRY NOT TO HURT--YOU--URP.
THE RAYS FROM THE SHACK-- THEY'RE STILL ACTIVE, CHANGING-- TRANSFORMING YOU--
--INTO A SAMAURI WARRIOR!
INU NEKO MIMASHIPA!
SWISH!
AFTER THAT FLIGHT, MY FLAME'S WEAK--
--I'M GOING TO HAVE TO TAKE YOU ON YOUR OWN TERMS, FRIEND--
--OR AT LEAST-- TRY TO!
HAI!

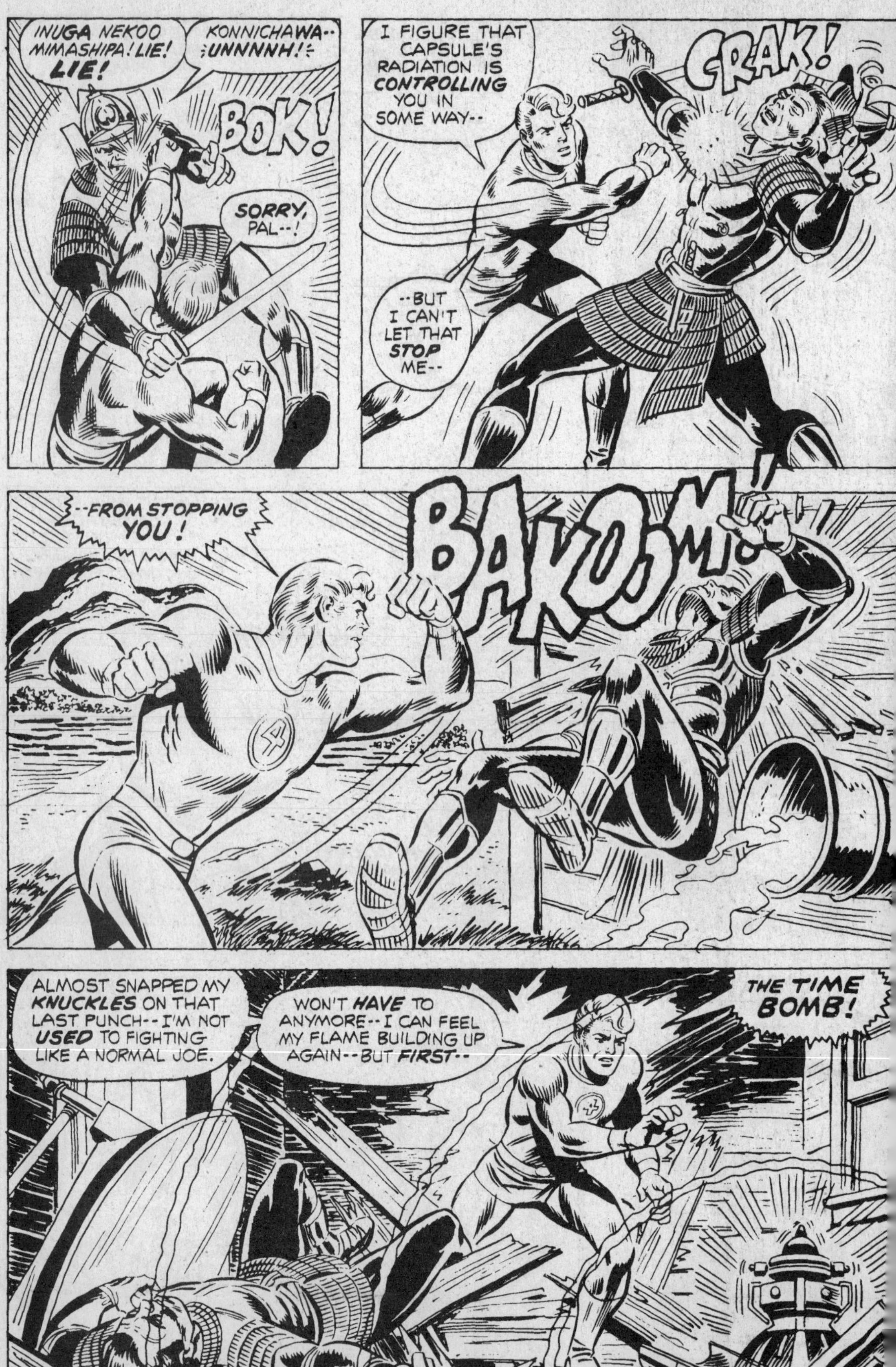
INUGA NEKOO MIMASHIPA! LIE! LIE!
KONNICHAWA-- UNNNNH!
BOK!
SORRY, PAL--!
I FIGURE THAT CAPSULE'S RADIATION IS CONTROLLING YOU IN SOME WAY--
CRAK!
--BUT I CAN'T LET THAT STOP ME--
--FROM STOPPING YOU!
BAKOOOM
ALMOST SNAPPED MY KNUCKLES ON THAT LAST PUNCH--I'M NOT USED TO FIGHTING LIKE A NORMAL JOE.
WON'T HAVE TO ANYMORE--I CAN FEEL MY FLAME BUILDING UP AGAIN--BUT FIRST--
THE TIME BOMB!

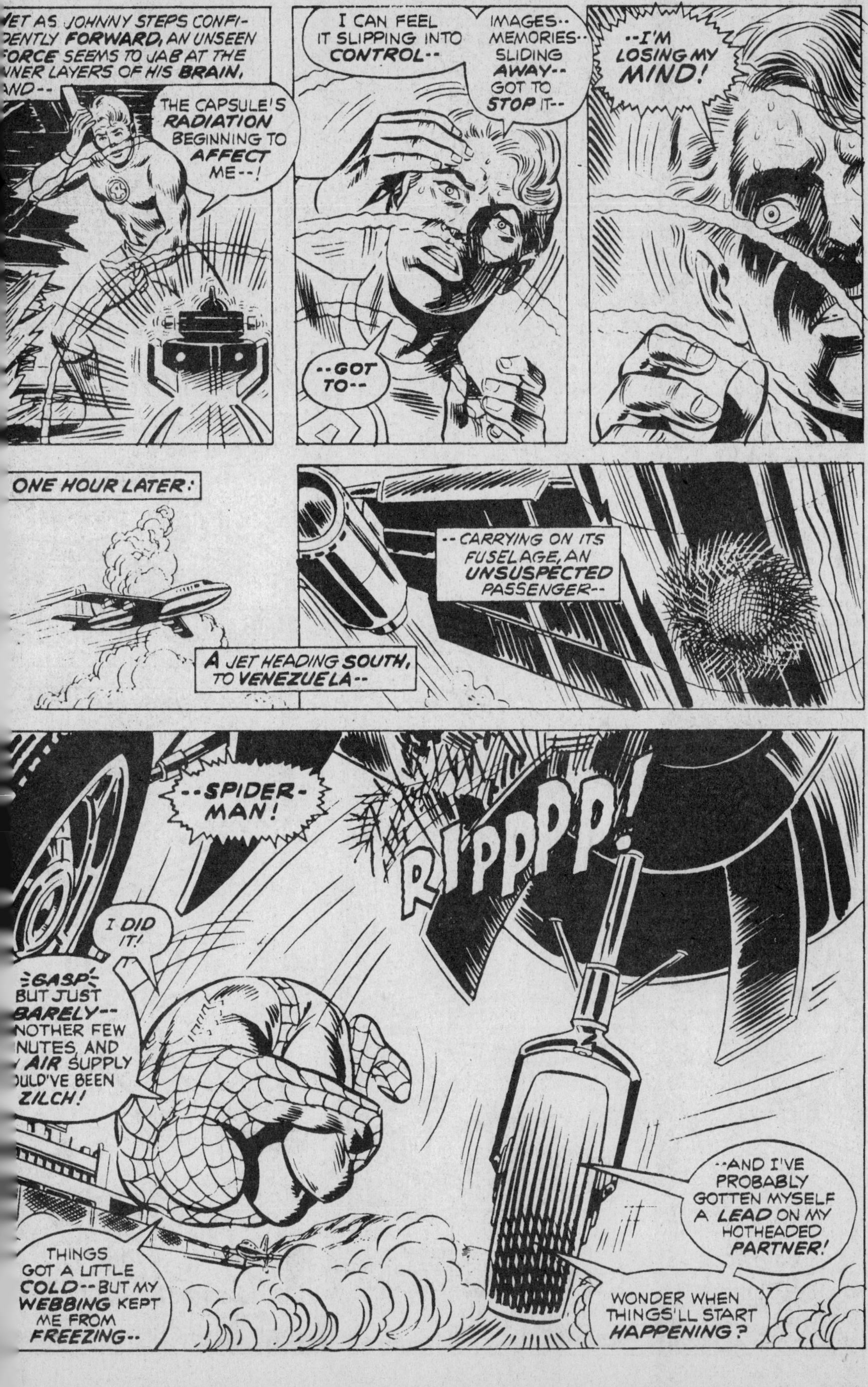
YET AS JOHNNY STEPS CONFIDENTLY FORWARD, AN UNSEEN FORCE SEEMS TO JAB AT THE INNER LAYERS OF HIS BRAIN, AND--
THE CAPSULE'S RADIATION BEGINNING TO AFFECT ME--!
I CAN FEEL IT SLIPPING INTO CONTROL--
IMAGES.. MEMORIES.. SLIDING AWAY-- GOT TO STOP IT--
--GOT TO--
--I'M LOSING MY MIND!
ONE HOUR LATER:
A JET HEADING SOUTH, TO VENEZUELA--
--CARRYING ON ITS FUSELAGE, AN UNSUSPECTED PASSENGER--
--SPIDER-MAN!
RIPPPP!
I DID IT!
GASP BUT JUST BARELY-- NOTHER FEW NUTES, AND AIR SUPPLY OULD'VE BEEN ZILCH!
THINGS GOT A LITTLE COLD--BUT MY WEBBING KEPT ME FROM FREEZING--
--AND I'VE PROBABLY GOTTEN MYSELF A LEAD ON MY HOTHEADED PARTNER!
WONDER WHEN THINGS'LL START HAPPENING?

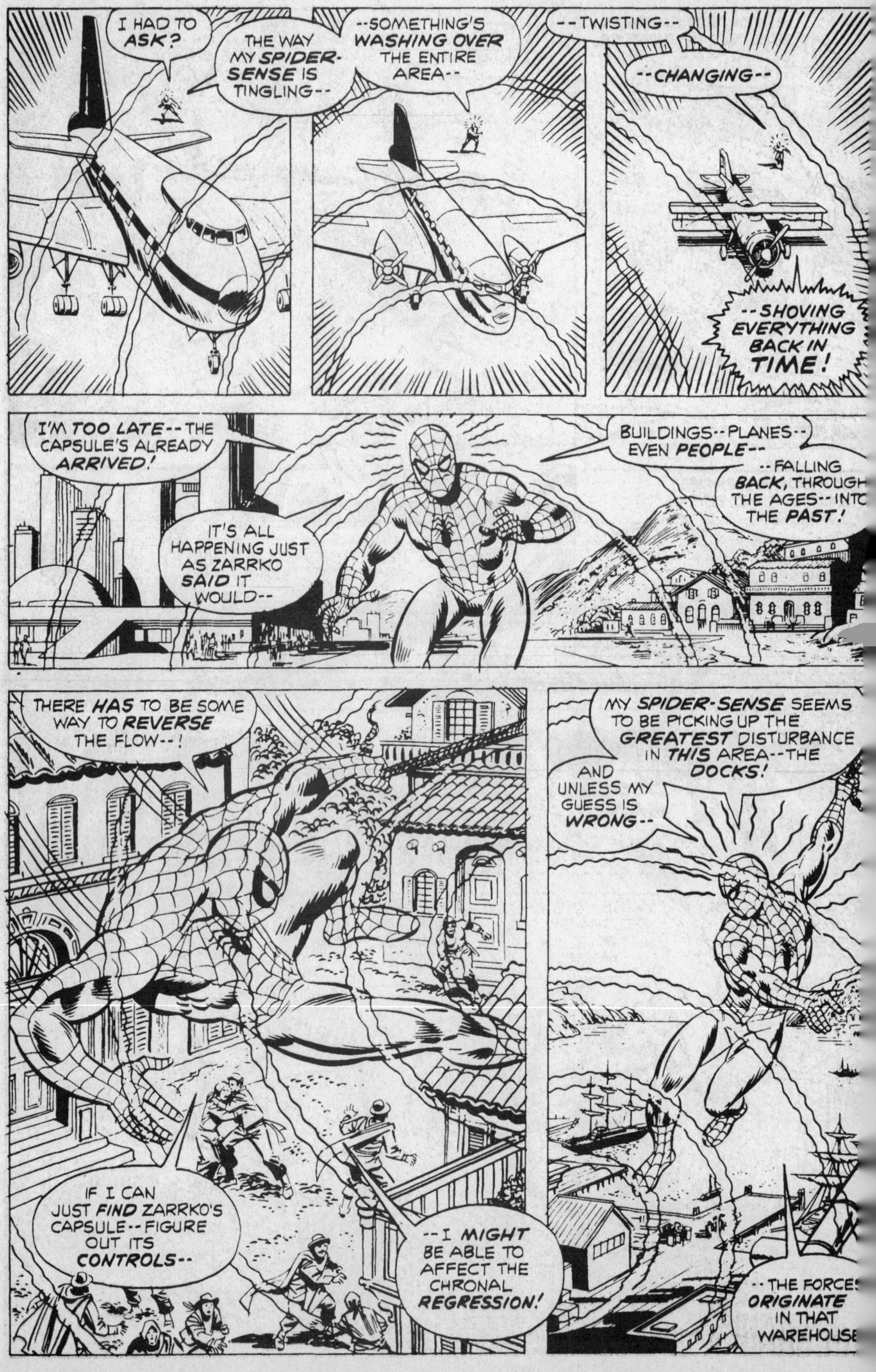
I HAD TO ASK?
THE WAY MY SPIDER-SENSE IS TINGLING--
--SOMETHING'S WASHING OVER THE ENTIRE AREA--
--TWISTING--
--CHANGING--
--SHOVING EVERYTHING BACK IN TIME!
I'M TOO LATE--THE CAPSULE'S ALREADY ARRIVED!
IT'S ALL HAPPENING JUST AS ZARRKO SAID IT WOULD--
BUILDINGS--PLANES--EVEN PEOPLE--
--FALLING BACK, THROUGH THE AGES--INTO THE PAST!
THERE HAS TO BE SOME WAY TO REVERSE THE FLOW--!
IF I CAN JUST FIND ZARRKO'S CAPSULE--FIGURE OUT ITS CONTROLS--
--I MIGHT BE ABLE TO AFFECT THE CHRONAL REGRESSION!
MY SPIDER-SENSE SEEMS TO BE PICKING UP THE GREATEST DISTURBANCE IN THIS AREA--THE DOCKS!
AND UNLESS MY GUESS IS WRONG--
--THE FORCES ORIGINATE IN THAT WAREHOUSE

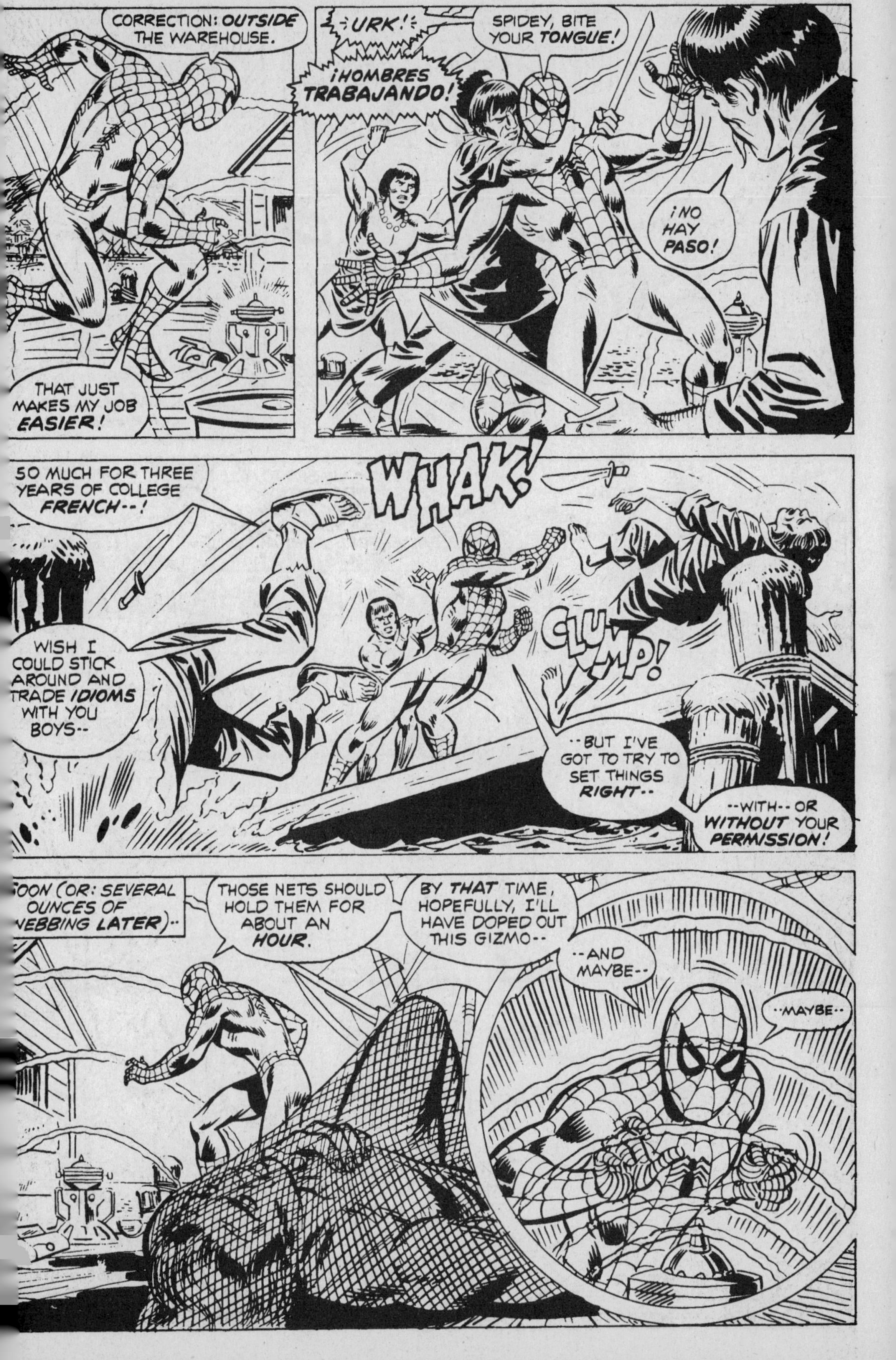
CORRECTION: OUTSIDE THE WAREHOUSE.
THAT JUST MAKES MY JOB EASIER!
-URK!-
¡HOMBRES TRABAJANDO!
SPIDEY, BITE YOUR TONGUE!
¡NO HAY PASO!
SO MUCH FOR THREE YEARS OF COLLEGE FRENCH--!
WHAK!
WISH I COULD STICK AROUND AND TRADE IDIOMS WITH YOU BOYS--
CLUMP!
--BUT I'VE GOT TO TRY TO SET THINGS RIGHT--
--WITH-- OR WITHOUT YOUR PERMISSION!
SOON (OR: SEVERAL OUNCES OF WEBBING LATER)--
THOSE NETS SHOULD HOLD THEM FOR ABOUT AN HOUR.
BY THAT TIME, HOPEFULLY, I'LL HAVE DOPED OUT THIS GIZMO--
--AND MAYBE--
--MAYBE--

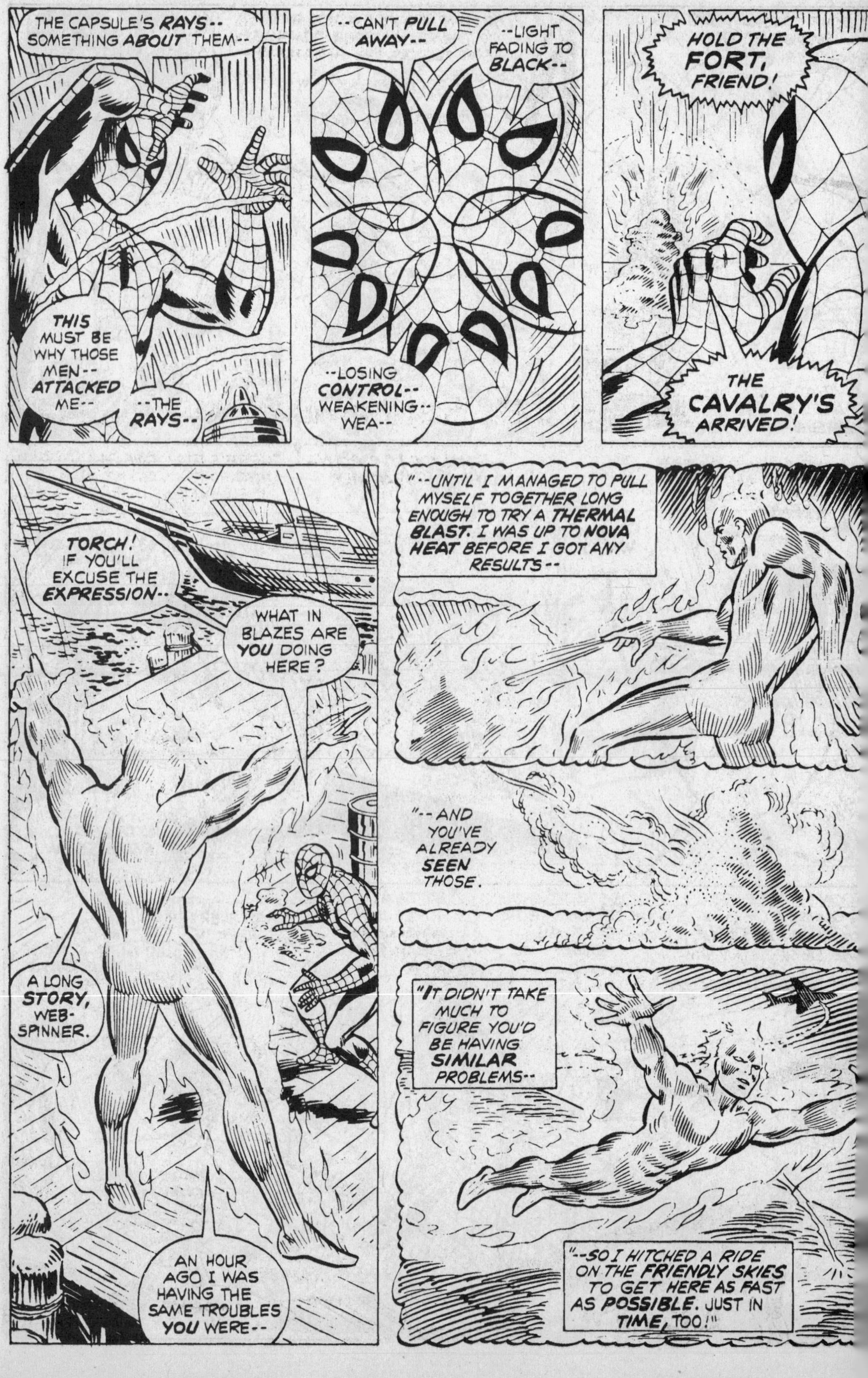

THE CAPSULE'S RAYS-- SOMETHING ABOUT THEM--
THIS MUST BE WHY THOSE MEN--ATTACKED ME--
--THE RAYS--
--CAN'T PULL AWAY--
--LIGHT FADING TO BLACK--
--LOSING CONTROL--WEAKENING--WEA--
HOLD THE FORT, FRIEND!
THE CAVALRY'S ARRIVED!
TORCH! IF YOU'LL EXCUSE THE EXPRESSION--
WHAT IN BLAZES ARE YOU DOING HERE?
A LONG STORY, WEB-SPINNER.
AN HOUR AGO I WAS HAVING THE SAME TROUBLES YOU WERE--
"--UNTIL I MANAGED TO PULL MYSELF TOGETHER LONG ENOUGH TO TRY A THERMAL BLAST. I WAS UP TO NOVA HEAT BEFORE I GOT ANY RESULTS--
"--AND YOU'VE ALREADY SEEN THOSE.
"IT DIDN'T TAKE MUCH TO FIGURE YOU'D BE HAVING SIMILAR PROBLEMS--
"--SO I HITCHED A RIDE ON THE FRIENDLY SKIES TO GET HERE AS FAST AS POSSIBLE. JUST IN TIME, TOO!"

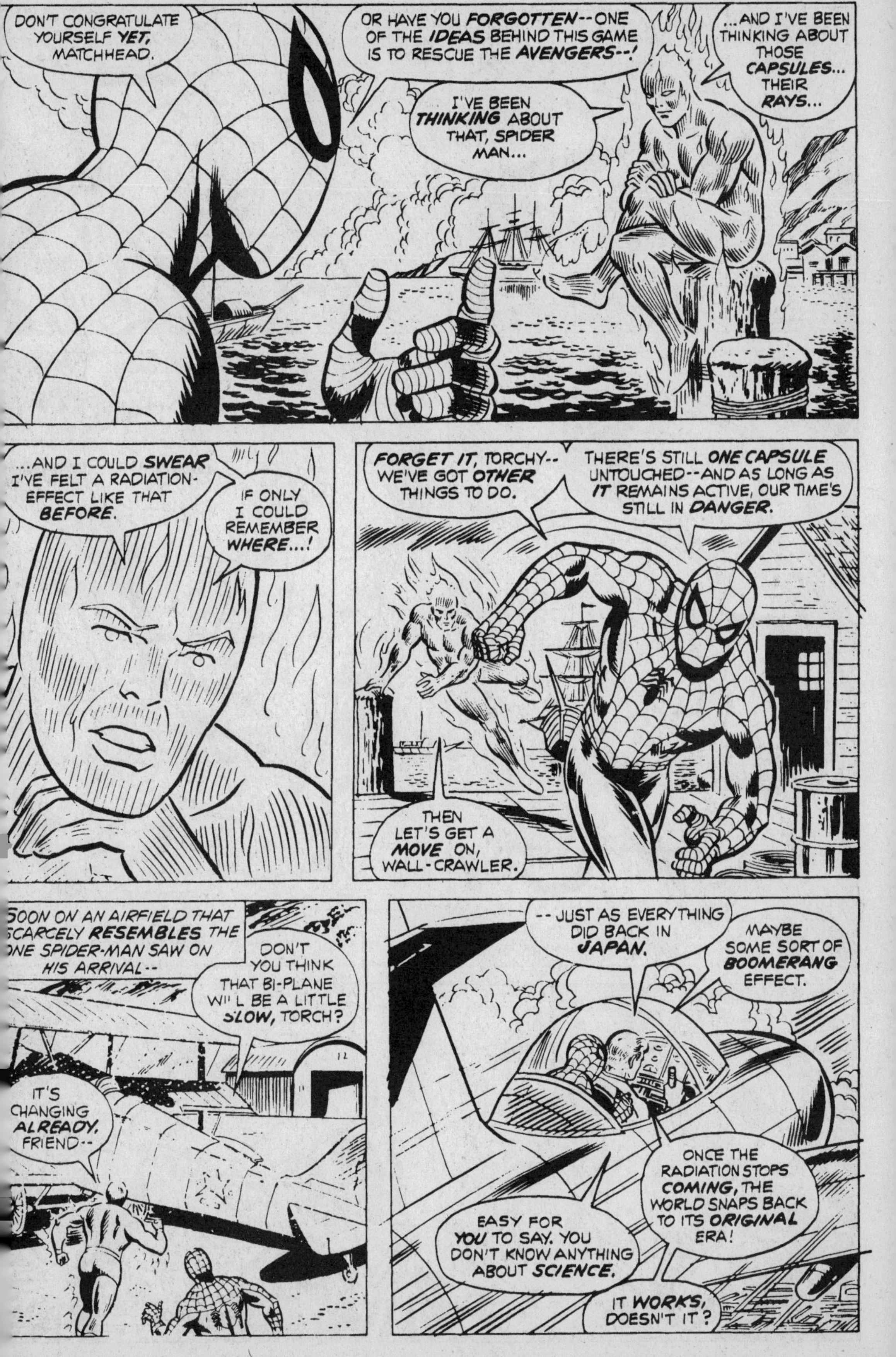
DON'T CONGRATULATE YOURSELF YET, MATCHHEAD.
OR HAVE YOU FORGOTTEN--ONE OF THE IDEAS BEHIND THIS GAME IS TO RESCUE THE AVENGERS--!
I'VE BEEN THINKING ABOUT THAT, SPIDER MAN...
...AND I'VE BEEN THINKING ABOUT THOSE CAPSULES... THEIR RAYS...
...AND I COULD SWEAR I'VE FELT A RADIATION-EFFECT LIKE THAT BEFORE.
IF ONLY I COULD REMEMBER WHERE...!
FORGET IT, TORCHY--WE'VE GOT OTHER THINGS TO DO.
THERE'S STILL ONE CAPSULE UNTOUCHED--AND AS LONG AS IT REMAINS ACTIVE, OUR TIME'S STILL IN DANGER.
THEN LET'S GET A MOVE ON, WALL-CRAWLER.
SOON ON AN AIRFIELD THAT SCARCELY RESEMBLES THE ONE SPIDER-MAN SAW ON HIS ARRIVAL--
DON'T YOU THINK THAT BI-PLANE WILL BE A LITTLE SLOW, TORCH?
IT'S CHANGING ALREADY, FRIEND--
--JUST AS EVERYTHING DID BACK IN JAPAN.
MAYBE SOME SORT OF BOOMERANG EFFECT.
ONCE THE RADIATION STOPS COMING, THE WORLD SNAPS BACK TO ITS ORIGINAL ERA!
EASY FOR YOU TO SAY. YOU DON'T KNOW ANYTHING ABOUT SCIENCE.
IT WORKS, DOESN'T IT?

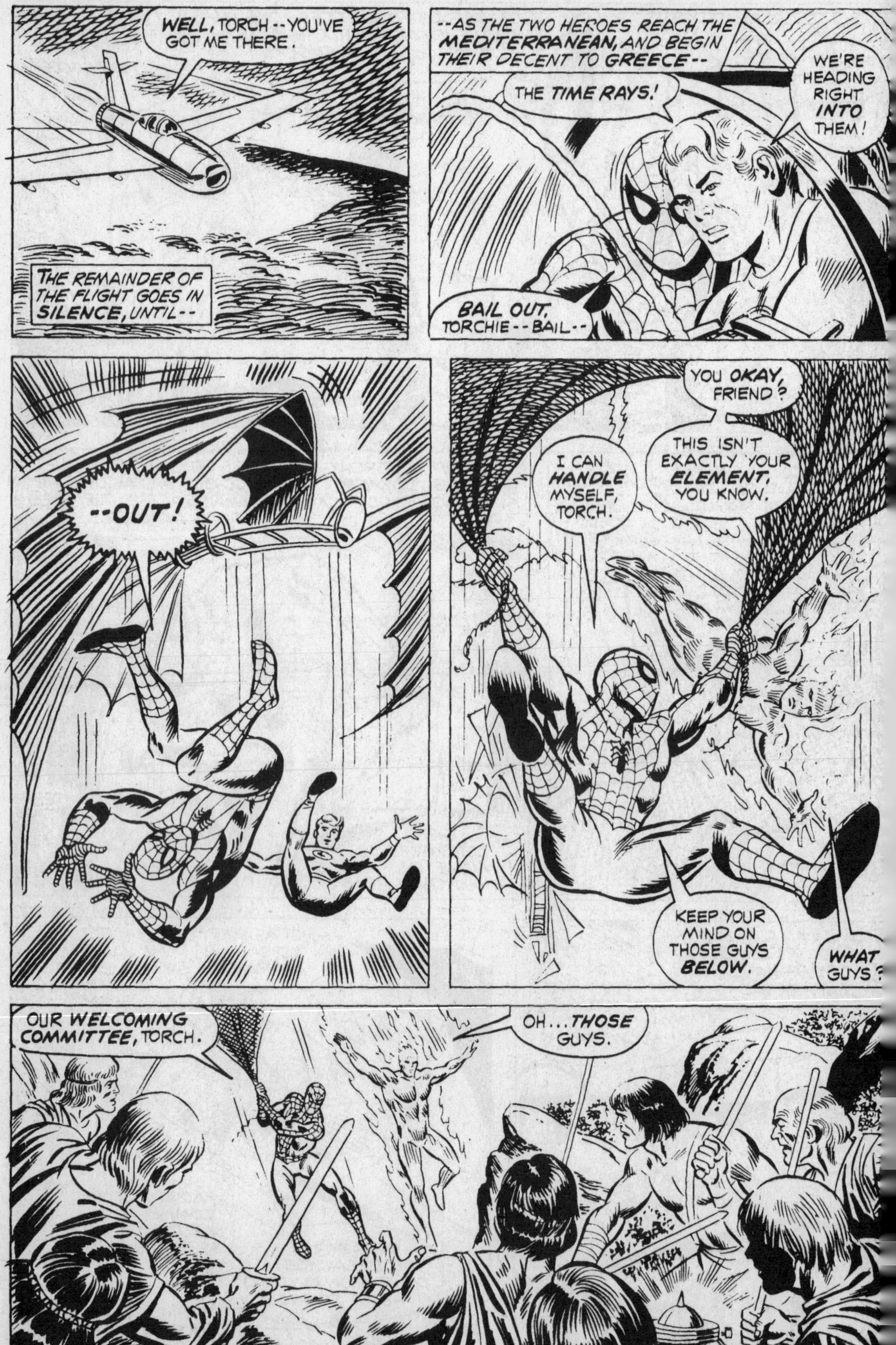
WELL, TORCH--YOU'VE GOT ME THERE.
THE REMAINDER OF THE FLIGHT GOES IN SILENCE, UNTIL--
--AS THE TWO HEROES REACH THE MEDITERRANEAN, AND BEGIN THEIR DECENT TO GREECE--
THE TIME RAYS!
WE'RE HEADING RIGHT INTO THEM!
BAIL OUT, TORCHIE--BAIL--
--OUT!
YOU OKAY, FRIEND?
THIS ISN'T EXACTLY YOUR ELEMENT, YOU KNOW.
I CAN HANDLE MYSELF, TORCH.
KEEP YOUR MIND ON THOSE GUYS BELOW.
WHAT GUYS?
OUR WELCOMING COMMITTEE, TORCH.
OH... THOSE GUYS.

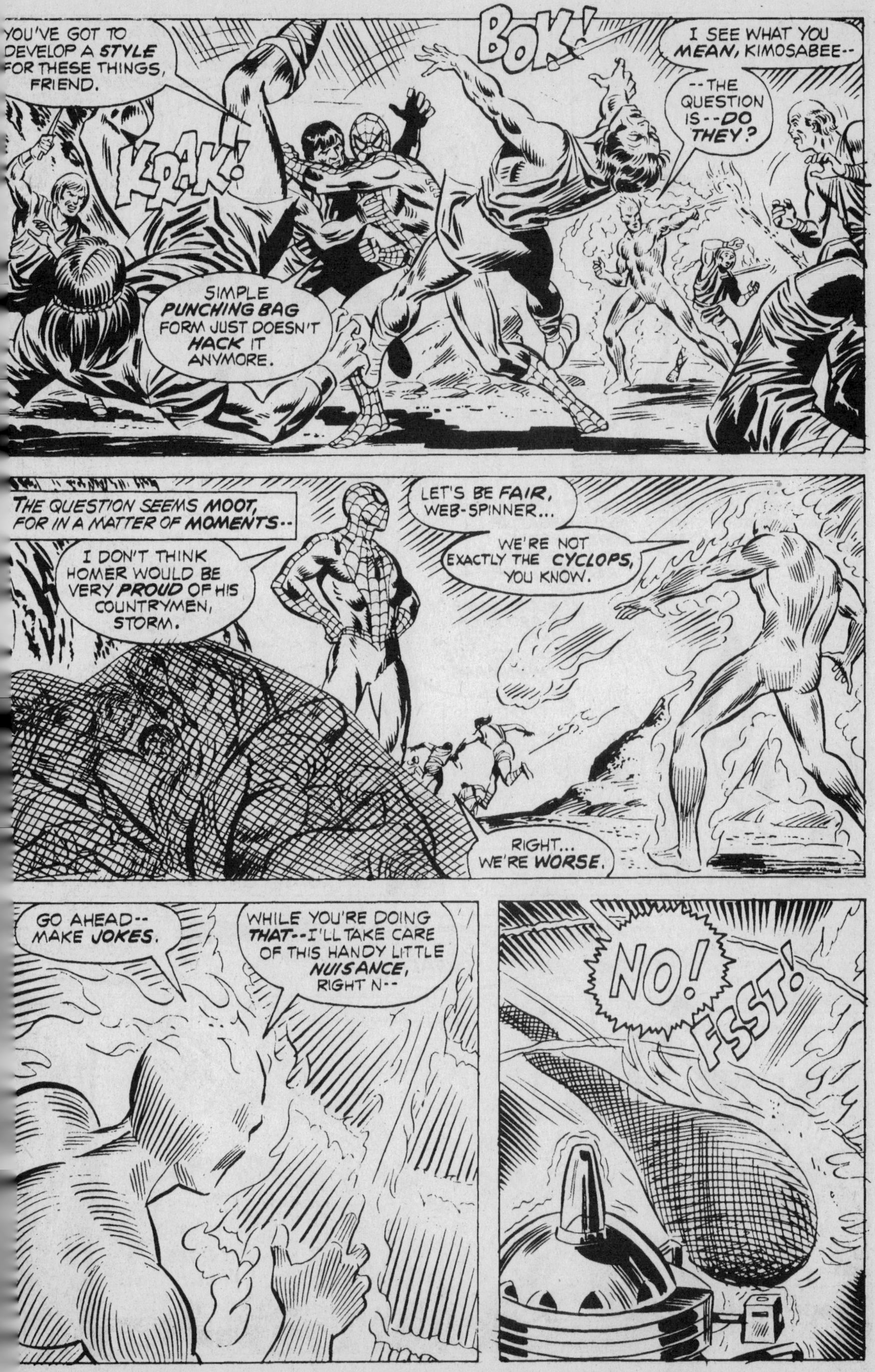

YOU'VE GOT TO DEVELOP A STYLE FOR THESE THINGS, FRIEND.
KRAAK!
SIMPLE PUNCHING BAG FORM JUST DOESN'T HACK IT ANYMORE.
BOK!
I SEE WHAT YOU MEAN, KIMOSABEE--
--THE QUESTION IS--DO THEY?
THE QUESTION SEEMS MOOT, FOR IN A MATTER OF MOMENTS--
I DON'T THINK HOMER WOULD BE VERY PROUD OF HIS COUNTRYMEN, STORM.
LET'S BE FAIR, WEB-SPINNER...
WE'RE NOT EXACTLY THE CYCLOPS, YOU KNOW.
RIGHT... WE'RE WORSE.
GO AHEAD-- MAKE JOKES.
WHILE YOU'RE DOING THAT--I'LL TAKE CARE OF THIS HANDY LITTLE NUISANCE, RIGHT N--
NO!
FSST!

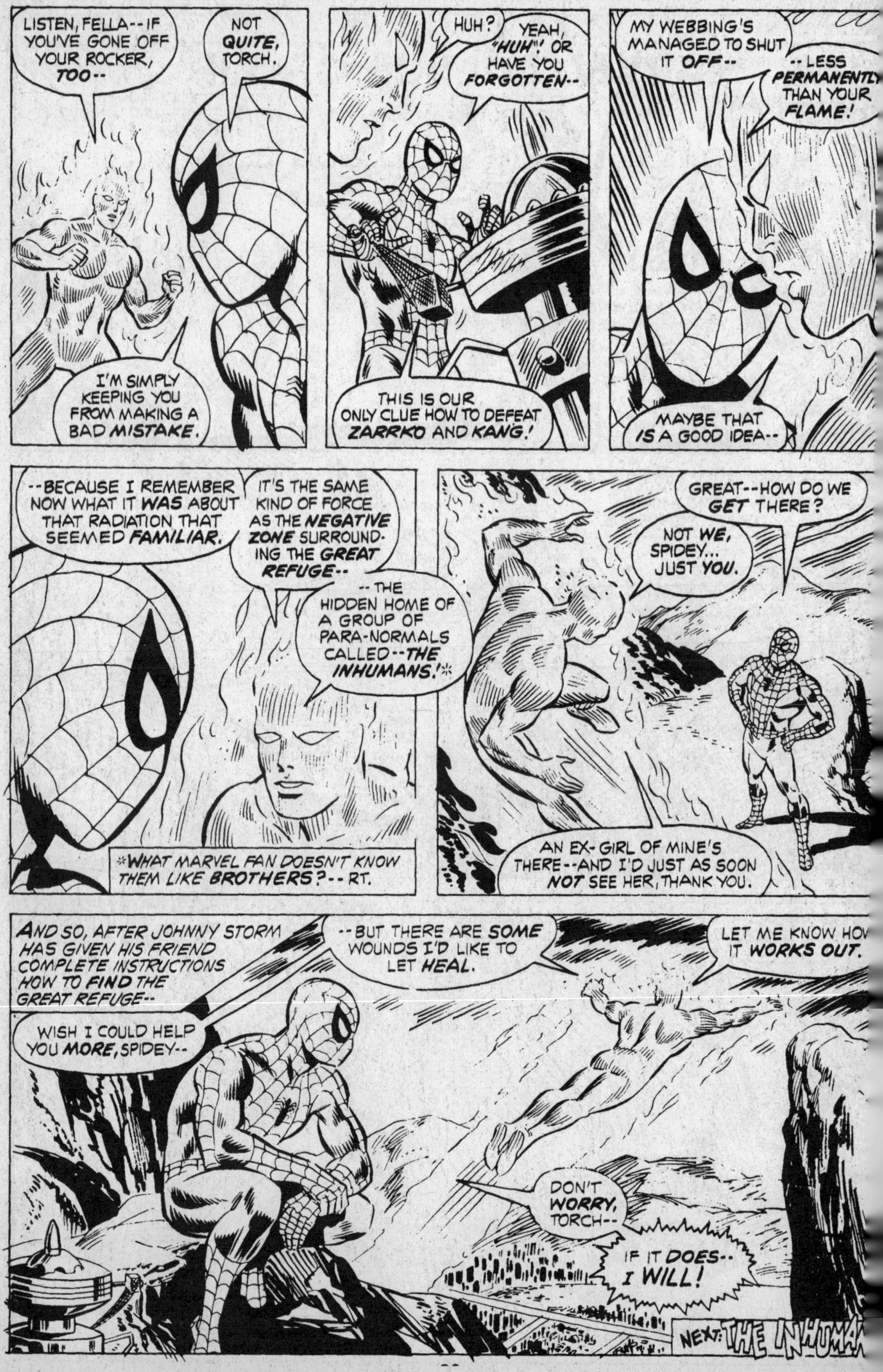
LISTEN, FELLA-- IF YOU'VE GONE OFF YOUR ROCKER, TOO--
NOT QUITE, TORCH.
I'M SIMPLY KEEPING YOU FROM MAKING A BAD MISTAKE.
HUH?
YEAH, "HUH"! OR HAVE YOU FORGOTTEN--
THIS IS OUR ONLY CLUE HOW TO DEFEAT ZARRKO AND KANG!
MY WEBBING'S MANAGED TO SHUT IT OFF--
--LESS PERMANENTLY THAN YOUR FLAME!
MAYBE THAT IS A GOOD IDEA--
--BECAUSE I REMEMBER NOW WHAT IT WAS ABOUT THAT RADIATION THAT SEEMED FAMILIAR.
IT'S THE SAME KIND OF FORCE AS THE NEGATIVE ZONE SURROUNDING THE GREAT REFUGE--
--THE HIDDEN HOME OF A GROUP OF PARA-NORMALS CALLED--THE INHUMANS!*
*WHAT MARVEL FAN DOESN'T KNOW THEM LIKE BROTHERS?-- RT.
GREAT--HOW DO WE GET THERE?
NOT WE, SPIDEY... JUST YOU.
AN EX-GIRL OF MINE'S THERE--AND I'D JUST AS SOON NOT SEE HER, THANK YOU.
AND SO, AFTER JOHNNY STORM HAS GIVEN HIS FRIEND COMPLETE INSTRUCTIONS HOW TO FIND THE GREAT REFUGE--
WISH I COULD HELP YOU MORE, SPIDEY--
--BUT THERE ARE SOME WOUNDS I'D LIKE TO LET HEAL.
LET ME KNOW HOW IT WORKS OUT.
DON'T WORRY, TORCH--
IF IT DOES-- I WILL!
NEXT: THE INHUMA

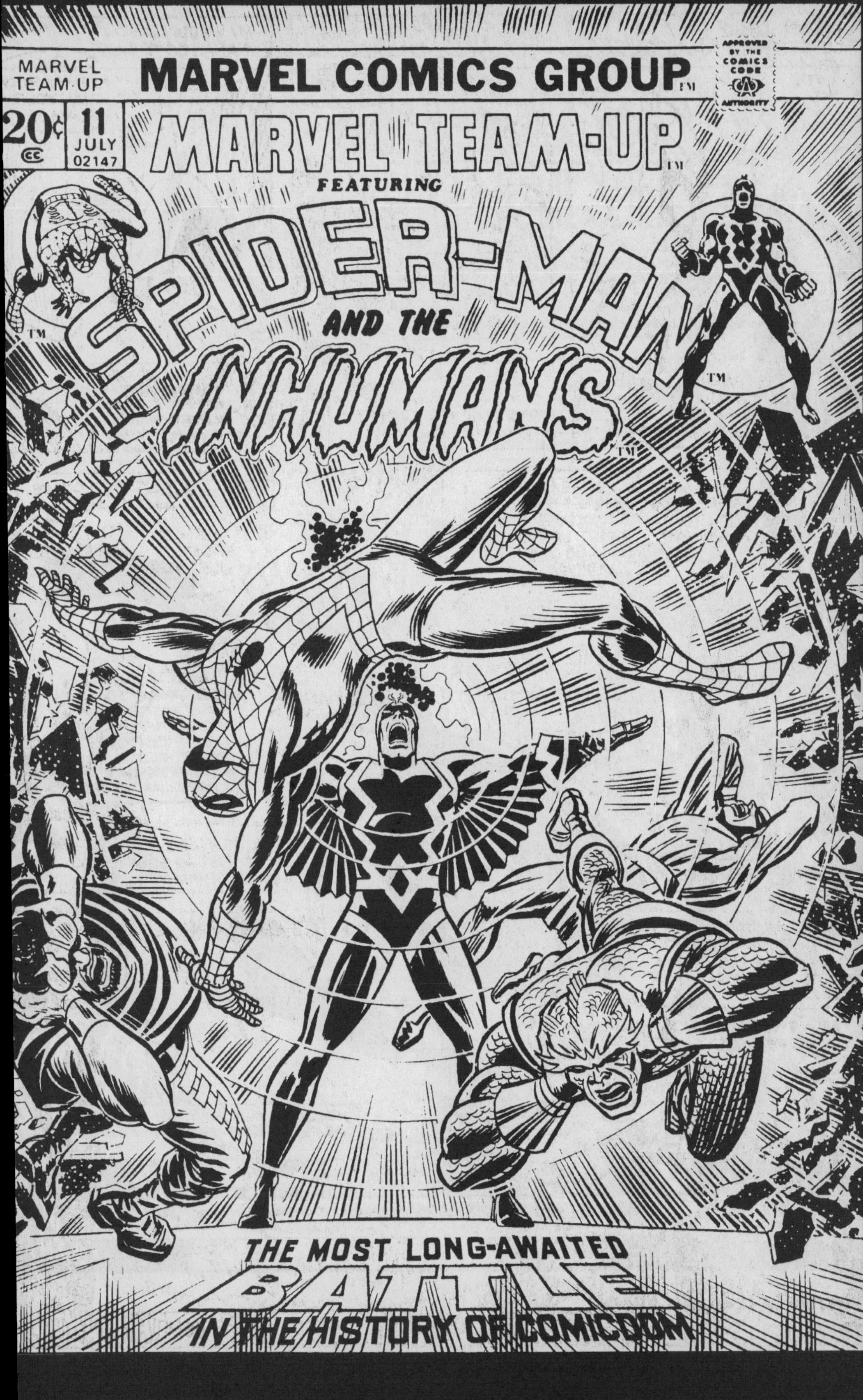
MARVEL TEAM-UP
MARVEL COMICS GROUP
APPROVED BY THE COMICS CODE AUTHORITY
20¢
11 JULY 02147
MARVEL TEAM-UP
FEATURING
SPIDER-MAN
AND THE
INHUMANS
THE MOST LONG-AWAITED
BATTLE
IN THE HISTORY OF COMICDOM

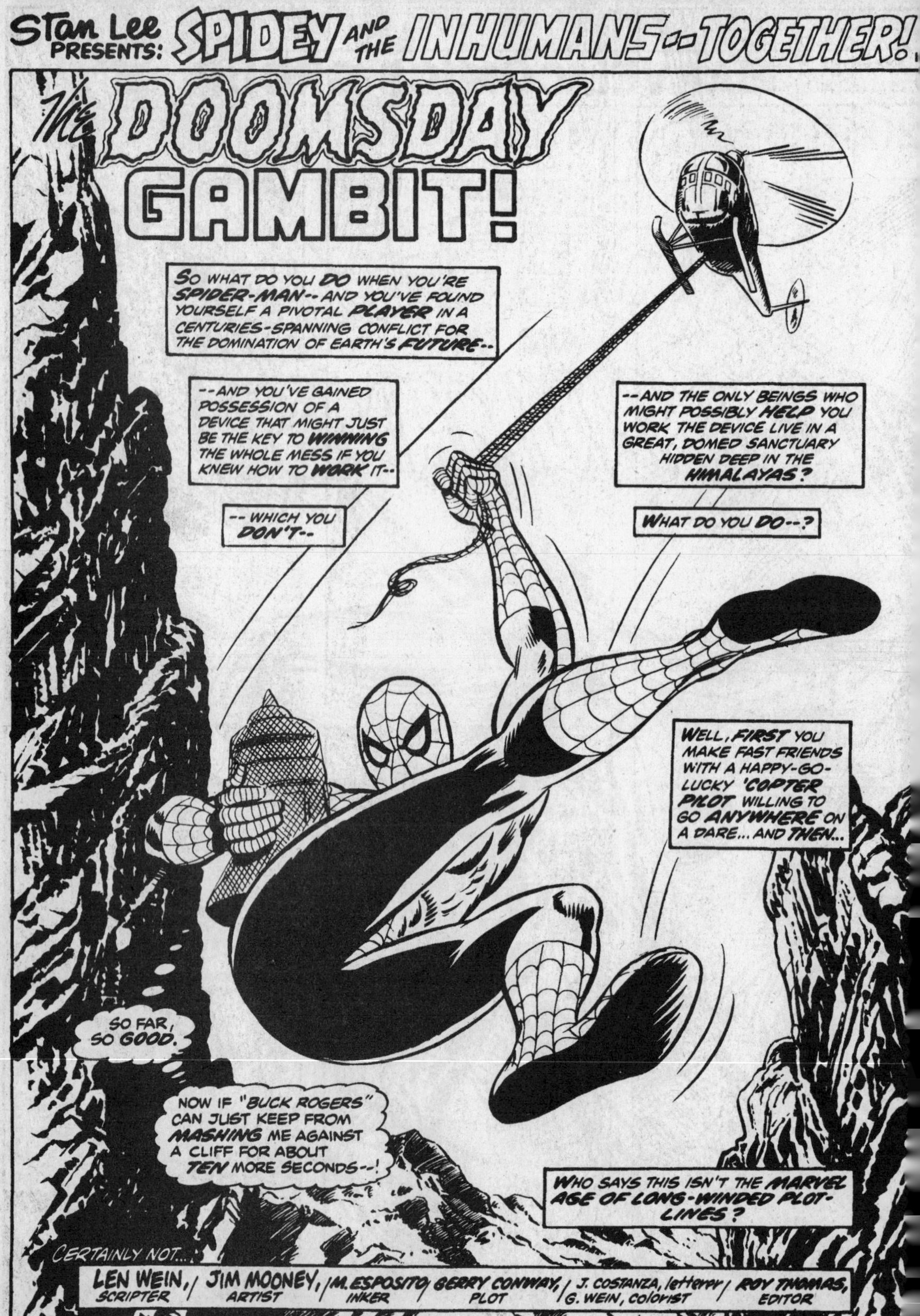
Stan Lee PRESENTS: SPIDEY AND THE INHUMANS--TOGETHER!
THE DOOMSDAY GAMBIT!
SO WHAT DO YOU DO WHEN YOU'RE SPIDER-MAN-- AND YOU'VE FOUND YOURSELF A PIVOTAL PLAYER IN A CENTURIES-SPANNING CONFLICT FOR THE DOMINATION OF EARTH'S FUTURE--
--AND YOU'VE GAINED POSSESSION OF A DEVICE THAT MIGHT JUST BE THE KEY TO WINNING THE WHOLE MESS IF YOU KNEW HOW TO WORK IT--
-- WHICH YOU DON'T--
--AND THE ONLY BEINGS WHO MIGHT POSSIBLY HELP YOU WORK THE DEVICE LIVE IN A GREAT, DOMED SANCTUARY HIDDEN DEEP IN THE HIMALAYAS?
WHAT DO YOU DO--?
WELL, FIRST YOU MAKE FAST FRIENDS WITH A HAPPY-GO-LUCKY 'COPTER PILOT WILLING TO GO ANYWHERE ON A DARE... AND THEN...
SO FAR, SO GOOD.
NOW IF "BUCK ROGERS" CAN JUST KEEP FROM MASHING ME AGAINST A CLIFF FOR ABOUT TEN MORE SECONDS--!
WHO SAYS THIS ISN'T THE MARVEL AGE OF LONG-WINDED PLOT-LINES?
CERTAINLY NOT...
LEN WEIN, SCRIPTER / JIM MOONEY, ARTIST / M. ESPOSITO INKER / GERRY CONWAY, PLOT / J. COSTANZA, letterer / G. WEIN, colorist / ROY THOMAS, EDITOR

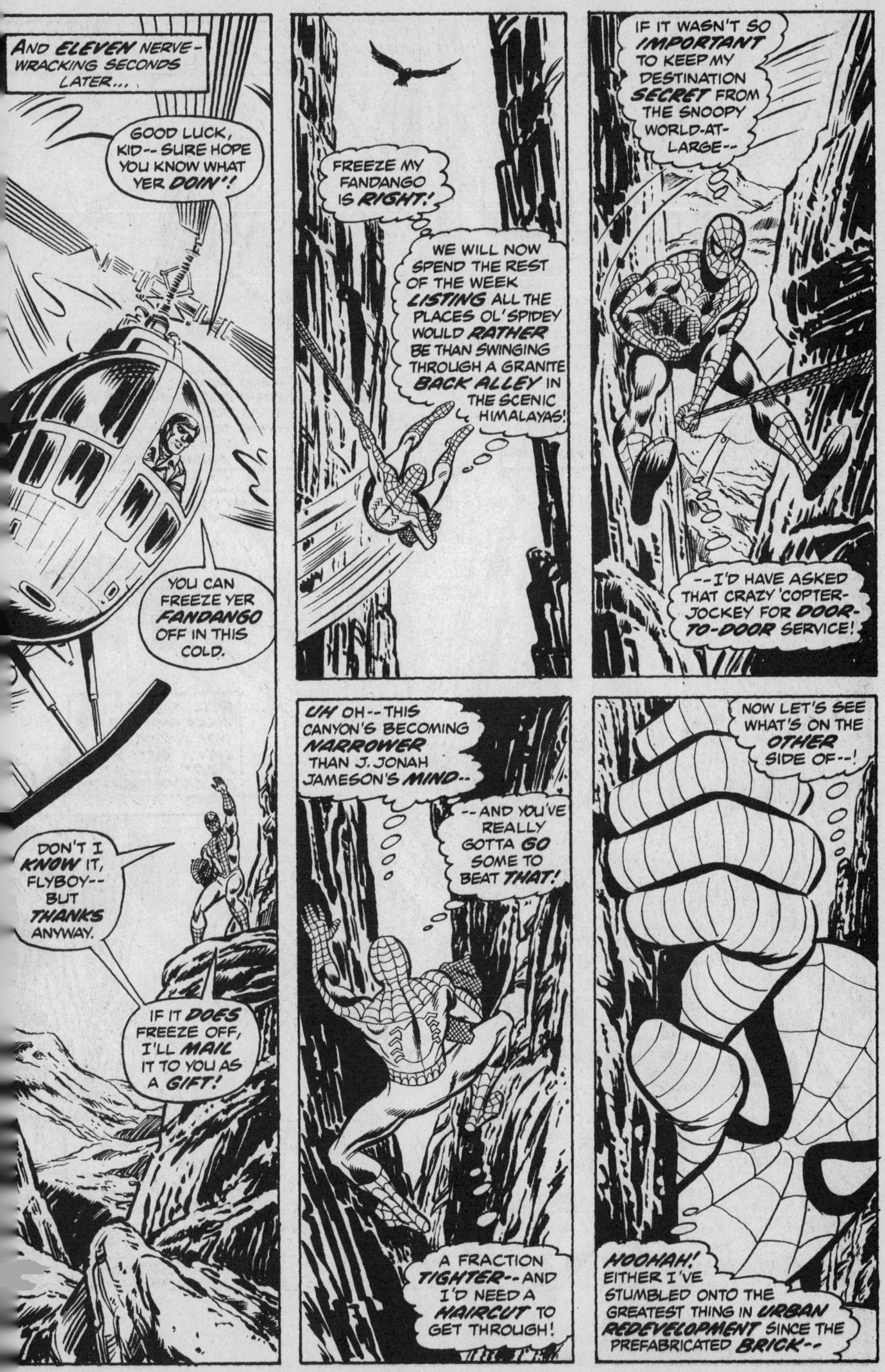
AND ELEVEN NERVE-WRACKING SECONDS LATER...
GOOD LUCK, KID-- SURE HOPE YOU KNOW WHAT YER DOIN'!
YOU CAN FREEZE YER FANDANGO OFF IN THIS COLD.
DON'T I KNOW IT, FLYBOY-- BUT THANKS ANYWAY.
IF IT DOES FREEZE OFF, I'LL MAIL IT TO YOU AS A GIFT!
FREEZE MY FANDANGO IS RIGHT!
WE WILL NOW SPEND THE REST OF THE WEEK LISTING ALL THE PLACES OL' SPIDEY WOULD RATHER BE THAN SWINGING THROUGH A GRANITE BACK ALLEY IN THE SCENIC HIMALAYAS!
IF IT WASN'T SO IMPORTANT TO KEEP MY DESTINATION SECRET FROM THE SNOOPY WORLD-AT-LARGE--
--I'D HAVE ASKED THAT CRAZY 'COPTER-JOCKEY FOR DOOR-TO-DOOR SERVICE!
UH OH--THIS CANYON'S BECOMING NARROWER THAN J. JONAH JAMESON'S MIND--
--AND YOU'VE REALLY GOTTA GO SOME TO BEAT THAT!
A FRACTION TIGHTER--AND I'D NEED A HAIRCUT TO GET THROUGH!
NOW LET'S SEE WHAT'S ON THE OTHER SIDE OF--!
HOOHAH! EITHER I'VE STUMBLED ONTO THE GREATEST THING IN URBAN REDEVELOPMENT SINCE THE PREFABRICATED BRICK--

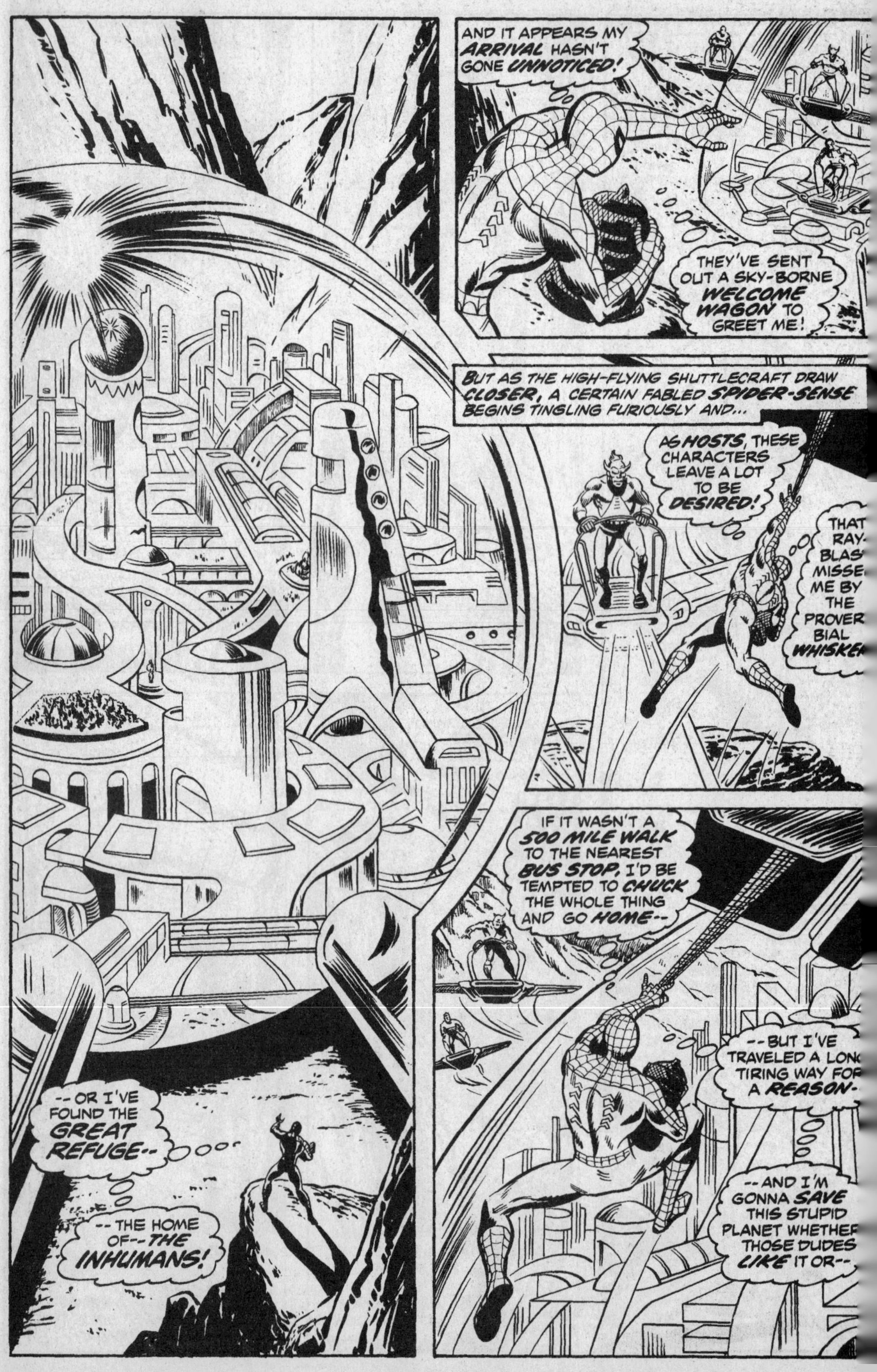

-- OR I'VE FOUND THE GREAT REFUGE--
-- THE HOME OF-- THE INHUMANS!
AND IT APPEARS MY ARRIVAL HASN'T GONE UNNOTICED!
THEY'VE SENT OUT A SKY-BORNE WELCOME WAGON TO GREET ME!
BUT AS THE HIGH-FLYING SHUTTLECRAFT DRAW CLOSER, A CERTAIN FABLED SPIDER-SENSE BEGINS TINGLING FURIOUSLY AND...
AS HOSTS, THESE CHARACTERS LEAVE A LOT TO BE DESIRED!
IF IT WASN'T A 500 MILE WALK TO THE NEAREST BUS STOP, I'D BE TEMPTED TO CHUCK THE WHOLE THING AND GO HOME--

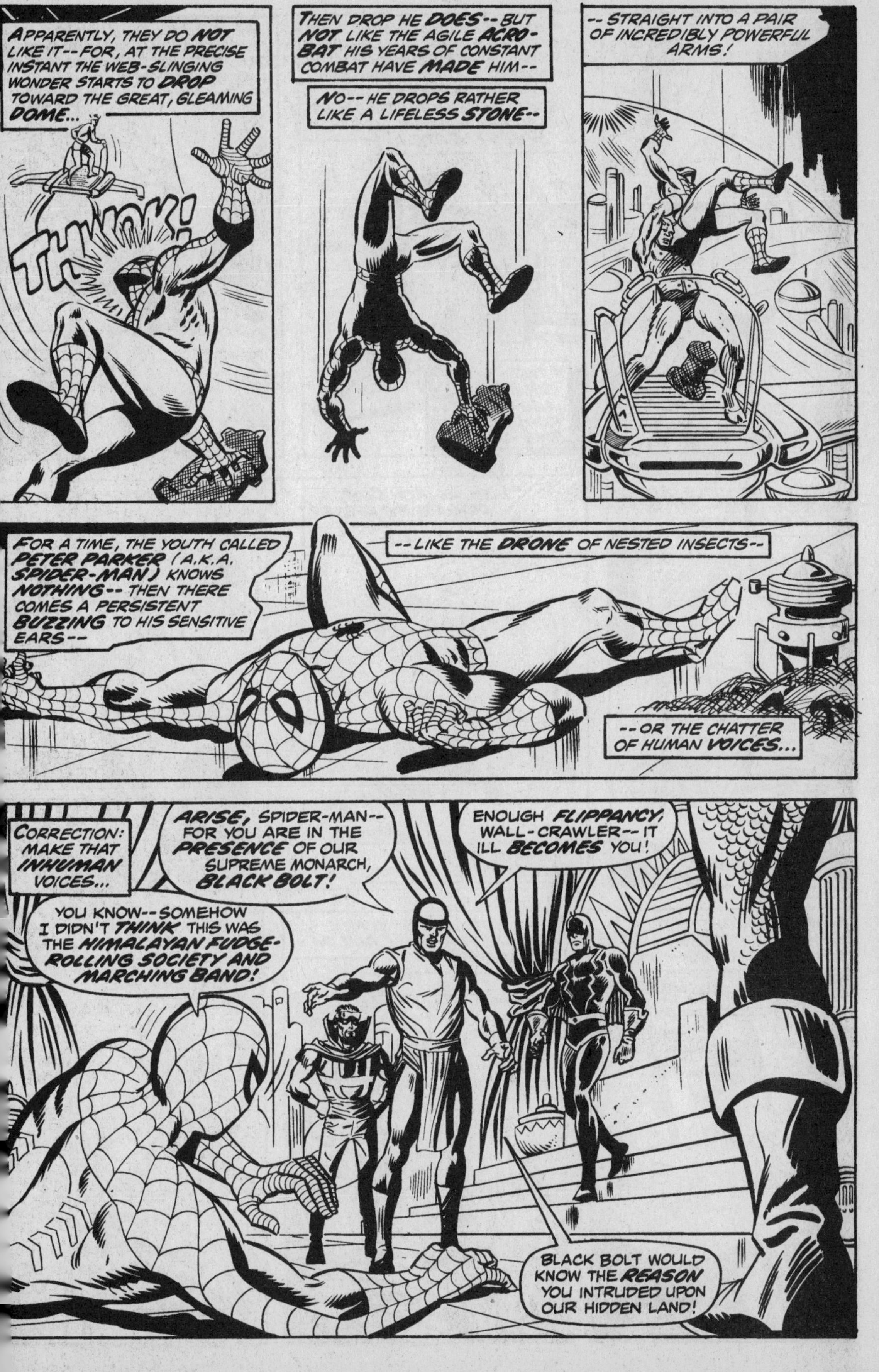

APPARENTLY, THEY DO NOT LIKE IT--FOR, AT THE PRECISE INSTANT THE WEB-SLINGING WONDER STARTS TO DROP TOWARD THE GREAT, GLEAMING DOME...
THWOK!
THEN DROP HE DOES--BUT NOT LIKE THE AGILE ACRO-BAT HIS YEARS OF CONSTANT COMBAT HAVE MADE HIM--
NO--HE DROPS RATHER LIKE A LIFELESS STONE--
--STRAIGHT INTO A PAIR OF INCREDIBLY POWERFUL ARMS!
FOR A TIME, THE YOUTH CALLED PETER PARKER (A.K.A. SPIDER-MAN) KNOWS NOTHING--THEN THERE COMES A PERSISTENT BUZZING TO HIS SENSITIVE EARS--
--LIKE THE DRONE OF NESTED INSECTS--
--OR THE CHATTER OF HUMAN VOICES...
CORRECTION: MAKE THAT INHUMAN VOICES...
ARISE, SPIDER-MAN--FOR YOU ARE IN THE PRESENCE OF OUR SUPREME MONARCH, BLACK BOLT!
YOU KNOW--SOMEHOW I DIDN'T THINK THIS WAS THE HIMALAYAN FUDGE-ROLLING SOCIETY AND MARCHING BAND!
ENOUGH FLIPPANCY, WALL-CRAWLER--IT ILL BECOMES YOU!
BLACK BOLT WOULD KNOW THE REASON YOU INTRUDED UPON OUR HIDDEN LAND!

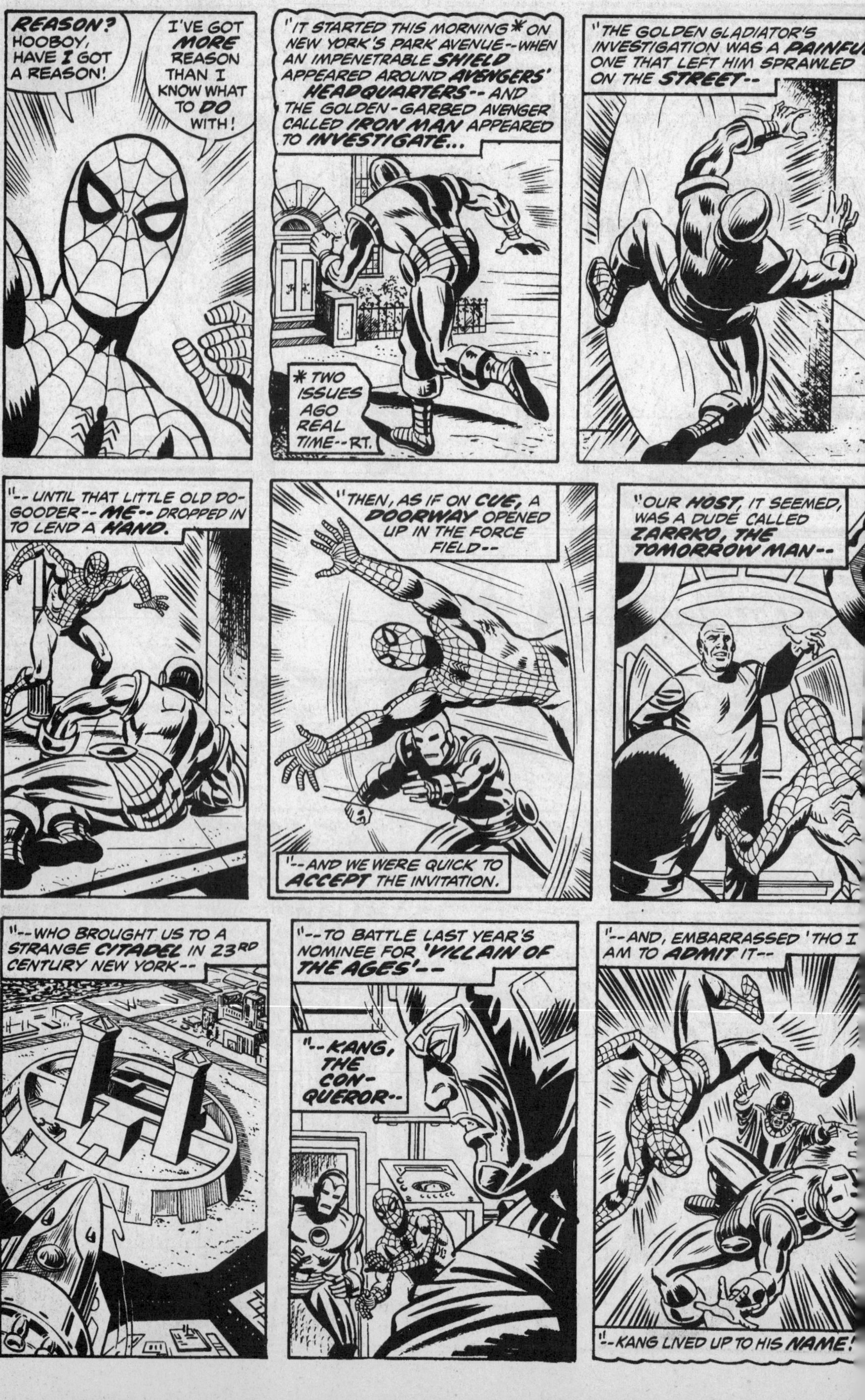
REASON? HOOBOY, HAVE I GOT A REASON!
I'VE GOT MORE REASON THAN I KNOW WHAT TO DO WITH!
"IT STARTED THIS MORNING* ON NEW YORK'S PARK AVENUE--WHEN AN IMPENETRABLE SHIELD APPEARED AROUND AVENGERS' HEADQUARTERS--AND THE GOLDEN-GARBED AVENGER CALLED IRON MAN APPEARED TO INVESTIGATE...
*TWO ISSUES AGO REAL TIME--RT.
"THE GOLDEN GLADIATOR'S INVESTIGATION WAS A PAINFUL ONE THAT LEFT HIM SPRAWLED ON THE STREET--
"--UNTIL THAT LITTLE OLD DO-GOODER--ME--DROPPED IN TO LEND A HAND.
"THEN, AS IF ON CUE, A DOORWAY OPENED UP IN THE FORCE FIELD--
"--AND WE WERE QUICK TO ACCEPT THE INVITATION.
"OUR HOST, IT SEEMED, WAS A DUDE CALLED ZARRKO, THE TOMORROW MAN--
"--WHO BROUGHT US TO A STRANGE CITADEL IN 23RD CENTURY NEW YORK--
"--TO BATTLE LAST YEAR'S NOMINEE FOR 'VILLAIN OF THE AGES'--
"--KANG, THE CON-QUEROR--
"--AND, EMBARRASSED 'THO I AM TO ADMIT IT--
"--KANG LIVED UP TO HIS NAME!

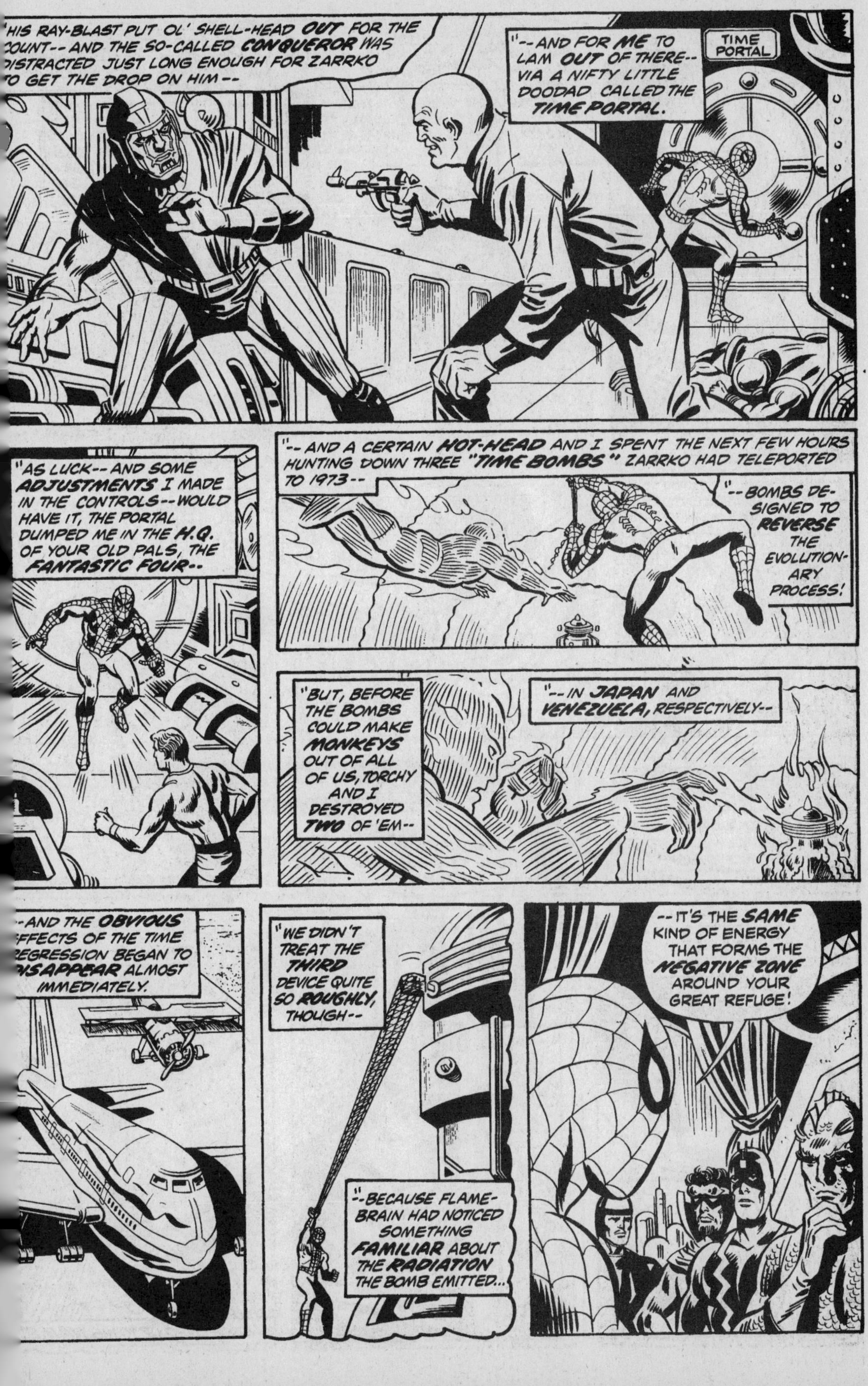
'HIS RAY-BLAST PUT OL' SHELL-HEAD OUT FOR THE COUNT-- AND THE SO-CALLED CONQUEROR WAS DISTRACTED JUST LONG ENOUGH FOR ZARRKO TO GET THE DROP ON HIM --
"-- AND FOR ME TO LAM OUT OF THERE-- VIA A NIFTY LITTLE DOODAD CALLED THE TIME PORTAL.
TIME PORTAL
"AS LUCK-- AND SOME ADJUSTMENTS I MADE IN THE CONTROLS--WOULD HAVE IT, THE PORTAL DUMPED ME IN THE H.Q. OF YOUR OLD PALS, THE FANTASTIC FOUR--
"-- AND A CERTAIN HOT-HEAD AND I SPENT THE NEXT FEW HOURS HUNTING DOWN THREE "TIME BOMBS" ZARRKO HAD TELEPORTED TO 1973--
"-- BOMBS DE-SIGNED TO REVERSE THE EVOLUTION-ARY PROCESS!
"BUT, BEFORE THE BOMBS COULD MAKE MONKEYS OUT OF ALL OF US, TORCHY AND I DESTROYED TWO OF 'EM--
"-- IN JAPAN AND VENEZUELA, RESPECTIVELY--
--AND THE OBVIOUS EFFECTS OF THE TIME REGRESSION BEGAN TO DISAPPEAR ALMOST IMMEDIATELY.
"WE DIDN'T TREAT THE THIRD DEVICE QUITE SO ROUGHLY, THOUGH--
"-BECAUSE FLAME-BRAIN HAD NOTICED SOMETHING FAMILIAR ABOUT THE RADIATION THE BOMB EMITTED...
-- IT'S THE SAME KIND OF ENERGY THAT FORMS THE NEGATIVE ZONE AROUND YOUR GREAT REFUGE!

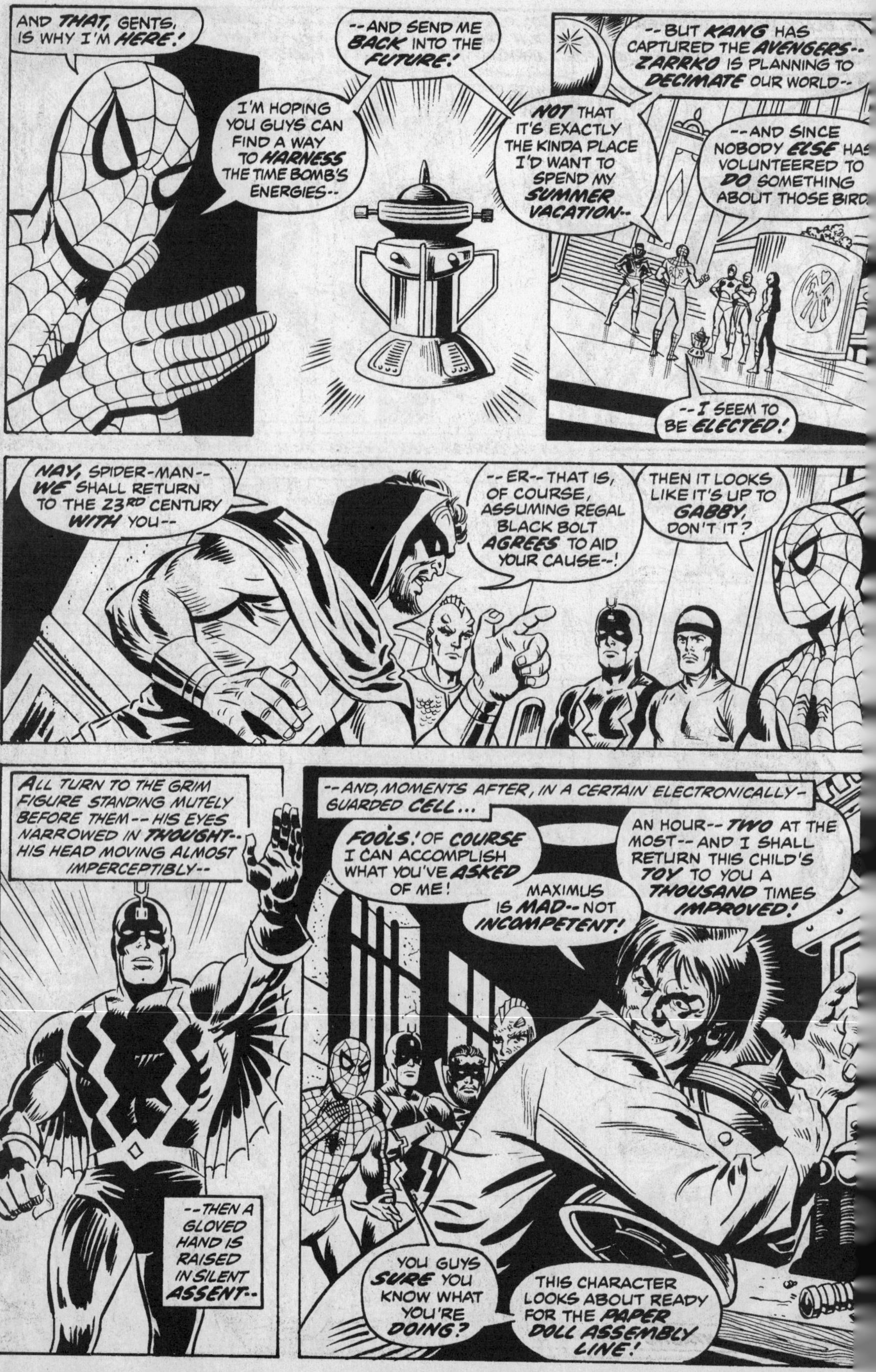
AND THAT, GENTS, IS WHY I'M HERE!
I'M HOPING YOU GUYS CAN FIND A WAY TO HARNESS THE TIME BOMB'S ENERGIES--
--AND SEND ME BACK INTO THE FUTURE!
NOT THAT IT'S EXACTLY THE KINDA PLACE I'D WANT TO SPEND MY SUMMER VACATION--
--BUT KANG HAS CAPTURED THE AVENGERS--ZARRKO IS PLANNING TO DECIMATE OUR WORLD--
--AND SINCE NOBODY ELSE HAS VOLUNTEERED TO DO SOMETHING ABOUT THOSE BIRD
--I SEEM TO BE ELECTED!
NAY, SPIDER-MAN--WE SHALL RETURN TO THE 23RD CENTURY WITH YOU--
--ER--THAT IS, OF COURSE, ASSUMING REGAL BLACK BOLT AGREES TO AID YOUR CAUSE--!
THEN IT LOOKS LIKE IT'S UP TO GABBY, DON'T IT?
ALL TURN TO THE GRIM FIGURE STANDING MUTELY BEFORE THEM--HIS EYES NARROWED IN THOUGHT--HIS HEAD MOVING ALMOST IMPERCEPTIBLY--
--THEN A GLOVED HAND IS RAISED IN SILENT ASSENT--
--AND, MOMENTS AFTER, IN A CERTAIN ELECTRONICALLY-GUARDED CELL...
FOOLS! OF COURSE I CAN ACCOMPLISH WHAT YOU'VE ASKED OF ME!
MAXIMUS IS MAD--NOT INCOMPETENT!
AN HOUR--TWO AT THE MOST--AND I SHALL RETURN THIS CHILD'S TOY TO YOU A THOUSAND TIMES IMPROVED!
YOU GUYS SURE YOU KNOW WHAT YOU'RE DOING?
THIS CHARACTER LOOKS ABOUT READY FOR THE PAPER DOLL ASSEMBLY LINE!

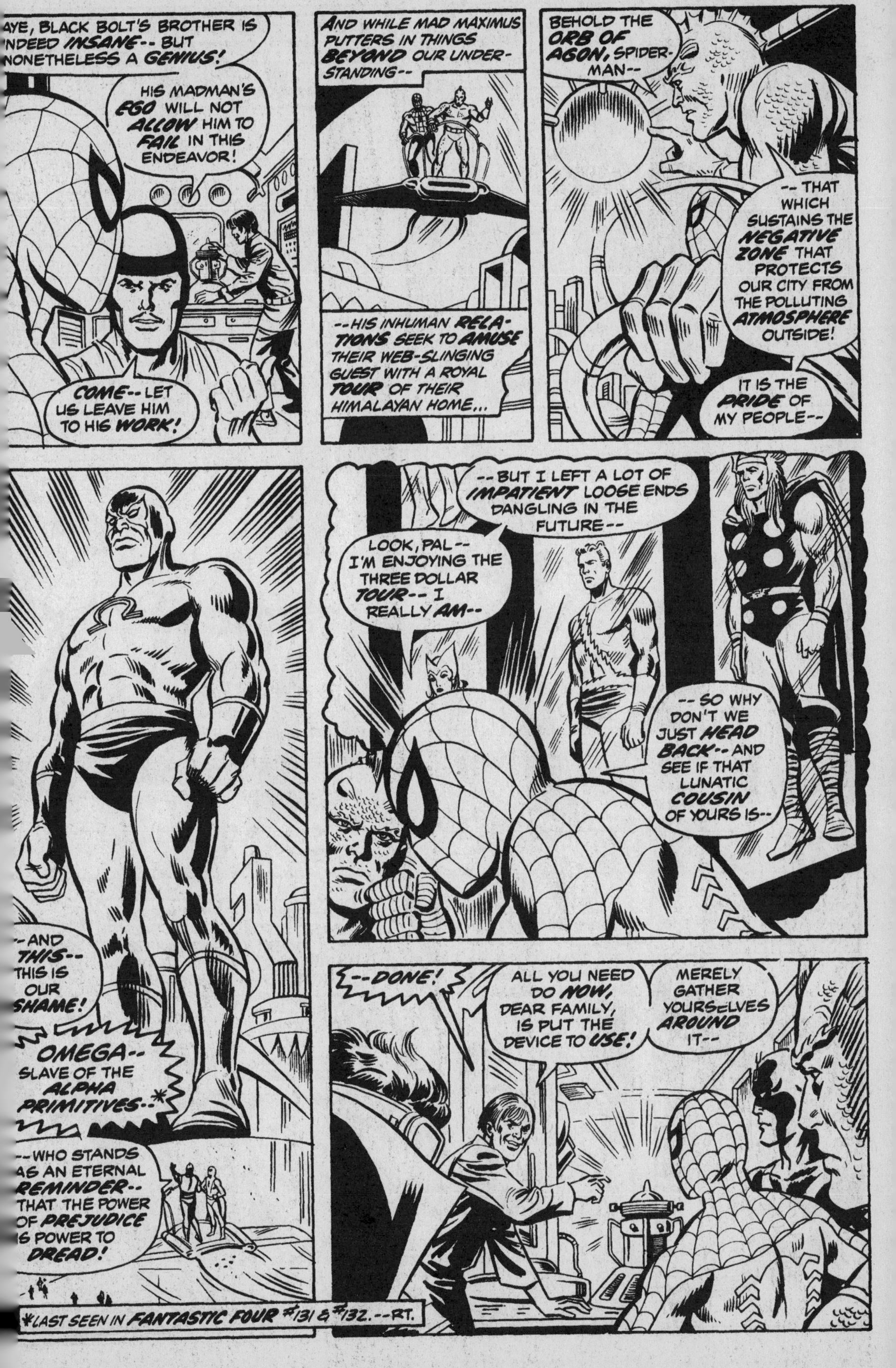
AYE, BLACK BOLT'S BROTHER IS INDEED INSANE-- BUT NONETHELESS A GENIUS!
HIS MADMAN'S EGO WILL NOT ALLOW HIM TO FAIL IN THIS ENDEAVOR!
COME-- LET US LEAVE HIM TO HIS WORK!
AND WHILE MAD MAXIMUS PUTTERS IN THINGS BEYOND OUR UNDER-STANDING--
--HIS INHUMAN RELA-TIONS SEEK TO AMUSE THEIR WEB-SLINGING GUEST WITH A ROYAL TOUR OF THEIR HIMALAYAN HOME...
BEHOLD THE ORB OF AGON, SPIDER-MAN--
-- THAT WHICH SUSTAINS THE NEGATIVE ZONE THAT PROTECTS OUR CITY FROM THE POLLUTING ATMOSPHERE OUTSIDE!
IT IS THE PRIDE OF MY PEOPLE--
--AND THIS-- THIS IS OUR SHAME!
OMEGA-- SLAVE OF THE ALPHA PRIMITIVES--*
--WHO STANDS AS AN ETERNAL REMINDER-- THAT THE POWER OF PREJUDICE IS POWER TO DREAD!
*LAST SEEN IN FANTASTIC FOUR #131 & #132.--RT.
LOOK, PAL-- I'M ENJOYING THE THREE DOLLAR TOUR-- I REALLY AM--
-- BUT I LEFT A LOT OF IMPATIENT LOOSE ENDS DANGLING IN THE FUTURE--
-- SO WHY DON'T WE JUST HEAD BACK-- AND SEE IF THAT LUNATIC COUSIN OF YOURS IS--
--DONE!
ALL YOU NEED DO NOW, DEAR FAMILY, IS PUT THE DEVICE TO USE!
MERELY GATHER YOURSELVES AROUND IT--

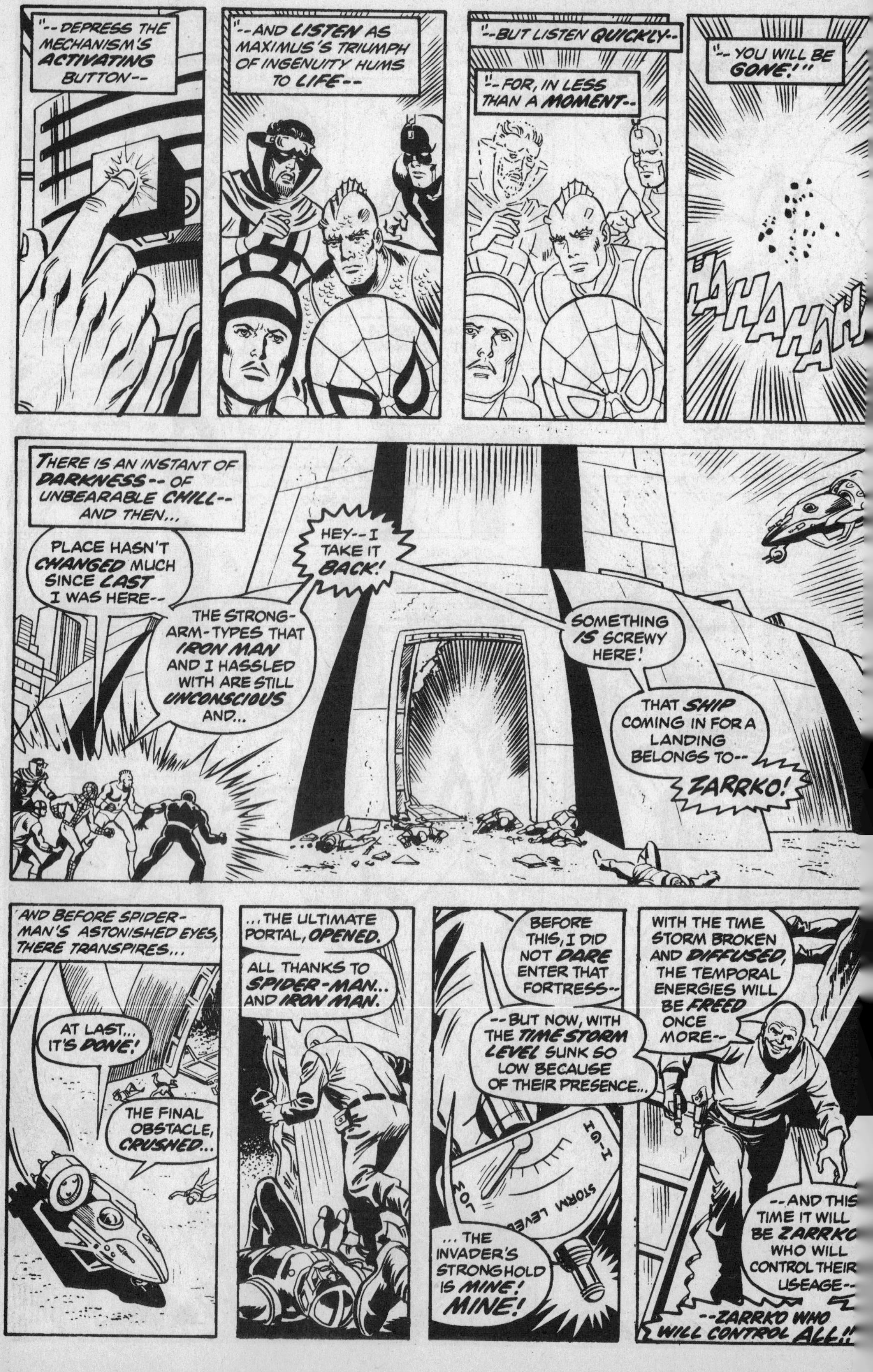
"--DEPRESS THE MECHANISM'S ACTIVATING BUTTON--
"--AND LISTEN AS MAXIMUS'S TRIUMPH OF INGENUITY HUMS TO LIFE--
"--BUT LISTEN QUICKLY--
"--FOR, IN LESS THAN A MOMENT--
"--YOU WILL BE GONE!"
HAHAHAH
THERE IS AN INSTANT OF DARKNESS-- OF UNBEARABLE CHILL-- AND THEN...
PLACE HASN'T CHANGED MUCH SINCE LAST I WAS HERE--
THE STRONG-ARM-TYPES THAT IRON MAN AND I HASSLED WITH ARE STILL UNCONSCIOUS AND...
HEY--I TAKE IT BACK!
SOMETHING IS SCREWY HERE!
THAT SHIP COMING IN FOR A LANDING BELONGS TO--
ZARRKO!
AND BEFORE SPIDER-MAN'S ASTONISHED EYES, THERE TRANSPIRES...
AT LAST... IT'S DONE!
THE FINAL OBSTACLE, CRUSHED...
...THE ULTIMATE PORTAL, OPENED.
ALL THANKS TO SPIDER-MAN... AND IRON MAN.
BEFORE THIS, I DID NOT DARE ENTER THAT FORTRESS--
--BUT NOW, WITH THE TIME STORM LEVEL SUNK SO LOW BECAUSE OF THEIR PRESENCE...
HIGH
STORM LEVEL
LOW
...THE INVADER'S STRONGHOLD IS MINE! MINE!
WITH THE TIME STORM BROKEN AND DIFFUSED, THE TEMPORAL ENERGIES WILL BE FREED ONCE MORE--
--AND THIS TIME IT WILL BE ZARRKO WHO WILL CONTROL THEIR USEAGE--
--ZARRKO WHO WILL CONTROL ALL!!

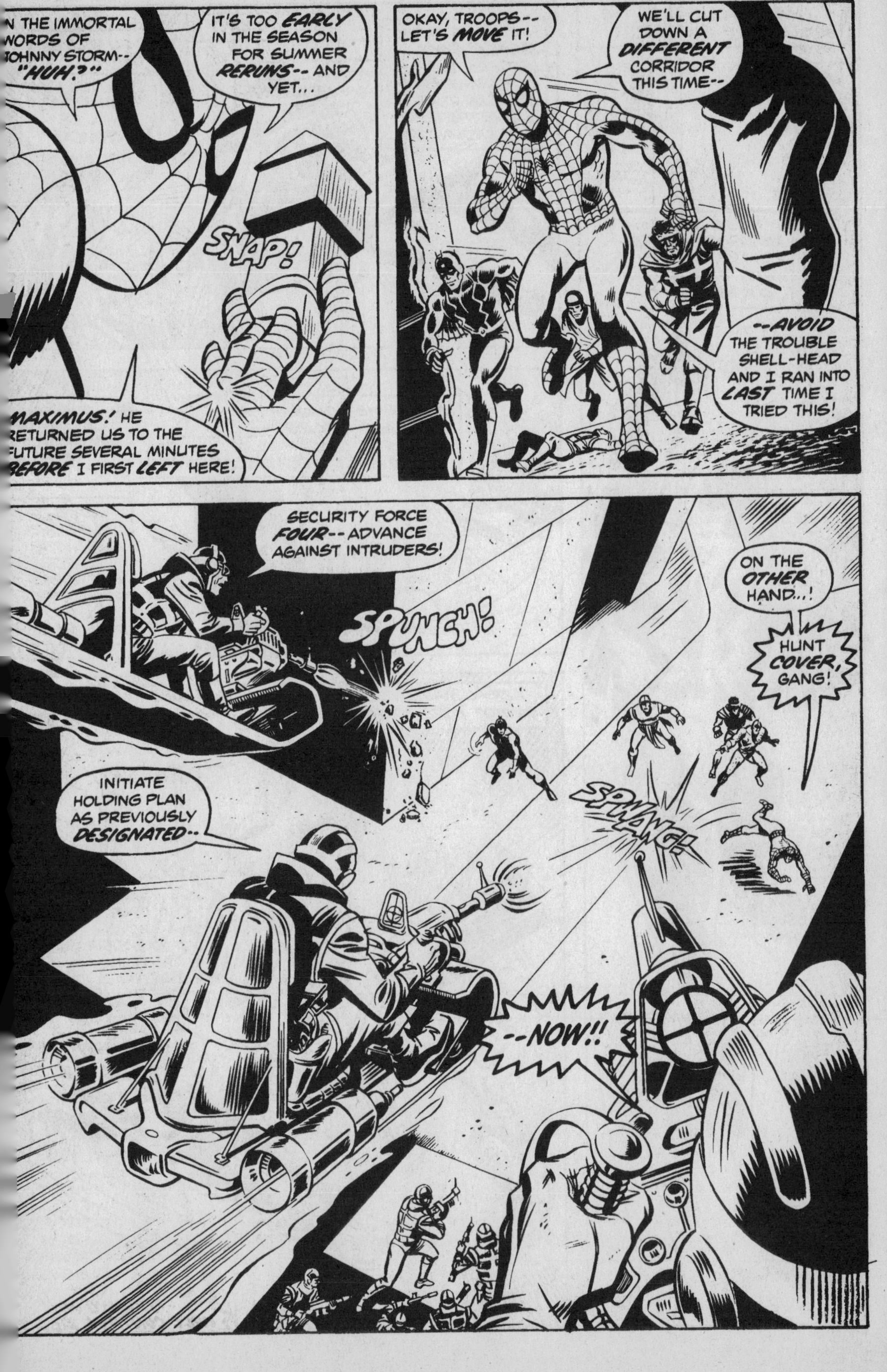
N THE IMMORTAL WORDS OF JOHNNY STORM-- "HUH?"
IT'S TOO EARLY IN THE SEASON FOR SUMMER RERUNS-- AND YET...
SNAP!
MAXIMUS! HE RETURNED US TO THE FUTURE SEVERAL MINUTES BEFORE I FIRST LEFT HERE!
OKAY, TROOPS-- LET'S MOVE IT!
WE'LL CUT DOWN A DIFFERENT CORRIDOR THIS TIME--
--AVOID THE TROUBLE SHELL-HEAD AND I RAN INTO LAST TIME I TRIED THIS!
SECURITY FORCE FOUR-- ADVANCE AGAINST INTRUDERS!
SPUNCH!
ON THE OTHER HAND...!
HUNT COVER, GANG!
INITIATE HOLDING PLAN AS PREVIOUSLY DESIGNATED--
SPANG!
--NOW!!

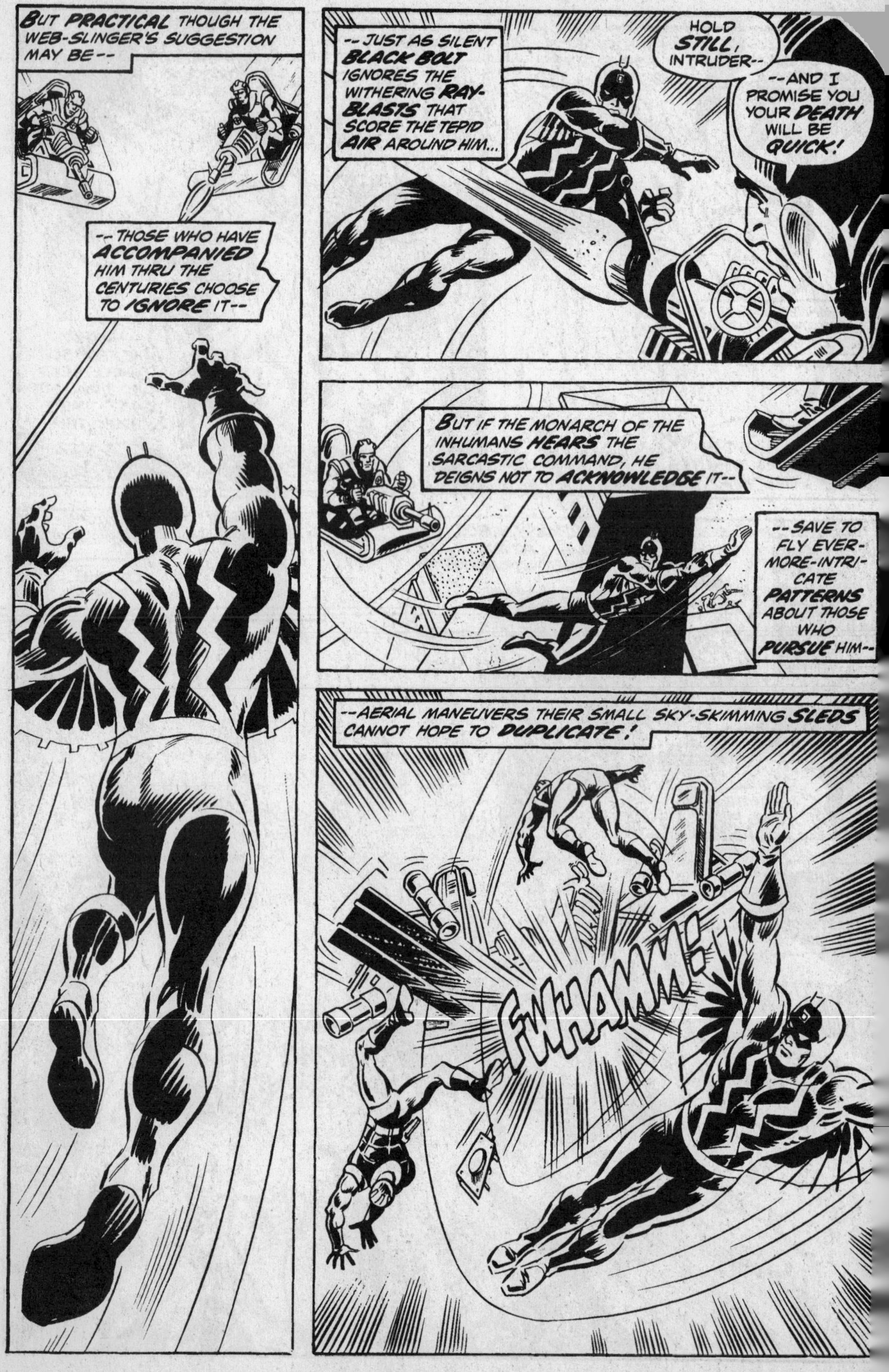

BUT PRACTICAL THOUGH THE WEB-SLINGER'S SUGGESTION MAY BE--
--THOSE WHO HAVE ACCOMPANIED HIM THRU THE CENTURIES CHOOSE TO IGNORE IT--
--JUST AS SILENT BLACK BOLT IGNORES THE WITHERING RAY-BLASTS THAT SCORE THE TEPID AIR AROUND HIM...
HOLD STILL, INTRUDER--
--AND I PROMISE YOU YOUR DEATH WILL BE QUICK!
BUT IF THE MONARCH OF THE INHUMANS HEARS THE SARCASTIC COMMAND, HE DEIGNS NOT TO ACKNOWLEDGE IT--
--SAVE TO FLY EVER-MORE-INTRICATE PATTERNS ABOUT THOSE WHO PURSUE HIM--
--AERIAL MANEUVERS THEIR SMALL SKY-SKIMMING SLEDS CANNOT HOPE TO DUPLICATE!
FWHAMM!

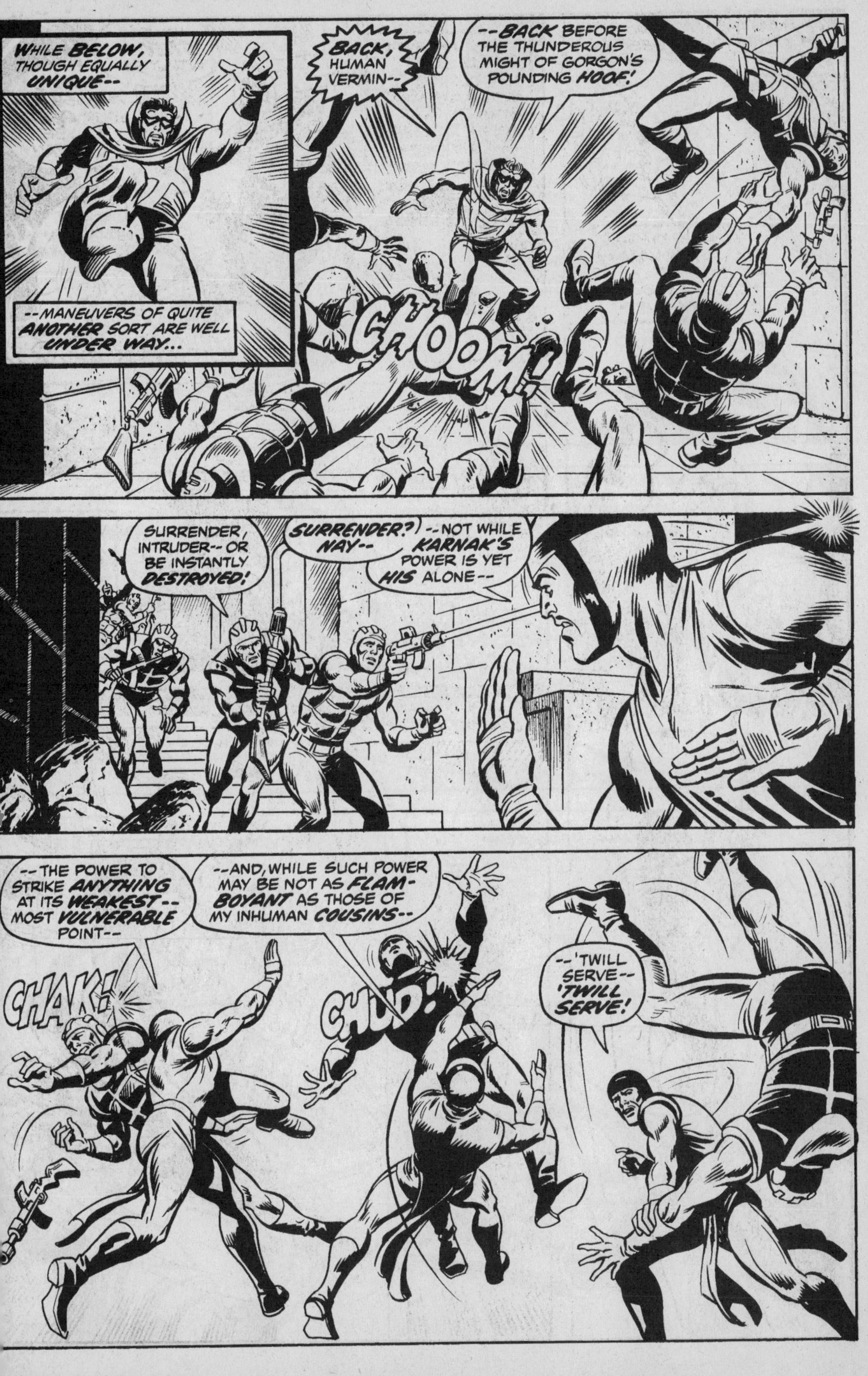
WHILE BELOW, THOUGH EQUALLY UNIQUE--
BACK, HUMAN VERMIN--
--BACK BEFORE THE THUNDEROUS MIGHT OF GORGON'S POUNDING HOOF!
--MANEUVERS OF QUITE ANOTHER SORT ARE WELL UNDER WAY...
CHOOOM!
SURRENDER, INTRUDER-- OR BE INSTANTLY DESTROYED!
SURRENDER? NAY--
--NOT WHILE KARNAK'S POWER IS YET HIS ALONE--
-- THE POWER TO STRIKE ANYTHING AT ITS WEAKEST -- MOST VULNERABLE POINT--
--AND, WHILE SUCH POWER MAY BE NOT AS FLAMBOYANT AS THOSE OF MY INHUMAN COUSINS--
CHAK!
CHUD!
--'TWILL SERVE-- 'TWILL SERVE!

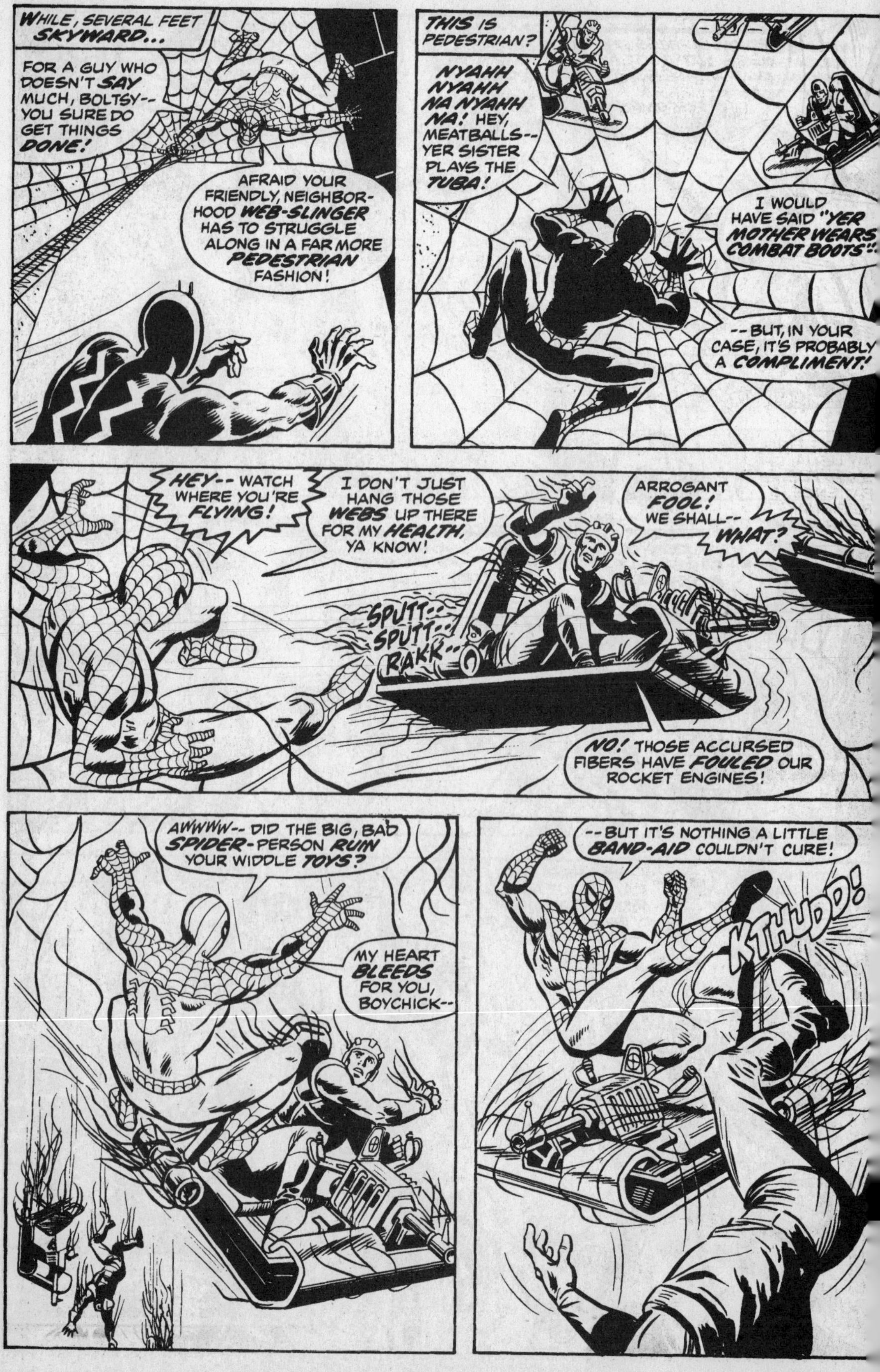
WHILE, SEVERAL FEET SKYWARD...
FOR A GUY WHO DOESN'T SAY MUCH, BOLTSY-- YOU SURE DO GET THINGS DONE!
AFRAID YOUR FRIENDLY, NEIGHBORHOOD WEB-SLINGER HAS TO STRUGGLE ALONG IN A FAR MORE PEDESTRIAN FASHION!
THIS IS PEDESTRIAN?
NYAHH NYAHH NA NYAHH NA! HEY, MEATBALLS-- YER SISTER PLAYS THE TUBA!
I WOULD HAVE SAID "YER MOTHER WEARS COMBAT BOOTS"--
--BUT, IN YOUR CASE, IT'S PROBABLY A COMPLIMENT!
HEY-- WATCH WHERE YOU'RE FLYING!
I DON'T JUST HANG THOSE WEBS UP THERE FOR MY HEALTH, YA KNOW!
ARROGANT FOOL! WE SHALL--
WHAT?
SPUTT-- SPUTT-- RAKK--
NO! THOSE ACCURSED FIBERS HAVE FOULED OUR ROCKET ENGINES!
AWWWW-- DID THE BIG, BAD SPIDER-PERSON RUIN YOUR WIDDLE TOYS?
MY HEART BLEEDS FOR YOU, BOYCHICK--
--BUT IT'S NOTHING A LITTLE BAND-AID COULDN'T CURE!
KTHUDD!

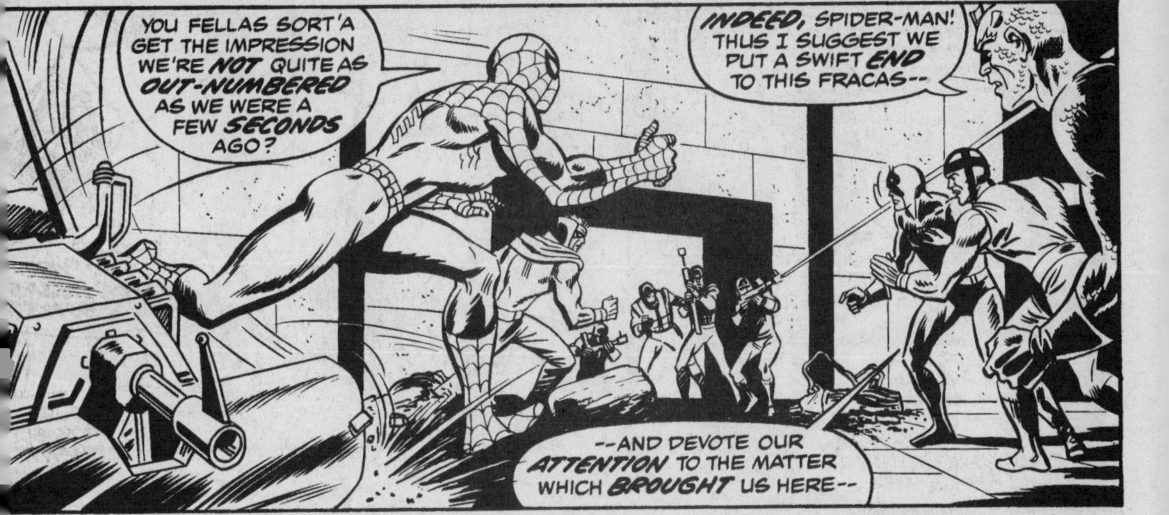
YOU FELLAS SORT'A GET THE IMPRESSION WE'RE NOT QUITE AS OUT-NUMBERED AS WE WERE A FEW SECONDS AGO?
INDEED, SPIDER-MAN! THUS I SUGGEST WE PUT A SWIFT END TO THIS FRACAS--
--AND DEVOTE OUR ATTENTION TO THE MATTER WHICH BROUGHT US HERE--

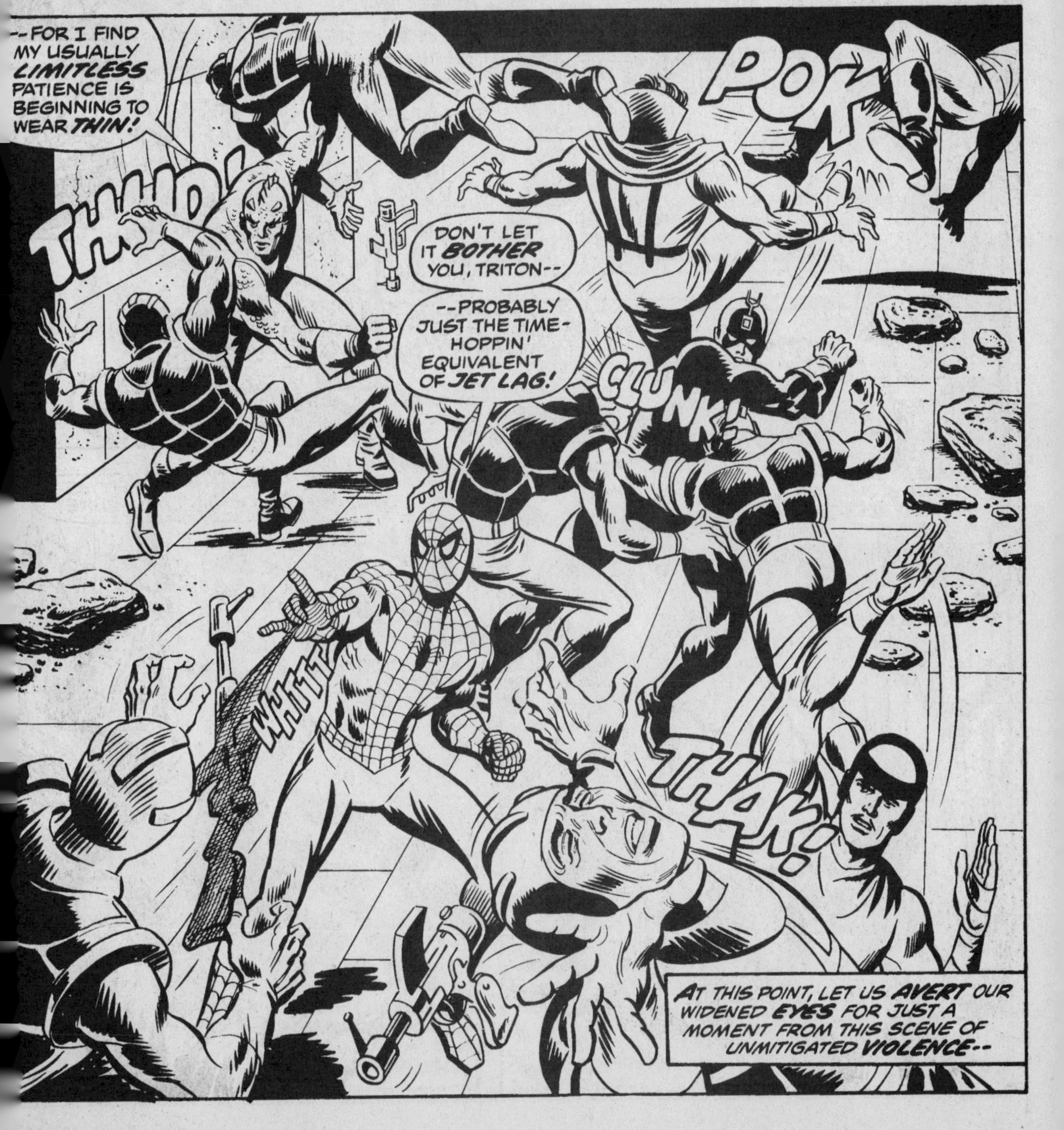
--FOR I FIND MY USUALLY LIMITLESS PATIENCE IS BEGINNING TO WEAR THIN!
POK!
THUD!
DON'T LET IT BOTHER YOU, TRITON--
--PROBABLY JUST THE TIME-HOPPIN' EQUIVALENT OF JET LAG!
CLUNK!
THAK!
AT THIS POINT, LET US AVERT OUR WIDENED EYES FOR JUST A MOMENT FROM THIS SCENE OF UNMITIGATED VIOLENCE--

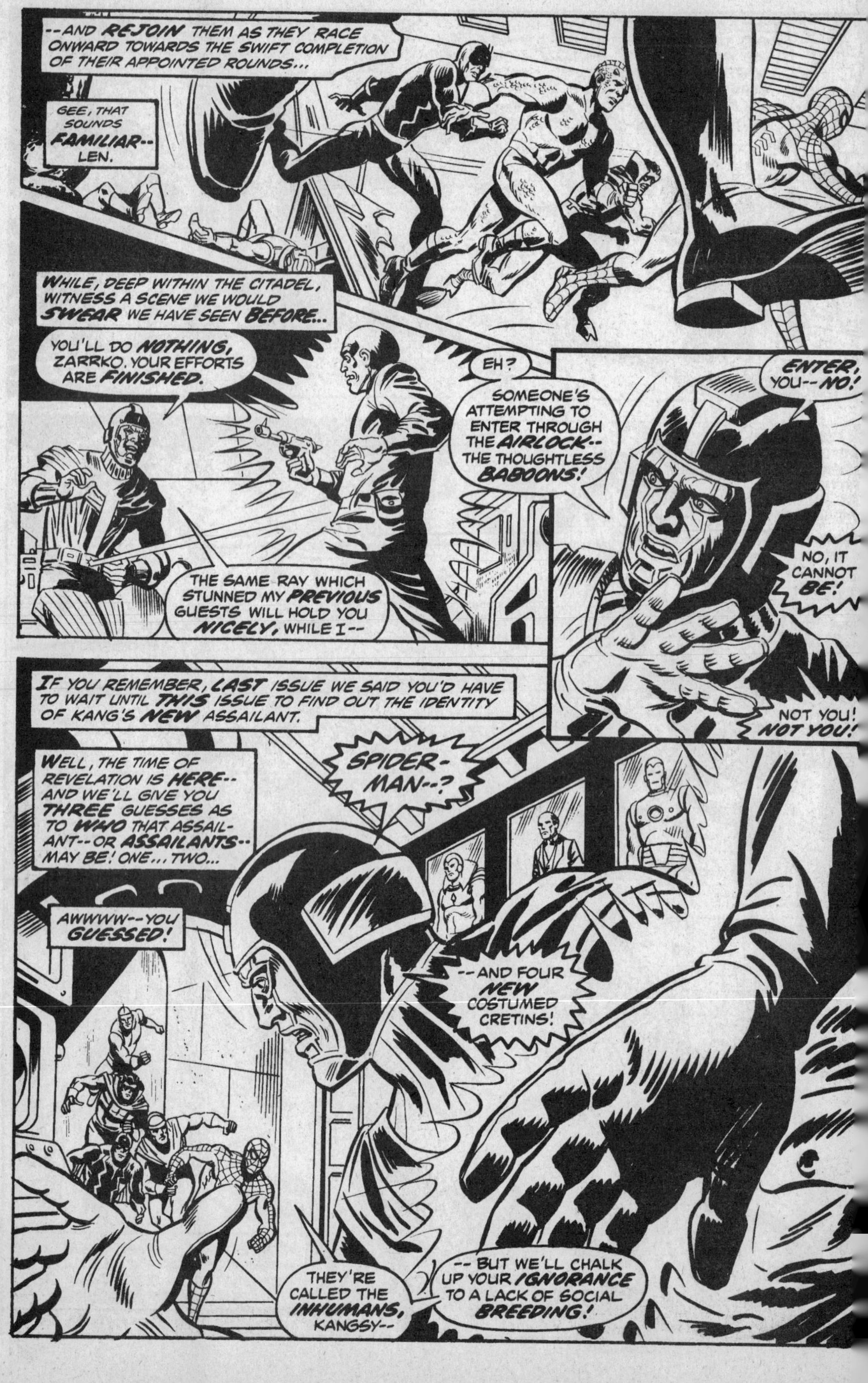
--AND REJOIN THEM AS THEY RACE ONWARD TOWARDS THE SWIFT COMPLETION OF THEIR APPOINTED ROUNDS...
GEE, THAT SOUNDS FAMILIAR-- LEN.
WHILE, DEEP WITHIN THE CITADEL, WITNESS A SCENE WE WOULD SWEAR WE HAVE SEEN BEFORE...
YOU'LL DO NOTHING, ZARRKO. YOUR EFFORTS ARE FINISHED.
EH?
SOMEONE'S ATTEMPTING TO ENTER THROUGH THE AIRLOCK-- THE THOUGHTLESS BABOONS!
THE SAME RAY WHICH STUNNED MY PREVIOUS GUESTS WILL HOLD YOU NICELY, WHILE I--
ENTER, YOU-- NO!
NO, IT CANNOT BE!
NOT YOU! NOT YOU!
IF YOU REMEMBER, LAST ISSUE WE SAID YOU'D HAVE TO WAIT UNTIL THIS ISSUE TO FIND OUT THE IDENTITY OF KANG'S NEW ASSAILANT.
WELL, THE TIME OF REVELATION IS HERE-- AND WE'LL GIVE YOU THREE GUESSES AS TO WHO THAT ASSAIL-ANT-- OR ASSAILANTS-- MAY BE! ONE... TWO...
SPIDER-MAN--?
AWWWW--YOU GUESSED!
--AND FOUR NEW COSTUMED CRETINS!
THEY'RE CALLED THE INHUMANS, KANGSY--
-- BUT WE'LL CHALK UP YOUR IGNORANCE TO A LACK OF SOCIAL BREEDING!

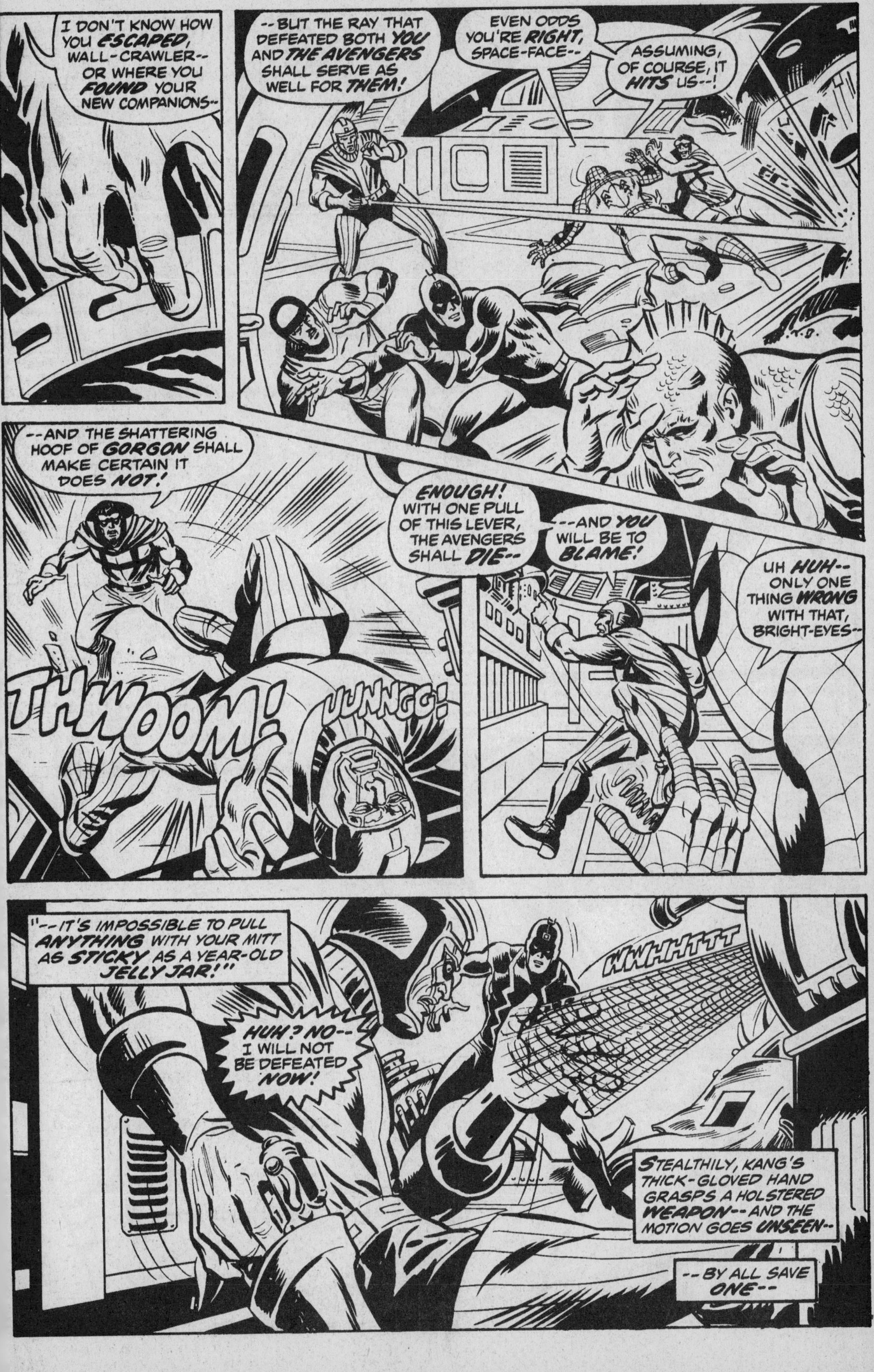

I DON'T KNOW HOW YOU ESCAPED, WALL-CRAWLER-- OR WHERE YOU FOUND YOUR NEW COMPANIONS--
--BUT THE RAY THAT DEFEATED BOTH YOU AND THE AVENGERS SHALL SERVE AS WELL FOR THEM!
EVEN ODDS YOU'RE RIGHT, SPACE-FACE--
ASSUMING, OF COURSE, IT HITS US--!
--AND THE SHATTERING HOOF OF GORGON SHALL MAKE CERTAIN IT DOES NOT!
THWOOM!
UUNNGG!
ENOUGH! WITH ONE PULL OF THIS LEVER, THE AVENGERS SHALL DIE--
--AND YOU WILL BE TO BLAME!
UH HUH-- ONLY ONE THING WRONG WITH THAT, BRIGHT-EYES--
"--IT'S IMPOSSIBLE TO PULL ANYTHING WITH YOUR MITT AS STICKY AS A YEAR-OLD JELLY JAR!"
WWHHHTTT
HUH? NO-- I WILL NOT BE DEFEATED NOW!
STEALTHILY, KANG'S THICK-GLOVED HAND GRASPS A HOLSTERED WEAPON--AND THE MOTION GOES UNSEEN--
--BY ALL SAVE ONE--

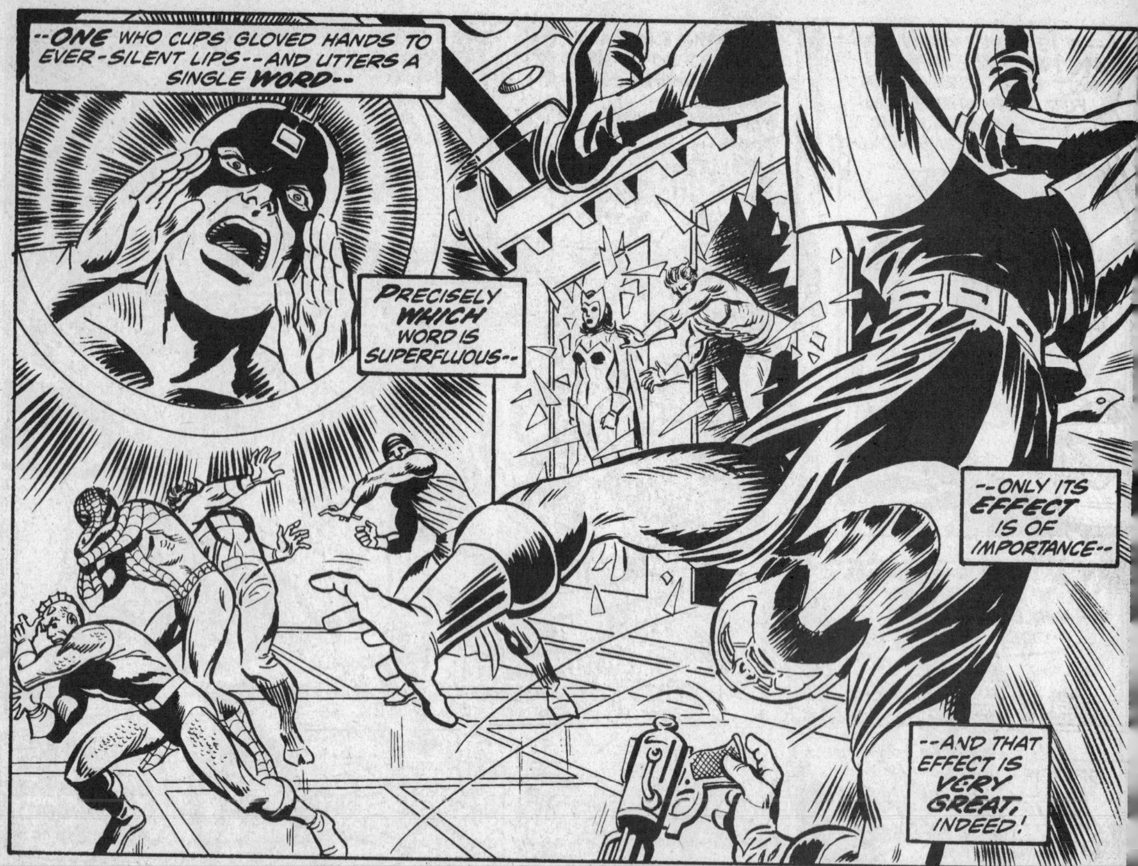
--ONE WHO CUPS GLOVED HANDS TO EVER-SILENT LIPS--AND UTTERS A SINGLE WORD--
PRECISELY WHICH WORD IS SUPERFLUOUS--
--ONLY ITS EFFECT IS OF IMPORTANCE--
--AND THAT EFFECT IS VERY GREAT, INDEED!

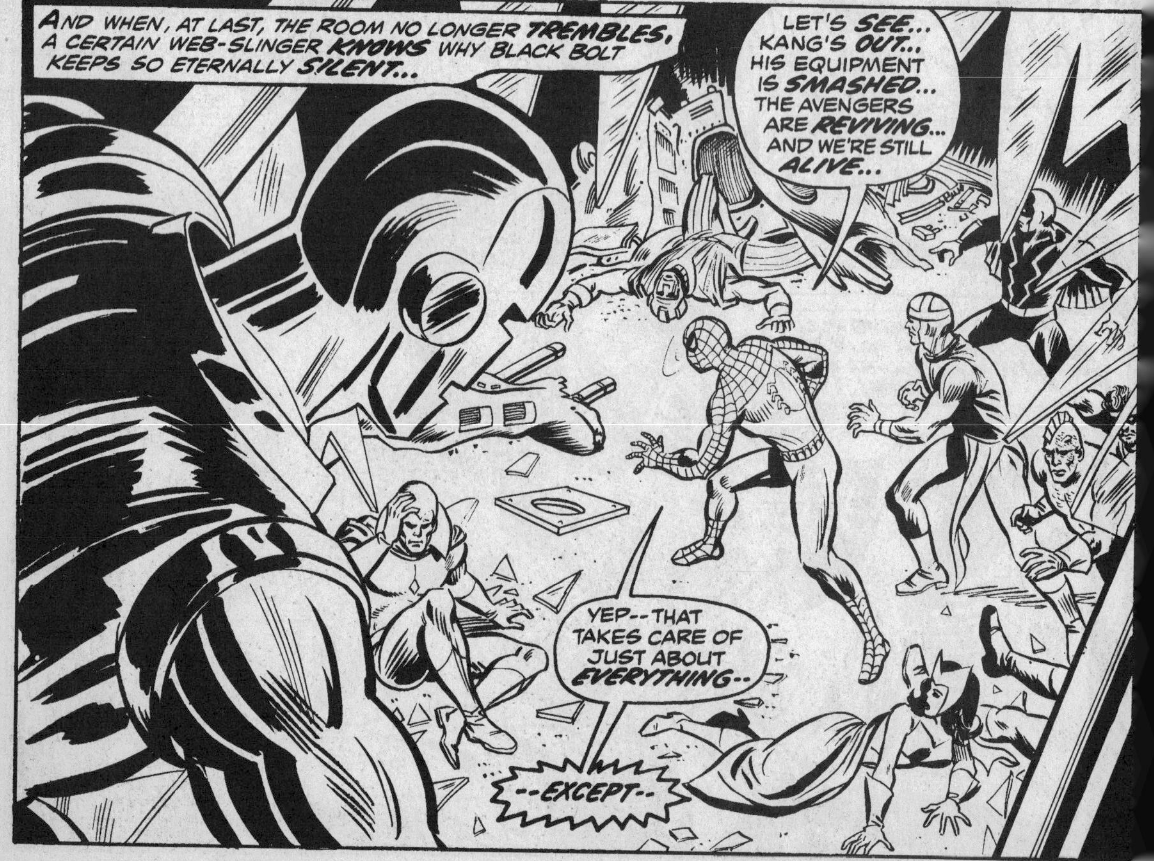
AND WHEN, AT LAST, THE ROOM NO LONGER TREMBLES, A CERTAIN WEB-SLINGER KNOWS WHY BLACK BOLT KEEPS SO ETERNALLY SILENT...
LET'S SEE... KANG'S OUT... HIS EQUIPMENT IS SMASHED... THE AVENGERS ARE REVIVING... AND WE'RE STILL ALIVE...
YEP--THAT TAKES CARE OF JUST ABOUT EVERYTHING--
--EXCEPT--

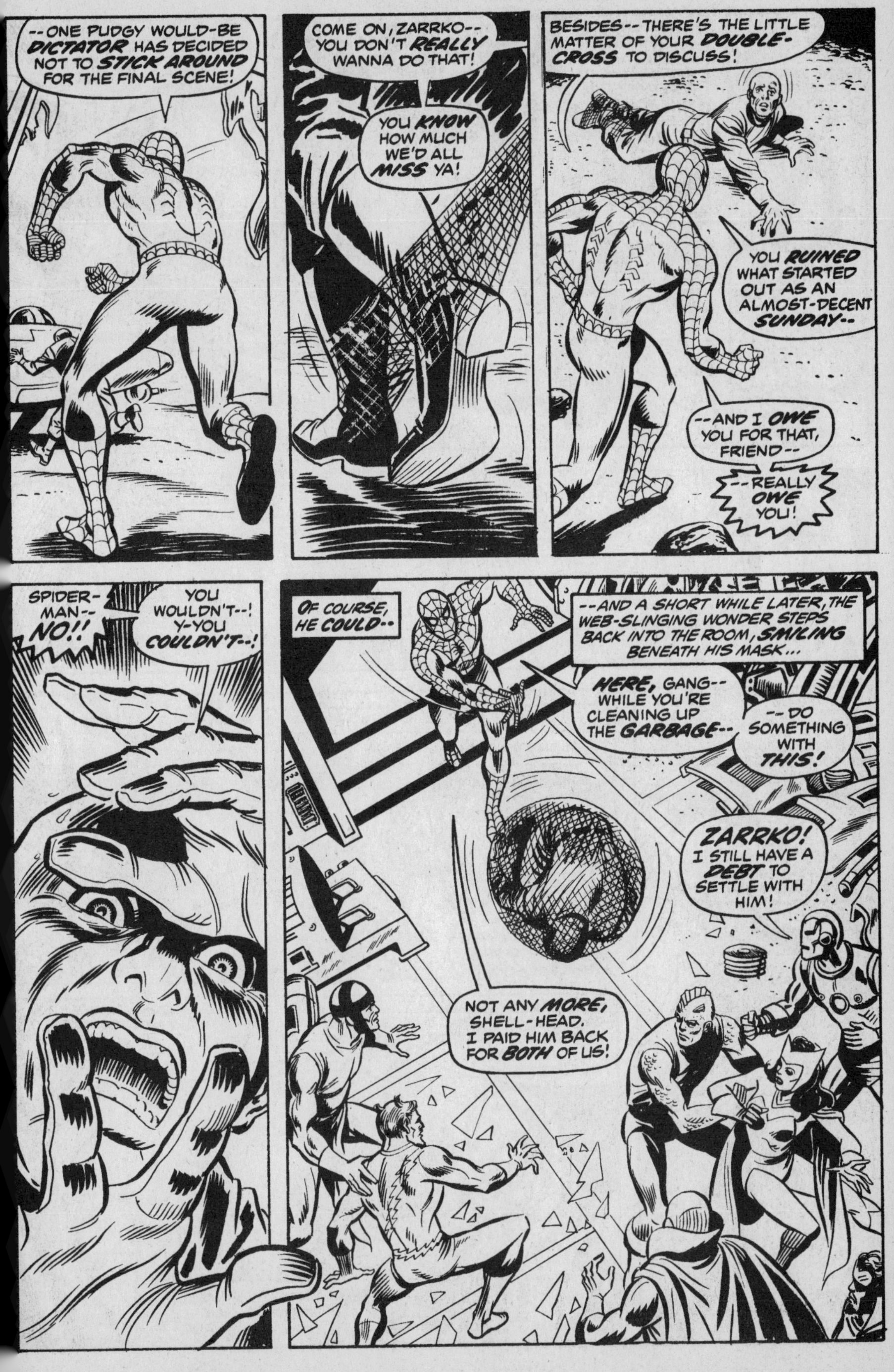
--ONE PUDGY WOULD-BE DICTATOR HAS DECIDED NOT TO STICK AROUND FOR THE FINAL SCENE!
COME ON, ZARRKO-- YOU DON'T REALLY WANNA DO THAT!
YOU KNOW HOW MUCH WE'D ALL MISS YA!
BESIDES--THERE'S THE LITTLE MATTER OF YOUR DOUBLE-CROSS TO DISCUSS!
YOU RUINED WHAT STARTED OUT AS AN ALMOST-DECENT SUNDAY--
--AND I OWE YOU FOR THAT, FRIEND--
--REALLY OWE YOU!
SPIDER-MAN--NO!!
YOU WOULDN'T--! Y-YOU COULDN'T--!
OF COURSE, HE COULD--
--AND A SHORT WHILE LATER, THE WEB-SLINGING WONDER STEPS BACK INTO THE ROOM, SMILING BENEATH HIS MASK...
HERE, GANG-- WHILE YOU'RE CLEANING UP THE GARBAGE--
--DO SOMETHING WITH THIS!
ZARRKO! I STILL HAVE A DEBT TO SETTLE WITH HIM!
NOT ANY MORE, SHELL-HEAD. I PAID HIM BACK FOR BOTH OF US!

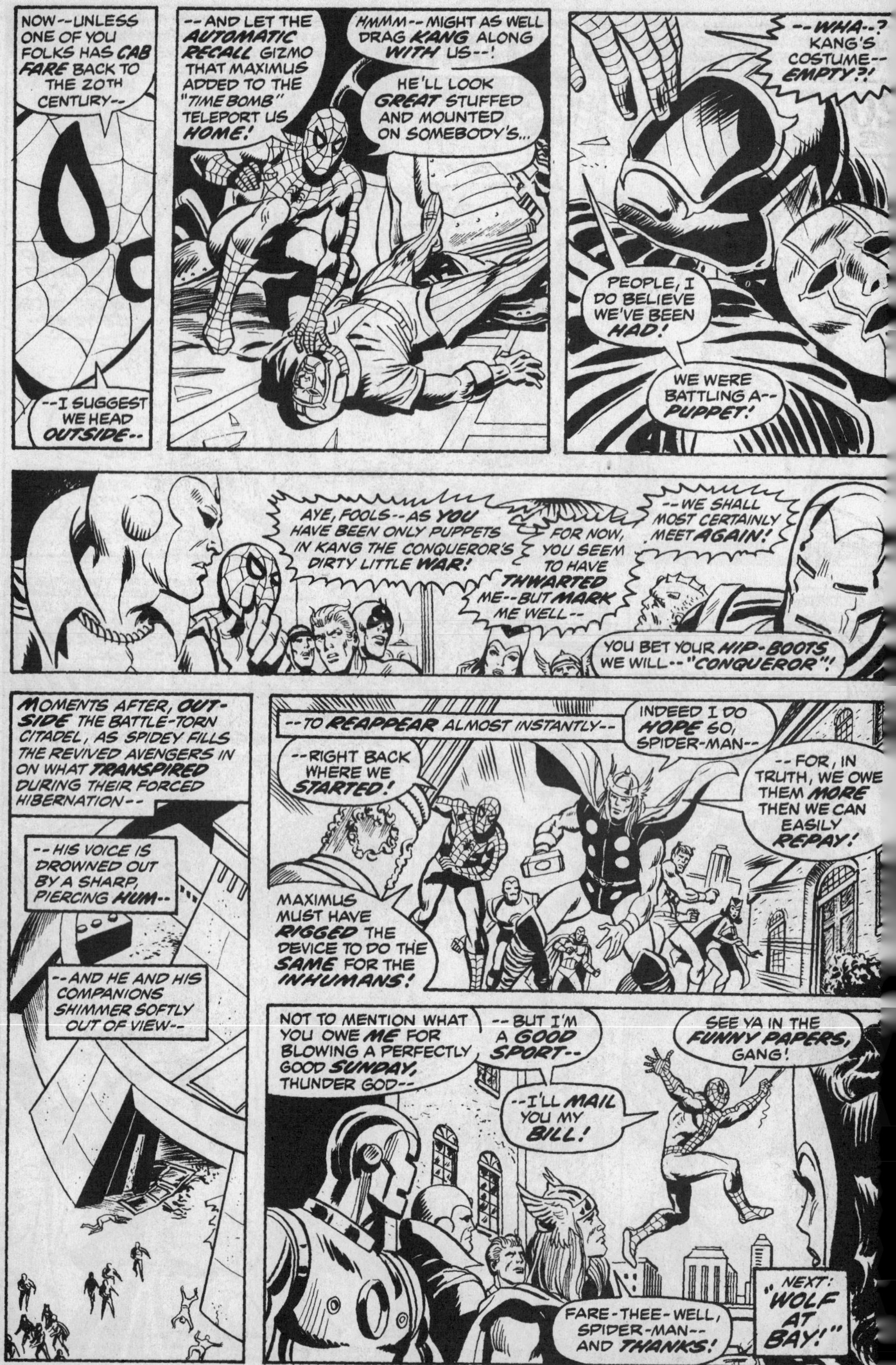
NOW--UNLESS ONE OF YOU FOLKS HAS CAB FARE BACK TO THE 20TH CENTURY--
--I SUGGEST WE HEAD OUTSIDE--
--AND LET THE AUTOMATIC RECALL GIZMO THAT MAXIMUS ADDED TO THE "TIME BOMB" TELEPORT US HOME!
HMMM--MIGHT AS WELL DRAG KANG ALONG WITH US--!
HE'LL LOOK GREAT STUFFED AND MOUNTED ON SOMEBODY'S...
--WHA--? KANG'S COSTUME--EMPTY?!
PEOPLE, I DO BELIEVE WE'VE BEEN HAD!
WE WERE BATTLING A--PUPPET!
AYE, FOOLS--AS YOU HAVE BEEN ONLY PUPPETS IN KANG THE CONQUEROR'S DIRTY LITTLE WAR!
FOR NOW, YOU SEEM TO HAVE THWARTED ME--BUT MARK ME WELL--
--WE SHALL MOST CERTAINLY MEET AGAIN!
YOU BET YOUR HIP-BOOTS WE WILL--"CONQUEROR"!
MOMENTS AFTER, OUTSIDE THE BATTLE-TORN CITADEL, AS SPIDEY FILLS THE REVIVED AVENGERS IN ON WHAT TRANSPIRED DURING THEIR FORCED HIBERNATION--
--HIS VOICE IS DROWNED OUT BY A SHARP, PIERCING HUM--
--AND HE AND HIS COMPANIONS SHIMMER SOFTLY OUT OF VIEW--
--TO REAPPEAR ALMOST INSTANTLY--
--RIGHT BACK WHERE WE STARTED!
MAXIMUS MUST HAVE RIGGED THE DEVICE TO DO THE SAME FOR THE INHUMANS!
INDEED I DO HOPE SO, SPIDER-MAN--
--FOR, IN TRUTH, WE OWE THEM MORE THEN WE CAN EASILY REPAY!
NOT TO MENTION WHAT YOU OWE ME FOR BLOWING A PERFECTLY GOOD SUNDAY, THUNDER GOD--
--BUT I'M A GOOD SPORT--
--I'LL MAIL YOU MY BILL!
SEE YA IN THE FUNNY PAPERS, GANG!
FARE-THEE-WELL, SPIDER-MAN--AND THANKS!
NEXT: "WOLF AT BAY!"

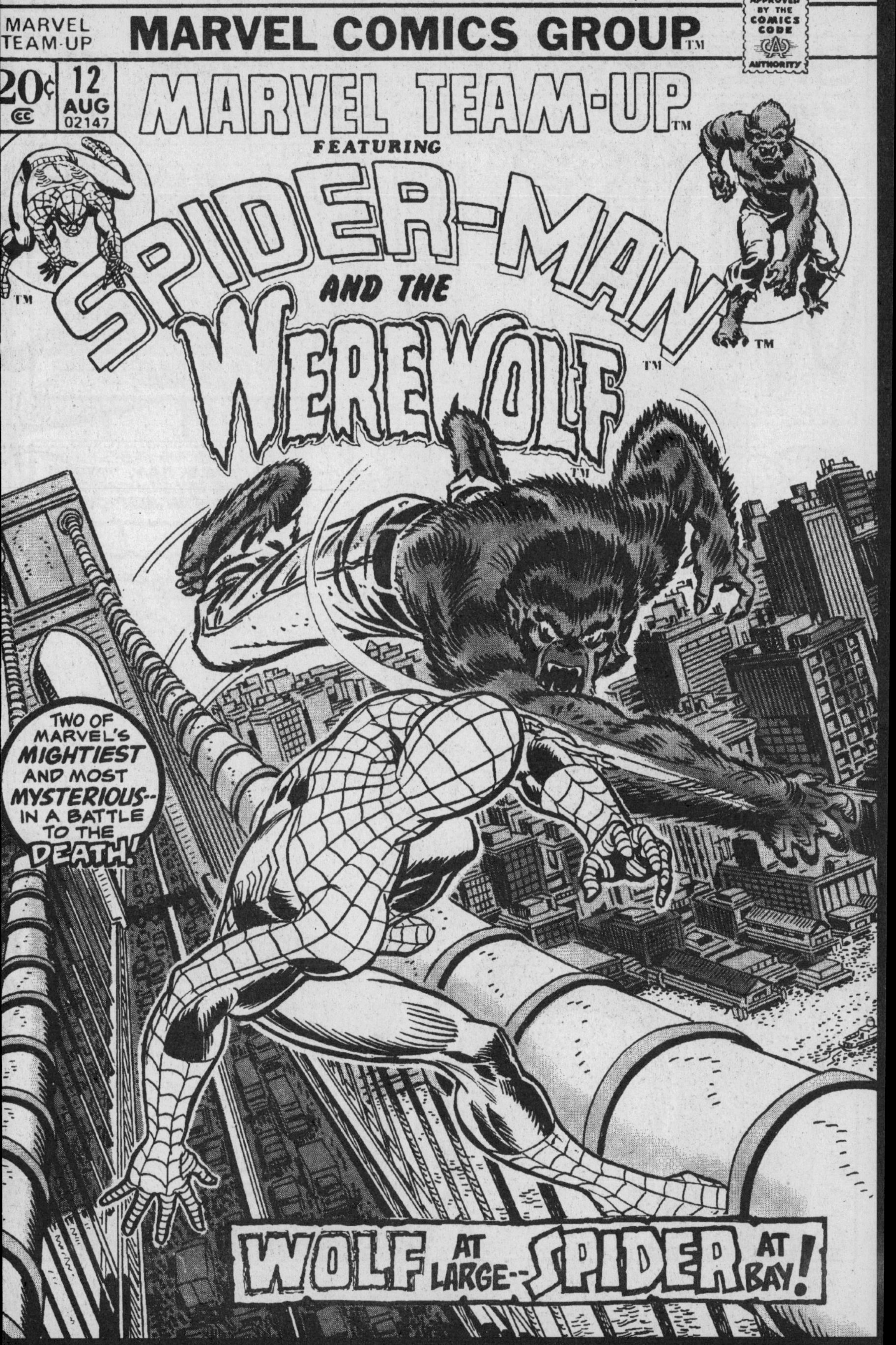

MARVEL TEAM-UP
MARVEL COMICS GROUP
APPROVED BY THE COMICS CODE AUTHORITY
20¢
12 AUG 02147
MARVEL TEAM-UP
FEATURING
SPIDER-MAN AND THE WEREWOLF
TWO OF MARVEL'S MIGHTIEST AND MOST MYSTERIOUS-- IN A BATTLE TO THE DEATH!
WOLF AT LARGE-- SPIDER AT BAY!

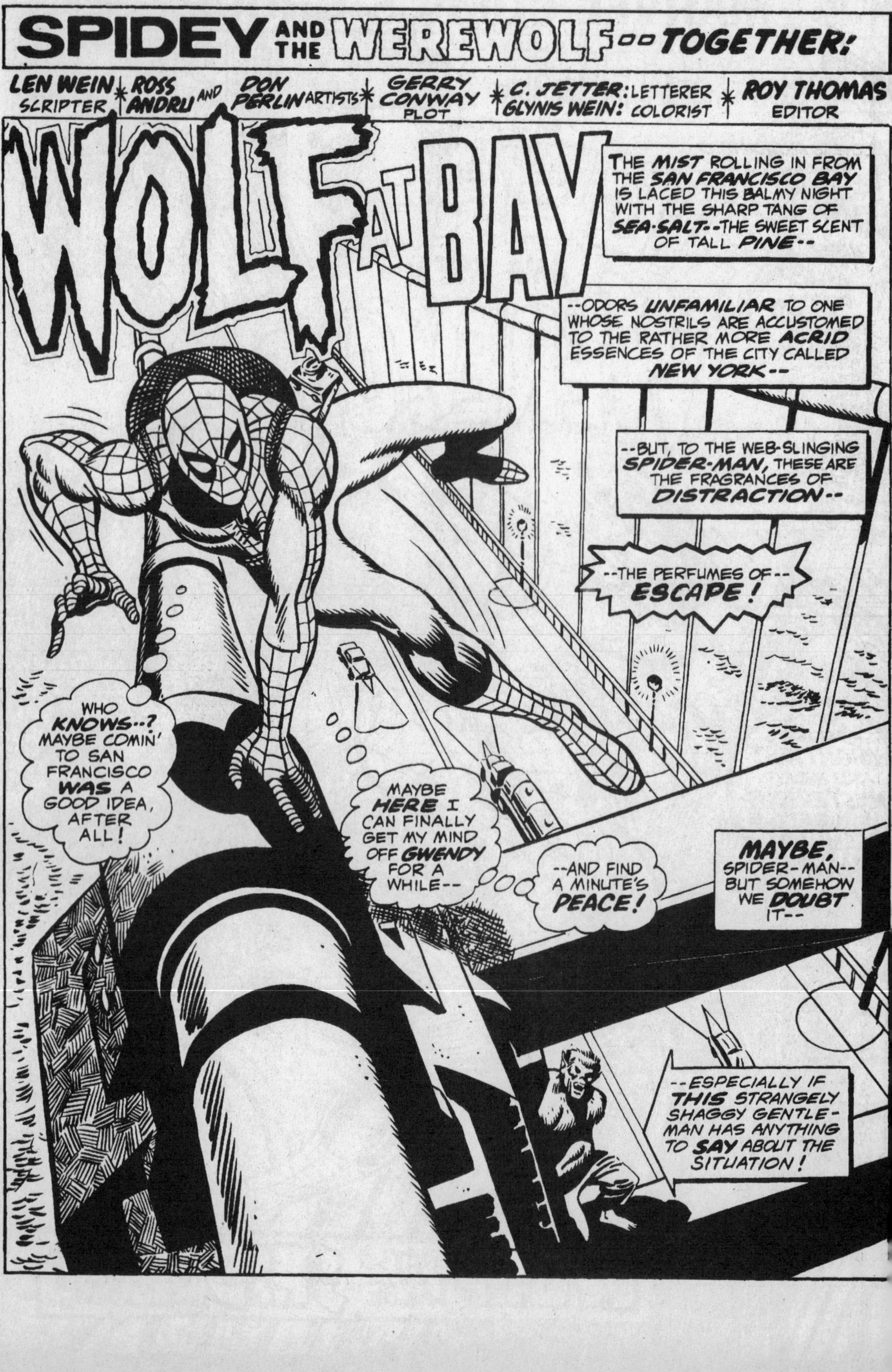

SPIDEY AND THE WEREWOLF -- TOGETHER!
LEN WEIN SCRIPTER * ROSS ANDRU AND DON PERLIN ARTISTS * GERRY CONWAY PLOT * C. JETTER: LETTERER GLYNIS WEIN: COLORIST * ROY THOMAS EDITOR
WOLF AT BAY
THE MIST ROLLING IN FROM THE SAN FRANCISCO BAY IS LACED THIS BALMY NIGHT WITH THE SHARP TANG OF SEA-SALT--THE SWEET SCENT OF TALL PINE--
--ODORS UNFAMILIAR TO ONE WHOSE NOSTRILS ARE ACCUSTOMED TO THE RATHER MORE ACRID ESSENCES OF THE CITY CALLED NEW YORK--
--BUT, TO THE WEB-SLINGING SPIDER-MAN, THESE ARE THE FRAGRANCES OF DISTRACTION--
--THE PERFUMES OF-- ESCAPE!
WHO KNOWS..? MAYBE COMIN' TO SAN FRANCISCO WAS A GOOD IDEA, AFTER ALL!
MAYBE HERE I CAN FINALLY GET MY MIND OFF GWENDY FOR A WHILE--
--AND FIND A MINUTE'S PEACE!
MAYBE, SPIDER-MAN--BUT SOMEHOW WE DOUBT IT--
--ESPECIALLY IF THIS STRANGELY SHAGGY GENTLEMAN HAS ANYTHING TO SAY ABOUT THE SITUATION!

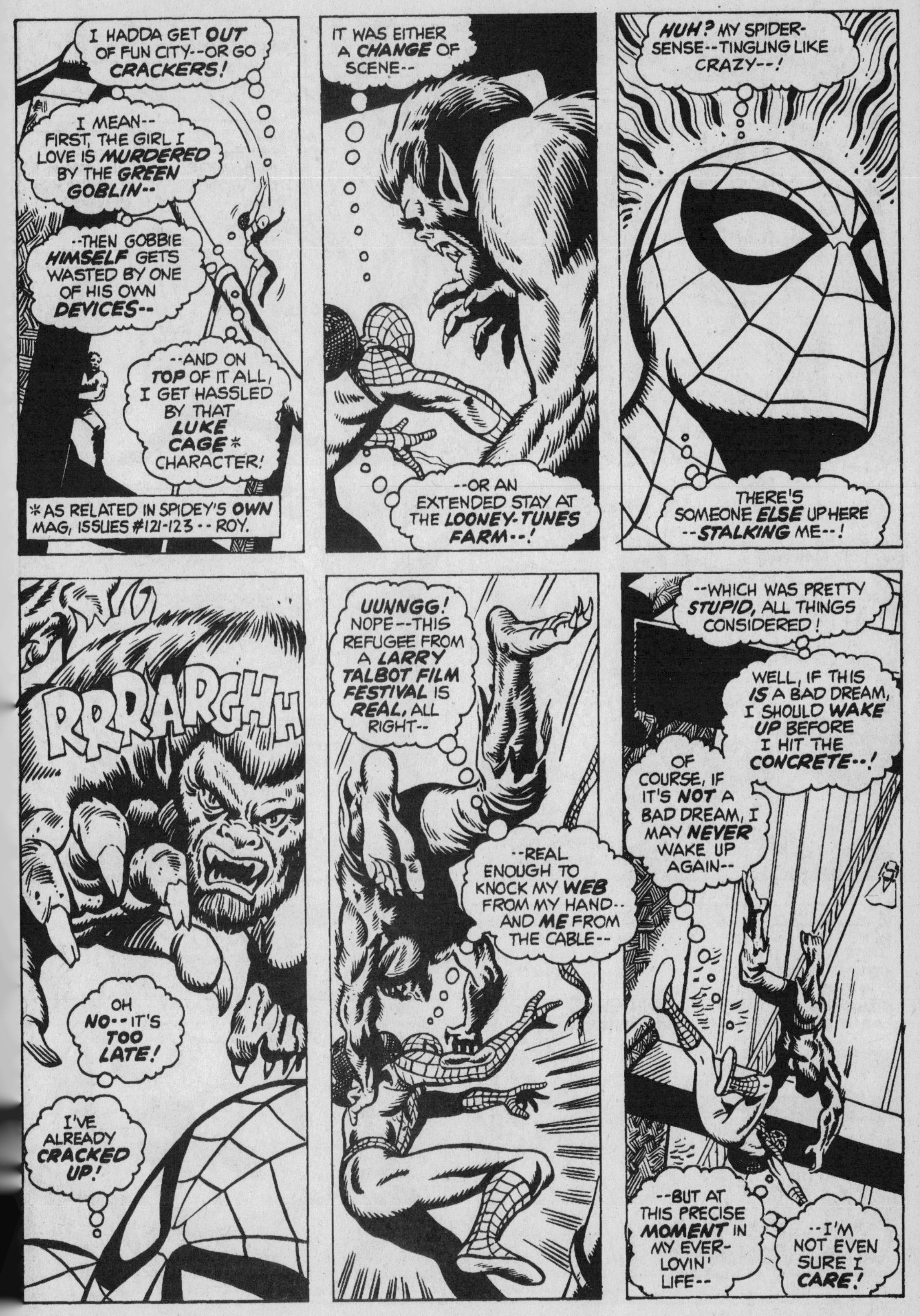
I HADDA GET OUT OF FUN CITY--OR GO CRACKERS!
I MEAN-- FIRST, THE GIRL I LOVE IS MURDERED BY THE GREEN GOBLIN--
--THEN GOBBIE HIMSELF GETS WASTED BY ONE OF HIS OWN DEVICES--
--AND ON TOP OF IT ALL, I GET HASSLED BY THAT LUKE CAGE* CHARACTER!
*AS RELATED IN SPIDEY'S OWN MAG, ISSUES #121-123 -- ROY.
IT WAS EITHER A CHANGE OF SCENE--
--OR AN EXTENDED STAY AT THE LOONEY-TUNES FARM--!
HUH? MY SPIDER-SENSE--TINGLING LIKE CRAZY--!
THERE'S SOMEONE ELSE UP HERE --STALKING ME--!
RRRARGHH
OH NO--IT'S TOO LATE!
I'VE ALREADY CRACKED UP!
UUNNGG! NOPE--THIS REFUGEE FROM A LARRY TALBOT FILM FESTIVAL IS REAL, ALL RIGHT--
--REAL ENOUGH TO KNOCK MY WEB FROM MY HAND-- AND ME FROM THE CABLE--
--WHICH WAS PRETTY STUPID, ALL THINGS CONSIDERED!
WELL, IF THIS IS A BAD DREAM, I SHOULD WAKE UP BEFORE I HIT THE CONCRETE--!
OF COURSE, IF IT'S NOT A BAD DREAM, I MAY NEVER WAKE UP AGAIN--
--BUT AT THIS PRECISE MOMENT IN MY EVER-LOVIN' LIFE--
--I'M NOT EVEN SURE I CARE!

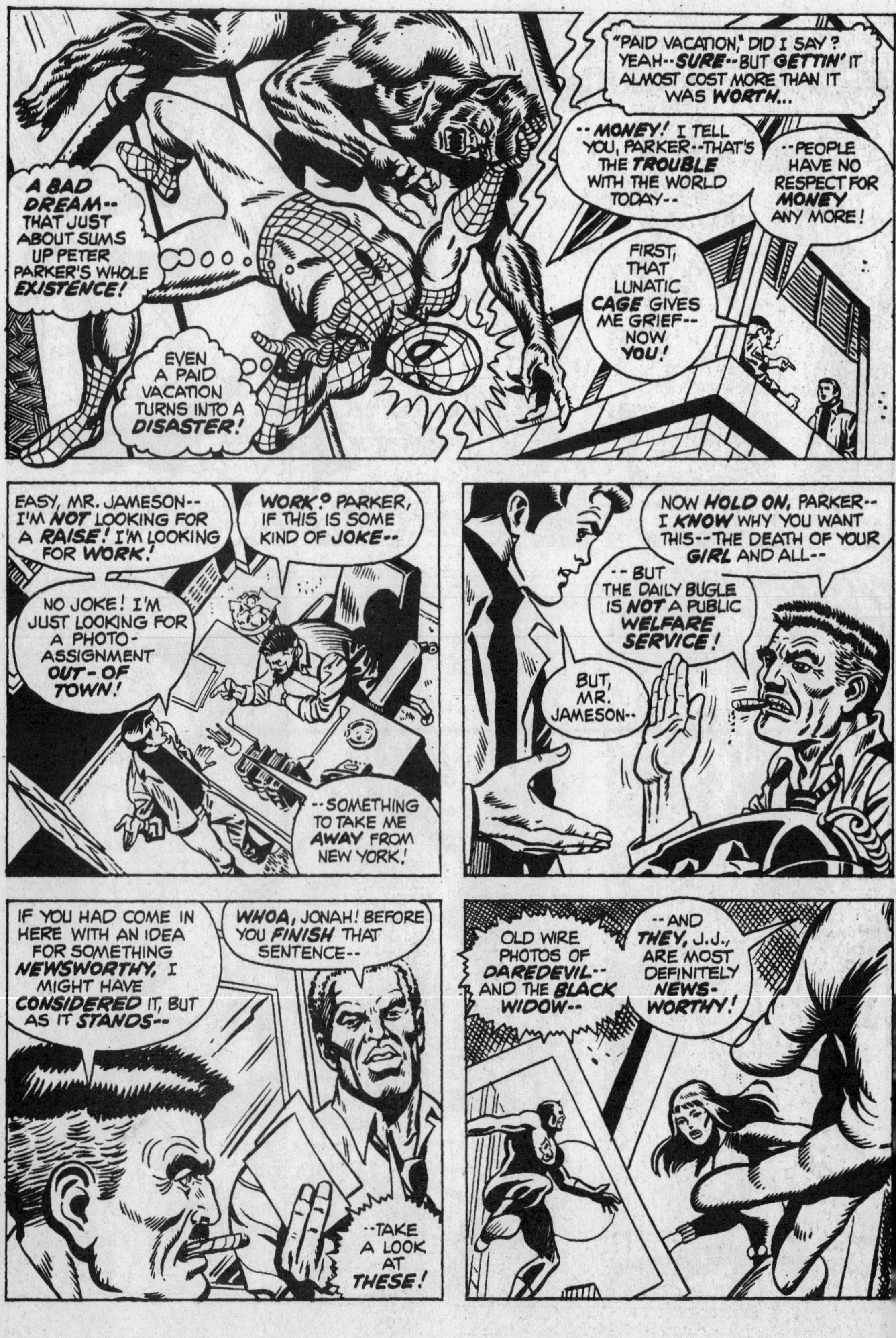
"PAID VACATION," DID I SAY? YEAH--SURE--BUT GETTIN' IT ALMOST COST MORE THAN IT WAS WORTH...
A BAD DREAM--THAT JUST ABOUT SUMS UP PETER PARKER'S WHOLE EXISTENCE!
EVEN A PAID VACATION TURNS INTO A DISASTER!
--MONEY! I TELL YOU, PARKER--THAT'S THE TROUBLE WITH THE WORLD TODAY--
--PEOPLE HAVE NO RESPECT FOR MONEY ANY MORE!
FIRST, THAT LUNATIC CAGE GIVES ME GRIEF--NOW YOU!
EASY, MR. JAMESON--I'M NOT LOOKING FOR A RAISE! I'M LOOKING FOR WORK!
WORK? PARKER, IF THIS IS SOME KIND OF JOKE--
NO JOKE! I'M JUST LOOKING FOR A PHOTO-ASSIGNMENT OUT-OF TOWN!
--SOMETHING TO TAKE ME AWAY FROM NEW YORK!
NOW HOLD ON, PARKER--I KNOW WHY YOU WANT THIS--THE DEATH OF YOUR GIRL AND ALL--
--BUT THE DAILY BUGLE IS NOT A PUBLIC WELFARE SERVICE!
BUT, MR. JAMESON--
IF YOU HAD COME IN HERE WITH AN IDEA FOR SOMETHING NEWSWORTHY, I MIGHT HAVE CONSIDERED IT, BUT AS IT STANDS--
WHOA, JONAH! BEFORE YOU FINISH THAT SENTENCE--
--TAKE A LOOK AT THESE!
OLD WIRE PHOTOS OF DAREDEVIL--AND THE BLACK WIDOW--
--AND THEY, J.J., ARE MOST DEFINITELY NEWS-WORTHY!

--AND *POPULAR* ENOUGH FOR US TO RUN A SPECIAL *SPREAD* ON THEM IN NEXT SUNDAY'S MAGAZINE SECTION--

--A SPREAD THAT'S GOING TO REQUIRE A BATCH OF *NEW PHOTOS* TO MAKE IT SING--!

SO--UNLESS YOU CAN THINK OF ANYONE MORE *QUALIFIED* THAN PETER TO *TAKE* THOSE PICTURES--?

ALL RIGHT, ROBERTSON-- YOU MADE YOUR *POINT!* PARKER HAS HIMSELF A *FREE RIDE!*

BUT IF HE COMES *BACK* HERE WITH ANYTHING LESS THAN *BRILLIANT*--!

DON'T *WORRY* ABOUT IT, MR. JAMESON--

WITH ANY *LUCK*, LITTLE PETER PARKER MIGHT *NOT* COME BACK FROM 'FRISCO AT *ALL!*

OF COURSE, I HADN'T EXACTLY *MEANT* THAT MAUDLIN THOUGHT TO WORK OUT QUITE *THIS* WAY--!

I'D RATHER DIG FOR *WORMS* IN THE *BIG APPLE*--

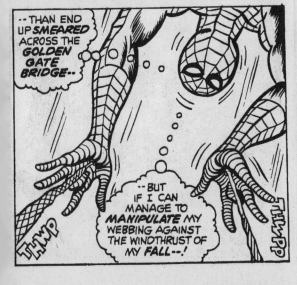

--THAN END UP *SMEARED* ACROSS THE *GOLDEN GATE BRIDGE*--

--BUT IF I CAN MANAGE TO *MANIPULATE* MY WEBBING AGAINST THE WINDTHRUST OF MY *FALL*--!

THWP

THWPP

BINGO! ONE INSTANT SPIDEY-*TRAMPOLINE*--

THWANGG

--GUARANTEED TO PUT A LITTLE *BOUNCE* IN YOUR LIFE--

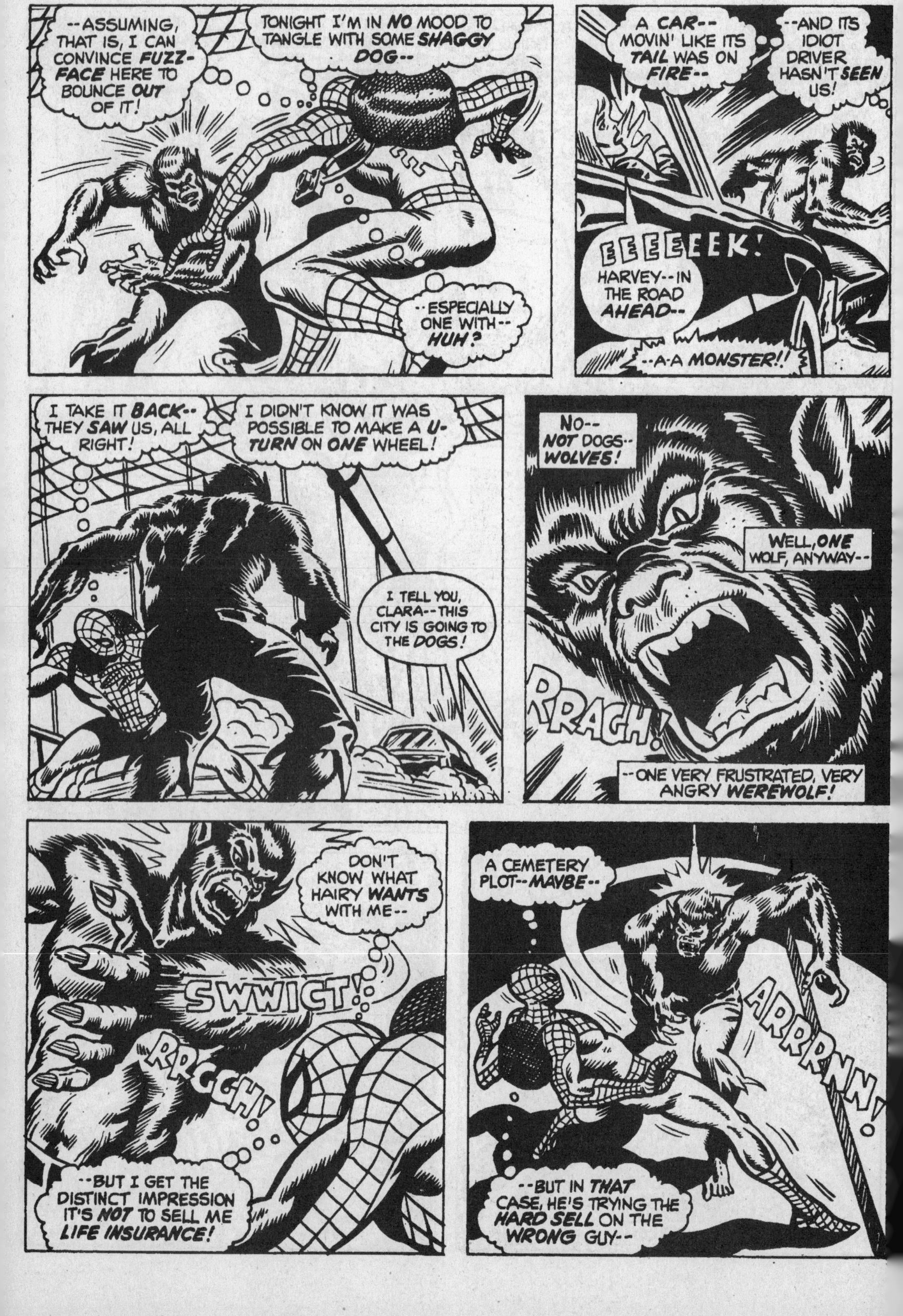
--ASSUMING, THAT IS, I CAN CONVINCE FUZZ-FACE HERE TO BOUNCE OUT OF IT!
TONIGHT I'M IN NO MOOD TO TANGLE WITH SOME SHAGGY DOG--
--ESPECIALLY ONE WITH--HUH?
A CAR--MOVIN' LIKE ITS TAIL WAS ON FIRE--
--AND ITS IDIOT DRIVER HASN'T SEEN US!
EEEEEEEK!
HARVEY--IN THE ROAD AHEAD--
--A-A MONSTER!!
I TAKE IT BACK--THEY SAW US, ALL RIGHT!
I DIDN'T KNOW IT WAS POSSIBLE TO MAKE A U-TURN ON ONE WHEEL!
I TELL YOU, CLARA--THIS CITY IS GOING TO THE DOGS!
NO--NOT DOGS--WOLVES!
WELL, ONE WOLF, ANYWAY--
RRAGH!
--ONE VERY FRUSTRATED, VERY ANGRY WEREWOLF!
DON'T KNOW WHAT HAIRY WANTS WITH ME--
SWWICT!
RRGGH!
--BUT I GET THE DISTINCT IMPRESSION IT'S NOT TO SELL ME LIFE INSURANCE!
A CEMETERY PLOT--MAYBE--
ARRRNN!
--BUT IN THAT CASE, HE'S TRYING THE HARD SELL ON THE WRONG GUY--

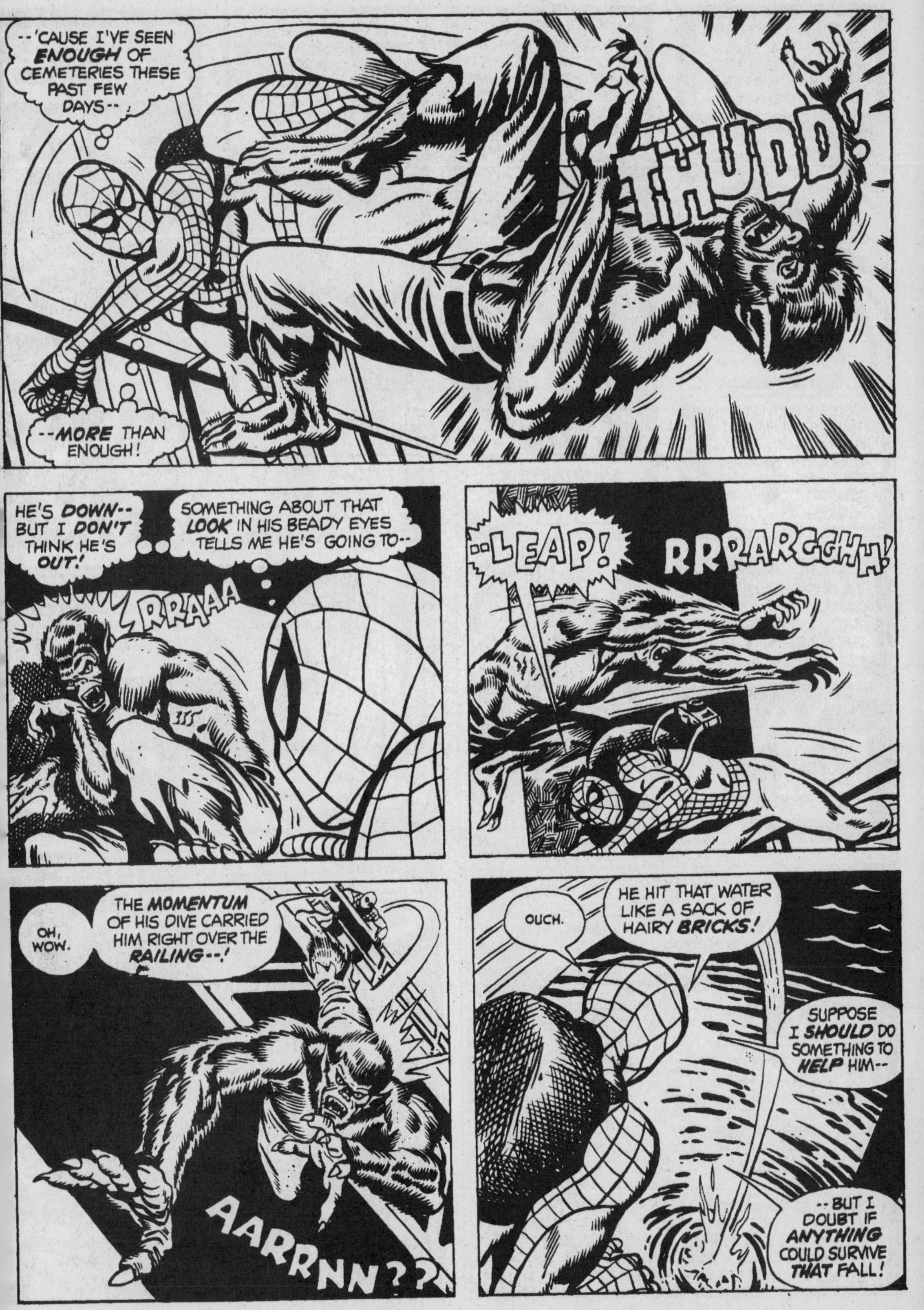

--'CAUSE I'VE SEEN ENOUGH OF CEMETERIES THESE PAST FEW DAYS--
THUDD!
--MORE THAN ENOUGH!
HE'S DOWN-- BUT I DON'T THINK HE'S OUT!
SOMETHING ABOUT THAT LOOK IN HIS BEADY EYES TELLS ME HE'S GOING TO--
RRAAA
--LEAP!
RRRARGGHH!
OH, WOW.
THE MOMENTUM OF HIS DIVE CARRIED HIM RIGHT OVER THE RAILING--!
AARRNN??
OUCH.
HE HIT THAT WATER LIKE A SACK OF HAIRY BRICKS!
SUPPOSE I SHOULD DO SOMETHING TO HELP HIM--
--BUT I DOUBT IF ANYTHING COULD SURVIVE THAT FALL!

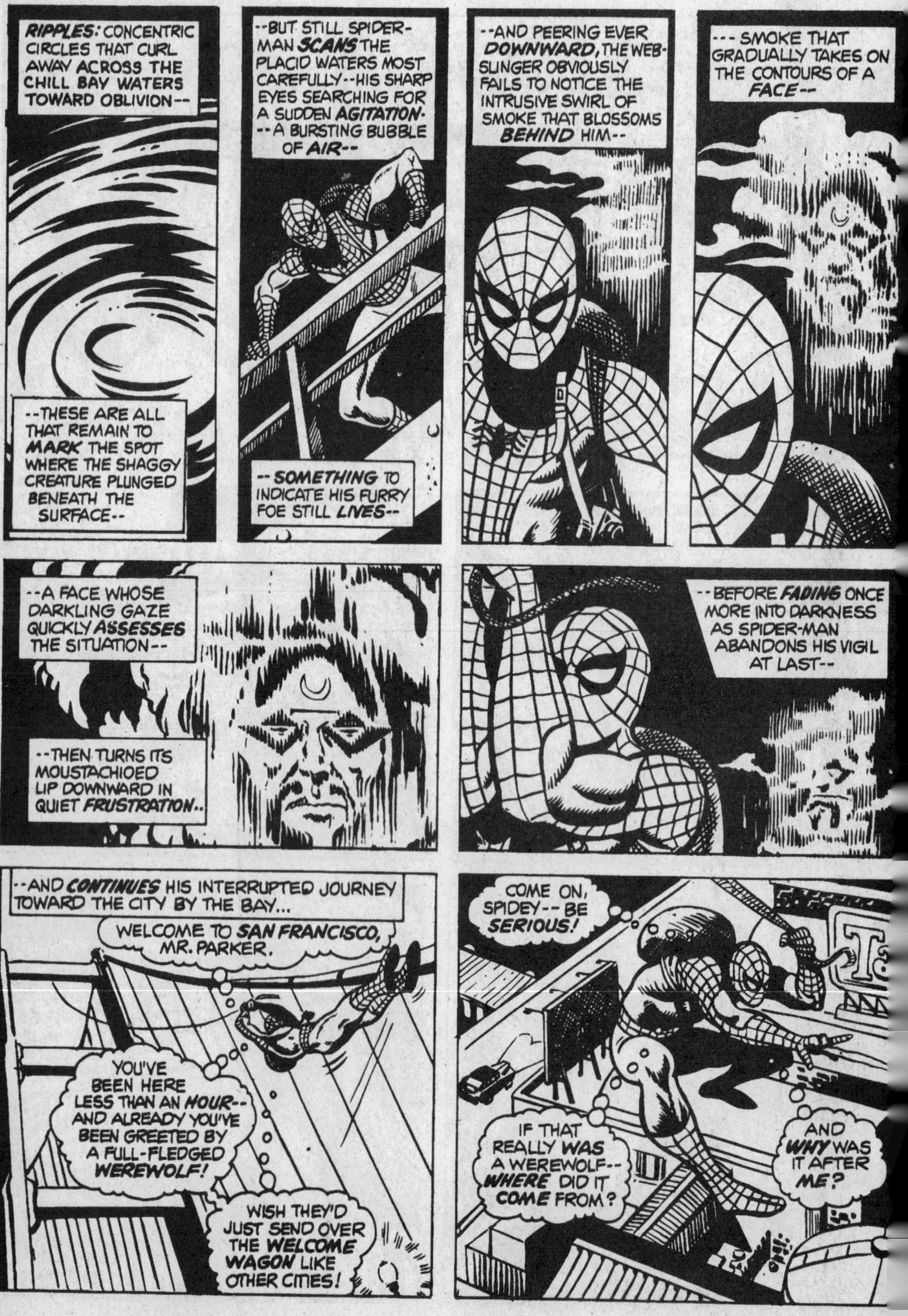
RIPPLES: CONCENTRIC CIRCLES THAT CURL AWAY ACROSS THE CHILL BAY WATERS TOWARD OBLIVION--
--THESE ARE ALL THAT REMAIN TO MARK THE SPOT WHERE THE SHAGGY CREATURE PLUNGED BENEATH THE SURFACE--
--BUT STILL SPIDER-MAN SCANS THE PLACID WATERS MOST CAREFULLY--HIS SHARP EYES SEARCHING FOR A SUDDEN AGITATION--A BURSTING BUBBLE OF AIR--
--SOMETHING TO INDICATE HIS FURRY FOE STILL LIVES--
--AND PEERING EVER DOWNWARD, THE WEB-SLINGER OBVIOUSLY FAILS TO NOTICE THE INTRUSIVE SWIRL OF SMOKE THAT BLOSSOMS BEHIND HIM--
--- SMOKE THAT GRADUALLY TAKES ON THE CONTOURS OF A FACE--
--A FACE WHOSE DARKLING GAZE QUICKLY ASSESSES THE SITUATION--
--THEN TURNS ITS MOUSTACHIOED LIP DOWNWARD IN QUIET FRUSTRATION..
--BEFORE FADING ONCE MORE INTO DARKNESS AS SPIDER-MAN ABANDONS HIS VIGIL AT LAST--
--AND CONTINUES HIS INTERRUPTED JOURNEY TOWARD THE CITY BY THE BAY...
WELCOME TO SAN FRANCISCO, MR. PARKER.
YOU'VE BEEN HERE LESS THAN AN HOUR--AND ALREADY YOU'VE BEEN GREETED BY A FULL-FLEDGED WEREWOLF!
WISH THEY'D JUST SEND OVER THE WELCOME WAGON LIKE OTHER CITIES!
COME ON, SPIDEY-- BE SERIOUS!
IF THAT REALLY WAS A WEREWOLF--WHERE DID IT COME FROM?
AND WHY WAS IT AFTER ME?

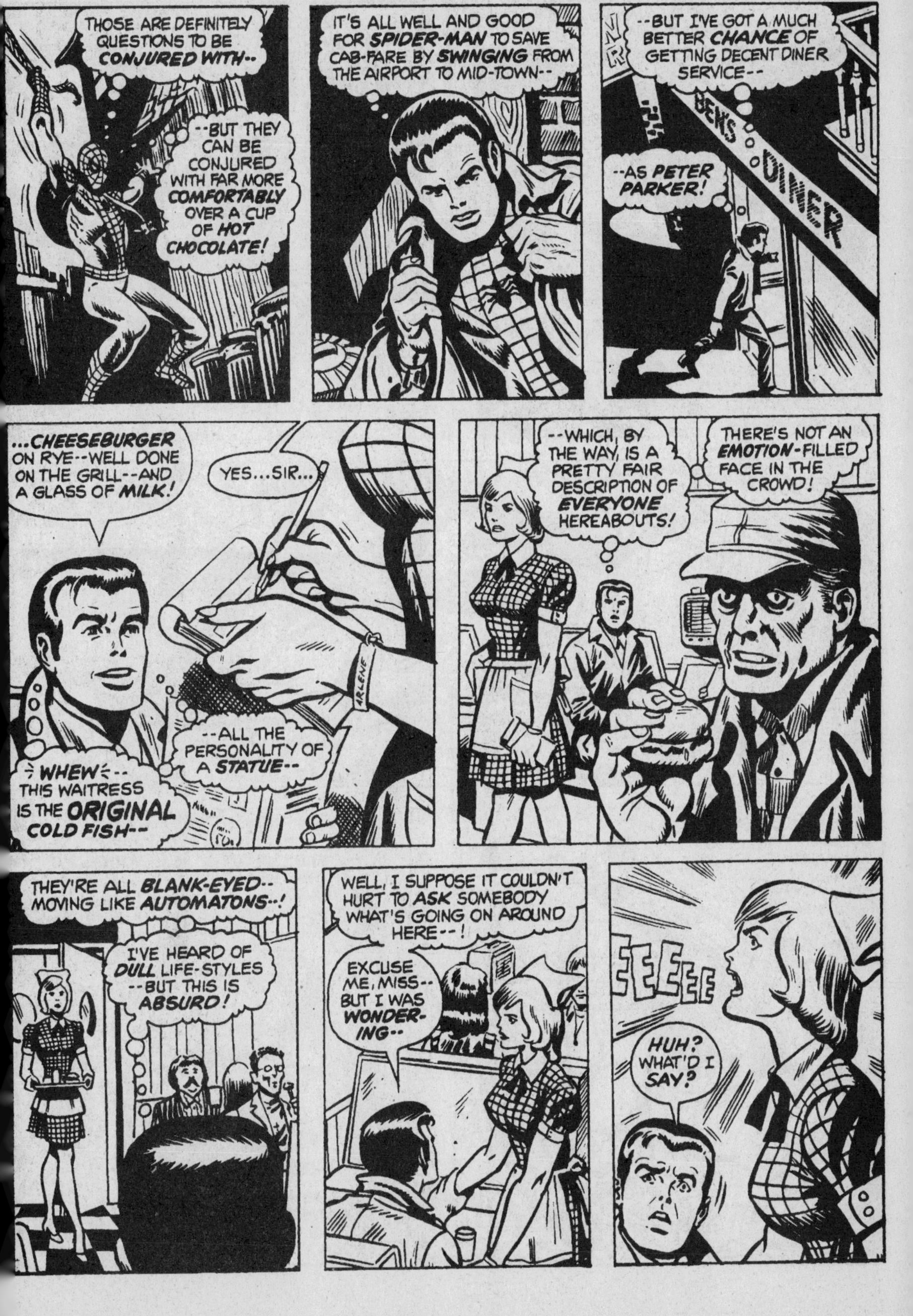
THOSE ARE DEFINITELY QUESTIONS TO BE CONJURED WITH--
--BUT THEY CAN BE CONJURED WITH FAR MORE COMFORTABLY OVER A CUP OF HOT CHOCOLATE!
IT'S ALL WELL AND GOOD FOR SPIDER-MAN TO SAVE CAB-FARE BY SWINGING FROM THE AIRPORT TO MID-TOWN--
--BUT I'VE GOT A MUCH BETTER CHANCE OF GETTING DECENT DINER SERVICE--
BEN'S DINER
--AS PETER PARKER!
...CHEESEBURGER ON RYE--WELL DONE ON THE GRILL--AND A GLASS OF MILK!
YES...SIR...
ARLENE
WHEW-- THIS WAITRESS IS THE ORIGINAL COLD FISH--
--ALL THE PERSONALITY OF A STATUE--
--WHICH, BY THE WAY, IS A PRETTY FAIR DESCRIPTION OF EVERYONE HEREABOUTS!
THERE'S NOT AN EMOTION-FILLED FACE IN THE CROWD!
THEY'RE ALL BLANK-EYED-- MOVING LIKE AUTOMATONS--!
I'VE HEARD OF DULL LIFE-STYLES --BUT THIS IS ABSURD!
WELL, I SUPPOSE IT COULDN'T HURT TO ASK SOMEBODY WHAT'S GOING ON AROUND HERE--!
EXCUSE ME, MISS-- BUT I WAS WONDER-ING--
EEEEEE
HUH? WHAT'D I SAY?

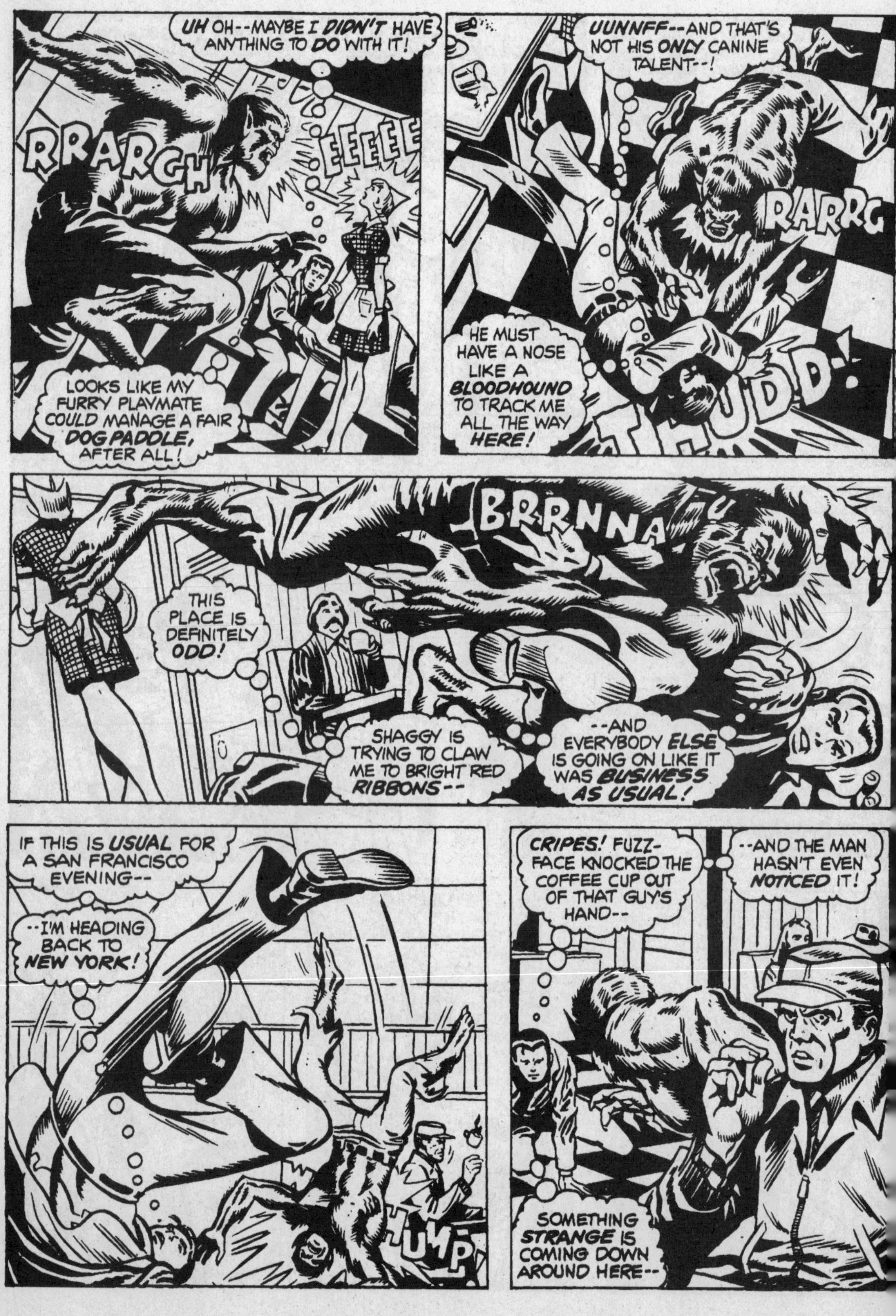

UH OH--MAYBE I DIDN'T HAVE ANYTHING TO DO WITH IT!
RRARGH
EEEEEE
LOOKS LIKE MY FURRY PLAYMATE COULD MANAGE A FAIR DOG PADDLE, AFTER ALL!
UUNNFF--AND THAT'S NOT HIS ONLY CANINE TALENT--!
RARRG
HE MUST HAVE A NOSE LIKE A BLOODHOUND TO TRACK ME ALL THE WAY HERE!
THUDD!
BRRNNA
THIS PLACE IS DEFINITELY ODD!
SHAGGY IS TRYING TO CLAW ME TO BRIGHT RED RIBBONS--
--AND EVERYBODY ELSE IS GOING ON LIKE IT WAS BUSINESS AS USUAL!
IF THIS IS USUAL FOR A SAN FRANCISCO EVENING--
--I'M HEADING BACK TO NEW YORK!
THUMP
CRIPES! FUZZ-FACE KNOCKED THE COFFEE CUP OUT OF THAT GUY'S HAND--
--AND THE MAN HASN'T EVEN NOTICED IT!
SOMETHING STRANGE IS COMING DOWN AROUND HERE--

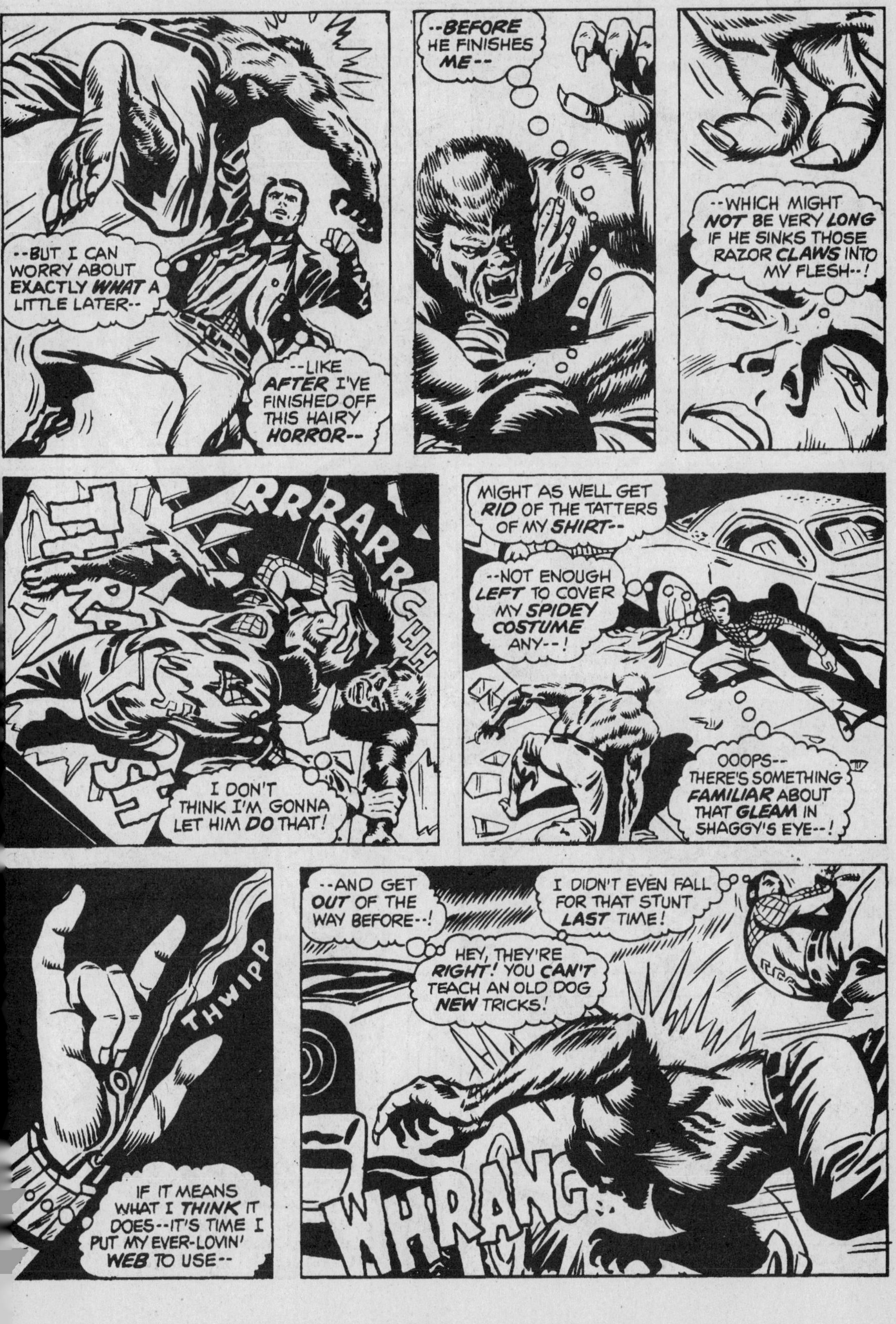
--BUT I CAN WORRY ABOUT EXACTLY WHAT A LITTLE LATER--
--LIKE AFTER I'VE FINISHED OFF THIS HAIRY HORROR--
--BEFORE HE FINISHES ME--
--WHICH MIGHT NOT BE VERY LONG IF HE SINKS THOSE RAZOR CLAWS INTO MY FLESH--!
RRRARRR
I DON'T THINK I'M GONNA LET HIM DO THAT!
MIGHT AS WELL GET RID OF THE TATTERS OF MY SHIRT--
--NOT ENOUGH LEFT TO COVER MY SPIDEY COSTUME ANY--!
OOOPS-- THERE'S SOMETHING FAMILIAR ABOUT THAT GLEAM IN SHAGGY'S EYE--!
THWIPP
IF IT MEANS WHAT I THINK IT DOES--IT'S TIME I PUT MY EVER-LOVIN' WEB TO USE--
--AND GET OUT OF THE WAY BEFORE--!
I DIDN'T EVEN FALL FOR THAT STUNT LAST TIME!
HEY, THEY'RE RIGHT! YOU CAN'T TEACH AN OLD DOG NEW TRICKS!
WHRANG

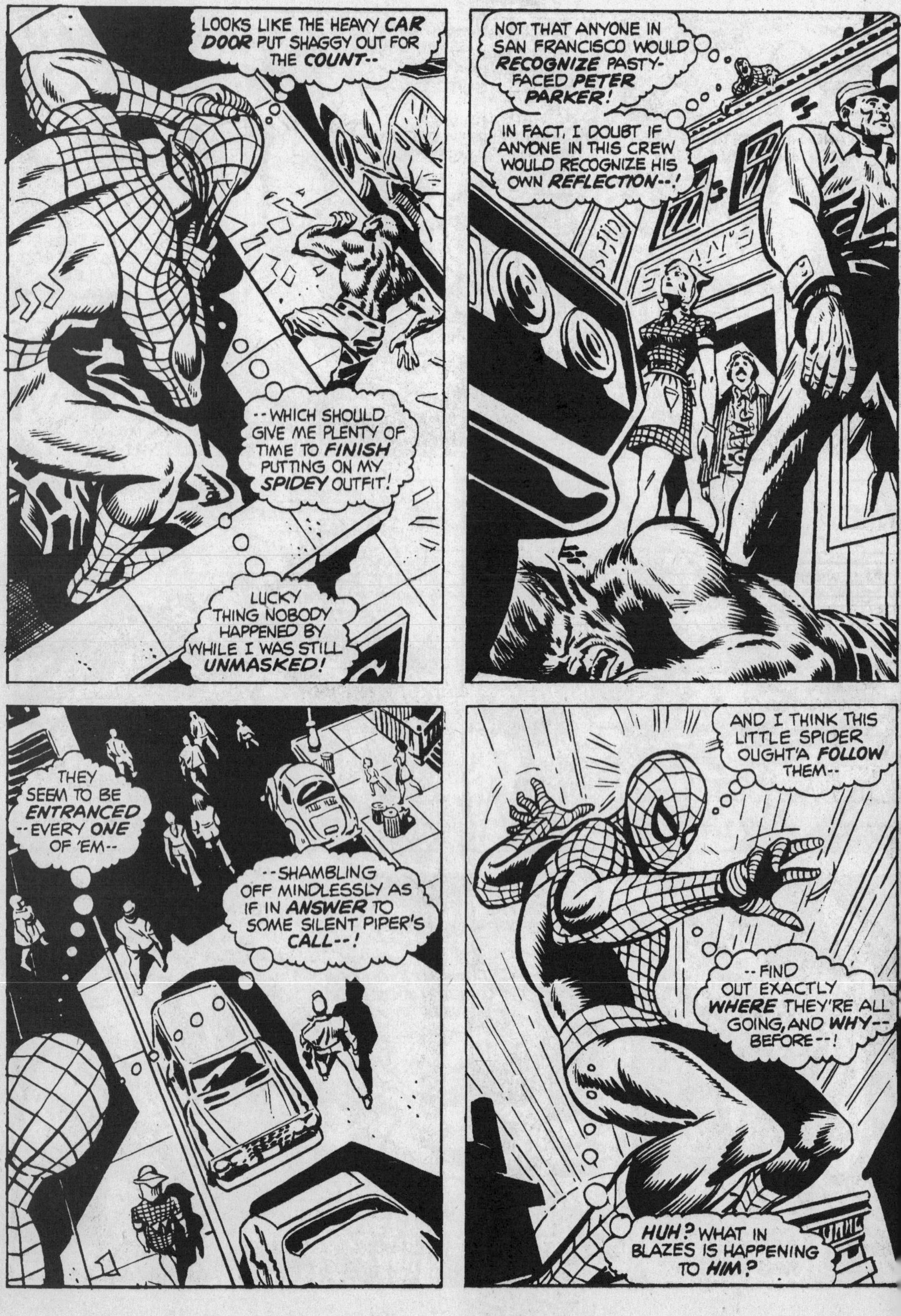
LOOKS LIKE THE HEAVY CAR DOOR PUT SHAGGY OUT FOR THE COUNT--
--WHICH SHOULD GIVE ME PLENTY OF TIME TO FINISH PUTTING ON MY SPIDEY OUTFIT!
LUCKY THING NOBODY HAPPENED BY WHILE I WAS STILL UNMASKED!
NOT THAT ANYONE IN SAN FRANCISCO WOULD RECOGNIZE PASTY-FACED PETER PARKER!
IN FACT, I DOUBT IF ANYONE IN THIS CREW WOULD RECOGNIZE HIS OWN REFLECTION--!
THEY SEEM TO BE ENTRANCED --EVERY ONE OF 'EM--
--SHAMBLING OFF MINDLESSLY AS IF IN ANSWER TO SOME SILENT PIPER'S CALL--!
AND I THINK THIS LITTLE SPIDER OUGHT'A FOLLOW THEM--
--FIND OUT EXACTLY WHERE THEY'RE ALL GOING, AND WHY-- BEFORE--!
HUH? WHAT IN BLAZES IS HAPPENING TO HIM?

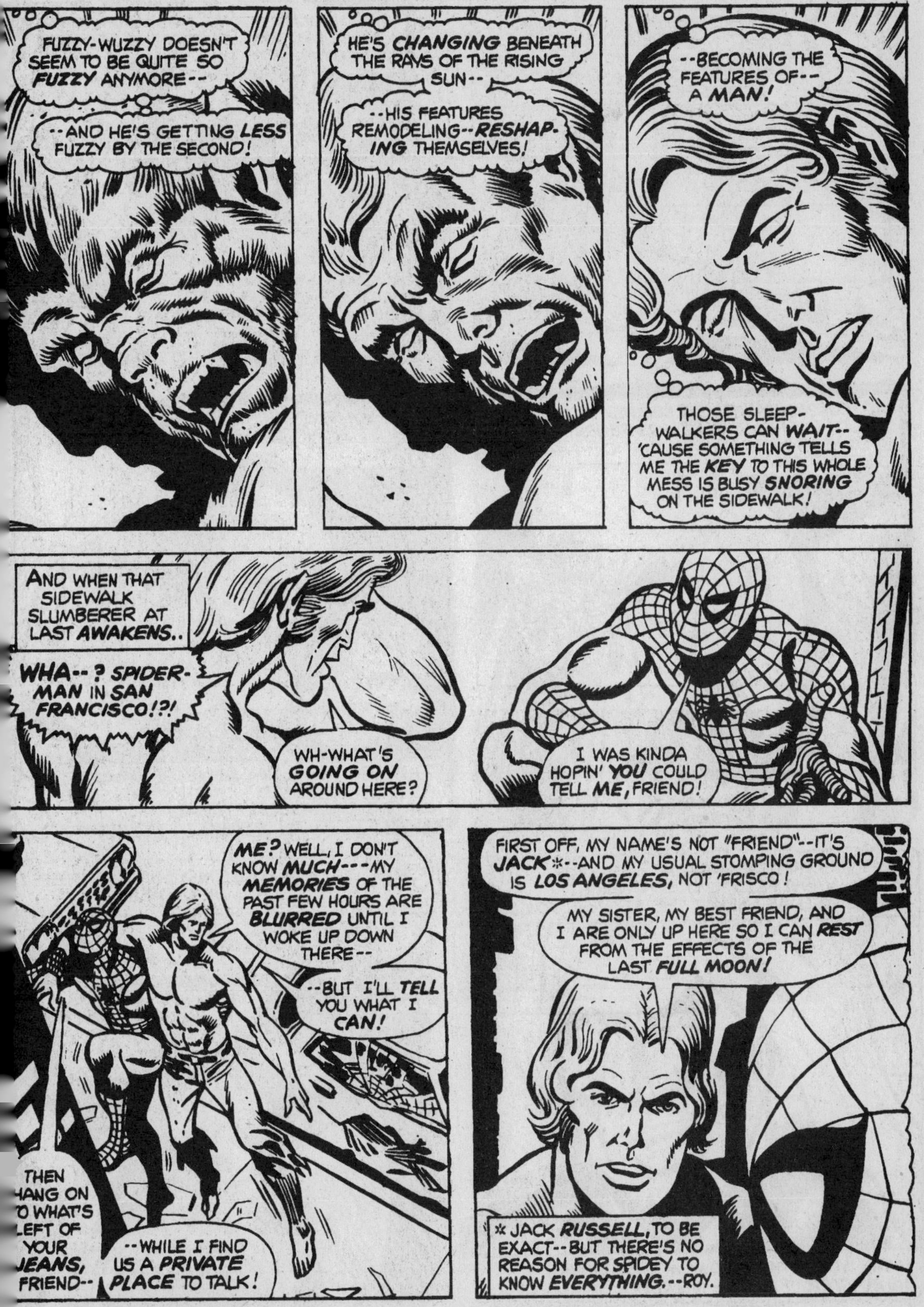
FUZZY-WUZZY DOESN'T SEEM TO BE QUITE SO FUZZY ANYMORE--
--AND HE'S GETTING LESS FUZZY BY THE SECOND!
HE'S CHANGING BENEATH THE RAYS OF THE RISING SUN--
--HIS FEATURES REMODELING--RESHAPING THEMSELVES!
--BECOMING THE FEATURES OF-- A MAN!
THOSE SLEEP-WALKERS CAN WAIT--'CAUSE SOMETHING TELLS ME THE KEY TO THIS WHOLE MESS IS BUSY SNORING ON THE SIDEWALK!
AND WHEN THAT SIDEWALK SLUMBERER AT LAST AWAKENS..
WHA--? SPIDER-MAN IN SAN FRANCISCO!?!
WH-WHAT'S GOING ON AROUND HERE?
I WAS KINDA HOPIN' YOU COULD TELL ME, FRIEND!
ME? WELL, I DON'T KNOW MUCH---MY MEMORIES OF THE PAST FEW HOURS ARE BLURRED UNTIL I WOKE UP DOWN THERE--
--BUT I'LL TELL YOU WHAT I CAN!
THEN HANG ON TO WHAT'S LEFT OF YOUR JEANS, FRIEND--
--WHILE I FIND US A PRIVATE PLACE TO TALK!
FIRST OFF, MY NAME'S NOT "FRIEND"--IT'S JACK*--AND MY USUAL STOMPING GROUND IS LOS ANGELES, NOT 'FRISCO!
MY SISTER, MY BEST FRIEND, AND I ARE ONLY UP HERE SO I CAN REST FROM THE EFFECTS OF THE LAST FULL MOON!
*JACK RUSSELL, TO BE EXACT--BUT THERE'S NO REASON FOR SPIDEY TO KNOW EVERYTHING.--ROY.

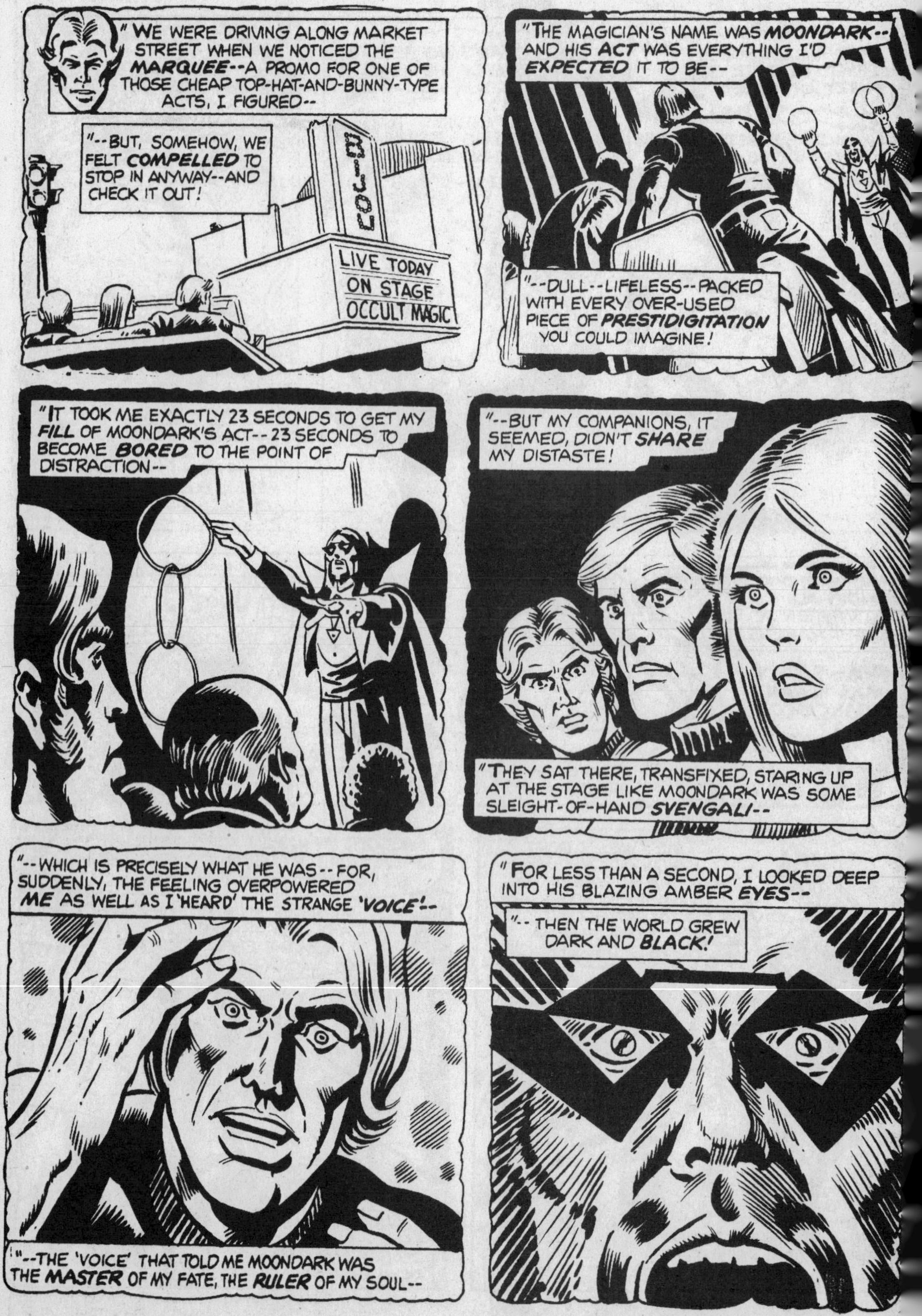
"WE WERE DRIVING ALONG MARKET STREET WHEN WE NOTICED THE MARQUEE--A PROMO FOR ONE OF THOSE CHEAP TOP-HAT-AND-BUNNY-TYPE ACTS, I FIGURED--
"--BUT, SOMEHOW, WE FELT COMPELLED TO STOP IN ANYWAY--AND CHECK IT OUT!
BIJOU
LIVE TODAY
ON STAGE
OCCULT MAGIC
"THE MAGICIAN'S NAME WAS MOONDARK--AND HIS ACT WAS EVERYTHING I'D EXPECTED IT TO BE--
"--DULL--LIFELESS--PACKED WITH EVERY OVER-USED PIECE OF PRESTIDIGITATION YOU COULD IMAGINE!
"IT TOOK ME EXACTLY 23 SECONDS TO GET MY FILL OF MOONDARK'S ACT--23 SECONDS TO BECOME BORED TO THE POINT OF DISTRACTION--
"--BUT MY COMPANIONS, IT SEEMED, DIDN'T SHARE MY DISTASTE!
"THEY SAT THERE, TRANSFIXED, STARING UP AT THE STAGE LIKE MOONDARK WAS SOME SLEIGHT-OF-HAND SVENGALI--
"--WHICH IS PRECISELY WHAT HE WAS--FOR, SUDDENLY, THE FEELING OVERPOWERED ME AS WELL AS I 'HEARD' THE STRANGE 'VOICE'--
"--THE 'VOICE' THAT TOLD ME MOONDARK WAS THE MASTER OF MY FATE, THE RULER OF MY SOUL--
"FOR LESS THAN A SECOND, I LOOKED DEEP INTO HIS BLAZING AMBER EYES--
"--THEN THE WORLD GREW DARK AND BLACK!

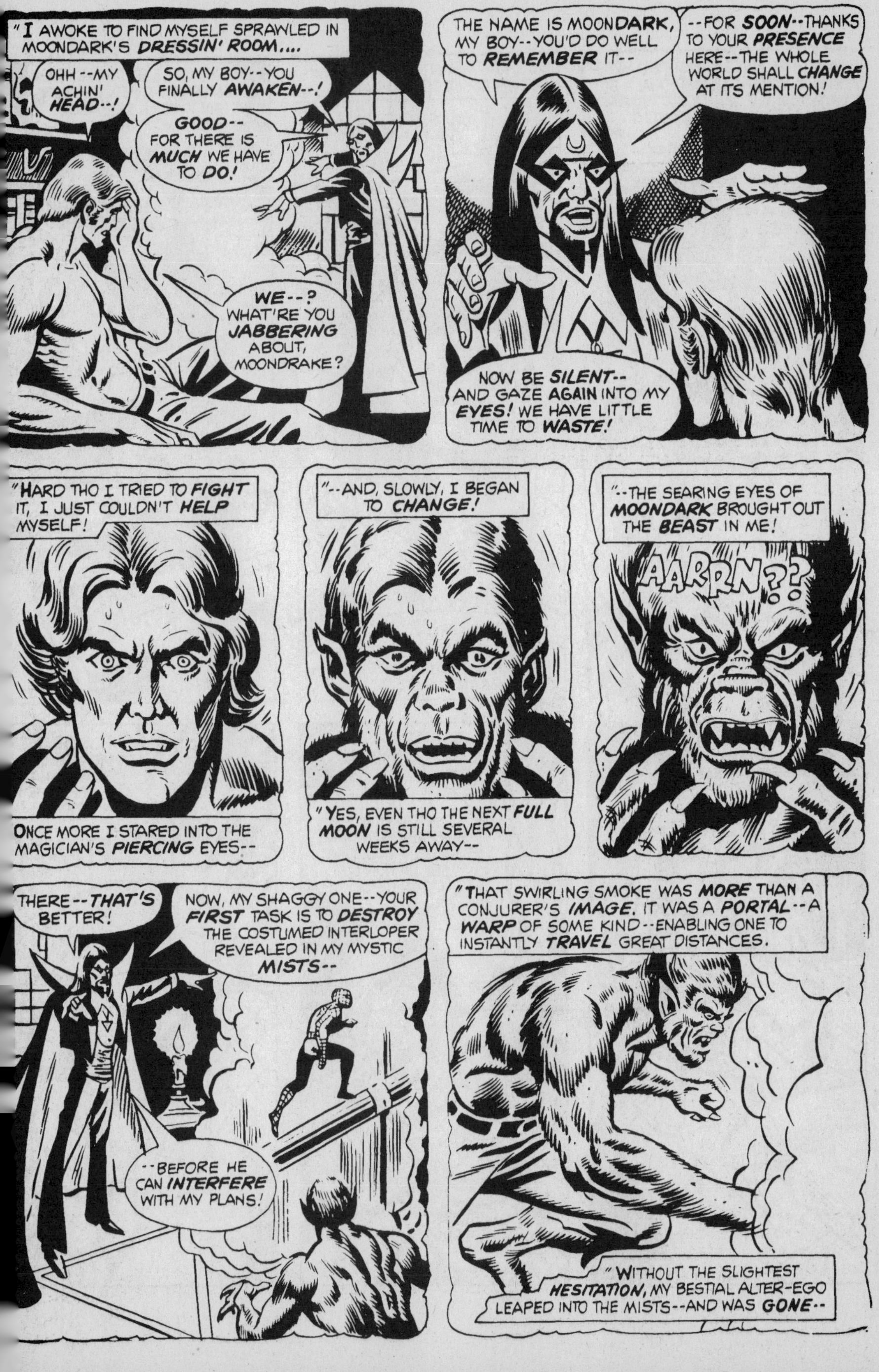

"I AWOKE TO FIND MYSELF SPRAWLED IN MOONDARK'S DRESSIN' ROOM....
OHH--MY ACHIN' HEAD--!
SO, MY BOY--YOU FINALLY AWAKEN--!
GOOD-- FOR THERE IS MUCH WE HAVE TO DO!
WE--? WHAT'RE YOU JABBERING ABOUT, MOONDRAKE?
THE NAME IS MOONDARK, MY BOY--YOU'D DO WELL TO REMEMBER IT--
--FOR SOON--THANKS TO YOUR PRESENCE HERE--THE WHOLE WORLD SHALL CHANGE AT ITS MENTION!
NOW BE SILENT-- AND GAZE AGAIN INTO MY EYES! WE HAVE LITTLE TIME TO WASTE!
"HARD THO I TRIED TO FIGHT IT, I JUST COULDN'T HELP MYSELF!
ONCE MORE I STARED INTO THE MAGICIAN'S PIERCING EYES--
"--AND, SLOWLY, I BEGAN TO CHANGE!
"YES, EVEN THO THE NEXT FULL MOON IS STILL SEVERAL WEEKS AWAY--
"--THE SEARING EYES OF MOONDARK BROUGHT OUT THE BEAST IN ME!
AARRN??
THERE--THAT'S BETTER!
NOW, MY SHAGGY ONE--YOUR FIRST TASK IS TO DESTROY THE COSTUMED INTERLOPER REVEALED IN MY MYSTIC MISTS--
--BEFORE HE CAN INTERFERE WITH MY PLANS!
"THAT SWIRLING SMOKE WAS MORE THAN A CONJURER'S IMAGE. IT WAS A PORTAL--A WARP OF SOME KIND--ENABLING ONE TO INSTANTLY TRAVEL GREAT DISTANCES.
"WITHOUT THE SLIGHTEST HESITATION, MY BESTIAL ALTER-EGO LEAPED INTO THE MISTS--AND WAS GONE--

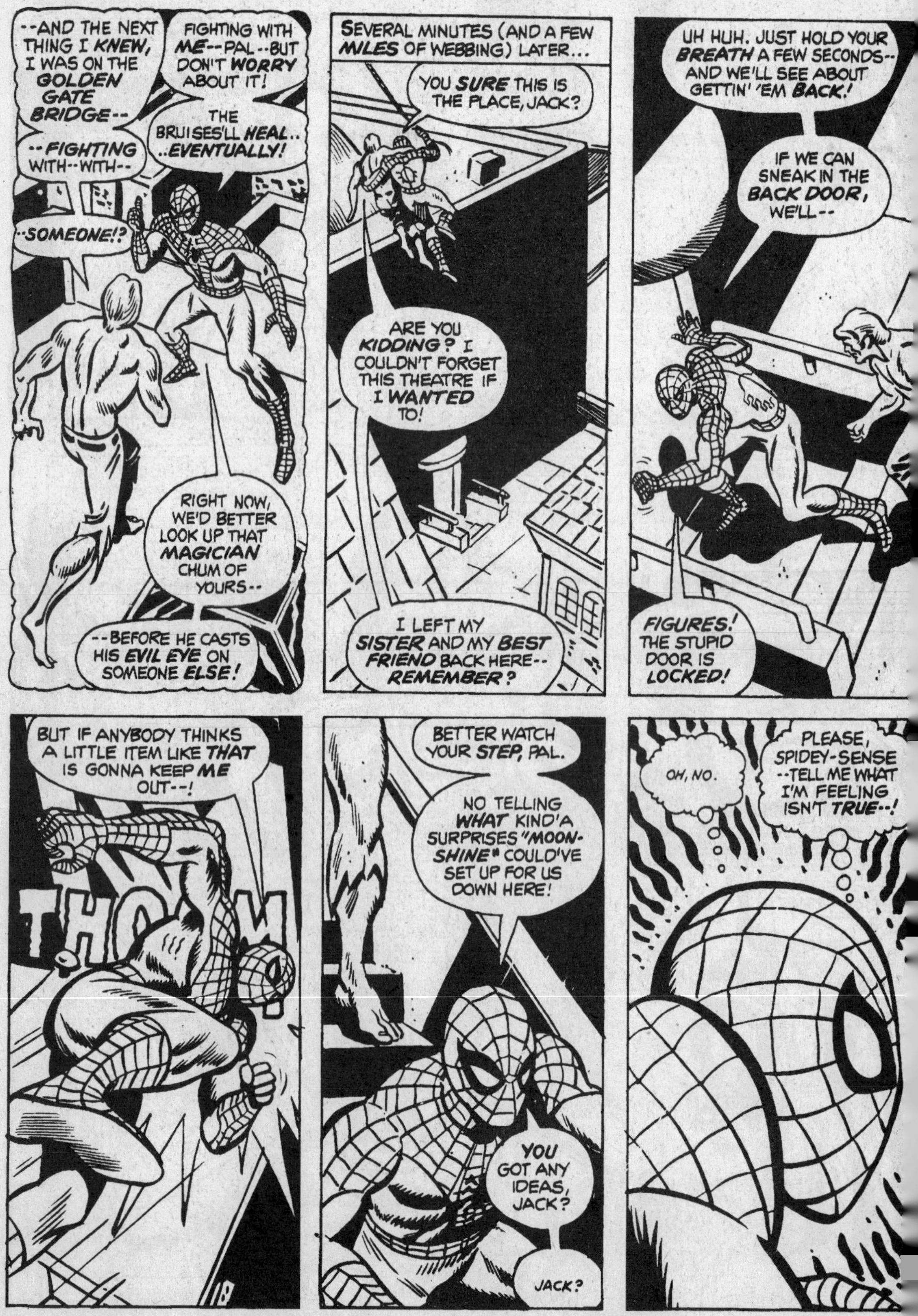
--AND THE NEXT THING I KNEW, I WAS ON THE GOLDEN GATE BRIDGE--
--FIGHTING WITH--WITH--
--SOMEONE!?
FIGHTING WITH ME--PAL--BUT DON'T WORRY ABOUT IT!
THE BRUISES'LL HEAL.. ..EVENTUALLY!
RIGHT NOW, WE'D BETTER LOOK UP THAT MAGICIAN CHUM OF YOURS--
--BEFORE HE CASTS HIS EVIL EYE ON SOMEONE ELSE!
SEVERAL MINUTES (AND A FEW MILES OF WEBBING) LATER...
YOU SURE THIS IS THE PLACE, JACK?
ARE YOU KIDDING? I COULDN'T FORGET THIS THEATRE IF I WANTED TO!
I LEFT MY SISTER AND MY BEST FRIEND BACK HERE-- REMEMBER?
UH HUH. JUST HOLD YOUR BREATH A FEW SECONDS-- AND WE'LL SEE ABOUT GETTIN' 'EM BACK!
IF WE CAN SNEAK IN THE BACK DOOR, WE'LL--
FIGURES! THE STUPID DOOR IS LOCKED!
BUT IF ANYBODY THINKS A LITTLE ITEM LIKE THAT IS GONNA KEEP ME OUT--!
THOOM
BETTER WATCH YOUR STEP, PAL.
NO TELLING WHAT KIND'A SURPRISES "MOONSHINE" COULD'VE SET UP FOR US DOWN HERE!
YOU GOT ANY IDEAS, JACK?
JACK?
OH, NO.
PLEASE, SPIDEY-SENSE --TELL ME WHAT I'M FEELING ISN'T TRUE--!
18

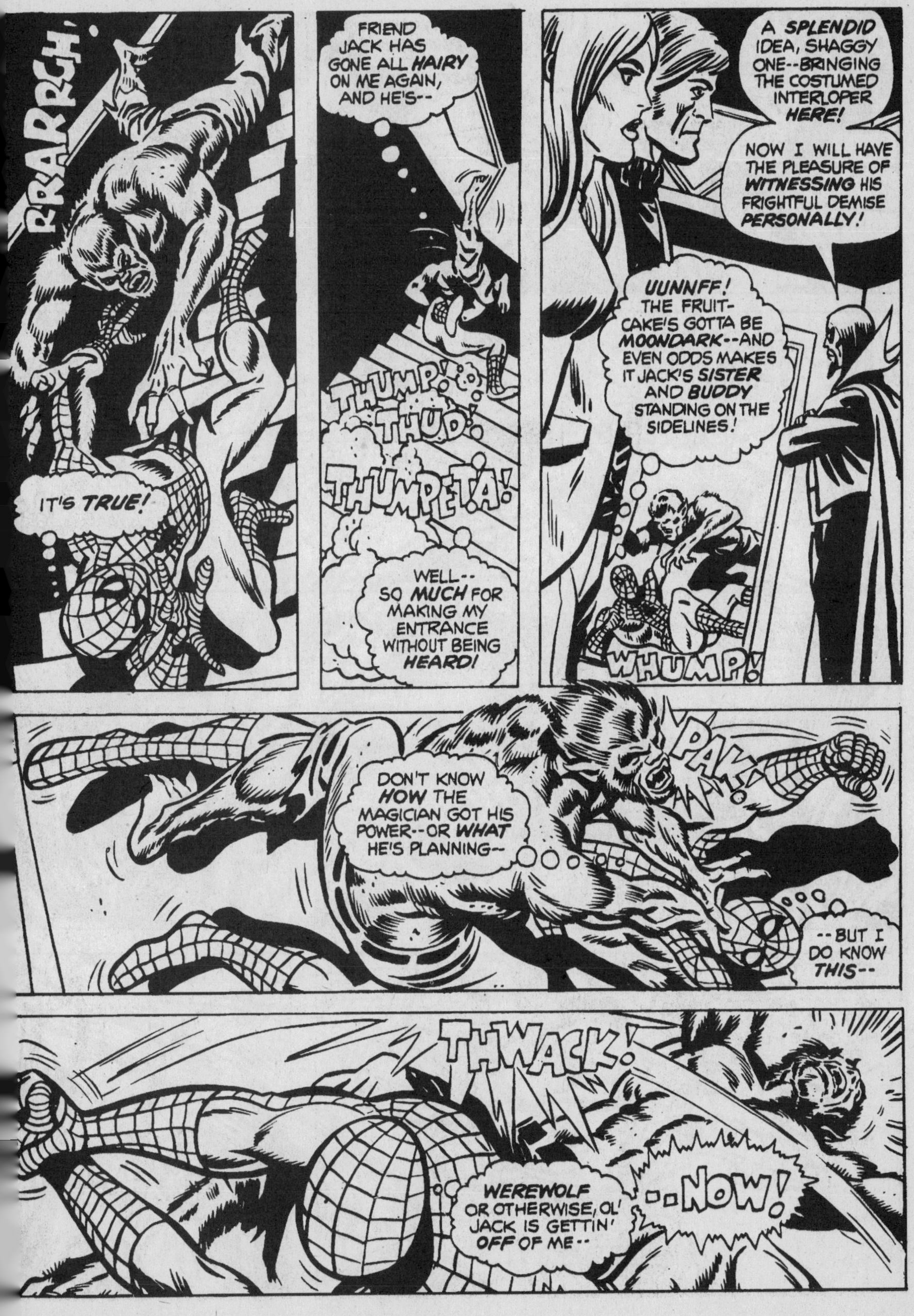

RRARRGH!
IT'S TRUE!
FRIEND JACK HAS GONE ALL HAIRY ON ME AGAIN, AND HE'S--
THUMP! THUD! THUMPETA!
WELL-- SO MUCH FOR MAKING MY ENTRANCE WITHOUT BEING HEARD!
A SPLENDID IDEA, SHAGGY ONE--BRINGING THE COSTUMED INTERLOPER HERE!
NOW I WILL HAVE THE PLEASURE OF WITNESSING HIS FRIGHTFUL DEMISE PERSONALLY!
UUNNFF! THE FRUIT-CAKE'S GOTTA BE MOONDARK--AND EVEN ODDS MAKES IT JACK'S SISTER AND BUDDY STANDING ON THE SIDELINES!
WHUMP!
PAW!
DON'T KNOW HOW THE MAGICIAN GOT HIS POWER--OR WHAT HE'S PLANNING--
--BUT I DO KNOW THIS--
THWACK!
WEREWOLF OR OTHERWISE, OL' JACK IS GETTIN' OFF OF ME--
..NOW!

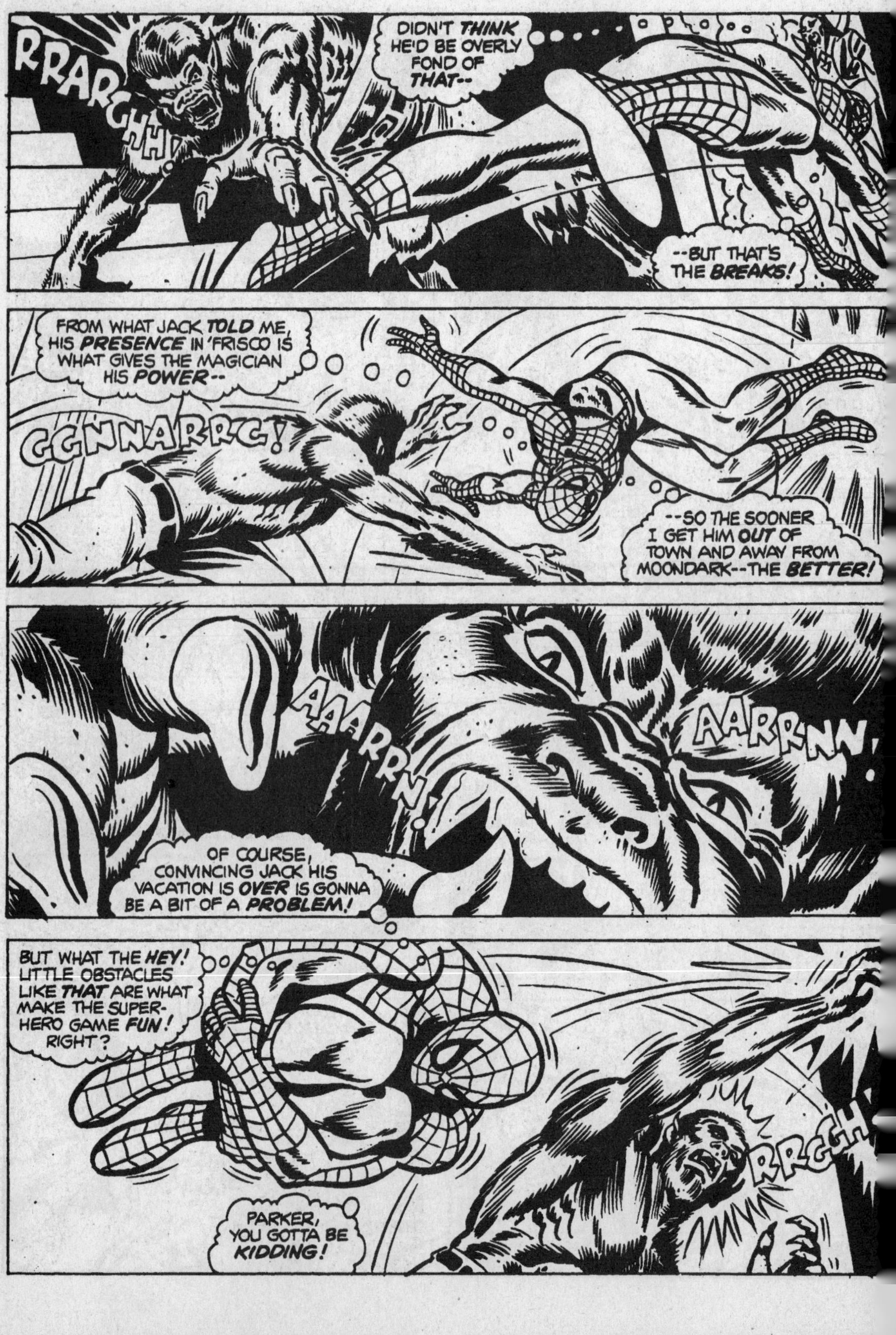
RRARGHH!
DIDN'T THINK HE'D BE OVERLY FOND OF THAT--
--BUT THAT'S THE BREAKS!
FROM WHAT JACK TOLD ME, HIS PRESENCE IN 'FRISCO IS WHAT GIVES THE MAGICIAN HIS POWER--
GGNNARRRG!
--SO THE SOONER I GET HIM OUT OF TOWN AND AWAY FROM MOONDARK--THE BETTER!
AAARRN!
AARRNN!
OF COURSE, CONVINCING JACK HIS VACATION IS OVER IS GONNA BE A BIT OF A PROBLEM!
BUT WHAT THE HEY! LITTLE OBSTACLES LIKE THAT ARE WHAT MAKE THE SUPER-HERO GAME FUN! RIGHT?
RRRGGH
PARKER, YOU GOTTA BE KIDDING!

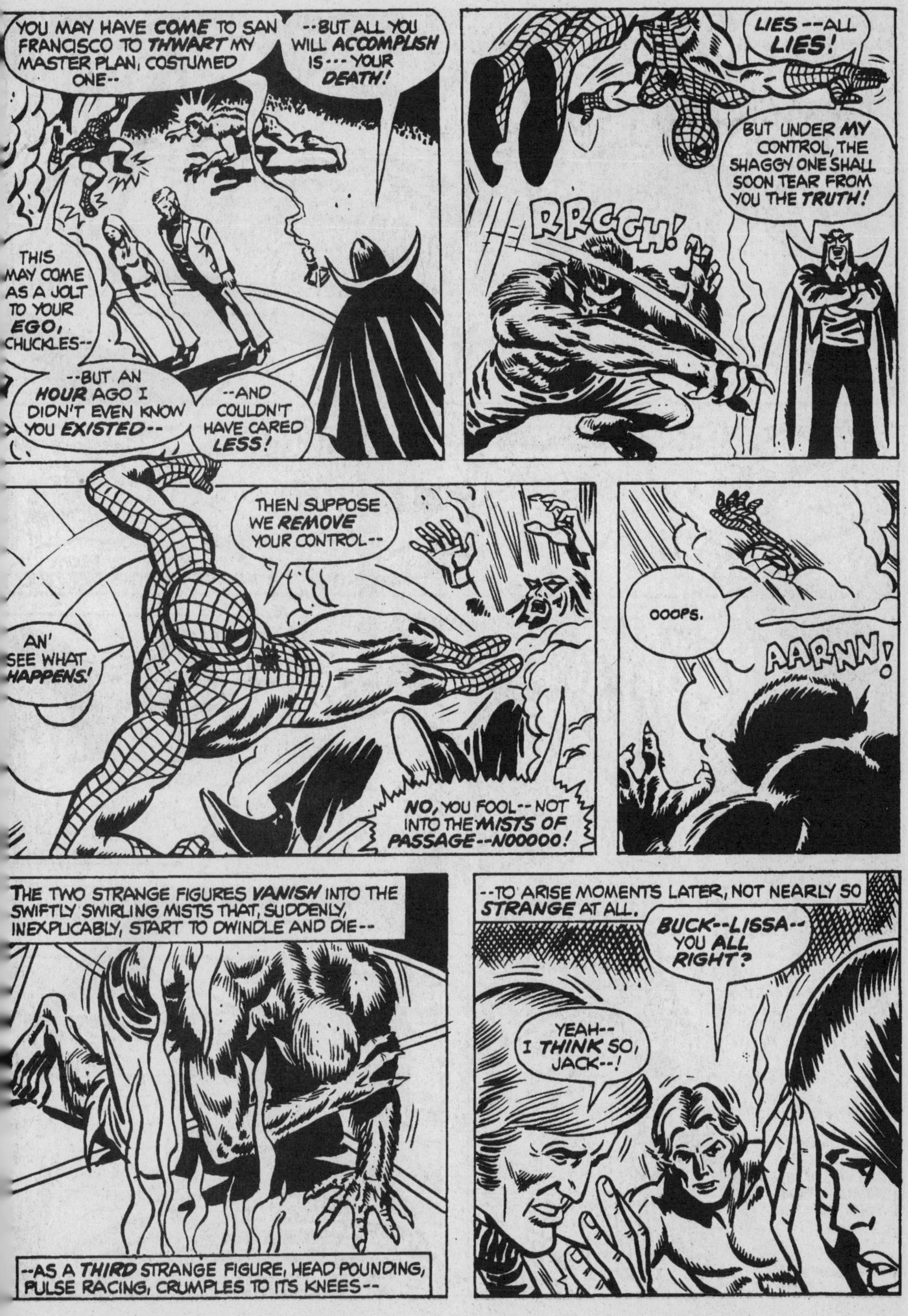
YOU MAY HAVE COME TO SAN FRANCISCO TO THWART MY MASTER PLAN, COSTUMED ONE--
--BUT ALL YOU WILL ACCOMPLISH IS--- YOUR DEATH!
THIS MAY COME AS A JOLT TO YOUR EGO, CHUCKLES--
--BUT AN HOUR AGO I DIDN'T EVEN KNOW YOU EXISTED--
--AND COULDN'T HAVE CARED LESS!
LIES--ALL LIES!
BUT UNDER MY CONTROL, THE SHAGGY ONE SHALL SOON TEAR FROM YOU THE TRUTH!
RRGGH!
THEN SUPPOSE WE REMOVE YOUR CONTROL--
AN' SEE WHAT HAPPENS!
NO, YOU FOOL--NOT INTO THE MISTS OF PASSAGE--NOOOOO!
OOOPS.
AARNN!
THE TWO STRANGE FIGURES VANISH INTO THE SWIFTLY SWIRLING MISTS THAT, SUDDENLY, INEXPLICABLY, START TO DWINDLE AND DIE--
--AS A THIRD STRANGE FIGURE, HEAD POUNDING, PULSE RACING, CRUMPLES TO ITS KNEES--
--TO ARISE MOMENTS LATER, NOT NEARLY SO STRANGE AT ALL.
BUCK--LISSA--YOU ALL RIGHT?
YEAH--I THINK SO, JACK--!

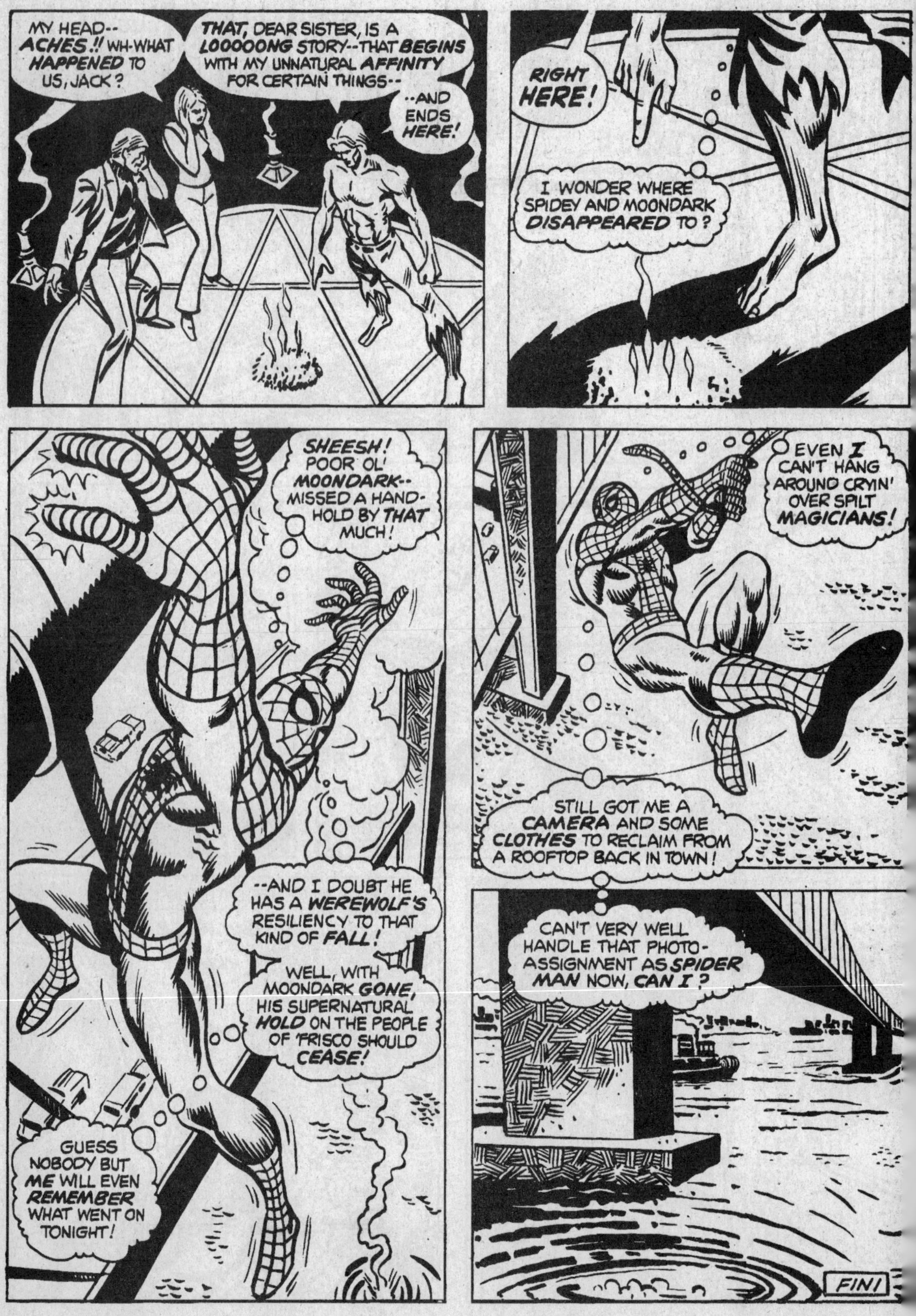
MY HEAD-- ACHES!! WH-WHAT HAPPENED TO US, JACK?
THAT, DEAR SISTER, IS A LOOOOONG STORY--THAT BEGINS WITH MY UNNATURAL AFFINITY FOR CERTAIN THINGS--
--AND ENDS HERE!
RIGHT HERE!
I WONDER WHERE SPIDEY AND MOONDARK DISAPPEARED TO?
SHEESH! POOR OL' MOONDARK-- MISSED A HAND-HOLD BY THAT MUCH!
--AND I DOUBT HE HAS A WEREWOLF'S RESILIENCY TO THAT KIND OF FALL!
WELL, WITH MOONDARK GONE, HIS SUPERNATURAL HOLD ON THE PEOPLE OF 'FRISCO SHOULD CEASE!
GUESS NOBODY BUT ME WILL EVEN REMEMBER WHAT WENT ON TONIGHT!
EVEN I CAN'T HANG AROUND CRYIN' OVER SPILT MAGICIANS!
STILL GOT ME A CAMERA AND SOME CLOTHES TO RECLAIM FROM A ROOFTOP BACK IN TOWN!
CAN'T VERY WELL HANDLE THAT PHOTO-ASSIGNMENT AS SPIDER MAN NOW, CAN I?
FINI

MARVEL TEAM-UP
MARVEL COMICS GROUP
APPROVED BY THE COMICS CODE AUTHORITY
20¢ 13 SEPT 02147
MARVEL TEAM-UP
FEATURING
SPIDER-MAN
AND
CAPTAIN AMERICA
FIRE! FIRE! THEY MUST BE DESTROYED!
SO SPEAKS THE GREY GARGOYLE!
TWO OF MARVEL'S MIGHTIEST HEROES IN NON-STOP ACTION --TOGETHER!

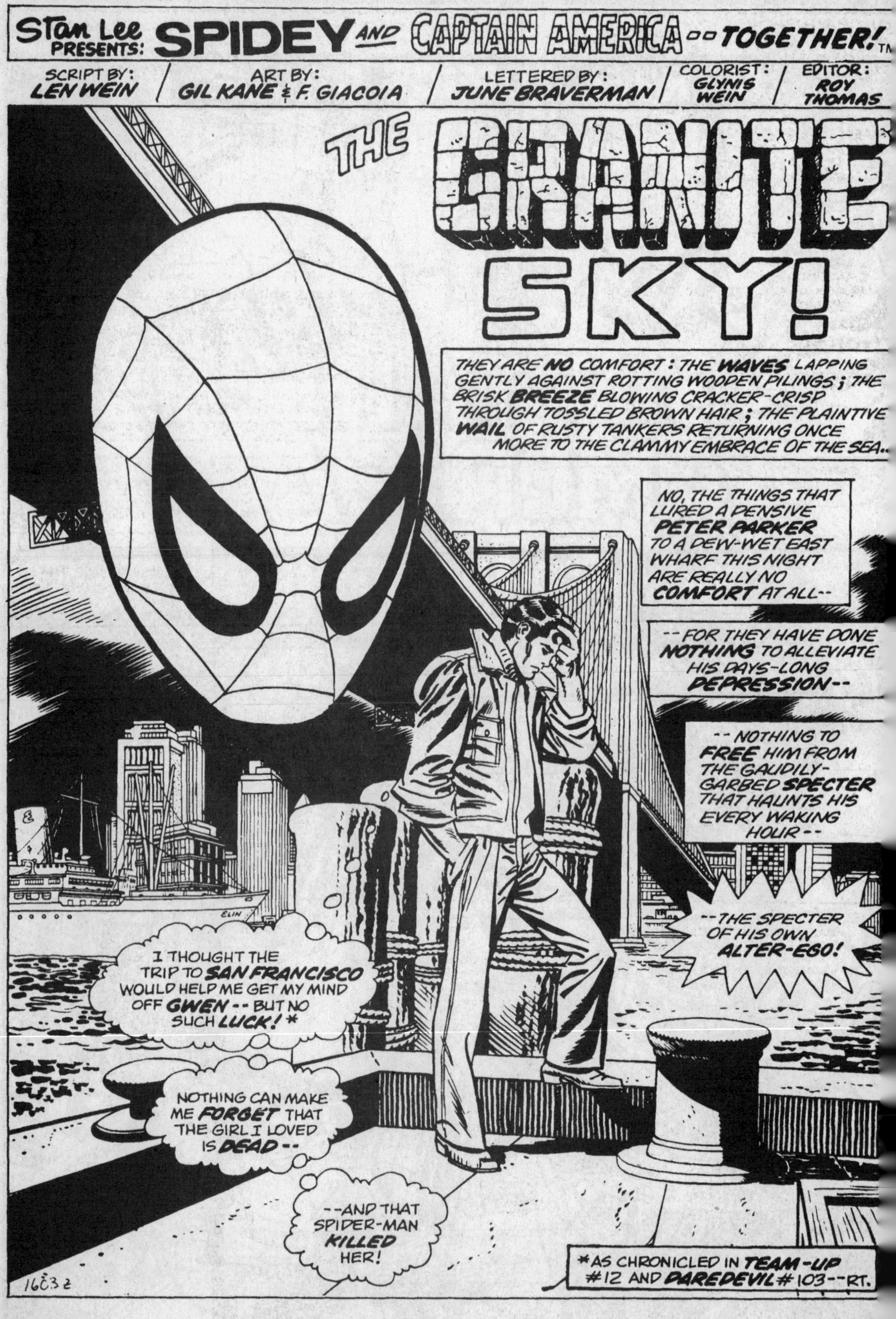
STAN LEE PRESENTS: SPIDEY AND CAPTAIN AMERICA -- TOGETHER!™
SCRIPT BY: LEN WEIN
ART BY: GIL KANE & F. GIACOIA
LETTERED BY: JUNE BRAVERMAN
COLORIST: GLYNIS WEIN
EDITOR: ROY THOMAS
THE GRANITE SKY!
THEY ARE NO COMFORT: THE WAVES LAPPING GENTLY AGAINST ROTTING WOODEN PILINGS; THE BRISK BREEZE BLOWING CRACKER-CRISP THROUGH TOSSLED BROWN HAIR; THE PLAINTIVE WAIL OF RUSTY TANKERS RETURNING ONCE MORE TO THE CLAMMY EMBRACE OF THE SEA..
NO, THE THINGS THAT LURED A PENSIVE PETER PARKER TO A DEW-WET EAST WHARF THIS NIGHT ARE REALLY NO COMFORT AT ALL--
--FOR THEY HAVE DONE NOTHING TO ALLEVIATE HIS DAYS-LONG DEPRESSION--
--NOTHING TO FREE HIM FROM THE GAUDILY-GARBED SPECTER THAT HAUNTS HIS EVERY WAKING HOUR--
--THE SPECTER OF HIS OWN ALTER-EGO!
I THOUGHT THE TRIP TO SAN FRANCISCO WOULD HELP ME GET MY MIND OFF GWEN -- BUT NO SUCH LUCK! *
NOTHING CAN MAKE ME FORGET THAT THE GIRL I LOVED IS DEAD--
--AND THAT SPIDER-MAN KILLED HER!
*AS CHRONICLED IN TEAM-UP #12 AND DAREDEVIL #103--RT.

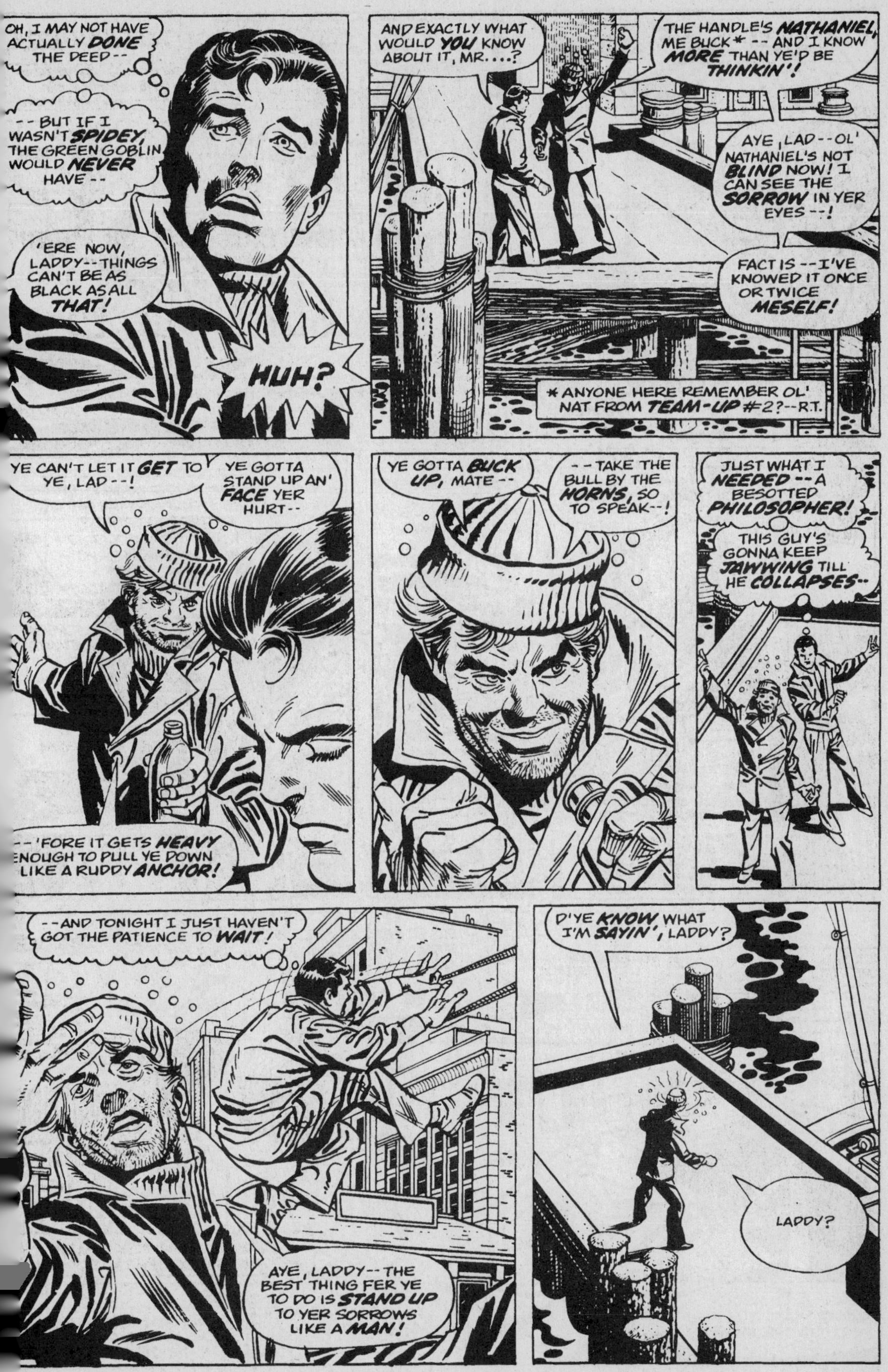

OH, I MAY NOT HAVE ACTUALLY DONE THE DEED--
--BUT IF I WASN'T SPIDEY, THE GREEN GOBLIN WOULD NEVER HAVE--
'ERE NOW, LADDY--THINGS CAN'T BE AS BLACK AS ALL THAT!
HUH?
AND EXACTLY WHAT WOULD YOU KNOW ABOUT IT, MR....?
THE HANDLE'S NATHANIEL, ME BUCK* -- AND I KNOW MORE THAN YE'D BE THINKIN'!
AYE, LAD--OL' NATHANIEL'S NOT BLIND NOW! I CAN SEE THE SORROW IN YER EYES--!
FACT IS--I'VE KNOWED IT ONCE OR TWICE MESELF!
*ANYONE HERE REMEMBER OL' NAT FROM TEAM-UP #2?--R.T.
YE CAN'T LET IT GET TO YE, LAD--!
YE GOTTA STAND UP AN' FACE YER HURT--
--'FORE IT GETS HEAVY ENOUGH TO PULL YE DOWN LIKE A RUDDY ANCHOR!
YE GOTTA BUCK UP, MATE--
--TAKE THE BULL BY THE HORNS, SO TO SPEAK--!
JUST WHAT I NEEDED--A BESOTTED PHILOSOPHER!
THIS GUY'S GONNA KEEP JAWWING TILL HE COLLAPSES--
--AND TONIGHT I JUST HAVEN'T GOT THE PATIENCE TO WAIT!
AYE, LADDY--THE BEST THING FER YE TO DO IS STAND UP TO YER SORROWS LIKE A MAN!
D'YE KNOW WHAT I'M SAYIN', LADDY?
LADDY?

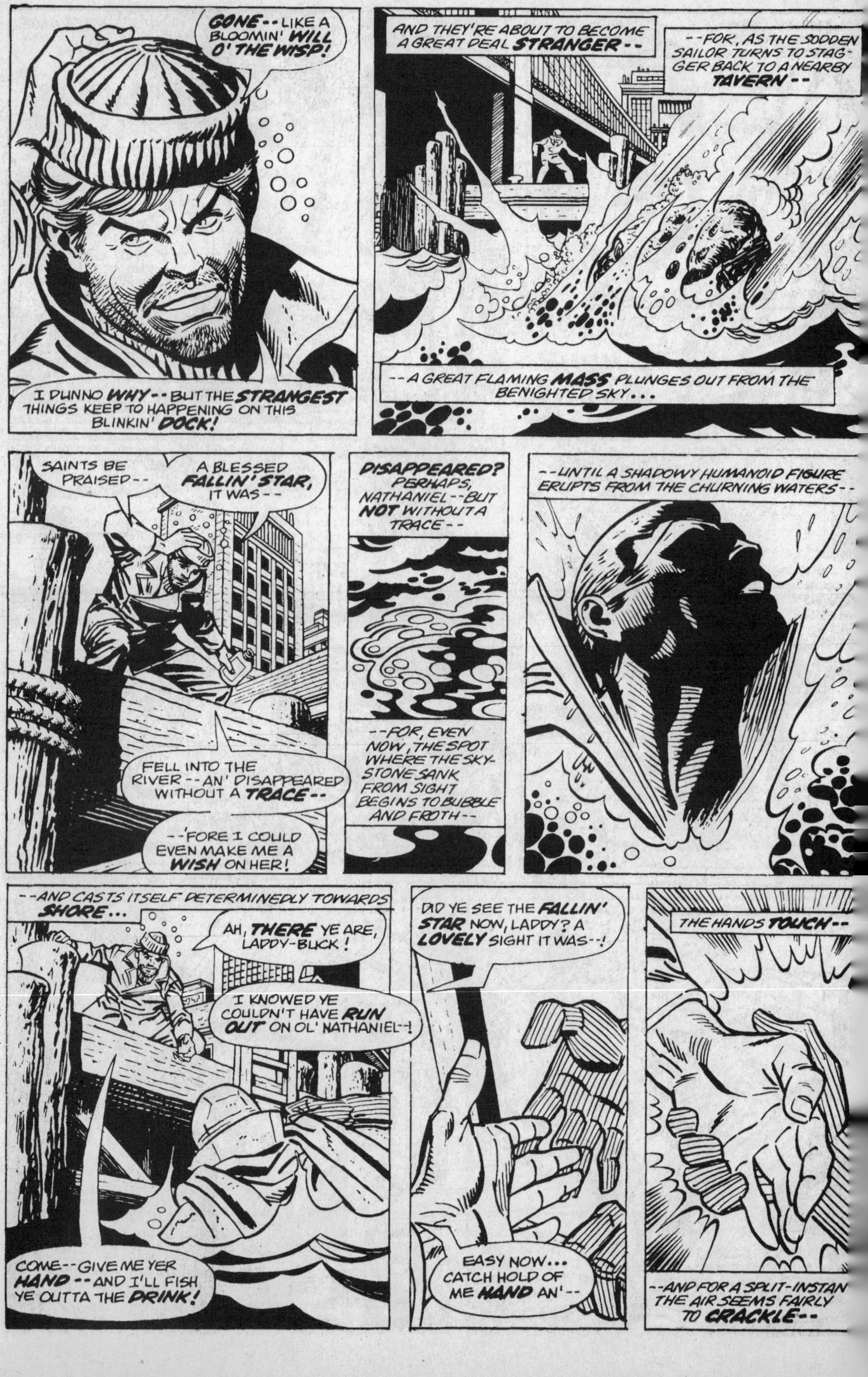
GONE--LIKE A BLOOMIN' WILL O' THE WISP!
I DUNNO WHY--BUT THE STRANGEST THINGS KEEP TO HAPPENING ON THIS BLINKIN' DOCK!
AND THEY'RE ABOUT TO BECOME A GREAT DEAL STRANGER--
--FOR, AS THE SODDEN SAILOR TURNS TO STAGGER BACK TO A NEARBY TAVERN--
--A GREAT FLAMING MASS PLUNGES OUT FROM THE BENIGHTED SKY...
SAINTS BE PRAISED--
A BLESSED FALLIN' STAR, IT WAS--
FELL INTO THE RIVER--AN' DISAPPEARED WITHOUT A TRACE--
--'FORE I COULD EVEN MAKE ME A WISH ON HER!
DISAPPEARED? PERHAPS, NATHANIEL--BUT NOT WITHOUT A TRACE--
--FOR, EVEN NOW, THE SPOT WHERE THE SKY-STONE SANK FROM SIGHT BEGINS TO BUBBLE AND FROTH--
--UNTIL A SHADOWY HUMANOID FIGURE ERUPTS FROM THE CHURNING WATERS--
--AND CASTS ITSELF DETERMINEDLY TOWARDS SHORE...
AH, THERE YE ARE, LADDY-BUCK!
I KNOWED YE COULDN'T HAVE RUN OUT ON OL' NATHANIEL--!
COME--GIVE ME YER HAND--AND I'LL FISH YE OUTTA THE DRINK!
DID YE SEE THE FALLIN' STAR NOW, LADDY? A LOVELY SIGHT IT WAS--!
EASY NOW... CATCH HOLD OF ME HAND AN'--
THE HANDS TOUCH--
--AND FOR A SPLIT-INSTAN THE AIR SEEMS FAIRLY TO CRACKLE--

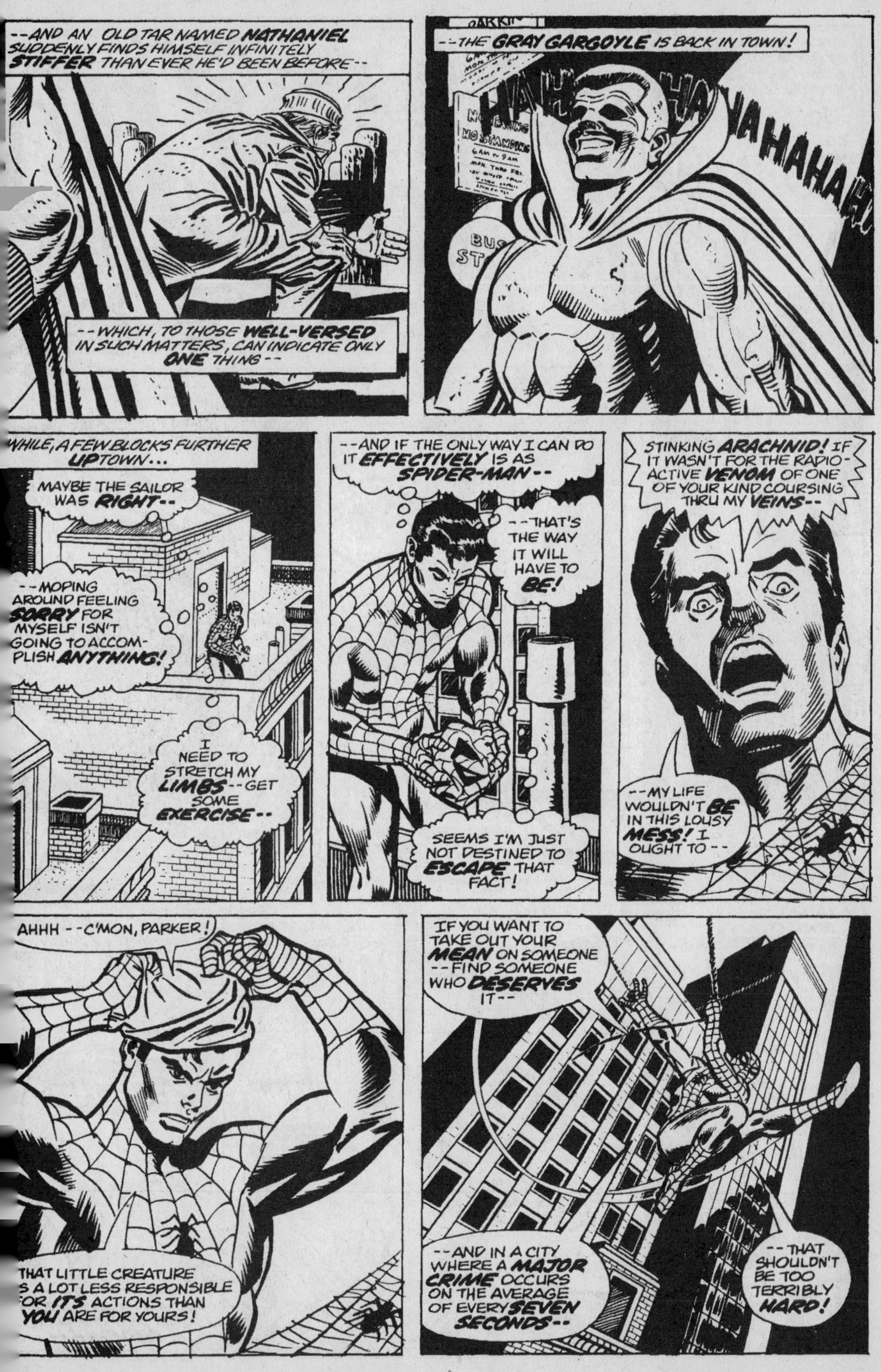
--AND AN OLD TAR NAMED NATHANIEL SUDDENLY FINDS HIMSELF INFINITELY STIFFER THAN EVER HE'D BEEN BEFORE--
--WHICH, TO THOSE WELL-VERSED IN SUCH MATTERS, CAN INDICATE ONLY ONE THING--
--THE GRAY GARGOYLE IS BACK IN TOWN!
HAHAHAHAHAHAHAHAH
NO STANDING
6AM TO 9AM
MON. THRU FRI.
BUS ST
WHILE, A FEW BLOCKS FURTHER UPTOWN...
MAYBE THE SAILOR WAS RIGHT--
--MOPING AROUND FEELING SORRY FOR MYSELF ISN'T GOING TO ACCOMPLISH ANYTHING!
I NEED TO STRETCH MY LIMBS--GET SOME EXERCISE--
--AND IF THE ONLY WAY I CAN DO IT EFFECTIVELY IS AS SPIDER-MAN--
--THAT'S THE WAY IT WILL HAVE TO BE!
SEEMS I'M JUST NOT DESTINED TO ESCAPE THAT FACT!
STINKING ARACHNID! IF IT WASN'T FOR THE RADIO-ACTIVE VENOM OF ONE OF YOUR KIND COURSING THRU MY VEINS--
--MY LIFE WOULDN'T BE IN THIS LOUSY MESS! I OUGHT TO--
AHHH--C'MON, PARKER!
THAT LITTLE CREATURE IS A LOT LESS RESPONSIBLE FOR IT'S ACTIONS THAN YOU ARE FOR YOURS!
IF YOU WANT TO TAKE OUT YOUR MEAN ON SOMEONE --FIND SOMEONE WHO DESERVES IT--
--AND IN A CITY WHERE A MAJOR CRIME OCCURS ON THE AVERAGE OF EVERY SEVEN SECONDS--
--THAT SHOULDN'T BE TOO TERRIBLY HARD!

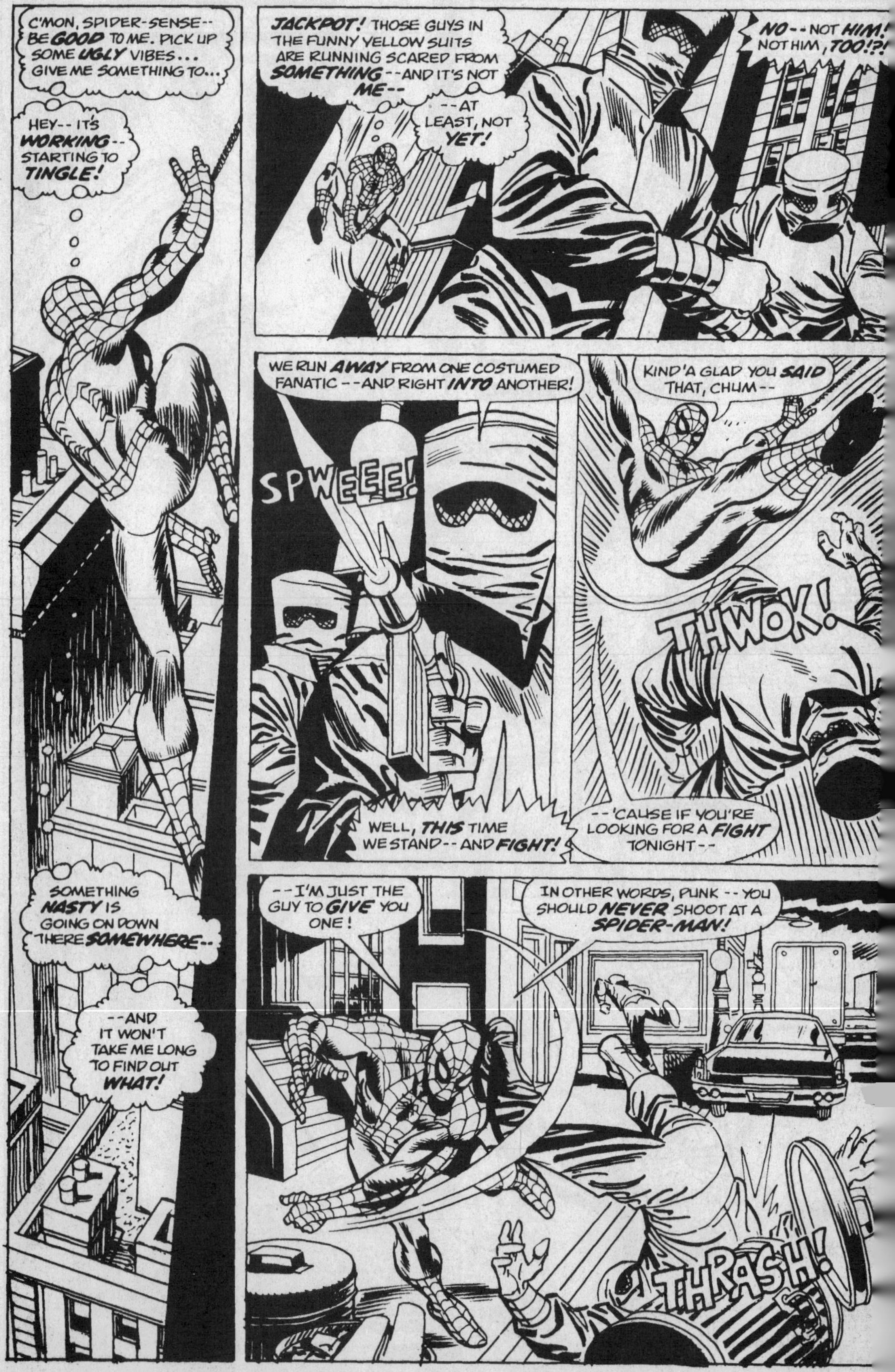
C'MON, SPIDER-SENSE-- BE GOOD TO ME. PICK UP SOME UGLY VIBES... GIVE ME SOMETHING TO...
HEY-- IT'S WORKING-- STARTING TO TINGLE!
SOMETHING NASTY IS GOING ON DOWN THERE SOMEWHERE--
--AND IT WON'T TAKE ME LONG TO FIND OUT WHAT!
JACKPOT! THOSE GUYS IN THE FUNNY YELLOW SUITS ARE RUNNING SCARED FROM SOMETHING--AND IT'S NOT ME--
--AT LEAST, NOT YET!
NO--NOT HIM! NOT HIM, TOO!?!
WE RUN AWAY FROM ONE COSTUMED FANATIC--AND RIGHT INTO ANOTHER!
SPWEEEE!
WELL, THIS TIME WE STAND--AND FIGHT!
KIND'A GLAD YOU SAID THAT, CHUM--
THWOK!
--'CAUSE IF YOU'RE LOOKING FOR A FIGHT TONIGHT--
--I'M JUST THE GUY TO GIVE YOU ONE!
IN OTHER WORDS, PUNK--YOU SHOULD NEVER SHOOT AT A SPIDER-MAN!
THRASH!

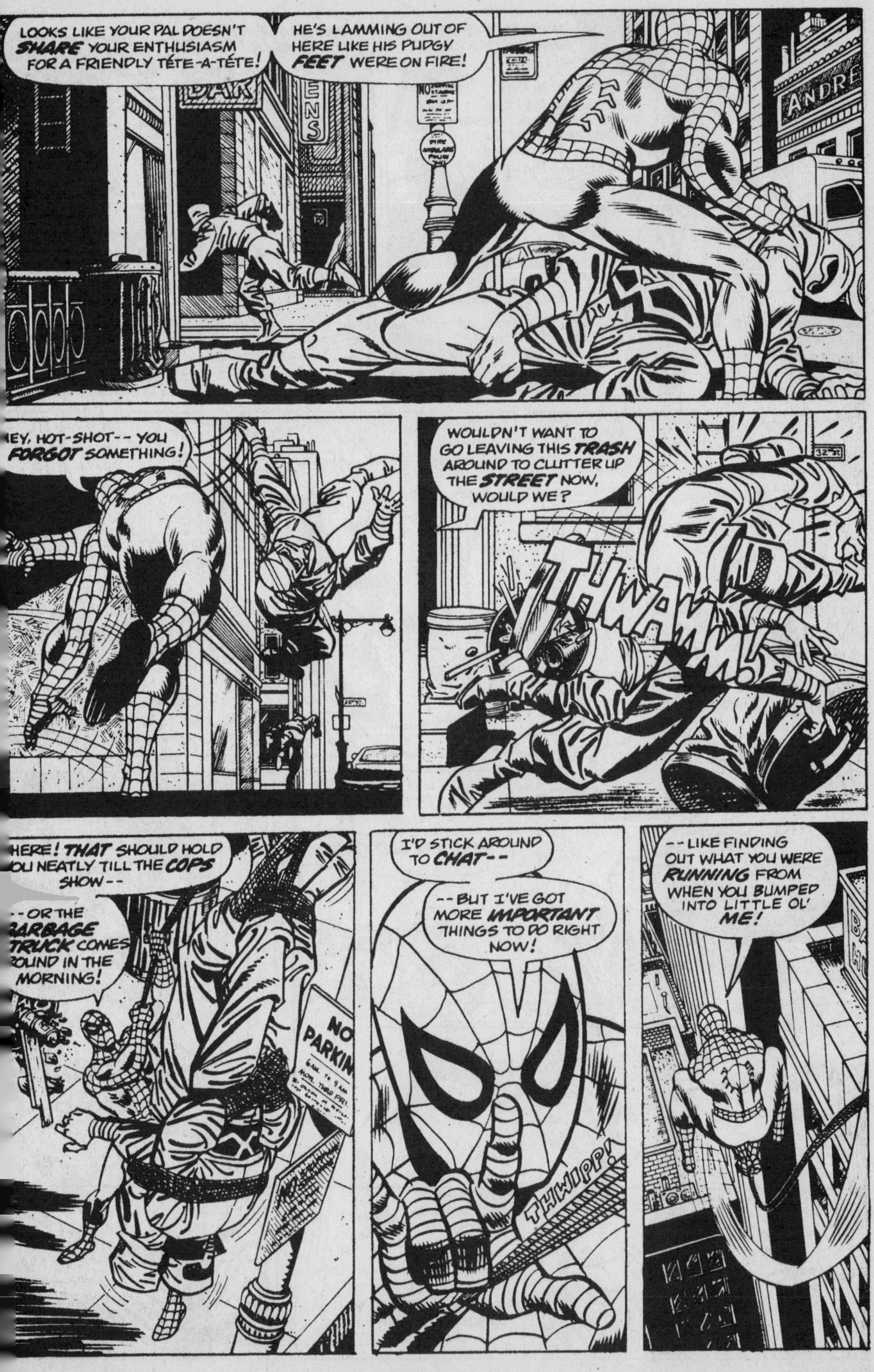

LOOKS LIKE YOUR PAL DOESN'T SHARE YOUR ENTHUSIASM FOR A FRIENDLY TÉTE-A-TÉTE!
HE'S LAMMING OUT OF HERE LIKE HIS PUDGY FEET WERE ON FIRE!
ANDRE
HEY, HOT-SHOT-- YOU FORGOT SOMETHING!
WOULDN'T WANT TO GO LEAVING THIS TRASH AROUND TO CLUTTER UP THE STREET NOW, WOULD WE?
32ND ST
THWAMM!
HERE! THAT SHOULD HOLD YOU NEATLY TILL THE COPS SHOW--
--OR THE GARBAGE TRUCK COMES AROUND IN THE MORNING!
NO PARKING
I'D STICK AROUND TO CHAT--
--BUT I'VE GOT MORE IMPORTANT THINGS TO DO RIGHT NOW!
THWIPP!
--LIKE FINDING OUT WHAT YOU WERE RUNNING FROM WHEN YOU BUMPED INTO LITTLE OL' ME!

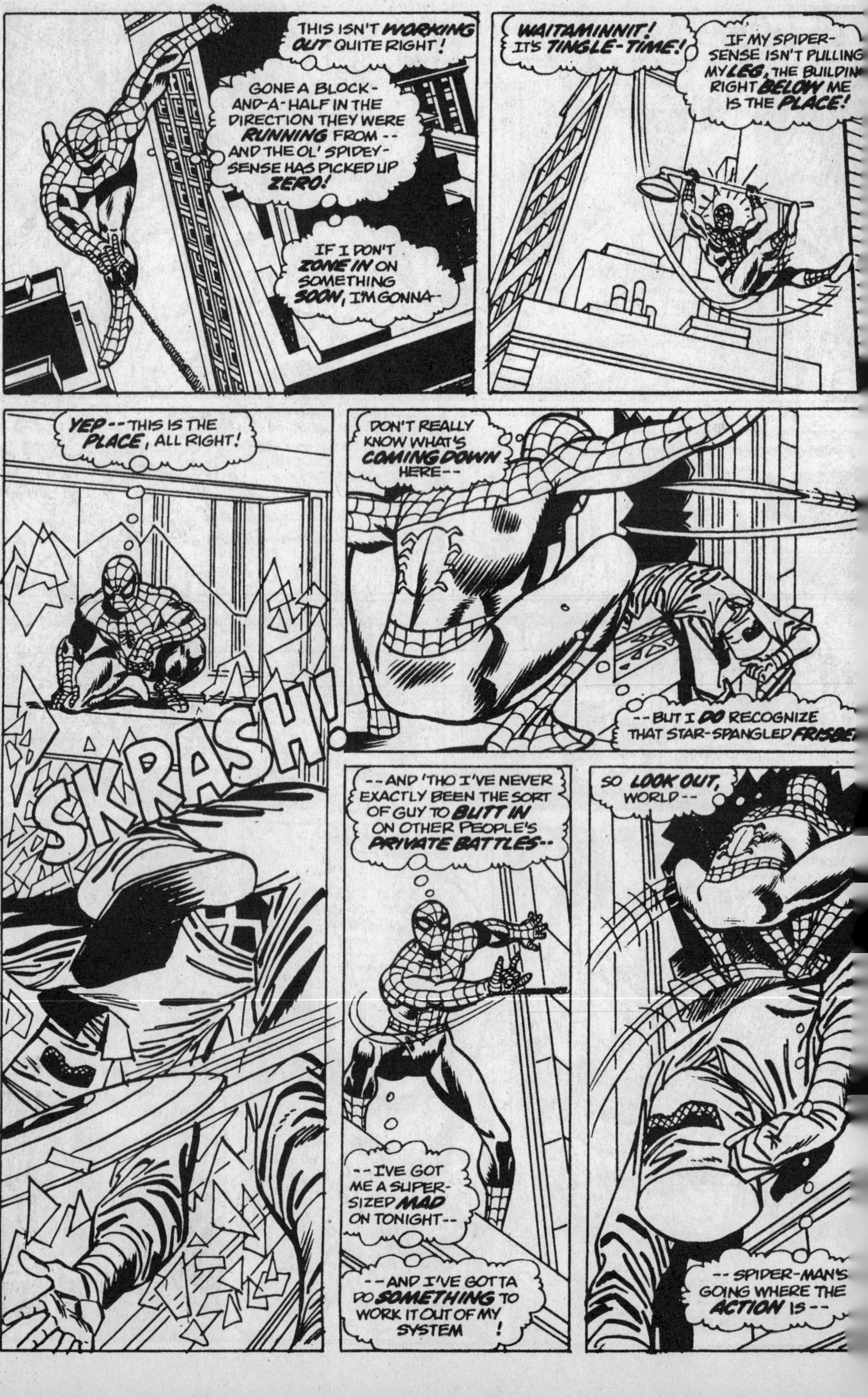
THIS ISN'T WORKING OUT QUITE RIGHT!
GONE A BLOCK-AND-A-HALF IN THE DIRECTION THEY WERE RUNNING FROM -- AND THE OL' SPIDEY-SENSE HAS PICKED UP ZERO!
IF I DON'T ZONE IN ON SOMETHING SOON, I'M GONNA--
WAITAMINNIT! IT'S TINGLE-TIME!
IF MY SPIDER-SENSE ISN'T PULLING MY LEG, THE BUILDING RIGHT BELOW ME IS THE PLACE!
YEP -- THIS IS THE PLACE, ALL RIGHT!
SKRASH!
DON'T REALLY KNOW WHAT'S COMING DOWN HERE--
-- BUT I DO RECOGNIZE THAT STAR-SPANGLED FRISBEE
-- AND 'THO I'VE NEVER EXACTLY BEEN THE SORT OF GUY TO BUTT IN ON OTHER PEOPLE'S PRIVATE BATTLES--
-- I'VE GOT ME A SUPER-SIZED MAD ON TONIGHT--
-- AND I'VE GOTTA DO SOMETHING TO WORK IT OUT OF MY SYSTEM!
SO LOOK OUT, WORLD --
-- SPIDER-MAN'S GOING WHERE THE ACTION IS --

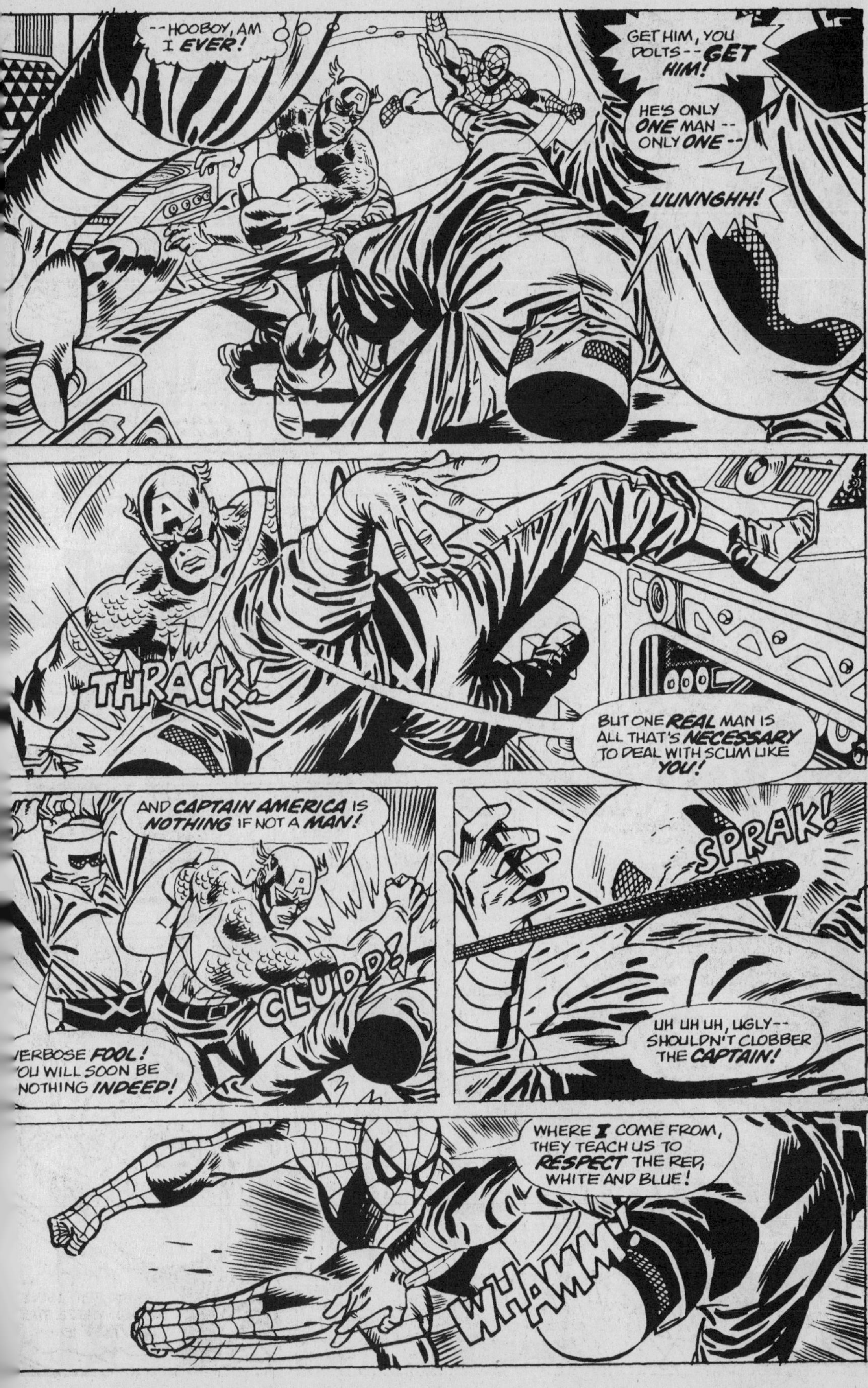

--HOOBOY, AM I EVER!
GET HIM, YOU DOLTS--GET HIM!
HE'S ONLY ONE MAN--ONLY ONE--
UUNNGHH!
THRACK!
BUT ONE REAL MAN IS ALL THAT'S NECESSARY TO DEAL WITH SCUM LIKE YOU!
AND CAPTAIN AMERICA IS NOTHING IF NOT A MAN!
CLUDD!
VERBOSE FOOL! YOU WILL SOON BE NOTHING INDEED!
SPRAK!
UH UH UH, UGLY--SHOULDN'T CLOBBER THE CAPTAIN!
WHERE I COME FROM, THEY TEACH US TO RESPECT THE RED, WHITE AND BLUE!
WHAMM!

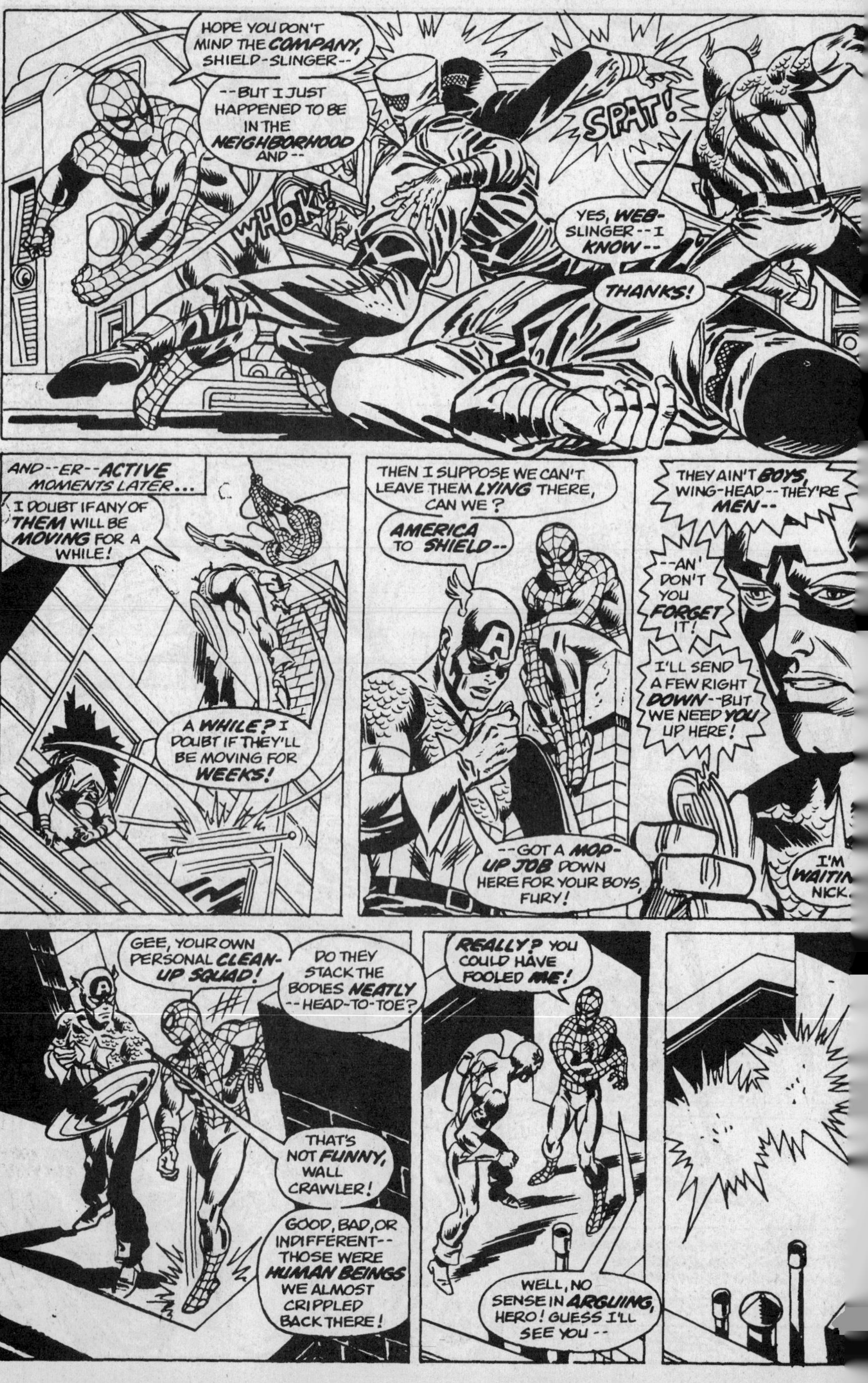
HOPE YOU DON'T MIND THE COMPANY, SHIELD-SLINGER--
--BUT I JUST HAPPENED TO BE IN THE NEIGHBORHOOD AND--
WHOK!
SPAT!
YES, WEB-SLINGER--I KNOW--
THANKS!
AND--ER--ACTIVE MOMENTS LATER...
I DOUBT IF ANY OF THEM WILL BE MOVING FOR A WHILE!
A WHILE? I DOUBT IF THEY'LL BE MOVING FOR WEEKS!
THEN I SUPPOSE WE CAN'T LEAVE THEM LYING THERE, CAN WE?
AMERICA TO SHIELD--
--GOT A MOP-UP JOB DOWN HERE FOR YOUR BOYS, FURY!
THEY AIN'T BOYS, WING-HEAD--THEY'RE MEN--
--AN' DON'T YOU FORGET IT!
I'LL SEND A FEW RIGHT DOWN--BUT WE NEED YOU UP HERE!
I'M WAITIN NICK.
GEE, YOUR OWN PERSONAL CLEAN-UP SQUAD!
DO THEY STACK THE BODIES NEATLY--HEAD-TO-TOE?
THAT'S NOT FUNNY, WALL CRAWLER!
GOOD, BAD, OR INDIFFERENT--THOSE WERE HUMAN BEINGS WE ALMOST CRIPPLED BACK THERE!
REALLY? YOU COULD HAVE FOOLED ME!
WELL, NO SENSE IN ARGUING, HERO! GUESS I'LL SEE YOU--

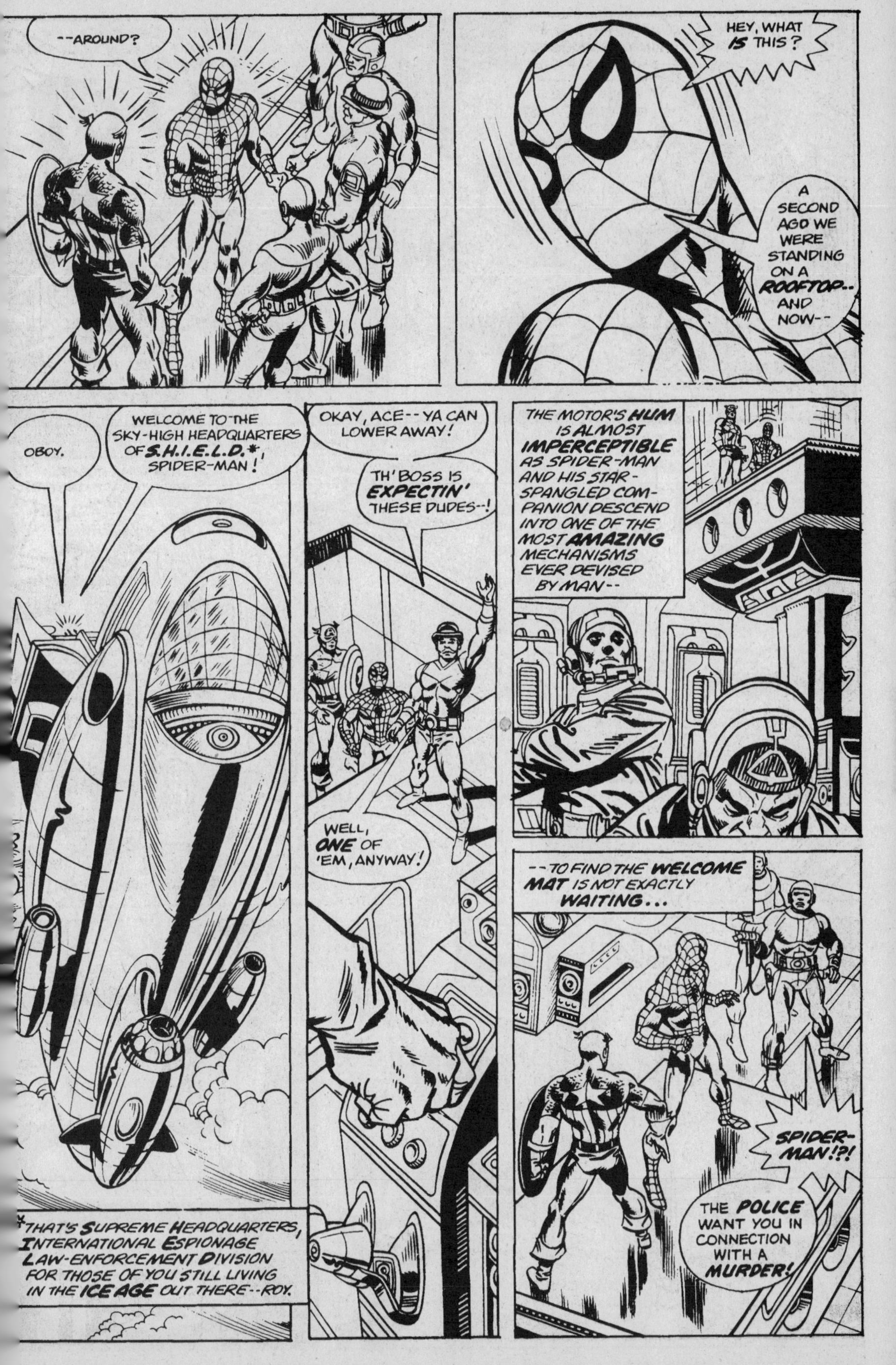
--AROUND?
HEY, WHAT IS THIS?
A SECOND AGO WE WERE STANDING ON A ROOFTOP-- AND NOW--
OBOY.
WELCOME TO THE SKY-HIGH HEADQUARTERS OF S.H.I.E.L.D.*, SPIDER-MAN!
*THAT'S SUPREME HEADQUARTERS, INTERNATIONAL ESPIONAGE LAW-ENFORCEMENT DIVISION FOR THOSE OF YOU STILL LIVING IN THE ICE AGE OUT THERE--ROY.
OKAY, ACE--YA CAN LOWER AWAY!
TH' BOSS IS EXPECTIN' THESE DUDES--!
WELL, ONE OF 'EM, ANYWAY!
THE MOTOR'S HUM IS ALMOST IMPERCEPTIBLE AS SPIDER-MAN AND HIS STAR-SPANGLED COMPANION DESCEND INTO ONE OF THE MOST AMAZING MECHANISMS EVER DEVISED BY MAN--
--TO FIND THE WELCOME MAT IS NOT EXACTLY WAITING...
SPIDER-MAN!?!
THE POLICE WANT YOU IN CONNECTION WITH A MURDER!

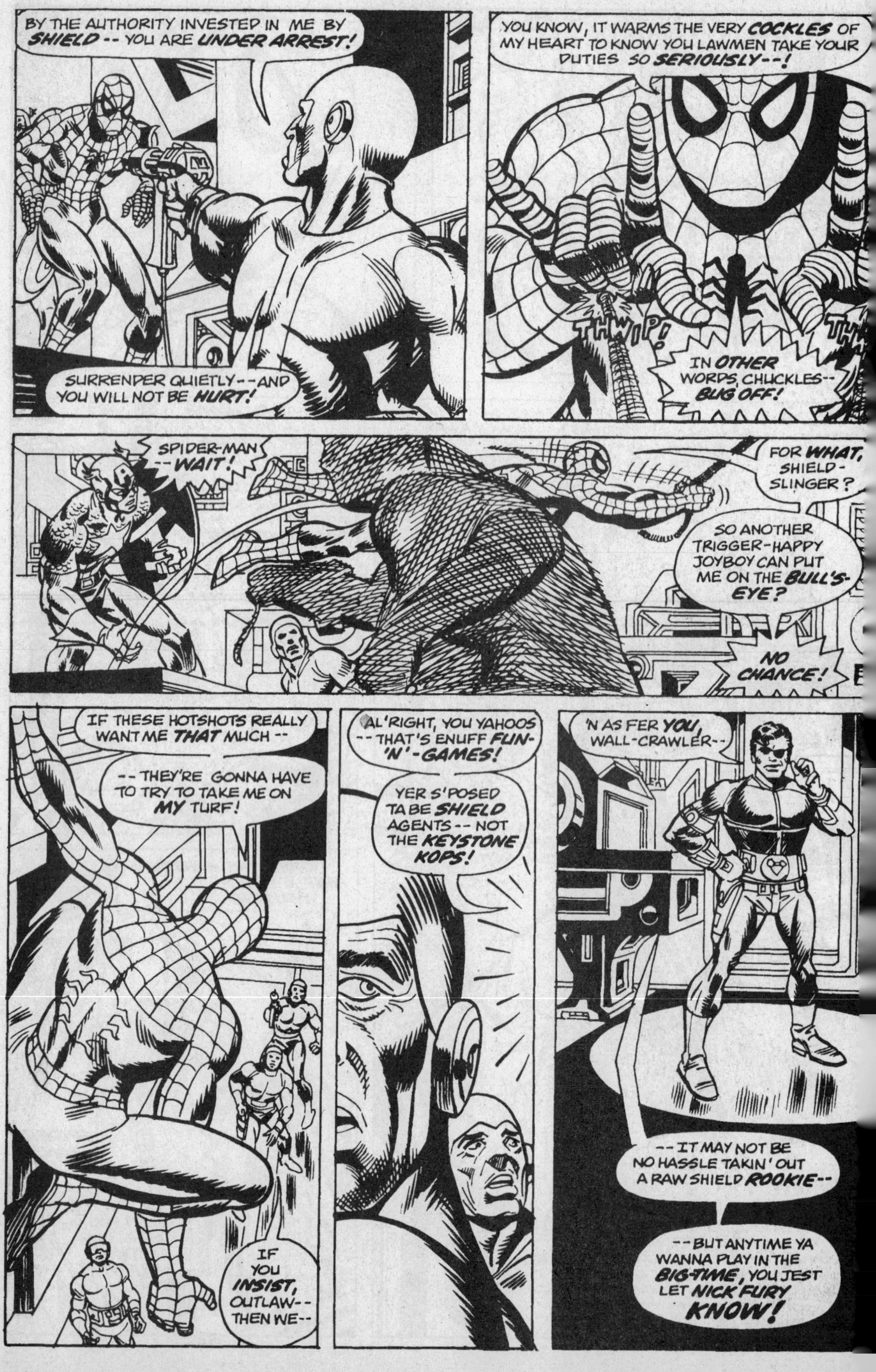
BY THE AUTHORITY INVESTED IN ME BY SHIELD -- YOU ARE UNDER ARREST!
SURRENDER QUIETLY--AND YOU WILL NOT BE HURT!
YOU KNOW, IT WARMS THE VERY COCKLES OF MY HEART TO KNOW YOU LAWMEN TAKE YOUR DUTIES SO SERIOUSLY--!
THWIP!
IN OTHER WORDS, CHUCKLES-- BUG OFF!
SPIDER-MAN --WAIT!
FOR WHAT, SHIELD-SLINGER?
SO ANOTHER TRIGGER-HAPPY JOYBOY CAN PUT ME ON THE BULL'S-EYE?
NO CHANCE!
IF THESE HOTSHOTS REALLY WANT ME THAT MUCH --
-- THEY'RE GONNA HAVE TO TRY TO TAKE ME ON MY TURF!
IF YOU INSIST, OUTLAW-- THEN WE--
AL'RIGHT, YOU YAHOOS -- THAT'S ENUFF FUN-'N'-GAMES!
YER S'POSED TA BE SHIELD AGENTS -- NOT THE KEYSTONE KOPS!
'N AS FER YOU, WALL-CRAWLER--
--IT MAY NOT BE NO HASSLE TAKIN' OUT A RAW SHIELD ROOKIE--
--BUT ANYTIME YA WANNA PLAY IN THE BIG-TIME, YOU JEST LET NICK FURY KNOW!

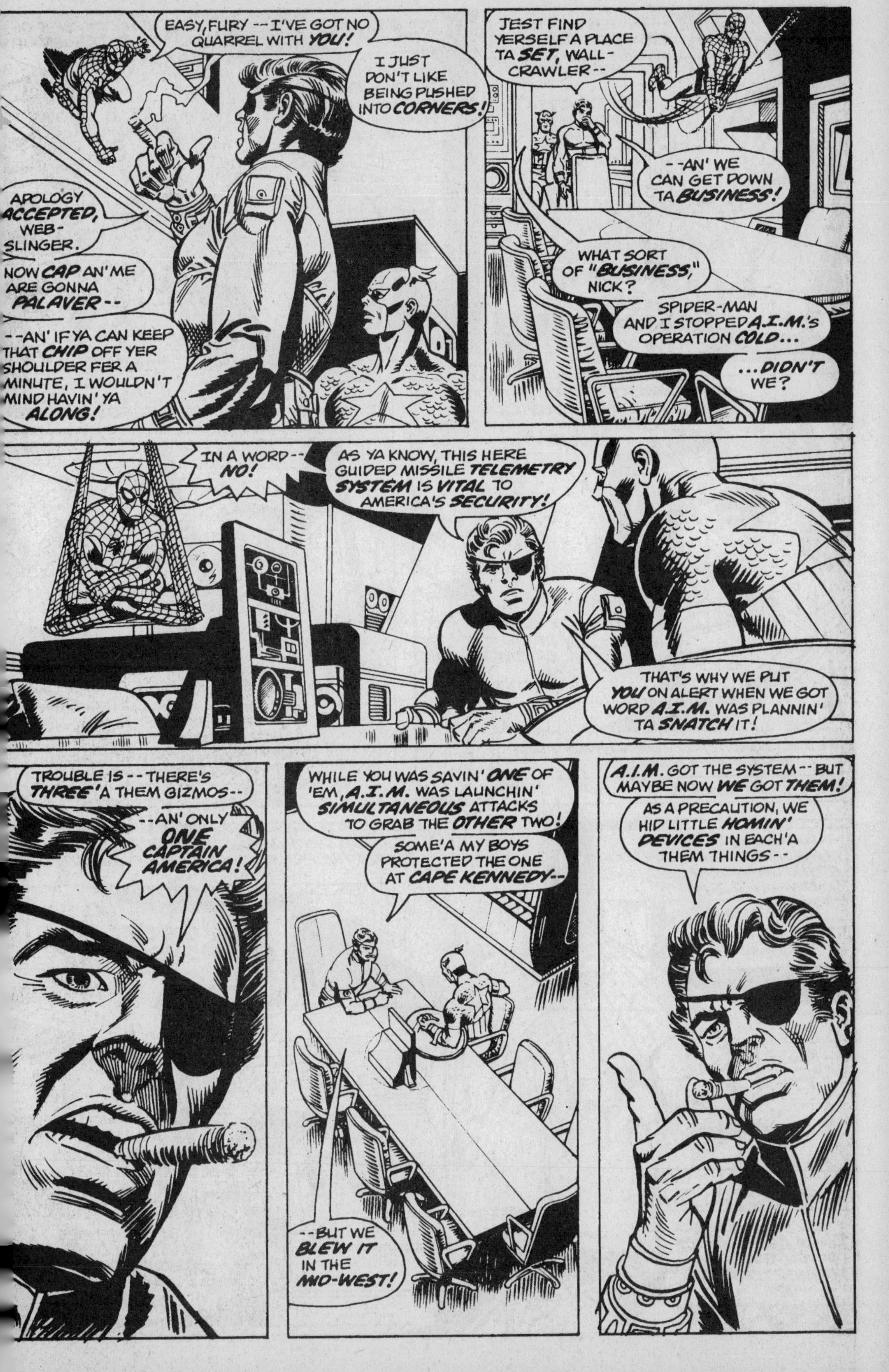
EASY, FURY -- I'VE GOT NO QUARREL WITH YOU!
I JUST DON'T LIKE BEING PUSHED INTO CORNERS!
APOLOGY ACCEPTED, WEB-SLINGER.
NOW CAP AN' ME ARE GONNA PALAVER --
--AN' IF YA CAN KEEP THAT CHIP OFF YER SHOULDER FER A MINUTE, I WOULDN'T MIND HAVIN' YA ALONG!
JEST FIND YERSELF A PLACE TA SET, WALL-CRAWLER --
--AN' WE CAN GET DOWN TA BUSINESS!
WHAT SORT OF "BUSINESS," NICK?
SPIDER-MAN AND I STOPPED A.I.M.'s OPERATION COLD...
...DIDN'T WE?
IN A WORD-- NO!
AS YA KNOW, THIS HERE GUIDED MISSILE TELEMETRY SYSTEM IS VITAL TO AMERICA'S SECURITY!
THAT'S WHY WE PUT YOU ON ALERT WHEN WE GOT WORD A.I.M. WAS PLANNIN' TA SNATCH IT!
TROUBLE IS -- THERE'S THREE 'A THEM GIZMOS --
--AN' ONLY ONE CAPTAIN AMERICA!
WHILE YOU WAS SAVIN' ONE OF 'EM, A.I.M. WAS LAUNCHIN' SIMULTANEOUS ATTACKS TO GRAB THE OTHER TWO!
SOME'A MY BOYS PROTECTED THE ONE AT CAPE KENNEDY --
--BUT WE BLEW IT IN THE MID-WEST!
A.I.M. GOT THE SYSTEM -- BUT MAYBE NOW WE GOT THEM!
AS A PRECAUTION, WE HID LITTLE HOMIN' DEVICES IN EACH'A THEM THINGS --

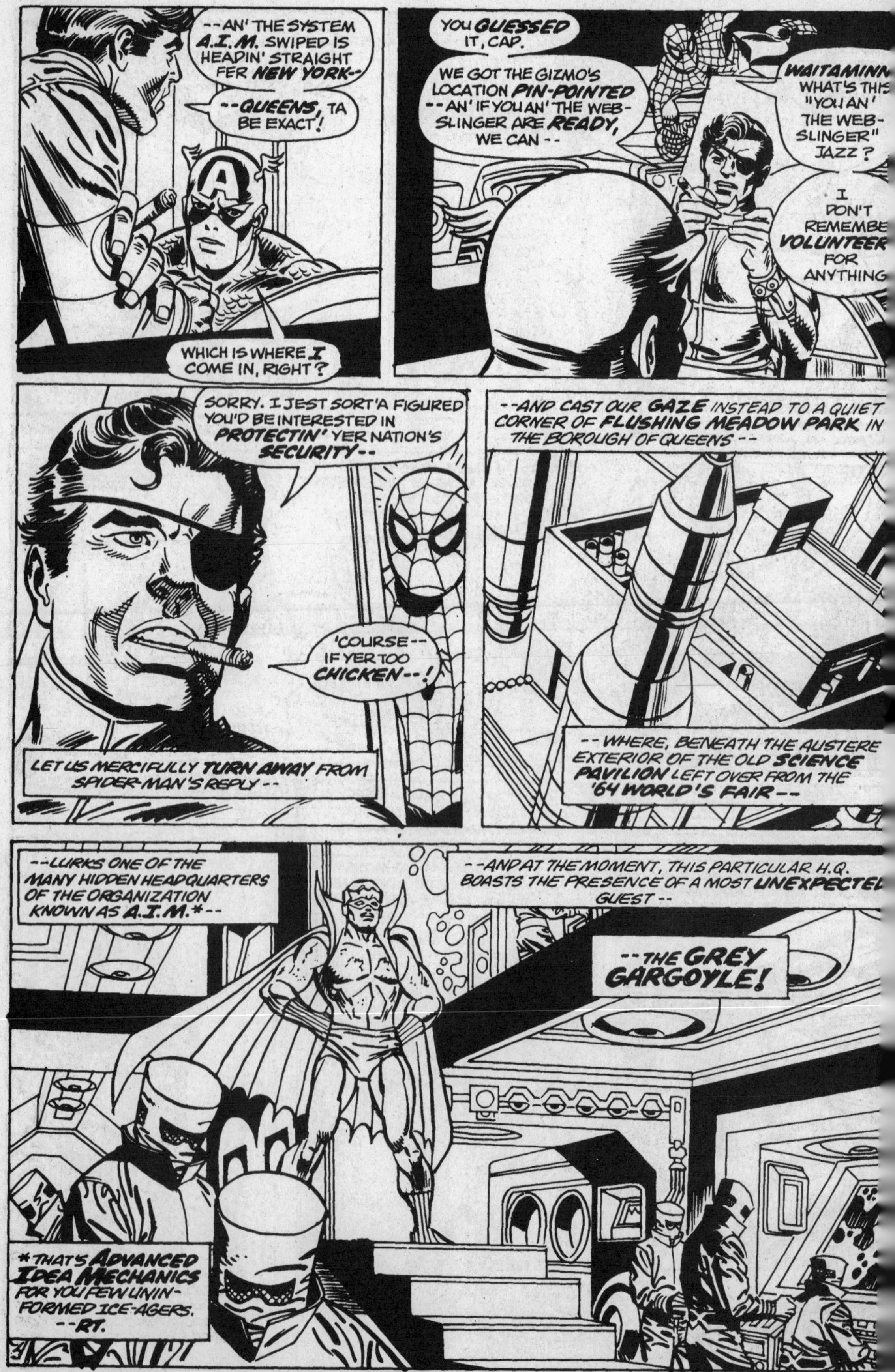
--AN' THE SYSTEM A.I.M. SWIPED IS HEADIN' STRAIGHT FER NEW YORK--
--QUEENS, TA BE EXACT!
WHICH IS WHERE I COME IN, RIGHT?
YOU GUESSED IT, CAP.
WE GOT THE GIZMO'S LOCATION PIN-POINTED --AN' IF YOU AN' THE WEB-SLINGER ARE READY, WE CAN --
WAITAMINN WHAT'S THIS "YOU AN' THE WEB-SLINGER" JAZZ?
I DON'T REMEMBE VOLUNTEER FOR ANYTHING
SORRY. I JEST SORT'A FIGURED YOU'D BE INTERESTED IN PROTECTIN' YER NATION'S SECURITY--
'COURSE-- IF YER TOO CHICKEN--!
LET US MERCIFULLY TURN AWAY FROM SPIDER-MAN'S REPLY--
--AND CAST OUR GAZE INSTEAD TO A QUIET CORNER OF FLUSHING MEADOW PARK IN THE BOROUGH OF QUEENS--
--WHERE, BENEATH THE AUSTERE EXTERIOR OF THE OLD SCIENCE PAVILION LEFT OVER FROM THE '64 WORLD'S FAIR--
--LURKS ONE OF THE MANY HIDDEN HEADQUARTERS OF THE ORGANIZATION KNOWN AS A.I.M.*--
--AND AT THE MOMENT, THIS PARTICULAR H.Q. BOASTS THE PRESENCE OF A MOST UNEXPECTED GUEST--
--THE GREY GARGOYLE!
*THAT'S ADVANCED IDEA MECHANICS FOR YOU FEW UNINFORMED ICE-AGERS. --RT.

CAN'T YOUR UNDERLINGS WORK ANY FASTER, PRIME-4?

OUR "LAUNCH WINDOW" IS ONLY HOURS AWAY -- AND WE CANNOT AFFORD TO MISS IT!

THE PROJECT IS PROGRESSING SWIFTER THAN IT APPEARS, STONE ONE!

IT MAY WELL BE COMPLETED AHEAD OF SCHEDULE.

SPLENDID! A FEW SHORT HOURS, THEN -- AND I SHALL HAVE MY REVENGE AGAINST THE WORLD --

-- AND CAPTAIN AMERICA IN PARTICULAR!

" I WILL NOT FORGET HOW HE TRICKED ME WHEN LAST WE MET --

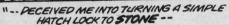

" -- DECEIVED ME INTO TURNING A SIMPLE HATCH LOCK TO STONE --

" THUS IMPRISONING ME IN A GREAT GRANITE MISSILE -- WHILE THAT ACCURSED AVENGER AND HIS COMPANION, THE FALCON, MADE GOOD THEIR ESCAPE --

" -- IMPRISONING ME JUST LONG ENOUGH FOR COLONEL NICK FURY, THE DIRECTOR OF SHIELD TO COMPLETE A DESPERATE COUNT-DOWN --

" -- AND LAUNCH THE MISSILE SPACEWARD --

" -- WITH MYSELF STILL INSIDE! *

* THE PRECEDING FLASHBACK HAS BEEN BROUGHT TO YOU THROUGH THE COURTESY OF CAPTAIN AMERICA #142.
--R.T.

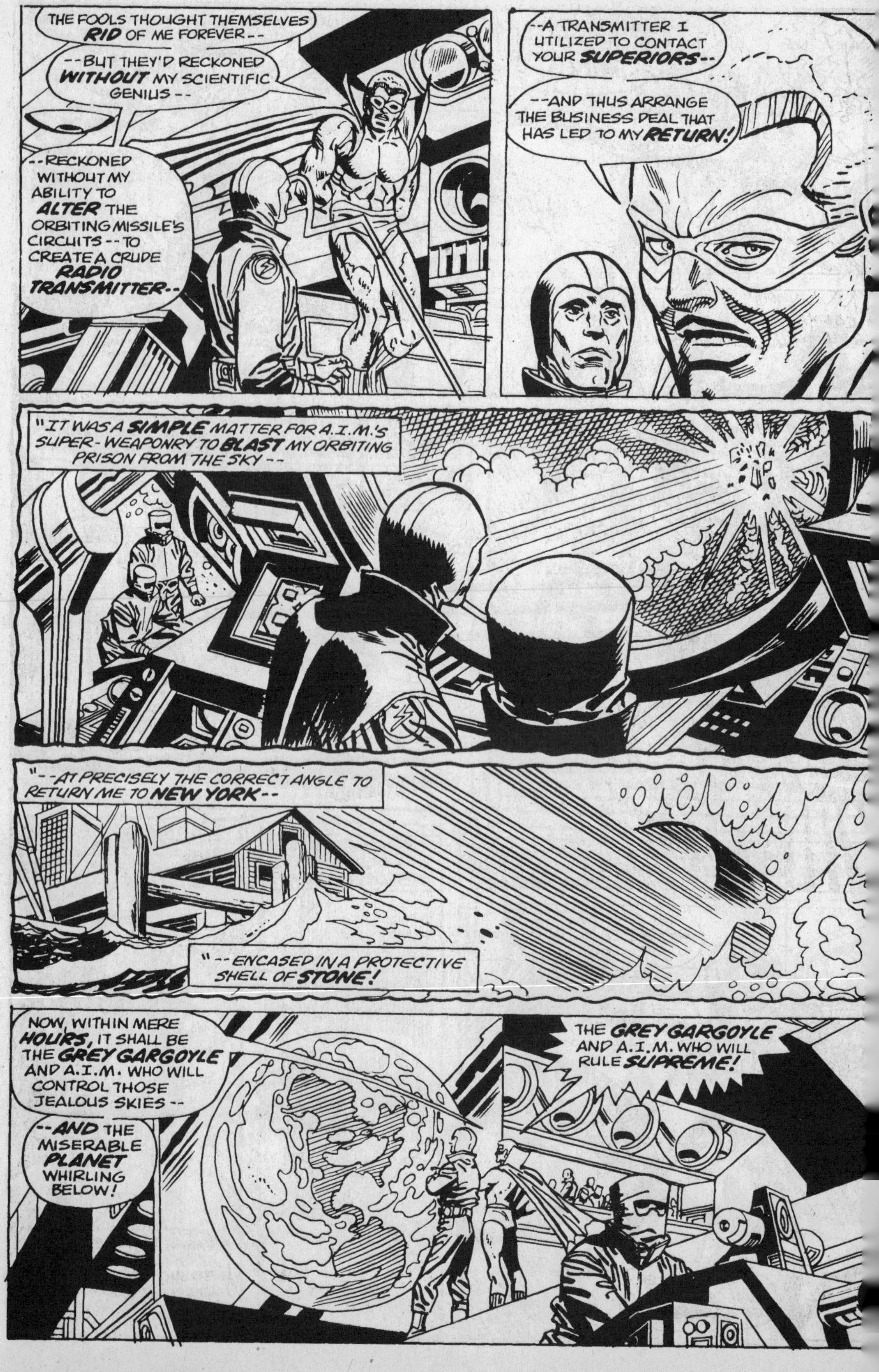
THE FOOLS THOUGHT THEMSELVES RID OF ME FOREVER--
--BUT THEY'D RECKONED WITHOUT MY SCIENTIFIC GENIUS--
--RECKONED WITHOUT MY ABILITY TO ALTER THE ORBITING MISSILE'S CIRCUITS--TO CREATE A CRUDE RADIO TRANSMITTER--
--A TRANSMITTER I UTILIZED TO CONTACT YOUR SUPERIORS--
--AND THUS ARRANGE THE BUSINESS DEAL THAT HAS LED TO MY RETURN!
"IT WAS A SIMPLE MATTER FOR A.I.M.'S SUPER-WEAPONRY TO BLAST MY ORBITING PRISON FROM THE SKY--
"--AT PRECISELY THE CORRECT ANGLE TO RETURN ME TO NEW YORK--
"--ENCASED IN A PROTECTIVE SHELL OF STONE!
NOW, WITHIN MERE HOURS, IT SHALL BE THE GREY GARGOYLE AND A.I.M. WHO WILL CONTROL THOSE JEALOUS SKIES--
--AND THE MISERABLE PLANET WHIRLING BELOW!
THE GREY GARGOYLE AND A.I.M. WHO WILL RULE SUPREME!

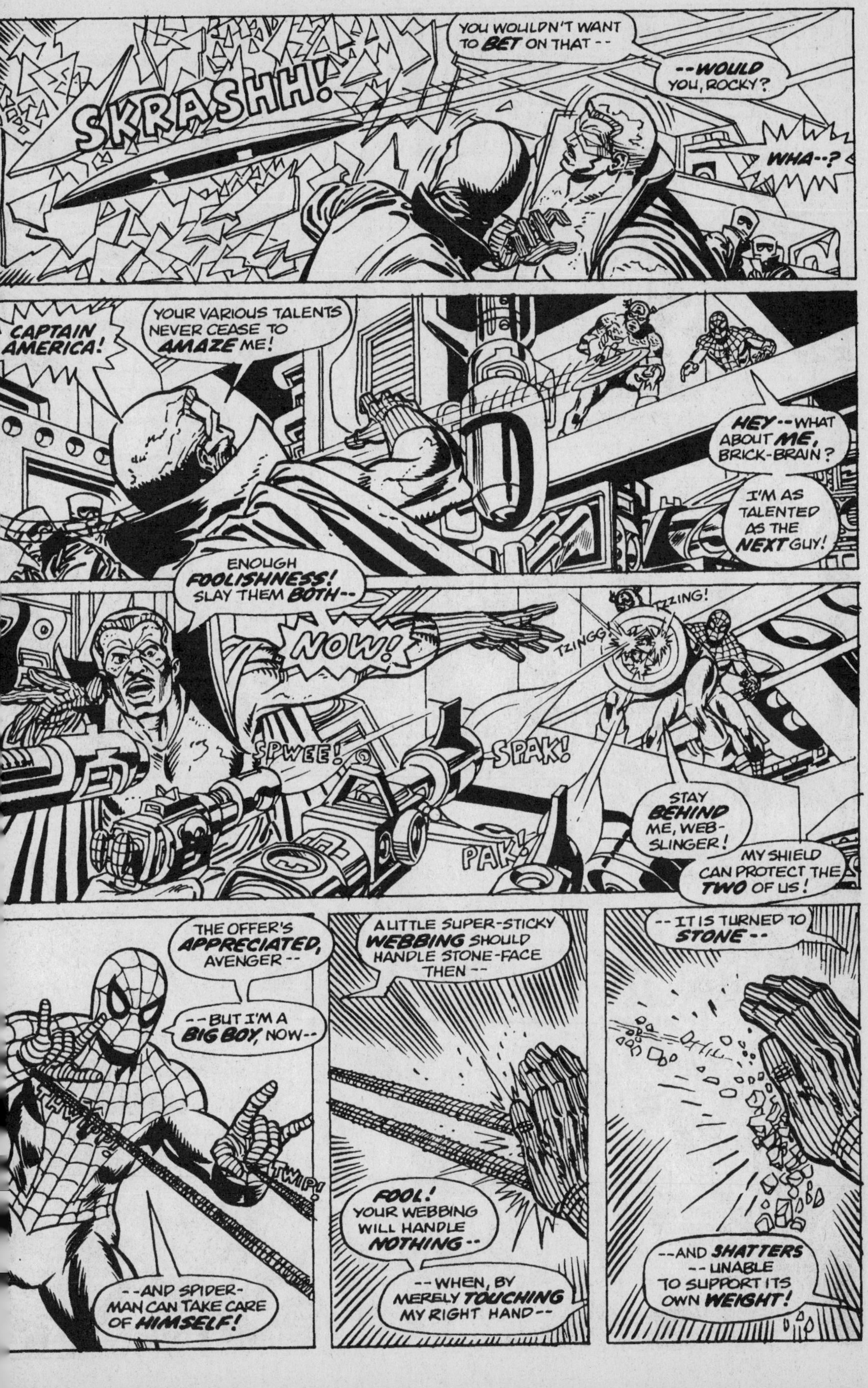
SKRASHH!
YOU WOULDN'T WANT TO BET ON THAT --
--WOULD YOU, ROCKY?
WHA--?
CAPTAIN AMERICA!
YOUR VARIOUS TALENTS NEVER CEASE TO AMAZE ME!
HEY--WHAT ABOUT ME, BRICK-BRAIN?
I'M AS TALENTED AS THE NEXT GUY!
ENOUGH FOOLISHNESS! SLAY THEM BOTH--
NOW!
TZZING!
TZINGG!
SPWEE!
SPAK!
PAK!
STAY BEHIND ME, WEB-SLINGER!
MY SHIELD CAN PROTECT THE TWO OF US!
THE OFFER'S APPRECIATED, AVENGER--
--BUT I'M A BIG BOY, NOW--
TWIP!
--AND SPIDER-MAN CAN TAKE CARE OF HIMSELF!
A LITTLE SUPER-STICKY WEBBING SHOULD HANDLE STONE-FACE THEN--
FOOL! YOUR WEBBING WILL HANDLE NOTHING--
--WHEN, BY MERELY TOUCHING MY RIGHT HAND--
--IT IS TURNED TO STONE--
--AND SHATTERS --UNABLE TO SUPPORT ITS OWN WEIGHT!

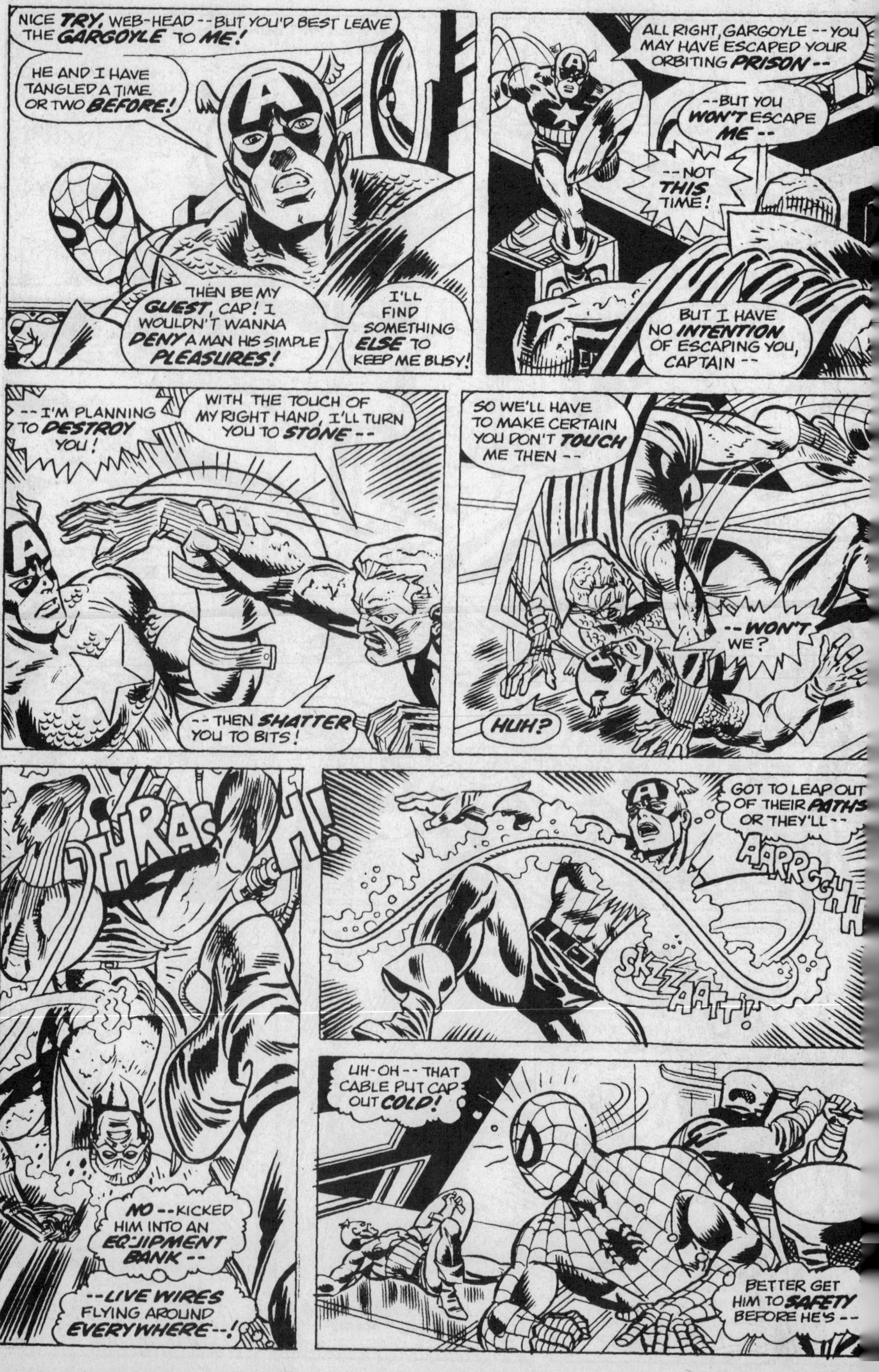
NICE TRY, WEB-HEAD -- BUT YOU'D BEST LEAVE THE GARGOYLE TO ME!
HE AND I HAVE TANGLED A TIME OR TWO BEFORE!
THEN BE MY GUEST, CAP! I WOULDN'T WANNA DENY A MAN HIS SIMPLE PLEASURES!
I'LL FIND SOMETHING ELSE TO KEEP ME BUSY!
ALL RIGHT, GARGOYLE -- YOU MAY HAVE ESCAPED YOUR ORBITING PRISON --
--BUT YOU WON'T ESCAPE ME --
-- NOT THIS TIME!
BUT I HAVE NO INTENTION OF ESCAPING YOU, CAPTAIN --
-- I'M PLANNING TO DESTROY YOU!
WITH THE TOUCH OF MY RIGHT HAND, I'LL TURN YOU TO STONE --
-- THEN SHATTER YOU TO BITS!
SO WE'LL HAVE TO MAKE CERTAIN YOU DON'T TOUCH ME THEN --
-- WON'T WE?
HUH?
THRASH!
GOT TO LEAP OUT OF THEIR PATHS OR THEY'LL --
AARRGGHH
SKZZAATT!
NO -- KICKED HIM INTO AN EQUIPMENT BANK --
-- LIVE WIRES FLYING AROUND EVERYWHERE --!
UH-OH -- THAT CABLE PUT CAP OUT COLD!
BETTER GET HIM TO SAFETY BEFORE HE'S --

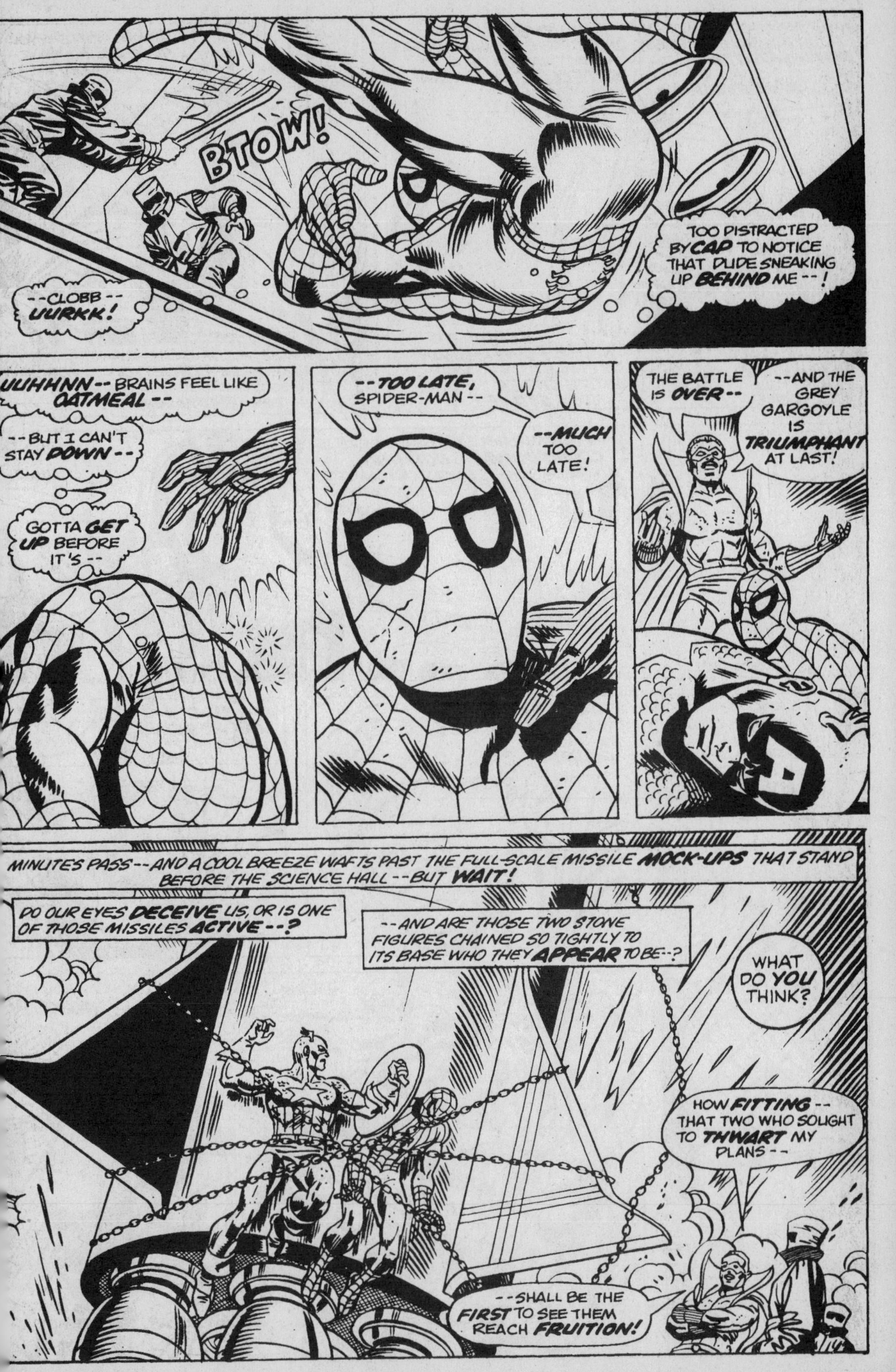
BTOW!
TOO DISTRACTED BY CAP TO NOTICE THAT DUDE SNEAKING UP BEHIND ME--!
--CLOBB-- UURKK!
UUHHNN--BRAINS FEEL LIKE OATMEAL--
--BUT I CAN'T STAY DOWN--
GOTTA GET UP BEFORE IT'S--
--TOO LATE, SPIDER-MAN--
--MUCH TOO LATE!
THE BATTLE IS OVER--
--AND THE GREY GARGOYLE IS TRIUMPHANT AT LAST!
MINUTES PASS--AND A COOL BREEZE WAFTS PAST THE FULL-SCALE MISSILE MOCK-UPS THAT STAND BEFORE THE SCIENCE HALL--BUT WAIT!
DO OUR EYES DECEIVE US, OR IS ONE OF THOSE MISSILES ACTIVE--?
--AND ARE THOSE TWO STONE FIGURES CHAINED SO TIGHTLY TO ITS BASE WHO THEY APPEAR TO BE--?
WHAT DO YOU THINK?
HOW FITTING--THAT TWO WHO SOUGHT TO THWART MY PLANS--
--SHALL BE THE FIRST TO SEE THEM REACH FRUITION!

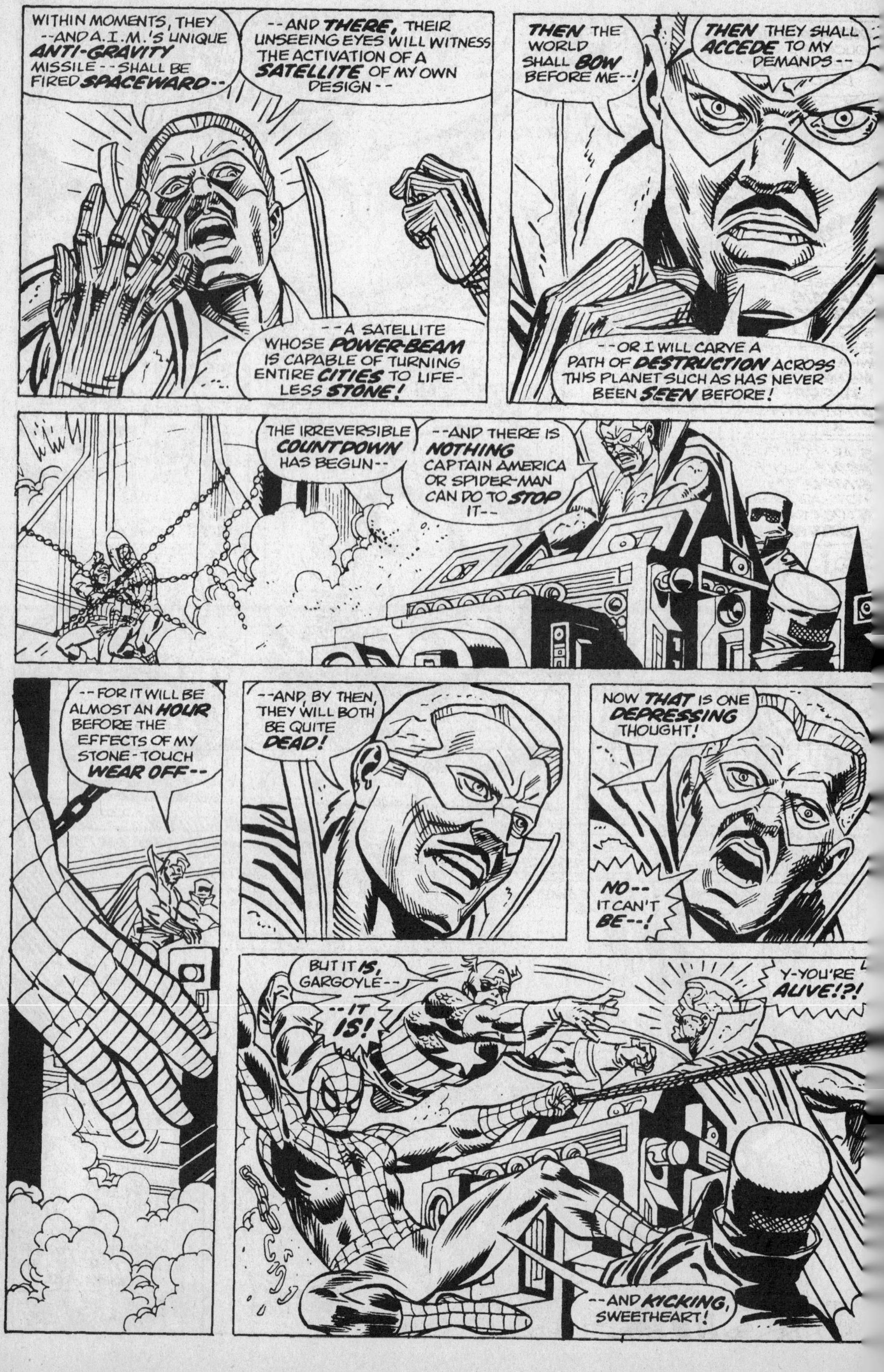

WITHIN MOMENTS, THEY --AND A.I.M.'S UNIQUE ANTI-GRAVITY MISSILE--SHALL BE FIRED SPACEWARD--
--AND THERE, THEIR UNSEEING EYES WILL WITNESS THE ACTIVATION OF A SATELLITE OF MY OWN DESIGN--
--A SATELLITE WHOSE POWER-BEAM IS CAPABLE OF TURNING ENTIRE CITIES TO LIFE-LESS STONE!
THEN THE WORLD SHALL BOW BEFORE ME--!
THEN THEY SHALL ACCEDE TO MY DEMANDS--
--OR I WILL CARVE A PATH OF DESTRUCTION ACROSS THIS PLANET SUCH AS HAS NEVER BEEN SEEN BEFORE!
THE IRREVERSIBLE COUNTDOWN HAS BEGUN--
--AND THERE IS NOTHING CAPTAIN AMERICA OR SPIDER-MAN CAN DO TO STOP IT--
--FOR IT WILL BE ALMOST AN HOUR BEFORE THE EFFECTS OF MY STONE-TOUCH WEAR OFF--
--AND, BY THEN, THEY WILL BOTH BE QUITE DEAD!
NOW THAT IS ONE DEPRESSING THOUGHT!
NO--IT CAN'T BE--!
BUT IT IS, GARGOYLE--
--IT IS!
Y-YOU'RE ALIVE!?!
--AND KICKING, SWEETHEART!

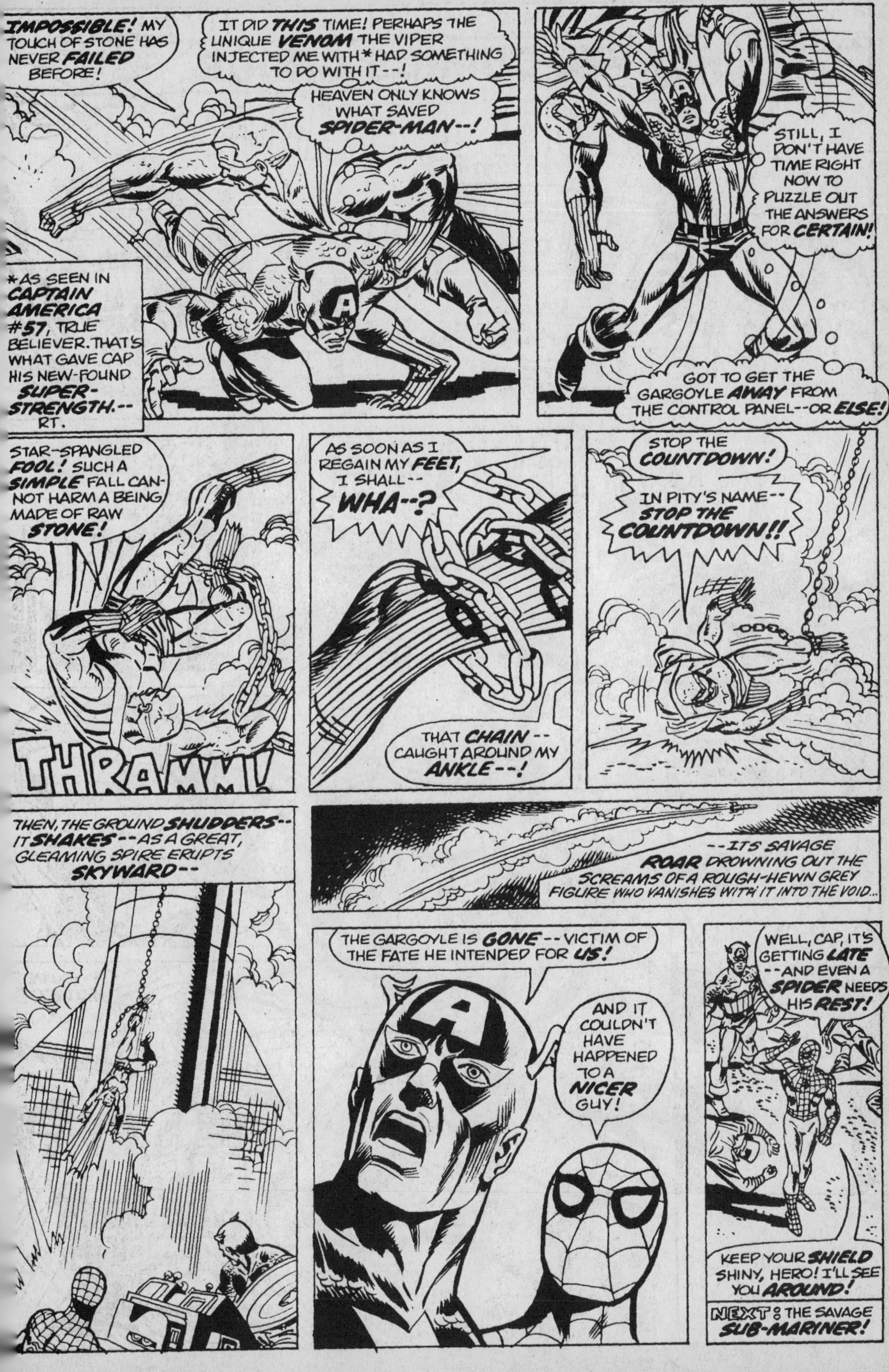
IMPOSSIBLE! MY TOUCH OF STONE HAS NEVER FAILED BEFORE!
IT DID THIS TIME! PERHAPS THE UNIQUE VENOM THE VIPER INJECTED ME WITH* HAD SOMETHING TO DO WITH IT--!
HEAVEN ONLY KNOWS WHAT SAVED SPIDER-MAN--!
*AS SEEN IN CAPTAIN AMERICA #57, TRUE BELIEVER. THAT'S WHAT GAVE CAP HIS NEW-FOUND SUPER-STRENGTH.--RT.
STILL, I DON'T HAVE TIME RIGHT NOW TO PUZZLE OUT THE ANSWERS FOR CERTAIN!
GOT TO GET THE GARGOYLE AWAY FROM THE CONTROL PANEL--OR ELSE!
STAR-SPANGLED FOOL! SUCH A SIMPLE FALL CANNOT HARM A BEING MADE OF RAW STONE!
THRAMM!
AS SOON AS I REGAIN MY FEET, I SHALL--
WHA--?
THAT CHAIN--CAUGHT AROUND MY ANKLE--!
STOP THE COUNTDOWN!
IN PITY'S NAME--STOP THE COUNTDOWN!!
THEN, THE GROUND SHUDDERS--IT SHAKES--AS A GREAT, GLEAMING SPIRE ERUPTS SKYWARD--
--ITS SAVAGE ROAR DROWNING OUT THE SCREAMS OF A ROUGH-HEWN GREY FIGURE WHO VANISHES WITH IT INTO THE VOID...
THE GARGOYLE IS GONE--VICTIM OF THE FATE HE INTENDED FOR US!
AND IT COULDN'T HAVE HAPPENED TO A NICER GUY!
WELL, CAP, IT'S GETTING LATE--AND EVEN A SPIDER NEEDS HIS REST!
KEEP YOUR SHIELD SHINY, HERO! I'LL SEE YOU AROUND!
NEXT: THE SAVAGE SUB-MARINER!

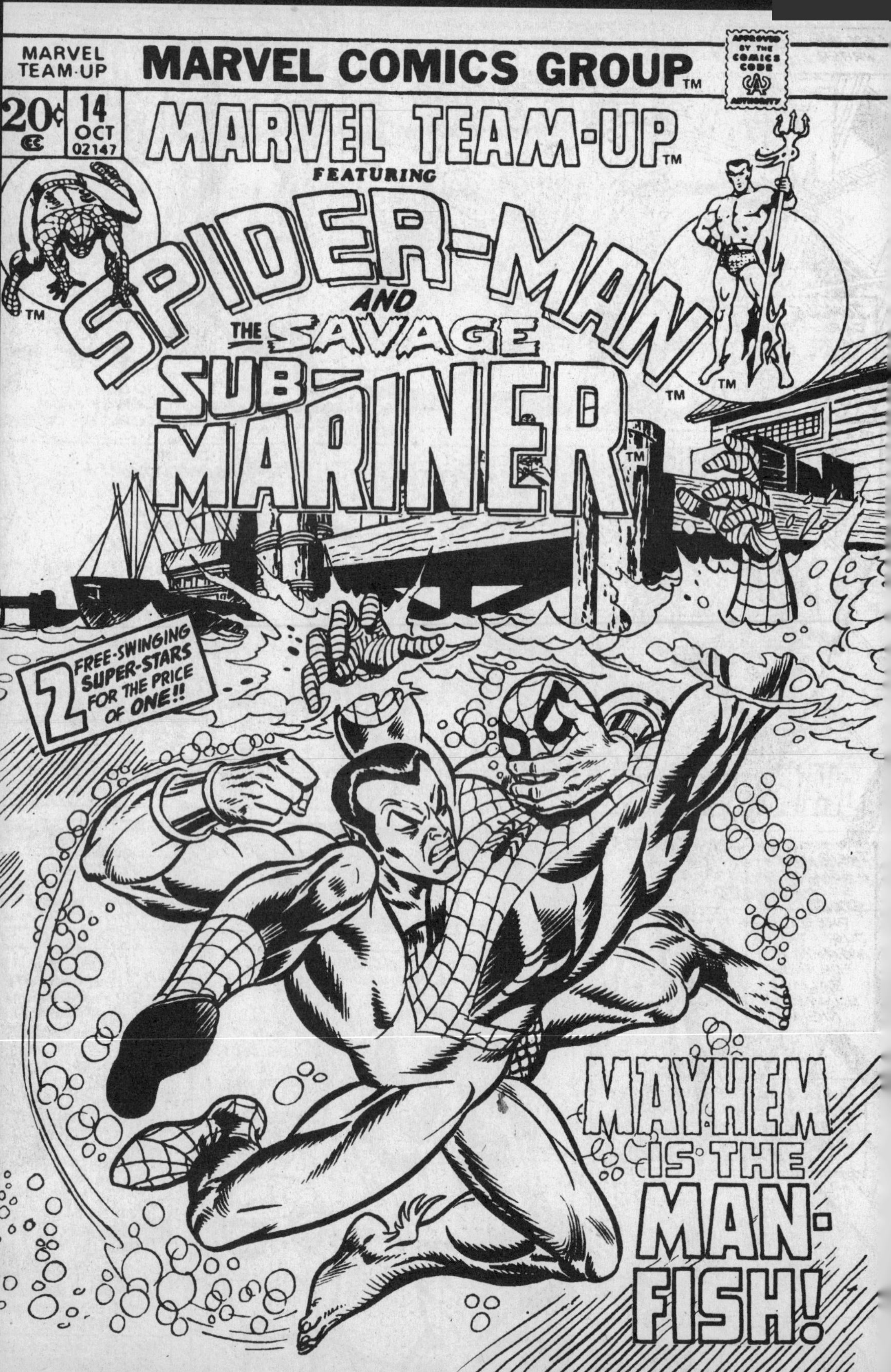
MARVEL TEAM-UP
MARVEL COMICS GROUP
APPROVED BY THE COMICS CODE AUTHORITY
20¢
14 OCT 02147
MARVEL TEAM-UP
FEATURING
SPIDER-MAN AND THE SAVAGE SUB-MARINER
2 FREE-SWINGING SUPER-STARS FOR THE PRICE OF ONE!!
MAYHEM IS THE MAN-FISH!

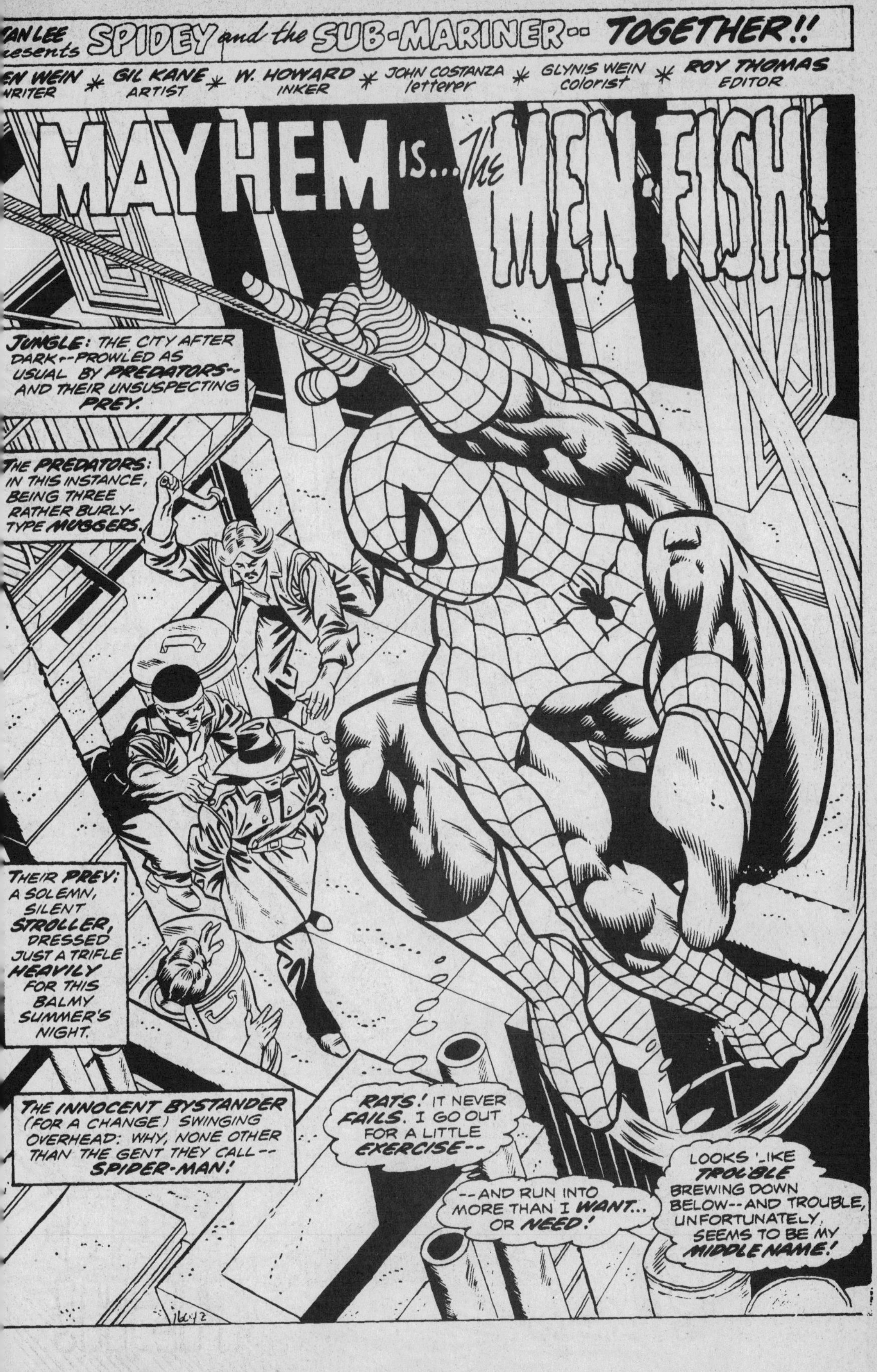
STAN LEE presents SPIDEY and the SUB-MARINER -- TOGETHER!!
LEN WEIN WRITER * GIL KANE ARTIST * W. HOWARD INKER * JOHN COSTANZA letterer * GLYNIS WEIN colorist * ROY THOMAS EDITOR
MAYHEM IS... THE MEN-FISH!
JUNGLE: THE CITY AFTER DARK--PROWLED AS USUAL BY PREDATORS--AND THEIR UNSUSPECTING PREY.
THE PREDATORS: IN THIS INSTANCE, BEING THREE RATHER BURLY-TYPE MUGGERS.
THEIR PREY: A SOLEMN, SILENT STROLLER, DRESSED JUST A TRIFLE HEAVILY FOR THIS BALMY SUMMER'S NIGHT.
THE INNOCENT BYSTANDER (FOR A CHANGE) SWINGING OVERHEAD: WHY, NONE OTHER THAN THE GENT THEY CALL--SPIDER-MAN!
RATS! IT NEVER FAILS. I GO OUT FOR A LITTLE EXERCISE--
--AND RUN INTO MORE THAN I WANT... OR NEED!
LOOKS LIKE TROUBLE BREWING DOWN BELOW--AND TROUBLE, UNFORTUNATELY, SEEMS TO BE MY MIDDLE NAME!
16-12

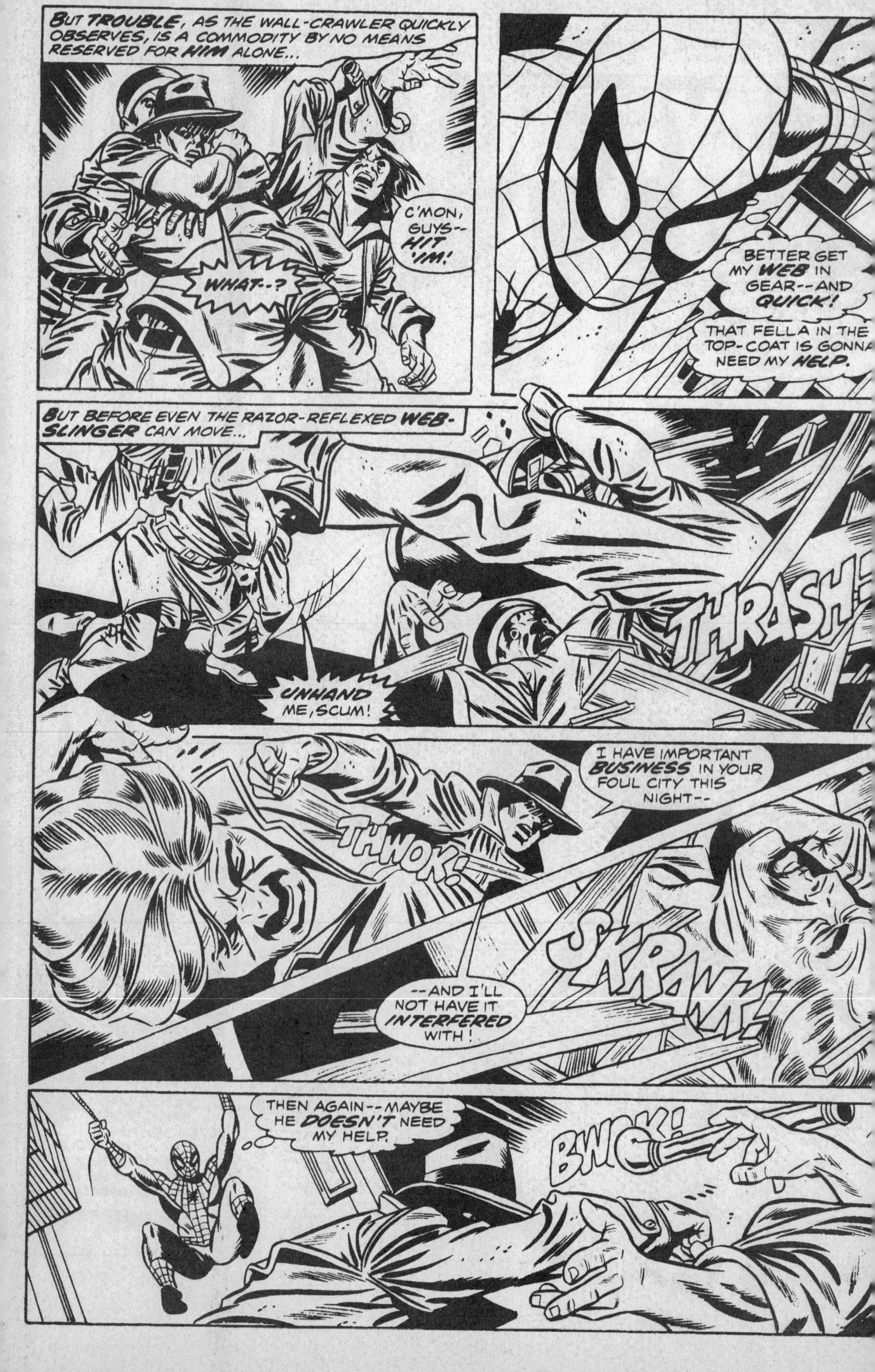

BUT TROUBLE, AS THE WALL-CRAWLER QUICKLY OBSERVES, IS A COMMODITY BY NO MEANS RESERVED FOR HIM ALONE...
C'MON, GUYS-- HIT 'IM!
WHAT--?
BETTER GET MY WEB IN GEAR--AND QUICK!
THAT FELLA IN THE TOP-COAT IS GONNA NEED MY HELP.
BUT BEFORE EVEN THE RAZOR-REFLEXED WEB-SLINGER CAN MOVE...
THRASH!
UNHAND ME, SCUM!
I HAVE IMPORTANT BUSINESS IN YOUR FOUL CITY THIS NIGHT--
THWOK!
SKRANK!
--AND I'LL NOT HAVE IT INTERFERED WITH!
THEN AGAIN--MAYBE HE DOESN'T NEED MY HELP.
BWOK!

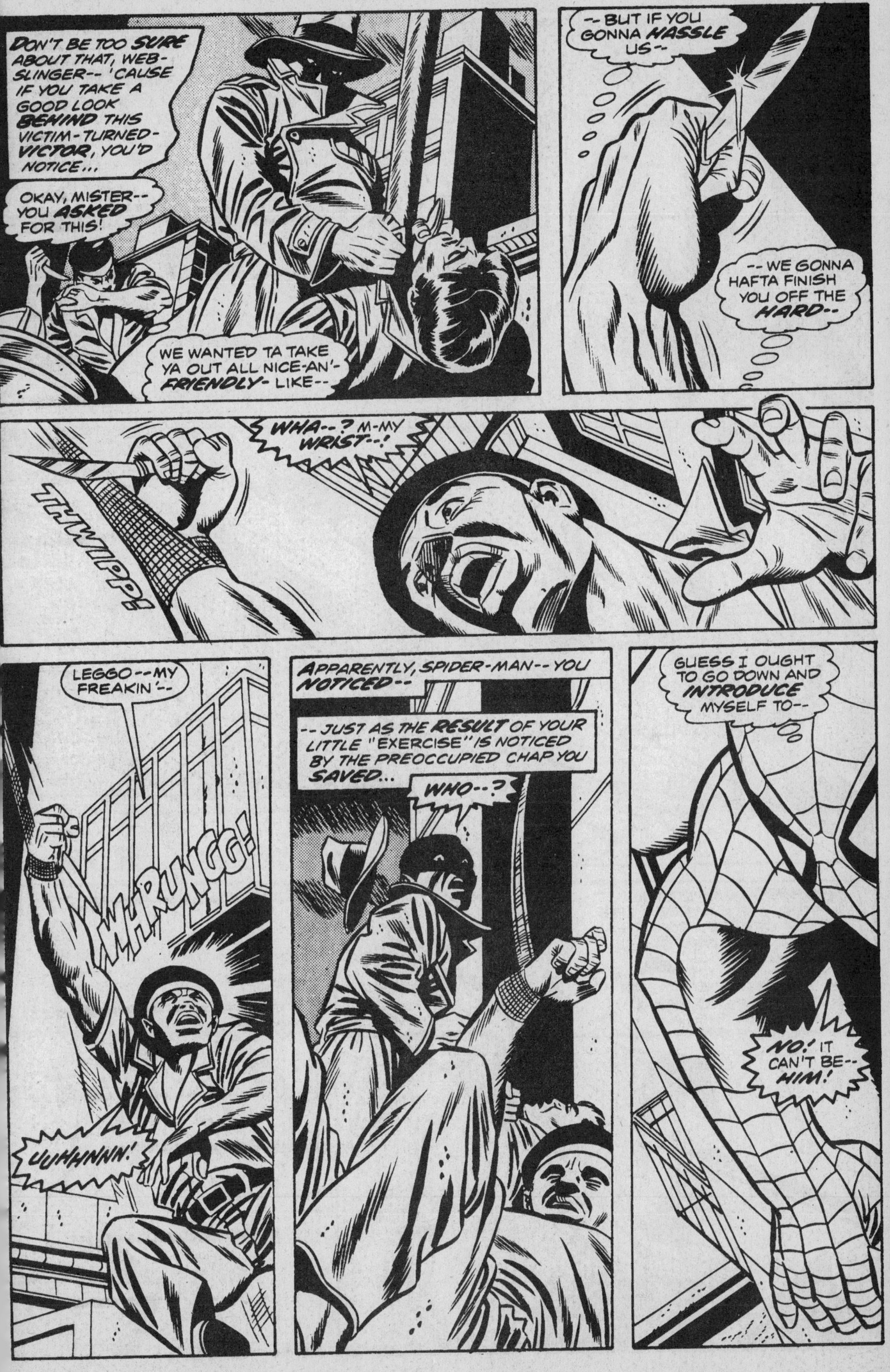
DON'T BE TOO SURE ABOUT THAT, WEB-SLINGER-- 'CAUSE IF YOU TAKE A GOOD LOOK BEHIND THIS VICTIM-TURNED-VICTOR, YOU'D NOTICE...
OKAY, MISTER-- YOU ASKED FOR THIS!
WE WANTED TA TAKE YA OUT ALL NICE-AN'-FRIENDLY-LIKE--
--BUT IF YOU GONNA HASSLE US--
--WE GONNA HAFTA FINISH YOU OFF THE HARD--
THWIPP!
WHA--? M-MY WRIST--!
LEGGO--MY FREAKIN'--
WHRUNGG!
UUHHNNN!
APPARENTLY, SPIDER-MAN--YOU NOTICED--
--JUST AS THE RESULT OF YOUR LITTLE "EXERCISE" IS NOTICED BY THE PREOCCUPIED CHAP YOU SAVED...
WHO--?
GUESS I OUGHT TO GO DOWN AND INTRODUCE MYSELF TO--
NO! IT CAN'T BE--HIM!

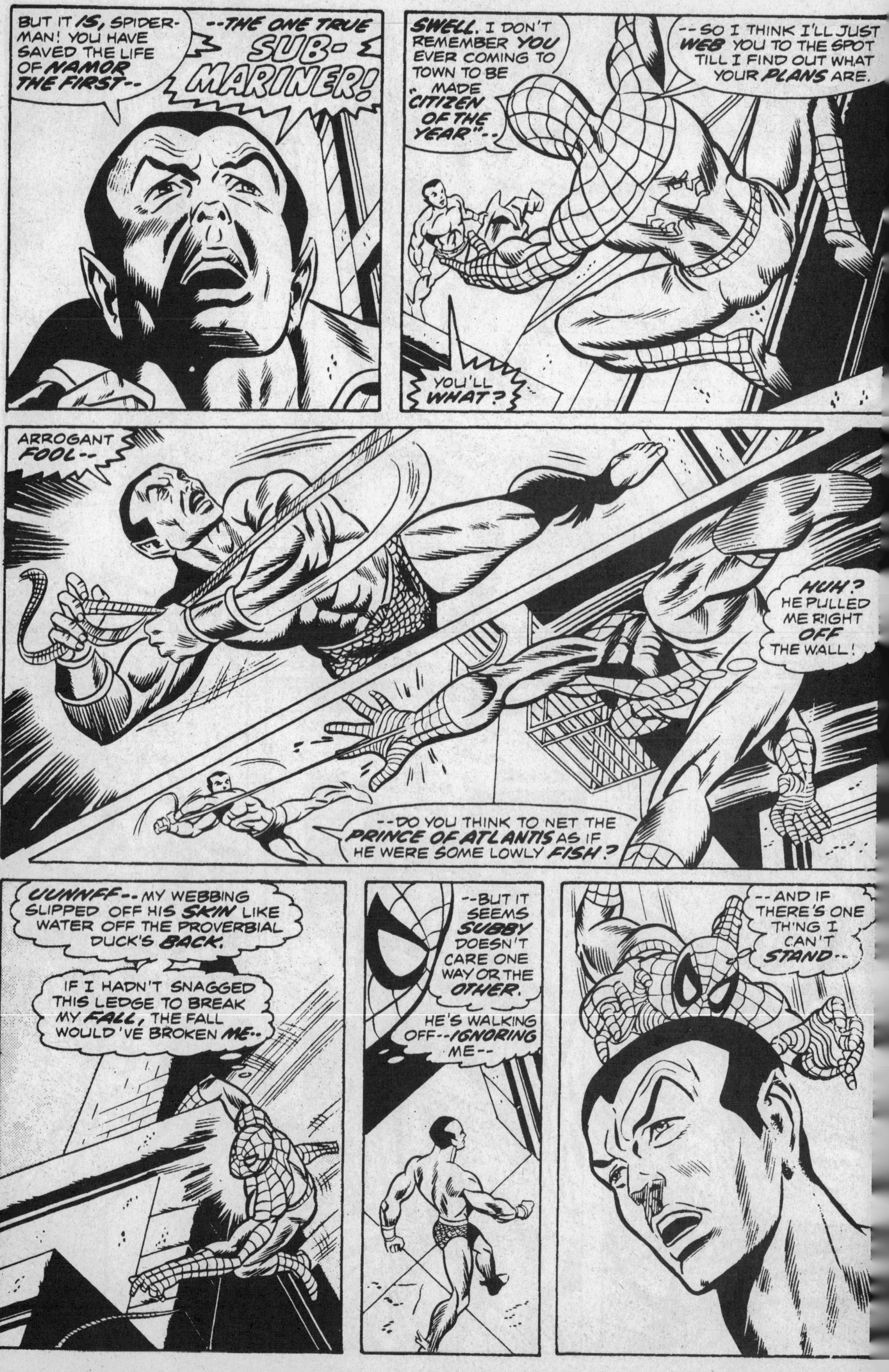

BUT IT IS, SPIDER-MAN! YOU HAVE SAVED THE LIFE OF NAMOR THE FIRST--
--THE ONE TRUE SUB-MARINER!
SWELL. I DON'T REMEMBER YOU EVER COMING TO TOWN TO BE "MADE CITIZEN OF THE YEAR"--
--SO I THINK I'LL JUST WEB YOU TO THE SPOT TILL I FIND OUT WHAT YOUR PLANS ARE.
YOU'LL WHAT?
ARROGANT FOOL--
HUH? HE PULLED ME RIGHT OFF THE WALL!
--DO YOU THINK TO NET THE PRINCE OF ATLANTIS AS IF HE WERE SOME LOWLY FISH?
UUNNFF-- MY WEBBING SLIPPED OFF HIS SKIN LIKE WATER OFF THE PROVERBIAL DUCK'S BACK.
IF I HADN'T SNAGGED THIS LEDGE TO BREAK MY FALL, THE FALL WOULD'VE BROKEN ME..
--BUT IT SEEMS SUBBY DOESN'T CARE ONE WAY OR THE OTHER.
HE'S WALKING OFF--IGNORING ME--
--AND IF THERE'S ONE THING I CAN'T STAND..

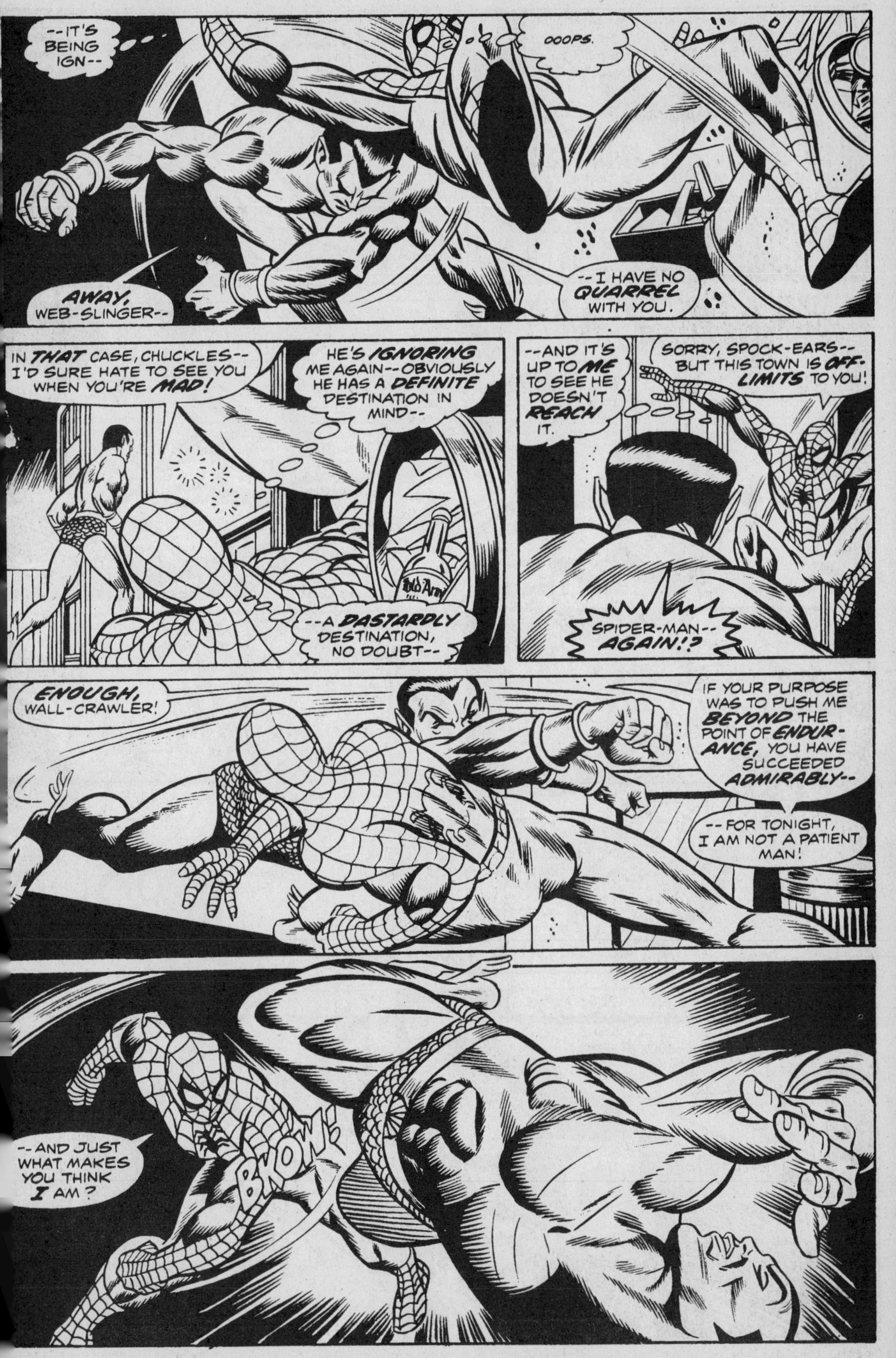
--IT'S BEING IGN--
OOOPS.
AWAY, WEB-SLINGER--
--I HAVE NO QUARREL WITH YOU.
IN THAT CASE, CHUCKLES--I'D SURE HATE TO SEE YOU WHEN YOU'RE MAD!
HE'S IGNORING ME AGAIN--OBVIOUSLY HE HAS A DEFINITE DESTINATION IN MIND--
--A DASTARDLY DESTINATION, NO DOUBT--
--AND IT'S UP TO ME TO SEE HE DOESN'T REACH IT.
SORRY, SPOCK-EARS--BUT THIS TOWN IS OFF-LIMITS TO YOU!
SPIDER-MAN--AGAIN!?
ENOUGH, WALL-CRAWLER!
IF YOUR PURPOSE WAS TO PUSH ME BEYOND THE POINT OF ENDUR-ANCE, YOU HAVE SUCCEEDED ADMIRABLY--
--FOR TONIGHT, I AM NOT A PATIENT MAN!
--AND JUST WHAT MAKES YOU THINK I AM?
BKOW!

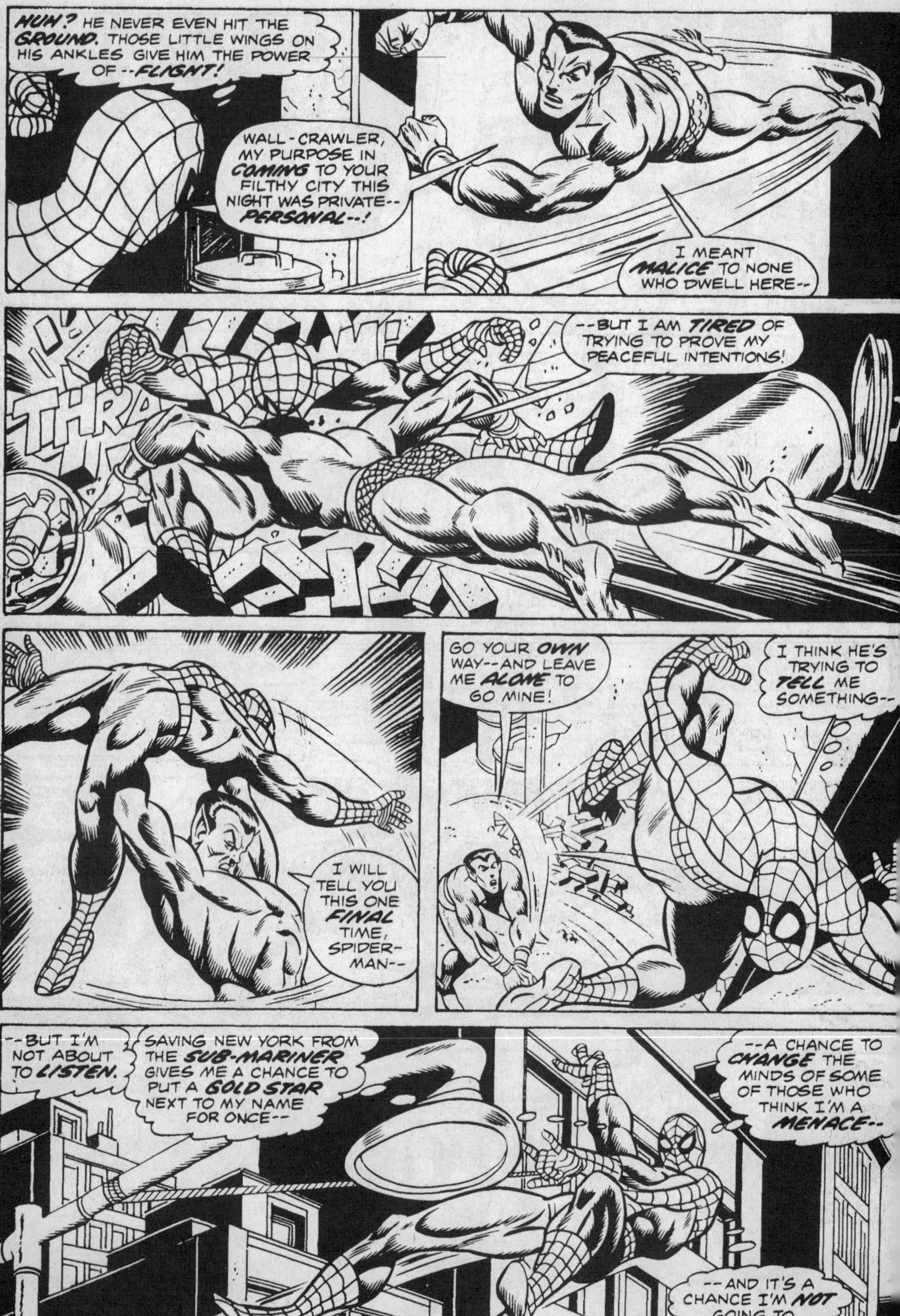
HUH? HE NEVER EVEN HIT THE GROUND. THOSE LITTLE WINGS ON HIS ANKLES GIVE HIM THE POWER OF --FLIGHT!
WALL-CRAWLER, MY PURPOSE IN COMING TO YOUR FILTHY CITY THIS NIGHT WAS PRIVATE-- PERSONAL--!
I MEANT MALICE TO NONE WHO DWELL HERE--
THRA
--BUT I AM TIRED OF TRYING TO PROVE MY PEACEFUL INTENTIONS!
I WILL TELL YOU THIS ONE FINAL TIME, SPIDER-MAN--
GO YOUR OWN WAY--AND LEAVE ME ALONE TO GO MINE!
I THINK HE'S TRYING TO TELL ME SOMETHING--
--BUT I'M NOT ABOUT TO LISTEN.
SAVING NEW YORK FROM THE SUB-MARINER GIVES ME A CHANCE TO PUT A GOLD STAR NEXT TO MY NAME FOR ONCE--
--A CHANCE TO CHANGE THE MINDS OF SOME OF THOSE WHO THINK I'M A MENACE--
--AND IT'S A CHANCE I'M NOT GOING TO BLOW!

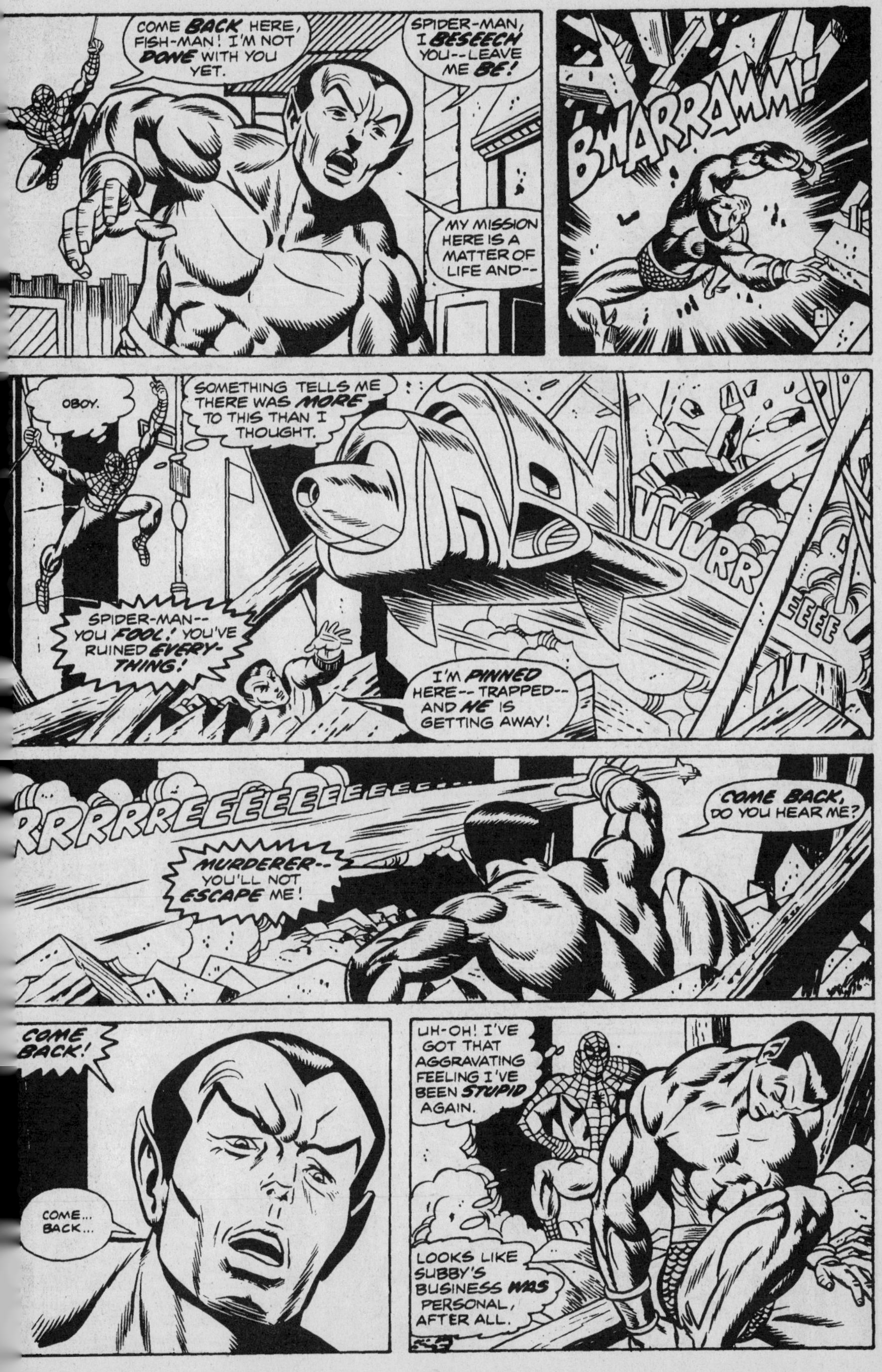
COME BACK HERE, FISH-MAN! I'M NOT DONE WITH YOU YET.
SPIDER-MAN, I BESEECH YOU--LEAVE ME BE!
MY MISSION HERE IS A MATTER OF LIFE AND--
BWARRAMM!
OBOY.
SOMETHING TELLS ME THERE WAS MORE TO THIS THAN I THOUGHT.
VVVRRREEEE
SPIDER-MAN-- YOU FOOL! YOU'VE RUINED EVERY-THING!
I'M PINNED HERE-- TRAPPED-- AND HE IS GETTING AWAY!
RRRRRREEEEEEEEEEE...
COME BACK, DO YOU HEAR ME?
MURDERER-- YOU'LL NOT ESCAPE ME!
COME BACK!
COME... BACK...
UH-OH! I'VE GOT THAT AGGRAVATING FEELING I'VE BEEN STUPID AGAIN.
LOOKS LIKE SUBBY'S BUSINESS WAS PERSONAL, AFTER ALL.

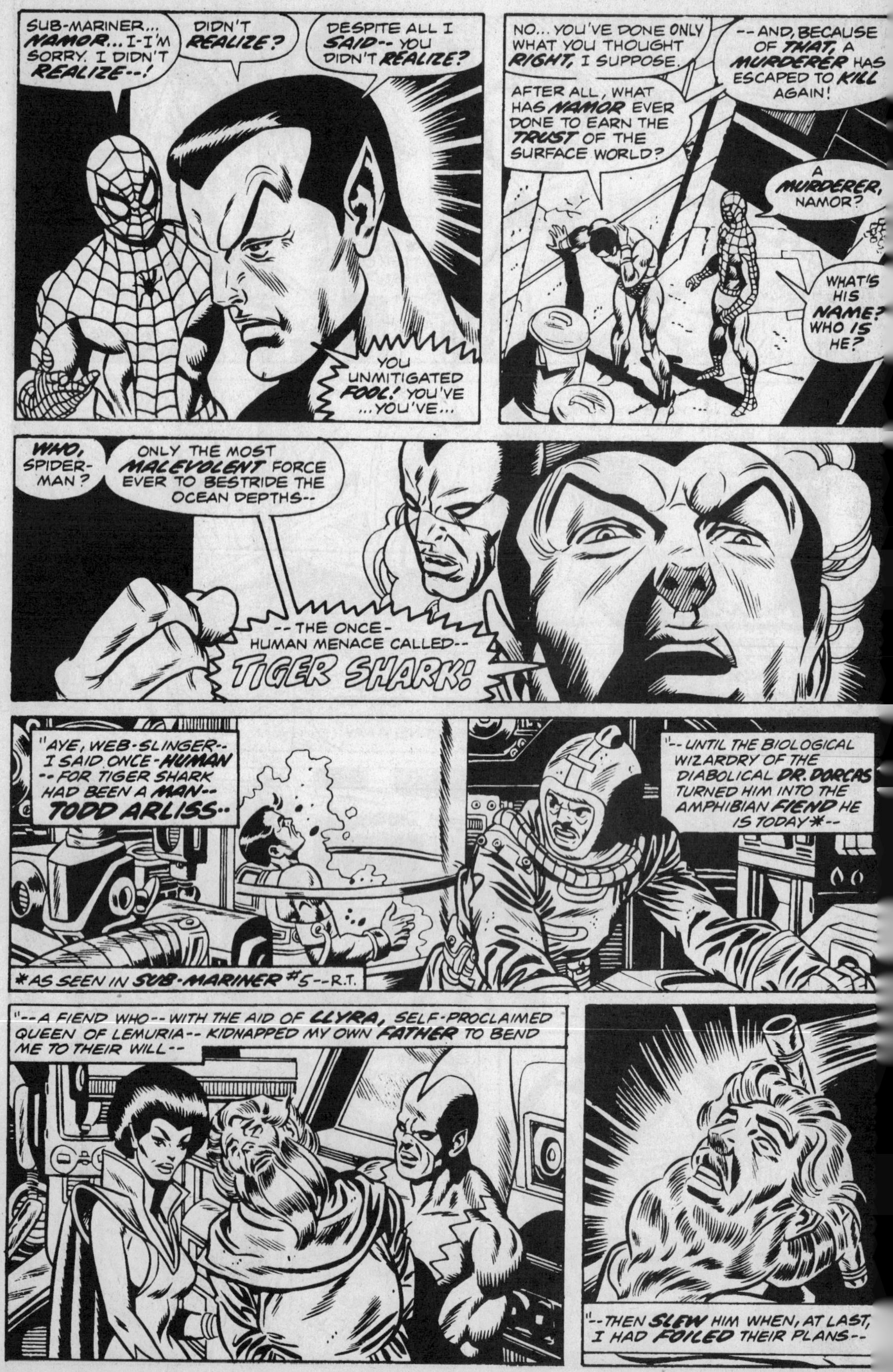

SUB-MARINER... NAMOR... I-I'M SORRY. I DIDN'T REALIZE--!
DIDN'T REALIZE?
DESPITE ALL I SAID-- YOU DIDN'T REALIZE?
YOU UNMITIGATED FOOL! YOU'VE ...YOU'VE...
NO... YOU'VE DONE ONLY WHAT YOU THOUGHT RIGHT, I SUPPOSE.
AFTER ALL, WHAT HAS NAMOR EVER DONE TO EARN THE TRUST OF THE SURFACE WORLD?
--AND, BECAUSE OF THAT, A MURDERER HAS ESCAPED TO KILL AGAIN!
A MURDERER, NAMOR?
WHAT'S HIS NAME? WHO IS HE?
WHO, SPIDER-MAN?
ONLY THE MOST MALEVOLENT FORCE EVER TO BESTRIDE THE OCEAN DEPTHS--
--THE ONCE-HUMAN MENACE CALLED--
TIGER SHARK!
"AYE, WEB-SLINGER-- I SAID ONCE-HUMAN --FOR TIGER SHARK HAD BEEN A MAN-- TODD ARLISS--
"--UNTIL THE BIOLOGICAL WIZARDRY OF THE DIABOLICAL DR. DORCAS TURNED HIM INTO THE AMPHIBIAN FIEND HE IS TODAY*--
*AS SEEN IN SUB-MARINER #5--R.T.
"--A FIEND WHO--WITH THE AID OF LLYRA, SELF-PROCLAIMED QUEEN OF LEMURIA--KIDNAPPED MY OWN FATHER TO BEND ME TO THEIR WILL--
"--THEN SLEW HIM WHEN, AT LAST, I HAD FOILED THEIR PLANS--

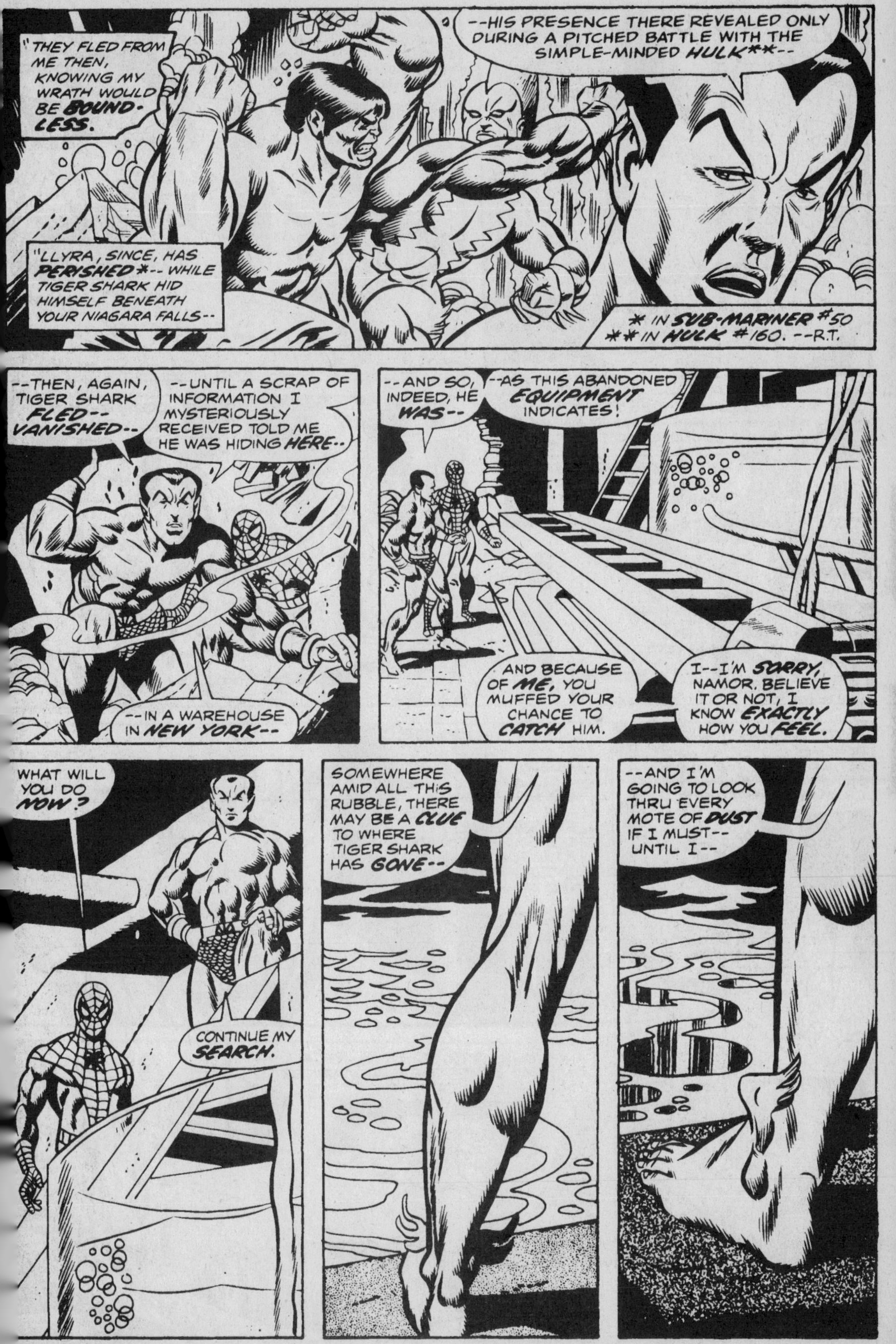

"THEY FLED FROM ME THEN, KNOWING MY WRATH WOULD BE BOUNDLESS.
--HIS PRESENCE THERE REVEALED ONLY DURING A PITCHED BATTLE WITH THE SIMPLE-MINDED HULK**--
"LLYRA, SINCE, HAS PERISHED*-- WHILE TIGER SHARK HID HIMSELF BENEATH YOUR NIAGARA FALLS--
* IN SUB-MARINER #50
** IN HULK #160. --R.T.
--THEN, AGAIN, TIGER SHARK FLED-- VANISHED--
--UNTIL A SCRAP OF INFORMATION I MYSTERIOUSLY RECEIVED TOLD ME HE WAS HIDING HERE--
--IN A WAREHOUSE IN NEW YORK--
--AND SO, INDEED, HE WAS--
--AS THIS ABANDONED EQUIPMENT INDICATES!
AND BECAUSE OF ME, YOU MUFFED YOUR CHANCE TO CATCH HIM.
I--I'M SORRY, NAMOR. BELIEVE IT OR NOT, I KNOW EXACTLY HOW YOU FEEL.
WHAT WILL YOU DO NOW?
CONTINUE MY SEARCH.
SOMEWHERE AMID ALL THIS RUBBLE, THERE MAY BE A CLUE TO WHERE TIGER SHARK HAS GONE--
--AND I'M GOING TO LOOK THRU EVERY MOTE OF DUST IF I MUST-- UNTIL I--

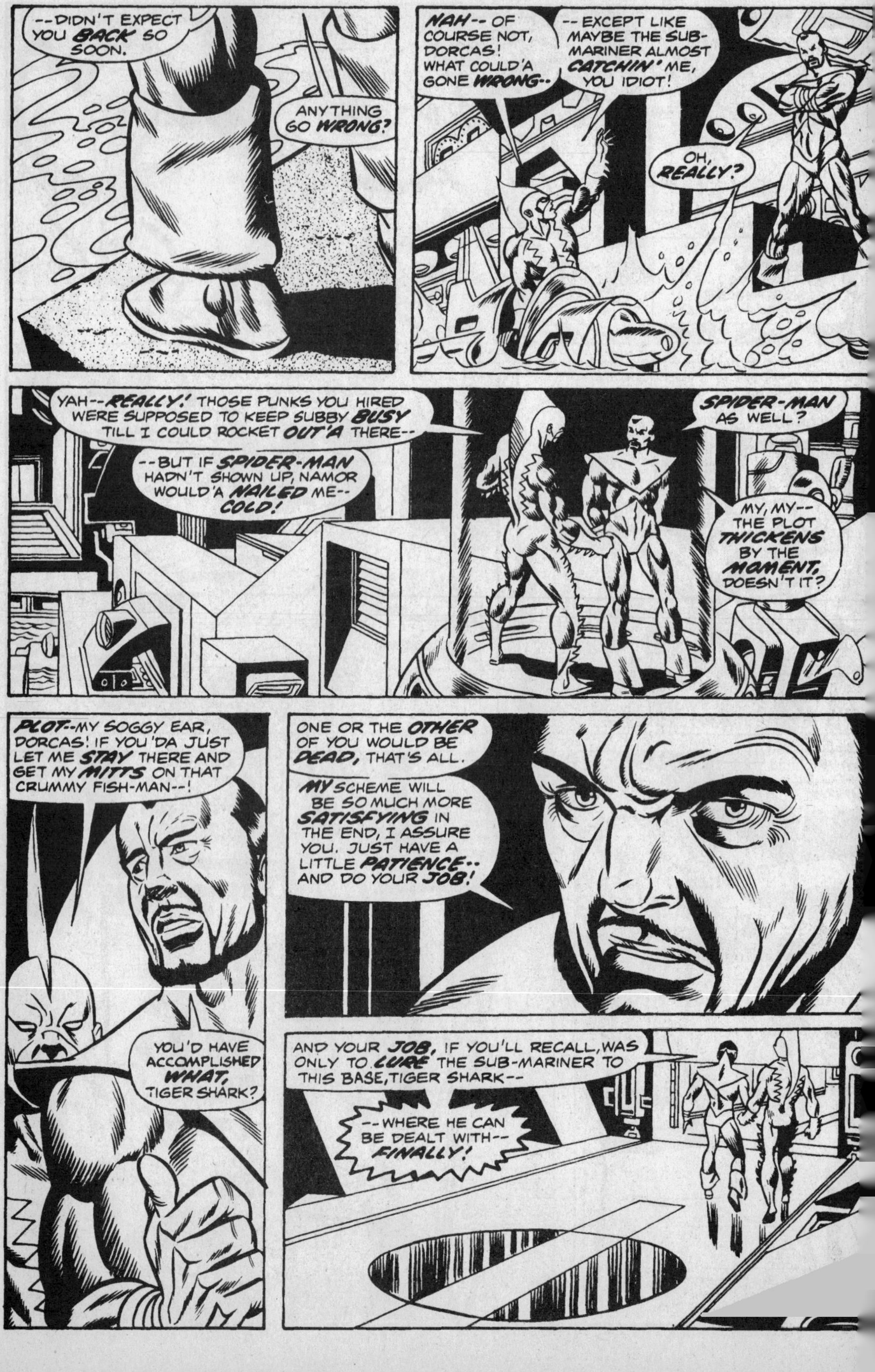
--DIDN'T EXPECT YOU BACK SO SOON.
ANYTHING GO WRONG?
NAH-- OF COURSE NOT, DORCAS! WHAT COULD'A GONE WRONG--
-- EXCEPT LIKE MAYBE THE SUB-MARINER ALMOST CATCHIN' ME, YOU IDIOT!
OH, REALLY?
YAH--REALLY! THOSE PUNKS YOU HIRED WERE SUPPOSED TO KEEP SUBBY BUSY TILL I COULD ROCKET OUT'A THERE--
--BUT IF SPIDER-MAN HADN'T SHOWN UP, NAMOR WOULD'A NAILED ME-- COLD!
SPIDER-MAN AS WELL?
MY, MY-- THE PLOT THICKENS BY THE MOMENT, DOESN'T IT?
PLOT--MY SOGGY EAR, DORCAS! IF YOU'DA JUST LET ME STAY THERE AND GET MY MITTS ON THAT CRUMMY FISH-MAN--!
YOU'D HAVE ACCOMPLISHED WHAT, TIGER SHARK?
ONE OR THE OTHER OF YOU WOULD BE DEAD, THAT'S ALL.
MY SCHEME WILL BE SO MUCH MORE SATISFYING IN THE END, I ASSURE YOU. JUST HAVE A LITTLE PATIENCE.. AND DO YOUR JOB!
AND YOUR JOB, IF YOU'LL RECALL, WAS ONLY TO LURE THE SUB-MARINER TO THIS BASE, TIGER SHARK--
--WHERE HE CAN BE DEALT WITH-- FINALLY!

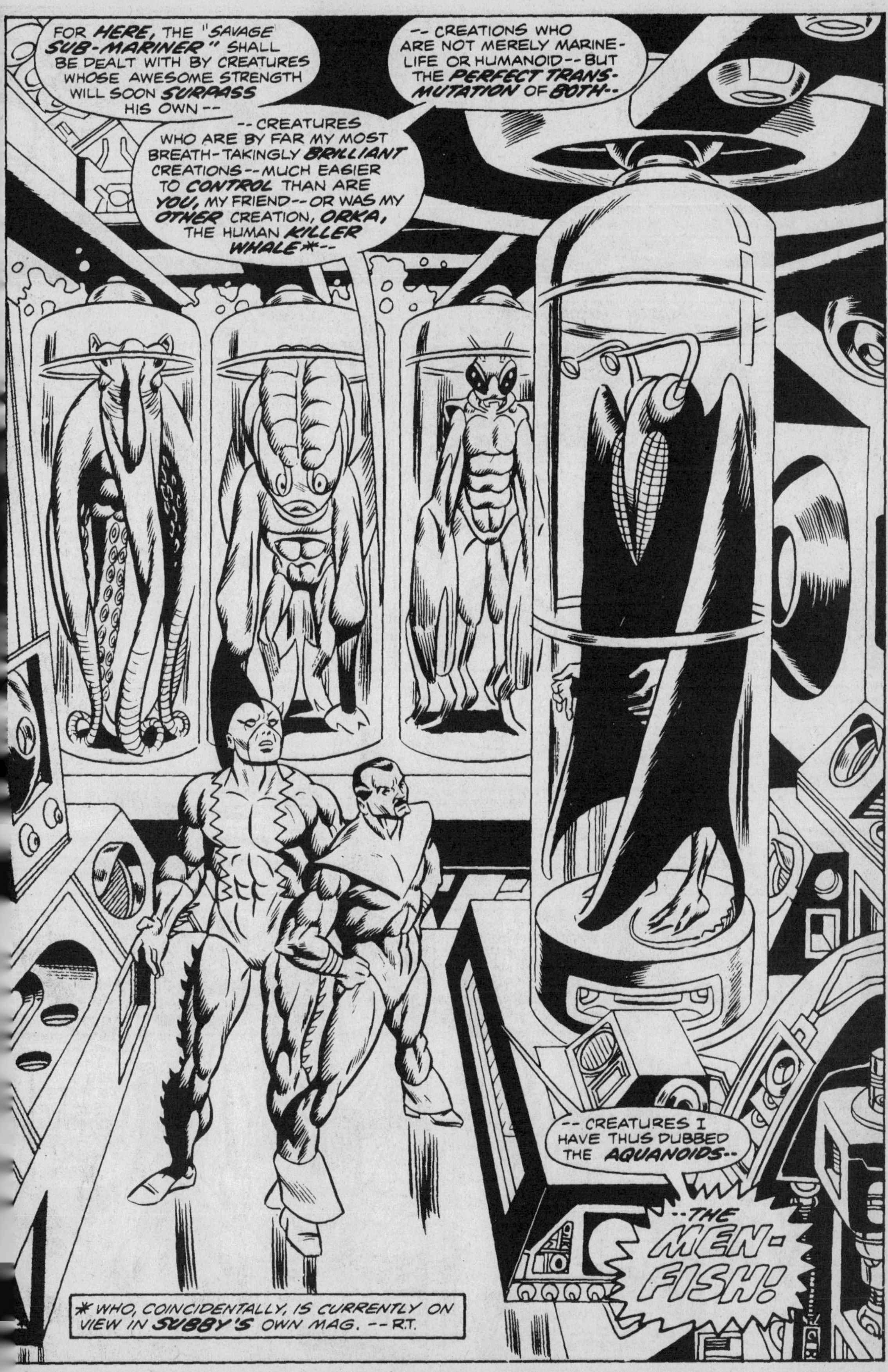

FOR HERE, THE "SAVAGE SUB-MARINER" SHALL BE DEALT WITH BY CREATURES WHOSE AWESOME STRENGTH WILL SOON SURPASS HIS OWN --
-- CREATURES WHO ARE BY FAR MY MOST BREATH-TAKINGLY BRILLIANT CREATIONS--MUCH EASIER TO CONTROL THAN ARE YOU, MY FRIEND--OR WAS MY OTHER CREATION, ORKA, THE HUMAN KILLER WHALE*--
-- CREATIONS WHO ARE NOT MERELY MARINE-LIFE OR HUMANOID--BUT THE PERFECT TRANS-MUTATION OF BOTH--
-- CREATURES I HAVE THUS DUBBED THE AQUANOIDS--
--THE MEN-FISH!
* WHO, COINCIDENTALLY, IS CURRENTLY ON VIEW IN SUBBY'S OWN MAG. --R.T.

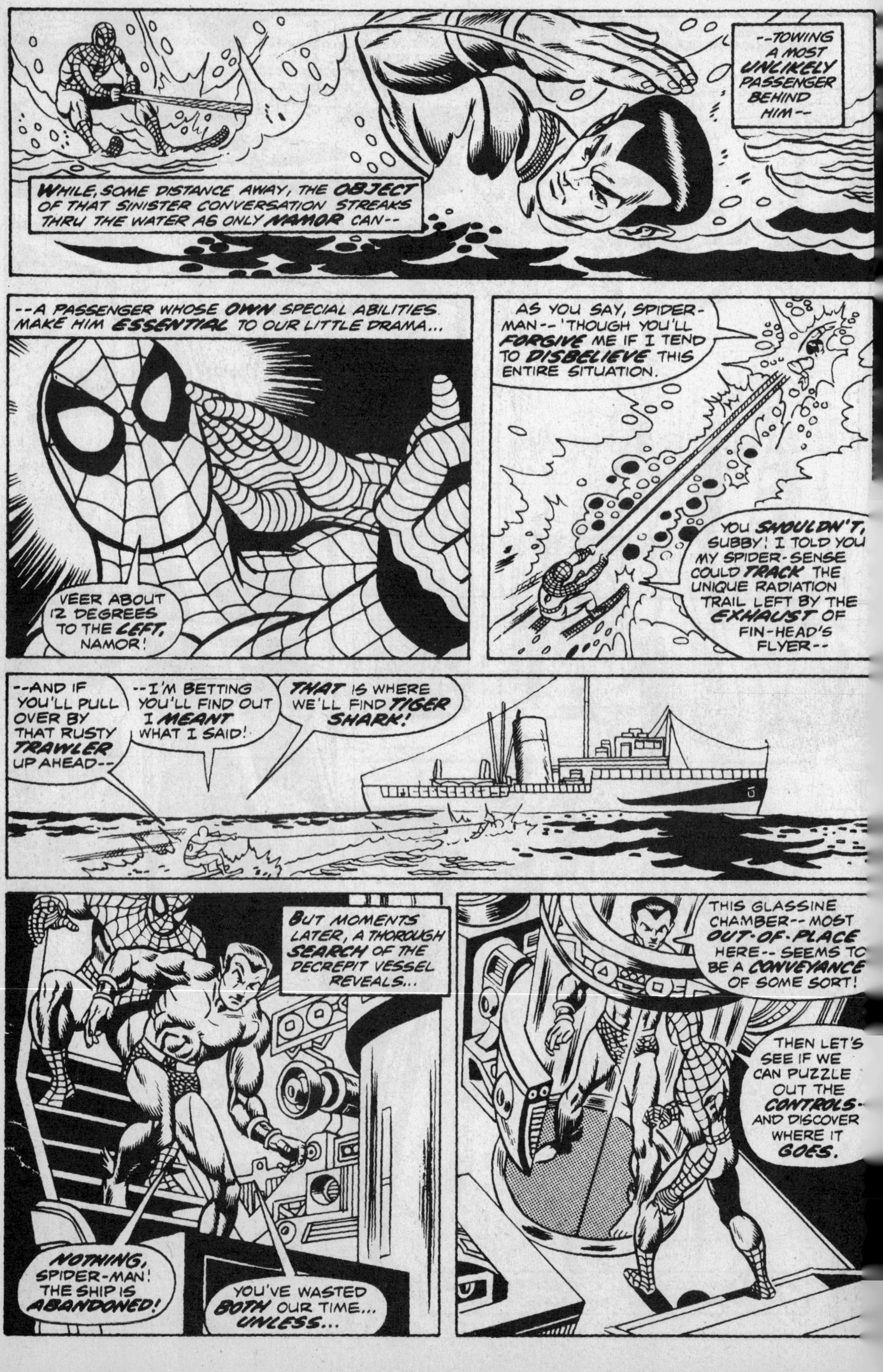

--TOWING A MOST UNLIKELY PASSENGER BEHIND HIM--
WHILE, SOME DISTANCE AWAY, THE OBJECT OF THAT SINISTER CONVERSATION STREAKS THRU THE WATER AS ONLY NAMOR CAN--
--A PASSENGER WHOSE OWN SPECIAL ABILITIES MAKE HIM ESSENTIAL TO OUR LITTLE DRAMA...
VEER ABOUT 12 DEGREES TO THE LEFT, NAMOR!
AS YOU SAY, SPIDER-MAN--'THOUGH YOU'LL FORGIVE ME IF I TEND TO DISBELIEVE THIS ENTIRE SITUATION.
YOU SHOULDN'T, SUBBY! I TOLD YOU MY SPIDER-SENSE COULD TRACK THE UNIQUE RADIATION TRAIL LEFT BY THE EXHAUST OF FIN-HEAD'S FLYER--
--AND IF YOU'LL PULL OVER BY THAT RUSTY TRAWLER UP AHEAD--
--I'M BETTING YOU'LL FIND OUT I MEANT WHAT I SAID!
THAT IS WHERE WE'LL FIND TIGER SHARK!
BUT MOMENTS LATER, A THOROUGH SEARCH OF THE DECREPIT VESSEL REVEALS...
NOTHING, SPIDER-MAN! THE SHIP IS ABANDONED!
YOU'VE WASTED BOTH OUR TIME... UNLESS...
THIS GLASSINE CHAMBER--MOST OUT-OF-PLACE HERE--SEEMS TO BE A CONVEYANCE OF SOME SORT!
THEN LET'S SEE IF WE CAN PUZZLE OUT THE CONTROLS-- AND DISCOVER WHERE IT GOES.

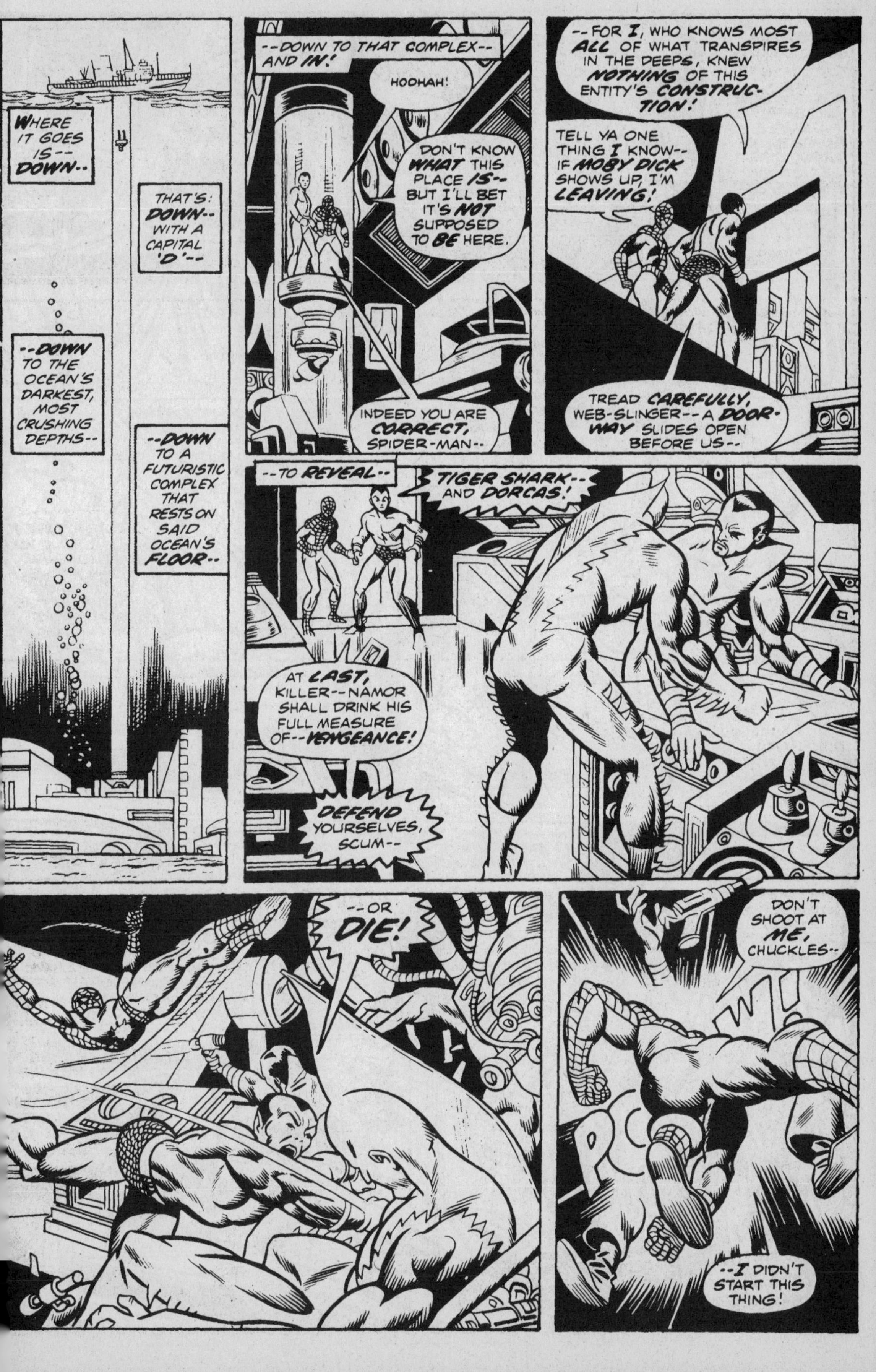
WHERE IT GOES IS-- DOWN--
THAT'S: DOWN-- WITH A CAPITAL 'D'--
--DOWN TO THE OCEAN'S DARKEST, MOST CRUSHING DEPTHS--
--DOWN TO A FUTURISTIC COMPLEX THAT RESTS ON SAID OCEAN'S FLOOR--
--DOWN TO THAT COMPLEX-- AND IN!
HOOHAH!
DON'T KNOW WHAT THIS PLACE IS-- BUT I'LL BET IT'S NOT SUPPOSED TO BE HERE.
INDEED YOU ARE CORRECT, SPIDER-MAN--
--FOR I, WHO KNOWS MOST ALL OF WHAT TRANSPIRES IN THE DEEPS, KNEW NOTHING OF THIS ENTITY'S CONSTRUCTION!
TELL YA ONE THING I KNOW-- IF MOBY DICK SHOWS UP, I'M LEAVING!
TREAD CAREFULLY, WEB-SLINGER-- A DOORWAY SLIDES OPEN BEFORE US--
--TO REVEAL--
TIGER SHARK-- AND DORCAS!
AT LAST, KILLER--NAMOR SHALL DRINK HIS FULL MEASURE OF--VENGEANCE!
DEFEND YOURSELVES, SCUM--
--OR DIE!
DON'T SHOOT AT ME, CHUCKLES--
--I DIDN'T START THIS THING!

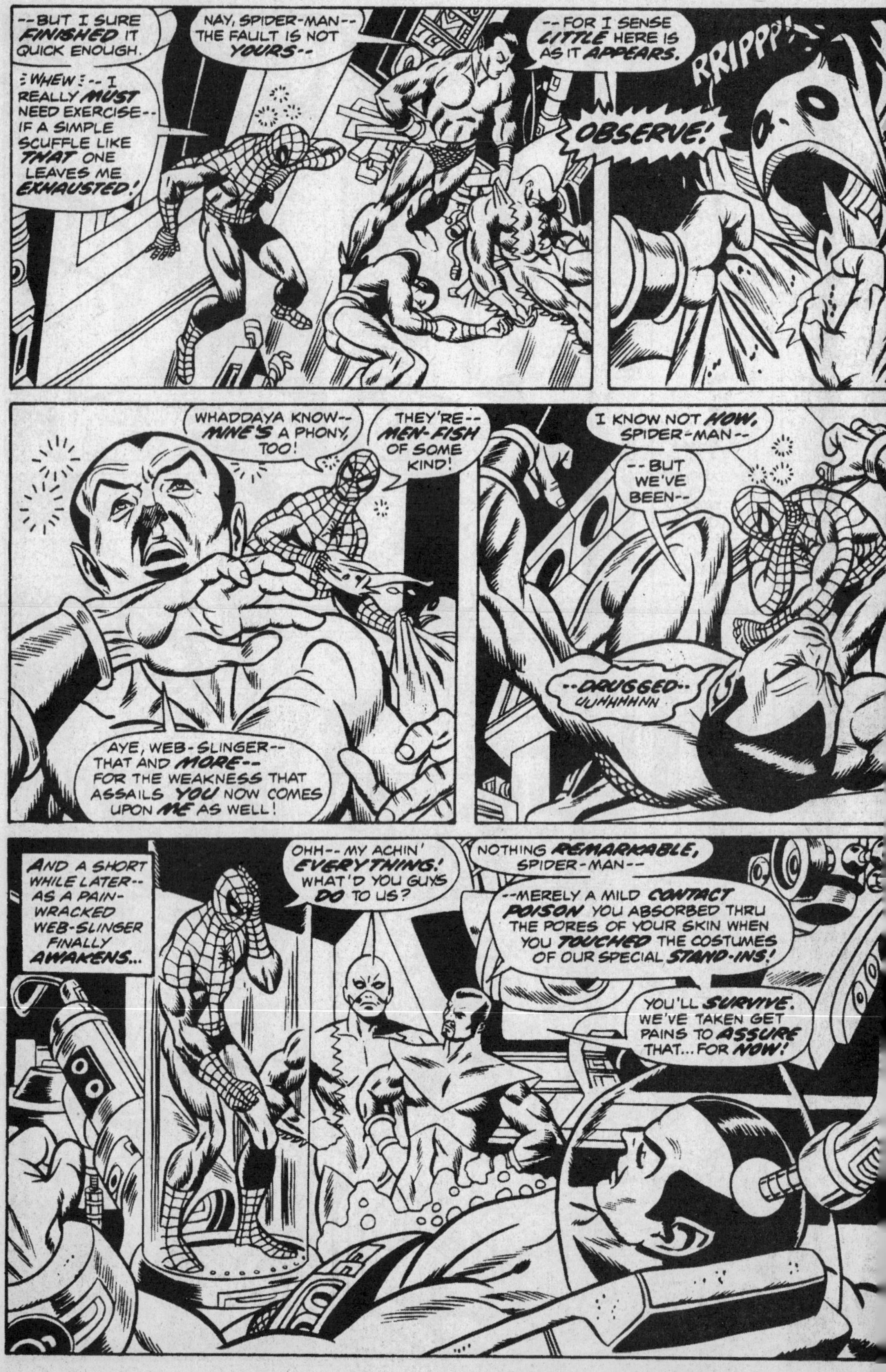
--BUT I SURE FINISHED IT QUICK ENOUGH.
WHEW --I REALLY MUST NEED EXERCISE--IF A SIMPLE SCUFFLE LIKE THAT ONE LEAVES ME EXHAUSTED!
NAY, SPIDER-MAN--THE FAULT IS NOT YOURS--
--FOR I SENSE LITTLE HERE IS AS IT APPEARS.
RRIPPP!
OBSERVE!
WHADDAYA KNOW--MINE'S A PHONY, TOO!
THEY'RE--MEN-FISH OF SOME KIND!
AYE, WEB-SLINGER--THAT AND MORE--FOR THE WEAKNESS THAT ASSAILS YOU NOW COMES UPON ME AS WELL!
I KNOW NOT NOW, SPIDER-MAN--
--BUT WE'VE BEEN--
--DRUGGED-- UUHHHHNN
AND A SHORT WHILE LATER--AS A PAIN-WRACKED WEB-SLINGER FINALLY AWAKENS...
OHH--MY ACHIN' EVERYTHING! WHAT'D YOU GUYS DO TO US?
NOTHING REMARKABLE, SPIDER-MAN--
--MERELY A MILD CONTACT POISON YOU ABSORBED THRU THE PORES OF YOUR SKIN WHEN YOU TOUCHED THE COSTUMES OF OUR SPECIAL STAND-INS!
YOU'LL SURVIVE. WE'VE TAKEN GET PAINS TO ASSURE THAT...FOR NOW!

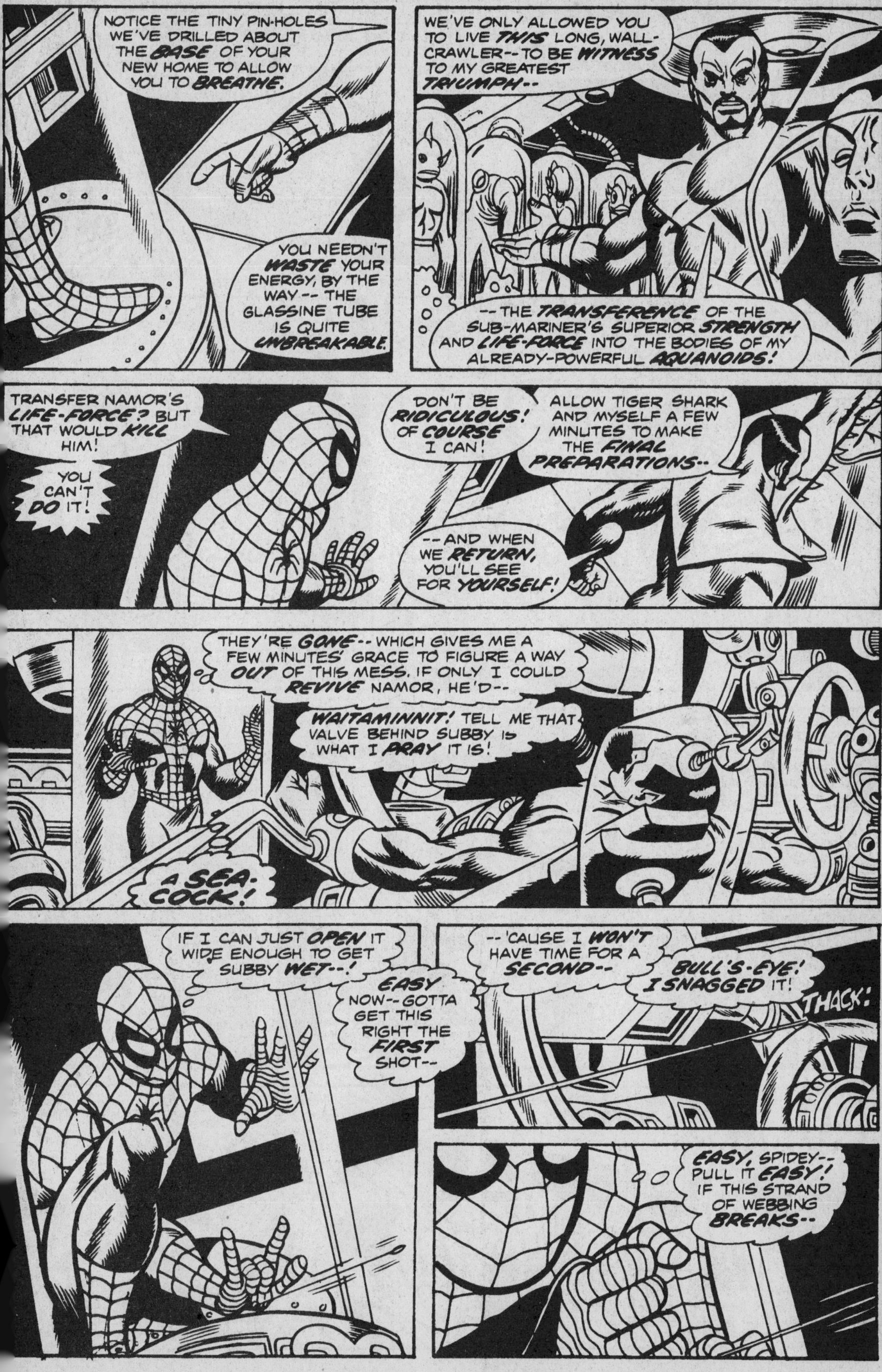
NOTICE THE TINY PIN-HOLES WE'VE DRILLED ABOUT THE BASE OF YOUR NEW HOME TO ALLOW YOU TO BREATHE.
YOU NEEDN'T WASTE YOUR ENERGY, BY THE WAY -- THE GLASSINE TUBE IS QUITE UNBREAKABLE.
WE'VE ONLY ALLOWED YOU TO LIVE THIS LONG, WALL-CRAWLER -- TO BE WITNESS TO MY GREATEST TRIUMPH --
-- THE TRANSFERENCE OF THE SUB-MARINER'S SUPERIOR STRENGTH AND LIFE-FORCE INTO THE BODIES OF MY ALREADY-POWERFUL AQUANOIDS!
TRANSFER NAMOR'S LIFE-FORCE? BUT THAT WOULD KILL HIM!
YOU CAN'T DO IT!
DON'T BE RIDICULOUS! OF COURSE I CAN!
ALLOW TIGER SHARK AND MYSELF A FEW MINUTES TO MAKE THE FINAL PREPARATIONS --
-- AND WHEN WE RETURN, YOU'LL SEE FOR YOURSELF!
THEY'RE GONE -- WHICH GIVES ME A FEW MINUTES' GRACE TO FIGURE A WAY OUT OF THIS MESS. IF ONLY I COULD REVIVE NAMOR, HE'D --
WAITAMINNIT! TELL ME THAT VALVE BEHIND SUBBY IS WHAT I PRAY IT IS!
A SEA-COCK!
IF I CAN JUST OPEN IT WIDE ENOUGH TO GET SUBBY WET -- !
EASY NOW -- GOTTA GET THIS RIGHT THE FIRST SHOT --
-- 'CAUSE I WON'T HAVE TIME FOR A SECOND --
BULL'S-EYE! I SNAGGED IT!
THACK!
EASY, SPIDEY -- PULL IT EASY! IF THIS STRAND OF WEBBING BREAKS --

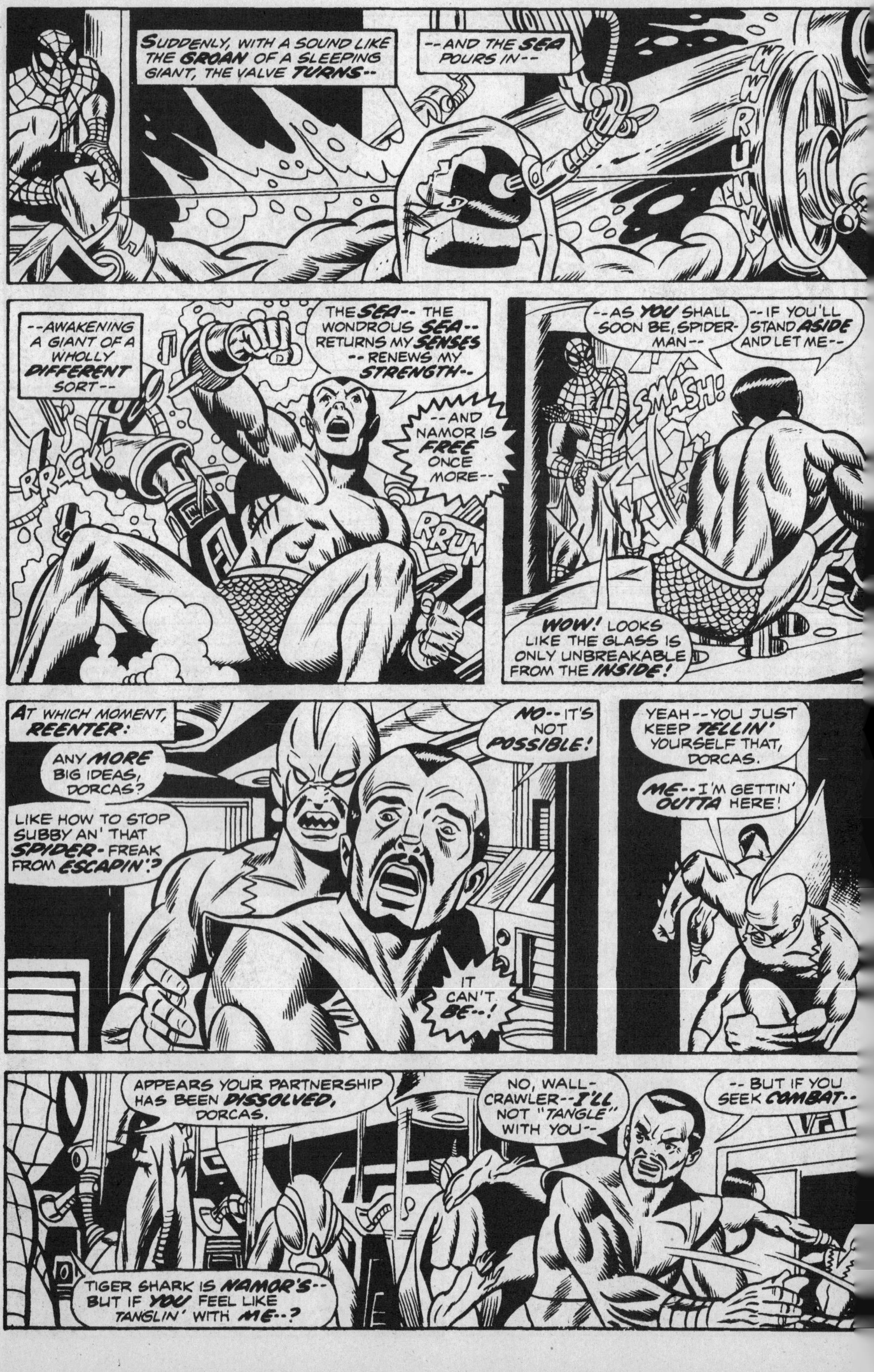
SUDDENLY, WITH A SOUND LIKE THE GROAN OF A SLEEPING GIANT, THE VALVE TURNS--
--AND THE SEA POURS IN--
WWWRRUNNK
--AWAKENING A GIANT OF A WHOLLY DIFFERENT SORT--
THE SEA-- THE WONDROUS SEA-- RETURNS MY SENSES --RENEWS MY STRENGTH--
--AND NAMOR IS FREE ONCE MORE--
RRACK!
RRUN
--AS YOU SHALL SOON BE, SPIDER-MAN--
--IF YOU'LL STAND ASIDE AND LET ME--
SMASH!
WOW! LOOKS LIKE THE GLASS IS ONLY UNBREAKABLE FROM THE INSIDE!
AT WHICH MOMENT, REENTER:
ANY MORE BIG IDEAS, DORCAS?
LIKE HOW TO STOP SUBBY AN' THAT SPIDER-FREAK FROM ESCAPIN'?
NO-- IT'S NOT POSSIBLE!
IT CAN'T BE--!
YEAH --YOU JUST KEEP TELLIN' YOURSELF THAT, DORCAS.
ME-- I'M GETTIN' OUTTA HERE!
APPEARS YOUR PARTNERSHIP HAS BEEN DISSOLVED, DORCAS.
TIGER SHARK IS NAMOR'S-- BUT IF YOU FEEL LIKE TANGLIN' WITH ME--?
NO, WALL-CRAWLER--I'LL NOT "TANGLE" WITH YOU--
-- BUT IF YOU SEEK COMBAT--

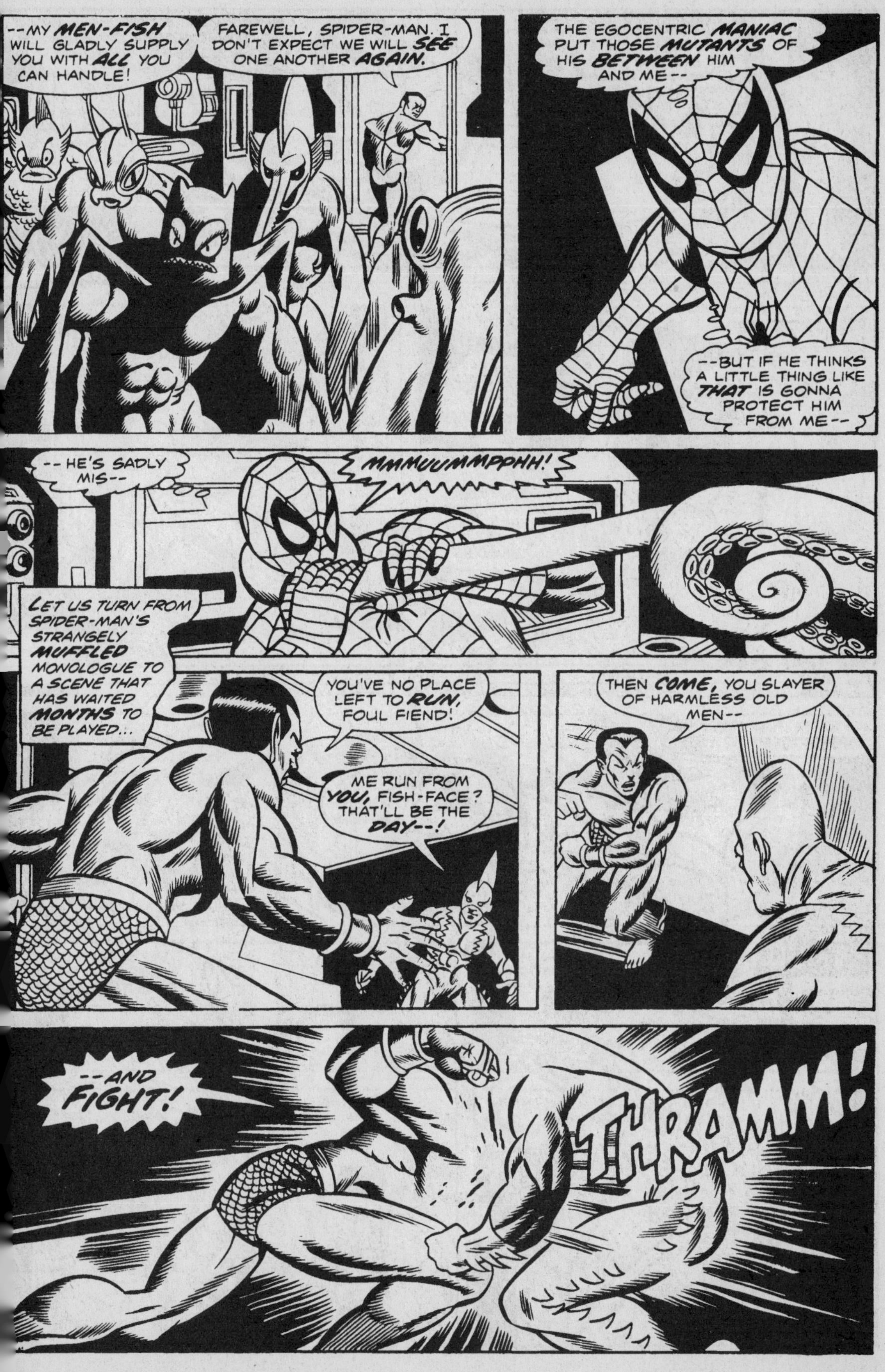
--MY MEN-FISH WILL GLADLY SUPPLY YOU WITH ALL YOU CAN HANDLE!
FAREWELL, SPIDER-MAN. I DON'T EXPECT WE WILL SEE ONE ANOTHER AGAIN.
THE EGOCENTRIC MANIAC PUT THOSE MUTANTS OF HIS BETWEEN HIM AND ME--
--BUT IF HE THINKS A LITTLE THING LIKE THAT IS GONNA PROTECT HIM FROM ME--
--HE'S SADLY MIS--
MMMUUMMPPHH!
LET US TURN FROM SPIDER-MAN'S STRANGELY MUFFLED MONOLOGUE TO A SCENE THAT HAS WAITED MONTHS TO BE PLAYED...
YOU'VE NO PLACE LEFT TO RUN, FOUL FIEND!
ME RUN FROM YOU, FISH-FACE? THAT'LL BE THE DAY--!
THEN COME, YOU SLAYER OF HARMLESS OLD MEN--
--AND FIGHT!
THRAMM!

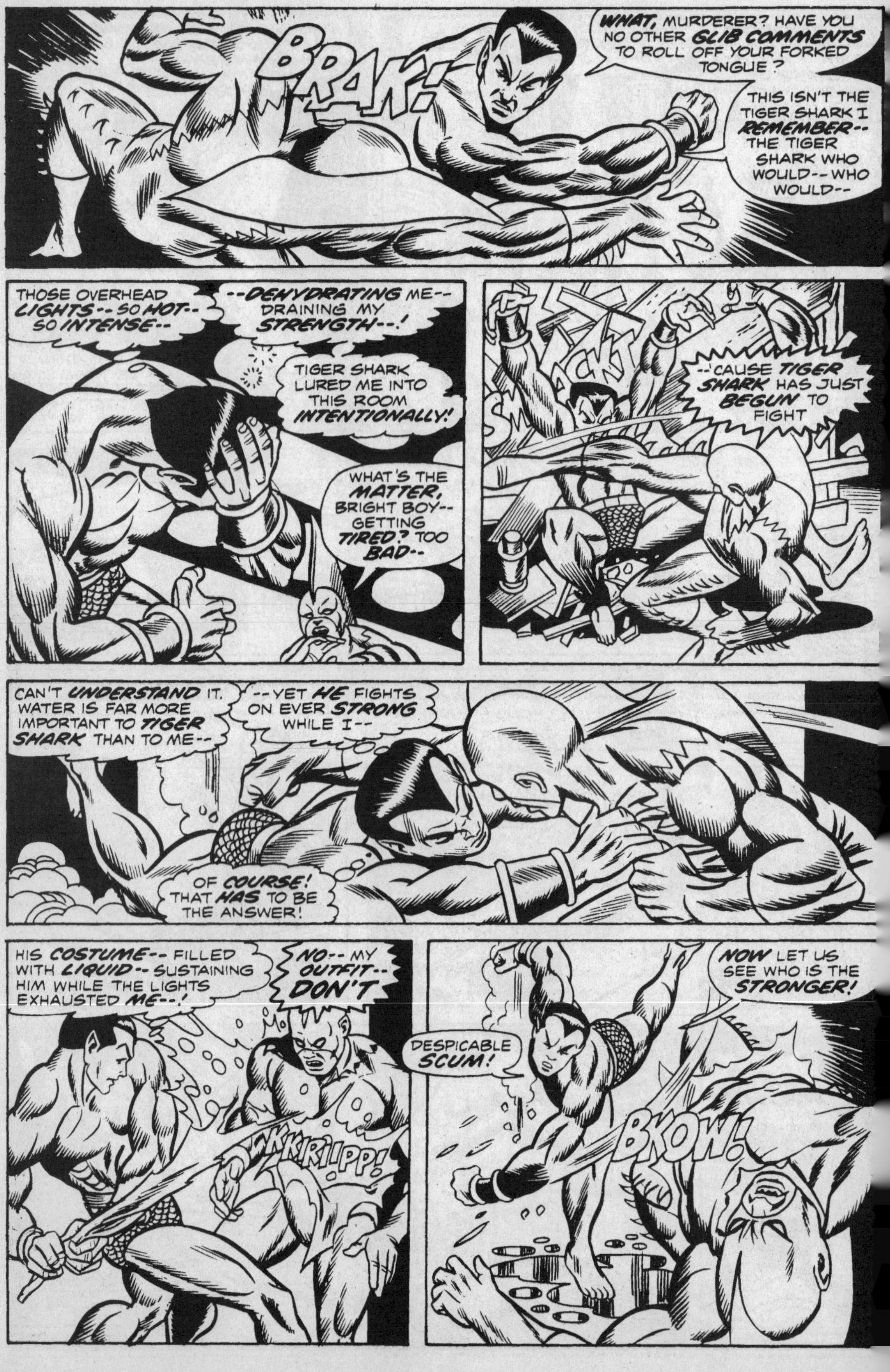
BRAK!
WHAT, MURDERER? HAVE YOU NO OTHER GLIB COMMENTS TO ROLL OFF YOUR FORKED TONGUE?
THIS ISN'T THE TIGER SHARK I REMEMBER-- THE TIGER SHARK WHO WOULD--WHO WOULD--
THOSE OVERHEAD LIGHTS--SO HOT--SO INTENSE--
--DEHYDRATING ME-- DRAINING MY STRENGTH--!
TIGER SHARK LURED ME INTO THIS ROOM INTENTIONALLY!
WHAT'S THE MATTER, BRIGHT BOY-- GETTING TIRED? TOO BAD--
--CAUSE TIGER SHARK HAS JUST BEGUN TO FIGHT
CAN'T UNDERSTAND IT. WATER IS FAR MORE IMPORTANT TO TIGER SHARK THAN TO ME--
--YET HE FIGHTS ON EVER STRONG WHILE I--
OF COURSE! THAT HAS TO BE THE ANSWER!
HIS COSTUME-- FILLED WITH LIQUID--SUSTAINING HIM WHILE THE LIGHTS EXHAUSTED ME--!
NO--MY OUTFIT-- DON'T
KKRIIPP!
NOW LET US SEE WHO IS THE STRONGER!
DESPICABLE SCUM!
BKOW!

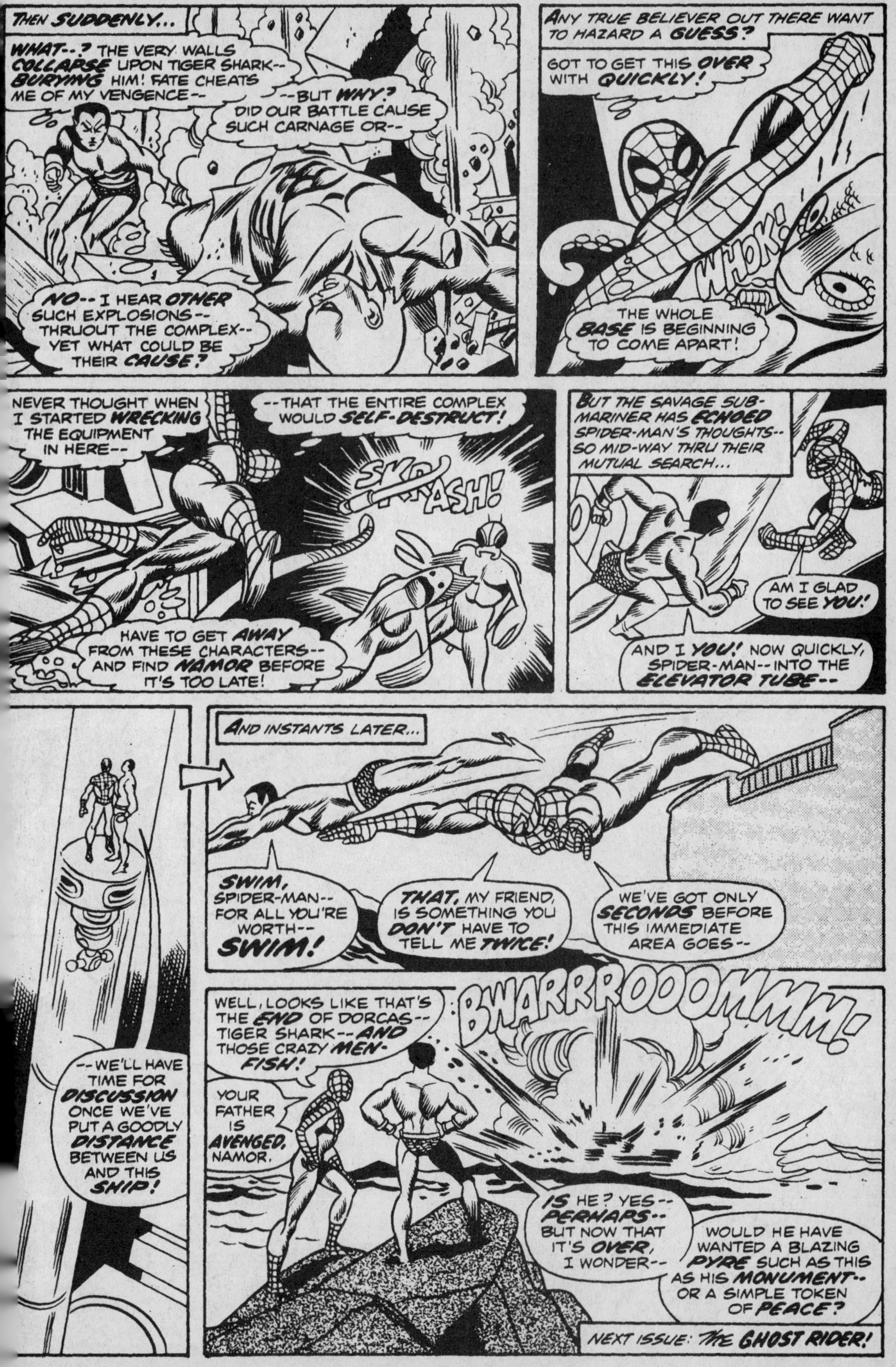
THEN SUDDENLY...
WHAT--? THE VERY WALLS COLLAPSE UPON TIGER SHARK--BURYING HIM! FATE CHEATS ME OF MY VENGENCE--
--BUT WHY? DID OUR BATTLE CAUSE SUCH CARNAGE OR--
NO--I HEAR OTHER SUCH EXPLOSIONS--THRUOUT THE COMPLEX--YET WHAT COULD BE THEIR CAUSE?
ANY TRUE BELIEVER OUT THERE WANT TO HAZARD A GUESS?
GOT TO GET THIS OVER WITH QUICKLY!
WHOK!
THE WHOLE BASE IS BEGINNING TO COME APART!
NEVER THOUGHT WHEN I STARTED WRECKING THE EQUIPMENT IN HERE--
--THAT THE ENTIRE COMPLEX WOULD SELF-DESTRUCT!
SKRASH!
HAVE TO GET AWAY FROM THESE CHARACTERS--AND FIND NAMOR BEFORE IT'S TOO LATE!
BUT THE SAVAGE SUB-MARINER HAS ECHOED SPIDER-MAN'S THOUGHTS--SO MID-WAY THRU THEIR MUTUAL SEARCH...
AM I GLAD TO SEE YOU!
AND I YOU! NOW QUICKLY, SPIDER-MAN--INTO THE ELEVATOR TUBE--
--WE'LL HAVE TIME FOR DISCUSSION ONCE WE'VE PUT A GOODLY DISTANCE BETWEEN US AND THIS SHIP!
AND INSTANTS LATER...
SWIM, SPIDER-MAN--FOR ALL YOU'RE WORTH--SWIM!
THAT, MY FRIEND, IS SOMETHING YOU DON'T HAVE TO TELL ME TWICE!
WE'VE GOT ONLY SECONDS BEFORE THIS IMMEDIATE AREA GOES--
WELL, LOOKS LIKE THAT'S THE END OF DORCAS--TIGER SHARK--AND THOSE CRAZY MEN-FISH!
BWARRROOOMMMM!
YOUR FATHER IS AVENGED, NAMOR.
IS HE? YES--PERHAPS--BUT NOW THAT IT'S OVER, I WONDER--
WOULD HE HAVE WANTED A BLAZING PYRE SUCH AS THIS AS HIS MONUMENT--OR A SIMPLE TOKEN OF PEACE?
NEXT ISSUE: THE GHOST RIDER!

MARVEL TEAM-UP
MARVEL COMICS GROUP™
APPROVED BY THE COMICS CODE AUTHORITY
20¢ CC
15 NOV 02147
MARVEL TEAM-UP™
FEATURING
SPIDER-MAN™
AND THE
GHOST RIDER™
GOOD LORD! I'LL NEVER STOP THIS TRAIN-- IN TIME!
SPIDER-MAN! REACH OUT-- GRAB MY HAND-- OR YOU'VE HAD IT!!
42nd St
NO! GET OFF THE TRACKS-- BEFORE YOU'RE KILLED, TOO!
IT'S-- TOO LATE FOR ME! TOO LATE!

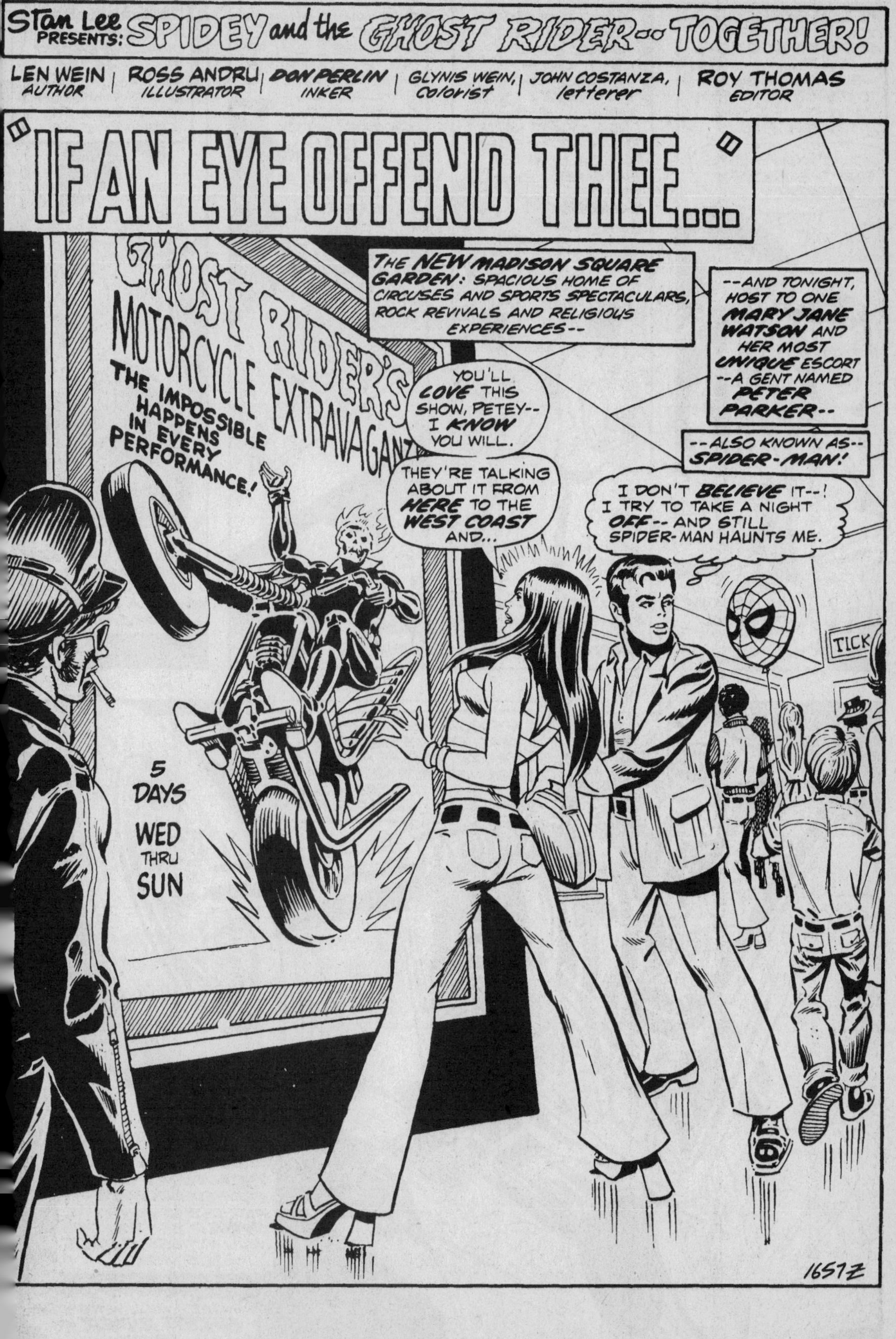

Stan Lee PRESENTS: SPIDEY and the GHOST RIDER -- TOGETHER!
LEN WEIN AUTHOR | ROSS ANDRU ILLUSTRATOR | DON PERLIN INKER | GLYNIS WEIN, colorist | JOHN COSTANZA, letterer | ROY THOMAS EDITOR
"IF AN EYE OFFEND THEE..."
GHOST RIDER'S MOTORCYCLE EXTRAVAGANZ
THE IMPOSSIBLE HAPPENS IN EVERY PERFORMANCE!
5 DAYS WED THRU SUN
THE NEW MADISON SQUARE GARDEN: SPACIOUS HOME OF CIRCUSES AND SPORTS SPECTACULARS, ROCK REVIVALS AND RELIGIOUS EXPERIENCES--
--AND TONIGHT, HOST TO ONE MARY JANE WATSON AND HER MOST UNIQUE ESCORT --A GENT NAMED PETER PARKER--
--ALSO KNOWN AS-- SPIDER-MAN!
YOU'LL LOVE THIS SHOW, PETEY-- I KNOW YOU WILL.
THEY'RE TALKING ABOUT IT FROM HERE TO THE WEST COAST AND...
I DON'T BELIEVE IT--! I TRY TO TAKE A NIGHT OFF-- AND STILL SPIDER-MAN HAUNTS ME.
TICK
1651Z

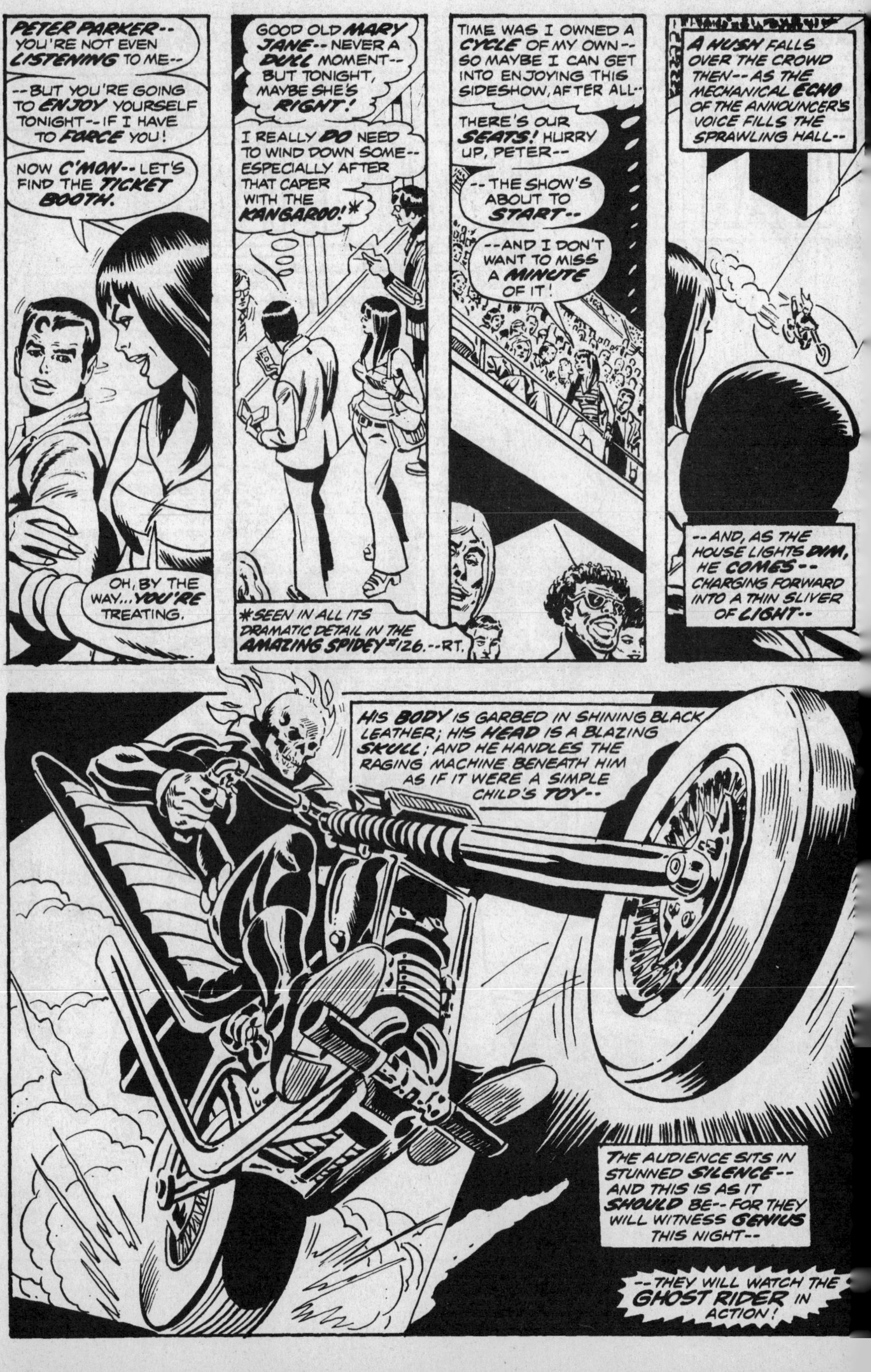
PETER PARKER-- YOU'RE NOT EVEN LISTENING TO ME--
--BUT YOU'RE GOING TO ENJOY YOURSELF TONIGHT--IF I HAVE TO FORCE YOU!
NOW C'MON--LET'S FIND THE TICKET BOOTH.
OH, BY THE WAY...YOU'RE TREATING.
GOOD OLD MARY JANE--NEVER A DULL MOMENT--BUT TONIGHT, MAYBE SHE'S RIGHT!
I REALLY DO NEED TO WIND DOWN SOME--ESPECIALLY AFTER THAT CAPER WITH THE KANGAROO!*
*SEEN IN ALL ITS DRAMATIC DETAIL IN THE AMAZING SPIDEY #126.--RT.
TIME WAS I OWNED A CYCLE OF MY OWN--SO MAYBE I CAN GET INTO ENJOYING THIS SIDESHOW, AFTER ALL--
THERE'S OUR SEATS! HURRY UP, PETER--
--THE SHOW'S ABOUT TO START--
--AND I DON'T WANT TO MISS A MINUTE OF IT!
A HUSH FALLS OVER THE CROWD THEN--AS THE MECHANICAL ECHO OF THE ANNOUNCER'S VOICE FILLS THE SPRAWLING HALL--
--AND, AS THE HOUSE LIGHTS DIM, HE COMES--CHARGING FORWARD INTO A THIN SLIVER OF LIGHT--
HIS BODY IS GARBED IN SHINING BLACK LEATHER; HIS HEAD IS A BLAZING SKULL; AND HE HANDLES THE RAGING MACHINE BENEATH HIM AS IF IT WERE A SIMPLE CHILD'S TOY--
THE AUDIENCE SITS IN STUNNED SILENCE--AND THIS IS AS IT SHOULD BE--FOR THEY WILL WITNESS GENIUS THIS NIGHT--
--THEY WILL WATCH THE GHOST RIDER IN ACTION!

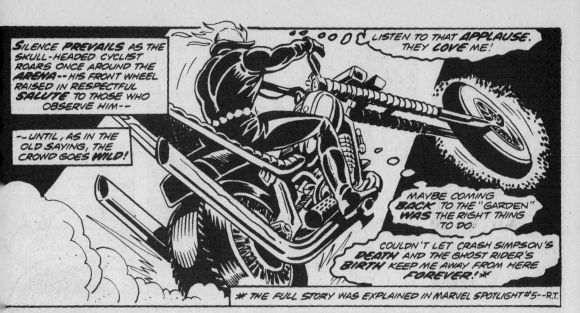

SILENCE *PREVAILS* AS THE SKULL-HEADED CYCLIST ROARS ONCE AROUND THE *ARENA*--HIS FRONT WHEEL RAISED IN RESPECTFUL *SALUTE* TO THOSE WHO OBSERVE HIM--

--UNTIL, AS IN THE OLD SAYING, THE CROWD GOES *WILD!*

LISTEN TO THAT *APPLAUSE.* THEY *LOVE* ME!

MAYBE COMING *BACK* TO THE "GARDEN" *WAS* THE RIGHT THING TO DO.

COULDN'T LET CRASH SIMPSON'S *DEATH* AND THE GHOST RIDER'S *BIRTH* KEEP ME AWAY FROM HERE *FOREVER!**

* THE FULL STORY WAS EXPLAINED IN MARVEL SPOTLIGHT #5--R.T.

WHILE, IN THE GRANDSTANDS...

HEY... THIS ISN'T GONNA BE *HALF* AS BAD AS I *THOUGHT*--!

DON'T KNOW *HOW* HE MANAGES THE *MAKE-UP*--

--BUT THAT *GHOST RIDER* IS ONE *IMPRESSIVE* GENT!

AND HE'S ABOUT TO BECOME A GOOD DEAL *MORE* IMPRESSIVE, PETER--AS HIS CYCLING SKILLS ARE TESTED BY...

BUT WHY DON'T WE LET THE *ANNOUNCER* EXPLAIN IT?

...*NOW,* FOR THE *FIRST* TIME ANYWHERE, JOHNNY BLAZE-- THE *GHOST RIDER*--WILL RISK, NOT ONLY HIS *OWN* LIFE, BUT THE LIVES OF *FOUR OTHERS*--

--IN AN EXHIBITION OF MOTORCYCLE *WIZARDRY* THAT WILL ASTOUND AND AMAZE YOU!

LADIES AND GENTLEMEN, IF YOU WILL PLEASE REMAIN SEATED AND SILENT, WE PRESENT...

...THE *GHOST RIDER*... AND THE *HEADSMAN'S RUN!*

WRROOMM

WRROOMM

WRROOMM!

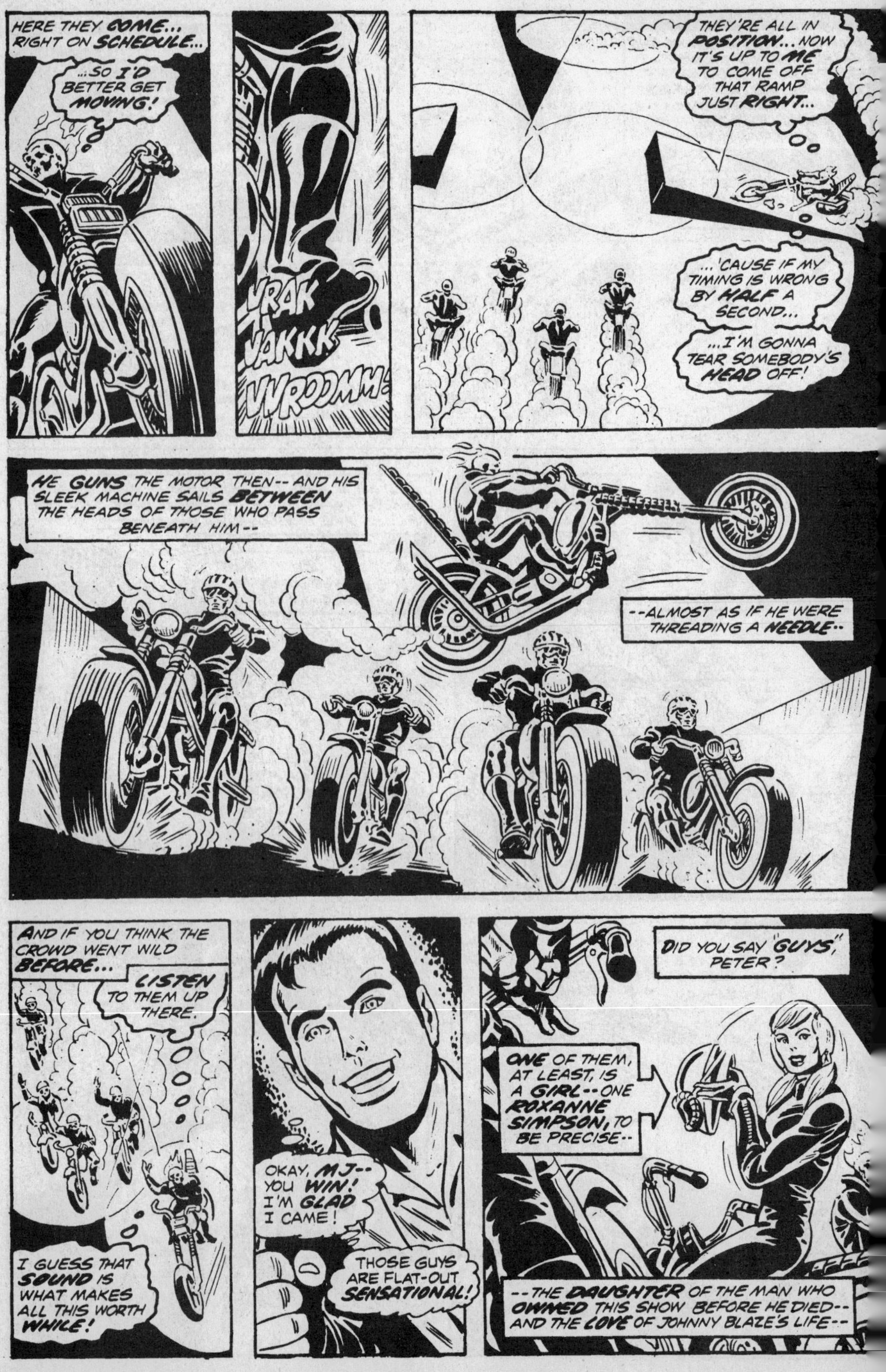
HERE THEY COME... RIGHT ON SCHEDULE...
...SO I'D BETTER GET MOVING!
VRAK
VAKKK
VVROOMM!
THEY'RE ALL IN POSITION... NOW IT'S UP TO ME TO COME OFF THAT RAMP JUST RIGHT...
...'CAUSE IF MY TIMING IS WRONG BY HALF A SECOND...
...I'M GONNA TEAR SOMEBODY'S HEAD OFF!
HE GUNS THE MOTOR THEN-- AND HIS SLEEK MACHINE SAILS BETWEEN THE HEADS OF THOSE WHO PASS BENEATH HIM--
--ALMOST AS IF HE WERE THREADING A NEEDLE--
AND IF YOU THINK THE CROWD WENT WILD BEFORE...
LISTEN TO THEM UP THERE.
I GUESS THAT SOUND IS WHAT MAKES ALL THIS WORTH WHILE!
OKAY, MJ-- YOU WIN! I'M GLAD I CAME!
THOSE GUYS ARE FLAT-OUT SENSATIONAL!
DID YOU SAY "GUYS", PETER?
ONE OF THEM, AT LEAST, IS A GIRL--ONE ROXANNE SIMPSON, TO BE PRECISE--
--THE DAUGHTER OF THE MAN WHO OWNED THIS SHOW BEFORE HE DIED-- AND THE LOVE OF JOHNNY BLAZE'S LIFE--

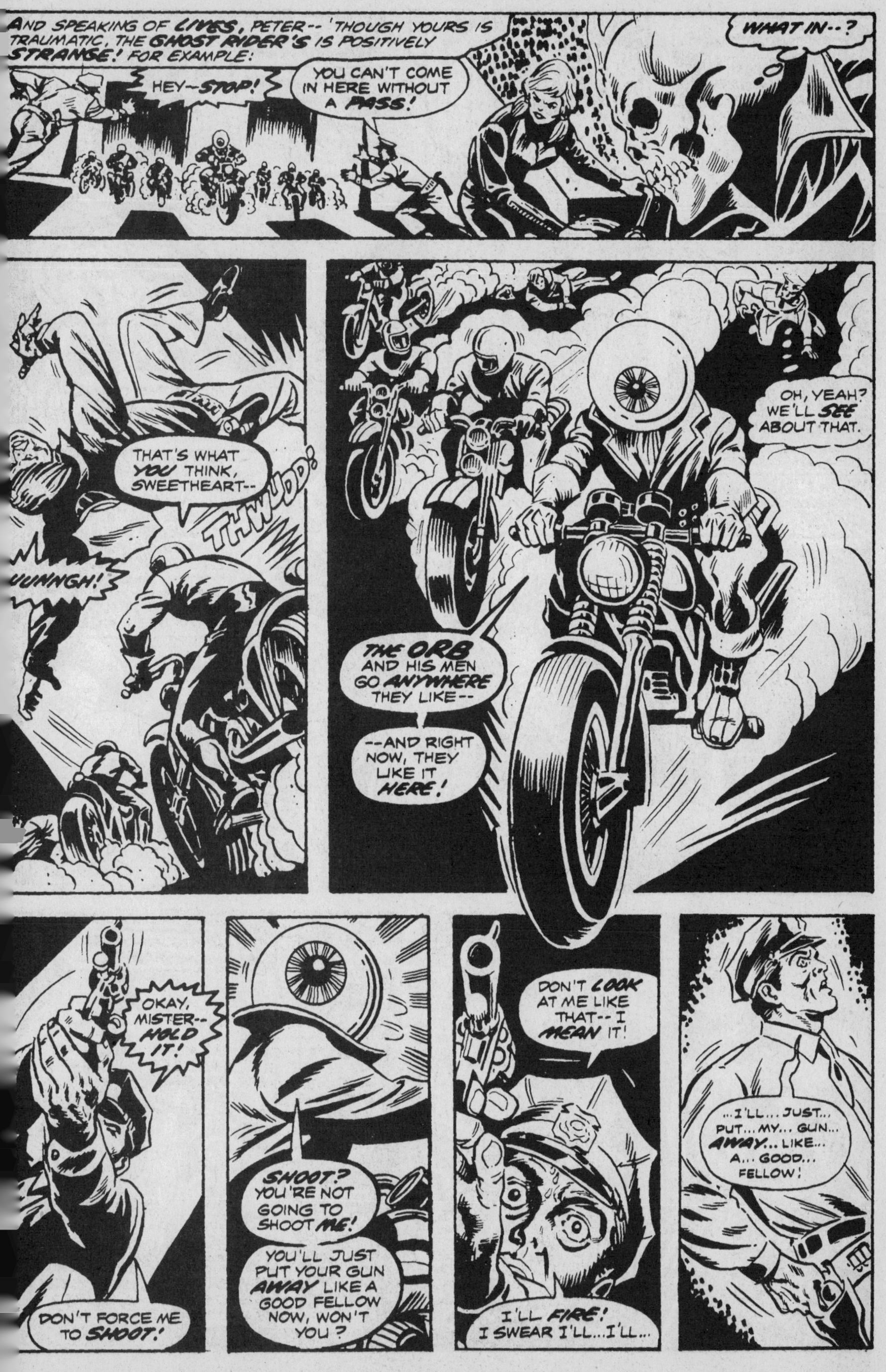

AND SPEAKING OF LIVES, PETER-- 'THOUGH YOURS IS TRAUMATIC, THE GHOST RIDER'S IS POSITIVELY STRANGE! FOR EXAMPLE:
HEY--STOP!
YOU CAN'T COME IN HERE WITHOUT A PASS!
WHAT IN--?
THAT'S WHAT YOU THINK, SWEETHEART--
THWUDD!
UUNNGH!
THE ORB AND HIS MEN GO ANYWHERE THEY LIKE--
--AND RIGHT NOW, THEY LIKE IT HERE!
OH, YEAH? WE'LL SEE ABOUT THAT.
OKAY, MISTER-- HOLD IT!
DON'T FORCE ME TO SHOOT!
SHOOT? YOU'RE NOT GOING TO SHOOT ME!
YOU'LL JUST PUT YOUR GUN AWAY LIKE A GOOD FELLOW NOW, WON'T YOU?
DON'T LOOK AT ME LIKE THAT-- I MEAN IT!
I'LL FIRE! I SWEAR I'LL...I'LL...
...I'LL... JUST... PUT... MY... GUN... AWAY... LIKE... A... GOOD... FELLOW!

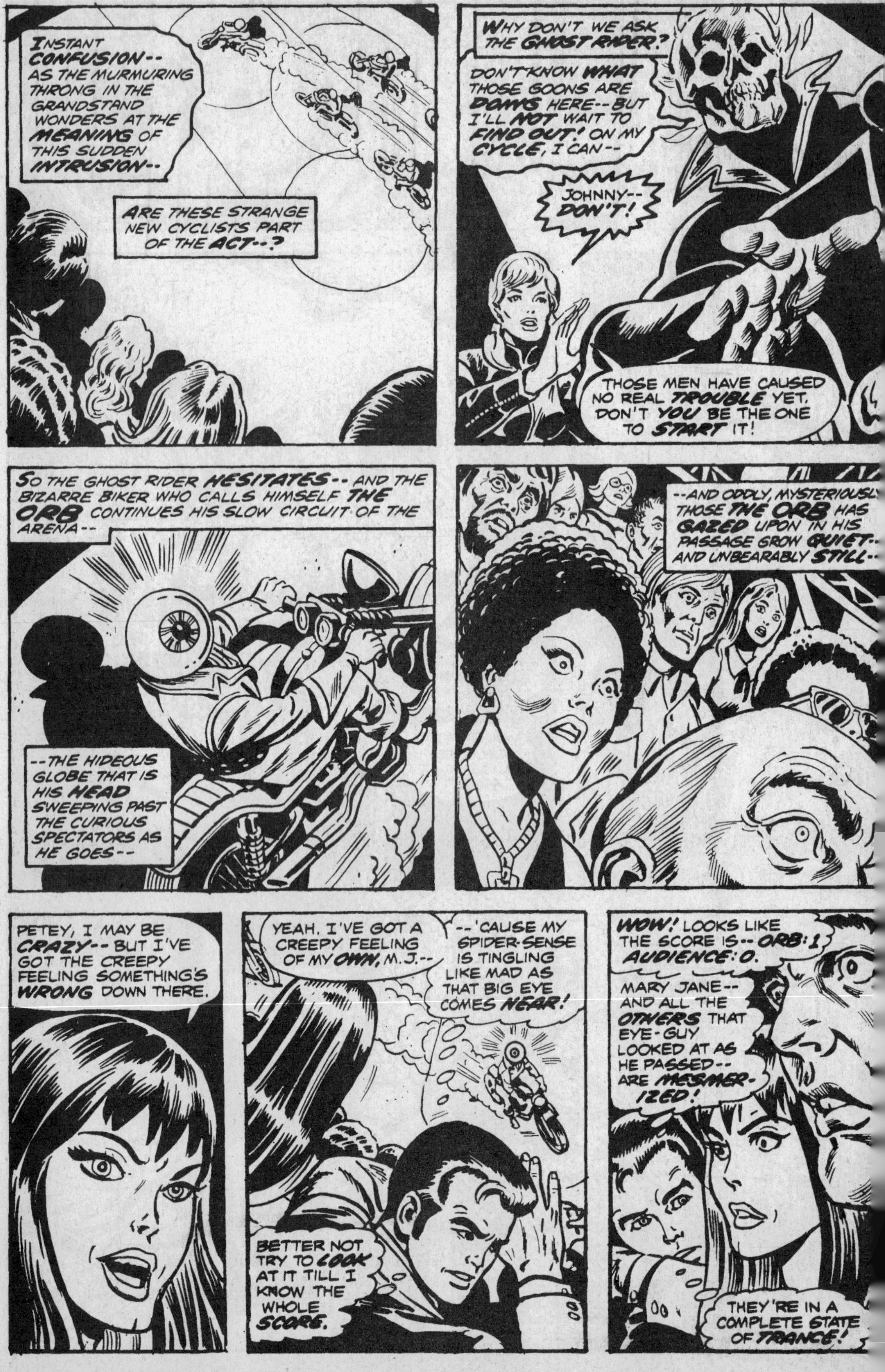

INSTANT CONFUSION-- AS THE MURMURING THRONG IN THE GRANDSTAND WONDERS AT THE MEANING OF THIS SUDDEN INTRUSION--
ARE THESE STRANGE NEW CYCLISTS PART OF THE ACT--?
WHY DON'T WE ASK THE GHOST RIDER?
DON'T KNOW WHAT THOSE GOONS ARE DOING HERE--BUT I'LL NOT WAIT TO FIND OUT! ON MY CYCLE, I CAN--
JOHNNY-- DON'T!
THOSE MEN HAVE CAUSED NO REAL TROUBLE YET. DON'T YOU BE THE ONE TO START IT!
SO THE GHOST RIDER HESITATES-- AND THE BIZARRE BIKER WHO CALLS HIMSELF THE ORB CONTINUES HIS SLOW CIRCUIT OF THE ARENA--
--THE HIDEOUS GLOBE THAT IS HIS HEAD SWEEPING PAST THE CURIOUS SPECTATORS AS HE GOES--
--AND ODDLY, MYSTERIOUSL THOSE THE ORB HAS GAZED UPON IN HIS PASSAGE GROW QUIET-- AND UNBEARABLY STILL--
PETEY, I MAY BE CRAZY-- BUT I'VE GOT THE CREEPY FEELING SOMETHING'S WRONG DOWN THERE.
YEAH. I'VE GOT A CREEPY FEELING OF MY OWN, M.J.--
--'CAUSE MY SPIDER-SENSE IS TINGLING LIKE MAD AS THAT BIG EYE COMES NEAR!
BETTER NOT TRY TO LOOK AT IT TILL I KNOW THE WHOLE SCORE.
WOW! LOOKS LIKE THE SCORE IS-- ORB: 1 AUDIENCE: 0.
MARY JANE-- AND ALL THE OTHERS THAT EYE-GUY LOOKED AT AS HE PASSED-- ARE MESMER-IZED!
THEY'RE IN A COMPLETE STATE OF TRANCE!

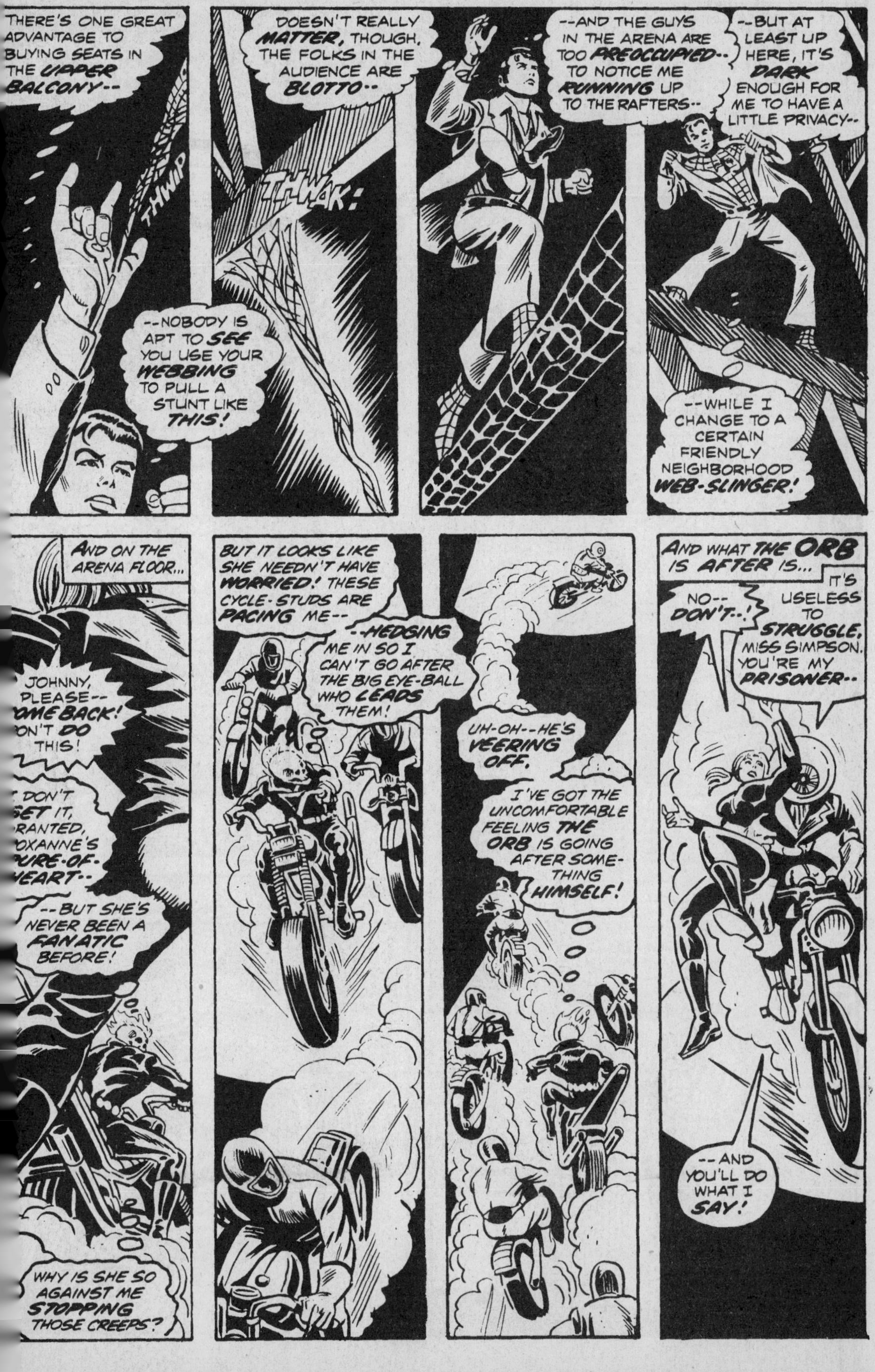
THERE'S ONE GREAT ADVANTAGE TO BUYING SEATS IN THE UPPER BALCONY--
--NOBODY IS APT TO SEE YOU USE YOUR WEBBING TO PULL A STUNT LIKE THIS!
THWIP
DOESN'T REALLY MATTER, THOUGH, THE FOLKS IN THE AUDIENCE ARE BLOTTO--
THWAK!
--AND THE GUYS IN THE ARENA ARE TOO PREOCCUPIED-- TO NOTICE ME RUNNING UP TO THE RAFTERS--
--BUT AT LEAST UP HERE, IT'S DARK ENOUGH FOR ME TO HAVE A LITTLE PRIVACY--
--WHILE I CHANGE TO A CERTAIN FRIENDLY NEIGHBORHOOD WEB-SLINGER!
AND ON THE ARENA FLOOR...
JOHNNY, PLEASE-- OME BACK! ON'T DO THIS!
DON'T ET IT, RANTED, OXANNE'S URE-OF- EART--
--BUT SHE'S NEVER BEEN A FANATIC BEFORE!
WHY IS SHE SO AGAINST ME STOPPING THOSE CREEPS?
BUT IT LOOKS LIKE SHE NEEDN'T HAVE WORRIED! THESE CYCLE-STUDS ARE PACING ME--
--HEDGING ME IN SO I CAN'T GO AFTER THE BIG EYE-BALL WHO LEADS THEM!
UH-OH--HE'S VEERING OFF.
I'VE GOT THE UNCOMFORTABLE FEELING THE ORB IS GOING AFTER SOME-THING HIMSELF!
AND WHAT THE ORB IS AFTER IS...
NO-- DON'T--!
IT'S USELESS TO STRUGGLE, MISS SIMPSON. YOU'RE MY PRISONER--
--AND YOU'LL DO WHAT I SAY!

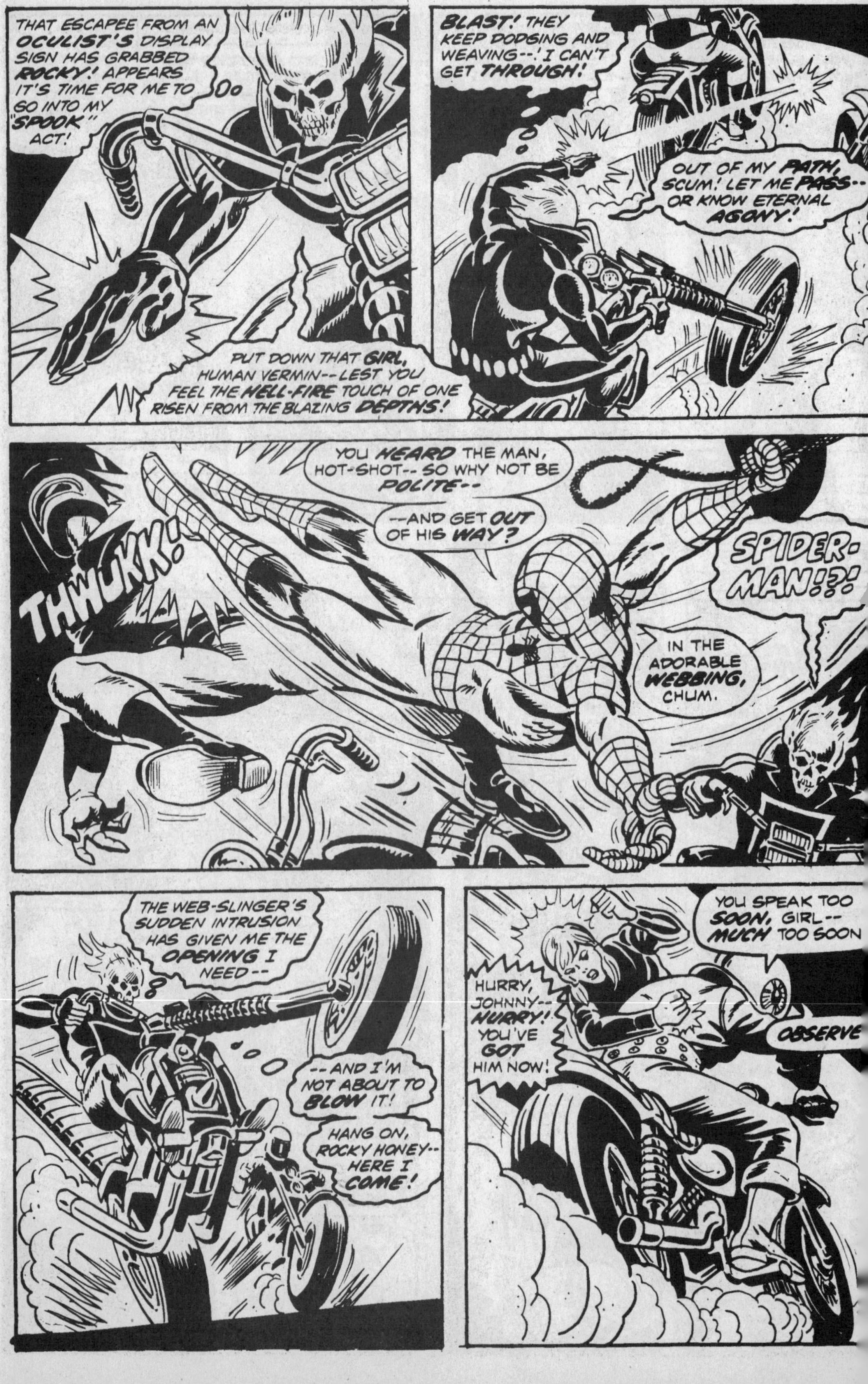
THAT ESCAPEE FROM AN OCULIST'S DISPLAY SIGN HAS GRABBED ROCKY! APPEARS IT'S TIME FOR ME TO GO INTO MY "SPOOK" ACT!
PUT DOWN THAT GIRL, HUMAN VERMIN--LEST YOU FEEL THE HELL-FIRE TOUCH OF ONE RISEN FROM THE BLAZING DEPTHS!
BLAST! THEY KEEP DODGING AND WEAVING--! I CAN'T GET THROUGH!
OUT OF MY PATH, SCUM! LET ME PASS--OR KNOW ETERNAL AGONY!
THWUKK!
YOU HEARD THE MAN, HOT-SHOT--SO WHY NOT BE POLITE--
--AND GET OUT OF HIS WAY?
SPIDER-MAN!?!
IN THE ADORABLE WEBBING, CHUM.
THE WEB-SLINGER'S SUDDEN INTRUSION HAS GIVEN ME THE OPENING I NEED--
--AND I'M NOT ABOUT TO BLOW IT!
HANG ON, ROCKY HONEY--HERE I COME!
HURRY, JOHNNY--HURRY! YOU'VE GOT HIM NOW!
YOU SPEAK TOO SOON, GIRL--MUCH TOO SOON
OBSERVE

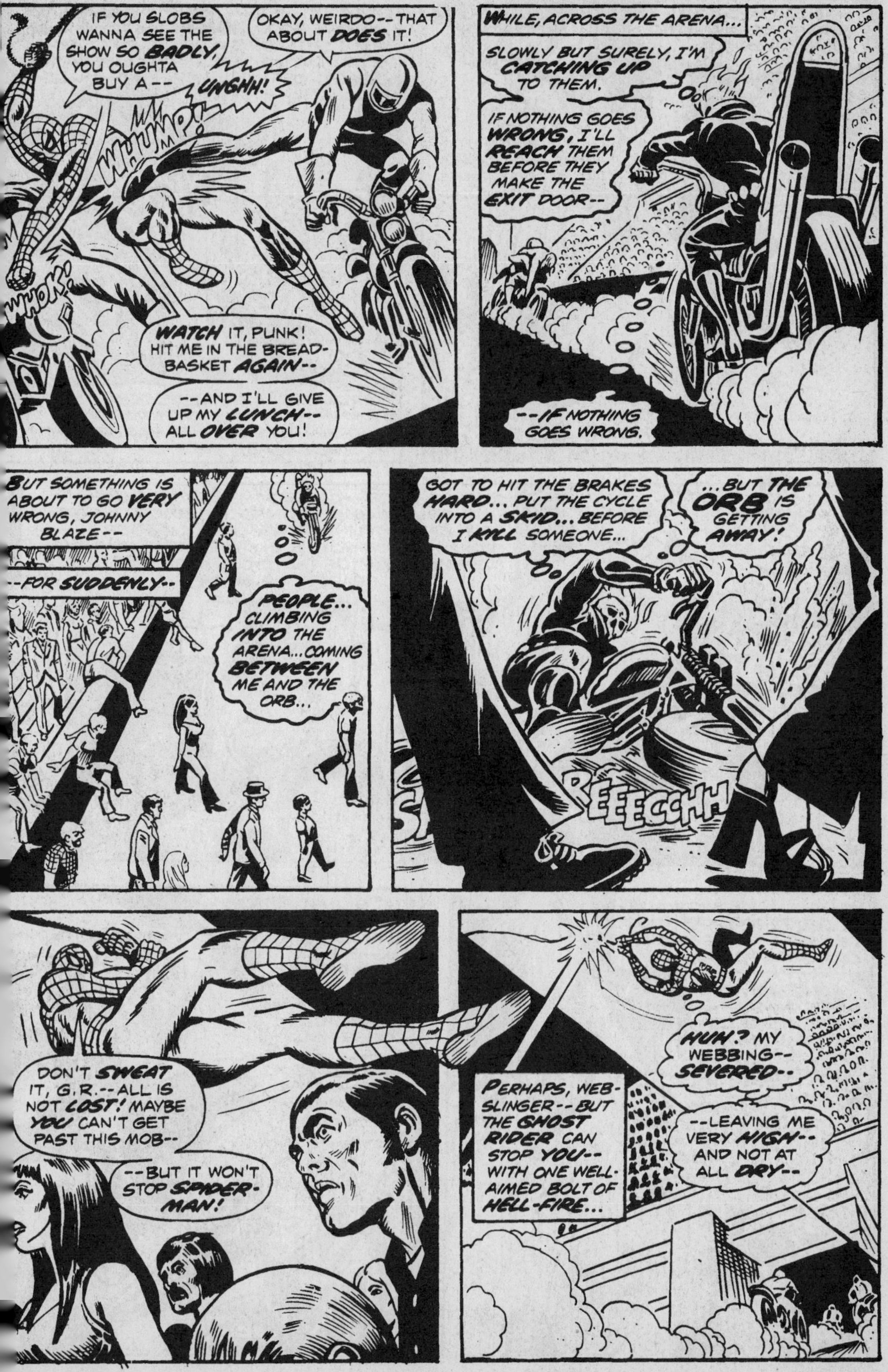

IF YOU SLOBS WANNA SEE THE SHOW SO BADLY, YOU OUGHTA BUY A--
OKAY, WEIRDO--THAT ABOUT DOES IT!
UNGHH!
WHUMP!
WHOK!
WATCH IT, PUNK! HIT ME IN THE BREAD-BASKET AGAIN--
--AND I'LL GIVE UP MY LUNCH--ALL OVER YOU!
WHILE, ACROSS THE ARENA...
SLOWLY BUT SURELY, I'M CATCHING UP TO THEM.
IF NOTHING GOES WRONG, I'LL REACH THEM BEFORE THEY MAKE THE EXIT DOOR--
--IF NOTHING GOES WRONG.
BUT SOMETHING IS ABOUT TO GO VERY WRONG, JOHNNY BLAZE--
--FOR SUDDENLY--
PEOPLE... CLIMBING INTO THE ARENA... COMING BETWEEN ME AND THE ORB...
GOT TO HIT THE BRAKES HARD... PUT THE CYCLE INTO A SKID... BEFORE I KILL SOMEONE...
...BUT THE ORB IS GETTING AWAY!
REEEECCHH
DON'T SWEAT IT, G.R.--ALL IS NOT LOST! MAYBE YOU CAN'T GET PAST THIS MOB--
--BUT IT WON'T STOP SPIDER-MAN!
HUH? MY WEBBING--SEVERED--
PERHAPS, WEB-SLINGER--BUT THE GHOST RIDER CAN STOP YOU--WITH ONE WELL-AIMED BOLT OF HELL-FIRE...
--LEAVING ME VERY HIGH--AND NOT AT ALL DRY--

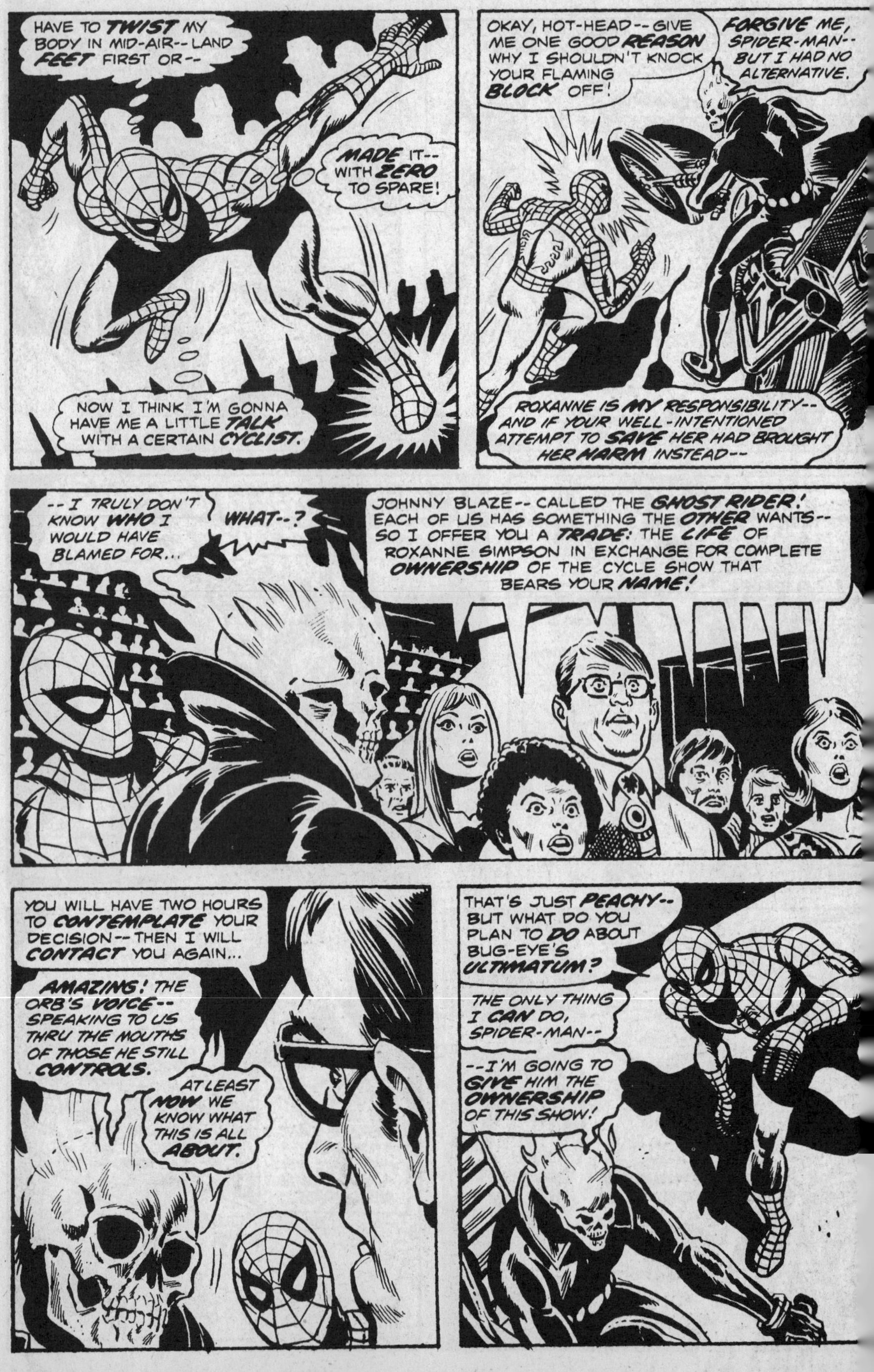

HAVE TO TWIST MY BODY IN MID-AIR-- LAND FEET FIRST OR--
MADE IT-- WITH ZERO TO SPARE!
NOW I THINK I'M GONNA HAVE ME A LITTLE TALK WITH A CERTAIN CYCLIST.
OKAY, HOT-HEAD-- GIVE ME ONE GOOD REASON WHY I SHOULDN'T KNOCK YOUR FLAMING BLOCK OFF!
FORGIVE ME, SPIDER-MAN-- BUT I HAD NO ALTERNATIVE.
ROXANNE IS MY RESPONSIBILITY-- AND IF YOUR WELL-INTENTIONED ATTEMPT TO SAVE HER HAD BROUGHT HER HARM INSTEAD--
--I TRULY DON'T KNOW WHO I WOULD HAVE BLAMED FOR...
WHAT--?
JOHNNY BLAZE-- CALLED THE GHOST RIDER! EACH OF US HAS SOMETHING THE OTHER WANTS-- SO I OFFER YOU A TRADE: THE LIFE OF ROXANNE SIMPSON IN EXCHANGE FOR COMPLETE OWNERSHIP OF THE CYCLE SHOW THAT BEARS YOUR NAME!
YOU WILL HAVE TWO HOURS TO CONTEMPLATE YOUR DECISION-- THEN I WILL CONTACT YOU AGAIN...
AMAZING! THE ORB'S VOICE-- SPEAKING TO US THRU THE MOUTHS OF THOSE HE STILL CONTROLS.
AT LEAST NOW WE KNOW WHAT THIS IS ALL ABOUT.
THAT'S JUST PEACHY-- BUT WHAT DO YOU PLAN TO DO ABOUT BUG-EYE'S ULTIMATUM?
THE ONLY THING I CAN DO, SPIDER-MAN--
--I'M GOING TO GIVE HIM THE OWNERSHIP OF THIS SHOW!

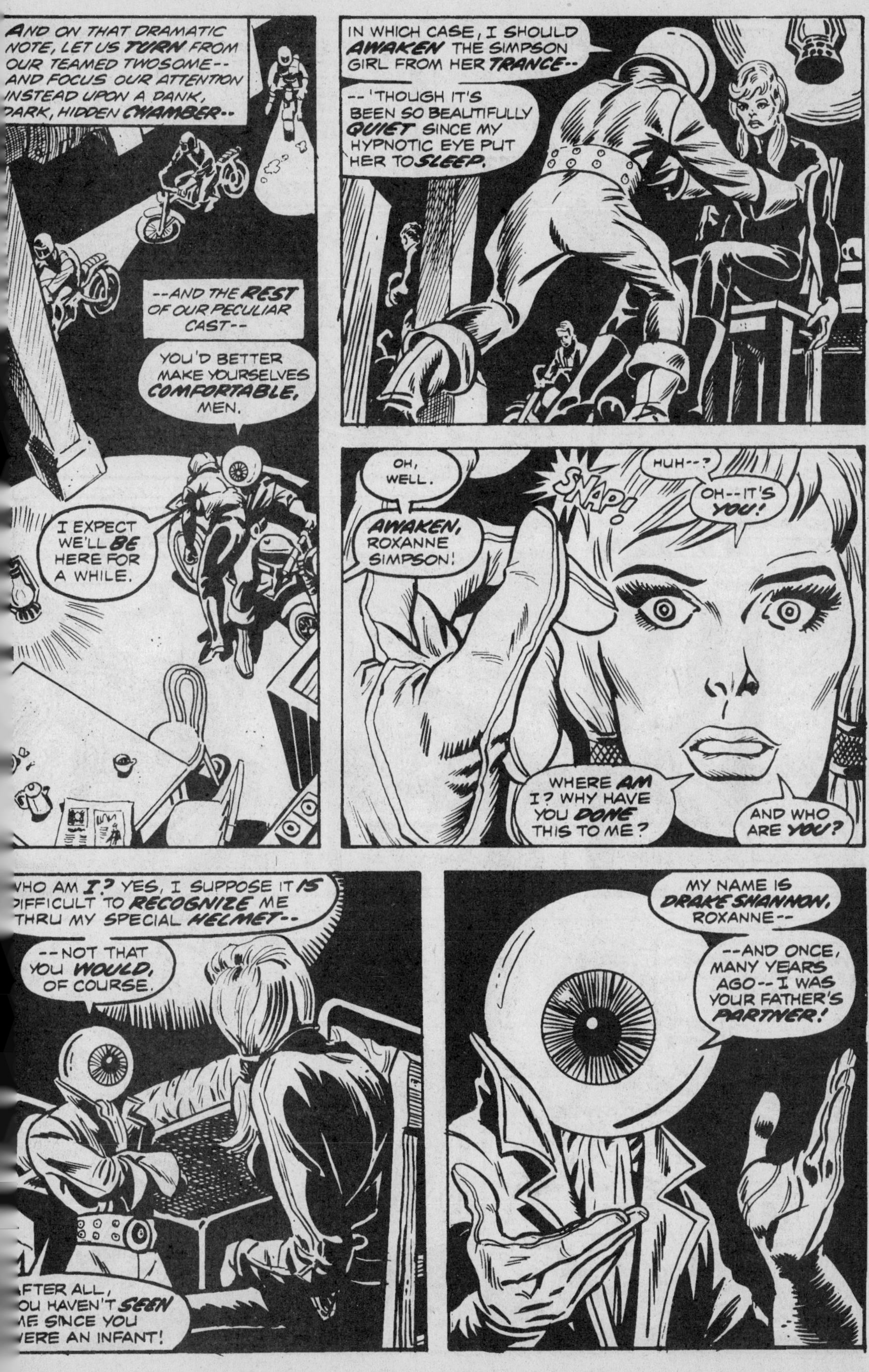
AND ON THAT DRAMATIC NOTE, LET US TURN FROM OUR TEAMED TWOSOME-- AND FOCUS OUR ATTENTION INSTEAD UPON A DANK, DARK, HIDDEN CHAMBER--
--AND THE REST OF OUR PECULIAR CAST--
YOU'D BETTER MAKE YOURSELVES COMFORTABLE, MEN.
I EXPECT WE'LL BE HERE FOR A WHILE.
IN WHICH CASE, I SHOULD AWAKEN THE SIMPSON GIRL FROM HER TRANCE--
--'THOUGH IT'S BEEN SO BEAUTIFULLY QUIET SINCE MY HYPNOTIC EYE PUT HER TO SLEEP.
OH, WELL.
AWAKEN, ROXANNE SIMPSON!
SNAP!
HUH--?
OH--IT'S YOU!
WHERE AM I? WHY HAVE YOU DONE THIS TO ME?
AND WHO ARE YOU?
WHO AM I? YES, I SUPPOSE IT IS DIFFICULT TO RECOGNIZE ME THRU MY SPECIAL HELMET--
--NOT THAT YOU WOULD, OF COURSE.
AFTER ALL, YOU HAVEN'T SEEN ME SINCE YOU WERE AN INFANT!
MY NAME IS DRAKE SHANNON, ROXANNE--
--AND ONCE, MANY YEARS AGO--I WAS YOUR FATHER'S PARTNER!

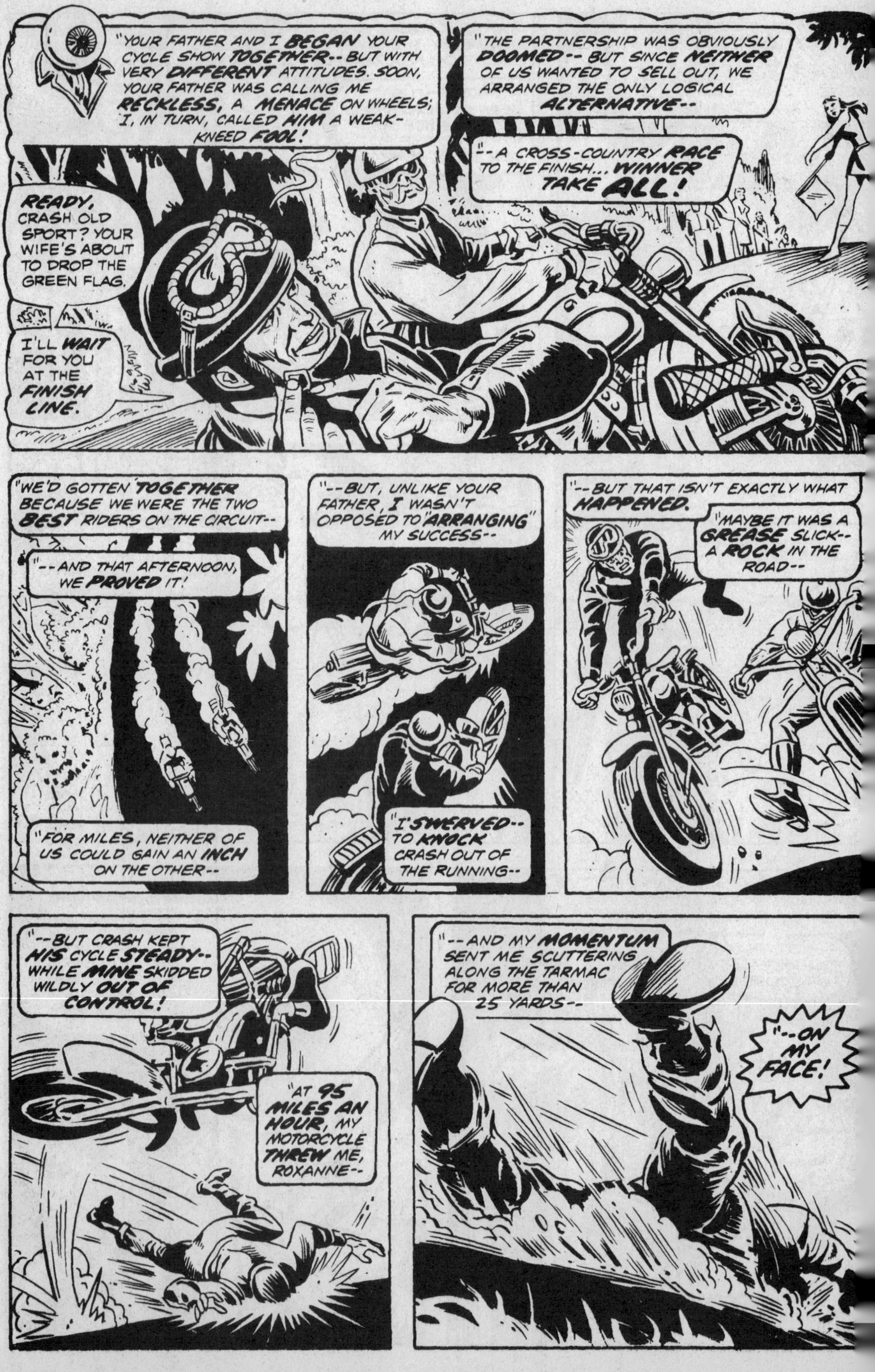
"YOUR FATHER AND I BEGAN YOUR CYCLE SHOW TOGETHER-- BUT WITH VERY DIFFERENT ATTITUDES. SOON, YOUR FATHER WAS CALLING ME RECKLESS, A MENACE ON WHEELS; I, IN TURN, CALLED HIM A WEAK-KNEED FOOL!
"THE PARTNERSHIP WAS OBVIOUSLY DOOMED-- BUT SINCE NEITHER OF US WANTED TO SELL OUT, WE ARRANGED THE ONLY LOGICAL ALTERNATIVE--
"--A CROSS-COUNTRY RACE TO THE FINISH... WINNER TAKE ALL!
READY, CRASH OLD SPORT? YOUR WIFE'S ABOUT TO DROP THE GREEN FLAG.
I'LL WAIT FOR YOU AT THE FINISH LINE.
"WE'D GOTTEN TOGETHER BECAUSE WE WERE THE TWO BEST RIDERS ON THE CIRCUIT--
"--AND THAT AFTERNOON, WE PROVED IT!
"FOR MILES, NEITHER OF US COULD GAIN AN INCH ON THE OTHER--
"--BUT, UNLIKE YOUR FATHER, I WASN'T OPPOSED TO "ARRANGING" MY SUCCESS--
"I SWERVED-- TO KNOCK CRASH OUT OF THE RUNNING--
"--BUT THAT ISN'T EXACTLY WHAT HAPPENED.
"MAYBE IT WAS A GREASE SLICK-- A ROCK IN THE ROAD--
"--BUT CRASH KEPT HIS CYCLE STEADY-- WHILE MINE SKIDDED WILDLY OUT OF CONTROL!
"AT 95 MILES AN HOUR, MY MOTORCYCLE THREW ME, ROXANNE--
"--AND MY MOMENTUM SENT ME SCUTTERING ALONG THE TARMAC FOR MORE THAN 25 YARDS--
"--ON MY FACE!

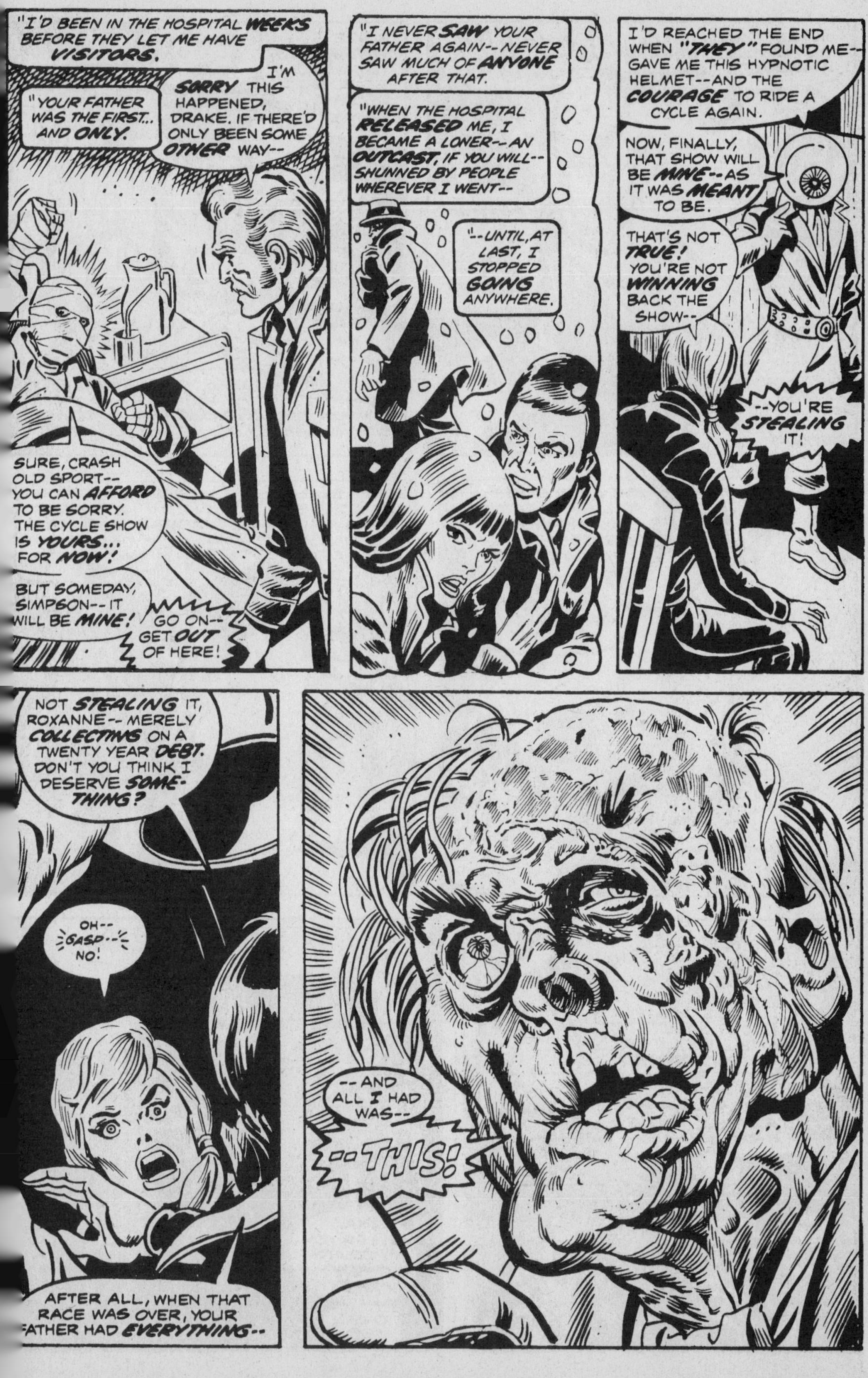
"I'D BEEN IN THE HOSPITAL WEEKS BEFORE THEY LET ME HAVE VISITORS.
"YOUR FATHER WAS THE FIRST... AND ONLY.
I'M SORRY THIS HAPPENED, DRAKE. IF THERE'D ONLY BEEN SOME OTHER WAY--
SURE, CRASH OLD SPORT-- YOU CAN AFFORD TO BE SORRY. THE CYCLE SHOW IS YOURS... FOR NOW!
BUT SOMEDAY, SIMPSON-- IT WILL BE MINE!
GO ON-- GET OUT OF HERE!
"I NEVER SAW YOUR FATHER AGAIN--NEVER SAW MUCH OF ANYONE AFTER THAT.
"WHEN THE HOSPITAL RELEASED ME, I BECAME A LONER--AN OUTCAST, IF YOU WILL-- SHUNNED BY PEOPLE WHEREVER I WENT--
"--UNTIL, AT LAST, I STOPPED GOING ANYWHERE.
I'D REACHED THE END WHEN "THEY" FOUND ME-- GAVE ME THIS HYPNOTIC HELMET--AND THE COURAGE TO RIDE A CYCLE AGAIN.
NOW, FINALLY, THAT SHOW WILL BE MINE--AS IT WAS MEANT TO BE.
THAT'S NOT TRUE! YOU'RE NOT WINNING BACK THE SHOW--
--YOU'RE STEALING IT!
NOT STEALING IT, ROXANNE-- MERELY COLLECTING ON A TWENTY YEAR DEBT. DON'T YOU THINK I DESERVE SOME-THING?
OH-- GASP-- NO!
AFTER ALL, WHEN THAT RACE WAS OVER, YOUR FATHER HAD EVERYTHING--
--AND ALL I HAD WAS--
--THIS!

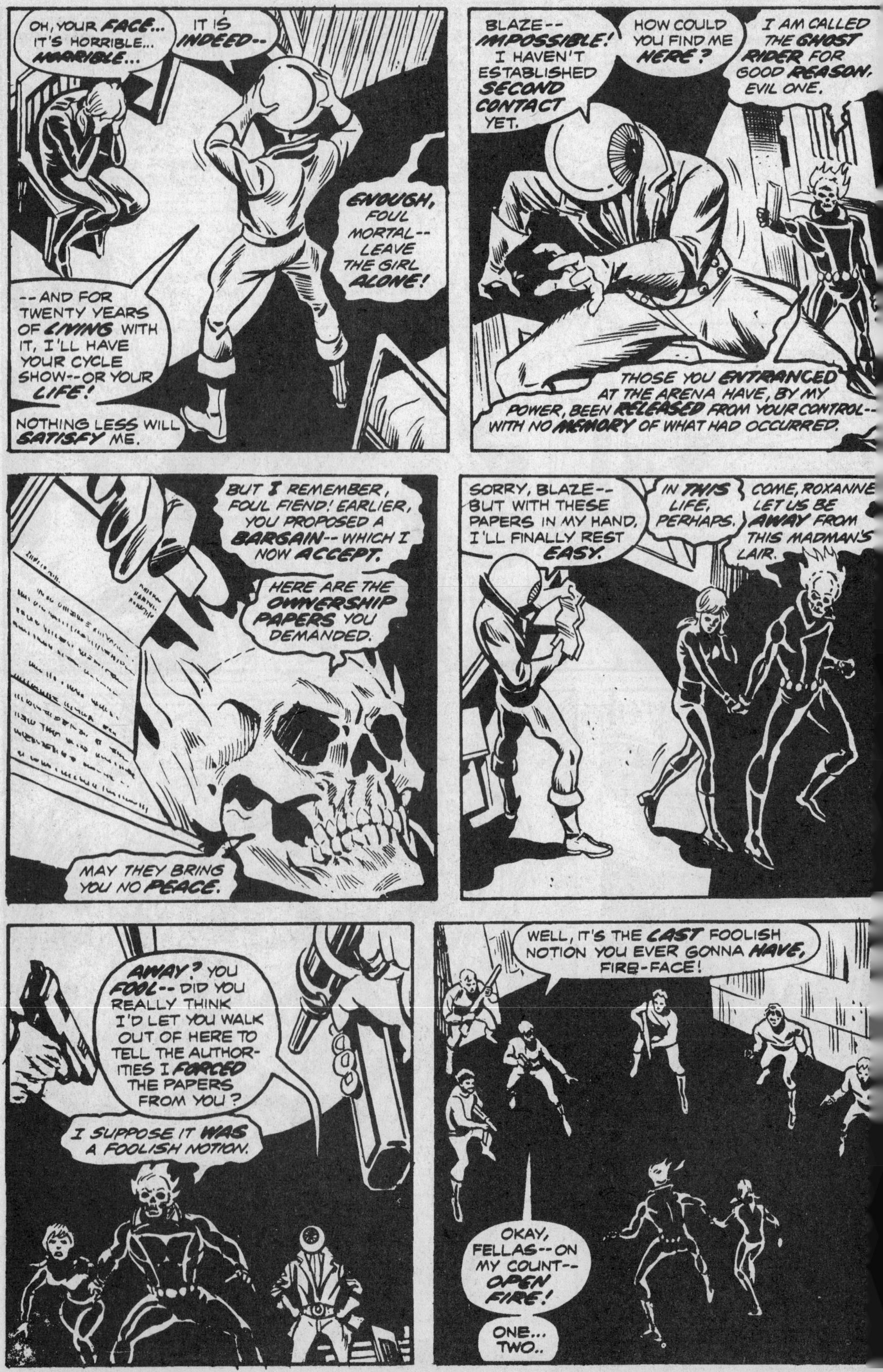

OH, YOUR FACE... IT'S HORRIBLE... HORRIBLE...
IT IS INDEED--
--AND FOR TWENTY YEARS OF LIVING WITH IT, I'LL HAVE YOUR CYCLE SHOW--OR YOUR LIFE!
NOTHING LESS WILL SATISFY ME.
ENOUGH, FOUL MORTAL-- LEAVE THE GIRL ALONE!
BLAZE-- IMPOSSIBLE! I HAVEN'T ESTABLISHED SECOND CONTACT YET.
HOW COULD YOU FIND ME HERE?
I AM CALLED THE GHOST RIDER FOR GOOD REASON, EVIL ONE.
THOSE YOU ENTRANCED AT THE ARENA HAVE, BY MY POWER, BEEN RELEASED FROM YOUR CONTROL-- WITH NO MEMORY OF WHAT HAD OCCURRED.
BUT I REMEMBER, FOUL FIEND! EARLIER, YOU PROPOSED A BARGAIN-- WHICH I NOW ACCEPT.
HERE ARE THE OWNERSHIP PAPERS YOU DEMANDED.
MAY THEY BRING YOU NO PEACE.
SORRY, BLAZE-- BUT WITH THESE PAPERS IN MY HAND, I'LL FINALLY REST EASY.
IN THIS LIFE, PERHAPS.
COME, ROXANNE LET US BE AWAY FROM THIS MADMAN'S LAIR.
AWAY? YOU FOOL-- DID YOU REALLY THINK I'D LET YOU WALK OUT OF HERE TO TELL THE AUTHORITIES I FORCED THE PAPERS FROM YOU?
I SUPPOSE IT WAS A FOOLISH NOTION.
WELL, IT'S THE LAST FOOLISH NOTION YOU EVER GONNA HAVE, FIRE-FACE!
OKAY, FELLAS--ON MY COUNT-- OPEN FIRE!
ONE... TWO..

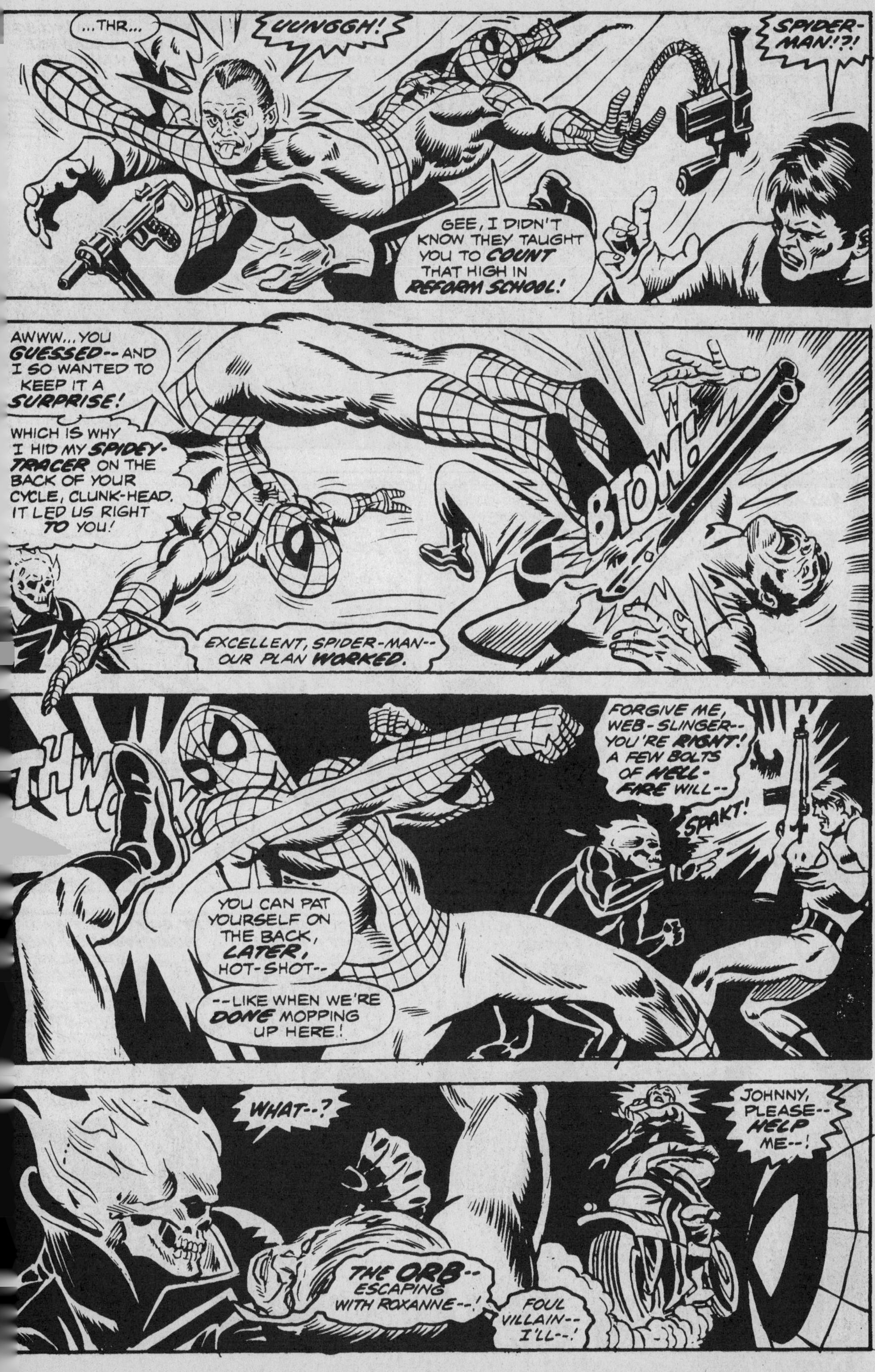
...THR...
UUNGGH!
SPIDER-MAN!?!
GEE, I DIDN'T KNOW THEY TAUGHT YOU TO COUNT THAT HIGH IN REFORM SCHOOL!
AWWW... YOU GUESSED-- AND I SO WANTED TO KEEP IT A SURPRISE!
WHICH IS WHY I HID MY SPIDEY-TRACER ON THE BACK OF YOUR CYCLE, CLUNK-HEAD. IT LED US RIGHT TO YOU!
BTOW!
EXCELLENT, SPIDER-MAN-- OUR PLAN WORKED.
THWACK
FORGIVE ME, WEB-SLINGER-- YOU'RE RIGHT! A FEW BOLTS OF HELL-FIRE WILL--
SPAKT!
YOU CAN PAT YOURSELF ON THE BACK, LATER, HOT-SHOT--
--LIKE WHEN WE'RE DONE MOPPING UP HERE!
WHAT--?
JOHNNY, PLEASE-- HELP ME--!
THE ORB-- ESCAPING WITH ROXANNE--!
FOUL VILLAIN-- I'LL--!

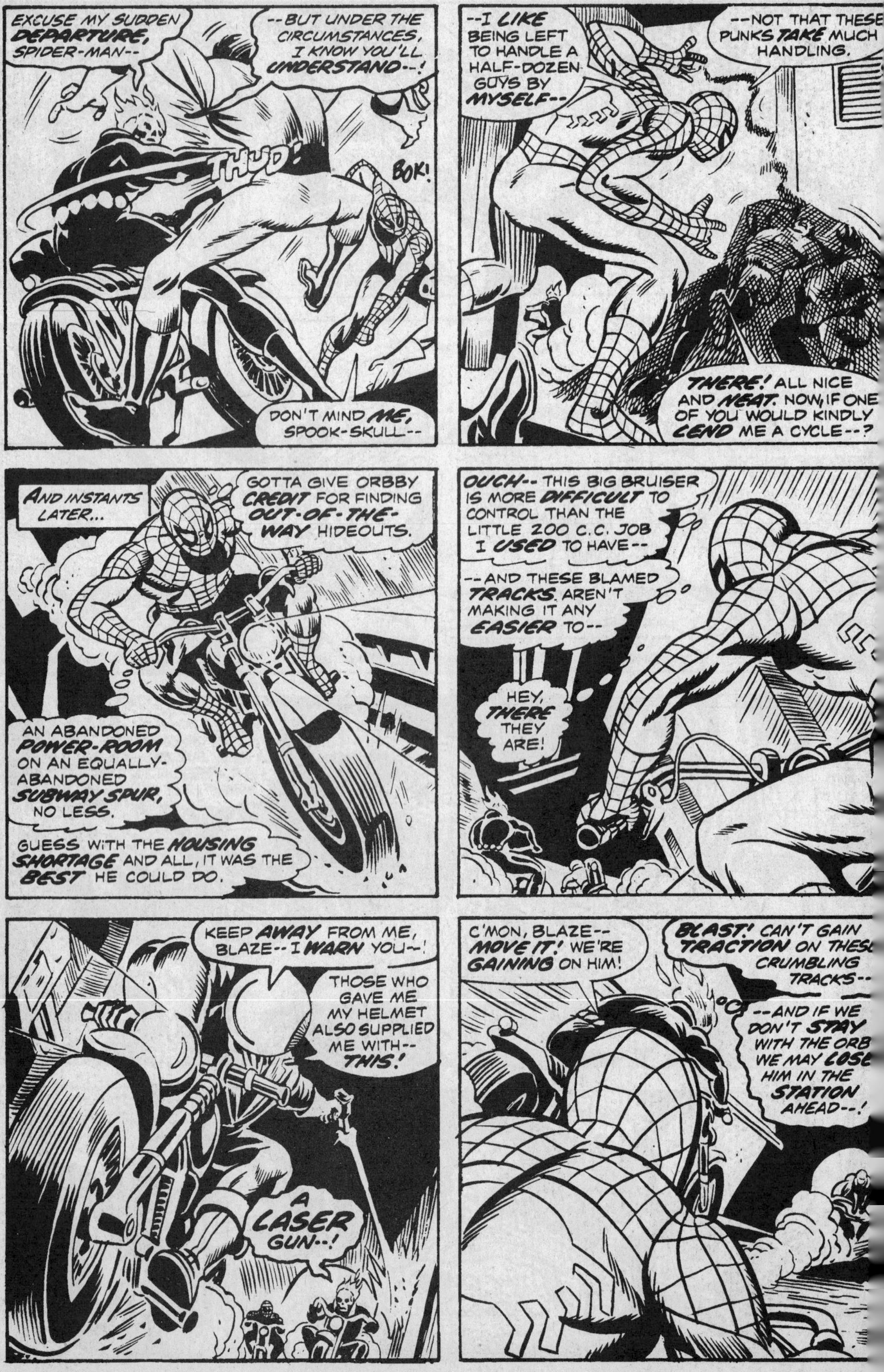
EXCUSE MY SUDDEN DEPARTURE, SPIDER-MAN--
--BUT UNDER THE CIRCUMSTANCES, I KNOW YOU'LL UNDERSTAND--!
THUD!
BOK!
DON'T MIND ME, SPOOK-SKULL--
--I LIKE BEING LEFT TO HANDLE A HALF-DOZEN GUYS BY MYSELF--
--NOT THAT THESE PUNKS TAKE MUCH HANDLING.
THERE! ALL NICE AND NEAT. NOW, IF ONE OF YOU WOULD KINDLY LEND ME A CYCLE--?
AND INSTANTS LATER...
GOTTA GIVE ORBBY CREDIT FOR FINDING OUT-OF-THE-WAY HIDEOUTS.
AN ABANDONED POWER-ROOM ON AN EQUALLY-ABANDONED SUBWAY SPUR, NO LESS.
GUESS WITH THE HOUSING SHORTAGE AND ALL, IT WAS THE BEST HE COULD DO.
OUCH-- THIS BIG BRUISER IS MORE DIFFICULT TO CONTROL THAN THE LITTLE 200 C.C. JOB I USED TO HAVE--
--AND THESE BLAMED TRACKS AREN'T MAKING IT ANY EASIER TO--
HEY, THERE THEY ARE!
KEEP AWAY FROM ME, BLAZE-- I WARN YOU--!
THOSE WHO GAVE ME MY HELMET ALSO SUPPLIED ME WITH-- THIS!
A LASER GUN--!
C'MON, BLAZE-- MOVE IT! WE'RE GAINING ON HIM!
BLAST! CAN'T GAIN TRACTION ON THESE CRUMBLING TRACKS--
--AND IF WE DON'T STAY WITH THE ORB WE MAY LOSE HIM IN THE STATION AHEAD--!

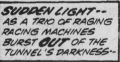

SUDDEN LIGHT-- AS A TRIO OF RAGING RACING MACHINES BURST *OUT* OF THE TUNNEL'S DARKNESS--

--AND *ONTO* THE GRITY, GARBAGE-STEWN PLAT-FORM--

--THEN, PAST STARTLED SPECTATORS, *UP* A LONG FLIGHT OF CHISELED MARBLE STAIRS--

--INTO *GRAND CENTRAL STATION!*

"CROSS-ROADS OF THE NATION," AN OLD *RADIO SHOW* CALLED IT--

--AND, TONIGHT, A *BATTLEGOUND* AS WELL--FOR THREE SEEMING *LUNATICS,* ROARING WILDLY EVER ONWARD--

--AND *WOE* BE UNTO ANYTHING--OR ANY-*ONE*--THAT STRAYS INTO THEIR PATH...

THE ORB HAS US *STYMIED,* WEB-SLINGER--!

AS LONG AS ROXANNE IS HIS *CAPTIVE,* THERE IS *LITTLE* WE CAN DO.

OH?

I FIGURE THERE'S *PLENTY* WE CAN DO-- IF OUR *TIMING* IS CORRECT.

TO COIN A CLICHÉ, HOT-HEAD-- "HERE'S MY *PLAN*..."

THUS, MOMENTS LATER, AS THE EYE-DOMED DESPERADO ATTEMPTS TO *DISSUADE* HIS RELENT-LESS PURSUERS...

STAY *AWAY* FROM ME, FOOLS--OR *DIE!*

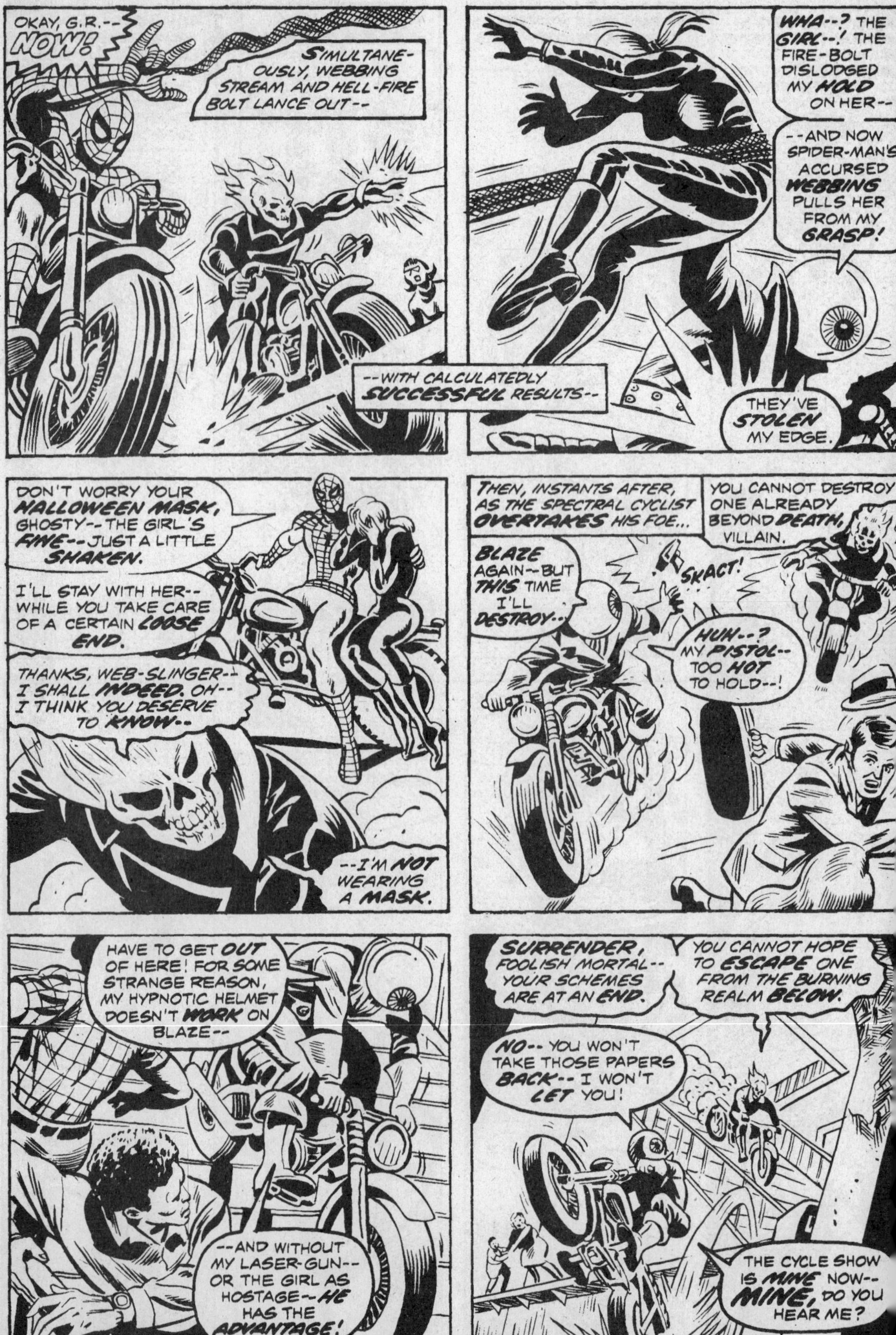
OKAY, G.R.-- NOW!
SIMULTANEOUSLY, WEBBING STREAM AND HELL-FIRE BOLT LANCE OUT--
--WITH CALCULATEDLY SUCCESSFUL RESULTS--
WHA--? THE GIRL--! THE FIRE-BOLT DISLODGED MY HOLD ON HER--
--AND NOW SPIDER-MAN'S ACCURSED WEBBING PULLS HER FROM MY GRASP!
THEY'VE STOLEN MY EDGE.
DON'T WORRY YOUR HALLOWEEN MASK, GHOSTY-- THE GIRL'S FINE-- JUST A LITTLE SHAKEN.
I'LL STAY WITH HER-- WHILE YOU TAKE CARE OF A CERTAIN LOOSE END.
THANKS, WEB-SLINGER-- I SHALL INDEED. OH-- I THINK YOU DESERVE TO KNOW--
--I'M NOT WEARING A MASK.
THEN, INSTANTS AFTER, AS THE SPECTRAL CYCLIST OVERTAKES HIS FOE...
BLAZE AGAIN-- BUT THIS TIME I'LL DESTROY--
SKACT!
YOU CANNOT DESTROY ONE ALREADY BEYOND DEATH, VILLAIN.
HUH--? MY PISTOL-- TOO HOT TO HOLD--!
HAVE TO GET OUT OF HERE! FOR SOME STRANGE REASON, MY HYPNOTIC HELMET DOESN'T WORK ON BLAZE--
--AND WITHOUT MY LASER-GUN-- OR THE GIRL AS HOSTAGE-- HE HAS THE ADVANTAGE!
SURRENDER, FOOLISH MORTAL-- YOUR SCHEMES ARE AT AN END.
YOU CANNOT HOPE TO ESCAPE ONE FROM THE BURNING REALM BELOW.
NO-- YOU WON'T TAKE THOSE PAPERS BACK-- I WON'T LET YOU!
THE CYCLE SHOW IS MINE NOW-- MINE, DO YOU HEAR ME?

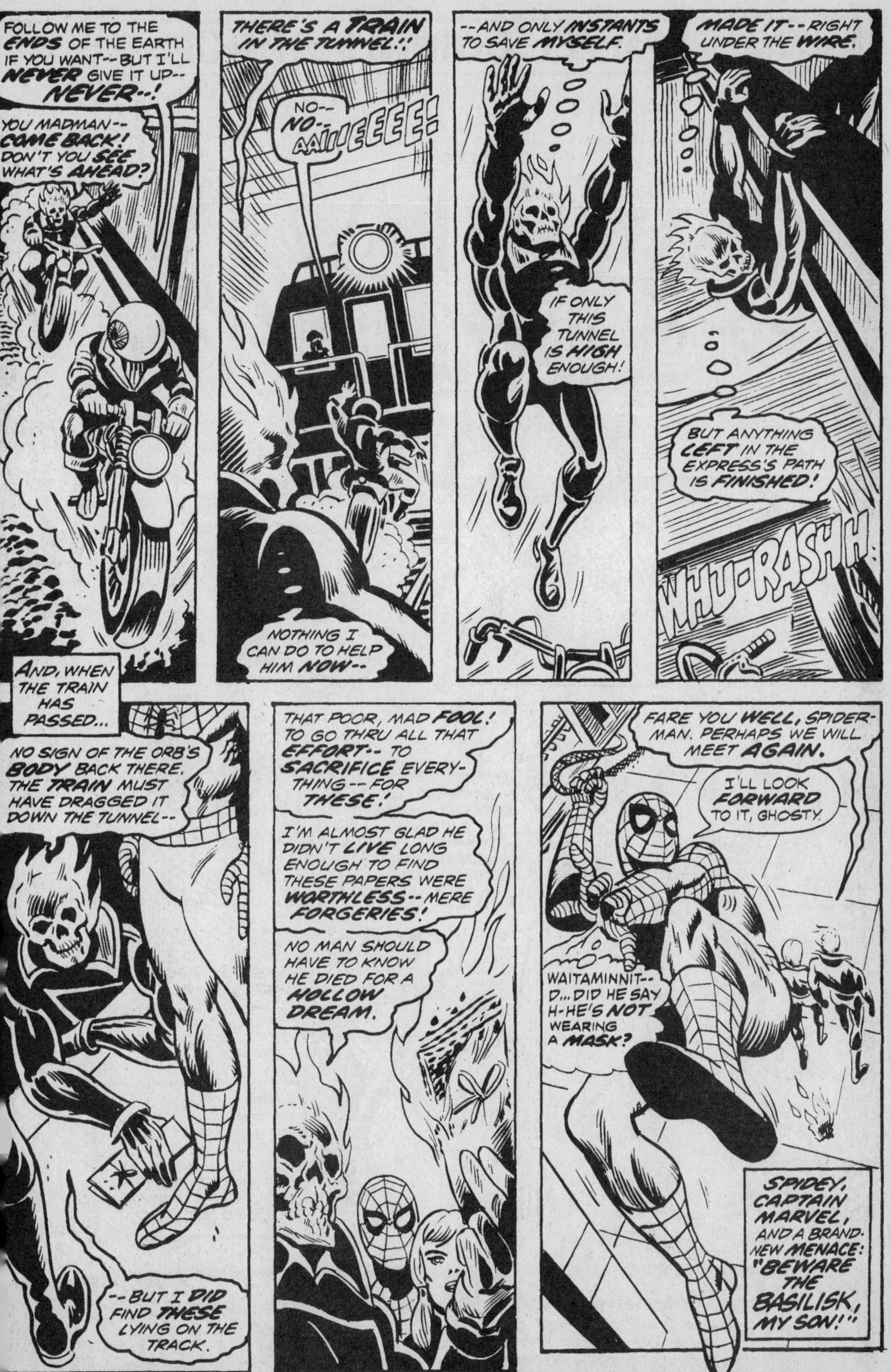
FOLLOW ME TO THE ENDS OF THE EARTH IF YOU WANT-- BUT I'LL NEVER GIVE IT UP-- NEVER--!
YOU MADMAN-- COME BACK! DON'T YOU SEE WHAT'S AHEAD?
THERE'S A TRAIN IN THE TUNNEL!
NO-- NO-- AAIIIEEEEE!
NOTHING I CAN DO TO HELP HIM NOW--
--AND ONLY INSTANTS TO SAVE MYSELF.
IF ONLY THIS TUNNEL IS HIGH ENOUGH!
MADE IT-- RIGHT UNDER THE WIRE.
BUT ANYTHING LEFT IN THE EXPRESS'S PATH IS FINISHED!
WHU-RASHH
AND, WHEN THE TRAIN HAS PASSED...
NO SIGN OF THE ORB'S BODY BACK THERE. THE TRAIN MUST HAVE DRAGGED IT DOWN THE TUNNEL--
--BUT I DID FIND THESE LYING ON THE TRACK.
THAT POOR, MAD FOOL! TO GO THRU ALL THAT EFFORT-- TO SACRIFICE EVERYTHING-- FOR THESE!
I'M ALMOST GLAD HE DIDN'T LIVE LONG ENOUGH TO FIND THESE PAPERS WERE WORTHLESS-- MERE FORGERIES!
NO MAN SHOULD HAVE TO KNOW HE DIED FOR A HOLLOW DREAM.
FARE YOU WELL, SPIDER-MAN. PERHAPS WE WILL MEET AGAIN.
I'LL LOOK FORWARD TO IT, GHOSTY.
WAITAMINNIT-- D...DID HE SAY H-HE'S NOT WEARING A MASK?
SPIDEY, CAPTAIN MARVEL, AND A BRAND-NEW MENACE: "BEWARE THE BASILISK, MY SON!"

MARVEL TEAM-UP
MARVEL COMICS GROUP
APPROVED BY THE COMICS CODE AUTHORITY
20¢
16 DEC 02147
MARVEL TEAM-UP
FEATURING
SPIDER-MAN AND CAPTAIN MARVEL
NOT EVEN SPIDER-MAN CAN SAVE YOU! MARVEL! NO POWER CAN MATCH--THE BASILISK!
*BASILISK. (a) IN MYTHOLOGY--A SERPENT WHOSE MEREST LOOK WAS FATAL! (b) IN THIS ISSUE--A FOE WHOSE DEADLY EYES CAN TURN A MAN TO STONE!
TWO OF THE WORLD'S MIGHTIEST HEROES, VS.
A POWER SUPERNATURAL!

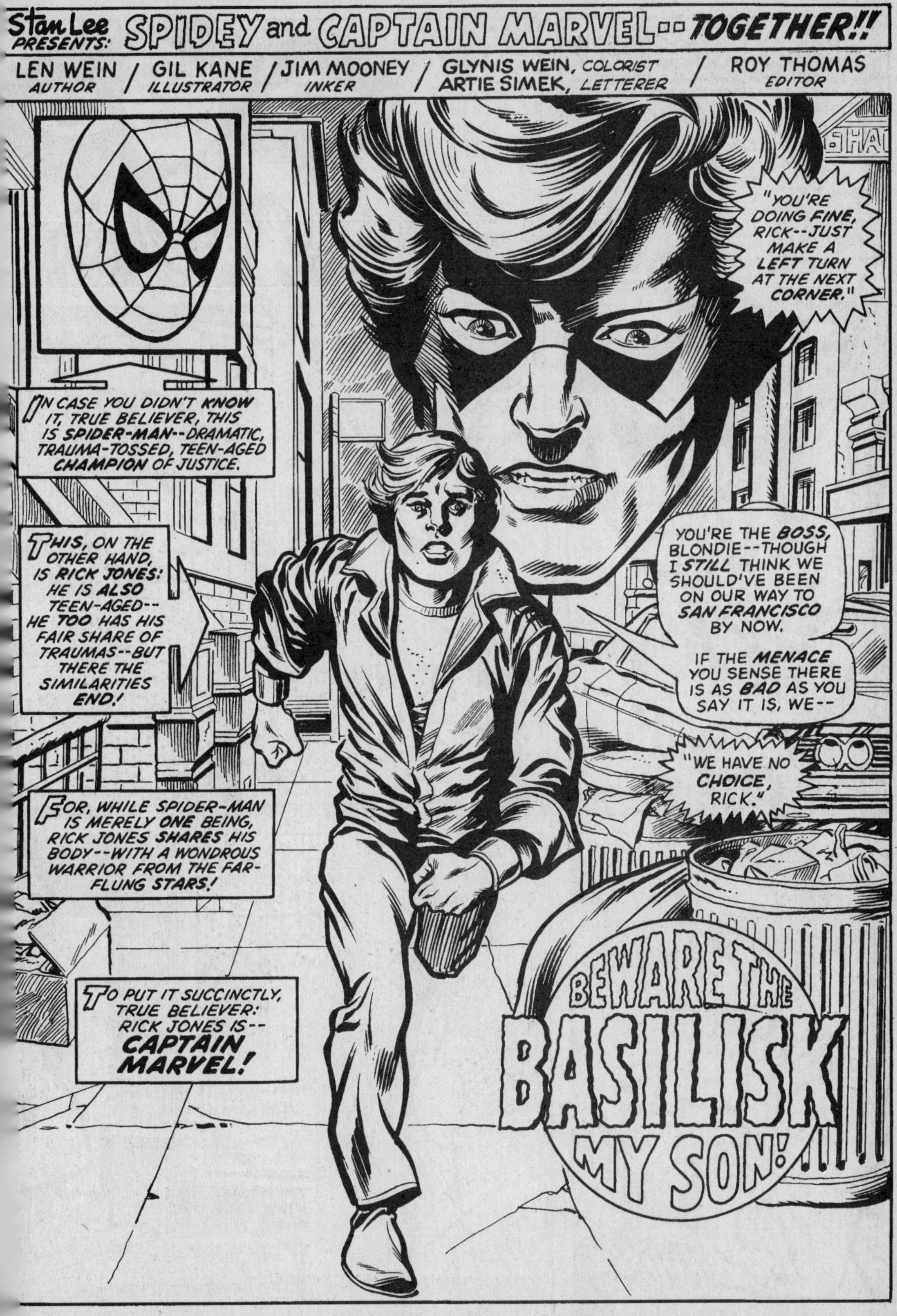

Stan Lee PRESENTS: SPIDEY and CAPTAIN MARVEL--TOGETHER!!
LEN WEIN AUTHOR / GIL KANE ILLUSTRATOR / JIM MOONEY INKER / GLYNIS WEIN, COLORIST ARTIE SIMEK, LETTERER / ROY THOMAS EDITOR
IN CASE YOU DIDN'T KNOW IT, TRUE BELIEVER, THIS IS SPIDER-MAN--DRAMATIC, TRAUMA-TOSSED, TEEN-AGED CHAMPION OF JUSTICE.
THIS, ON THE OTHER HAND, IS RICK JONES: HE IS ALSO TEEN-AGED--HE TOO HAS HIS FAIR SHARE OF TRAUMAS--BUT THERE THE SIMILARITIES END!
FOR, WHILE SPIDER-MAN IS MERELY ONE BEING, RICK JONES SHARES HIS BODY--WITH A WONDROUS WARRIOR FROM THE FAR-FLUNG STARS!
TO PUT IT SUCCINCTLY, TRUE BELIEVER: RICK JONES IS--CAPTAIN MARVEL!
"YOU'RE DOING FINE, RICK--JUST MAKE A LEFT TURN AT THE NEXT CORNER."
YOU'RE THE BOSS, BLONDIE--THOUGH I STILL THINK WE SHOULD'VE BEEN ON OUR WAY TO SAN FRANCISCO BY NOW.
IF THE MENACE YOU SENSE THERE IS AS BAD AS YOU SAY IT IS, WE--
"WE HAVE NO CHOICE, RICK."
BEWARE THE BASILISK MY SON!

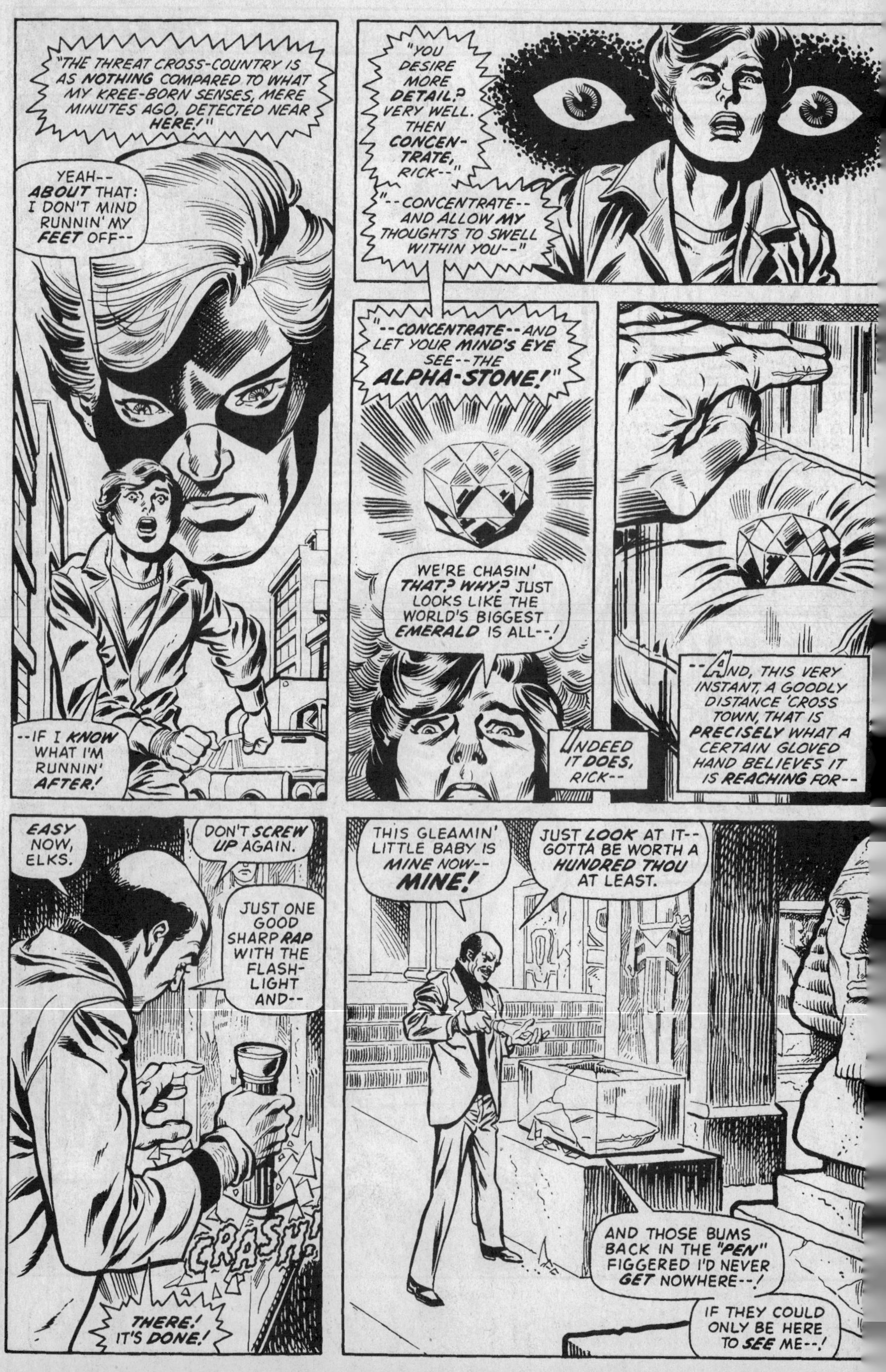
"THE THREAT CROSS-COUNTRY IS AS NOTHING COMPARED TO WHAT MY KREE-BORN SENSES, MERE MINUTES AGO, DETECTED NEAR HERE!"
YEAH-- ABOUT THAT: I DON'T MIND RUNNIN' MY FEET OFF--
--IF I KNOW WHAT I'M RUNNIN' AFTER!
"YOU DESIRE MORE DETAIL? VERY WELL. THEN CONCENTRATE, RICK--"
"--CONCENTRATE-- AND ALLOW MY THOUGHTS TO SWELL WITHIN YOU--"
"--CONCENTRATE--AND LET YOUR MIND'S EYE SEE--THE ALPHA-STONE!"
WE'RE CHASIN' THAT? WHY? JUST LOOKS LIKE THE WORLD'S BIGGEST EMERALD IS ALL--!
UNDEED IT DOES, RICK--
--AND, THIS VERY INSTANT, A GOODLY DISTANCE 'CROSS TOWN, THAT IS PRECISELY WHAT A CERTAIN GLOVED HAND BELIEVES IT IS REACHING FOR--
EASY NOW, ELKS.
DON'T SCREW UP AGAIN.
JUST ONE GOOD SHARP RAP WITH THE FLASH-LIGHT AND--
CRASH!
THERE! IT'S DONE!
THIS GLEAMIN' LITTLE BABY IS MINE NOW-- MINE!
JUST LOOK AT IT-- GOTTA BE WORTH A HUNDRED THOU AT LEAST.
AND THOSE BUMS BACK IN THE "PEN" FIGGERED I'D NEVER GET NOWHERE--!
IF THEY COULD ONLY BE HERE TO SEE ME--!

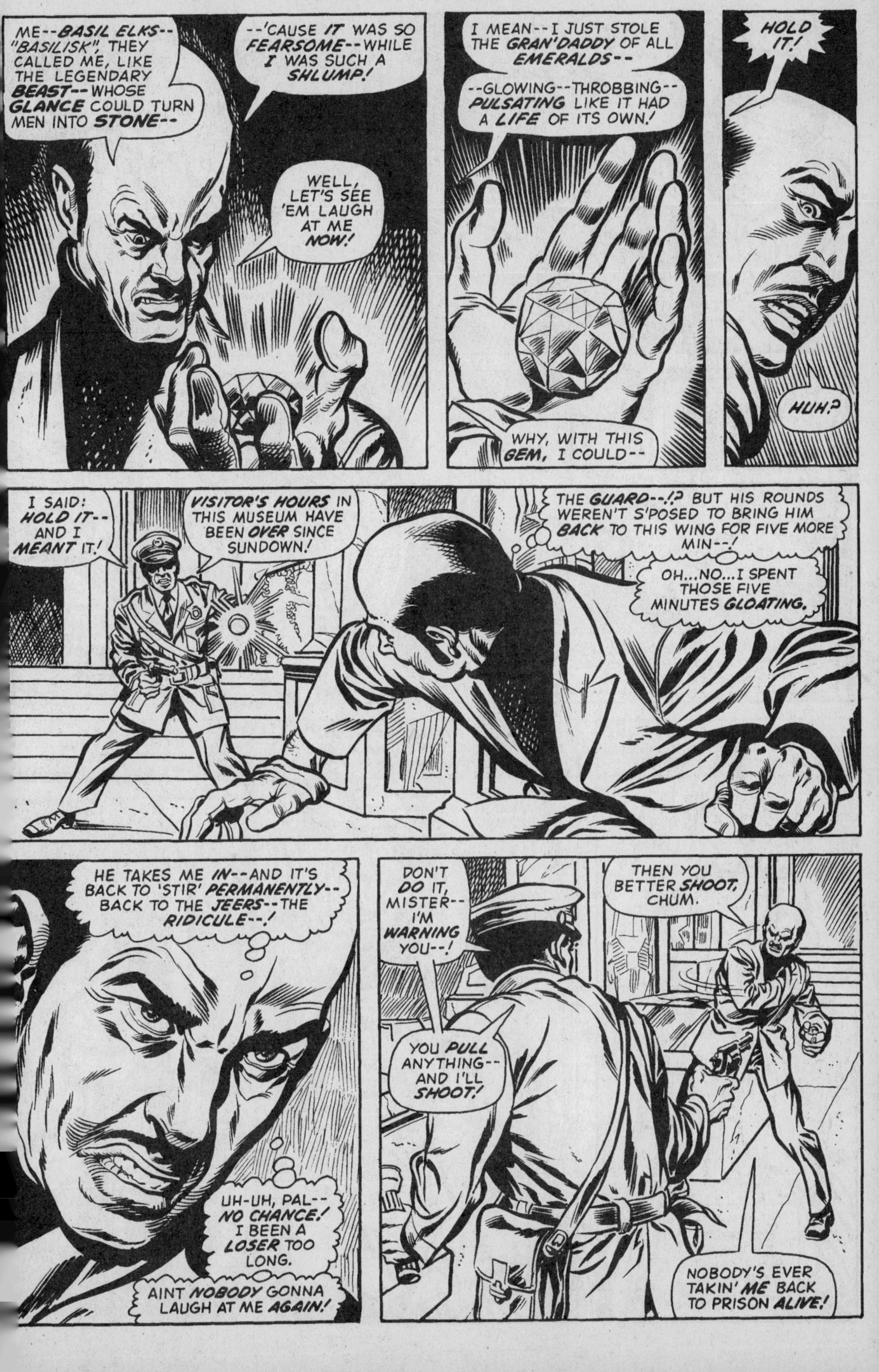
ME--BASIL ELKS--"BASILISK", THEY CALLED ME, LIKE THE LEGENDARY BEAST--WHOSE GLANCE COULD TURN MEN INTO STONE--
--'CAUSE IT WAS SO FEARSOME--WHILE I WAS SUCH A SHLUMP!
WELL, LET'S SEE 'EM LAUGH AT ME NOW!
I MEAN--I JUST STOLE THE GRAN'DADDY OF ALL EMERALDS--
--GLOWING--THROBBING--PULSATING LIKE IT HAD A LIFE OF ITS OWN!
WHY, WITH THIS GEM, I COULD--
HOLD IT!
HUH?
I SAID: HOLD IT--AND I MEANT IT!
VISITOR'S HOURS IN THIS MUSEUM HAVE BEEN OVER SINCE SUNDOWN!
THE GUARD--!? BUT HIS ROUNDS WEREN'T S'POSED TO BRING HIM BACK TO THIS WING FOR FIVE MORE MIN--!
OH...NO...I SPENT THOSE FIVE MINUTES GLOATING.
HE TAKES ME IN--AND IT'S BACK TO 'STIR' PERMANENTLY--BACK TO THE JEERS--THE RIDICULE--!
UH-UH, PAL--NO CHANCE! I BEEN A LOSER TOO LONG.
AINT NOBODY GONNA LAUGH AT ME AGAIN!
DON'T DO IT, MISTER--I'M WARNING YOU--!
YOU PULL ANYTHING--AND I'LL SHOOT!
THEN YOU BETTER SHOOT, CHUM.
NOBODY'S EVER TAKIN' ME BACK TO PRISON ALIVE!

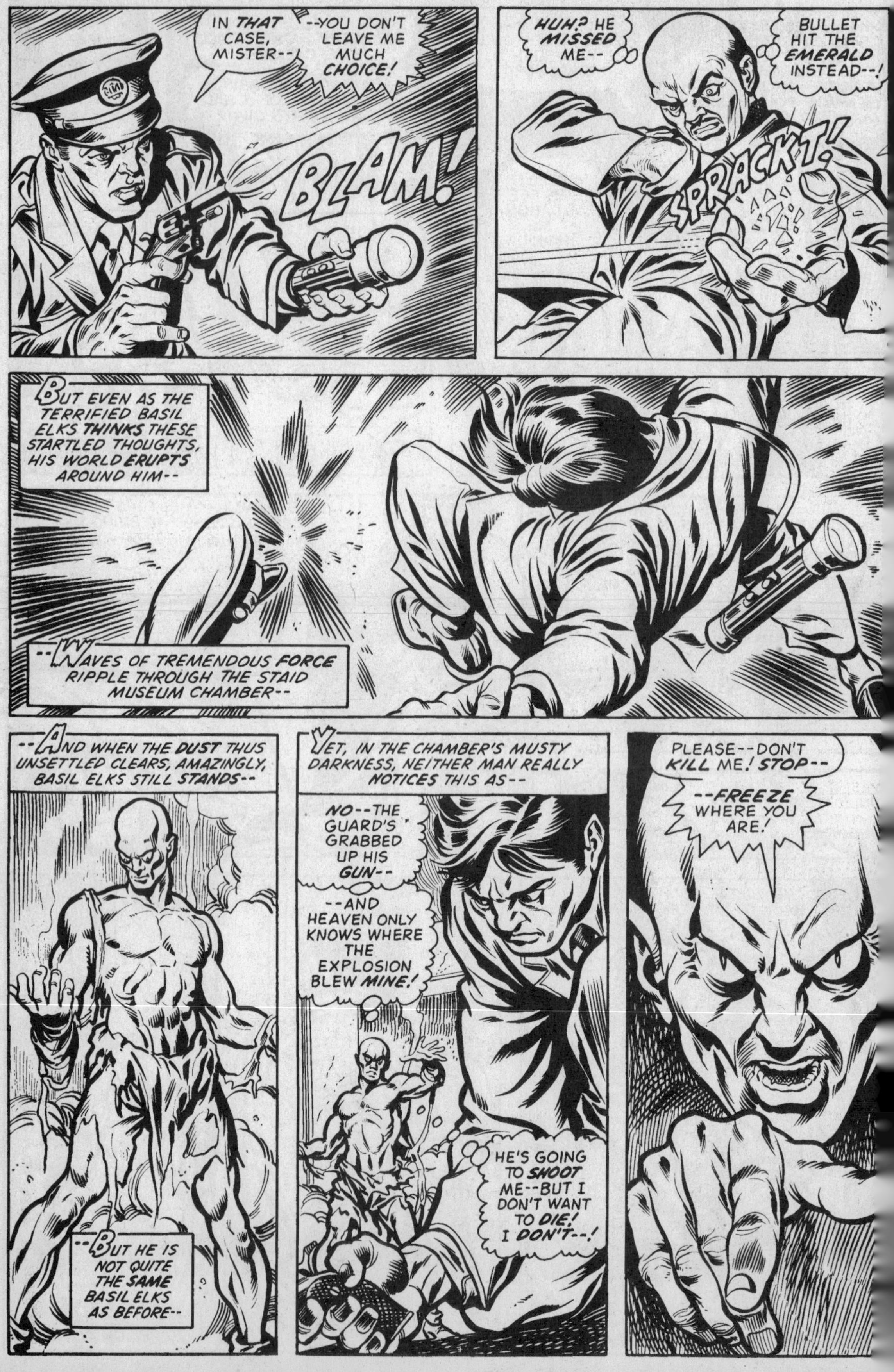

IN THAT CASE, MISTER--
--YOU DON'T LEAVE ME MUCH CHOICE!
BLAM!
HUH? HE MISSED ME--
BULLET HIT THE EMERALD INSTEAD--!
SPRACKT!
BUT EVEN AS THE TERRIFIED BASIL ELKS THINKS THESE STARTLED THOUGHTS, HIS WORLD ERUPTS AROUND HIM--
--WAVES OF TREMENDOUS FORCE RIPPLE THROUGH THE STAID MUSEUM CHAMBER--
--AND WHEN THE DUST THUS UNSETTLED CLEARS, AMAZINGLY, BASIL ELKS STILL STANDS--
--BUT HE IS NOT QUITE THE SAME BASIL ELKS AS BEFORE--
YET, IN THE CHAMBER'S MUSTY DARKNESS, NEITHER MAN REALLY NOTICES THIS AS--
NO--THE GUARD'S GRABBED UP HIS GUN--
--AND HEAVEN ONLY KNOWS WHERE THE EXPLOSION BLEW MINE!
HE'S GOING TO SHOOT ME--BUT I DON'T WANT TO DIE! I DON'T--!
PLEASE--DON'T KILL ME! STOP--
--FREEZE WHERE YOU ARE!

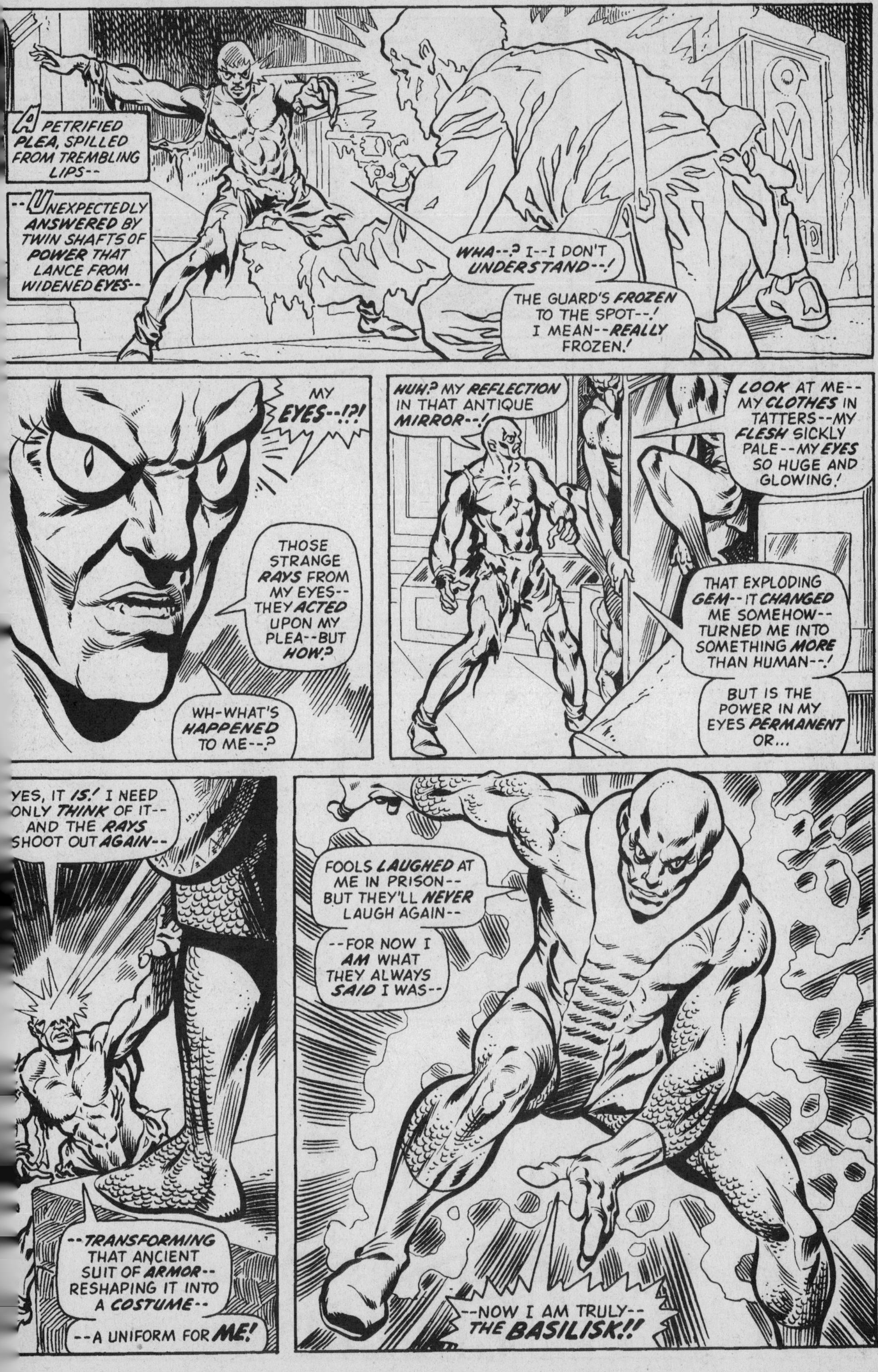

A PETRIFIED PLEA, SPILLED FROM TREMBLING LIPS--
--UNEXPECTEDLY ANSWERED BY TWIN SHAFTS OF POWER THAT LANCE FROM WIDENED EYES--
WHA--? I--I DON'T UNDERSTAND--!
THE GUARD'S FROZEN TO THE SPOT--! I MEAN--REALLY FROZEN!
MY EYES--!?!
THOSE STRANGE RAYS FROM MY EYES--THEY ACTED UPON MY PLEA--BUT HOW?
WH-WHAT'S HAPPENED TO ME--?
HUH? MY REFLECTION IN THAT ANTIQUE MIRROR--!
LOOK AT ME--MY CLOTHES IN TATTERS--MY FLESH SICKLY PALE--MY EYES SO HUGE AND GLOWING!
THAT EXPLODING GEM--IT CHANGED ME SOMEHOW--TURNED ME INTO SOMETHING MORE THAN HUMAN--!
BUT IS THE POWER IN MY EYES PERMANENT OR...
YES, IT IS! I NEED ONLY THINK OF IT--AND THE RAYS SHOOT OUT AGAIN--
--TRANSFORMING THAT ANCIENT SUIT OF ARMOR--RESHAPING IT INTO A COSTUME--
--A UNIFORM FOR ME!
FOOLS LAUGHED AT ME IN PRISON--BUT THEY'LL NEVER LAUGH AGAIN--
--FOR NOW I AM WHAT THEY ALWAYS SAID I WAS--
--NOW I AM TRULY--THE BASILISK!!

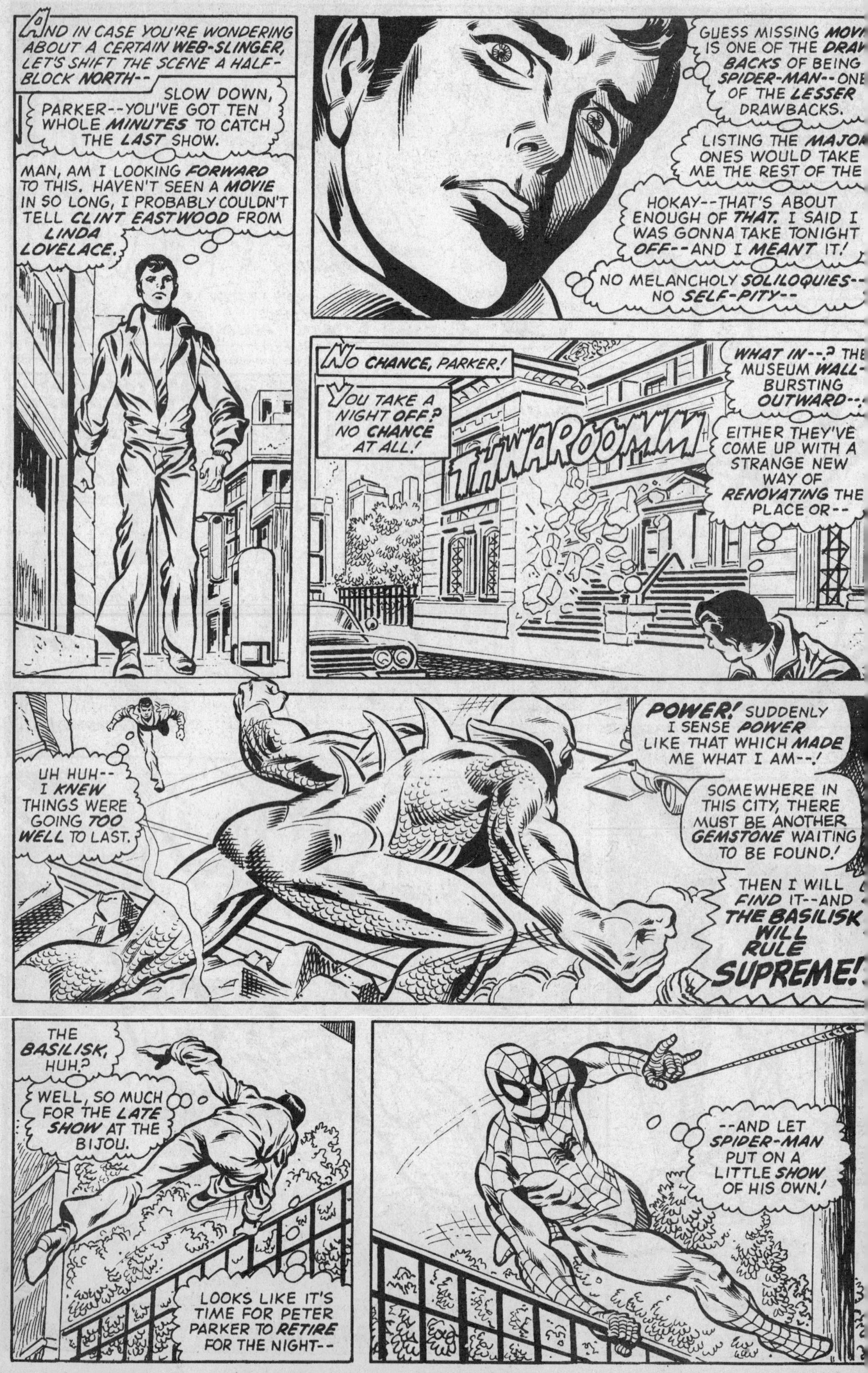
AND IN CASE YOU'RE WONDERING ABOUT A CERTAIN WEB-SLINGER, LET'S SHIFT THE SCENE A HALF-BLOCK NORTH--
SLOW DOWN, PARKER--YOU'VE GOT TEN WHOLE MINUTES TO CATCH THE LAST SHOW.
MAN, AM I LOOKING FORWARD TO THIS. HAVEN'T SEEN A MOVIE IN SO LONG, I PROBABLY COULDN'T TELL CLINT EASTWOOD FROM LINDA LOVELACE.
GUESS MISSING MOVI IS ONE OF THE DRAW BACKS OF BEING SPIDER-MAN--ONE OF THE LESSER DRAWBACKS.
LISTING THE MAJOR ONES WOULD TAKE ME THE REST OF THE
HOKAY--THAT'S ABOUT ENOUGH OF THAT. I SAID I WAS GONNA TAKE TONIGHT OFF--AND I MEANT IT!
NO MELANCHOLY SOLILOQUIES--NO SELF-PITY--
NO CHANCE, PARKER!
YOU TAKE A NIGHT OFF? NO CHANCE AT ALL!
THWAROOMM
WHAT IN--? THE MUSEUM WALL--BURSTING OUTWARD--!
EITHER THEY'VE COME UP WITH A STRANGE NEW WAY OF RENOVATING THE PLACE OR--
UH HUH--I KNEW THINGS WERE GOING TOO WELL TO LAST.
POWER! SUDDENLY I SENSE POWER LIKE THAT WHICH MADE ME WHAT I AM--!
SOMEWHERE IN THIS CITY, THERE MUST BE ANOTHER GEMSTONE WAITING TO BE FOUND!
THEN I WILL FIND IT--AND THE BASILISK WILL RULE SUPREME!
THE BASILISK, HUH?
WELL, SO MUCH FOR THE LATE SHOW AT THE BIJOU.
LOOKS LIKE IT'S TIME FOR PETER PARKER TO RETIRE FOR THE NIGHT--
--AND LET SPIDER-MAN PUT ON A LITTLE SHOW OF HIS OWN!

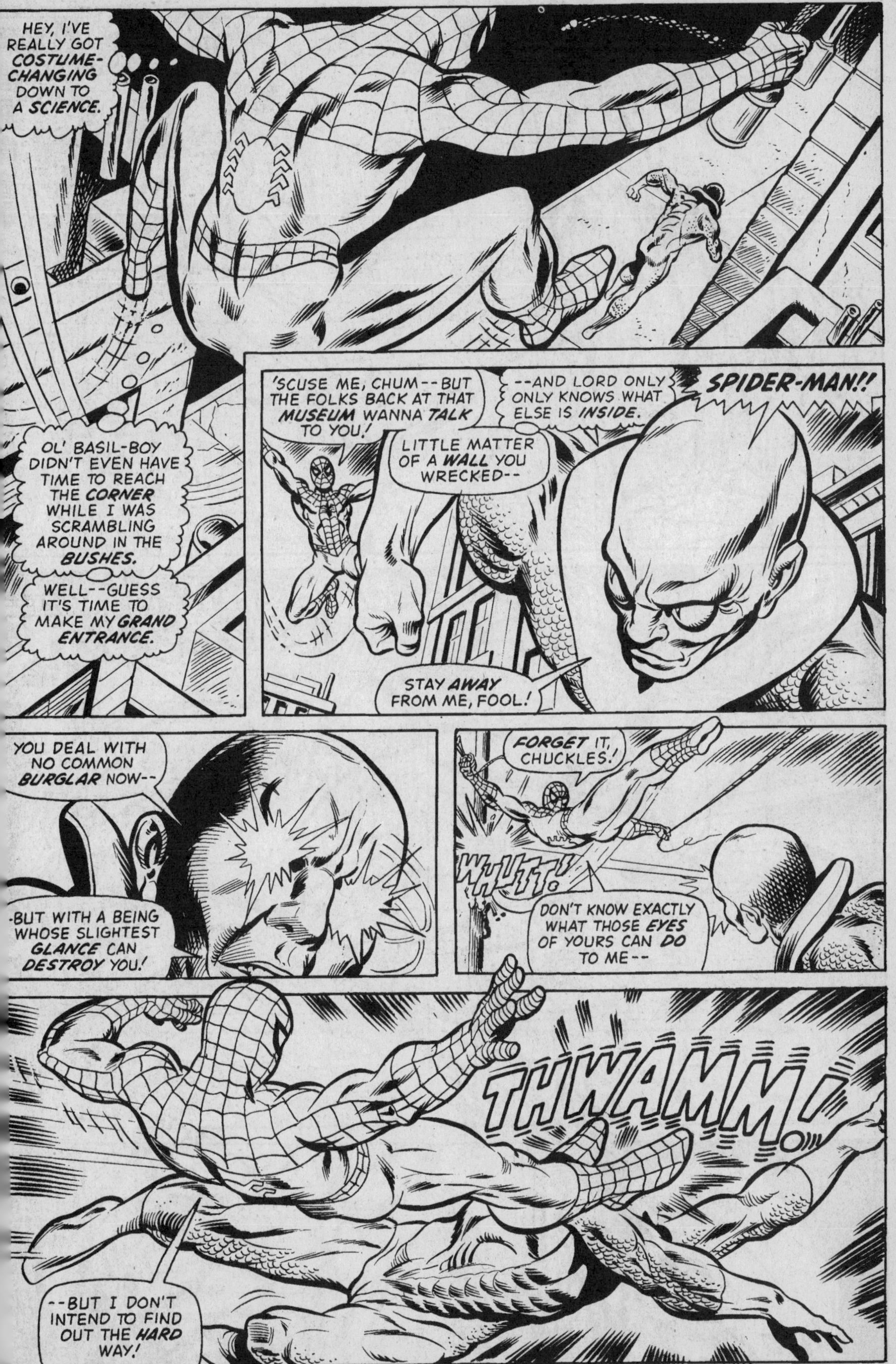
HEY, I'VE REALLY GOT COSTUME-CHANGING DOWN TO A SCIENCE.
OL' BASIL-BOY DIDN'T EVEN HAVE TIME TO REACH THE CORNER WHILE I WAS SCRAMBLING AROUND IN THE BUSHES.
WELL--GUESS IT'S TIME TO MAKE MY GRAND ENTRANCE.
'SCUSE ME, CHUM--BUT THE FOLKS BACK AT THAT MUSEUM WANNA TALK TO YOU!
LITTLE MATTER OF A WALL YOU WRECKED--
--AND LORD ONLY ONLY KNOWS WHAT ELSE IS INSIDE.
SPIDER-MAN!!
STAY AWAY FROM ME, FOOL!
YOU DEAL WITH NO COMMON BURGLAR NOW--
-BUT WITH A BEING WHOSE SLIGHTEST GLANCE CAN DESTROY YOU!
FORGET IT, CHUCKLES!
WHUTT!
DON'T KNOW EXACTLY WHAT THOSE EYES OF YOURS CAN DO TO ME--
THWAMM!
--BUT I DON'T INTEND TO FIND OUT THE HARD WAY!

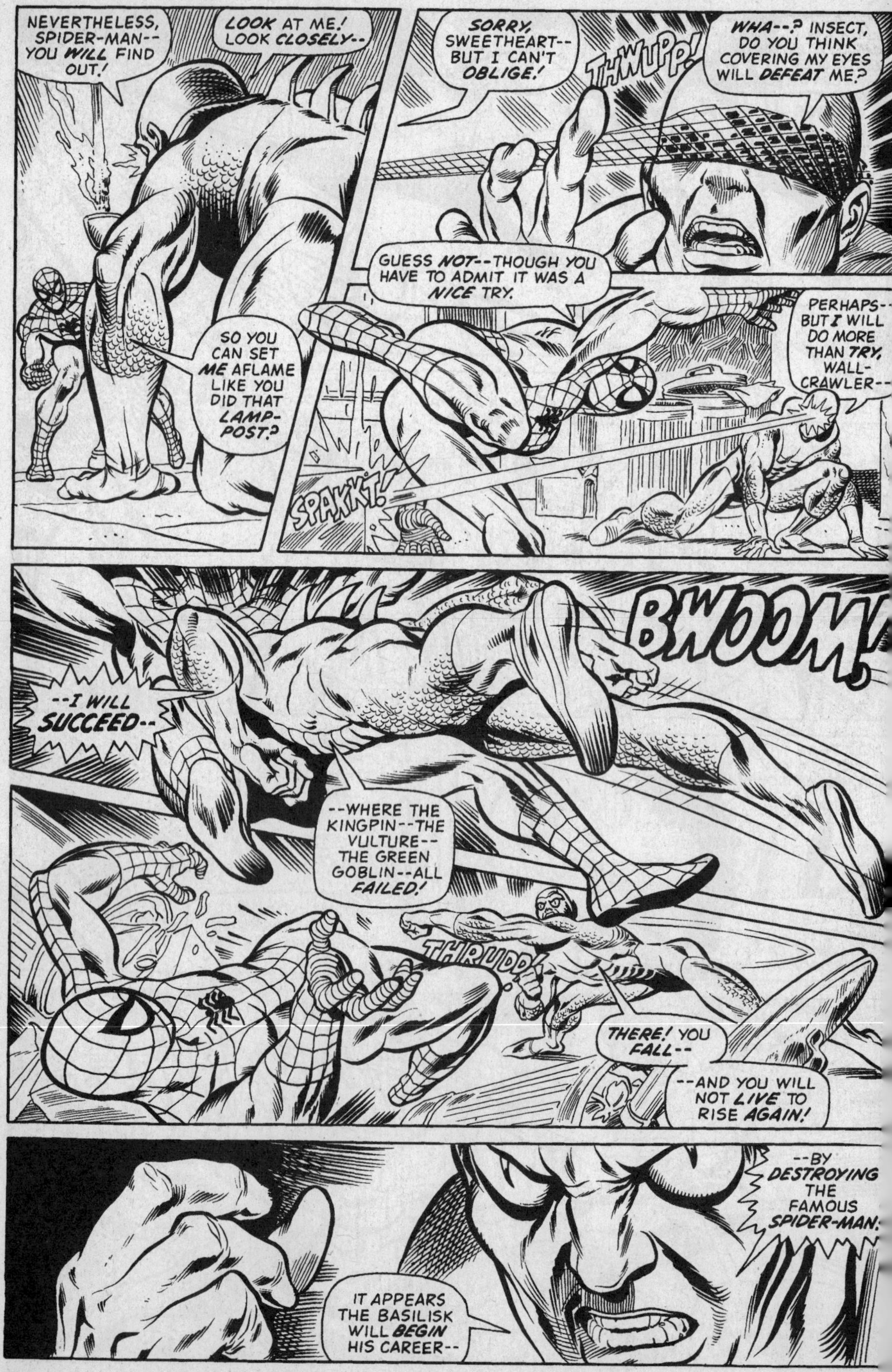
NEVERTHELESS, SPIDER-MAN--YOU WILL FIND OUT!
LOOK AT ME! LOOK CLOSELY--
SO YOU CAN SET ME AFLAME LIKE YOU DID THAT LAMP-POST?
SORRY, SWEETHEART--BUT I CAN'T OBLIGE!
THWUPP!
WHA--? INSECT, DO YOU THINK COVERING MY EYES WILL DEFEAT ME?
GUESS NOT--THOUGH YOU HAVE TO ADMIT IT WAS A NICE TRY.
PERHAPS--BUT I WILL DO MORE THAN TRY, WALL-CRAWLER--
SPAKKT!
BWOOM!
--I WILL SUCCEED--
--WHERE THE KINGPIN--THE VULTURE--THE GREEN GOBLIN--ALL FAILED!
THRUDD!
THERE! YOU FALL--
--AND YOU WILL NOT LIVE TO RISE AGAIN!
IT APPEARS THE BASILISK WILL BEGIN HIS CAREER--
--BY DESTROYING THE FAMOUS SPIDER-MAN!

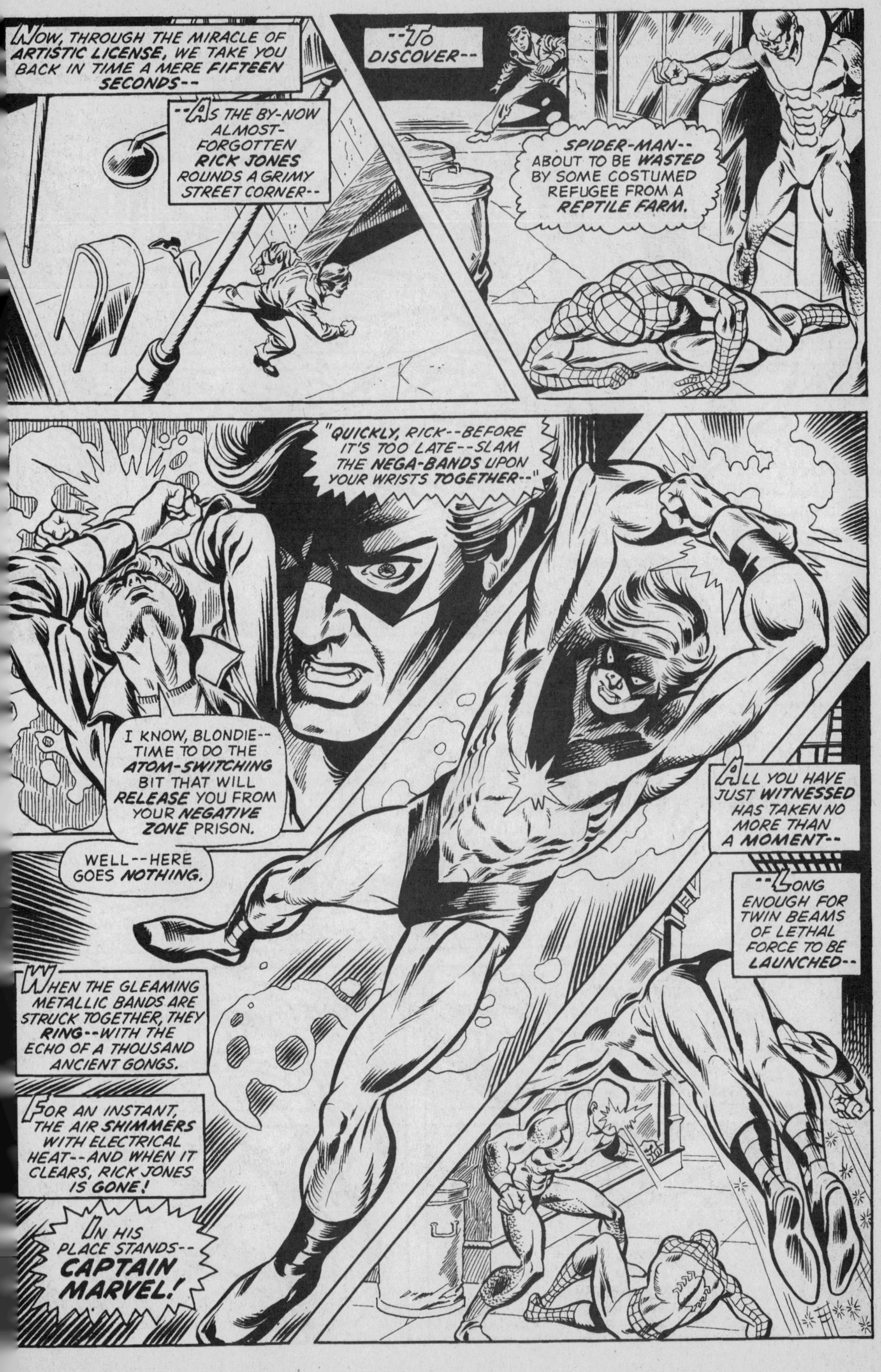
NOW, THROUGH THE MIRACLE OF ARTISTIC LICENSE, WE TAKE YOU BACK IN TIME A MERE FIFTEEN SECONDS--
--AS THE BY-NOW ALMOST-FORGOTTEN RICK JONES ROUNDS A GRIMY STREET CORNER--
--TO DISCOVER--
SPIDER-MAN--ABOUT TO BE WASTED BY SOME COSTUMED REFUGEE FROM A REPTILE FARM.
"QUICKLY, RICK--BEFORE IT'S TOO LATE--SLAM THE NEGA-BANDS UPON YOUR WRISTS TOGETHER--"
I KNOW, BLONDIE--TIME TO DO THE ATOM-SWITCHING BIT THAT WILL RELEASE YOU FROM YOUR NEGATIVE ZONE PRISON.
WELL--HERE GOES NOTHING.
WHEN THE GLEAMING METALLIC BANDS ARE STRUCK TOGETHER, THEY RING--WITH THE ECHO OF A THOUSAND ANCIENT GONGS.
FOR AN INSTANT, THE AIR SHIMMERS WITH ELECTRICAL HEAT--AND WHEN IT CLEARS, RICK JONES IS GONE!
IN HIS PLACE STANDS--CAPTAIN MARVEL!
ALL YOU HAVE JUST WITNESSED HAS TAKEN NO MORE THAN A MOMENT--
--LONG ENOUGH FOR TWIN BEAMS OF LETHAL FORCE TO BE LAUNCHED--

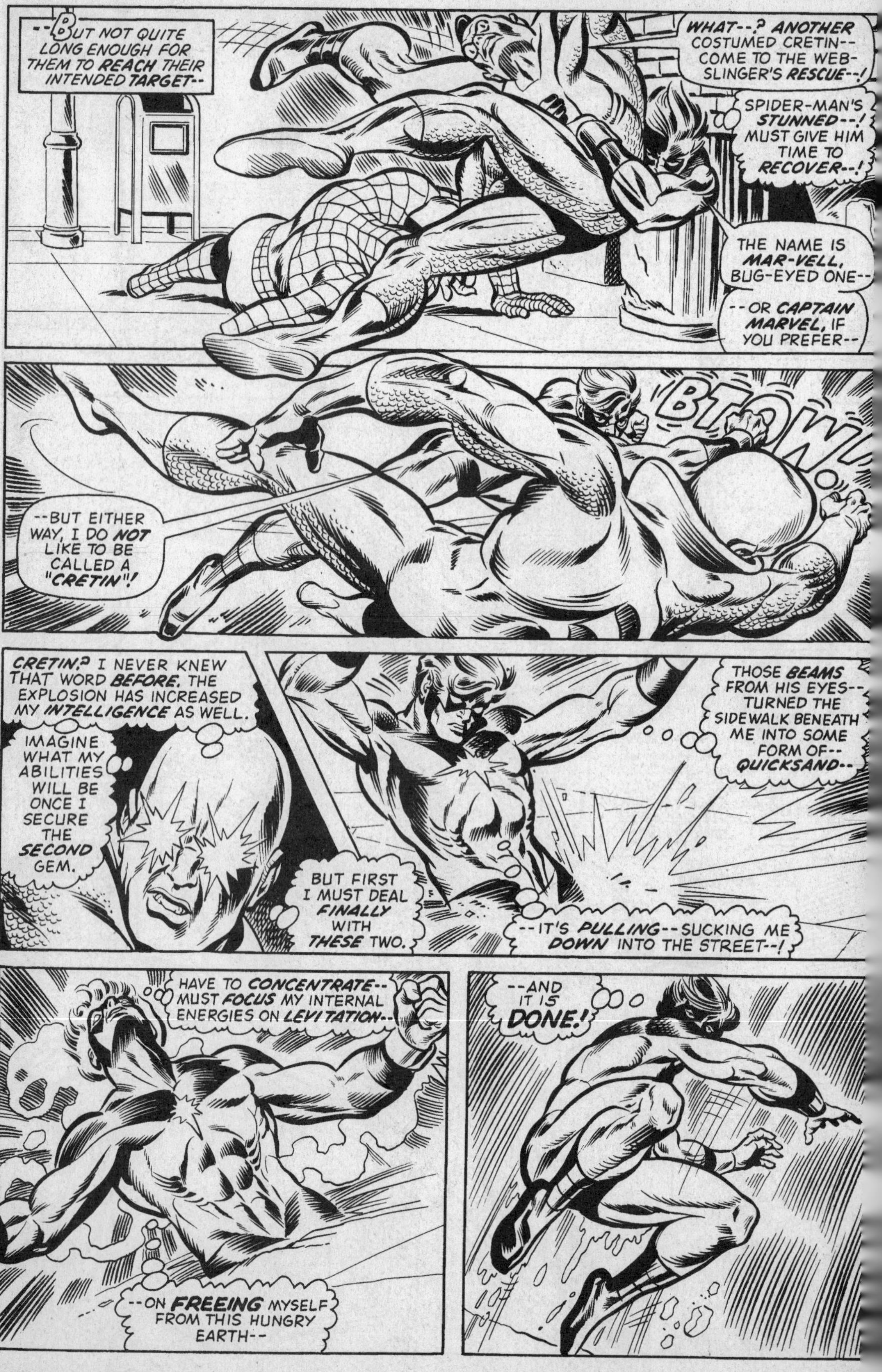
--BUT NOT QUITE LONG ENOUGH FOR THEM TO REACH THEIR INTENDED TARGET--
WHAT--? ANOTHER COSTUMED CRETIN--COME TO THE WEB-SLINGER'S RESCUE--!
SPIDER-MAN'S STUNNED--! MUST GIVE HIM TIME TO RECOVER--!
THE NAME IS MAR-VELL, BUG-EYED ONE--
--OR CAPTAIN MARVEL, IF YOU PREFER--
BTOWW
--BUT EITHER WAY, I DO NOT LIKE TO BE CALLED A "CRETIN"!
CRETIN? I NEVER KNEW THAT WORD BEFORE. THE EXPLOSION HAS INCREASED MY INTELLIGENCE AS WELL.
IMAGINE WHAT MY ABILITIES WILL BE ONCE I SECURE THE SECOND GEM.
BUT FIRST I MUST DEAL FINALLY WITH THESE TWO.
THOSE BEAMS FROM HIS EYES--TURNED THE SIDEWALK BENEATH ME INTO SOME FORM OF--QUICKSAND--!
--IT'S PULLING--SUCKING ME DOWN INTO THE STREET--!
HAVE TO CONCENTRATE--MUST FOCUS MY INTERNAL ENERGIES ON LEVITATION--
--ON FREEING MYSELF FROM THIS HUNGRY EARTH--
--AND IT IS DONE!

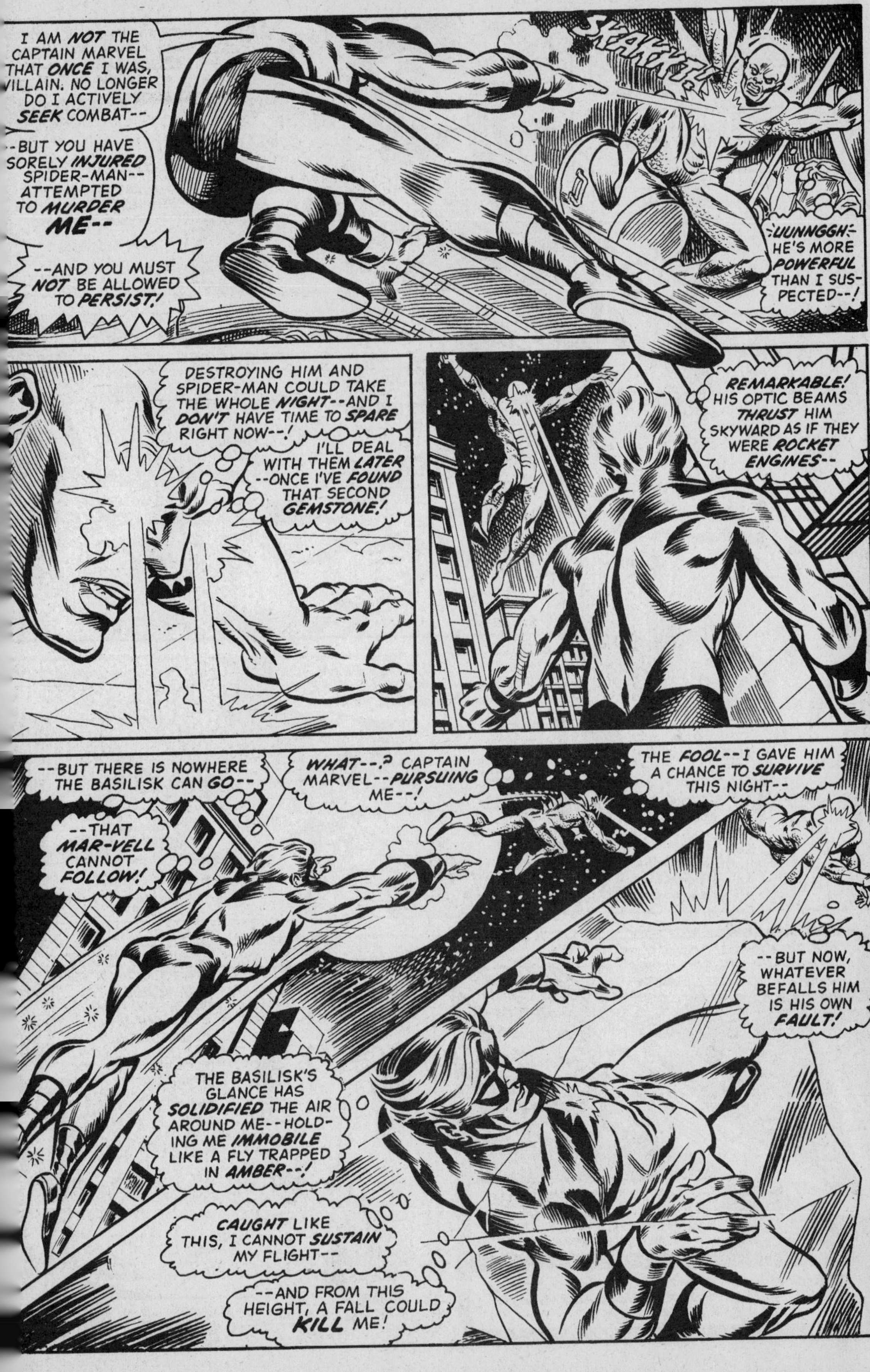
I AM NOT THE CAPTAIN MARVEL THAT ONCE I WAS, VILLAIN. NO LONGER DO I ACTIVELY SEEK COMBAT--
SKAKKT!
--BUT YOU HAVE SORELY INJURED SPIDER-MAN--ATTEMPTED TO MURDER ME--
--AND YOU MUST NOT BE ALLOWED TO PERSIST!
UUNNGGH! HE'S MORE POWERFUL THAN I SUSPECTED--!
DESTROYING HIM AND SPIDER-MAN COULD TAKE THE WHOLE NIGHT--AND I DON'T HAVE TIME TO SPARE RIGHT NOW--!
I'LL DEAL WITH THEM LATER --ONCE I'VE FOUND THAT SECOND GEMSTONE!
REMARKABLE! HIS OPTIC BEAMS THRUST HIM SKYWARD AS IF THEY WERE ROCKET ENGINES--
--BUT THERE IS NOWHERE THE BASILISK CAN GO--
--THAT MAR-VELL CANNOT FOLLOW!
WHAT--? CAPTAIN MARVEL--PURSUING ME--!
THE FOOL--I GAVE HIM A CHANCE TO SURVIVE THIS NIGHT--
--BUT NOW, WHATEVER BEFALLS HIM IS HIS OWN FAULT!
THE BASILISK'S GLANCE HAS SOLIDIFIED THE AIR AROUND ME--HOLDING ME IMMOBILE LIKE A FLY TRAPPED IN AMBER--!
CAUGHT LIKE THIS, I CANNOT SUSTAIN MY FLIGHT--
--AND FROM THIS HEIGHT, A FALL COULD KILL ME!

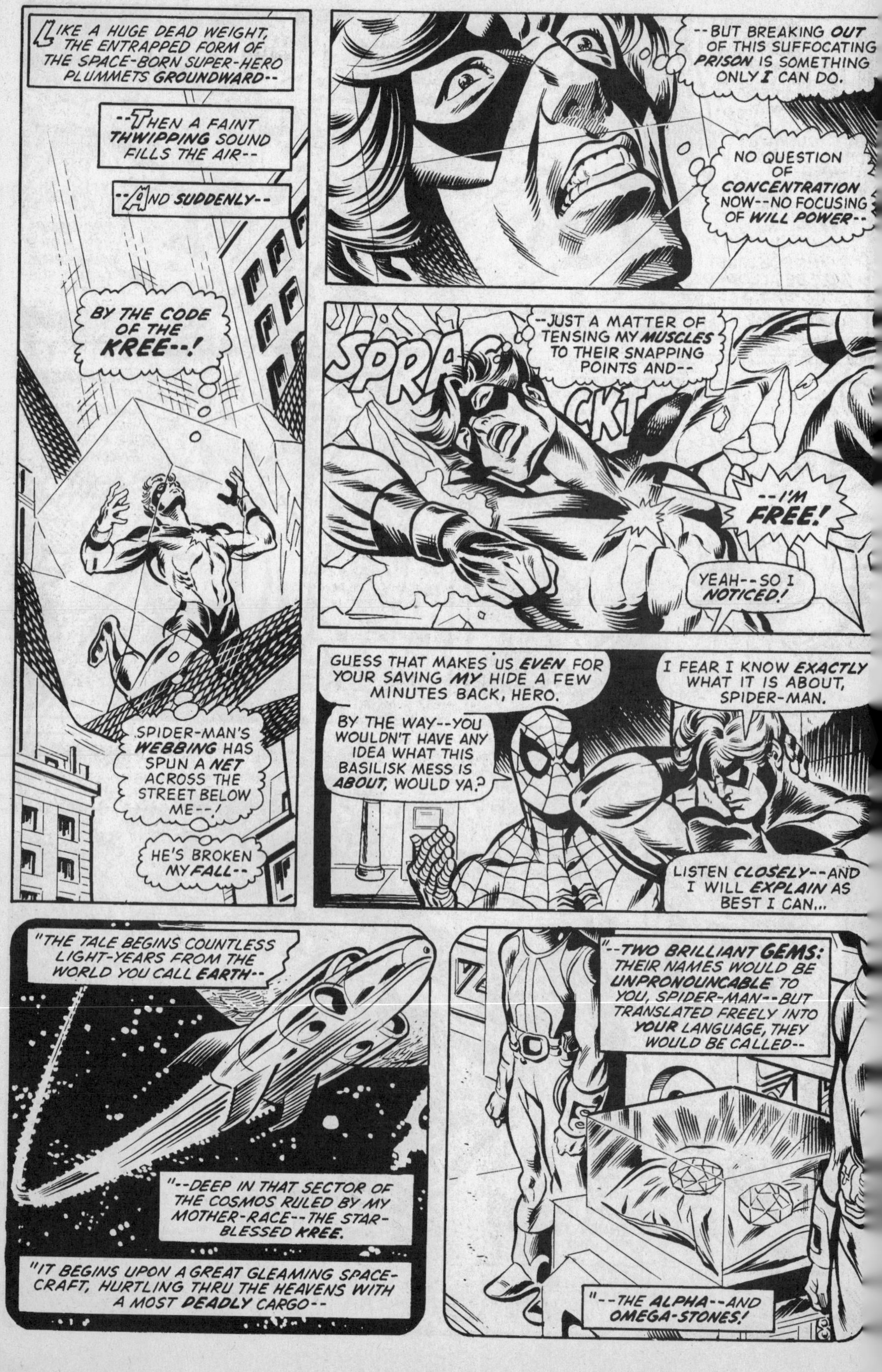
LIKE A HUGE DEAD WEIGHT, THE ENTRAPPED FORM OF THE SPACE-BORN SUPER-HERO PLUMMETS GROUNDWARD--
--THEN A FAINT THWIPPING SOUND FILLS THE AIR--
--AND SUDDENLY--
BY THE CODE OF THE KREE--!
SPIDER-MAN'S WEBBING HAS SPUN A NET ACROSS THE STREET BELOW ME--!
HE'S BROKEN MY FALL--
--BUT BREAKING OUT OF THIS SUFFOCATING PRISON IS SOMETHING ONLY I CAN DO.
NO QUESTION OF CONCENTRATION NOW--NO FOCUSING OF WILL POWER--
SPRACKT
--JUST A MATTER OF TENSING MY MUSCLES TO THEIR SNAPPING POINTS AND--
--I'M FREE!
YEAH--SO I NOTICED!
GUESS THAT MAKES US EVEN FOR YOUR SAVING MY HIDE A FEW MINUTES BACK, HERO.
BY THE WAY--YOU WOULDN'T HAVE ANY IDEA WHAT THIS BASILISK MESS IS ABOUT, WOULD YA?
I FEAR I KNOW EXACTLY WHAT IT IS ABOUT, SPIDER-MAN.
LISTEN CLOSELY--AND I WILL EXPLAIN AS BEST I CAN...
"THE TALE BEGINS COUNTLESS LIGHT-YEARS FROM THE WORLD YOU CALL EARTH--
"--DEEP IN THAT SECTOR OF THE COSMOS RULED BY MY MOTHER-RACE--THE STAR-BLESSED KREE.
"IT BEGINS UPON A GREAT GLEAMING SPACE-CRAFT, HURTLING THRU THE HEAVENS WITH A MOST DEADLY CARGO--
"--TWO BRILLIANT GEMS: THEIR NAMES WOULD BE UNPRONOUNCABLE TO YOU, SPIDER-MAN--BUT TRANSLATED FREELY INTO YOUR LANGUAGE, THEY WOULD BE CALLED--
"--THE ALPHA--AND OMEGA-STONES!

"THE SHIP WAS TAKING THE GEMS TO BE **DESTROYED** IN THE HEART OF A DISTANT SUN--WHEN THE **INCIDENT** OCCURRED."

"ONE OF THE CREWMEN, **MADDENED** BY LUST FOR **POSSESSION** OF THE STONES, **SLEW** THEIR GUARDS--"

"--AND SET ABOUT TO **STEAL** THEM.

"HE PLANNED TO **ESCAPE** THE KREE-SHIP IN A SMALL LIFE-CRAFT, SELL THE GEMS ON SOME FAR-FLUNG WORLD--AND LIVE IN **LUXURY** FOR THE REST OF HIS DAYS.

"HE DID NOT **LIVE** LONG ENOUGH TO CARRY THEM **OUT.**

"YOU SEE SPIDER-MAN, THOSE GEMS WERE TO BE OBLITERATED FOR A **REASON**-- FOR POWER SUCH AS THEY BESTOW IS MORE THAN EVEN A **KREE** CAN HANDLE WITH IMPUNITY.

"THOSE, AT LEAST, WERE HIS **INTENTIONS.**

"THE LIFE-CRAFT WAS STILL IN SIGHT OF THE MOTHER-SHIP WHEN IT **EXPLODED,** BRIGHTENING THE HEAVENS FOR AN INSTANT WITH A PAROXYSM OF **LIGHT.**

"THE GEMS WERE THOUGHT **DESTROYED** --BUT OBVIOUSLY THEY WERE **NOT.**

"FOR A TIME, THEY MUST HAVE **DRIFTED** THRU SPACE--THEN, BY THE GREATEST COINCIDENCE, LANDED **HERE**--

"--UPON **YOUR** WORLD."

SOMEHOW, A SHORT WHILE AGO, MY KREE-BRED SENSES DETECTED THE PRE-SENSE OF **ONE** GEM IN THE MUSEUM NEARBY-- THE **ALPHA-STONE** THAT SUPPLIES THE **BASILISK** WITH HIS POWER.

APPARENTLY, HE'S GONE IN SEARCH OF THE **SECOND** GEM--BUT HE MUST **NOT** BE ALLOWED TO **POSSESS** IT!

SAYING SO IS **ONE** THING-- BUT JUST WHAT DO YOU FIGURE WE CAN **DO** ABOUT IT?

WE **FOLLOW** HIM, SPIDER-MAN-- FOR MY SENSES ARE NOW **ATTUNED** TO THE BASILISK'S ALPHA-STONE-SPAWNED **VIBRATIONS.**

THEN **LEAD ON,** MAC-MARVEL. I'M **WITH** YA ALL THE WAY.

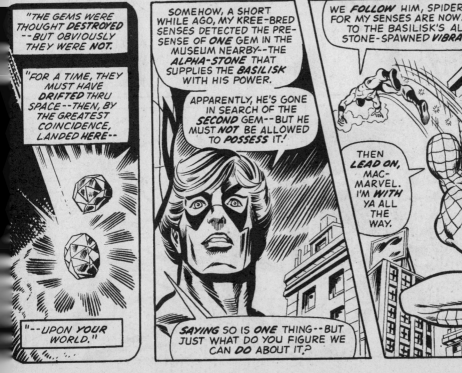

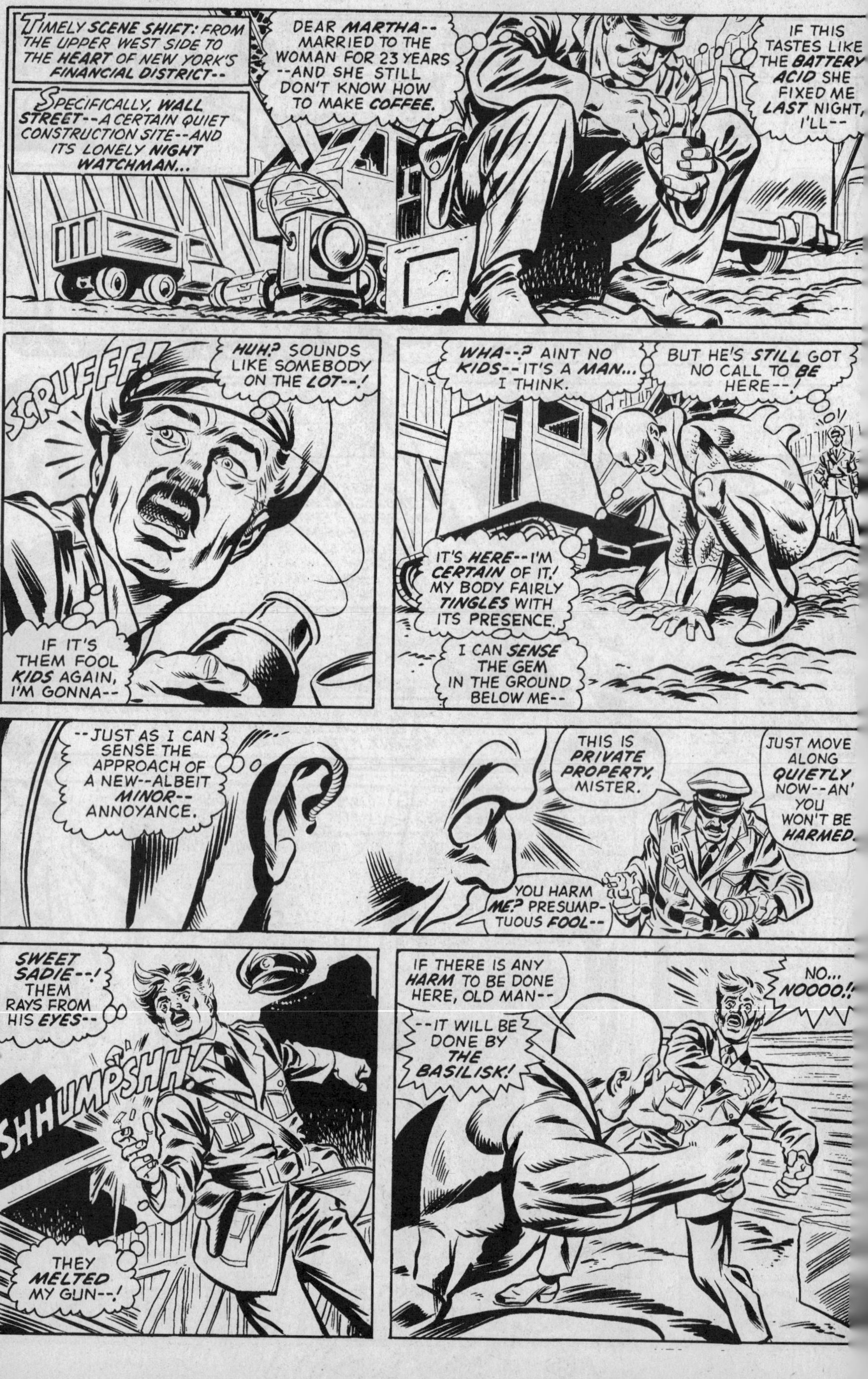
TIMELY SCENE SHIFT: FROM THE UPPER WEST SIDE TO THE HEART OF NEW YORK'S FINANCIAL DISTRICT--
SPECIFICALLY, WALL STREET--A CERTAIN QUIET CONSTRUCTION SITE--AND ITS LONELY NIGHT WATCHMAN...
DEAR MARTHA-- MARRIED TO THE WOMAN FOR 23 YEARS --AND SHE STILL DON'T KNOW HOW TO MAKE COFFEE.
IF THIS TASTES LIKE THE BATTERY ACID SHE FIXED ME LAST NIGHT, I'LL--
SCRUFFF!
HUH? SOUNDS LIKE SOMEBODY ON THE LOT--!
IF IT'S THEM FOOL KIDS AGAIN, I'M GONNA--
WHA--? AINT NO KIDS--IT'S A MAN... I THINK.
BUT HE'S STILL GOT NO CALL TO BE HERE--!
IT'S HERE--I'M CERTAIN OF IT! MY BODY FAIRLY TINGLES WITH ITS PRESENCE.
I CAN SENSE THE GEM IN THE GROUND BELOW ME--
--JUST AS I CAN SENSE THE APPROACH OF A NEW--ALBEIT MINOR--ANNOYANCE.
THIS IS PRIVATE PROPERTY, MISTER.
JUST MOVE ALONG QUIETLY NOW--AN' YOU WON'T BE HARMED.
YOU HARM ME? PRESUMPTUOUS FOOL--
SWEET SADIE--! THEM RAYS FROM HIS EYES--
SHHUMPSHH!
THEY MELTED MY GUN--!
IF THERE IS ANY HARM TO BE DONE HERE, OLD MAN--
--IT WILL BE DONE BY THE BASILISK!
NO... NOOOO!!

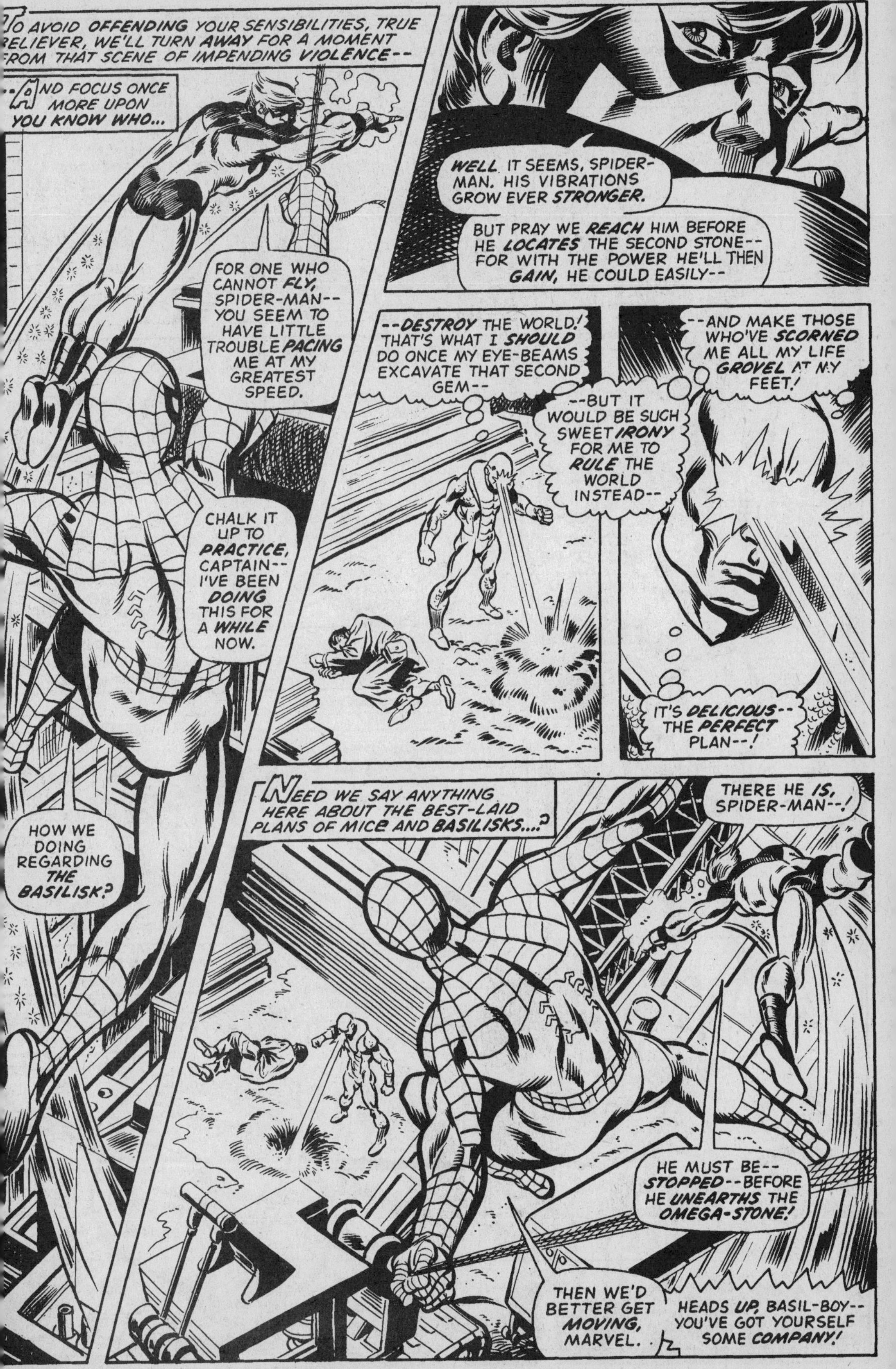
TO AVOID OFFENDING YOUR SENSIBILITIES, TRUE BELIEVER, WE'LL TURN AWAY FOR A MOMENT FROM THAT SCENE OF IMPENDING VIOLENCE--
--AND FOCUS ONCE MORE UPON YOU KNOW WHO...
FOR ONE WHO CANNOT FLY, SPIDER-MAN--YOU SEEM TO HAVE LITTLE TROUBLE PACING ME AT MY GREATEST SPEED.
CHALK IT UP TO PRACTICE, CAPTAIN--I'VE BEEN DOING THIS FOR A WHILE NOW.
HOW WE DOING REGARDING THE BASILISK?
WELL IT SEEMS, SPIDER-MAN. HIS VIBRATIONS GROW EVER STRONGER.
BUT PRAY WE REACH HIM BEFORE HE LOCATES THE SECOND STONE--FOR WITH THE POWER HE'LL THEN GAIN, HE COULD EASILY--
--DESTROY THE WORLD! THAT'S WHAT I SHOULD DO ONCE MY EYE-BEAMS EXCAVATE THAT SECOND GEM--
--BUT IT WOULD BE SUCH SWEET IRONY FOR ME TO RULE THE WORLD INSTEAD--
--AND MAKE THOSE WHO'VE SCORNED ME ALL MY LIFE GROVEL AT MY FEET!
IT'S DELICIOUS--THE PERFECT PLAN--!
NEED WE SAY ANYTHING HERE ABOUT THE BEST-LAID PLANS OF MICE AND BASILISKS...?
THERE HE IS, SPIDER-MAN--!
HE MUST BE--STOPPED--BEFORE HE UNEARTHS THE OMEGA-STONE!
THEN WE'D BETTER GET MOVING, MARVEL.
HEADS UP, BASIL-BOY--YOU'VE GOT YOURSELF SOME COMPANY!

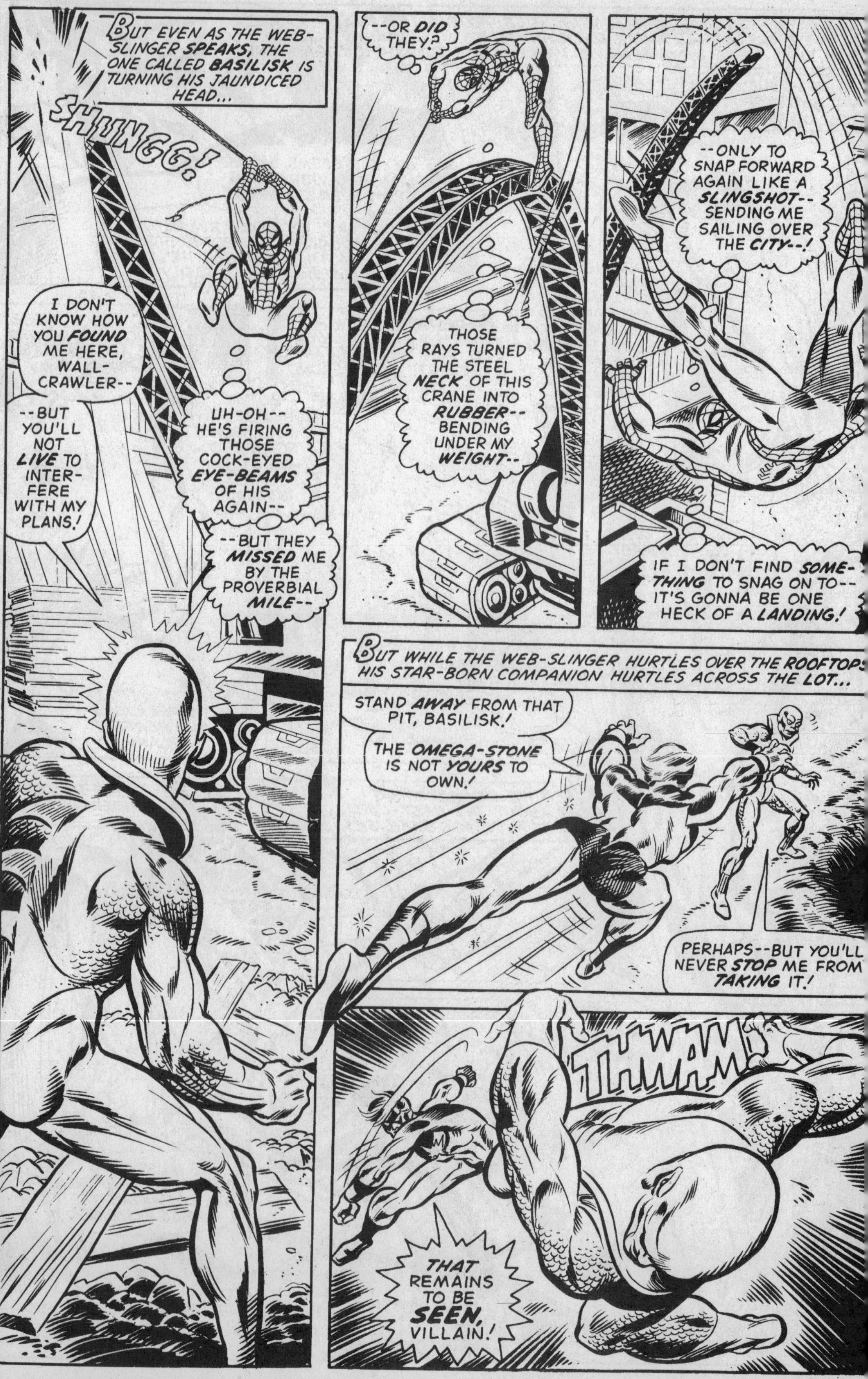
BUT EVEN AS THE WEB-SLINGER SPEAKS, THE ONE CALLED BASILISK IS TURNING HIS JAUNDICED HEAD...
SHUNGG!
I DON'T KNOW HOW YOU FOUND ME HERE, WALL-CRAWLER--
--BUT YOU'LL NOT LIVE TO INTERFERE WITH MY PLANS!
UH-OH-- HE'S FIRING THOSE COCK-EYED EYE-BEAMS OF HIS AGAIN--
--BUT THEY MISSED ME BY THE PROVERBIAL MILE--
--OR DID THEY?
THOSE RAYS TURNED THE STEEL NECK OF THIS CRANE INTO RUBBER-- BENDING UNDER MY WEIGHT--
--ONLY TO SNAP FORWARD AGAIN LIKE A SLINGSHOT-- SENDING ME SAILING OVER THE CITY--!
IF I DON'T FIND SOMETHING TO SNAG ON TO-- IT'S GONNA BE ONE HECK OF A LANDING!
BUT WHILE THE WEB-SLINGER HURTLES OVER THE ROOFTOPS HIS STAR-BORN COMPANION HURTLES ACROSS THE LOT...
STAND AWAY FROM THAT PIT, BASILISK!
THE OMEGA-STONE IS NOT YOURS TO OWN!
PERHAPS--BUT YOU'LL NEVER STOP ME FROM TAKING IT!
THWAM!
THAT REMAINS TO BE SEEN, VILLAIN!

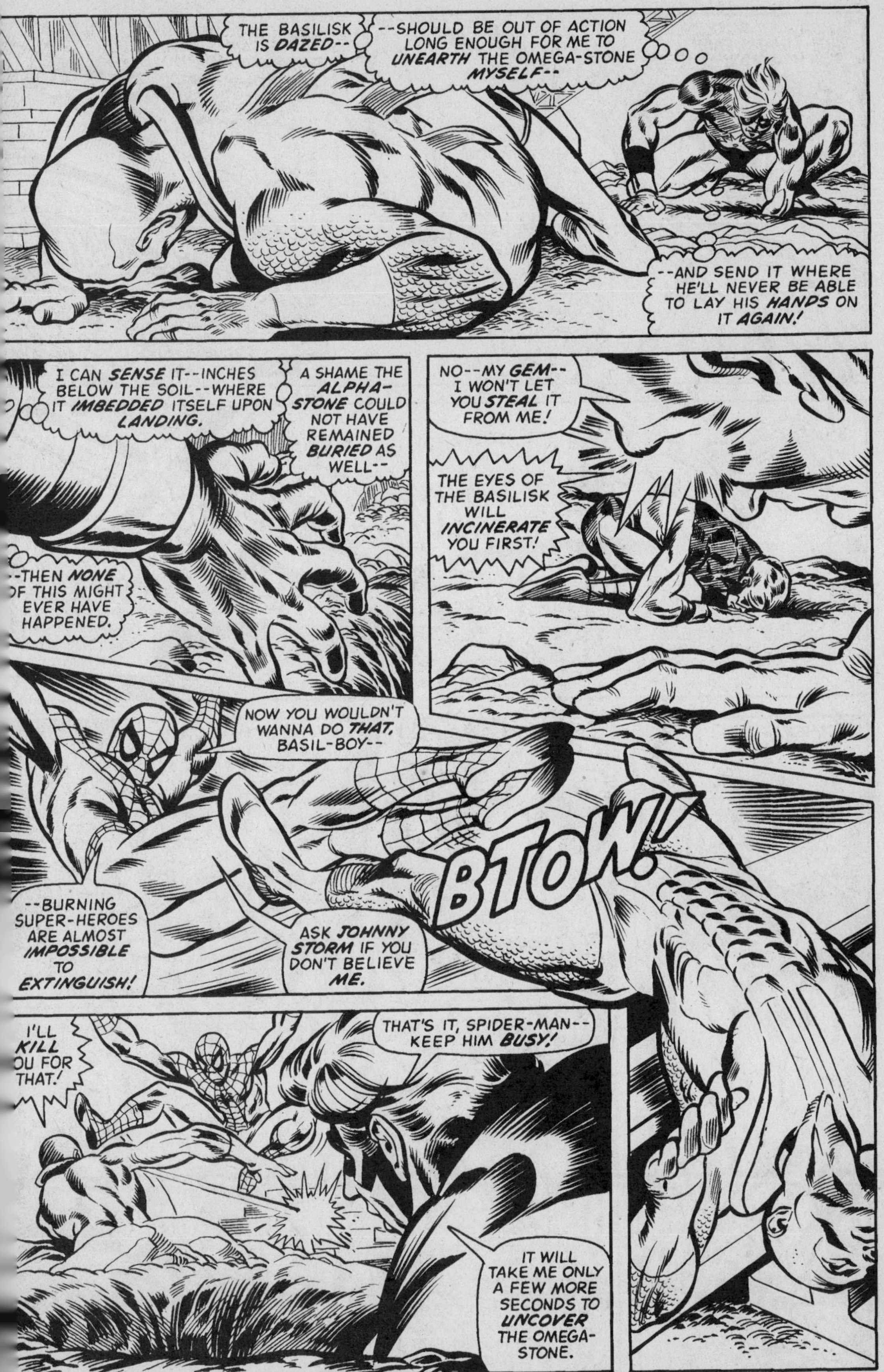
THE BASILISK IS DAZED--
--SHOULD BE OUT OF ACTION LONG ENOUGH FOR ME TO UNEARTH THE OMEGA-STONE MYSELF--
--AND SEND IT WHERE HE'LL NEVER BE ABLE TO LAY HIS HANDS ON IT AGAIN!
I CAN SENSE IT--INCHES BELOW THE SOIL--WHERE IT IMBEDDED ITSELF UPON LANDING.
A SHAME THE ALPHA-STONE COULD NOT HAVE REMAINED BURIED AS WELL--
--THEN NONE OF THIS MIGHT EVER HAVE HAPPENED.
NO--MY GEM--I WON'T LET YOU STEAL IT FROM ME!
THE EYES OF THE BASILISK WILL INCINERATE YOU FIRST!
NOW YOU WOULDN'T WANNA DO THAT, BASIL-BOY--
BTOW!
--BURNING SUPER-HEROES ARE ALMOST IMPOSSIBLE TO EXTINGUISH!
ASK JOHNNY STORM IF YOU DON'T BELIEVE ME.
I'LL KILL OU FOR THAT!
THAT'S IT, SPIDER-MAN--KEEP HIM BUSY!
IT WILL TAKE ME ONLY A FEW MORE SECONDS TO UNCOVER THE OMEGA-STONE.

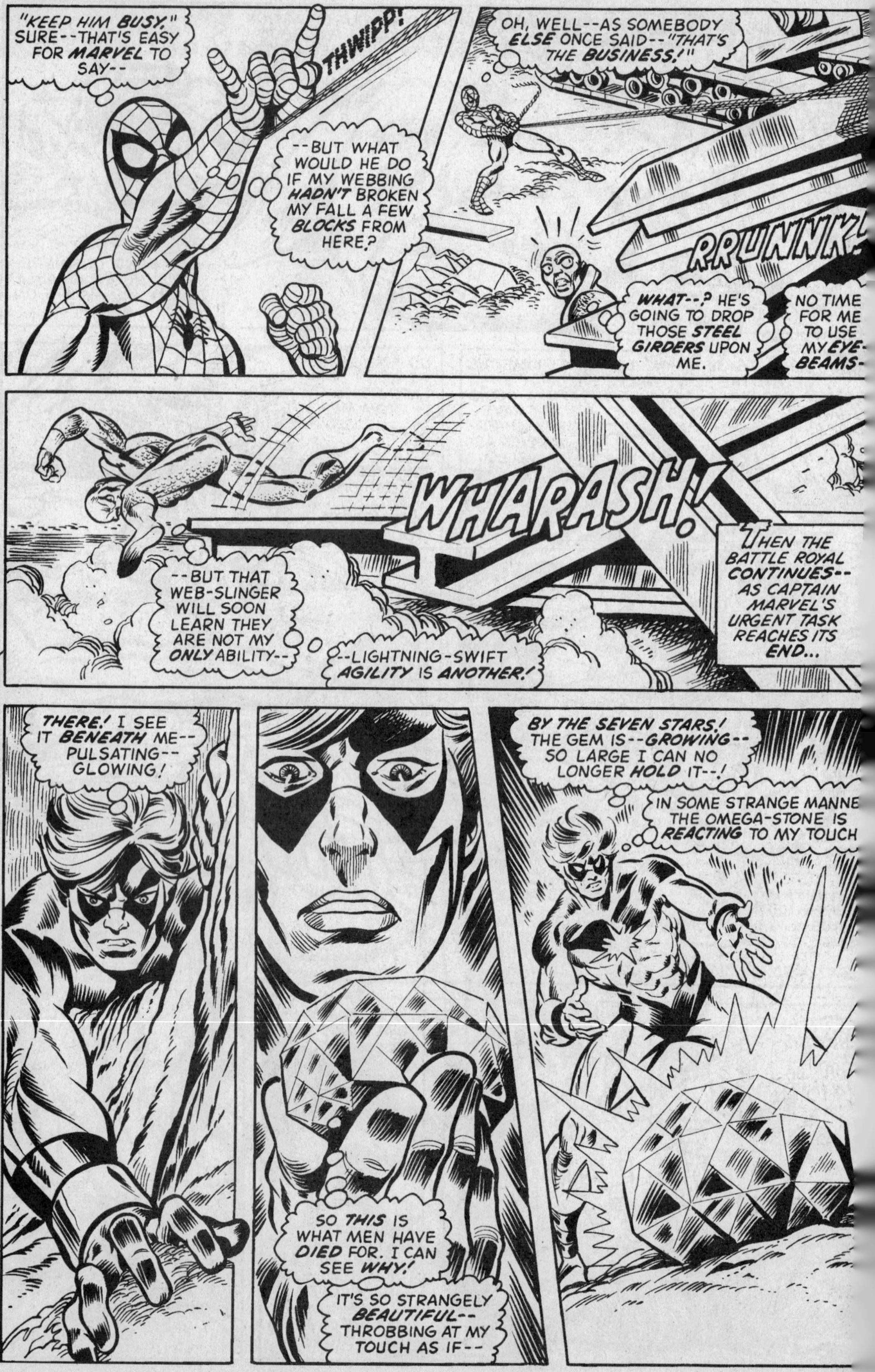
"KEEP HIM BUSY," SURE--THAT'S EASY FOR MARVEL TO SAY--
THWIPP!
--BUT WHAT WOULD HE DO IF MY WEBBING HADN'T BROKEN MY FALL A FEW BLOCKS FROM HERE?
OH, WELL--AS SOMEBODY ELSE ONCE SAID--"THAT'S THE BUSINESS!"
RRUNNK
WHAT--? HE'S GOING TO DROP THOSE STEEL GIRDERS UPON ME.
NO TIME FOR ME TO USE MY EYE-BEAMS-
WHARASH!
--BUT THAT WEB-SLINGER WILL SOON LEARN THEY ARE NOT MY ONLY ABILITY--
--LIGHTNING-SWIFT AGILITY IS ANOTHER!
THEN THE BATTLE ROYAL CONTINUES--AS CAPTAIN MARVEL'S URGENT TASK REACHES ITS END...
THERE! I SEE IT BENEATH ME--PULSATING--GLOWING!
SO THIS IS WHAT MEN HAVE DIED FOR. I CAN SEE WHY!
IT'S SO STRANGELY BEAUTIFUL--THROBBING AT MY TOUCH AS IF--
BY THE SEVEN STARS! THE GEM IS--GROWING--SO LARGE I CAN NO LONGER HOLD IT--!
IN SOME STRANGE MANNE THE OMEGA-STONE IS REACTING TO MY TOUCH

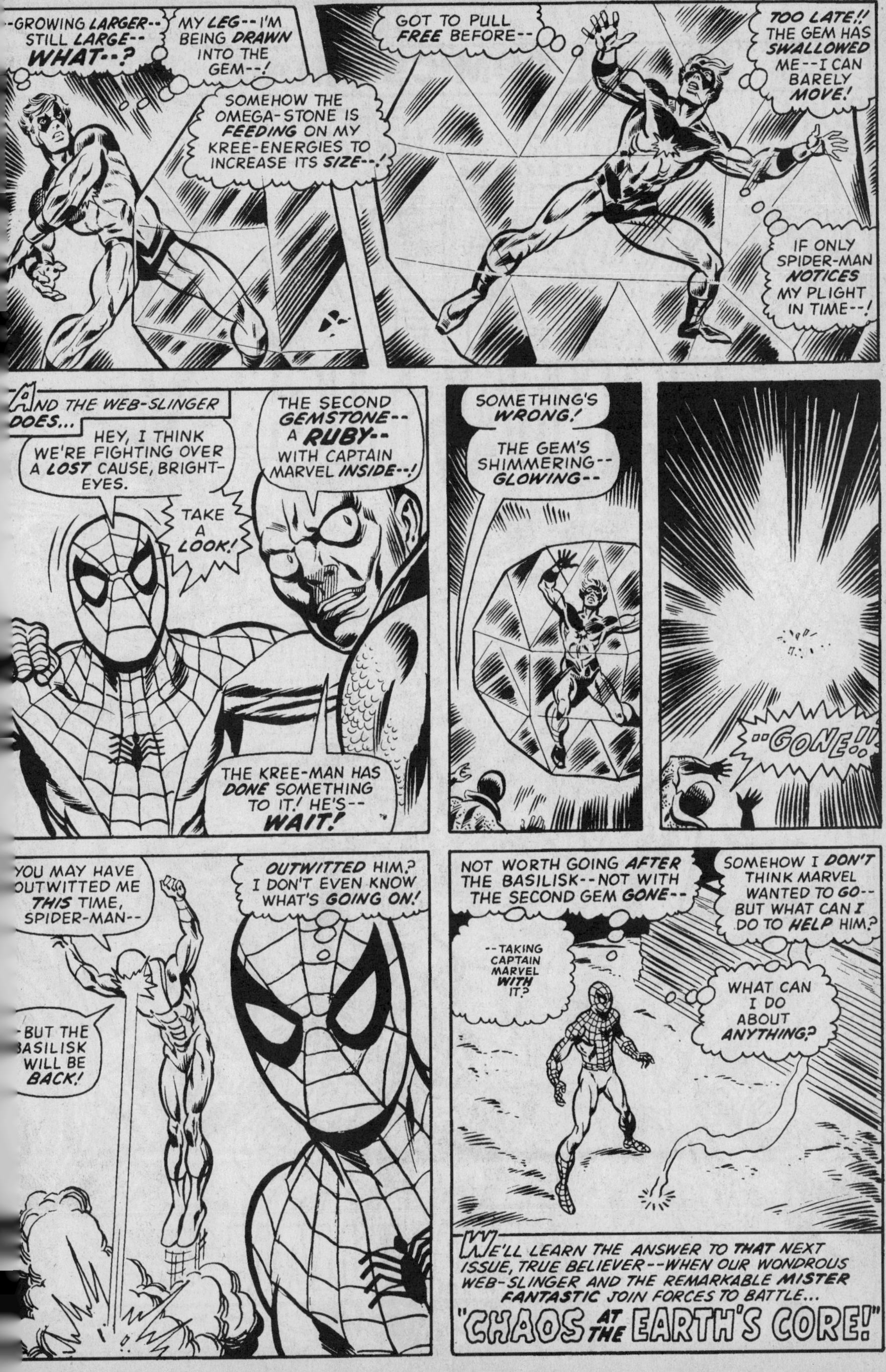
--GROWING LARGER--STILL LARGE--WHAT--?
MY LEG--I'M BEING DRAWN INTO THE GEM--!
SOMEHOW THE OMEGA-STONE IS FEEDING ON MY KREE-ENERGIES TO INCREASE ITS SIZE--!
GOT TO PULL FREE BEFORE--
TOO LATE!! THE GEM HAS SWALLOWED ME--I CAN BARELY MOVE!
IF ONLY SPIDER-MAN NOTICES MY PLIGHT IN TIME--!
AND THE WEB-SLINGER DOES...
HEY, I THINK WE'RE FIGHTING OVER A LOST CAUSE, BRIGHT-EYES.
TAKE A LOOK!
THE SECOND GEMSTONE--A RUBY--WITH CAPTAIN MARVEL INSIDE--!
THE KREE-MAN HAS DONE SOMETHING TO IT! HE'S--WAIT!
SOMETHING'S WRONG!
THE GEM'S SHIMMERING--GLOWING--
--GONE!!
YOU MAY HAVE OUTWITTED ME THIS TIME, SPIDER-MAN--
-BUT THE BASILISK WILL BE BACK!
OUTWITTED HIM? I DON'T EVEN KNOW WHAT'S GOING ON!
NOT WORTH GOING AFTER THE BASILISK--NOT WITH THE SECOND GEM GONE--
--TAKING CAPTAIN MARVEL WITH IT?
SOMEHOW I DON'T THINK MARVEL WANTED TO GO--BUT WHAT CAN I DO TO HELP HIM?
WHAT CAN I DO ABOUT ANYTHING?
WE'LL LEARN THE ANSWER TO THAT NEXT ISSUE, TRUE BELIEVER--WHEN OUR WONDROUS WEB-SLINGER AND THE REMARKABLE MISTER FANTASTIC JOIN FORCES TO BATTLE...
"CHAOS AT THE EARTH'S CORE!"

MARVEL TEAM-UP
MARVEL COMICS GROUP
APPROVED BY THE COMICS CODE AUTHORITY
20¢
17 JAN 02147
MARVEL TEAM-UP
FEATURING
SPIDER-MAN AND MISTER FANTASTIC
THE MOLE MAN STRIKES BACK!

Stan Lee PRESENTS: SPIDEY AND MR. FANTASTIC--TOGETHER!™

LEN WEIN WRITER * GIL KANE ARTIST * EVERYBODY! INKERS * GLYNIS WEIN COLORIST * JEAN IZZO LETTERER * ROY THOMAS EDITOR

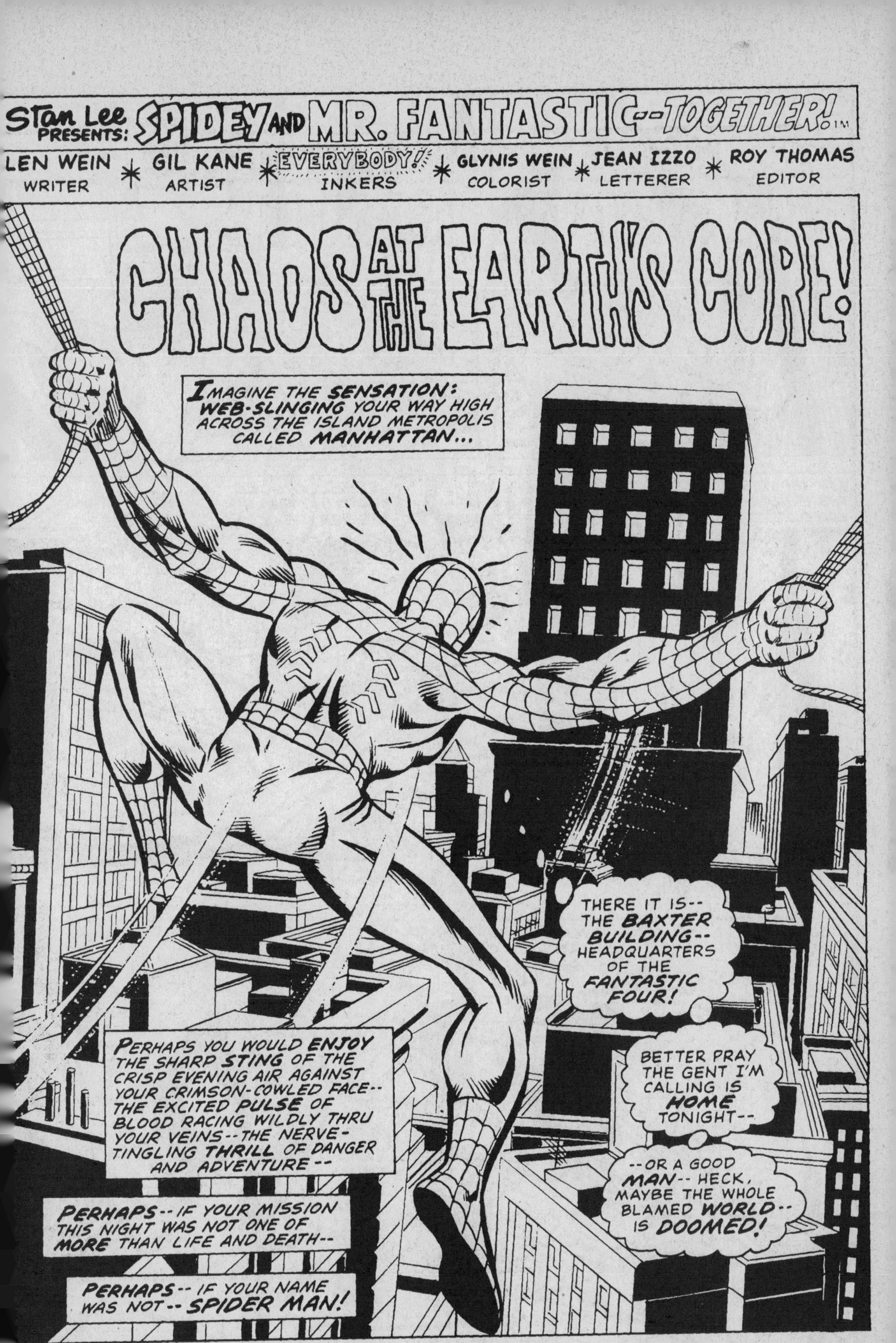

CHAOS AT THE EARTH'S CORE!
IMAGINE THE SENSATION: WEB-SLINGING YOUR WAY HIGH ACROSS THE ISLAND METROPOLIS CALLED MANHATTAN...
THERE IT IS-- THE BAXTER BUILDING-- HEADQUARTERS OF THE FANTASTIC FOUR!
PERHAPS YOU WOULD ENJOY THE SHARP STING OF THE CRISP EVENING AIR AGAINST YOUR CRIMSON-COWLED FACE-- THE EXCITED PULSE OF BLOOD RACING WILDLY THRU YOUR VEINS--THE NERVE-TINGLING THRILL OF DANGER AND ADVENTURE--
BETTER PRAY THE GENT I'M CALLING IS HOME TONIGHT--
PERHAPS--IF YOUR MISSION THIS NIGHT WAS NOT ONE OF MORE THAN LIFE AND DEATH--
--OR A GOOD MAN-- HECK, MAYBE THE WHOLE BLAMED WORLD-- IS DOOMED!
PERHAPS-- IF YOUR NAME WAS NOT-- SPIDER MAN!

OKAY, NOW ALL I'VE GOTTA DO IS FIND A WAY *INTO* THIS--

HEY-- LOOKS LIKE SOMEBODY LEFT A *WINDOW* OPEN.

VERY *CARELESS* OF THEM--

--BUT I SUPPOSE THEY *DON'T* EXPECT MANY VISITORS TO DROP IN UNEXPECTEDLY ON THE *34TH FLOOR.*

WELL, SURPRISE, *SURPRISE*-- SOMEBODY JUST *HAS!*

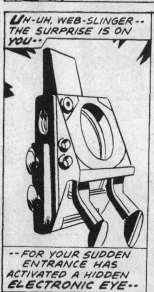

UH-UH, WEB-SLINGER-- THE SURPRISE IS ON *YOU*--

--FOR YOUR SUDDEN ENTRANCE HAS ACTIVATED A HIDDEN *ELECTRONIC EYE*--

--*TRIGGERING THE RELEASE OF*--

STEEL CABLES-- SHOOTING OUT OF THE VERY *WALLS!*

THEY SEEM DRAWN TO MY *BODY HEAT*-- TRYING TO WRAP ME IN A METALLIC *COCOON*--!

SORRY, LITTLE CABLES-- BUT IT JUST WON'T *WORK!*

NO MATTER HOW *HARD* YOU TRY-- YOU CAN'T TURN A SPIDER INTO A *BUTTER-FLY!*

SNAP!

RRAC!

ALL RIGHT, WALL-CRAWLER-- THAT'S *ENOUGH!*

KEEP IT UP AND YOU'LL TEAR THE WHOLE *PLACE* DOWN!

WHO--?

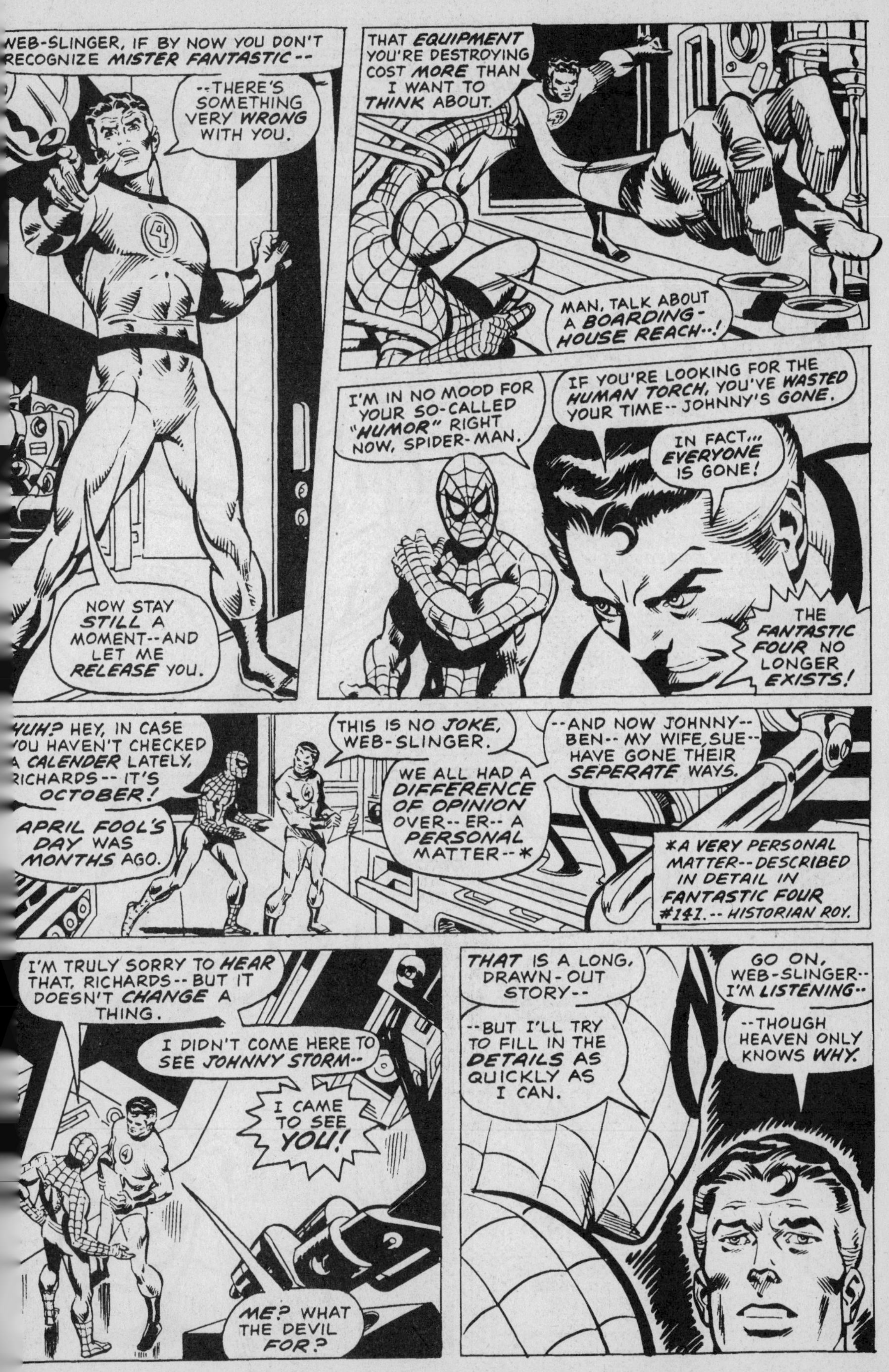
WEB-SLINGER, IF BY NOW YOU DON'T RECOGNIZE MISTER FANTASTIC--
--THERE'S SOMETHING VERY WRONG WITH YOU.
NOW STAY STILL A MOMENT--AND LET ME RELEASE YOU.
THAT EQUIPMENT YOU'RE DESTROYING COST MORE THAN I WANT TO THINK ABOUT.
MAN, TALK ABOUT A BOARDING-HOUSE REACH--!
I'M IN NO MOOD FOR YOUR SO-CALLED "HUMOR" RIGHT NOW, SPIDER-MAN.
IF YOU'RE LOOKING FOR THE HUMAN TORCH, YOU'VE WASTED YOUR TIME-- JOHNNY'S GONE.
IN FACT... EVERYONE IS GONE!
THE FANTASTIC FOUR NO LONGER EXISTS!
HUH? HEY, IN CASE YOU HAVEN'T CHECKED A CALENDER LATELY, RICHARDS -- IT'S OCTOBER!
APRIL FOOL'S DAY WAS MONTHS AGO.
THIS IS NO JOKE, WEB-SLINGER.
WE ALL HAD A DIFFERENCE OF OPINION OVER-- ER-- A PERSONAL MATTER--*
--AND NOW JOHNNY--BEN-- MY WIFE, SUE--HAVE GONE THEIR SEPERATE WAYS.
*A VERY PERSONAL MATTER--DESCRIBED IN DETAIL IN FANTASTIC FOUR #141.-- HISTORIAN ROY.
I'M TRULY SORRY TO HEAR THAT, RICHARDS-- BUT IT DOESN'T CHANGE A THING.
I DIDN'T COME HERE TO SEE JOHNNY STORM--
I CAME TO SEE YOU!
ME? WHAT THE DEVIL FOR?
THAT IS A LONG, DRAWN-OUT STORY--
--BUT I'LL TRY TO FILL IN THE DETAILS AS QUICKLY AS I CAN.
GO ON, WEB-SLINGER-- I'M LISTENING--
--THOUGH HEAVEN ONLY KNOWS WHY.

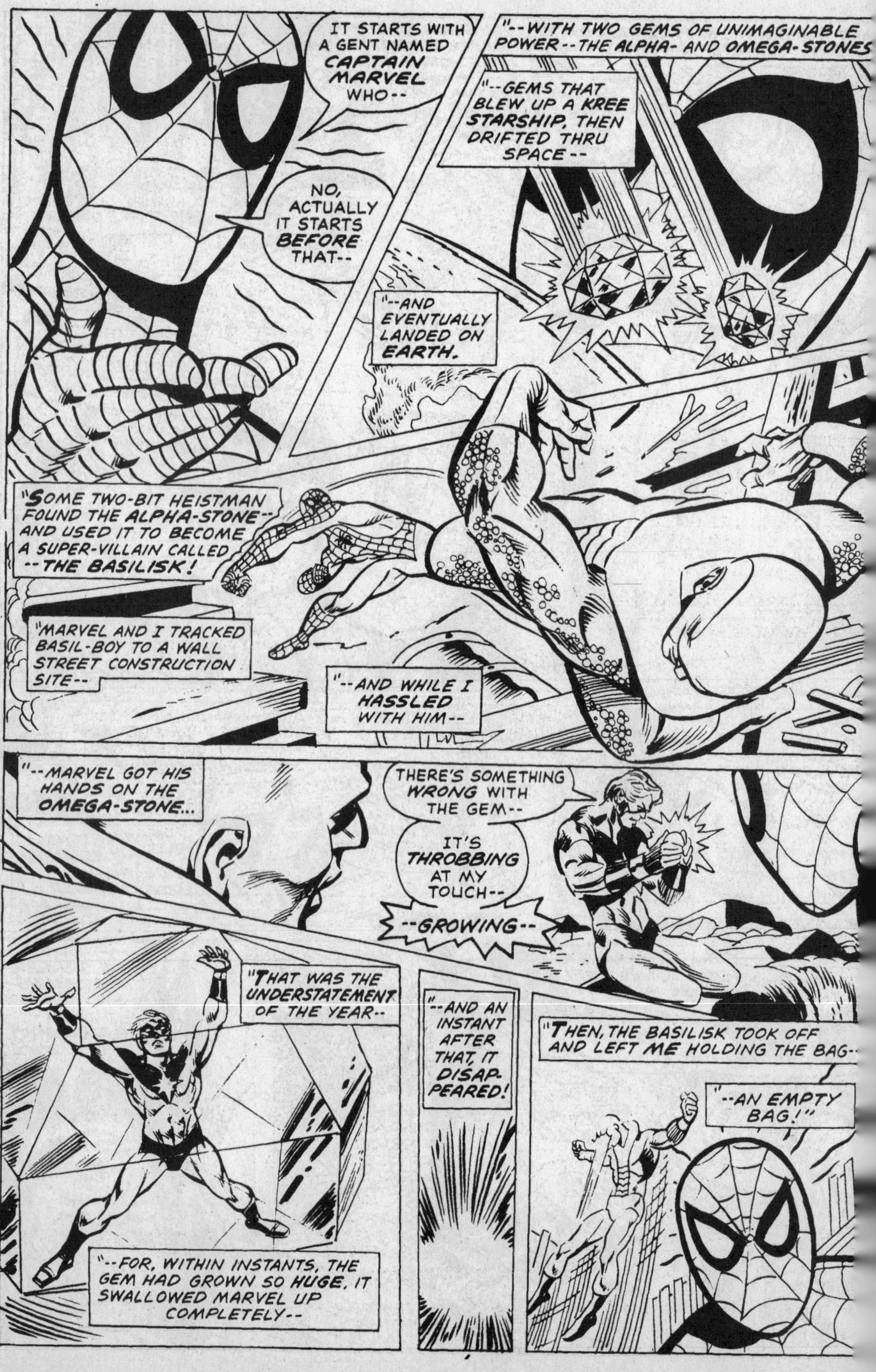
IT STARTS WITH A GENT NAMED CAPTAIN MARVEL WHO--
NO, ACTUALLY IT STARTS BEFORE THAT--
"--WITH TWO GEMS OF UNIMAGINABLE POWER--THE ALPHA- AND OMEGA-STONES
"--GEMS THAT BLEW UP A KREE STARSHIP, THEN DRIFTED THRU SPACE--
"--AND EVENTUALLY LANDED ON EARTH.
"SOME TWO-BIT HEISTMAN FOUND THE ALPHA-STONE-- AND USED IT TO BECOME A SUPER-VILLAIN CALLED --THE BASILISK!
"MARVEL AND I TRACKED BASIL-BOY TO A WALL STREET CONSTRUCTION SITE--
"--AND WHILE I HASSLED WITH HIM--
"--MARVEL GOT HIS HANDS ON THE OMEGA-STONE...
THERE'S SOMETHING WRONG WITH THE GEM--
IT'S THROBBING AT MY TOUCH--
--GROWING--
"THAT WAS THE UNDERSTATEMENT OF THE YEAR--
"--FOR, WITHIN INSTANTS, THE GEM HAD GROWN SO HUGE, IT SWALLOWED MARVEL UP COMPLETELY--
"--AND AN INSTANT AFTER THAT, IT DISAPPEARED!
"THEN, THE BASILISK TOOK OFF AND LEFT ME HOLDING THE BAG--
"--AN EMPTY BAG!"

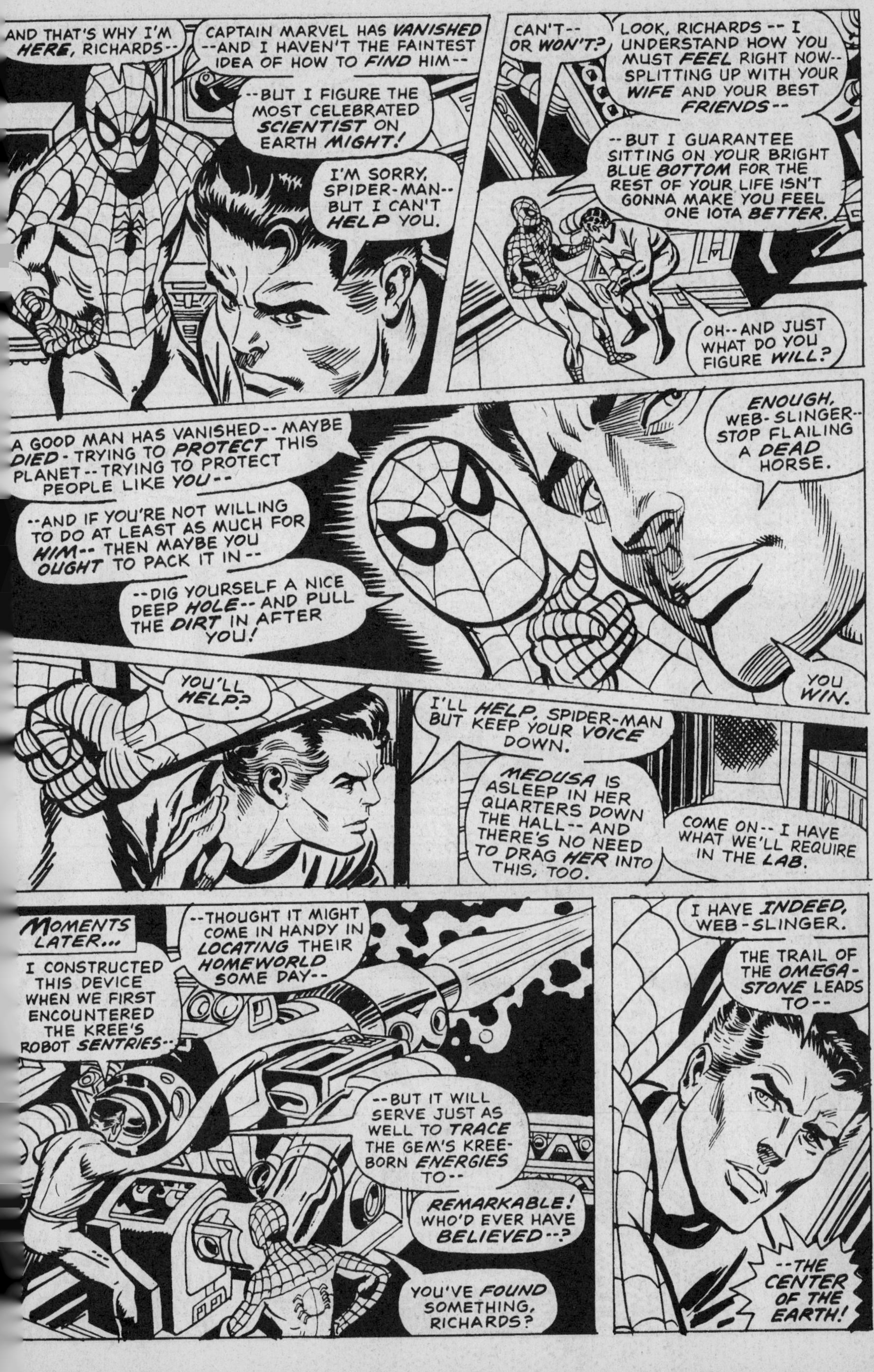
AND THAT'S WHY I'M HERE, RICHARDS--
CAPTAIN MARVEL HAS VANISHED --AND I HAVEN'T THE FAINTEST IDEA OF HOW TO FIND HIM--
--BUT I FIGURE THE MOST CELEBRATED SCIENTIST ON EARTH MIGHT!
I'M SORRY, SPIDER-MAN-- BUT I CAN'T HELP YOU.
CAN'T-- OR WON'T?
LOOK, RICHARDS -- I UNDERSTAND HOW YOU MUST FEEL RIGHT NOW-- SPLITTING UP WITH YOUR WIFE AND YOUR BEST FRIENDS--
--BUT I GUARANTEE SITTING ON YOUR BRIGHT BLUE BOTTOM FOR THE REST OF YOUR LIFE ISN'T GONNA MAKE YOU FEEL ONE IOTA BETTER.
OH--AND JUST WHAT DO YOU FIGURE WILL?
A GOOD MAN HAS VANISHED-- MAYBE DIED-- TRYING TO PROTECT THIS PLANET--TRYING TO PROTECT PEOPLE LIKE YOU--
--AND IF YOU'RE NOT WILLING TO DO AT LEAST AS MUCH FOR HIM-- THEN MAYBE YOU OUGHT TO PACK IT IN--
--DIG YOURSELF A NICE DEEP HOLE-- AND PULL THE DIRT IN AFTER YOU!
ENOUGH, WEB-SLINGER-- STOP FLAILING A DEAD HORSE.
YOU WIN.
YOU'LL HELP?
I'LL HELP, SPIDER-MAN BUT KEEP YOUR VOICE DOWN.
MEDUSA IS ASLEEP IN HER QUARTERS DOWN THE HALL-- AND THERE'S NO NEED TO DRAG HER INTO THIS, TOO.
COME ON-- I HAVE WHAT WE'LL REQUIRE IN THE LAB.
MOMENTS LATER...
I CONSTRUCTED THIS DEVICE WHEN WE FIRST ENCOUNTERED THE KREE'S ROBOT SENTRIES--
--THOUGHT IT MIGHT COME IN HANDY IN LOCATING THEIR HOMEWORLD SOME DAY--
--BUT IT WILL SERVE JUST AS WELL TO TRACE THE GEM'S KREE-BORN ENERGIES TO--
REMARKABLE! WHO'D EVER HAVE BELIEVED--?
YOU'VE FOUND SOMETHING, RICHARDS?
I HAVE INDEED, WEB-SLINGER.
THE TRAIL OF THE OMEGA-STONE LEADS TO--
--THE CENTER OF THE EARTH!

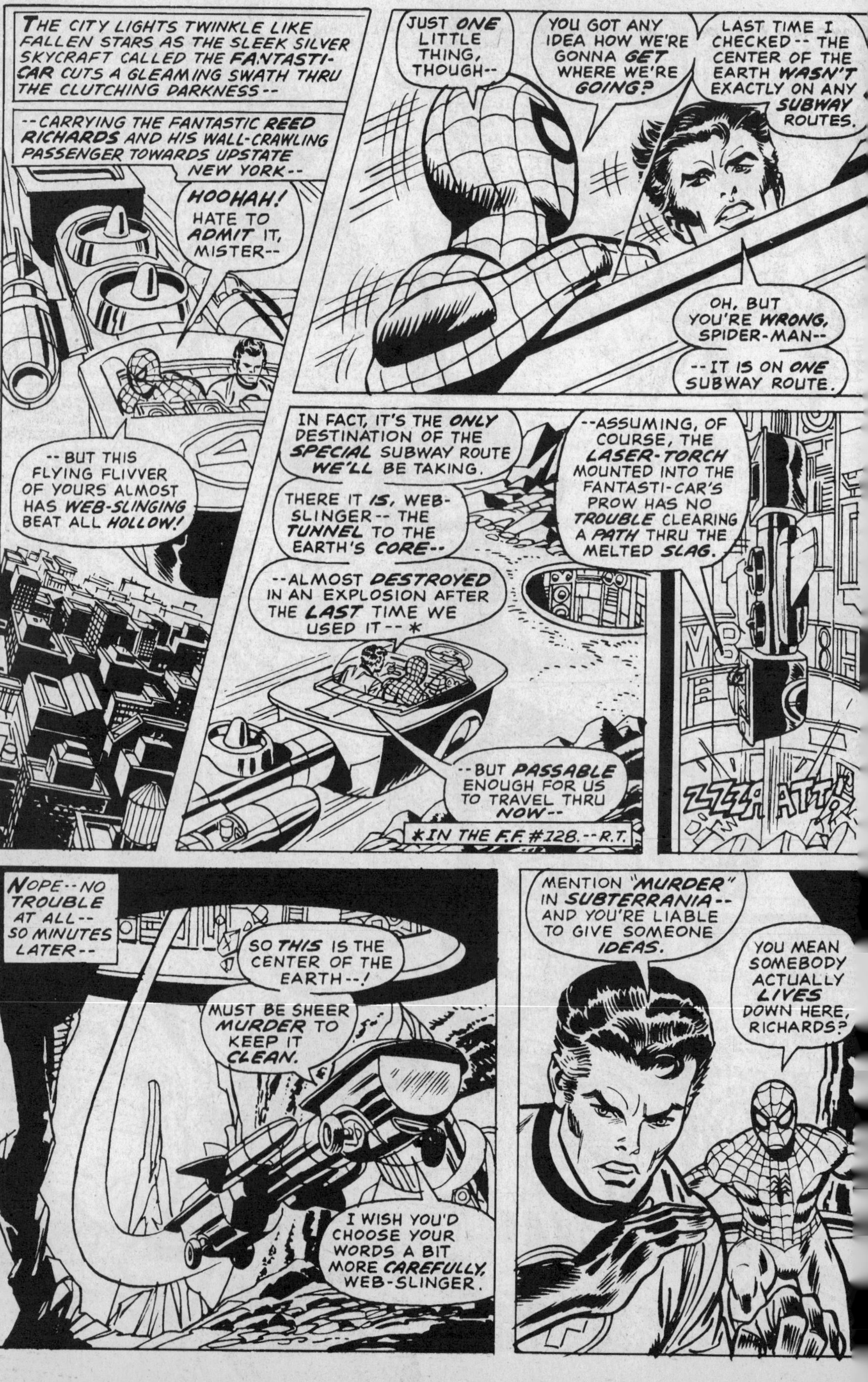
THE CITY LIGHTS TWINKLE LIKE FALLEN STARS AS THE SLEEK SILVER SKYCRAFT CALLED THE FANTASTI-CAR CUTS A GLEAMING SWATH THRU THE CLUTCHING DARKNESS--
--CARRYING THE FANTASTIC REED RICHARDS AND HIS WALL-CRAWLING PASSENGER TOWARDS UPSTATE NEW YORK--
HOOHAH! HATE TO ADMIT IT, MISTER--
--BUT THIS FLYING FLIVVER OF YOURS ALMOST HAS WEB-SLINGING BEAT ALL HOLLOW!
JUST ONE LITTLE THING, THOUGH--
YOU GOT ANY IDEA HOW WE'RE GONNA GET WHERE WE'RE GOING?
LAST TIME I CHECKED-- THE CENTER OF THE EARTH WASN'T EXACTLY ON ANY SUBWAY ROUTES.
OH, BUT YOU'RE WRONG, SPIDER-MAN--
--IT IS ON ONE SUBWAY ROUTE.
IN FACT, IT'S THE ONLY DESTINATION OF THE SPECIAL SUBWAY ROUTE WE'LL BE TAKING.
THERE IT IS, WEB-SLINGER-- THE TUNNEL TO THE EARTH'S CORE--
--ALMOST DESTROYED IN AN EXPLOSION AFTER THE LAST TIME WE USED IT-- *
--BUT PASSABLE ENOUGH FOR US TO TRAVEL THRU NOW--
*IN THE F.F. #128.--R.T.
--ASSUMING, OF COURSE, THE LASER-TORCH MOUNTED INTO THE FANTASTI-CAR'S PROW HAS NO TROUBLE CLEARING A PATH THRU THE MELTED SLAG.
ZZZRAT!
NOPE--NO TROUBLE AT ALL-- SO MINUTES LATER--
SO THIS IS THE CENTER OF THE EARTH--!
MUST BE SHEER MURDER TO KEEP IT CLEAN.
I WISH YOU'D CHOOSE YOUR WORDS A BIT MORE CAREFULLY, WEB-SLINGER.
MENTION "MURDER" IN SUBTERRANIA-- AND YOU'RE LIABLE TO GIVE SOMEONE IDEAS.
YOU MEAN SOMEBODY ACTUALLY LIVES DOWN HERE, RICHARDS?

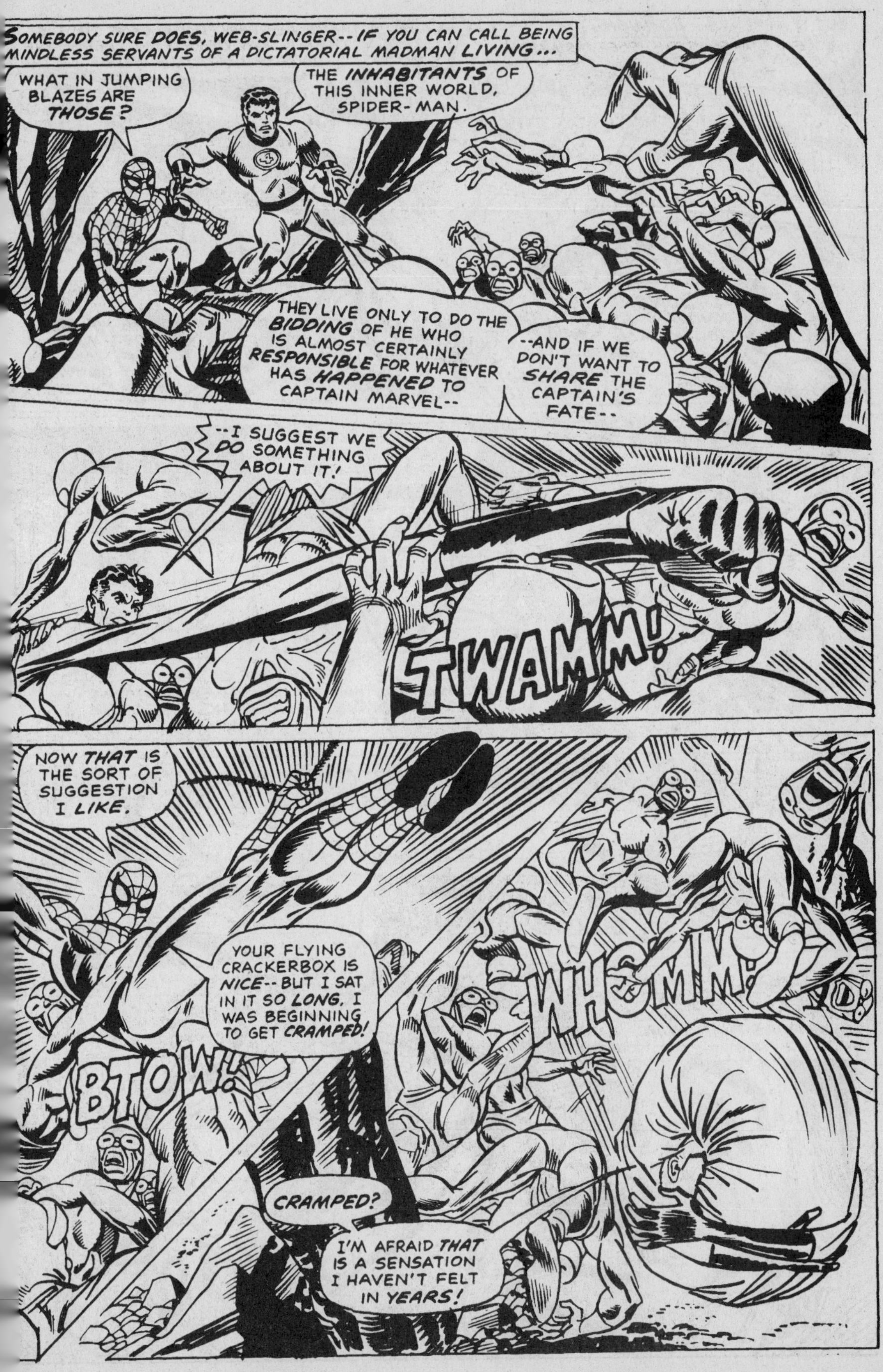
SOMEBODY SURE DOES, WEB-SLINGER--IF YOU CAN CALL BEING MINDLESS SERVANTS OF A DICTATORIAL MADMAN LIVING...
WHAT IN JUMPING BLAZES ARE THOSE?
THE INHABITANTS OF THIS INNER WORLD, SPIDER-MAN.
THEY LIVE ONLY TO DO THE BIDDING OF HE WHO IS ALMOST CERTAINLY RESPONSIBLE FOR WHATEVER HAS HAPPENED TO CAPTAIN MARVEL--
--AND IF WE DON'T WANT TO SHARE THE CAPTAIN'S FATE--
--I SUGGEST WE DO SOMETHING ABOUT IT!
TWAMM!
NOW THAT IS THE SORT OF SUGGESTION I LIKE.
YOUR FLYING CRACKERBOX IS NICE--BUT I SAT IN IT SO LONG, I WAS BEGINNING TO GET CRAMPED!
WHOMM!
BTOW!
CRAMPED?
I'M AFRAID THAT IS A SENSATION I HAVEN'T FELT IN YEARS!

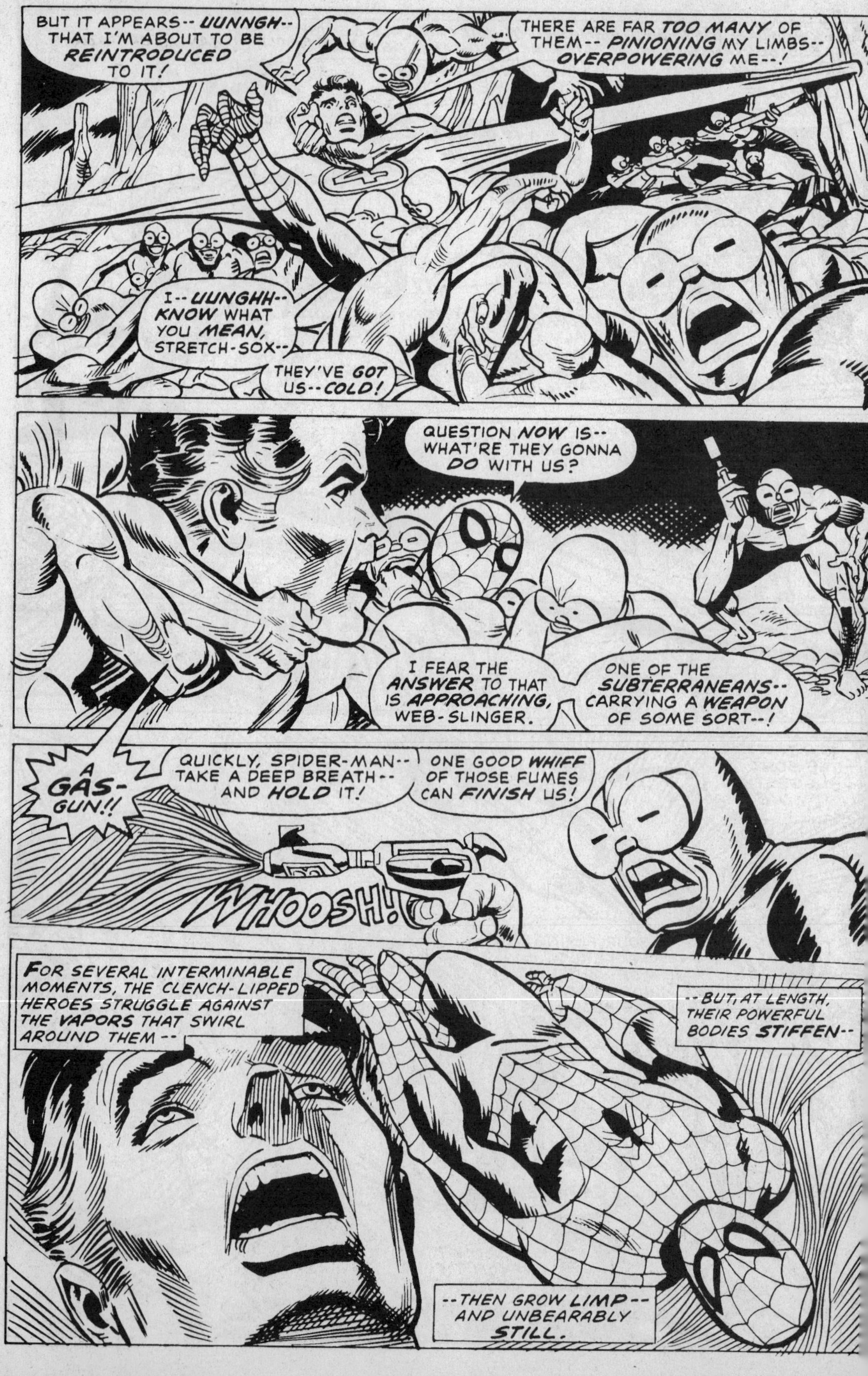

BUT IT APPEARS-- UUNNGH-- THAT I'M ABOUT TO BE REINTRODUCED TO IT!
THERE ARE FAR TOO MANY OF THEM-- PINIONING MY LIMBS-- OVERPOWERING ME--!
I-- UUNGHH-- KNOW WHAT YOU MEAN, STRETCH-SOX--
THEY'VE GOT US--COLD!
QUESTION NOW IS-- WHAT'RE THEY GONNA DO WITH US?
I FEAR THE ANSWER TO THAT IS APPROACHING, WEB-SLINGER.
ONE OF THE SUBTERRANEANS-- CARRYING A WEAPON OF SOME SORT--!
A GAS-GUN!!
QUICKLY, SPIDER-MAN-- TAKE A DEEP BREATH-- AND HOLD IT!
ONE GOOD WHIFF OF THOSE FUMES CAN FINISH US!
WHOOSH!
FOR SEVERAL INTERMINABLE MOMENTS, THE CLENCH-LIPPED HEROES STRUGGLE AGAINST THE VAPORS THAT SWIRL AROUND THEM --
--BUT, AT LENGTH, THEIR POWERFUL BODIES STIFFEN--
--THEN GROW LIMP-- AND UNBEARABLY STILL.

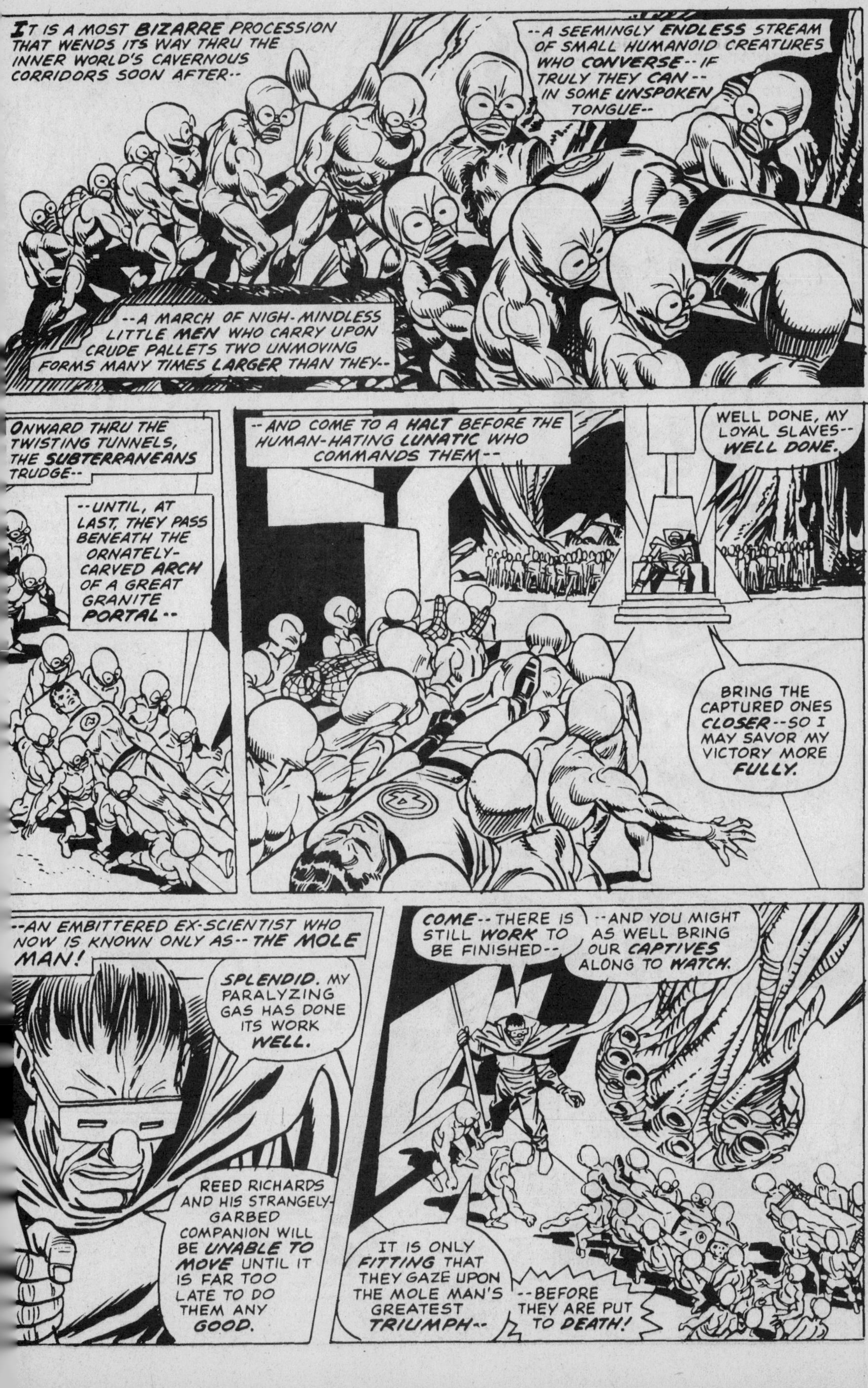

IT IS A MOST BIZARRE PROCESSION THAT WENDS ITS WAY THRU THE INNER WORLD'S CAVERNOUS CORRIDORS SOON AFTER--
--A SEEMINGLY ENDLESS STREAM OF SMALL HUMANOID CREATURES WHO CONVERSE--IF TRULY THEY CAN--IN SOME UNSPOKEN TONGUE--
--A MARCH OF NIGH-MINDLESS LITTLE MEN WHO CARRY UPON CRUDE PALLETS TWO UNMOVING FORMS MANY TIMES LARGER THAN THEY--
ONWARD THRU THE TWISTING TUNNELS, THE SUBTERRANEANS TRUDGE--
--UNTIL, AT LAST, THEY PASS BENEATH THE ORNATELY-CARVED ARCH OF A GREAT GRANITE PORTAL--
--AND COME TO A HALT BEFORE THE HUMAN-HATING LUNATIC WHO COMMANDS THEM--
WELL DONE, MY LOYAL SLAVES--WELL DONE.
BRING THE CAPTURED ONES CLOSER--SO I MAY SAVOR MY VICTORY MORE FULLY.
--AN EMBITTERED EX-SCIENTIST WHO NOW IS KNOWN ONLY AS--THE MOLE MAN!
SPLENDID. MY PARALYZING GAS HAS DONE ITS WORK WELL.
REED RICHARDS AND HIS STRANGELY-GARBED COMPANION WILL BE UNABLE TO MOVE UNTIL IT IS FAR TOO LATE TO DO THEM ANY GOOD.
COME--THERE IS STILL WORK TO BE FINISHED--
--AND YOU MIGHT AS WELL BRING OUR CAPTIVES ALONG TO WATCH.
IT IS ONLY FITTING THAT THEY GAZE UPON THE MOLE MAN'S GREATEST TRIUMPH--
--BEFORE THEY ARE PUT TO DEATH!

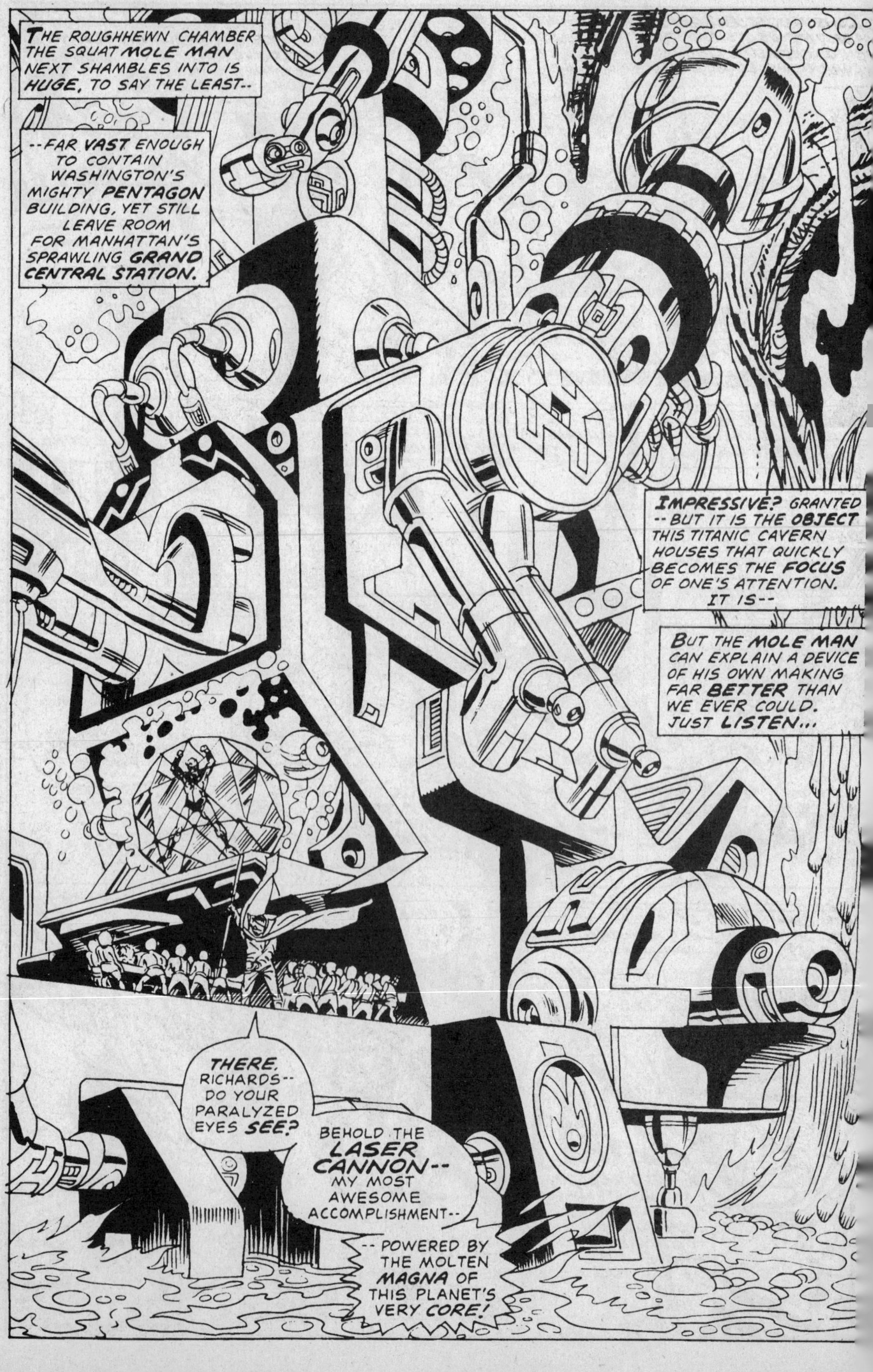
THE ROUGHHEWN CHAMBER THE SQUAT MOLE MAN NEXT SHAMBLES INTO IS HUGE, TO SAY THE LEAST--
--FAR VAST ENOUGH TO CONTAIN WASHINGTON'S MIGHTY PENTAGON BUILDING, YET STILL LEAVE ROOM FOR MANHATTAN'S SPRAWLING GRAND CENTRAL STATION.
IMPRESSIVE? GRANTED --BUT IT IS THE OBJECT THIS TITANIC CAVERN HOUSES THAT QUICKLY BECOMES THE FOCUS OF ONE'S ATTENTION. IT IS--
BUT THE MOLE MAN CAN EXPLAIN A DEVICE OF HIS OWN MAKING FAR BETTER THAN WE EVER COULD. JUST LISTEN...
THERE, RICHARDS-- DO YOUR PARALYZED EYES SEE?
BEHOLD THE LASER CANNON-- MY MOST AWESOME ACCOMPLISHMENT--
--POWERED BY THE MOLTEN MAGNA OF THIS PLANET'S VERY CORE!

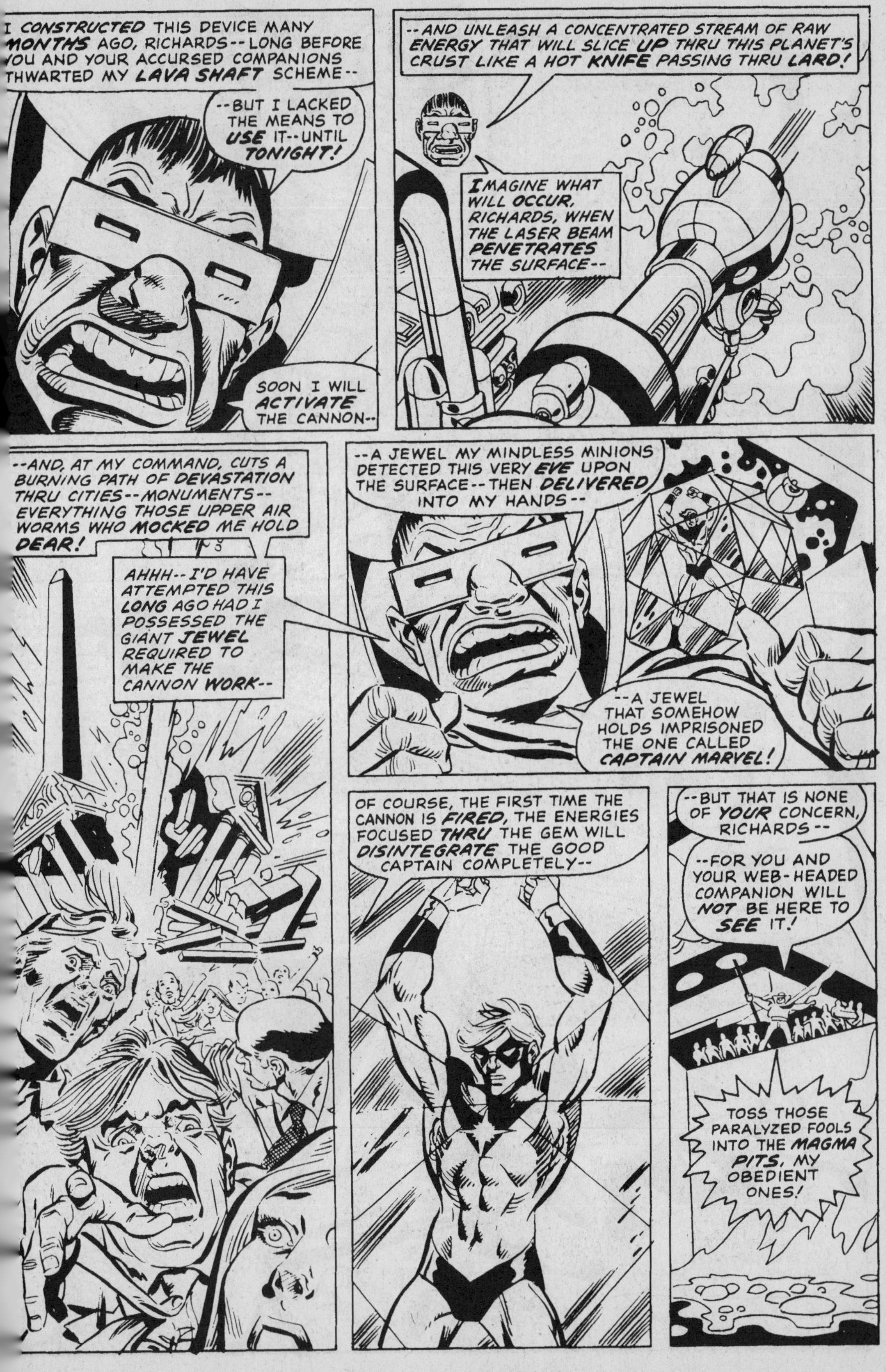
I CONSTRUCTED THIS DEVICE MANY MONTHS AGO, RICHARDS--LONG BEFORE YOU AND YOUR ACCURSED COMPANIONS THWARTED MY LAVA SHAFT SCHEME--
--BUT I LACKED THE MEANS TO USE IT--UNTIL TONIGHT!
SOON I WILL ACTIVATE THE CANNON--
--AND UNLEASH A CONCENTRATED STREAM OF RAW ENERGY THAT WILL SLICE UP THRU THIS PLANET'S CRUST LIKE A HOT KNIFE PASSING THRU LARD!
IMAGINE WHAT WILL OCCUR, RICHARDS, WHEN THE LASER BEAM PENETRATES THE SURFACE--
--AND, AT MY COMMAND, CUTS A BURNING PATH OF DEVASTATION THRU CITIES--MONUMENTS--EVERYTHING THOSE UPPER AIR WORMS WHO MOCKED ME HOLD DEAR!
AHHH--I'D HAVE ATTEMPTED THIS LONG AGO HAD I POSSESSED THE GIANT JEWEL REQUIRED TO MAKE THE CANNON WORK--
--A JEWEL MY MINDLESS MINIONS DETECTED THIS VERY EVE UPON THE SURFACE--THEN DELIVERED INTO MY HANDS--
--A JEWEL THAT SOMEHOW HOLDS IMPRISONED THE ONE CALLED CAPTAIN MARVEL!
OF COURSE, THE FIRST TIME THE CANNON IS FIRED, THE ENERGIES FOCUSED THRU THE GEM WILL DISINTEGRATE THE GOOD CAPTAIN COMPLETELY--
--BUT THAT IS NONE OF YOUR CONCERN, RICHARDS--
--FOR YOU AND YOUR WEB-HEADED COMPANION WILL NOT BE HERE TO SEE IT!
TOSS THOSE PARALYZED FOOLS INTO THE MAGMA PITS, MY OBEDIENT ONES!

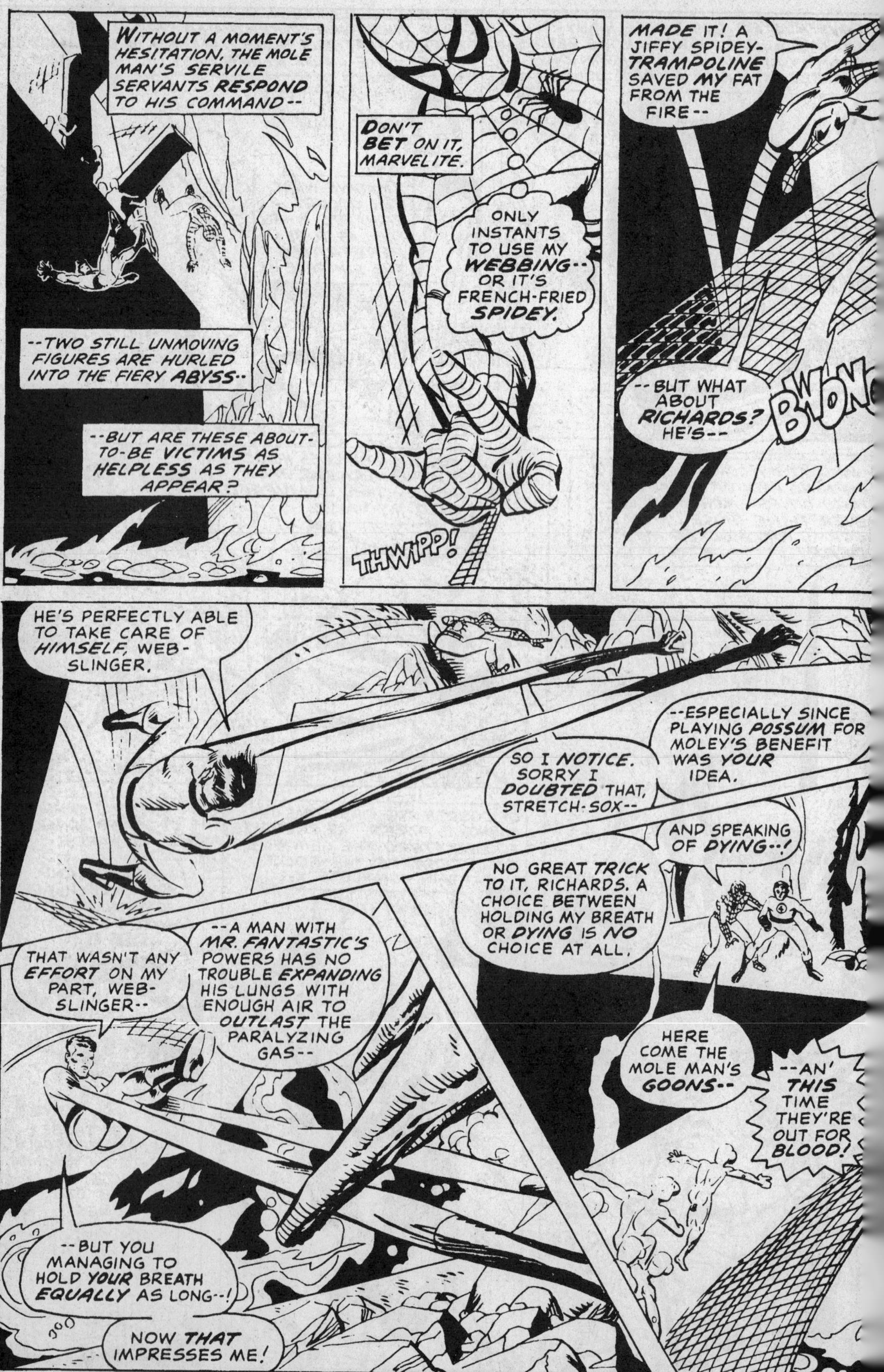
WITHOUT A MOMENT'S HESITATION, THE MOLE MAN'S SERVILE SERVANTS RESPOND TO HIS COMMAND--
--TWO STILL UNMOVING FIGURES ARE HURLED INTO THE FIERY ABYSS--
--BUT ARE THESE ABOUT-TO-BE VICTIMS AS HELPLESS AS THEY APPEAR?
DON'T BET ON IT, MARVELITE.
ONLY INSTANTS TO USE MY WEBBING-- OR IT'S FRENCH-FRIED SPIDEY.
THWIPP!
MADE IT! A JIFFY SPIDEY-TRAMPOLINE SAVED MY FAT FROM THE FIRE--
--BUT WHAT ABOUT RICHARDS? HE'S--
HE'S PERFECTLY ABLE TO TAKE CARE OF HIMSELF, WEB-SLINGER.
SO I NOTICE. SORRY I DOUBTED THAT, STRETCH-SOX--
--ESPECIALLY SINCE PLAYING POSSUM FOR MOLEY'S BENEFIT WAS YOUR IDEA.
THAT WASN'T ANY EFFORT ON MY PART, WEB-SLINGER--
--A MAN WITH MR. FANTASTIC'S POWERS HAS NO TROUBLE EXPANDING HIS LUNGS WITH ENOUGH AIR TO OUTLAST THE PARALYZING GAS--
--BUT YOU MANAGING TO HOLD YOUR BREATH EQUALLY AS LONG--!
NOW THAT IMPRESSES ME!
NO GREAT TRICK TO IT, RICHARDS. A CHOICE BETWEEN HOLDING MY BREATH OR DYING IS NO CHOICE AT ALL.
AND SPEAKING OF DYING--!
HERE COME THE MOLE MAN'S GOONS--
--AN' THIS TIME THEY'RE OUT FOR BLOOD!

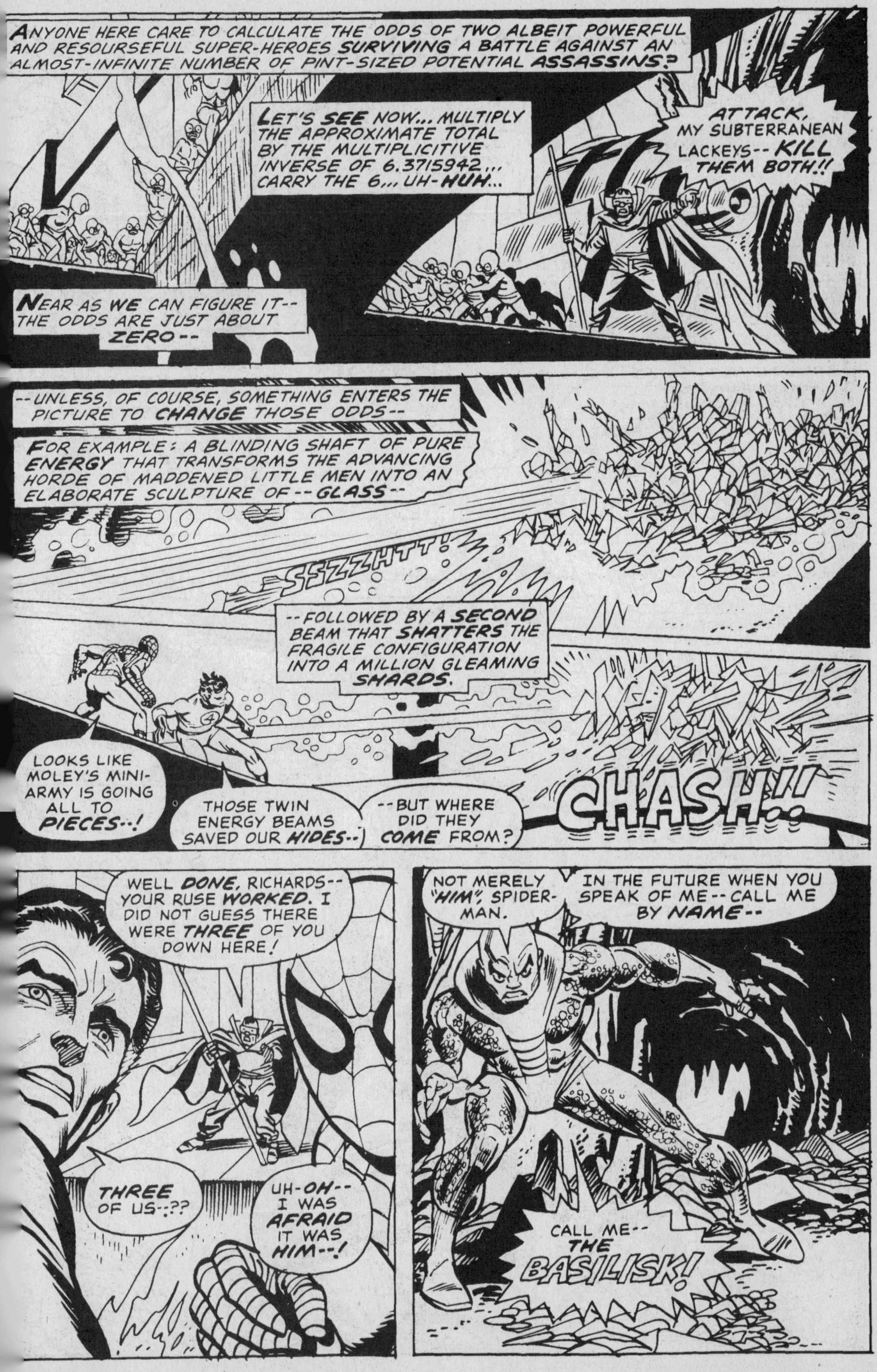
ANYONE HERE CARE TO CALCULATE THE ODDS OF TWO ALBEIT POWERFUL AND RESOURSEFUL SUPER-HEROES SURVIVING A BATTLE AGAINST AN ALMOST-INFINITE NUMBER OF PINT-SIZED POTENTIAL ASSASSINS?
LET'S SEE NOW... MULTIPLY THE APPROXIMATE TOTAL BY THE MULTIPLICITIVE INVERSE OF 6.3715942... CARRY THE 6... UH-HUH...
ATTACK, MY SUBTERRANEAN LACKEYS-- KILL THEM BOTH!!
NEAR AS WE CAN FIGURE IT-- THE ODDS ARE JUST ABOUT ZERO--
--UNLESS, OF COURSE, SOMETHING ENTERS THE PICTURE TO CHANGE THOSE ODDS--
FOR EXAMPLE: A BLINDING SHAFT OF PURE ENERGY THAT TRANSFORMS THE ADVANCING HORDE OF MADDENED LITTLE MEN INTO AN ELABORATE SCULPTURE OF --GLASS--
SEZZZHTTT!
--FOLLOWED BY A SECOND BEAM THAT SHATTERS THE FRAGILE CONFIGURATION INTO A MILLION GLEAMING SHARDS.
LOOKS LIKE MOLEY'S MINI-ARMY IS GOING ALL TO PIECES--!
THOSE TWIN ENERGY BEAMS SAVED OUR HIDES--
--BUT WHERE DID THEY COME FROM?
CHASH!!
WELL DONE, RICHARDS-- YOUR RUSE WORKED. I DID NOT GUESS THERE WERE THREE OF YOU DOWN HERE!
THREE OF US--??
UH-OH-- I WAS AFRAID IT WAS HIM--!
NOT MERELY "HIM", SPIDER-MAN.
IN THE FUTURE WHEN YOU SPEAK OF ME-- CALL ME BY NAME--
CALL ME-- THE BASILISK!

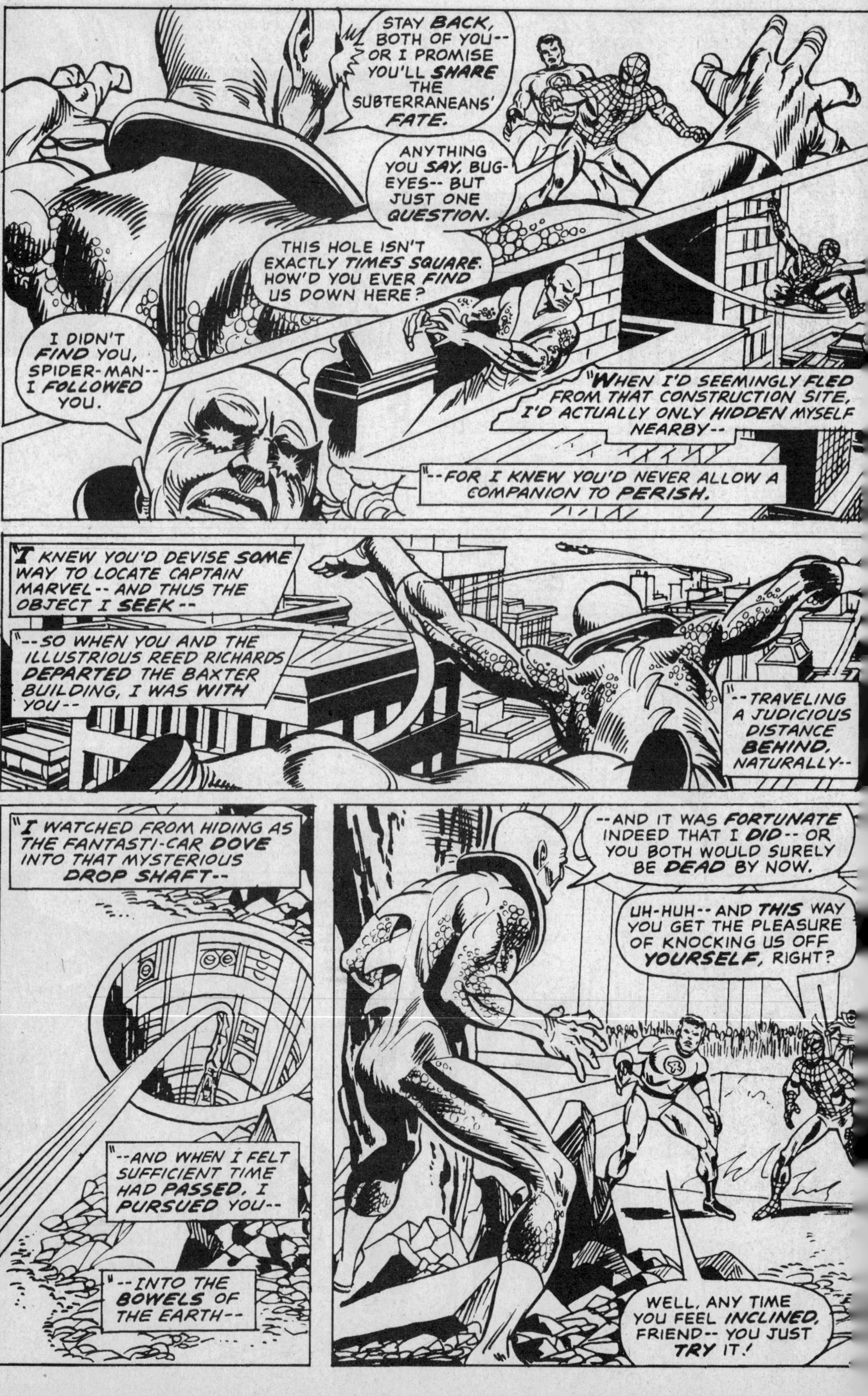
STAY BACK, BOTH OF YOU-- OR I PROMISE YOU'LL SHARE THE SUBTERRANEANS' FATE.
ANYTHING YOU SAY, BUG-EYES-- BUT JUST ONE QUESTION.
THIS HOLE ISN'T EXACTLY TIMES SQUARE. HOW'D YOU EVER FIND US DOWN HERE?
I DIDN'T FIND YOU, SPIDER-MAN-- I FOLLOWED YOU.
"WHEN I'D SEEMINGLY FLED FROM THAT CONSTRUCTION SITE, I'D ACTUALLY ONLY HIDDEN MYSELF NEARBY--
"--FOR I KNEW YOU'D NEVER ALLOW A COMPANION TO PERISH.
"I KNEW YOU'D DEVISE SOME WAY TO LOCATE CAPTAIN MARVEL-- AND THUS THE OBJECT I SEEK--
"--SO WHEN YOU AND THE ILLUSTRIOUS REED RICHARDS DEPARTED THE BAXTER BUILDING, I WAS WITH YOU--
"--TRAVELING A JUDICIOUS DISTANCE BEHIND, NATURALLY--
"I WATCHED FROM HIDING AS THE FANTASTI-CAR DOVE INTO THAT MYSTERIOUS DROP SHAFT--
"--AND WHEN I FELT SUFFICIENT TIME HAD PASSED, I PURSUED YOU--
"--INTO THE BOWELS OF THE EARTH--
--AND IT WAS FORTUNATE INDEED THAT I DID-- OR YOU BOTH WOULD SURELY BE DEAD BY NOW.
UH-HUH-- AND THIS WAY YOU GET THE PLEASURE OF KNOCKING US OFF YOURSELF, RIGHT?
WELL, ANY TIME YOU FEEL INCLINED, FRIEND-- YOU JUST TRY IT!

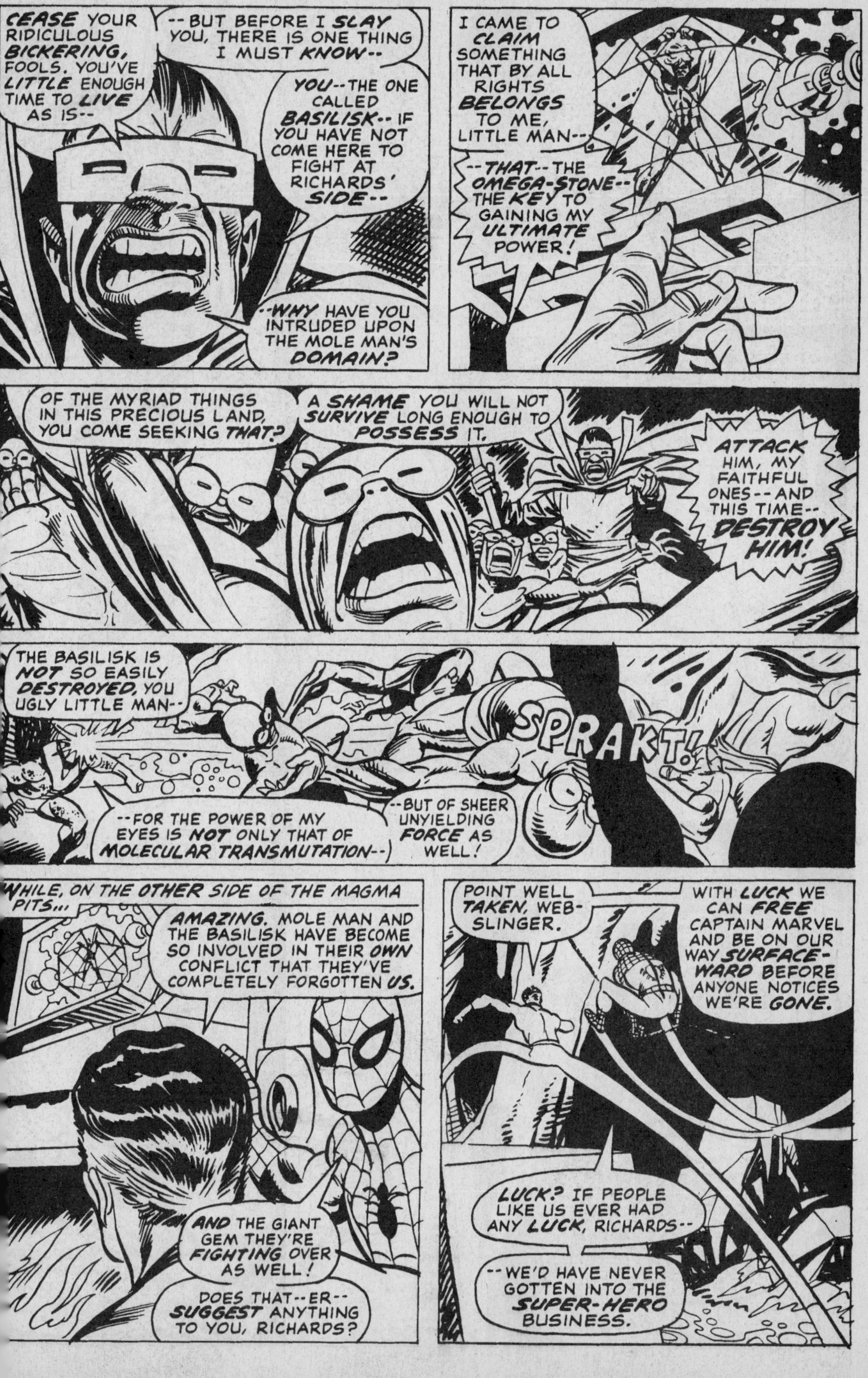
CEASE YOUR RIDICULOUS BICKERING, FOOLS. YOU'VE LITTLE ENOUGH TIME TO LIVE AS IS--
--BUT BEFORE I SLAY YOU, THERE IS ONE THING I MUST KNOW--
YOU--THE ONE CALLED BASILISK--IF YOU HAVE NOT COME HERE TO FIGHT AT RICHARDS' SIDE--
--WHY HAVE YOU INTRUDED UPON THE MOLE MAN'S DOMAIN?
I CAME TO CLAIM SOMETHING THAT BY ALL RIGHTS BELONGS TO ME, LITTLE MAN--
--THAT--THE OMEGA-STONE--THE KEY TO GAINING MY ULTIMATE POWER!
OF THE MYRIAD THINGS IN THIS PRECIOUS LAND, YOU COME SEEKING THAT?
A SHAME YOU WILL NOT SURVIVE LONG ENOUGH TO POSSESS IT.
ATTACK HIM, MY FAITHFUL ONES--AND THIS TIME--DESTROY HIM!
THE BASILISK IS NOT SO EASILY DESTROYED, YOU UGLY LITTLE MAN--
SPRAKT!
--FOR THE POWER OF MY EYES IS NOT ONLY THAT OF MOLECULAR TRANSMUTATION--
--BUT OF SHEER UNYIELDING FORCE AS WELL!
WHILE, ON THE OTHER SIDE OF THE MAGMA PITS...
AMAZING. MOLE MAN AND THE BASILISK HAVE BECOME SO INVOLVED IN THEIR OWN CONFLICT THAT THEY'VE COMPLETELY FORGOTTEN US.
AND THE GIANT GEM THEY'RE FIGHTING OVER AS WELL!
DOES THAT--ER--SUGGEST ANYTHING TO YOU, RICHARDS?
POINT WELL TAKEN, WEB-SLINGER.
WITH LUCK WE CAN FREE CAPTAIN MARVEL AND BE ON OUR WAY SURFACE-WARD BEFORE ANYONE NOTICES WE'RE GONE.
LUCK? IF PEOPLE LIKE US EVER HAD ANY LUCK, RICHARDS--
--WE'D HAVE NEVER GOTTEN INTO THE SUPER-HERO BUSINESS.

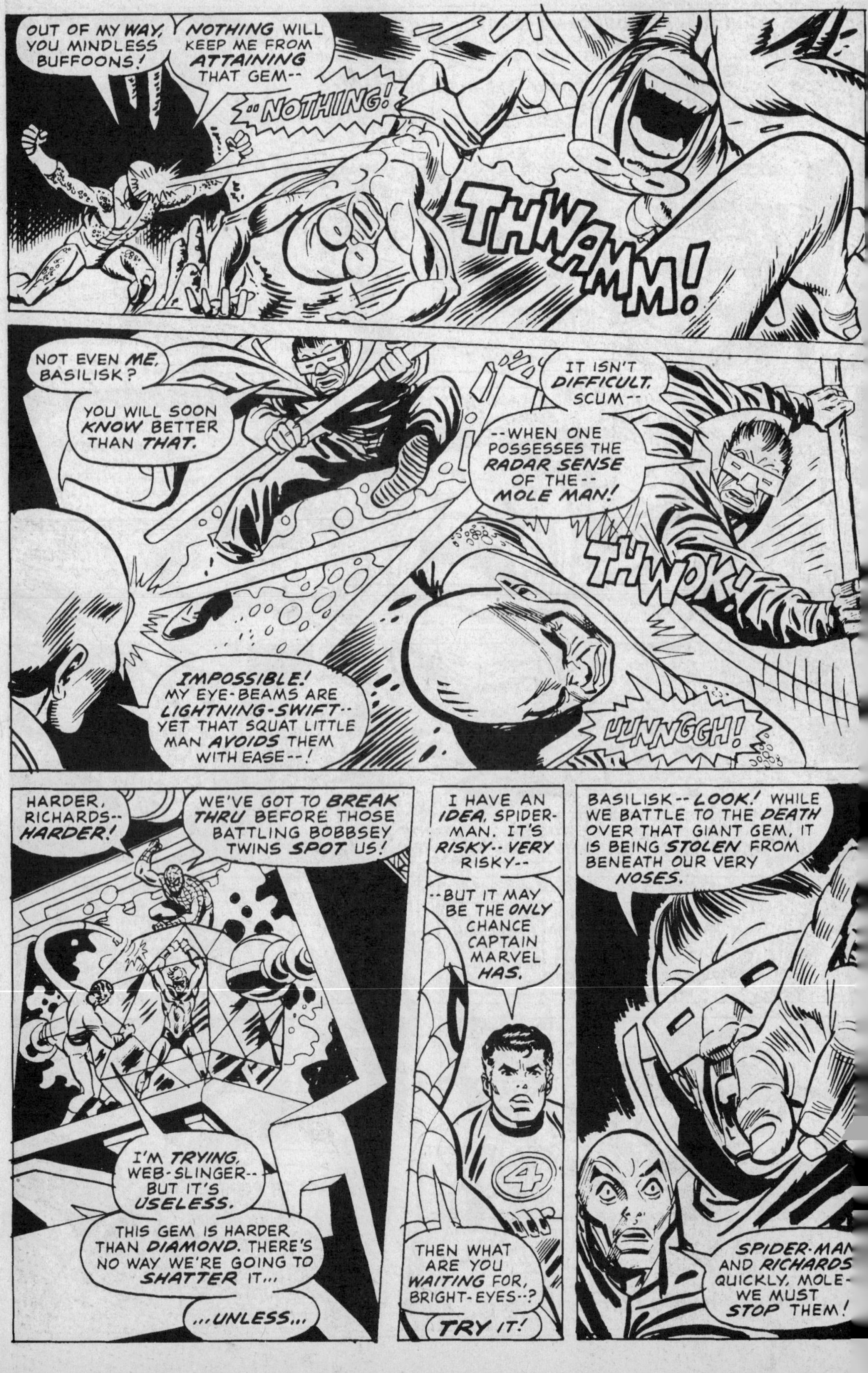
OUT OF MY WAY, YOU MINDLESS BUFFOONS!
NOTHING WILL KEEP ME FROM ATTAINING THAT GEM--
--NOTHING!
THWAMM!
NOT EVEN ME, BASILISK?
YOU WILL SOON KNOW BETTER THAN THAT.
IT ISN'T DIFFICULT, SCUM--
--WHEN ONE POSSESSES THE RADAR SENSE OF THE-- MOLE MAN!
THWOK!
IMPOSSIBLE! MY EYE-BEAMS ARE LIGHTNING-SWIFT-- YET THAT SQUAT LITTLE MAN AVOIDS THEM WITH EASE--!
UUNNGGH!
HARDER, RICHARDS-- HARDER!
WE'VE GOT TO BREAK THRU BEFORE THOSE BATTLING BOBBSEY TWINS SPOT US!
I'M TRYING, WEB-SLINGER-- BUT IT'S USELESS.
THIS GEM IS HARDER THAN DIAMOND. THERE'S NO WAY WE'RE GOING TO SHATTER IT...
...UNLESS...
I HAVE AN IDEA, SPIDER-MAN. IT'S RISKY-- VERY RISKY--
--BUT IT MAY BE THE ONLY CHANCE CAPTAIN MARVEL HAS.
THEN WHAT ARE YOU WAITING FOR, BRIGHT-EYES--?
TRY IT!
BASILISK--LOOK! WHILE WE BATTLE TO THE DEATH OVER THAT GIANT GEM, IT IS BEING STOLEN FROM BENEATH OUR VERY NOSES.
SPIDER-MAN AND RICHARDS! QUICKLY, MOLE-- WE MUST STOP THEM!

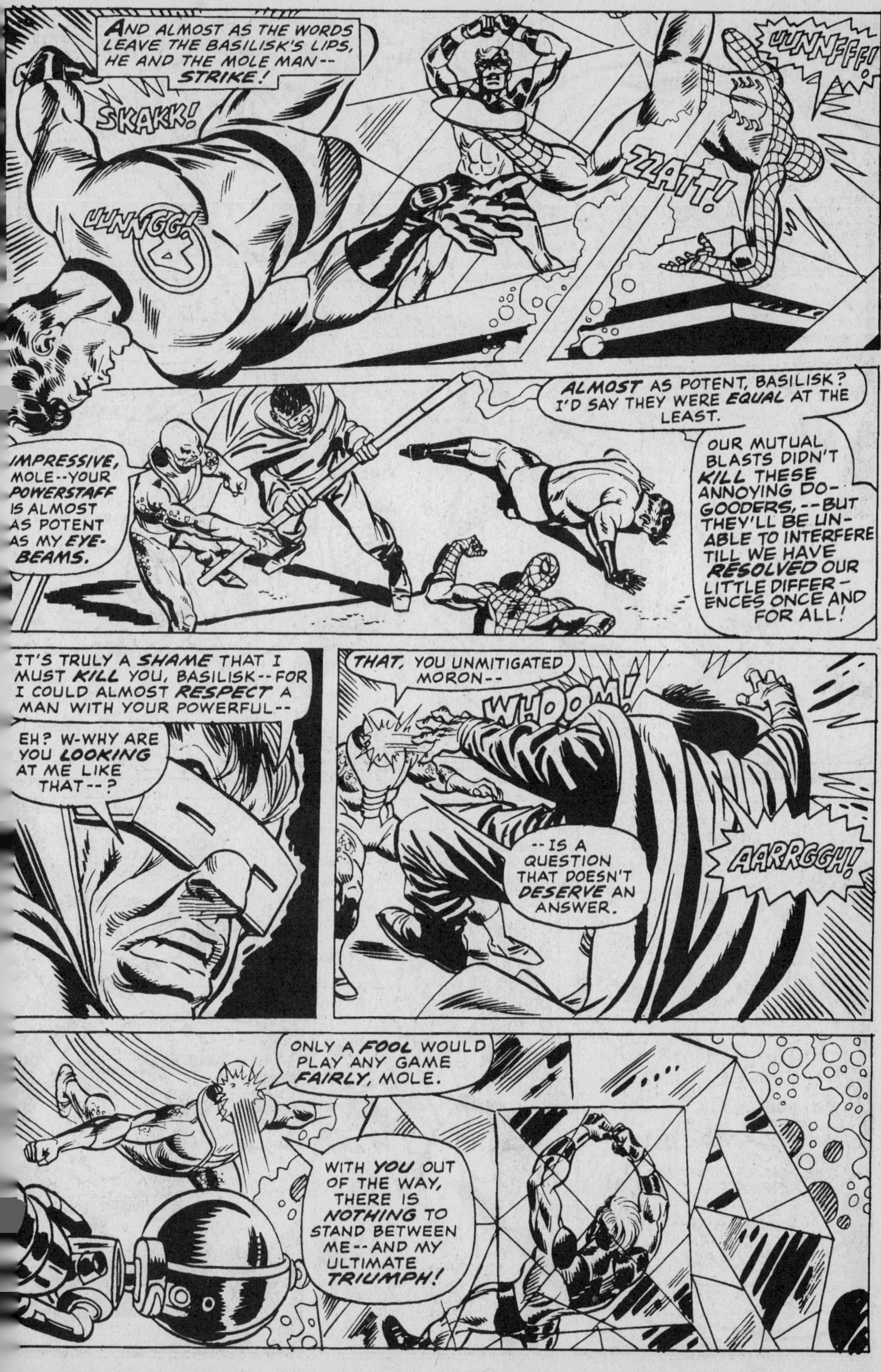
AND ALMOST AS THE WORDS LEAVE THE BASILISK'S LIPS, HE AND THE MOLE MAN-- STRIKE!
SKAKK!
UNNGG!
ZZATT!
UUNNFFF!
IMPRESSIVE, MOLE--YOUR POWERSTAFF IS ALMOST AS POTENT AS MY EYE-BEAMS.
ALMOST AS POTENT, BASILISK? I'D SAY THEY WERE EQUAL AT THE LEAST.
OUR MUTUAL BLASTS DIDN'T KILL THESE ANNOYING DO-GOODERS,--BUT THEY'LL BE UN-ABLE TO INTERFERE TILL WE HAVE RESOLVED OUR LITTLE DIFFER-ENCES ONCE AND FOR ALL!
IT'S TRULY A SHAME THAT I MUST KILL YOU, BASILISK--FOR I COULD ALMOST RESPECT A MAN WITH YOUR POWERFUL--
EH? W-WHY ARE YOU LOOKING AT ME LIKE THAT--?
THAT, YOU UNMITIGATED MORON--
WHOOM!
--IS A QUESTION THAT DOESN'T DESERVE AN ANSWER.
AARRGGH!
ONLY A FOOL WOULD PLAY ANY GAME FAIRLY, MOLE.
WITH YOU OUT OF THE WAY, THERE IS NOTHING TO STAND BETWEEN ME--AND MY ULTIMATE TRIUMPH!
...

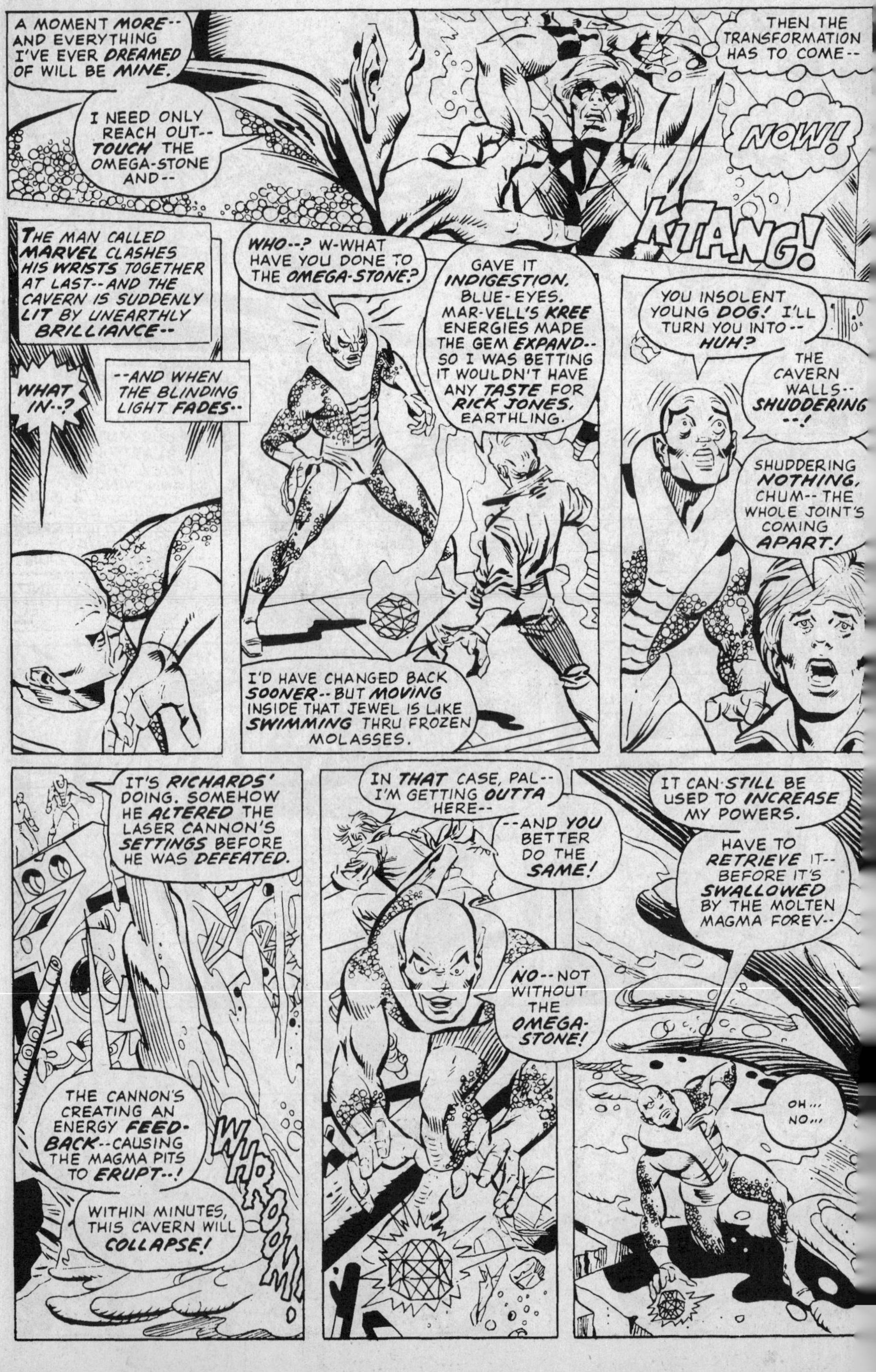

A MOMENT MORE-- AND EVERYTHING I'VE EVER DREAMED OF WILL BE MINE.
I NEED ONLY REACH OUT-- TOUCH THE OMEGA-STONE AND--
THEN THE TRANSFORMATION HAS TO COME--
NOW!
KTANG!
THE MAN CALLED MARVEL CLASHES HIS WRISTS TOGETHER AT LAST--AND THE CAVERN IS SUDDENLY LIT BY UNEARTHLY BRILLIANCE--
WHAT IN--?
--AND WHEN THE BLINDING LIGHT FADES--
WHO--? W-WHAT HAVE YOU DONE TO THE OMEGA-STONE?
GAVE IT INDIGESTION, BLUE-EYES. MAR-VELL'S KREE ENERGIES MADE THE GEM EXPAND-- SO I WAS BETTING IT WOULDN'T HAVE ANY TASTE FOR RICK JONES, EARTHLING.
I'D HAVE CHANGED BACK SOONER--BUT MOVING INSIDE THAT JEWEL IS LIKE SWIMMING THRU FROZEN MOLASSES.
YOU INSOLENT YOUNG DOG! I'LL TURN YOU INTO-- HUH?
THE CAVERN WALLS-- SHUDDERING--!
SHUDDERING NOTHING, CHUM-- THE WHOLE JOINT'S COMING APART!
IT'S RICHARDS' DOING. SOMEHOW HE ALTERED THE LASER CANNON'S SETTINGS BEFORE HE WAS DEFEATED.
THE CANNON'S CREATING AN ENERGY FEED-BACK--CAUSING THE MAGMA PITS TO ERUPT--!
WITHIN MINUTES, THIS CAVERN WILL COLLAPSE!
WHROOM!
IN THAT CASE, PAL-- I'M GETTING OUTTA HERE--
--AND YOU BETTER DO THE SAME!
NO--NOT WITHOUT THE OMEGA-STONE!
IT CAN STILL BE USED TO INCREASE MY POWERS.
HAVE TO RETRIEVE IT-- BEFORE IT'S SWALLOWED BY THE MOLTEN MAGMA FOREV--
OH... NO...

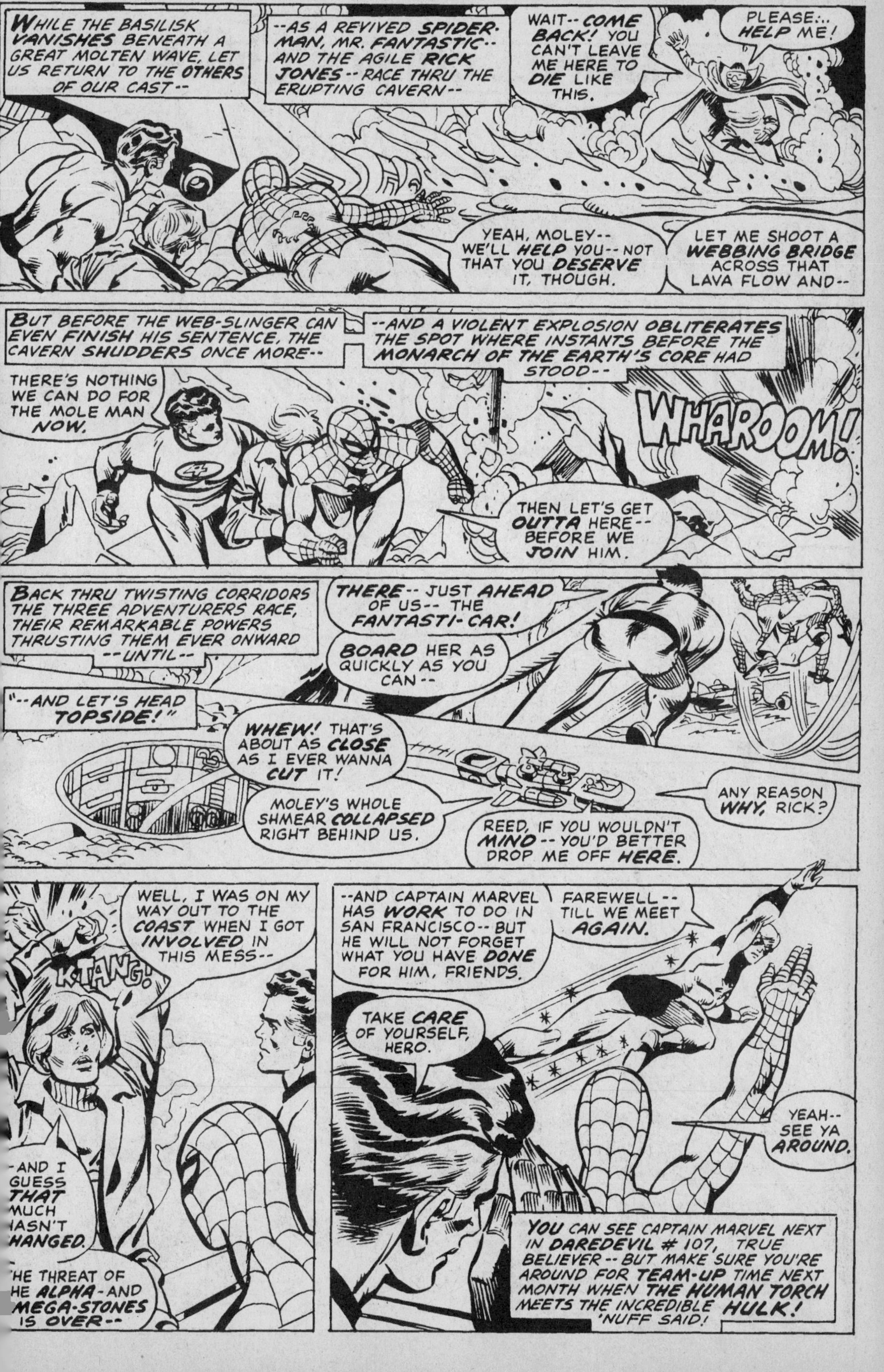

WHILE THE BASILISK VANISHES BENEATH A GREAT MOLTEN WAVE, LET US RETURN TO THE OTHERS OF OUR CAST--
--AS A REVIVED SPIDER-MAN, MR. FANTASTIC--AND THE AGILE RICK JONES--RACE THRU THE ERUPTING CAVERN--
WAIT--COME BACK! YOU CAN'T LEAVE ME HERE TO DIE LIKE THIS.
PLEASE... HELP ME!
YEAH, MOLEY-- WE'LL HELP YOU--NOT THAT YOU DESERVE IT, THOUGH.
LET ME SHOOT A WEBBING BRIDGE ACROSS THAT LAVA FLOW AND--
BUT BEFORE THE WEB-SLINGER CAN EVEN FINISH HIS SENTENCE, THE CAVERN SHUDDERS ONCE MORE--
--AND A VIOLENT EXPLOSION OBLITERATES THE SPOT WHERE INSTANTS BEFORE THE MONARCH OF THE EARTH'S CORE HAD STOOD--
THERE'S NOTHING WE CAN DO FOR THE MOLE MAN NOW.
WHAROOM!
THEN LET'S GET OUTTA HERE-- BEFORE WE JOIN HIM.
BACK THRU TWISTING CORRIDORS THE THREE ADVENTURERS RACE, THEIR REMARKABLE POWERS THRUSTING THEM EVER ONWARD --UNTIL--
THERE-- JUST AHEAD OF US-- THE FANTASTI-CAR!
BOARD HER AS QUICKLY AS YOU CAN--
"--AND LET'S HEAD TOPSIDE!"
WHEW! THAT'S ABOUT AS CLOSE AS I EVER WANNA CUT IT!
MOLEY'S WHOLE SHMEAR COLLAPSED RIGHT BEHIND US.
ANY REASON WHY, RICK?
REED, IF YOU WOULDN'T MIND--YOU'D BETTER DROP ME OFF HERE.
WELL, I WAS ON MY WAY OUT TO THE COAST WHEN I GOT INVOLVED IN THIS MESS--
K'TANG!
-AND I GUESS THAT MUCH HASN'T HANGED.
THE THREAT OF HE ALPHA- AND MEGA-STONES IS OVER--
--AND CAPTAIN MARVEL HAS WORK TO DO IN SAN FRANCISCO--BUT HE WILL NOT FORGET WHAT YOU HAVE DONE FOR HIM, FRIENDS.
FAREWELL-- TILL WE MEET AGAIN.
TAKE CARE OF YOURSELF, HERO.
YEAH-- SEE YA AROUND.
YOU CAN SEE CAPTAIN MARVEL NEXT IN DAREDEVIL #107, TRUE BELIEVER--BUT MAKE SURE YOU'RE AROUND FOR TEAM-UP TIME NEXT MONTH WHEN THE HUMAN TORCH MEETS THE INCREDIBLE HULK! 'NUFF SAID!

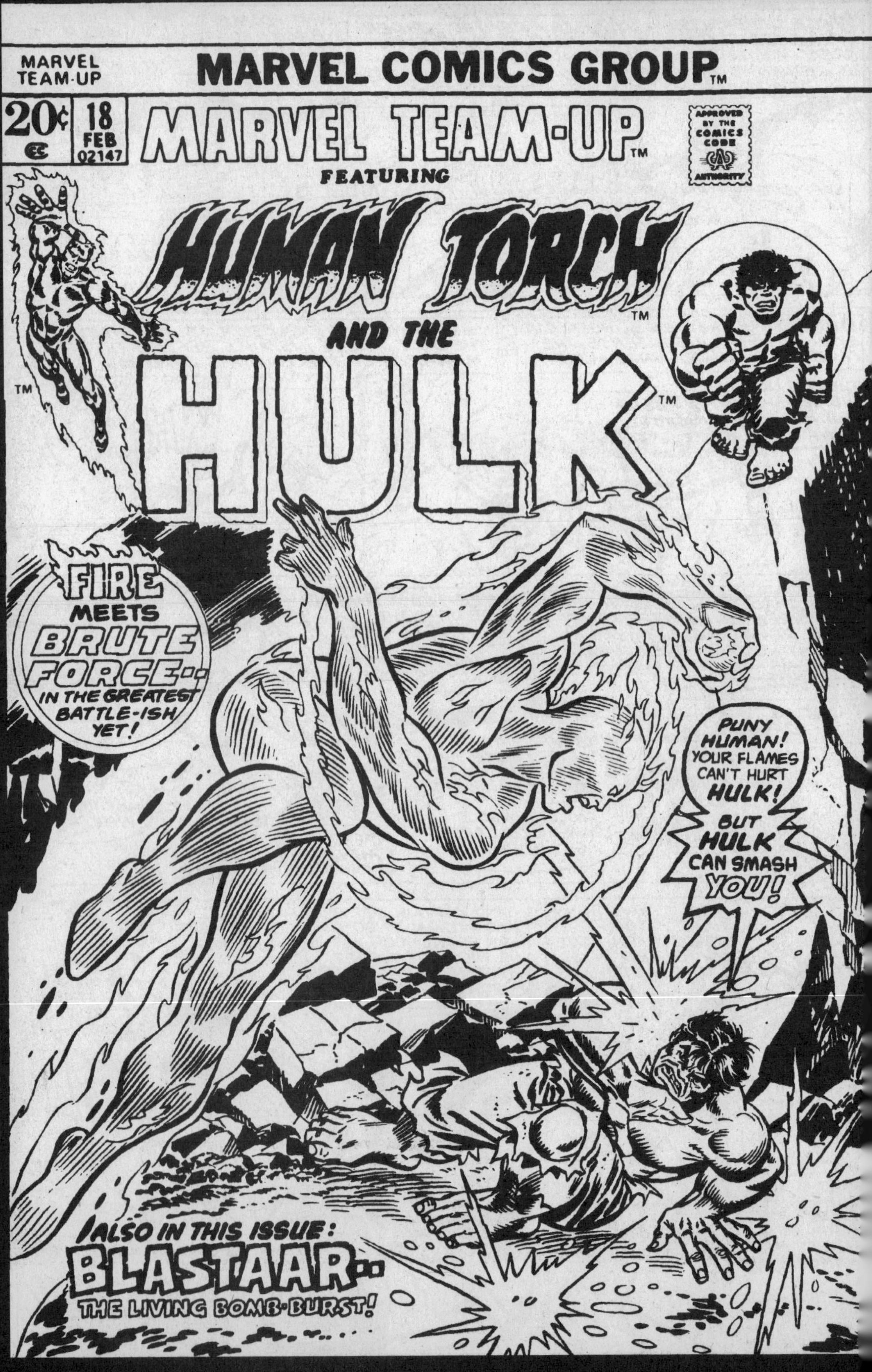
MARVEL TEAM-UP
MARVEL COMICS GROUP TM
20¢ CC
18 FEB 02147
MARVEL TEAM-UP TM
APPROVED BY THE COMICS CODE AUTHORITY
FEATURING
HUMAN TORCH TM
AND THE
HULK TM
TM
FIRE MEETS BRUTE FORCE.. IN THE GREATEST BATTLE-ISH YET!
PUNY HUMAN! YOUR FLAMES CAN'T HURT HULK!
BUT HULK CAN SMASH YOU!
ALSO IN THIS ISSUE: BLASTAAR.. THE LIVING BOMB-BURST!

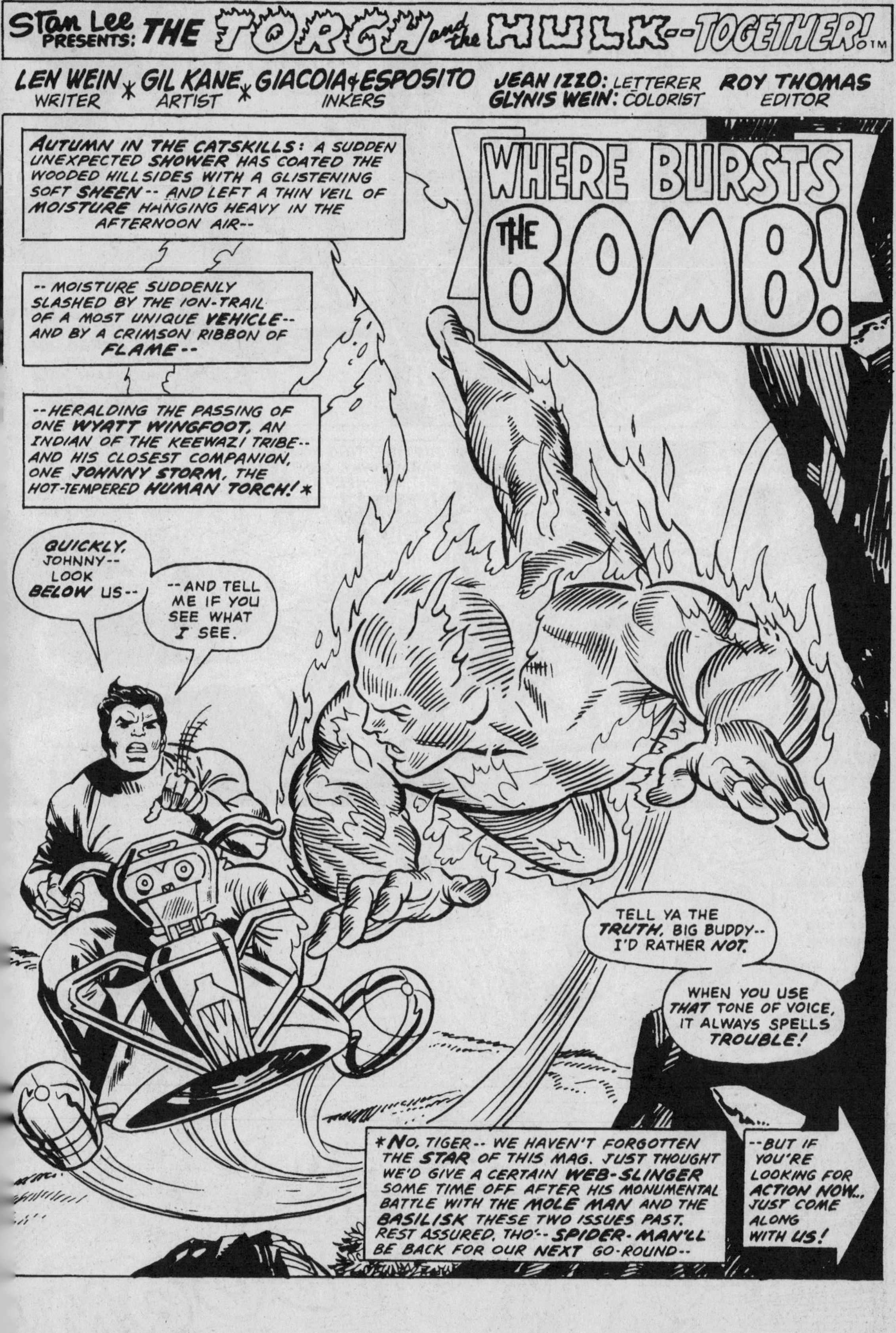

Stan Lee PRESENTS: THE TORCH and the HULK--TOGETHER!
LEN WEIN WRITER * GIL KANE ARTIST * GIACOIA & ESPOSITO INKERS
JEAN IZZO: LETTERER
GLYNIS WEIN: COLORIST
ROY THOMAS EDITOR
AUTUMN IN THE CATSKILLS: A SUDDEN UNEXPECTED SHOWER HAS COATED THE WOODED HILLSIDES WITH A GLISTENING SOFT SHEEN -- AND LEFT A THIN VEIL OF MOISTURE HANGING HEAVY IN THE AFTERNOON AIR--
WHERE BURSTS THE BOMB!
-- MOISTURE SUDDENLY SLASHED BY THE ION-TRAIL OF A MOST UNIQUE VEHICLE-- AND BY A CRIMSON RIBBON OF FLAME--
--HERALDING THE PASSING OF ONE WYATT WINGFOOT, AN INDIAN OF THE KEEWAZI TRIBE-- AND HIS CLOSEST COMPANION, ONE JOHNNY STORM, THE HOT-TEMPERED HUMAN TORCH! *
QUICKLY, JOHNNY-- LOOK BELOW US--
--AND TELL ME IF YOU SEE WHAT I SEE.
TELL YA THE TRUTH, BIG BUDDY-- I'D RATHER NOT.
WHEN YOU USE THAT TONE OF VOICE, IT ALWAYS SPELLS TROUBLE!
* NO, TIGER-- WE HAVEN'T FORGOTTEN THE STAR OF THIS MAG. JUST THOUGHT WE'D GIVE A CERTAIN WEB-SLINGER SOME TIME OFF AFTER HIS MONUMENTAL BATTLE WITH THE MOLE MAN AND THE BASILISK THESE TWO ISSUES PAST. REST ASSURED, THO'-- SPIDER-MAN'LL BE BACK FOR OUR NEXT GO-ROUND--
--BUT IF YOU'RE LOOKING FOR ACTION NOW.. JUST COME ALONG WITH US!

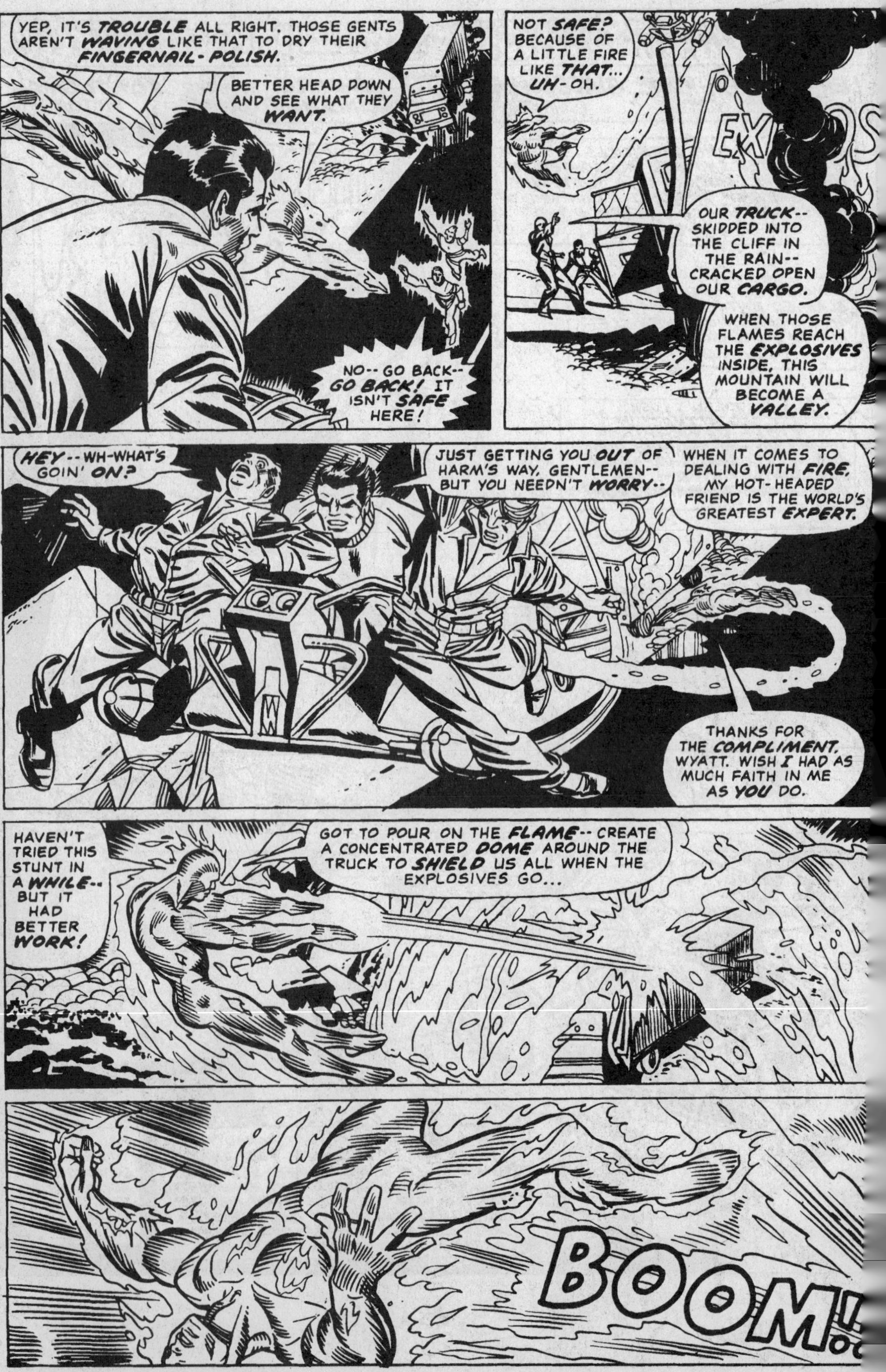
YEP, IT'S TROUBLE ALL RIGHT. THOSE GENTS AREN'T WAVING LIKE THAT TO DRY THEIR FINGERNAIL-POLISH.
BETTER HEAD DOWN AND SEE WHAT THEY WANT.
NO-- GO BACK-- GO BACK! IT ISN'T SAFE HERE!
NOT SAFE? BECAUSE OF A LITTLE FIRE LIKE THAT... UH-OH.
OUR TRUCK-- SKIDDED INTO THE CLIFF IN THE RAIN-- CRACKED OPEN OUR CARGO.
WHEN THOSE FLAMES REACH THE EXPLOSIVES INSIDE, THIS MOUNTAIN WILL BECOME A VALLEY.
HEY-- WH-WHAT'S GOIN' ON?
JUST GETTING YOU OUT OF HARM'S WAY, GENTLEMEN-- BUT YOU NEEDN'T WORRY--
WHEN IT COMES TO DEALING WITH FIRE, MY HOT-HEADED FRIEND IS THE WORLD'S GREATEST EXPERT.
THANKS FOR THE COMPLIMENT, WYATT. WISH I HAD AS MUCH FAITH IN ME AS YOU DO.
HAVEN'T TRIED THIS STUNT IN A WHILE-- BUT IT HAD BETTER WORK!
GOT TO POUR ON THE FLAME-- CREATE A CONCENTRATED DOME AROUND THE TRUCK TO SHIELD US ALL WHEN THE EXPLOSIVES GO...
BOOM!

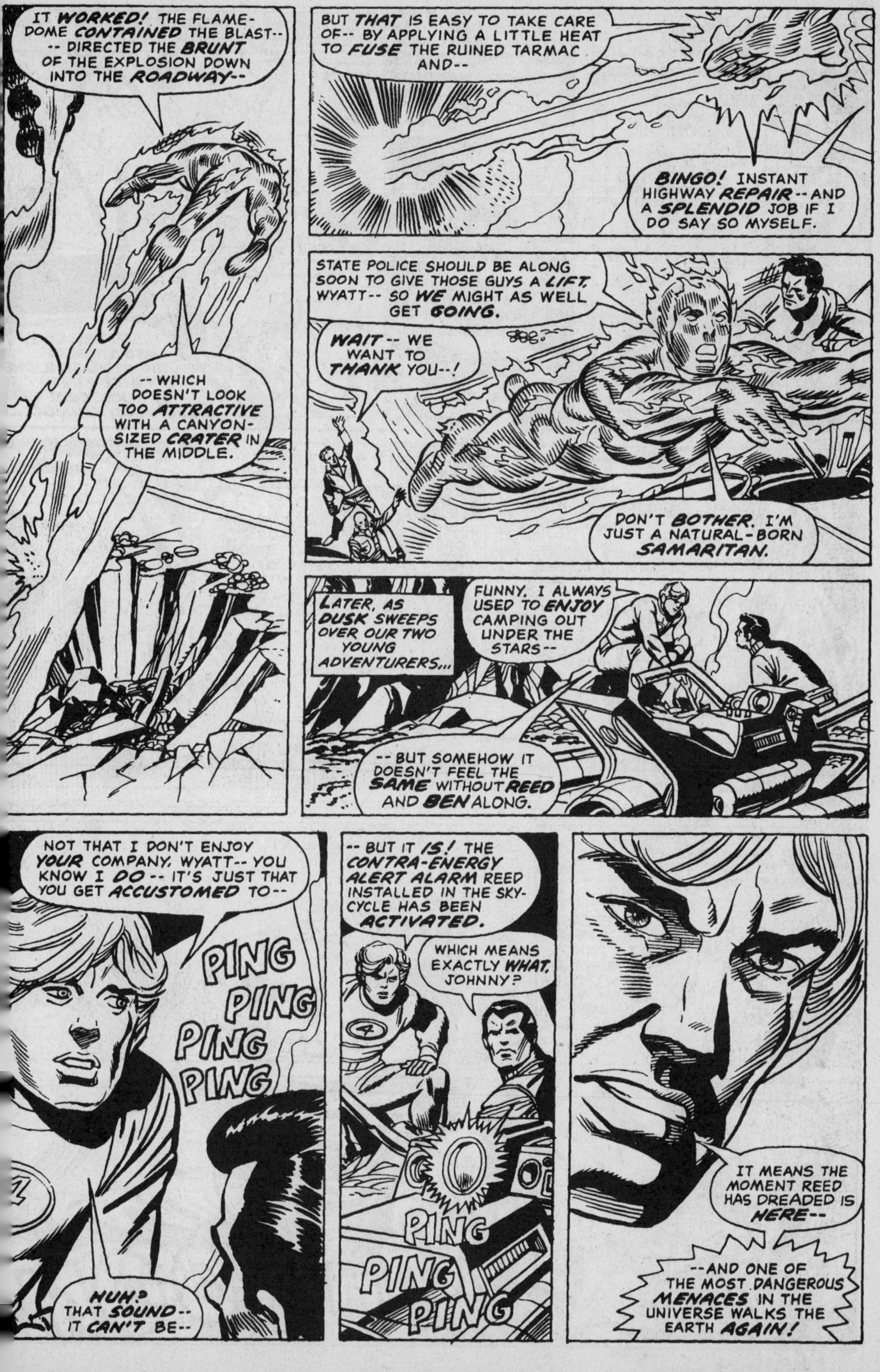
IT WORKED! THE FLAME-DOME CONTAINED THE BLAST-- -- DIRECTED THE BRUNT OF THE EXPLOSION DOWN INTO THE ROADWAY--
BUT THAT IS EASY TO TAKE CARE OF-- BY APPLYING A LITTLE HEAT TO FUSE THE RUINED TARMAC AND--
-- WHICH DOESN'T LOOK TOO ATTRACTIVE WITH A CANYON-SIZED CRATER IN THE MIDDLE.
BINGO! INSTANT HIGHWAY REPAIR -- AND A SPLENDID JOB IF I DO SAY SO MYSELF.
STATE POLICE SHOULD BE ALONG SOON TO GIVE THOSE GUYS A LIFT, WYATT-- SO WE MIGHT AS WELL GET GOING.
WAIT -- WE WANT TO THANK YOU--!
DON'T BOTHER. I'M JUST A NATURAL-BORN SAMARITAN.
LATER, AS DUSK SWEEPS OVER OUR TWO YOUNG ADVENTURERS...
FUNNY. I ALWAYS USED TO ENJOY CAMPING OUT UNDER THE STARS--
-- BUT SOMEHOW IT DOESN'T FEEL THE SAME WITHOUT REED AND BEN ALONG.
NOT THAT I DON'T ENJOY YOUR COMPANY, WYATT-- YOU KNOW I DO -- IT'S JUST THAT YOU GET ACCUSTOMED TO--
PING PING PING PING
HUH? THAT SOUND-- IT CAN'T BE--
-- BUT IT IS! THE CONTRA-ENERGY ALERT ALARM REED INSTALLED IN THE SKY-CYCLE HAS BEEN ACTIVATED.
WHICH MEANS EXACTLY WHAT, JOHNNY?
PING PING PING
IT MEANS THE MOMENT REED HAS DREADED IS HERE--
--AND ONE OF THE MOST DANGEROUS MENACES IN THE UNIVERSE WALKS THE EARTH AGAIN!

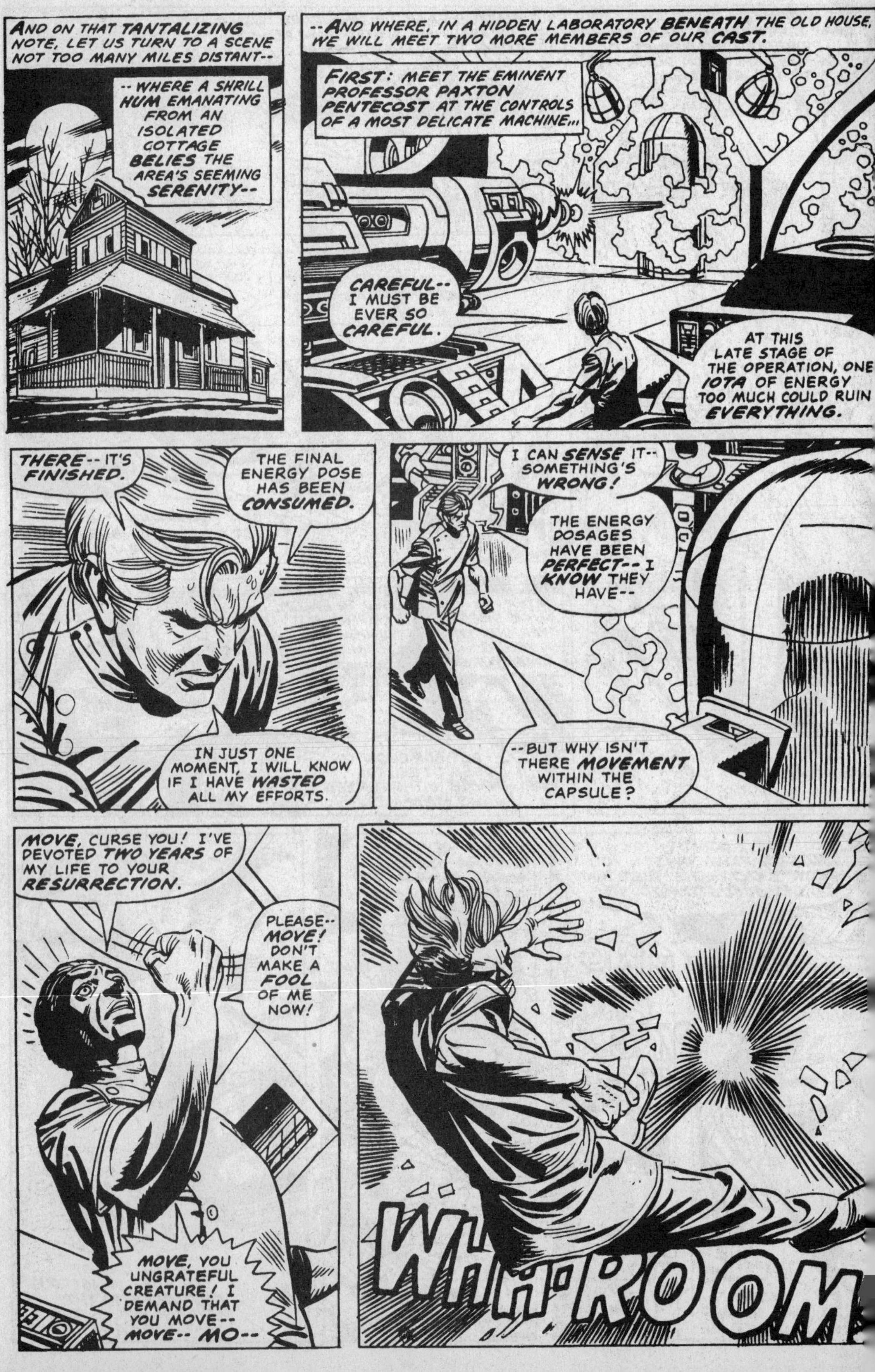
AND ON THAT TANTALIZING NOTE, LET US TURN TO A SCENE NOT TOO MANY MILES DISTANT--
--WHERE A SHRILL HUM EMANATING FROM AN ISOLATED COTTAGE BELIES THE AREA'S SEEMING SERENITY--
--AND WHERE, IN A HIDDEN LABORATORY BENEATH THE OLD HOUSE, WE WILL MEET TWO MORE MEMBERS OF OUR CAST.
FIRST: MEET THE EMINENT PROFESSOR PAXTON PENTECOST AT THE CONTROLS OF A MOST DELICATE MACHINE...
CAREFUL-- I MUST BE EVER SO CAREFUL.
AT THIS LATE STAGE OF THE OPERATION, ONE IOTA OF ENERGY TOO MUCH COULD RUIN EVERYTHING.
THERE--IT'S FINISHED.
THE FINAL ENERGY DOSE HAS BEEN CONSUMED.
IN JUST ONE MOMENT, I WILL KNOW IF I HAVE WASTED ALL MY EFFORTS.
I CAN SENSE IT-- SOMETHING'S WRONG!
THE ENERGY DOSAGES HAVE BEEN PERFECT-- I KNOW THEY HAVE--
--BUT WHY ISN'T THERE MOVEMENT WITHIN THE CAPSULE?
MOVE, CURSE YOU! I'VE DEVOTED TWO YEARS OF MY LIFE TO YOUR RESURRECTION.
PLEASE-- MOVE! DON'T MAKE A FOOL OF ME NOW!
MOVE, YOU UNGRATEFUL CREATURE! I DEMAND THAT YOU MOVE-- MOVE-- MO--
WHH-ROOOM

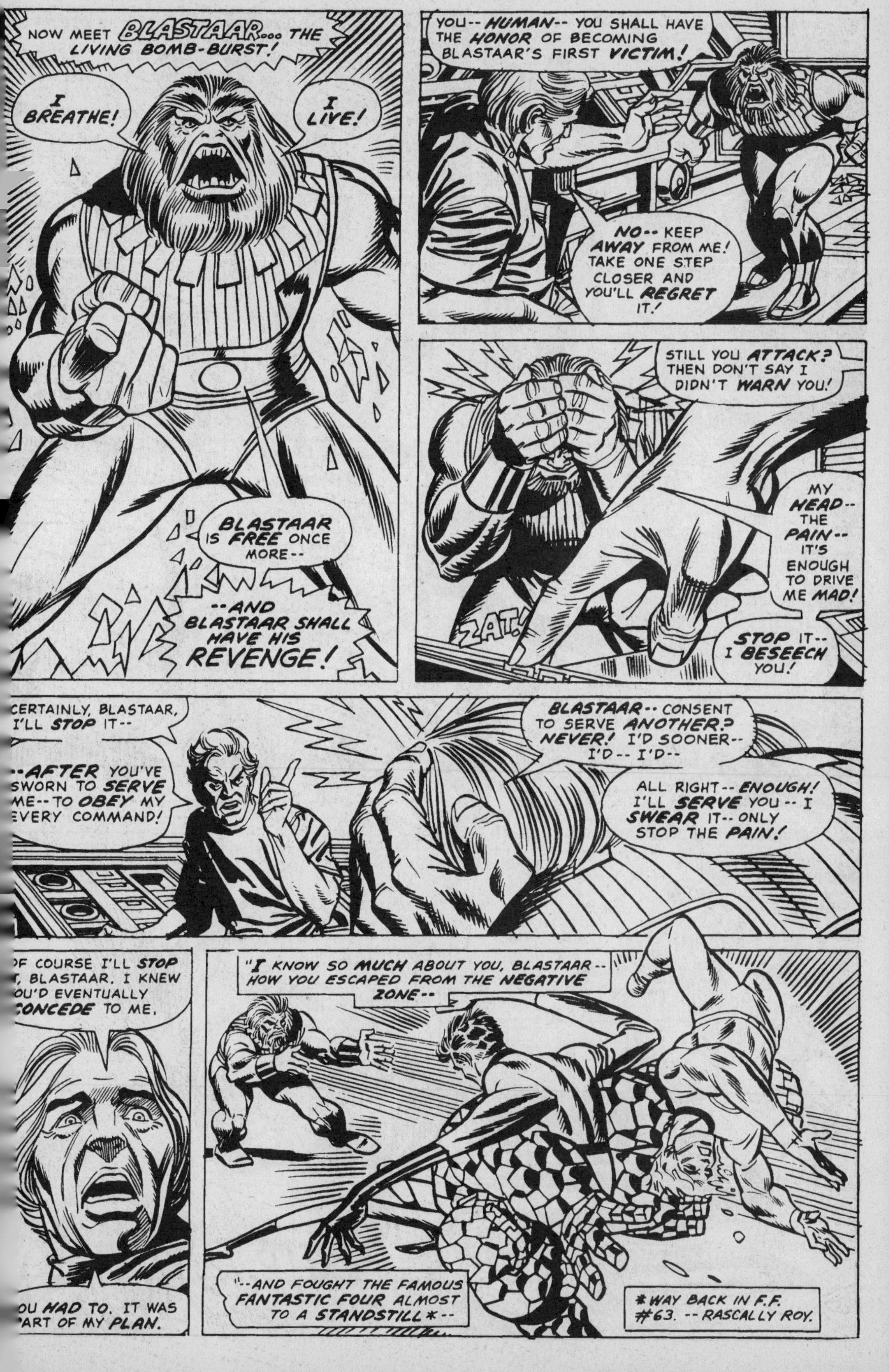
NOW MEET BLASTAAR... THE LIVING BOMB-BURST!
I BREATHE!
I LIVE!
BLASTAAR IS FREE ONCE MORE--
--AND BLASTAAR SHALL HAVE HIS REVENGE!
YOU-- HUMAN-- YOU SHALL HAVE THE HONOR OF BECOMING BLASTAAR'S FIRST VICTIM!
NO-- KEEP AWAY FROM ME! TAKE ONE STEP CLOSER AND YOU'LL REGRET IT!
STILL YOU ATTACK? THEN DON'T SAY I DIDN'T WARN YOU!
MY HEAD-- THE PAIN-- IT'S ENOUGH TO DRIVE ME MAD!
ZAT!
STOP IT-- I BESEECH YOU!
CERTAINLY, BLASTAAR, I'LL STOP IT--
--AFTER YOU'VE SWORN TO SERVE ME-- TO OBEY MY EVERY COMMAND!
BLASTAAR-- CONSENT TO SERVE ANOTHER? NEVER! I'D SOONER-- I'D-- I'D--
ALL RIGHT-- ENOUGH! I'LL SERVE YOU-- I SWEAR IT-- ONLY STOP THE PAIN!
OF COURSE I'LL STOP IT, BLASTAAR. I KNEW YOU'D EVENTUALLY CONCEDE TO ME.
YOU HAD TO. IT WAS PART OF MY PLAN.
"I KNOW SO MUCH ABOUT YOU, BLASTAAR-- HOW YOU ESCAPED FROM THE NEGATIVE ZONE--
"--AND FOUGHT THE FAMOUS FANTASTIC FOUR ALMOST TO A STANDSTILL*--
*WAY BACK IN F.F. #63. -- RASCALLY ROY.

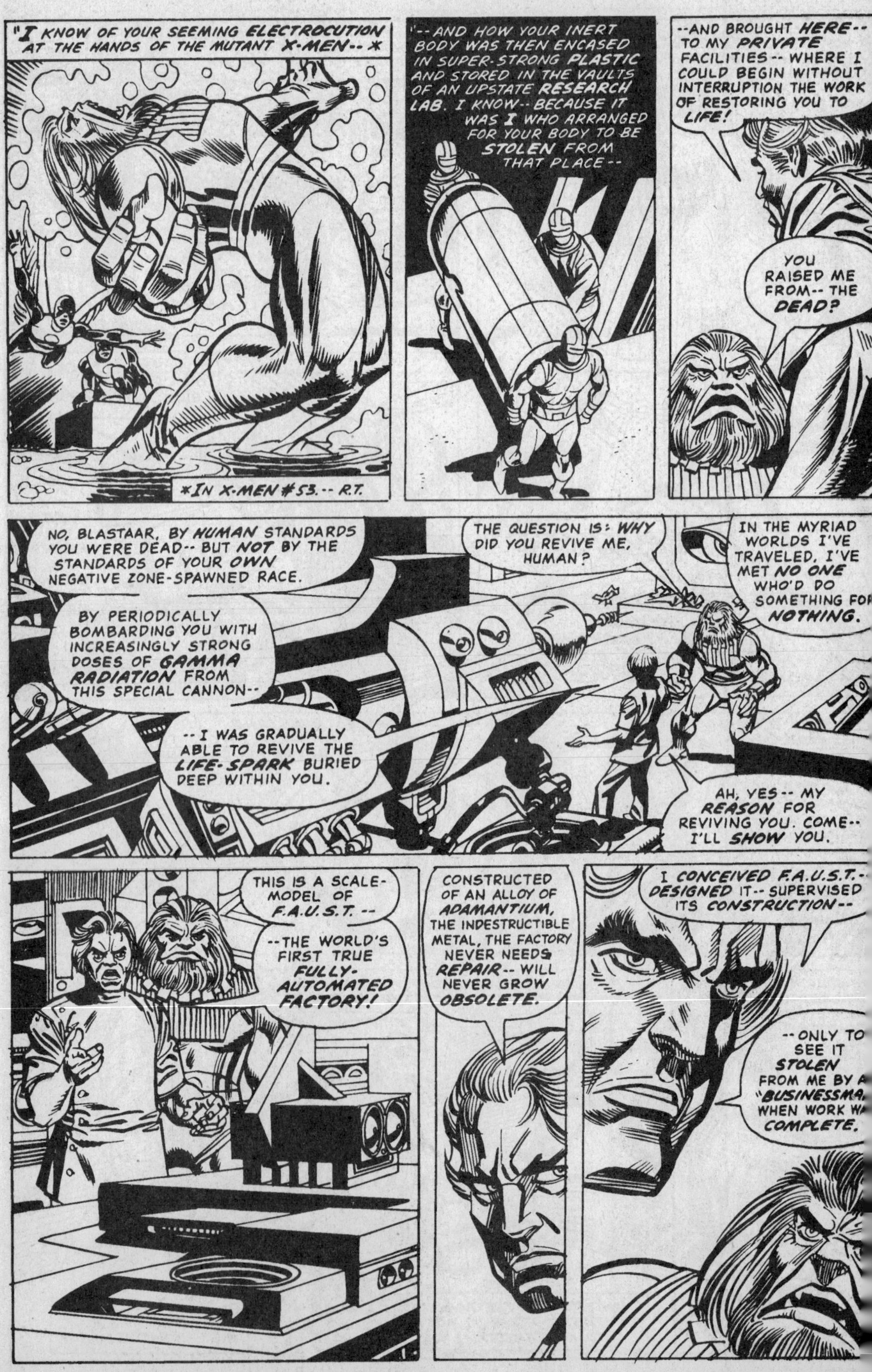

"I KNOW OF YOUR SEEMING ELECTROCUTION AT THE HANDS OF THE MUTANT X-MEN-- *
*IN X-MEN #53.--R.T.
"--AND HOW YOUR INERT BODY WAS THEN ENCASED IN SUPER-STRONG PLASTIC AND STORED IN THE VAULTS OF AN UPSTATE RESEARCH LAB. I KNOW--BECAUSE IT WAS I WHO ARRANGED FOR YOUR BODY TO BE STOLEN FROM THAT PLACE--
--AND BROUGHT HERE--TO MY PRIVATE FACILITIES--WHERE I COULD BEGIN WITHOUT INTERRUPTION THE WORK OF RESTORING YOU TO LIFE!
YOU RAISED ME FROM--THE DEAD?
NO, BLASTAAR, BY HUMAN STANDARDS YOU WERE DEAD--BUT NOT BY THE STANDARDS OF YOUR OWN NEGATIVE ZONE-SPAWNED RACE.
BY PERIODICALLY BOMBARDING YOU WITH INCREASINGLY STRONG DOSES OF GAMMA RADIATION FROM THIS SPECIAL CANNON--
--I WAS GRADUALLY ABLE TO REVIVE THE LIFE-SPARK BURIED DEEP WITHIN YOU.
THE QUESTION IS: WHY DID YOU REVIVE ME, HUMAN?
IN THE MYRIAD WORLDS I'VE TRAVELED, I'VE MET NO ONE WHO'D DO SOMETHING FOR NOTHING.
AH, YES--MY REASON FOR REVIVING YOU. COME--I'LL SHOW YOU.
THIS IS A SCALE-MODEL OF F.A.U.S.T.--
--THE WORLD'S FIRST TRUE FULLY-AUTOMATED FACTORY!
CONSTRUCTED OF AN ALLOY OF ADAMANTIUM, THE INDESTRUCTIBLE METAL, THE FACTORY NEVER NEEDS REPAIR--WILL NEVER GROW OBSOLETE.
I CONCEIVED F.A.U.S.T.--DESIGNED IT--SUPERVISED ITS CONSTRUCTION--
--ONLY TO SEE IT STOLEN FROM ME BY A "BUSINESSMA WHEN WORK WA COMPLETE.

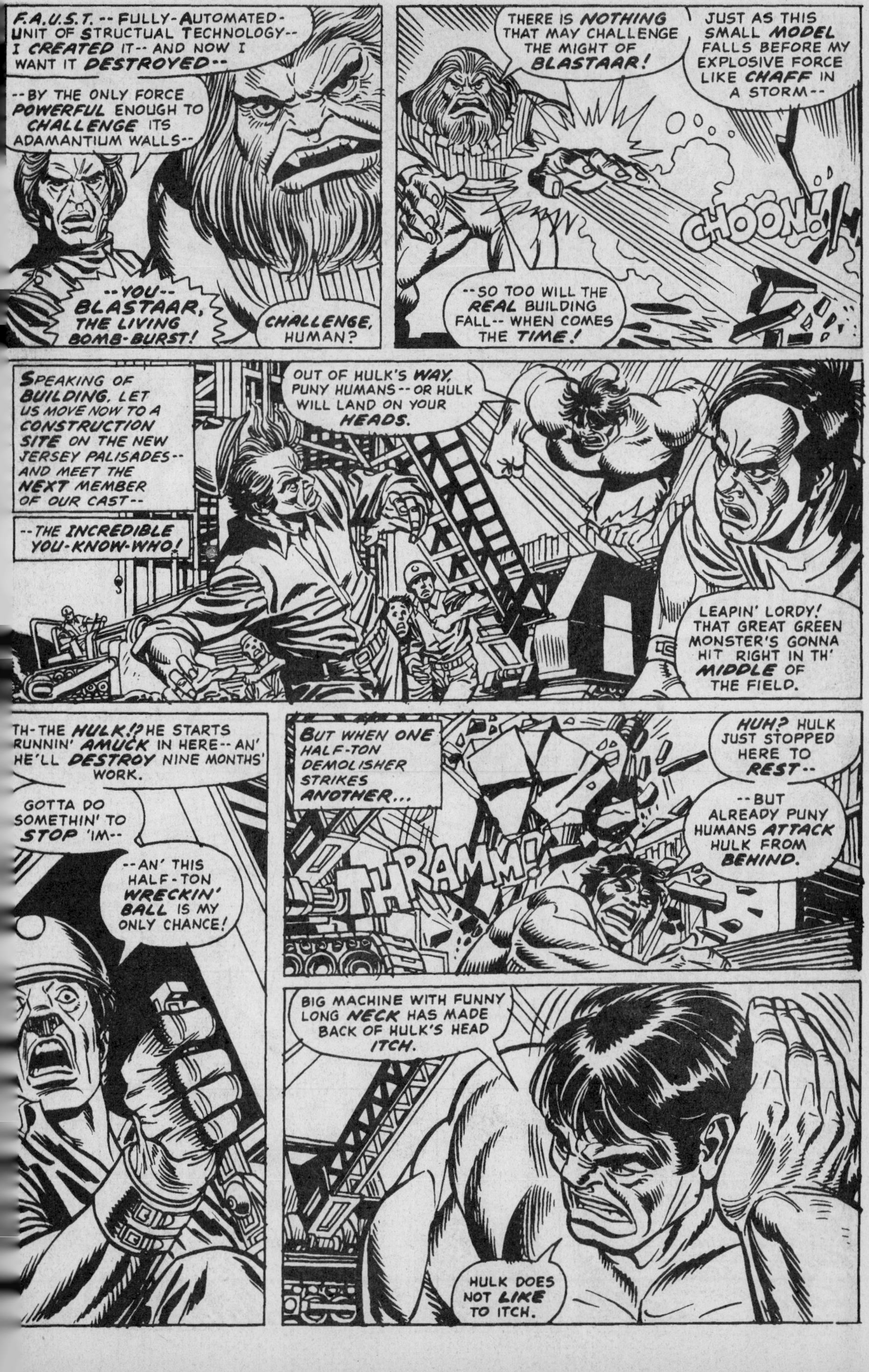

F.A.U.S.T. -- FULLY-AUTOMATED-UNIT OF STRUCTUAL TECHNOLOGY-- I CREATED IT-- AND NOW I WANT IT DESTROYED--
--BY THE ONLY FORCE POWERFUL ENOUGH TO CHALLENGE ITS ADAMANTIUM WALLS--
--YOU-- BLASTAAR, THE LIVING BOMB-BURST!
CHALLENGE, HUMAN?
THERE IS NOTHING THAT MAY CHALLENGE THE MIGHT OF BLASTAAR!
JUST AS THIS SMALL MODEL FALLS BEFORE MY EXPLOSIVE FORCE LIKE CHAFF IN A STORM--
CHOOM!
--SO TOO WILL THE REAL BUILDING FALL-- WHEN COMES THE TIME!
SPEAKING OF BUILDING, LET US MOVE NOW TO A CONSTRUCTION SITE ON THE NEW JERSEY PALISADES-- AND MEET THE NEXT MEMBER OF OUR CAST--
--THE INCREDIBLE YOU-KNOW-WHO!
OUT OF HULK'S WAY, PUNY HUMANS--OR HULK WILL LAND ON YOUR HEADS.
LEAPIN' LORDY! THAT GREAT GREEN MONSTER'S GONNA HIT RIGHT IN TH' MIDDLE OF THE FIELD.
TH-THE HULK!? HE STARTS RUNNIN' AMUCK IN HERE-- AN' HE'LL DESTROY NINE MONTHS' WORK.
GOTTA DO SOMETHIN' TO STOP 'IM--
--AN' THIS HALF-TON WRECKIN' BALL IS MY ONLY CHANCE!
BUT WHEN ONE HALF-TON DEMOLISHER STRIKES ANOTHER...
THRAMM!
HUH? HULK JUST STOPPED HERE TO REST--
--BUT ALREADY PUNY HUMANS ATTACK HULK FROM BEHIND.
BIG MACHINE WITH FUNNY LONG NECK HAS MADE BACK OF HULK'S HEAD ITCH.
HULK DOES NOT LIKE TO ITCH.

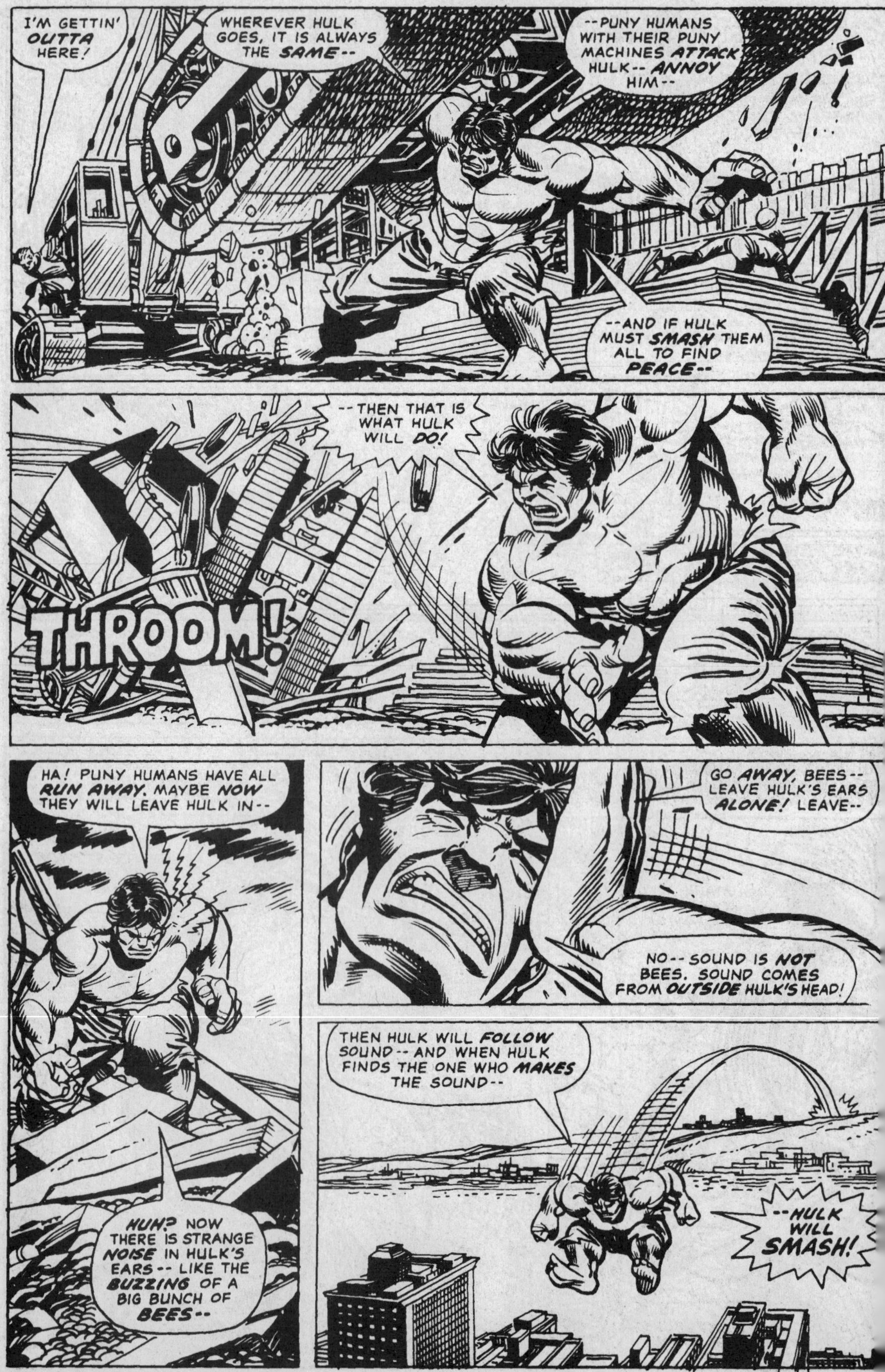
I'M GETTIN' OUTTA HERE!
WHEREVER HULK GOES, IT IS ALWAYS THE SAME--
--PUNY HUMANS WITH THEIR PUNY MACHINES ATTACK HULK-- ANNOY HIM--
--AND IF HULK MUST SMASH THEM ALL TO FIND PEACE--
--THEN THAT IS WHAT HULK WILL DO!
THROOM!
HA! PUNY HUMANS HAVE ALL RUN AWAY. MAYBE NOW THEY WILL LEAVE HULK IN--
HUH? NOW THERE IS STRANGE NOISE IN HULK'S EARS-- LIKE THE BUZZING OF A BIG BUNCH OF BEES--
GO AWAY, BEES-- LEAVE HULK'S EARS ALONE! LEAVE--
NO-- SOUND IS NOT BEES. SOUND COMES FROM OUTSIDE HULK'S HEAD!
THEN HULK WILL FOLLOW SOUND-- AND WHEN HULK FINDS THE ONE WHO MAKES THE SOUND--
--HULK WILL SMASH!

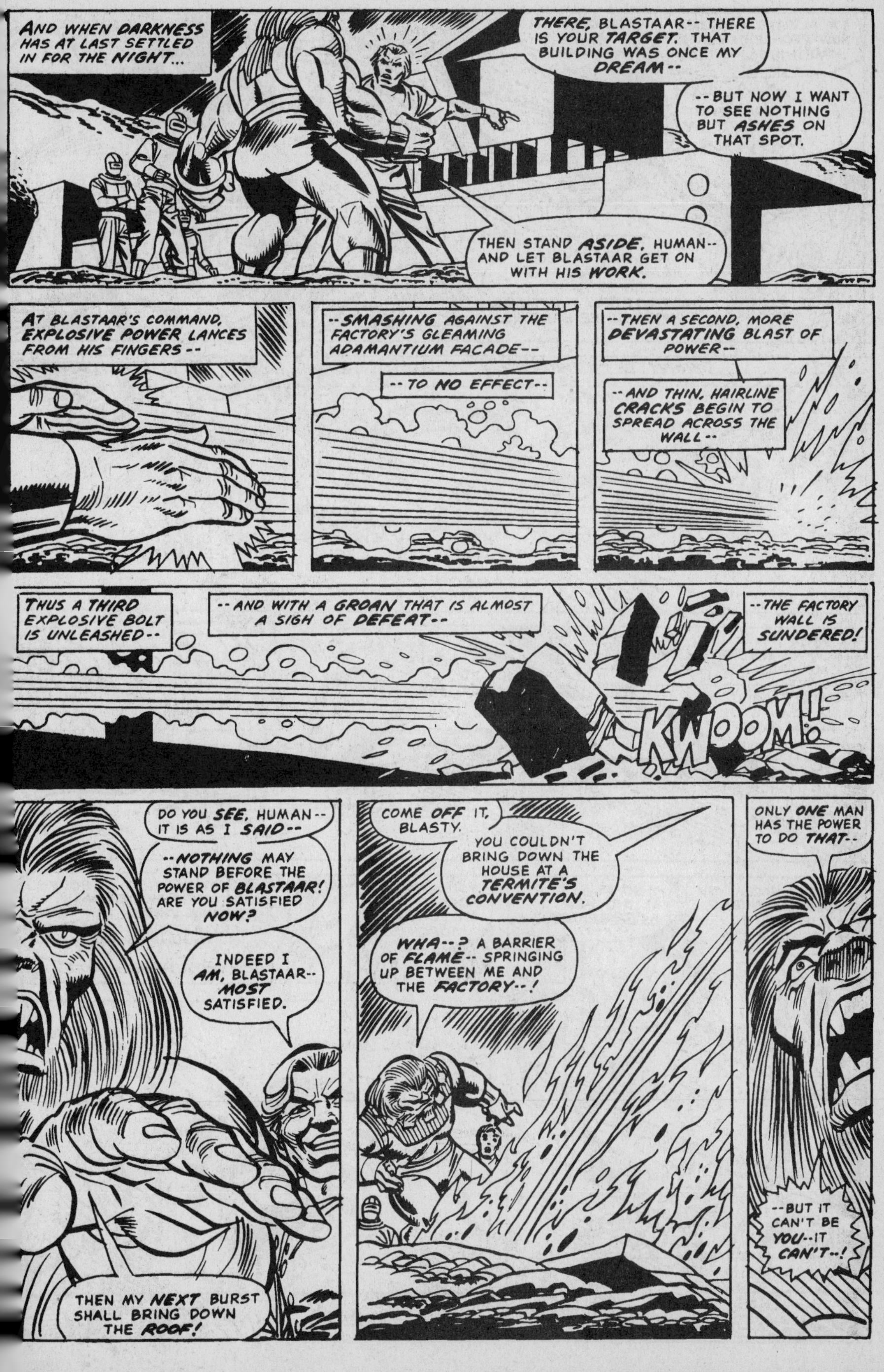

AND WHEN DARKNESS HAS AT LAST SETTLED IN FOR THE NIGHT...
THERE, BLASTAAR-- THERE IS YOUR TARGET. THAT BUILDING WAS ONCE MY DREAM--
--BUT NOW I WANT TO SEE NOTHING BUT ASHES ON THAT SPOT.
THEN STAND ASIDE, HUMAN-- AND LET BLASTAAR GET ON WITH HIS WORK.
AT BLASTAAR'S COMMAND, EXPLOSIVE POWER LANCES FROM HIS FINGERS--
--SMASHING AGAINST THE FACTORY'S GLEAMING ADAMANTIUM FACADE--
--TO NO EFFECT--
--THEN A SECOND, MORE DEVASTATING BLAST OF POWER--
--AND THIN, HAIRLINE CRACKS BEGIN TO SPREAD ACROSS THE WALL--
THUS A THIRD EXPLOSIVE BOLT IS UNLEASHED--
--AND WITH A GROAN THAT IS ALMOST A SIGH OF DEFEAT--
--THE FACTORY WALL IS SUNDERED!
KWOOM!
DO YOU SEE, HUMAN-- IT IS AS I SAID--
--NOTHING MAY STAND BEFORE THE POWER OF BLASTAAR! ARE YOU SATISFIED NOW?
INDEED I AM, BLASTAAR-- MOST SATISFIED.
THEN MY NEXT BURST SHALL BRING DOWN THE ROOF!
COME OFF IT, BLASTY.
YOU COULDN'T BRING DOWN THE HOUSE AT A TERMITE'S CONVENTION.
WHA--? A BARRIER OF FLAME-- SPRINGING UP BETWEEN ME AND THE FACTORY--!
ONLY ONE MAN HAS THE POWER TO DO THAT--
--BUT IT CAN'T BE YOU--IT CAN'T--!

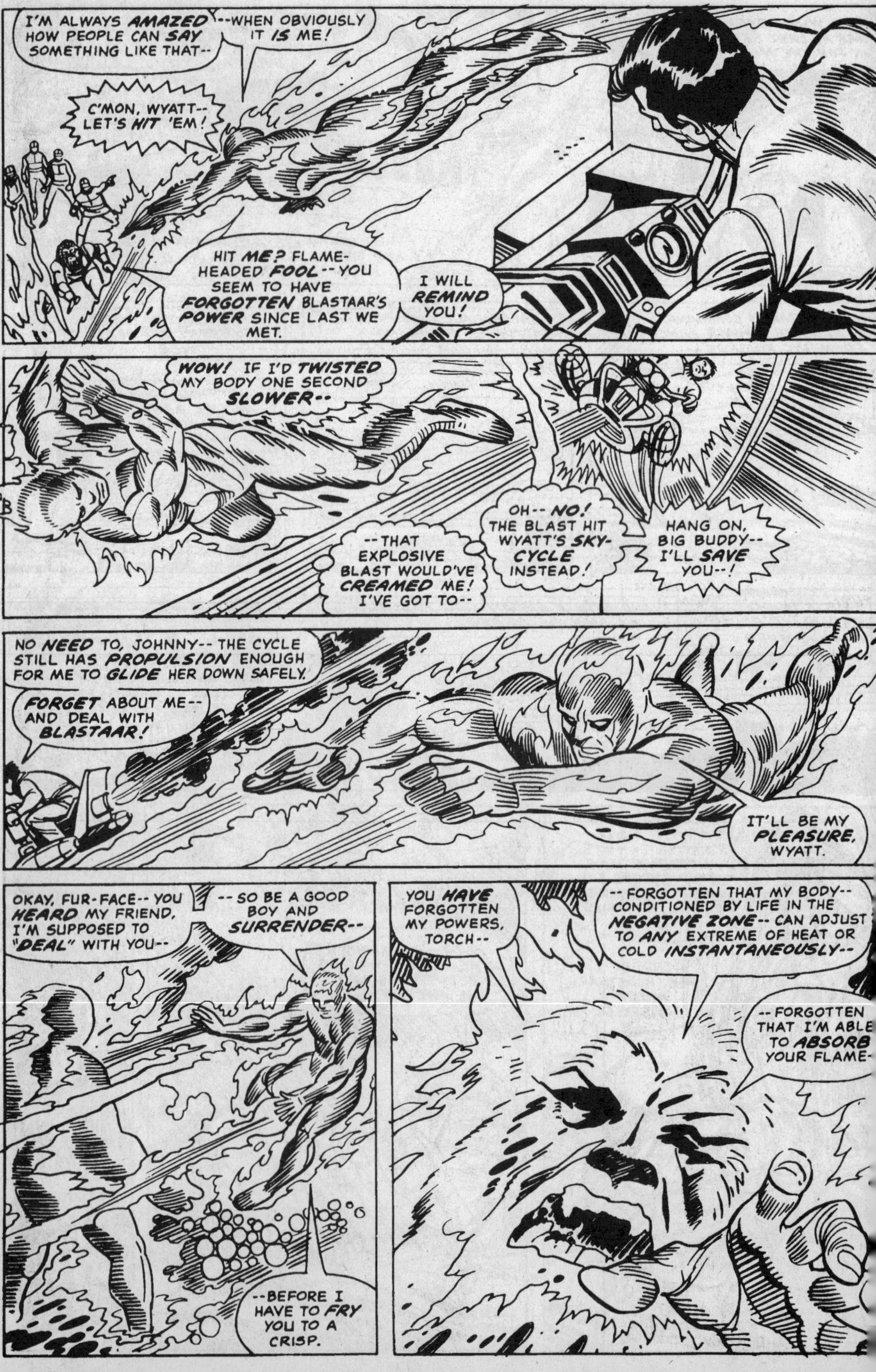
I'M ALWAYS AMAZED HOW PEOPLE CAN SAY SOMETHING LIKE THAT--
--WHEN OBVIOUSLY IT IS ME!
C'MON, WYATT-- LET'S HIT 'EM!
HIT ME? FLAME-HEADED FOOL--YOU SEEM TO HAVE FORGOTTEN BLASTAAR'S POWER SINCE LAST WE MET.
I WILL REMIND YOU!
WOW! IF I'D TWISTED MY BODY ONE SECOND SLOWER--
--THAT EXPLOSIVE BLAST WOULD'VE CREAMED ME! I'VE GOT TO--
OH--NO! THE BLAST HIT WYATT'S SKY-CYCLE INSTEAD!
HANG ON, BIG BUDDY-- I'LL SAVE YOU--!
NO NEED TO, JOHNNY-- THE CYCLE STILL HAS PROPULSION ENOUGH FOR ME TO GLIDE HER DOWN SAFELY.
FORGET ABOUT ME-- AND DEAL WITH BLASTAAR!
IT'LL BE MY PLEASURE, WYATT.
OKAY, FUR-FACE-- YOU HEARD MY FRIEND, I'M SUPPOSED TO "DEAL" WITH YOU--
--SO BE A GOOD BOY AND SURRENDER--
--BEFORE I HAVE TO FRY YOU TO A CRISP.
YOU HAVE FORGOTTEN MY POWERS, TORCH--
--FORGOTTEN THAT MY BODY--CONDITIONED BY LIFE IN THE NEGATIVE ZONE--CAN ADJUST TO ANY EXTREME OF HEAT OR COLD INSTANTANEOUSLY--
--FORGOTTEN THAT I'M ABLE TO ABSORB YOUR FLAME-

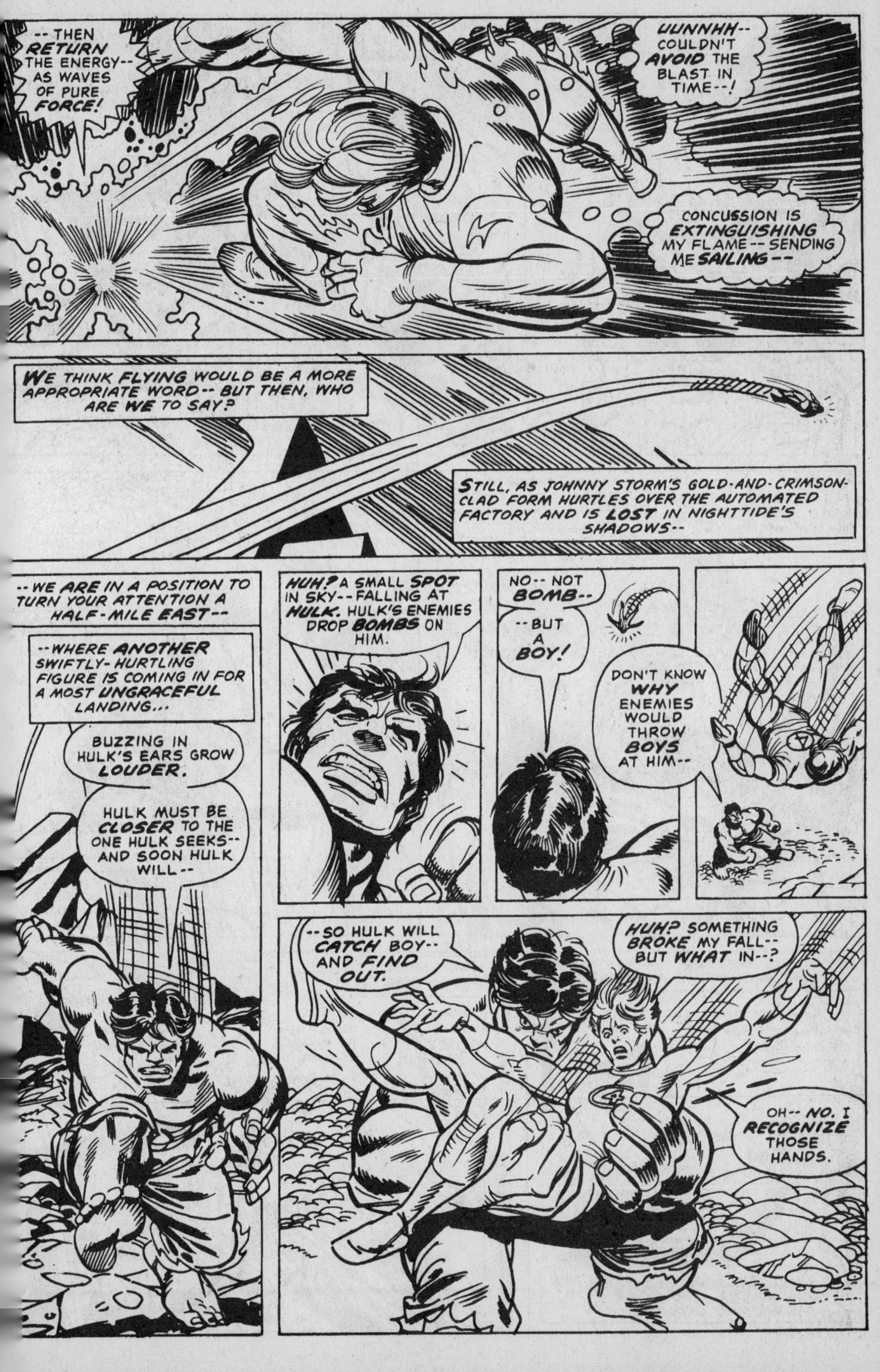
-- THEN RETURN THE ENERGY-- AS WAVES OF PURE FORCE!
UUNNHH-- COULDN'T AVOID THE BLAST IN TIME--!
CONCUSSION IS EXTINGUISHING MY FLAME -- SENDING ME SAILING --
WE THINK FLYING WOULD BE A MORE APPROPRIATE WORD-- BUT THEN, WHO ARE WE TO SAY?
STILL, AS JOHNNY STORM'S GOLD-AND-CRIMSON-CLAD FORM HURTLES OVER THE AUTOMATED FACTORY AND IS LOST IN NIGHTTIDE'S SHADOWS--
-- WE ARE IN A POSITION TO TURN YOUR ATTENTION A HALF-MILE EAST--
--WHERE ANOTHER SWIFTLY-HURTLING FIGURE IS COMING IN FOR A MOST UNGRACEFUL LANDING...
BUZZING IN HULK'S EARS GROW LOUDER.
HULK MUST BE CLOSER TO THE ONE HULK SEEKS-- AND SOON HULK WILL--
HUH? A SMALL SPOT IN SKY--FALLING AT HULK. HULK'S ENEMIES DROP BOMBS ON HIM.
NO-- NOT BOMB--
--BUT A BOY!
DON'T KNOW WHY ENEMIES WOULD THROW BOYS AT HIM--
--SO HULK WILL CATCH BOY-- AND FIND OUT.
HUH? SOMETHING BROKE MY FALL-- BUT WHAT IN--?
OH-- NO. I RECOGNIZE THOSE HANDS.

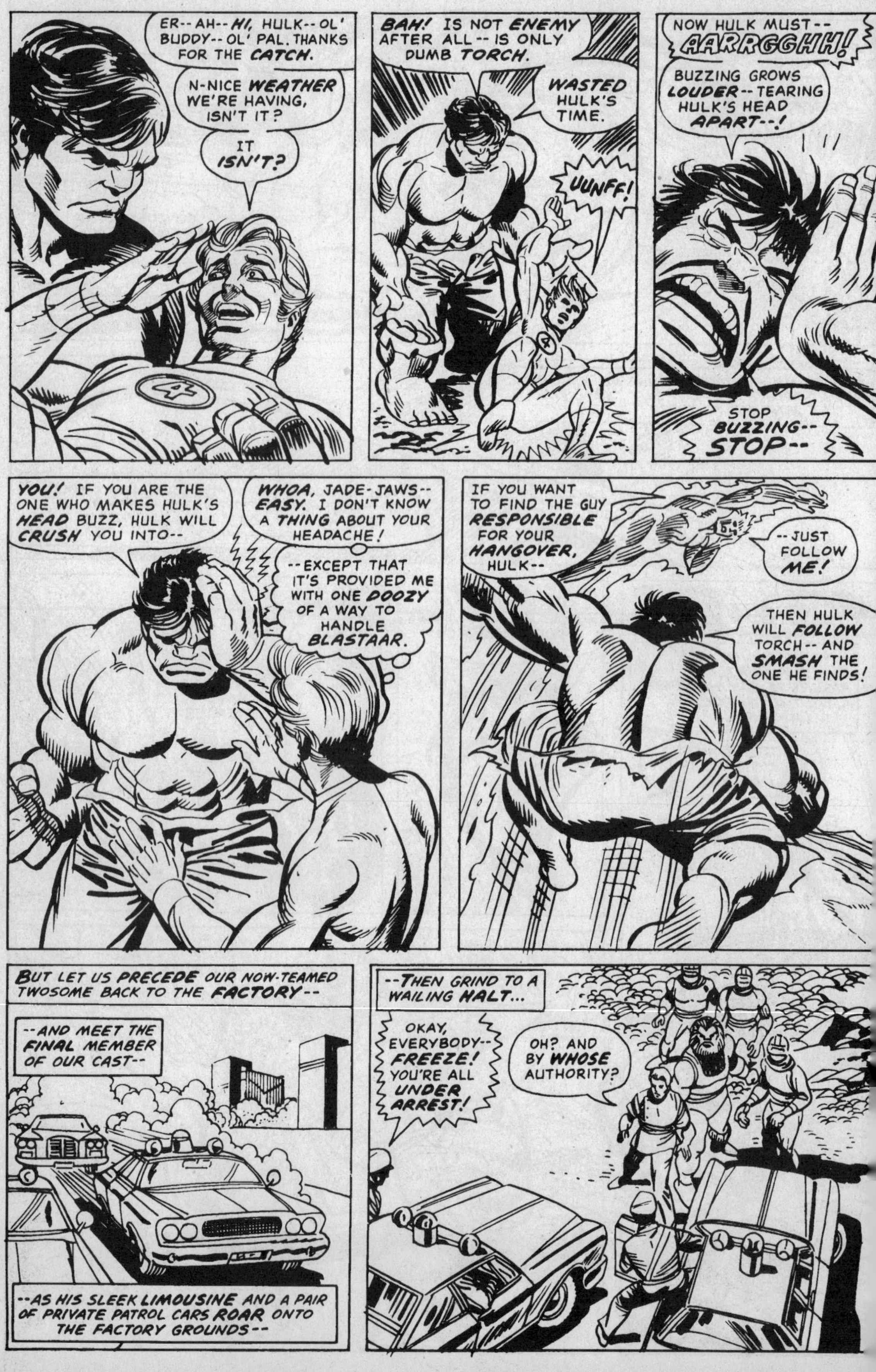
ER--AH--HI, HULK--OL' BUDDY--OL' PAL. THANKS FOR THE CATCH.
N-NICE WEATHER WE'RE HAVING, ISN'T IT?
IT ISN'T?
BAH! IS NOT ENEMY AFTER ALL--IS ONLY DUMB TORCH.
WASTED HULK'S TIME.
UUNFF!
NOW HULK MUST--
AARRGGHH!
BUZZING GROWS LOUDER--TEARING HULK'S HEAD APART--!
STOP BUZZING--STOP--
YOU! IF YOU ARE THE ONE WHO MAKES HULK'S HEAD BUZZ, HULK WILL CRUSH YOU INTO--
WHOA, JADE-JAWS--EASY. I DON'T KNOW A THING ABOUT YOUR HEADACHE!
--EXCEPT THAT IT'S PROVIDED ME WITH ONE DOOZY OF A WAY TO HANDLE BLASTAAR.
IF YOU WANT TO FIND THE GUY RESPONSIBLE FOR YOUR HANGOVER, HULK--
--JUST FOLLOW ME!
THEN HULK WILL FOLLOW TORCH--AND SMASH THE ONE HE FINDS!
BUT LET US PRECEDE OUR NOW-TEAMED TWOSOME BACK TO THE FACTORY--
--AND MEET THE FINAL MEMBER OF OUR CAST--
--AS HIS SLEEK LIMOUSINE AND A PAIR OF PRIVATE PATROL CARS ROAR ONTO THE FACTORY GROUNDS--
--THEN GRIND TO A WAILING HALT...
OKAY, EVERYBODY--FREEZE! YOU'RE ALL UNDER ARREST!
OH? AND BY WHOSE AUTHORITY?

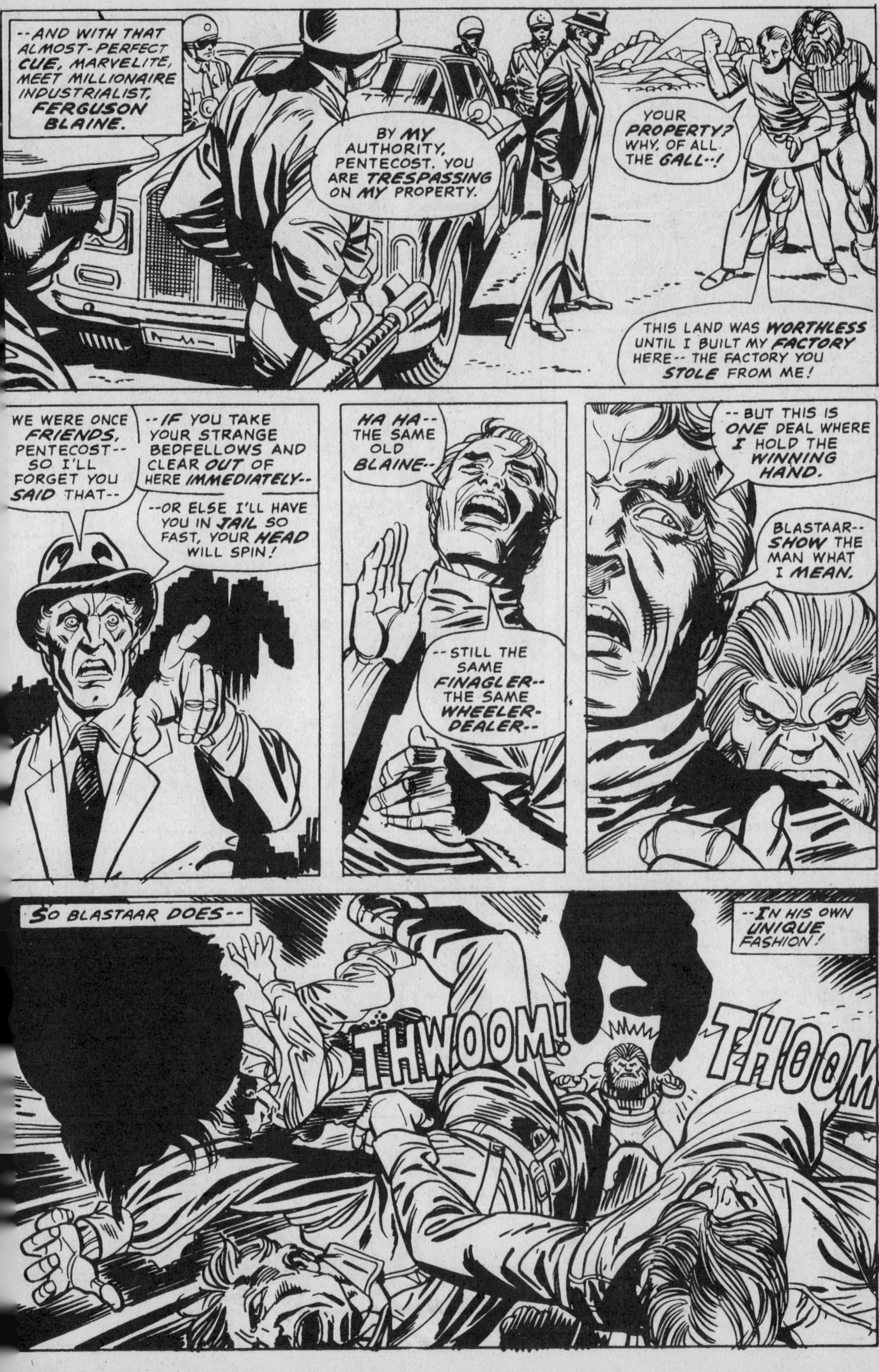
--AND WITH THAT ALMOST-PERFECT CUE, MARVELITE, MEET MILLIONAIRE INDUSTRIALIST, FERGUSON BLAINE.
BY MY AUTHORITY, PENTECOST. YOU ARE TRESPASSING ON MY PROPERTY.
YOUR PROPERTY? WHY, OF ALL THE GALL--!
THIS LAND WAS WORTHLESS UNTIL I BUILT MY FACTORY HERE-- THE FACTORY YOU STOLE FROM ME!
WE WERE ONCE FRIENDS, PENTECOST-- SO I'LL FORGET YOU SAID THAT--
--IF YOU TAKE YOUR STRANGE BEDFELLOWS AND CLEAR OUT OF HERE IMMEDIATELY--
--OR ELSE I'LL HAVE YOU IN JAIL SO FAST, YOUR HEAD WILL SPIN!
HA HA-- THE SAME OLD BLAINE--
--STILL THE SAME FINAGLER-- THE SAME WHEELER-DEALER--
-- BUT THIS IS ONE DEAL WHERE I HOLD THE WINNING HAND.
BLASTAAR-- SHOW THE MAN WHAT I MEAN.
SO BLASTAAR DOES--
--IN HIS OWN UNIQUE FASHION!
THWOOM!
THOOM

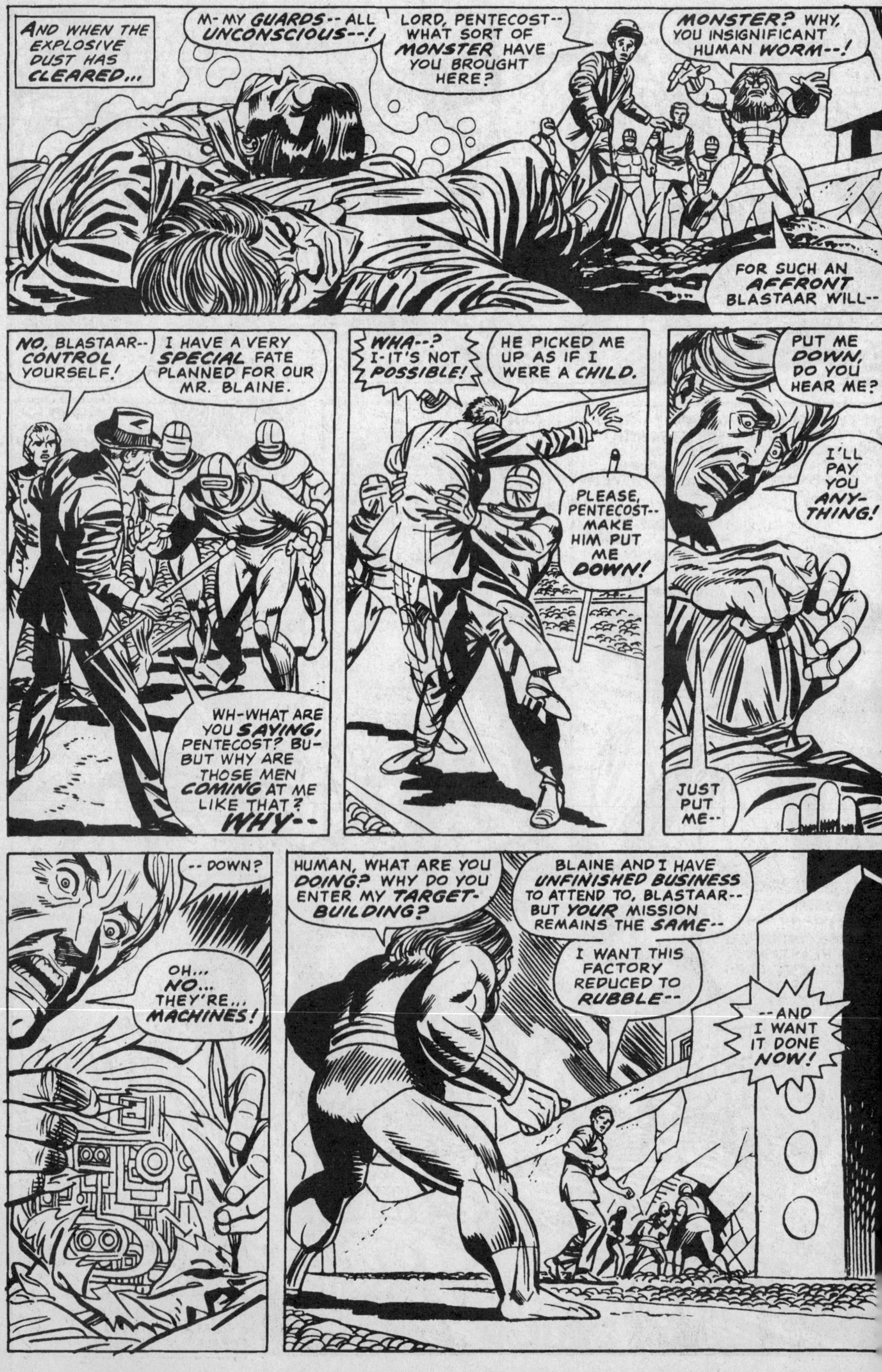
AND WHEN THE EXPLOSIVE DUST HAS CLEARED...
M-MY GUARDS-- ALL UNCONSCIOUS--!
LORD, PENTECOST-- WHAT SORT OF MONSTER HAVE YOU BROUGHT HERE?
MONSTER? WHY, YOU INSIGNIFICANT HUMAN WORM--!
FOR SUCH AN AFFRONT BLASTAAR WILL--
NO, BLASTAAR-- CONTROL YOURSELF!
I HAVE A VERY SPECIAL FATE PLANNED FOR OUR MR. BLAINE.
WH-WHAT ARE YOU SAYING, PENTECOST? BU-BUT WHY ARE THOSE MEN COMING AT ME LIKE THAT? WHY--
WHA--? I-IT'S NOT POSSIBLE!
HE PICKED ME UP AS IF I WERE A CHILD.
PLEASE, PENTECOST-- MAKE HIM PUT ME DOWN!
PUT ME DOWN, DO YOU HEAR ME?
I'LL PAY YOU ANY-THING!
JUST PUT ME--
-- DOWN?
OH... NO... THEY'RE... MACHINES!
HUMAN, WHAT ARE YOU DOING? WHY DO YOU ENTER MY TARGET-BUILDING?
BLAINE AND I HAVE UNFINISHED BUSINESS TO ATTEND TO, BLASTAAR-- BUT YOUR MISSION REMAINS THE SAME--
I WANT THIS FACTORY REDUCED TO RUBBLE--
--AND I WANT IT DONE NOW!

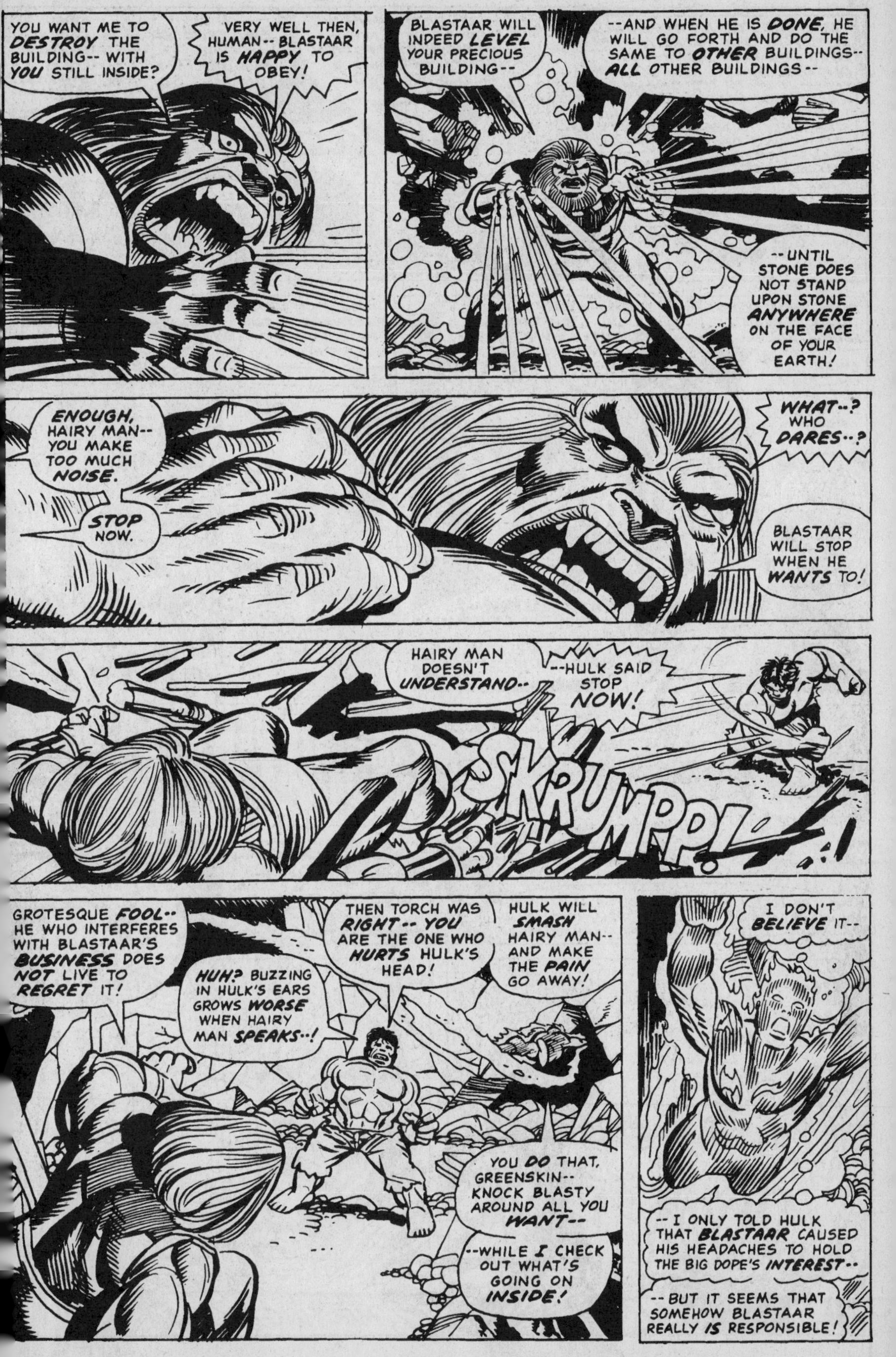
YOU WANT ME TO DESTROY THE BUILDING-- WITH YOU STILL INSIDE?
VERY WELL THEN, HUMAN-- BLASTAAR IS HAPPY TO OBEY!
BLASTAAR WILL INDEED LEVEL YOUR PRECIOUS BUILDING--
--AND WHEN HE IS DONE, HE WILL GO FORTH AND DO THE SAME TO OTHER BUILDINGS-- ALL OTHER BUILDINGS--
--UNTIL STONE DOES NOT STAND UPON STONE ANYWHERE ON THE FACE OF YOUR EARTH!
ENOUGH, HAIRY MAN-- YOU MAKE TOO MUCH NOISE.
STOP NOW.
WHAT--? WHO DARES--?
BLASTAAR WILL STOP WHEN HE WANTS TO!
HAIRY MAN DOESN'T UNDERSTAND--
--HULK SAID STOP NOW!
SKRUMPP!
GROTESQUE FOOL-- HE WHO INTERFERES WITH BLASTAAR'S BUSINESS DOES NOT LIVE TO REGRET IT!
HUH? BUZZING IN HULK'S EARS GROWS WORSE WHEN HAIRY MAN SPEAKS--!
THEN TORCH WAS RIGHT-- YOU ARE THE ONE WHO HURTS HULK'S HEAD!
HULK WILL SMASH HAIRY MAN-- AND MAKE THE PAIN GO AWAY!
YOU DO THAT, GREENSKIN-- KNOCK BLASTY AROUND ALL YOU WANT--
--WHILE I CHECK OUT WHAT'S GOING ON INSIDE!
I DON'T BELIEVE IT--
--I ONLY TOLD HULK THAT BLASTAAR CAUSED HIS HEADACHES TO HOLD THE BIG DOPE'S INTEREST--
--BUT IT SEEMS THAT SOMEHOW BLASTAAR REALLY IS RESPONSIBLE!

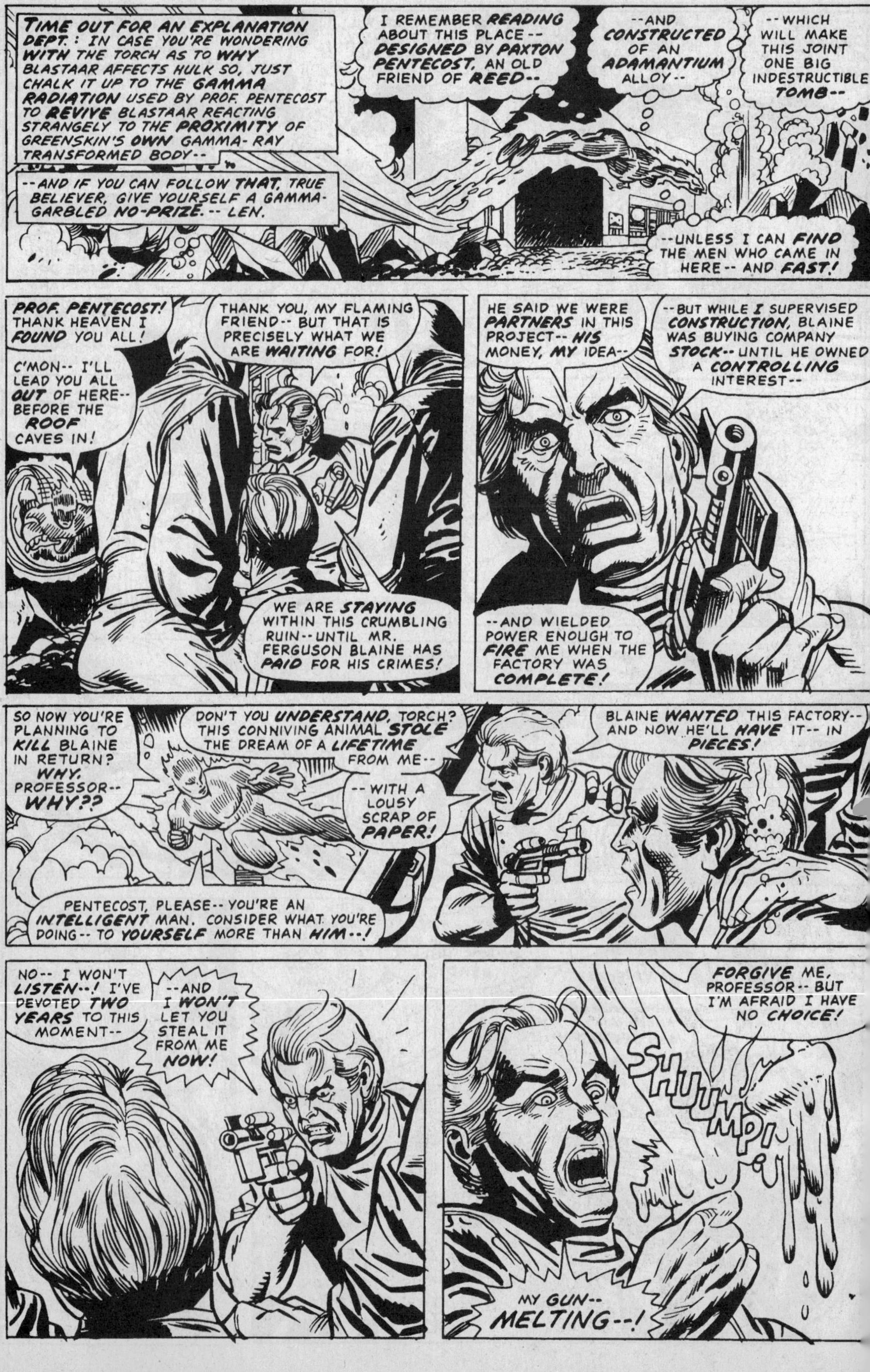

TIME OUT FOR AN EXPLANATION DEPT.: IN CASE YOU'RE WONDERING WITH THE TORCH AS TO WHY BLASTAAR AFFECTS HULK SO, JUST CHALK IT UP TO THE GAMMA RADIATION USED BY PROF. PENTECOST TO REVIVE BLASTAAR REACTING STRANGELY TO THE PROXIMITY OF GREENSKIN'S OWN GAMMA-RAY TRANSFORMED BODY--
--AND IF YOU CAN FOLLOW THAT, TRUE BELIEVER, GIVE YOURSELF A GAMMA-GARBLED NO-PRIZE. --LEN.
I REMEMBER READING ABOUT THIS PLACE-- DESIGNED BY PAXTON PENTECOST, AN OLD FRIEND OF REED--
--AND CONSTRUCTED OF AN ADAMANTIUM ALLOY--
--WHICH WILL MAKE THIS JOINT ONE BIG INDESTRUCTIBLE TOMB--
--UNLESS I CAN FIND THE MEN WHO CAME IN HERE-- AND FAST!
PROF. PENTECOST! THANK HEAVEN I FOUND YOU ALL!
C'MON-- I'LL LEAD YOU ALL OUT OF HERE-- BEFORE THE ROOF CAVES IN!
THANK YOU, MY FLAMING FRIEND-- BUT THAT IS PRECISELY WHAT WE ARE WAITING FOR!
WE ARE STAYING WITHIN THIS CRUMBLING RUIN--UNTIL MR. FERGUSON BLAINE HAS PAID FOR HIS CRIMES!
HE SAID WE WERE PARTNERS IN THIS PROJECT-- HIS MONEY, MY IDEA--
--BUT WHILE I SUPERVISED CONSTRUCTION, BLAINE WAS BUYING COMPANY STOCK-- UNTIL HE OWNED A CONTROLLING INTEREST--
--AND WIELDED POWER ENOUGH TO FIRE ME WHEN THE FACTORY WAS COMPLETE!
SO NOW YOU'RE PLANNING TO KILL BLAINE IN RETURN? WHY, PROFESSOR-- WHY??
DON'T YOU UNDERSTAND, TORCH? THIS CONNIVING ANIMAL STOLE THE DREAM OF A LIFETIME FROM ME--
--WITH A LOUSY SCRAP OF PAPER!
BLAINE WANTED THIS FACTORY-- AND NOW HE'LL HAVE IT-- IN PIECES!
PENTECOST, PLEASE-- YOU'RE AN INTELLIGENT MAN. CONSIDER WHAT YOU'RE DOING-- TO YOURSELF MORE THAN HIM--!
NO-- I WON'T LISTEN--! I'VE DEVOTED TWO YEARS TO THIS MOMENT--
--AND I WON'T LET YOU STEAL IT FROM ME NOW!
FORGIVE ME, PROFESSOR-- BUT I'M AFRAID I HAVE NO CHOICE!
SHUUMP!
MY GUN-- MELTING--!

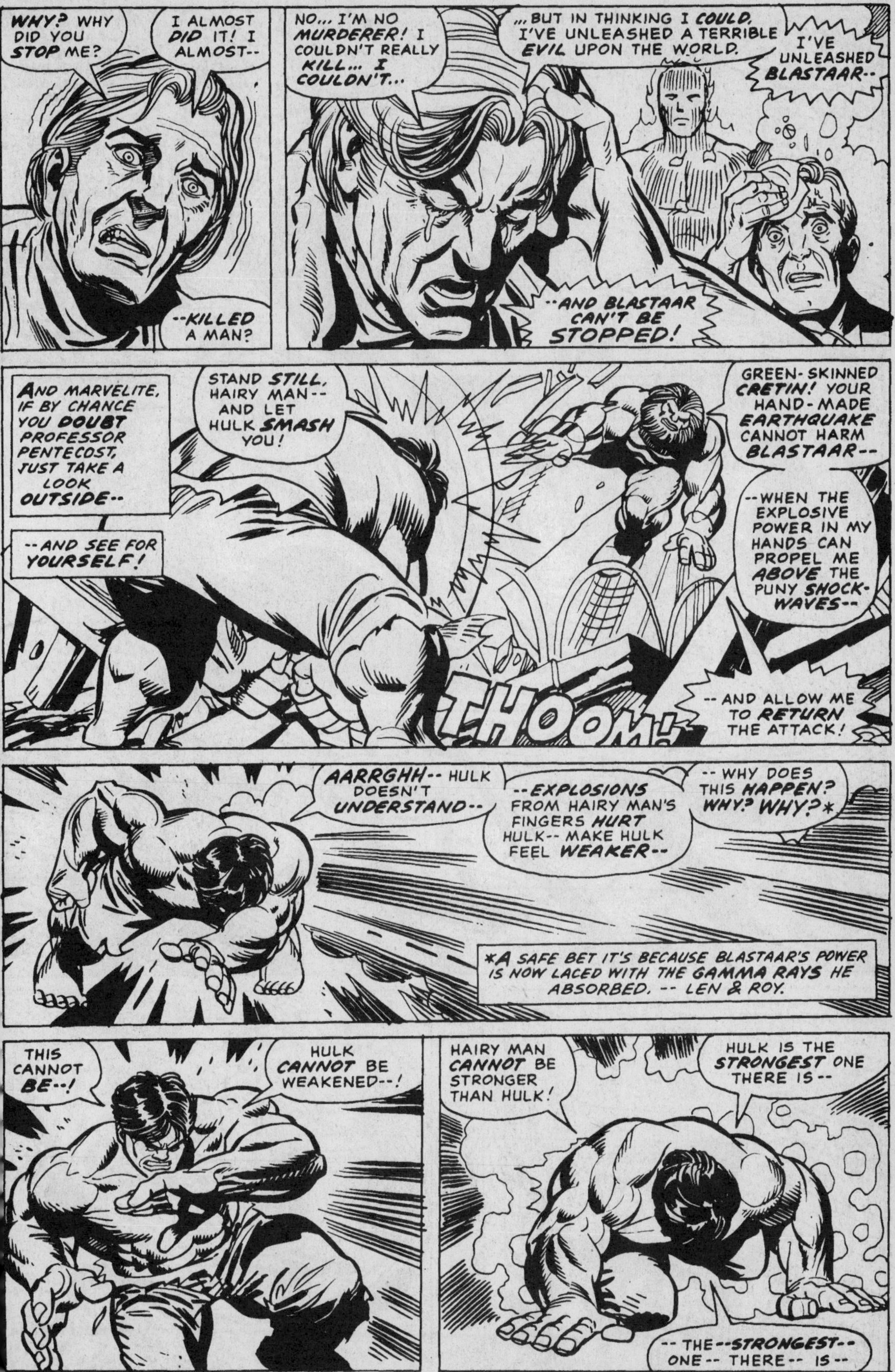
WHY? WHY DID YOU STOP ME?
I ALMOST DID IT! I ALMOST--
--KILLED A MAN?
NO... I'M NO MURDERER! I COULDN'T REALLY KILL... I COULDN'T...
...BUT IN THINKING I COULD, I'VE UNLEASHED A TERRIBLE EVIL UPON THE WORLD.
I'VE UNLEASHED BLASTAAR--
--AND BLASTAAR CAN'T BE STOPPED!
AND MARVELITE, IF BY CHANCE YOU DOUBT PROFESSOR PENTECOST, JUST TAKE A LOOK OUTSIDE--
--AND SEE FOR YOURSELF!
STAND STILL, HAIRY MAN--AND LET HULK SMASH YOU!
GREEN-SKINNED CRETIN! YOUR HAND-MADE EARTHQUAKE CANNOT HARM BLASTAAR--
--WHEN THE EXPLOSIVE POWER IN MY HANDS CAN PROPEL ME ABOVE THE PUNY SHOCK-WAVES--
THOOM!
--AND ALLOW ME TO RETURN THE ATTACK!
AARRGHH-- HULK DOESN'T UNDERSTAND--
--EXPLOSIONS FROM HAIRY MAN'S FINGERS HURT HULK-- MAKE HULK FEEL WEAKER--
-- WHY DOES THIS HAPPEN? WHY? WHY?*
*A SAFE BET IT'S BECAUSE BLASTAAR'S POWER IS NOW LACED WITH THE GAMMA RAYS HE ABSORBED. -- LEN & ROY.
THIS CANNOT BE--!
HULK CANNOT BE WEAKENED--!
HAIRY MAN CANNOT BE STRONGER THAN HULK!
HULK IS THE STRONGEST ONE THERE IS--
-- THE --STRONGEST-- ONE -- THERE -- IS --

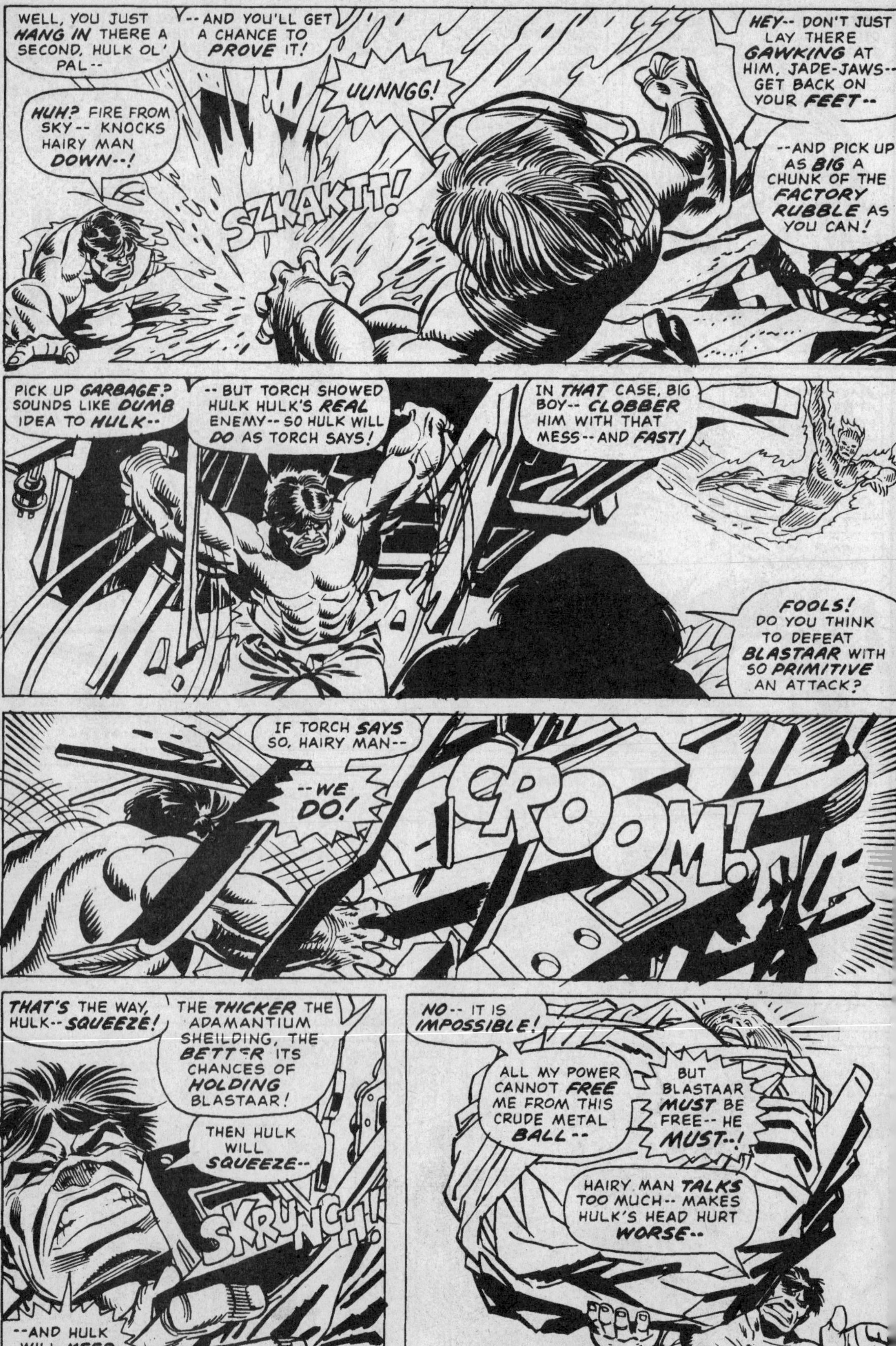
WELL, YOU JUST HANG IN THERE A SECOND, HULK OL' PAL--
--AND YOU'LL GET A CHANCE TO PROVE IT!
HEY-- DON'T JUST LAY THERE GAWKING AT HIM, JADE-JAWS-- GET BACK ON YOUR FEET--
UUNNGG!
HUH? FIRE FROM SKY-- KNOCKS HAIRY MAN DOWN--!
--AND PICK UP AS BIG A CHUNK OF THE FACTORY RUBBLE AS YOU CAN!
SZKAKTT!
PICK UP GARBAGE? SOUNDS LIKE DUMB IDEA TO HULK--
--BUT TORCH SHOWED HULK HULK'S REAL ENEMY--SO HULK WILL DO AS TORCH SAYS!
IN THAT CASE, BIG BOY-- CLOBBER HIM WITH THAT MESS--AND FAST!
FOOLS! DO YOU THINK TO DEFEAT BLASTAAR WITH SO PRIMITIVE AN ATTACK?
IF TORCH SAYS SO, HAIRY MAN--
--WE DO!
CROOM!
THAT'S THE WAY, HULK--SQUEEZE!
THE THICKER THE ADAMANTIUM SHEILDING, THE BETTER ITS CHANCES OF HOLDING BLASTAAR!
THEN HULK WILL SQUEEZE--
SKRUNCH!
--AND HULK WILL KEEP SQUEEZING!
NO-- IT IS IMPOSSIBLE!
ALL MY POWER CANNOT FREE ME FROM THIS CRUDE METAL BALL--
BUT BLASTAAR MUST BE FREE-- HE MUST--!
HAIRY MAN TALKS TOO MUCH-- MAKES HULK'S HEAD HURT WORSE--

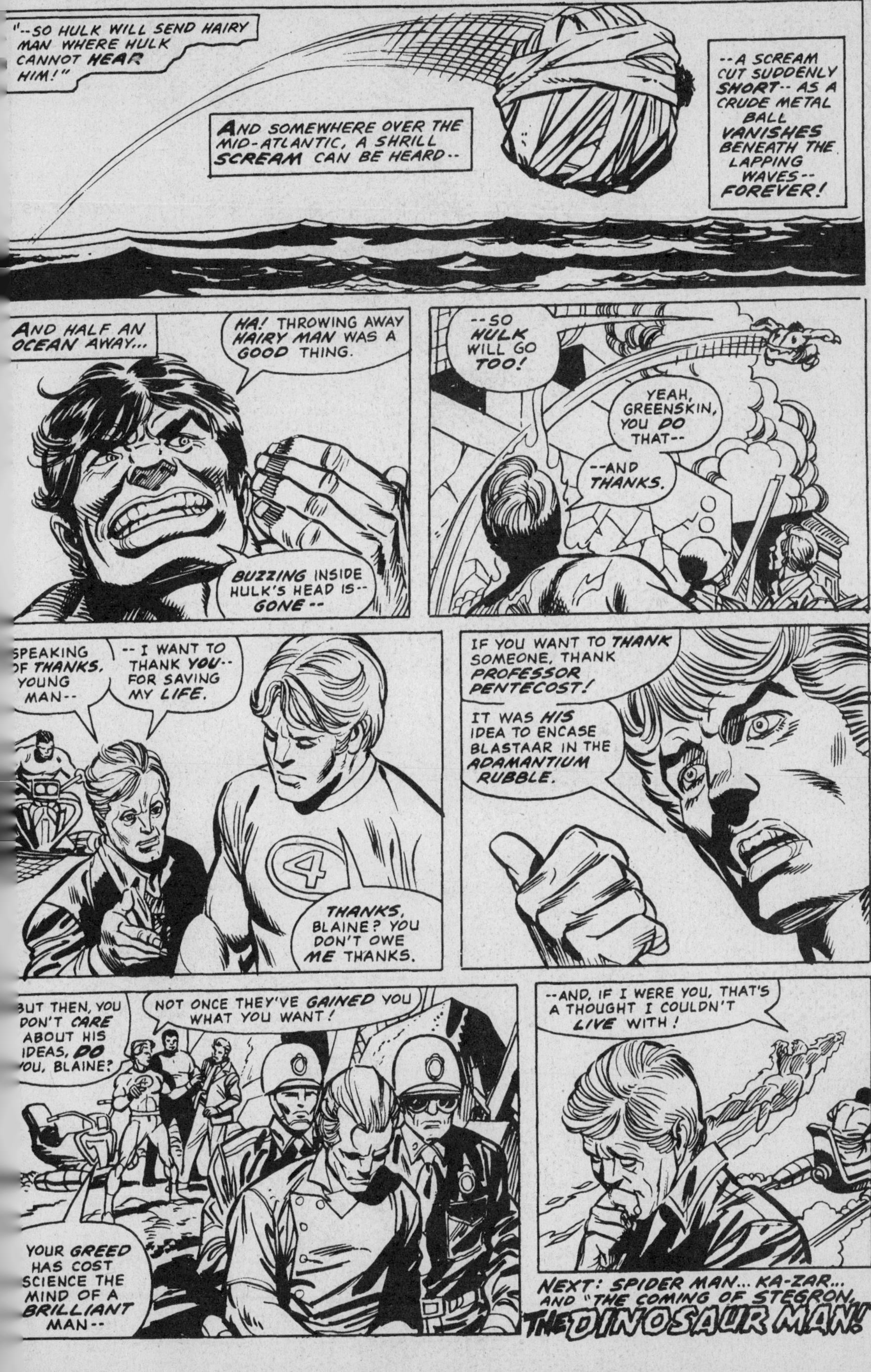
"--SO HULK WILL SEND HAIRY MAN WHERE HULK CANNOT HEAR HIM!"
AND SOMEWHERE OVER THE MID-ATLANTIC, A SHRILL SCREAM CAN BE HEARD--
--A SCREAM CUT SUDDENLY SHORT-- AS A CRUDE METAL BALL VANISHES BENEATH THE LAPPING WAVES-- FOREVER!
AND HALF AN OCEAN AWAY...
HA! THROWING AWAY HAIRY MAN WAS A GOOD THING.
BUZZING INSIDE HULK'S HEAD IS-- GONE--
--SO HULK WILL GO TOO!
YEAH, GREENSKIN, YOU DO THAT--
--AND THANKS.
SPEAKING OF THANKS, YOUNG MAN--
-- I WANT TO THANK YOU-- FOR SAVING MY LIFE.
THANKS, BLAINE? YOU DON'T OWE ME THANKS.
IF YOU WANT TO THANK SOMEONE, THANK PROFESSOR PENTECOST!
IT WAS HIS IDEA TO ENCASE BLASTAAR IN THE ADAMANTIUM RUBBLE.
BUT THEN, YOU DON'T CARE ABOUT HIS IDEAS, DO YOU, BLAINE?
NOT ONCE THEY'VE GAINED YOU WHAT YOU WANT!
YOUR GREED HAS COST SCIENCE THE MIND OF A BRILLIANT MAN--
--AND, IF I WERE YOU, THAT'S A THOUGHT I COULDN'T LIVE WITH!
NEXT: SPIDER MAN... KA-ZAR... AND "THE COMING OF STEGRON, THE DINOSAUR MAN!"

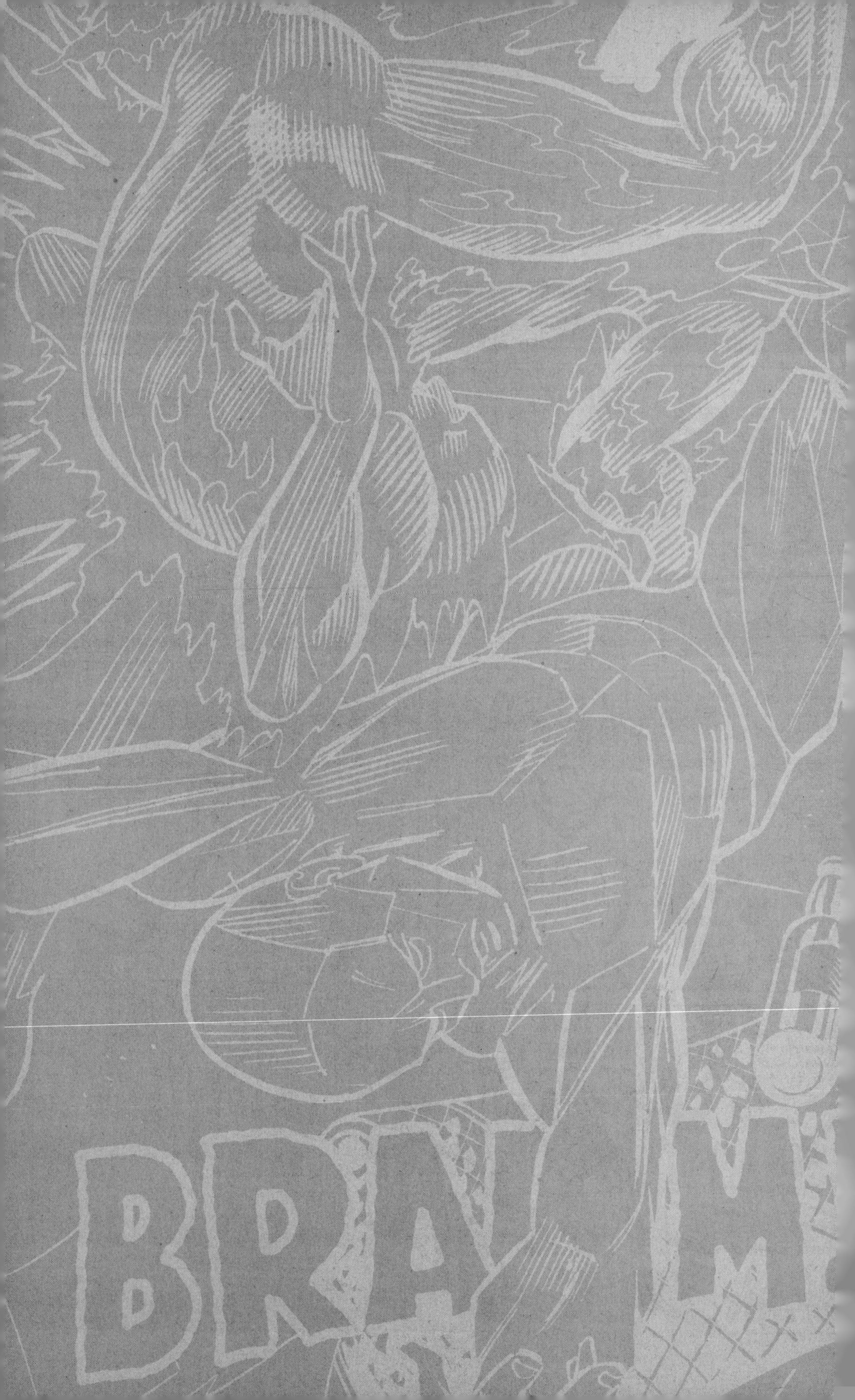

MARVEL TEAM-UP
MARVEL COMICS GROUP
APPROVED BY THE COMICS CODE AUTHORITY
20¢
19 MAR 02147
MARVEL TEAM-UP
FEATURING
SPIDER-MAN
AND
LORD OF THE HIDDEN JUNGLE
KA-ZAR
SLAUGHTER IN THE SAVAGE LAND!
Featuring: THE COMING OF
STEGRON, THE DINOSAUR MAN!

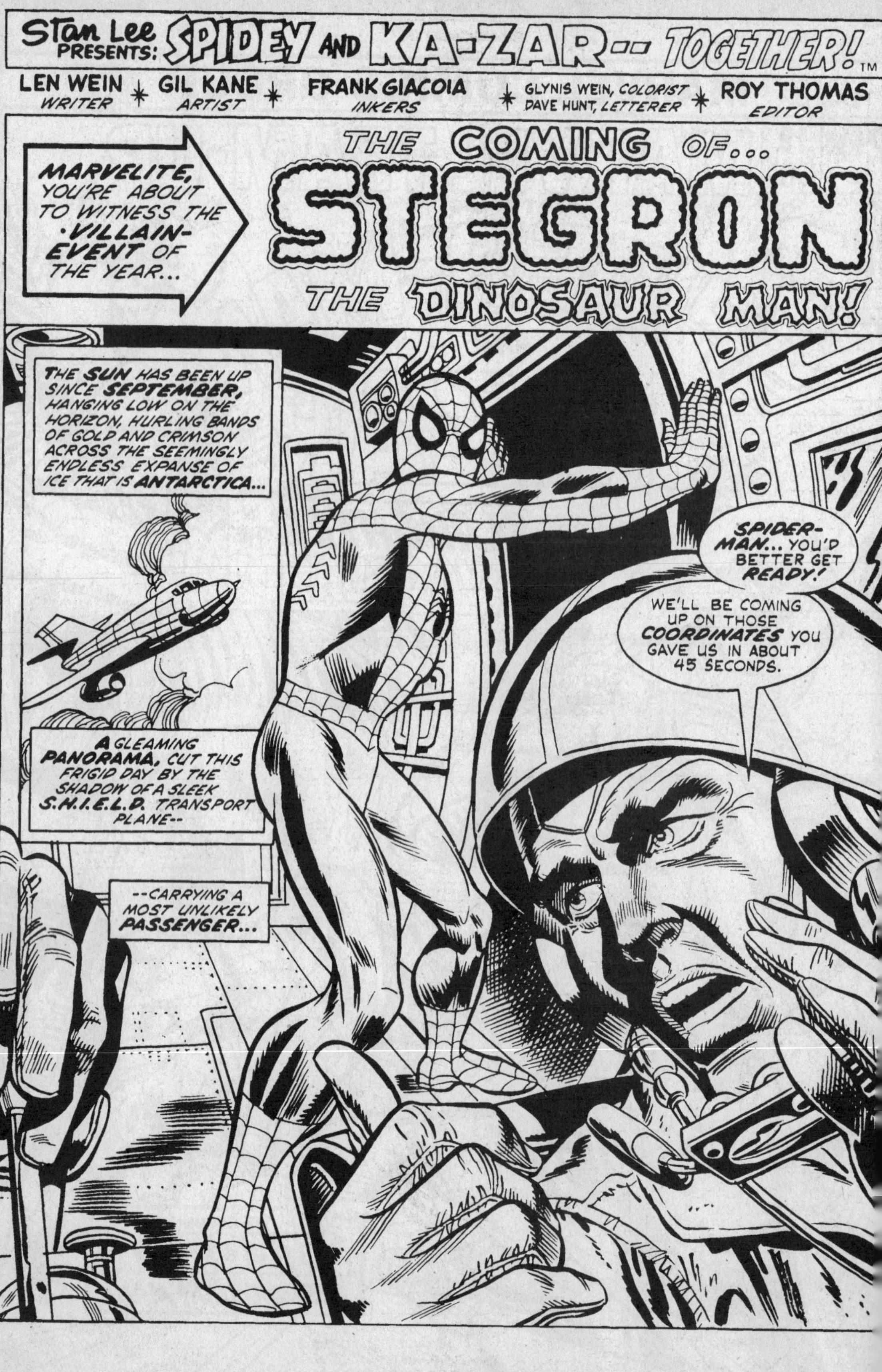
STAN LEE PRESENTS: SPIDEY AND KA-ZAR-- TOGETHER! TM
LEN WEIN WRITER ✦ GIL KANE ARTIST ✦ FRANK GIACOIA INKERS ✦ GLYNIS WEIN, COLORIST DAVE HUNT, LETTERER ✦ ROY THOMAS EDITOR
MARVELITE, YOU'RE ABOUT TO WITNESS THE ·VILLAIN-EVENT OF THE YEAR...
THE COMING OF... STEGRON THE DINOSAUR MAN!
THE SUN HAS BEEN UP SINCE SEPTEMBER, HANGING LOW ON THE HORIZON, HURLING BANDS OF GOLD AND CRIMSON ACROSS THE SEEMINGLY ENDLESS EXPANSE OF ICE THAT IS ANTARCTICA...
A GLEAMING PANORAMA, CUT THIS FRIGID DAY BY THE SHADOW OF A SLEEK S.H.I.E.L.D. TRANSPORT PLANE--
--CARRYING A MOST UNLIKELY PASSENGER...
SPIDER-MAN... YOU'D BETTER GET READY!
WE'LL BE COMING UP ON THOSE COORDINATES YOU GAVE US IN ABOUT 45 SECONDS.

C'MON, WEB-SLINGER-- HAUL IT! THERE'S NO TIME TO WASTE.

YOU'LL FIND A PARACHUTE SLUNG UNDER THE CARGO RACK.

PARACHUTE? THANKS, FELLA--

--BUT I DON'T THINK I'LL NEED ONE.

TAKE CARE NOW, HEAR?

"HARRY, H-HE DIDN'T JUST DO WHAT I THINK HE DID... DID HE?"

"NAH, CHARLIE, HE COULDN'T HAVE, HE ...JUST... COULDN'T ...HAVE..."

BETTER GET THIS LITTLE STUNT RIGHT THE FIRST TIME--

--OR I'M GONNA MAKE ONE HECK OF A PANCAKE LANDING.

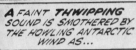

A FAINT THWIPPING SOUND IS SMOTHERED BY THE HOWLING ANTARCTIC WIND AS...

THE TEMPERATURE DOWN HERE ON AN AVERAGE DAY IS ABOUT 20 BELOW ZERO--

--AND EVEN THRU THE SPECIAL INSULATION I DEVISED FOR MY COSTUME--BROTHER, I CAN FEEL--!

HEY, THERE IT IS-- THE ETERNAL VEIL OF MIST THAT HIDES THE SECRET ENTRANCE TO-- THE SAVAGE LAND!

PRESTO... ONE WEB-WOVEN SPIDEY-PARACHUTE... GUARANTEED NOT TO WEAR--TEAR-- OR SPILL SPIDERS THRU THE AIR...

...I HOPE.

IF THE COORDINATES I REMEMBERED FROM MY TRIP HERE WITH J. JONAH JAMESON AREN'T CORRECT--*

--THERE'S GONNA BE ONE FLASH-FROZEN WEB-SLINGER STUCK IN THE ICE A FEW MINUTES FROM NOW.

*ANYBODY HERE RECALL THAT BOLD EXPEDITION FROM SPIDER-MAN #103-104? --BRING-'EM-BACK-ALIVE ROY.

HOW DO I GET MYSELF INTO THESE THINGS?

NEXT TIME I VOLUNTEER TO DO A FAVOR FOR A FRIEND, WILL SOMEBODY PLEASE KICK ME...?

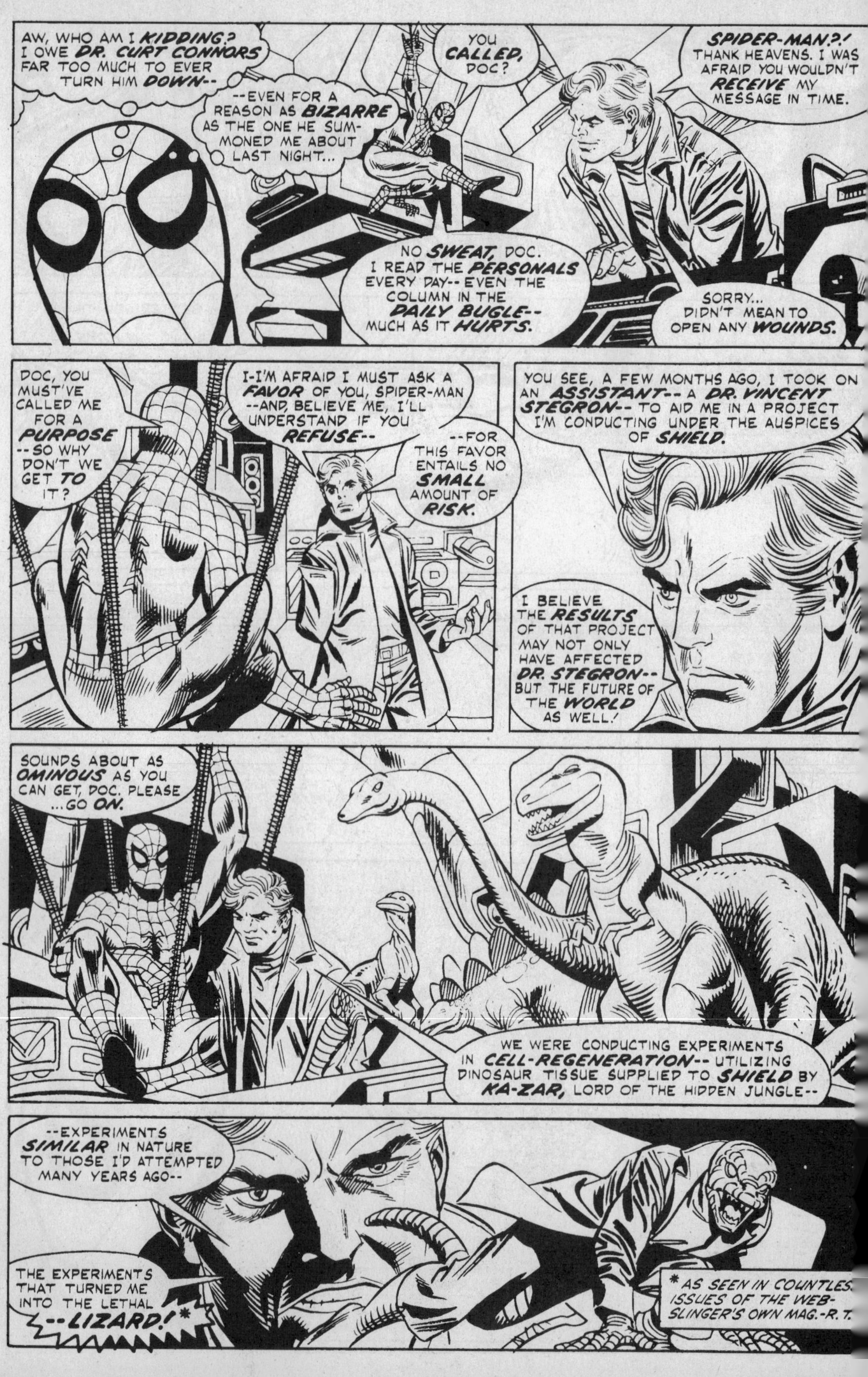
AW, WHO AM I KIDDING? I OWE DR. CURT CONNORS FAR TOO MUCH TO EVER TURN HIM DOWN--
--EVEN FOR A REASON AS BIZARRE AS THE ONE HE SUMMONED ME ABOUT LAST NIGHT...
YOU CALLED, DOC?
SPIDER-MAN?! THANK HEAVENS. I WAS AFRAID YOU WOULDN'T RECEIVE MY MESSAGE IN TIME.
NO SWEAT, DOC. I READ THE PERSONALS EVERY DAY-- EVEN THE COLUMN IN THE DAILY BUGLE-- MUCH AS IT HURTS.
SORRY... DIDN'T MEAN TO OPEN ANY WOUNDS.
DOC, YOU MUST'VE CALLED ME FOR A PURPOSE --SO WHY DON'T WE GET TO IT?
I-I'M AFRAID I MUST ASK A FAVOR OF YOU, SPIDER-MAN --AND, BELIEVE ME, I'LL UNDERSTAND IF YOU REFUSE--
--FOR THIS FAVOR ENTAILS NO SMALL AMOUNT OF RISK.
YOU SEE, A FEW MONTHS AGO, I TOOK ON AN ASSISTANT-- A DR. VINCENT STEGRON-- TO AID ME IN A PROJECT I'M CONDUCTING UNDER THE AUSPICES OF SHIELD.
I BELIEVE THE RESULTS OF THAT PROJECT MAY NOT ONLY HAVE AFFECTED DR. STEGRON-- BUT THE FUTURE OF THE WORLD AS WELL!
SOUNDS ABOUT AS OMINOUS AS YOU CAN GET, DOC. PLEASE ...GO ON.
WE WERE CONDUCTING EXPERIMENTS IN CELL-REGENERATION-- UTILIZING DINOSAUR TISSUE SUPPLIED TO SHIELD BY KA-ZAR, LORD OF THE HIDDEN JUNGLE--
--EXPERIMENTS SIMILAR IN NATURE TO THOSE I'D ATTEMPTED MANY YEARS AGO--
THE EXPERIMENTS THAT TURNED ME INTO THE LETHAL --LIZARD!*
*AS SEEN IN COUNTLESS ISSUES OF THE WEB-SLINGER'S OWN MAG.-R.T.

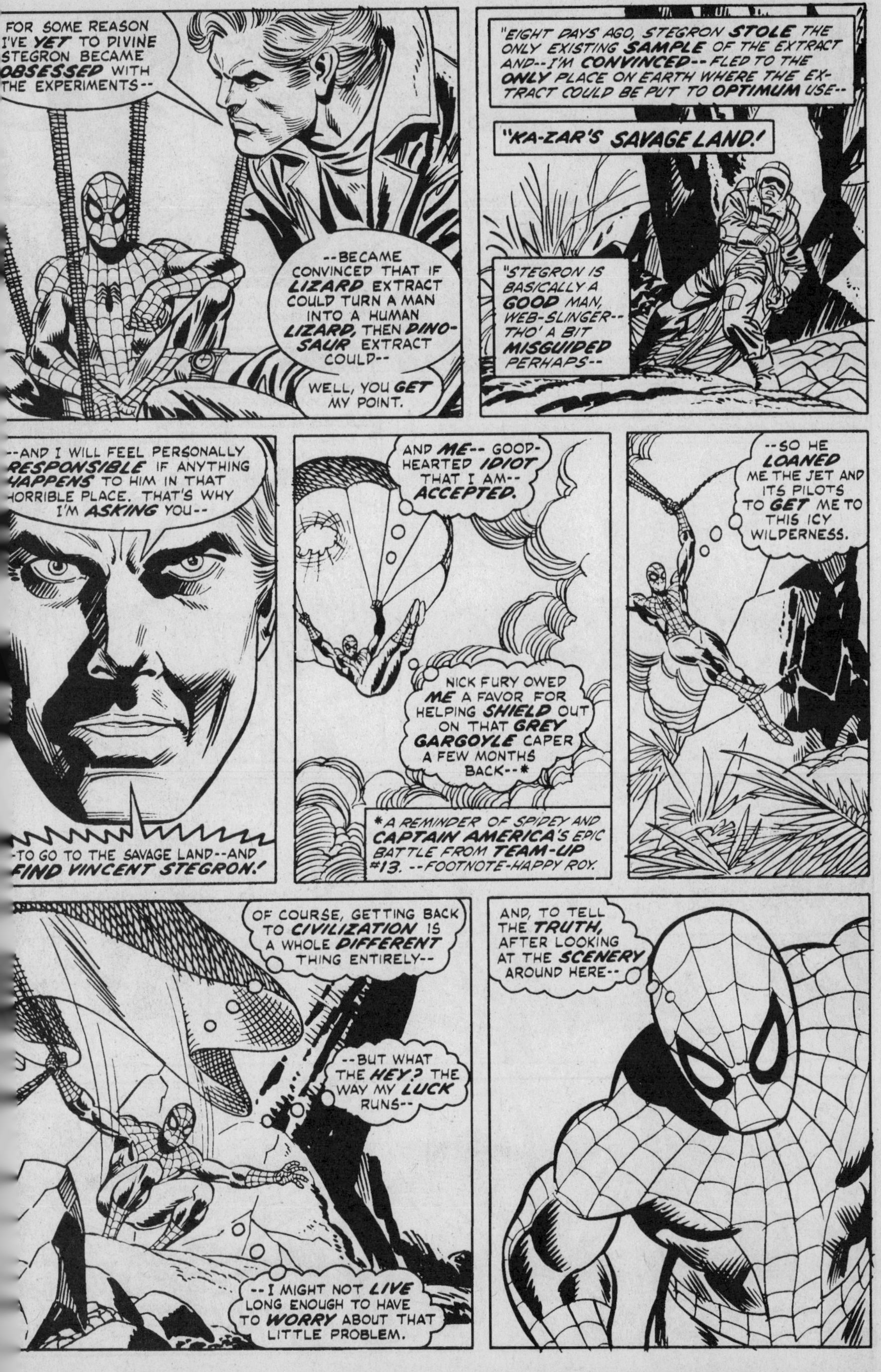
FOR SOME REASON I'VE YET TO DIVINE STEGRON BECAME OBSESSED WITH THE EXPERIMENTS--
--BECAME CONVINCED THAT IF LIZARD EXTRACT COULD TURN A MAN INTO A HUMAN LIZARD, THEN DINO-SAUR EXTRACT COULD--
WELL, YOU GET MY POINT.
"EIGHT DAYS AGO, STEGRON STOLE THE ONLY EXISTING SAMPLE OF THE EXTRACT AND--I'M CONVINCED--FLED TO THE ONLY PLACE ON EARTH WHERE THE EX-TRACT COULD BE PUT TO OPTIMUM USE--
"KA-ZAR'S SAVAGE LAND!
"STEGRON IS BASICALLY A GOOD MAN, WEB-SLINGER--THO' A BIT MISGUIDED PERHAPS--
--AND I WILL FEEL PERSONALLY RESPONSIBLE IF ANYTHING HAPPENS TO HIM IN THAT HORRIBLE PLACE. THAT'S WHY I'M ASKING YOU--
-TO GO TO THE SAVAGE LAND--AND FIND VINCENT STEGRON!
AND ME-- GOOD-HEARTED IDIOT THAT I AM-- ACCEPTED.
NICK FURY OWED ME A FAVOR FOR HELPING SHIELD OUT ON THAT GREY GARGOYLE CAPER A FEW MONTHS BACK--*
*A REMINDER OF SPIDEY AND CAPTAIN AMERICA'S EPIC BATTLE FROM TEAM-UP #13. --FOOTNOTE-HAPPY ROY.
--SO HE LOANED ME THE JET AND ITS PILOTS TO GET ME TO THIS ICY WILDERNESS.
OF COURSE, GETTING BACK TO CIVILIZATION IS A WHOLE DIFFERENT THING ENTIRELY--
--BUT WHAT THE HEY? THE WAY MY LUCK RUNS--
--I MIGHT NOT LIVE LONG ENOUGH TO HAVE TO WORRY ABOUT THAT LITTLE PROBLEM.
AND, TO TELL THE TRUTH, AFTER LOOKING AT THE SCENERY AROUND HERE--

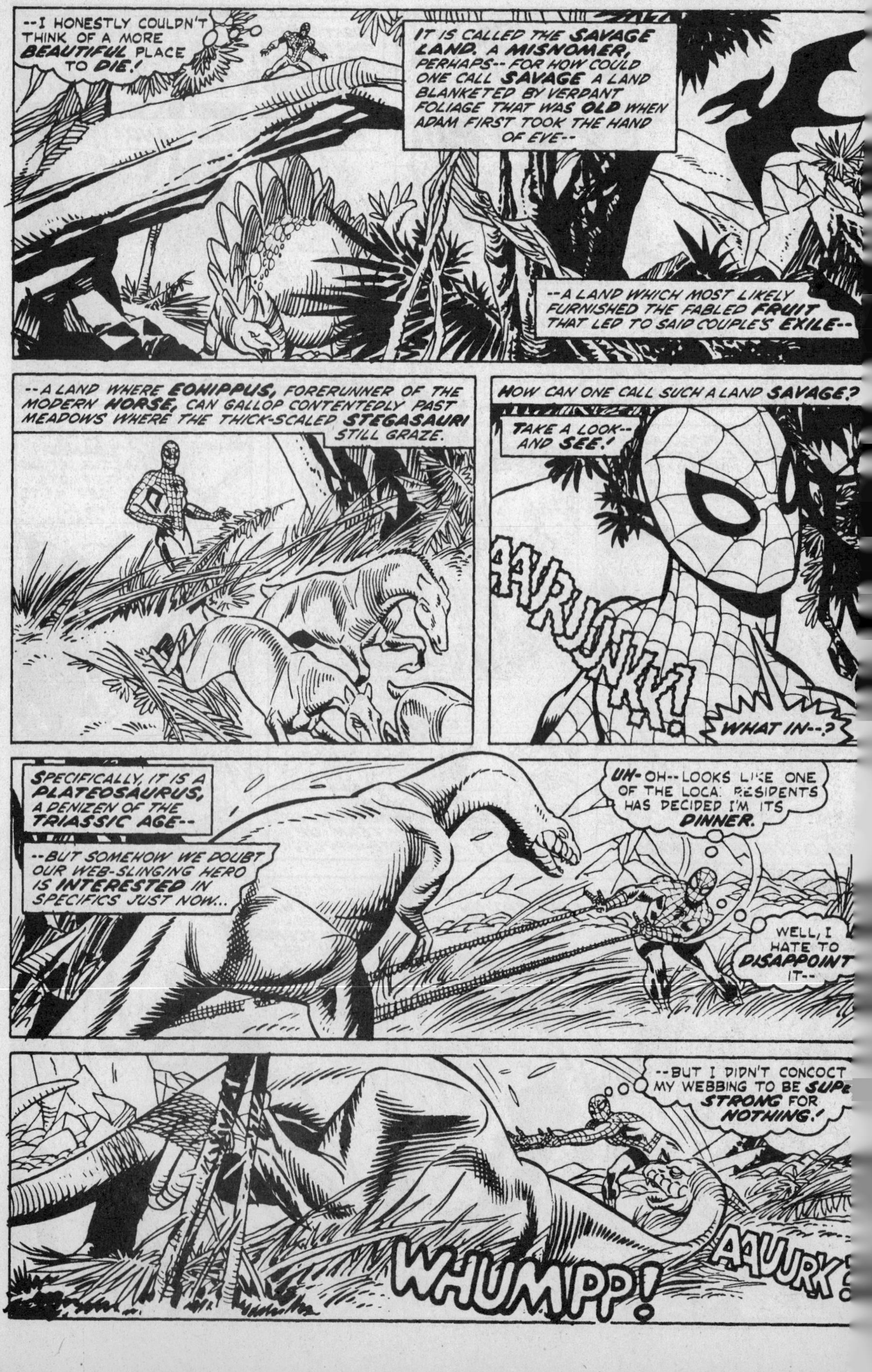
--I HONESTLY COULDN'T THINK OF A MORE BEAUTIFUL PLACE TO DIE!
IT IS CALLED THE SAVAGE LAND. A MISNOMER, PERHAPS-- FOR HOW COULD ONE CALL SAVAGE A LAND BLANKETED BY VERDANT FOLIAGE THAT WAS OLD WHEN ADAM FIRST TOOK THE HAND OF EVE--
--A LAND WHICH MOST LIKELY FURNISHED THE FABLED FRUIT THAT LED TO SAID COUPLE'S EXILE--
--A LAND WHERE EOHIPPUS, FORERUNNER OF THE MODERN HORSE, CAN GALLOP CONTENTEDLY PAST MEADOWS WHERE THE THICK-SCALED STEGASAURI STILL GRAZE.
HOW CAN ONE CALL SUCH A LAND SAVAGE?
TAKE A LOOK-- AND SEE!
AAVRUNKK!
WHAT IN--?
SPECIFICALLY, IT IS A PLATEOSAURUS, A DENIZEN OF THE TRIASSIC AGE--
--BUT SOMEHOW WE DOUBT OUR WEB-SLINGING HERO IS INTERESTED IN SPECIFICS JUST NOW...
UH-OH-- LOOKS LIKE ONE OF THE LOCAL RESIDENTS HAS DECIDED I'M ITS DINNER.
WELL, I HATE TO DISAPPOINT IT--
--BUT I DIDN'T CONCOCT MY WEBBING TO BE SUPE STRONG FOR NOTHING!
WHUMPP!
AAURK!

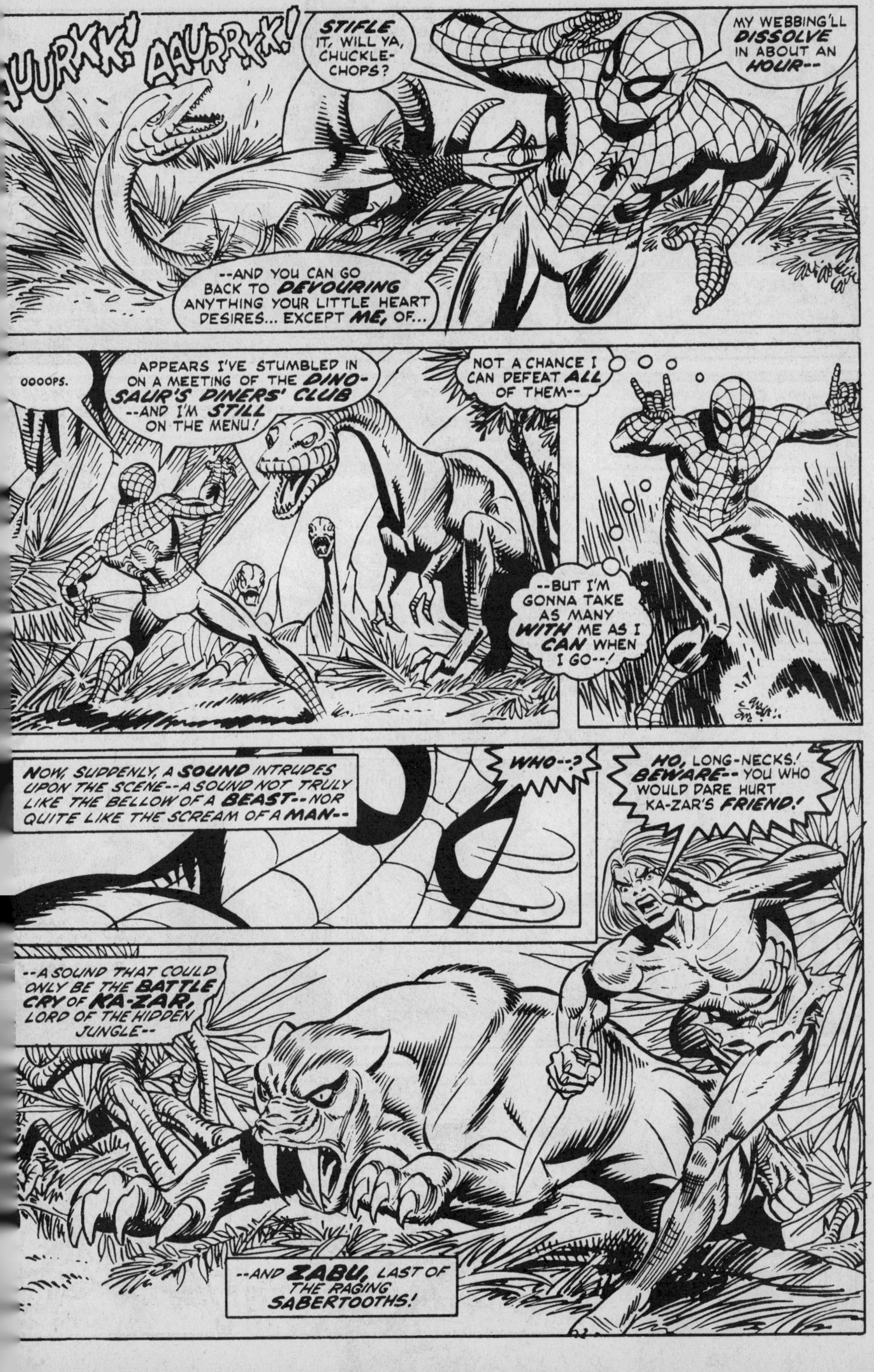
UURKK! AAURRKK!
STIFLE IT, WILL YA, CHUCKLE-CHOPS?
MY WEBBING'LL DISSOLVE IN ABOUT AN HOUR--
--AND YOU CAN GO BACK TO DEVOURING ANYTHING YOUR LITTLE HEART DESIRES... EXCEPT ME, OF...
OOOOPS.
APPEARS I'VE STUMBLED IN ON A MEETING OF THE DINO-SAUR'S DINERS' CLUB --AND I'M STILL ON THE MENU!
NOT A CHANCE I CAN DEFEAT ALL OF THEM--
--BUT I'M GONNA TAKE AS MANY WITH ME AS I CAN WHEN I GO--!
NOW, SUDDENLY, A SOUND INTRUDES UPON THE SCENE--A SOUND NOT TRULY LIKE THE BELLOW OF A BEAST--NOR QUITE LIKE THE SCREAM OF A MAN--
WHO--?
HO, LONG-NECKS! BEWARE-- YOU WHO WOULD DARE HURT KA-ZAR'S FRIEND!
--A SOUND THAT COULD ONLY BE THE BATTLE CRY OF KA-ZAR, LORD OF THE HIDDEN JUNGLE--
--AND ZABU, LAST OF THE RAGING SABERTOOTHS!

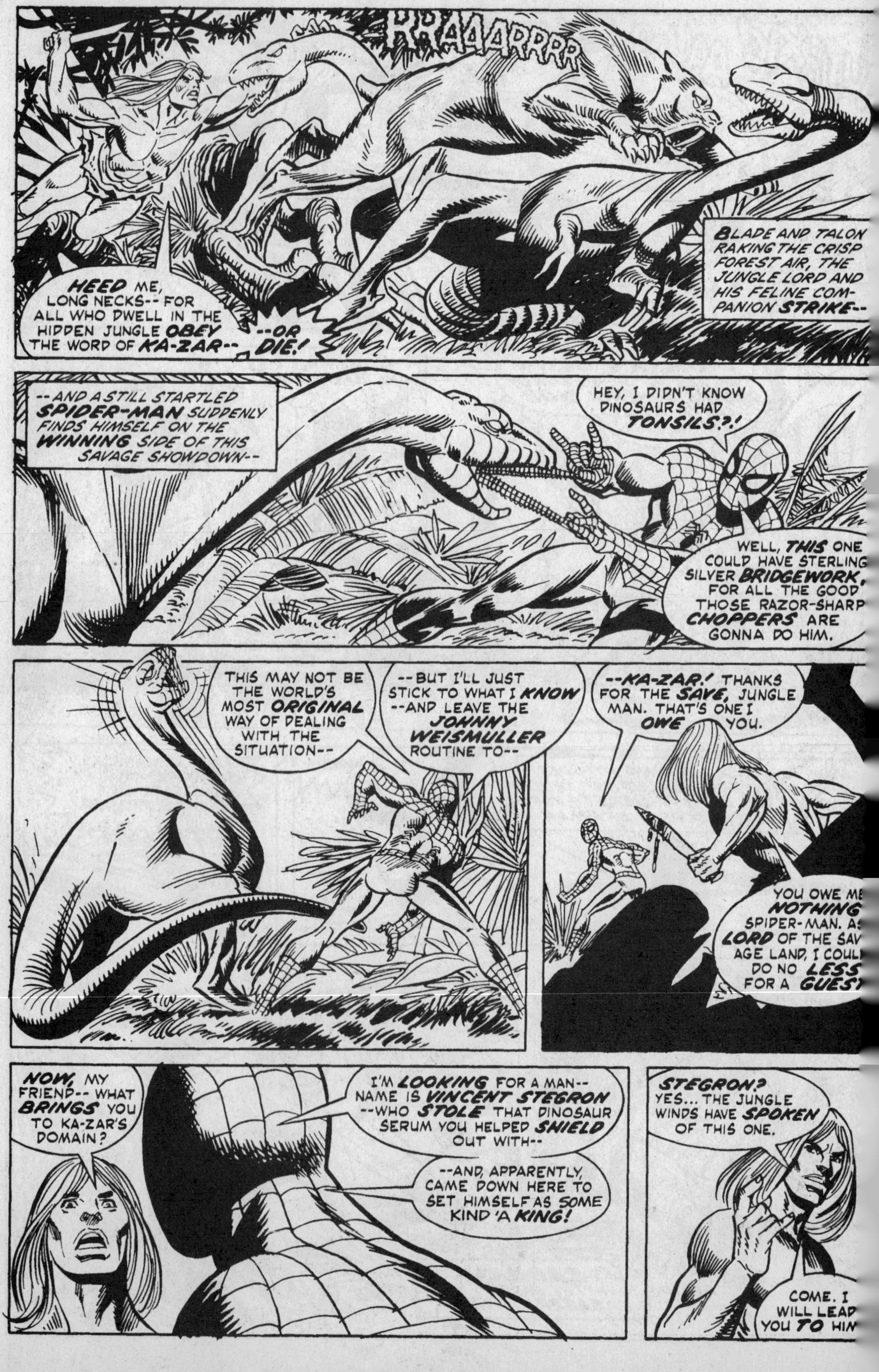
KRAAAARRRR
HEED ME, LONG NECKS-- FOR ALL WHO DWELL IN THE HIDDEN JUNGLE OBEY THE WORD OF KA-ZAR--
--OR DIE!
BLADE AND TALON RAKING THE CRISP FOREST AIR, THE JUNGLE LORD AND HIS FELINE COMPANION STRIKE--
--AND A STILL STARTLED SPIDER-MAN SUDDENLY FINDS HIMSELF ON THE WINNING SIDE OF THIS SAVAGE SHOWDOWN--
HEY, I DIDN'T KNOW DINOSAURS HAD TONSILS?!
WELL, THIS ONE COULD HAVE STERLING SILVER BRIDGEWORK, FOR ALL THE GOOD THOSE RAZOR-SHARP CHOPPERS ARE GONNA DO HIM.
THIS MAY NOT BE THE WORLD'S MOST ORIGINAL WAY OF DEALING WITH THE SITUATION--
--BUT I'LL JUST STICK TO WHAT I KNOW --AND LEAVE THE JOHNNY WEISMULLER ROUTINE TO--
--KA-ZAR! THANKS FOR THE SAVE, JUNGLE MAN. THAT'S ONE I OWE YOU.
YOU OWE ME NOTHING SPIDER-MAN. AS LORD OF THE SAV AGE LAND, I COUL DO NO LESS FOR A GUES
NOW, MY FRIEND-- WHAT BRINGS YOU TO KA-ZAR'S DOMAIN?
I'M LOOKING FOR A MAN-- NAME IS VINCENT STEGRON --WHO STOLE THAT DINOSAUR SERUM YOU HELPED SHIELD OUT WITH--
--AND, APPARENTLY, CAME DOWN HERE TO SET HIMSELF AS SOME KIND 'A KING!
STEGRON? YES... THE JUNGLE WINDS HAVE SPOKEN OF THIS ONE.
COME. I WILL LEAD YOU TO HIM

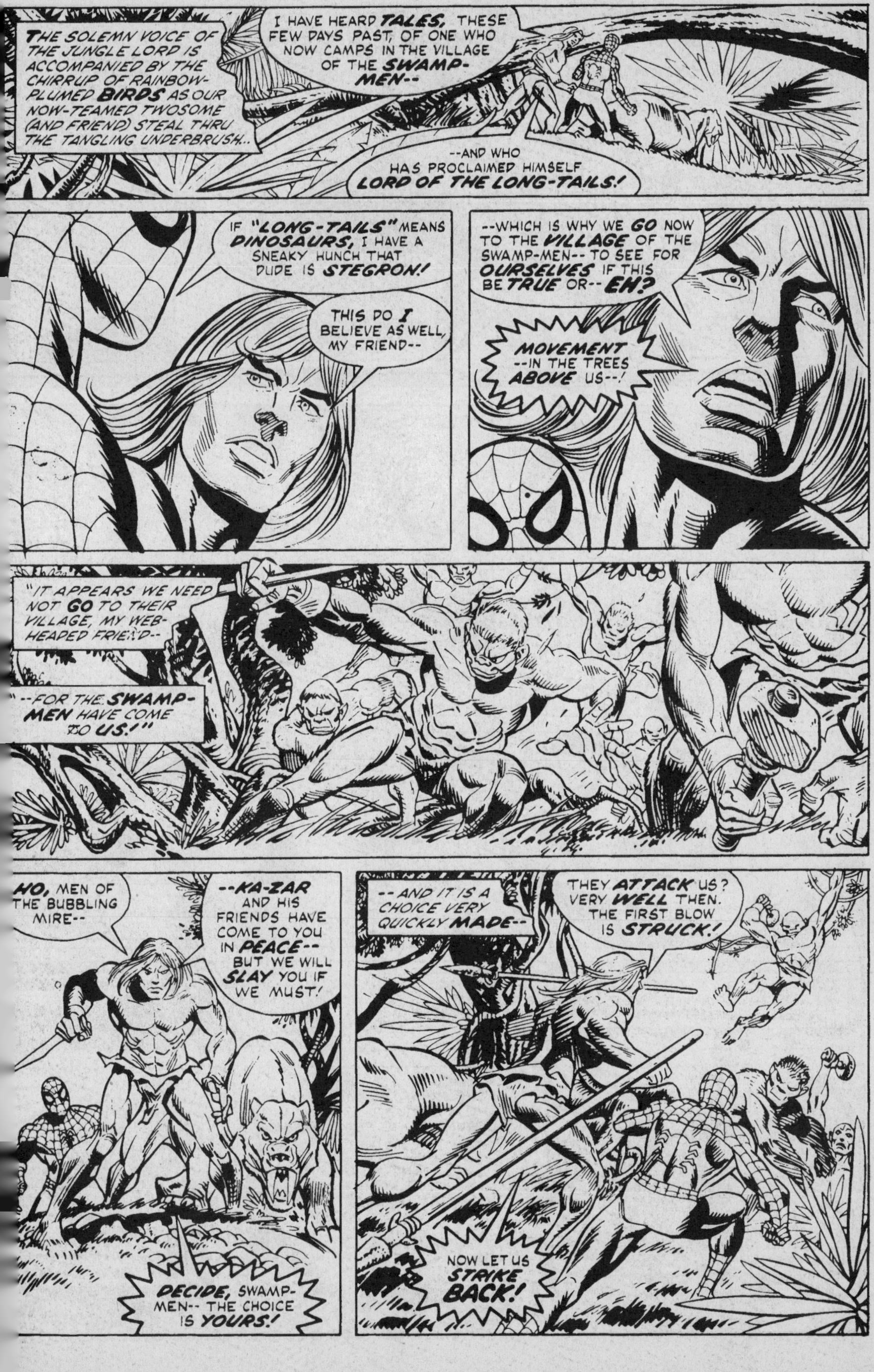
THE SOLEMN VOICE OF THE JUNGLE LORD IS ACCOMPANIED BY THE CHIRRUP OF RAINBOW-PLUMED BIRDS AS OUR NOW-TEAMED TWOSOME (AND FRIEND) STEAL THRU THE TANGLING UNDERBRUSH...
I HAVE HEARD TALES, THESE FEW DAYS PAST, OF ONE WHO NOW CAMPS IN THE VILLAGE OF THE SWAMP-MEN--
--AND WHO HAS PROCLAIMED HIMSELF LORD OF THE LONG-TAILS!
IF "LONG-TAILS" MEANS DINOSAURS, I HAVE A SNEAKY HUNCH THAT DUDE IS STEGRON!
THIS DO I BELIEVE AS WELL, MY FRIEND--
--WHICH IS WHY WE GO NOW TO THE VILLAGE OF THE SWAMP-MEN-- TO SEE FOR OURSELVES IF THIS BE TRUE OR-- EH?
MOVEMENT --IN THE TREES ABOVE US--!
"IT APPEARS WE NEED NOT GO TO THEIR VILLAGE, MY WEB-HEADED FRIEND--
--FOR THE SWAMP-MEN HAVE COME TO US!"
HO, MEN OF THE BUBBLING MIRE--
--KA-ZAR AND HIS FRIENDS HAVE COME TO YOU IN PEACE-- BUT WE WILL SLAY YOU IF WE MUST!
DECIDE, SWAMP-MEN-- THE CHOICE IS YOURS!
--AND IT IS A CHOICE VERY QUICKLY MADE--
THEY ATTACK US? VERY WELL THEN. THE FIRST BLOW IS STRUCK!
NOW LET US STRIKE BACK!

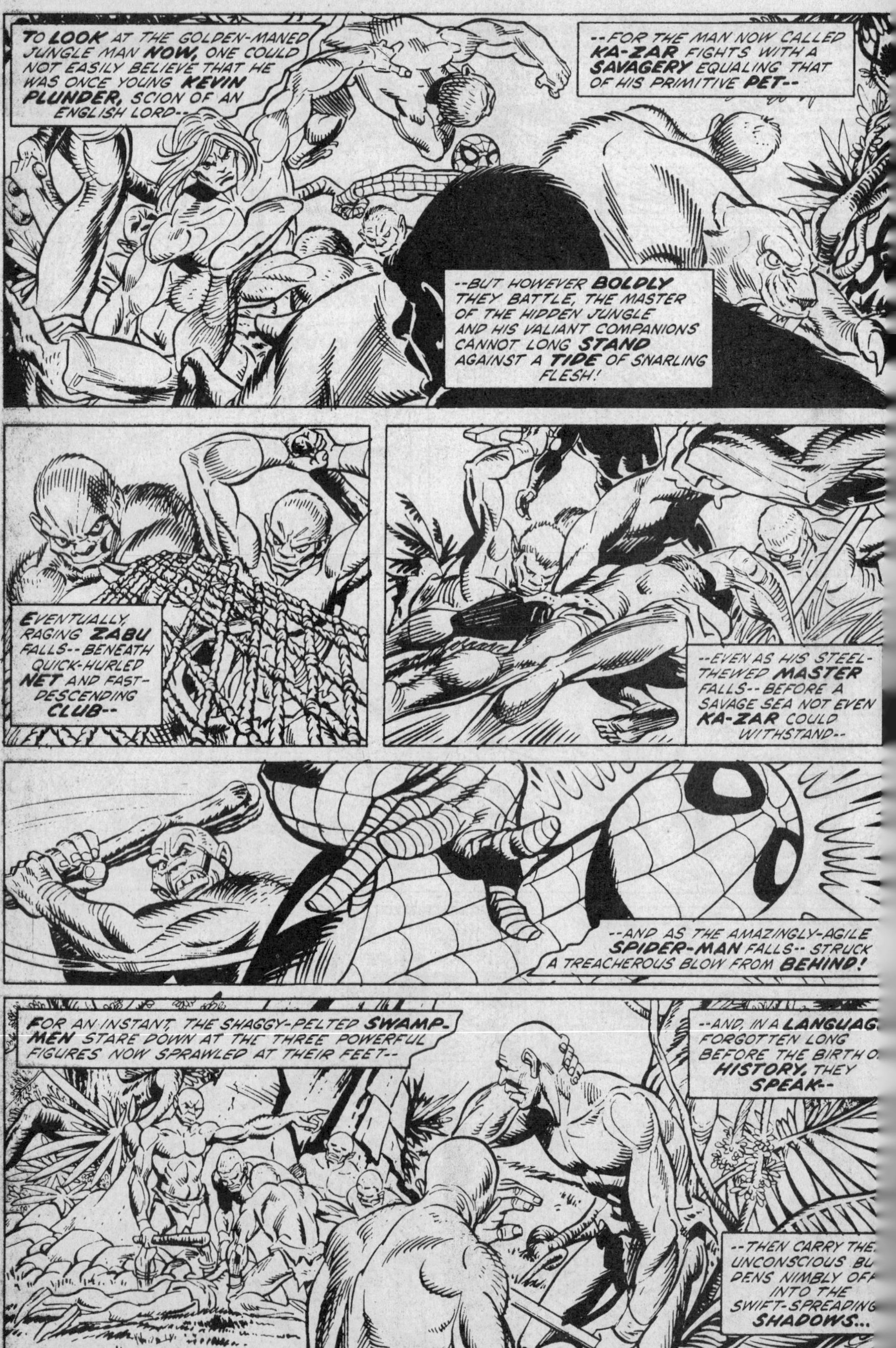
TO LOOK AT THE GOLDEN-MANED JUNGLE MAN NOW, ONE COULD NOT EASILY BELIEVE THAT HE WAS ONCE YOUNG KEVIN PLUNDER, SCION OF AN ENGLISH LORD--
--FOR THE MAN NOW CALLED KA-ZAR FIGHTS WITH A SAVAGERY EQUALING THAT OF HIS PRIMITIVE PET--
--BUT HOWEVER BOLDLY THEY BATTLE, THE MASTER OF THE HIDDEN JUNGLE AND HIS VALIANT COMPANIONS CANNOT LONG STAND AGAINST A TIDE OF SNARLING FLESH!
EVENTUALLY, RAGING ZABU FALLS--BENEATH QUICK-HURLED NET AND FAST-DESCENDING CLUB--
--EVEN AS HIS STEEL-THEWED MASTER FALLS--BEFORE A SAVAGE SEA NOT EVEN KA-ZAR COULD WITHSTAND--
--AND AS THE AMAZINGLY-AGILE SPIDER-MAN FALLS--STRUCK A TREACHEROUS BLOW FROM BEHIND!
FOR AN INSTANT, THE SHAGGY-PELTED SWAMP-MEN STARE DOWN AT THE THREE POWERFUL FIGURES NOW SPRAWLED AT THEIR FEET--
--AND, IN A LANGUAG FORGOTTEN LONG BEFORE THE BIRTH O HISTORY, THEY SPEAK--
--THEN CARRY THE UNCONSCIOUS BU DENS NIMBLY OFF INTO THE SWIFT-SPREADING SHADOWS...

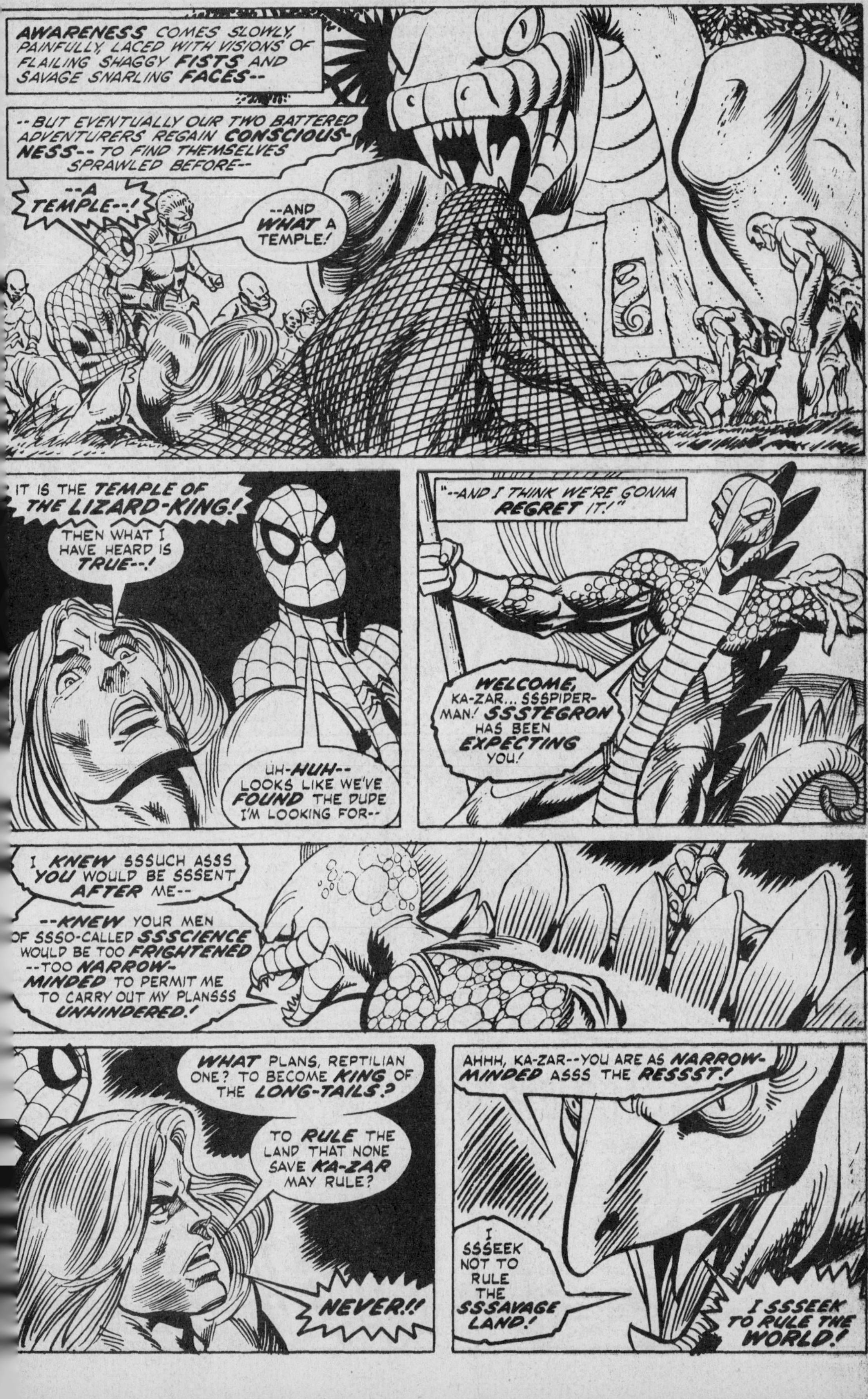
AWARENESS COMES SLOWLY, PAINFULLY, LACED WITH VISIONS OF FLAILING SHAGGY FISTS AND SAVAGE SNARLING FACES--
--BUT EVENTUALLY OUR TWO BATTERED ADVENTURERS REGAIN CONSCIOUSNESS-- TO FIND THEMSELVES SPRAWLED BEFORE--
--A TEMPLE--!
--AND WHAT A TEMPLE!
IT IS THE TEMPLE OF THE LIZARD-KING!
THEN WHAT I HAVE HEARD IS TRUE--!
UH-HUH-- LOOKS LIKE WE'VE FOUND THE DUDE I'M LOOKING FOR--
"--AND I THINK WE'RE GONNA REGRET IT!"
WELCOME, KA-ZAR... SSSPIDER-MAN! SSSTEGRON HAS BEEN EXPECTING YOU!
I KNEW SSSUCH ASSS YOU WOULD BE SSSENT AFTER ME--
--KNEW YOUR MEN OF SSSO-CALLED SSSCIENCE WOULD BE TOO FRIGHTENED --TOO NARROW-MINDED TO PERMIT ME TO CARRY OUT MY PLANSSS UNHINDERED!
WHAT PLANS, REPTILIAN ONE? TO BECOME KING OF THE LONG-TAILS?
TO RULE THE LAND THAT NONE SAVE KA-ZAR MAY RULE?
NEVER!!
AHHH, KA-ZAR--YOU ARE AS NARROW-MINDED ASSS THE RESSST!
I SSSEEK NOT TO RULE THE SSSAVAGE LAND!
I SSSEEK TO RULE THE WORLD!

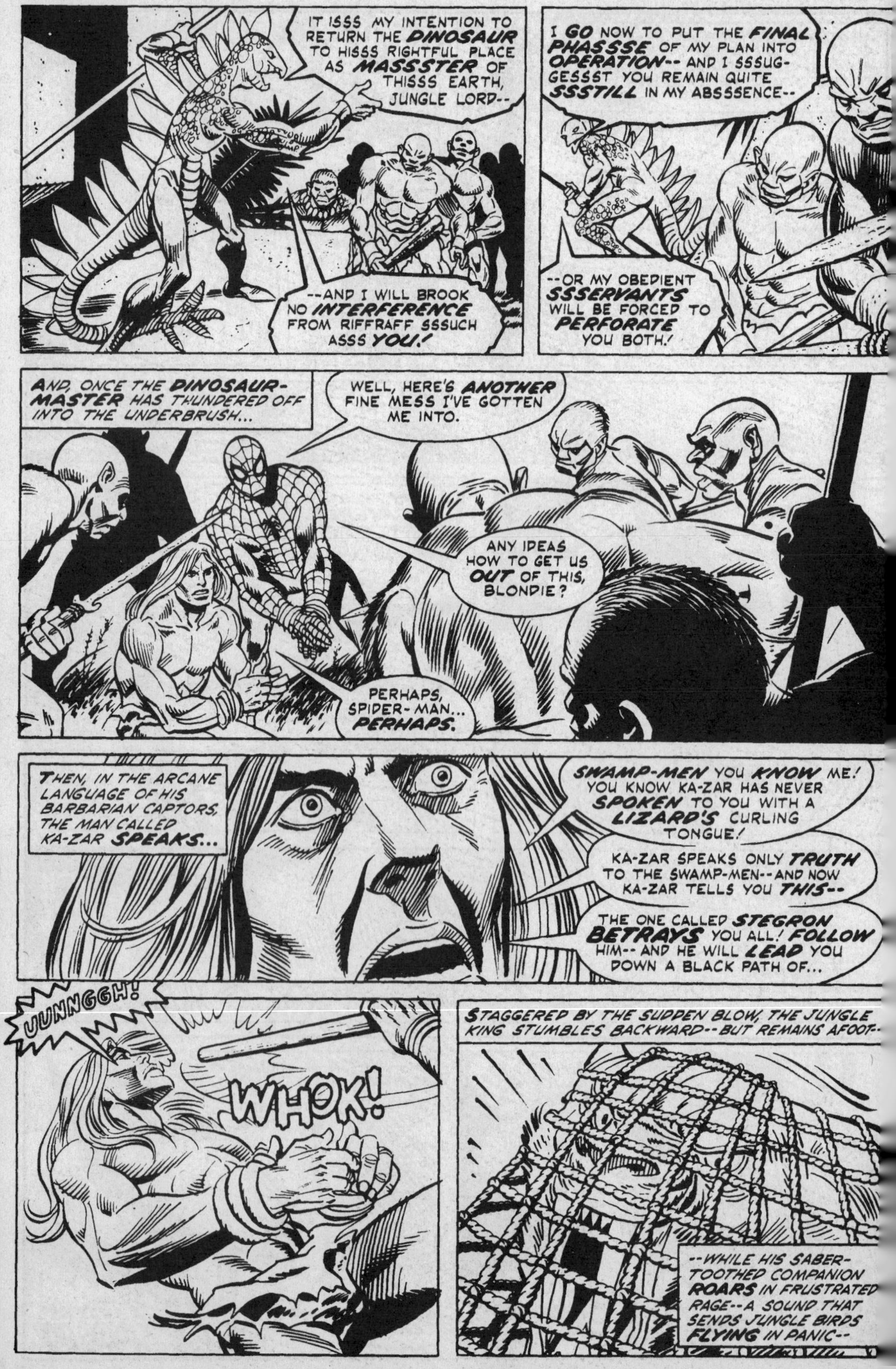
IT ISSS MY INTENTION TO RETURN THE DINOSAUR TO HISSS RIGHTFUL PLACE AS MASSSTER OF THISSS EARTH, JUNGLE LORD--
--AND I WILL BROOK NO INTERFERENCE FROM RIFFRAFF SSSUCH ASSS YOU!
I GO NOW TO PUT THE FINAL PHASSSE OF MY PLAN INTO OPERATION-- AND I SSSUGGESSST YOU REMAIN QUITE SSSTILL IN MY ABSSSENCE--
--OR MY OBEDIENT SSSERVANTS WILL BE FORCED TO PERFORATE YOU BOTH!
AND, ONCE THE DINOSAUR-MASTER HAS THUNDERED OFF INTO THE UNDERBRUSH...
WELL, HERE'S ANOTHER FINE MESS I'VE GOTTEN ME INTO.
ANY IDEAS HOW TO GET US OUT OF THIS, BLONDIE?
PERHAPS, SPIDER-MAN... PERHAPS.
THEN, IN THE ARCANE LANGUAGE OF HIS BARBARIAN CAPTORS, THE MAN CALLED KA-ZAR SPEAKS...
SWAMP-MEN YOU KNOW ME! YOU KNOW KA-ZAR HAS NEVER SPOKEN TO YOU WITH A LIZARD'S CURLING TONGUE!
KA-ZAR SPEAKS ONLY TRUTH TO THE SWAMP-MEN--AND NOW KA-ZAR TELLS YOU THIS--
THE ONE CALLED STEGRON BETRAYS YOU ALL! FOLLOW HIM-- AND HE WILL LEAD YOU DOWN A BLACK PATH OF...
UUNNGGH!
WHOK!
STAGGERED BY THE SUDDEN BLOW, THE JUNGLE KING STUMBLES BACKWARD--BUT REMAINS AFOOT--
--WHILE HIS SABER-TOOTHED COMPANION ROARS IN FRUSTRATED RAGE--A SOUND THAT SENDS JUNGLE BIRDS FLYING IN PANIC--

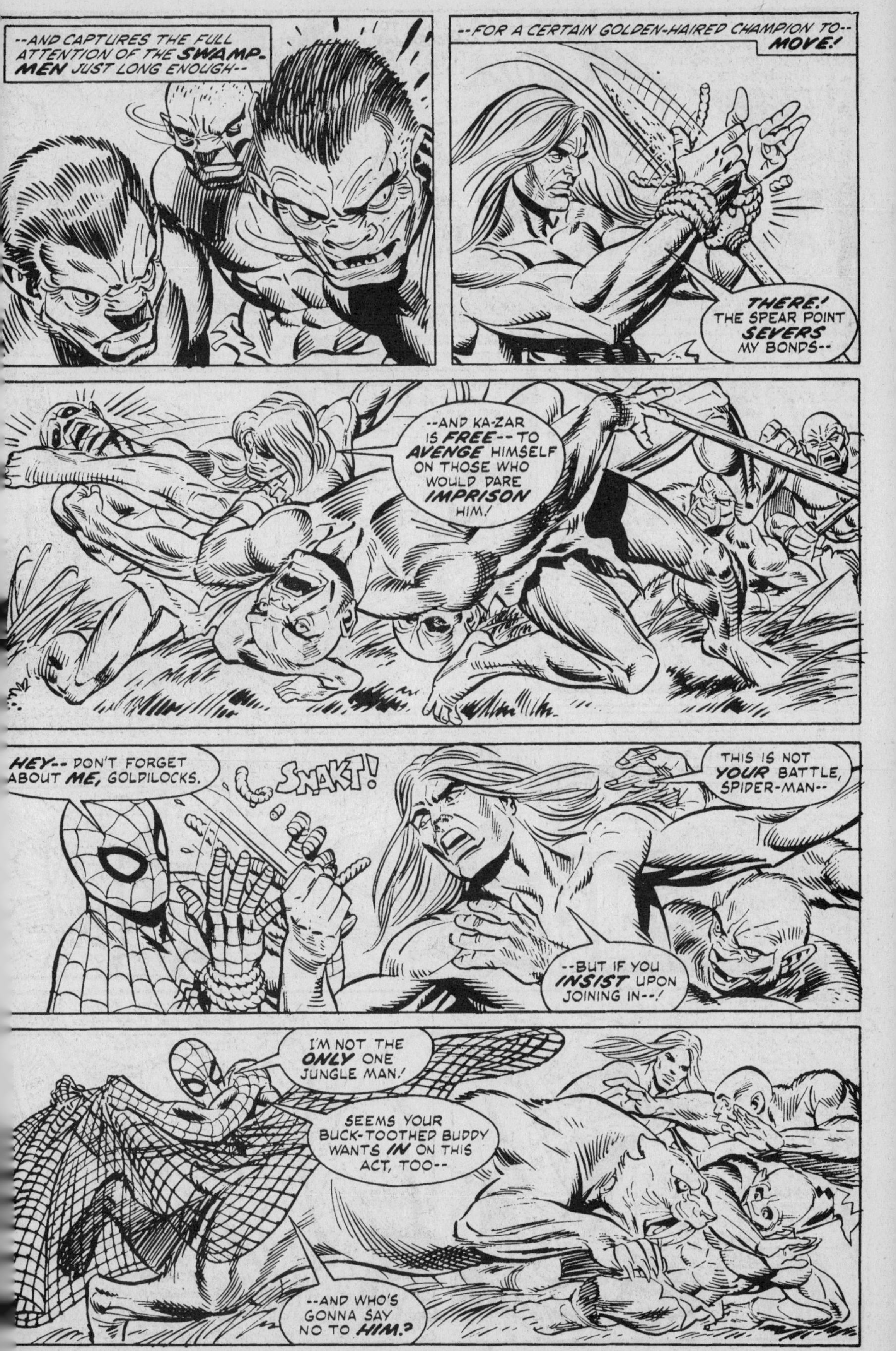
--AND CAPTURES THE FULL ATTENTION OF THE SWAMP-MEN JUST LONG ENOUGH--
--FOR A CERTAIN GOLDEN-HAIRED CHAMPION TO--MOVE!
THERE! THE SPEAR POINT SEVERS MY BONDS--
--AND KA-ZAR IS FREE--TO AVENGE HIMSELF ON THOSE WHO WOULD DARE IMPRISON HIM!
HEY-- DON'T FORGET ABOUT ME, GOLDILOCKS.
SNAKT!
THIS IS NOT YOUR BATTLE, SPIDER-MAN--
--BUT IF YOU INSIST UPON JOINING IN--!
I'M NOT THE ONLY ONE JUNGLE MAN!
SEEMS YOUR BUCK-TOOTHED BUDDY WANTS IN ON THIS ACT, TOO--
--AND WHO'S GONNA SAY NO TO HIM?

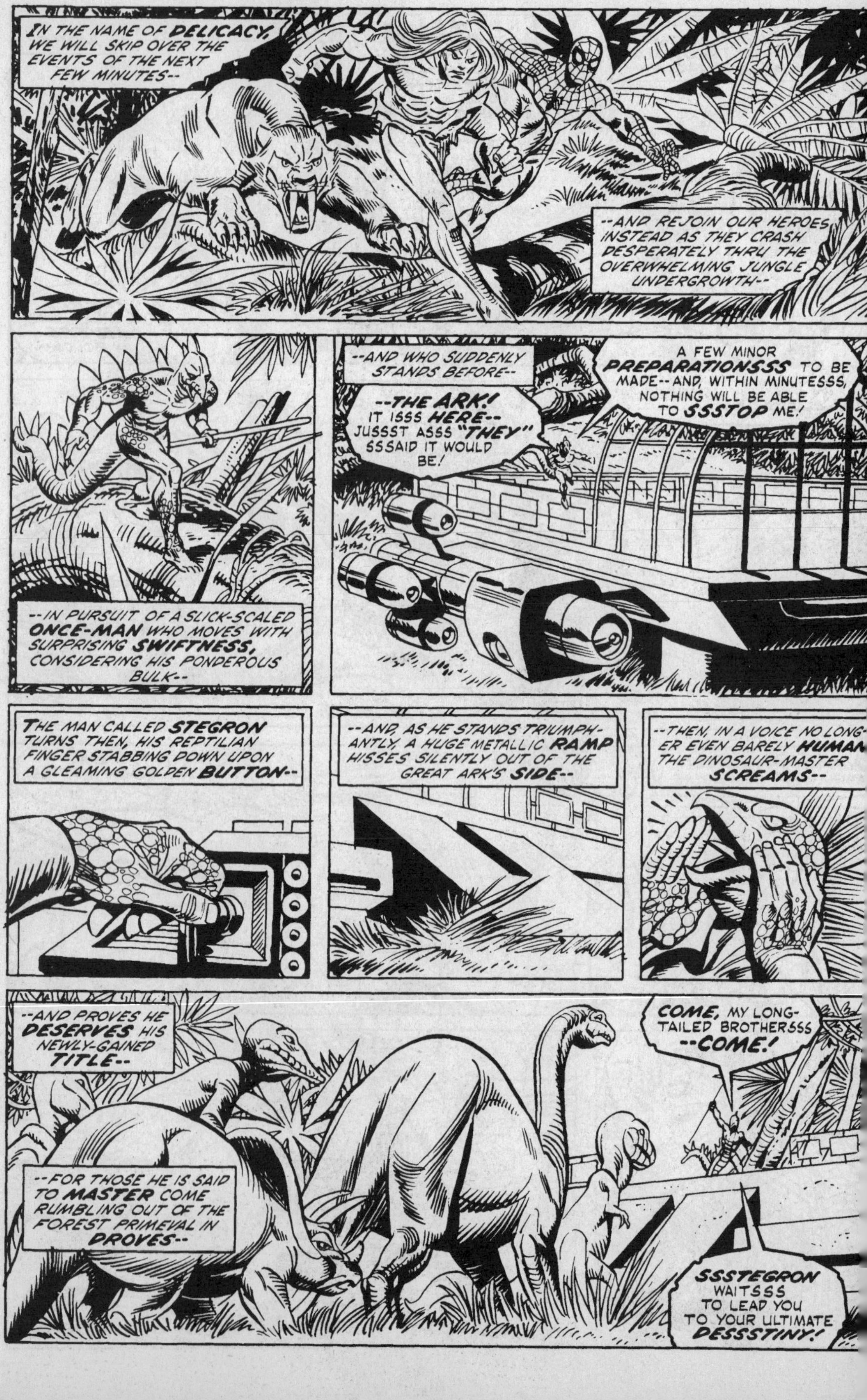
IN THE NAME OF DELICACY, WE WILL SKIP OVER THE EVENTS OF THE NEXT FEW MINUTES--
--AND REJOIN OUR HEROES INSTEAD AS THEY CRASH DESPERATELY THRU THE OVERWHELMING JUNGLE UNDERGROWTH--
--IN PURSUIT OF A SLICK-SCALED ONCE-MAN WHO MOVES WITH SURPRISING SWIFTNESS, CONSIDERING HIS PONDEROUS BULK--
--AND WHO SUDDENLY STANDS BEFORE--
--THE ARK! IT ISSS HERE-- JUSSST ASSS "THEY" SSSAID IT WOULD BE!
A FEW MINOR PREPARATIONSSS TO BE MADE--AND, WITHIN MINUTESSS, NOTHING WILL BE ABLE TO SSSTOP ME!
THE MAN CALLED STEGRON TURNS THEN, HIS REPTILIAN FINGER STABBING DOWN UPON A GLEAMING GOLDEN BUTTON--
--AND, AS HE STANDS TRIUMPH-ANTLY, A HUGE METALLIC RAMP HISSES SILENTLY OUT OF THE GREAT ARK'S SIDE--
--THEN, IN A VOICE NO LONG-ER EVEN BARELY HUMAN THE DINOSAUR-MASTER SCREAMS--
--AND PROVES HE DESERVES HIS NEWLY-GAINED TITLE--
COME, MY LONG-TAILED BROTHERSSS --COME!
--FOR THOSE HE IS SAID TO MASTER COME RUMBLING OUT OF THE FOREST PRIMEVAL IN DROVES--
SSSTEGRON WAITSSS TO LEAD YOU TO YOUR ULTIMATE DESSSTINY!

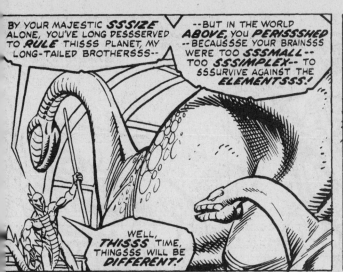

BY YOUR MAJESTIC **SS-SIZE** ALONE, YOU'VE LONG **DESSSERVED** TO **RULE** THISSS PLANET, MY LONG-TAILED **BROTHERSSS**--

--BUT IN THE WORLD **ABOVE**, YOU **PERISSSSHED** --BECAUSSSE YOUR **BRAINSSS** WERE TOO **SSSMALL**-- TOO **SSSIMPLEX**-- TO SSSURVIVE AGAINST THE **ELEMENTSSS**!

WELL, **THISSS** TIME, **THINGSSS** WILL BE **DIFFERENT**!

THISSS TIME, YOU **HAVE** A BRAIN TO LEAD YOU--

--A **SSSUPERIOR** BRAIN--**MY BRAIN**-- AND TOGETHER WE WILL--

··**EH?**

HATE TO **DISAPPOINT** YOU, STEGGY--

--BUT IF **YOU'RE** IN COMMAND OF THIS LITTLE OPERATION, YOUR LONG-TAILED CHUMS **STILL** HAVE NO BRAIN TO LEAD THEM!

SSSPIDER-MAN... AND **KA-ZAR**!

NO! I'VE COME **TOO FAR** FOR THEM TO **RUIN** EVERYTHING **NOW**!

ONCE AGAIN, THE CREATURE CALLED **STEGRON** RAISES HIS GROUND-GRAVEL VOICE IN **INHUMAN ADJURATION**--

--AND THOSE OF HIS SUBJECTS WHO HAVE NOT YET BOARDED THE ARK'S GREAT RAMP **TURN** SUDDENLY--

--AND **STAMPEDE** OFF INTO THE UNDERBRUSH!

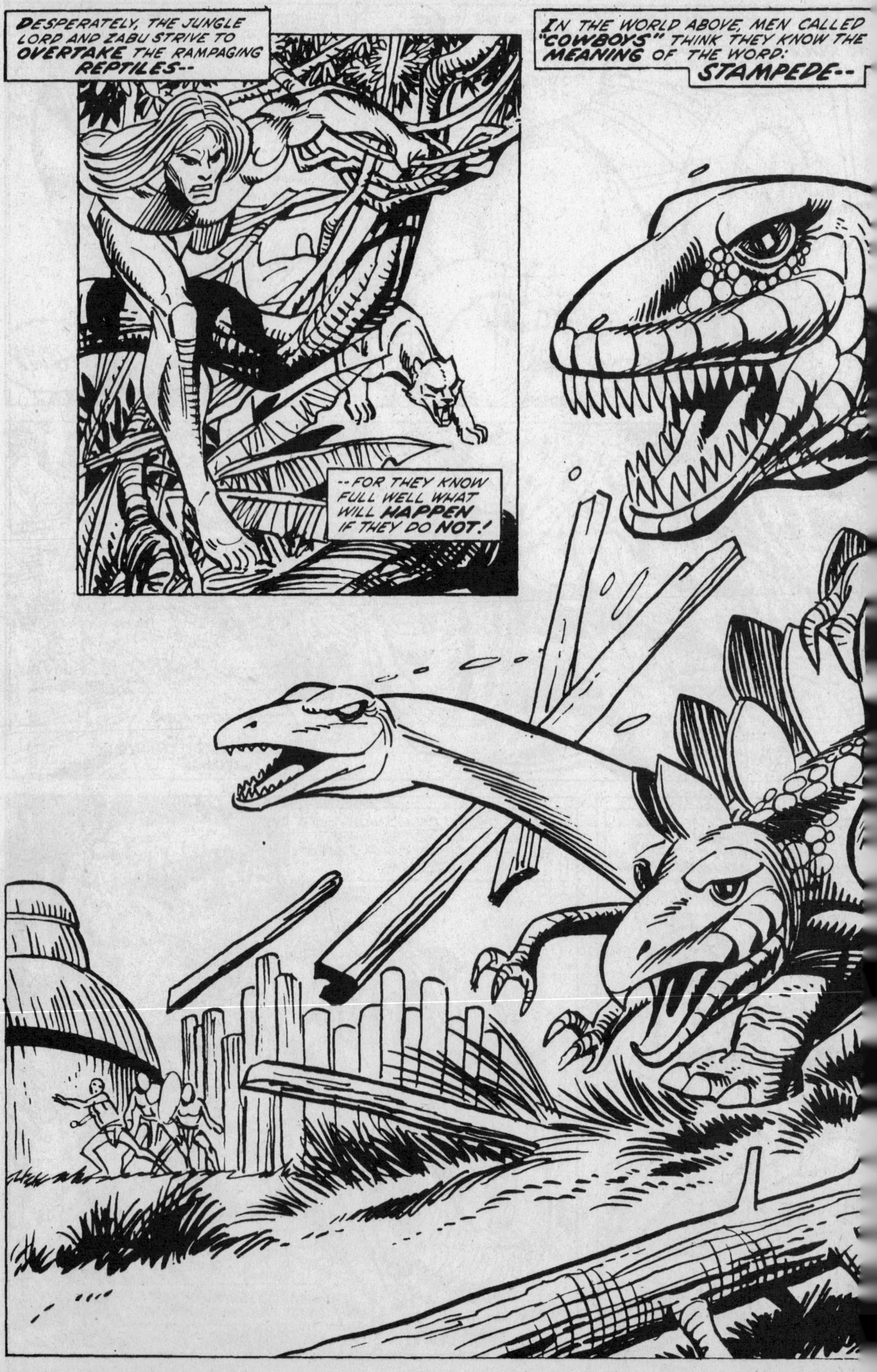
DESPERATELY, THE JUNGLE LORD AND ZABU STRIVE TO OVERTAKE THE RAMPAGING REPTILES--
--FOR THEY KNOW FULL WELL WHAT WILL HAPPEN IF THEY DO NOT!
IN THE WORLD ABOVE, MEN CALLED "COWBOYS" THINK THEY KNOW THE MEANING OF THE WORD:
STAMPEDE--

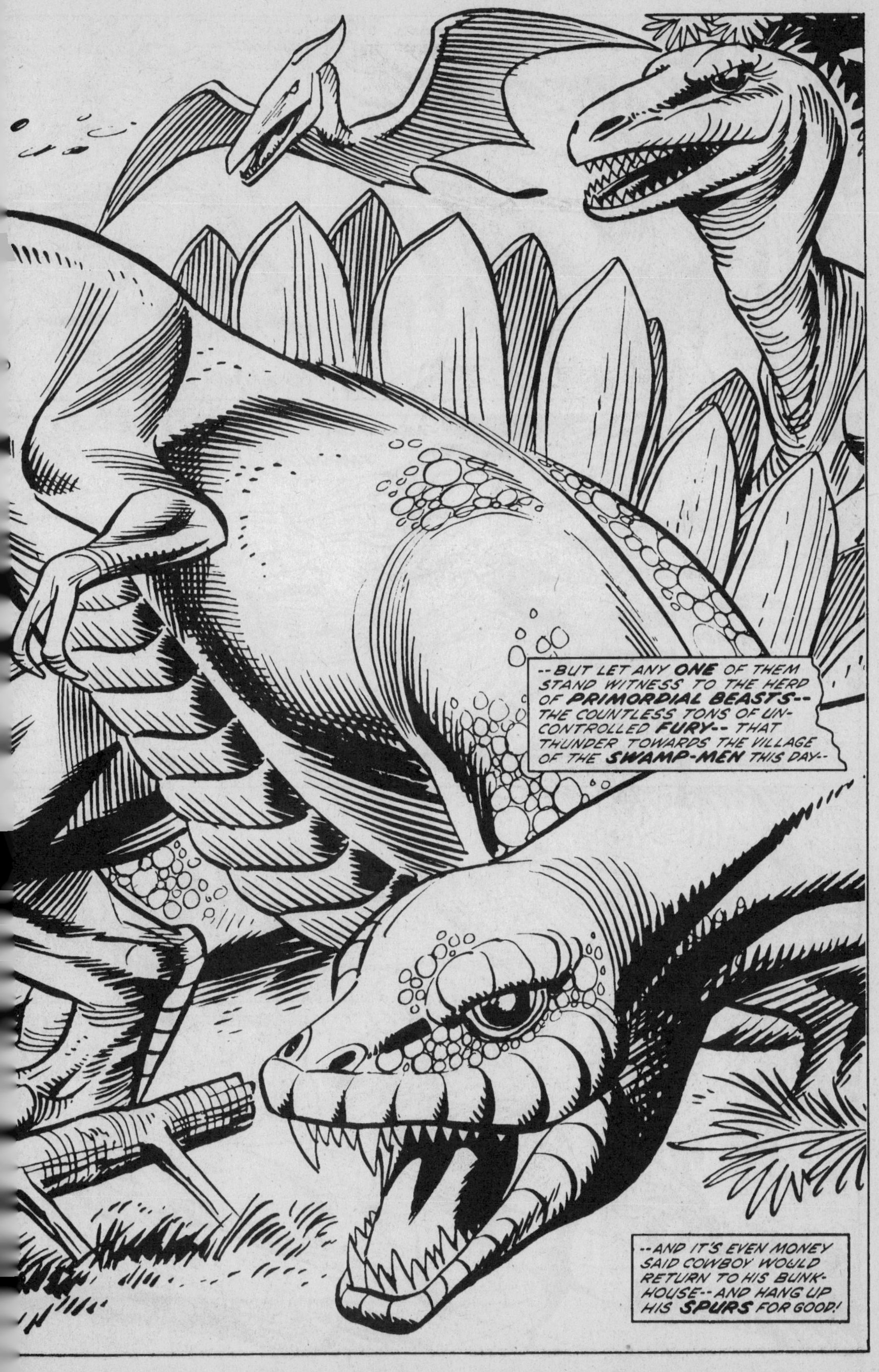
--BUT LET ANY ONE OF THEM STAND WITNESS TO THE HERD OF PRIMORDIAL BEASTS-- THE COUNTLESS TONS OF UNCONTROLLED FURY-- THAT THUNDER TOWARDS THE VILLAGE OF THE SWAMP-MEN THIS DAY--
--AND IT'S EVEN MONEY SAID COWBOY WOULD RETURN TO HIS BUNK-HOUSE--AND HANG UP HIS SPURS FOR GOOD!

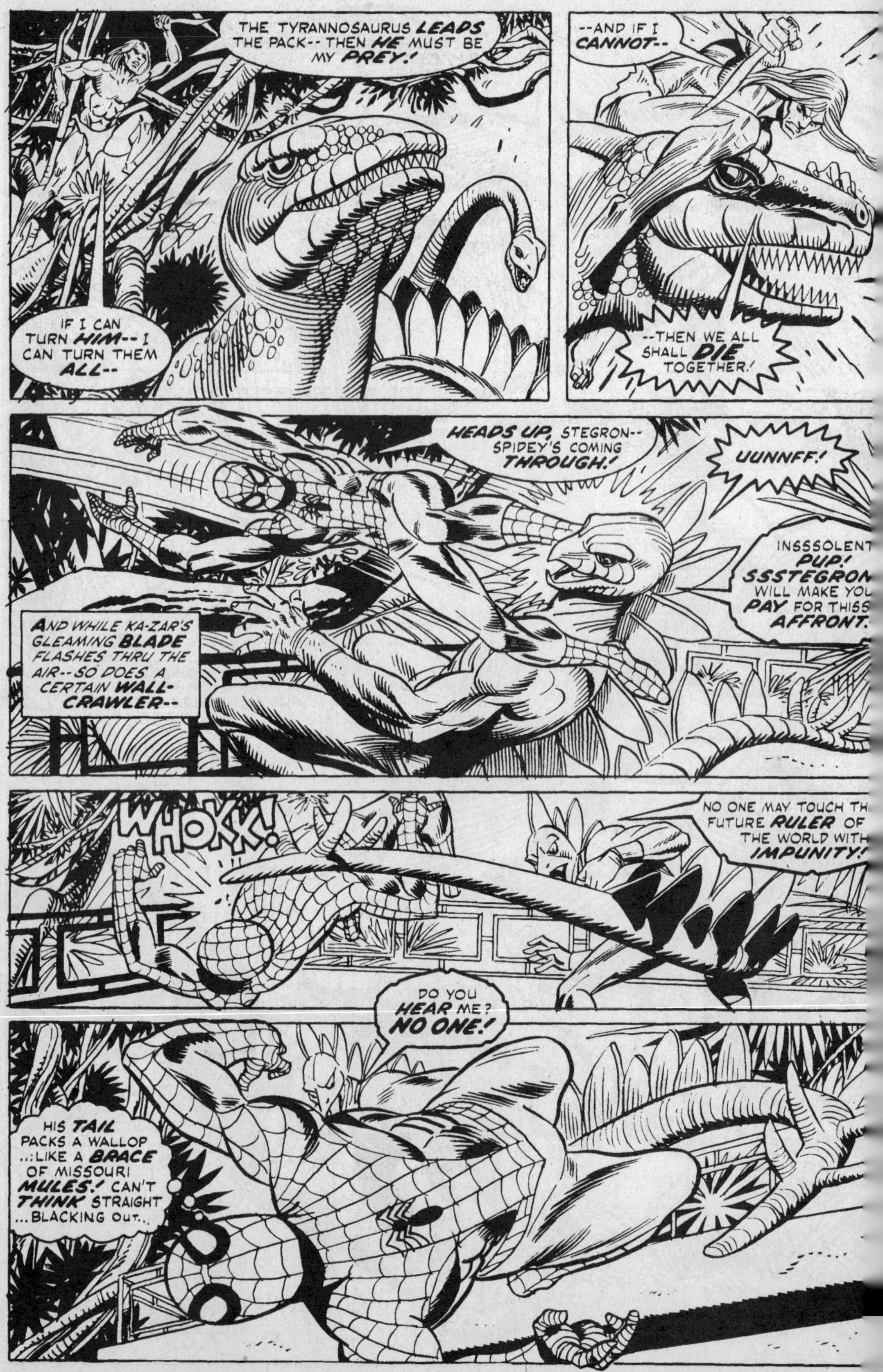

THE TYRANNOSAURUS LEADS THE PACK-- THEN HE MUST BE MY PREY!
IF I CAN TURN HIM-- I CAN TURN THEM ALL--
--AND IF I CANNOT--
--THEN WE ALL SHALL DIE TOGETHER!
AND WHILE KA-ZAR'S GLEAMING BLADE FLASHES THRU THE AIR--SO DOES A CERTAIN WALL-CRAWLER--
HEADS UP, STEGRON-- SPIDEY'S COMING THROUGH!
UUNNFF!
INSSSOLENT PUP! SSSTEGRON WILL MAKE YOU PAY FOR THISS AFFRONT.
WHOKK!
NO ONE MAY TOUCH TH FUTURE RULER OF THE WORLD WITH IMPUNITY!
DO YOU HEAR ME? NO ONE!
HIS TAIL PACKS A WALLOP ...LIKE A BRACE OF MISSOURI MULES! CAN'T THINK STRAIGHT ...BLACKING OUT...

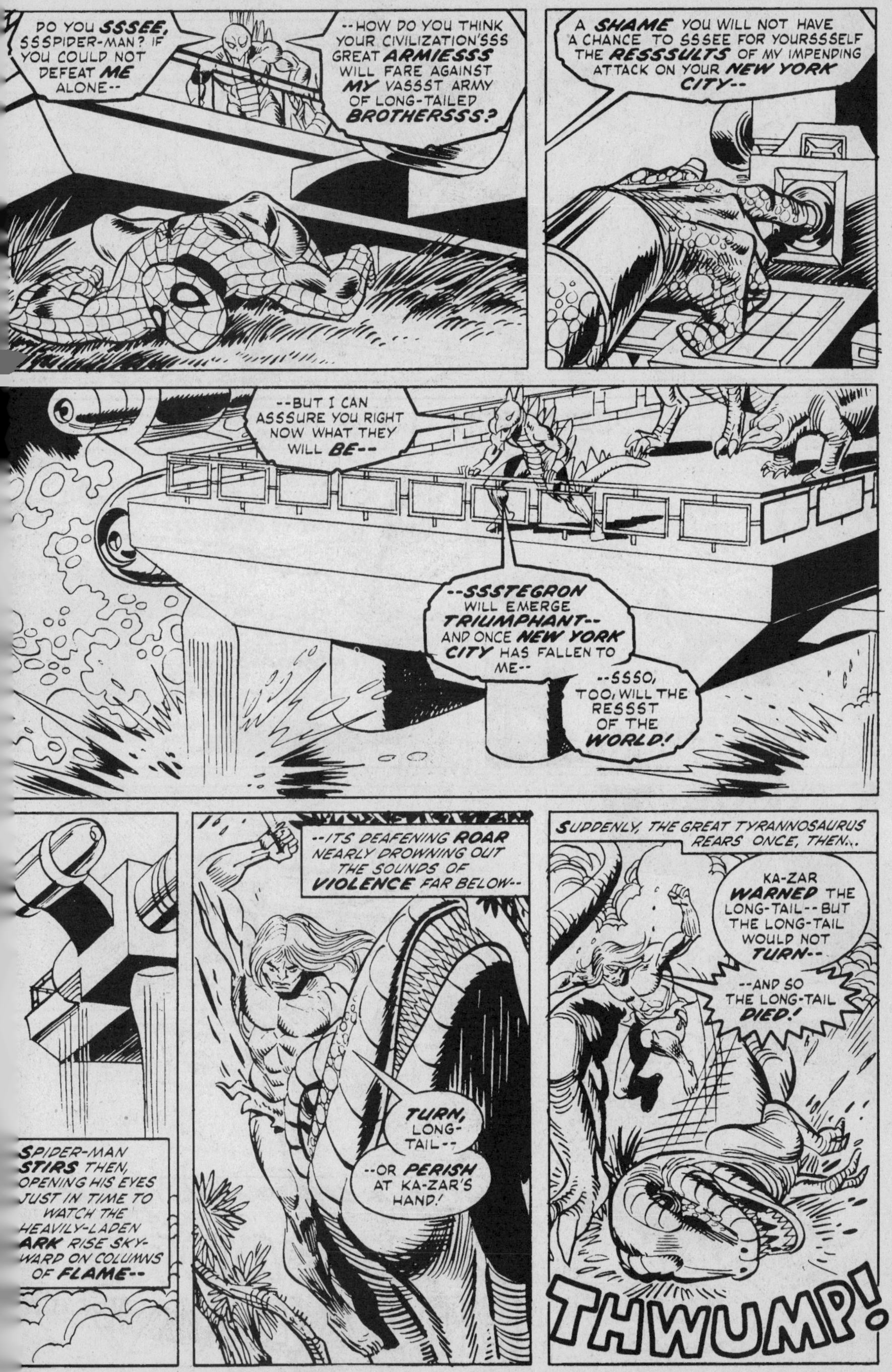

DO YOU SSSEE, SSSPIDER-MAN? IF YOU COULD NOT DEFEAT ME ALONE--
--HOW DO YOU THINK YOUR CIVILIZATION'SSS GREAT ARMIESSS WILL FARE AGAINST MY VASSST ARMY OF LONG-TAILED BROTHERSSS?
A SHAME YOU WILL NOT HAVE A CHANCE TO SSSEE FOR YOURSSSELF THE RESSSULTS OF MY IMPENDING ATTACK ON YOUR NEW YORK CITY--
--BUT I CAN ASSSURE YOU RIGHT NOW WHAT THEY WILL BE--
--SSSTEGRON WILL EMERGE TRIUMPHANT-- AND ONCE NEW YORK CITY HAS FALLEN TO ME--
--SSSO, TOO, WILL THE RESSST OF THE WORLD!
SPIDER-MAN STIRS THEN, OPENING HIS EYES JUST IN TIME TO WATCH THE HEAVILY-LADEN ARK RISE SKY-WARD ON COLUMNS OF FLAME--
--ITS DEAFENING ROAR NEARLY DROWNING OUT THE SOUNDS OF VIOLENCE FAR BELOW--
TURN, LONG-TAIL--
--OR PERISH AT KA-ZAR'S HAND!
SUDDENLY, THE GREAT TYRANNOSAURUS REARS ONCE, THEN...
KA-ZAR WARNED THE LONG-TAIL--BUT THE LONG-TAIL WOULD NOT TURN--
--AND SO THE LONG-TAIL DIED!
THWUMP!

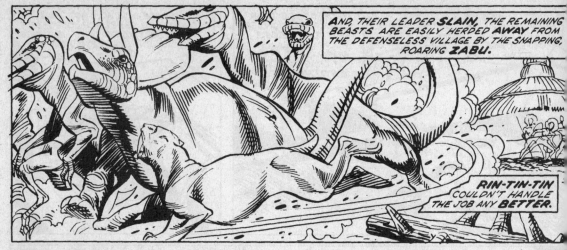

AND, THEIR LEADER *SLAIN*, THE REMAINING BEASTS ARE EASILY HERDED *AWAY* FROM THE DEFENSELESS VILLAGE BY THE SNAPPING, ROARING *ZABU*.

RIN-TIN-TIN COULDN'T HANDLE THE JOB ANY *BETTER.*

THE IMMEDIATE MENACE *ENDED*, KA-ZAR SUDDENLY NOTICES--

STEGRON'S FLYING SHIP-- GETTING *AWAY*--

--OR *IS* IT?

IF THAT SMALL FORM DANGLING BENEATH THE *WING-LIZARD* IS WHO I *THINK* IT IS--

"--STEGRON MAY BE DEFEATED *WITHOUT* KA-ZAR'S HELP!"

SOME DAY, I'M GONNA *TELL* SOMEBODY HOW I SPENT THIS AFTERNOON -- AND THEY'RE GONNA HAVE ME *COMMITED!*

BUT IF HITCHING A RIDE ON A *PTERODACTYL* IS THE ONLY WAY TO *CATCH* STEGGY'S *ARK*--

--WHAT *ELSE* CAN I DO?

*HOO*HAH! MY WEBBING'S SNAGGED THE *BOTTOM* OF STEGGY'S SHIP-- AND SINCE MY BUZZARD-BEAKED *CABBY* HAS FLOWN OFF--

--FROM HERE ON OUT, *I'M GOING WHEREVER STEGRON GOES!*

SO WHY DO I HAVE THE ANNOYING FEELING THAT WHEREVER *THAT* MAY BE--

--I'M NOT GONNA *LIKE* IT!

NEXT ISSUE: SPIDER-MAN... THE BLACK PANTHER... VERSUS THE MENACE OF STEGRON AND

DINOSAURS ON BROADWAY!

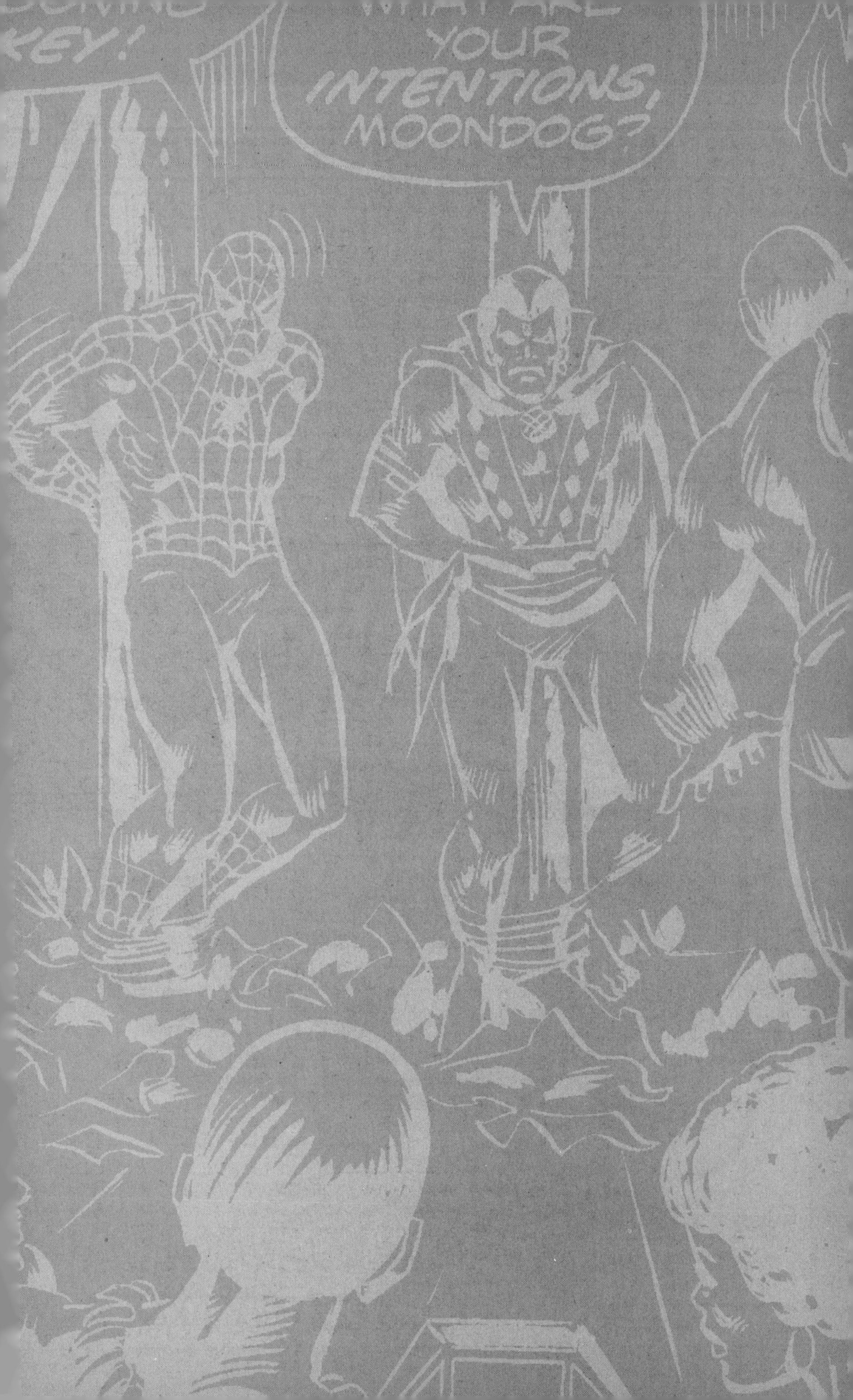
YOUR INTENTIONS, MOONDOG?

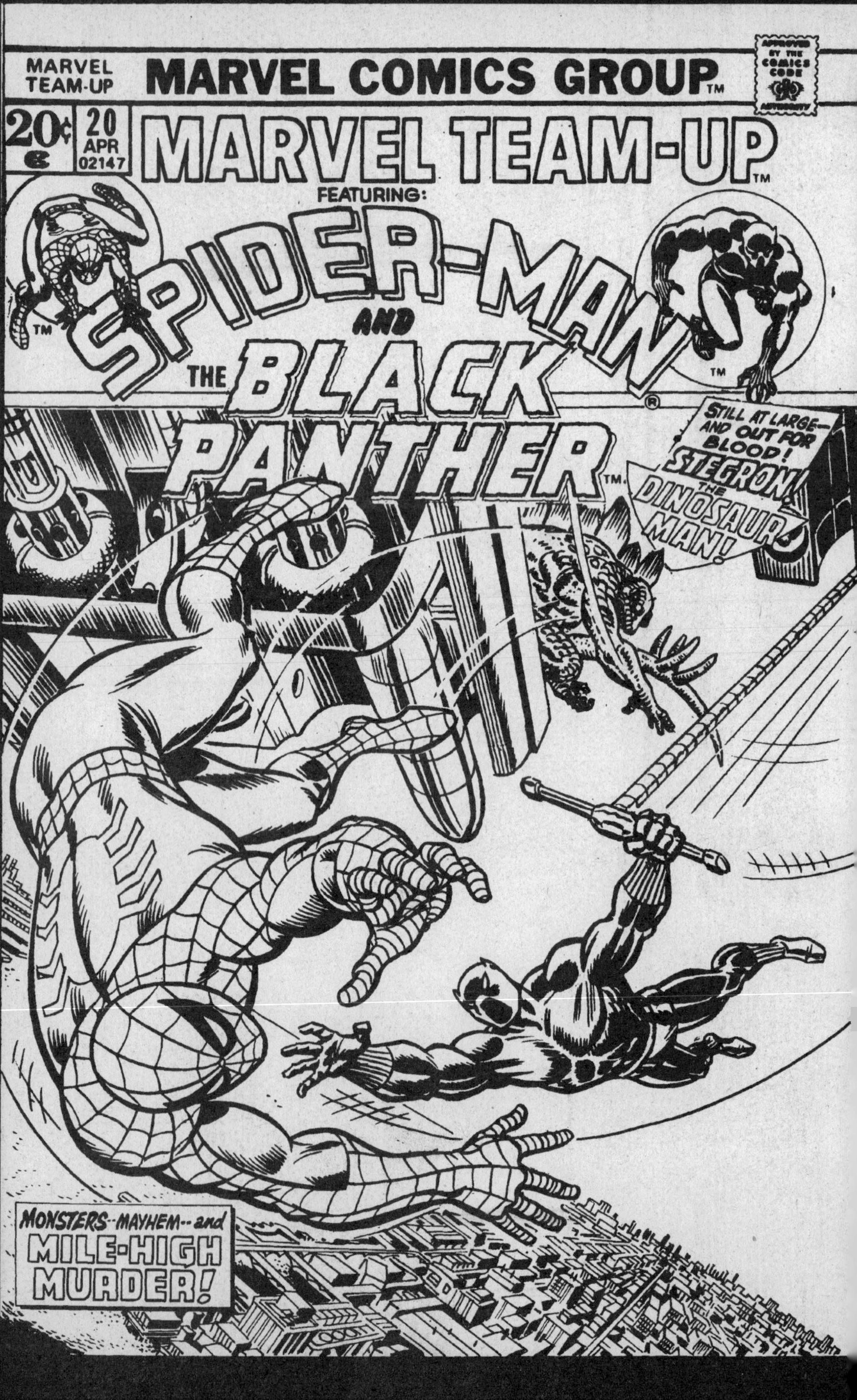
MARVEL TEAM-UP
MARVEL COMICS GROUP
APPROVED BY THE COMICS CODE AUTHORITY
20¢
20 APR 02147
MARVEL TEAM-UP
FEATURING:
SPIDER-MAN
AND
THE BLACK PANTHER
STILL AT LARGE-- AND OUT FOR BLOOD! STEGRON! THE DINOSAUR MAN!
MONSTERS--MAYHEM--and
MILE-HIGH MURDER!

STAN LEE PRESENTS: SPIDEY and the BLACK PANTHER™ -- TOGETHER!

LEN WEIN, WRITER * SAL BUSCEMA, ARTIST * GIACOIA & ESPOSITO, INKERS * GLYNIS WEIN, COLORIST * ARTIE SIMEK, LETTERER * ROY THOMAS, EDITOR

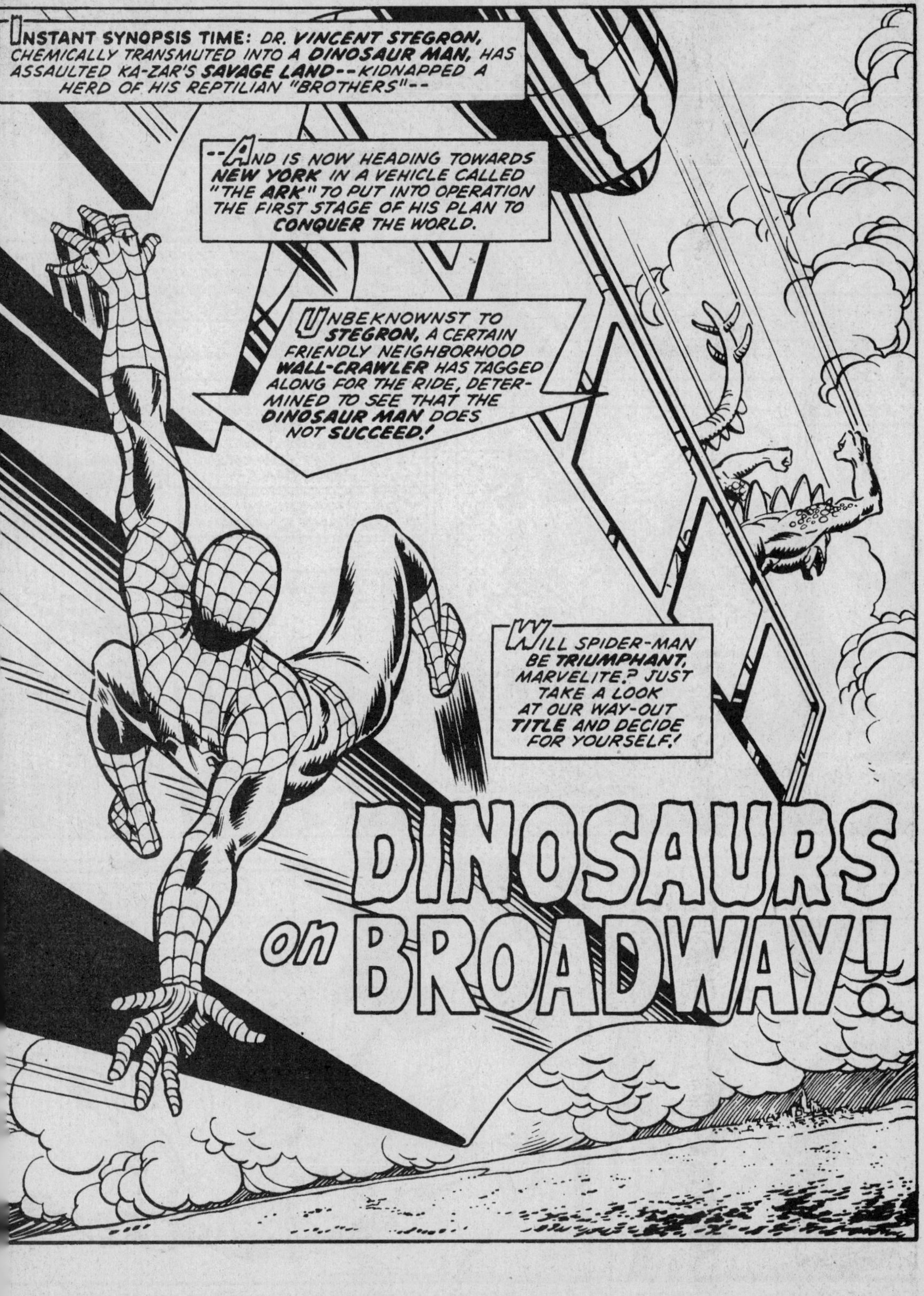
INSTANT SYNOPSIS TIME: DR. VINCENT STEGRON, CHEMICALLY TRANSMUTED INTO A DINOSAUR MAN, HAS ASSAULTED KA-ZAR'S SAVAGE LAND--KIDNAPPED A HERD OF HIS REPTILIAN "BROTHERS"--
--AND IS NOW HEADING TOWARDS NEW YORK IN A VEHICLE CALLED "THE ARK" TO PUT INTO OPERATION THE FIRST STAGE OF HIS PLAN TO CONQUER THE WORLD.
UNBEKNOWNST TO STEGRON, A CERTAIN FRIENDLY NEIGHBORHOOD WALL-CRAWLER HAS TAGGED ALONG FOR THE RIDE, DETERMINED TO SEE THAT THE DINOSAUR MAN DOES NOT SUCCEED!
WILL SPIDER-MAN BE TRIUMPHANT, MARVELITE? JUST TAKE A LOOK AT OUR WAY-OUT TITLE AND DECIDE FOR YOURSELF!
DINOSAURS on BROADWAY!

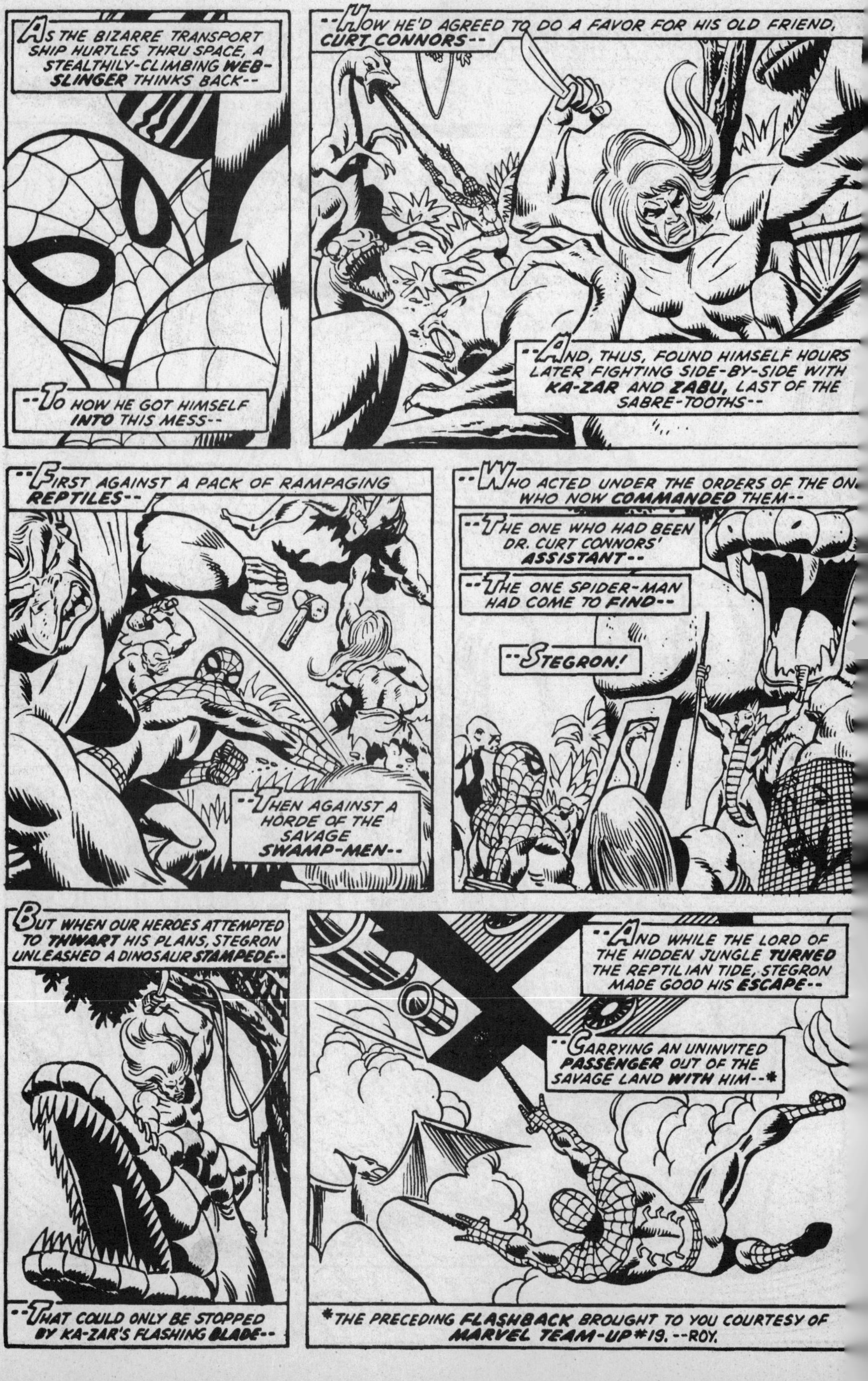
AS THE BIZARRE TRANSPORT SHIP HURTLES THRU SPACE, A STEALTHILY-CLIMBING WEB-SLINGER THINKS BACK--
--TO HOW HE GOT HIMSELF INTO THIS MESS--
--HOW HE'D AGREED TO DO A FAVOR FOR HIS OLD FRIEND, CURT CONNORS--
--AND, THUS, FOUND HIMSELF HOURS LATER FIGHTING SIDE-BY-SIDE WITH KA-ZAR AND ZABU, LAST OF THE SABRE-TOOTHS--
--FIRST AGAINST A PACK OF RAMPAGING REPTILES--
--THEN AGAINST A HORDE OF THE SAVAGE SWAMP-MEN--
--WHO ACTED UNDER THE ORDERS OF THE ONE WHO NOW COMMANDED THEM--
--THE ONE WHO HAD BEEN DR. CURT CONNORS' ASSISTANT--
--THE ONE SPIDER-MAN HAD COME TO FIND--
--STEGRON!
BUT WHEN OUR HEROES ATTEMPTED TO THWART HIS PLANS, STEGRON UNLEASHED A DINOSAUR STAMPEDE--
--THAT COULD ONLY BE STOPPED BY KA-ZAR'S FLASHING BLADE--
--AND WHILE THE LORD OF THE HIDDEN JUNGLE TURNED THE REPTILIAN TIDE, STEGRON MADE GOOD HIS ESCAPE--
--CARRYING AN UNINVITED PASSENGER OUT OF THE SAVAGE LAND WITH HIM--*
*THE PRECEDING FLASHBACK BROUGHT TO YOU COURTESY OF MARVEL TEAM-UP #19. --ROY.

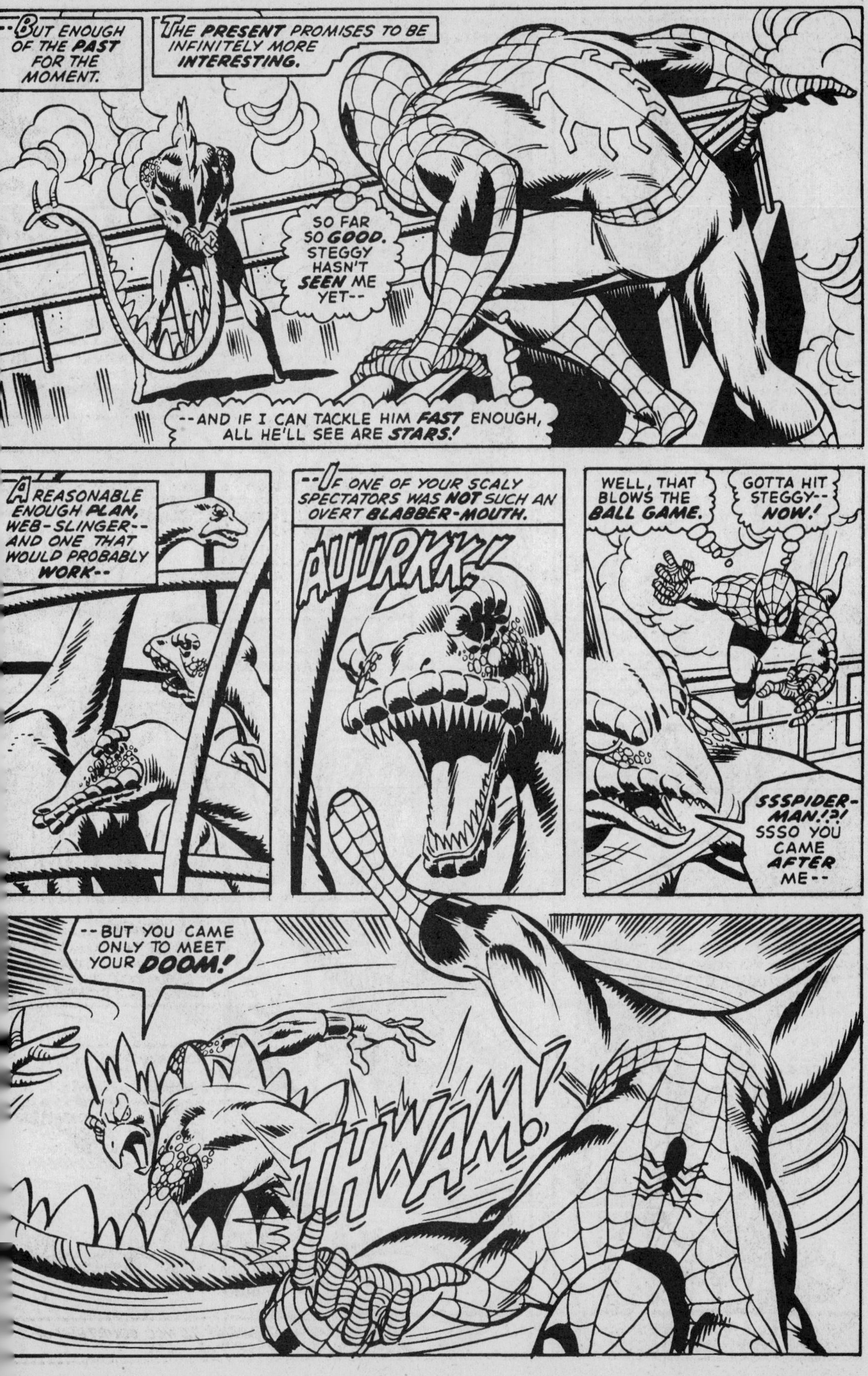
--BUT ENOUGH OF THE PAST FOR THE MOMENT.
THE PRESENT PROMISES TO BE INFINITELY MORE INTERESTING.
SO FAR SO GOOD. STEGGY HASN'T SEEN ME YET--
--AND IF I CAN TACKLE HIM FAST ENOUGH, ALL HE'LL SEE ARE STARS!
A REASONABLE ENOUGH PLAN, WEB-SLINGER--AND ONE THAT WOULD PROBABLY WORK--
--IF ONE OF YOUR SCALY SPECTATORS WAS NOT SUCH AN OVERT BLABBER-MOUTH.
AUURKK!
WELL, THAT BLOWS THE BALL GAME.
GOTTA HIT STEGGY-- NOW!
SSSPIDER-MAN!?! SSSO YOU CAME AFTER ME--
--BUT YOU CAME ONLY TO MEET YOUR DOOM!
THWAM!

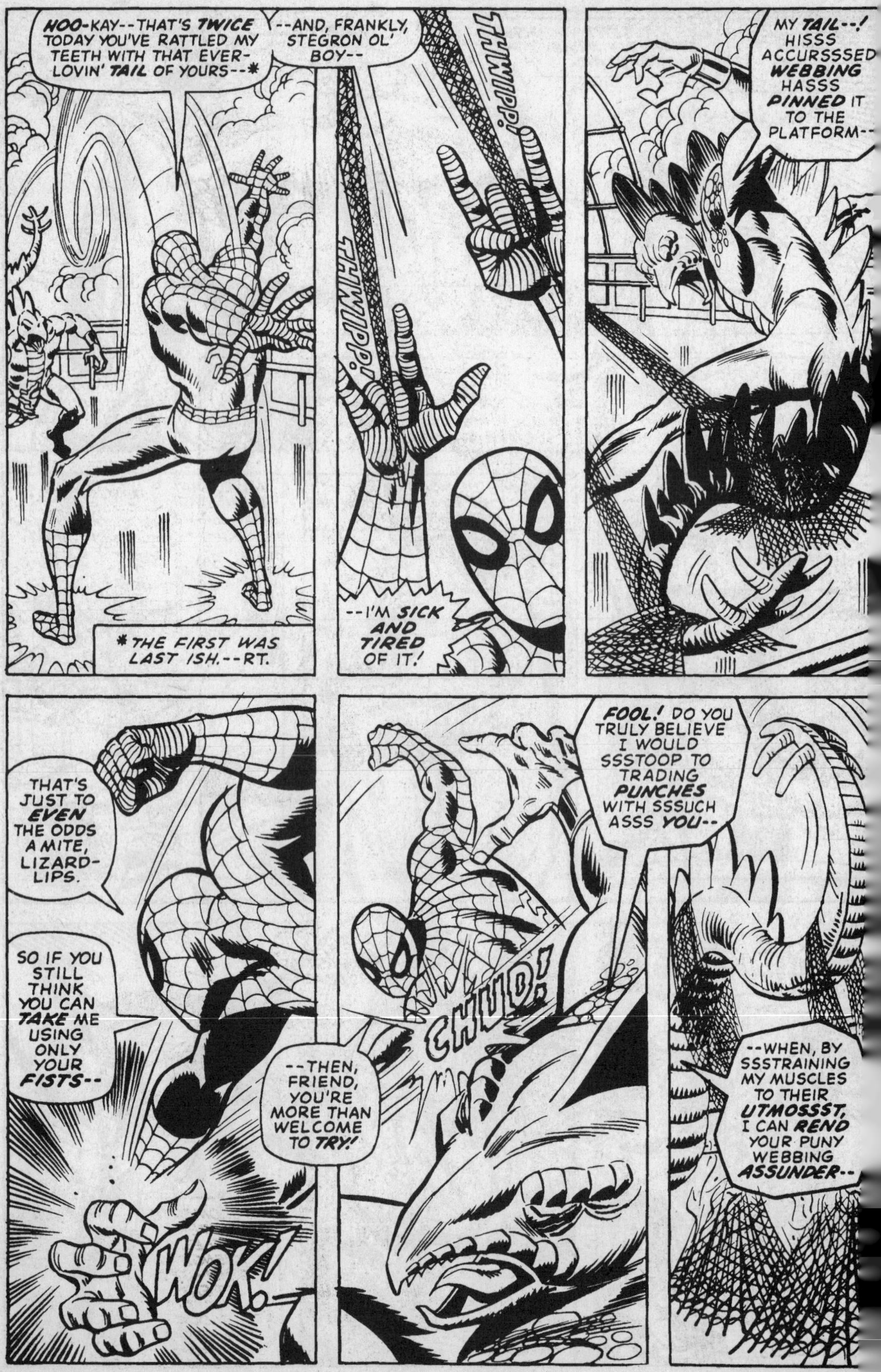

HOO-KAY--THAT'S TWICE TODAY YOU'VE RATTLED MY TEETH WITH THAT EVER-LOVIN' TAIL OF YOURS--*
*THE FIRST WAS LAST ISH.--RT.
--AND, FRANKLY, STEGRON OL' BOY--
THWIPP!
THWIPP!
--I'M SICK AND TIRED OF IT!
MY TAIL--! HISSS ACCURSSSED WEBBING HASSS PINNED IT TO THE PLATFORM--
THAT'S JUST TO EVEN THE ODDS A MITE, LIZARD-LIPS.
SO IF YOU STILL THINK YOU CAN TAKE ME USING ONLY YOUR FISTS--
WOK!
--THEN, FRIEND, YOU'RE MORE THAN WELCOME TO TRY!
CHUD!
FOOL! DO YOU TRULY BELIEVE I WOULD SSSTOOP TO TRADING PUNCHES WITH SSSUCH ASSS YOU--
--WHEN, BY SSSTRAINING MY MUSCLES TO THEIR UTMOSSST, I CAN REND YOUR PUNY WEBBING ASSUNDER--

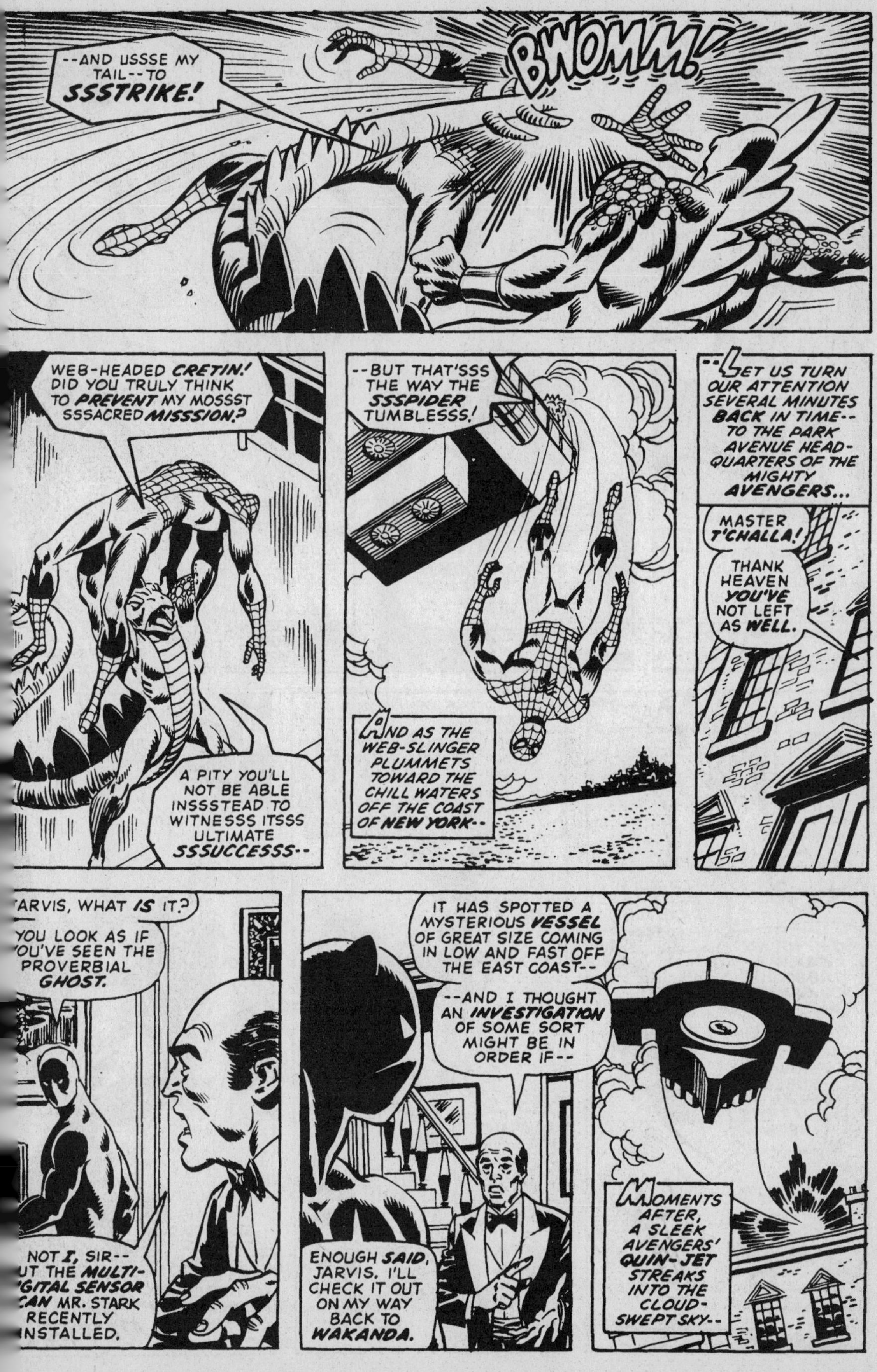

--AND USSSE MY TAIL--TO SSSTRIKE!
BWOMM!
WEB-HEADED CRETIN! DID YOU TRULY THINK TO PREVENT MY MOSSST SSSACRED MISSSION?
A PITY YOU'LL NOT BE ABLE INSSSTEAD TO WITNESSS ITSSS ULTIMATE SSSUCCESSS--
--BUT THAT'SSS THE WAY THE SSSPIDER TUMBLESSS!
AND AS THE WEB-SLINGER PLUMMETS TOWARD THE CHILL WATERS OFF THE COAST OF NEW YORK--
--LET US TURN OUR ATTENTION SEVERAL MINUTES BACK IN TIME--TO THE PARK AVENUE HEAD-QUARTERS OF THE MIGHTY AVENGERS...
MASTER T'CHALLA!
THANK HEAVEN YOU'VE NOT LEFT AS WELL.
JARVIS, WHAT IS IT?
YOU LOOK AS IF YOU'VE SEEN THE PROVERBIAL GHOST.
NOT I, SIR--BUT THE MULTI-DIGITAL SENSOR SCAN MR. STARK RECENTLY INSTALLED.
IT HAS SPOTTED A MYSTERIOUS VESSEL OF GREAT SIZE COMING IN LOW AND FAST OFF THE EAST COAST--
--AND I THOUGHT AN INVESTIGATION OF SOME SORT MIGHT BE IN ORDER IF--
ENOUGH SAID, JARVIS. I'LL CHECK IT OUT ON MY WAY BACK TO WAKANDA.
MOMENTS AFTER, A SLEEK AVENGERS' QUIN-JET STREAKS INTO THE CLOUD-SWEPT SKY--

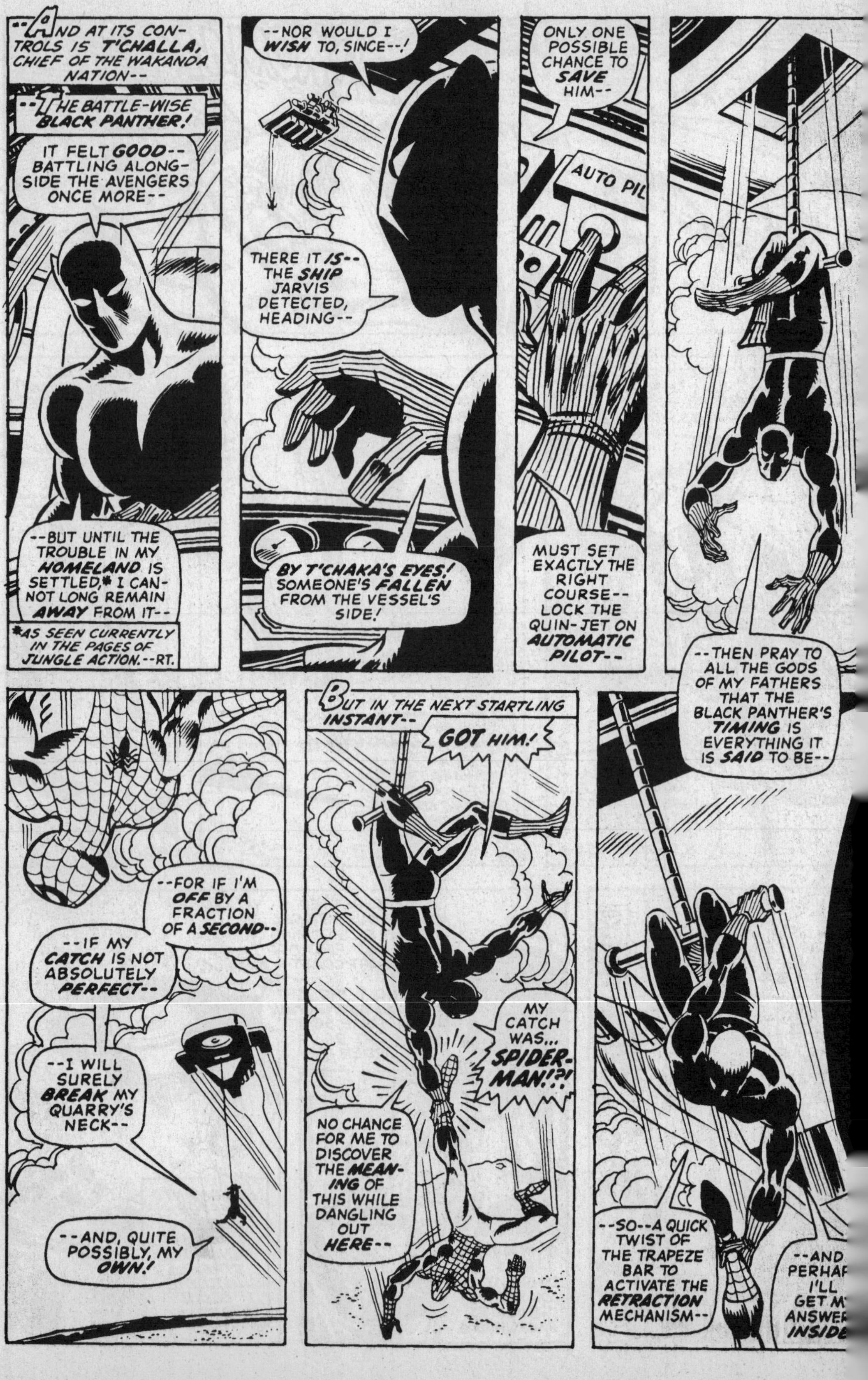
--AND AT ITS CONTROLS IS T'CHALLA, CHIEF OF THE WAKANDA NATION--
--THE BATTLE-WISE BLACK PANTHER!
IT FELT GOOD--BATTLING ALONGSIDE THE AVENGERS ONCE MORE--
--BUT UNTIL THE TROUBLE IN MY HOMELAND IS SETTLED,* I CANNOT LONG REMAIN AWAY FROM IT--
*AS SEEN CURRENTLY IN THE PAGES OF JUNGLE ACTION.--RT.
--NOR WOULD I WISH TO, SINCE--!
THERE IT IS--THE SHIP JARVIS DETECTED, HEADING--
BY T'CHAKA'S EYES! SOMEONE'S FALLEN FROM THE VESSEL'S SIDE!
ONLY ONE POSSIBLE CHANCE TO SAVE HIM--
AUTO PIL
MUST SET EXACTLY THE RIGHT COURSE--LOCK THE QUIN-JET ON AUTOMATIC PILOT--
--THEN PRAY TO ALL THE GODS OF MY FATHERS THAT THE BLACK PANTHER'S TIMING IS EVERYTHING IT IS SAID TO BE--
--FOR IF I'M OFF BY A FRACTION OF A SECOND--
--IF MY CATCH IS NOT ABSOLUTELY PERFECT--
--I WILL SURELY BREAK MY QUARRY'S NECK--
--AND, QUITE POSSIBLY, MY OWN!
BUT IN THE NEXT STARTLING INSTANT--
GOT HIM!
MY CATCH WAS... SPIDER-MAN!?!
NO CHANCE FOR ME TO DISCOVER THE MEANING OF THIS WHILE DANGLING OUT HERE--
--SO--A QUICK TWIST OF THE TRAPEZE BAR TO ACTIVATE THE RETRACTION MECHANISM--
--AND PERHAP I'LL GET M ANSWER INSIDE

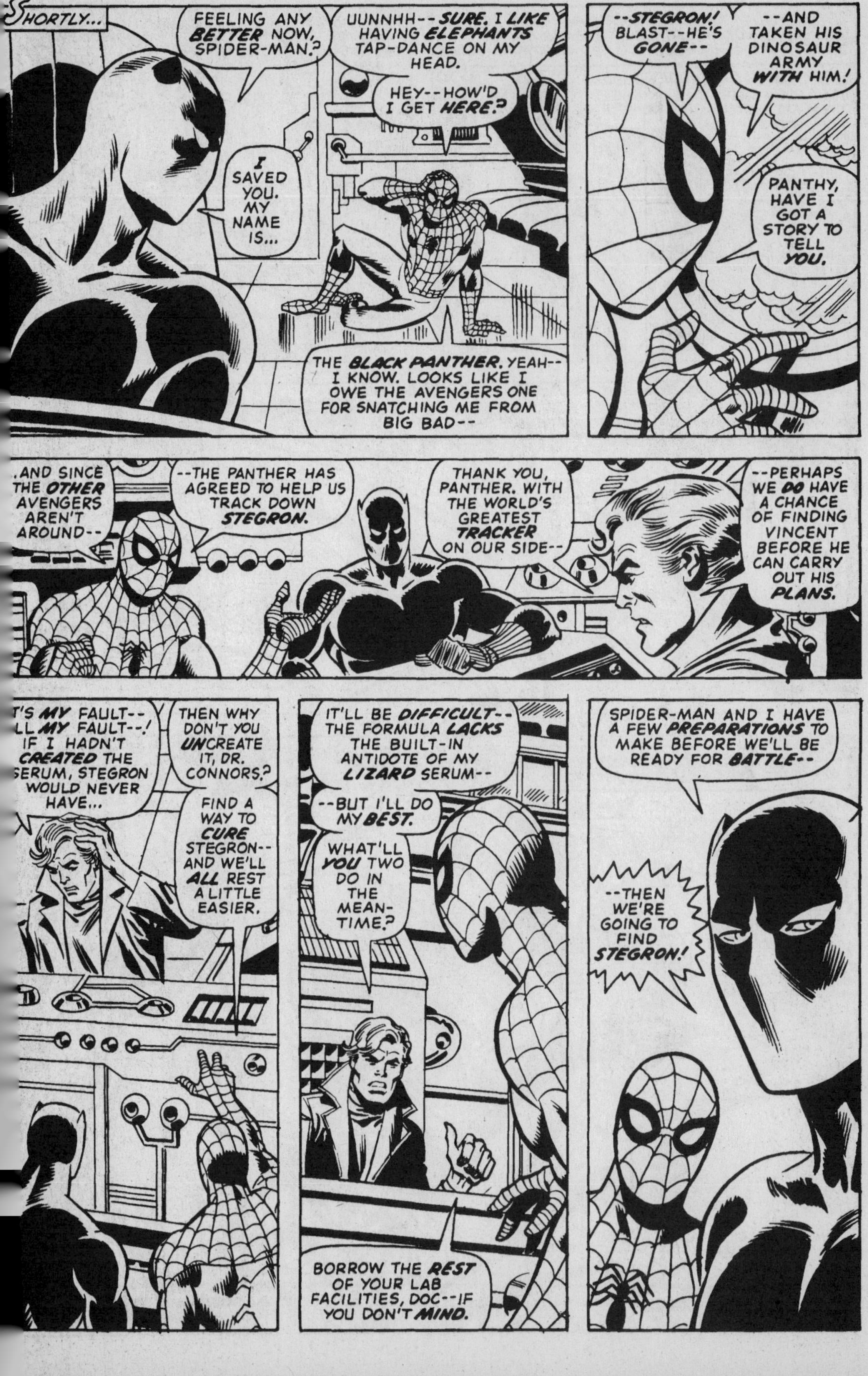
SHORTLY...
FEELING ANY BETTER NOW, SPIDER-MAN?
UUNNHH--SURE. I LIKE HAVING ELEPHANTS TAP-DANCE ON MY HEAD.
HEY--HOW'D I GET HERE?
I SAVED YOU. MY NAME IS...
THE BLACK PANTHER. YEAH--I KNOW. LOOKS LIKE I OWE THE AVENGERS ONE FOR SNATCHING ME FROM BIG BAD--
--STEGRON! BLAST--HE'S GONE--
--AND TAKEN HIS DINOSAUR ARMY WITH HIM!
PANTHY, HAVE I GOT A STORY TO TELL YOU.
.AND SINCE THE OTHER AVENGERS AREN'T AROUND--
--THE PANTHER HAS AGREED TO HELP US TRACK DOWN STEGRON.
THANK YOU, PANTHER. WITH THE WORLD'S GREATEST TRACKER ON OUR SIDE--
--PERHAPS WE DO HAVE A CHANCE OF FINDING VINCENT BEFORE HE CAN CARRY OUT HIS PLANS.
T'S MY FAULT--LL MY FAULT--! IF I HADN'T CREATED THE SERUM, STEGRON WOULD NEVER HAVE...
THEN WHY DON'T YOU UNCREATE IT, DR. CONNORS?
FIND A WAY TO CURE STEGRON--AND WE'LL ALL REST A LITTLE EASIER.
IT'LL BE DIFFICULT--THE FORMULA LACKS THE BUILT-IN ANTIDOTE OF MY LIZARD SERUM--
--BUT I'LL DO MY BEST.
WHAT'LL YOU TWO DO IN THE MEAN-TIME?
BORROW THE REST OF YOUR LAB FACILITIES, DOC--IF YOU DON'T MIND.
SPIDER-MAN AND I HAVE A FEW PREPARATIONS TO MAKE BEFORE WE'LL BE READY FOR BATTLE--
--THEN WE'RE GOING TO FIND STEGRON!

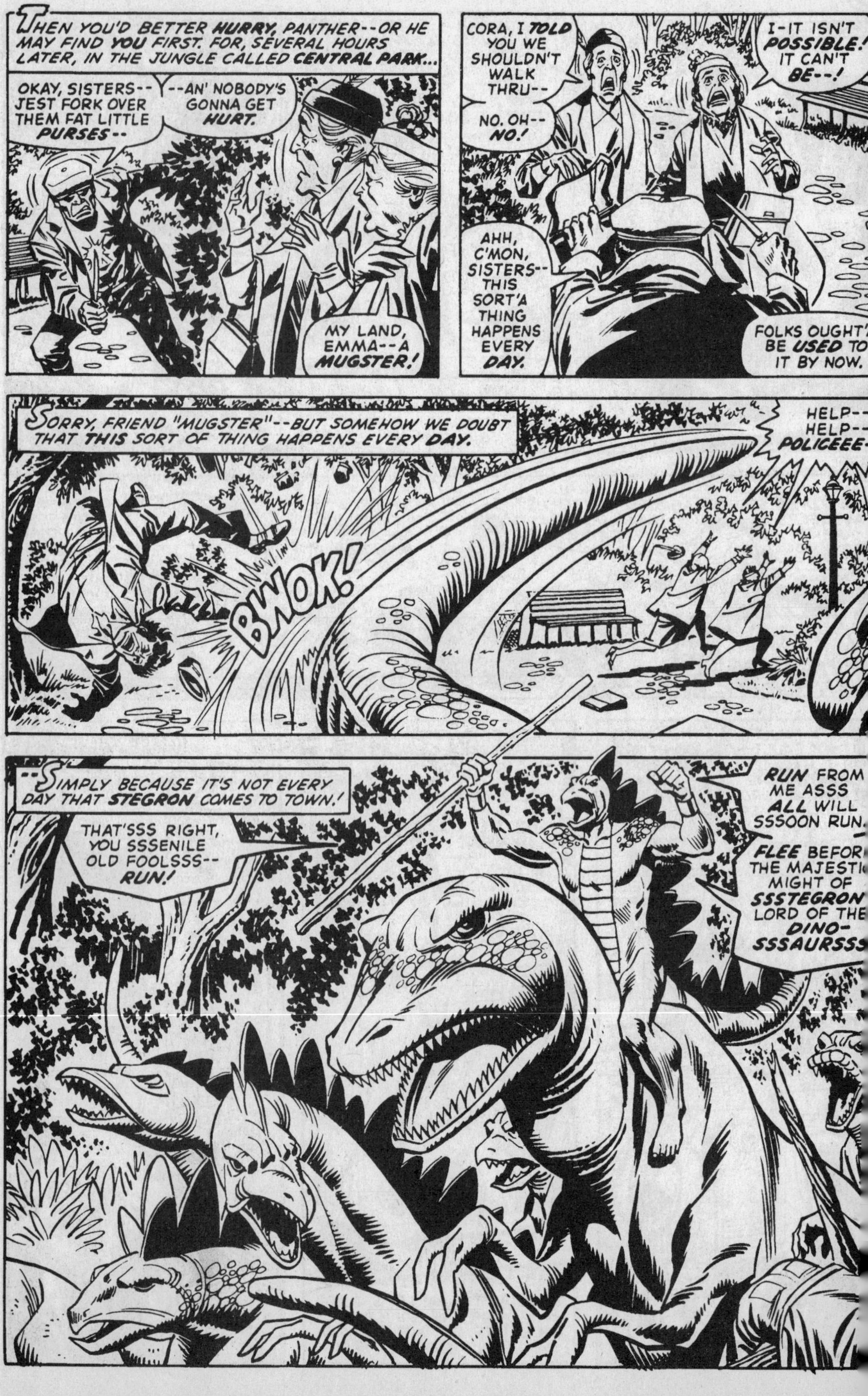
THEN YOU'D BETTER HURRY, PANTHER--OR HE MAY FIND YOU FIRST. FOR, SEVERAL HOURS LATER, IN THE JUNGLE CALLED CENTRAL PARK...
OKAY, SISTERS--JEST FORK OVER THEM FAT LITTLE PURSES--
--AN' NOBODY'S GONNA GET HURT.
MY LAND, EMMA--A MUGSTER!
CORA, I TOLD YOU WE SHOULDN'T WALK THRU--
NO. OH--NO!
I-IT ISN'T POSSIBLE! IT CAN'T BE--!
AHH, C'MON, SISTERS--THIS SORT'A THING HAPPENS EVERY DAY.
FOLKS OUGHT'A BE USED TO IT BY NOW.
SORRY, FRIEND "MUGSTER"--BUT SOMEHOW WE DOUBT THAT THIS SORT OF THING HAPPENS EVERY DAY.
BWOK!
HELP--HELP--POLICEEE-
--SIMPLY BECAUSE IT'S NOT EVERY DAY THAT STEGRON COMES TO TOWN!
THAT'SSS RIGHT, YOU SSSENILE OLD FOOLSSS--RUN!
RUN FROM ME ASSS ALL WILL SSSOON RUN.
FLEE BEFORE THE MAJESTIC MIGHT OF SSSTEGRON LORD OF THE DINO-SSSAURSSS

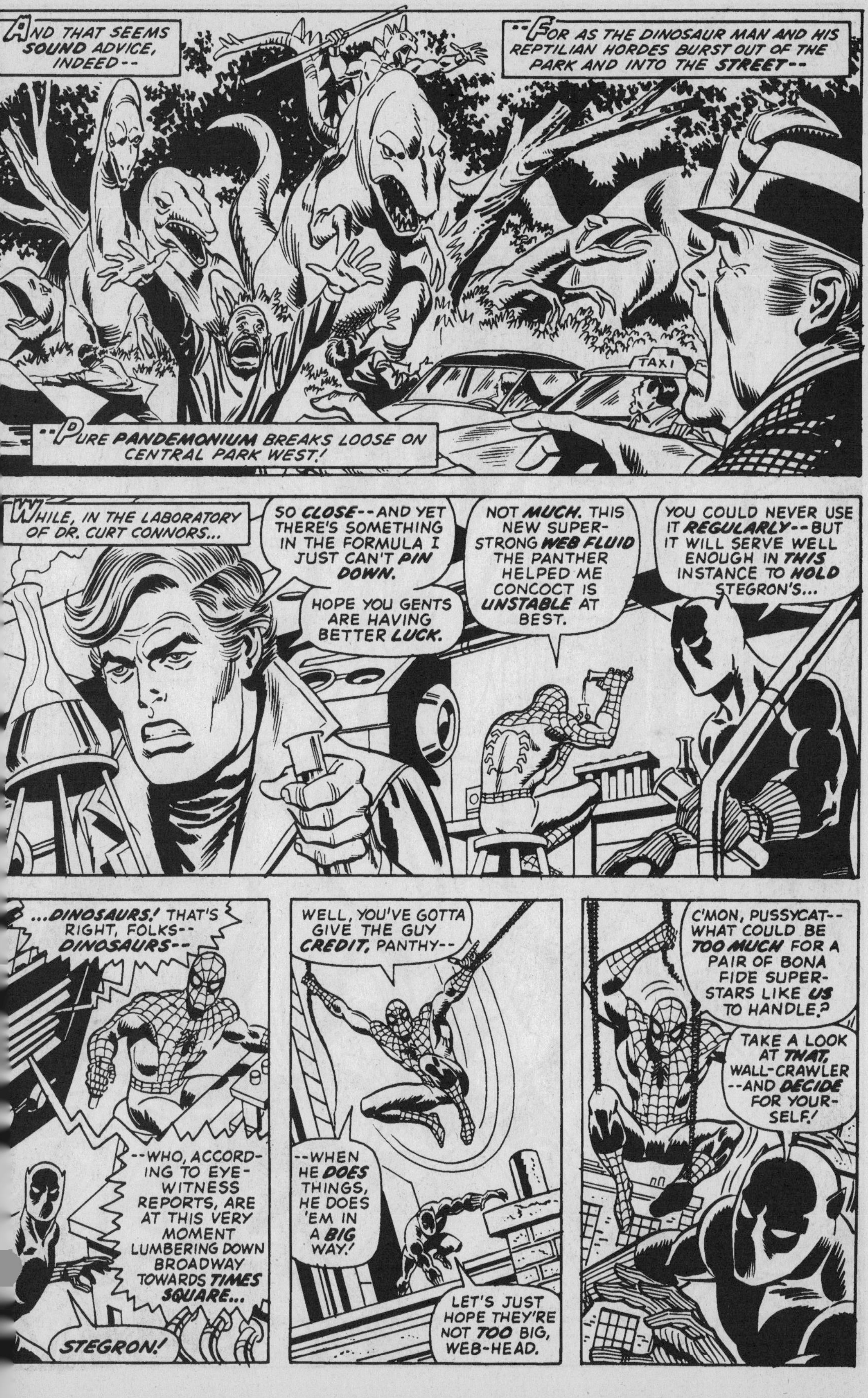

AND THAT SEEMS SOUND ADVICE, INDEED--
--FOR AS THE DINOSAUR MAN AND HIS REPTILIAN HORDES BURST OUT OF THE PARK AND INTO THE STREET--
TAXI
--PURE PANDEMONIUM BREAKS LOOSE ON CENTRAL PARK WEST!
WHILE, IN THE LABORATORY OF DR. CURT CONNORS...
SO CLOSE--AND YET THERE'S SOMETHING IN THE FORMULA I JUST CAN'T PIN DOWN.
HOPE YOU GENTS ARE HAVING BETTER LUCK.
NOT MUCH. THIS NEW SUPER-STRONG WEB FLUID THE PANTHER HELPED ME CONCOCT IS UNSTABLE AT BEST.
YOU COULD NEVER USE IT REGULARLY--BUT IT WILL SERVE WELL ENOUGH IN THIS INSTANCE TO HOLD STEGRON'S...
...DINOSAURS! THAT'S RIGHT, FOLKS--DINOSAURS--
--WHO, ACCORDING TO EYE-WITNESS REPORTS, ARE AT THIS VERY MOMENT LUMBERING DOWN BROADWAY TOWARDS TIMES SQUARE...
STEGRON!
WELL, YOU'VE GOTTA GIVE THE GUY CREDIT, PANTHY--
--WHEN HE DOES THINGS, HE DOES 'EM IN A BIG WAY!
LET'S JUST HOPE THEY'RE NOT TOO BIG, WEB-HEAD.
C'MON, PUSSYCAT--WHAT COULD BE TOO MUCH FOR A PAIR OF BONA FIDE SUPER-STARS LIKE US TO HANDLE?
TAKE A LOOK AT THAT, WALL-CRAWLER--AND DECIDE FOR YOURSELF!

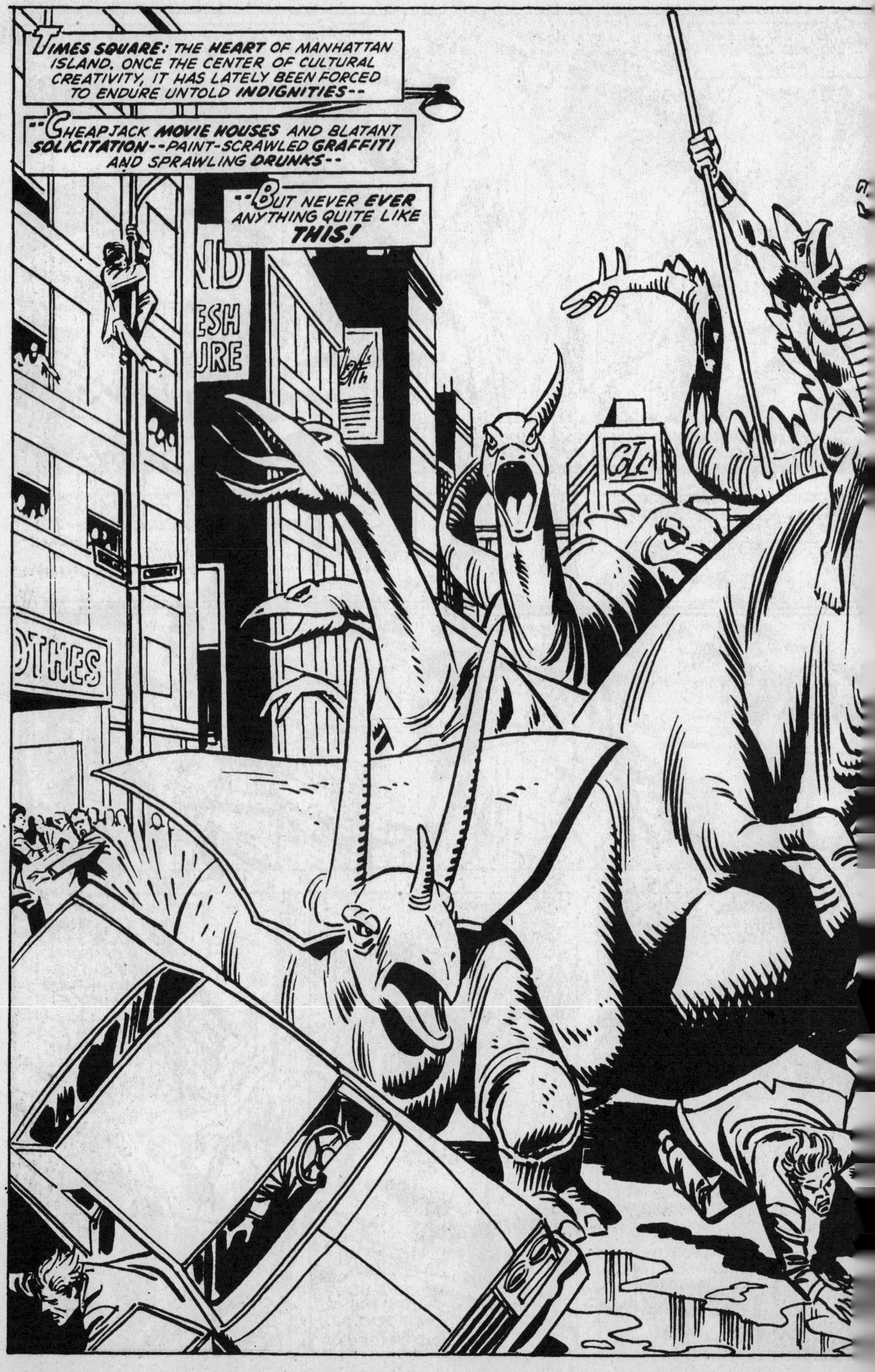
TIMES SQUARE: THE HEART OF MANHATTAN ISLAND. ONCE THE CENTER OF CULTURAL CREATIVITY, IT HAS LATELY BEEN FORCED TO ENDURE UNTOLD INDIGNITIES--
--CHEAPJACK MOVIE HOUSES AND BLATANT SOLICITATION--PAINT-SCRAWLED GRAFFITI AND SPRAWLING DRUNKS--
--BUT NEVER EVER ANYTHING QUITE LIKE THIS!
OTHES

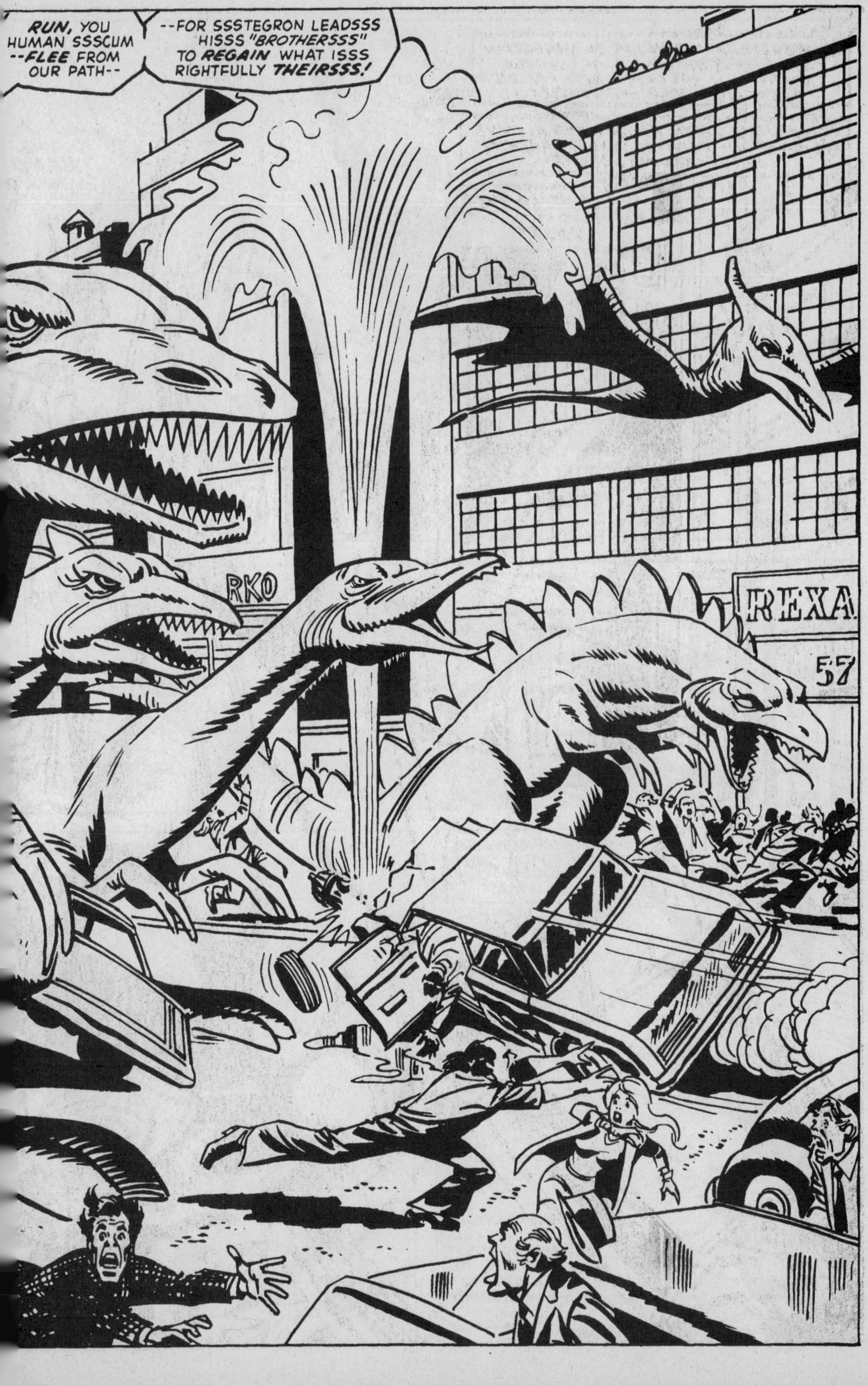

RUN, YOU HUMAN SSSCUM --FLEE FROM OUR PATH--
--FOR SSSTEGRON LEADSSS HISSS "BROTHERSSS" TO REGAIN WHAT ISSS RIGHTFULLY THEIRSSS!
RKO
REXA
57

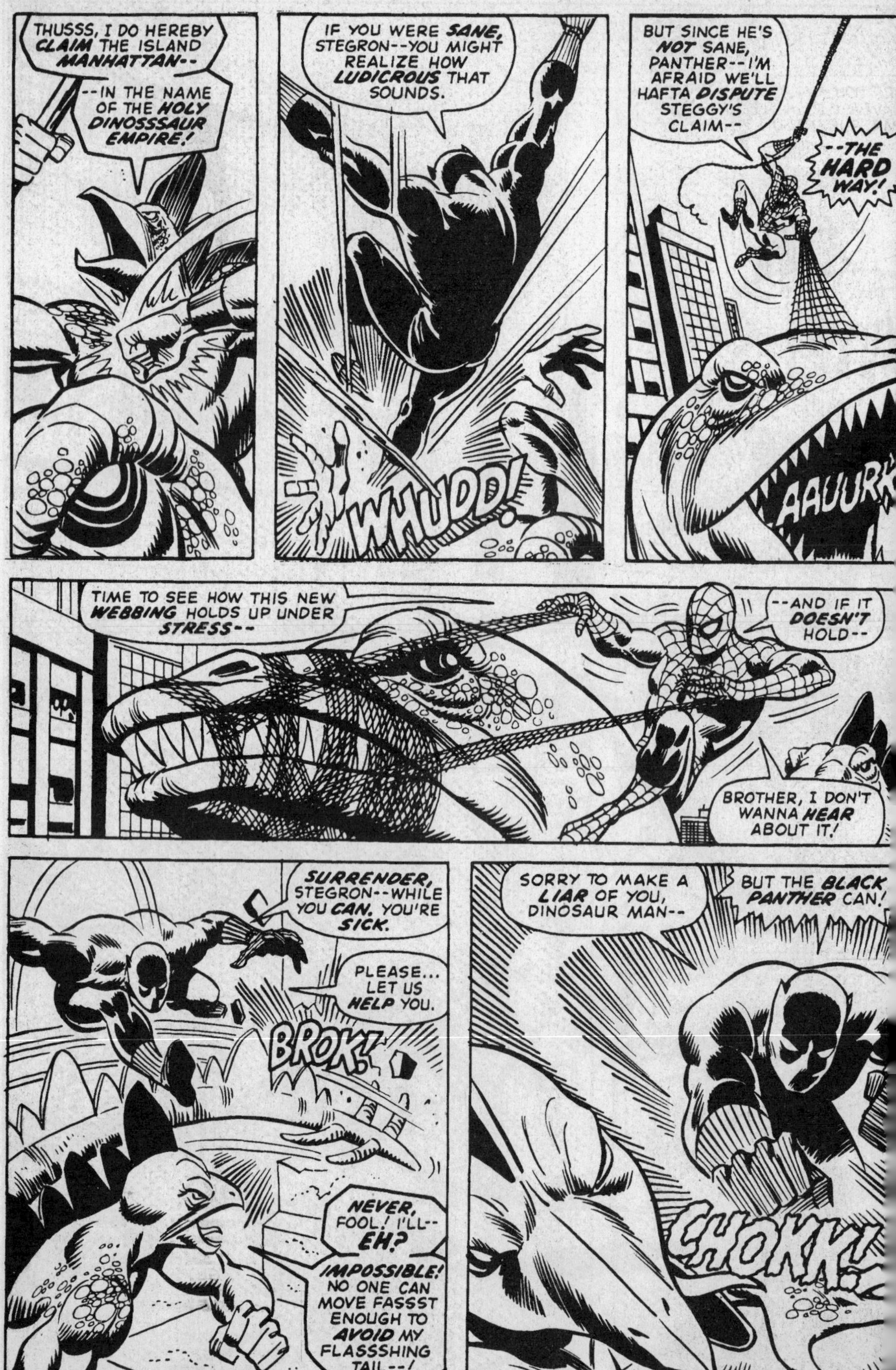
THUSSS, I DO HEREBY CLAIM THE ISLAND MANHATTAN--
--IN THE NAME OF THE HOLY DINOSSSAUR EMPIRE!
IF YOU WERE SANE, STEGRON--YOU MIGHT REALIZE HOW LUDICROUS THAT SOUNDS.
WHUDD!
BUT SINCE HE'S NOT SANE, PANTHER--I'M AFRAID WE'LL HAFTA DISPUTE STEGGY'S CLAIM--
--THE HARD WAY!
AAUURK
TIME TO SEE HOW THIS NEW WEBBING HOLDS UP UNDER STRESS--
--AND IF IT DOESN'T HOLD--
BROTHER, I DON'T WANNA HEAR ABOUT IT!
SURRENDER, STEGRON--WHILE YOU CAN. YOU'RE SICK.
PLEASE... LET US HELP YOU.
BROK!
NEVER, FOOL! I'LL--EH?
IMPOSSIBLE! NO ONE CAN MOVE FASSST ENOUGH TO AVOID MY FLASSSHING TAIL--!
SORRY TO MAKE A LIAR OF YOU, DINOSAUR MAN--
BUT THE BLACK PANTHER CAN!
CHOKK!

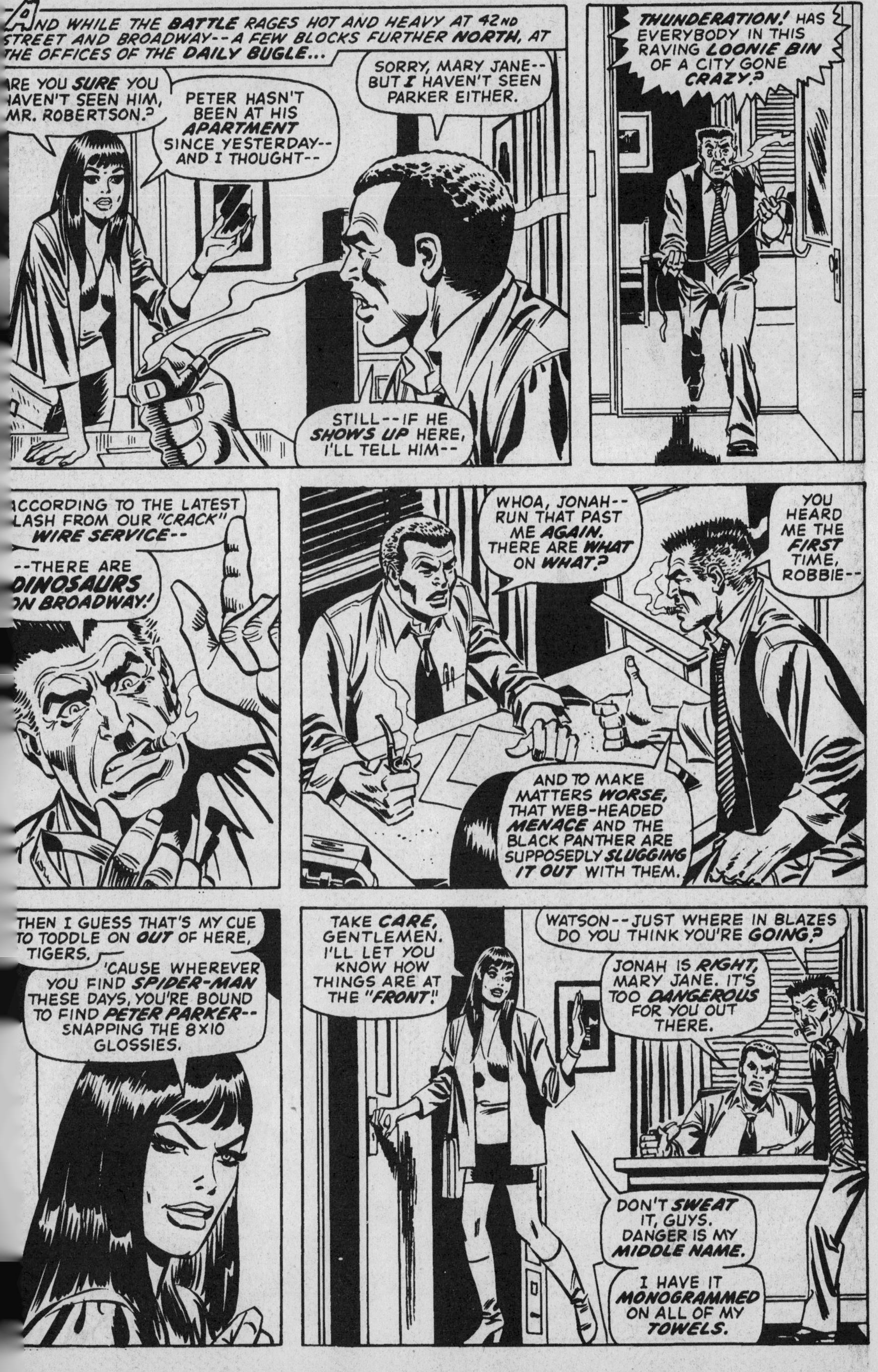
AND WHILE THE BATTLE RAGES HOT AND HEAVY AT 42ND STREET AND BROADWAY--A FEW BLOCKS FURTHER NORTH, AT THE OFFICES OF THE DAILY BUGLE...
ARE YOU SURE YOU HAVEN'T SEEN HIM, MR. ROBERTSON?
PETER HASN'T BEEN AT HIS APARTMENT SINCE YESTERDAY--AND I THOUGHT--
SORRY, MARY JANE--BUT I HAVEN'T SEEN PARKER EITHER.
STILL--IF HE SHOWS UP HERE, I'LL TELL HIM--
THUNDERATION! HAS EVERYBODY IN THIS RAVING LOONIE BIN OF A CITY GONE CRAZY?
ACCORDING TO THE LATEST LASH FROM OUR "CRACK" WIRE SERVICE--
--THERE ARE DINOSAURS ON BROADWAY!
WHOA, JONAH--RUN THAT PAST ME AGAIN. THERE ARE WHAT ON WHAT?
YOU HEARD ME THE FIRST TIME, ROBBIE--
AND TO MAKE MATTERS WORSE, THAT WEB-HEADED MENACE AND THE BLACK PANTHER ARE SUPPOSEDLY SLUGGING IT OUT WITH THEM.
THEN I GUESS THAT'S MY CUE TO TODDLE ON OUT OF HERE, TIGERS.
'CAUSE WHEREVER YOU FIND SPIDER-MAN THESE DAYS, YOU'RE BOUND TO FIND PETER PARKER--SNAPPING THE 8X10 GLOSSIES.
TAKE CARE, GENTLEMEN. I'LL LET YOU KNOW HOW THINGS ARE AT THE "FRONT"!
WATSON--JUST WHERE IN BLAZES DO YOU THINK YOU'RE GOING?
JONAH IS RIGHT, MARY JANE. IT'S TOO DANGEROUS FOR YOU OUT THERE.
DON'T SWEAT IT, GUYS. DANGER IS MY MIDDLE NAME.
I HAVE IT MONOGRAMMED ON ALL OF MY TOWELS.

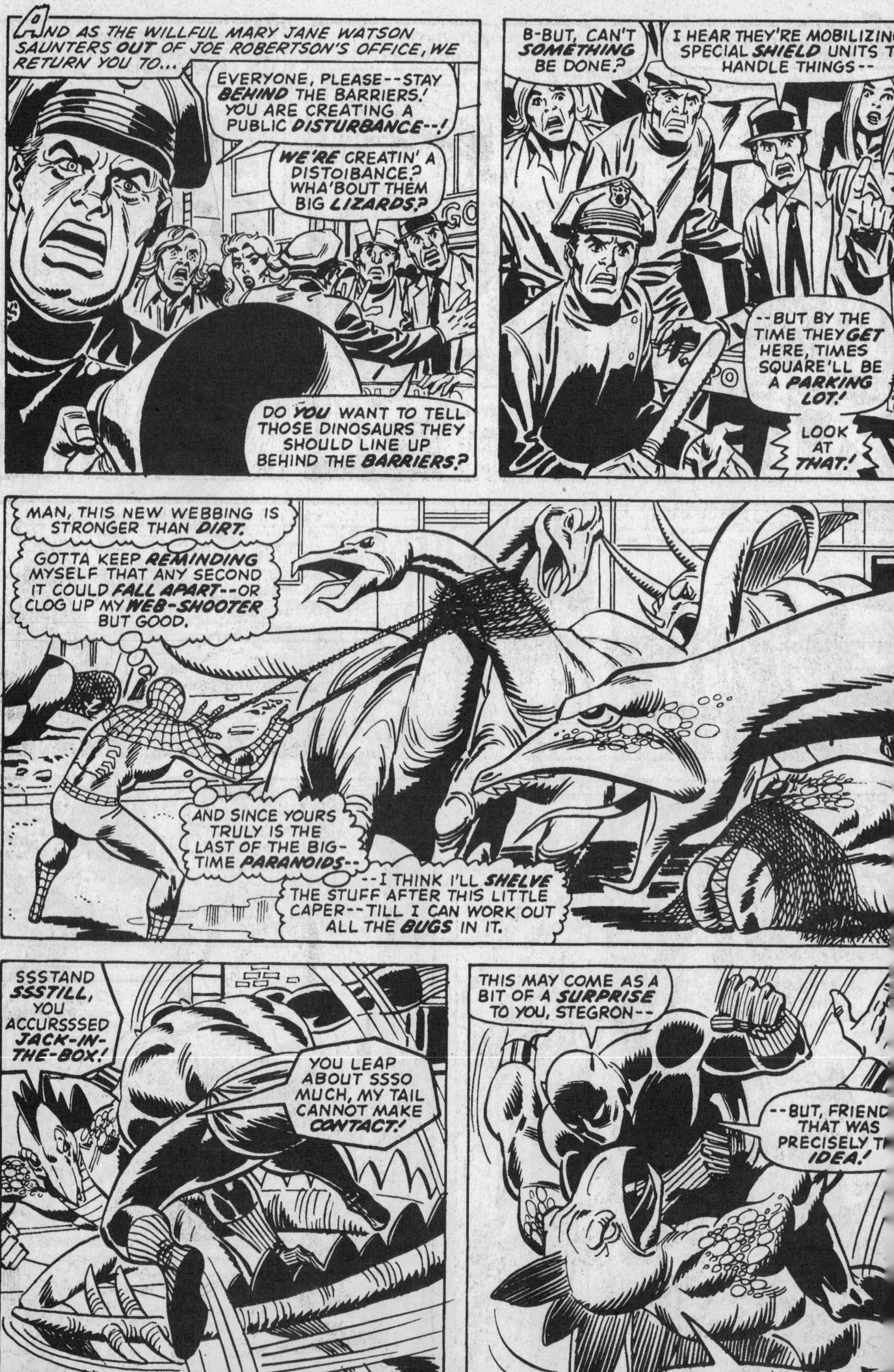
AND AS THE WILLFUL MARY JANE WATSON SAUNTERS OUT OF JOE ROBERTSON'S OFFICE, WE RETURN YOU TO...
EVERYONE, PLEASE--STAY BEHIND THE BARRIERS! YOU ARE CREATING A PUBLIC DISTURBANCE--!
WE'RE CREATIN' A DISTOIBANCE? WHA'BOUT THEM BIG LIZARDS?
DO YOU WANT TO TELL THOSE DINOSAURS THEY SHOULD LINE UP BEHIND THE BARRIERS?
B-BUT, CAN'T SOMETHING BE DONE?
I HEAR THEY'RE MOBILIZING SPECIAL SHIELD UNITS TO HANDLE THINGS--
--BUT BY THE TIME THEY GET HERE, TIMES SQUARE'LL BE A PARKING LOT!
LOOK AT THAT!
MAN, THIS NEW WEBBING IS STRONGER THAN DIRT.
GOTTA KEEP REMINDING MYSELF THAT ANY SECOND IT COULD FALL APART--OR CLOG UP MY WEB-SHOOTER BUT GOOD.
AND SINCE YOURS TRULY IS THE LAST OF THE BIG-TIME PARANOIDS--
--I THINK I'LL SHELVE THE STUFF AFTER THIS LITTLE CAPER--TILL I CAN WORK OUT ALL THE BUGS IN IT.
SSSTAND SSSTILL, YOU ACCURSSSED JACK-IN-THE-BOX!
YOU LEAP ABOUT SSSO MUCH, MY TAIL CANNOT MAKE CONTACT!
THIS MAY COME AS A BIT OF A SURPRISE TO YOU, STEGRON--
--BUT, FRIEND THAT WAS PRECISELY T IDEA!
UUNNFF!

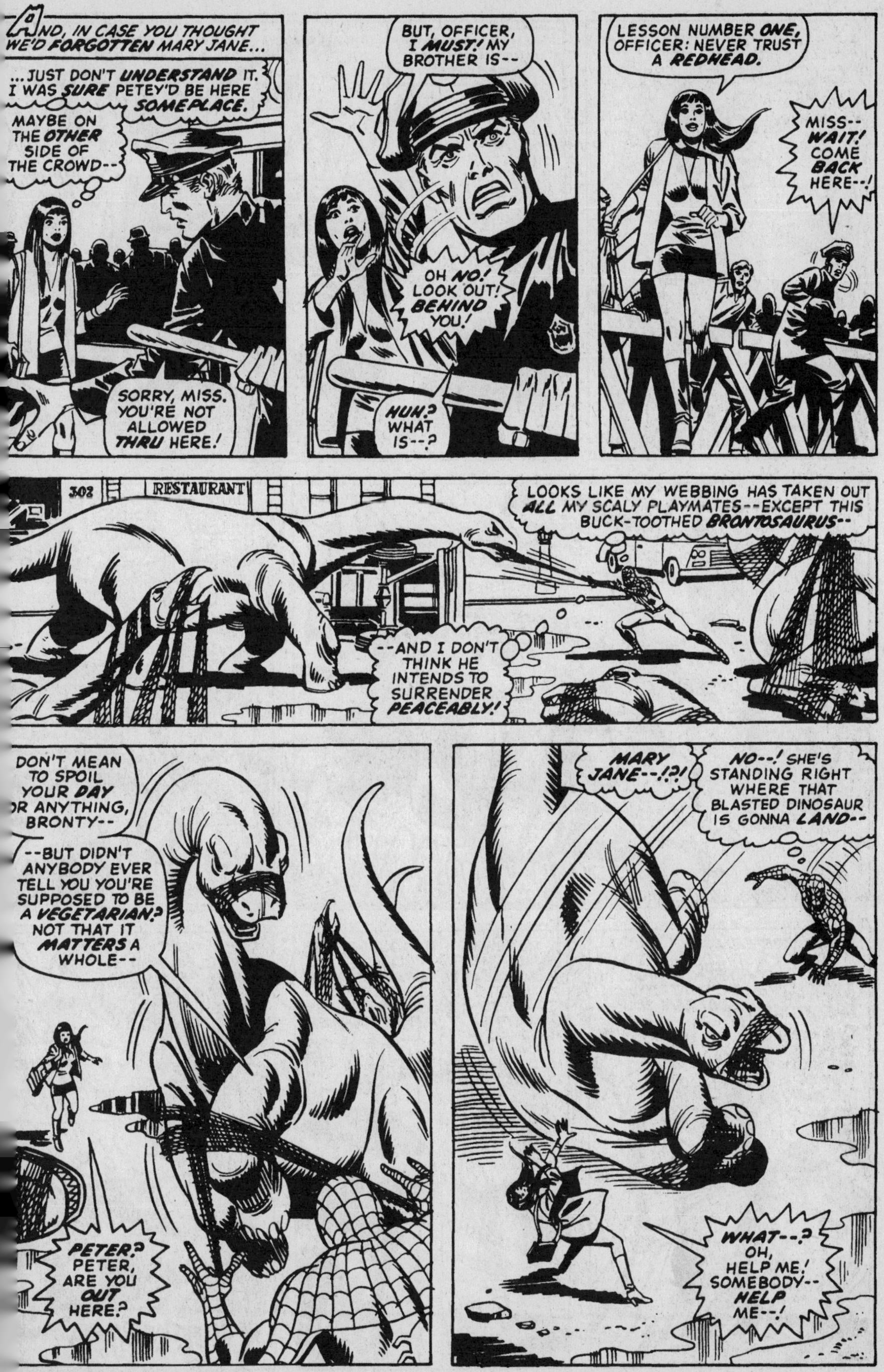
AND, IN CASE YOU THOUGHT WE'D FORGOTTEN MARY JANE...
...JUST DON'T UNDERSTAND IT. I WAS SURE PETEY'D BE HERE SOMEPLACE.
MAYBE ON THE OTHER SIDE OF THE CROWD--
SORRY, MISS. YOU'RE NOT ALLOWED THRU HERE!
BUT, OFFICER, I MUST! MY BROTHER IS--
OH NO! LOOK OUT! BEHIND YOU!
HUH? WHAT IS--?
LESSON NUMBER ONE, OFFICER: NEVER TRUST A REDHEAD.
MISS--WAIT! COME BACK HERE--!
302
RESTAURANT
LOOKS LIKE MY WEBBING HAS TAKEN OUT ALL MY SCALY PLAYMATES--EXCEPT THIS BUCK-TOOTHED BRONTOSAURUS--
--AND I DON'T THINK HE INTENDS TO SURRENDER PEACEABLY!
DON'T MEAN TO SPOIL YOUR DAY OR ANYTHING, BRONTY--
--BUT DIDN'T ANYBODY EVER TELL YOU YOU'RE SUPPOSED TO BE A VEGETARIAN? NOT THAT IT MATTERS A WHOLE--
PETER? PETER, ARE YOU OUT HERE?
MARY JANE--!?!
NO--! SHE'S STANDING RIGHT WHERE THAT BLASTED DINOSAUR IS GONNA LAND--
WHAT--? OH, HELP ME! SOMEBODY--HELP ME--!

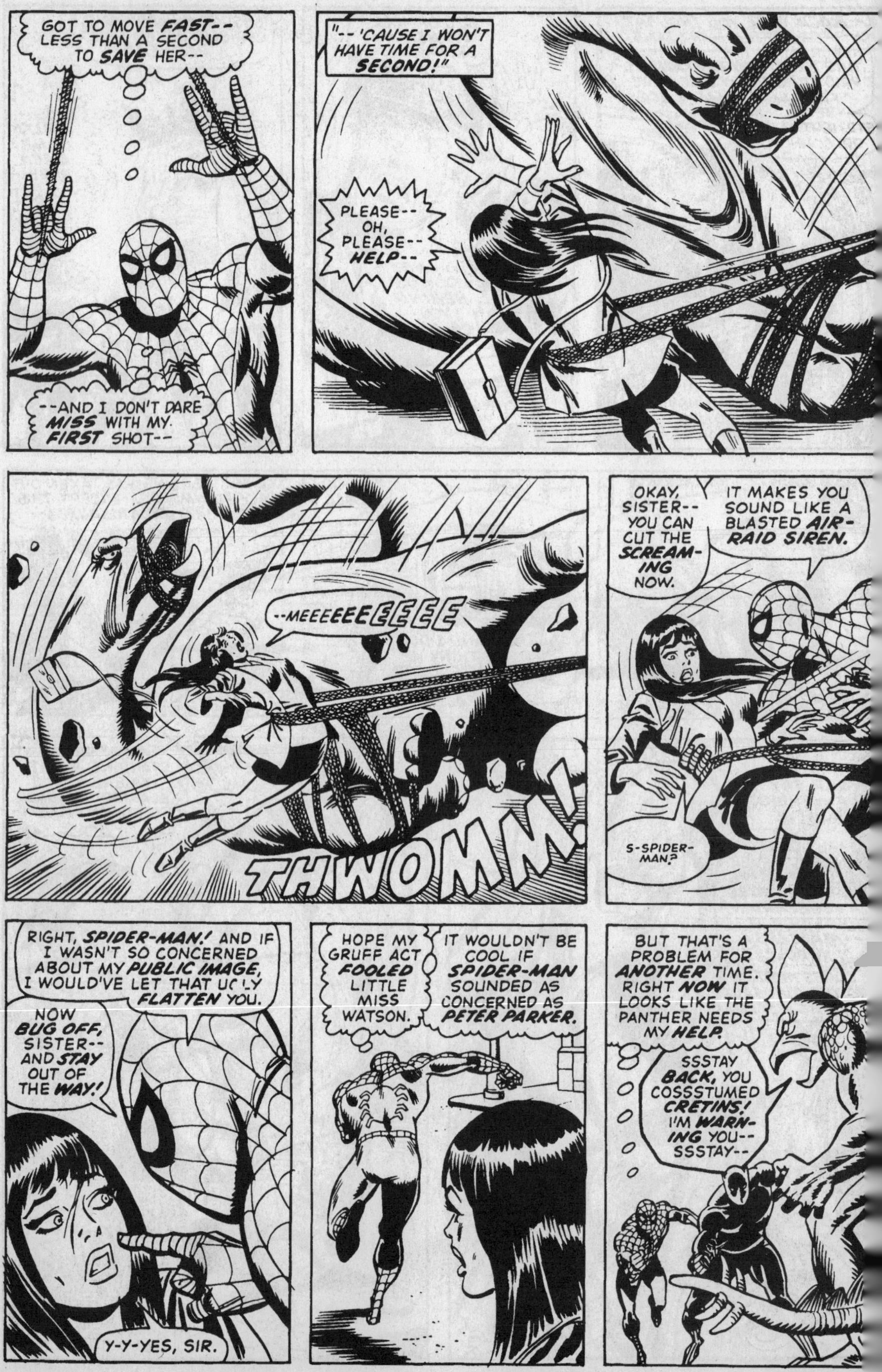
GOT TO MOVE FAST-- LESS THAN A SECOND TO SAVE HER--
--AND I DON'T DARE MISS WITH MY FIRST SHOT--
"--'CAUSE I WON'T HAVE TIME FOR A SECOND!"
PLEASE-- OH, PLEASE-- HELP--
--MEEEEEEEEEE
THWOMM!
OKAY, SISTER-- YOU CAN CUT THE SCREAMING NOW.
IT MAKES YOU SOUND LIKE A BLASTED AIR-RAID SIREN.
S-SPIDER-MAN?
RIGHT, SPIDER-MAN! AND IF I WASN'T SO CONCERNED ABOUT MY PUBLIC IMAGE, I WOULD'VE LET THAT UGLY FLATTEN YOU.
NOW BUG OFF, SISTER-- AND STAY OUT OF THE WAY!
Y-Y-YES, SIR.
HOPE MY GRUFF ACT FOOLED LITTLE MISS WATSON.
IT WOULDN'T BE COOL IF SPIDER-MAN SOUNDED AS CONCERNED AS PETER PARKER.
BUT THAT'S A PROBLEM FOR ANOTHER TIME. RIGHT NOW IT LOOKS LIKE THE PANTHER NEEDS MY HELP.
SSSTAY BACK, YOU COSSSTUMED CRETINS! I'M WARNING YOU-- SSSTAY--

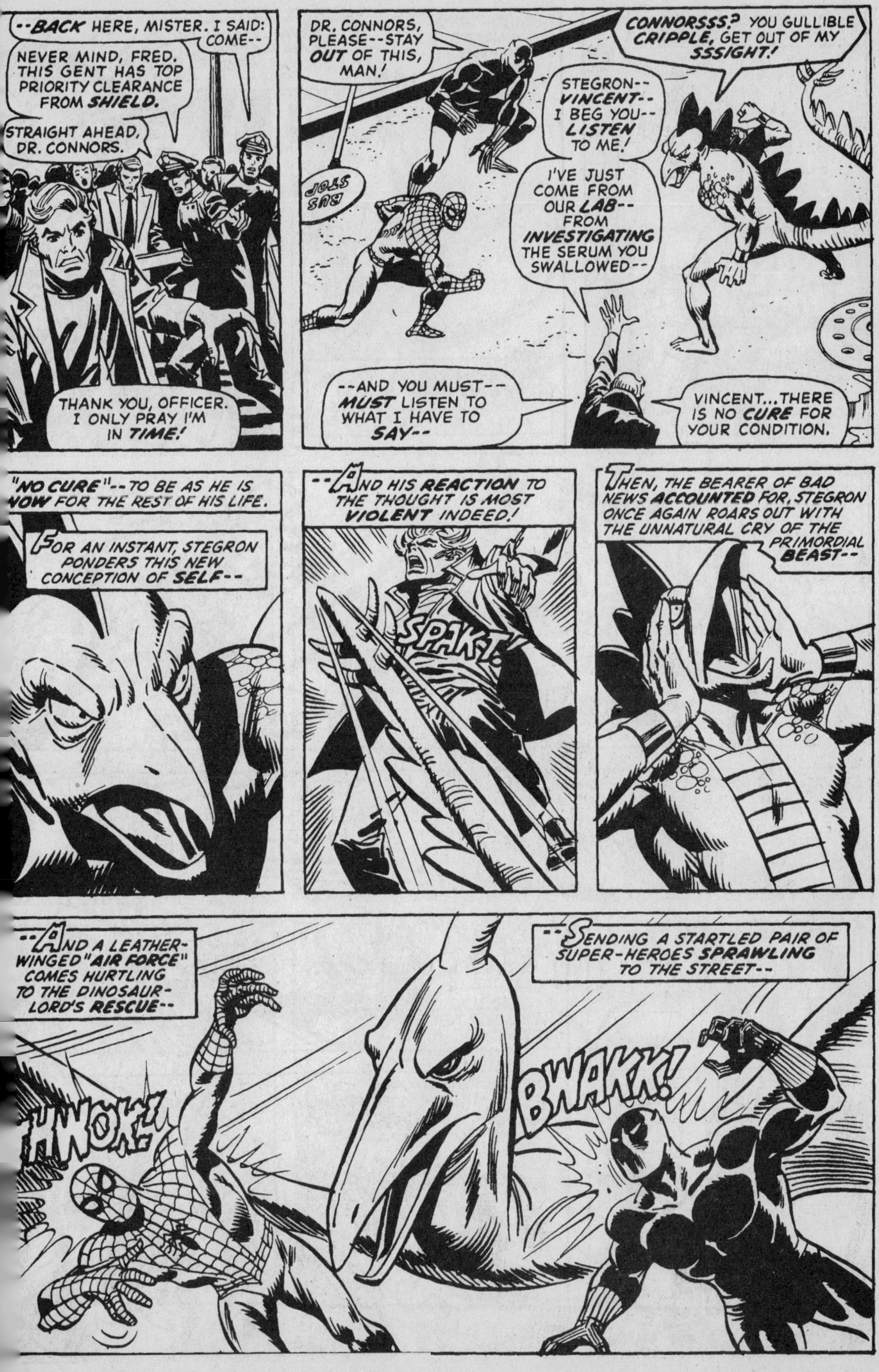
--BACK HERE, MISTER. I SAID: COME--
NEVER MIND, FRED. THIS GENT HAS TOP PRIORITY CLEARANCE FROM SHIELD.
STRAIGHT AHEAD, DR. CONNORS.
THANK YOU, OFFICER. I ONLY PRAY I'M IN TIME!
DR. CONNORS, PLEASE--STAY OUT OF THIS, MAN!
BUS STOP
CONNORSSS? YOU GULLIBLE CRIPPLE, GET OUT OF MY SSSIGHT!
STEGRON-- VINCENT-- I BEG YOU-- LISTEN TO ME!
I'VE JUST COME FROM OUR LAB-- FROM INVESTIGATING THE SERUM YOU SWALLOWED--
--AND YOU MUST-- MUST LISTEN TO WHAT I HAVE TO SAY--
VINCENT...THERE IS NO CURE FOR YOUR CONDITION.
"NO CURE"--TO BE AS HE IS NOW FOR THE REST OF HIS LIFE.
FOR AN INSTANT, STEGRON PONDERS THIS NEW CONCEPTION OF SELF--
--AND HIS REACTION TO THE THOUGHT IS MOST VIOLENT INDEED!
SPAKT
THEN, THE BEARER OF BAD NEWS ACCOUNTED FOR, STEGRON ONCE AGAIN ROARS OUT WITH THE UNNATURAL CRY OF THE PRIMORDIAL BEAST--
--AND A LEATHER-WINGED "AIR FORCE" COMES HURTLING TO THE DINOSAUR-LORD'S RESCUE--
--SENDING A STARTLED PAIR OF SUPER-HEROES SPRAWLING TO THE STREET--
HWOK!
BWAKK!

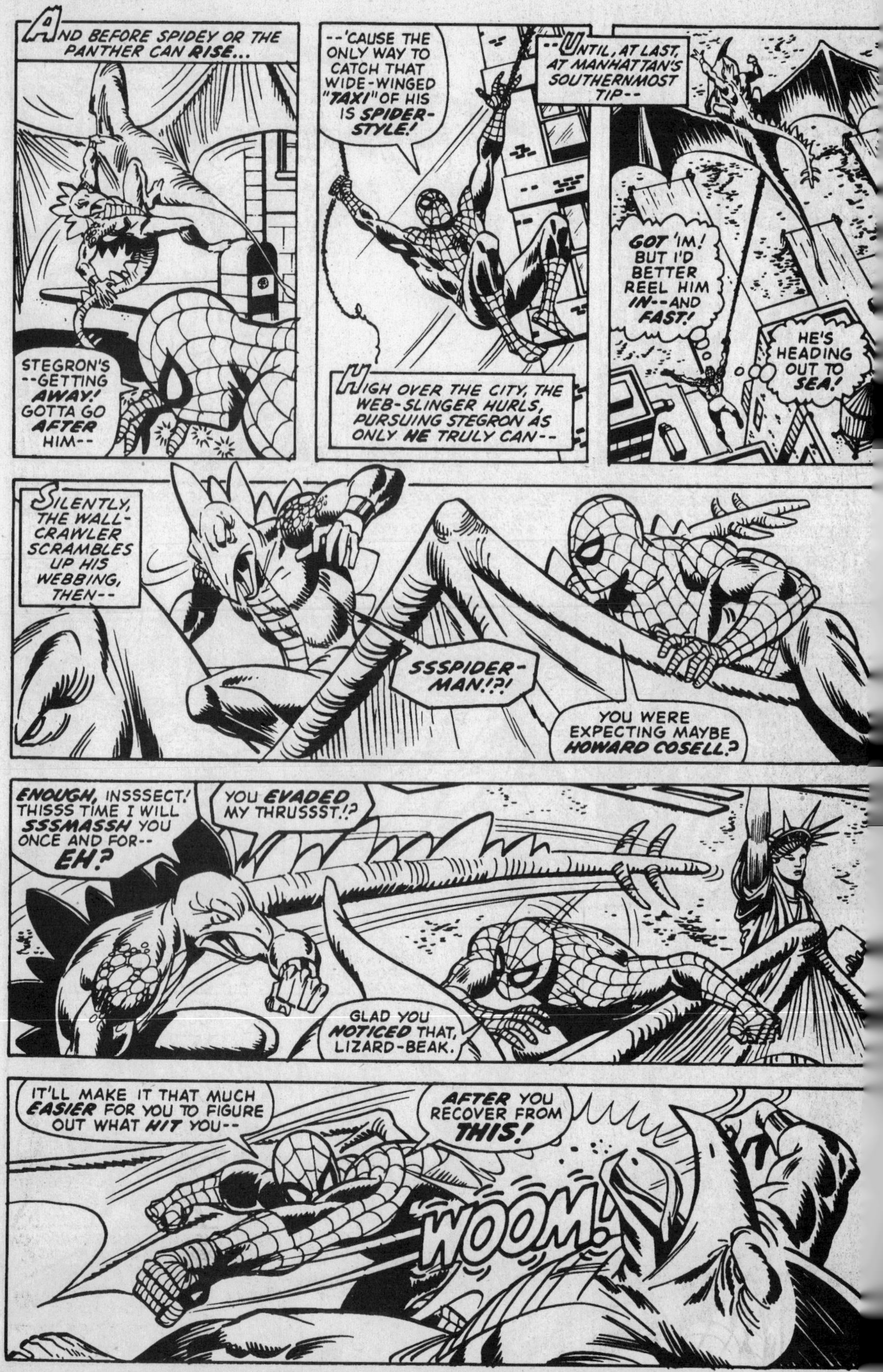
AND BEFORE SPIDEY OR THE PANTHER CAN RISE...
STEGRON'S --GETTING AWAY! GOTTA GO AFTER HIM--
--'CAUSE THE ONLY WAY TO CATCH THAT WIDE-WINGED "TAXI" OF HIS IS SPIDER-STYLE!
HIGH OVER THE CITY, THE WEB-SLINGER HURLS, PURSUING STEGRON AS ONLY HE TRULY CAN--
--UNTIL, AT LAST, AT MANHATTAN'S SOUTHERNMOST TIP--
GOT 'IM! BUT I'D BETTER REEL HIM IN--AND FAST!
HE'S HEADING OUT TO SEA!
SILENTLY, THE WALL-CRAWLER SCRAMBLES UP HIS WEBBING, THEN--
SSSPIDER-MAN!?!
YOU WERE EXPECTING MAYBE HOWARD COSELL?
ENOUGH, INSSSECT! THISSS TIME I WILL SSSMASSH YOU ONCE AND FOR-- EH?
YOU EVADED MY THRUSSST.!?
GLAD YOU NOTICED THAT, LIZARD-BEAK.
IT'LL MAKE IT THAT MUCH EASIER FOR YOU TO FIGURE OUT WHAT HIT YOU--
AFTER YOU RECOVER FROM THIS!
WOOOM!

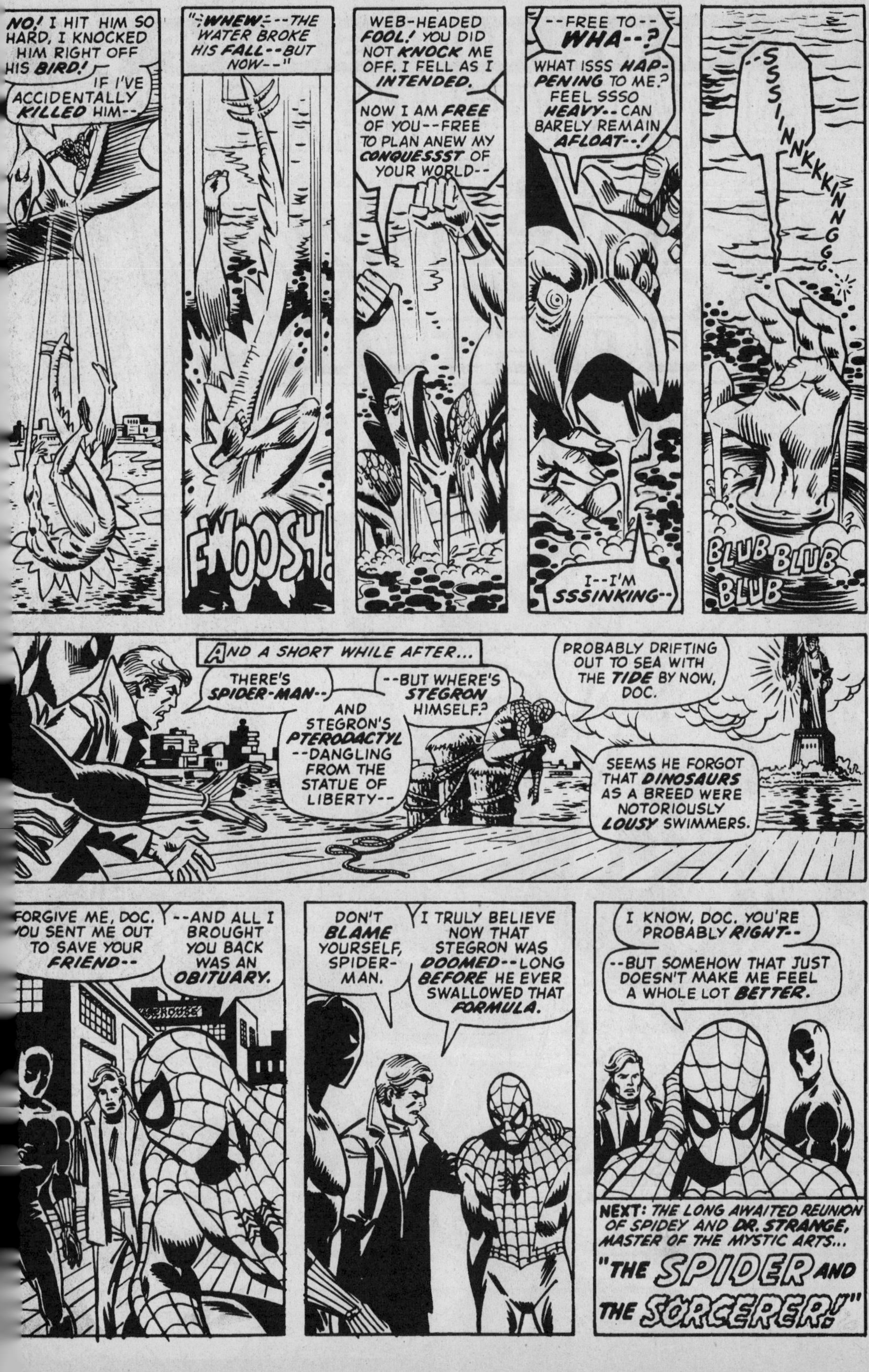

NO! I HIT HIM SO HARD, I KNOCKED HIM RIGHT OFF HIS BIRD!
IF I'VE ACCIDENTALLY KILLED HIM--
"WHEW!--THE WATER BROKE HIS FALL--BUT NOW--"
FWOOSH!
WEB-HEADED FOOL! YOU DID NOT KNOCK ME OFF. I FELL AS I INTENDED.
NOW I AM FREE OF YOU--FREE TO PLAN ANEW MY CONQUESSST OF YOUR WORLD--
--FREE TO--WHA--?
WHAT ISSS HAPPENING TO ME? FEEL SSSO HEAVY--CAN BARELY REMAIN AFLOAT--!
I--I'M SSSINKING--
SSSINNKKKINNGGG...
BLUB BLUB BLUB
AND A SHORT WHILE AFTER...
THERE'S SPIDER-MAN--
--BUT WHERE'S STEGRON HIMSELF?
AND STEGRON'S PTERODACTYL--DANGLING FROM THE STATUE OF LIBERTY--
PROBABLY DRIFTING OUT TO SEA WITH THE TIDE BY NOW, DOC.
SEEMS HE FORGOT THAT DINOSAURS AS A BREED WERE NOTORIOUSLY LOUSY SWIMMERS.
FORGIVE ME, DOC. YOU SENT ME OUT TO SAVE YOUR FRIEND--
--AND ALL I BROUGHT YOU BACK WAS AN OBITUARY.
DON'T BLAME YOURSELF, SPIDER-MAN.
I TRULY BELIEVE NOW THAT STEGRON WAS DOOMED--LONG BEFORE HE EVER SWALLOWED THAT FORMULA.
I KNOW, DOC. YOU'RE PROBABLY RIGHT--
--BUT SOMEHOW THAT JUST DOESN'T MAKE ME FEEL A WHOLE LOT BETTER.
NEXT: THE LONG AWAITED REUNION OF SPIDEY AND DR. STRANGE, MASTER OF THE MYSTIC ARTS...
"THE SPIDER AND THE SORCERER!"

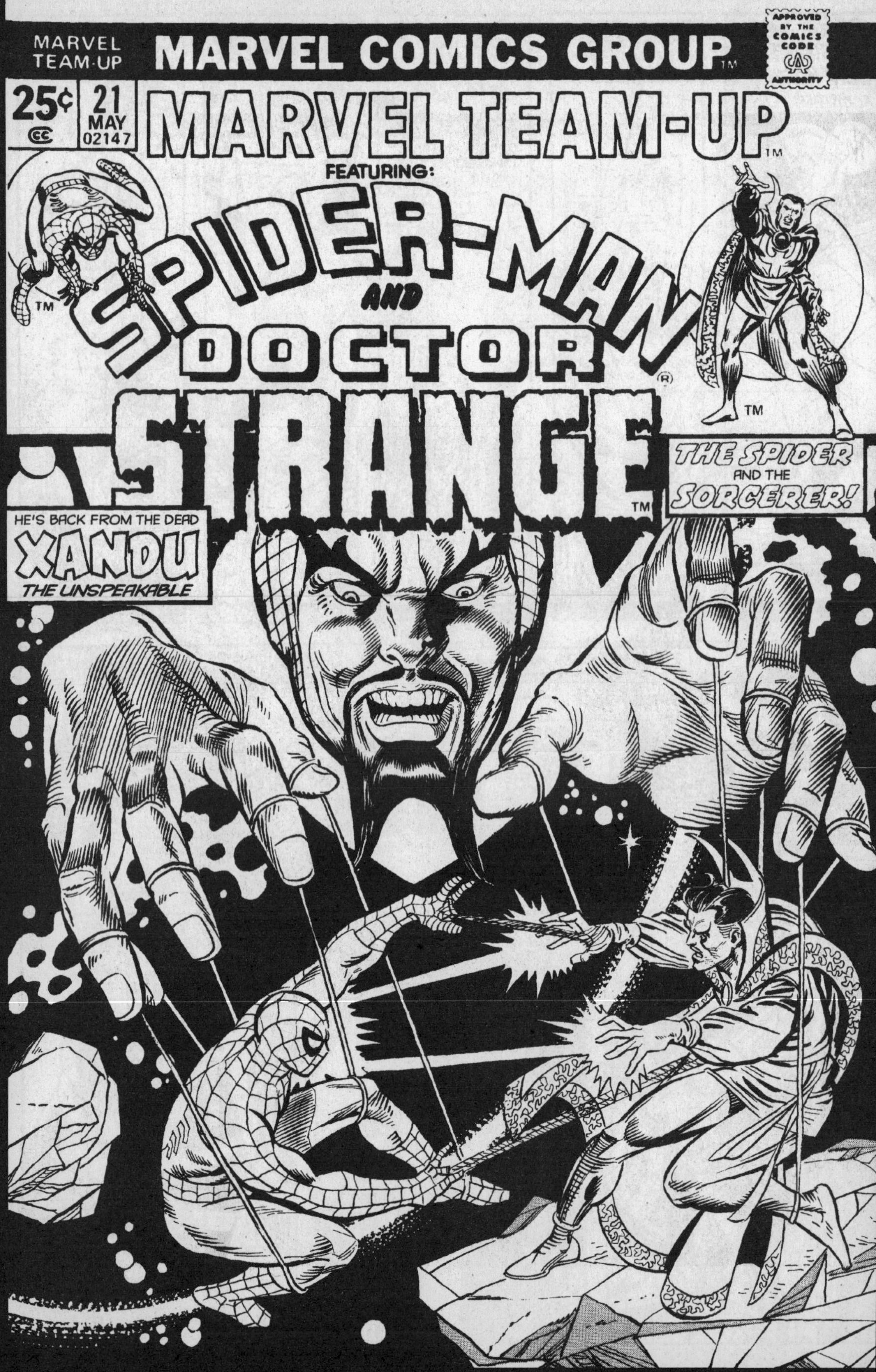

MARVEL TEAM-UP
MARVEL COMICS GROUP
APPROVED BY THE COMICS CODE AUTHORITY
25¢
21 MAY 02147
MARVEL TEAM-UP
FEATURING:
SPIDER-MAN AND DOCTOR STRANGE
THE SPIDER AND THE SORCERER!
HE'S BACK FROM THE DEAD
XANDU
THE UNSPEAKABLE

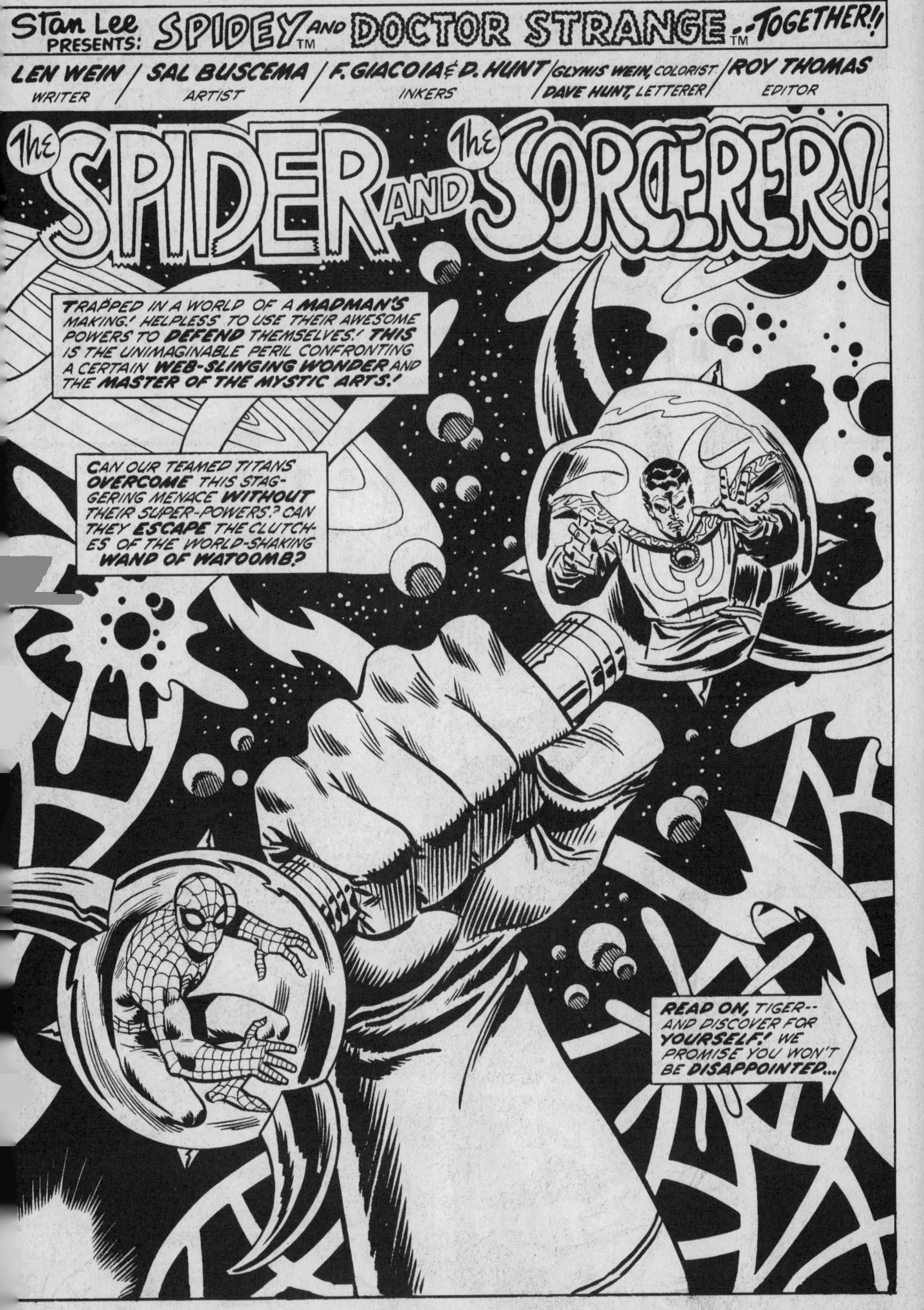

Stan Lee PRESENTS: SPIDEY AND DOCTOR STRANGE --TOGETHER!!
LEN WEIN WRITER / SAL BUSCEMA ARTIST / F. GIACOIA & D. HUNT INKERS / GLYNIS WEIN, COLORIST DAVE HUNT, LETTERER / ROY THOMAS EDITOR
THE SPIDER AND THE SORCERER!
TRAPPED IN A WORLD OF A MADMAN'S MAKING! HELPLESS TO USE THEIR AWESOME POWERS TO DEFEND THEMSELVES! THIS IS THE UNIMAGINABLE PERIL CONFRONTING A CERTAIN WEB-SLINGING WONDER AND THE MASTER OF THE MYSTIC ARTS!
CAN OUR TEAMED TITANS OVERCOME THIS STAGGERING MENACE WITHOUT THEIR SUPER-POWERS? CAN THEY ESCAPE THE CLUTCHES OF THE WORLD-SHAKING WAND OF WATOOMB?
READ ON, TIGER-- AND DISCOVER FOR YOURSELF! WE PROMISE YOU WON'T BE DISAPPOINTED...

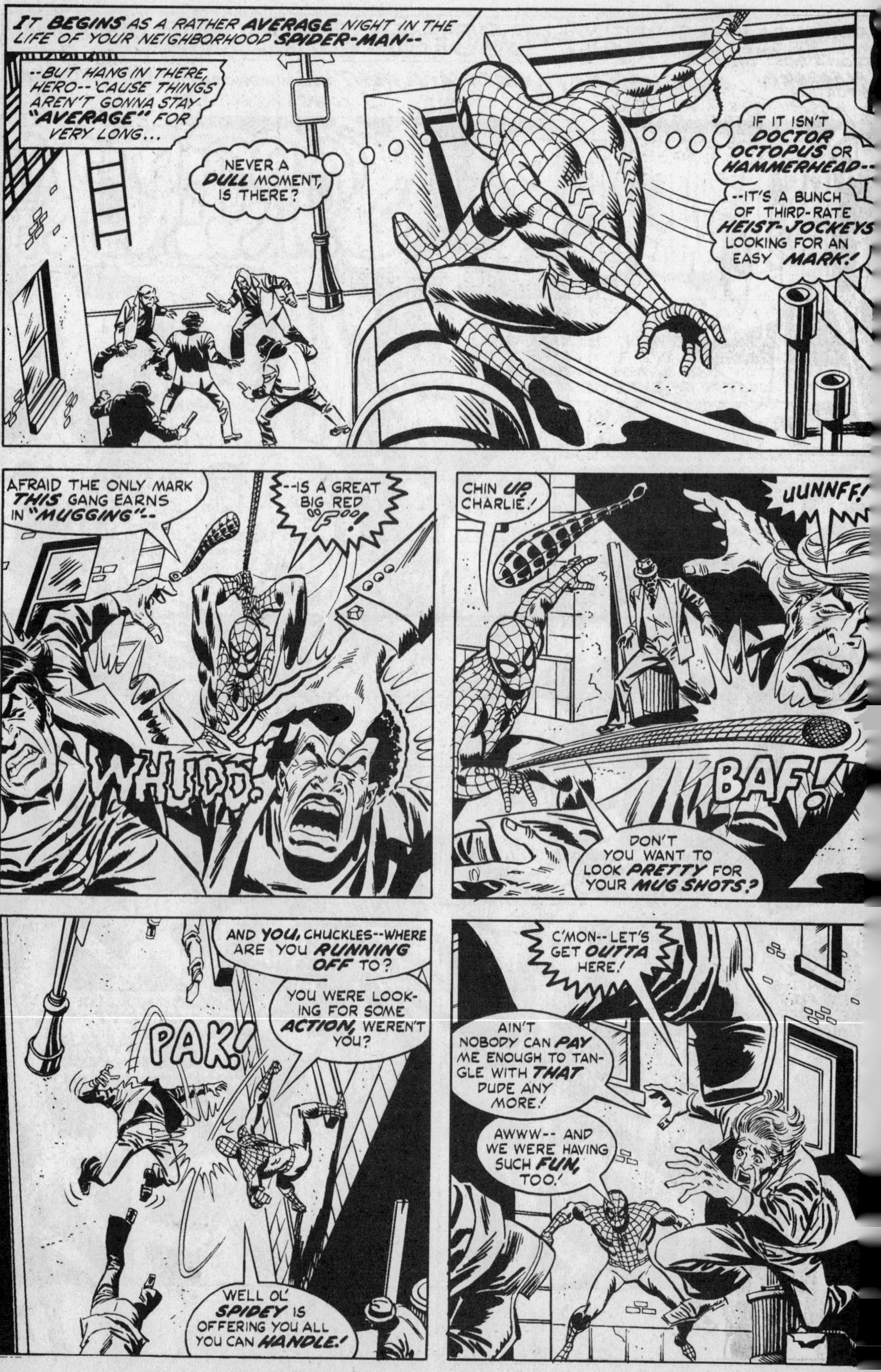
IT BEGINS AS A RATHER AVERAGE NIGHT IN THE LIFE OF YOUR NEIGHBORHOOD SPIDER-MAN--
--BUT HANG IN THERE, HERO--'CAUSE THINGS AREN'T GONNA STAY "AVERAGE" FOR VERY LONG...
NEVER A DULL MOMENT, IS THERE?
IF IT ISN'T DOCTOR OCTOPUS OR HAMMERHEAD--
--IT'S A BUNCH OF THIRD-RATE HEIST-JOCKEYS LOOKING FOR AN EASY MARK!
AFRAID THE ONLY MARK THIS GANG EARNS IN "MUGGING"--
--IS A GREAT BIG RED "F"!
WHUDD!
CHIN UP, CHARLIE!
UUNNFF!
BAF!
DON'T YOU WANT TO LOOK PRETTY FOR YOUR MUG SHOTS?
AND YOU, CHUCKLES--WHERE ARE YOU RUNNING OFF TO?
YOU WERE LOOKING FOR SOME ACTION, WEREN'T YOU?
PAK!
WELL OL' SPIDEY IS OFFERING YOU ALL YOU CAN HANDLE!
C'MON--LET'S GET OUTTA HERE!
AIN'T NOBODY CAN PAY ME ENOUGH TO TANGLE WITH THAT DUDE ANY MORE!
AWWW-- AND WE WERE HAVING SUCH FUN, TOO!

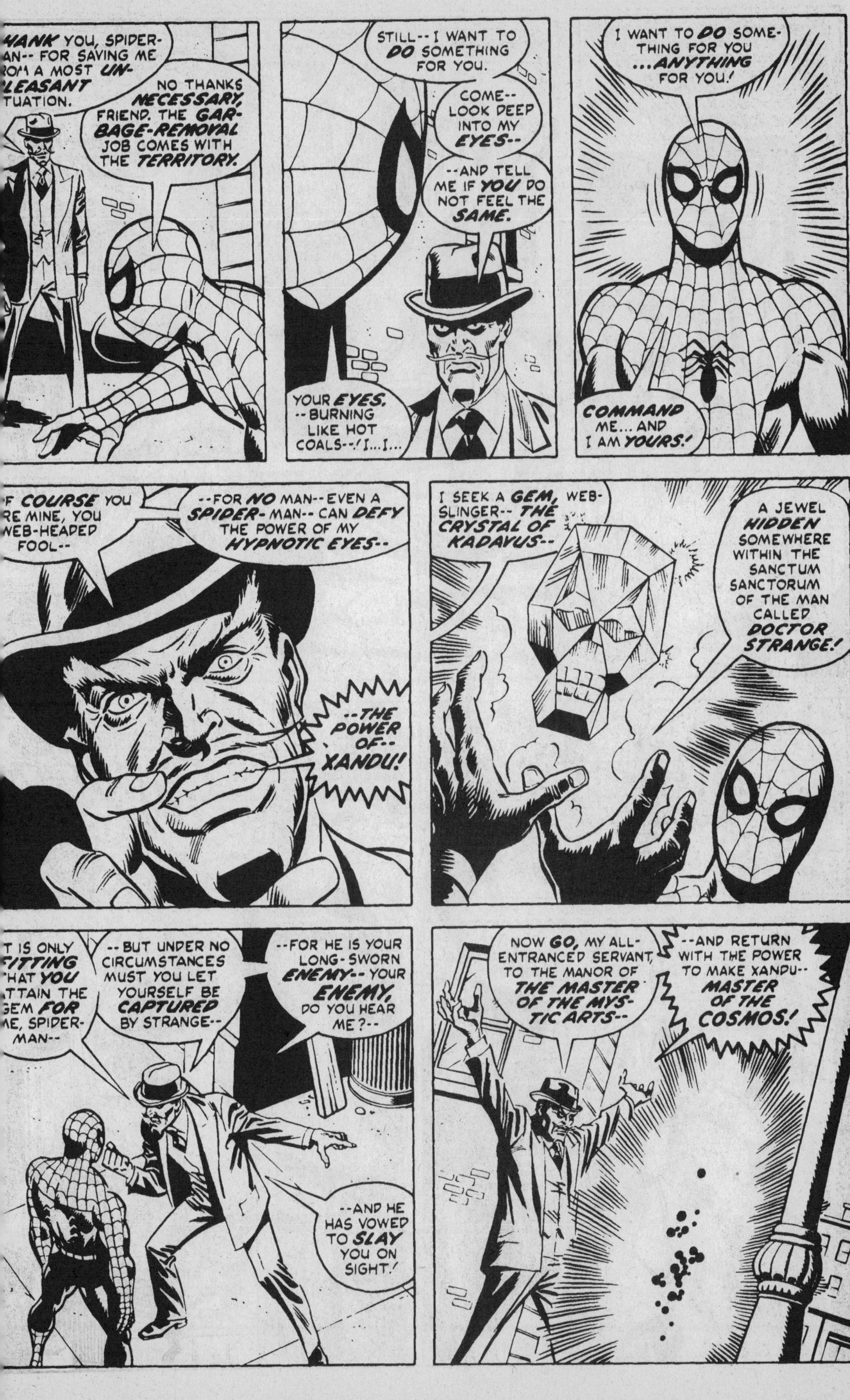
HANK YOU, SPIDER-
AN-- FOR SAVING ME
ROM A MOST UN-
LEASANT
TUATION.
NO THANKS NECESSARY, FRIEND. THE GARBAGE-REMOVAL JOB COMES WITH THE TERRITORY.
STILL--I WANT TO DO SOMETHING FOR YOU.
COME--LOOK DEEP INTO MY EYES--
--AND TELL ME IF YOU DO NOT FEEL THE SAME.
YOUR EYES. --BURNING LIKE HOT COALS--! I...I...
I WANT TO DO SOMETHING FOR YOU ...ANYTHING FOR YOU!
COMMAND ME... AND I AM YOURS!
F COURSE YOU
RE MINE, YOU
WEB-HEADED
FOOL--
--FOR NO MAN--EVEN A SPIDER-MAN--CAN DEFY THE POWER OF MY HYPNOTIC EYES--
--THE POWER OF--XANDU!
I SEEK A GEM, WEB-SLINGER--THE CRYSTAL OF KADAVUS--
A JEWEL HIDDEN SOMEWHERE WITHIN THE SANCTUM SANCTORUM OF THE MAN CALLED DOCTOR STRANGE!
T IS ONLY
FITTING
THAT YOU
TTAIN THE
GEM FOR
ME, SPIDER-
MAN--
--BUT UNDER NO CIRCUMSTANCES MUST YOU LET YOURSELF BE CAPTURED BY STRANGE--
--FOR HE IS YOUR LONG-SWORN ENEMY--YOUR ENEMY, DO YOU HEAR ME?--
--AND HE HAS VOWED TO SLAY YOU ON SIGHT!
NOW GO, MY ALL-ENTRANCED SERVANT, TO THE MANOR OF THE MASTER OF THE MYSTIC ARTS--
--AND RETURN WITH THE POWER TO MAKE XANDU--MASTER OF THE COSMOS!

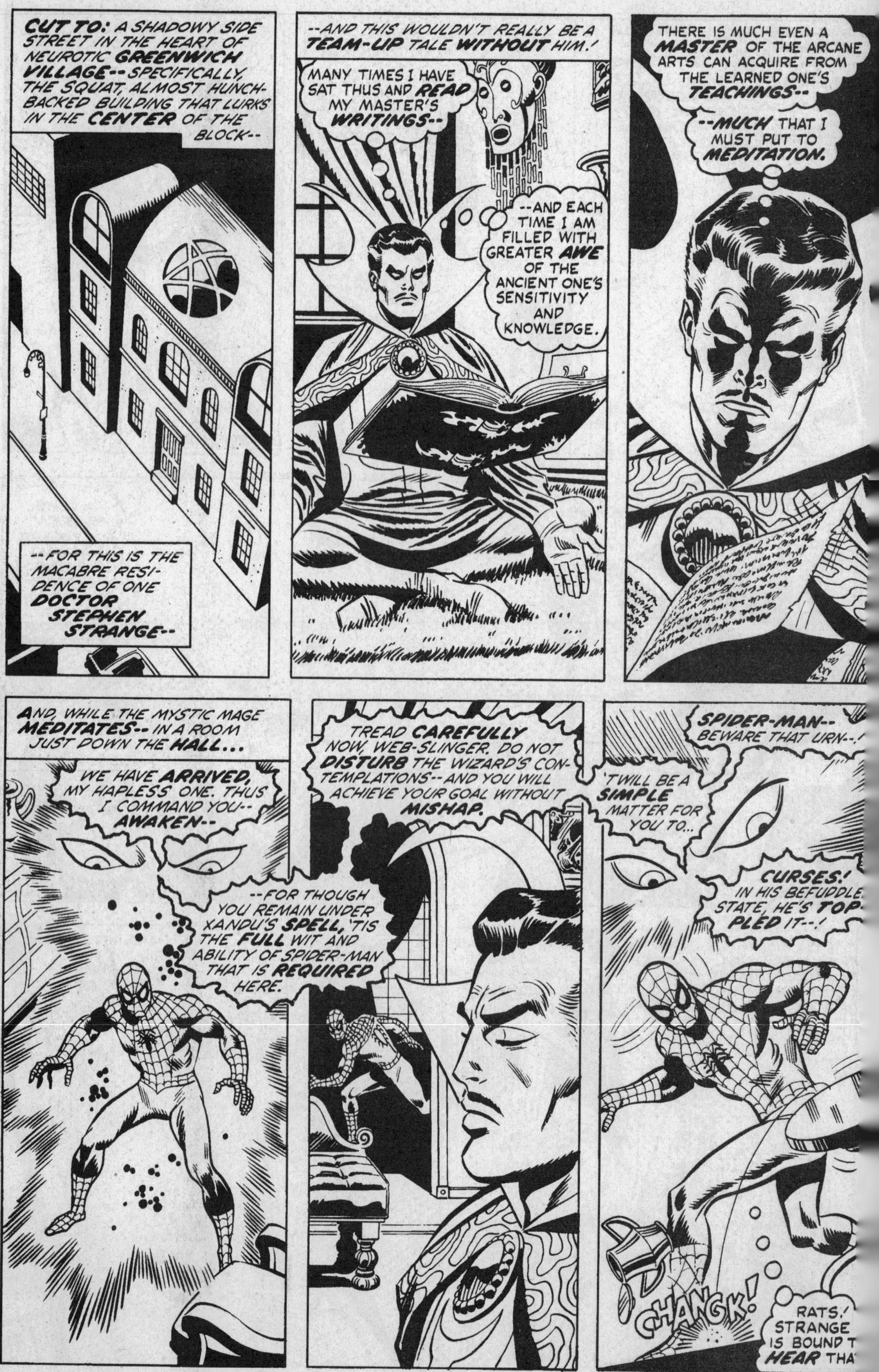
CUT TO: A SHADOWY SIDE STREET IN THE HEART OF NEUROTIC GREENWICH VILLAGE--SPECIFICALLY, THE SQUAT, ALMOST HUNCH-BACKED BUILDING THAT LURKS IN THE CENTER OF THE BLOCK--
--FOR THIS IS THE MACABRE RESI-DENCE OF ONE DOCTOR STEPHEN STRANGE--
--AND THIS WOULDN'T REALLY BE A TEAM-UP TALE WITHOUT HIM!
MANY TIMES I HAVE SAT THUS AND READ MY MASTER'S WRITINGS--
--AND EACH TIME I AM FILLED WITH GREATER AWE OF THE ANCIENT ONE'S SENSITIVITY AND KNOWLEDGE.
THERE IS MUCH EVEN A MASTER OF THE ARCANE ARTS CAN ACQUIRE FROM THE LEARNED ONE'S TEACHINGS--
--MUCH THAT I MUST PUT TO MEDITATION.
AND, WHILE THE MYSTIC MAGE MEDITATES--IN A ROOM JUST DOWN THE HALL...
WE HAVE ARRIVED, MY HAPLESS ONE. THUS I COMMAND YOU--AWAKEN--
--FOR THOUGH YOU REMAIN UNDER XANDU'S SPELL, 'TIS THE FULL WIT AND ABILITY OF SPIDER-MAN THAT IS REQUIRED HERE.
TREAD CAREFULLY NOW, WEB-SLINGER. DO NOT DISTURB THE WIZARD'S CON-TEMPLATIONS--AND YOU WILL ACHIEVE YOUR GOAL WITHOUT MISHAP.
'TWILL BE A SIMPLE MATTER FOR YOU TO...
SPIDER-MAN--BEWARE THAT URN--!
CURSES! IN HIS BEFUDDLE STATE, HE'S TOP-PLED IT--!
CHANGK!
RATS! STRANGE IS BOUND T HEAR THA

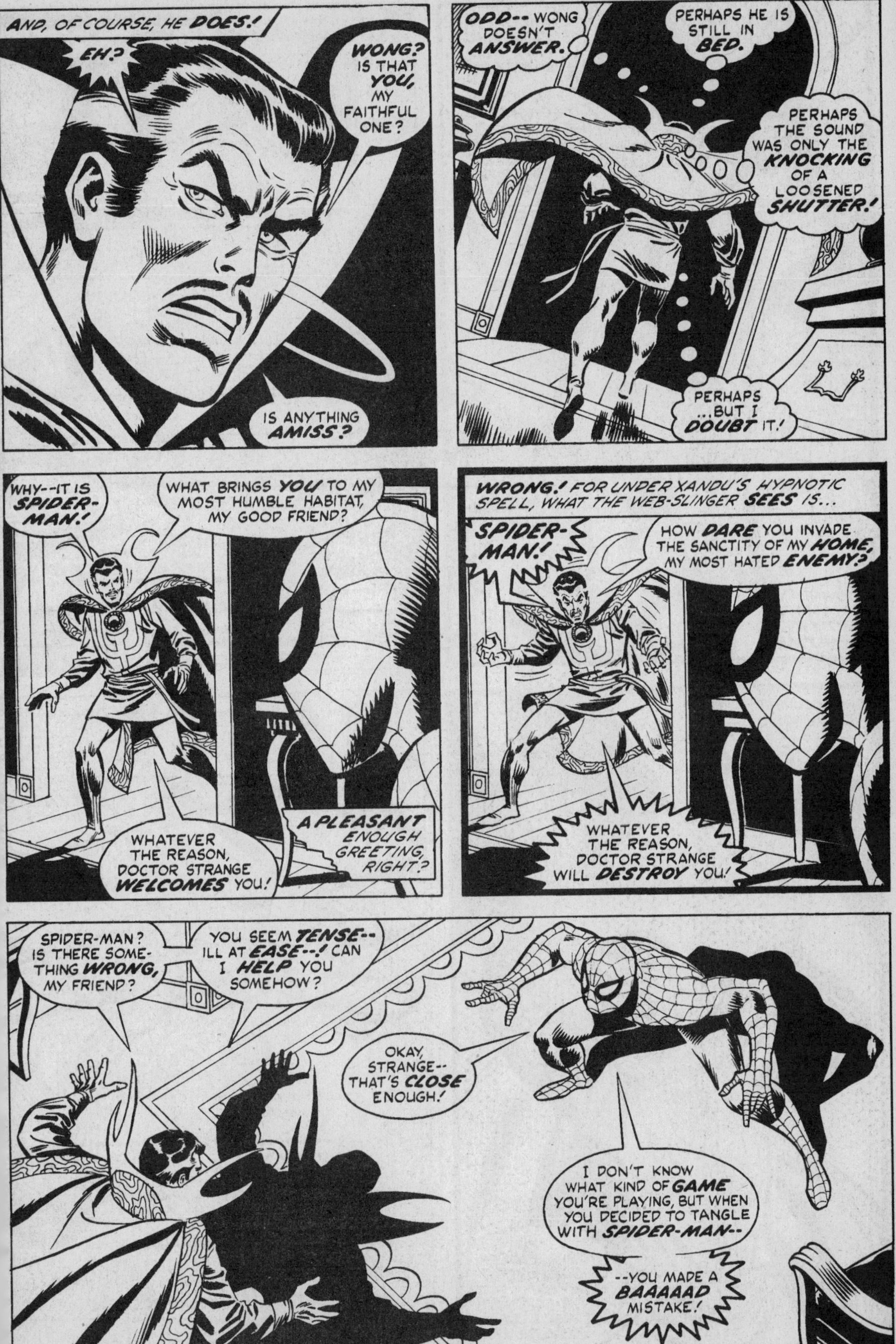
AND, OF COURSE, HE DOES!
EH?
WONG? IS THAT YOU, MY FAITHFUL ONE?
IS ANYTHING AMISS?
ODD-- WONG DOESN'T ANSWER.
PERHAPS HE IS STILL IN BED.
PERHAPS THE SOUND WAS ONLY THE KNOCKING OF A LOOSENED SHUTTER!
PERHAPS ...BUT I DOUBT IT!
WHY--IT IS SPIDER-MAN!
WHAT BRINGS YOU TO MY MOST HUMBLE HABITAT, MY GOOD FRIEND?
WHATEVER THE REASON, DOCTOR STRANGE WELCOMES YOU!
A PLEASANT ENOUGH GREETING, RIGHT?
WRONG! FOR UNDER XANDU'S HYPNOTIC SPELL, WHAT THE WEB-SLINGER SEES IS...
SPIDER-MAN!
HOW DARE YOU INVADE THE SANCTITY OF MY HOME, MY MOST HATED ENEMY?
WHATEVER THE REASON, DOCTOR STRANGE WILL DESTROY YOU!
SPIDER-MAN? IS THERE SOMETHING WRONG, MY FRIEND?
YOU SEEM TENSE-- ILL AT EASE--! CAN I HELP YOU SOMEHOW?
OKAY, STRANGE-- THAT'S CLOSE ENOUGH!
I DON'T KNOW WHAT KIND OF GAME YOU'RE PLAYING, BUT WHEN YOU DECIDED TO TANGLE WITH SPIDER-MAN--
--YOU MADE A BAAAAAD MISTAKE!

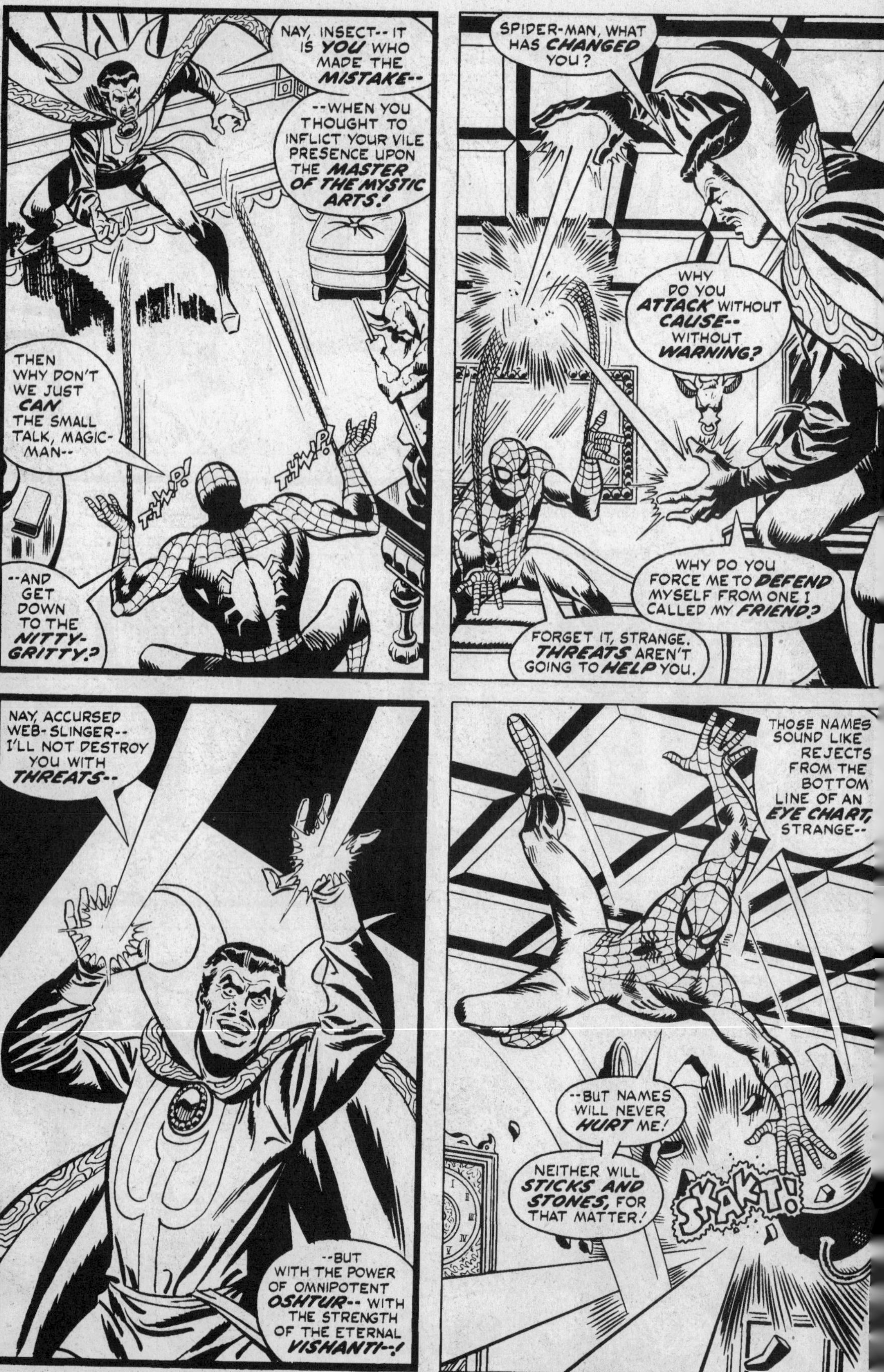
NAY, INSECT-- IT IS YOU WHO MADE THE MISTAKE--
--WHEN YOU THOUGHT TO INFLICT YOUR VILE PRESENCE UPON THE MASTER OF THE MYSTIC ARTS!
THEN WHY DON'T WE JUST CAN THE SMALL TALK, MAGIC-MAN--
THWIP!
THWIP!
--AND GET DOWN TO THE NITTY-GRITTY?
SPIDER-MAN, WHAT HAS CHANGED YOU?
WHY DO YOU ATTACK WITHOUT CAUSE-- WITHOUT WARNING?
WHY DO YOU FORCE ME TO DEFEND MYSELF FROM ONE I CALLED MY FRIEND?
FORGET IT, STRANGE. THREATS AREN'T GOING TO HELP YOU.
NAY, ACCURSED WEB-SLINGER-- I'LL NOT DESTROY YOU WITH THREATS--
--BUT WITH THE POWER OF OMNIPOTENT OSHTUR-- WITH THE STRENGTH OF THE ETERNAL VISHANTI--!
THOSE NAMES SOUND LIKE REJECTS FROM THE BOTTOM LINE OF AN EYE CHART, STRANGE--
--BUT NAMES WILL NEVER HURT ME!
NEITHER WILL STICKS AND STONES, FOR THAT MATTER!
SKAKT!

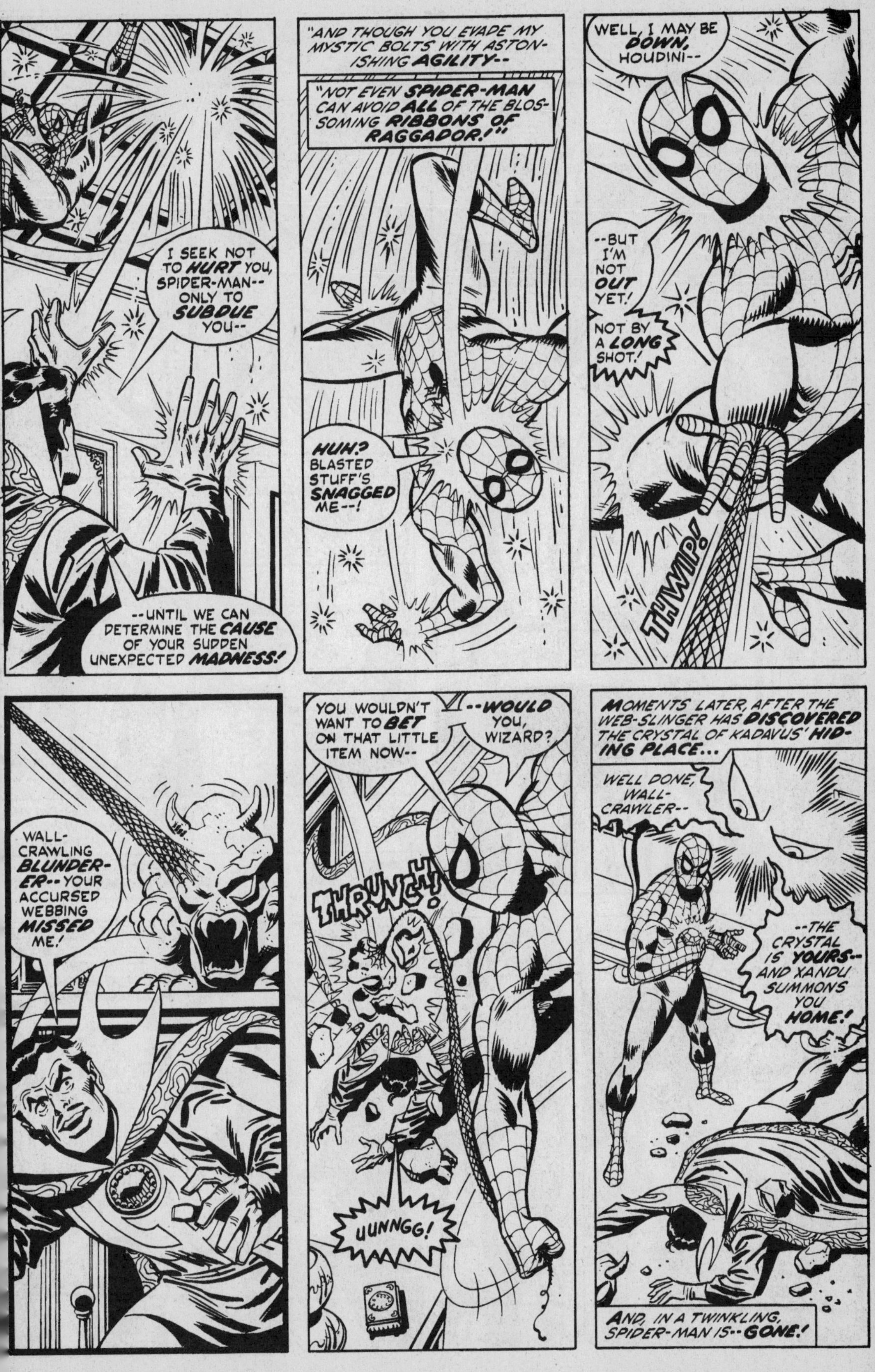
I SEEK NOT TO HURT YOU, SPIDER-MAN-- ONLY TO SUBDUE YOU--
--UNTIL WE CAN DETERMINE THE CAUSE OF YOUR SUDDEN UNEXPECTED MADNESS!
"AND THOUGH YOU EVADE MY MYSTIC BOLTS WITH ASTON-ISHING AGILITY--
"NOT EVEN SPIDER-MAN CAN AVOID ALL OF THE BLOS-SOMING RIBBONS OF RAGGADOR!"
HUH? BLASTED STUFF'S SNAGGED ME--!
WELL, I MAY BE DOWN, HOUDINI--
--BUT I'M NOT OUT YET!
NOT BY A LONG SHOT!
THWIP!
WALL-CRAWLING BLUNDER-ER-- YOUR ACCURSED WEBBING MISSED ME!
YOU WOULDN'T WANT TO BET ON THAT LITTLE ITEM NOW--
--WOULD YOU, WIZARD?
THRUNCH!
UUNNGG!
MOMENTS LATER, AFTER THE WEB-SLINGER HAS DISCOVERED THE CRYSTAL OF KADAVUS' HID-ING PLACE...
WELL DONE, WALL-CRAWLER--
--THE CRYSTAL IS YOURS-- AND XANDU SUMMONS YOU HOME!
AND, IN A TWINKLING, SPIDER-MAN IS--GONE!

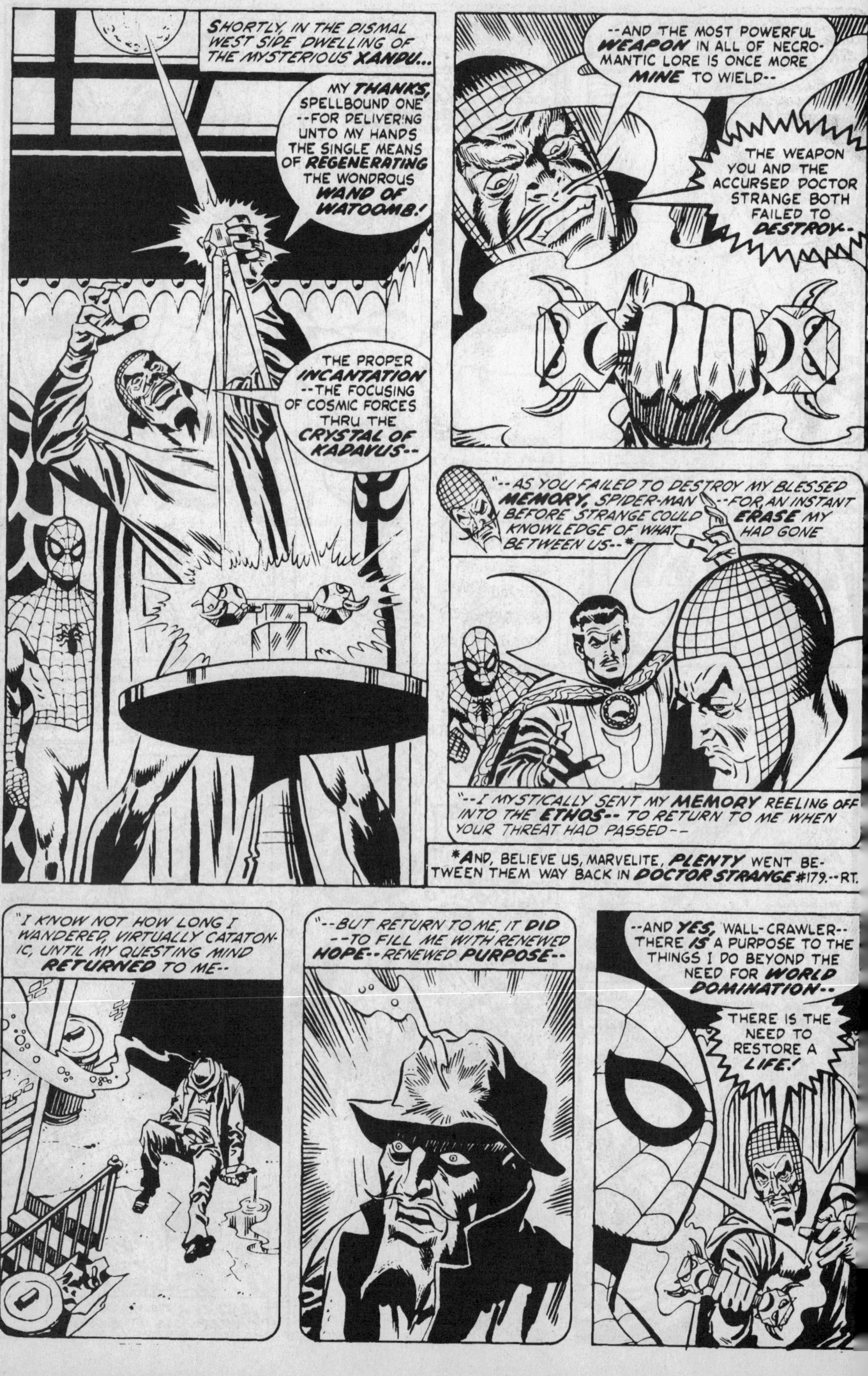

SHORTLY, IN THE DISMAL WEST SIDE DWELLING OF THE MYSTERIOUS XANDU...
MY THANKS, SPELLBOUND ONE --FOR DELIVERING UNTO MY HANDS THE SINGLE MEANS OF REGENERATING THE WONDROUS WAND OF WATOOMB!
THE PROPER INCANTATION --THE FOCUSING OF COSMIC FORCES THRU THE CRYSTAL OF KADAVUS--
--AND THE MOST POWERFUL WEAPON IN ALL OF NECRO-MANTIC LORE IS ONCE MORE MINE TO WIELD--
THE WEAPON YOU AND THE ACCURSED DOCTOR STRANGE BOTH FAILED TO DESTROY--
"--AS YOU FAILED TO DESTROY MY BLESSED MEMORY, SPIDER-MAN --FOR, AN INSTANT BEFORE STRANGE COULD ERASE MY KNOWLEDGE OF WHAT HAD GONE BETWEEN US--*
"--I MYSTICALLY SENT MY MEMORY REELING OFF INTO THE ETHOS-- TO RETURN TO ME WHEN YOUR THREAT HAD PASSED--
*AND, BELIEVE US, MARVELITE, PLENTY WENT BETWEEN THEM WAY BACK IN DOCTOR STRANGE #179.--RT.
"I KNOW NOT HOW LONG I WANDERED, VIRTUALLY CATATONIC, UNTIL MY QUESTING MIND RETURNED TO ME--
"--BUT RETURN TO ME, IT DID --TO FILL ME WITH RENEWED HOPE--RENEWED PURPOSE--
--AND YES, WALL-CRAWLER-- THERE IS A PURPOSE TO THE THINGS I DO BEYOND THE NEED FOR WORLD DOMINATION--
THERE IS THE NEED TO RESTORE A LIFE!

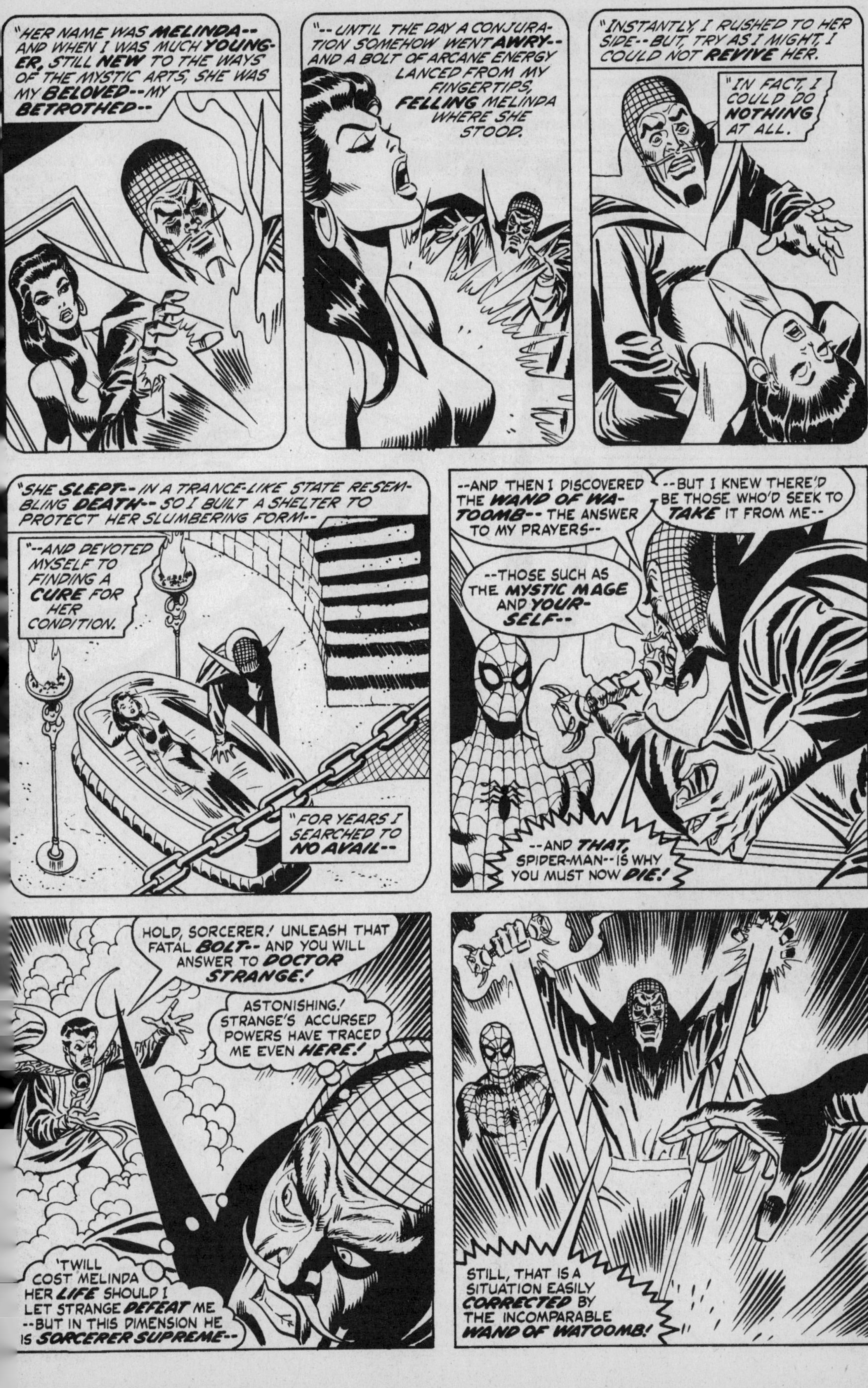
"HER NAME WAS MELINDA-- AND WHEN I WAS MUCH YOUNGER, STILL NEW TO THE WAYS OF THE MYSTIC ARTS, SHE WAS MY BELOVED--MY BETROTHED--
"--UNTIL THE DAY A CONJURATION SOMEHOW WENT AWRY-- AND A BOLT OF ARCANE ENERGY LANCED FROM MY FINGERTIPS, FELLING MELINDA WHERE SHE STOOD.
"INSTANTLY, I RUSHED TO HER SIDE--BUT, TRY AS I MIGHT, I COULD NOT REVIVE HER.
"IN FACT, I COULD DO NOTHING AT ALL.
"SHE SLEPT--IN A TRANCE-LIKE STATE RESEMBLING DEATH--SO I BUILT A SHELTER TO PROTECT HER SLUMBERING FORM--
"--AND DEVOTED MYSELF TO FINDING A CURE FOR HER CONDITION.
"FOR YEARS I SEARCHED TO NO AVAIL--
--AND THEN I DISCOVERED THE WAND OF WATOOMB--THE ANSWER TO MY PRAYERS--
--BUT I KNEW THERE'D BE THOSE WHO'D SEEK TO TAKE IT FROM ME--
--THOSE SUCH AS THE MYSTIC MAGE AND YOURSELF--
--AND THAT, SPIDER-MAN--IS WHY YOU MUST NOW DIE!
HOLD, SORCERER! UNLEASH THAT FATAL BOLT--AND YOU WILL ANSWER TO DOCTOR STRANGE!
ASTONISHING! STRANGE'S ACCURSED POWERS HAVE TRACED ME EVEN HERE!
'TWILL COST MELINDA HER LIFE SHOULD I LET STRANGE DEFEAT ME --BUT IN THIS DIMENSION HE IS SORCERER SUPREME--
STILL, THAT IS A SITUATION EASILY CORRECTED BY THE INCOMPARABLE WAND OF WATOOMB!

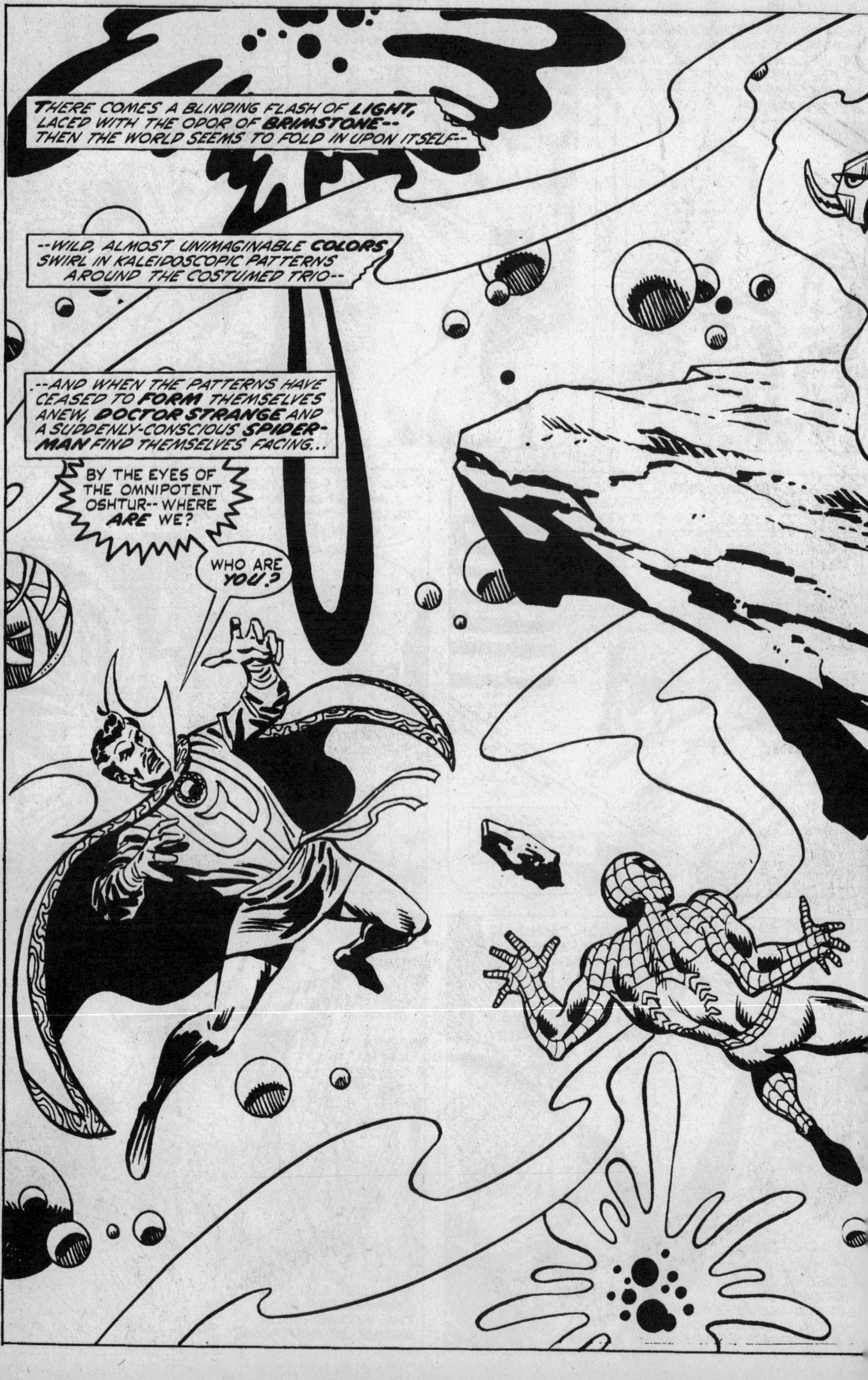
THERE COMES A BLINDING FLASH OF LIGHT, LACED WITH THE ODOR OF BRIMSTONE-- THEN THE WORLD SEEMS TO FOLD IN UPON ITSELF--
--WILD, ALMOST UNIMAGINABLE COLORS SWIRL IN KALEIDOSCOPIC PATTERNS AROUND THE COSTUMED TRIO--
--AND WHEN THE PATTERNS HAVE CEASED TO FORM THEMSELVES ANEW, DOCTOR STRANGE AND A SUDDENLY-CONSCIOUS SPIDER-MAN FIND THEMSELVES FACING...
BY THE EYES OF THE OMNIPOTENT OSHTUR-- WHERE ARE WE?
WHO ARE YOU.?

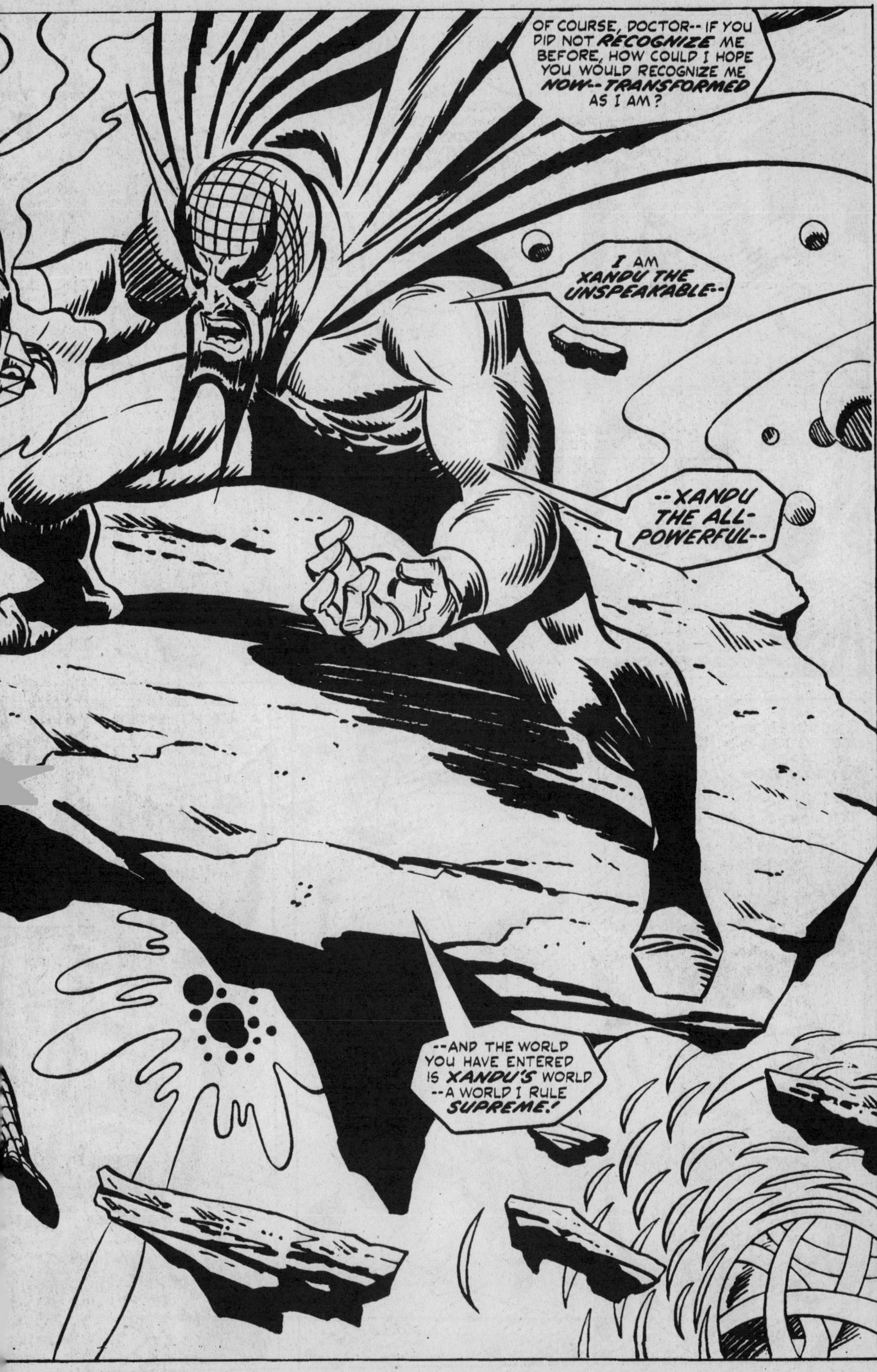
OF COURSE, DOCTOR-- IF YOU DID NOT RECOGNIZE ME BEFORE, HOW COULD I HOPE YOU WOULD RECOGNIZE ME NOW--TRANSFORMED AS I AM?
I AM XANDU THE UNSPEAKABLE--
--XANDU THE ALL-POWERFUL--
--AND THE WORLD YOU HAVE ENTERED IS XANDU'S WORLD --A WORLD I RULE SUPREME!

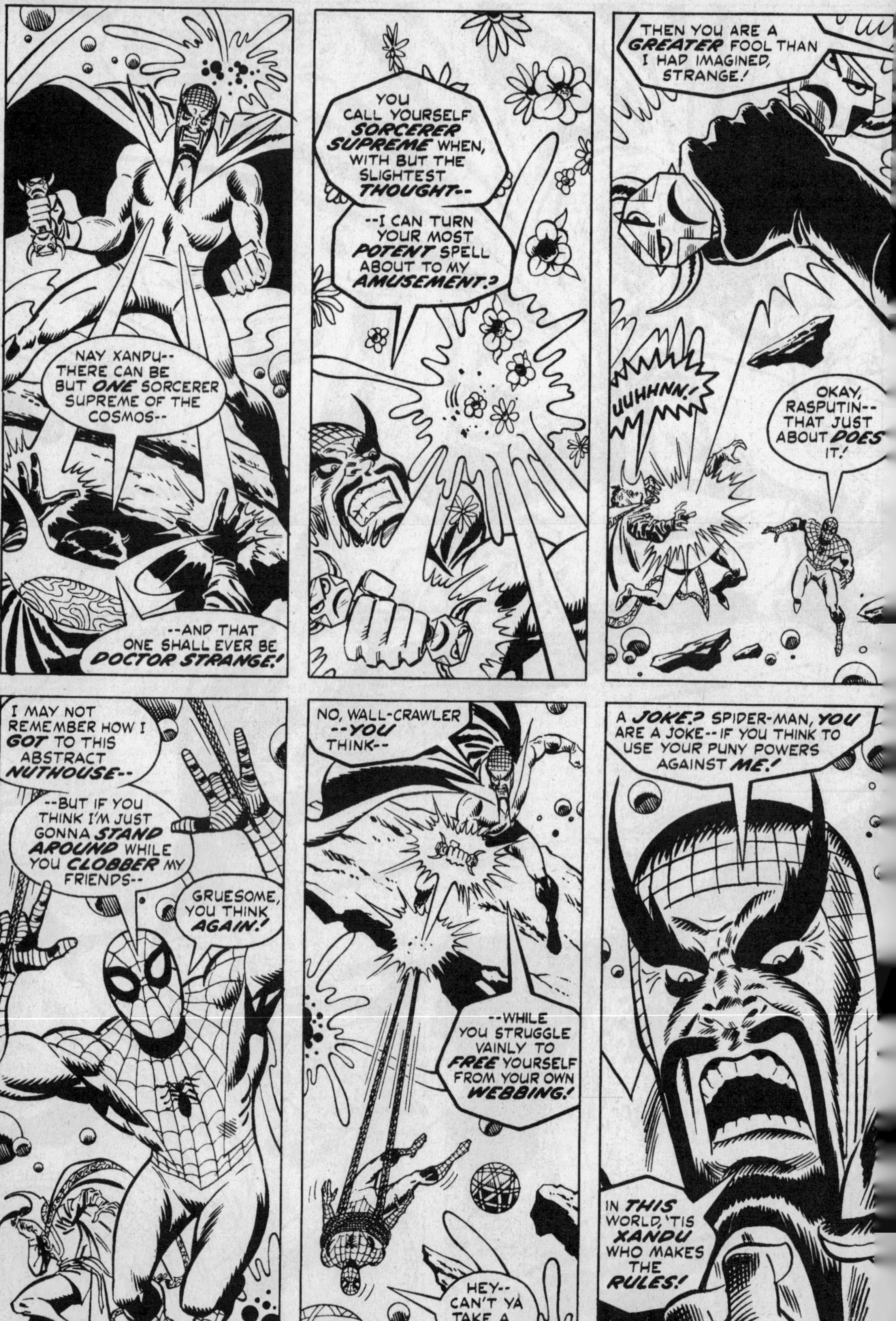
NAY XANDU-- THERE CAN BE BUT ONE SORCERER SUPREME OF THE COSMOS--
--AND THAT ONE SHALL EVER BE DOCTOR STRANGE!
YOU CALL YOURSELF SORCERER SUPREME WHEN, WITH BUT THE SLIGHTEST THOUGHT--
--I CAN TURN YOUR MOST POTENT SPELL ABOUT TO MY AMUSEMENT?
THEN YOU ARE A GREATER FOOL THAN I HAD IMAGINED, STRANGE!
UUHHHNN!
OKAY, RASPUTIN-- THAT JUST ABOUT DOES IT!
I MAY NOT REMEMBER HOW I GOT TO THIS ABSTRACT NUTHOUSE--
--BUT IF YOU THINK I'M JUST GONNA STAND AROUND WHILE YOU CLOBBER MY FRIENDS--
GRUESOME, YOU THINK AGAIN!
NO, WALL-CRAWLER --YOU THINK--
--WHILE YOU STRUGGLE VAINLY TO FREE YOURSELF FROM YOUR OWN WEBBING!
HEY-- CAN'T YA TAKE A JOKE?
A JOKE? SPIDER-MAN, YOU ARE A JOKE-- IF YOU THINK TO USE YOUR PUNY POWERS AGAINST ME!
IN THIS WORLD, 'TIS XANDU WHO MAKES THE RULES!

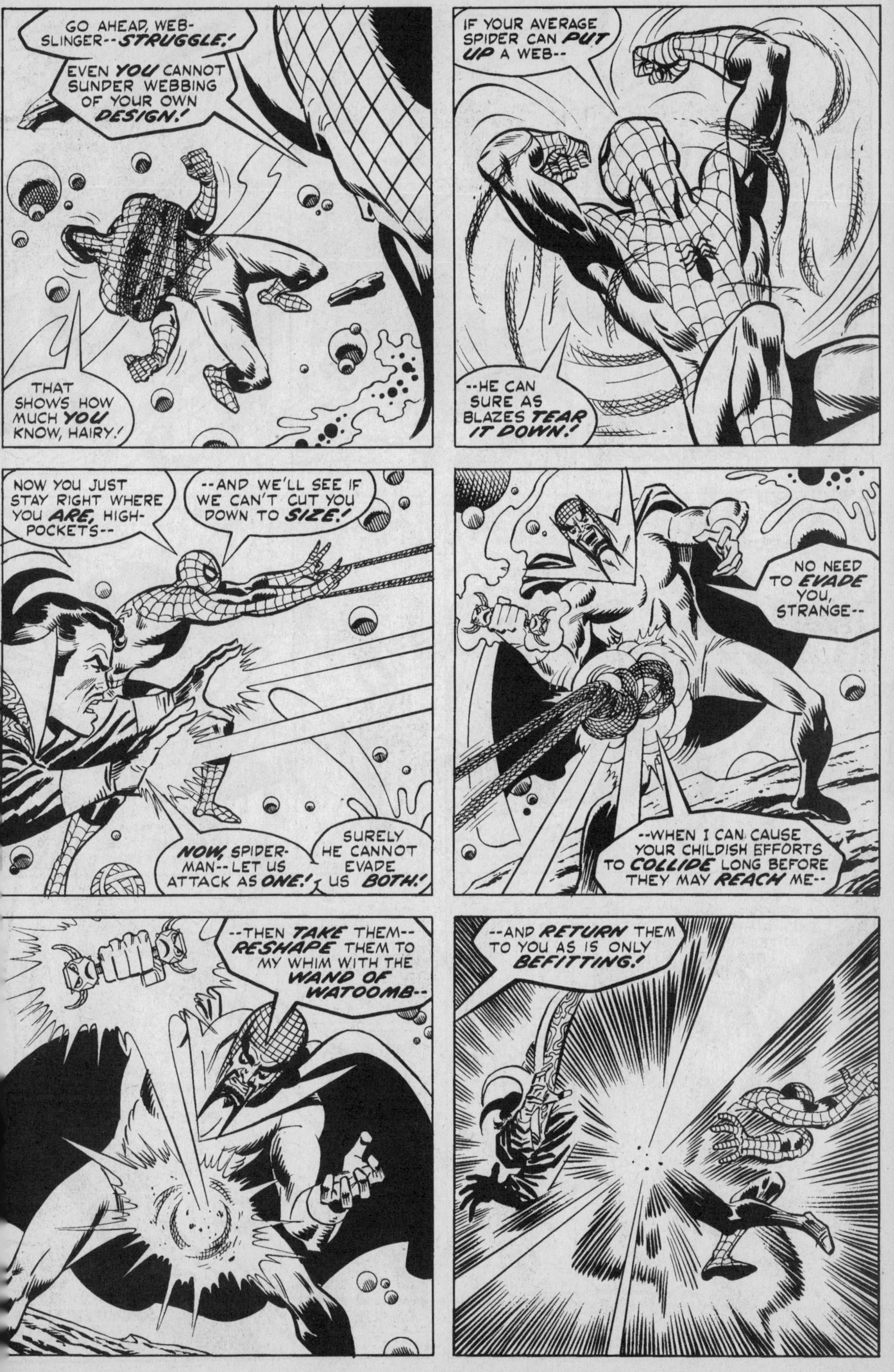
GO AHEAD, WEB-SLINGER--STRUGGLE!
EVEN YOU CANNOT SUNDER WEBBING OF YOUR OWN DESIGN!
THAT SHOWS HOW MUCH YOU KNOW, HAIRY!
IF YOUR AVERAGE SPIDER CAN PUT UP A WEB--
--HE CAN SURE AS BLAZES TEAR IT DOWN!
NOW YOU JUST STAY RIGHT WHERE YOU ARE, HIGH-POCKETS--
--AND WE'LL SEE IF WE CAN'T CUT YOU DOWN TO SIZE!
NOW, SPIDER-MAN--LET US ATTACK AS ONE!
SURELY HE CANNOT EVADE US BOTH!
NO NEED TO EVADE YOU, STRANGE--
--WHEN I CAN CAUSE YOUR CHILDISH EFFORTS TO COLLIDE LONG BEFORE THEY MAY REACH ME--
--THEN TAKE THEM--RESHAPE THEM TO MY WHIM WITH THE WAND OF WATOOMB--
--AND RETURN THEM TO YOU AS IS ONLY BEFITTING!

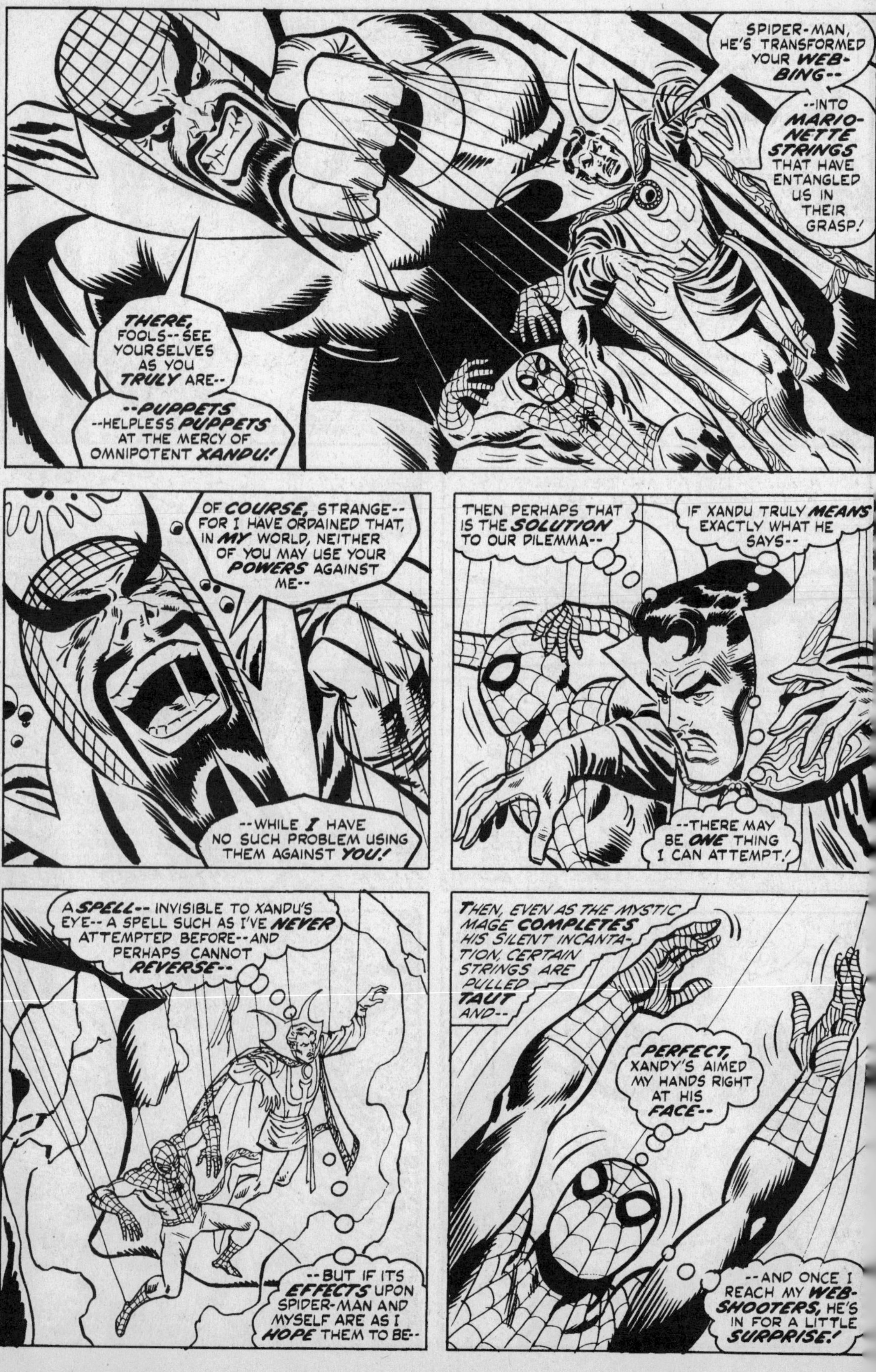
SPIDER-MAN, HE'S TRANSFORMED YOUR WEB-BING--
--INTO MARIO-NETTE STRINGS THAT HAVE ENTANGLED US IN THEIR GRASP!
THERE, FOOLS--SEE YOURSELVES AS YOU TRULY ARE--
--PUPPETS --HELPLESS PUPPETS AT THE MERCY OF OMNIPOTENT XANDU!
OF COURSE, STRANGE-- FOR I HAVE ORDAINED THAT, IN MY WORLD, NEITHER OF YOU MAY USE YOUR POWERS AGAINST ME--
--WHILE I HAVE NO SUCH PROBLEM USING THEM AGAINST YOU!
THEN PERHAPS THAT IS THE SOLUTION TO OUR DILEMMA--
IF XANDU TRULY MEANS EXACTLY WHAT HE SAYS--
--THERE MAY BE ONE THING I CAN ATTEMPT!
A SPELL-- INVISIBLE TO XANDU'S EYE-- A SPELL SUCH AS I'VE NEVER ATTEMPTED BEFORE--AND PERHAPS CANNOT REVERSE--
--BUT IF ITS EFFECTS UPON SPIDER-MAN AND MYSELF ARE AS I HOPE THEM TO BE--
THEN, EVEN AS THE MYSTIC MAGE COMPLETES HIS SILENT INCANTA-TION, CERTAIN STRINGS ARE PULLED TAUT AND--
PERFECT, XANDY'S AIMED MY HANDS RIGHT AT HIS FACE--
--AND ONCE I REACH MY WEB-SHOOTERS, HE'S IN FOR A LITTLE SURPRISE!

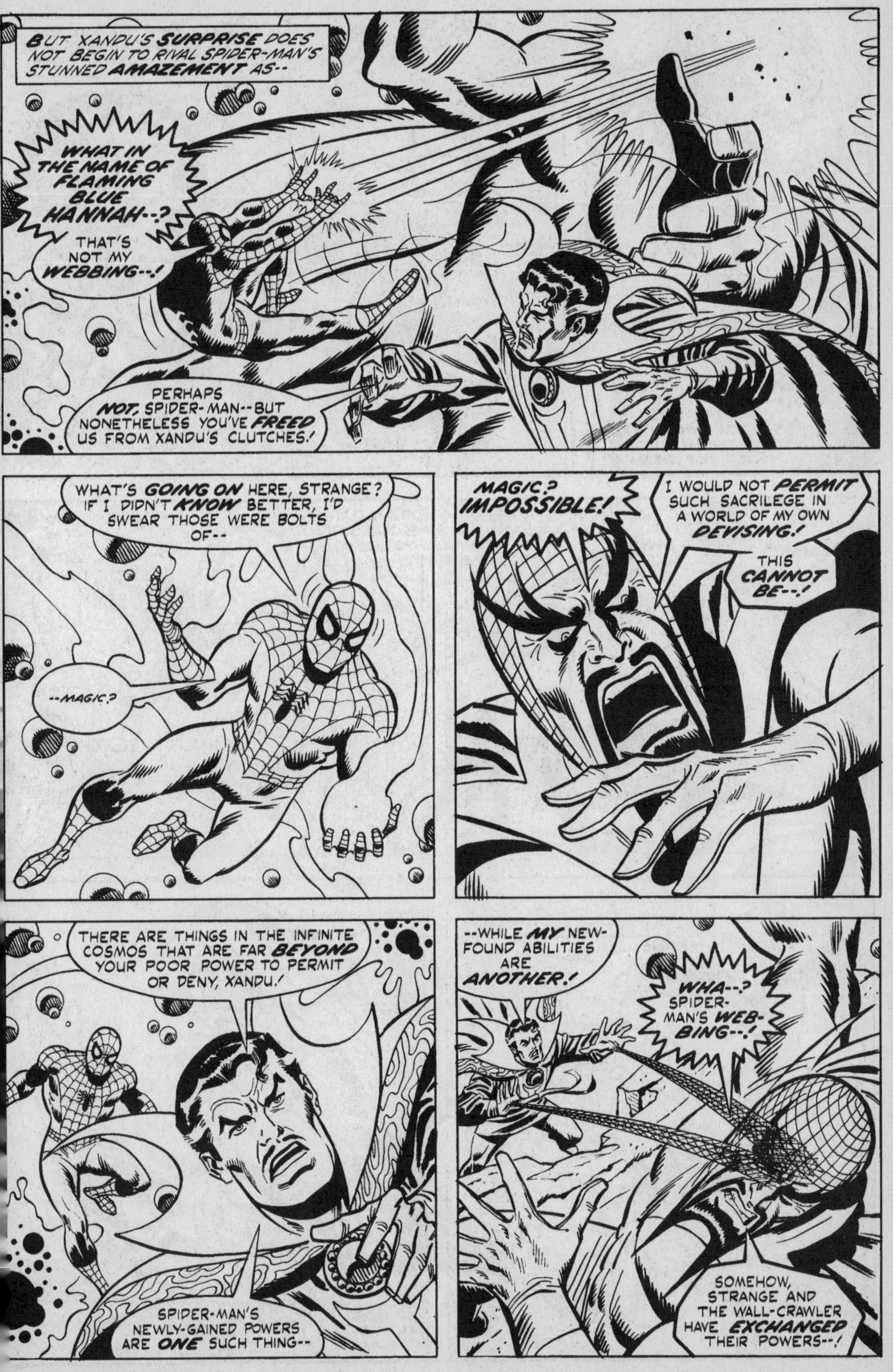
BUT XANDU'S SURPRISE DOES NOT BEGIN TO RIVAL SPIDER-MAN'S STUNNED AMAZEMENT AS--
WHAT IN THE NAME OF FLAMING BLUE HANNAH--?
THAT'S NOT MY WEBBING--!
PERHAPS NOT, SPIDER-MAN--BUT NONETHELESS YOU'VE FREED US FROM XANDU'S CLUTCHES!
WHAT'S GOING ON HERE, STRANGE? IF I DIDN'T KNOW BETTER, I'D SWEAR THOSE WERE BOLTS OF--
--MAGIC?
MAGIC? IMPOSSIBLE!
I WOULD NOT PERMIT SUCH SACRILEGE IN A WORLD OF MY OWN DEVISING!
THIS CANNOT BE--!
THERE ARE THINGS IN THE INFINITE COSMOS THAT ARE FAR BEYOND YOUR POOR POWER TO PERMIT OR DENY, XANDU!
SPIDER-MAN'S NEWLY-GAINED POWERS ARE ONE SUCH THING--
--WHILE MY NEW-FOUND ABILITIES ARE ANOTHER!
WHA--? SPIDER-MAN'S WEB-BING--!
SOMEHOW, STRANGE AND THE WALL-CRAWLER HAVE EXCHANGED THEIR POWERS--!

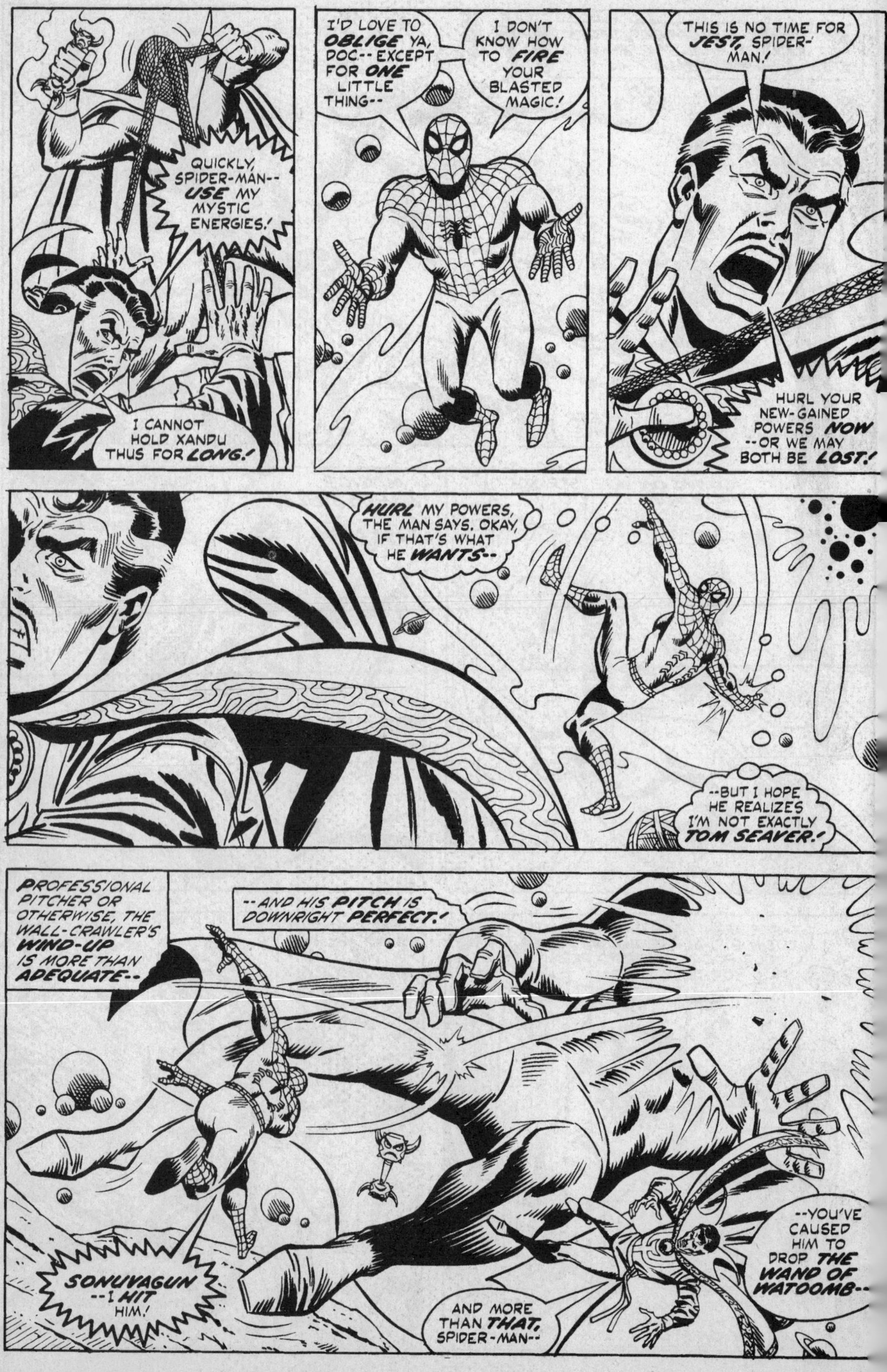
QUICKLY, SPIDER-MAN-- USE MY MYSTIC ENERGIES!
I CANNOT HOLD XANDU THUS FOR LONG!
I'D LOVE TO OBLIGE YA, DOC-- EXCEPT FOR ONE LITTLE THING--
I DON'T KNOW HOW TO FIRE YOUR BLASTED MAGIC!
THIS IS NO TIME FOR JEST, SPIDER-MAN!
HURL YOUR NEW-GAINED POWERS NOW --OR WE MAY BOTH BE LOST!
HURL MY POWERS, THE MAN SAYS. OKAY, IF THAT'S WHAT HE WANTS--
--BUT I HOPE HE REALIZES I'M NOT EXACTLY TOM SEAVER!
PROFESSIONAL PITCHER OR OTHERWISE, THE WALL-CRAWLER'S WIND-UP IS MORE THAN ADEQUATE--
--AND HIS PITCH IS DOWNRIGHT PERFECT!
SONUVAGUN --I HIT HIM!
AND MORE THAN THAT, SPIDER-MAN--
--YOU'VE CAUSED HIM TO DROP THE WAND OF WATOOMB--

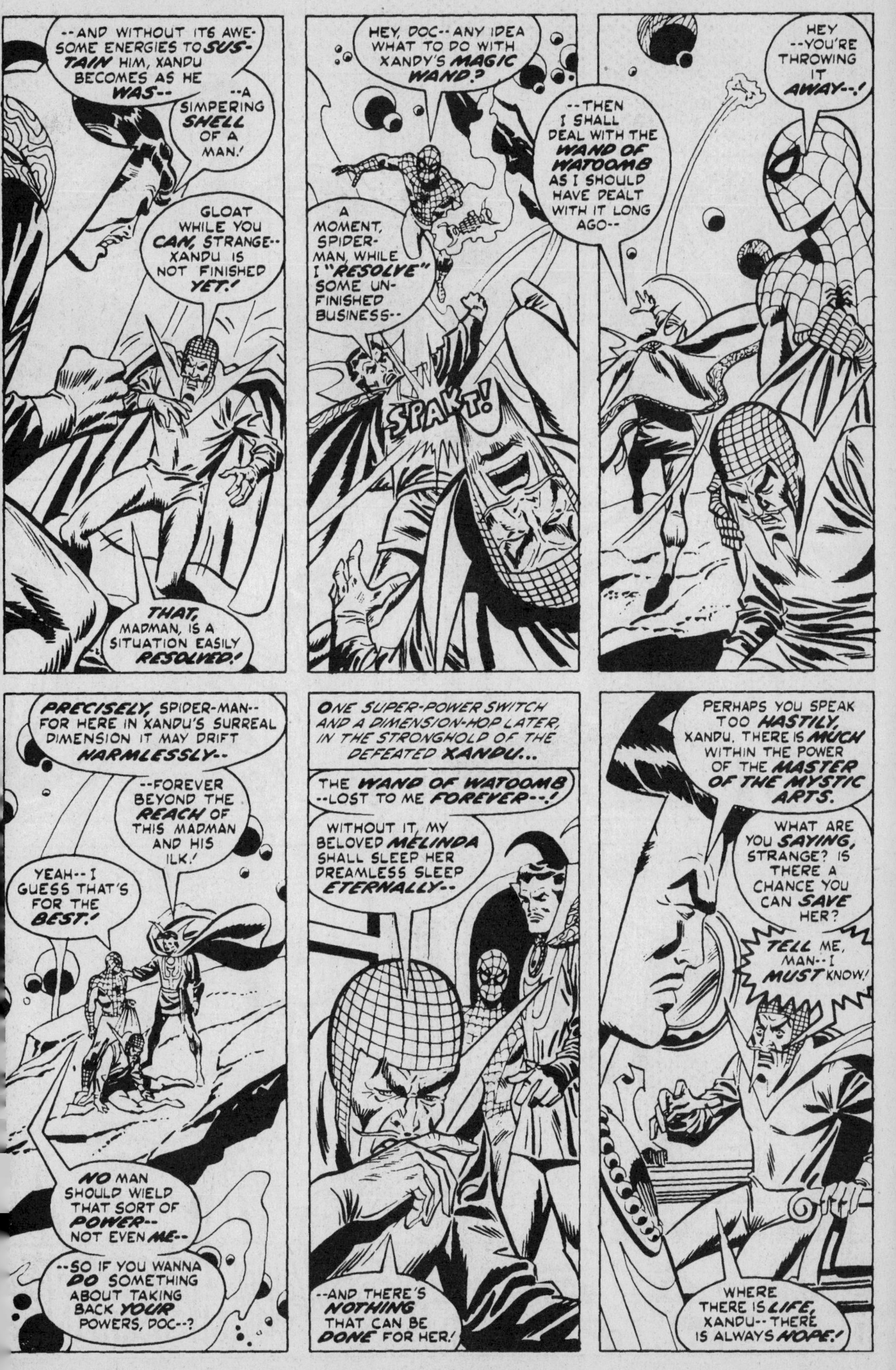
--AND WITHOUT ITS AWESOME ENERGIES TO SUSTAIN HIM, XANDU BECOMES AS HE WAS--
--A SIMPERING SHELL OF A MAN!
GLOAT WHILE YOU CAN, STRANGE-- XANDU IS NOT FINISHED YET!
THAT, MADMAN, IS A SITUATION EASILY RESOLVED!
HEY, DOC--ANY IDEA WHAT TO DO WITH XANDY'S MAGIC WAND?
A MOMENT, SPIDER-MAN, WHILE I "RESOLVE" SOME UNFINISHED BUSINESS--
SPAKT!
--THEN I SHALL DEAL WITH THE WAND OF WATOOMB AS I SHOULD HAVE DEALT WITH IT LONG AGO--
HEY --YOU'RE THROWING IT AWAY--!
PRECISELY, SPIDER-MAN-- FOR HERE IN XANDU'S SURREAL DIMENSION IT MAY DRIFT HARMLESSLY--
--FOREVER BEYOND THE REACH OF THIS MADMAN AND HIS ILK!
YEAH--I GUESS THAT'S FOR THE BEST!
NO MAN SHOULD WIELD THAT SORT OF POWER-- NOT EVEN ME--
--SO IF YOU WANNA DO SOMETHING ABOUT TAKING BACK YOUR POWERS, DOC--?
ONE SUPER-POWER SWITCH AND A DIMENSION-HOP LATER, IN THE STRONGHOLD OF THE DEFEATED XANDU...
THE WAND OF WATOOMB --LOST TO ME FOREVER--!
WITHOUT IT, MY BELOVED MELINDA SHALL SLEEP HER DREAMLESS SLEEP ETERNALLY--
--AND THERE'S NOTHING THAT CAN BE DONE FOR HER!
PERHAPS YOU SPEAK TOO HASTILY, XANDU. THERE IS MUCH WITHIN THE POWER OF THE MASTER OF THE MYSTIC ARTS.
WHAT ARE YOU SAYING, STRANGE? IS THERE A CHANCE YOU CAN SAVE HER?
TELL ME, MAN--I MUST KNOW!
WHERE THERE IS LIFE, XANDU-- THERE IS ALWAYS HOPE!

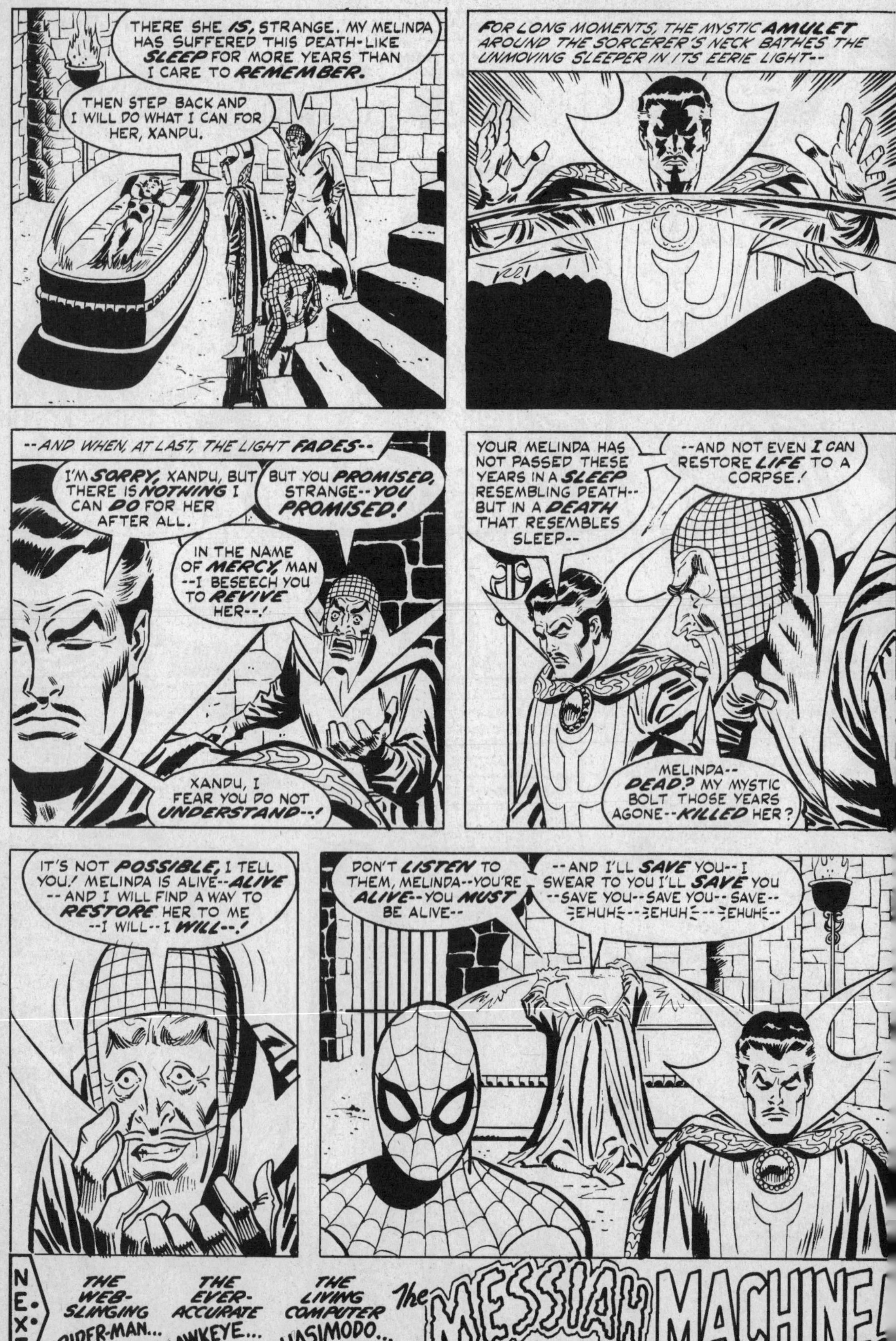

THERE SHE IS, STRANGE. MY MELINDA HAS SUFFERED THIS DEATH-LIKE SLEEP FOR MORE YEARS THAN I CARE TO REMEMBER.
THEN STEP BACK AND I WILL DO WHAT I CAN FOR HER, XANDU.
FOR LONG MOMENTS, THE MYSTIC AMULET AROUND THE SORCERER'S NECK BATHES THE UNMOVING SLEEPER IN ITS EERIE LIGHT--
--AND WHEN, AT LAST, THE LIGHT FADES--
I'M SORRY, XANDU, BUT THERE IS NOTHING I CAN DO FOR HER AFTER ALL.
BUT YOU PROMISED, STRANGE--YOU PROMISED!
IN THE NAME OF MERCY, MAN --I BESEECH YOU TO REVIVE HER--!
XANDU, I FEAR YOU DO NOT UNDERSTAND--!
YOUR MELINDA HAS NOT PASSED THESE YEARS IN A SLEEP RESEMBLING DEATH-- BUT IN A DEATH THAT RESEMBLES SLEEP--
--AND NOT EVEN I CAN RESTORE LIFE TO A CORPSE!
MELINDA-- DEAD? MY MYSTIC BOLT THOSE YEARS AGONE--KILLED HER?
IT'S NOT POSSIBLE, I TELL YOU! MELINDA IS ALIVE--ALIVE --AND I WILL FIND A WAY TO RESTORE HER TO ME --I WILL--I WILL--!
DON'T LISTEN TO THEM, MELINDA--YOU'RE ALIVE--YOU MUST BE ALIVE--
--AND I'LL SAVE YOU--I SWEAR TO YOU I'LL SAVE YOU --SAVE YOU--SAVE YOU--SAVE-- EHUH-- EHUH-- EHUH--
NEXT
THE WEB-SLINGING SPIDER-MAN...
THE EVER-ACCURATE HAWKEYE...
THE LIVING COMPUTER QUASIMODO...
The MESSIAH MACHINE!

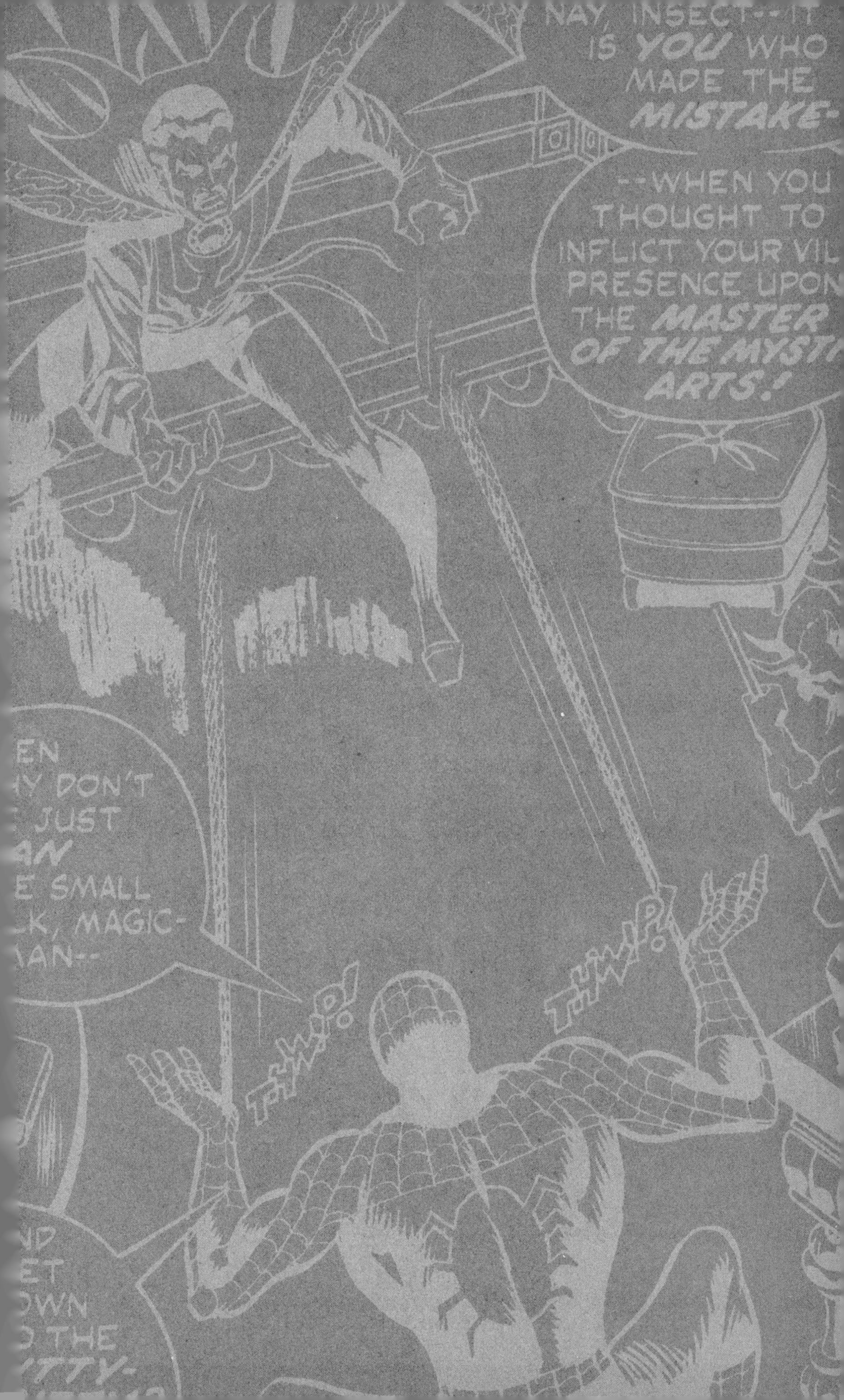
NAY, INSECT--IT IS YOU WHO MADE THE MISTAKE-
--WHEN YOU THOUGHT TO INFLICT YOUR VIL PRESENCE UPON THE MASTER OF THE MYST ARTS!
DON'T JUST
SMALL
MAGIC-
THWIP!
THWIP!

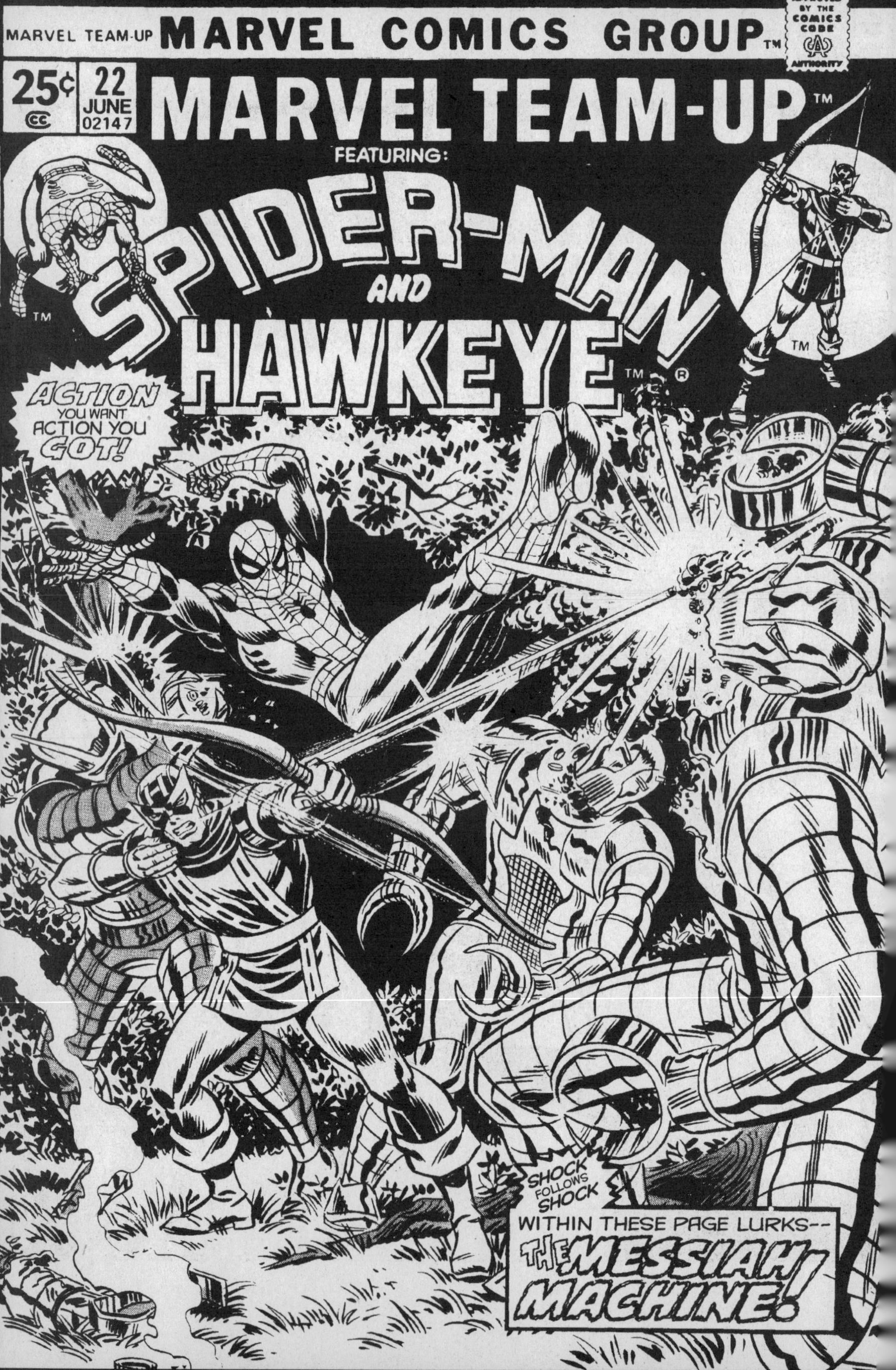
MARVEL TEAM-UP MARVEL COMICS GROUP™
APPROVED BY THE COMICS CODE AUTHORITY
25¢
22 JUNE 02147
MARVEL TEAM-UP™
FEATURING:
SPIDER-MAN™ AND HAWKEYE™®
ACTION YOU WANT ACTION YOU GOT!
SHOCK FOLLOWS SHOCK
WITHIN THESE PAGE LURKS--
THE MESSIAH MACHINE!

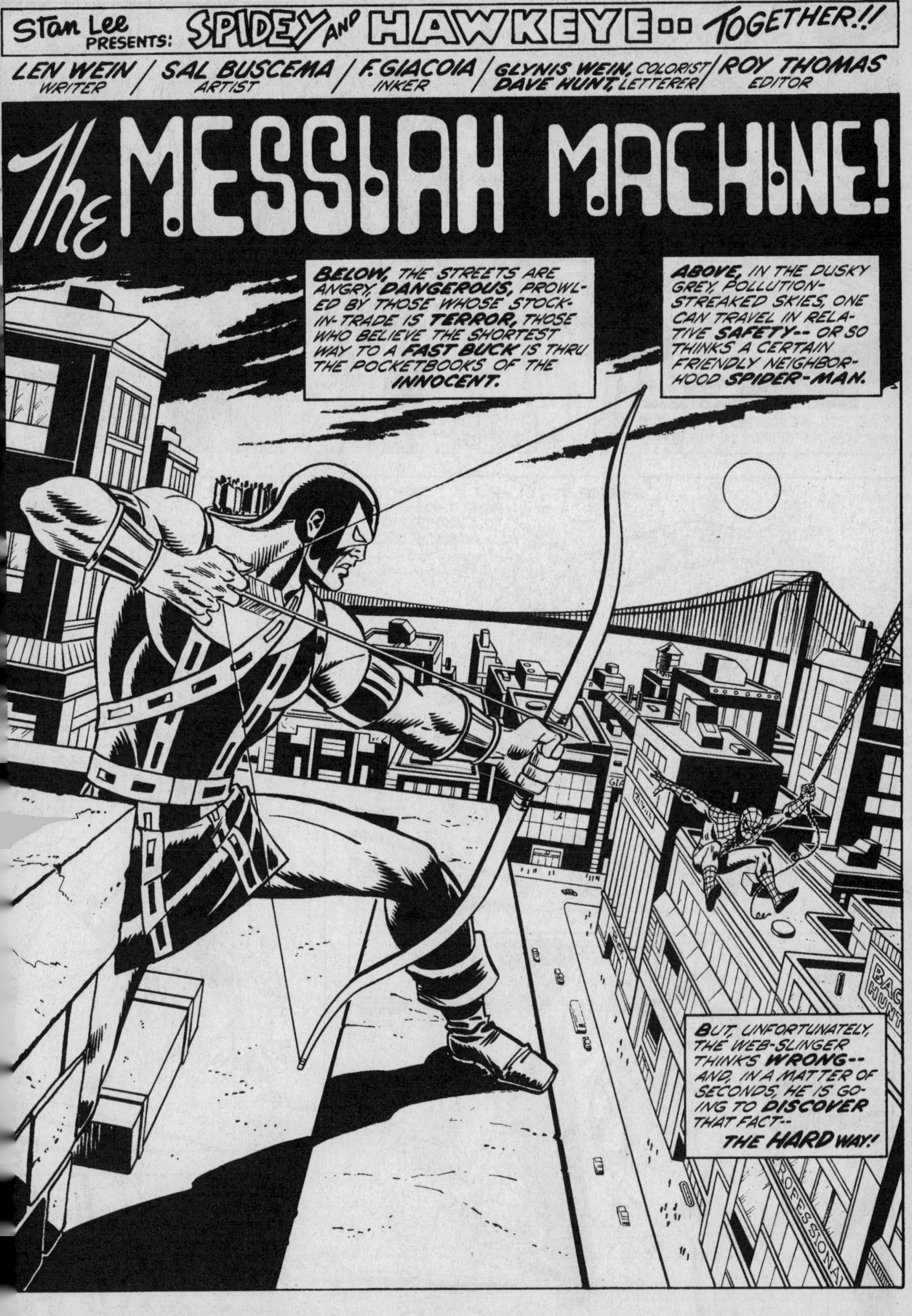

Stan Lee PRESENTS: SPIDEY AND HAWKEYE.. TOGETHER!!
LEN WEIN WRITER / SAL BUSCEMA ARTIST / F. GIACOIA INKER / GLYNIS WEIN, COLORIST DAVE HUNT, LETTERER / ROY THOMAS EDITOR
THE MESSIAH MACHINE!
BELOW, THE STREETS ARE ANGRY, DANGEROUS, PROWLED BY THOSE WHOSE STOCK-IN-TRADE IS TERROR, THOSE WHO BELIEVE THE SHORTEST WAY TO A FAST BUCK IS THRU THE POCKETBOOKS OF THE INNOCENT.
ABOVE, IN THE DUSKY GREY, POLLUTION-STREAKED SKIES, ONE CAN TRAVEL IN RELATIVE SAFETY-- OR SO THINKS A CERTAIN FRIENDLY NEIGHBORHOOD SPIDER-MAN.
BUT, UNFORTUNATELY, THE WEB-SLINGER THINKS WRONG-- AND, IN A MATTER OF SECONDS, HE IS GOING TO DISCOVER THAT FACT-- THE HARD WAY!

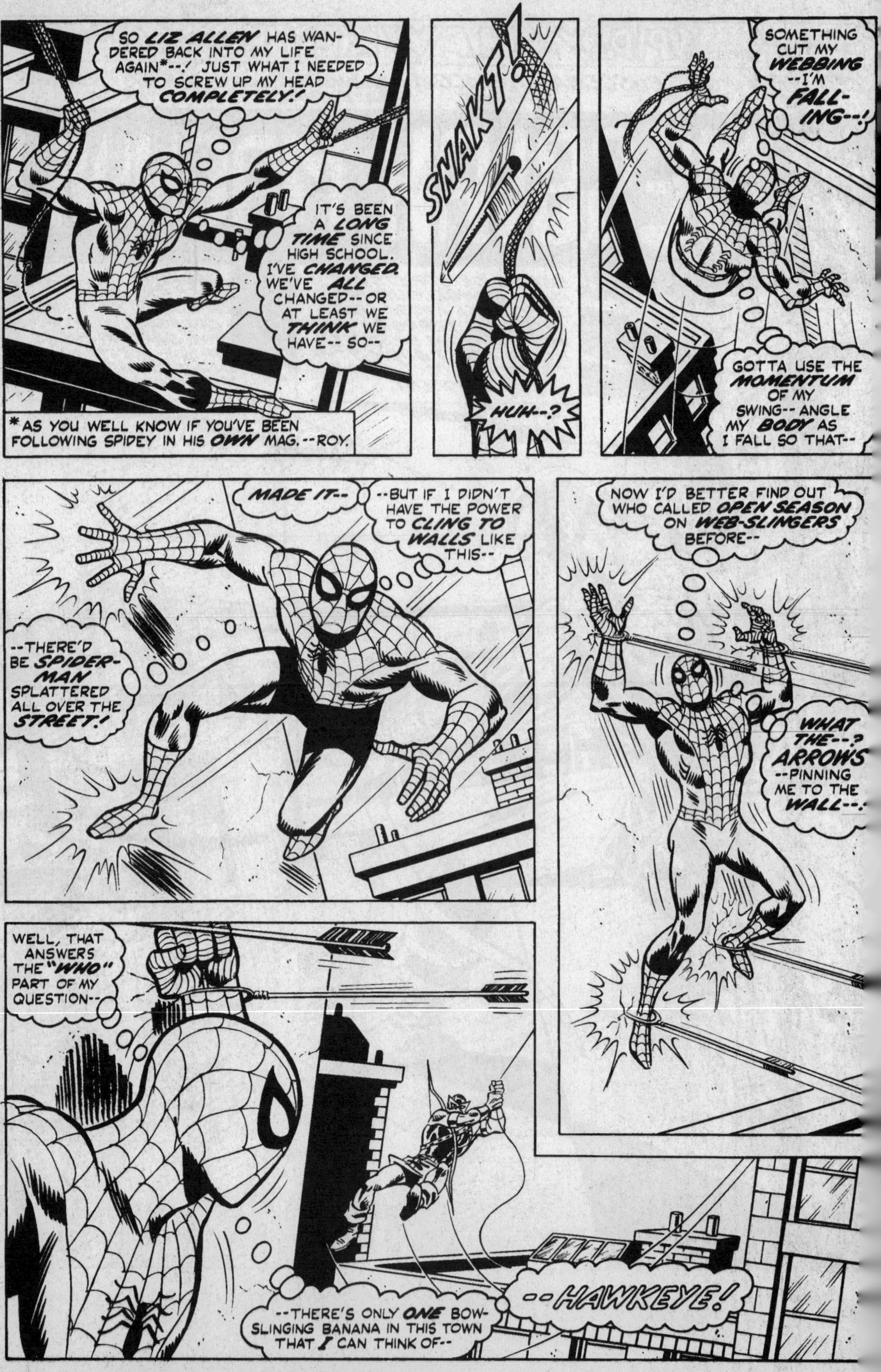

SO LIZ ALLEN HAS WANDERED BACK INTO MY LIFE AGAIN*--! JUST WHAT I NEEDED TO SCREW UP MY HEAD COMPLETELY!
IT'S BEEN A LONG TIME SINCE HIGH SCHOOL. I'VE CHANGED. WE'VE ALL CHANGED--OR AT LEAST WE THINK WE HAVE-- SO--
*AS YOU WELL KNOW IF YOU'VE BEEN FOLLOWING SPIDEY IN HIS OWN MAG.--ROY.
SNAKT!
HUH--?
SOMETHING CUT MY WEBBING --I'M FALL-ING--!
GOTTA USE THE MOMENTUM OF MY SWING-- ANGLE MY BODY AS I FALL SO THAT--
MADE IT--
--BUT IF I DIDN'T HAVE THE POWER TO CLING TO WALLS LIKE THIS--
--THERE'D BE SPIDER-MAN SPLATTERED ALL OVER THE STREET!
NOW I'D BETTER FIND OUT WHO CALLED OPEN SEASON ON WEB-SLINGERS BEFORE--
WHAT THE--? ARROWS --PINNING ME TO THE WALL--!
WELL, THAT ANSWERS THE "WHO" PART OF MY QUESTION--
--THERE'S ONLY ONE BOW-SLINGING BANANA IN THIS TOWN THAT I CAN THINK OF--
--HAWKEYE!

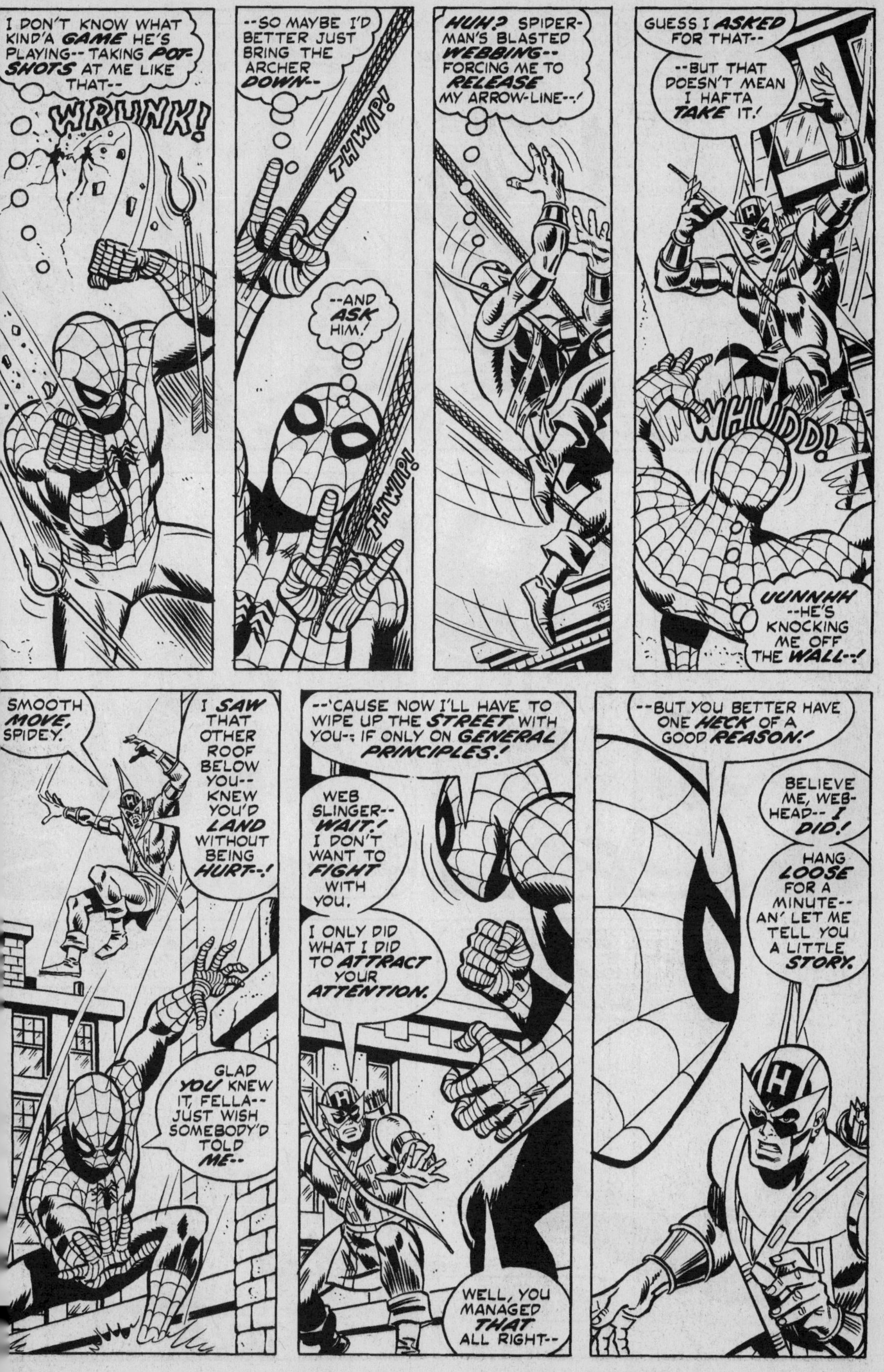

I DON'T KNOW WHAT KIND'A GAME HE'S PLAYING-- TAKING POT-SHOTS AT ME LIKE THAT--
WRUNK!
--SO MAYBE I'D BETTER JUST BRING THE ARCHER DOWN--
THWIP!
--AND ASK HIM!
THWIP!
HUH? SPIDER-MAN'S BLASTED WEBBING--FORCING ME TO RELEASE MY ARROW-LINE--!
GUESS I ASKED FOR THAT--
--BUT THAT DOESN'T MEAN I HAFTA TAKE IT!
WHUDD!
UUNNHH --HE'S KNOCKING ME OFF THE WALL--!
SMOOTH MOVE, SPIDEY.
I SAW THAT OTHER ROOF BELOW YOU-- KNEW YOU'D LAND WITHOUT BEING HURT--!
GLAD YOU KNEW IT, FELLA-- JUST WISH SOMEBODY'D TOLD ME--
--'CAUSE NOW I'LL HAVE TO WIPE UP THE STREET WITH YOU--; IF ONLY ON GENERAL PRINCIPLES!
WEB SLINGER-- WAIT! I DON'T WANT TO FIGHT WITH YOU.
I ONLY DID WHAT I DID TO ATTRACT YOUR ATTENTION.
WELL, YOU MANAGED THAT ALL RIGHT--
--BUT YOU BETTER HAVE ONE HECK OF A GOOD REASON!
BELIEVE ME, WEB-HEAD-- I DID!
HANG LOOSE FOR A MINUTE-- AN' LET ME TELL YOU A LITTLE STORY.

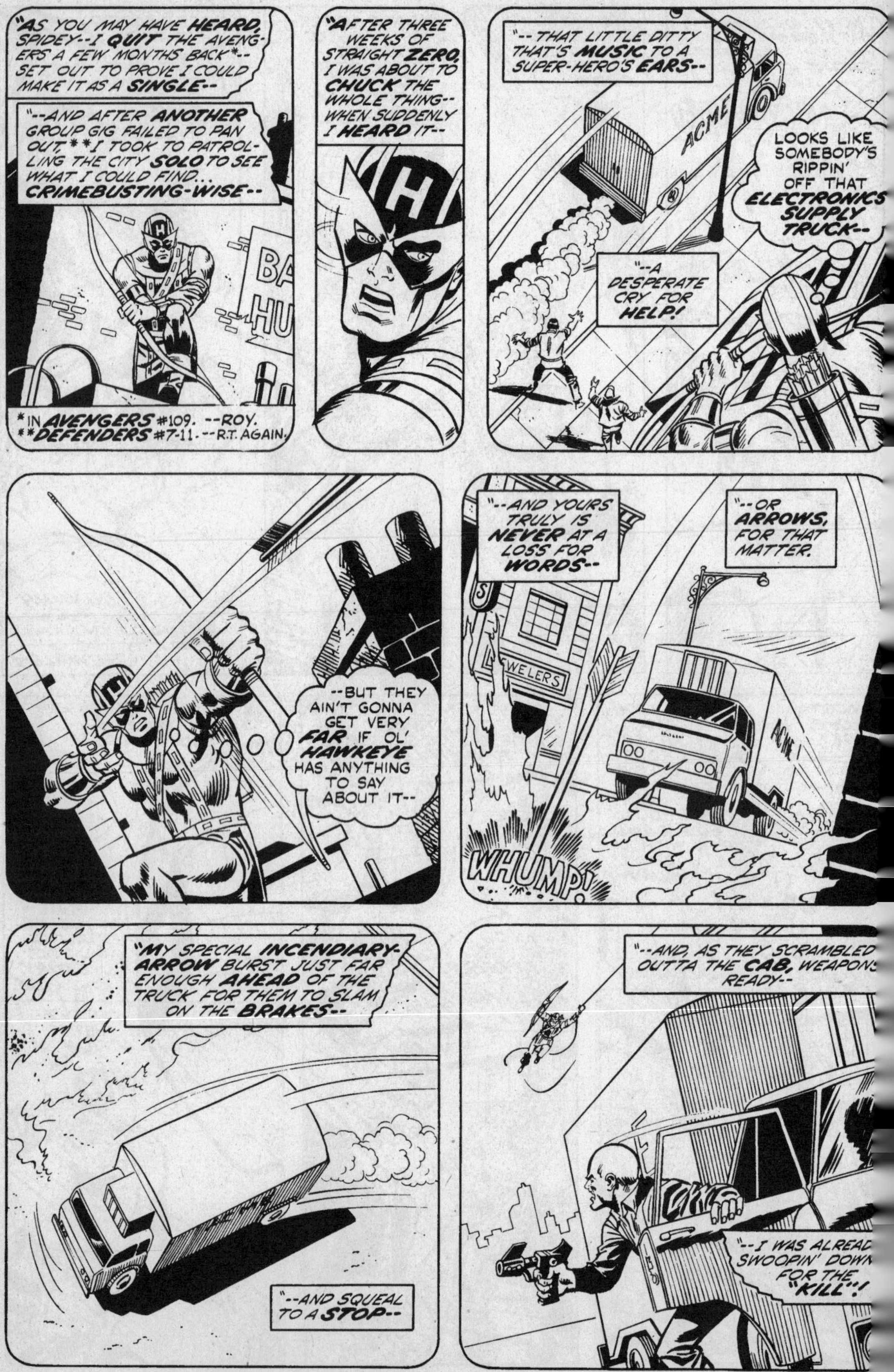
"AS YOU MAY HAVE HEARD, SPIDEY--I QUIT THE AVENGERS A FEW MONTHS BACK*--SET OUT TO PROVE I COULD MAKE IT AS A SINGLE--
"--AND AFTER ANOTHER GROUP GIG FAILED TO PAN OUT,** I TOOK TO PATROLLING THE CITY SOLO TO SEE WHAT I COULD FIND... CRIMEBUSTING-WISE--
*IN AVENGERS #109. --ROY.
**DEFENDERS #7-11. --R.T. AGAIN.
"AFTER THREE WEEKS OF STRAIGHT ZERO, I WAS ABOUT TO CHUCK THE WHOLE THING--WHEN SUDDENLY I HEARD IT--
"--THAT LITTLE DITTY THAT'S MUSIC TO A SUPER-HERO'S EARS--
ACME
LOOKS LIKE SOMEBODY'S RIPPIN' OFF THAT ELECTRONICS SUPPLY TRUCK--
"--A DESPERATE CRY FOR HELP!
--BUT THEY AIN'T GONNA GET VERY FAR IF OL' HAWKEYE HAS ANYTHING TO SAY ABOUT IT--
"--AND YOURS TRULY IS NEVER AT A LOSS FOR WORDS--
"--OR ARROWS, FOR THAT MATTER.
WELERS
ACME
WHUMP!
"MY SPECIAL INCENDIARY-ARROW BURST JUST FAR ENOUGH AHEAD OF THE TRUCK FOR THEM TO SLAM ON THE BRAKES--
"--AND SQUEAL TO A STOP--
"--AND, AS THEY SCRAMBLED OUTTA THE CAB, WEAPONS READY--
"--I WAS ALREAD SWOOPIN' DOWN FOR THE "KILL"!

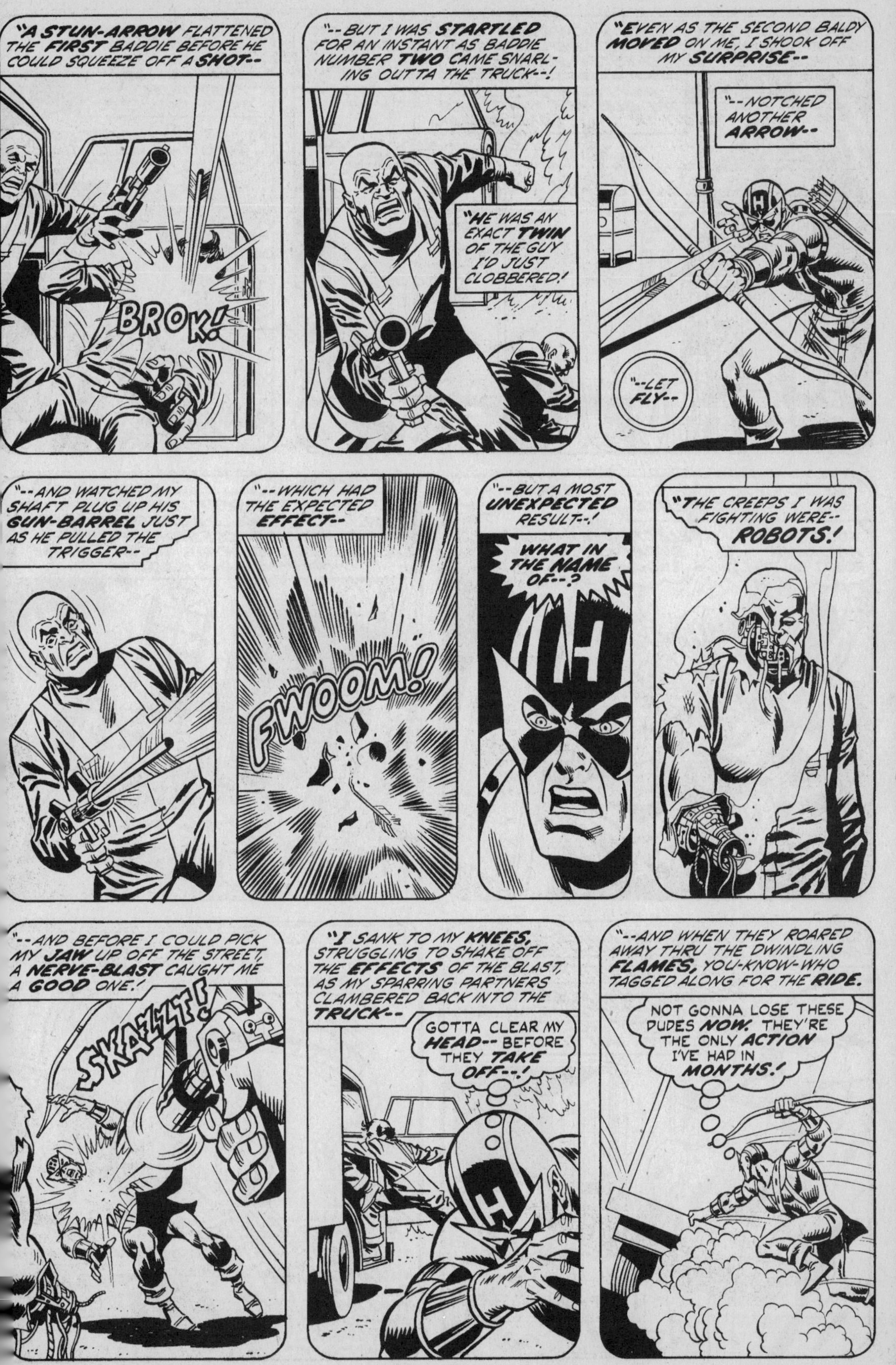
"A STUN-ARROW FLATTENED THE FIRST BADDIE BEFORE HE COULD SQUEEZE OFF A SHOT--
BROK!
"--BUT I WAS STARTLED FOR AN INSTANT AS BADDIE NUMBER TWO CAME SNARLING OUTTA THE TRUCK--!
"HE WAS AN EXACT TWIN OF THE GUY I'D JUST CLOBBERED!
"EVEN AS THE SECOND BALDY MOVED ON ME, I SHOOK OFF MY SURPRISE--
"--NOTCHED ANOTHER ARROW--
"--LET FLY--
"--AND WATCHED MY SHAFT PLUG UP HIS GUN-BARREL JUST AS HE PULLED THE TRIGGER--
"--WHICH HAD THE EXPECTED EFFECT--
FWOOM!
"--BUT A MOST UNEXPECTED RESULT--!
WHAT IN THE NAME OF--?
"THE CREEPS I WAS FIGHTING WERE-- ROBOTS!
"--AND BEFORE I COULD PICK MY JAW UP OFF THE STREET, A NERVE-BLAST CAUGHT ME A GOOD ONE!
SKAZZT!
"I SANK TO MY KNEES, STRUGGLING TO SHAKE OFF THE EFFECTS OF THE BLAST, AS MY SPARRING PARTNERS CLAMBERED BACK INTO THE TRUCK--
GOTTA CLEAR MY HEAD-- BEFORE THEY TAKE OFF--!
"--AND WHEN THEY ROARED AWAY THRU THE DWINDLING FLAMES, YOU-KNOW-WHO TAGGED ALONG FOR THE RIDE.
NOT GONNA LOSE THESE DUDES NOW. THEY'RE THE ONLY ACTION I'VE HAD IN MONTHS.!

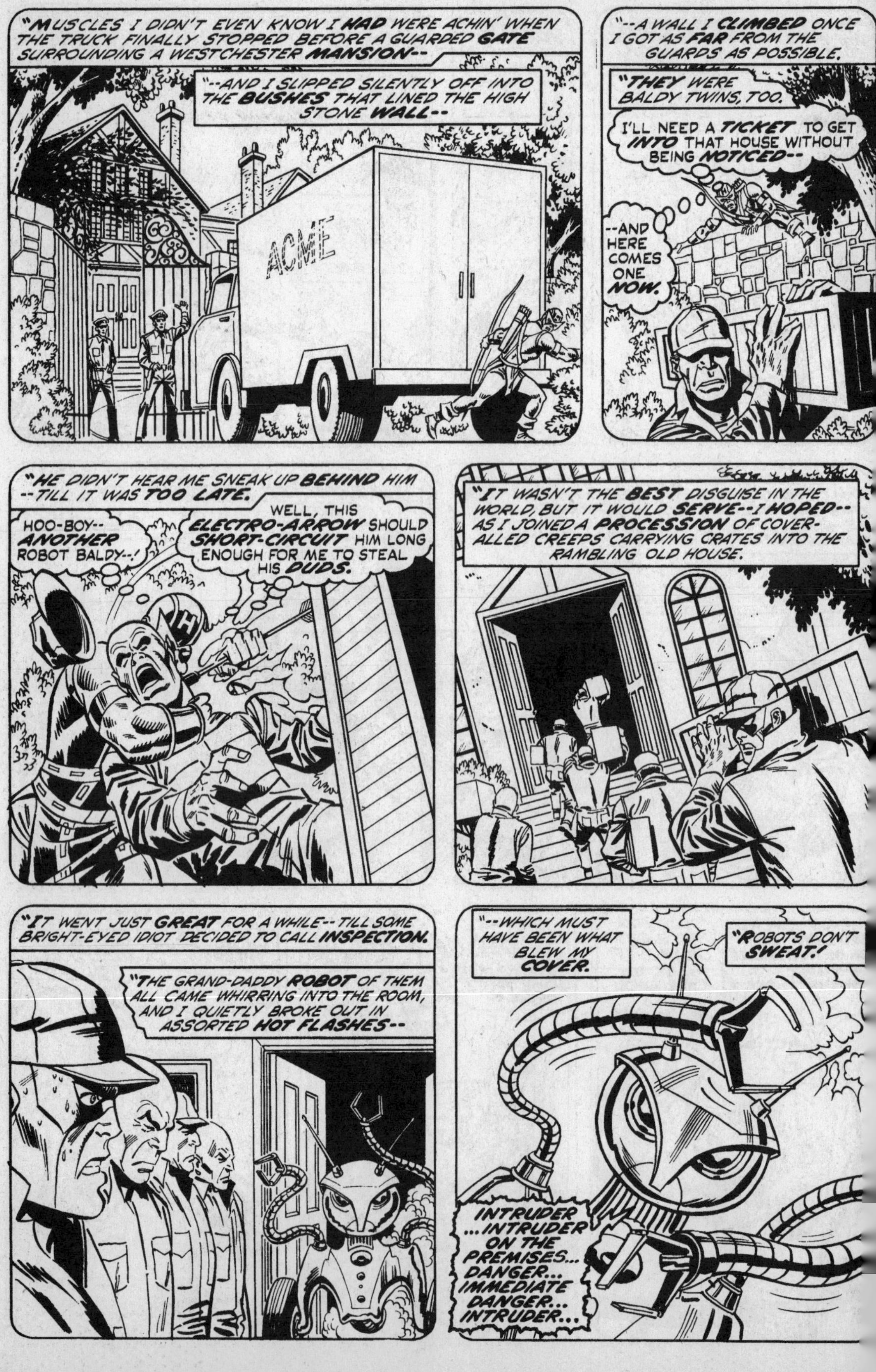
"MUSCLES I DIDN'T EVEN KNOW I HAD WERE ACHIN' WHEN THE TRUCK FINALLY STOPPED BEFORE A GUARDED GATE SURROUNDING A WESTCHESTER MANSION--
"--AND I SLIPPED SILENTLY OFF INTO THE BUSHES THAT LINED THE HIGH STONE WALL--
ACME
"--A WALL I CLIMBED ONCE I GOT AS FAR FROM THE GUARDS AS POSSIBLE.
"THEY WERE BALDY TWINS, TOO.
I'LL NEED A TICKET TO GET INTO THAT HOUSE WITHOUT BEING NOTICED--
--AND HERE COMES ONE NOW.
"HE DIDN'T HEAR ME SNEAK UP BEHIND HIM --TILL IT WAS TOO LATE.
HOO-BOY-- ANOTHER ROBOT BALDY--!
WELL, THIS ELECTRO-ARROW SHOULD SHORT-CIRCUIT HIM LONG ENOUGH FOR ME TO STEAL HIS DUDS.
"IT WASN'T THE BEST DISGUISE IN THE WORLD, BUT IT WOULD SERVE--I HOPED-- AS I JOINED A PROCESSION OF COVER-ALLED CREEPS CARRYING CRATES INTO THE RAMBLING OLD HOUSE.
"IT WENT JUST GREAT FOR A WHILE--TILL SOME BRIGHT-EYED IDIOT DECIDED TO CALL INSPECTION.
"THE GRAND-DADDY ROBOT OF THEM ALL CAME WHIRRING INTO THE ROOM, AND I QUIETLY BROKE OUT IN ASSORTED HOT FLASHES--
"--WHICH MUST HAVE BEEN WHAT BLEW MY COVER.
"ROBOTS DON'T SWEAT.'
INTRUDER ...INTRUDER ON THE PREMISES... DANGER... IMMEDIATE DANGER... INTRUDER...

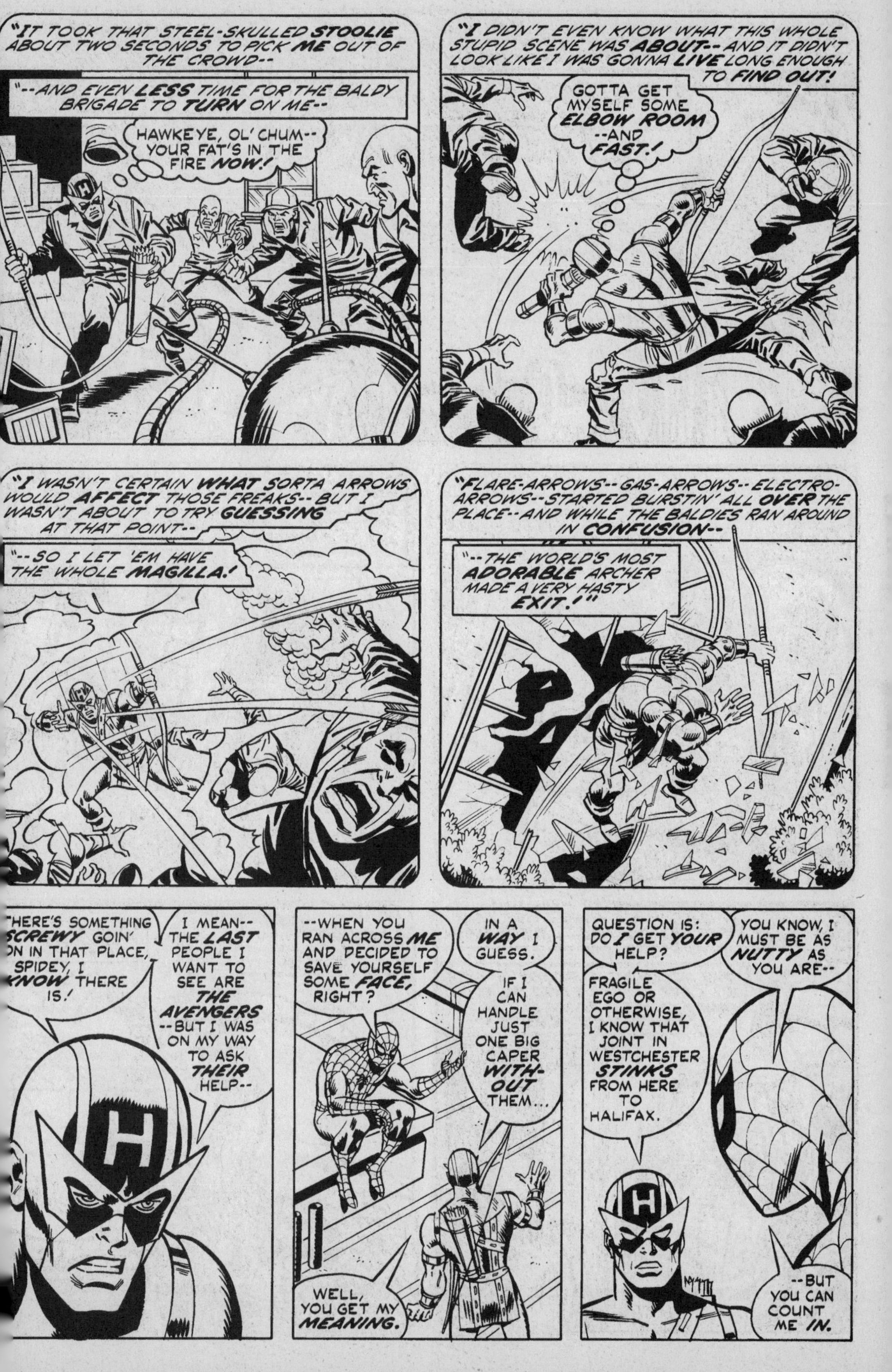

"IT TOOK THAT STEEL-SKULLED STOOLIE ABOUT TWO SECONDS TO PICK ME OUT OF THE CROWD--
"--AND EVEN LESS TIME FOR THE BALDY BRIGADE TO TURN ON ME--
HAWKEYE, OL' CHUM-- YOUR FAT'S IN THE FIRE NOW!
"I DIDN'T EVEN KNOW WHAT THIS WHOLE STUPID SCENE WAS ABOUT-- AND IT DIDN'T LOOK LIKE I WAS GONNA LIVE LONG ENOUGH TO FIND OUT!
GOTTA GET MYSELF SOME ELBOW ROOM --AND FAST!
"I WASN'T CERTAIN WHAT SORTA ARROWS WOULD AFFECT THOSE FREAKS-- BUT I WASN'T ABOUT TO TRY GUESSING AT THAT POINT--
"--SO I LET 'EM HAVE THE WHOLE MAGILLA!
"FLARE-ARROWS-- GAS-ARROWS-- ELECTRO-ARROWS--STARTED BURSTIN' ALL OVER THE PLACE--AND WHILE THE BALDIES RAN AROUND IN CONFUSION--
"--THE WORLD'S MOST ADORABLE ARCHER MADE A VERY HASTY EXIT!"
THERE'S SOMETHING SCREWY GOIN' ON IN THAT PLACE, SPIDEY, I KNOW THERE IS!
I MEAN-- THE LAST PEOPLE I WANT TO SEE ARE THE AVENGERS --BUT I WAS ON MY WAY TO ASK THEIR HELP--
--WHEN YOU RAN ACROSS ME AND DECIDED TO SAVE YOURSELF SOME FACE, RIGHT?
IN A WAY I GUESS.
IF I CAN HANDLE JUST ONE BIG CAPER WITH-OUT THEM...
WELL, YOU GET MY MEANING.
QUESTION IS: DO I GET YOUR HELP?
FRAGILE EGO OR OTHERWISE, I KNOW THAT JOINT IN WESTCHESTER STINKS FROM HERE TO HALIFAX.
YOU KNOW, I MUST BE AS NUTTY AS YOU ARE--
--BUT YOU CAN COUNT ME IN.

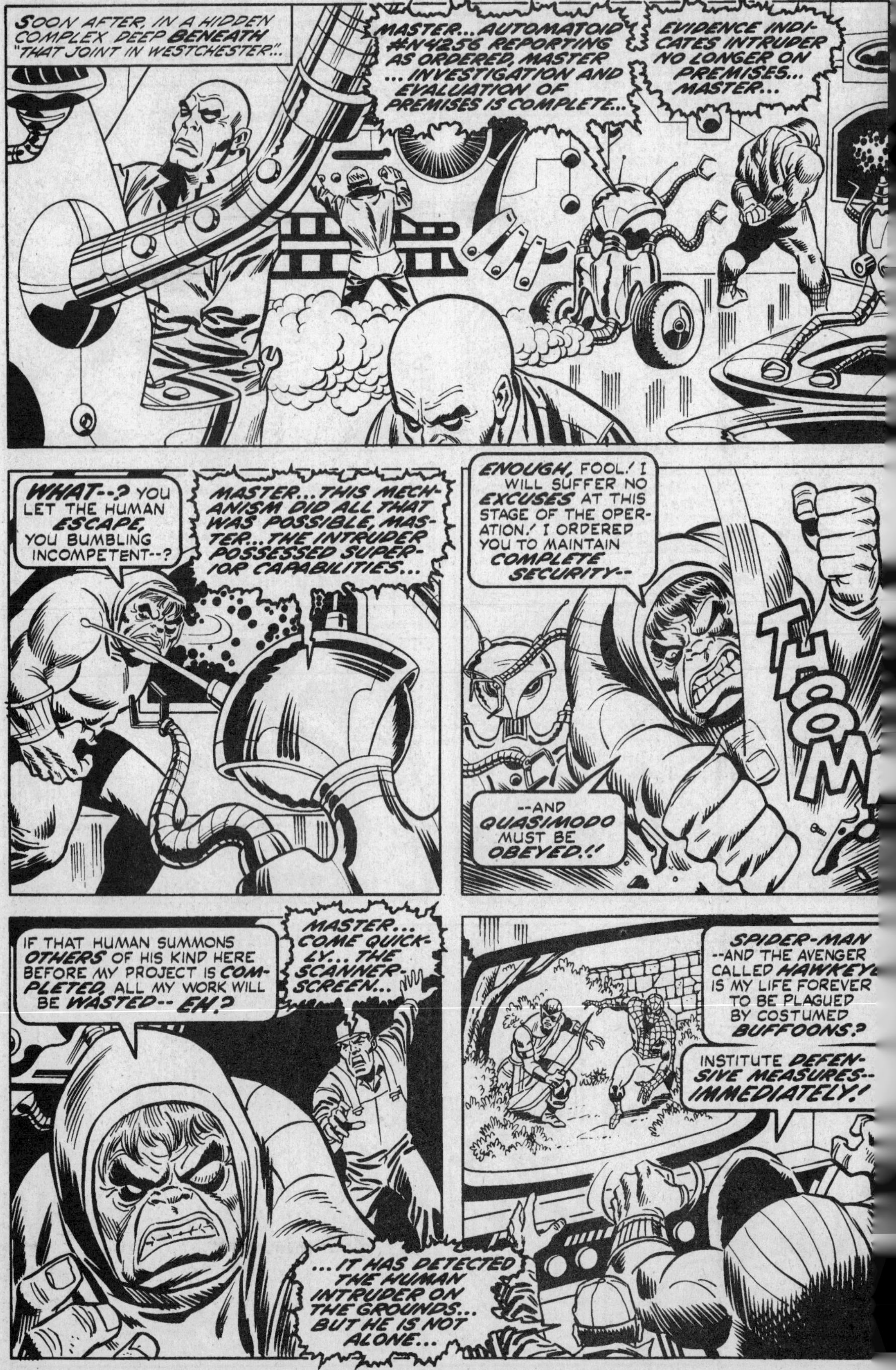
SOON AFTER, IN A HIDDEN COMPLEX DEEP BENEATH "THAT JOINT IN WESTCHESTER"...
MASTER... AUTOMATOID #N4256 REPORTING AS ORDERED, MASTER ...INVESTIGATION AND EVALUATION OF PREMISES IS COMPLETE...
EVIDENCE INDICATES INTRUDER NO LONGER ON PREMISES... MASTER...
WHAT--? YOU LET THE HUMAN ESCAPE, YOU BUMBLING INCOMPETENT--?
MASTER...THIS MECHANISM DID ALL THAT WAS POSSIBLE, MASTER...THE INTRUDER POSSESSED SUPERIOR CAPABILITIES...
ENOUGH, FOOL! I WILL SUFFER NO EXCUSES AT THIS STAGE OF THE OPERATION! I ORDERED YOU TO MAINTAIN COMPLETE SECURITY--
THOOM!
--AND QUASIMODO MUST BE OBEYED!!
IF THAT HUMAN SUMMONS OTHERS OF HIS KIND HERE BEFORE MY PROJECT IS COMPLETED, ALL MY WORK WILL BE WASTED-- EH?
MASTER... COME QUICKLY... THE SCANNER-SCREEN...
...IT HAS DETECTED THE HUMAN INTRUDER ON THE GROUNDS... BUT HE IS NOT ALONE...
SPIDER-MAN --AND THE AVENGER CALLED HAWKEYE! IS MY LIFE FOREVER TO BE PLAGUED BY COSTUMED BUFFOONS?
INSTITUTE DEFENSIVE MEASURES-- IMMEDIATELY!

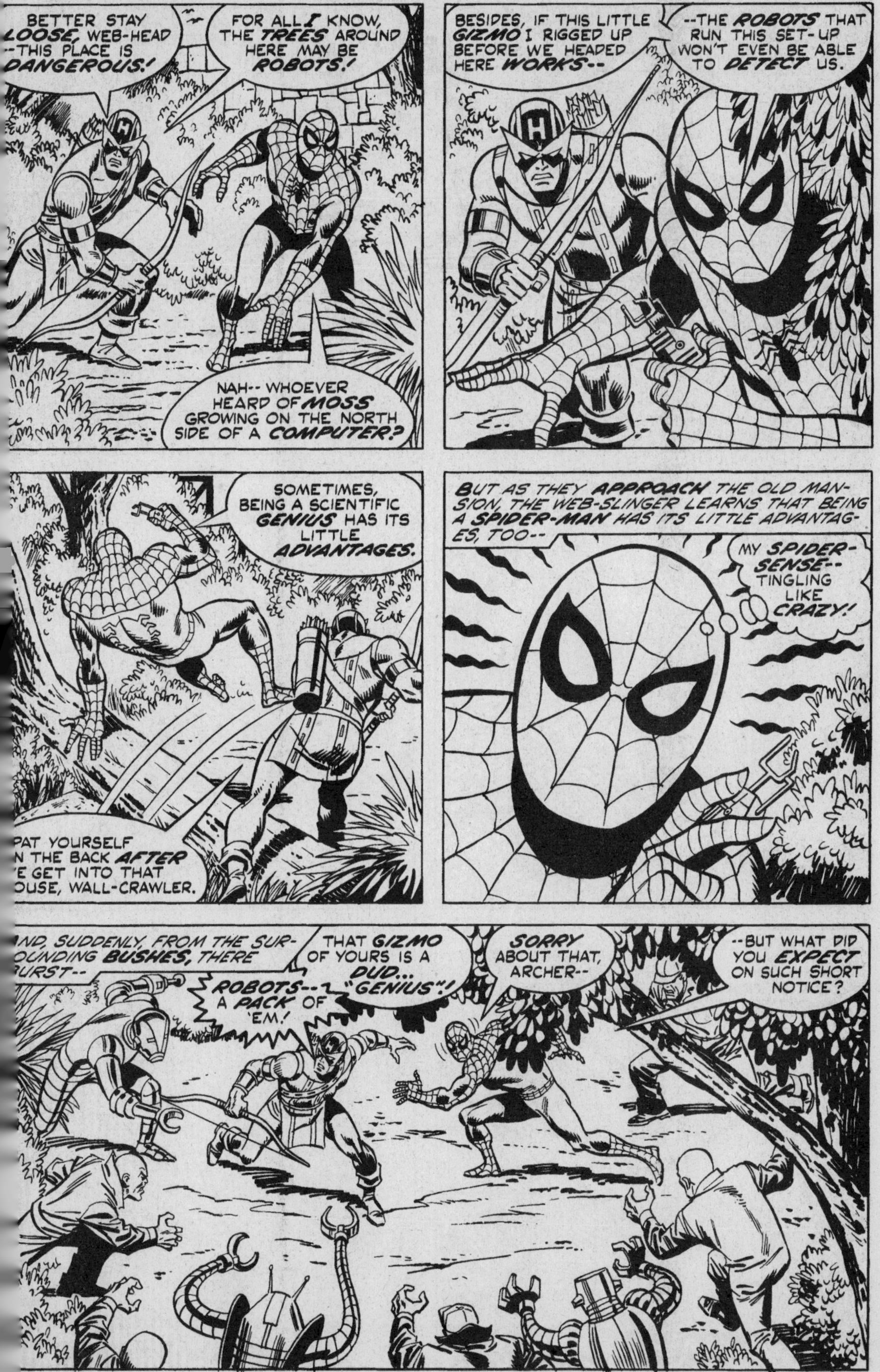
BETTER STAY LOOSE, WEB-HEAD --THIS PLACE IS DANGEROUS.!
FOR ALL I KNOW, THE TREES AROUND HERE MAY BE ROBOTS.!
NAH-- WHOEVER HEARD OF MOSS GROWING ON THE NORTH SIDE OF A COMPUTER?
BESIDES, IF THIS LITTLE GIZMO I RIGGED UP BEFORE WE HEADED HERE WORKS--
--THE ROBOTS THAT RUN THIS SET-UP WON'T EVEN BE ABLE TO DETECT US.
SOMETIMES, BEING A SCIENTIFIC GENIUS HAS ITS LITTLE ADVANTAGES.
PAT YOURSELF N THE BACK AFTER E GET INTO THAT OUSE, WALL-CRAWLER.
BUT AS THEY APPROACH THE OLD MANSION, THE WEB-SLINGER LEARNS THAT BEING A SPIDER-MAN HAS ITS LITTLE ADVANTAGES, TOO--
MY SPIDER-SENSE-- TINGLING LIKE CRAZY!
ND, SUDDENLY, FROM THE SURROUNDING BUSHES, THERE URST--
ROBOTS-- A PACK OF 'EM!
THAT GIZMO OF YOURS IS A DUD... "GENIUS"!
SORRY ABOUT THAT, ARCHER--
--BUT WHAT DID YOU EXPECT ON SUCH SHORT NOTICE?

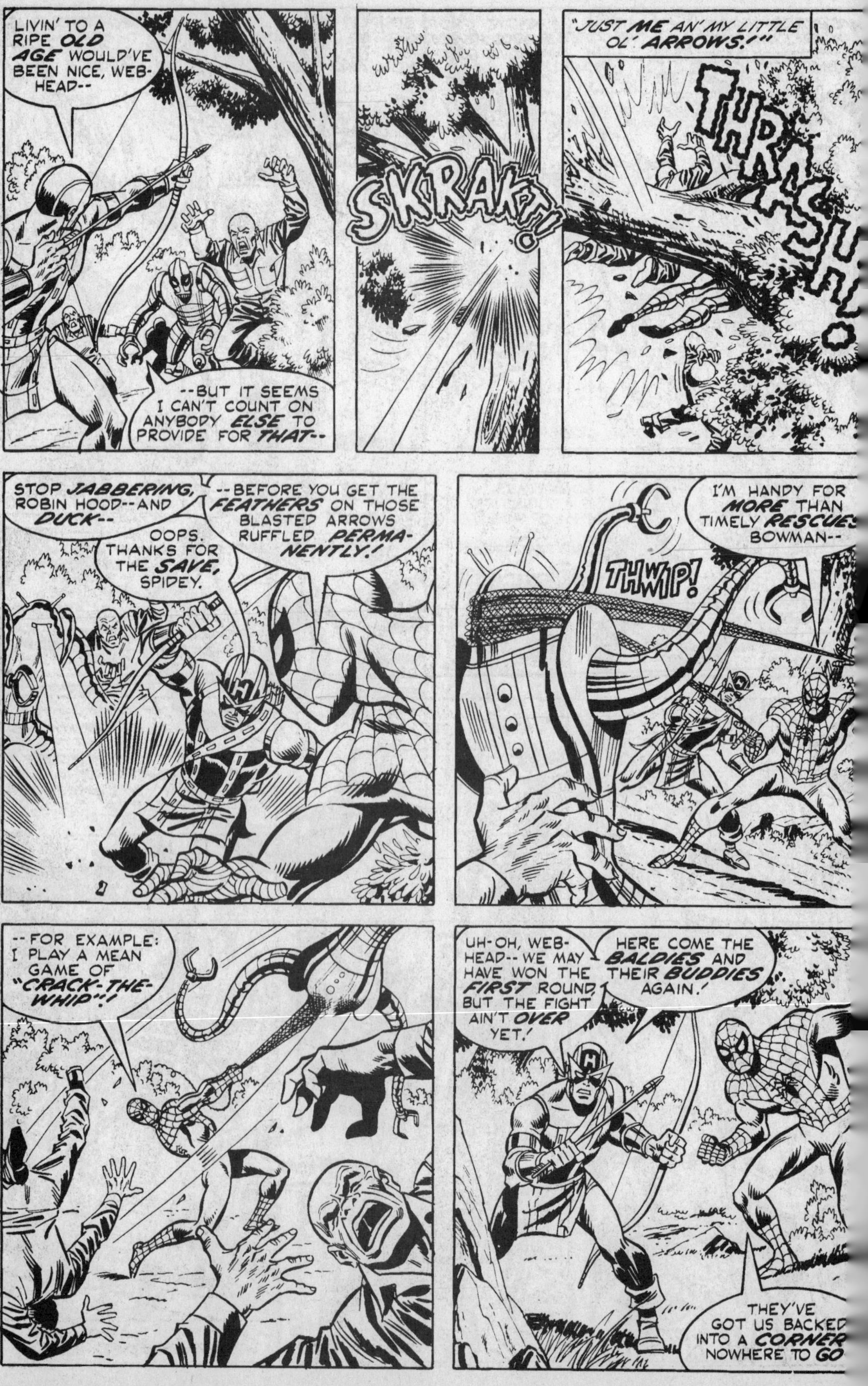
LIVIN' TO A RIPE OLD AGE WOULD'VE BEEN NICE, WEB-HEAD--
--BUT IT SEEMS I CAN'T COUNT ON ANYBODY ELSE TO PROVIDE FOR THAT--
SKRAKT!
"JUST ME AN' MY LITTLE OL' ARROWS!"
STOP JABBERING, ROBIN HOOD--AND DUCK--
--BEFORE YOU GET THE FEATHERS ON THOSE BLASTED ARROWS RUFFLED PERMA-NENTLY!
OOPS. THANKS FOR THE SAVE, SPIDEY.
I'M HANDY FOR MORE THAN TIMELY RESCUES BOWMAN--
THWIP!
--FOR EXAMPLE: I PLAY A MEAN GAME OF "CRACK-THE-WHIP"!
UH-OH, WEB-HEAD-- WE MAY HAVE WON THE FIRST ROUND, BUT THE FIGHT AIN'T OVER YET.
HERE COME THE BALDIES AND THEIR BUDDIES AGAIN.
THEY'VE GOT US BACKED INTO A CORNER NOWHERE TO GO

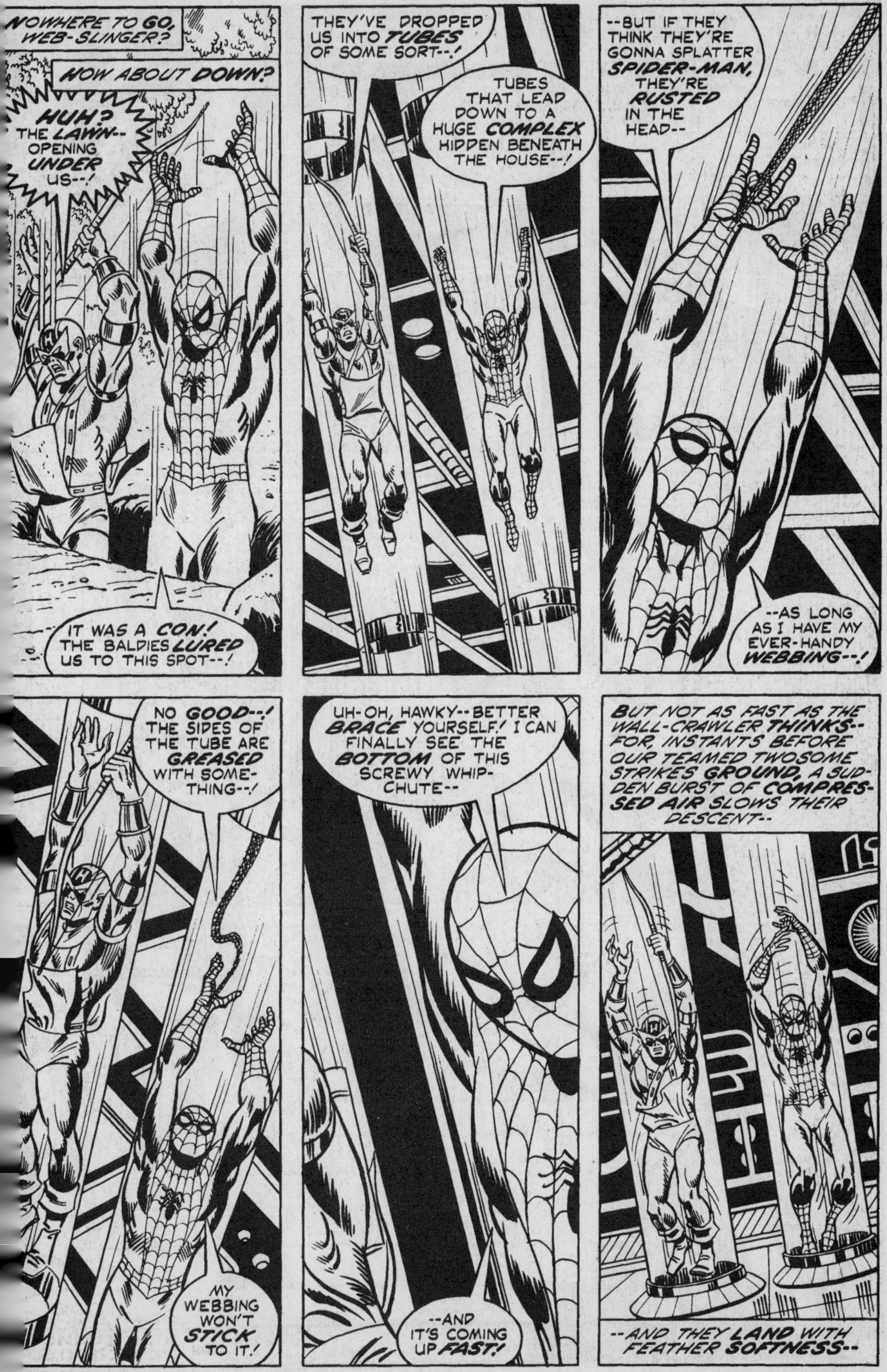
NOWHERE TO GO, WEB-SLINGER?
HOW ABOUT DOWN?
HUH? THE LAWN-- OPENING UNDER US--!
IT WAS A CON! THE BALDIES LURED US TO THIS SPOT--!
THEY'VE DROPPED US INTO TUBES OF SOME SORT--!
TUBES THAT LEAD DOWN TO A HUGE COMPLEX HIDDEN BENEATH THE HOUSE--!
--BUT IF THEY THINK THEY'RE GONNA SPLATTER SPIDER-MAN, THEY'RE RUSTED IN THE HEAD--
--AS LONG AS I HAVE MY EVER-HANDY WEBBING--!
NO GOOD--! THE SIDES OF THE TUBE ARE GREASED WITH SOME-THING--!
MY WEBBING WON'T STICK TO IT!
UH-OH, HAWKY--BETTER BRACE YOURSELF! I CAN FINALLY SEE THE BOTTOM OF THIS SCREWY WHIP-CHUTE--
--AND IT'S COMING UP FAST!
BUT NOT AS FAST AS THE WALL-CRAWLER THINKS--FOR, INSTANTS BEFORE OUR TEAMED TWOSOME STRIKES GROUND, A SUDDEN BURST OF COMPRESSED AIR SLOWS THEIR DESCENT--
--AND THEY LAND WITH FEATHER SOFTNESS--

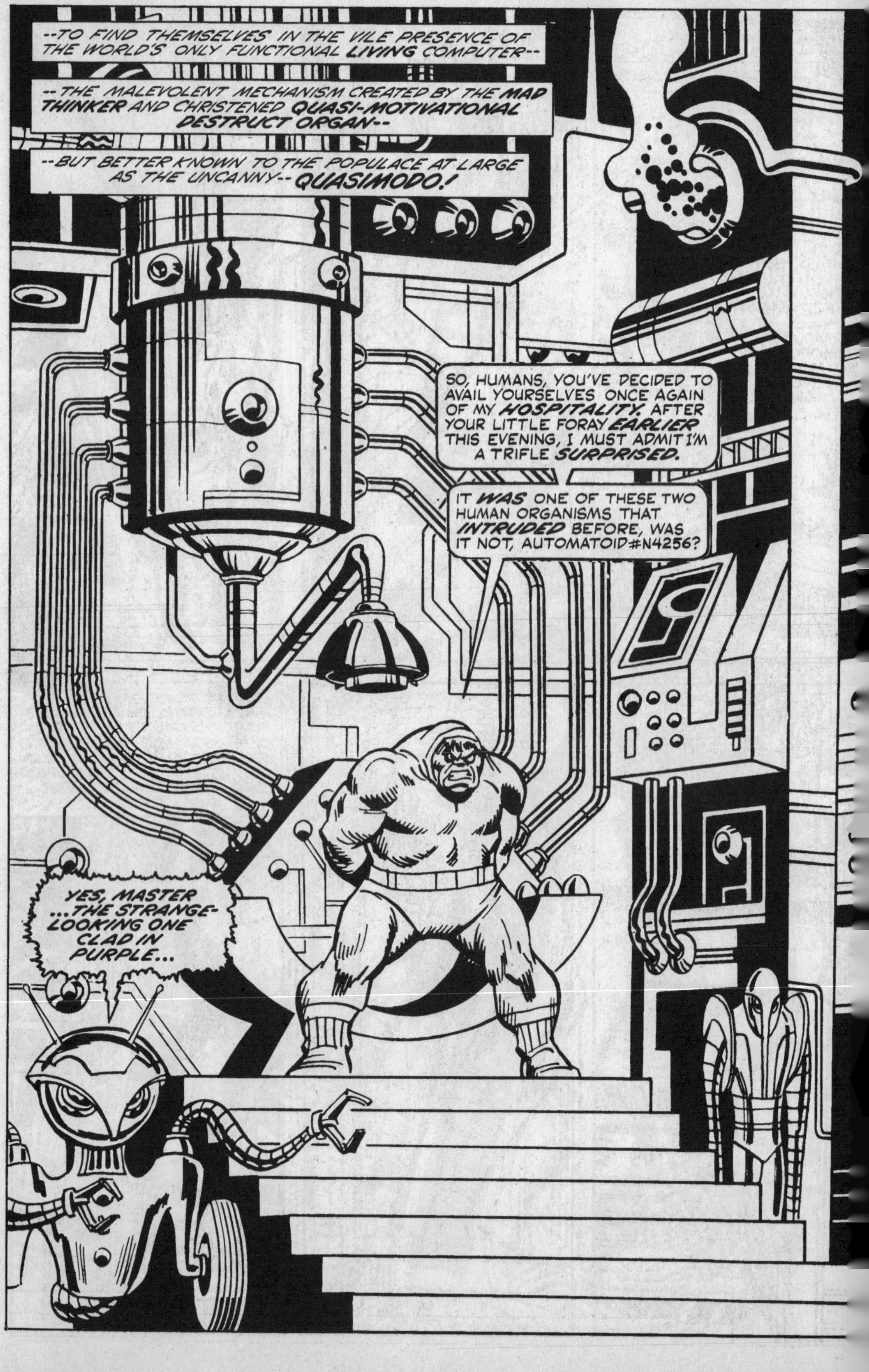
--TO FIND THEMSELVES IN THE VILE PRESENCE OF THE WORLD'S ONLY FUNCTIONAL LIVING COMPUTER--
--THE MALEVOLENT MECHANISM CREATED BY THE MAD THINKER AND CHRISTENED QUASI-MOTIVATIONAL DESTRUCT ORGAN--
--BUT BETTER KNOWN TO THE POPULACE AT LARGE AS THE UNCANNY-- QUASIMODO!
SO, HUMANS, YOU'VE DECIDED TO AVAIL YOURSELVES ONCE AGAIN OF MY HOSPITALITY. AFTER YOUR LITTLE FORAY EARLIER THIS EVENING, I MUST ADMIT I'M A TRIFLE SURPRISED.
IT WAS ONE OF THESE TWO HUMAN ORGANISMS THAT INTRUDED BEFORE, WAS IT NOT, AUTOMATOID#N4256?
YES, MASTER ...THE STRANGE-LOOKING ONE CLAD IN PURPLE...

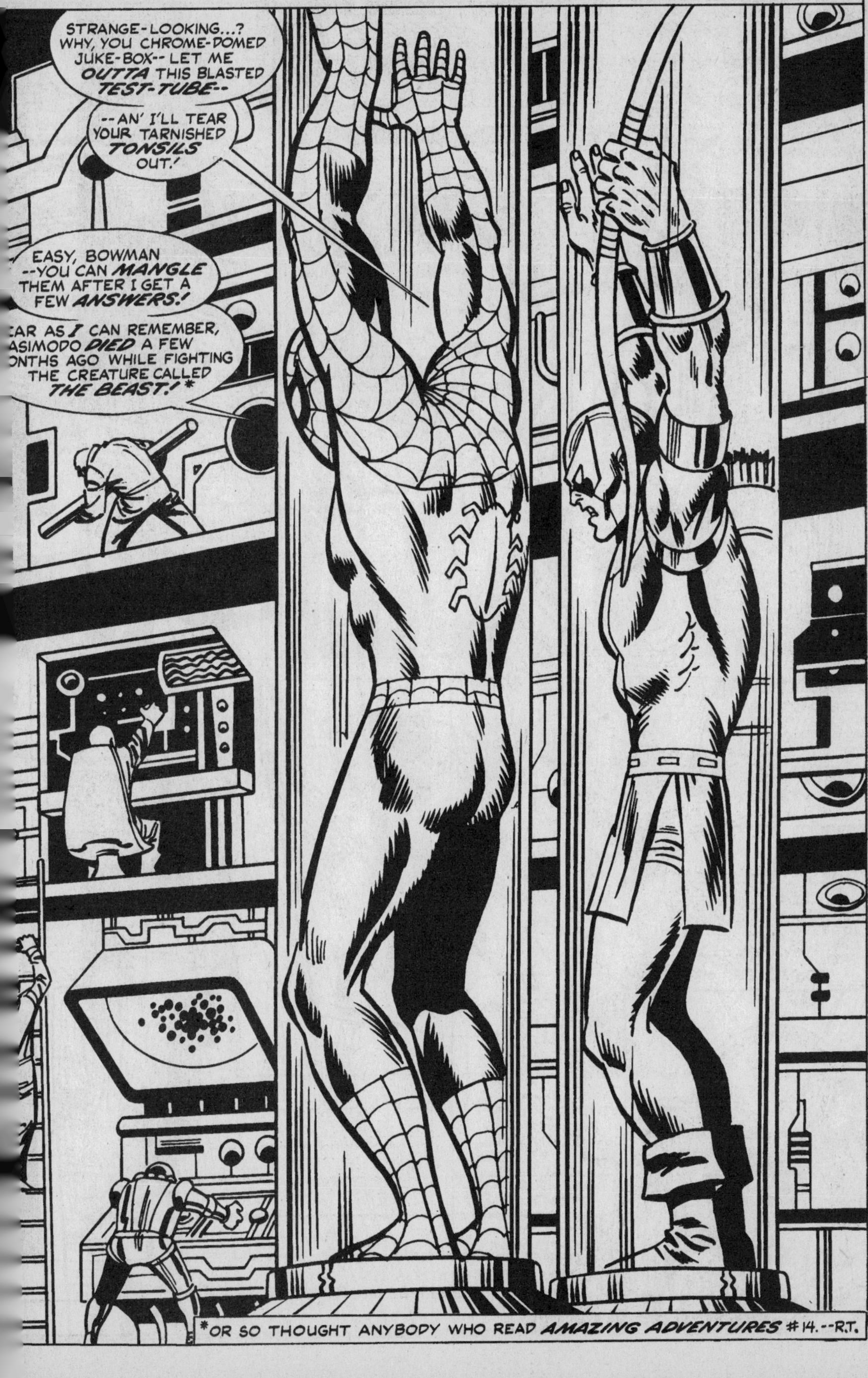
STRANGE-LOOKING...? WHY, YOU CHROME-DOMED JUKE-BOX-- LET ME OUTTA THIS BLASTED TEST-TUBE--
--AN' I'LL TEAR YOUR TARNISHED TONSILS OUT!
EASY, BOWMAN --YOU CAN MANGLE THEM AFTER I GET A FEW ANSWERS!
AR AS I CAN REMEMBER, ASIMODO DIED A FEW ONTHS AGO WHILE FIGHTING THE CREATURE CALLED THE BEAST! *
*OR SO THOUGHT ANYBODY WHO READ AMAZING ADVENTURES #14.--R.T.

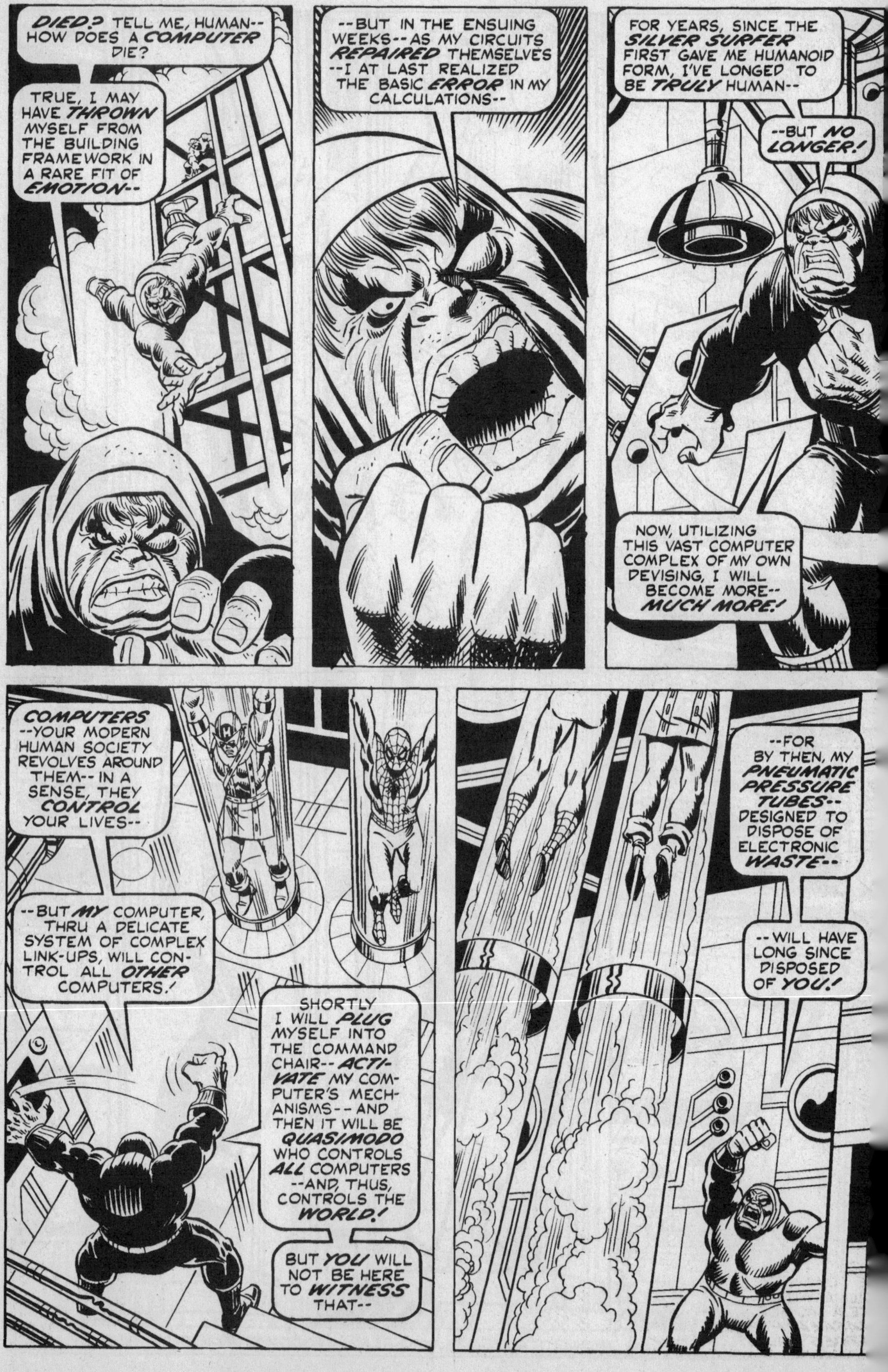

DIED? TELL ME, HUMAN-- HOW DOES A COMPUTER DIE?
TRUE, I MAY HAVE THROWN MYSELF FROM THE BUILDING FRAMEWORK IN A RARE FIT OF EMOTION--
--BUT IN THE ENSUING WEEKS--AS MY CIRCUITS REPAIRED THEMSELVES --I AT LAST REALIZED THE BASIC ERROR IN MY CALCULATIONS--
FOR YEARS, SINCE THE SILVER SURFER FIRST GAVE ME HUMANOID FORM, I'VE LONGED TO BE TRULY HUMAN--
--BUT NO LONGER!
NOW, UTILIZING THIS VAST COMPUTER COMPLEX OF MY OWN DEVISING, I WILL BECOME MORE-- MUCH MORE!
COMPUTERS --YOUR MODERN HUMAN SOCIETY REVOLVES AROUND THEM-- IN A SENSE, THEY CONTROL YOUR LIVES--
--BUT MY COMPUTER, THRU A DELICATE SYSTEM OF COMPLEX LINK-UPS, WILL CONTROL ALL OTHER COMPUTERS!
SHORTLY I WILL PLUG MYSELF INTO THE COMMAND CHAIR-- ACTIVATE MY COMPUTER'S MECHANISMS-- AND THEN IT WILL BE QUASIMODO WHO CONTROLS ALL COMPUTERS --AND, THUS, CONTROLS THE WORLD!
BUT YOU WILL NOT BE HERE TO WITNESS THAT--
--FOR BY THEN, MY PNEUMATIC PRESSURE TUBES-- DESIGNED TO DISPOSE OF ELECTRONIC WASTE--
--WILL HAVE LONG SINCE DISPOSED OF YOU!

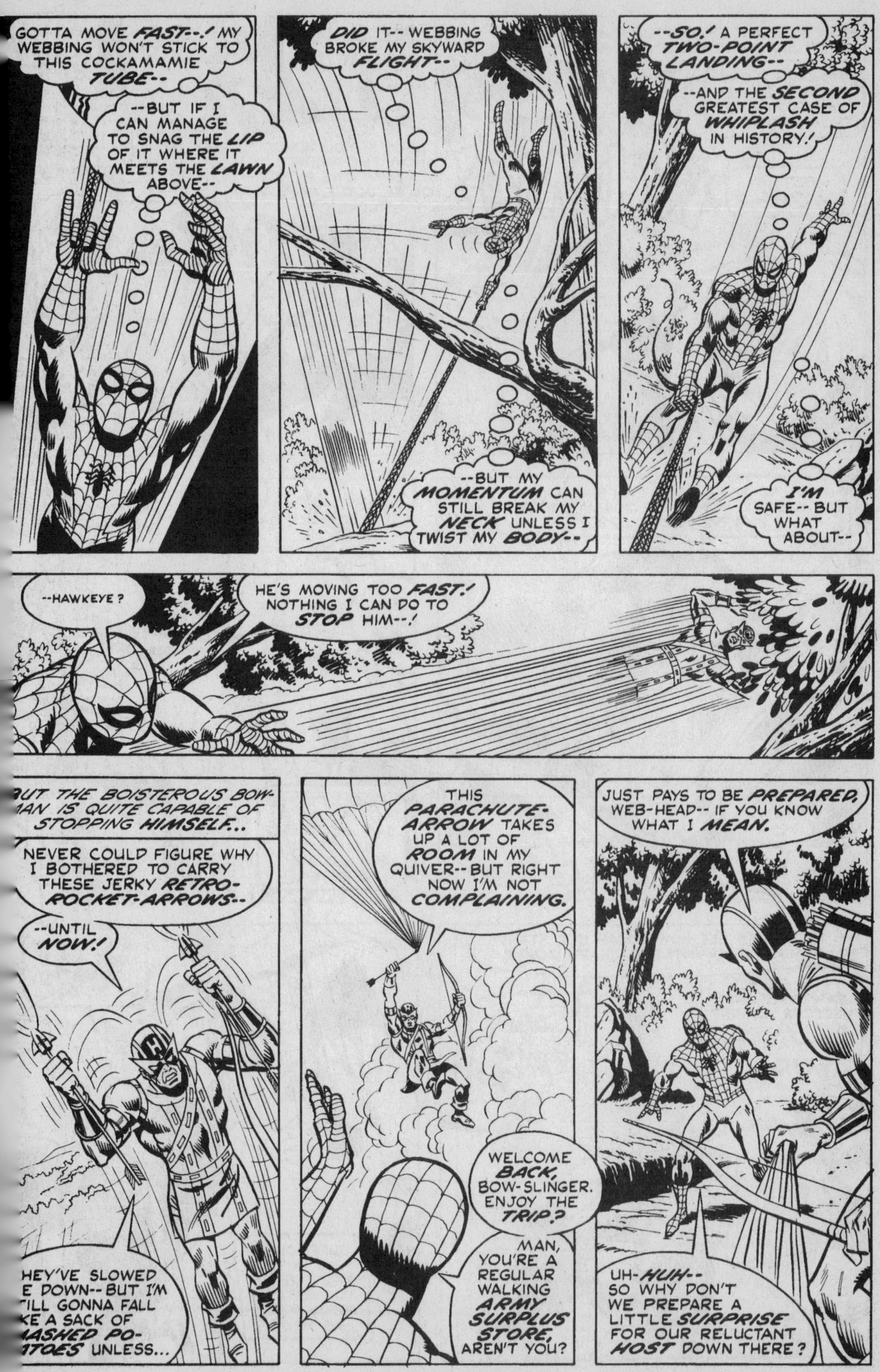
GOTTA MOVE FAST--! MY WEBBING WON'T STICK TO THIS COCKAMAMIE TUBE--
--BUT IF I CAN MANAGE TO SNAG THE LIP OF IT WHERE IT MEETS THE LAWN ABOVE--
DID IT-- WEBBING BROKE MY SKYWARD FLIGHT--
--BUT MY MOMENTUM CAN STILL BREAK MY NECK UNLESS I TWIST MY BODY--
--SO! A PERFECT TWO-POINT LANDING--
--AND THE SECOND GREATEST CASE OF WHIPLASH IN HISTORY!
I'M SAFE-- BUT WHAT ABOUT--
--HAWKEYE?
HE'S MOVING TOO FAST! NOTHING I CAN DO TO STOP HIM--!
UT THE BOISTEROUS BOW-MAN IS QUITE CAPABLE OF STOPPING HIMSELF...
NEVER COULD FIGURE WHY I BOTHERED TO CARRY THESE JERKY RETRO-ROCKET-ARROWS--
--UNTIL NOW!
HEY'VE SLOWED E DOWN-- BUT I'M ILL GONNA FALL KE A SACK OF ASHED PO-ATOES UNLESS...
THIS PARACHUTE-ARROW TAKES UP A LOT OF ROOM IN MY QUIVER-- BUT RIGHT NOW I'M NOT COMPLAINING.
WELCOME BACK, BOW-SLINGER. ENJOY THE TRIP?
MAN, YOU'RE A REGULAR WALKING ARMY SURPLUS STORE, AREN'T YOU?
JUST PAYS TO BE PREPARED, WEB-HEAD-- IF YOU KNOW WHAT I MEAN.
UH-HUH-- SO WHY DON'T WE PREPARE A LITTLE SURPRISE FOR OUR RELUCTANT HOST DOWN THERE?

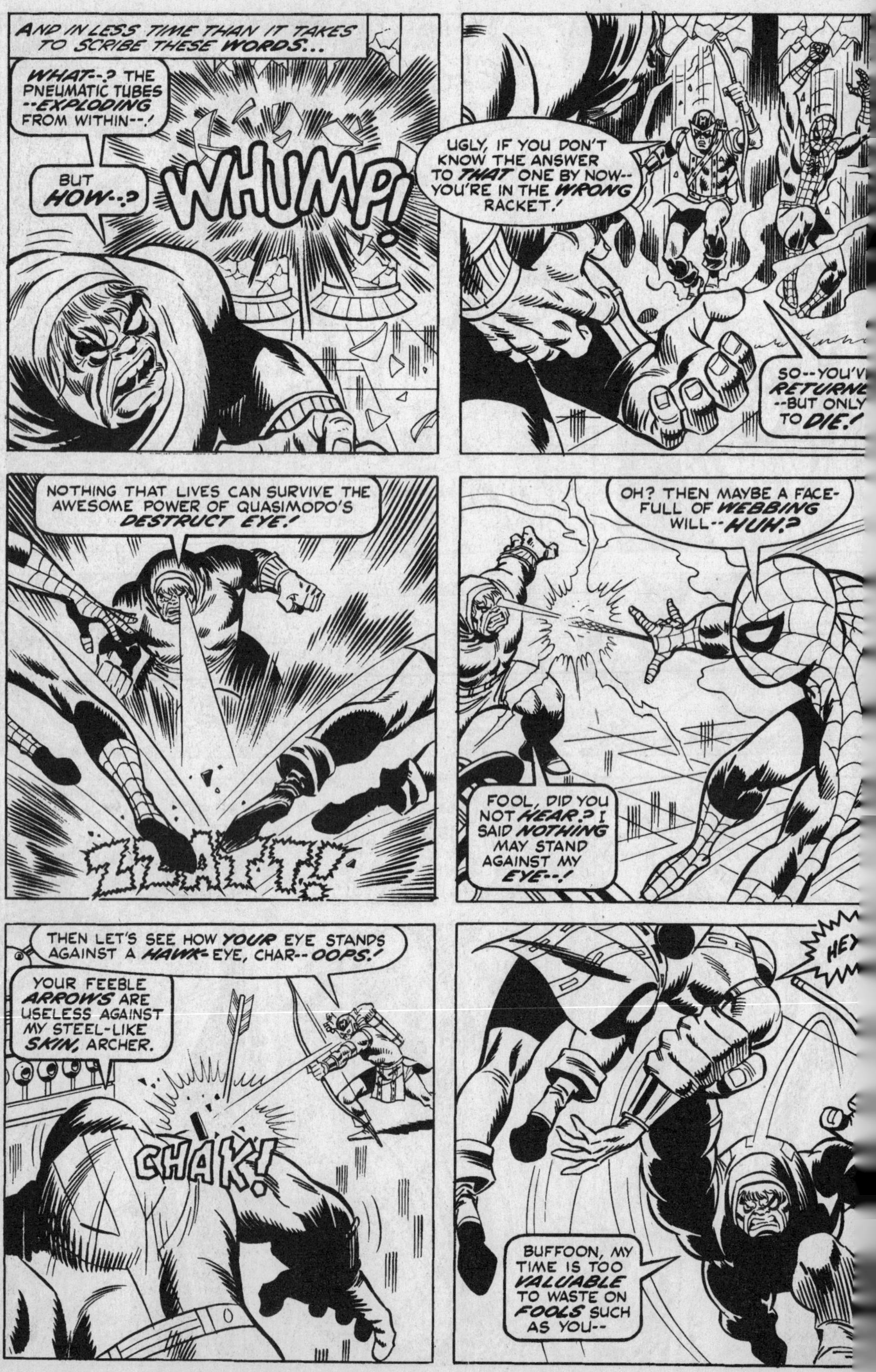
AND IN LESS TIME THAN IT TAKES TO SCRIBE THESE WORDS...
WHAT--? THE PNEUMATIC TUBES --EXPLODING FROM WITHIN--!
BUT HOW--?
WHUMP!
UGLY, IF YOU DON'T KNOW THE ANSWER TO THAT ONE BY NOW--YOU'RE IN THE WRONG RACKET.!
SO--YOU'V RETURNE --BUT ONLY TO DIE!
NOTHING THAT LIVES CAN SURVIVE THE AWESOME POWER OF QUASIMODO'S DESTRUCT EYE!
ZZAKT!
OH? THEN MAYBE A FACE-FULL OF WEBBING WILL--HUH?
FOOL, DID YOU NOT HEAR? I SAID NOTHING MAY STAND AGAINST MY EYE--!
THEN LET'S SEE HOW YOUR EYE STANDS AGAINST A HAWK-EYE, CHAR--OOPS!
YOUR FEEBLE ARROWS ARE USELESS AGAINST MY STEEL-LIKE SKIN, ARCHER.
CHAK!
HEY
BUFFOON, MY TIME IS TOO VALUABLE TO WASTE ON FOOLS SUCH AS YOU--

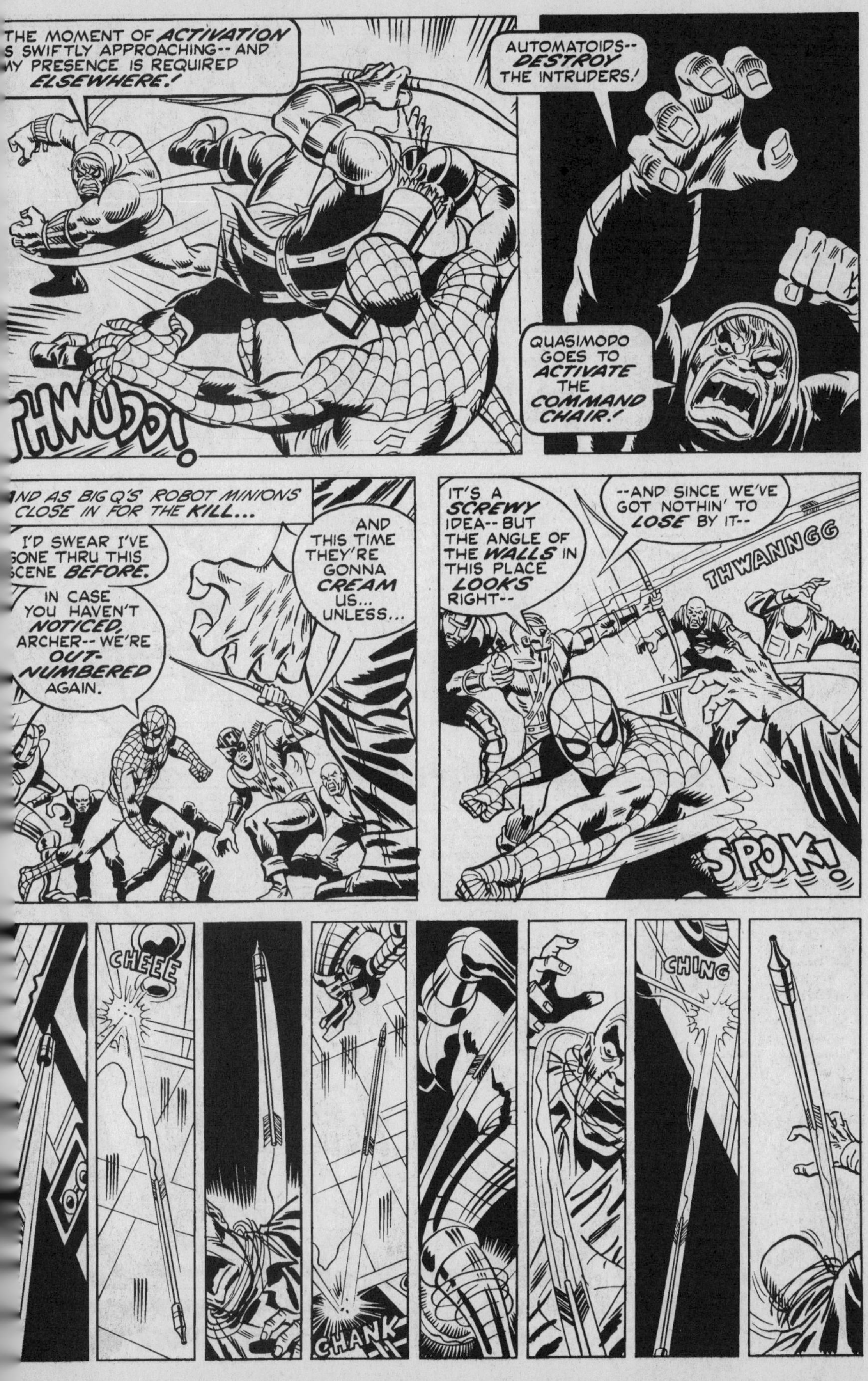
THE MOMENT OF ACTIVATION
S SWIFTLY APPROACHING-- AND
MY PRESENCE IS REQUIRED
ELSEWHERE!
THWUDD!
AUTOMATOIDS--
DESTROY
THE INTRUDERS!
QUASIMODO
GOES TO
ACTIVATE
THE
COMMAND
CHAIR!
AND AS BIG Q'S ROBOT MINIONS
CLOSE IN FOR THE KILL...
I'D SWEAR I'VE
GONE THRU THIS
SCENE BEFORE.
IN CASE
YOU HAVEN'T
NOTICED,
ARCHER-- WE'RE
OUT-
NUMBERED
AGAIN.
AND
THIS TIME
THEY'RE
GONNA
CREAM
US...
UNLESS...
IT'S A
SCREWY
IDEA-- BUT
THE ANGLE OF
THE WALLS IN
THIS PLACE
LOOKS
RIGHT--
--AND SINCE WE'VE
GOT NOTHIN' TO
LOSE BY IT--
THWANNGG
SPOK!
CHEEE
CHANK
CHING

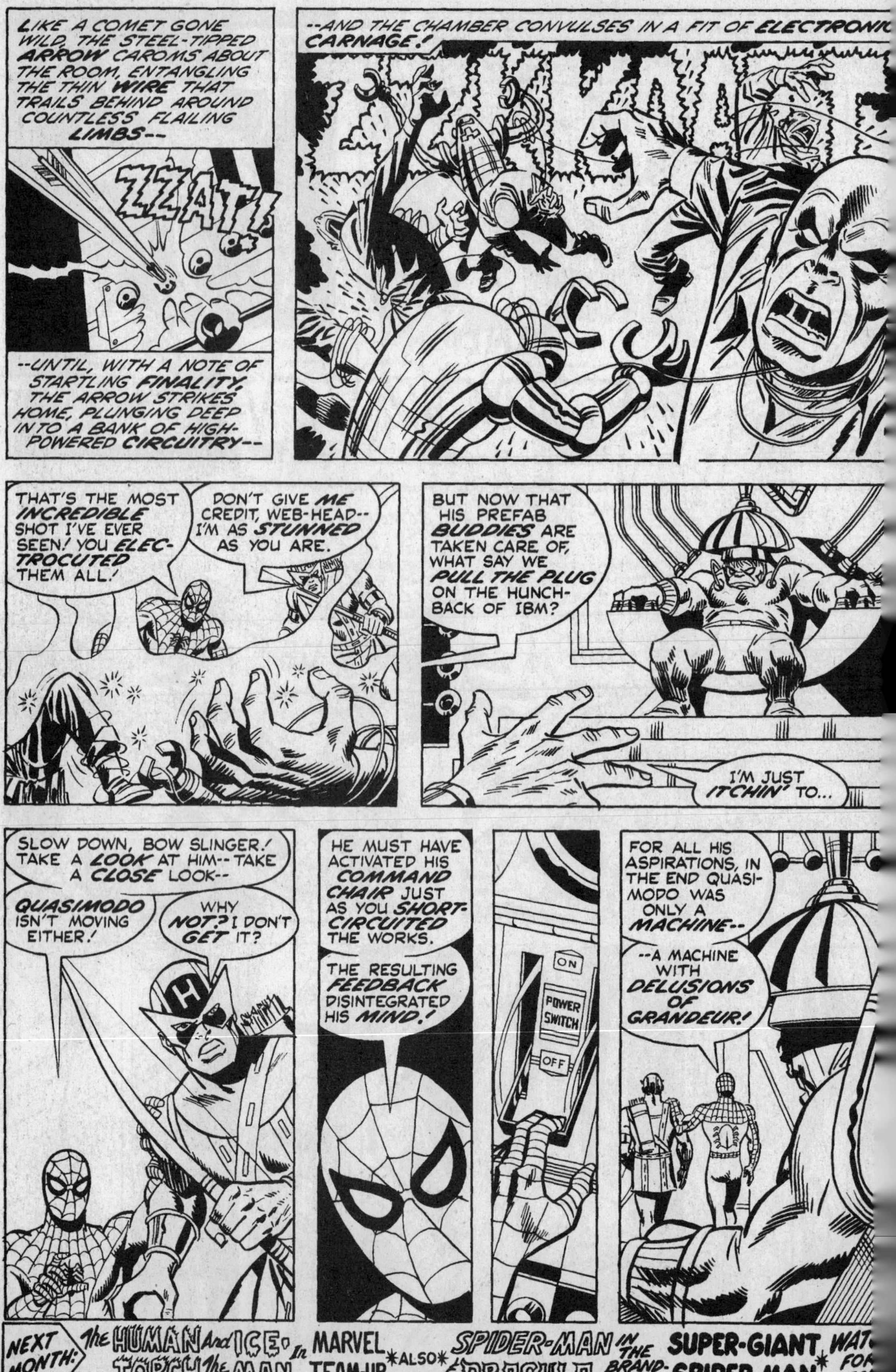
LIKE A COMET GONE WILD, THE STEEL-TIPPED ARROW CAROMS ABOUT THE ROOM, ENTANGLING THE THIN WIRE THAT TRAILS BEHIND AROUND COUNTLESS FLAILING LIMBS--
ZZAT!
--UNTIL, WITH A NOTE OF STARTLING FINALITY, THE ARROW STRIKES HOME, PLUNGING DEEP INTO A BANK OF HIGH-POWERED CIRCUITRY--
--AND THE CHAMBER CONVULSES IN A FIT OF ELECTRONIC CARNAGE!
THAT'S THE MOST INCREDIBLE SHOT I'VE EVER SEEN! YOU ELECTROCUTED THEM ALL!
DON'T GIVE ME CREDIT, WEB-HEAD-- I'M AS STUNNED AS YOU ARE.
BUT NOW THAT HIS PREFAB BUDDIES ARE TAKEN CARE OF, WHAT SAY WE PULL THE PLUG ON THE HUNCH-BACK OF IBM?
I'M JUST ITCHIN' TO...
SLOW DOWN, BOW SLINGER! TAKE A LOOK AT HIM--TAKE A CLOSE LOOK--
QUASIMODO ISN'T MOVING EITHER!
WHY NOT? I DON'T GET IT?
HE MUST HAVE ACTIVATED HIS COMMAND CHAIR JUST AS YOU SHORT-CIRCUITED THE WORKS.
THE RESULTING FEEDBACK DISINTEGRATED HIS MIND!
ON
POWER SWITCH
OFF
FOR ALL HIS ASPIRATIONS, IN THE END QUASIMODO WAS ONLY A MACHINE--
--A MACHINE WITH DELUSIONS OF GRANDEUR!
NEXT MONTH: The HUMAN TORCH And the ICE-MAN In MARVEL TEAM-UP *ALSO* SPIDER-MAN & DRACULA IN THE BRAND-NEW SUPER-GIANT SPIDER-MAN*

MARVEL TEAM-UP
MARVEL COMICS GROUP
APPROVED BY THE COMICS CODE AUTHORITY
25¢ 23 JULY 02147
MARVEL TEAM-UP
FEATURING
HUMAN TORCH
AND
ICEMAN
FIRE VS ICE IN THE BATTLE OF THE CENTURY
THIS TIME YOU'VE HAD IT, TORCH! HERE'S WHERE I PUT YOU IN COLD STORAGE-- FOR KEEPS!
NOT AFTER MY NEXT FIREBALL MELTS YOU DOWN TO SIZE!
CO-STARRING THE UNCANNY X-MEN AND THE MARAUDING MENACE KNOWN AS-- EQUINOX!

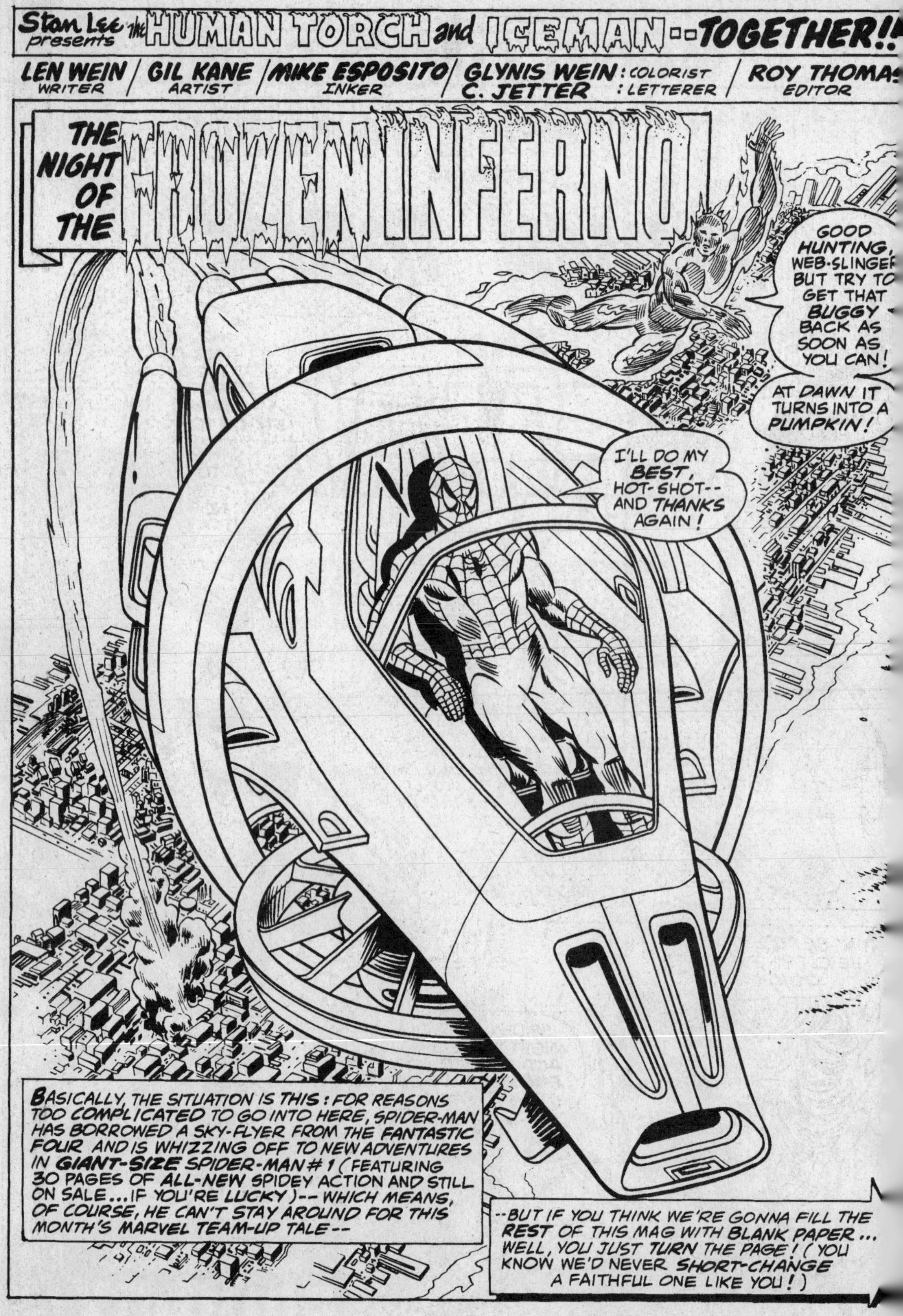
Stan Lee presents the HUMAN TORCH and ICEMAN--TOGETHER!!
LEN WEIN WRITER / GIL KANE ARTIST / MIKE ESPOSITO INKER / GLYNIS WEIN : COLORIST C. JETTER : LETTERER / ROY THOMAS EDITOR
THE NIGHT OF THE FROZEN INFERNO!
GOOD HUNTING, WEB-SLINGER BUT TRY TO GET THAT BUGGY BACK AS SOON AS YOU CAN!
AT DAWN IT TURNS INTO A PUMPKIN!
I'LL DO MY BEST, HOT-SHOT-- AND THANKS AGAIN!
BASICALLY, THE SITUATION IS THIS: FOR REASONS TOO COMPLICATED TO GO INTO HERE, SPIDER-MAN HAS BORROWED A SKY-FLYER FROM THE FANTASTIC FOUR AND IS WHIZZING OFF TO NEW ADVENTURES IN GIANT-SIZE SPIDER-MAN #1 (FEATURING 30 PAGES OF ALL-NEW SPIDEY ACTION AND STILL ON SALE...IF YOU'RE LUCKY)-- WHICH MEANS, OF COURSE, HE CAN'T STAY AROUND FOR THIS MONTH'S MARVEL TEAM-UP TALE--
--BUT IF YOU THINK WE'RE GONNA FILL THE REST OF THIS MAG WITH BLANK PAPER... WELL, YOU JUST TURN THE PAGE! (YOU KNOW WE'D NEVER SHORT-CHANGE A FAITHFUL ONE LIKE YOU!)

WELL, SO MUCH FOR *THAT!* NOW THAT I'M SURE THE WEB-SLINGER WON'T *BOUNCE* THAT BUGGY OFF THE SIDE OF SOME *BUILDING*--

-- I MIGHT AS WELL HEAD *HOME!*

NOT THAT THERE'S ANYONE TO COME HOME *TO,* OF COURSE.

REED, BEN AND MEDUSA ARE ALL *OUT* FOR THE EVENING--

--LEAVING LITTLE *JOHNNY STORM* TO MIND THE STORE--

WHICH IS ABOUT AS *EXCITING* AS BEING A JUDGE AT A *TURNIP-PICKING* CONTEST!

MAN, I *DO* HAVE A MAD ON TONIGHT, DON'T I?

WONDER *WHY?*

GRANTED, I'VE BEEN INDULGING IN A LOT OF AMATEUR *HEAD-SHRINKING* TONIGHT--

--TRYING TO SOLVE THE *PROBLEMS* REED AND SUE ARE HAVING--

--TRYING TO FIGURE OUT EXACTLY *WHAT* MY FEELINGS ARE TOWARDS *CRYSTAL* THESE DAYS, BUT...

CRIPES-- JUST LOOK AT WHAT I'M *DOING!*

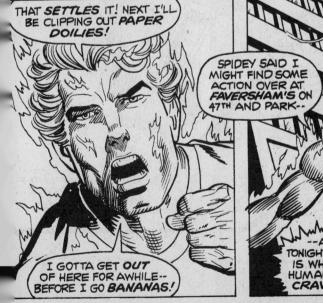

THAT *SETTLES* IT! NEXT I'LL BE CLIPPING OUT *PAPER DOILIES!*

I GOTTA GET *OUT* OF HERE FOR AWHILE-- BEFORE I GO *BANANAS!*

SPIDEY SAID I MIGHT FIND SOME ACTION OVER AT *FAVERSHAM'S* ON 47TH AND PARK--

--AND TONIGHT, *ACTION* IS WHAT THE HUMAN TORCH *CRAVES*--

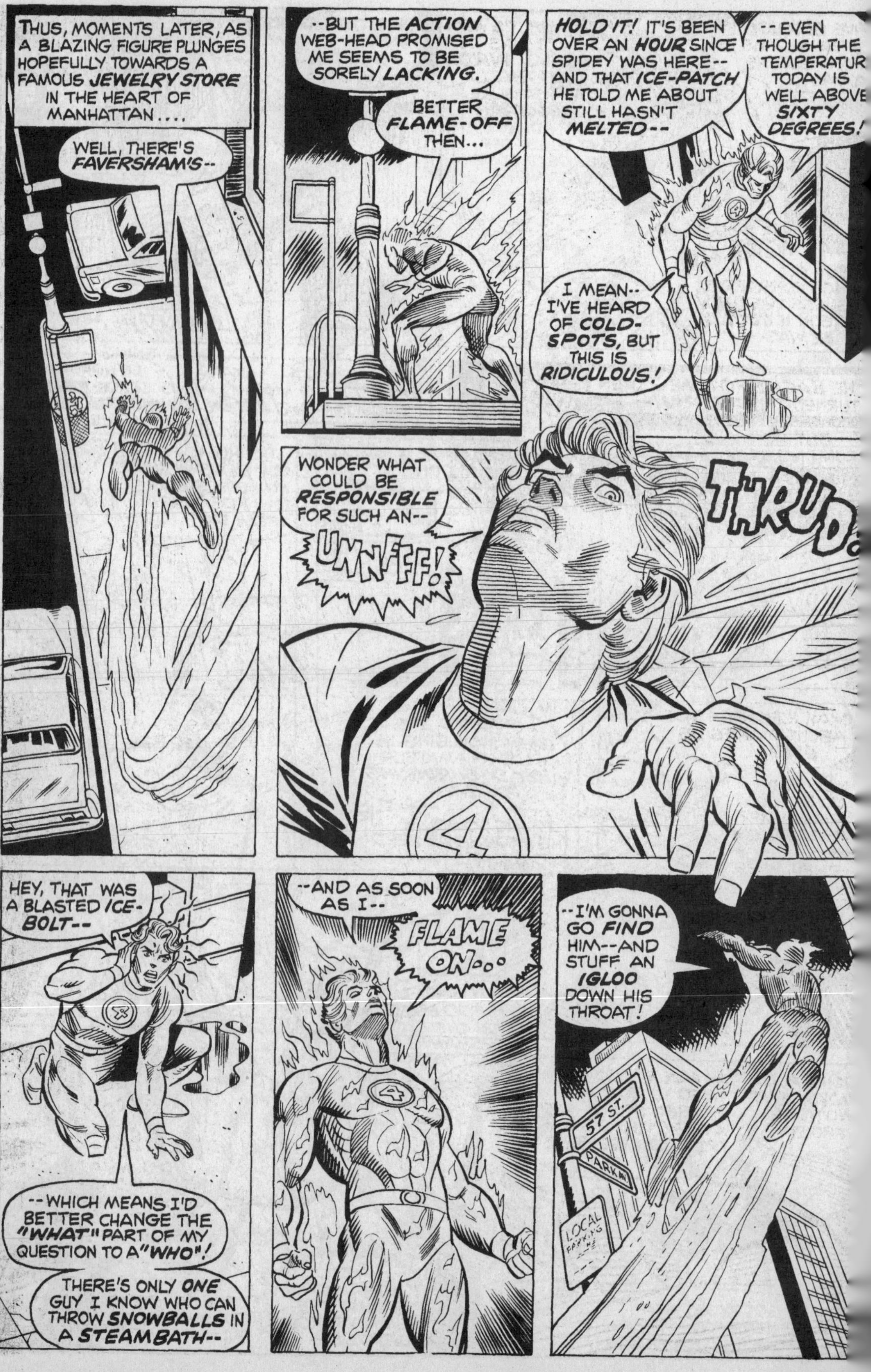
THUS, MOMENTS LATER, AS A BLAZING FIGURE PLUNGES HOPEFULLY TOWARDS A FAMOUS JEWELRY STORE IN THE HEART OF MANHATTAN....
WELL, THERE'S FAVERSHAM'S--
--BUT THE ACTION WEB-HEAD PROMISED ME SEEMS TO BE SORELY LACKING.
BETTER FLAME-OFF THEN...
HOLD IT! IT'S BEEN OVER AN HOUR SINCE SPIDEY WAS HERE-- AND THAT ICE-PATCH HE TOLD ME ABOUT STILL HASN'T MELTED--
--EVEN THOUGH THE TEMPERATUR TODAY IS WELL ABOVE SIXTY DEGREES!
I MEAN-- I'VE HEARD OF COLD-SPOTS, BUT THIS IS RIDICULOUS!
WONDER WHAT COULD BE RESPONSIBLE FOR SUCH AN--
UNNFFF!
THRUD
HEY, THAT WAS A BLASTED ICE-BOLT--
--WHICH MEANS I'D BETTER CHANGE THE "WHAT" PART OF MY QUESTION TO A "WHO"!
THERE'S ONLY ONE GUY I KNOW WHO CAN THROW SNOWBALLS IN A STEAMBATH--
--AND AS SOON AS I--
FLAME ON...
--I'M GONNA GO FIND HIM--AND STUFF AN IGLOO DOWN HIS THROAT!
57 ST.
PARK AV
LOCAL

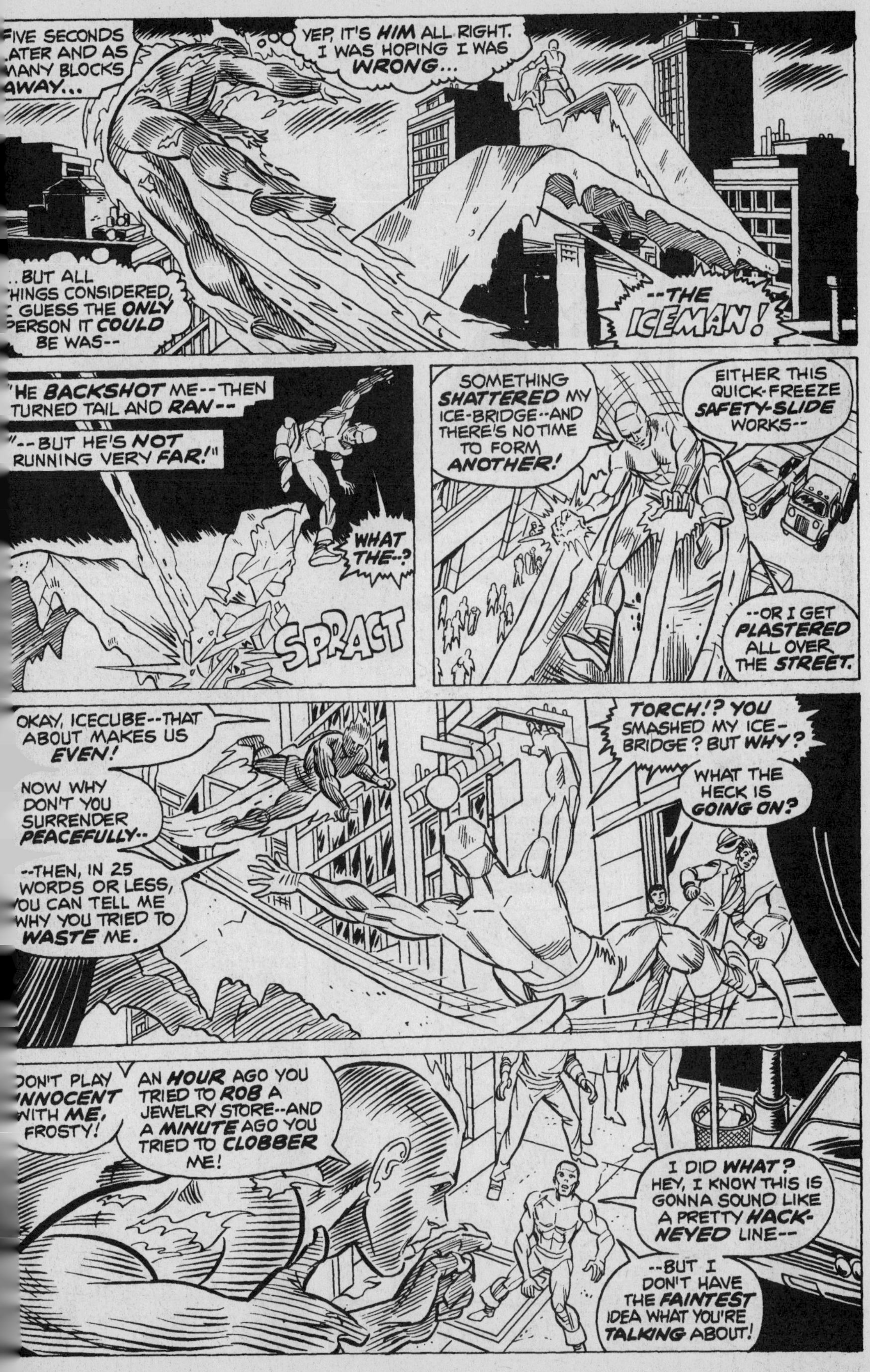
FIVE SECONDS LATER AND AS MANY BLOCKS AWAY...
YEP, IT'S HIM ALL RIGHT. I WAS HOPING I WAS WRONG...
...BUT ALL THINGS CONSIDERED, I GUESS THE ONLY PERSON IT COULD BE WAS--
--THE ICEMAN!
"HE BACKSHOT ME--THEN TURNED TAIL AND RAN--
"--BUT HE'S NOT RUNNING VERY FAR!"
WHAT THE--?
SPRACT
SOMETHING SHATTERED MY ICE-BRIDGE--AND THERE'S NO TIME TO FORM ANOTHER!
EITHER THIS QUICK-FREEZE SAFETY-SLIDE WORKS--
--OR I GET PLASTERED ALL OVER THE STREET.
OKAY, ICECUBE--THAT ABOUT MAKES US EVEN!
NOW WHY DON'T YOU SURRENDER PEACEFULLY--
--THEN, IN 25 WORDS OR LESS, YOU CAN TELL ME WHY YOU TRIED TO WASTE ME.
TORCH!? YOU SMASHED MY ICE-BRIDGE? BUT WHY?
WHAT THE HECK IS GOING ON?
DON'T PLAY INNOCENT WITH ME, FROSTY!
AN HOUR AGO YOU TRIED TO ROB A JEWELRY STORE--AND A MINUTE AGO YOU TRIED TO CLOBBER ME!
I DID WHAT? HEY, I KNOW THIS IS GONNA SOUND LIKE A PRETTY HACK-NEYED LINE--
--BUT I DON'T HAVE THE FAINTEST IDEA WHAT YOU'RE TALKING ABOUT!

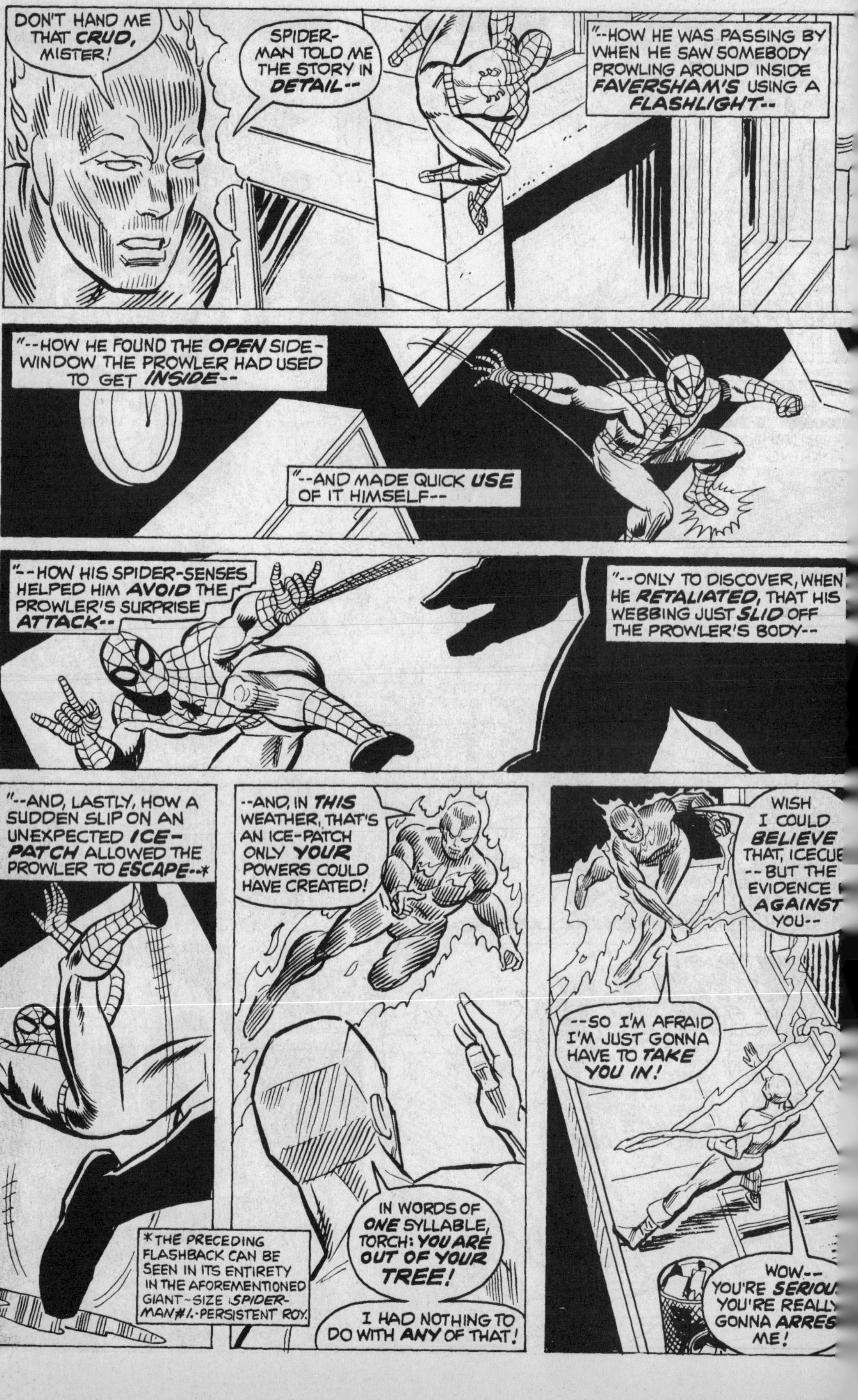

DON'T HAND ME THAT CRUD, MISTER!
SPIDER-MAN TOLD ME THE STORY IN DETAIL--
"--HOW HE WAS PASSING BY WHEN HE SAW SOMEBODY PROWLING AROUND INSIDE FAVERSHAM'S USING A FLASHLIGHT--
"--HOW HE FOUND THE OPEN SIDE-WINDOW THE PROWLER HAD USED TO GET INSIDE--
"--AND MADE QUICK USE OF IT HIMSELF--
"--HOW HIS SPIDER-SENSES HELPED HIM AVOID THE PROWLER'S SURPRISE ATTACK--
"--ONLY TO DISCOVER, WHEN HE RETALIATED, THAT HIS WEBBING JUST SLID OFF THE PROWLER'S BODY--
"--AND, LASTLY, HOW A SUDDEN SLIP ON AN UNEXPECTED ICE-PATCH ALLOWED THE PROWLER TO ESCAPE--*
--AND, IN THIS WEATHER, THAT'S AN ICE-PATCH ONLY YOUR POWERS COULD HAVE CREATED!
*THE PRECEDING FLASHBACK CAN BE SEEN IN ITS ENTIRETY IN THE AFOREMENTIONED GIANT-SIZE SPIDER-MAN #1.-PERSISTENT ROY.
IN WORDS OF ONE SYLLABLE, TORCH: YOU ARE OUT OF YOUR TREE!
I HAD NOTHING TO DO WITH ANY OF THAT!
WISH I COULD BELIEVE THAT, ICECU
--BUT THE EVIDENCE
AGAINST YOU--
--SO I'M AFRAID I'M JUST GONNA HAVE TO TAKE YOU IN!
WOW-- YOU'RE SERIOU
YOU'RE REALL
GONNA ARRES
ME!

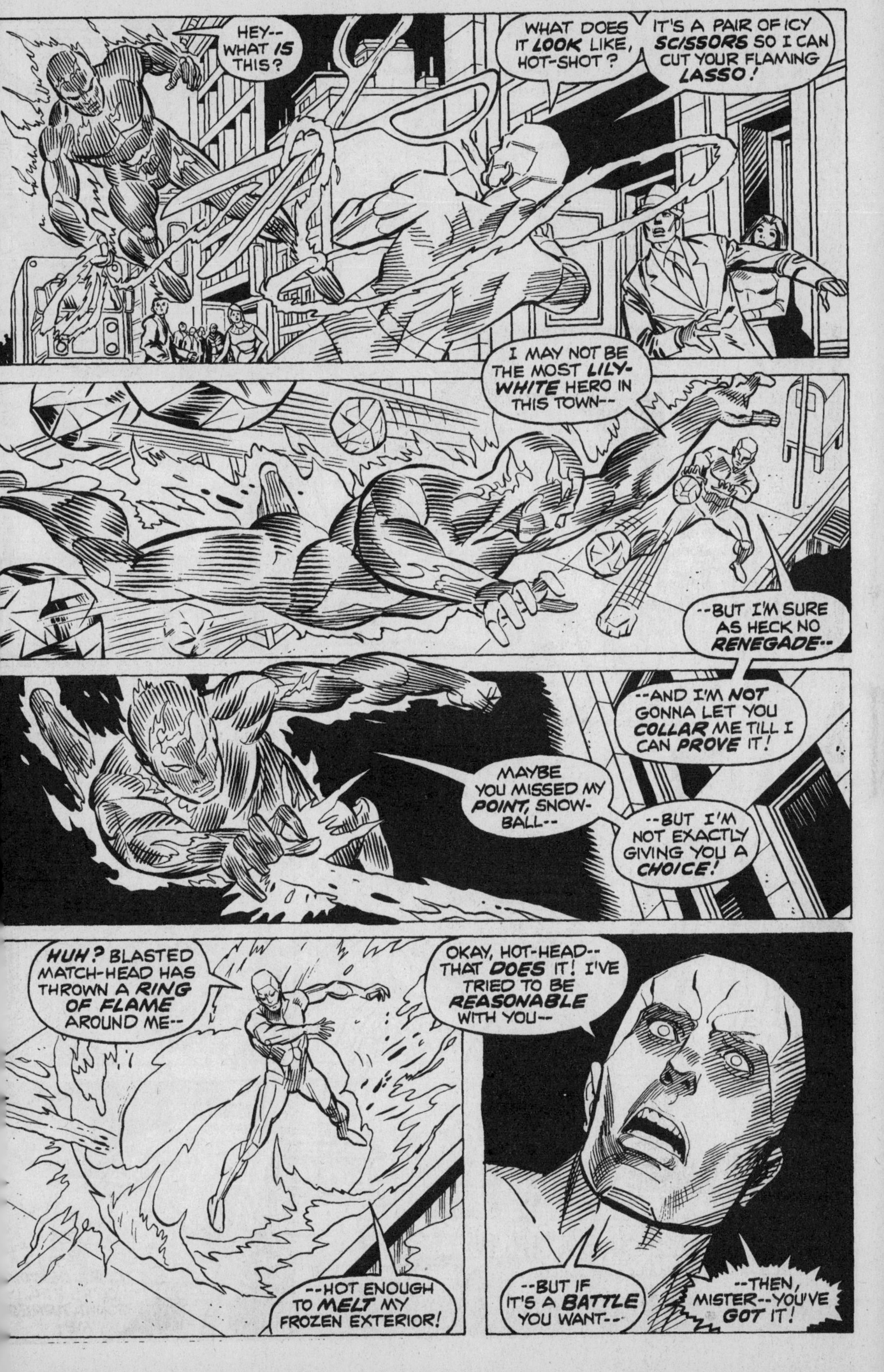
HEY-- WHAT IS THIS?
WHAT DOES IT LOOK LIKE, HOT-SHOT?
IT'S A PAIR OF ICY SCISSORS SO I CAN CUT YOUR FLAMING LASSO!
I MAY NOT BE THE MOST LILY-WHITE HERO IN THIS TOWN--
--BUT I'M SURE AS HECK NO RENEGADE--
--AND I'M NOT GONNA LET YOU COLLAR ME TILL I CAN PROVE IT!
MAYBE YOU MISSED MY POINT, SNOW-BALL--
--BUT I'M NOT EXACTLY GIVING YOU A CHOICE!
HUH? BLASTED MATCH-HEAD HAS THROWN A RING OF FLAME AROUND ME--
--HOT ENOUGH TO MELT MY FROZEN EXTERIOR!
OKAY, HOT-HEAD-- THAT DOES IT! I'VE TRIED TO BE REASONABLE WITH YOU--
--BUT IF IT'S A BATTLE YOU WANT--
--THEN, MISTER--YOU'VE GOT IT!

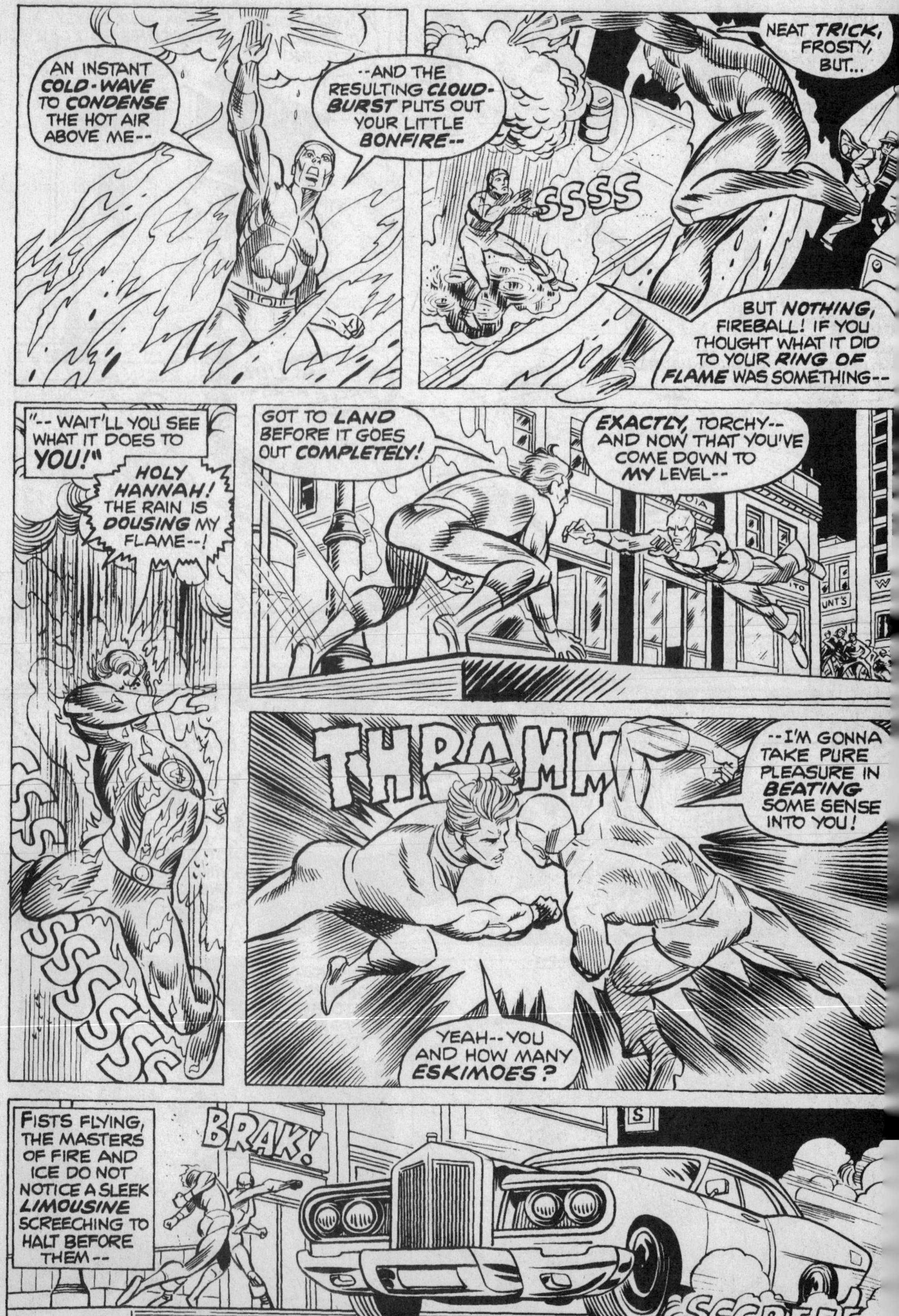
AN INSTANT COLD-WAVE TO CONDENSE THE HOT AIR ABOVE ME--
--AND THE RESULTING CLOUD-BURST PUTS OUT YOUR LITTLE BONFIRE--
SSSS
NEAT TRICK, FROSTY, BUT...
BUT NOTHING, FIREBALL! IF YOU THOUGHT WHAT IT DID TO YOUR RING OF FLAME WAS SOMETHING--
"--WAIT'LL YOU SEE WHAT IT DOES TO YOU!"
HOLY HANNAH! THE RAIN IS DOUSING MY FLAME--!
SSSSSSS
GOT TO LAND BEFORE IT GOES OUT COMPLETELY!
EXACTLY, TORCHY-- AND NOW THAT YOU'VE COME DOWN TO MY LEVEL--
THRAMM
--I'M GONNA TAKE PURE PLEASURE IN BEATING SOME SENSE INTO YOU!
YEAH--YOU AND HOW MANY ESKIMOES?
FISTS FLYING, THE MASTERS OF FIRE AND ICE DO NOT NOTICE A SLEEK LIMOUSINE SCREECHING TO HALT BEFORE THEM--
BRAK!
SSCREEEE

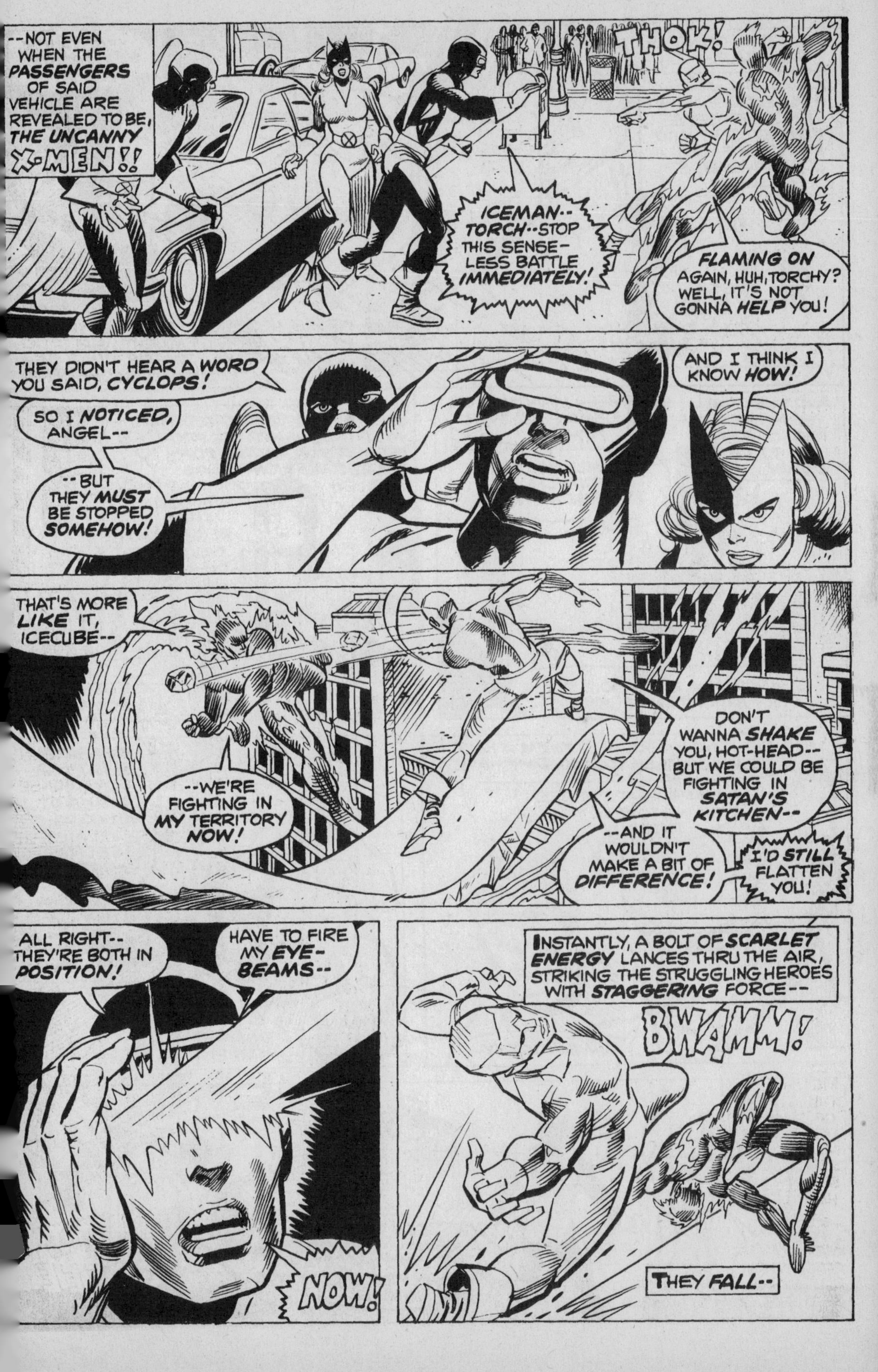
--NOT EVEN WHEN THE PASSENGERS OF SAID VEHICLE ARE REVEALED TO BE, THE UNCANNY X-MEN!!
THOK!
ICEMAN-- TORCH--STOP THIS SENSE-LESS BATTLE IMMEDIATELY!
FLAMING ON AGAIN, HUH, TORCHY? WELL, IT'S NOT GONNA HELP YOU!
THEY DIDN'T HEAR A WORD YOU SAID, CYCLOPS!
SO I NOTICED, ANGEL--
--BUT THEY MUST BE STOPPED SOMEHOW!
AND I THINK I KNOW HOW!
THAT'S MORE LIKE IT, ICECUBE--
--WE'RE FIGHTING IN MY TERRITORY NOW!
DON'T WANNA SHAKE YOU, HOT-HEAD-- BUT WE COULD BE FIGHTING IN SATAN'S KITCHEN--
--AND IT WOULDN'T MAKE A BIT OF DIFFERENCE!
I'D STILL FLATTEN YOU!
ALL RIGHT-- THEY'RE BOTH IN POSITION!
HAVE TO FIRE MY EYE-BEAMS--
NOW!
INSTANTLY, A BOLT OF SCARLET ENERGY LANCES THRU THE AIR, STRIKING THE STRUGGLING HEROES WITH STAGGERING FORCE--
BWAMM!
THEY FALL--

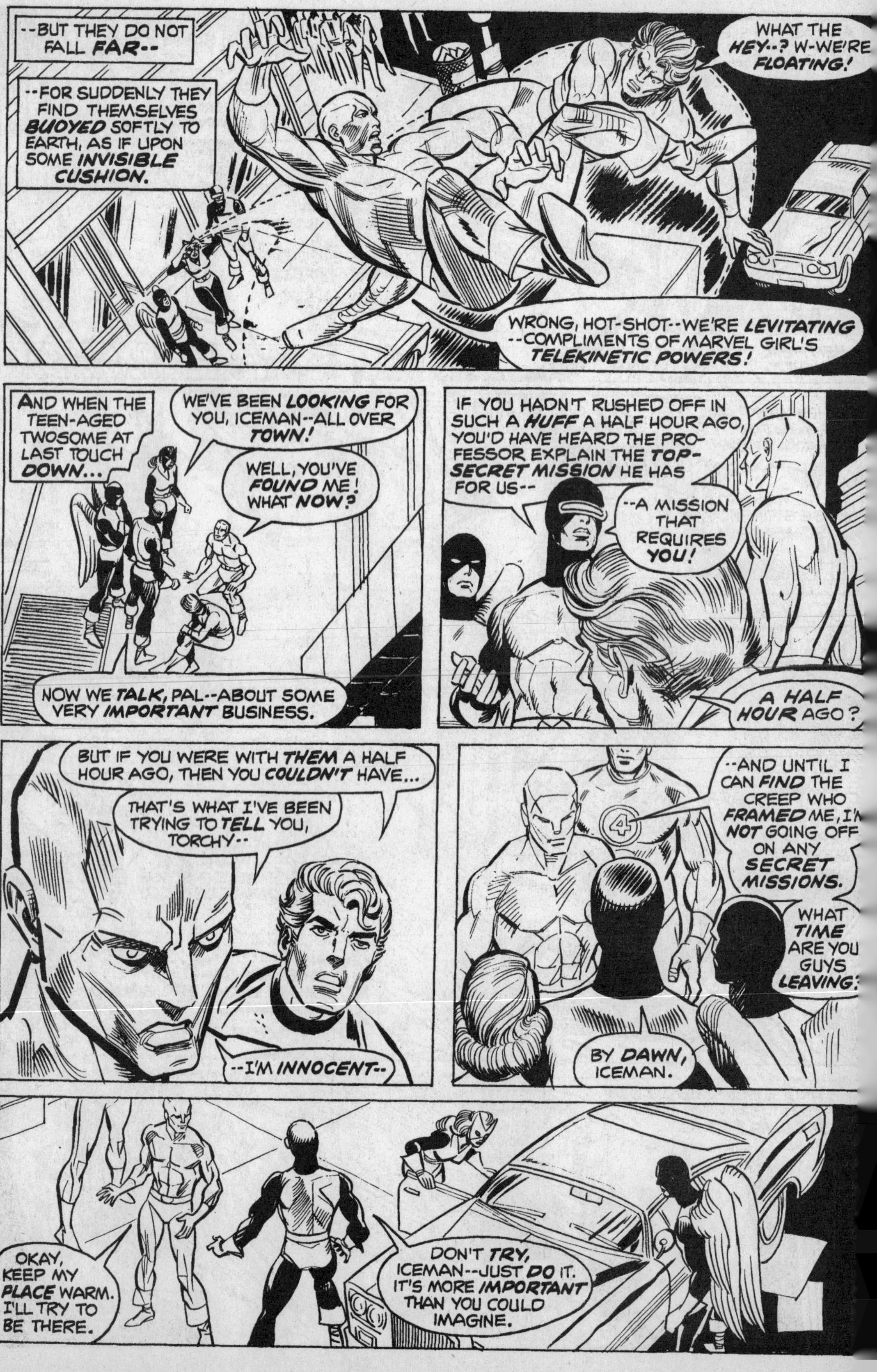
--BUT THEY DO NOT FALL FAR--
--FOR SUDDENLY THEY FIND THEMSELVES BUOYED SOFTLY TO EARTH, AS IF UPON SOME INVISIBLE CUSHION.
WHAT THE HEY--? W-WE'RE FLOATING!
WRONG, HOT-SHOT--WE'RE LEVITATING --COMPLIMENTS OF MARVEL GIRL'S TELEKINETIC POWERS!
AND WHEN THE TEEN-AGED TWOSOME AT LAST TOUCH DOWN...
WE'VE BEEN LOOKING FOR YOU, ICEMAN--ALL OVER TOWN!
WELL, YOU'VE FOUND ME! WHAT NOW?
NOW WE TALK, PAL--ABOUT SOME VERY IMPORTANT BUSINESS.
IF YOU HADN'T RUSHED OFF IN SUCH A HUFF A HALF HOUR AGO, YOU'D HAVE HEARD THE PROFESSOR EXPLAIN THE TOP-SECRET MISSION HE HAS FOR US--
--A MISSION THAT REQUIRES YOU!
A HALF HOUR AGO?
BUT IF YOU WERE WITH THEM A HALF HOUR AGO, THEN YOU COULDN'T HAVE...
THAT'S WHAT I'VE BEEN TRYING TO TELL YOU, TORCHY--
--I'M INNOCENT--
--AND UNTIL I CAN FIND THE CREEP WHO FRAMED ME, I'M NOT GOING OFF ON ANY SECRET MISSIONS.
WHAT TIME ARE YOU GUYS LEAVING?
BY DAWN, ICEMAN.
OKAY, KEEP MY PLACE WARM. I'LL TRY TO BE THERE.
DON'T TRY, ICEMAN--JUST DO IT. IT'S MORE IMPORTANT THAN YOU COULD IMAGINE.

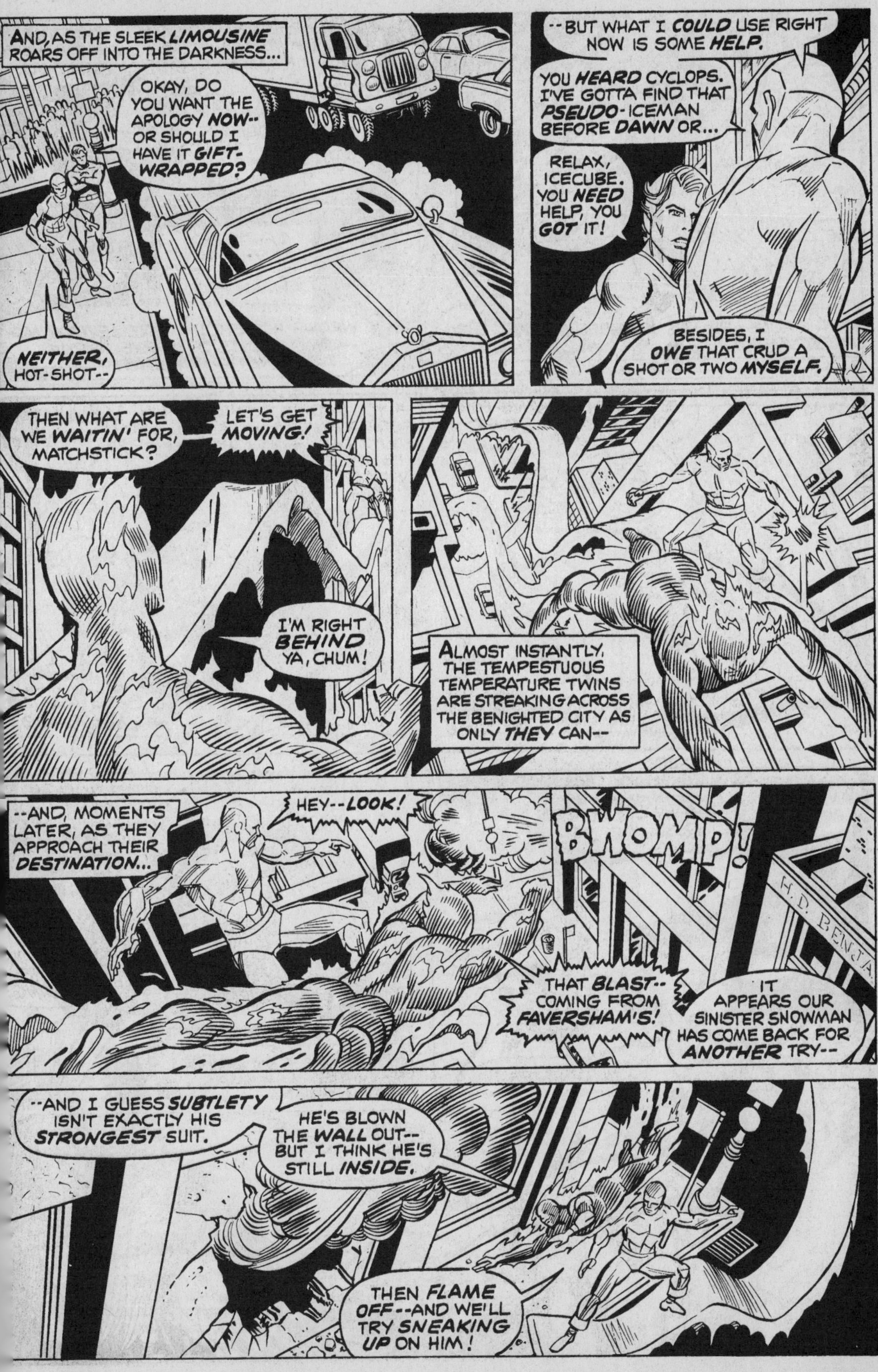
AND, AS THE SLEEK LIMOUSINE ROARS OFF INTO THE DARKNESS...
OKAY, DO YOU WANT THE APOLOGY NOW-- OR SHOULD I HAVE IT GIFT-WRAPPED?
NEITHER, HOT-SHOT--
--BUT WHAT I COULD USE RIGHT NOW IS SOME HELP.
YOU HEARD CYCLOPS. I'VE GOTTA FIND THAT PSEUDO-ICEMAN BEFORE DAWN OR...
RELAX, ICECUBE. YOU NEED HELP, YOU GOT IT!
BESIDES, I OWE THAT CRUD A SHOT OR TWO MYSELF.
THEN WHAT ARE WE WAITIN' FOR, MATCHSTICK?
LET'S GET MOVING!
I'M RIGHT BEHIND YA, CHUM!
ALMOST INSTANTLY, THE TEMPESTUOUS TEMPERATURE TWINS ARE STREAKING ACROSS THE BENIGHTED CITY AS ONLY THEY CAN--
--AND, MOMENTS LATER, AS THEY APPROACH THEIR DESTINATION...
HEY--LOOK!
BWOMP!
H. D. BENJA
THAT BLAST-- COMING FROM FAVERSHAM'S!
IT APPEARS OUR SINISTER SNOWMAN HAS COME BACK FOR ANOTHER TRY--
--AND I GUESS SUBTLETY ISN'T EXACTLY HIS STRONGEST SUIT.
HE'S BLOWN THE WALL OUT-- BUT I THINK HE'S STILL INSIDE.
THEN FLAME OFF--AND WE'LL TRY SNEAKING UP ON HIM!

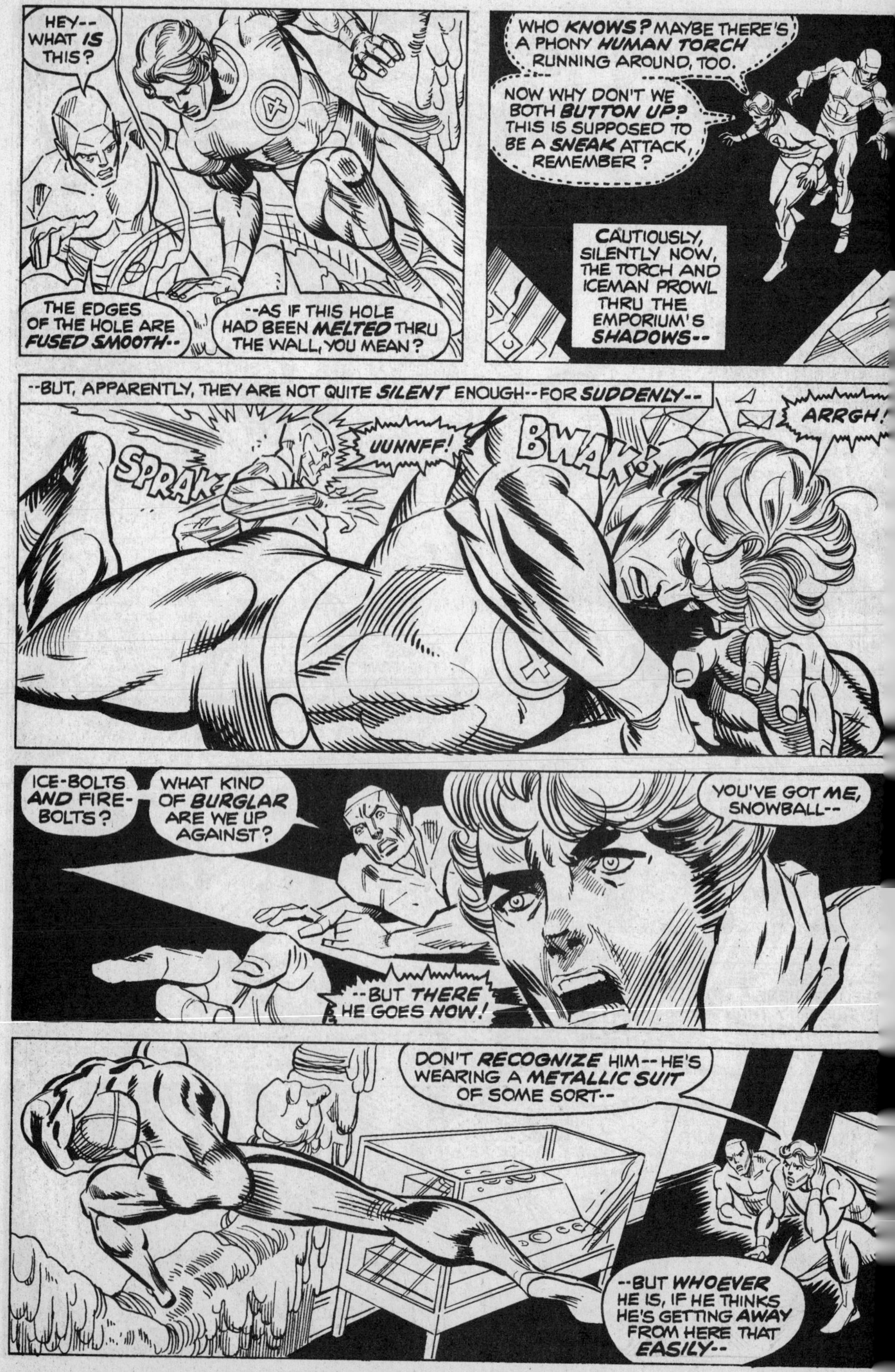
HEY--
WHAT IS
THIS?
THE EDGES
OF THE HOLE ARE
FUSED SMOOTH--
--AS IF THIS HOLE
HAD BEEN MELTED THRU
THE WALL, YOU MEAN?
WHO KNOWS? MAYBE THERE'S
A PHONY HUMAN TORCH
RUNNING AROUND, TOO.
NOW WHY DON'T WE
BOTH BUTTON UP?
THIS IS SUPPOSED TO
BE A SNEAK ATTACK,
REMEMBER?
CAUTIOUSLY,
SILENTLY NOW,
THE TORCH AND
ICEMAN PROWL
THRU THE
EMPORIUM'S
SHADOWS--
--BUT, APPARENTLY, THEY ARE NOT QUITE SILENT ENOUGH--FOR SUDDENLY--
SPRAK
UUNNFF!
BWAK!
ARRGH!
ICE-BOLTS
AND FIRE-
BOLTS?
WHAT KIND
OF BURGLAR
ARE WE UP
AGAINST?
YOU'VE GOT ME,
SNOWBALL--
--BUT THERE
HE GOES NOW!
DON'T RECOGNIZE HIM--HE'S
WEARING A METALLIC SUIT
OF SOME SORT--
--BUT WHOEVER
HE IS, IF HE THINKS
HE'S GETTING AWAY
FROM HERE THAT
EASILY--

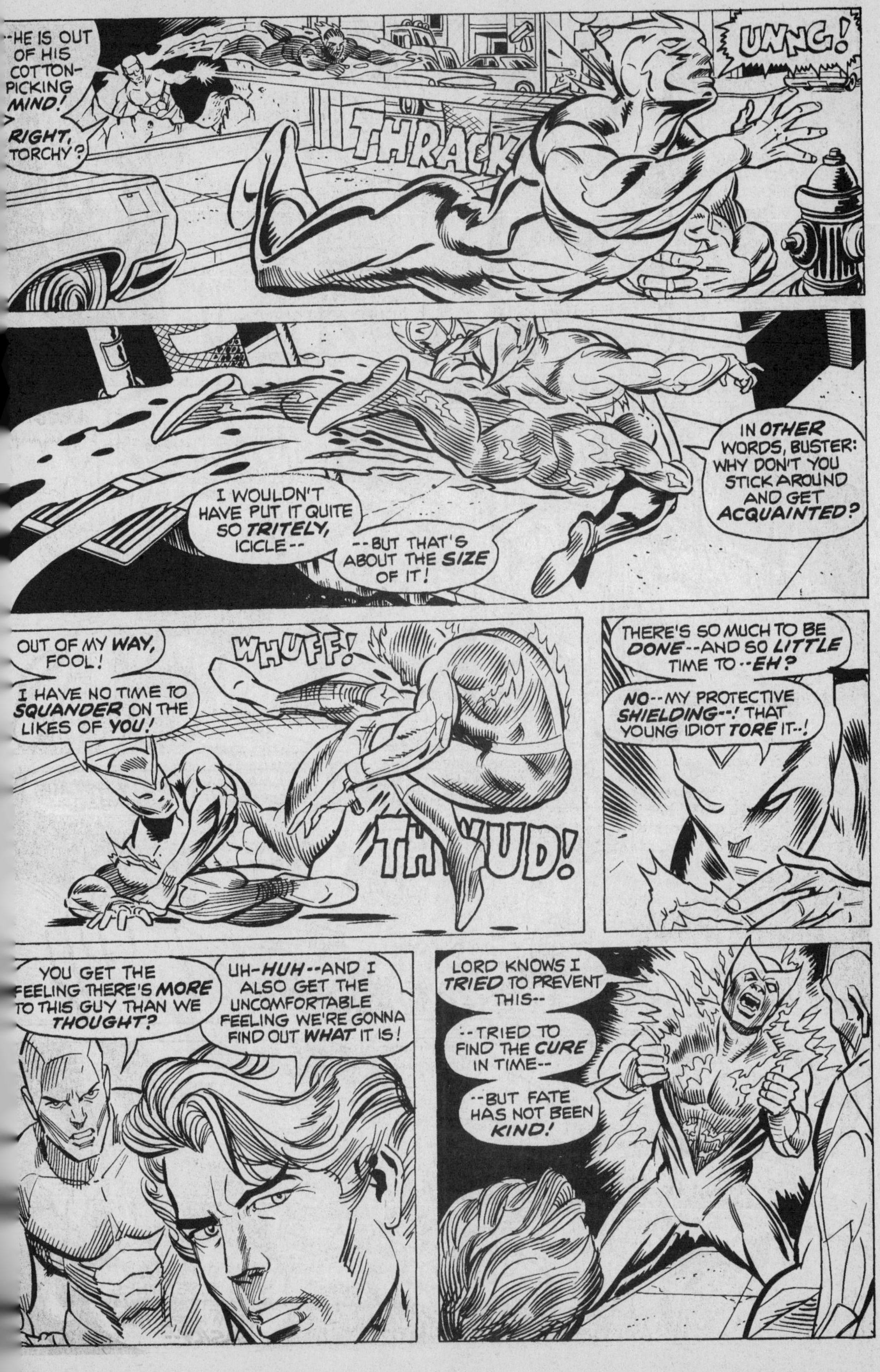
--HE IS OUT OF HIS COTTON-PICKING MIND!
RIGHT, TORCHY?
UNNG!
THRACK
I WOULDN'T HAVE PUT IT QUITE SO TRITELY, ICICLE--
--BUT THAT'S ABOUT THE SIZE OF IT!
IN OTHER WORDS, BUSTER: WHY DON'T YOU STICK AROUND AND GET ACQUAINTED?
OUT OF MY WAY, FOOL!
I HAVE NO TIME TO SQUANDER ON THE LIKES OF YOU!
WHUFF!
THUD!
THERE'S SO MUCH TO BE DONE--AND SO LITTLE TIME TO--EH?
NO--MY PROTECTIVE SHIELDING--! THAT YOUNG IDIOT TORE IT--!
YOU GET THE FEELING THERE'S MORE TO THIS GUY THAN WE THOUGHT?
UH-HUH--AND I ALSO GET THE UNCOMFORTABLE FEELING WE'RE GONNA FIND OUT WHAT IT IS!
LORD KNOWS I TRIED TO PREVENT THIS--
--TRIED TO FIND THE CURE IN TIME--
--BUT FATE HAS NOT BEEN KIND!

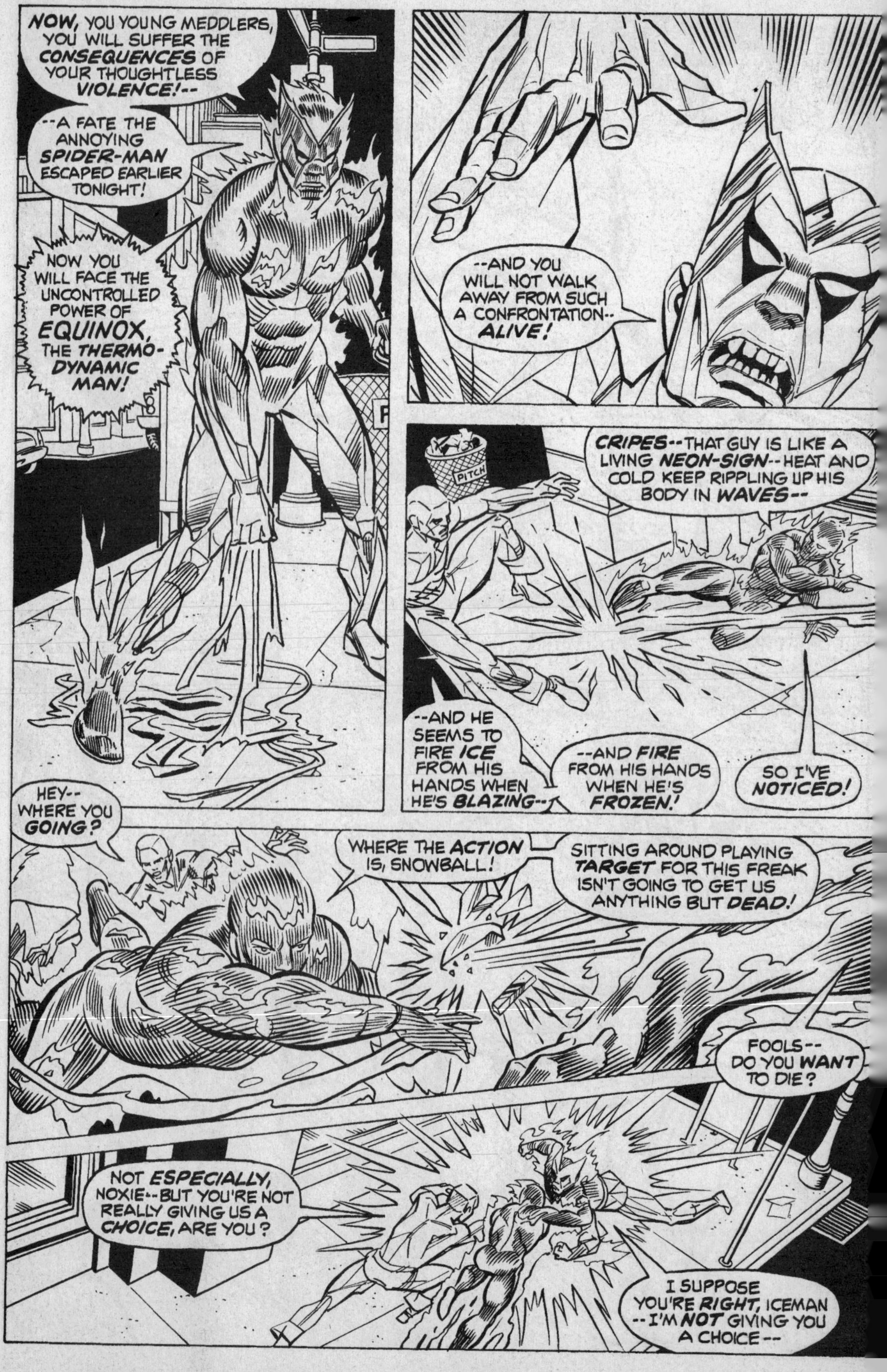

NOW, YOU YOUNG MEDDLERS, YOU WILL SUFFER THE CONSEQUENCES OF YOUR THOUGHTLESS VIOLENCE!--
--A FATE THE ANNOYING SPIDER-MAN ESCAPED EARLIER TONIGHT!
NOW YOU WILL FACE THE UNCONTROLLED POWER OF EQUINOX, THE THERMO-DYNAMIC MAN!
--AND YOU WILL NOT WALK AWAY FROM SUCH A CONFRONTATION-- ALIVE!
CRIPES--THAT GUY IS LIKE A LIVING NEON-SIGN--HEAT AND COLD KEEP RIPPLING UP HIS BODY IN WAVES--
PITCH
--AND HE SEEMS TO FIRE ICE FROM HIS HANDS WHEN HE'S BLAZING--
--AND FIRE FROM HIS HANDS WHEN HE'S FROZEN!
SO I'VE NOTICED!
HEY-- WHERE YOU GOING?
WHERE THE ACTION IS, SNOWBALL!
SITTING AROUND PLAYING TARGET FOR THIS FREAK ISN'T GOING TO GET US ANYTHING BUT DEAD!
FOOLS-- DO YOU WANT TO DIE?
NOT ESPECIALLY, NOXIE--BUT YOU'RE NOT REALLY GIVING US A CHOICE, ARE YOU?
I SUPPOSE YOU'RE RIGHT, ICEMAN --I'M NOT GIVING YOU A CHOICE--

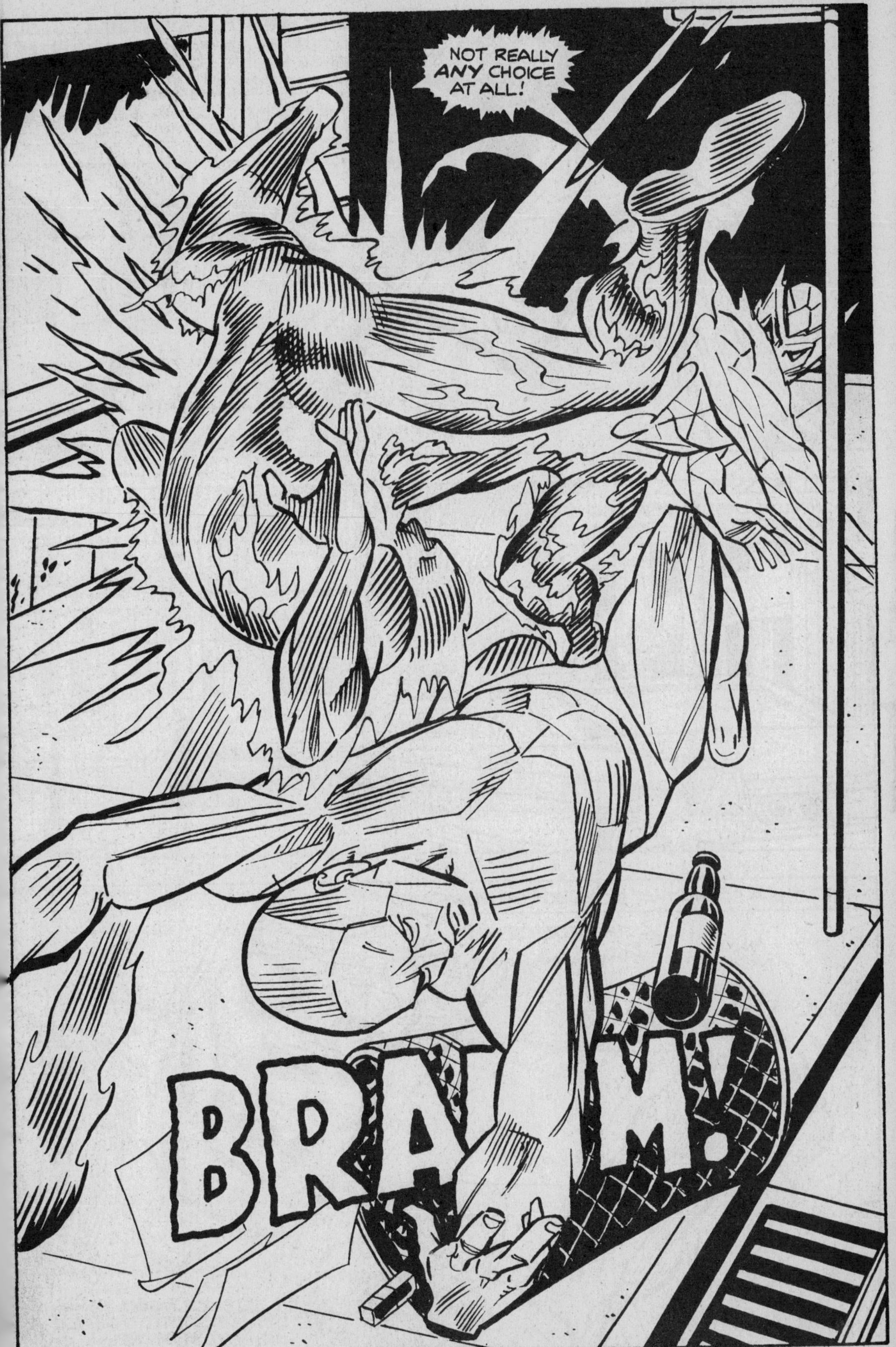
NOT REALLY ANY CHOICE AT ALL!
BRAM!

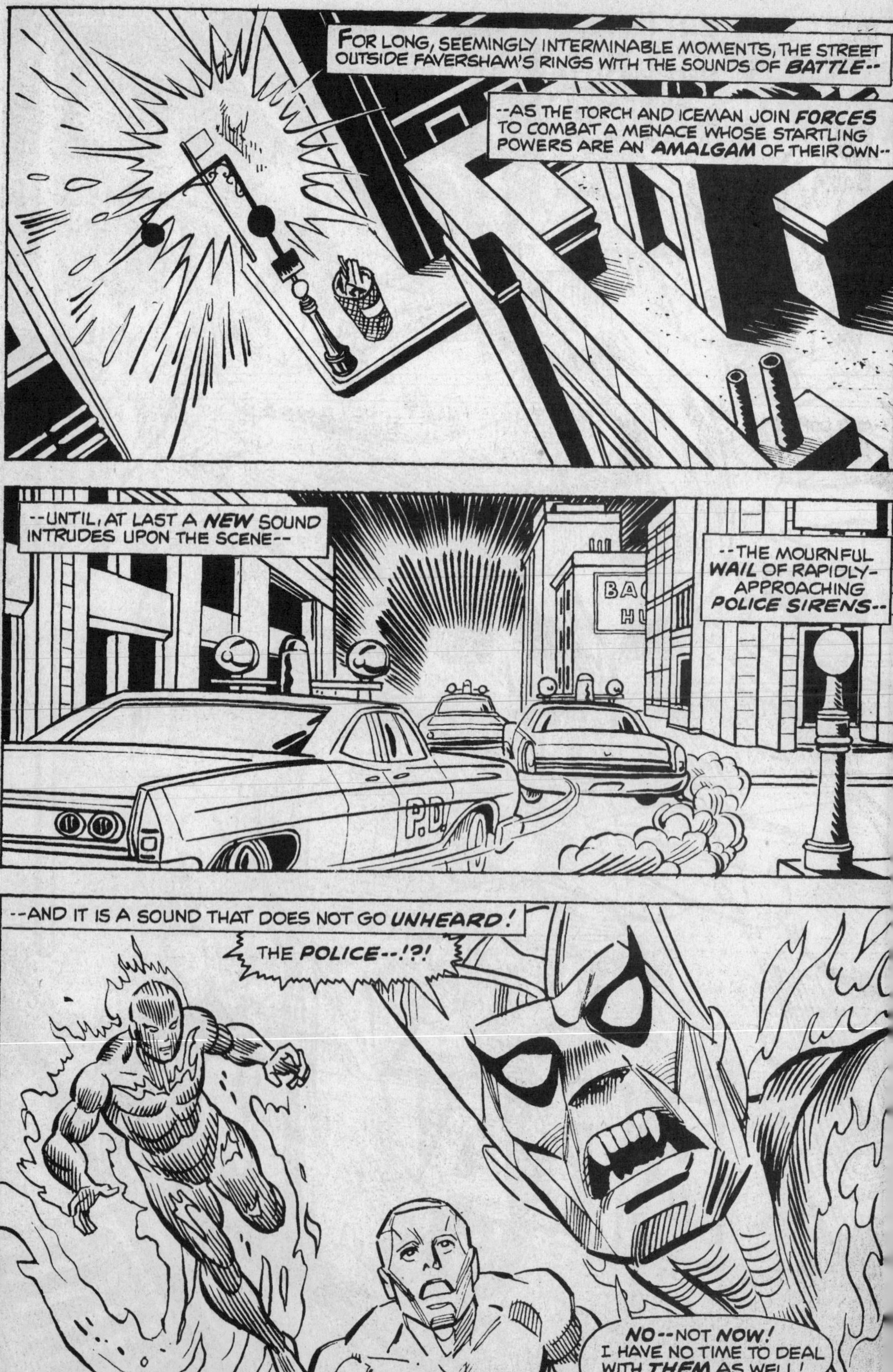
FOR LONG, SEEMINGLY INTERMINABLE MOMENTS, THE STREET OUTSIDE FAVERSHAM'S RINGS WITH THE SOUNDS OF BATTLE--
--AS THE TORCH AND ICEMAN JOIN FORCES TO COMBAT A MENACE WHOSE STARTLING POWERS ARE AN AMALGAM OF THEIR OWN--
--UNTIL, AT LAST A NEW SOUND INTRUDES UPON THE SCENE--
--THE MOURNFUL WAIL OF RAPIDLY-APPROACHING POLICE SIRENS--
P.D.
--AND IT IS A SOUND THAT DOES NOT GO UNHEARD!
THE POLICE--!?!
NO--NOT NOW! I HAVE NO TIME TO DEAL WITH THEM AS WELL!

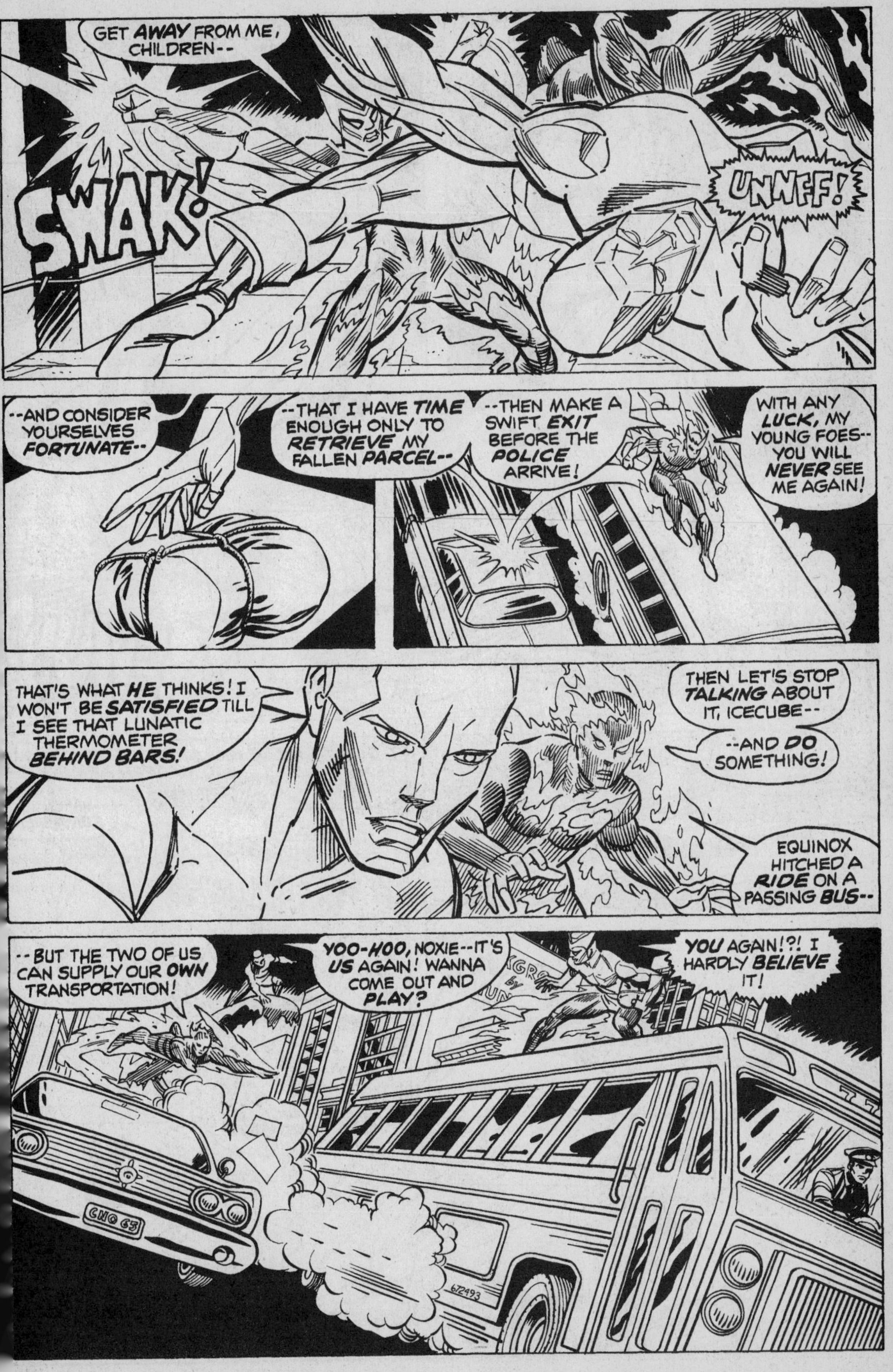
GET AWAY FROM ME, CHILDREN--
SWAK!
UNNFF!
--AND CONSIDER YOURSELVES FORTUNATE--
--THAT I HAVE TIME ENOUGH ONLY TO RETRIEVE MY FALLEN PARCEL--
--THEN MAKE A SWIFT EXIT BEFORE THE POLICE ARRIVE!
WITH ANY LUCK, MY YOUNG FOES--YOU WILL NEVER SEE ME AGAIN!
THAT'S WHAT HE THINKS! I WON'T BE SATISFIED TILL I SEE THAT LUNATIC THERMOMETER BEHIND BARS!
THEN LET'S STOP TALKING ABOUT IT, ICECUBE--
--AND DO SOMETHING!
EQUINOX HITCHED A RIDE ON A PASSING BUS--
--BUT THE TWO OF US CAN SUPPLY OUR OWN TRANSPORTATION!
YOO-HOO, NOXIE--IT'S US AGAIN! WANNA COME OUT AND PLAY?
YOU AGAIN!?! I HARDLY BELIEVE IT!
CNQ 65
672493

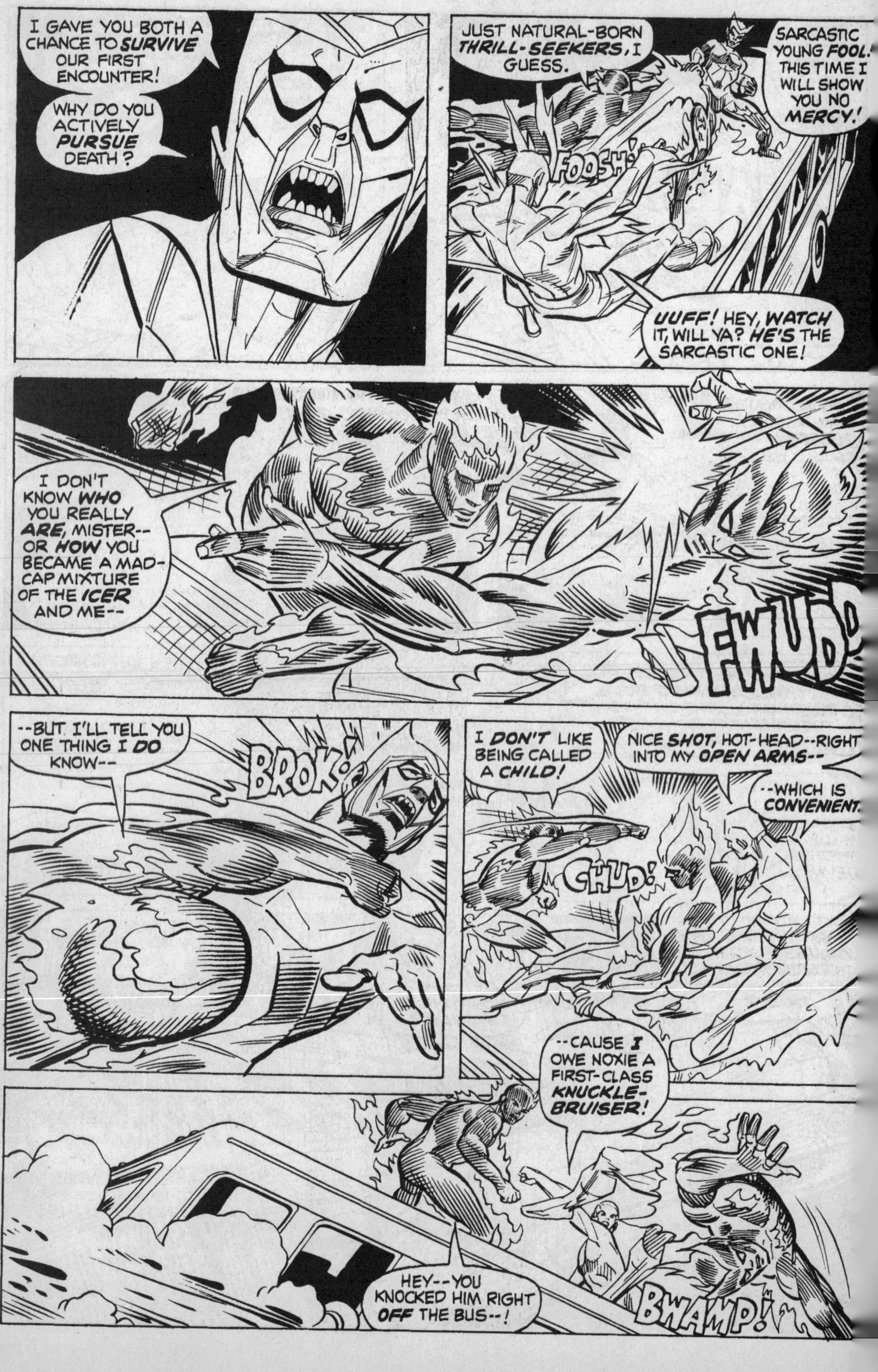
I GAVE YOU BOTH A CHANCE TO SURVIVE OUR FIRST ENCOUNTER!
WHY DO YOU ACTIVELY PURSUE DEATH?
JUST NATURAL-BORN THRILL-SEEKERS, I GUESS.
SARCASTIC YOUNG FOOL! THIS TIME I WILL SHOW YOU NO MERCY!
FOOSH!
UUFF! HEY, WATCH IT, WILL YA? HE'S THE SARCASTIC ONE!
I DON'T KNOW WHO YOU REALLY ARE, MISTER-- OR HOW YOU BECAME A MAD-CAP MIXTURE OF THE ICER AND ME--
FWUD
--BUT I'LL TELL YOU ONE THING I DO KNOW--
BROK
I DON'T LIKE BEING CALLED A CHILD!
NICE SHOT, HOT-HEAD--RIGHT INTO MY OPEN ARMS--
--WHICH IS CONVENIENT.
CHUD!
--CAUSE I OWE NOXIE A FIRST-CLASS KNUCKLE-BRUISER!
HEY--YOU KNOCKED HIM RIGHT OFF THE BUS--!
BWAMP!

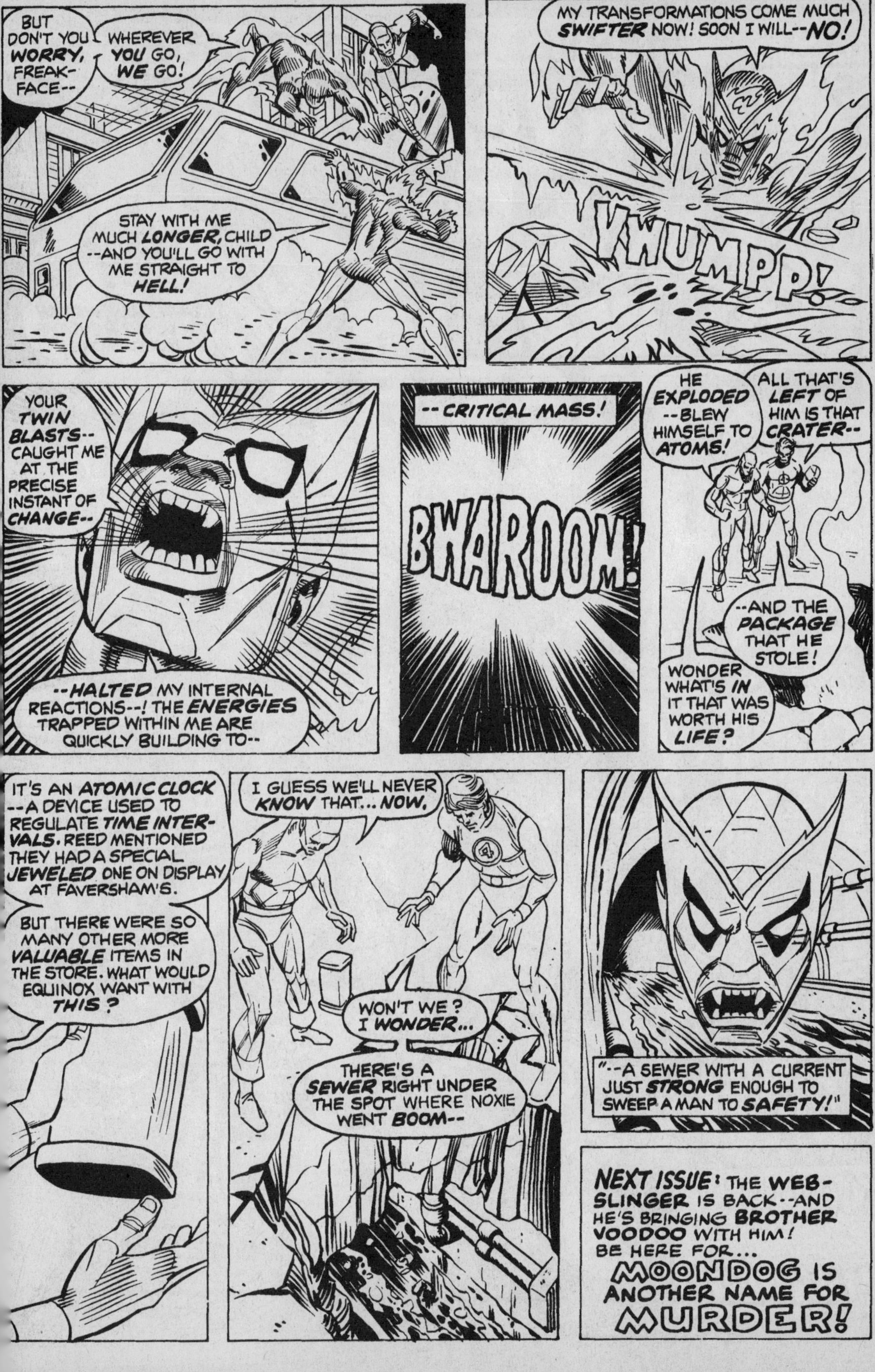

BUT DON'T YOU WORRY, FREAK-FACE--
WHEREVER YOU GO, WE GO!
STAY WITH ME MUCH LONGER, CHILD --AND YOU'LL GO WITH ME STRAIGHT TO HELL!
MY TRANSFORMATIONS COME MUCH SWIFTER NOW! SOON I WILL--NO!
VWUMPP!
YOUR TWIN BLASTS--CAUGHT ME AT THE PRECISE INSTANT OF CHANGE--
--HALTED MY INTERNAL REACTIONS--! THE ENERGIES TRAPPED WITHIN ME ARE QUICKLY BUILDING TO--
--CRITICAL MASS!
BWAROOM!
HE EXPLODED --BLEW HIMSELF TO ATOMS!
ALL THAT'S LEFT OF HIM IS THAT CRATER--
--AND THE PACKAGE THAT HE STOLE!
WONDER WHAT'S IN IT THAT WAS WORTH HIS LIFE?
IT'S AN ATOMIC CLOCK --A DEVICE USED TO REGULATE TIME INTERVALS. REED MENTIONED THEY HAD A SPECIAL JEWELED ONE ON DISPLAY AT FAVERSHAM'S.
BUT THERE WERE SO MANY OTHER MORE VALUABLE ITEMS IN THE STORE. WHAT WOULD EQUINOX WANT WITH THIS?
I GUESS WE'LL NEVER KNOW THAT... NOW.
WON'T WE? I WONDER...
THERE'S A SEWER RIGHT UNDER THE SPOT WHERE NOXIE WENT BOOM--
"--A SEWER WITH A CURRENT JUST STRONG ENOUGH TO SWEEP A MAN TO SAFETY!"
NEXT ISSUE: THE WEB-SLINGER IS BACK--AND HE'S BRINGING BROTHER VOODOO WITH HIM! BE HERE FOR...
MOONDOG IS ANOTHER NAME FOR MURDER!

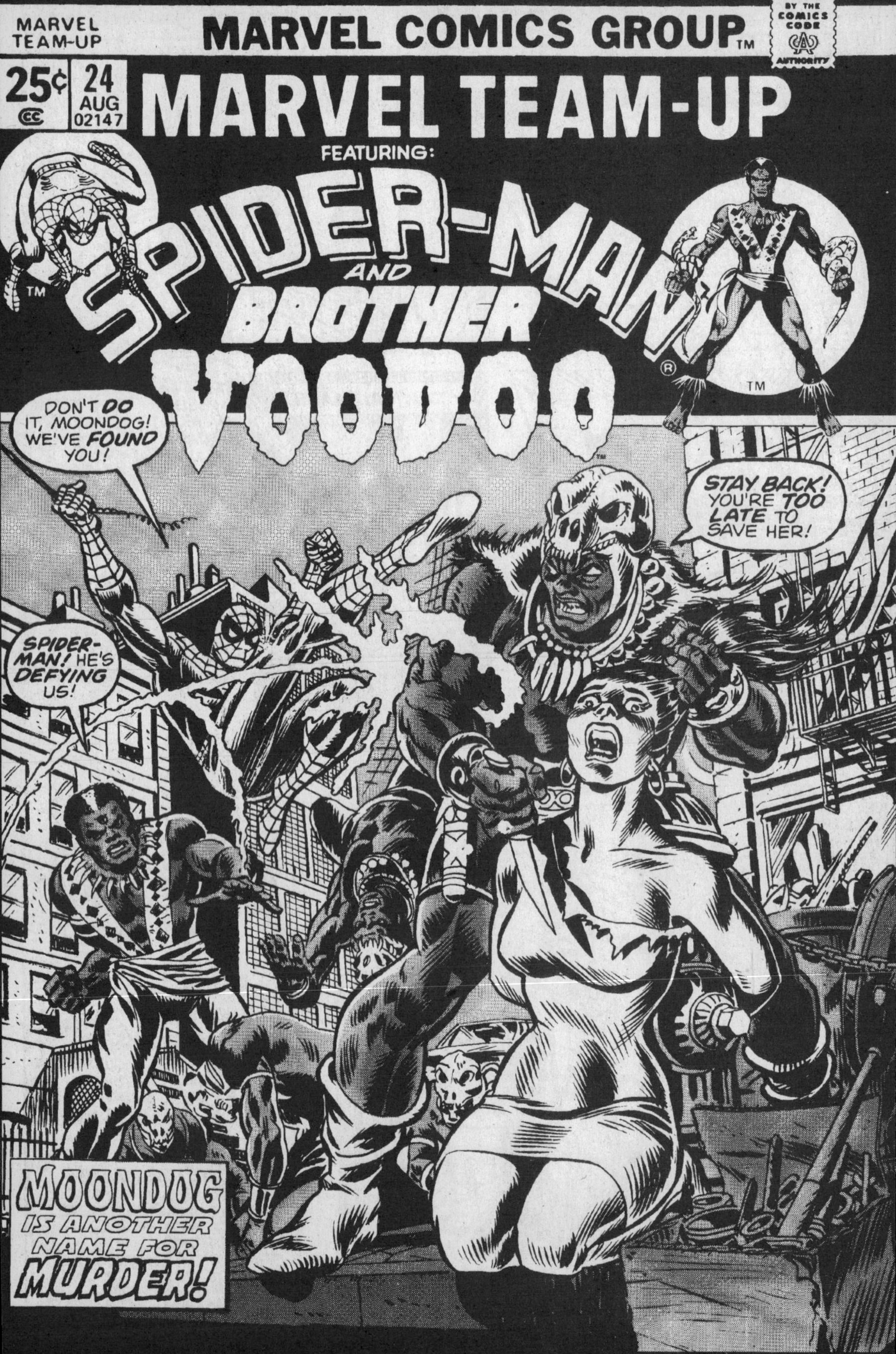
MARVEL TEAM-UP
MARVEL COMICS GROUP
APPROVED BY THE COMICS CODE AUTHORITY
25¢
24 AUG 02147
MARVEL TEAM-UP
FEATURING:
SPIDER-MAN AND BROTHER VOODOO
DON'T DO IT, MOONDOG! WE'VE FOUND YOU!
STAY BACK! YOU'RE TOO LATE TO SAVE HER!
SPIDER-MAN! HE'S DEFYING US!
MOONDOG IS ANOTHER NAME FOR MURDER!

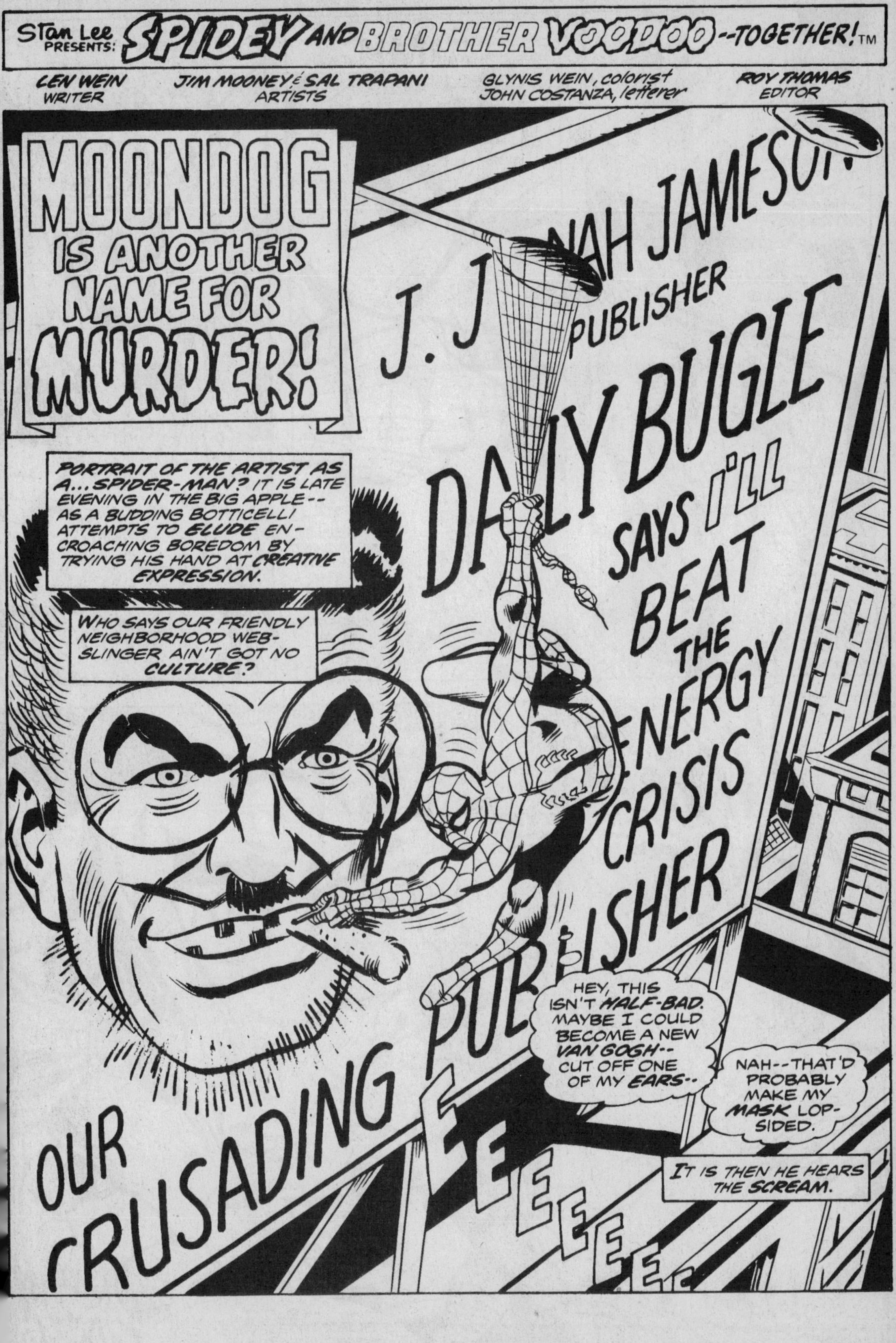

Stan Lee PRESENTS: SPIDEY AND BROTHER VOODOO--TOGETHER!™
LEN WEIN WRITER
JIM MOONEY & SAL TRAPANI ARTISTS
GLYNIS WEIN, colorist
JOHN COSTANZA, letterer
ROY THOMAS EDITOR
MOONDOG IS ANOTHER NAME FOR MURDER!
PORTRAIT OF THE ARTIST AS A... SPIDER-MAN? IT IS LATE EVENING IN THE BIG APPLE-- AS A BUDDING BOTTICELLI ATTEMPTS TO ELUDE EN-CROACHING BOREDOM BY TRYING HIS HAND AT CREATIVE EXPRESSION.
WHO SAYS OUR FRIENDLY NEIGHBORHOOD WEB-SLINGER AIN'T GOT NO CULTURE?
J. J NAH JAMESON PUBLISHER
DA LY BUGLE
SAYS I'LL BEAT THE ENERGY CRISIS
OUR CRUSADING PUB ISHER
HEY, THIS ISN'T HALF-BAD. MAYBE I COULD BECOME A NEW VAN GOGH-- CUT OFF ONE OF MY EARS--
NAH--THAT'D PROBABLY MAKE MY MASK LOP-SIDED.
EEEEEEE
IT IS THEN HE HEARS THE SCREAM.

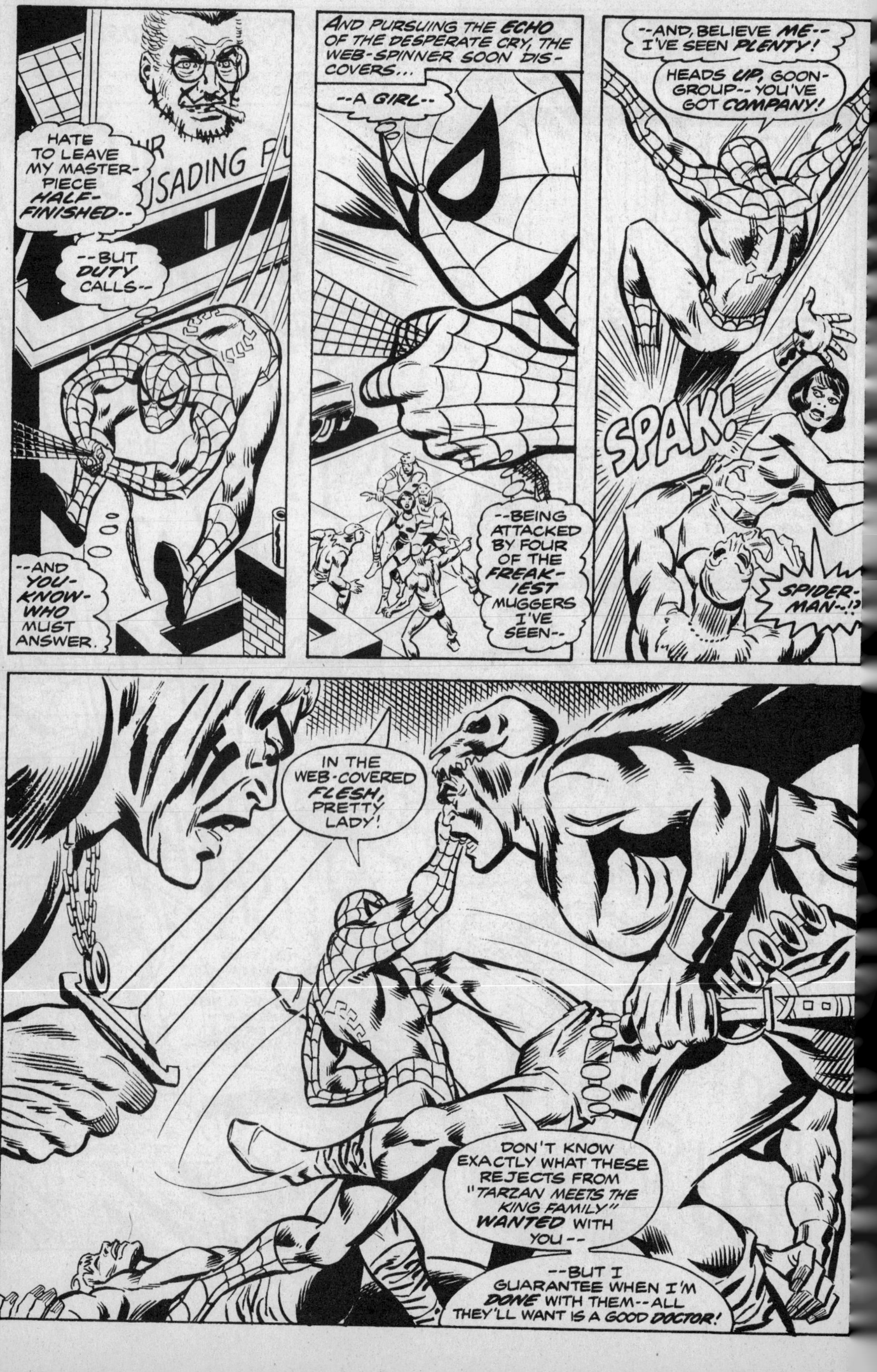

HATE TO LEAVE MY MASTER-PIECE HALF-FINISHED--
--BUT DUTY CALLS--
--AND YOU-KNOW-WHO MUST ANSWER.
AND PURSUING THE ECHO OF THE DESPERATE CRY, THE WEB-SPINNER SOON DIS-COVERS...
--A GIRL--
--BEING ATTACKED BY FOUR OF THE FREAK-IEST MUGGERS I'VE SEEN--
--AND, BELIEVE ME-- I'VE SEEN PLENTY!
HEADS UP, GOON-GROUP-- YOU'VE GOT COMPANY!
SPAK!
SPIDER-MAN--!?
IN THE WEB-COVERED FLESH, PRETTY LADY!
DON'T KNOW EXACTLY WHAT THESE REJECTS FROM "TARZAN MEETS THE KING FAMILY" WANTED WITH YOU--
--BUT I GUARANTEE WHEN I'M DONE WITH THEM--ALL THEY'LL WANT IS A GOOD DOCTOR!

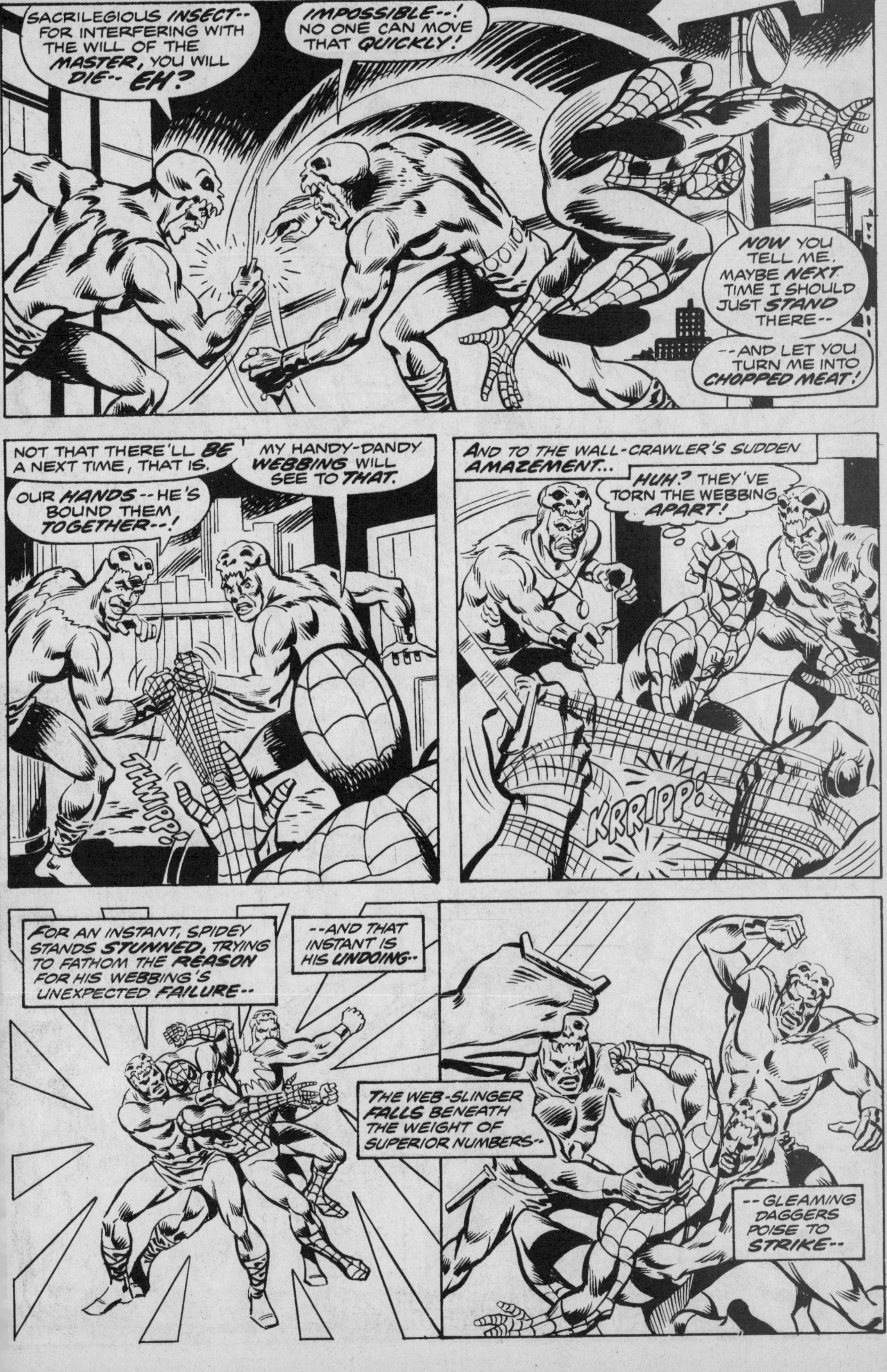
SACRILEGIOUS INSECT-- FOR INTERFERING WITH THE WILL OF THE MASTER, YOU WILL DIE-- EH?
IMPOSSIBLE--! NO ONE CAN MOVE THAT QUICKLY!
NOW YOU TELL ME. MAYBE NEXT TIME I SHOULD JUST STAND THERE--
--AND LET YOU TURN ME INTO CHOPPED MEAT!
NOT THAT THERE'LL BE A NEXT TIME, THAT IS.
MY HANDY-DANDY WEBBING WILL SEE TO THAT.
OUR HANDS--HE'S BOUND THEM TOGETHER--!
THWIPP!
AND TO THE WALL-CRAWLER'S SUDDEN AMAZEMENT...
HUH? THEY'VE TORN THE WEBBING APART!
KRRIPP!
FOR AN INSTANT, SPIDEY STANDS STUNNED, TRYING TO FATHOM THE REASON FOR HIS WEBBING'S UNEXPECTED FAILURE--
--AND THAT INSTANT IS HIS UNDOING--
THE WEB-SLINGER FALLS BENEATH THE WEIGHT OF SUPERIOR NUMBERS--
--GLEAMING DAGGERS POISE TO STRIKE--

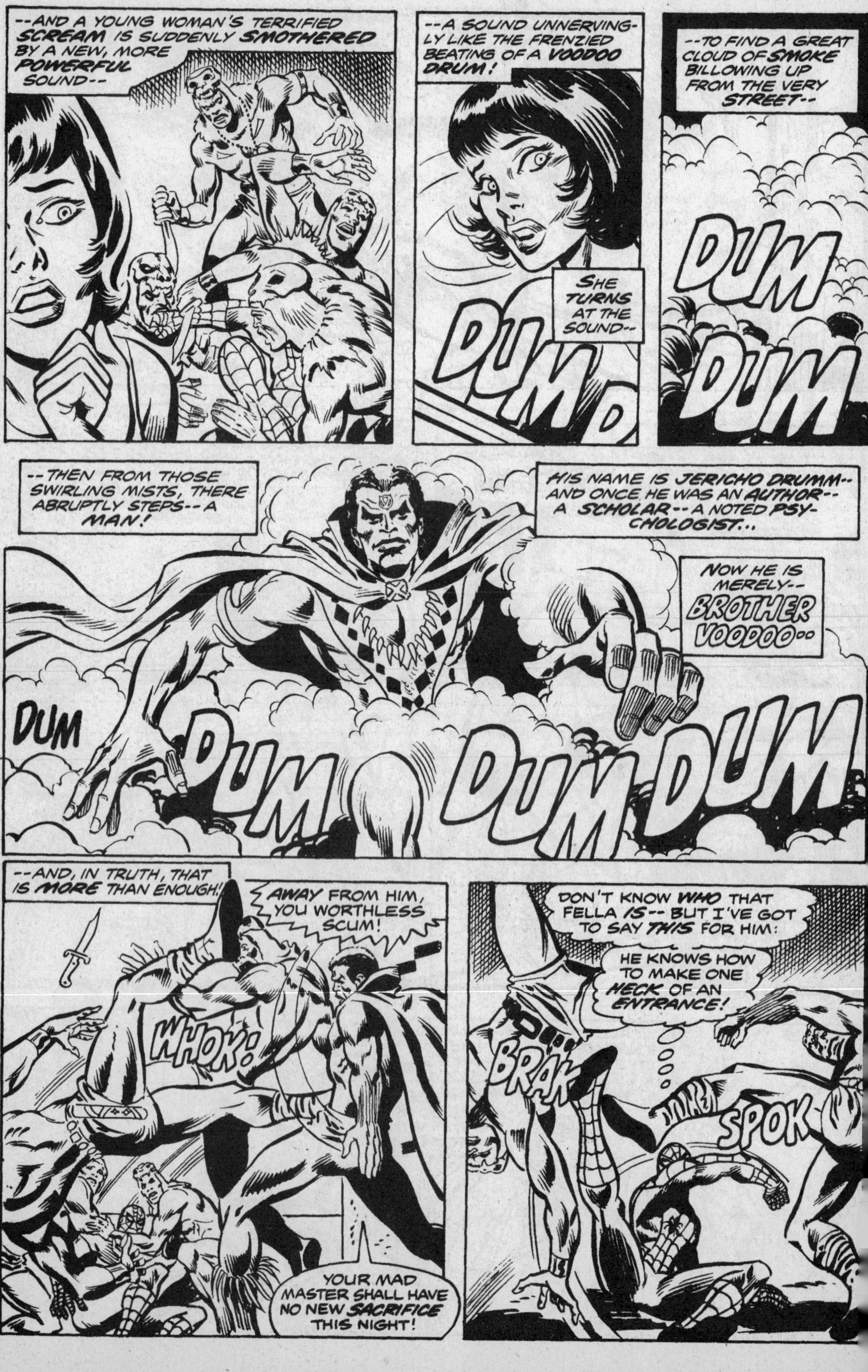
--AND A YOUNG WOMAN'S TERRIFIED SCREAM IS SUDDENLY SMOTHERED BY A NEW, MORE POWERFUL SOUND--
--A SOUND UNNERVINGLY LIKE THE FRENZIED BEATING OF A VOODOO DRUM!
SHE TURNS AT THE SOUND--
DUM
--TO FIND A GREAT CLOUD OF SMOKE BILLOWING UP FROM THE VERY STREET--
DUM
DUM
--THEN FROM THOSE SWIRLING MISTS, THERE ABRUPTLY STEPS--A MAN!
HIS NAME IS JERICHO DRUMM--AND ONCE HE WAS AN AUTHOR--A SCHOLAR--A NOTED PSYCHOLOGIST...
NOW HE IS MERELY--BROTHER VOODOO..
DUM
DUM
DUM
DUM
--AND, IN TRUTH, THAT IS MORE THAN ENOUGH!
AWAY FROM HIM, YOU WORTHLESS SCUM!
WHOK!
YOUR MAD MASTER SHALL HAVE NO NEW SACRIFICE THIS NIGHT!
DON'T KNOW WHO THAT FELLA IS--BUT I'VE GOT TO SAY THIS FOR HIM:
HE KNOWS HOW TO MAKE ONE HECK OF AN ENTRANCE!
BRAK
SPOK

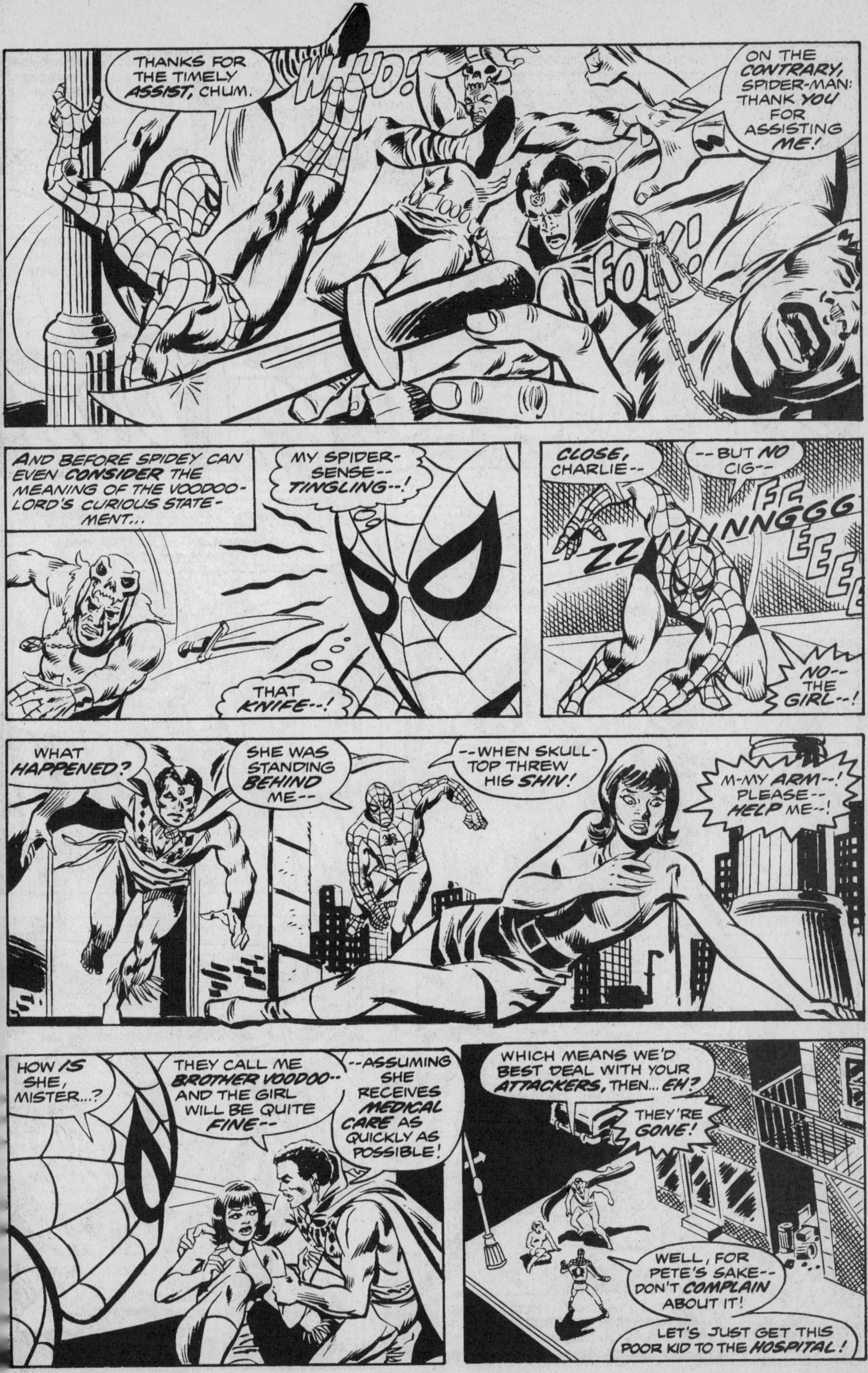
THANKS FOR THE TIMELY ASSIST, CHUM.
WHUD!
ON THE CONTRARY, SPIDER-MAN: THANK YOU FOR ASSISTING ME!
FOOM!
AND BEFORE SPIDEY CAN EVEN CONSIDER THE MEANING OF THE VOODOO-LORD'S CURIOUS STATEMENT...
MY SPIDER-SENSE-- TINGLING--!
THAT KNIFE--!
CLOSE, CHARLIE--
--BUT NO CIG--
FFNNGGG
ZZ
EEEE
NO-- THE GIRL--!
WHAT HAPPENED?
SHE WAS STANDING BEHIND ME--
--WHEN SKULL-TOP THREW HIS SHIV!
M-MY ARM--! PLEASE-- HELP ME--!
HOW IS SHE, MISTER...?
THEY CALL ME BROTHER VOODOO-- AND THE GIRL WILL BE QUITE FINE--
--ASSUMING SHE RECEIVES MEDICAL CARE AS QUICKLY AS POSSIBLE!
WHICH MEANS WE'D BEST DEAL WITH YOUR ATTACKERS, THEN... EH?
THEY'RE GONE!
WELL, FOR PETE'S SAKE-- DON'T COMPLAIN ABOUT IT!
LET'S JUST GET THIS POOR KID TO THE HOSPITAL!

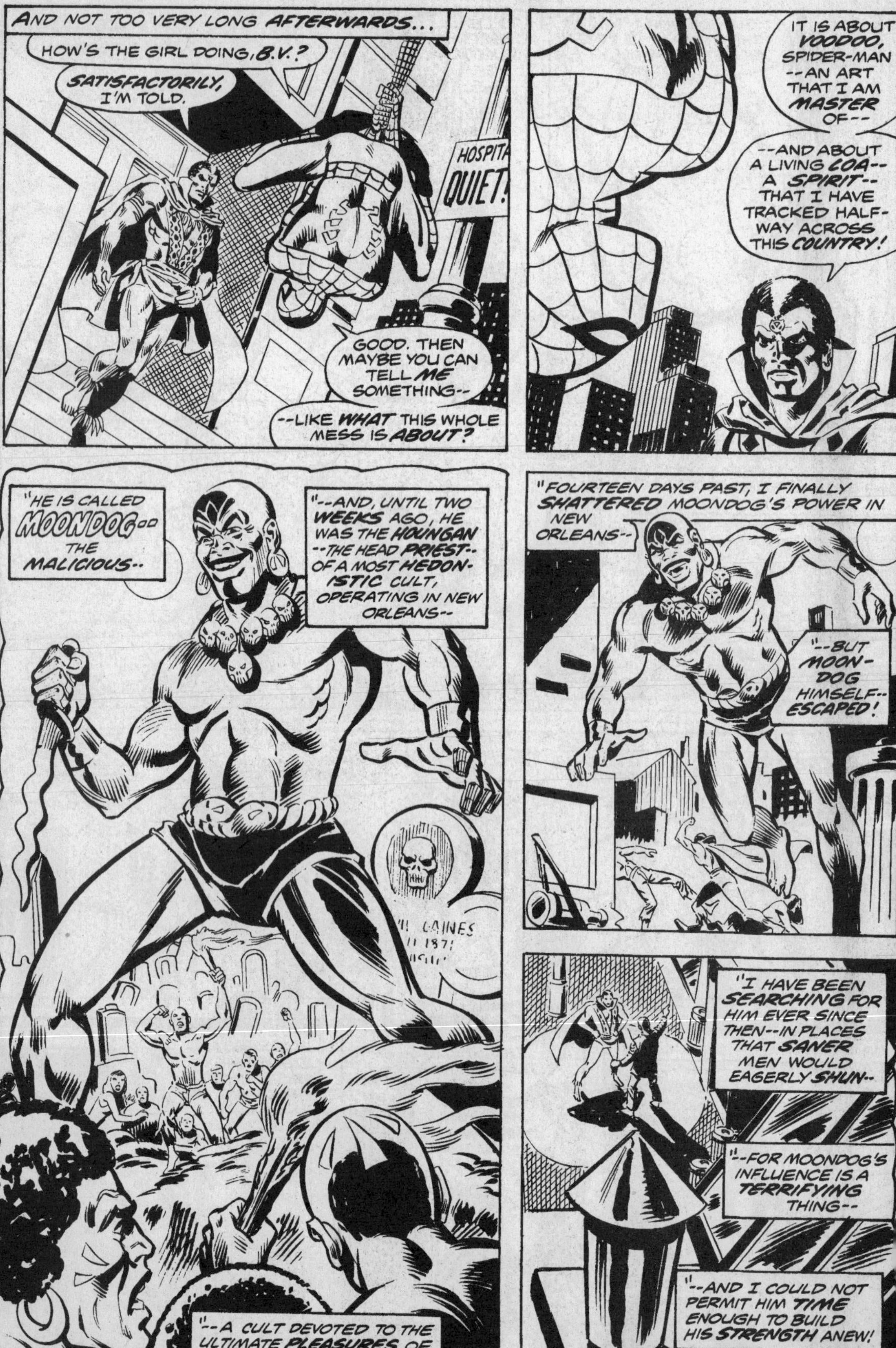
AND NOT TOO VERY LONG AFTERWARDS...
HOW'S THE GIRL DOING, B.V.?
SATISFACTORILY, I'M TOLD.
HOSPITA
QUIET!
GOOD. THEN MAYBE YOU CAN TELL ME SOMETHING--
--LIKE WHAT THIS WHOLE MESS IS ABOUT?
IT IS ABOUT VOODOO, SPIDER-MAN --AN ART THAT I AM MASTER OF--
--AND ABOUT A LIVING COA-- A SPIRIT-- THAT I HAVE TRACKED HALF-WAY ACROSS THIS COUNTRY!
"HE IS CALLED MOONDOG-- THE MALICIOUS--
"--AND, UNTIL TWO WEEKS AGO, HE WAS THE HOUNGAN --THE HEAD PRIEST-- OF A MOST HEDONISTIC CULT, OPERATING IN NEW ORLEANS--
"--A CULT DEVOTED TO THE ULTIMATE PLEASURES OF LIFE-- AND OF DEATH!
"FOURTEEN DAYS PAST, I FINALLY SHATTERED MOONDOG'S POWER IN NEW ORLEANS--
"--BUT MOONDOG HIMSELF-- ESCAPED!
"I HAVE BEEN SEARCHING FOR HIM EVER SINCE THEN--IN PLACES THAT SANER MEN WOULD EAGERLY SHUN--
"--FOR MOONDOG'S INFLUENCE IS A TERRIFYING THING--
"--AND I COULD NOT PERMIT HIM TIME ENOUGH TO BUILD HIS STRENGTH ANEW!

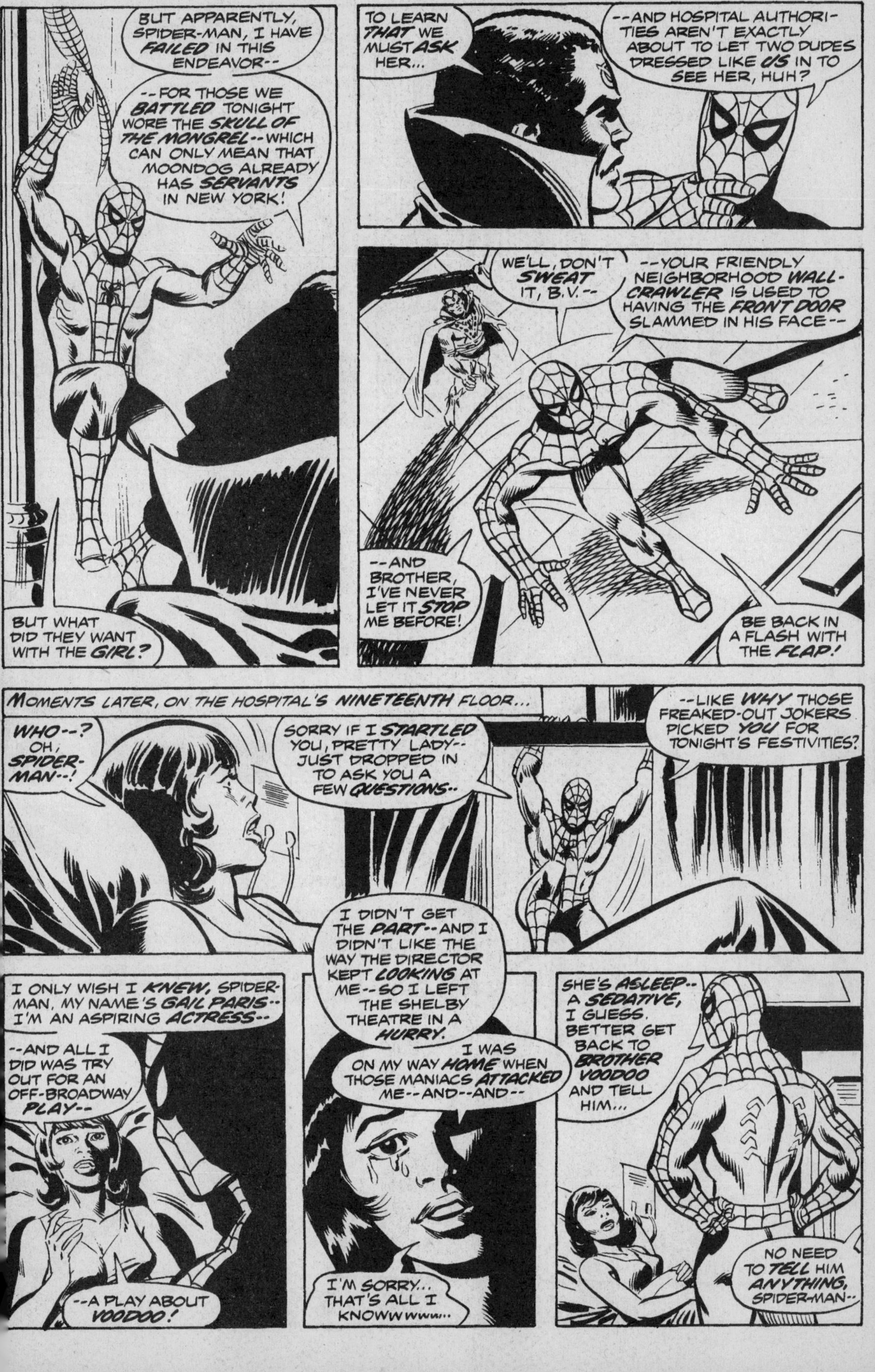
BUT APPARENTLY, SPIDER-MAN, I HAVE FAILED IN THIS ENDEAVOR--
--FOR THOSE WE BATTLED TONIGHT WORE THE SKULL OF THE MONGREL--WHICH CAN ONLY MEAN THAT MOONDOG ALREADY HAS SERVANTS IN NEW YORK!
BUT WHAT DID THEY WANT WITH THE GIRL?
TO LEARN THAT WE MUST ASK HER...
--AND HOSPITAL AUTHORITIES AREN'T EXACTLY ABOUT TO LET TWO DUDES DRESSED LIKE US IN TO SEE HER, HUH?
WE'LL, DON'T SWEAT IT, B.V.--
--YOUR FRIENDLY NEIGHBORHOOD WALL-CRAWLER IS USED TO HAVING THE FRONT DOOR SLAMMED IN HIS FACE--
--AND BROTHER, I'VE NEVER LET IT STOP ME BEFORE!
BE BACK IN A FLASH WITH THE FLAP!
MOMENTS LATER, ON THE HOSPITAL'S NINETEENTH FLOOR...
WHO--? OH, SPIDER-MAN--!
SORRY IF I STARTLED YOU, PRETTY LADY--JUST DROPPED IN TO ASK YOU A FEW QUESTIONS--
--LIKE WHY THOSE FREAKED-OUT JOKERS PICKED YOU FOR TONIGHT'S FESTIVITIES?
I ONLY WISH I KNEW, SPIDER-MAN. MY NAME'S GAIL PARIS--I'M AN ASPIRING ACTRESS--
--AND ALL I DID WAS TRY OUT FOR AN OFF-BROADWAY PLAY--
--A PLAY ABOUT VOODOO!
I DIDN'T GET THE PART--AND I DIDN'T LIKE THE WAY THE DIRECTOR KEPT LOOKING AT ME--SO I LEFT THE SHELBY THEATRE IN A HURRY.
I WAS ON MY WAY HOME WHEN THOSE MANIACS ATTACKED ME--AND--AND--
I'M SORRY... THAT'S ALL I KNOWWWWW...
SHE'S ASLEEP--A SEDATIVE, I GUESS. BETTER GET BACK TO BROTHER VOODOO AND TELL HIM...
NO NEED TO TELL HIM ANYTHING, SPIDER-MAN--

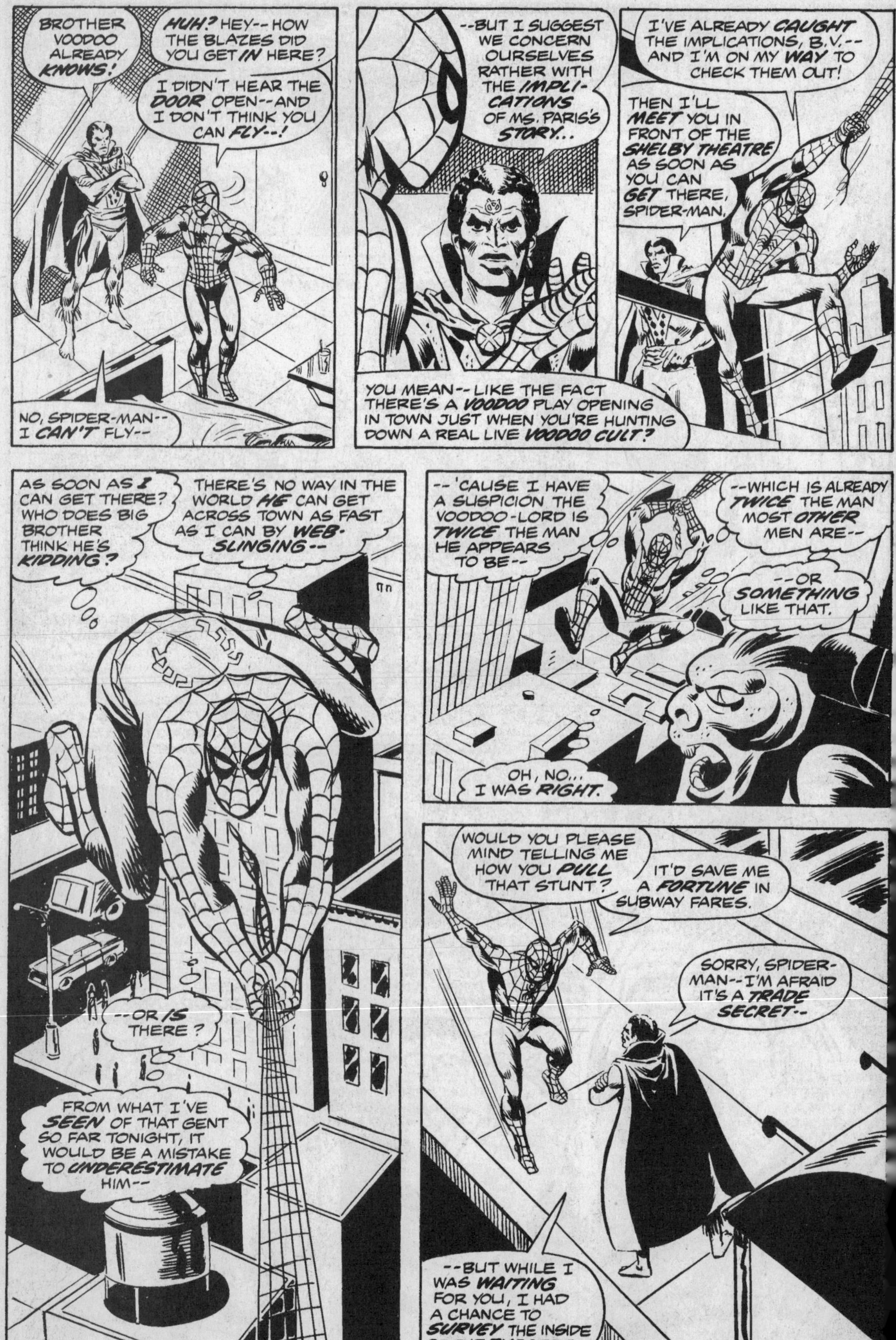

BROTHER VOODOO ALREADY KNOWS!
HUH? HEY-- HOW THE BLAZES DID YOU GET IN HERE?
I DIDN'T HEAR THE DOOR OPEN--AND I DON'T THINK YOU CAN FLY--!
NO, SPIDER-MAN-- I CAN'T FLY--
--BUT I SUGGEST WE CONCERN OURSELVES RATHER WITH THE IMPLICATIONS OF MS. PARIS'S STORY...
YOU MEAN--LIKE THE FACT THERE'S A VOODOO PLAY OPENING IN TOWN JUST WHEN YOU'RE HUNTING DOWN A REAL LIVE VOODOO CULT?
I'VE ALREADY CAUGHT THE IMPLICATIONS, B.V.-- AND I'M ON MY WAY TO CHECK THEM OUT!
THEN I'LL MEET YOU IN FRONT OF THE SHELBY THEATRE AS SOON AS YOU CAN GET THERE, SPIDER-MAN.
AS SOON AS I CAN GET THERE? WHO DOES BIG BROTHER THINK HE'S KIDDING?
THERE'S NO WAY IN THE WORLD HE CAN GET ACROSS TOWN AS FAST AS I CAN BY WEB-SLINGING--
--OR IS THERE?
FROM WHAT I'VE SEEN OF THAT GENT SO FAR TONIGHT, IT WOULD BE A MISTAKE TO UNDERESTIMATE HIM--
--'CAUSE I HAVE A SUSPICION THE VOODOO-LORD IS TWICE THE MAN HE APPEARS TO BE--
--WHICH IS ALREADY TWICE THE MAN MOST OTHER MEN ARE--
--OR SOMETHING LIKE THAT.
OH, NO... I WAS RIGHT.
WOULD YOU PLEASE MIND TELLING ME HOW YOU PULL THAT STUNT?
IT'D SAVE ME A FORTUNE IN SUBWAY FARES.
SORRY, SPIDER-MAN--I'M AFRAID IT'S A TRADE SECRET--
--BUT WHILE I WAS WAITING FOR YOU, I HAD A CHANCE TO SURVEY THE INSIDE OF THE THEATRE.

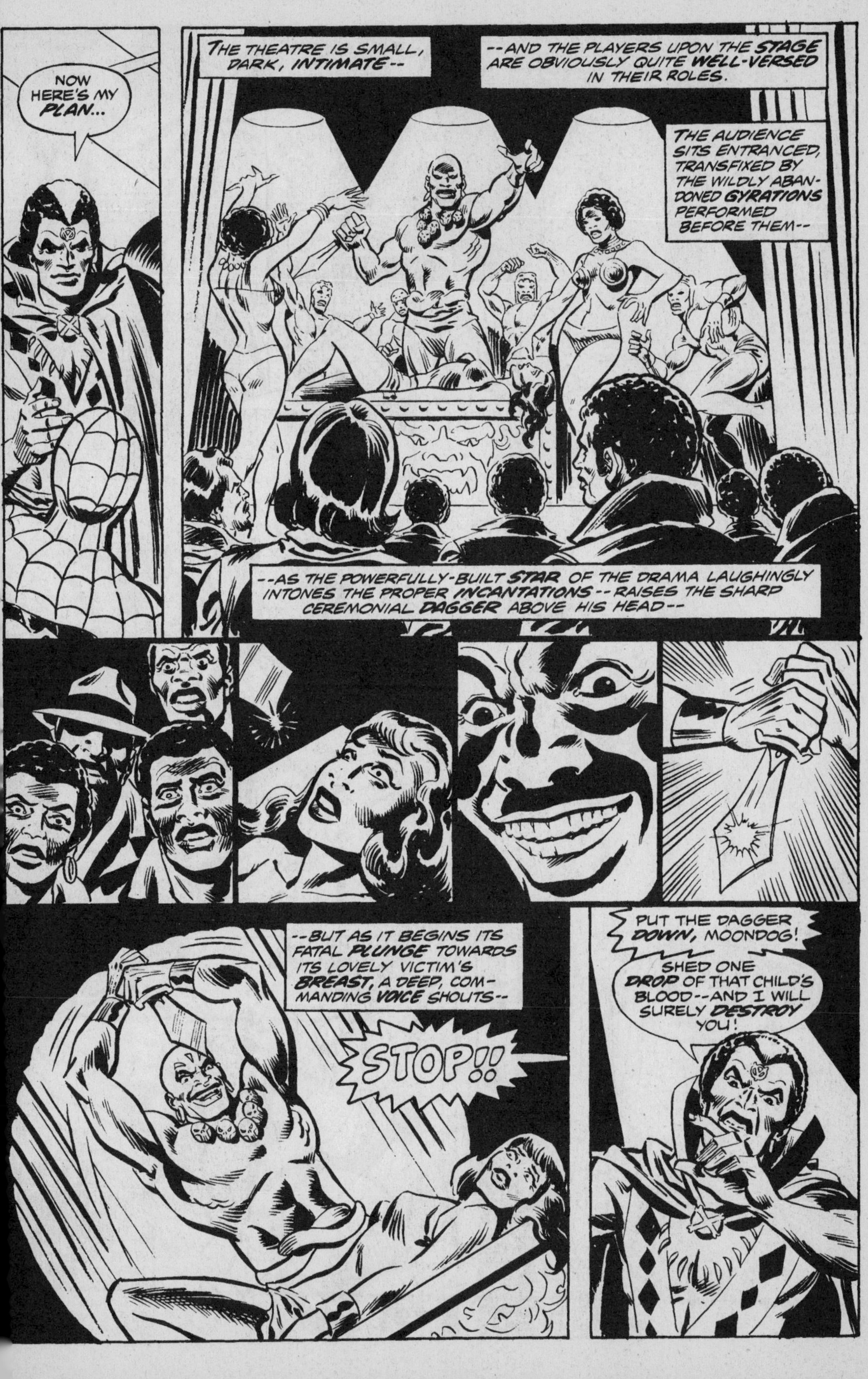
NOW HERE'S MY PLAN...
THE THEATRE IS SMALL, DARK, INTIMATE--
--AND THE PLAYERS UPON THE STAGE ARE OBVIOUSLY QUITE WELL-VERSED IN THEIR ROLES.
THE AUDIENCE SITS ENTRANCED, TRANSFIXED BY THE WILDLY ABANDONED GYRATIONS PERFORMED BEFORE THEM--
--AS THE POWERFULLY-BUILT STAR OF THE DRAMA LAUGHINGLY INTONES THE PROPER INCANTATIONS--RAISES THE SHARP CEREMONIAL DAGGER ABOVE HIS HEAD--
--BUT AS IT BEGINS ITS FATAL PLUNGE TOWARDS ITS LOVELY VICTIM'S BREAST, A DEEP, COMMANDING VOICE SHOUTS--
STOP!!
PUT THE DAGGER DOWN, MOONDOG!
SHED ONE DROP OF THAT CHILD'S BLOOD--AND I WILL SURELY DESTROY YOU!

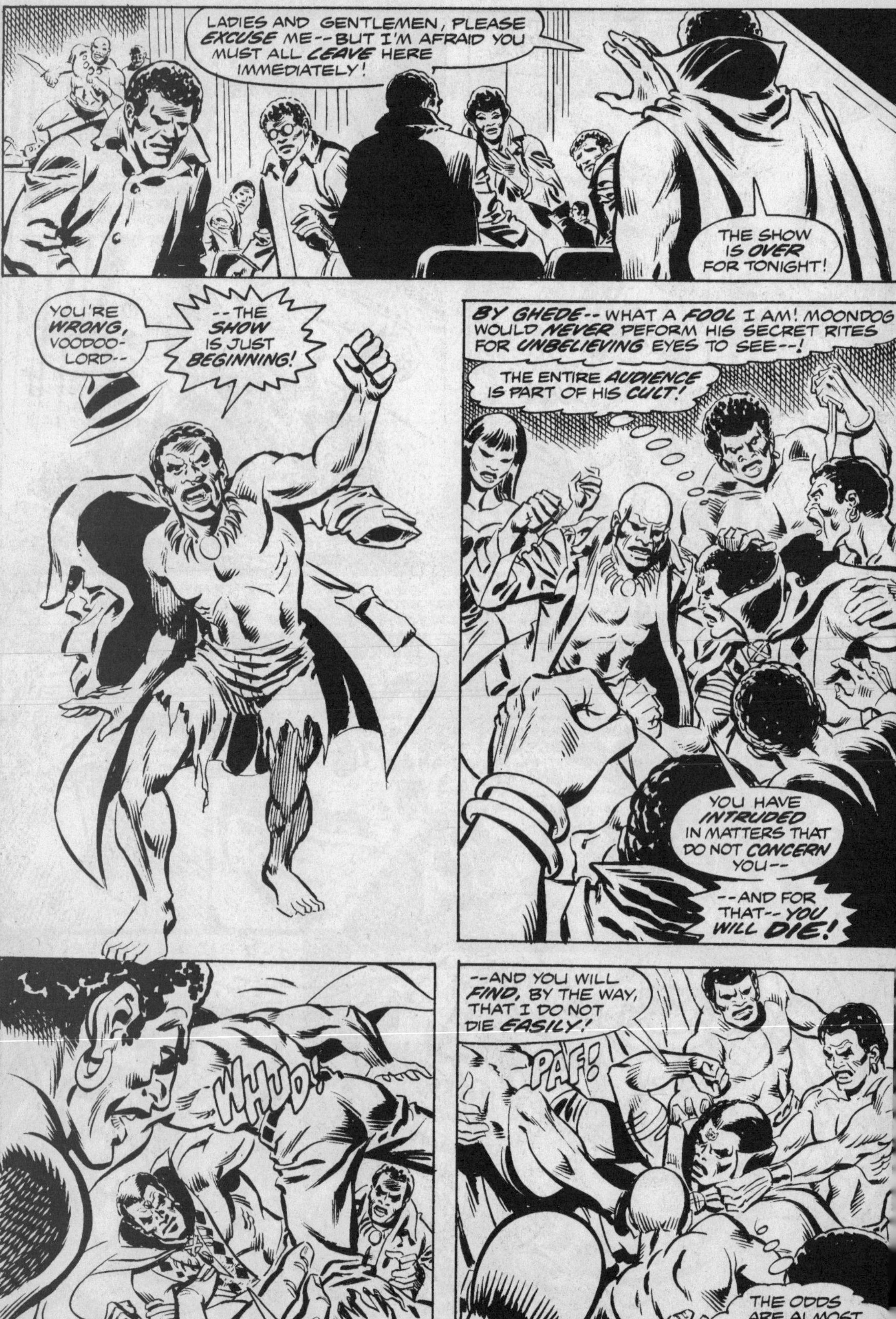
LADIES AND GENTLEMEN, PLEASE EXCUSE ME--BUT I'M AFRAID YOU MUST ALL LEAVE HERE IMMEDIATELY!
THE SHOW IS OVER FOR TONIGHT!
YOU'RE WRONG, VOODOO-LORD--
--THE SHOW IS JUST BEGINNING!
BY GHEDE-- WHAT A FOOL I AM! MOONDOG WOULD NEVER PEFORM HIS SECRET RITES FOR UNBELIEVING EYES TO SEE--!
THE ENTIRE AUDIENCE IS PART OF HIS CULT!
YOU HAVE INTRUDED IN MATTERS THAT DO NOT CONCERN YOU--
--AND FOR THAT--YOU WILL DIE!
WHUD!
WHATEVER CONCERNS VOODOO CONCERNS ME, DOLT--
--AND YOU WILL FIND, BY THE WAY, THAT I DO NOT DIE EASILY!
PAF!
THE ODDS ARE ALMOST OVERWHELMING --BUT I MUST KEEP STALLING FOR TIME UNTIL--

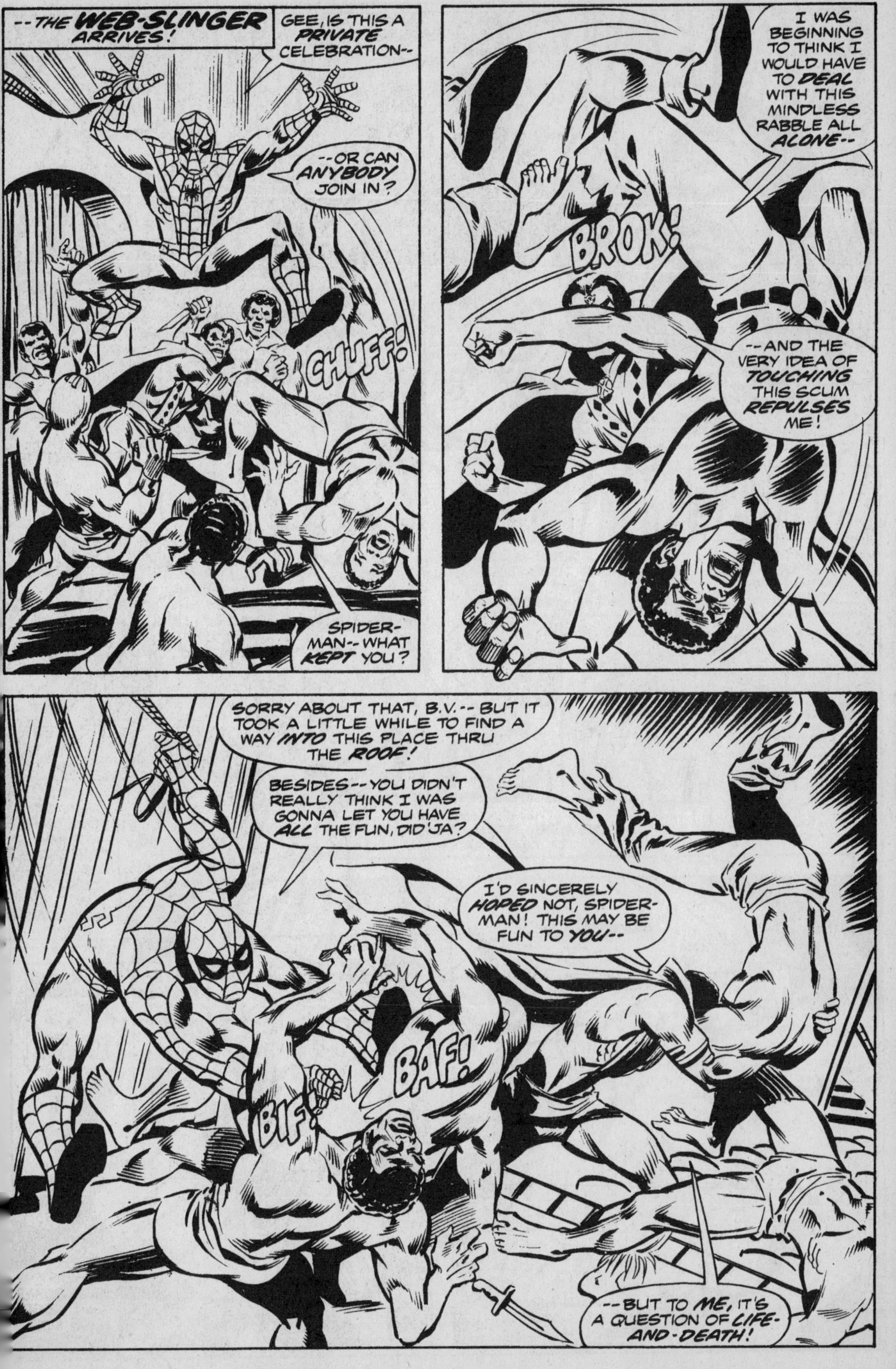
--THE WEB-SLINGER ARRIVES!
GEE, IS THIS A PRIVATE CELEBRATION--
--OR CAN ANYBODY JOIN IN?
CHUFF!
SPIDER-MAN--WHAT KEPT YOU?
I WAS BEGINNING TO THINK I WOULD HAVE TO DEAL WITH THIS MINDLESS RABBLE ALL ALONE--
BROK!
--AND THE VERY IDEA OF TOUCHING THIS SCUM REPULSES ME!
SORRY ABOUT THAT, B.V.--BUT IT TOOK A LITTLE WHILE TO FIND A WAY INTO THIS PLACE THRU THE ROOF!
BESIDES--YOU DIDN'T REALLY THINK I WAS GONNA LET YOU HAVE ALL THE FUN, DID'JA?
I'D SINCERELY HOPED NOT, SPIDER-MAN! THIS MAY BE FUN TO YOU--
BAF!
BIF!
--BUT TO ME, IT'S A QUESTION OF LIFE-AND-DEATH!

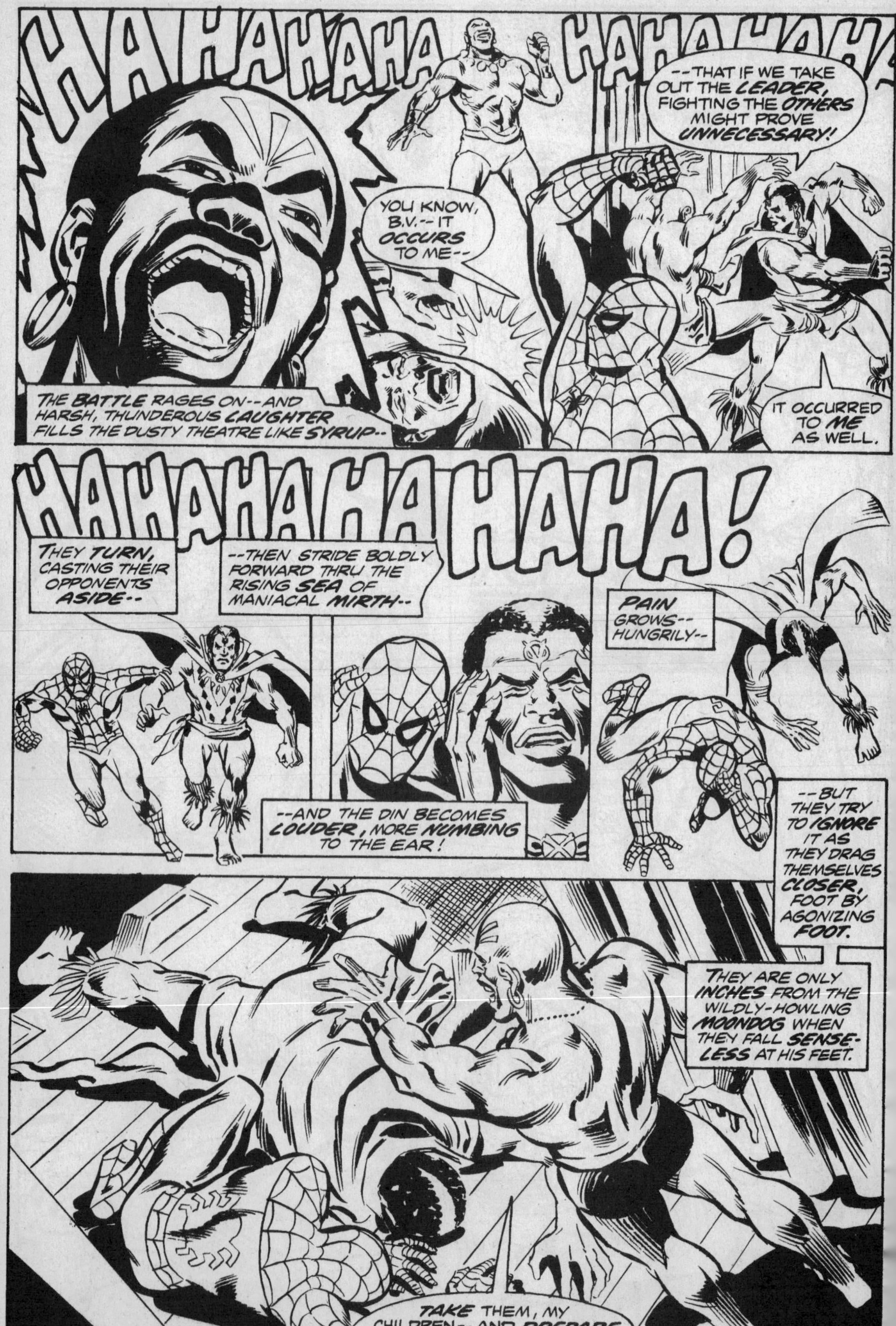

HAHAHAHA
HAHAHAHA
--THAT IF WE TAKE OUT THE LEADER, FIGHTING THE OTHERS MIGHT PROVE UNNECESSARY!
YOU KNOW, B.V.--IT OCCURS TO ME--
THE BATTLE RAGES ON--AND HARSH, THUNDEROUS LAUGHTER FILLS THE DUSTY THEATRE LIKE SYRUP--
IT OCCURRED TO ME AS WELL.
HAHAHAHAHAHAHA!
THEY TURN, CASTING THEIR OPPONENTS ASIDE--
--THEN STRIDE BOLDLY FORWARD THRU THE RISING SEA OF MANIACAL MIRTH--
--AND THE DIN BECOMES LOUDER, MORE NUMBING TO THE EAR!
PAIN GROWS--HUNGRILY--
--BUT THEY TRY TO IGNORE IT AS THEY DRAG THEMSELVES CLOSER, FOOT BY AGONIZING FOOT.
THEY ARE ONLY INCHES FROM THE WILDLY-HOWLING MOONDOG WHEN THEY FALL SENSELESS AT HIS FEET.
TAKE THEM, MY CHILDREN--AND PREPARE THEM FOR WHAT COMES NEXT!

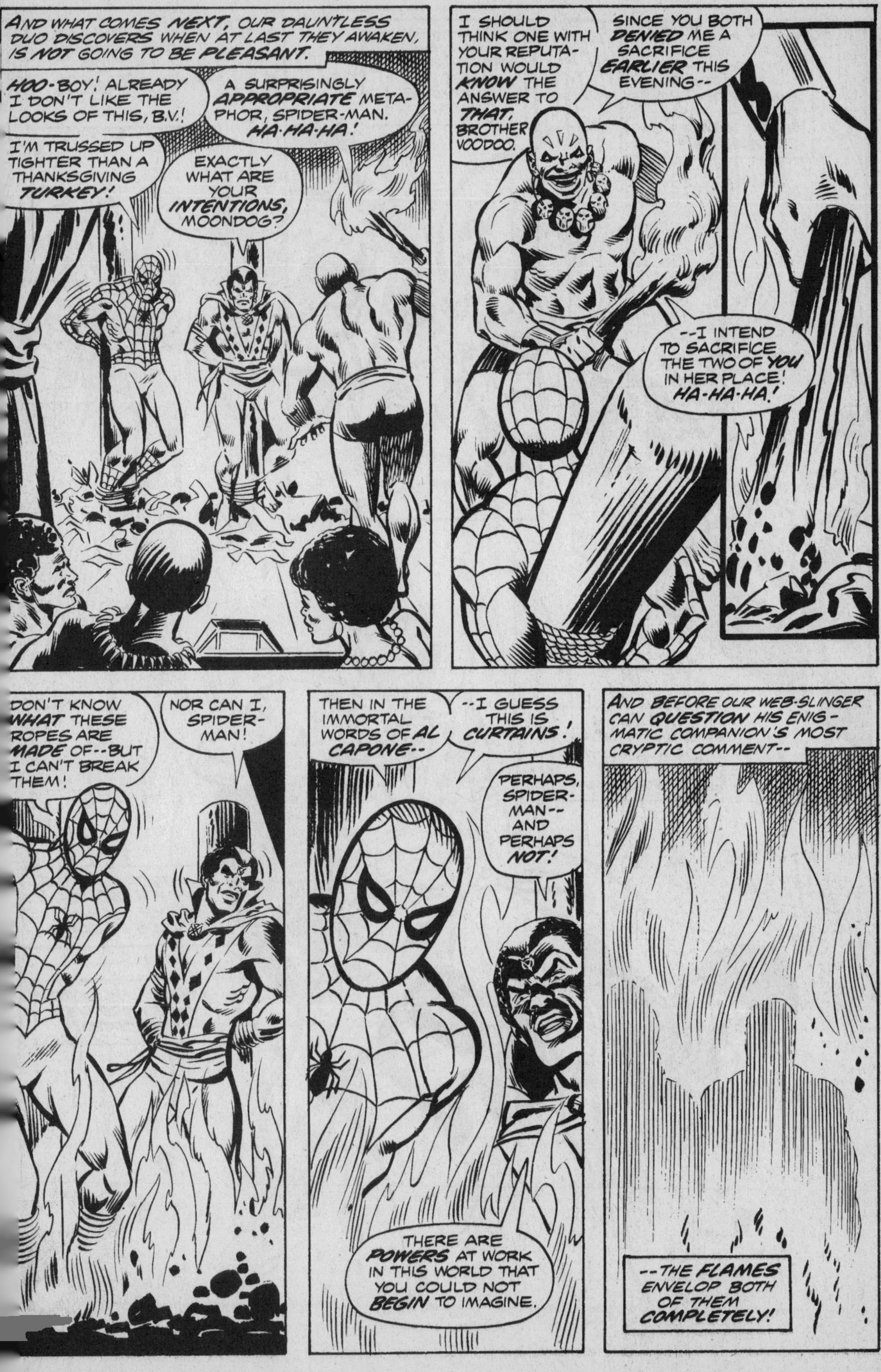
AND WHAT COMES NEXT, OUR DAUNTLESS DUO DISCOVERS WHEN AT LAST THEY AWAKEN, IS NOT GOING TO BE PLEASANT.
HOO-BOY! ALREADY I DON'T LIKE THE LOOKS OF THIS, B.V.!
I'M TRUSSED UP TIGHTER THAN A THANKSGIVING TURKEY!
A SURPRISINGLY APPROPRIATE METAPHOR, SPIDER-MAN. HA-HA-HA!
EXACTLY WHAT ARE YOUR INTENTIONS, MOONDOG?
I SHOULD THINK ONE WITH YOUR REPUTATION WOULD KNOW THE ANSWER TO THAT, BROTHER VOODOO.
SINCE YOU BOTH DENIED ME A SACRIFICE EARLIER THIS EVENING--
--I INTEND TO SACRIFICE THE TWO OF YOU IN HER PLACE! HA-HA-HA!
DON'T KNOW WHAT THESE ROPES ARE MADE OF--BUT I CAN'T BREAK THEM!
NOR CAN I, SPIDER-MAN!
THEN IN THE IMMORTAL WORDS OF AL CAPONE--
--I GUESS THIS IS CURTAINS!
PERHAPS, SPIDER-MAN--AND PERHAPS NOT!
THERE ARE POWERS AT WORK IN THIS WORLD THAT YOU COULD NOT BEGIN TO IMAGINE.
AND BEFORE OUR WEB-SLINGER CAN QUESTION HIS ENIGMATIC COMPANION'S MOST CRYPTIC COMMENT--
--THE FLAMES ENVELOP BOTH OF THEM COMPLETELY!

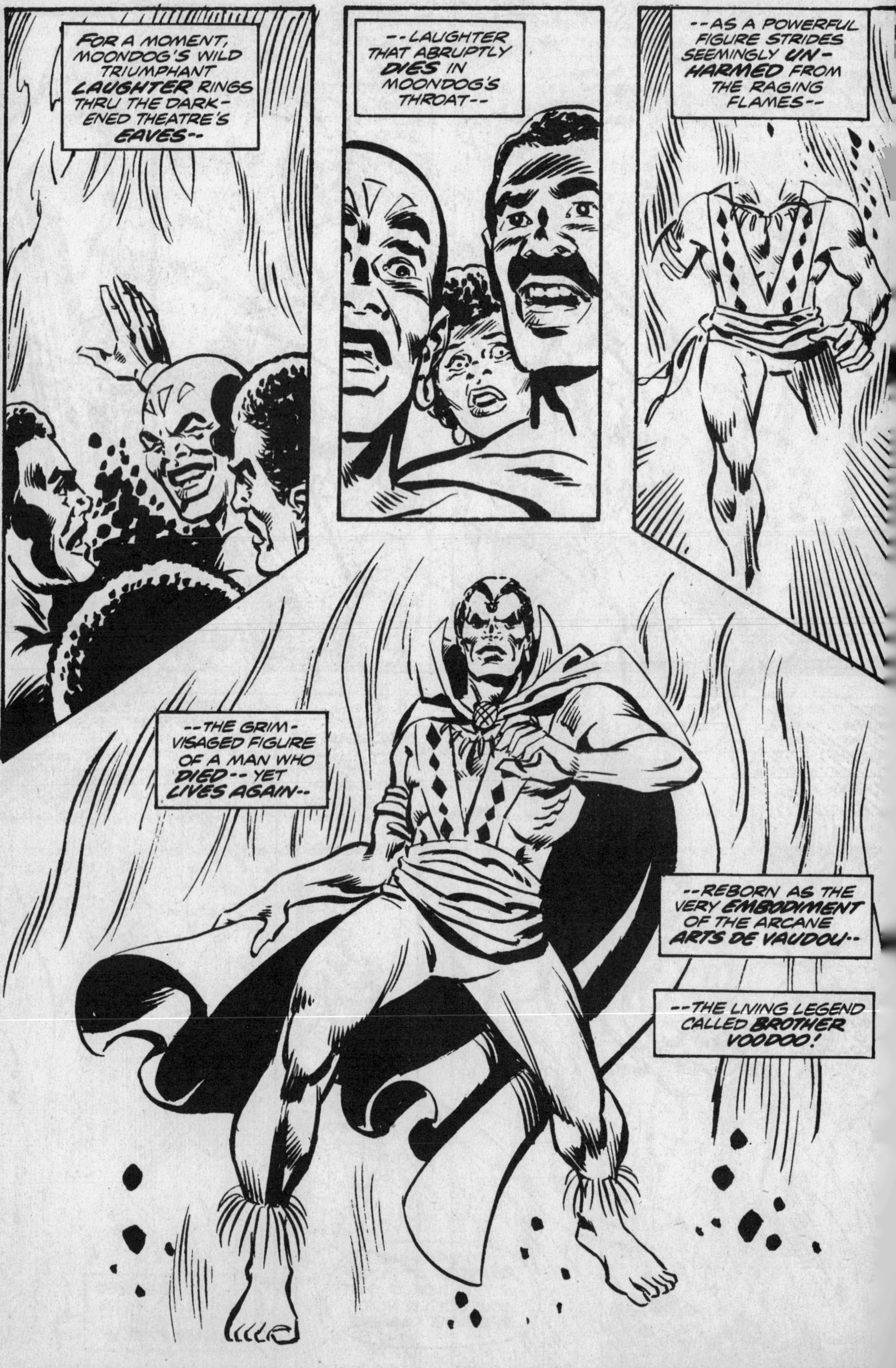
FOR A MOMENT, MOONDOG'S WILD TRIUMPHANT LAUGHTER RINGS THRU THE DARK-ENED THEATRE'S EAVES--
--LAUGHTER THAT ABRUPTLY DIES IN MOONDOG'S THROAT--
--AS A POWERFUL FIGURE STRIDES SEEMINGLY UN-HARMED FROM THE RAGING FLAMES--
--THE GRIM-VISAGED FIGURE OF A MAN WHO DIED--YET LIVES AGAIN--
--REBORN AS THE VERY EMBODIMENT OF THE ARCANE ARTS DE VAUDOU--
--THE LIVING LEGEND CALLED BROTHER VOODOO!

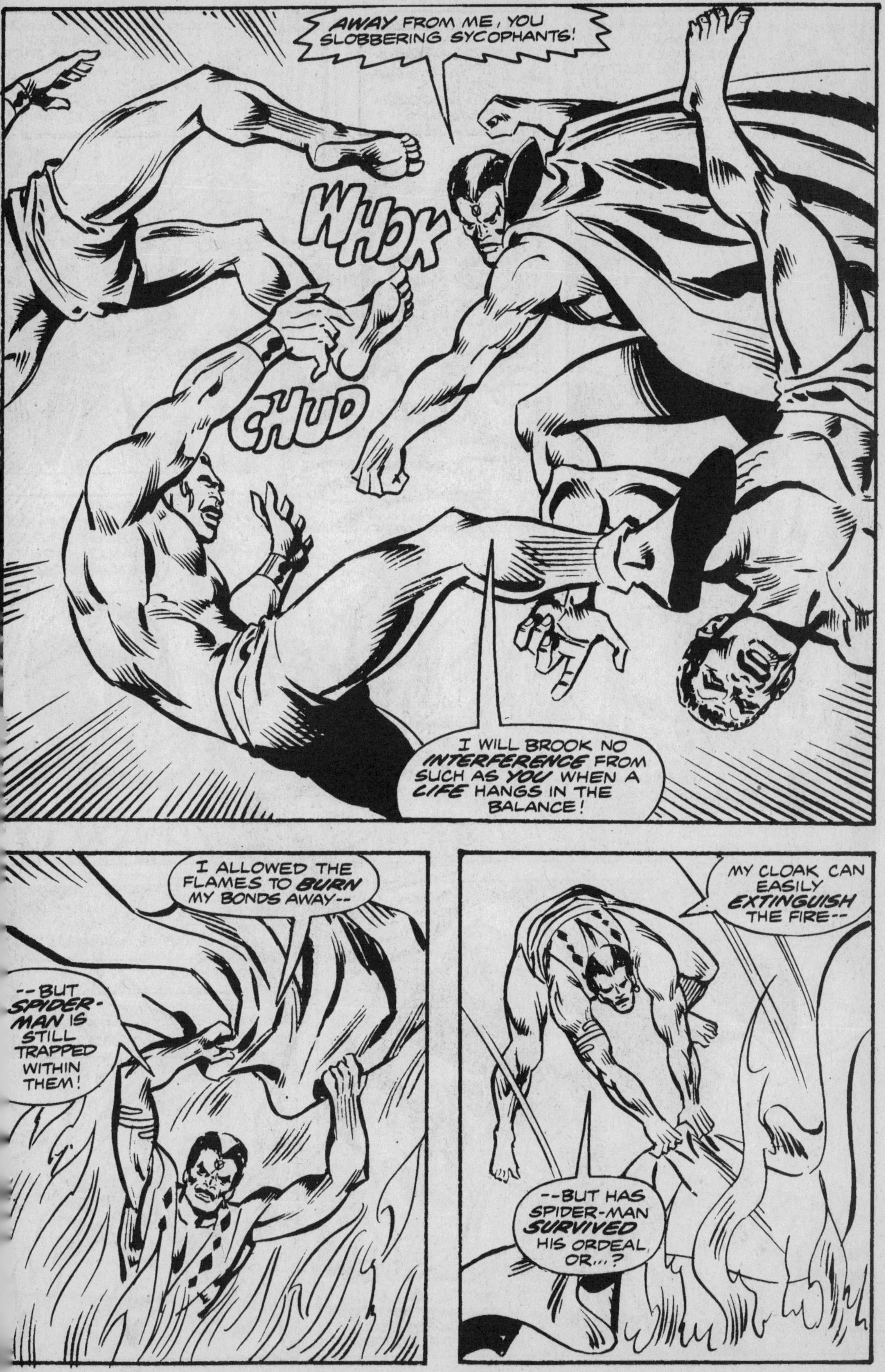
AWAY FROM ME, YOU SLOBBERING SYCOPHANTS!
WHOK
CHUD
I WILL BROOK NO INTERFERENCE FROM SUCH AS YOU WHEN A LIFE HANGS IN THE BALANCE!
I ALLOWED THE FLAMES TO BURN MY BONDS AWAY--
--BUT SPIDER-MAN IS STILL TRAPPED WITHIN THEM!
MY CLOAK CAN EASILY EXTINGUISH THE FIRE--
--BUT HAS SPIDER-MAN SURVIVED HIS ORDEAL OR...?

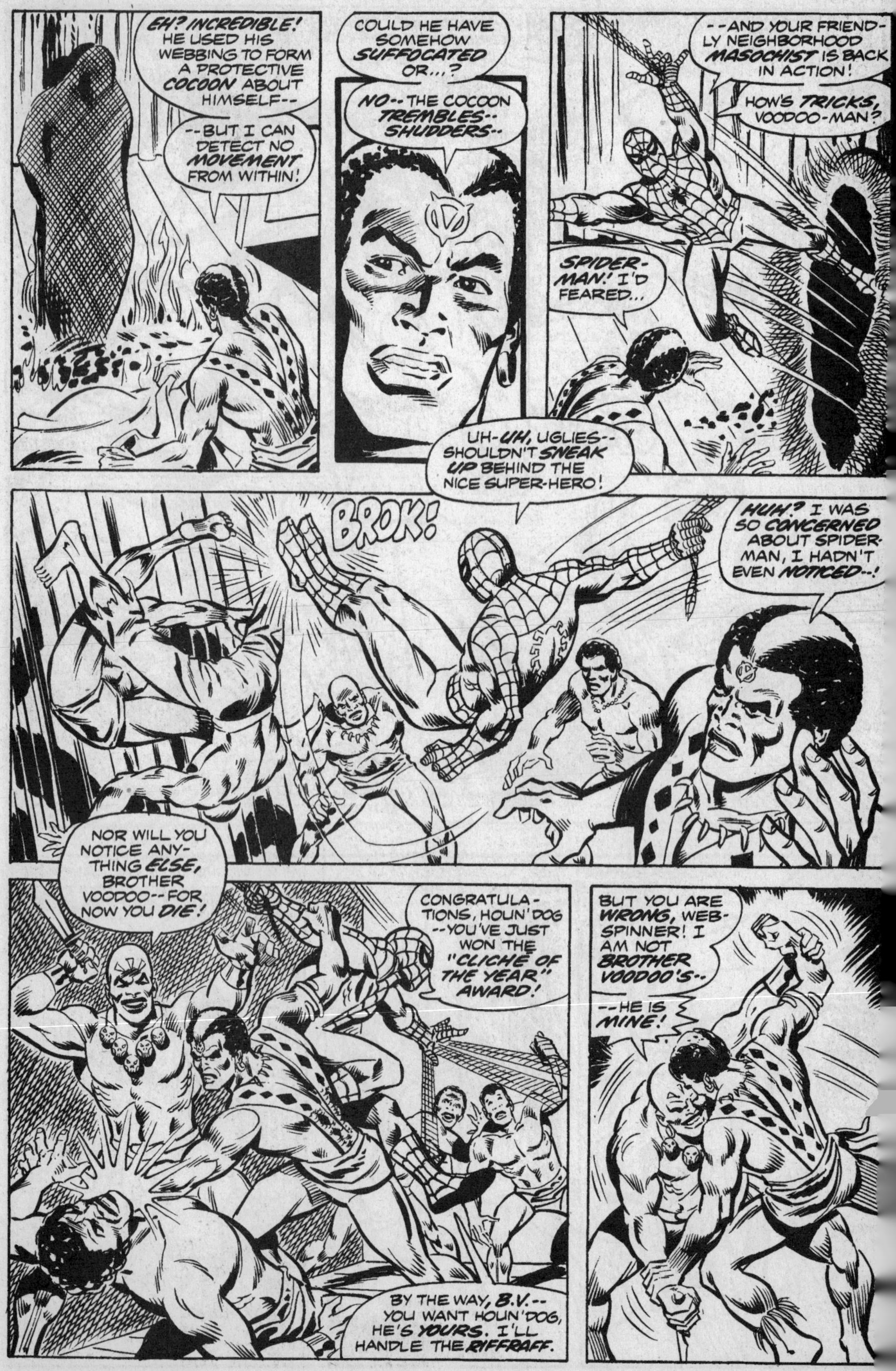
EH? INCREDIBLE! HE USED HIS WEBBING TO FORM A PROTECTIVE COCOON ABOUT HIMSELF--
--BUT I CAN DETECT NO MOVEMENT FROM WITHIN!
COULD HE HAVE SOMEHOW SUFFOCATED OR...?
NO--THE COCOON TREMBLES--SHUDDERS--
--AND YOUR FRIENDLY NEIGHBORHOOD MASOCHIST IS BACK IN ACTION!
HOW'S TRICKS, VOODOO-MAN?
SPIDER-MAN! I'D FEARED...
UH-UH, UGLIES--SHOULDN'T SNEAK UP BEHIND THE NICE SUPER-HERO!
BROK!
HUH? I WAS SO CONCERNED ABOUT SPIDER-MAN, I HADN'T EVEN NOTICED--!
NOR WILL YOU NOTICE ANYTHING ELSE, BROTHER VOODOO--FOR NOW YOU DIE!
CONGRATULATIONS, HOUN' DOG--YOU'VE JUST WON THE "CLICHÉ OF THE YEAR" AWARD!
BY THE WAY, B.V.--YOU WANT HOUN' DOG, HE'S YOURS. I'LL HANDLE THE RIFFRAFF.
BUT YOU ARE WRONG, WEB-SPINNER! I AM NOT BROTHER VOODOO'S--
--HE IS MINE!

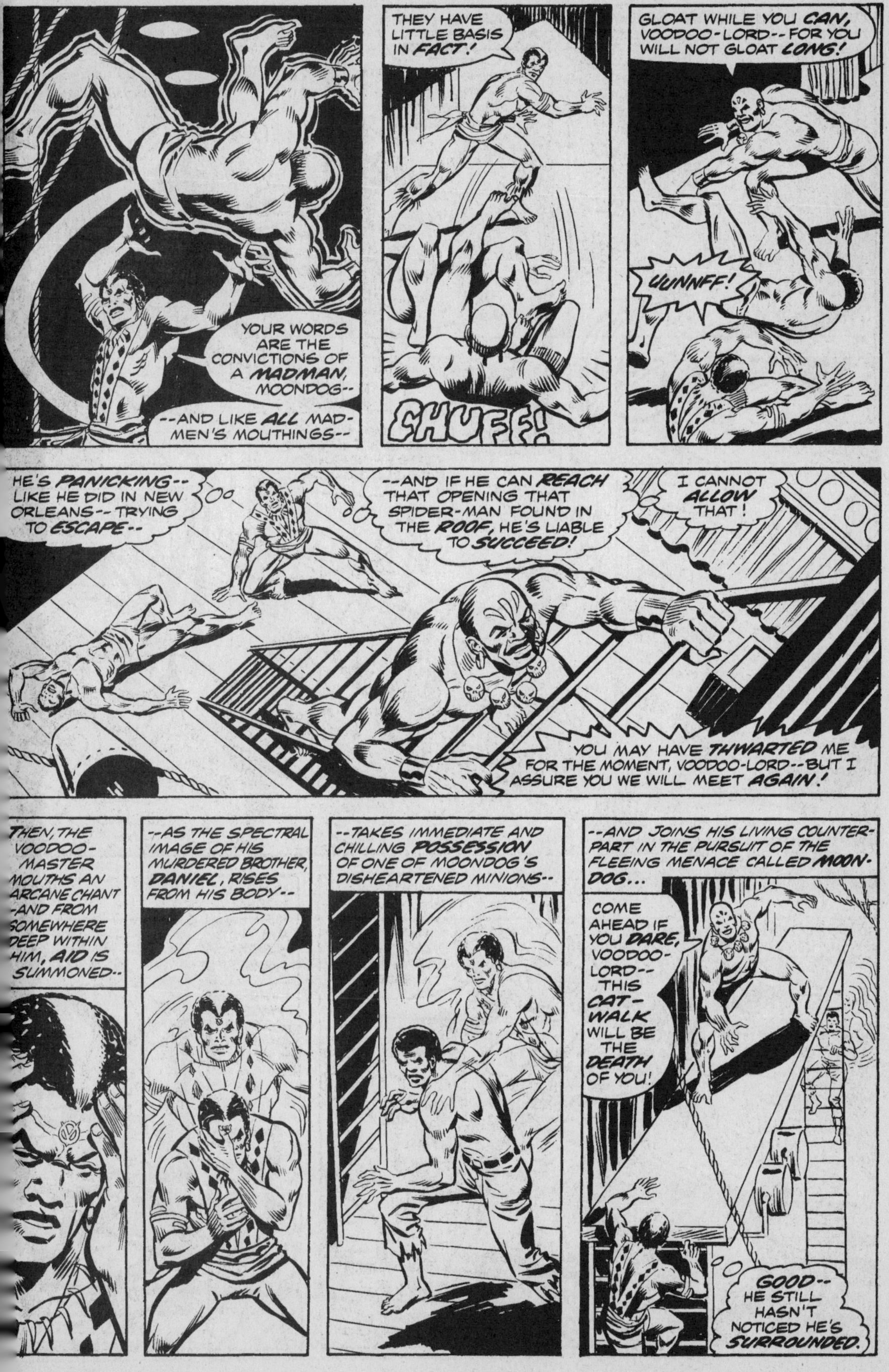
YOUR WORDS ARE THE CONVICTIONS OF A MADMAN, MOONDOG--
--AND LIKE ALL MADMEN'S MOUTHINGS--
THEY HAVE LITTLE BASIS IN FACT!
CHUFF!
GLOAT WHILE YOU CAN, VOODOO-LORD--FOR YOU WILL NOT GLOAT LONG!
UUNNFF!
HE'S PANICKING--LIKE HE DID IN NEW ORLEANS--TRYING TO ESCAPE--
--AND IF HE CAN REACH THAT OPENING THAT SPIDER-MAN FOUND IN THE ROOF, HE'S LIABLE TO SUCCEED!
I CANNOT ALLOW THAT!
YOU MAY HAVE THWARTED ME FOR THE MOMENT, VOODOO-LORD--BUT I ASSURE YOU WE WILL MEET AGAIN!
THEN, THE VOODOO-MASTER MOUTHS AN ARCANE CHANT -AND FROM SOMEWHERE DEEP WITHIN HIM, AID IS SUMMONED--
--AS THE SPECTRAL IMAGE OF HIS MURDERED BROTHER, DANIEL, RISES FROM HIS BODY--
--TAKES IMMEDIATE AND CHILLING POSSESSION OF ONE OF MOONDOG'S DISHEARTENED MINIONS--
--AND JOINS HIS LIVING COUNTERPART IN THE PURSUIT OF THE FLEEING MENACE CALLED MOONDOG...
COME AHEAD IF YOU DARE, VOODOO-LORD--THIS CATWALK WILL BE THE DEATH OF YOU!
GOOD--HE STILL HASN'T NOTICED HE'S SURROUNDED.

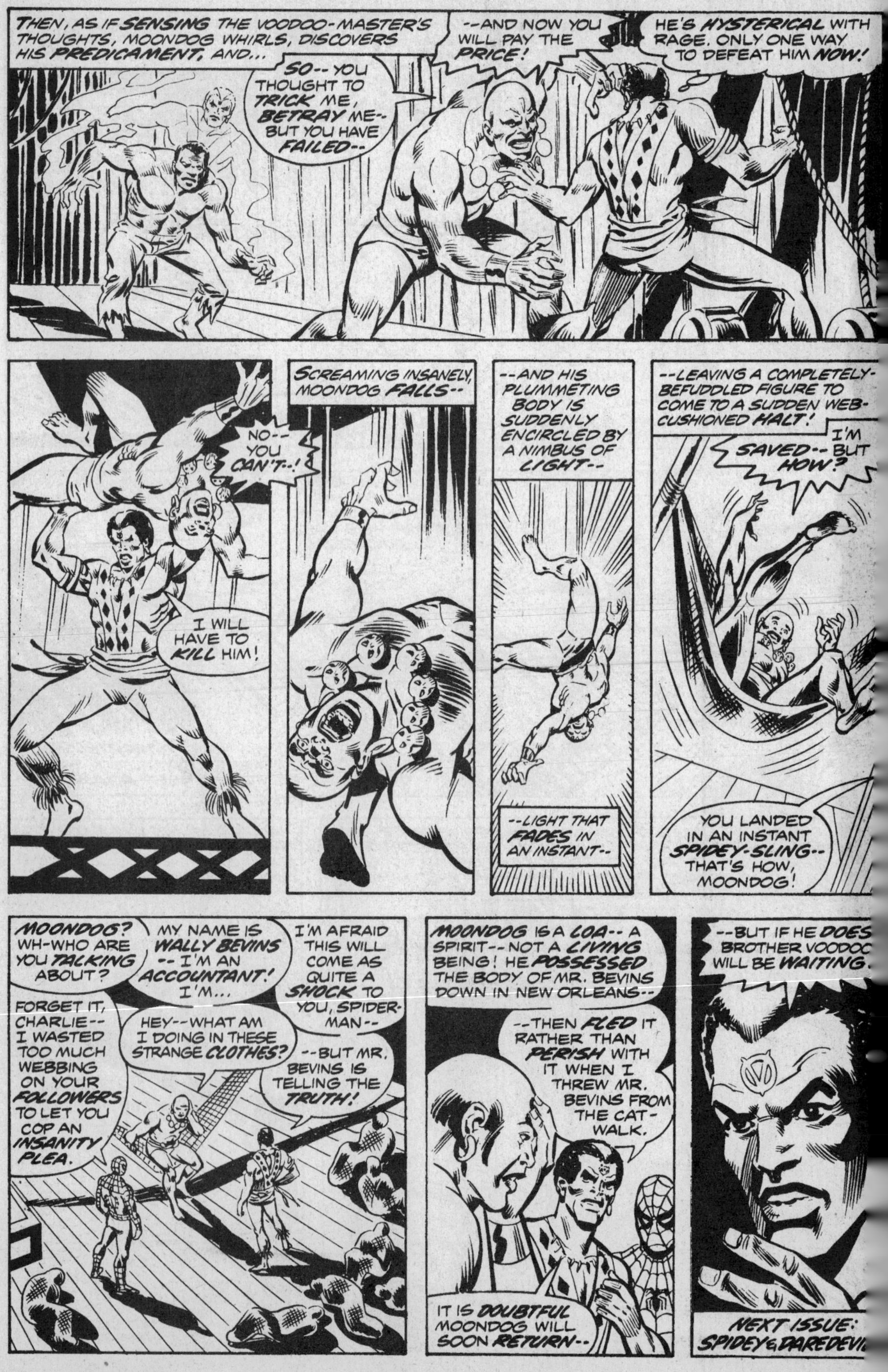
THEN, AS IF SENSING THE VOODOO-MASTER'S THOUGHTS, MOONDOG WHIRLS, DISCOVERS HIS PREDICAMENT, AND...
SO-- YOU THOUGHT TO TRICK ME, BETRAY ME-- BUT YOU HAVE FAILED--
--AND NOW YOU WILL PAY THE PRICE!
HE'S HYSTERICAL WITH RAGE. ONLY ONE WAY TO DEFEAT HIM NOW!
NO-- YOU CAN'T--!
I WILL HAVE TO KILL HIM!
SCREAMING INSANELY, MOONDOG FALLS--
--AND HIS PLUMMETING BODY IS SUDDENLY ENCIRCLED BY A NIMBUS OF LIGHT--
--LIGHT THAT FADES IN AN INSTANT--
--LEAVING A COMPLETELY-BEFUDDLED FIGURE TO COME TO A SUDDEN WEB-CUSHIONED HALT!
SAVED-- BUT HOW?
I'M
YOU LANDED IN AN INSTANT SPIDEY-SLING-- THAT'S HOW, MOONDOG!
MOONDOG? WH-WHO ARE YOU TALKING ABOUT?
MY NAME IS WALLY BEVINS -- I'M AN ACCOUNTANT! I'M...
I'M AFRAID THIS WILL COME AS QUITE A SHOCK TO YOU, SPIDER-MAN--
FORGET IT, CHARLIE-- I WASTED TOO MUCH WEBBING ON YOUR FOLLOWERS TO LET YOU COP AN INSANITY PLEA.
HEY--WHAT AM I DOING IN THESE STRANGE CLOTHES?
--BUT MR. BEVINS IS TELLING THE TRUTH!
MOONDOG IS A LOA-- A SPIRIT-- NOT A LIVING BEING! HE POSSESSED THE BODY OF MR. BEVINS DOWN IN NEW ORLEANS--
--THEN FLED IT RATHER THAN PERISH WITH IT WHEN I THREW MR. BEVINS FROM THE CAT-WALK.
IT IS DOUBTFUL MOONDOG WILL SOON RETURN--
--BUT IF HE DOES BROTHER VOODOO WILL BE WAITING.
NEXT ISSUE: SPIDEY & DAREDEVIL